EDITORIAL BOARD

UNIVERSITY CASEBOOK SERIES®

EMPLOYMENT DISCRIMINATION

LAW AND THEORY

FOURTH EDITION

GEORGE A. RUTHERGLEN
John Barbee Minor Distinguished Professor of Law
University of Virginia

JOHN J. DONOHUE III
C. Wendell and Edith M. Carlsmith Professor of Law
Stanford Law School

FOUNDATION PRESS

444 Cedar Street, Suite 700
St. Paul, MN 55101
1-877-888-1330

Printed in the United States of America

ISBN: 978-1-63460-338-6

PREFACE

Decisions of the Supreme Court continue to alter the landscape of employment discrimination law, on issues as different as the burden of proving retaliation to reasonable accommodation of pregnancy and reasonable accommodation of religious garb. Still further changes stem from the implications of constitutional law, which continues to exercise a pervasive influence over interpretation of the statutes against employment discrimination. The constitutional standards for affirmative action, addressed in the context of higher education, signal further restrictions on affirmative action in employment. In the opposite direction, recognition of a constitutional right to gay marriage supports expansion of the prohibition against sex discrimination to reach discrimination on the basis of sexual orientation and gender identity. So, too, the burst of public allegations of sexual misconduct by public figures and corporate executives raise the question whether the prohibition against sexual harassment has been adequately enforced.

These developments call for reassessment of the contents of a basic course on employment discrimination. Decisions that took a salient place in earlier editions of this casebook now appear in a different light and, in a number of instances, require that excerpts from them be condensed and that more space be given to recent cases. This edition of the casebook, like earlier editions, tries to take account of the different directions in which the law might go. A complete account of what the law is now must take account of what it might be tomorrow. Uncertainty and indeterminacy in this field should not be regarded as vices to be avoided, but challenges for the clarification of legal doctrine and a demonstration of the continued vitality of this field.

While taking account of these complexities, we have tried to preserve the relative simplicity and compact coverage of an introductory casebook to an area of law that continues to grow more detailed and nuanced. Keeping the larger questions in view, and the controversial arguments that surround them on all sides, remains our goal. This new edition takes account of changes in the law, both obvious and subtle, tries to relate them to basic principles of fairness regardless of group membership, the need to allow employers to maintain efficient practices in the workplace, and the demands on the courts to articulate sound rules of interpretation and enforcement.

GEORGE A. RUTHERGLEN

JOHN J. DONOHUE III

April 15, 2018

SUMMARY OF CONTENTS

TABLE OF CONTENTS

TABLE OF CASES

The principal cases are in bold type.

UNIVERSITY CASEBOOK SERIES®

EMPLOYMENT DISCRIMINATION

LAW AND THEORY

FOURTH EDITION

CHAPTER 1

INTRODUCTION

A. HISTORICAL PERSPECTIVE

1. **Reconstruction.** Employment discrimination law forms part of the larger body of civil rights law, and its origins can therefore be traced to the constitutional amendments passed in the immediate aftermath of the Civil War. These Reconstruction amendments broadly prohibited racial discrimination in several different forms: the Thirteenth Amendment abolished slavery; the Fourteenth Amendment required the states to observe the requirements of due process and equal protection; and the Fifteenth Amendment prohibited racial discrimination in voting. The meaning of these amendments, and particularly the Fourteenth Amendment, has had a long and contentious history, eventually resulting in the constitutional prohibitions against racial discrimination by government that are familiar to us today.

All of the Reconstruction amendments also explicitly empowered Congress to enforce their provisions by appropriate legislation, and Congress did not hesitate to use its newly granted powers. Several of the civil rights acts passed during Reconstruction were held unconstitutional, but several survived into the modern era. Two of these statutes are important both in their own right and as the vehicle for claims of employment discrimination. Section 1981, first enacted as part of the Civil Rights Act of 1866, prohibits racial discrimination in all forms of contracting, whether by private individuals or by the government, and § 1983, enacted in the Civil Rights Act of 1871, creates a general cause of action for any deprivation of federal rights under color of state law. The first of these statutes, § 1981, provides a remedy for discrimination in private employment and the second, § 1983, covers discrimination by state and local government.

Neither the Reconstruction amendments nor the Reconstruction civil rights acts reached their present form in any straightforward manner. When Reconstruction ended in 1876, the constitutional prohibitions against discrimination received a narrow interpretation, as did the statutes implementing them (when the latter were not declared wholly or partially invalid as beyond the power of Congress). The case that has come to stand for the abandonment of the nation's commitment to racial equality is Plessy v. Ferguson, 163 U.S. 537 (1896), which established the doctrine of "separate but equal" and the accompanying regime of Jim Crow laws in the South. Other decisions did as much to undo the work of Reconstruction, but *Plessy* stands out because it became the target of the wave of civil rights litigation that culminated in Brown v. Board of Education, 347 U.S. 483 (1954).

2. The Civil Rights Era. *Brown* marked the beginning of the modern era of civil rights law, overruling *Plessy* and replacing it with a broadly defined principle against discrimination. Exactly what the contours of this principle are, and how it is to be enforced, are questions that have remained at the center of civil rights law ever since. The immediate aim of *Brown*—desegregation of the public schools—was not accomplished until over a decade later. The single most important legal development that made *Brown* effective was the passage of the Civil Rights Act of 1964. In Title VI, this act authorized the withdrawal of federal funds from school districts that failed to desegregate. An accompanying set of provisions, in Title VII, created the first effective federal prohibition against employment discrimination. Title VII forms the foundation of employment discrimination law as we know it today.

Title VII extended the constitutional prohibition from *Brown* along several different dimensions: from discrimination by government to discrimination by private employers; from discrimination on the basis of race and national origin to discrimination on the basis of sex; and from intentional discrimination to neutral practices with discriminatory effects. The first extension required Title VII to go beyond the "state action" doctrine, which limits the coverage of the Fifth and Fourteenth Amendments to actions by government, and in the employment context, almost entirely to public employment. Congress accomplished this extension by invoking its power under the Commerce Clause, avoiding decisions following Reconstruction that had narrowly construed its power to enforce the Fourteenth Amendment against private actors. The Commerce Clause contains no such limitation and easily reaches virtually every form of employment. The second extension also depended on Congress's exercise of its power over commerce because, at the time Title VII was enacted, there was no robust constitutional prohibition against sex discrimination. Constitutional decisions that subjected sex-based classifications by government to heightened scrutiny under the Equal Protection Clause were not handed down until several years after the enactment of Title VII. The third extension, to neutral practices with discriminatory effects, was less apparent at the time that Title VII was enacted, but emerged as decisions interpreting Title VII diverged from those interpreting the Constitution. In the landmark decision in Griggs v. Duke Power Co., 401 U.S. 424 (1971), the Supreme Court held that Title VII prohibited tests and other qualifications for employment that have a disparate impact on the basis of race, even if such practices were not motivated by an intent to discriminate. Another landmark case, Washington v. Davis, 426 U.S. 229 (1976), reached exactly the opposite conclusion under the Constitution, holding that it prohibited only intentional discrimination. The precise meaning and significance of these decisions will be explored later in this book. The difference between statutory and constitutional law on this issue, however, has now become established.

With the passage of Title VII, Congress enacted both a broad prohibition against discrimination in employment and created a model for prohibitions against discrimination on other grounds. Title VII itself took this second step, as we have seen, by prohibiting discrimination on the basis of sex. It also prohibited discrimination on the basis of religion, which, although based in the First Amendment, raised distinctive issues of government interference with religion, whether to aid or to hinder adherents of different religious faiths. Accordingly, the prohibitions against discrimination on the basis of sex and religion depart from the prohibitions against discrimination on the basis of race and national origin. Some of the departures are accomplished by explicit provisions in the statute, and others by interpretation. Thus, there are special provisions in the statute concerned with discrimination on the basis of pregnancy and others concerned with religious institutions and religious practices. Such provisions raise the question whether the model of racial discrimination should be uniformly applied to discrimination on other grounds.

This question became still more acute with the enactment of the Age Discrimination in Employment Act (ADEA) soon after Title VII and the enactment of the Americans with Disabilities Act (ADA) decades later. These acts reach grounds of discrimination that receive no special treatment at all under the Constitution. Government discrimination on the basis of age or disability requires only a rational relationship to some legitimate government interest to survive judicial review under the Constitution. Massachusetts Board of Retirement v. Murgia, 427 U.S. 307, 312–14 (1976) (age); City of Cleburne v. Cleburne Living Center, 473 U.S. 432, 442–47 (1985) (disability). Yet the main prohibitions in the ADEA and the ADA closely follow those in Title VII, leaving any necessary adjustments to be made for these different forms of discrimination in exceptions and other special provisions in the statutes themselves, or through judicial interpretation. In the ADEA, statutory provisions and accompanying regulations on permissible forms of age discrimination, particularly in pension plans and in voluntary retirement plans, have become extraordinarily complex and have no precedent under Title VII. So, too, under the ADA, the provisions on reasonable accommodation of disabled workers have become a major source of litigation, unlike any corresponding provision in Title VII. This latter development has occurred despite the fact that the language of reasonable accommodation was first used in Title VII to protect religious practices from restrictions imposed by employers.

Beneath all of these doctrinal complexities lies a fundamental question of policy: To what extent can changing or highly variable characteristics, such as age and disability, be treated like the unchanging characteristic of race? The ADEA, for instance, does not protect a group whose members have suffered systematic disadvantages in the past; on the contrary, it protects a class of individual, everyone at least 40 years old, who once was younger and who now has lived into middle age. With this change in scope comes the need for a change in justification. Much the same can be said of the ADA. The individuals protected by this statute need not always have been disabled and their disability need not be hereditary, so that only in rare cases have they suffered the cumulative effects of discrimination in previous generations. Moreover, the range of covered disabilities itself is defined in the broadest possible terms, so that those protected by the statute represent an extremely heterogeneous group. They do not share any single, readily identifiable characteristic, like skin color, that is common among members of a racial minority. Discrimination against the disabled takes more varied forms and requires more individualized treatment than discrimination on the basis of race. The provisions of the ADA accordingly require greater case-by-case consideration of who is covered by the statute and whether they have been victims of discrimination.

As Congress assumed a more active role in expanding the constitutional prohibition against discrimination first recognized in *Brown v. Board of Education*, the Supreme Court did likewise in interpreting the statutes that Congress had enacted. The theory of disparate impact, extending the prohibition in Title VII to practices with discriminatory effects, was initially the product of judicial interpretation. The details of this theory of liability and the defenses to it were worked out in a series of cases and eventually codified, with important modifications, by the Civil Rights Act of 1991. The same process of interpretation and codification also worked itself out in the development of different standards for proving intentional discrimination. Here, too, a series of judicial decisions eventually resulted in amendments enacted in the Civil Rights Act of 1991.

A more dramatic example of the same process appears in the curious history of the Civil Rights Act of 1866, better known in its codified form as § 1981. This statute was first enacted immediately after the Civil War, and, after a long period of neglect, it was revived by the Warren Court. Section 1981 prohibits employment discrimination as part of a more general prohibition against discrimination in any form of contracting. It provides that "[a]ll persons within the jurisdiction of the United States shall have the same right in every State and Territory to make and enforce contracts . . . as is enjoyed by white citizens . . . ." Because this statute served as a predecessor to the Fourteenth Amendment, it was thought for over a century to apply, just like that amendment, only to discrimination by government. In Jones v. Alfred H. Mayer Co., 392 U.S. 409 (1968), the Warren Court radically revised this understanding of the statute and extended it to private discrimination. This decision, although controversial at the time, was soon extended to claims of employment discrimination and eventually was accepted by Congress in amendments codifying this interpretation in the Civil Rights Act of 1991.

These developments, in several different areas of employment discrimination law, illustrate how legislative and judicial activity combine to form the law as it continues to evolve to this day. The enactment of the ADEA and the ADA have also played a part in this process, as the courts have been called upon to modify the prohibitions first formulated to address racial discrimination in order to confront these new grounds of discrimination. Congress has often responded to such decisions with its own elaboration of the statute's meaning, in amendments either adopting or, in some cases, rejecting judicial interpretations of the statute. Such exchanges between Congress and the courts, of course, are a far cry from the process of constitutional interpretation, which is dominated by the judiciary. Even if Congress contributes to the meaning and implementation of the Constitution, the Supreme Court always has the last word in deciding issues of constitutionality. In employment discrimination law, with its basis in statutes like Title VII, these institutional roles are reversed. Much of the interest of the subject lies in precisely how Congress has responded to judicial decisions seeking to implement the statutory prohibitions that it has enacted. We begin with two decisions articulating theories of liability, first, for claims of discrimination generally, and second, for claims of sex discrimination in particular.

3. **Bibliography.** The history of employment discrimination law has been thoroughly explored in books and articles devoted to this topic. Hugh Davis Graham, The Civil Rights Era: Origins and Development of National Policy 1960–72 (1990); Charles Whalen & Barbara Whalen, The Longest Debate: A Legislative History of the 1964 Civil Rights Act (1985); David Freeman Engstrom, The Lost Origins of American Fair Employment Law: Regulatory Choice and the Making of Modern Civil Rights, 1943–1972, 63 Stan. L. Rev. 1071 (2011); Daniel B. Rodriguez & Barry R. Weingast, The Positive Political Theory of Legislative History: New Perspectives on the 1964 Civil Rights Act and Its Interpretation, 151 U. Pa. L. Rev. 1417 (2003); George P. Sape & Thomas J. Hart, Title VII Reconsidered: The Equal Employment Opportunity Act of 1972, 40 Geo. Wash. L. Rev. 824 (1972); Francis J. Vaas, Title VII: Legislative History, 7 B.C. Indus. & Com. L. Rev. 431 (1966).

A number of articles re-examined Title VII on the occasion of the fiftieth anniversary of its enactment. In a Nation of Widening Opportunities? The Civil Rights Act at Fifty (Samual Bagenstos & Ellen Katz eds. 2014); Alfred Brophy & Steven L. Nelson, The 50th Anniversary of the Civil Rights Act of 1964 & Voting Rights Act of 1965: An Interdisciplinary Dialogue, 22 Wash. & Lee J. C.R. & Soc. Just. 273 (2016); Symposium, The Civil Rights Act of 1964 at 50: Past, Present, and Future, 95 B.U. L. Rev. 683 (2015); Symposium, The Civil Rights Act at Fifty, 66 Stan. L. Rev. 1195–1421 (2014); Symposium, The Civil Rights Act at Fifty, 10 Stan. J. C.R. & C.L. 159 (2014); Symposium, 50th Anniversary of Title VII, 14 Nev. L.J. 661–830 (2014); The 50th

Anniversary of the Civil Rights Act of 1964: A Written Symposium, 74 La. L. Rev 1039 (2014); Symposium, The Civil Rights Act at 50 Years, 2014 U. Chi. Legal F. 1–753; 2014 Symposium, Revisiting Sex: Gender & Sex Discrimination Fifty Years After the Civil Rights Act, 91 Denv. U. L. Rev. 779 (2014). See also Michael Selmi, The Evolution of Employment Discrimination Law: Changed Doctrine for Changed Social Conditions, 2014 Wis. L. Rev. 937 (2014); Drew S. Days, Childress Lecture and Symposium, 49 St. Louis U. L.J. 981 (2005).

B. THEORIES OF DISCRIMINATION

This first case introduces many of the major issues that dominate the law of employment discrimination: What constitutes intentional discrimination? How can it be proved through the use of statistical evidence? What weight is to be given to the effects of past discrimination that predated the enactment of Title VII? Do the seniority rights of other employees limit an employer's liability for otherwise discriminatory practices? All of these questions arise from the factual background of a pervasive distinction between jobs in the trucking industry at the time: "line driver" jobs that involved routes between major cities and were generally better paid and "city driver" jobs (and related service jobs) that involved routes within cities on a more regular schedule but with lower pay. The line drivers were almost all white, while the city drivers were a representative mix of white and minority drivers. As you read this case, consider how much of this pattern of employment resulted from past discrimination and how much from present discrimination. What difference does that make in the employer's and the union's liability under Title VII?

International Brotherhood of Teamsters v. United States

431 U.S. 324 (1977).

■ MR. JUSTICE STEWART delivered the opinion of the Court.

This litigation brings here several important questions under Title VII of the Civil Rights Act of 1964. The issues grow out of alleged unlawful employment practices engaged in by an employer and a union. The employer is a common carrier of motor freight with nationwide operations, and the union represents a large group of its employees. The District Court and the Court of Appeals held that the employer had violated Title VII by engaging in a pattern and practice of employment discrimination against Negroes and Spanish-surnamed Americans, and that the union had violated the Act by agreeing with the employer to create and maintain a seniority system that perpetuated the effects of past racial and ethnic discrimination. In addition to the basic questions presented by these two rulings, other subsidiary issues must be resolved if violations of Title VII occurred—issues concerning the nature of the relief to which aggrieved individuals may be entitled.

I

The United States brought an action in a Tennessee federal court against the petitioner T.I.M.E.-D.C., Inc. (company), pursuant to § 707(a) of the Civil Rights Act of 1964, 42 U.S.C. § 2000e–6(a). The complaint charged that the company had followed discriminatory hiring, assignment, and promotion policies against Negroes at its terminal in Nashville, Tenn. The Government brought a second action against the company almost three years later in a Federal District Court in Texas, charging a pattern and practice of employment discrimination against Negroes and Spanish-surnamed persons throughout the company's transportation system. The petitioner International Brotherhood of Teamsters (union) was joined as a defendant in that suit. The two actions were consolidated for trial in the Northern District of Texas.

The central claim in both lawsuits was that the company had engaged in a pattern or practice of discriminating against minorities in hiring so-called line drivers. Those Negroes and Spanish-surnamed persons who had been hired, the Government alleged, were given lower paying, less desirable jobs as servicemen or local city drivers, and were thereafter discriminated against with respect to promotions and transfers.[3] In this connection the complaint also challenged the seniority system established by the collective-bargaining agreements between the employer and the union. The Government sought a general injunctive remedy and specific "make whole" relief for all individual discriminatees, which would allow them an opportunity to transfer to line-driver jobs with full company seniority for all purposes.

The cases went to trial and the District Court found that the Government had shown "by a preponderance of the evidence that T.I.M.E.-D.C. and its predecessor companies were engaged in a plan and practice of discrimination in violation of Title VII." The court further found that the seniority system contained in the collective-bargaining contracts between the company and the union violated Title VII because it "[operated] to impede the free transfer of minority groups into and within the company." Both the company and the union were enjoined from committing further violations of Title VII.

The Court of Appeals for the Fifth Circuit agreed with the basic conclusions of the District Court: that the company had engaged in a pattern or practice of employment discrimination and that the seniority

[3] *Line drivers*, also known as over-the-road drivers, engage in long-distance hauling between company terminals. They compose a separate bargaining unit at the company. Other distinct bargaining units include *servicemen*, who service trucks, unhook tractors and trailers, and perform similar tasks; and *city operations*, composed of dockmen, hostlers, and city drivers who pick up and deliver freight within the immediate area of a particular terminal. All of these employees were represented by the petitioner union.

system in the collective bargaining agreements violated Title VII as applied to victims of prior discrimination.

II

In this Court, the company and the union contend that their conduct did not violate Title VII in any respect, asserting first that the evidence introduced at trial was insufficient to show that the company engaged in a "pattern or practice" of employment discrimination. The union further contends that the seniority system contained in the collective-bargaining agreements in no way violated Title VII. If these contentions are correct, it is unnecessary, of course, to reach any of the issues concerning remedies that so occupied the attention of the Court of Appeals.

A

Consideration of the question whether the company engaged in a pattern or practice of discriminatory hiring practices involves controlling legal principles that are relatively clear. The Government's theory of discrimination was simply that the company, in violation of § 703(a) of Title VII, regularly and purposefully treated Negroes and Spanish-surnamed Americans less favorably than white persons. The disparity in treatment allegedly involved the refusal to recruit, hire, transfer, or promote minority group members on an equal basis with white people, particularly with respect to line-driving positions. The ultimate factual issues are thus simply whether there was a pattern or practice of such disparate treatment and, if so, whether the differences were "racially premised."[15] McDonnell Douglas Corp. v. Green, 411 U.S. 792, 805 n.18.

As the plaintiff, the Government bore the initial burden of making out a prima facie case of discrimination. Albemarle Paper Co. v. Moody, 422 U.S. 405, 425; McDonnell Douglas Corp. v. Green, supra, at 802. And, because it alleged a systemwide pattern or practice of resistance to the full enjoyment of Title VII rights, the Government ultimately had to prove more than the mere occurrence of isolated or "accidental" or sporadic discriminatory acts. It had to establish by a preponderance of

---

[15] "Disparate treatment" such as is alleged in the present case is the most easily understood type of discrimination. The employer simply treats some people less favorably than others because of their race, color, religion, sex, or national origin. Proof of discriminatory motive is critical, although it can in some situations be inferred from the mere fact of differences in treatment. See, e.g., Arlington Heights v. Metropolitan Housing Dev. Corp., 429 U.S. 252, 265–66. Undoubtedly disparate treatment was the most obvious evil Congress had in mind when it enacted Title VII. See, e.g., 110 Cong. Rec. 13088 (1964) (remarks of Sen. Humphrey) ("What the bill does . . . is simply to make it an illegal practice to use race as a factor in denying employment. It provides that men and women shall be employed on the basis of their qualifications, not as Catholic citizens, not as Protestant citizens, not as Jewish citizens, not as colored citizens, but as citizens of the United States").

Claims of disparate treatment may be distinguished from claims that stress "disparate impact." The latter involve employment practices that are facially neutral in their treatment of different groups but that in fact fall more harshly on one group than another and cannot be justified by business necessity. Proof of discriminatory motive, we have held, is not required under a disparate-impact theory. Compare, e.g., Griggs v. Duke Power Co., 401 U.S. 424, 430–32, with McDonnell Douglas Corp. v. Green, 411 U.S. 792, 802–06. Either theory may, of course, be applied to a particular set of facts.

the evidence that racial discrimination was the company's standard operating procedure—the regular rather than the unusual practice.[16]

We agree with the District Court and the Court of Appeals that the Government carried its burden of proof. As of March 31, 1971, shortly after the Government filed its complaint alleging systemwide discrimination, the company had 6,472 employees. Of these, 314 (5%) were Negroes and 257 (4%) were Spanish-surnamed Americans. Of the 1,828 line drivers, however, there were only 8 (0.4%) Negroes and 5 (0.3%) Spanish-surnamed persons, and all of the Negroes had been hired after the litigation had commenced. With one exception—a man who worked as a line driver at the Chicago terminal from 1950 to 1959—the company and its predecessors did not employ a Negro on a regular basis as a line driver until 1969. And, as the Government showed, even in 1971 there were terminals in areas of substantial Negro population where all of the company's line drivers were white.[17] A great majority of the Negroes (83%) and Spanish-surnamed Americans (78%) who did work for the company held the lower paying city operations and serviceman jobs, whereas only 39% of the nonminority employees held jobs in those categories.

The Government bolstered its statistical evidence with the testimony of individuals who recounted over 40 specific instances of discrimination. Upon the basis of this testimony the District Court found that "[numerous] qualified black and Spanish-surnamed American applicants who sought line driving jobs at the company over the years, either had their requests ignored, were given false or misleading information about requirements, opportunities, and application procedures, or were not considered and hired on the same basis that whites were considered and hired." Minority employees who wanted to transfer to line-driver jobs met with similar difficulties.[19]

---

[16] The "pattern or practice" language in § 707(a) of Title VII, was not intended as a term of art, and the words reflect only their usual meaning.

[17] In Atlanta, for instance, Negroes composed 22.35% of the population in the surrounding metropolitan area and 51.31% of the population in the city proper. The company's Atlanta terminal employed 57 line drivers. All were white. In Los Angeles, 10.84% of the greater metropolitan population and 17.88% of the city population were Negro. But at the company's two Los Angeles terminals there was not a single Negro among the 374 line drivers. The proof showed similar disparities in San Francisco, Denver, Nashville, Chicago, Dallas, and at several other terminals.

[19] Two examples are illustrative:

George Taylor, a Negro, worked for the company as a city driver in Los Angeles, beginning in late 1966. In 1968, after hearing that a white city driver had transferred to a line-driver job, he told the terminal manager that he also would like to consider line driving. The manager replied that there would be "a lot of problems on the road . . . with different people, Caucasian, et cetera," and stated: "I don't feel that the company is ready for this right now. . . . Give us a little time. It will come around, you know." Mr. Taylor made similar requests some months later and got similar responses. He was never offered a line-driving job or an application.

Feliberto Trujillo worked as a dockman at the company's Denver terminal. When he applied for a line-driver job in 1967, he was told by a personnel officer that he had one strike against him. He asked what that was and was told: "You're a Chicano, and as far as we know, there isn't a Chicano driver in the system."

The company's principal response to this evidence is that statistics can never in and of themselves prove the existence of a pattern or practice of discrimination, or even establish a prima facie case shifting to the employer the burden of rebutting the inference raised by the figures. But, as even our brief summary of the evidence shows, this was not a case in which the Government relied on "statistics alone." The individuals who testified about their personal experiences with the company brought the cold numbers convincingly to life.

In any event, our cases make it unmistakably clear that "[s]tatistical analyses have served and will continue to serve an important role" in cases in which the existence of discrimination is a disputed issue. . . . We have repeatedly approved the use of statistical proof, where it reached proportions comparable to those in this case, to establish a prima facie case of racial discrimination in jury selection cases. . . . Statistics are equally competent in proving employment discrimination.[20] We caution only that statistics are not irrefutable; they come in infinite variety and, like any other kind of evidence, they may be rebutted. In short, their usefulness depends on all of the surrounding facts and circumstances.

In addition to its general protest against the use of statistics in Title VII cases, the company claims that in this case the statistics revealing racial imbalance are misleading because they fail to take into account the company's particular business situation as of the effective date of Title

---

[20] Petitioners argue that statistics, at least those comparing the racial composition of an employer's work force to the composition of the population at large, should never be given decisive weight in a Title VII case because to do so would conflict with § 703(j) of the Act, 42 U.S.C. § 2000e–2(j). That section provides:

> "Nothing contained in this subchapter shall be interpreted to require any employer . . . to grant preferential treatment to any individual or to any group because of the race . . . or national origin of such individual or group on account of an imbalance which may exist with respect to the total number or percentage of persons of any race . . . or national origin employed by any employer . . . in comparison with the total number or percentage of persons of such race . . . or national origin in any community, State, section, or other area, or in the available work force in any community, State, section, or other area."

The argument fails in this case because the statistical evidence was not offered or used to support an erroneous theory that Title VII requires an employer's work force to be racially balanced. Statistics showing racial or ethnic imbalance are probative in a case such as this one only because such imbalance is often a telltale sign of purposeful discrimination; absent explanation, it is ordinarily to be expected that nondiscriminatory hiring practices will in time result in a work force more or less representative of the racial and ethnic composition of the population in the community from which employees are hired. Evidence of long-lasting and gross disparity between the composition of a work force and that of the general population thus may be significant even though § 703(j) makes clear that Title VII imposes no requirement that a work force mirror the general population. See, e.g., United States v. Sheet Metal Workers Local 36, 416 F.2d 123, 127 n.7 (8th Cir.). Considerations such as small sample size may, of course, detract from the value of such evidence, see, e.g., Mayor of Philadelphia v. Educational Equality League, 415 U.S. 605, 620–21, and evidence showing that the figures for the general population might not accurately reflect the pool of qualified job applicants would also be relevant.

> "Since the passage of the Civil Rights Act of 1964, the courts have frequently relied upon statistical evidence to prove a violation. . . . In many cases the only available avenue of proof is the use of racial statistics to uncover clandestine and covert discrimination by the employer or union involved." United States v. Ironworkers Local 86, 443 F.2d at 551.

VII. The company concedes that its line drivers were virtually all white in July 1965, but it claims that thereafter business conditions were such that its work force dropped. Its argument is that low personnel turnover, rather than post-Act discrimination, accounts for more recent statistical disparities. It points to substantial minority hiring in later years, especially after 1971, as showing that any pre-Act patterns of discrimination were broken.

The argument would be a forceful one if this were an employer who, at the time of suit, had done virtually no new hiring since the effective date of Title VII. But it is not. Although the company's total number of employees apparently dropped somewhat during the late 1960's, the record shows that many line drivers continued to be hired throughout this period, and that almost all of them were white. To be sure, there were improvements in the company's hiring practices. The Court of Appeals commented that "T.I.M.E.-D.C.'s recent minority hiring progress stands as a laudable good faith effort to eradicate the effects of past discrimination in the area of hiring and initial assignment." But the District Court and the Court of Appeals found upon substantial evidence that the company had engaged in a course of discrimination that continued well after the effective date of Title VII. The company's later changes in its hiring and promotion policies could be of little comfort to the victims of the earlier post-Act discrimination, and could not erase its previous illegal conduct or its obligation to afford relief to those who suffered because of it. Cf. Albemarle Paper Co. v. Moody, 422 U.S., at 413–23.[23]

The District Court and the Court of Appeals, on the basis of substantial evidence, held that the Government had proved a prima facie case of systematic and purposeful employment discrimination, continuing well beyond the effective date of Title VII. The company's attempts to rebut that conclusion were held to be inadequate.[24] For the

[23] The company's narrower attacks upon the statistical evidence—that there was no precise delineation of the areas referred to in the general population statistics, that the Government did not demonstrate that minority populations were located close to terminals or that transportation was available, that the statistics failed to show what portion of the minority population was suited by age, health, or other qualifications to hold trucking jobs, etc.—are equally lacking in force. At best, these attacks go only to the accuracy of the comparison between the composition of the company's work force at various terminals and the general population of the surrounding communities. They detract little from the Government's further showing that Negroes and Spanish-surnamed Americans who were hired were overwhelmingly excluded from line-driver jobs. Such employees were willing to work, had access to the terminal, were healthy and of working age, and often were at least sufficiently qualified to hold city-driver jobs. Yet they became line drivers with far less frequency than whites. See, e. g., Pretrial Stipulation 14, summarized in 517 F.2d, at 312 n.24 (of 2,919 whites who held driving jobs in 1971, 1,802 (62%) were line drivers and 1,117 (38%) were city drivers; of 180 Negroes and Spanish-surnamed Americans who held driving jobs, 13 (7%) were line drivers and 167 (93%) were city drivers). In any event, fine tuning of the statistics could not have obscured the glaring absence of minority line drivers. As the Court of Appeals remarked, the company's inability to rebut the inference of discrimination came not from a misuse of statistics but from "the inexorable zero."

[24] The company's evidence, apart from the showing of recent changes in hiring and promotion policies, consisted mainly of general statements that it hired only the best qualified

reasons we have summarized, there is no warrant for this Court to disturb the findings of the District Court and the Court of Appeals on this basic issue.

II

. . .

B

The District Court and the Court of Appeals also found that the seniority system contained in the collective-bargaining agreements between the company and the union operated to violate Title VII of the Act.

For purposes of calculating benefits, such as vacations, pensions, and other fringe benefits, an employee's seniority under this system runs from the date he joins the company, and takes into account his total service in all jobs and bargaining units. For competitive purposes, however, such as determining the order in which employees may bid for particular jobs, are laid off, or are recalled from layoff, it is bargaining unit seniority that controls. Thus, a line driver's seniority, for purposes of bidding for particular runs and protection against layoff, takes into account only the length of time he has been a line driver at a particular terminal. The practical effect is that a city driver or serviceman who transfers to a line-driver job must forfeit all the competitive seniority he has accumulated in his previous bargaining unit and start at the bottom of the line drivers' "board."

The vice of this arrangement, as found by the District Court and the Court of Appeals, was that it "locked" minority workers into inferior jobs and perpetuated prior discrimination by discouraging transfers to jobs as line drivers. While the disincentive applied to all workers, including whites, it was Negroes and Spanish-surnamed persons who, those courts found, suffered the most because many of them had been denied the equal opportunity to become line drivers when they were initially hired, whereas whites either had not sought or were refused line-driver positions for reasons unrelated to their race or national origin.

The linchpin of the theory embraced by the District Court and the Court of Appeals was that a discriminatee who must forfeit his competitive seniority in order finally to obtain a line-driver job will never be able to "catch up" to the seniority level of his contemporary who was

---

applicants. But "affirmations of good faith in making individual selections are insufficient to dispel a prima facie case of systematic exclusion." Alexander v. Louisiana, 405 U.S. 625, 632.

The company also attempted to show that all of the witnesses who testified to specific instances of discrimination either were not discriminated against or suffered no injury. The Court of Appeals correctly ruled that the trial judge was not bound to accept this testimony and that it committed no error by relying instead on the other overpowering evidence in the case. The Court of Appeals was also correct in the view that individual proof concerning each class member's specific injury was appropriately left to proceedings to determine individual relief. In a suit brought by the Government under § 707(a) of the Act the District Court's initial concern is in deciding whether the Government has proved that the defendant has engaged in a pattern or practice of discriminatory conduct.

not subject to discrimination.[27] Accordingly, this continued, built-in disadvantage to the prior discriminatee who transfers to a line-driver job was held to constitute a continuing violation of Title VII, for which both the employer and the union who jointly created and maintain the seniority system were liable.

The union, while acknowledging that the seniority system may in some sense perpetuate the effects of prior discrimination, asserts that the system is immunized from a finding of illegality by reason of § 703(h) of Title VII, 42 U.S.C. § 2000e–2(h), which provides in part:

> "Notwithstanding any other provision of this subchapter, it shall not be an unlawful employment practice for an employer to apply different standards of compensation, or different terms, conditions, or privileges of employment pursuant to a bona fide seniority . . . system, . . . provided that such differences are not the result of an intention to discriminate because of race . . . or national origin. . . ."

. . . The issues thus joined are open ones in this Court.[28] We considered § 703(h) in Franks v. Bowman Transportation Co., 424 U.S. 747, but there decided only that § 703(h) does not bar the award of retroactive seniority to job applicants who seek relief from an employer's post-Act hiring discrimination. We stated that "the thrust of [§ 703(h)] is directed toward defining what is and what is not an illegal discriminatory practice in instances in which the post-Act operation of a seniority system is challenged as perpetuating the effects of discrimination occurring prior to the effective date of the Act." 424 U.S., at 761. Beyond noting the general purpose of the statute, however, we did not undertake the task of statutory construction required in this litigation.

(1)

Because the company discriminated both before and after the enactment of Title VII, the seniority system is said to have operated to perpetuate the effects of both pre- and post-Act discrimination. Post-Act

---

[27] An example would be a Negro who was qualified to be a line driver in 1958 but who, because of his race, was assigned instead a job as a city driver, and is allowed to become a line driver only in 1971. Because he loses his competitive seniority when he transfers jobs, he is forever junior to white line drivers hired between 1958 and 1970. The whites, rather than the Negro, will henceforth enjoy the preferable runs and the greater protection against layoff. Although the original discrimination occurred in 1958—before the effective date of Title VII—the seniority system operates to carry the effects of the earlier discrimination into the present.

[28] Concededly, the view that § 703(h) does not immunize seniority systems that perpetuate the effects of prior discrimination has much support. It was apparently first adopted in Quarles v. Philip Morris, Inc., 279 F. Supp. 505 (E.D. Va. 1968). The court there held that "a departmental seniority system *that has its genesis in racial discrimination* is not a *bona fide* seniority system." Id. at 517 (first emphasis added). The *Quarles* view has since enjoyed wholesale adoption in the Courts of Appeals. . . . Insofar as the result in *Quarles* and in the cases that followed it depended upon findings that the seniority systems were themselves "racially discriminatory" or had their "genesis in racial discrimination," 279 F. Supp., at 517, the decisions can be viewed as resting upon the proposition that a seniority system that perpetuates the effects of pre-Act discrimination cannot be bona fide if an intent to discriminate entered into its very adoption.

discriminatees, however, may obtain full "make whole" relief, including retroactive seniority under *Franks v. Bowman*, supra, without attacking the legality of the seniority system as applied to them. *Franks* made clear and the union acknowledges that retroactive seniority may be awarded as relief from an employer's discriminatory hiring and assignment policies even if the seniority system agreement itself makes no provision for such relief. 424 U.S., at 778–79. Here the Government has proved that the company engaged in a post-Act pattern of discriminatory hiring, assignment, transfer, and promotion policies. Any Negro or Spanish-surnamed American injured by those policies may receive all appropriate relief as a direct remedy for this discrimination.[30]

(2)

What remains for review is the judgment that the seniority system unlawfully perpetuated the effects of *pre*-Act discrimination. We must decide, in short, whether § 703(h) validates otherwise bona fide seniority systems that afford no constructive seniority to victims discriminated against prior to the effective date of Title VII, and it is to that issue that we now turn.

The primary purpose of Title VII was "to assure equality of employment opportunities and to eliminate those discriminatory practices and devices which have fostered racially stratified job environments to the disadvantage of minority citizens." McDonnell Douglas Corp. v. Green, 411 U.S., at 800. To achieve this purpose, Congress "proscribe[d] not only overt discrimination but also practices that are fair in form, but discriminatory in operation." Id. at 431. Thus, the Court has repeatedly held that a prima facie Title VII violation may be established by policies or practices that are neutral on their face and in intent but that nonetheless discriminate in effect against a particular group.

One kind of practice "fair in form, but discriminatory in operation" is that which perpetuates the effects of prior discrimination. As the Court held in *Griggs*: "Under the Act, practices, procedures, or tests neutral on their face, and even neutral in terms of intent, cannot be maintained if they operate to 'freeze' the status quo of prior discriminatory employment practices."

Were it not for § 703(h), the seniority system in this case would seem to fall under the *Griggs* rationale. The heart of the system is its allocation

---

[30] The legality of the seniority system insofar as it perpetuates post-Act discrimination nonetheless remains at issue in this case, in light of the injunction entered against the union. Our decision today in United Air Lines, Inc. v. Evans, is largely dispositive of this issue. *Evans* holds that the operation of a seniority system is not unlawful under Title VII even though it perpetuates post-Act discrimination that has not been the subject of a timely charge by the discriminatee. Here, of course, the Government has sued to remedy the post-Act discrimination directly, and there is no claim that any relief would be time barred. But this is simply an additional reason not to hold the seniority system unlawful, since such a holding would in no way enlarge the relief to be awarded. See Franks v. Bowman Transportation Co., 424 U.S. 747, 778–79. Section 703(h) on its face immunizes all bona fide seniority systems, and does not distinguish between the perpetuation of pre- and post-Act discrimination.

of the choicest jobs, the greatest protection against layoffs, and other advantages to those employees who have been line drivers for the longest time. Where, because of the employer's prior intentional discrimination, the line drivers with the longest tenure are without exception white, the advantages of the seniority system flow disproportionately to them and away from Negro and Spanish-surnamed employees who might by now have enjoyed those advantages had not the employer discriminated before the passage of the Act. This disproportionate distribution of advantages does in a very real sense "operate to 'freeze' the status quo of prior discriminatory employment practices." But both the literal terms of § 703(h) and the legislative history of Title VII demonstrate that Congress considered this very effect of many seniority systems and extended a measure of immunity to them. . . .

To be sure, § 703(h) does not immunize all seniority systems. It refers only to "bona fide" systems, and a proviso requires that any differences in treatment not be "the result of an intention to discriminate because of race . . . or national origin. . . ." But our reading of the legislative history compels us to reject the Government's broad argument that no seniority system that tends to perpetuate pre-Act discrimination can be "bona fide." To accept the argument would require us to hold that a seniority system becomes illegal simply because it allows the full exercise of the pre-Act seniority rights of employees of a company that discriminated before Title VII was enacted. It would place an affirmative obligation on the parties to the seniority agreement to subordinate those rights in favor of the claims of pre-Act discriminatees without seniority. The consequence would be a perversion of the congressional purpose. We cannot accept the invitation to disembowel § 703(h) by reading the words "bona fide" as the Government would have us do.[38] Accordingly, we hold that an otherwise neutral, legitimate seniority system does not become unlawful under Title VII simply because it may perpetuate pre-Act discrimination. Congress did not intend to make it illegal for employees with vested seniority rights to continue to exercise those rights, even at the expense of pre-Act discriminatees. . . .

(3)

The seniority system in this litigation is entirely bona fide. It applies equally to all races and ethnic groups. To the extent that it "locks" employees into non-line-driver jobs, it does so for all. The city drivers and servicemen who are discouraged from transferring to line-driver jobs are not all Negroes or Spanish-surnamed Americans; to the contrary, the

[38] For the same reason, we reject the contention that the proviso in § 703(h), which bars differences in treatment resulting from "an intention to discriminate," applies to any application of a seniority system that may perpetuate past discrimination. In this regard the language of the Justice Department memorandum introduced at the legislative hearings is especially pertinent: "It is perfectly clear that when a worker is laid off or denied a chance for promotion because under established seniority rules he is 'low man on the totem pole' he is not being discriminated against because of his race. . . . Any differences in treatment based on established seniority rights would not be based on race and would not be forbidden by the title." 110 Cong. Rec. 7207 (1964).

overwhelming majority are white. The placing of line drivers in a separate bargaining unit from other employees is rational, in accord with the industry practice, and consistent with National Labor Relation Board precedents. It is conceded that the seniority system did not have its genesis in racial discrimination, and that it was negotiated and has been maintained free from any illegal purpose. In these circumstances, the single fact that the system extends no retroactive seniority to pre-Act discriminatees does not make it unlawful.

Because the seniority system was protected by § 703(h), the union's conduct in agreeing to and maintaining the system did not violate Title VII. On remand, the District Court's injunction against the union must be vacated. . . .

■ JUSTICE MARSHALL, with whom JUSTICE BRENNAN joins, concurring in part and dissenting in part.

I agree with the Court that the United States proved that petitioner T.I.M.E.-D.C. was guilty of a pattern or practice of discriminating against blacks and Spanish-surnamed Americans in hiring line drivers. I also agree that incumbent minority-group employees who show that they applied for a line-driving job or that they would have applied but for the company's unlawful acts are presumptively entitled to the full measure of relief set forth in our decision last Term in Franks v. Bowman Transportation Co., 424 U.S. 747 (1976). But I do not agree that Title VII permits petitioners to treat Negro and Spanish-surnamed line drivers differently from other drivers who were hired by the company at the same time simply because the former drivers were prevented by the company from acquiring seniority over the road. I therefore dissent from that aspect of the Court's holding, and from the limitations on the scope of the remedy that follow from it.

As the Court quite properly acknowledges, the seniority provision at issue here clearly would violate Title VII absent § 703(h), which exempts at least some seniority systems from the reach of the Act. Title VII prohibits an employer from "classify[ing] his employees . . . in any way which would deprive or tend to deprive any individual of employment opportunities or otherwise adversely affect his status as an employee because of such individual's race, color, religion, sex or national origin." 42 U.S.C. § 2000e–2(a)(2). "Under the Act, practices, procedures, or tests neutral on their face, and even neutral in terms of intent, cannot be maintained *if they operate to 'freeze' the status quo of prior discriminatory employment practices*." Griggs v. Duke Power Co., 401 U.S. 424, 430 (1971) (emphasis added). Petitioners' seniority system does precisely that: It awards the choicest jobs and other benefits to those possessing a credential—seniority—which, due to past discrimination, blacks and Spanish-surnamed employees were prevented from acquiring. Consequently, "[e]very time a Negro worker hired under the old segregated system bids against a white worker in his job slot, the old racial classification reasserts itself, and the Negro suffers anew for his employer's previous bias." Local 189, United Papermakers & Paperworkers v. United States, 416 F.2d 980, 988 (CA5 1969) (Wisdom, J.), cert. denied, 397 U.S. 919 (1970). . . .

NOTES ON *TEAMSTERS V. UNITED STATES*

1. **Legal Theories of Discrimination.** In footnote 15, the Supreme Court observes that claims of discrimination come in two kinds: claims of "disparate treatment" or intentional discrimination and claims of "disparate impact" or discriminatory effects. *Teamsters* involved a claim of intentional discrimination: the trucking companies and the Teamsters Union took account of race and national origin in excluding African-Americans and Hispanics from positions as line drivers. Claims of intentional discrimination can be further subdivided into individual and class-wide claims. Individual claims are the more common of the two, and as the term implies, are brought on behalf of a single plaintiff or a small group of plaintiffs. Because these claims are so narrowly focused, they do not require the use of statistical evidence and can instead be based entirely on anecdotal evidence concerned with the situation of the individual plaintiffs. Class-wide claims, like those in *Teamsters*, depend upon proof of systematic discrimination against an entire class of employees or applicants for employment.

Teamsters presents particularly stark evidence of class-wide intentional discrimination, "the inexorable zero" of nearly complete absence of African-Americans and Hispanics in positions as line drivers. Without any elaborate statistical analysis, these numbers yield an inference of discrimination: that such an extreme imbalance in the representation of minorities among line drivers, as compared to city drivers, could only be caused by some form of discrimination. The Supreme Court does not frame the inference in quite this way, preferring a comparison of line drivers with general population figures, but again reaching the same conclusion: that the disparity between the number of minorities who were line drivers and the number who lived in the cities where trucking terminals were located yields an inference of discrimination. Which of these comparisons is the more appropriate? Which is easier to establish using publicly available statistics?

Note that the Court itself does not offer a definitive resolution of these questions, observing only that "statistics are not irrefutable; they come in infinite variety and, like any other kind of evidence, they may be rebutted." A more detailed analysis of statistical evidence is taken up in Chapter 3. In *Teamsters* itself, the defendants offered neither their own statistical evidence, showing the absence of any disparity, nor any explanation for the disparity established by the plaintiffs. The defendants also failed to rebut the inference of intentional discrimination in the individual cases presented by the plaintiffs. What choice did that leave the Court in analyzing the evidence available in the record?

The only claim in *Teamsters* was for intentional discrimination, and the statistical evidence was limited to proving that claim. It also could have been used, however, to establish a claim of disparate impact or discriminatory effects. Chapter 3 also will consider such claims in greater detail. For the present, it is worth reflecting on whether such claims are easier, or harder, for a plaintiff to establish than claims of intentional discrimination. When will an inference of disparate impact be available when an inference of disparate treatment is not? Does the answer depend upon the quality of the statistical evidence presented by the plaintiff—whether it meets standards similar to those required for social science research—or simply on the magnitude of the disparity revealed by the data?

2. **Affirmative Action.** The use of statistical evidence to prove discrimination also raises issues of affirmative action. The defendants in *Teamsters* argued that any such use of statistical evidence amounted to an attempt to impose affirmative action upon employers, contrary to the terms of § 703(j), in which Congress disclaimed any intent to require affirmative action in Title VII. This provision, quoted in footnote 20 in *Teamsters*, was meant to defuse criticism of the statute on the ground that it would, in effect, require employers to adopt racial quotas in order to avoid liability for discrimination. In response to the defendants' objection based on this provision, the Court defended the relevance of statistical evidence with this observation: "[A]bsent explanation, it is ordinarily to be expected that nondiscriminatory hiring practices will in time result in a work force more or less representative of the racial and ethnic composition of the population in the community from which employees are hired." Does this response fairly meet the substance of the defendants' objection? Or does it embrace proportional representation as a long-term goal of Title VII? Alternatively, does it express anything more than a pious hope that enforcement of Title VII eventually will result in a more equal distribution of jobs? Or does the Court take back all of these implications with the initial qualifying phrase, "absent explanation"?

3. **Seniority.** In stark contrast to the findings of discrimination in hiring and promotions, the Supreme Court found no discrimination in the seniority system. Its reason for doing so rests squarely on a provision in Title VII protecting seniority systems and the accompanying expectations of incumbent employees to exercise their seniority rights. This provision is found, along with several other qualifications to Title VII's general prohibition against discrimination, in § 703(h). The Court's holding preserved the seniority system even though it operated "to 'freeze' the status quo of prior discriminatory employment practices." Consequently, as Justice Marshall emphasized in his dissent on this issue, an entire generation of minority employees were frozen into positions as line drivers that placed them lower on the seniority ladder than whites who benefited from discrimination before the effective date of Title VII. Does this result make sense?

The black and Hispanic truck drivers who were denied positions as line drivers before the effective date of Title VII had no claim of discrimination that could be remedied under the statute. Only if they were victims of discrimination after the effective date of Title VII could they claim that they were denied their statutory rights. This conclusion may be regrettable, but it follows directly from what Title VII accomplished: it made previously legitimate forms of private discrimination illegal. Only illegal discrimination, after the effective date of the statute, could support a remedy for victims of discrimination.

What is less obvious is the scope of the remedies available to victims of such illegal discrimination. Virtually all the blacks and Hispanics who eventually became line drivers did so as a result of the decision in *Teamsters*. Their seniority, as the Supreme Court held in another part of its opinion discussed in Chapter 8, began to accrue only from the date that they suffered illegal discrimination. This date necessarily came after the effective date of Title VII itself, leaving them perpetually lower on the seniority ladder than whites who had been hired before the statute took effect. It is this consequence of the decision that Justice Marshall objects to: favoring whites who were the beneficiaries of past discrimination over blacks who were the victims not just of permissible discrimination before the effective date of Title VII, but of illegal discrimination thereafter.

Is the compromise, limiting the remedies available to victims of illegal discrimination, at all justifiable? Or is it simply a necessary consequence of the transition from a regime in which discrimination was tolerated or encouraged to one in which it is explicitly prohibited? National labor organizations, such as the A.F.L.-C.I.O., supported the passage of Title VII, but they did so with the interests of their members in mind. The protection of seniority systems in § 703(h) was entirely consistent with their position. See Hugh Davis Graham, The Civil Rights Era: Origins and Development of National Policy 1960–1972 139–41, 147, 150–52 (1990). As Senator Clark, one of the prominent supporters of Title VII, emphasized in the debate on this issue, "both organized labor and business want Title VII," and "it is clear that [Title VII] would not affect seniority at all." 110 Cong. Rec. 7205 (1964). Does this position represent a compromise between the interests of labor unions and those of minority groups? Or is it a straightforward application of the principle of nondiscrimination as colorblindness? If it is a compromise, does it strike the correct balance between the interests of incumbent employees and those of victims of discrimination? Does the acceptability and effectiveness of laws against discrimination depend as much on the reaction of other employees as it does on litigation by the victims of discrimination themselves? For an early and influential statement of the case for compromise on the issue of seniority, see Harry T. Edwards, Race Discrimination in Employment: What Price Equality?, 1976 U. Ill. L.F. 572.

Price Waterhouse v. Hopkins

490 U.S. 228 (1989).

■ JUSTICE BRENNAN announced the judgment of the Court and delivered an opinion, in which JUSTICE MARSHALL, JUSTICE BLACKMUN, and JUSTICE STEVENS join.

Ann Hopkins was a senior manager in an office of Price Waterhouse when she was proposed for partnership in 1982. She was neither offered nor denied admission to the partnership; instead, her candidacy was held for reconsideration the following year. When the partners in her office later refused to repropose her for partnership, she sued Price Waterhouse under Title VII of the Civil Rights Act of 1964, charging that the firm had discriminated against her on the basis of sex in its decisions regarding partnership. Judge Gesell in the Federal District Court for the District of Columbia ruled in her favor on the question of liability and the Court of Appeals for the District of Columbia Circuit affirmed. We granted certiorari to resolve a conflict among the Courts of Appeals concerning the respective burdens of proof of a defendant and plaintiff in a suit under Title VII when it has been shown that an employment decision resulted from a mixture of legitimate and illegitimate motives.

I

At Price Waterhouse, a nationwide professional accounting partnership, a senior manager becomes a candidate for partnership when the partners in her local office submit her name as a candidate. All of the other partners in the firm are then invited to submit written comments on each candidate—either on a "long" or a "short" form, depending on the partner's degree of exposure to the candidate. Not every partner in the firm submits comments on every candidate. After reviewing the comments and interviewing the partners who submitted them, the firm's Admissions Committee makes a recommendation to the Policy Board. This recommendation will be either that the firm accept the candidate for partnership, put her application on "hold," or deny her the promotion outright. The Policy Board then decides whether to submit the candidate's name to the entire partnership for a vote, to "hold" her candidacy, or to reject her. The recommendation of the Admissions Committee, and the decision of the Policy Board, are not controlled by fixed guidelines: a certain number of positive comments from partners will not guarantee a candidate's admission to the partnership, nor will a specific quantity of negative comments necessarily defeat her application. Price Waterhouse places no limit on the number of persons whom it will admit to the partnership in any given year.

Ann Hopkins had worked at Price Waterhouse's Office of Government Services in Washington, D.C., for five years when the partners in that office proposed her as a candidate for partnership. Of the 662 partners at the firm at that time, 7 were women. Of the 88 persons proposed for partnership that year, only 1—Hopkins—was a woman. Forty-seven of these candidates were admitted to the partnership, 21 were rejected, and 20—including Hopkins—were "held" for reconsideration the following year. Thirteen of the 32 partners who had submitted comments on Hopkins supported her bid for partnership. Three partners recommended that her candidacy be placed on hold, eight stated that they did not have an informed opinion about her, and eight recommended that she be denied partnership.

In a jointly prepared statement supporting her candidacy, the partners in Hopkins' office showcased her successful 2-year effort to secure a $25 million contract with the Department of State, labeling it "an outstanding performance" and one that Hopkins carried out "virtually at the partner level." Despite Price Waterhouse's attempt at trial to minimize her contribution to this project, Judge Gesell specifically found that Hopkins had "played a key role in Price Waterhouse's successful effort to win a multi-million dollar contract with the Department of State." Indeed, he went on, "[n]one of the other partnership candidates at Price Waterhouse that year had a comparable record in terms of successfully securing major contracts for the partnership."

The partners in Hopkins' office praised her character as well as her accomplishments, describing her in their joint statement as "an outstanding professional" who had a "deft touch," a "strong character, independence and integrity." Clients appear to have agreed with these assessments. At trial, one official from the State Department described her as "extremely competent, intelligent," "strong and forthright, very productive, energetic and creative." Another high-ranking official praised Hopkins' decisiveness, broadmindedness, and "intellectual clarity"; she was, in his words, "a stimulating conversationalist." Evaluations such as these led Judge Gesell to conclude that Hopkins "had no difficulty dealing with clients and her clients appear to have been very pleased with her work" and that she "was generally viewed as a highly competent project leader who worked long hours, pushed vigorously to meet deadlines and demanded much from the multidisciplinary staffs with which she worked."

On too many occasions, however, Hopkins' aggressiveness apparently spilled over into abrasiveness. Staff members seem to have borne the brunt of Hopkins' brusqueness. Long before her bid for partnership, partners evaluating her work had counseled her to improve her relations with staff members. Although later evaluations indicate an improvement, Hopkins' perceived shortcomings in this important area eventually doomed her bid for partnership. Virtually all of the partners' negative remarks about Hopkins—even those of partners supporting her—had to do with her "interpersonal skills." Both "[s]upporters and opponents of her candidacy," stressed Judge Gesell, "indicated that she was sometimes overly aggressive, unduly harsh, difficult to work with and impatient with staff."

There were clear signs, though, that some of the partners reacted negatively to Hopkins' personality because she was a woman. One partner described her as "macho"; another suggested that she "overcompensated for being a woman"; a third advised her to take "a course at charm school." Several partners criticized her use of profanity; in response, one partner suggested that those partners objected to her swearing only "because it's a lady using foul language." Another supporter explained that Hopkins "ha[d] matured from a tough-talking somewhat masculine hard-nosed mgr to an authoritative, formidable, but much more appealing lady ptr candidate." But it was the man who, as

Judge Gesell found, bore responsibility for explaining to Hopkins the reasons for the Policy Board's decision to place her candidacy on hold who delivered the coup de grace: in order to improve her chances for partnership, Thomas Beyer advised, Hopkins should "walk more femininely, talk more femininely, dress more femininely, wear make-up, have her hair styled, and wear jewelry."

Dr. Susan Fiske, a social psychologist and Associate Professor of Psychology at Carnegie-Mellon University, testified at trial that the partnership selection process at Price Waterhouse was likely influenced by sex stereotyping. Her testimony focused not only on the overtly sex-based comments of partners but also on gender-neutral remarks, made by partners who knew Hopkins only slightly, that were intensely critical of her. One partner, for example, baldly stated that Hopkins was "universally disliked" by staff, and another described her as "consistently annoying and irritating"; yet these were people who had had very little contact with Hopkins. According to Fiske, Hopkins' uniqueness (as the only woman in the pool of candidates) and the subjectivity of the evaluations made it likely that sharply critical remarks such as these were the product of sex stereotyping—although Fiske admitted that she could not say with certainty whether any particular comment was the result of stereotyping. Fiske based her opinion on a review of the submitted comments, explaining that it was commonly accepted practice for social psychologists to reach this kind of conclusion without having met any of the people involved in the decisionmaking process.

In previous years, other female candidates for partnership also had been evaluated in sex-based terms. As a general matter, Judge Gesell concluded, "[c]andidates were viewed favorably if partners believed they maintained their femin[in]ity while becoming effective professional managers"; in this environment, "[t]o be identified as a 'women's lib[b]er' was regarded as [a] negative comment." In fact, the judge found that in previous years "[o]ne partner repeatedly commented that he could not consider any woman seriously as a partnership candidate and believed that women were not even capable of functioning as senior managers—yet the firm took no action to discourage his comments and recorded his vote in the overall summary of the evaluations."

Judge Gesell found that Price Waterhouse legitimately emphasized interpersonal skills in its partnership decisions, and also found that the firm had not fabricated its complaints about Hopkins' interpersonal skills as a pretext for discrimination. Moreover, he concluded, the firm did not give decisive emphasis to such traits only because Hopkins was a woman; although there were male candidates who lacked these skills but who were admitted to partnership, the judge found that these candidates possessed other, positive traits that Hopkins lacked. The judge went on to decide, however, that some of the partners' remarks about Hopkins stemmed from an impermissibly cabined view of the proper behavior of women, and that Price Waterhouse had done nothing to disavow reliance on such comments. He held that Price Waterhouse had unlawfully discriminated against Hopkins on the basis of sex by consciously giving credence and effect to partners' comments that resulted from sex stereotyping. Noting that Price Waterhouse could avoid equitable relief by proving by clear and convincing evidence that it would have placed Hopkins' candidacy on hold even absent this discrimination, the judge decided that the firm had not carried this heavy burden.

The Court of Appeals affirmed the District Court's ultimate conclusion, but departed from its analysis in one particular: it held that even if a plaintiff proves that discrimination played a role in an employment decision, the defendant will not be found liable if it proves, by clear and convincing evidence, that it would have made the same decision in the absence of discrimination. Under this approach, an employer is not deemed to have violated Title VII if it proves that it would have made the same decision in the absence of an impermissible motive, whereas under the District Court's approach, the employer's proof in that respect only avoids equitable relief. We decide today that the Court of Appeals had the better approach, but that both courts erred in requiring the employer to make its proof by clear and convincing evidence.

II

The specification of the standard of causation under Title VII is a decision about the kind of conduct that violates that statute. According to Price Waterhouse, an employer violates Title VII only if it gives decisive consideration to an employee's gender, race, national origin, or religion in making a decision that affects that employee. On Price Waterhouse's theory, even if a plaintiff shows that her gender played a part in an employment decision, it is still her burden to show that the decision would have been different if the employer had not discriminated. In Hopkins' view, on the other hand, an employer violates the statute whenever it allows one of these attributes to play any part in an employment decision. Once a plaintiff shows that this occurred, according to Hopkins, the employer's proof that it would have made the same decision in the absence of discrimination can serve to limit equitable relief but not to avoid a finding of liability. . . .

A

In passing Title VII, Congress made the simple but momentous announcement that sex, race, religion, and national origin are not relevant to the selection, evaluation, or compensation of employees.[32] Yet, the statute does not purport to limit the other qualities and characteristics that employers may take into account in making employment decisions. The converse, therefore, of "for cause" legislation, Title VII eliminates certain bases for distinguishing among employees while otherwise preserving employers' freedom of choice. This balance

[32] We disregard, for purposes of this discussion, the special context of affirmative action.

between employee rights and employer prerogatives turns out to be decisive in the case before us.

Congress' intent to forbid employers to take gender into account in making employment decisions appears on the face of the statute. In now-familiar language, the statute forbids an employer to "fail or refuse to hire or to discharge any individual, or otherwise to discriminate with respect to his compensation, terms, conditions, or privileges of employment," or to "limit, segregate, or classify his employees or applicants for employment in any way which would deprive or tend to deprive any individual of employment opportunities or otherwise adversely affect his status as an employee, *because of* such individual's . . . sex." 42 U.S.C. §§ 2000e–2(a)(1), (2) (emphasis added). We take these words to mean that gender must be irrelevant to employment decisions. . . .

We need not leave our common sense at the doorstep when we interpret a statute. It is difficult for us to imagine that, in the simple words "because of," Congress meant to obligate a plaintiff to identify the precise causal role played by legitimate and illegitimate motivations in the employment decision she challenges. We conclude, instead, that Congress meant to obligate her to prove that the employer relied upon sex-based considerations in coming to its decision.

Our interpretation of the words "because of" also is supported by the fact that Title VII does identify one circumstance in which an employer may take gender into account in making an employment decision, namely, when gender is a "bona fide occupational qualification (BFOQ) reasonably necessary to the normal operation of th[e] particular business or enterprise." 42 U.S.C. § 2000e–2(e). The only plausible inference to draw from this provision is that, in all other circumstances, a person's gender may not be considered in making decisions that affect her. Indeed, Title VII even forbids employers to make gender an indirect stumbling block to employment opportunities. An employer may not, we have held, condition employment opportunities on the satisfaction of facially neutral tests or qualifications that have a disproportionate, adverse impact on members of protected groups when those tests or qualifications are not required for performance of the job. See Watson v. Fort Worth Bank & Trust, 487 U.S. 977 (1988); Griggs v. Duke Power Co., 401 U.S. 424 (1971).

To say that an employer may not take gender into account is not, however, the end of the matter, for that describes only one aspect of Title VII. The other important aspect of the statute is its preservation of an employer's remaining freedom of choice. We conclude that the preservation of this freedom means that an employer shall not be liable if it can prove that, even if it had not taken gender into account, it would have come to the same decision regarding a particular person. The statute's maintenance of employer prerogatives is evident from the statute itself and from its history, both in Congress and in this Court.

To begin with, the existence of the BFOQ exception shows Congress' unwillingness to require employers to change the very nature of their operations in response to the statute. And our emphasis on "business necessity" in disparate-impact cases, see *Watson* and *Griggs*, and on "legitimate, nondiscriminatory reason[s]" in disparate-treatment cases, see McDonnell Douglas Corp. v. Green, 411 U.S. 792, 802 (1973); Texas Dept. of Community Affairs v. Burdine, 450 U.S. 248 (1981), results from our awareness of Title VII's balance between employee rights and employer prerogatives. In *McDonnell Douglas*, we described as follows Title VII's goal to eradicate discrimination while preserving workplace efficiency: "The broad, overriding interest, shared by employer, employee, and consumer, is efficient and trustworthy workmanship assured through fair and racially neutral employment and personnel decisions. In the implementation of such decisions, it is abundantly clear that Title VII tolerates no racial discrimination, subtle or otherwise." 411 U.S., at 801.

When an employer ignored the attributes enumerated in the statute, Congress hoped, it naturally would focus on the qualifications of the applicant or employee. The intent to drive employers to focus on qualifications rather than on race, religion, sex, or national origin is the theme of a good deal of the statute's legislative history. An interpretive memorandum entered into the Congressional Record by Senators Case and Clark, comanagers of the bill in the Senate, is representative of this general theme. According to their memorandum, Title VII " 'expressly protects the employer's right to insist that any prospective applicant, Negro or white, must meet the applicable job qualifications. Indeed, the very purpose of Title VII is to promote hiring on the basis of job qualifications, rather than on the basis of race or color.' "[9] 110 Cong. Rec. 7247 (1964), quoted in Griggs v. Duke Power Co., supra, 401 U.S., at 434. The memorandum went on: "To discriminate is to make a distinction, to make a difference in treatment or favor, and those distinctions or differences in treatment or favor which are prohibited by § 704 are those which are based on any five of the forbidden criteria: race, color, religion, sex, and national origin. Any other criterion or qualification for employment is not affected by this title." 110 Cong. Rec. 7213 (1964).

---

[9] Many of the legislators' statements, such as the memorandum quoted in text, focused specifically on race rather than on gender or religion or national origin. We do not, however, limit their statements to the context of race, but instead we take them as general statements on the meaning of Title VII. The somewhat bizarre path by which "sex" came to be included as a forbidden criterion for employment—it was included in an attempt to defeat the bill, see C. & B. Whalen, The Longest Debate: A Legislative History of the 1964 Civil Rights Act 115–17 (1985)—does not persuade us that the legislators' statements pertaining to race are irrelevant to cases alleging gender discrimination. The amendment that added "sex" as one of the forbidden criteria for employment was passed, of course, and the statute on its face treats each of the enumerated categories exactly the same.

By the same token, our specific references to gender throughout this opinion, and the principles we announce, apply with equal force to discrimination based on race, religion, or national origin.

Many other legislators made statements to a similar effect; we see no need to set out each remark in full here. The central point is this: while an employer may not take gender into account in making an employment decision (except in those very narrow circumstances in which gender is a BFOQ), it is free to decide against a woman for other reasons. We think these principles require that, once a plaintiff in a Title VII case shows that gender played a motivating part in an employment decision, the defendant may avoid a finding of liability only by proving that it would have made the same decision even if it had not allowed gender to play such a role. This balance of burdens is the direct result of Title VII's balance of rights. . . .

C

In saying that gender played a motivating part in an employment decision, we mean that, if we asked the employer at the moment of the decision what its reasons were and if we received a truthful response, one of those reasons would be that the applicant or employee was a woman. In the specific context of sex stereotyping, an employer who acts on the basis of a belief that a woman cannot be aggressive, or that she must not be, has acted on the basis of gender.

Although the parties do not overtly dispute this last proposition, the placement by Price Waterhouse of "sex stereotyping" in quotation marks throughout its brief seems to us an insinuation either that such stereotyping was not present in this case or that it lacks legal relevance. We reject both possibilities. As to the existence of sex stereotyping in this case, we are not inclined to quarrel with the District Court's conclusion that a number of the partners' comments showed sex stereotyping at work. As for the legal relevance of sex stereotyping, we are beyond the day when an employer could evaluate employees by assuming or insisting that they matched the stereotype associated with their group, for " '[i]n forbidding employers to discriminate against individuals because of their sex, Congress intended to strike at the entire spectrum of disparate treatment of men and women resulting from sex stereotypes.' " Los Angeles Dept. of Water and Power v. Manhart, 435 U.S. 702, 707, n. 13 (1978), quoting Sprogis v. United Air Lines, Inc., 444 F.2d 1194, 1198 (7th Cir. 1971). An employer who objects to aggressiveness in women but whose positions require this trait places women in an intolerable and impermissible catch 22: out of a job if they behave aggressively and out of a job if they do not. Title VII lifts women out of this bind.

Remarks at work that are based on sex stereotypes do not inevitably prove that gender played a part in a particular employment decision. The plaintiff must show that the employer actually relied on her gender in making its decision. In making this showing, stereotyped remarks can certainly be evidence that gender played a part. In any event, the stereotyping in this case did not simply consist of stray remarks. On the contrary, Hopkins proved that Price Waterhouse invited partners to submit comments; that some of the comments stemmed from sex stereotypes; that an important part of the Policy Board's decision on Hopkins was an assessment of the submitted comments; and that Price Waterhouse in no way disclaimed reliance on the sex-linked evaluations. This is not, as Price Waterhouse suggests, "discrimination in the air"; rather, it is, as Hopkins puts it, "discrimination brought to ground and visited upon" an employee. By focusing on Hopkins' specific proof, however, we do not suggest a limitation on the possible ways of proving that stereotyping played a motivating role in an employment decision, and we refrain from deciding here which specific facts, "standing alone," would or would not establish a plaintiff's case, since such a decision is unnecessary in this case. . . .

IV

The District Court found that sex stereotyping "was permitted to play a part" in the evaluation of Hopkins as a candidate for partnership. Price Waterhouse disputes both that stereotyping occurred and that it played any part in the decision to place Hopkins' candidacy on hold. In the firm's view, in other words, the District Court's factual conclusions are clearly erroneous. We do not agree.

In finding that some of the partners' comments reflected sex stereotyping, the District Court relied in part on Dr. Fiske's expert testimony. Without directly impugning Dr. Fiske's credentials or qualifications, Price Waterhouse insinuates that a social psychologist is unable to identify sex stereotyping in evaluations without investigating whether those evaluations have a basis in reality. This argument comes too late. At trial, counsel for Price Waterhouse twice assured the court that he did not question Dr. Fiske's expertise and failed to challenge the legitimacy of her discipline. Without contradiction from Price Waterhouse, Fiske testified that she discerned sex stereotyping in the partners' evaluations of Hopkins and she further explained that it was part of her business to identify stereotyping in written documents. We are not inclined to accept petitioner's belated and unsubstantiated characterization of Dr. Fiske's testimony as "gossamer evidence" based only on "intuitive hunches" and of her detection of sex stereotyping as "intuitively divined." Nor are we disposed to adopt the dissent's dismissive attitude toward Dr. Fiske's field of study and toward her own professional integrity.

Indeed, we are tempted to say that Dr. Fiske's expert testimony was merely icing on Hopkins' cake. It takes no special training to discern sex stereotyping in a description of an aggressive female employee as requiring "a course at charm school." Nor, turning to Thomas Beyer's memorable advice to Hopkins, does it require expertise in psychology to know that, if an employee's flawed "interpersonal skills" can be corrected by a soft-hued suit or a new shade of lipstick, perhaps it is the employee's sex and not her interpersonal skills that has drawn the criticism.

Price Waterhouse also charges that Hopkins produced no evidence that sex stereotyping played a role in the decision to place her candidacy on hold. As we have stressed, however, Hopkins showed that the partnership solicited evaluations from all of the firm's partners; that it generally relied very heavily on such evaluations in making its decision; that some of the partners' comments were the product of stereotyping; and that the firm in no way disclaimed reliance on those particular comments, either in Hopkins' case or in the past. Certainly a plausible—and, one might say, inevitable—conclusion to draw from this set of circumstances is that the Policy Board in making its decision did in fact take into account all of the partners' comments, including the comments that were motivated by stereotypical notions about women's proper deportment.

Price Waterhouse concedes that the proof in NLRB v. Transportation Management Corp., 462 U.S. 393 (1983), adequately showed that the employer there had relied on an impermissible motivation in firing the plaintiff. But the only evidence in that case that a discriminatory motive contributed to the plaintiff's discharge was that the employer harbored a grudge toward the plaintiff on account of his union activity; there was, contrary to Price Waterhouse's suggestion, no direct evidence that that grudge had played a role in the decision, and, in fact, the employer had given other reasons in explaining the plaintiff's discharge. See 462 U.S., at 396. If the partnership considers that proof sufficient, we do not know why it takes such vehement issue with Hopkins' proof.

Nor is the finding that sex stereotyping played a part in the Policy Board's decision undermined by the fact that many of the suspect comments were made by supporters rather than detractors of Hopkins. A negative comment, even when made in the context of a generally favorable review, nevertheless may influence the decisionmaker to think less highly of the candidate; the Policy Board, in fact, did not simply tally the "yeses" and "noes" regarding a candidate, but carefully reviewed the content of the submitted comments. The additional suggestion that the comments were made by "persons outside the decisionmaking chain"—and therefore could not have harmed Hopkins—simply ignores the critical role that partners' comments played in the Policy Board's partnership decisions.

Price Waterhouse appears to think that we cannot affirm the factual findings of the trial court without deciding that, instead of being overbearing and aggressive and curt, Hopkins is, in fact, kind and considerate and patient. If this is indeed its impression, petitioner misunderstands the theory on which Hopkins prevailed. The District Judge acknowledged that Hopkins' conduct justified complaints about her behavior as a senior manager. But he also concluded that the reactions of at least some of the partners were reactions to her as a woman manager. Where an evaluation is based on a subjective assessment of a person's strengths and weaknesses, it is simply not true that each evaluator will focus on, or even mention, the same weaknesses. Thus, even if we knew that Hopkins had "personality problems," this would not tell us that the partners who cast their evaluations of Hopkins in sex-based terms would have criticized her as sharply (or criticized her at all) if she had been a man. It is not our job to review the evidence and decide that the negative reactions to Hopkins were based on reality; our perception of Hopkins' character is irrelevant. We sit not to determine whether Ms. Hopkins is nice, but to decide whether the partners reacted negatively to her personality because she is a woman.

V

We hold that when a plaintiff in a Title VII case proves that her gender played a motivating part in an employment decision, the defendant may avoid a finding of liability only by proving by a preponderance of the evidence that it would have made the same decision even if it had not taken the plaintiff's gender into account. Because the courts below erred by deciding that the defendant must make this proof by clear and convincing evidence, we reverse the Court of Appeals' judgment against Price Waterhouse on liability and remand the case to that court for further proceedings.

It is so ordered.

■ JUSTICE WHITE, concurring in the judgment.

. . . [A]s Justice O'Connor states, her burden was to show that the unlawful motive was a substantial factor in the adverse employment action. The District Court, as its opinion was construed by the Court of Appeals, so found, and I agree that the finding was supported by the record. The burden of persuasion then should have shifted to Price Waterhouse to prove "by a preponderance of the evidence that it would have reached the same decision . . . in the absence of" the unlawful motive. Mt. Healthy, supra, 429 U.S., at 287. . . . This would even more plainly be the case where the employer denies any illegitimate motive in the first place but the court finds that illegitimate, as well as legitimate, factors motivated the adverse action.*

■ JUSTICE O'CONNOR, concurring in the judgment.

I agree with the plurality that, on the facts presented in this case, the burden of persuasion should shift to the employer to demonstrate by a preponderance of the evidence that it would have reached the same decision concerning Ann Hopkins' candidacy absent consideration of her gender. I further agree that this burden shift is properly part of the liability phase of the litigation. I thus concur in the judgment of the Court. . . .

■ JUSTICE KENNEDY, with whom the CHIEF JUSTICE and JUSTICE SCALIA join, dissenting.

[In the first two parts of his opinion, Justice Kennedy argues that Title VII must be interpreted so that "there is no violation of the statute

* I agree with the plurality that if the employer carries this burden, there has been no violation of Title VII.

absent but-for causation" and that the burden of proof on this issue is entirely on the plaintiff. In the remainder of his opinion, he then applies this standard of liability to the facts of this case.]

III

The ultimate question in every individual disparate-treatment case is whether discrimination caused the particular decision at issue. Some of the plurality's comments with respect to the District Court's findings in this case, however, are potentially misleading. As the plurality notes, the District Court based its liability determination on expert evidence that some evaluations of respondent Hopkins were based on unconscious sex stereotypes,[5] and on the fact that Price Waterhouse failed to disclaim reliance on these comments when it conducted the partnership review. The District Court also based liability on Price Waterhouse's failure to "make partners sensitive to the dangers [of stereotyping], to discourage comments tainted by sexism, or to investigate comments to determine whether they were influenced by stereotypes."

Although the District Court's version of Title VII liability is improper under any of today's opinions, I think it important to stress that Title VII creates no independent cause of action for sex stereotyping. Evidence of use by decisionmakers of sex stereotypes is, of course, quite relevant to the question of discriminatory intent. The ultimate question, however, is whether discrimination caused the plaintiff's harm. Our cases do not support the suggestion that failure to "disclaim reliance" on stereotypical comments itself violates Title VII. Neither do they support creation of a "duty to sensitize." As the dissenting judge in the Court of Appeals observed, acceptance of such theories would turn Title VII "from a prohibition of discriminatory conduct into an engine for rooting out sexist thoughts." 825 F.2d 458, 477 (1987) (Williams, J., dissenting).

Employment discrimination claims require factfinders to make difficult and sensitive decisions. Sometimes this may mean that no finding of discrimination is justified even though a qualified employee is passed over by a less than admirable employer. In other cases, Title VII's protections properly extend to plaintiffs who are by no means model employees. As Justice BRENNAN notes, courts do not sit to determine whether litigants are nice. In this case, Hopkins plainly presented a strong case both of her own professional qualifications and of the

[5] The plaintiff who engages the services of Dr. Susan Fiske should have no trouble showing that sex discrimination played a part in any decision. Price Waterhouse chose not to object to Fiske's testimony, and at this late stage we are constrained to accept it, but I think the plurality's enthusiasm for Fiske's conclusions unwarranted. Fiske purported to discern stereotyping in comments that were gender neutral—e.g., "overbearing and abrasive"—without any knowledge of the comments' basis in reality and without having met the speaker or subject. "To an expert of Dr. Fiske's qualifications, it seems plain that no woman could be overbearing, arrogant, or abrasive: any observations to that effect would necessarily be discounted as the product of stereotyping. If analysis like this is to prevail in federal courts, no employer can base any adverse action as to a woman on such attributes." 825 F.2d 458, 477 (1987) (Williams, J., dissenting). Today's opinions cannot be read as requiring factfinders to credit testimony based on this type of analysis.

presence of discrimination in Price Waterhouse's partnership process. Had the District Court found on this record that sex discrimination caused the adverse decision, I doubt it would have been reversible error. Cf. Aikens, supra, 460 U.S., at 714, n. 2. That decision was for the finder of fact, however, and the District Court made plain that sex discrimination was not a but-for cause of the decision to place Hopkins' partnership candidacy on hold. Attempts to evade tough decisions by erecting novel theories of liability or multitiered systems of shifting burdens are misguided.

IV

The language of Title VII and our well-considered precedents require this plaintiff to establish that the decision to place her candidacy on hold was made "because of" sex. Here the District Court found that the "comments of the individual partners and the expert evidence of Dr. Fiske do not prove an intentional discriminatory motive or purpose," and that "[b]ecause plaintiff has considerable problems dealing with staff and peers, the Court cannot say that she would have been elected to partnership if the Policy Board's decision had not been tainted by sexually based evaluations." Hopkins thus failed to meet the requisite standard of proof after a full trial. I would remand the case for entry of judgment in favor of Price Waterhouse. . . .

NOTES ON *PRICE WATERHOUSE V. HOPKINS*

1. **Mixed-Motive Cases.** The decision in *Price Waterhouse* mainly concerned the standard of proof in mixed-motive cases: those in which the evidence establishes that the employer relied both on a discriminatory reason and on a legitimate reason for taking action adverse to the plaintiff. This aspect of the decision is discussed in greater detail in Chapter 2, where it is placed in the context of earlier decisions on standards of proof under Title VII and later decisions and statutory amendments that altered the standards set forth in the plurality and concurring opinions. All of the opinions in *Price Waterhouse*, including the dissenting opinion, agreed that some of the partners who refused to promote Hopkins engaged in sex discrimination. The only dispute was over whether their discrimination caused her to be denied the promotion. The comments that follow address this preliminary question. In what sense did these partners engage in sex discrimination?

2. **Sex-Based Stereotypes.** Theories of sex discrimination, both legal and economic, generally follow theories of race discrimination. The legal prohibitions against sex discrimination are modeled on those for race discrimination, and the economic consequences of discrimination, limiting the jobs available to women and the amount that they are paid, resemble the disadvantages suffered by racial minorities. Even so, differences in emphasis and application inevitably arise. Cases such as *Teamsters* tend to submerge the differences between different forms of discrimination because race and national origin discrimination, which were both at issue in that case, receive such similar treatment, both in the legal system and in society at large. Yet,

as Chapter 6 discusses, discrimination on the basis of national origin raises its own distinctive problems. The model of race, in other words, cannot be applied without adjustments to other forms of discrimination.

Sex discrimination brings out these differences most dramatically in issues directly related to sexual activity, childbearing, and family life. To take an example first made prominent by Richard Wasserstrom, race-segregated bathrooms are taken to be an emblem of discrimination in the Jim Crow South. Sex-segregated bathrooms, by contrast, are treated as an acceptable means of preserving the privacy of men and women. Richard A. Wasserstrom, Racism, Sexism, and Preferential Treatment: An Approach to the Topics, 24 U.C.L.A. L. Rev. 581 (1977). The rationale for this practice, which is nearly universally observed in this country, does not rest solely on the physical differences between women and men—what might narrowly be called their "sexual differences"—but on the differences between their social roles—what might be called their "gender roles." Sexual differences, of course, have some inherent significance. The physical differences between women and men require different medical treatment. But sexual differences acquire much of their significance through gender roles. Physical privacy of men and women would not need to be protected if it was not related to pervasive differences in the gender roles of men and women, and in particular, those involving dating, marriage, and raising children. Of course, this is not to say that gender roles justify sex discrimination. Wasserstrom, for instance, thought that they did not, even in the case of sex-segregated bathrooms.

What gender roles do justify is the question whether sex discrimination should be treated just like race discrimination. As a matter of legal theory, Title VII treats the two forms of discrimination the same way most of the time, but not always. As the plurality opinion in *Price Waterhouse* points out, Title VII creates an exception for any "bona fide occupational qualification" (or BFOQ) on the basis of sex. This exception also applies to national origin and religion, leaving race as the only form of discrimination not subject to an explicit exception on this ground. As Chapter 5 discusses, the BFOQ for sex has been narrowly interpreted, so that it applies only in exceptional circumstances. Yet these exceptional circumstances, like the example of sex-segregated bathrooms, require some distinction to be made between permissible sex-based classifications and impermissible sex-based stereotypes. The comments in *Price Waterhouse* about the need for Hopkins to act "more like a lady" crossed the line from permissible to impermissible. That conclusion was obvious to all the justices, even those who dissented. Justifying that conclusion, however, is more difficult than reaching it.

Do we need economic theories to explain what was wrong with the comments in *Price Waterhouse*? Do such comments work systematically to the disadvantage of women? Was Hopkins placed in the position that no matter what she did she would have been criticized? If she had not been aggressive, she would not have generated business for the firm; but since she was aggressive, she was criticized for behaving too much like a man. Is Hopkins claiming simply that sex-based stereotypes limited her ability to succeed in her chosen profession? If so, could an effeminate man raise an analogous claim for being criticized for behaving too much like a woman? The economic theories do not explain what these sex-based stereotypes are, but instead presuppose that individuals bring them to the marketplace and act on them in making employment decisions.

3. **Feminist Theories.** Feminists have offered a wide range of theories that seek to explain how sexual stereotypes arose, why they persist, and what is wrong with them. Some are mainstream theories that build upon traditional economic and social science research. An exemplary study using these methods is Claudia Goldin, Understanding the Gender Gap: An Economic History of American Women (1990). Goldin offers an extended and detailed account of the increasing employment of women in our society, finding that it is closely correlated with economic development but recognizing the prevalence of continued occupational segregation on the basis of sex. Other theorists have argued that liberal political theory, with its emphasis on individual rights to personal freedom, private property, and participation in democratic government, must be modified to take account of the fact that such rights were traditionally exercised only by men and that it is necessary to remedy the systematic inequality suffered by women, both in private and in public life. Susan Moller Okin, for instance, criticizes John Rawls for formulating a theory of justice that neglects the unequal status of women within the family and the consequent impediments that women face in seeking positions and rewards outside the home. See Susan Moller Okin, Justice, Gender, and the Family (1989); John Rawls, A Theory of Justice (rev. ed. 1999); see also Martha C. Nussbaum, Sex and Social Justice (1999).

Many specifically legal theorists have further elaborated on the model of liberal equality, insisting that women be treated, to the extent possible, just like men. A leading defense of this point of view is Herma Hill Kay, Models of Equality, 1985 U. Ill. L. Rev. 39. Kay recognizes the need for the law to take account of the immutable reproductive differences between women and men, but insists on strictly equal treatment in all other respects on the model of colorblind racial equality. Other legal scholars have criticized this approach, on the ground that it assimilates women to a standard of equal treatment defined to favor men. If jobs, for instance, are defined by reference to a traditional family in which the husband works full time outside the home and his wife works full time within the home, women will gain little from formal equality defined wholly in male terms. A few examples of this alternative approach are Joan Williams, Canaries in the Mine: Work/Family Conflict and the Law, 70 Fordham L. Rev. 2221 (2002); Mary Becker, Prince Charming, Abstract Equality, 1987 Sup. Ct. Rev. 201. Criticism of liberalism along these lines often goes a step further and finds in the entire legal system an attempt to entrench patriarchy as the default standard for social interaction. On this view, the existing law of sex discrimination amounts to only a thinly veiled attempt to legitimize the dominance of men over women. A leading statement of this position is Catherine MacKinnon, Towards a Feminist Theory of the State (1989). Other feminist scholars could be added to this list, as could scholars who take issue with the entire project of feminist equality. A broad sample of writings on this topic can be found in Feminist Legal Theory (Frances E. Olsen ed., 1995).

What all these writings have in common is a focus on gender roles in the crucial areas of sex, children, and the family, and how these have determined and limited the opportunities of women in public life, including their opportunities for employment. The consequences of gender roles can be grouped into two broad categories: those that directly limit the employment of women because they have greater responsibilities within the home, and particularly in raising children; and those that indirectly limit their role in public life by establishing and reinforcing sex-based stereotypes. It is the latter that was at issue in *Price Waterhouse*. The stereotypical comments that were directed at Hopkins cannot be explained on any narrowly economic theory, but apparently resulted from social roles first learned and then maintained through gender roles in the family. Division of labor in that setting has pervasive consequences in forming the beliefs and expectations that determine decisions about employment and other formal economic relationships, or so feminists have argued. Does that argument explain why the partners in Price Waterhouse felt free to offer their stereotypical evaluations of Hopkins, after Title VII had prohibited sex discrimination in employment? Does it also explain what is wrong with stereotypical comments made in support of a decision to hire, fire, or promote a female employee? Do the same explanations hold for freestanding comments, not directly related to any such decision?

For articles that further examine the relationship between gender roles and sex discrimination, see Mary Anne Case, Disaggregating Gender from Sex and Sexual Orientation: The Effeminate Man in the Law and Feminist Jurisprudence, 105 Yale L.J. 1 (1995); Mary Anne Case, All the World's the Men's Room, 74 U. Chi. L. Rev. 1655 (2007); Robert C. Post et al., Prejudicial Appearances: The Logic of American Antidiscrimination Law (2001); Kimberly A. Yuracko, Gender Nonconformity and the Law (2016); Kimberly A. Yuracko, Trait Discrimination as Sex Discrimination: An Argument Against Neutrality, 83 Tex. L. Rev. 167 (2004).

4. ***Jespersen v. Harrah's Operating Co., Inc.*** The application of *Price Waterhouse* to claims of discrimination in dress and appearance was taken up in the widely noted decision in Jespersen v. Harrah's Operating Co., Inc., 444 F.3d 1104 (9th Cir. 2006) (en banc). The plaintiff in that case worked as a bartender in a casino and like all the bartenders, both male and female, she was required to conform to a detailed dress and grooming code. Under this code, female bartenders were required to wear makeup while male bartenders were forbidden from doing so. The plaintiff claimed that this requirement discriminated against women on two different theories: first, that it imposed a greater burden on women than men; and second, that it amounted to sex stereotyping under *Price Waterhouse*. The Ninth Circuit, sitting en banc, upheld summary judgment against the plaintiff on both theories, although over substantial dissents.

On the unequal burden theory, the court held that the dress and grooming code imposed burdens on both women and men. For instance, women could wear their hair longer than men. The majority rejected the plaintiff's request to take judicial notice of the fact that wearing makeup was more burdensome for women than was any corresponding requirement for men and concluded that sex-differentiated standards, without more, did not violate Title VII. A dissenting opinion disagreed on the issue of judicial notice and would have found sufficient evidence that wearing makeup was substantially more burdensome for women.

On the sex-stereotyping theory, the majority found that the dress and grooming code was unisex for the most part, requiring all bartenders to wear the same clothes, and it did not inhibit the plaintiff's ability to perform her job. Nor was the makeup requirement degrading or sexually provocative; it did not tend to treat women as sex objects; and it did not constitute any kind of sexual harassment. Another dissenting opinion would have found that the requirement that the women wear full makeup presented sufficient evidence of an impermissible stereotype.

This decision has elicited numerous comments, almost all of them critical of the majority's position. Many of the major articles are collected in two symposiums: Makeup, Identity Performance & Discrimination, 14 Duke J. Gender L. & Pol'y 1 (2007); Gender Stereotyping: Expanding the Boundaries of Title VII, 10 Emp. Rts. & Emp. Pol'y 271 (2006).

5. Discrimination Based on Appearance. In her book, The Beauty Bias: The Injustice of Appearance in Life and Law (Oxford University Press 2010), Deborah Rhode observes that appearance-based discrimination has a disproportionate impact on women. While men also suffer discrimination based on traits such as height and weight, women face more exacting standards of physical attractiveness, which affect them in both their personal and professional lives. Rhode emphasizes cases in which perceptions of women's competence are tied to their physical attractiveness, either because they are thought to be too attractive or not attractive enough. Discrimination based on appearance can have a substantial impact on hiring and promotion decisions, leading Rhode to offer two ways in which the law can mitigate the effects of appearance bias. First, there is the possibility of prohibiting appearance-based discrimination, except in instances where such discrimination is justified by some showing of business necessity. Alternatively, current laws against discrimination should be interpreted more broadly to cover more cases like *Jespersen*, in which the plaintiff proves that discrimination based on appearance falls more harshly on one sex rather than the other.

This book was based on her earlier article, Deborah L. Rhode, The Injustice of Appearance, 61 Stan. L. Rev. 1033 (2009). For other works on issues of appearance, see Mark S. Bandsuch, Dressing Up Title VII's Analysis of Workplace Appearance Policies, 40 Colum. Hum. Rts. L. Rev. 287 (2009); M. Neil Browne, Obesity as a Protected Category: The Complexity of Personal Responsibility for Physical Attributes, 14 Mich. St. U. J. Med. & L. 1 (2010); Anna Kirkland, FAT Rights: Dilemmas of Difference and Personhood (2008); Susan Schweik, The Ugly Laws: Disability in Public (2009); Yofi Tirosh, The Right to be Fat, 7 Yale J. Health Pol'y L. & Ethics 264 (2012).

6. Distinctive Problems of Discrimination on Different Grounds. As the preceding discussion reveals, each form of discrimination, based on different grounds such as race, sex, age, or disability, raises distinctive issues. This point has been widely appreciated, so much so that even the colorblind theory of racial equality—that race should be eliminated from decisions about employment, with the possible exception of affirmative action—has become problematic. See Reva B. Siegel, Discrimination in the Eyes of the Law: How "Color Blindness" Discourse Disrupts and Rationalizes Social Stratification, 88 Cal. L. Rev. 77 (2000). Critical race scholars have argued that colorblindness represents the white majority's view of racial equality, but that alternative views that reflect the distinctive experience of minority groups must also be taken into account. These scholars have taken the methods of Critical Legal Studies, a movement in legal thought that offered a general critique of the prevailing models of legal reasoning, and applied them to civil rights law. For an example of this, see Kimberle Williams Crenshaw, Race, Reform, and Retrenchment: Transformation and Legitimation in Antidiscrimination Law, 101 Harv. L. Rev. 1331 (1988).

If the need for alternative viewpoints is apparent with respect to race, it is still more obvious with respect to other grounds of discrimination. These reveal the essentially contested nature of the concept of discrimination, along two separate dimensions: first, the extent to which the reigning conception of equality on the model of colorblindness is adequate in and of itself; and second, the extent to which it can be adjusted to account for discrimination on such grounds as sex, religion, age, and disability. The treatment of sex-based stereotypes under Title VII simply opens the door to addressing these questions. Are sex-based stereotypes any different from race-based stereotypes, and if so, in what ways? Is the exception for BFOQs on the basis of sex at all justifiable, and if it is, should it be amended to apply to race?

Research examining how men and women perform differently in certain contexts illustrates some of the complex issues in identifying sex discrimination. An important study analyzed a series of experiments in which groups of men and women were tasked with solving mazes to earn monetary compensation. The authors found that competitive contexts (namely a tournament structure) improved the performance of men, regardless of whether they were in a single or mixed gender group. Women only showed similar improvements in single gender groups and had no significant performance improvement in mixed gender competitions. Moreover, when allowed to select their preferred level of difficulty (payment per maze solved increased with difficulty), men tended to select more difficult mazes. This result suggests that men may feel more competent at this specific task, potentially explaining the sex-dependent responses to competition. Uri Gneezy, Muriel Niederle, & Aldo Rustichini, Performance in Competitive Environments: Gender Differences, 118 Q.J. Econ. 1049 (2003). Does the possibility of differing performances based on context have any bearing on whether an exception for BFOQs on the basis of sex is appropriate?

Questions regarding the comparability of different forms of discrimination multiply as grounds for discrimination themselves multiply from seemingly immutable characteristics such as race, national origin, and sex and reach changeable or variable characteristics, such as religion, age, and disability. Scholars from the groups targeted by all these forms of discrimination—with the curious exception of victims of age discrimination—have offered their own perspective on the extent and nature of the discrimination practiced against them. Disability rights advocates, for instance, present a powerful argument for the stigma experienced by disabled individuals, particularly in seeking employment and other positions of public prominence. This casebook begins, as this chapter does, by considering characteristics similar to race, but the implications of the analysis for characteristics dissimilar to race should not be neglected. Indeed, those implications become a dominant theme in the later chapters of this book.

7. **Bibliography.** A number of articles have addressed the specific issues raised by *Price Waterhouse*. For articles on the "glass ceiling," the barriers faced by women in promotions to higher level jobs, see Edward S. Adams, Using Evaluations to Break Down the Male Corporate Hierarchy: A Full Circle Approach, 73 U. Colo. L. Rev. 117 (2002); Marianne Bertrand & Kevin F. Hallock, The Gender Gap in Top Corporate Jobs, 55 Ind. & Lab. Rel. Rev. 3 (2001); Tristin K. Green, Work Culture and Discrimination, 93 Cal. L. Rev. 623 (2005); Christine Jolls, Is There a Glass Ceiling?, 25 Harv. Women's L.J. 1 (2002); Symposium, Shattering the Glass Ceiling: The Status of Women in the Workplace and the Change Needed for Equality, 36 St. Louis U. Pub. L. Rev. 1 (2017). For a critical account of the arguments currently offered for breaking down these barriers, see Kingsley R. Browne, Sex and Temperament in Modern Society: A Darwinian View of the Glass Ceiling and the Gender Gap, 37 Ariz. L. Rev. 971 (1995).

For articles on proof of mixed motives and the use of expert witnesses, see Julie E. Blend, Using Expert Witnesses in Employment Litigation, 17 Rev. Litig. 27 (1998); John V. Jansonius & Andrew M. Gould, Expert Witnesses in Employment Litigation: The Role of Reliability in Assessing Admissibility, 50 Baylor L. Rev. 267 (1998); Symposium, The Burgeoning *Mt. Healthy* Mixed-Motive Defense to Civil Rights and Employment Discrimination Claims, 51 Mercer L. Rev. 583 (2000).

For clear evidence of the presence of sex-based discrimination in hiring and promotion, see Claudia Goldin & Cecelia Rouse, The Impact of "Blind" Auditions on Female Musicians, 90 American Econ. Rev. 715 (2000); David Neumark, Roy J. Bank, & Kyle D. Van Nort, Sex Discrimination in Restaurant Hiring: An Audit Study, 111 Q.J. Econ. 915 (1996).

A common theme in recent scholarship has been the persistence of inequality despite the presence of prohibitions against discrimination. A steady stream of articles has continued to cast doubt on the concept of discrimination as a vehicle for achieving equality and has instead proposed alternatives to it. Michelle Adams, Radical Integration, 94 Cal. L. Rev. 261 (2006); Ian Ayres & Jennifer Gerarda Brown, Mark(et)ing Nondiscrimination: Privatizing ENDA with a Certification Mark, 104 Mich. L. Rev. 1639 (2006); Samuel R. Bagenstos, The Structural Turn and the Limits of Antidiscrimination Law, 94 Cal. L. Rev. 1 (2006); Jack M. Balkin & Reva B. Siegel, The American Civil Rights Tradition: Anticlassification or Antisubordination?, 58 U. Miami L. Rev. 9 (2003); Katharine T. Bartlett,

Making Good on Good Intentions, 95 Va. L. Rev. 1893 (2009); Lauren B. Edelman, Aaron C. Smyth & Asad Rahim, Legal Discrimination: Empirical Sociolegal and Critical Race Perspectives on Antidiscrimination Law, 12 Ann. Rev. L. & Soc. Science 395 (2016); Reva B. Siegel, Discrimination in the Eyes of the Law: How "Color Blindness" Discourse Disrupts and Rationalizes Social Stratification, 88 Cal. L. Rev. 77 (2000); Sandra F. Sperino, Rethinking Discrimination Law, 110 Mich. L. Rev. 69 (2011); Susan P. Sturm, Second Generation Employment Discrimination: A Structural Approach, 101 Colum. L. Rev. 458 (2001); Julie Suk, Equal by Comparison: Unsettling Assumptions of Antidiscrimination Law, 55 Am. J. Comp. L. 295 (2007). For articles concentrating on the intersection of discrimination, race, and class, see Symposium, Civil Rights and the Low Wage Worker, 2009 U. Chi. Legal F. 1; Symposium, Race and Socioeconomic Class: Examining an Increasingly Complex Tapestry, 72 L. & Contemp. Prob. 1 (2009); Symposium, The Rights and Wrongs of Discrimination, 43 San Diego L. Rev. 733 (2006); Symposium, A New Legal Realist Perspective on Employment Discrimination, 31 L. & Soc. Inquiry 797 (2006).

NOTES ON ECONOMIC AND POLITICAL THEORIES OF DISCRIMINATION

The plaintiff in an employment discrimination case must rely on a theory of liability to prevail against the defendant. This is a creation entirely of legal doctrine, which identifies the elements of the plaintiff's case, any defenses available to the defendant, the nature of each party's burden of proof, and the overall substantive structure of the case. Economists and other social scientists use theories for a quite different purpose: to explain why discrimination is found in labor markets in the first place, why it has persisted, what its consequences are, and whether attempts to eradicate it are likely to be successful. These theories are descriptive and explanatory—(seeking to understand the phenomenon of discrimination)—while legal theories are normative and prescriptive—(seeking to identify when liability should be imposed for discrimination). Yet there must be some general connection between these very different kinds of theories, if only to have some confidence that legal prohibitions against discrimination actually accomplish what they set out to do: to prevent adverse action against minorities and other disfavored groups.

Two economic theories have dominated the analysis of discrimination in labor markets, one based on "tastes for discrimination" and the other based on "statistical discrimination." Alternative theories have developed insights from sociology and psychology, most prominently in the law review literature in the theory of discrimination based on "status" or on "implicit bias." The two key elements of this body of work focus on what has motivated the differential treatment of, for example, whites and blacks, and what are the institutional elements of the labor market that determine the degree to which the employer is subject to competitive pressure. A brief discussion of these elements and their application to *Teamsters* will illustrate both some of the key insights and the significant uncertainties surrounding the main economic theories.

1. Becker's Model of Tastes for Discrimination in Competitive Markets. The theory of tastes for discrimination, formulated by Gary Becker, defines such tastes as a desire to avoid transactions involving members of a disfavored group. An individual with a taste for discrimination acts as if he would pay to avoid certain transactions. Gary S. Becker, The Economics of Discrimination (2d ed. 1971). Thus a white worker with a taste for discrimination against blacks would have to be paid more to work in a job in which she associated with blacks. This discriminatory white worker would accept less pay to work in a job in which she didn't have to associate with black workers. The difference in compensation is a measure of the magnitude of her taste for discrimination. Employers, customers, and suppliers could also have tastes for discrimination, as, of course, could members of racial and ethnic minorities; they could prefer to deal only with members of their own group. Becker takes no position on why people develop tastes for discrimination. What counts for him is not the motive with which individuals act but their willingness to pay to avoid dealing with members of other groups. An employer, for instance, might be unwilling to hire black employees, either out of prejudice against them or out of misconceptions about their ability. What counts for Becker is the employer's unwillingness to deal with them.

In thinking about the complete exclusion of minority workers from jobs as line drivers but not as city drivers, let's begin with the assumption that the discrimination in *Teamsters* emanates from the discriminatory preferences of white drivers (although it might equally well have emanated from those of white owners and managers). It follows from Becker's theory that employers would have a monetary incentive to respond to such tastes for discrimination by engaging in segregation, by hiring employees entirely of one race or another or by hiring employees from different races in different departments. Hiring a workforce composed entirely of black employees could be the lowest cost alternative if other employers discriminated against blacks, but customers and suppliers did not. Discrimination by other employers would drive the wages of black employees down (as compared to white employees) and enable the nondiscriminatory employer to gain a competitive advantage by reducing his overall wage bill. By hiring only black employees, he would also avoid the premium he would have to pay whites in order to get them to work with blacks. His next-best alternative would be to hire only whites. Although he would not receive the discount available from hiring black workers, he would again avoid the premium he would have to pay to white workers in an integrated establishment. Integration, paradoxically enough, would be the least desirable option available to a nondiscriminatory employer (considering only monetary profits). He could gain the advantage neither of an entirely black work force at discounted wages nor an entirely white work force without the premium caused by integration.

This example, which explores only the application of Becker's theory to discriminatory fellow employees, reveals both its strengths and its weaknesses. Its strength is that it can offer an explanation for the occupational segregation found in *Teamsters*. The trucking companies could reduce their wage bill by hiring only whites as line drivers and avoid the premium necessary to compensate them for working with blacks. Its weakness is that it requires further elaboration to explain why the position of city driver wasn't also segregated. It also fails to explain why more employers did not hire an entirely black work force to gain the competitive advantage of the generally lower pay that blacks would accept because of discrimination by employers like those in *Teamsters*.

2. Taste-Based Discrimination in Noncompetitive Markets. Unfortunately, the opinion in *Teamsters* does not provide enough details about the nature of the two job categories and the effect of the institutional structures in a highly regulated and heavily unionized industry, which trucking then was. If line and city drivers really are drawn from the same pool of truck drivers with similar skills, then it is difficult to see why one would be segregated and the other integrated. One might venture the hypothesis that an overall limit on the supply of white truck drivers, or alternatively of African-American and Hispanic truck drivers, forced the trucking companies to integrate the city driver position. But this story would not hold in a competitive environment because new trucking companies could enter the market and hire away workers to form entirely segregated departments of city drivers at lower cost. For that matter, nothing would prevent such companies from hiring an entirely minority work force, both as city drivers and as line drivers. These companies would have a cost advantage over the existing companies and, all other things being equal, could compete to drive the existing companies out of business.

These factors suggest that competitive pressures were not very powerful in *Teamsters*. The heavily regulated trucking industry was unlikely to face competition from new entrants, and the effective control of the labor market by the powerful Teamsters Union meant that there was probably an excess of workers at the prevailing wage, which would enable discriminatory preferences to be indulged without fear of the increased costs incurred in a competitive environment. While the *Teamsters* case was filed in the South, raising the specter of the rigid racial apartheid of Jim Crow, it is worth noting that the company's pattern of exclusion of black line drivers was as thorough in Los Angeles as it was in Atlanta.

The question, then, is whether the type of persistent discrimination identified in *Teamsters* can persist, as Becker's theory implies, only in the absence of freely competitive markets. According to Becker's theory, individuals with tastes for discrimination eventually will be forced to pay for such tastes, leaving them at a disadvantage in any market in which competition occurs based solely on price. A discriminatory white worker demands a premium to work in an integrated job. Other workers, both black and white, without tastes for discrimination are willing to work for less in the same job. If there are enough of them, they will force the discriminatory white worker to abandon either her search for a job or her taste for discrimination. The same holds for discriminatory employers. For this reason, some economists have argued that the best way to eliminate discrimination is not through a prohibition against discrimination, enforced through cumbersome litigation as in *Teamsters*, but rather by enhancing competition, by reducing economic regulation, unionization, and minimum wages, and encouraging entry and free trade to the greatest extent possible.

But even if such a market orientation were the best approach to limiting discrimination, there are still situations in which the market can encourage discriminatory practices. If customers have a strong taste for discrimination, any firm that fails to cater to those tastes will be penalized in a competitive market. In these circumstances, law can clearly play a role in reducing discrimination by removing the competitive disadvantages faced by firms that refuse to discriminate, as the courts did in preventing airlines from hiring only pretty, young, unmarried women as flight attendants (as some airlines did in responding to the preferences of their largely male business travelers at the time of adoption of the 1964 Civil Rights Act). Economists, who tend to take preferences as given, note that this legal approach does tend to lower consumer satisfaction, by depriving consumers of the benefits from indulging their discriminatory preferences. Nevertheless, even as a matter of overall efficiency, this loss to consumers might well be offset by gains to employees and employers by opening up jobs to a broader array of otherwise qualified and interested applicants. Two further issues need to be explored in thinking about the ability of competitive markets to curtail discrimination. First, there are times when reliance on race in employee selection—or "statistical discrimination"—can lower labor costs or increase profits by catering to discriminatory preferences. Second, as we think about the primary evil that Title VII was intended to address—the stark and widespread racial exclusions in the Jim Crow South—we must consider why that discrimination was so pervasive and persistent. It was found even in largely competitive settings and could not be attributed to the economic regulation and unionization present in *Teamsters*. We address these issues in turn.

3. **Statistical Discrimination.** A statistical theory of discrimination, proposed by Edmund S. Phelps and Kenneth Arrow, tries to account for the persistence of discrimination by offering an explanation of why employers, even those who harbor no animus against any group, might still have a profit incentive to treat racial minorities unfavorably relative to whites. Kenneth J. Arrow, The Theory of Discrimination, in Discrimination in Labor Markets 3 (Orley Ashenfelter & Albert Rees eds., 1973); Edmund S. Phelps, The Statistical Theory of Racism and Sexism, 62 Am. Econ. Rev. 659 (1972); Dennis J. Aigner & Glen G. Cain, Statistical Theories of Discrimination in Labor Markets, 30 Indus. & Lab. Rel. Rev. 175 (1977). While there are two variants to this theory, the one that has gained most prominence posits that employers discriminate against members of minority groups because of difficulties in evaluating their productivity. If employers find it more difficult, and therefore more costly, to determine the productivity of minority workers, they will be deterred from hiring them at the same rate or at the same pay as other workers. These difficulties might arise because the same objective qualifications of minority workers, such as education or performance on standardized tests, yield less reliable information about their ability to perform the job. The variability in productivity of minority workers might be greater than for white workers even if their average

productivity were the same. So, too, evaluation of personal interviews might be more difficult for an employer not experienced in dealing with members of minority groups. Reasons such as these could prompt some employers to discount the value of the minority workers, who would be seen as riskier employment prospects than workers from other groups whose performance could be more accurately predicted or evaluated.

This theory of statistical discrimination corresponds to a sophisticated version of discrimination as stereotyping. It does not assert that employers believe all members of minority groups to be unqualified, or even to be less qualified on average than other workers. It only asserts that employers believe that the true qualifications of minority workers are more difficult to ascertain. The interesting element of this theory is that it predicts that, even when blacks are as productive as whites on average, the lower precision in evaluating black productivity causes black workers to earn less than whites. This is true even in a competitive market, because the lower precision in evaluating black workers is a cost to employers that will lower the demand for their services. So long as the relative difficulty of evaluating minority workers continues, employers have a reason to discriminate against them. Unlike the theory of tastes for discrimination, the theory of statistical discrimination need not appeal to external restraints on competition to explain the continued persistence of discrimination. The theory itself explains why discrimination has not been driven out of the labor markets through competition, and indeed, why it might become entrenched through a pattern of mutually reinforcing decisions. Minority workers would have less incentive to make additional investments in education, training, or other forms of human capital, if they expected to be treated only as well as the average minority worker. Employers would then have less reason to hire minority workers, which in turn would give those workers still less reason to acquire the human capital necessary to be hired, which would further reinforce the expectations of employers about their performance.

There is a second version of the statistical discrimination model that is less concerned about the precision of the productivity estimates of black and white workers, and more concerned with the differences in mean productivity levels between these groups. In this model, blacks are less productive on average for any given observable trait, perhaps because of poorer schools or other obstacles to acquiring qualifications or experience. While the first model is a story about different variances within groups, the second is a story about different means between groups. While either version of statistical discrimination would be prohibited by antidiscrimination law, economists tend to be less concerned about statistical discrimination because it always assumes that workers are paid their expected productivity on the basis of available information. In that sense, all workers are treated fairly both as groups and as individuals.

It is difficult to tell a persuasive story of statistical discrimination in *Teamsters*. The theory does not readily explain why employers would be willing to hire African-Americans and Hispanics as city drivers, but not as line drivers. The qualifications for each position appear to be the same and only ad hoc assumptions about differences between the two positions would suggest that employers would be more reluctant to hire minority workers for one position rather than the other. The ability of employers to evaluate workers for both positions appears to be the same. If employers could evaluate minority workers as city drivers, they seem equally capable of evaluating them as line drivers. Perhaps the risks involved in the two positions were different, so that an unskilled line driver was more likely to be involved in an accident, or damage cargo, or otherwise cause a loss to the employer. If so, employers might have had a reason to take the reliability of line drivers more seriously than city drivers and so preferred white workers for that reason. No such reason, however, appears from the facts of the case, which led the Supreme Court in the opposite direction, to assume that both line drivers and city drivers were essentially unskilled positions that could be filled by anyone with a driver's license.

Indeed, the story of greater variance in estimating the abilities of black workers would appear to conflict with the best available empirical evidence. Two major studies by the National Academy of Sciences evaluated the fairness and efficacy of the General Aptitude Test Battery (GATB), used by the United States Employment Service to refer job candidates to private sector employers. These studies found the GATB to be a valid predictor of job performance for a wide range of occupations and that the relationship between test scores and productivity is quite comparable for whites and blacks. Fairness in Employment Testing: Validity, Generalization, Minority Issues, and the General Aptitude Test Battery (John Hartigan and Alexandra Wigdor, eds., 1989); Performance Assessment for the Workplace (Alexandra Wigdor and Bert F. Green, eds., 1991).

A recent study strongly suggests that employers are using race as a proxy for productivity in the way that the second model of statistical discrimination suggests. David Autor and David Scarborough, Will Job Testing Harm Minority Workers?, 123 Q.J. Econ. 219 (2008). Autor and Scarborough examined the case of a national retail firm whose 1,363 stores switched from informal applicant screening to reliance on a standardized test of personality attributes. Consistent with much prior evidence, blacks did significantly worse on the test than whites did, which should immediately raise concerns that the switch to the test would dampen the hiring of blacks. The authors found, however, that "testing had no measurable impact on minority hiring, and productivity gains [from the better screening provided by the test] were uniformly large among minorities and non-minorities." The likely explanation for this result was that the firm had previously engaged in the second type of statistical discrimination. The firm had assumed that blacks on average were not as productive as whites in its operations. When the test was introduced, it confirmed that black productivity was lower on average, but it also improved the overall quality of the employees who were hired. This improvement extended to both black and white employees and the overall level of black employment remained unchanged. Before introducing the test, the firm apparently had engaged in statistical discrimination, even though it was not permitted to do so under Title VII, and after introducing the test, the firm maintained the same racial configuration of employment by other means.

Those studies raise important questions about the use of tests, and other seemingly neutral selection devices, that perpetuate the effects of discrimination. The theory of disparate impact under Title VII, discussed but not applied in *Teamsters*, addresses such questions and is discussed in detail in Chapter 3.

4. Explaining Persistent Racial Discrimination in the Jim Crow South. Neither the Becker model based on tastes for discrimination nor the model of statistical discrimination conform well with the empirical evidence of enduring racial discrimination. In the leading study of discrimination in the southern labor markets, James J. Heckman and Brooke S. Payner found that blacks were entirely excluded from jobs in the textile industry. James J. Heckman & Brooke S. Payner, Determining the Impact of Federal Antidiscrimination Policy on the Economic Status of Blacks, 79 Am. Econ. Rev. 138 (1989). These were mainly low-skilled jobs that were plentiful in the South because textiles were the primary manufacturing product there throughout most of the twentieth century. Moreover, the ultimate purchasers of the product were far removed from the manufacturing process and so remained unaware of who was employed in making it. Consumer discrimination, therefore, could not explain the virtually complete absence of blacks from this industry. While discrimination by fellow workers might explain exclusion from a particular plant, it would only lead to segregation, not the complete exclusion of blacks from the industry.

Statistical discrimination also fails to explain such complete exclusion of black workers. Even if black workers had lower average productivity than white workers, most of them would have been as productive as a large fraction of white workers. The distribution of skills among black and white workers would have overlapped to a large degree. Indeed, the evidence concerning the most compelling model of statistical discrimination leads to the conclusion that employers who engaged in this practice essentially paid blacks what they were worth on average. Employers do not refuse to hire blacks at all. Thus, the statistical theory of discrimination is entirely inconsistent with what motivated the adoption of Title VII in the first place—the massive exclusion of blacks from jobs for which they were qualified. Consequently, when Title VII was adopted, blacks flooded into industries—like the southern textile industry—that they had been excluded from for at least half a century, and the earnings of blacks rose sharply relative to the earnings of whites in the first decade following the adoption of the Civil Rights Act of 1964. John J. Donohue & James J. Heckman, Continuous Versus Episodic Change: The Impact of Civil Rights Policy on the Economic Status of Blacks, 29 J. Econ. Lit. 1603 (1991).

The persistence of discrimination in the South before the passage of Title VII raises the question of whether a kind of cartel could be maintained in an otherwise competitive market, creating an institutional structure that could resist market pressures that would otherwise undermine discrimination. Richard Epstein has argued that racist southern governments were the force that perpetuated this exclusionary cartel and kept the market from working. Richard Epstein, Forbidden Grounds: The Case against Employment Discrimination Laws (1992). Certainly, these governments did not show any solicitude for the safety and well-being of their black citizens and often were systematically hostile to them. Interestingly, Epstein concedes that Title VII was needed to break the stranglehold of racist southern governments and to allow the market to work. This leads him to argue that Title VII can now be repealed and that blacks will be protected as long as competitive markets are maintained and strengthened. Alternative theories of discrimination do not take such a hopeful view of the responsiveness of market participants to competition: that once employers abandoned pervasive forms of private discrimination, they would not return to such practices after laws like Title VII were repealed. Indeed, the statistical theory of discrimination suggests the opposite conclusion: that even minor differences in the perceived qualifications of minority workers would lead to a reinforcing pattern of discrimination. Employers might first deny jobs to minority workers based on the higher variability or the lower average qualifications that employers think they have. This would then cause other minority workers to be deterred from obtaining such qualifications in the first place, leading to still more statistical discrimination by employers. Epstein assumes that competition would be sufficient to prevent such a self-fulfilling prophecy, just as he supposes that it would make most tastes for discrimination too costly for employers to indulge. The evidence for this assumption is lacking.

5. **Racial Discrimination After Title VII.** Federal antidiscrimination law was broadened by the Equal Employment Opportunity Act (EEOA) of 1972 and by the Civil Rights Act of 1991. Kenneth Chay attempted to determine whether the EEOA provided additional independent stimulus beyond the original 1964 law. Chay was able to predict that the EEOA would have different impacts across industries and between the South and the rest of the country. This was because the EEOA lowered coverage of firms to those with 15 employees and would affect a large share of employment in sectors with smaller employers. It would also be more potent in the South since smaller employers in the rest of the country were already largely covered by state fair employment practice (FEP) laws. Based on his careful empirical work, Chay concludes that the EEOA increased the demand for black workers among small employers not previously covered by FEP laws. Kenneth Chay, the Impact of Federal Civil Rights Policy on Black Economic Progress: Evidence from the Equal Employment Opportunity Act of 1972, 51 I.L.R. Rev. 608 (1998).

On the other hand, Paul Oyer and Scott Schaefer concluded in a series of papers that there was little support for the view that the 1991 law stimulated black or female employment. Paul Oyer and Scott Schaefer, Layoffs and Litigation, 31 RAND J. Econ. 345 (2000); Paul Oyer and Scott Schaefer, Litigation Costs and Returns to Experience, 92 Am. Econ. Rev. 683 (2002); Paul Oyer and Scott Schaefer, Sorting, Quotas, and the Civil Rights Act of 1991: Who Hires When It's Hard to Fire?, 45 J.L. & Econ. 41 (2002).

Indeed, James Heckman, who was a major opponent of the view that labor markets in the 1960s fully protected workers against discrimination, has argued that the labor market is doing a much better job today at rewarding skills than it did a half century ago. Heckman looks to factors besides market discrimination (i.e., those that promote skill formation) to explain the modern black-white earnings gap. Pedro Carneiro, James J. Heckman, and Dimitriy V. Masterov, Labor Market Discrimination and Racial Differences in Premarket Factors, 48 J.L. & Econ. 1 (2005).

Heckman's analysis of the current black-white wage gap is informed by the work of Derek A. Neal and William R. Johnson. Neal and Johnson note that many studies find that the black-white wage gap cannot be explained by variables such as age, years of education, or marital status, suggesting that the contribution of discrimination is sizeable. They argue that years of education may exaggerate the true skill level attained by blacks, given the poorer-quality schools that many blacks attend. Neal and Johnson begin by noting that the unadjusted wage gap (after accounting for age) is –24.4% between black and white men and –18.5% between black and white women. When they control for the Armed Forces Qualification Test (AFQT) as a measure of acquired skills that one brings to the labor market, the estimated gap falls sharply to –7.2% for men and becomes positive, although not statistically significant, at +3.5% for women. Neal and Johnson contend that the AFQT score can explain a very large portion of the black-white wage gap for men, and essentially all of the gap for women.

The Neal and Johnson finding is sensitive to a methodological choice: should one control for years of education in addition to controlling for AFQT score? Neal and Johnson argue that one should not, since the test better captures ability. Others have argued that additional education confers added human capital beyond what is reflected in the AFQT. When years of education is added to the list of control variables, the unexplained racial wage gap re-emerges.

Neal and Johnson's analysis could also be compromised if the AFQT were racially biased, although a National Academy of Sciences report rejected this charge, or if statistical discrimination leads to black underinvestment in skills. Neal and Johnson find that the return to AFQT scores is significantly higher for black men (although not for black women), which they argue provides enough of an incentive to develop human capital to undermine the argument based on statistical discrimination. Derek A. Neal and William R. Johnson, the Role of Premarket Factors in Black-White Wage Differences, 104 J. Pol. Econ. 869 (1996).

6. **Status Discrimination.** Alternative theories have tried to fill such gaps in the prevailing economic theories by establishing why the market did not undermine massive racial exclusion and why legal intervention was necessary. One, based on status, tries to account for discrimination as the result of competition for the necessarily scarce resource of status. In Richard McAdams's version of the theory, individuals and groups compete in a zero-sum game for status, defined as relative position within society. Richard H. McAdams, Cooperation and Conflict: The Economics of Group Status Production and Race Discrimination, 108 Harv. L. Rev. 1003 (1995); Richard H. McAdams, Relative Preferences, 102 Yale L.J. 1 (1992). It follows from this definition that a gain in status for any person or group necessarily requires a loss for someone else. Status, in this sense, is closely tied to the commonly held view of discrimination as a form of stigma. Victims of

discrimination are meant to be stigmatized and assigned a lower status, while those who engage in discrimination seek a corresponding increase in status. Thus, on the facts of *Teamsters*, white line drivers seek to enhance their status by excluding minority drivers from this position. The status model seeks to explain both racial exclusion and—importantly—anticompetitive practices that preserve this exclusion. Under this model, whites adopt independent norms that discourage the pursuit of profitable business opportunities that would undermine racial exclusion.

Status undeniably plays a role in discrimination, yet articulating precisely how it does so remains a difficult task. Like the theory of tastes for discrimination, it provides a plausible explanation in *Teamsters* for the exclusion of African-Americans and Hispanics from jobs as line drivers, but it requires further elaboration to explain how they were hired as city drivers. The trucking companies and the unions were careful to maintain separate seniority lists for each position, so that even white city drivers were discouraged from transferring to positions as line drivers. Any city driver who did so lost his accumulated seniority from his work as a city driver. On the evidence available in *Teamsters*, there was no natural progression of whites from city drivers to line drivers, leaving only minority city drivers in a dead-end job. White city drivers could find themselves in the same position as minority city drivers, sharing whatever status that position had.

7. Implicit Bias. Another theory relies upon findings in cognitive psychology that people harbor "implicit bias" based on a variety of individual traits. This form of discrimination occurs subliminally without an individual necessarily even being aware of it. The empirical studies in this field typically ask subjects to associate members of different groups with desirable or undesirable characteristics. Thus in one kind of experiment, the subject is confronted with faces that appear to be African-American or white and then asked to decide whether they fit with words like "good" or "bad." The subject usually takes longer to associate African-Americans with qualities like "good" rather than "bad." Marianne Bertrand, Dolly Chugh & Sendhil Mullainathan, Implicit Discrimination, 95 Am. Econ. Ass'n Papers and Proceedings 94 (2005). The response times, however, are designed to be quite short, so that subjects do not conceal their initial reactions. Exactly how to generalize from such rapid responses to more considered decisions, typical of those in the workplace, has proved to be a contentious issue.

Some scholars conclude that these studies establish the pervasiveness of discrimination in everyday interactions, with an inevitable effect on employment decisions. Samuel R. Bagenstos, Implicit Bias, Science, and Antidiscrimination Law, 1 Harv. L. & Pol'y Rev. 477 (2007); Melissa Hart, Subjective Decisionmaking and Unconscious Discrimination, 56 Ala. L. Rev. 741 (2005); Tanya K. Hernandez, One Path for Post Racial Employment Discrimination Cases—The Implicit Association Test Research as Social Framework Evidence, 32 J. L. & Inequality 307 (2014); Linda Hamilton Krieger, Behavioral Realism in Employment Discrimination Law: Implicit Bias and Disparate Treatment, 94 Cal. L. Rev. 997, 1027–29 (2006); Joan C. Williams, Double Jeopardy? An Empirical Study with Implications for the Debates Over Implicit Bias and Intersectionality, 37 Harv. J.L. & Gender

185 (2014). Professor Bagenstos, however, has expressed doubts about whether implicit bias has helped the case for laws against discrimination. See Implicit Bias's Failure, 39_Berkeley J. Emp. & Lab. L. ___ (2018). Other scholars have proposed mechanisms for countering this type of unconscious bias. Christine Jolls & Cass R. Sunstein, Debiasing Through Law, 35 J. Legal Stud. 199 (2006); Cass R. Sunstein & Christine Jolls, The Law of Implicit Bias, 94 Cal. L. Rev. 969 (2006). In the context of economic theories of discrimination, the existence of implicit bias would provide a psychological basis for tastes for discrimination and for statistical discrimination. Tastes for discrimination would be based on psychological mechanisms that operated against members of disfavored groups. Statistical discrimination would result from the additional difficulties that implicit bias placed in the way of accurately evaluating the qualifications of the same individuals. Implicit bias would also provide a psychological explanation for the persistence of discrimination. Market forces would have to operate against ingrained tendencies towards misjudgment.

Plausible as the connection may be between subliminal processes and patterns of discrimination, some scholars find the evidence to be lacking for any link between implicit bias and the conscious choices made in employment decisions. Philip E. Tetlock, Gregory Mitchell & L. Jason Anastasopoulos, Detecting and Punishing Unconscious Bias, 42 J. Legal Stud. 83 (2013); Gregory Mitchell, Second Thoughts, 40 McGeorge L. Rev. 687 (2009); Gregory Mitchell & Philip E. Tetlock, Facts Do Matter: A Reply to Bagenstos, 37 Hofstra L. Rev. 737 (2009); John Monahan, Laurens Walker & Gregory Mitchell, Contextual Evidence of Gender Discrimination: The Ascendance of "Social Frameworks," 94 Va. L. Rev. 1715 (2008). Employers and their managers might well check their unconscious tendencies toward bias when they decide to hire, fire, or demote employees. A psychological theory based on empirical evidence of implicit bias also must be committed to empirical verification of its effect on conscious decisions. It also must explain how to sort out discriminatory decisions from those that are free of discrimination. If implicit bias is as widespread as these studies indicate, it would affect all employment decisions, not to mention those of the judges and juries who decide employment discrimination cases. To be serviceable as a theory of legal liability, it must identify those decisions so contaminated by implicit bias that they must be prohibited. Just as the economic theories of discrimination leave open the question of why discrimination has continued, the alternative theories leave open the question of which forms of discrimination must be remedied.

Implicit bias has also appeared as a central issue in the certification of class actions, as illustrated by *Wal-Mart Stores, Inc. v. Dukes*, 564 U.S. 338 (2011), which appears as a major case in Chapter 7. For additional articles on implicit bias as evidence of discrimination, see Hart Blanton et al., Strong Claims and Weak Evidence: Reassessing the Predictive Validity of the IAT, 94 J. App. Psych. 567 (2009); Marybeth Herald, Situations, Frames, and Stereotypes: Cognitive Barriers on the Road to Nondiscrimination, 17 Mich. J. Gender & L. 39 (2010); Elizabeth Hirsh & Christopher J. Lyons, Perceiving Discrimination on the Job: Legal Consciousness, Workplace Context, and the

Construction of Race Discrimination, 44 Law & Soc'y Rev. 269 (2010); Jerry Kang & Kristin Lane, Seeing Through Colorblindness: Implicit Bias and the Law, 58 UCLA L. Rev. 465 (2010); Monique R. Payne-Pikus, John Hagan & Robert L. Nelson, Experiencing Discrimination: Race and Retention in America's Largest Law Firms, 44 Law & Soc'y Rev. 553 (2010); Patrick S. Shin, Liability for Unconscious Discrimination? A Thought Experiment in the Theory of Employment Discrimination Law, 62 Hastings L.J. 67 (2010).

8. **Sex Discrimination.** The economic theories of discrimination can be applied, with only minor modifications, to explain the persistence of sex discrimination. Tastes for sex discrimination involve an unwillingness to associate with women in certain contexts. Statistical discrimination involves an inability to evaluate the qualifications of women with as much accuracy as those of men. Status discrimination against women seeks to maintain them in a subordinate position. Nevertheless, the incompleteness of all of these theories as applied to race becomes all the more apparent when applied to sex. Almost everyone regularly associates with members of the opposite sex, so that general tastes for discrimination, or general unfamiliarity with how women or men behave, cannot be assumed without further explanation. Women and men may come from different planets, as some popular writers assert, but the planets themselves interact closely and continuously. The status theory of discrimination could be directly applied to subordination of women, but doing so requires evidence that women generally lose status, as measured by some independent standard, in their interactions with men. As with race discrimination, these deficiencies in the economic theories of sex discrimination could benefit from further theoretical refinement and greater empirical validation.

9. **The Relevance of Economic Theories of Discrimination.** Does this brief survey of economic theories of discrimination only confirm Holmes's observation that "general propositions do not decide concrete cases?" The attempt of any theory to explain the existence of discrimination in any concrete case will be heavily influenced by the circumstances in which it arose. If this is true, how much should these economic theories influence the framing and interpretation of the legal theories of discrimination under Title VII? The theory of tastes for discrimination emphasizes anticompetitive practices as the condition for continued discrimination. The statistical theory of discrimination emphasizes inaccuracies in assessing the ability of workers from disfavored groups. The alternative theories based on status emphasize rivalry between groups and those based on implicit bias theory emphasize underlying psychological tendencies. Do these different theories dictate different agendas for employment discrimination law or can the objectives singled out by each theory all be pursued simultaneously? Must the law simply get on with the task of ending discrimination without waiting for a completely convincing account of why it arose in the first place?

Needless to say, economics is not the only source of theories seeking to explain the existence of discrimination or to offer recommendations on how to eliminate it. The status theory of discrimination goes beyond economics in any narrowly defined sense to consider advantages and benefits that cannot easily be quantified or exchanged. It appeals more to sociology than to economics. The implicit bias theory relies even more directly upon psychology. As the notes following the next case indicate, legal theorists have also exploited the resources of these other disciplines to frame theories of discrimination that augment or supplant a strictly economic approach. These theories respond to the felt need to explain the persistence of discrimination in American life, even if the stark patterns of segregation typical of the Jim Crow South or the facts of *Teamsters* have disappeared. The national consensus condemns discrimination in such public and obvious forms, on the model of equality as colorblindness, but the practices increasingly challenged in litigation take place much more frequently behind closed doors. For an account of how class claims of discrimination gave way to individual claims, see John J. Donohue III & Peter Siegelman, The Changing Nature of Employment Discrimination Litigation, 43 Stan. L. Rev. 983 (1991).

10. Normative Theories of Discrimination. The first systematic theoretical justification for Title VII was offered in Owen M. Fiss, A Theory of Fair Employment Laws, 38 U. Chi. L. Rev. 235 (1971). He relied primarily upon the justification offered for constitutional prohibitions against racial discrimination, emphasizing the stigmatic and cumulative effects of such discrimination. He argued that the same effects were present in markets for employment and justified government regulation for the same reasons. The most comprehensive general theoretical critique of employment discrimination law appeared much later in Richard A. Epstein, Forbidden Grounds: The Case Against Employment Discrimination Laws (1992). Epstein, as noted earlier, began from the same basis in constitutional law as Fiss, but would have limited permanent prohibitions only to discrimination by the government, which he believed to be the principal cause of pervasive discrimination in our society. Epstein's views elicited extensive commentary and criticism, much of it collected in Symposium, A Critique of Epstein's Forbidden Grounds, 31 San Diego L. Rev. 1 (1994).

Deborah Hellman has led a group of scholars who have developed the philosophical foundations of laws against discrimination. Her book, When Is Discrimination Wrong? (2008), seeks the foundations in demeaning distinctions on the basis of race, sex, and other personal characteristics. She distinguishes between wrongful discrimination and other wrongful conduct, and she considers and rejects competing accounts, based on merit, irrationality, or caste. Other authors have sought to justify laws against discrimination based on preventing "bottlenecks" that restrict individual choice, Joseph Fishkin, Bottlenecks, A New Theory of Equal Opportunity (2014), or preventing comparative harm to the victims of discrimination, Kasper Lipper-Rasmussen, Born Free and Equal?: A Philosophical Inquiry into the Nature of Discrimination (2014), or eliminating pervasive, abiding, and substantial relative disadvantage between certain groups. Tarunabh Khaitan, A Theory of Discrimination Law (2015). For comments on these and other justifications for laws against discrimination, see Larry Alexander, What Makes Wrongful Discrimination Wrong? Biases, Preferences, Stereotypes, and Proxies, 141 U. Pa. L. Rev. 149 (1992); Richard Thompson Ford, Rethinking Rights After the Second Reconstruction, 123 Yale L. J. 2942 (2014); John Hasnas, Equal Opportunity, Affirmative Action, and the

Anti-Discrimination Principle: The Philosophical Basis for the Legal Prohibition of Discrimination, 71 Fordham L. Rev. 423 (2002); Philosophical Foundations of Discrimination Law (Deborah Hellman & Sophia Moreau, eds. 2013).

11. Bibliography. Articles on the economic analysis of discrimination have examined its causes and consequences and proposed alternative remedies. Among the descriptive articles are: Marianne Bertrand & Sendhil Mullainathan, Desegregation and Black Dropout Rates: Are Emily and Greg More Employable Than Lakisha and Jamal? A Field Experiment on Labor Market Discrimination, 94 Am. Econ. Rev. 991 (2004); Devon W. Carbado & Mitu Gulati, Race to the Top of the Corporate Ladder: What Minorities Do When They Get There, 61 Wash. & Lee L. Rev. 1643 (2004); Major G. Coleman, Racial Discrimination in the Workplace: Does Market Structure Make a Difference?, 43 Indus. Rel. 660 (2004); Michael Conlin & Patrick Emerson, Discrimination in Hiring Versus Retention and Promotion: An Empirical Analysis of Within-Firm Treatment of Players in the NFL, 22 J. L. Econ. & Org. 115 (2006); Jonah Gelbach, Jonathan Klick & Leslie Wexler, Passive Discrimination: When Does It Make Sense to Pay Too Little?, 76 U. Chi. L. Rev. 797 (2009); Jacob E. Gerson, Markets and Discrimination, 82 N.Y.U. L. Rev. 689 (2007); Brant T. Lee, The Network Economic Effects of Whiteness, 53 Am. U. L. Rev. 1259 (2004); Camille Gear Rich, Performing Racial and Ethnic Identity: Discrimination by Proxy and the Future of Title VII, 79 N.Y.U. L. Rev. 1134 (2004); Stephen L. Ross & John Yinger, Uncovering Discrimination: A Comparison of the Methods Used by Scholars and Civil Rights Enforcement Officials, 8 Am. L. & Econ. Rev. 562 (2006); Kevin M. Woodson, Human Capital Discrimination, Law Firm Inequality, and the Limits of Title VII, 38 Cardozo L. Rev. 183 (2016).

In addition, several anthologies and symposiums have collected articles on these issues. John J. Donohue III, Foundations of Employment Discrimination Law (Foundation 2d ed. 2003); Symposium, Visions of Equality: The Future of Title VII, 92 Mich. L. Rev. 2311 2644 (1994); Symposium, The Law and Economics of Racial Discrimination in Employment, 79 Geo. L.J. 1619 (1991); Symposium, Inequality in the Workplace, 70 Int'l Lab. Rev. 3 (2017).

CHAPTER 2

Individual Claims of Intentional Discrimination

A. Statutory Definitions of Discrimination

A central question under the laws against employment discrimination concerns the definition of prohibited discrimination. This question initially is one of statutory drafting and interpretation, but it has proved to be so complicated and contentious that it has resisted resolution in a single statutory provision or judicial decision. As elsewhere in this field, Title VII has provided the model for other statutes. Its central prohibition is § 703(a), which defines prohibited discrimination by employers in the following terms:

> (a) It shall be an unlawful employment practice for an employer—
>
> (1) to fail or refuse to hire or to discharge any individual, or otherwise to discriminate against any individual with respect to his compensation, terms, conditions, or privileges of employment, because of such individual's race, color, religion, sex, or national origin; or
>
> (2) to limit, segregate, or classify his employees or applicants for employment in any way which would deprive or tend to deprive any individual of employment opportunities or otherwise adversely affect his status as an employee, because of such individual's race, color, religion, sex, or national origin.

42 U.S.C. § 2000e–2(a). Similar prohibitions, although framed in less elaborate terms, apply to other covered defendants under Title VII: unions, employment agencies, and joint labor-management committees. § 703(b), (c), (d), 42 U.S.C. § 2000e–2(b), (c), (d).

The disputes over Title VII have not concerned the variation in wording of these provisions but the fundamental nature of what they prohibit: discrimination in subsection (a)(1) and the related concept of segregation in subsection (a)(2). Both of these subsections elaborate upon these concepts by enumerating examples of covered employment decisions, such as "to fail or refuse to hire or to discharge any individual," followed by open-ended categories, like "otherwise to discriminate," and multiple grounds of discrimination, such as race, national origin, and color. While seemingly redundant, these provisions apparently were designed to prevent evasive action to avoid compliance with the statute. Employers could not argue that they met their statutory obligations by eliminating discrimination from some employment practices, but not others—in hiring but not in discharges—or by replacing discrimination on one ground with discrimination on another—relying on national origin or color but not on race.

This purpose has become a dominant theme in cases interpreting the statutory prohibitions, although it has been pursued by different means than those addressed by the statutory language. Instead of elaborating on the statutory definitions of discrimination, the cases interpreting Title VII have resorted to the device of allocating the burden of proof between the parties in order to specify what the statutory prohibitions actually mean in practice. Recall that the burden of proof has two components: the burden of production and the burden of persuasion.

The burden of production requires a party to come forward with evidence from which a reasonable inference can be drawn to a conclusion in her favor. It determines whether a party has submitted sufficient evidence to survive a motion for summary judgment and, in cases tried to a jury, whether a motion for judgment as a matter of law (formerly known as a motion for directed verdict or for judgment notwithstanding the verdict) must be entered for the opposing party. The burden of persuasion, by contrast, applies only when the case has been tried and submitted to the jury (or the judge in a case tried without a jury). It instructs the jury to decide for the party with the burden of persuasion only if the jury is convinced by a preponderance of the evidence to find the facts in favor of that party.

The Civil Rights Act of 1991 elaborated on and, to some extent, clarified these issues with provisions that defined what the plaintiff must prove in order to establish a violation of the statute. The Act added a new subsection, § 703(m), that provides:

> Except as otherwise provided in [Title VII], an unlawful employment practice is established when the complaining party demonstrates that race, color, religion, sex, or national origin was a motivating factor for any employment practice, even though other factors also motivated the practice.

42 U.S.C. § 2000e–2(m). This provision requires a plaintiff to prove that a prohibited reason, such as race or sex, entered into an adverse employment decision as "a motivating factor," even if other factors also entered into the decision. Not all cases fit this model of proof, as the initial qualifying phrase in this provision indicates. Claims of disparate impact do not require proof of intentional discrimination and some forms of intentional discrimination do not support a claim under Title VII, such as those involving affirmative action or bona fide occupational qualifications on the basis of sex, national origin, or religion. For all other claims, § 703(m) specifies what the plaintiff must "demonstrate" in order to establish a violation of Title VII. Section 701(m), another provision added by the Civil Rights Act of 1991, specifically defines "demonstrates" to mean "meets the burden of production and persuasion." 42 U.S.C. § 2000e(m).

These provisions follow the ordinary rule in civil litigation that the burden of production and the burden of persuasion are on the plaintiff. After the plaintiff has established a violation of the statute, however, the burden of proof generally shifts to the defendant, as recognized in the provisions on remedies under Title VII. The most important of these is § 706(g)(2)(B), 42 U.S.C. § 2000e–5(g)(2)(B), which limits the defendant's liability for compensatory relief. This provision applies to mixed motive cases, and as discussed later in this chapter, was added by the Civil Rights Act of 1991 to revise the allocation of the burden of proof established in Price Waterhouse v. Hopkins, 490 U.S. 228 (1989).

This chapter begins, however, with other decisions of the Supreme Court on the burden of proof. These decisions shift onto the defendant some of the burden of proof normally borne by the plaintiff to establish a violation of Title VII. These decisions were not revised by subsequent amendments to Title VII and continue to raise a variety of questions. The initial questions are: How much of the burden of proof is placed upon the defendant? And how heavy is it to carry? The ultimate question, which still has not received a definite answer, is: What does this shift in the burden of proof accomplish? We start with the most widely cited case on this subject.

B. THE *MCDONNELL DOUGLAS* FRAMEWORK

McDonnell Douglas Corp. v. Green

411 U.S. 792 (1973).

■ JUSTICE POWELL delivered the opinion of the Court.

The case before us raises significant questions as to the proper order and nature of proof in actions under Title VII of the Civil Rights Act of 1964, 78 Stat. 253, 42 U.S.C. § 2000e et seq.

Petitioner, McDonnell Douglas Corp., is an aerospace and aircraft manufacturer headquartered in St. Louis, Missouri, where it employs over 30,000 people. Respondent, a black citizen of St. Louis, worked for petitioner as a mechanic and laboratory technician from 1956 until August 28, 1964 when he was laid off in the course of a general reduction in petitioner's work force.

Respondent, a long-time activist in the civil rights movement, protested vigorously that his discharge and the general hiring practices of petitioner were racially motivated. As part of this protest, respondent and other members of the Congress on Racial Equality illegally stalled their cars on the main roads leading to petitioner's plant for the purpose of blocking access to it at the time of the morning shift change. The District Judge described the plan for, and respondent's participation in, the "stall-in" as follows:

> "[F]ive teams, each consisting of four cars would 'tie up' five main access roads into McDonnell at the time of the morning rush hour. The drivers of the cars were instructed to line up next to each other completely blocking the intersections or roads. The drivers were also instructed to stop their cars, turn off the engines, pull the emergency brake, raise all windows, lock the doors, and remain in their cars until the police arrived. The plan was to have the cars remain in position for one hour.
>
> Acting under the 'stall in' plan, plaintiff [respondent in the present action] drove his car onto Brown Road, a McDonnell access road, at approximately 7:00 a.m., at the start of the morning rush hour. Plaintiff was aware of the traffic problems that would result. He stopped his car with the intent to block traffic. The police arrived shortly and requested plaintiff to move his car. He refused to move his car voluntarily. Plaintiff's car was towed away by the police, and he was arrested for obstructing traffic. Plaintiff pleaded guilty to the charge of obstructing traffic and was fined."

On July 2, 1965, a "lock-in" took place wherein a chain and padlock were placed on the front door of a building to prevent the occupants, certain of petitioner's employees, from leaving. Though respondent apparently knew beforehand of the "lock-in," the full extent of his involvement remains uncertain.[3]

Some three weeks following the "lock-in," on July 25, 1965, petitioner publicly advertised for qualified mechanics, respondent's trade, and respondent promptly applied for re-employment. Petitioner turned down respondent, basing its rejection on respondent's participation in the "stall-in" and "lock-in." Shortly thereafter, respondent filed a formal complaint with the Equal Employment Opportunity Commission, claiming that petitioner had refused to rehire him because of his race and persistent involvement in the civil rights movement, in violation of §§ 703(a)(1) and 704(a) of the Civil Rights Act of 1964, 42 U.S.C. §§ 2000e–2(a)(1) and 2000e–3(a). The former section generally prohibits racial discrimination in any employment decision while the latter forbids discrimination against applicants or employees for attempting to protest or correct allegedly discriminatory conditions of employment.

The Commission made no finding on respondent's allegation of racial bias under § 703(a)(1), but it did find reasonable cause to believe petitioner had violated § 704(a) by refusing to rehire respondent because

---

[3] . . . The Court of Appeals majority, however, found that the record did "not support the trial court's conclusion that Green 'actively cooperated' in chaining the doors of the downtown St. Louis building during the 'lock-in' demonstration." 463 F.2d, at 341. See also concurring opinion of Judge Lay. Id. at 345. Judge Johnsen, in dissent, agreed with the District Court that the "chaining and padlocking [were] carried out as planned, [and that] Green had in fact given it . . . approval and authorization." Id. at 348. In view of respondent's admitted participation in the unlawful "stall-in," we find it unnecessary to resolve the contradictory contentions surrounding this "lock-in."

of his civil rights activity. After the Commission unsuccessfully attempted to conciliate the dispute, it advised respondent in March 1968, of his right to institute a civil action in federal court within 30 days.

On April 15, 1968, respondent brought the present action, claiming initially a violation of § 704(a) and, in an amended complaint, a violation of § 703(a)(1) as well. The District Court dismissed the latter claim of racial discrimination in petitioner's hiring procedures on the ground that the Commission had failed to make a determination of reasonable cause to believe that a violation of that section had been committed. The District Court also found that petitioner's refusal to rehire respondent was based solely on his participation in the illegal demonstrations and not on his legitimate civil rights activities. The court concluded that nothing in Title VII or § 704 protected "such activity as employed by the plaintiff in the 'stall in' and 'lock in' demonstrations."

On appeal, the Eighth Circuit affirmed that unlawful protests were not protected activities under § 704(a), but reversed the dismissal of respondent's § 703(a)(1) claim relating to racially discriminatory hiring practices, holding that a prior Commission determination of reasonable cause was not a jurisdictional prerequisite to raising a claim under that section in federal court. The court ordered the case remanded for trial of respondent's claim under § 703(a)(1).

I

We agree with the Court of Appeals that absence of a Commission finding of reasonable cause cannot bar suit under an appropriate section of Title VII and that the District Judge erred in dismissing respondent's claim of racial discrimination under § 703(a)(1). Respondent satisfied the jurisdictional prerequisites to a federal action (i) by filing timely charges of employment discrimination with the Commission and (ii) by receiving and acting upon the Commission's statutory notice of the right to sue, 42 U.S.C. §§ 2000e–5(a) and 2000e–5(e). The Act does not restrict a complainant's right to sue to those charges as to which the Commission has made findings of reasonable cause, and we will not engraft on the statute a requirement which may inhibit the review of claims of employment discrimination in the federal courts. The Commission itself does not consider the absence of a "reasonable cause" determination as providing employer immunity from similar charges in a federal court, 29 CFR § 1601.30, and the courts of appeal have held that, in view of the large volume of complaints before the Commission and the non-adversarial character of many of its proceedings, "court actions under Title VII are de novo proceedings and . . . a Commission 'no reasonable cause' finding does not bar a lawsuit in the case." Robinson v. Lorillard Corp., 444 F.2d 791, 800 (4th Cir. 1971). . . .

II

The critical issue before us concerns the order and allocation of proof in a private, non-class action challenging employment discrimination.

The language of Title VII makes plain the purpose of Congress to assure equality of employment opportunities and to eliminate those discriminatory practices and devices which have fostered racially stratified job environments to the disadvantage of minority citizens. . . .

There are societal as well as personal interests on both sides of this equation. The broad, overriding interest, shared by employer, employee, and consumer, is efficient and trustworthy workmanship assured through fair and racially neutral employment and personnel decisions. In the implementation of such decisions, it is abundantly clear that Title VII tolerates no racial discrimination, subtle or otherwise.

In this case respondent, the complainant below, charges that he was denied employment "because of his involvement in civil rights activities" and "because of his race and color." Petitioner denied discrimination of any kind, asserting that its failure to re-employ respondent was based upon and justified by his participation in the unlawful conduct against it. Thus, the issue at the trial on remand is framed by those opposing factual contentions. The two opinions of the Court of Appeals and the several opinions of the three judges of that court attempted, with a notable lack of harmony, to state the applicable rules as to burden of proof and how this shifts upon the making of a prima facie case. We now address this problem.

The complainant in a Title VII trial must carry the initial burden under the statute of establishing a prima facie case of racial discrimination. This may be done by showing (i) that he belongs to a racial minority; (ii) that he applied and was qualified for a job for which the employer was seeking applicants; (iii) that, despite his qualifications, he was rejected; and (iv) that, after his rejection, the position remained open and the employer continued to seek applicants from persons of complainant's qualifications.[13] In the instant case, we agree with the Court of Appeals that respondent proved a prima facie case. Petitioner sought mechanics, respondent's trade, and continued to do so after respondent's rejection. Petitioner, moreover, does not dispute respondent's qualifications and acknowledges that his past work performance in petitioner's employ was "satisfactory."

The burden then must shift to the employer to articulate some legitimate, nondiscriminatory reason for the employee's rejection. We need not attempt in the instant case to detail every matter which fairly could be recognized as a reasonable basis for a refusal to hire. Here petitioner has assigned respondent's participation in unlawful conduct against it as the cause for his rejection. We think that this suffices to discharge petitioner's burden of proof at this stage and to meet respondent's prima facie case of discrimination.

---

[13] The facts necessarily will vary in Title VII cases, and the specification above of the prima facie proof required from respondent is not necessarily applicable in every respect to differing factual situations.

The Court of Appeals intimated, however, that petitioner's stated reason for refusing to rehire respondent was a "subjective" rather than objective criterion which "carr[ies] little weight in rebutting charges of discrimination." This was among the statements which caused the dissenting judge to read the opinion as taking "the position that such unlawful acts as Green committed against McDonnell would not legally entitle McDonnell to refuse to hire him, even though no racial motivation was involved. . . ." Regardless of whether this was the intended import of the opinion, we think the court below seriously underestimated the rebuttal weight to which petitioner's reasons were entitled. Respondent admittedly had taken part in a carefully planned "stall-in," designed to tie up access to and egress from petitioner's plant at a peak traffic hour. Nothing in Title VII compels an employer to absolve and rehire one who has engaged in such deliberate, unlawful activity against it. In upholding, under the National Labor Relations Act, the discharge of employees who had seized and forcibly retained an employer's factory buildings in an illegal sit-down strike, the Court noted pertinently:

> "We are unable to conclude that Congress intended to compel employers to retain persons in their employ regardless of their unlawful conduct—to invest those who go on strike with an immunity from discharge for acts of trespass or violence against the employer's property. . . . Apart from the question of the constitutional validity of an enactment of that sort, it is enough to say that such a legislative intention should be found in some definite and unmistakable expression." NLRB v. Fansteel Corp., 306 U.S. 240, 255 (1939).

Petitioner's reason for rejection thus suffices to meet the prima facie case, but the inquiry must not end here. While Title VII does not, without more, compel rehiring of respondent, neither does it permit petitioner to use respondent's conduct as a pretext for the sort of discrimination prohibited by § 703(a)(1). On remand, respondent must, as the Court of Appeals recognized, be afforded a fair opportunity to show that petitioner's stated reason for respondent's rejection was in fact pretext. Especially relevant to such a showing would be evidence that white employees involved in acts against petitioner of comparable seriousness to the "stall-in" were nevertheless retained or rehired. Petitioner may justifiably refuse to rehire one who was engaged in unlawful, disruptive acts against it, but only if this criterion is applied alike to members of all races.

Other evidence that may be relevant to any showing of pretext includes facts as to the petitioner's treatment of respondent during his prior term of employment; petitioner's reaction, if any, to respondent's legitimate civil rights activities; and petitioner's general policy and practice with respect to minority employment. On the latter point, statistics as to petitioner's employment policy and practice may be helpful to a determination of whether petitioner's refusal to rehire respondent in this case conformed to a general pattern of discrimination against blacks. . . . In short, on the retrial respondent must be given a full and fair opportunity to demonstrate by competent evidence that the presumptively valid reasons for his rejection were in fact a cover-up for a racially discriminatory decision.

The court below appeared to rely upon Griggs v. Duke Power Co., 401 U.S. 424 (1971), in which the Court stated: "If an employment practice which operates to exclude Negroes cannot be shown to be related to job performance, the practice is prohibited." But *Griggs* differs from the instant case in important respects. It dealt with standardized testing devices which, however neutral on their face, operated to exclude many blacks who were capable of performing effectively in the desired positions. *Griggs* was rightly concerned that childhood deficiencies in the education and background of minority citizens, resulting from forces beyond their control, not be allowed to work a cumulative and invidious burden on such citizens for the remainder of their lives. Respondent, however, appears in different clothing. He had engaged in a seriously disruptive act against the very one from whom he now seeks employment. And petitioner does not seek his exclusion on the basis of a testing device which overstates what is necessary for competent performance, or through some sweeping disqualification of all those with any past record of unlawful behavior, however remote, insubstantial, or unrelated to applicant's personal qualifications as an employee. Petitioner assertedly rejected respondent for unlawful conduct against it and, in the absence of proof of pretext or discriminatory application of such a reason, this cannot be thought the kind of "artificial, arbitrary, and unnecessary barriers to employment" which the Court found to be the intention of Congress to remove. Id. at 431.[21]

III

In sum, respondent should have been allowed to pursue his claim under § 703(a)(1). If the evidence on retrial is substantially in accord with that before us in this case, we think that respondent carried his burden of establishing a prima facie case of racial discrimination and that petitioner successfully rebutted that case. But this does not end the matter. On retrial, respondent must be afforded a fair opportunity to demonstrate that petitioner's assigned reason for refusing to re-employ was a pretext or discriminatory in its application. If the District Judge so

[21] It is, of course, a predictive evaluation, resistant to empirical proof, whether "an applicant's past participation in unlawful conduct directed at his prospective employer might indicate the applicant's lack of a responsible attitude toward performing work for that employer." 463 F.2d at 353. But in this case, given the seriousness and harmful potential of respondent's participation in the "stall-in" and the accompanying inconvenience to other employees, it cannot be said that petitioner's refusal to employ lacked a rational and neutral business justification. As the Court has noted elsewhere: "Past conduct may well relate to present fitness; past loyalty may have a reasonable relationship to present and future trust." Garner v. Los Angeles Board, 341 U.S. 716, 720 (1951).

finds, he must order a prompt and appropriate remedy. In the absence of such a finding, petitioner's refusal to rehire must stand.

The judgment is vacated and the cause is hereby remanded to the District Court for further proceedings consistent with this opinion.

So ordered.

NOTES ON *MCDONNELL DOUGLAS CORP. V. GREEN*

1. **Procedural Background.** Plaintiffs can sue under Title VII only after they have first exhausted their administrative remedies. § 706(c)–(f). These come in two forms: remedies under state and local law, if it has established an agency to enforce claims of employment discrimination, and remedies before the federal Equal Employment Opportunity Commission (EEOC). As *McDonnell Douglas* holds, decisions made by such administrative agencies are not binding upon the court. At most, they serve as evidence that the court can take into account in making its own decision. The purpose of the exhaustion requirement is not to force the plaintiff to accept an administrative resolution of his claim, but to provide the parties with an opportunity to resolve it without the expense of litigation. In claims brought by private plaintiffs, like Green, the EEOC has no adjudicative powers but can only investigate the claim, determine whether it is supported by reasonable cause, and attempt to achieve conciliation between the parties. § 706(b). State and local agencies can, depending upon state law, adjudicate claims of discrimination, but a plaintiff is not required to accept their decisions or even to seek judicial review of them in state court in order to preserve his claim under Title VII. (His rights to pursue a claim under state law and the binding effect of a decision of a state court present more complicated questions, addressed in Chapter 7 on procedures.) *McDonnell Douglas* recognized the power of courts to consider a Title VII claim independently of any prior administrative decision, effectively making the federal courts the principal vehicle for enforcing and interpreting the statute.

2. **Historical Background.** *McDonnell Douglas* itself arose from a civil rights protest, and the plaintiff was a well-known civil rights activist. This fact situation is hardly typical of contemporary employment discrimination litigation, which usually concerns only the interests of the immediate plaintiff. Apart from the rare test case, plaintiffs today usually seek only to vindicate their own rights, rather than to change the law or to reform society. Yet the origins of the law in this field can be traced back directly to the civil rights movement, as the previous chapter explained.

This case provides a concrete illustration of the connection between protests designed to increase the employment opportunities of blacks and the legal protection afforded to those who participate in these activities. Title VII affords such protection most directly by prohibiting employers from retaliating against individuals who "oppose" discriminatory practices. This prohibition, found in § 704(a), formed the basis for an additional claim by Green that was not considered by the Supreme Court. A later section of this chapter considers the nature of such claims, but it is important to note that if Green recovered on his claim under § 703(a), there would have been no need to reach this claim.

3. Nature of the Plaintiff's Claim. Green's claim of discrimination under § 703(a) was unusual in several respects. First, it was a claim of discrimination in *rehiring*, without any allegation that he had been wrongly terminated from his job previously. Second, for this reason, there was no question that he possessed the minimal qualifications for the position that he sought. He had previously performed it in a satisfactory manner. And third, the employer's reason for refusing to rehire him had nothing to do with his ability to perform the job, either in a minimally satisfactory manner or as compared to other applicants for the job. Modern cases, by contrast, are far more likely to concern discharges than hiring, let alone the unusual circumstances of rehiring. Employers are also likely to offer reasons directly related to the job for discharging the plaintiff, either because his performance was unsatisfactory or because his position was no longer needed in the employer's operations.

As John J. Donohue III and Peter Siegelman first pointed out, claims of discrimination in hiring approximated those of discrimination in termination in the era in which *McDonnell Douglas* was decided. A little more than a decade later, discharge claims outnumbered hiring claims by a ratio of 6 to 1. The Changing Nature of Employment Discrimination Litigation, 43 Stan. L. Rev. 983, 1015 (1991). This change in the nature of claims signals a more profound change in what the law seeks, and to some extent, succeeds in accomplishing: not to increase opportunities for those who seek employment, but to preserve opportunities for those who already have jobs or have recently lost them. Employment discrimination law has become less a vehicle for altering the status quo than for maintaining it.

4. The Plaintiff's "Prima Facie" Case. The effect of these changes on legal doctrine has been no less profound. Several of the elements of the plaintiff's "prima facie" case under *McDonnell Douglas* have become either easily satisfied or completely beside the point in the current form of employment discrimination litigation. Recall what these elements are. The plaintiff must show "(i) that he belongs to a racial minority; (ii) that he applied and was qualified for a job for which the employer was seeking applicants; (iii) that, despite his qualifications, he was rejected; and (iv) that, after his rejection, the position remained open and the employer continued to seek applicants from persons of complainant's qualifications."

The first element, membership in a minority group, is either too easily satisfied or not satisfied at all, seemingly removing reverse discrimination claims from the coverage of Title VII. Like most members of racial minorities, Green could easily establish that he was black. But, even if he were not, he could still assert a claim under Title VII, which protects "any individual" from discrimination. If there were any doubt about this issue, it was resolved in McDonald v. Santa Fe Trail Transportation Co., 427 U.S. 273 (1976), where two white employees were dismissed for misappropriating property from a shipment of one of Santa Fe's customers. A black employee allegedly engaged in the same activity, but was retained. After the lower courts dismissed the plaintiff's case, the Supreme Court reversed, relying on legislative history revealing that Title VII was intended to "cover white men and white women and all Americans." The political appeal of this principle of colorblindness, presenting Title VII as legislation that benefits everyone, is undeniable. Can it be reconciled with the underlying aim of Title VII mainly to benefit racial minorities, or other disfavored groups, such as women? Whatever the answer to this question, the Supreme Court could not have meant to resolve it in a passing reference in *McDonnell Douglas*.

The second element of the plaintiff's prima facie case, that the plaintiff "applied and was qualified for a job for which the employer was seeking applicants," also is either too easily satisfied or not satisfied at all. The existence of an application for employment is readily proved in most cases, but in the most common case today, involving a discharge or termination, the existence of an application is not even at issue. So, too, in layoff cases, the employer's underlying reason for its decision is that it can no longer afford to fund the plaintiff's position and therefore is no longer seeking applications for it. The Supreme Court confronted the need to adapt this element for discharge cases in a decision under the Age Discrimination in Employment Act, O'Connor v. Consolidated Coin Caterers Corp., 517 U.S. 308 (1996). This decision is discussed more fully in the chapter on age discrimination, but in the course of its opinion, the Court quoted with seeming approval the court of appeals' reformulation of this element of the plaintiff's prima facie case: "at the time of his discharge or demotion, he was performing his job at a level that met his employer's legitimate expectations."[1]

Another aspect of this element has also given rise to litigation: whether the plaintiff was qualified for the job. Does this requirement refer to minimal qualifications for the job or to the best qualifications among all the applicants? If the former, then the plaintiff's burden is relatively light. If the latter, then it is significantly heavier, requiring the plaintiff to rebut the reason usually offered by the defendant for denying the job to the plaintiff in the first place. The fourth element of the plaintiff's prima facie case is framed in terms that suggest that the plaintiff need only prove minimal qualifications. That element requires proof that "the employer continued to seek applicants from persons of complainant's qualifications," implying that the plaintiff need not be the best qualified for the job. This implication was confirmed in United States Postal Service Board of Governors v. Aikens, 460 U.S. 711 (1983). The parties there argued over whether the plaintiff had the burden of proving more than minimal qualifications, but because the case had been fully tried, the Supreme Court found that this issue had dropped from the case:

> But when the defendant fails to persuade the district court to dismiss the action for lack of a prima facie case, and responds to the plaintiff's proof by offering evidence of the reason for the

[1] To the extent the Court expressed doubts about this formulation, it was over whether *McDonnell Douglas* applied to age discrimination claims at all. The adaptation of this element for discharge cases was not questioned.

plaintiff's rejection, the factfinder must then decide whether the rejection was discriminatory within the meaning of Title VII.

The last two elements of the plaintiff's case follow the same pattern as the first two. The third, that the plaintiff was rejected, is virtually a precondition for the plaintiff to bring suit at all. The fourth, that the position remained open, is either easily satisfied if someone else was selected in place of the plaintiff, or completely irrelevant when, as discussed earlier, the plaintiff is laid off and his position is abolished.

These points all support the observation in *McDonnell Douglas* that its formulation of the plaintiff's prima facie case was not meant to be exclusive and that the plaintiff can prove his case by other means. Direct evidence of discrimination, such as racist comments by supervisors or managers, can be used in addition to or instead of proof of the elements of the prima facie case. In many instances, such direct evidence will be far more persuasive evidence of discrimination than the circumstantial evidence discussed in *McDonnell Douglas*. If alternative, more persuasive methods of proof are always available to the plaintiff, what does the prima facie case accomplish? How often is it decisive, or even important, in resolving individual claims of intentional discrimination? These questions lead to the further issue of how much of the burden of proof is actually shifted to the defendant.

5. The Defendant's Rebuttal Burden. The defendant's burden under *McDonnell Douglas* is only "to articulate some legitimate, nondiscriminatory reason for the plaintiff's rejection." Taking the term "articulate" to mean only offering evidence, the burden that shifts to the defendant is only a burden of production: to present evidence from which a reasonable inference can be drawn that the plaintiff was rejected for a legitimate, nondiscriminatory reason. Later cases, discussed in the sections that follow, make clear that the defendant's burden is only one of producing evidence. The defendant must only present evidence from which a reasonable inference of a legitimate, nondiscriminatory reason can be drawn for the plaintiff's rejection.

Does the term "legitimate" add anything to the defendant's burden? Or does it just emphasize the nondiscriminatory nature of the reason that must be offered? A great advantage of prohibitions against discrimination is that they constitute only a limited form of regulation. They tell employers what they cannot consider in making their personnel decisions, but they leave employers otherwise free to exercise business judgment. The heavy hand of government regulation falls only on employers who engage in discrimination on the grounds prohibited by law. Under Title VII, an employer is free to offer no reason, or any reason, for rejecting the plaintiff, so long as it does not involve race, color, national origin, sex, or religion. Must these reasons be legitimate in some other sense? Presumably if these reasons were not legitimate, for instance, if they constituted unlawful opposition to union activity, the employer would be liable under a separate statute like the National Labor Relations Act. Must the employer also be liable under Title VII?

If the employer can appeal to a wide range of reasons in carrying its rebuttal burden, how often will the employer fail to meet its burden of production? McDonnell Douglas rejected Green because he had participated in a "stall-in" and had allegedly participated also in a "lock-in," both intended to disrupt the company's operations. The court of appeals characterized these reasons as "subjective" and therefore of little weight. In what sense were they "subjective": because they were not quantifiable, like a test score; because they were not made according to previously stated rules or policies of the company; because they involved the exercise of judgment by company officials; or because they involved conduct directed at the company itself? Should reasons that are subjective in any of these senses be given closer scrutiny? If so, under the Supreme Court's opinion, when should such scrutiny occur: at the defendant's stage of the case in offering a "legitimate, nondiscriminatory reason" or at the plaintiff's stage in proving pretext?

6. The Plaintiff's Burden of Proving Pretext. Assuming the parties each carry their initial burdens, the plaintiff must then prove pretext: as the opinion states, "that the presumptively valid reasons for his rejection were in fact a cover-up for a racially discriminatory decision." Is there any difference between proof of pretext in this sense and proof simply of intentional discrimination? If so, does the opinion in *McDonnell Douglas* identify what the difference is? If not, what does the entire structure of shifting burdens of production accomplish?

Again, as subsequent cases have made clear, the burden upon the plaintiff to prove pretext is both a burden of production and a burden of persuasion. Once the defendant's burden of production is met, the entire burden of proof then returns to the plaintiff. Thus the plaintiff must produce evidence from which a reasonable inference can be drawn that the defendant's offered reason was not the real reason for his rejection, but that discrimination was. The plaintiff must then also persuade the finder of fact to draw that inference by a preponderance of the evidence. Is this any different from the plaintiff's burden of proving intentional discrimination entirely without the benefit of *McDonnell Douglas*? Does the plaintiff gain anything because the burden of producing evidence of a legitimate, nondiscriminatory reason has been shifted to the defendant? Subsequent cases have explored this question in detail. For an account of the difficulties many plaintiffs face in making out claims of employment discrimination, see Peter Siegelman, The Compromised Worker & The Limits of Employment Discrimination Law, 64 Buff. L. Rev. 565 (2016). For a completely different way of encouraging employment of disfavored applicants, see Samuel Estreicher, Achieving Antidiscrimination Objectives through "Safe Harbor" Rules in Cases of Chronic Hiring Aversion, 2 J. Law & Pub. Aff. 1 (2017).

Some writers have been critical of this entire approach to discrimination, arguing that much of it is implicit, unconscious, reckless, or negligent. See Stephanie Bornstein, Reckless Discrimination, 105 Calif. L. Rev. 1055 (2017); Erik James Girvan & Grace M. Deason, Social Science in Law: A Psychological Case for Abandoning the "Discriminatory Motive" Under Title VII, 60 Cleveland St. L. Rev. 1057 (2013); Linda Hamilton Krieger, The Content of Our Categories: A Cognitive Bias Approach to Discrimination and Equal Employment Opportunity, 47 Stan. L. Rev. 1161 (1995); Charles Lawrence, The Id, the Ego, and Equal Protection: Reckoning with Unconscious Discrimination, 39 Stan. L. Rev. 317 (1987); Noah D. Zatz, Putting Intent in Its Place: A New Direction for Title VII, Calif. Lab. & Empl. L. Rev. 8 (July 2014). Does this argument for expanding the scope of prohibitions against intentional discrimination reflect ambiguities in the concept of discrimination itself, in the difficulty of obtaining direct evidence of discrimination, or in the organizational structure of most employers? For one view about how all three of these issues combine to complicate the search for intentional discrimination, see George Rutherglen, Reconsidering Burdens of Proof: Ideology, Evidence, and Intent in Individual Claims of Employment Discrimination, 1 Va. J. Soc. Pol'y & L. 43 (1993).

7. **Bibliography.** *McDonnell Douglas* has generated a literature all its own. For some of the earlier articles, see Robert Belton, Burdens of Pleading and Proof in Discrimination Cases: Toward a Theory of Procedural Justice, 34 Vand. L. Rev. 1205 (1981); Jessica A. Clarke, Protected Class Gatekeeping, 92 N.Y.U. L. Rev. 101 (2017); e. christi cunningham, The Rise of Identity Politics I: The Myth of the Protected Class in Title VII Disparate Treatment Cases, 30 Conn. L. Rev. 441 (1998); Sandra F. Sperino, Beyond *McDonnell Douglas*, 34 Berkeley J. Emp. & Lab. L. 257 (2013); Michael J. Zimmer, Systemic Empathy, 34 Colum. Hum. Rts. L. Rev. 575 (2003); Colloquy on *McDonnell Douglas*, 52 Drake L. Rev. 383 (2004); Symposium, Presumptions and Burdens of Proof, Annual Institute for Humane Studies, 17 Harv. J.L. & Pub. Pol'y 613 (1994).

Furnco Construction Corp. v. Waters

438 U.S. 567 (1978).

■ JUSTICE REHNQUIST delivered the opinion of the Court.

Respondents are three black bricklayers who sought employment with petitioner Furnco Construction Corp. Two of the three were never offered employment. The third was employed only long after he initially applied. Upon adverse findings entered after a bench trial, the District Court for the Northern District of Illinois held that respondents had not proved a claim under either the "disparate treatment" theory of McDonnell Douglas Corp. v. Green, 411 U.S. 792 (1973), or the "disparate impact" theory of Griggs v. Duke Power Co., 401 U.S. 424 (1971). The Court of Appeals for the Seventh Circuit, concluding that under *McDonnell Douglas* respondents had made out a prima facie case which had not been effectively rebutted, reversed the judgment of the District Court. 551 F.2d 1085 (7th Cir. 1977). We granted certiorari to consider important questions raised by this case regarding the exact scope of the prima facie case under *McDonnell Douglas* and the nature of the evidence necessary to rebut such a case. Having concluded that the Court of Appeals erred in its treatment of the latter question, we reverse and remand to that court for further proceedings consistent with this opinion.

I

A few facts in this case are not in serious dispute. Petitioner Furnco, an employer within the meaning of §§ 701 (b) and (h) of Title VII of the

1964 Civil Rights Act, specializes in refractory installation in steel mills and, more particularly, the rehabilitation or relining of blast furnaces with what is called in the trade "firebrick." Furnco does not, however, maintain a permanent force of bricklayers. Rather, it hires a superintendent for a specific job and then delegates to him the task of securing a competent work force. In August 1971, Furnco contracted with Interlake, Inc., to reline one of its blast furnaces. Joseph Dacies, who had been a job superintendent for Furnco since 1965, was placed in charge of the job and given the attendant hiring responsibilities. He did not accept applications at the jobsite, but instead hired only persons whom he knew to be experienced and competent in this type of work or persons who had been recommended to him as similarly skilled. He hired his first four bricklayers, all of whom were white, on two successive days in August, the 26th and 27th, and two in September, the 7th and 8th. On September 9 he hired the first black bricklayer. By September 13, he had hired 8 more bricklayers, 1 of whom was black; by September 17, 7 more had been employed, another of whom was black; and by September 23, 17 more were on the payroll, again with 1 black included in that number. From October 12 to 18, he hired 6 bricklayers, all of whom were black, including respondent Smith, who had worked for Dacies previously and had applied at the jobsite somewhat earlier. Respondents Samuels and Nemhard were not hired, though they were fully qualified and had also attempted to secure employment by appearing at the jobsite gate. Out of the total of 1,819 man-days worked on the Interlake job, 242, or 13.3%, were worked by black bricklayers.

Many of the remaining facts found by the District Court and the inferences to be drawn therefrom are in some dispute between the parties, but none was expressly found by the Court of Appeals to be clearly erroneous. The District Court elaborated at some length as to the "critical" necessity of insuring that only experienced and highly qualified fire-bricklayers were employed. Improper or untimely work would result in substantial losses both to Interlake, which was forced to shut down its furnace and lay off employees during the relining job, and to Furnco, which was paid for this work at a fixed price and for a fixed time period. In addition, not only might shoddy work slow this work process down, but it also might necessitate costly future maintenance work with its attendant loss of production and employee layoffs; diminish Furnco's reputation and ability to secure similar work in the future; and perhaps even create serious safety hazards, leading to explosions and the like. These considerations justified Furnco's refusal to engage in on-the-job training or to hire at the gate, a hiring process which would not provide an adequate method of matching qualified applications to job requirements and assuring that the applicants are sufficiently skilled and capable. Furthermore, there was no evidence that these policies and practices were a pretext to exclude black bricklayers or were otherwise illegitimate or had a disproportionate impact or effect on black bricklayers. From late 1969 through late 1973, 5.7% of the bricklayers in the relevant labor force were minority group members, see 41 CFR § 60–11 et seq. (1977), while, as mentioned before, 13.3% of the man-days on Furnco's Interlake job were worked by black bricklayers.

Because of the above considerations and following the established practice in the industry, most of the firebricklayers hired by Dacies were persons known by him to be experienced and competent in this type of work. The others were hired after being recommended as skilled in this type of work by his general foreman, an employee (a black), another Furnco superintendent in the area, and Furnco's General Manager John Wright. Wright had not only instructed Dacies to employ, as far as possible, at least 16% black bricklayers, a policy due to Furnco's self-imposed affirmative-action plan to insure that black bricklayers were employed by Furnco in Cook County in numbers substantially in excess of their percentage in the local union, but he had also recommended, in an effort to show good faith, that Dacies hire several specific bricklayers, who had previously filed a discrimination suit against Furnco, negotiations for the settlement of which had only recently broken down. . . .

From these factual findings, the District Court concluded that respondents had failed to make out a Title VII claim under the doctrine of Griggs v. Duke Power Co., 401 U.S. 424 (1971). Furnco's policy of not hiring at the gate was racially neutral on its face and there was no showing that it had a disproportionate impact or effect. It also held that respondents had failed to prove a case of discrimination under McDonnell Douglas Corp. v. Green, 411 U.S. 792 (1973). It is not entirely clear whether the court thought respondents had failed to make out a prima facie case of discrimination under *McDonnell Douglas*, but the court left no doubt that it thought Furnco's hiring practices and policies were justified as a "business necessity" in that they were required for the safe and efficient operation of Furnco's business, and were "not used as a pretext to exclude Negroes." Thus, even if a prima facie case had been made out, it had been effectively rebutted.

> "Not only have Plaintiffs entirely failed to establish that Furnco's employment practices on the Interlake job discriminated against them on the basis of race or constituted retaliatory conduct but Defendant has proven what it was not required to. By its cross-examination and direct evidence, Furnco has proven beyond all reasonable doubt that it did not engage in either racial discrimination or retaliatory conduct in its employment practices in regard to bricklayers on the Interlake job."

The Court of Appeals reversed, holding that respondents had made out a prima facie case under *McDonnell Douglas*, which Furnco had not effectively rebutted. Because of the "historical inequality of treatment of black workers" and the fact that the record failed to reveal that any white persons had applied at the gate, the Court of Appeals rejected Furnco's argument that discrimination had not been shown because a white appearing at the jobsite would have fared no better than respondents. That court also disagreed with Furnco's contention, which the District Court had adopted, that "the importance of selecting people whose capability had been demonstrated to defendant's brick superintendent is a 'legitimate, nondiscriminatory reason' for defendant's refusal to consider plaintiffs." Instead, the appellate court proceeded to devise what it thought would be an appropriate hiring procedure for Furnco, saying that "[it] seems to us that there is a reasonable middle ground between immediate hiring decisions on the spot and seeking out employees from among those known to the superintendent." This middle course, according to the Court of Appeals, was to take written applications, with inquiry as to qualifications and experience, and then check, evaluate, and compare those claims against the qualifications and experience of other bricklayers with whom the superintendent was already acquainted. We granted certiorari to consider whether the Court of Appeals had gone too far in substituting its own judgment as to proper hiring practices in the case of an employer which claimed the practices it had chosen did not violate Title VII.

II

A

We agree with the Court of Appeals that the proper approach was the analysis contained in *McDonnell Douglas*. We also think the Court of Appeals was justified in concluding that as a matter of law respondents made out a prima facie case of discrimination under *McDonnell Douglas*. In that case we held that a plaintiff could make out a prima facie claim by showing:

> "(i) that he belongs to a racial minority; (ii) that he applied and was qualified for a job for which the employer was seeking applicants; (iii) that, despite his qualifications, he was rejected; and (iv) that, after his rejection, the position remained open and the employer continued to seek applicants from persons of complainant's qualifications." 411 U.S., at 802 (footnote omitted).

This, of course, was not intended to be an inflexible rule, as the Court went on to note that "[the] facts necessarily will vary in Title VII cases, and the specification . . . of the prima facie proof required from respondent is not necessarily applicable in every respect to differing factual situations." Id. at 802 n.13. See Teamsters v. United States, 431 U.S. 324, 358 (1977). But *McDonnell Douglas* did make clear that a Title VII plaintiff carries the initial burden of showing actions taken by the employer from which one can infer, if such actions remain unexplained, that it is more likely than not that such actions were "based on a discriminatory criterion illegal under the Act." And here respondents carried that initial burden by proving they were members of a racial minority; they did everything within their power to apply for employment; Furnco has conceded that they were qualified in every respect for the jobs which were about to be open; they were not offered employment, although Smith later was; and the employer continued to seek persons of similar qualifications.

B

We think the Court of Appeals went awry, however, in apparently equating a prima facie showing under *McDonnell Douglas* with an ultimate finding of fact as to discriminatory refusal to hire under Title VII; the two are quite different and that difference has a direct bearing on the proper resolution of this case. The Court of Appeals, as we read its opinion, thought Furnco's hiring procedures not only must be reasonably related to the achievement of some legitimate purpose, but also must be the method which allows the employer to consider the qualifications of the largest number of minority applicants. We think the imposition of that second requirement simply finds no support either in the nature of the prima facie case or the purpose of Title VII.

The central focus of the inquiry in a case such as this is always whether the employer is treating "some people less favorably than others because of their race, color, religion, sex, or national origin." Teamsters v. United States, supra, at 335 n.15. The method suggested in *McDonnell Douglas* for pursuing this inquiry, however, was never intended to be rigid, mechanized, or ritualistic. Rather, it is merely a sensible, orderly way to evaluate the evidence in light of common experience as it bears on the critical question of discrimination. A prima facie case under *McDonnell Douglas* raises an inference of discrimination only because we presume these acts, if otherwise unexplained, are more likely than not based on the consideration of impermissible factors. And we are willing to presume this largely because we know from our experience that more often than not people do not act in a totally arbitrary manner, without any underlying reasons, especially in a business setting. Thus, when all legitimate reasons for rejecting an applicant have been eliminated as possible reasons for the employer's actions, it is more likely than not the employer, who we generally assume acts only with some reason, based his decision on an impermissible consideration such as race.

When the prima facie case is understood in the light of the opinion in *McDonnell Douglas*, it is apparent that the burden which shifts to the employer is merely that of proving that he based his employment decision on a legitimate consideration, and not an illegitimate one such as race. To prove that, he need not prove that he pursued the course which would both enable him to achieve his own business goal and allow him to consider the most employment applications. Title VII prohibits him from having as a goal a work force selected by any proscribed discriminatory practice, but it does not impose a duty to adopt a hiring procedure that maximizes hiring of minority employees. To dispel the adverse inference from a prima facie showing under *McDonnell Douglas*, the employer need only "articulate some legitimate, nondiscriminatory reason for the employee's rejection."

The dangers of embarking on a course such as that charted by the Court of Appeals here, where the court requires businesses to adopt what it perceives to be the "best" hiring procedures, are nowhere more evident than in the record of this very case. Not only does the record not reveal that the court's suggested hiring procedure would work satisfactorily, but also there is nothing in the record to indicate that it would be any less "haphazard, arbitrary, and subjective" than Furnco's method, which the Court of Appeals criticized as deficient for exactly those reasons. Courts are generally less competent than employers to restructure business practices, and unless mandated to do so by Congress they should not attempt it.

This is not to say, of course, that proof of a justification which is reasonably related to the achievement of some legitimate goal necessarily ends the inquiry. The plaintiff must be given the opportunity to introduce evidence that the proffered justification is merely a pretext for discrimination. And as we noted in *McDonnell Douglas*, this evidence might take a variety of forms. But the Court of Appeals, although stating its disagreement with the District Court's conclusion that the employer's hiring practices were a "legitimate, nondiscriminatory reason" for refusing to hire respondents, premised its disagreement on a view which we have discussed and rejected above. It did not conclude that the practices were a pretext for discrimination, but only that different practices would have enabled the employer to at least consider, and perhaps to hire, more minority employees. But courts may not impose such a remedy on an employer at least until a violation of Title VII has been proved, and here none had been under the reasoning of either the District Court or the Court of Appeals.

C

The Court of Appeals was also critical of petitioner's effort to employ statistics in this type of case. While the matter is not free from doubt, it appears that the court thought that once a *McDonnell Douglas* prima facie showing had been made out, statistics of a racially balanced work force were totally irrelevant to the question of motive. That would undoubtedly be a correct view of the matter if the *McDonnell Douglas* prima facie showing were the equivalent of an ultimate finding by the trier of fact that the original rejection of the applicant was racially motivated: A racially balanced work force cannot immunize an employer from liability for specific acts of discrimination. . . . It is clear beyond cavil that the obligation imposed by Title VII is to provide an equal opportunity for each applicant regardless of race, without regard to whether members of the applicant's race are already proportionately represented in the work force. . . .

A *McDonnell Douglas* prima facie showing is not the equivalent of a factual finding of discrimination, however. Rather, it is simply proof of actions taken by the employer from which we infer discriminatory animus because experience has proved that in the absence of any other explanation it is more likely than not that those actions were bottomed on impermissible considerations. When the prima facie showing is understood in this manner, the employer must be allowed some latitude to introduce evidence which bears on his motive. Proof that his work force was racially balanced or that it contained a disproportionately high percentage of minority employees is not wholly irrelevant on the issue of intent when that issue is yet to be decided. We cannot say that such proof would have absolutely no probative value in determining whether the otherwise unexplained rejection of the minority applicants was discriminatorily motivated. Thus, although we agree with the Court of Appeals that in this case such proof neither was nor could have been sufficient to conclusively demonstrate that Furnco's actions were not discriminatorily motivated, the District Court was entitled to consider the racial mix of the work force when trying to make the determination as to motivation. The Court of Appeals should likewise give similar consideration to the proffered statistical proof in any further proceedings in this case. . . .

It is so ordered.

[Justice Marshall dissented, joined by Justice Brennan, on the ground that the employer's hiring practices might have had a disparate impact on blacks and that that question should have been left open on remand.]

NOTES ON *FURNCO CONSTRUCTION CO. V. WATERS*

1. **Consequences of the "Prima Facie" Case.** According to the Supreme Court, the court of appeals erred in giving too much weight to the plaintiff's success in making out a "prima facie" case. The court of appeals erred "in apparently equating a prima facie showing under *McDonnell Douglas* with an ultimate finding of fact as to discriminatory refusal to hire under Title VII." Because it is so easy for the plaintiff to make out a prima facie case under *McDonnell Douglas* in most cases, the difference between an inference of discrimination and a finding of discrimination is exceedingly important. If the court of appeals' view were accepted, most individual claims of intentional discrimination would be litigated on the issue of remedies, not on the issue of violation. The plaintiff would have succeeded in establishing a violation of Title VII and the only remaining issue would be the remedies that the plaintiff was entitled to.

The court of appeals might have been led to this conclusion because at least three distinct meanings of the "prima facie" case can be distinguished. First, it might refer to evidence from which a reasonable inference of discrimination might be drawn. In a case tried to a jury, in the absence of countervailing evidence, the jury *may* find discrimination. Second, the term might refer to evidence from which an inference of discrimination *must* be drawn. The evidence, if believed and if not contradicted by further evidence, requires the jury to find discrimination. Or third, the term might refer to evidence from which a finding of discrimination has been drawn (whether it had to be drawn or not) and which entitles the plaintiff to relief in the absence of any further evidence. All of these variations on a prima facie case can be counteracted by opposing evidence, negating respectively, the inference of discrimination, the presumption of discrimination, or the presumption that the plaintiff is entitled to relief.

The Supreme Court seemed to endorse the first of these meanings, while the court of appeals seemed to endorse the third. Yet each of these interpretations results in further complications. Did the Supreme Court mean to suggest that every time a plaintiff makes out a prima facie case under *McDonnell Douglas*, the case must go to trial and must be submitted to the jury (or to the judge as trier of fact in a case tried without a jury)? In other words, does the prima facie case require the defendant's motion for summary judgment or motion for judgment as a matter of law to be denied? This consequence is not quite as drastic as requiring a finding of discrimination, but it leaves control over most individual claims of intentional discrimination in the hands of the jury. The court of appeals' seeming endorsement of the third interpretation of a prima facie case equates it with a finding of discrimination. But there is little in its decision concerned with the issue of remedies, which would follow on a finding of discrimination. The court of appeals, instead, seems to be concerned entirely with the defendant's burden to produce a "legitimate, nondiscriminatory reason" on the issue of liability. Doesn't the decision in this case really turn on this latter issue? If so, why invoke the confusing terminology of a "prima facie" case at all?

2. **The Defendant's Rebuttal Burden Re-examined.** How broad is the range of reasons that the defendant can offer under the heading of a "legitimate, nondiscriminatory reason"? Furnco asserted that its practice of using the subjective judgment of a supervisor was the most reliable means of selecting "firebrick" workers for a job that required skilled labor, subject to tight constraints of cost, time, and safety. Why would a supervisor's subjective evaluations be the best means of selecting these workers? Wasn't there a danger that he would select his friends and that, in doing so, he would discriminate against members of minority groups? How could Furnco monitor the supervisor's selection of employees to meet its own needs for skilled workers on the job? To prevent discrimination?

The court of appeals evidently was suspicious of a selection process that relied on the nearly unfettered discretion of a single supervisor and that did not advertise the open positions among minority workers. What is wrong with the more formal application process that it would have required? Would this process have compromised Furnco's ability to hire efficient and trustworthy workers? The Supreme Court plainly believed that the employer was in a better position to assess what was in its best interests. Even so, however, a court seems to be in a better position to determine how to prevent hidden forms of discrimination. How is that issue resolved under the structure of proof in *McDonnell Douglas*?

3. **Evidence of Pretext.** Although the plaintiff has the entire burden of proof, both of production and persuasion, on the issue of pretext, the defendant can also submit evidence on this issue. Indeed, it is generally true

that a party can—and to the extent possible, will—submit evidence on every material issue in litigation, whether or not it has the burden of proof on that issue. A party always gains by submitting favorable evidence on any disputed issue. In this case, Furnco Construction submitted evidence of its attempts to engage in affirmative action to rebut any finding of pretext.

How convincing is this evidence? Furnco had instructed the hiring supervisor to employ a work force that was at least 16 percent black, greater than the percentage of blacks in the local union. This policy was partly motivated by a pending lawsuit against Furnco brought by other black bricklayers, some of whom were recommended by Furnco's general manager for employment on the current project in an effort to facilitate settlement negotiations over their lawsuit. Yet most of the blacks who were hired for the current project were hired very late in the process, after all the whites had been hired. Does such "hurry-up" affirmative action count for, or against, Furnco's argument that its hiring policies were otherwise nondiscriminatory?

Empirical studies indicate that affirmative action has resulted in increased employment of minority workers only when it has been part of an intense and concerted effort to eliminate discrimination. Jonathan S. Leonard, The Impact of Affirmative Action Regulation and Equal Employment Law on Black Employment, 4 J. Econ. Perspectives 47 (1990). Do these findings suggest that ad hoc affirmative action plans, like that apparently adopted by Furnco, represent only superficial attempts at increasing minority employment? Or do such efforts represent the best possible outcome from enforcing the laws against employment discrimination? Particularly if these plans are adopted to forestall claims of discrimination, they result in increased minority employment without the substantial costs of litigation. In this case, Furnco had already been subjected to one lawsuit alleging discrimination against black workers. Did its affirmative action plan come too late to be credible or did it, in effect, extend the benefit of the litigation on behalf of a few individuals to all black bricklayers who might seek employment with the company? Note that the Supreme Court is careful in its opinion to identify evidence of Furnco's affirmative action plan only as relevant to the issue of pretext, not a complete defense to the plaintiffs' claim of intentional discrimination.

4. ***Ash v. Tyson Foods, Inc.*** In Ash v. Tyson Foods, Inc., 546 U.S. 454 (2006) (per curiam), the Supreme Court again cautioned the lower federal courts against invoking per se rules in evaluating evidence of intentional discrimination. The Court held that the court of appeals had erred in ruling on post-trial motions in two related cases, affirming a motion for judgment as a matter of law against one plaintiff and ordering a new trial as to another plaintiff. The court of appeals was mistaken, according to the Supreme Court, in discounting the effect of the word "boy" as a disparaging reference to black employees and in rejecting the plaintiffs' evidence of pretext. On the latter issue, the Court disapproved of a requirement that pretext be established through comparing qualifications only when "the disparity in qualifications is so apparent as virtually to jump off the page and slap you in

the face." The Court vacated and remanded the decision of the court of appeals for reconsideration of the evidence independently of these mistakes.

5. *Swierkiewicz v. Sorema, N.A.* What are the implications for pleading of the structure of proof established by *McDonnell Douglas*? In Swierkiewicz v. Sorema N.A., 534 U.S. 506 (2002), the Supreme Court held that it was almost none. The plaintiff in this case alleged that he had been discharged because of his national origin and because of his age, the latter in violation of the Age Discrimination in Employment Act. He also alleged the specific circumstances surrounding his termination, but he did not allege the elements of a prima facie case under *McDonnell Douglas*. The Court held that the complaint was sufficient because the Federal Rules of Civil Procedure require only simplified notice pleading, absent some specific exceptions, none of which apply to claims of discrimination. The Court also emphasized that "the *McDonnell Douglas* framework does not apply in every employment discrimination case."

In the cases in which the framework does apply, would the plaintiff nevertheless be better off alleging the elements of the prima facie case? Does the plaintiff lose anything by adding these allegations? How would the plaintiff know that *McDonnell Douglas* is applicable at the outset of a case, before any discovery has been undertaken? Would adding the allegations commit the plaintiff to relying on *McDonnell Douglas* when there might be other means of proving discrimination?

The continuing influence of *Swierkiewicz* has been called into question in light of subsequent decisions imposing a requirement upon pleading generally that the plaintiff's complaint "state a claim to relief that is plausible on its face." Bell Atlantic Corp. v. Twombly, 550 U.S. 544, 570 (2007); Ashcroft v. Iqbal, 556 U.S. 662 (2009). *Compare* Fowler v. UPMC Shadyside, 578 F.3d 203, 211 (3d Cir. 2009) (concluding that *Swierkiewicz*, has been repudiated to the extent that it relies on principles of liberal pleading) *with* Swanson v. Citibank, N.A., 614 F.3d 400, 404 (7th Cir. 2010) (concluding that *Swierkiewicz* was preserved because it was cited with approval in *Twombly*).

6. Bibliography. For articles specifically addressing the issues raised by *Furnco* and related cases, see Elizabeth Bartholet, Proof of Discriminatory Intent Under Title VII: *United States Postal Service Board of Governors v. Aikens*, 70 Cal. L. Rev. 1201 (1982); Tristin K. Green, Discrimination in Workplace Dynamics: Toward a Structural Account of Disparate Treatment Theory, 38 Harv. C.R.-C.L. L. Rev. 91 (2003); Charles A. Sullivan, Plausibly Pleading Employment Discrimination, 52 Wm. & Mary L. Rev. 1613 (2011); Suja A. Thomas, Oddball *Iqbal* and *Twombly* and Employment Discrimination, 2011 U. Ill. L. Rev. 215 (2011); Michael J. Zimmer & Charles A. Sullivan, The Structure of Title VII Individual Disparate Treatment Litigation: *Anderson v. City of Bessemer City*, Inferences of Discrimination, and Burdens of Proof, 9 Harv. Women's L.J. 25 (1986).

St. Mary's Honor Center v. Hicks

509 U.S. 502 (1993).

■ JUSTICE SCALIA delivered the opinion of the Court.

We granted certiorari to determine whether, in a suit against an employer alleging intentional racial discrimination in violation of § 703(a)(1) of Title VII of the Civil Rights Act of 1964, the trier of fact's rejection of the employer's asserted reasons for its actions mandates a finding for the plaintiff.

I

Petitioner St. Mary's Honor Center (St. Mary's) is a halfway house operated by the Missouri Department of Corrections and Human Resources (MDCHR). Respondent Melvin Hicks, a black man, was hired as a correctional officer at St. Mary's in August 1978 and was promoted to shift commander, one of six supervisory positions, in February 1980.

In 1983 MDCHR conducted an investigation of the administration of St. Mary's, which resulted in extensive supervisory changes in January 1984. Respondent retained his position, but John Powell became the new chief of custody (respondent's immediate supervisor) and petitioner Steve Long the new superintendent. Prior to these personnel changes respondent had enjoyed a satisfactory employment record, but soon thereafter became the subject of repeated, and increasingly severe, disciplinary actions. He was suspended for five days for violations of institutional rules by his subordinates on March 3, 1984. He received a letter of reprimand for alleged failure to conduct an adequate investigation of a brawl between inmates that occurred during his shift on March 21. He was later demoted from shift commander to correctional officer for his failure to ensure that his subordinates entered their use of a St. Mary's vehicle into the official log book on March 19, 1984. Finally, on June 7, 1984, he was discharged for threatening Powell during an exchange of heated words on April 19.

Respondent brought this suit in the United States District Court for the Eastern District of Missouri, alleging that petitioner St. Mary's violated § 703(a)(1) of Title VII, and that petitioner Long violated 42 U.S.C. § 1983, by demoting and then discharging him because of his race. After a full bench trial, the District Court found for petitioners. The United States Court of Appeals for the Eighth Circuit reversed and remanded, and we granted certiorari.

II

Section 703(a)(1) of Title VII of the Civil Rights Act of 1964 provides in relevant part:

> "It shall be an unlawful employment practice for an employer— . . . to discharge any individual, or otherwise to discriminate against any individual with respect to his compensation, terms,

> conditions, or privileges of employment, because of such individual's race. . . ."

With the goal of "progressively . . . sharpen[ing] the inquiry into the elusive factual question of intentional discrimination," Texas Dept. of Community Affairs v. Burdine, 450 U.S. 248, 255, n.8 (1981), our opinion in McDonnell Douglas Corp. v. Green, 411 U.S. 792 (1973), established an allocation of the burden of production and an order for the presentation of proof in Title VII discriminatory-treatment cases. The plaintiff in such a case, we said, must first establish, by a preponderance of the evidence, a "prima facie" case of racial discrimination. Petitioners do not challenge the District Court's finding that respondent satisfied the minimal requirements of such a prima facie case (set out in *McDonnell Douglas*) by proving (1) that he is black, (2) that he was qualified for the position of shift commander, (3) that he was demoted from that position and ultimately discharged, and (4) that the position remained open and was ultimately filled by a white man.

Under the *McDonnell Douglas* scheme, "[e]stablishment of the prima facie case in effect creates a presumption that the employer unlawfully discriminated against the employee." *Burdine*, supra, at 254. To establish a "presumption" is to say that a finding of the predicate fact (here, the prima facie case) produces "a required conclusion in the absence of explanation" (here, the finding of unlawful discrimination). 1 D. Louisell & C. Mueller, Federal Evidence § 67, p. 536 (1977). Thus, the *McDonnell Douglas* presumption places upon the defendant the burden of producing an explanation to rebut the prima facie case—i.e., the burden of "producing evidence" that the adverse employment actions were taken "for a legitimate, nondiscriminatory reason." *Burdine*, 450 U.S., at 254. "[T]he defendant must clearly set forth, through the introduction of admissible evidence," reasons for its actions which, *if believed by the trier of fact*, would support a finding that unlawful discrimination was not the cause of the employment action. Id. at 254–255, and n.8. It is important to note, however, that although the *McDonnell Douglas* presumption shifts the burden of production to the defendant, "[t]he ultimate burden of persuading the trier of fact that the defendant intentionally discriminated against the plaintiff remains at all times with the plaintiff," Id. at 253. In this regard it operates like all presumptions, as described in Rule 301 of the Federal Rules of Evidence:

> "In all civil actions and proceedings not otherwise provided for by Act of Congress or by these rules, a presumption imposes on the party against whom it is directed the burden of going forward with evidence to rebut or meet the presumption, but does not shift to such party the burden of proof in the sense of the risk of nonpersuasion, which remains throughout the trial upon the party on whom it was originally cast."

Respondent does not challenge the District Court's finding that petitioners sustained their burden of production by introducing evidence of two legitimate, nondiscriminatory reasons for their actions: the severity and the accumulation of rules violations committed by respondent. Our cases make clear that at that point the shifted burden of production became irrelevant: "If the defendant carries this burden of production, the presumption raised by the prima facie case is rebutted," *Burdine*, 450 U.S., at 255, and "drops from the case," Id. at 255, n.10. The plaintiff then has "the full and fair opportunity to demonstrate," through presentation of his own case and through cross-examination of the defendant's witnesses, "that the proffered reason was not the true reason for the employment decision," Id. at 256, and that race was. He retains that "ultimate burden of persuading the [trier of fact] that [he] has been the victim of intentional discrimination."

The District Court, acting as trier of fact in this bench trial, found that the reasons petitioners gave were not the real reasons for respondent's demotion and discharge. It found that respondent was the only supervisor disciplined for violations committed by his subordinates; that similar and even more serious violations committed by respondent's coworkers were either disregarded or treated more leniently; and that Powell manufactured the final verbal confrontation in order to provoke respondent into threatening him. It nonetheless held that respondent had failed to carry his ultimate burden of proving that his race was the determining factor in petitioners' decision first to demote and then to dismiss him.[2]

In short, the District Court concluded that "although [respondent] has proven the existence of a crusade to terminate him, he has not proven that the crusade was racially rather than personally motivated."

The Court of Appeals set this determination aside on the ground that "[o]nce [respondent] proved all of [petitioners'] proffered reasons for the adverse employment actions to be pretextual, [respondent] was entitled to judgment as a matter of law." The Court of Appeals reasoned:

> "Because all of defendants' proffered reasons were discredited, defendants were in a position of having offered no legitimate reason for their actions. In other words, defendants were in no better position than if they had remained silent, offering no rebuttal to an established inference that they had unlawfully discriminated against plaintiff on the basis of his race."

That is not so. By producing *evidence* (whether ultimately persuasive or not) of nondiscriminatory reasons, petitioners sustained their burden of production, and thus placed themselves in a "better position than if they had remained silent."

[2] Various considerations led it to this conclusion, including the fact that two blacks sat on the disciplinary review board that recommended disciplining respondent, that respondent's black subordinates who actually committed the violations were not disciplined, and that "the number of black employees at St. Mary's remained constant."

In the nature of things, the determination that a defendant has met its burden of production (and has thus rebutted any legal presumption of intentional discrimination) can involve no credibility assessment. For the burden-of-production determination necessarily *precedes* the credibility-assessment stage. At the close of the defendant's case, the court is asked to decide whether an issue of fact remains for the trier of fact to determine. None does if, on the evidence presented, (1) any rational person would have to find the existence of facts constituting a prima facie case, and (2) the defendant has failed to meet its burden of production—i.e., has failed to introduce evidence which, *taken as true*, would *permit* the conclusion that there was a nondiscriminatory reason for the adverse action. In that event, the court must award judgment to the plaintiff as a matter of law under Federal Rule of Civil Procedure 50(a)(1) (in the case of jury trials) or Federal Rule of Civil Procedure 52(c) (in the case of bench trials). See F. James & G. Hazard, Civil Procedure § 7.9, p. 327 (3d ed. 1985); 1 Louisell & Mueller, Federal Evidence § 70 at 568. If the defendant has failed to sustain its burden but reasonable minds could *differ* as to whether a preponderance of the evidence establishes the facts of a prima facie case, then a question of fact *does* remain, which the trier of fact will be called upon to answer.

If, on the other hand, the defendant has succeeded in carrying its burden of production, the *McDonnell Douglas* framework—with its presumptions and burdens—is no longer relevant. To resurrect it later, after the trier of fact has determined that what was "produced" to meet the burden of production is not credible, flies in the face of our holding in *Burdine* that to rebut the presumption "[t]he defendant need not persuade the court that it was actually motivated by the proffered reasons." The presumption, having fulfilled its role of forcing the defendant to come forward with some response, simply drops out of the picture. The defendant's "production" (whatever its persuasive effect) having been made, the trier of fact proceeds to decide the ultimate question: whether plaintiff has proven "that the defendant intentionally discriminated against [him]" because of his race. The factfinder's disbelief of the reasons put forward by the defendant (particularly if disbelief is accompanied by a suspicion of mendacity) may, together with the elements of the prima facie case, suffice to show intentional discrimination. Thus, rejection of the defendant's proffered reasons, will permit the trier of fact to infer the ultimate fact of intentional discrimination,[4] and the Court of Appeals was correct when it noted that, upon such rejection, "[n]o additional proof of discrimination is *required*," 970 F.2d, at 493 (emphasis added). But the Court of Appeals' holding that

[4] Contrary to the dissent's confusion-producing analysis, there is nothing whatever inconsistent between this statement and our later statements that (1) the plaintiff must show "both that the reason was false, and that discrimination was the real reason," and (2) "it is not enough . . . to disbelieve the employer." Even though (as we say here) rejection of the defendant's proffered reasons is enough at law to sustain a finding of discrimination, there must be a finding of discrimination.

rejection of the defendant's proffered reasons *compels* judgment for the plaintiff disregards the fundamental principle of Rule 301 that a presumption does not shift the burden of proof, and ignores our repeated admonition that the Title VII plaintiff at all times bears the "ultimate burden of persuasion."

III

Only one unfamiliar with our case-law will be upset by the dissent's alarum that we are today setting aside "settled precedent," "two decades of stable law in this Court," "a framework carefully crafted in precedents as old as 20 years," which "Congress is [aware]" of and has implicitly approved. Panic will certainly not break out among the courts of appeals, whose divergent views concerning the nature of the supposedly "stable law in this Court" are precisely what prompted us to take this case—a divergence in which the dissent's version of "settled precedent" cannot remotely be considered the "prevailing view." [Citations omitted.] We mean to answer the dissent's accusations in detail, by examining our cases, but at the outset it is worth noting the utter implausibility that we would ever have held what the dissent says we held.

As we have described, Title VII renders it unlawful "for an employer . . . to fail or refuse to hire or to discharge any individual, or otherwise to discriminate against any individual with respect to his compensation, terms, conditions, or privileges of employment, because of such individual's race, color, religion, sex, or national origin." 42 U.S.C. § 2000e–2(a)(1). Here (in the context of the now-permissible jury trials for Title VII causes of action) is what the dissent asserts we have held to be a proper assessment of liability for violation of this law: Assume that 40% of a business' work force are members of a particular minority group, a group which comprises only 10% of the relevant labor market. An applicant, who is a member of that group, applies for an opening for which he is minimally qualified, but is rejected by a hiring officer of that *same minority group*, and the search to fill the opening continues. The rejected applicant files suit for racial discrimination under Title VII, and before the suit comes to trial, the supervisor who conducted the company's hiring is fired. Under *McDonnell Douglas*, the plaintiff has a prima facie case, and under the dissent's interpretation of our law not only must the company come forward with some explanation for the refusal to hire (which it will have to try to confirm out of the mouth of its now antagonistic former employee), but the jury must be instructed that, if they find that explanation to be incorrect, they must assess damages against the company, *whether or not they believe the company was guilty of racial discrimination*. The disproportionate minority makeup of the company's work force and the fact that its hiring officer was of the same minority group as the plaintiff will be irrelevant, because the plaintiff's case can be proved "indirectly by showing that the employer's proffered explanation is unworthy of credence." Surely nothing short of inescapable prior *holdings* (the dissent does not pretend there are any) should make one assume that this is the law we have created.

We have no authority to impose liability upon an employer for alleged discriminatory employment practices unless an appropriate factfinder determines, according to proper procedures, *that the employer has unlawfully discriminated*. We may, according to traditional practice, establish certain modes and orders of proof, including an initial rebuttable presumption of the sort we described earlier in this opinion, which we believe *McDonnell Douglas* represents. But nothing in law would permit us to substitute for the required finding that the employer's action was the product of unlawful discrimination, the much different (and much lesser) finding that the employer's explanation of its action was not believable. The dissent's position amounts to precisely this, *unless* what is required to establish the *McDonnell Douglas* prima facie case is a degree of proof so high that it would, in absence of rebuttal, require a directed verdict for the plaintiff (for in that case proving the employer's rebuttal noncredible would leave the plaintiff's directed-verdict case in place, and compel a judgment in his favor). Quite obviously, however, what is required to establish the *McDonnell Douglas* prima facie case is infinitely less than what a directed verdict demands. The dissent is thus left with a position that has no support in the statute, no support in the reason of the matter, no support in any holding of this Court (that is not even contended), and support, if at all, only in the dicta of this Court's opinions. It is to those that we now turn—begrudgingly, since we think it generally undesirable, where holdings of the Court are not at issue, to dissect the sentences of the United States Reports as though they were the United States Code.

The principal case on which the dissent relies is *Burdine*. While there are some statements in that opinion that could be read to support the dissent's position, all but one of them bear a meaning consistent with our interpretation, and the one exception is simply incompatible with other language in the case. *Burdine* describes the situation that obtains after the employer has met its burden of adducing a nondiscriminatory reason as follows: "Third, should the defendant carry this burden, the plaintiff must then have an opportunity to prove by a preponderance of the evidence that the legitimate reasons offered by the defendant were not its true reasons, but were a pretext for discrimination." The dissent takes this to mean that if the plaintiff proves the asserted reason to be *false*, the plaintiff wins. But a reason cannot be proved to be "a pretext *for discrimination*" unless it is shown *both* that the reason was false, and that discrimination was the real reason. *Burdine*'s later allusions to proving or demonstrating simply "pretext" are reasonably understood to refer to the previously described pretext, i.e., "pretext for discrimination."

Burdine also says that when the employer has met its burden of production "the factual inquiry proceeds to a new level of specificity." The dissent takes this to mean that the factual inquiry reduces to whether the employer's asserted reason is true or false—if false, the defendant loses. But the "new level of specificity" may also (as we believe) refer to the fact that the inquiry now turns from the few generalized factors that establish a prima facie case to the specific proofs and rebuttals of discriminatory motivation the parties have introduced.

In the next sentence, *Burdine* says that "[p]lacing this burden of production on the defendant thus serves . . . to frame the factual issue with sufficient clarity so that the plaintiff will have a full and fair opportunity to demonstrate pretext." The dissent thinks this means that the only factual issue remaining in the case is whether the employer's reason is false. But since in our view "pretext" means "pretext for discrimination," we think the sentence must be understood as addressing the form rather than the substance of the defendant's production burden: The requirement that the employer "clearly set forth" its reasons gives the plaintiff a "full and fair" rebuttal opportunity.

A few sentences later, *Burdine* says: "[The plaintiff] now must have the opportunity to demonstrate that the proffered reason was not the true reason for the employment decision. This burden now merges with the ultimate burden of persuading the court that she has been the victim of intentional discrimination." Id. at 256. The dissent takes this "merger" to mean that the "the ultimate burden of persuading the court that she has been the victim of intentional discrimination" is *replaced* by the mere burden of "demonstrat[ing] that the proffered reason was not the true reason for the employment decision." But that would be a merger in which the little fish swallows the big one. Surely a more reasonable reading is that proving the employer's reason false becomes part of (and often considerably assists) the greater enterprise of proving that the real reason was intentional discrimination.

Finally, in the next sentence *Burdine* says: "[The plaintiff] may succeed in this [i.e., in persuading the court that she has been the victim of intentional discrimination] either directly by persuading the court that a discriminatory reason more likely motivated the employer or indirectly by showing that the employer's proffered explanation is unworthy of credence. See McDonnell Douglas, 411 U.S., at 804–805." We must agree with the dissent on this one: The words bear no other meaning but that the falsity of the employer's explanation is *alone enough* to compel judgment for the plaintiff. The problem is that that dictum contradicts or renders inexplicable numerous other statements, both in *Burdine* itself and in our later case-law—commencing with the very citation of authority *Burdine* uses to support the proposition. *McDonnell Douglas* does not say, at the cited pages or elsewhere, that all the plaintiff need do is disprove the employer's asserted reason. In fact, it says just the opposite: "[O]n the retrial respondent must be given a full and fair opportunity to demonstrate by competent evidence that the presumptively valid reasons for his rejection *were in fact a coverup for a racially discriminatory decision*." 411 U.S., at 805 (emphasis added). "We

. . . insist that respondent under § 703(a)(1) must be given a full and fair opportunity to demonstrate by competent evidence *that whatever the stated reasons for his rejection, the decision was in reality racially premised*." Id. at 805, n.18 (emphasis added). The statement in question also contradicts *Burdine*'s repeated assurance (indeed, its holding) regarding the burden of persuasion: "The ultimate burden of persuading the trier of fact that the defendant intentionally discriminated against the plaintiff remains at all times with the plaintiff. . . . The plaintiff retains the burden of persuasion." And lastly, the statement renders inexplicable *Burdine*'s explicit reliance, in describing the shifting burdens of *McDonnell Douglas*, upon authorities setting forth the classic law of presumptions we have described earlier, including Wigmore's Evidence, 450 U.S., at 253, 254, n.7, 255, n.8, James' and Hazard's Civil Procedure, Id. at 255, n.8, Federal Rule of Evidence 301, Maguire's Evidence, Common Sense and Common Law, and Thayer's Preliminary Treatise on Evidence, Id. at 255, n.10. In light of these inconsistencies, we think that the dictum at issue here must be regarded as an inadvertence, to the extent that it describes disproof of the defendant's reason as a totally independent, rather than an auxiliary, means of proving unlawful intent.

In sum, our interpretation of *Burdine* creates difficulty with one sentence; the dissent's interpretation causes many portions of the opinion to be incomprehensible or deceptive. But whatever doubt *Burdine* might have created was eliminated by *Aikens*. There we said, in language that cannot reasonably be mistaken, that "the ultimate question [is] discrimination vel non." 460 U.S., at 714. Once the defendant "responds to the plaintiff's proof by offering evidence of the reason for the plaintiff's rejection, the factfinder must then decide" *not* (as the dissent would have it) whether that evidence is credible, but "whether the rejection was discriminatory within the meaning of Title VII." At that stage, we said, "[t]he District Court was . . . in a position to decide the ultimate factual issue in the case," which is "whether the defendant intentionally discriminated against the plaintiff." Id. at 715 (brackets and internal quotation marks omitted). The *McDonnell Douglas* methodology was "never intended to be rigid, mechanized, or ritualistic." 460 U.S., at 715 (quoting *Furnco*, 438 U.S., at 577). Rather, once the defendant has responded to the plaintiff's prima facie case, "the district court has before it all the evidence it needs to decide" *not* (as the dissent would have it) whether defendant's response is credible, but "whether the defendant intentionally discriminated against the plaintiff. . . . On the state of the record at the close of the evidence, the District Court in this case should have proceeded to this specific question directly, just as district courts decide disputed questions of fact in other civil litigation." Id. at 715–716. *In confirmation of this* (rather than in contradiction of it), the Court then quotes the problematic passage from *Burdine*, which says that the plaintiff may carry her burden either directly "or indirectly by showing that the employer's proffered explanation is unworthy of credence." It then characterizes that passage as follows: "In short, the district court must decide which party's explanation of the employer's motivation it believes." It is not enough, in other words, to disbelieve the employer; the factfinder must *believe* the plaintiff's explanation of intentional discrimination. It is noteworthy that Justice Blackmun, although joining the Court's opinion in *Aikens*, wrote a separate concurrence for the sole purpose of saying that he understood the Court's opinion to be saying what the dissent today asserts. That concurrence was joined only by Justice Brennan. Justice Marshall would have none of that, but simply refused to join the Court's opinion, concurring without opinion in the judgment. We think there is little doubt what *Aikens* meant.

IV

We turn, finally, to the dire practical consequences that the respondents and the dissent claim our decision today will produce. What appears to trouble the dissent more than anything is that, in its view, our rule is adopted "for the benefit of employers who have been found to have given false evidence in a court of law," whom we "favo[r]" by "exempting them from responsibility for lies." As we shall explain, our rule in no way gives special favor to those employers whose evidence is disbelieved. But initially we must point out that there is no justification for assuming (as the dissent repeatedly does) that those employers whose evidence is disbelieved are perjurers and liars . . . even if these were typically cases in which an individual defendant's sworn assertion regarding a physical occurrence was pitted against an individual plaintiff's sworn assertion regarding the same physical occurrence, surely it would be imprudent to call the party whose assertion is (by a mere preponderance of the evidence) disbelieved, a perjurer and a liar. And in these Title VII cases, the defendant is ordinarily not an individual but a company, which must rely upon the statement of an employee—often a relatively low-level employee—as to the central fact; and that central fact is not a physical occurrence, but rather that employee's state of mind. To say that the company which in good faith introduces such testimony, or even the testifying employee himself, becomes a liar and a perjurer when the testimony is not believed, is nothing short of absurd. . . .

We reaffirm today what we said in *Aikens*:

> "[T]he question facing triers of fact in discrimination cases is both sensitive and difficult. The prohibitions against discrimination contained in the Civil Rights Act of 1964 reflect an important national policy. There will seldom be 'eyewitness' testimony as to the employer's mental processes. But none of this means that trial courts or reviewing courts should treat discrimination differently from other ultimate questions of fact. Nor should they make their inquiry even more difficult by applying legal rules which were devised to govern 'the basic allocation of burdens and order of presentation of proof,'

> *Burdine*, 450 U.S., at 252, in deciding this ultimate question." 460 U.S., at 716.

The judgment of the Court of Appeals is reversed, and the case is remanded for further proceedings consistent with this opinion.

It is so ordered.

■ JUSTICE SOUTER, with whom JUSTICE WHITE, JUSTICE BLACKMUN, and JUSTICE STEVENS join, dissenting.

. . . Proof of a prima facie case thus serves as a catalyst obligating the employer to step forward with an explanation for its actions. St. Mary's, in this case, used this opportunity to provide two reasons for its treatment of Hicks: the severity and accumulation of rule infractions he had allegedly committed.

The Court emphasizes that the employer's obligation at this stage is only a burden of production, and that, if the employer meets the burden, the presumption entitling the plaintiff to judgment "drops from the case." This much is certainly true, but the obligation also serves an important function neglected by the majority, in requiring the employer "to frame the factual issue with sufficient clarity so that the plaintiff will have a full and fair opportunity to demonstrate pretext." The employer, in other words, has a "burden of production" that gives it the right to choose the scope of the factual issues to be resolved by the factfinder. But investing the employer with this choice has no point unless the scope it chooses binds the employer as well as the plaintiff. Nor does it make sense to tell the employer, as this Court has done, that its explanation of legitimate reasons "must be clear and reasonably specific," if the factfinder can rely on a reason not clearly articulated, or on one not articulated at all, to rule in favor of the employer. Id. at 258; see id. at 255, n.9 ("An articulation not admitted into evidence will not suffice").

Once the employer chooses the battleground in this manner, "the factual inquiry proceeds to a new level of specificity." Id. at 255. During this final, more specific inquiry, the employer has no burden to prove that its proffered reasons are true; rather, the plaintiff must prove by a preponderance of the evidence that the proffered reasons are pretextual. *McDonnell Douglas* makes it clear that if the plaintiff fails to show "pretext," the challenged employment action "must stand." 411 U.S., at 807. If, on the other hand, the plaintiff carries his burden of showing "pretext," the court "must order a prompt and appropriate remedy." Or, as we said in *Burdine*: "[The plaintiff] now must have the opportunity to demonstrate that the proffered reason was not the true reason for the employment decision. This burden now merges with the ultimate burden of persuading the court that [the plaintiff] has been the victim of intentional discrimination." 450 U.S., at 256. *Burdine* drives home the point that the case has proceeded to "a new level of specificity" by explaining that the plaintiff can meet his burden of persuasion in either of two ways: "either directly by persuading the court that a discriminatory reason more likely motivated the employer or indirectly by showing that the employer's proffered explanation is unworthy of credence." Ibid.; see *Aikens*, 460 U.S., at 716 (quoting this language from *Burdine*); id. at 717–718 (Blackmun, J., joined by Brennan, J., concurring); see also Price Waterhouse v. Hopkins, 490 U.S. 228, 287–289 (1989) (Kennedy, J., dissenting) (discussing these "two alternative methods" and relying on Justice Blackmun's concurrence in *Aikens*). That the plaintiff can succeed simply by showing that "the employer's proffered explanation is unworthy of credence" indicates that the case has been narrowed to the question whether the employer's proffered reasons are pretextual. Thus, because Hicks carried his burden of persuasion by showing that St. Mary's proffered reasons were "unworthy of credence," the Court of Appeals properly concluded that he was entitled to judgment.[9] . . .

The majority's scheme greatly disfavors Title VII plaintiffs without the good luck to have direct evidence of discriminatory intent. The Court repeats the truism that the plaintiff has the "ultimate burden" of proving discrimination without ever facing the practical question of how the plaintiff without such direct evidence can meet this burden. *Burdine* provides the answer, telling us that such a plaintiff may succeed in meeting his ultimate burden of proving discrimination "indirectly by showing that the employer's proffered explanation is unworthy of credence." 450 U.S. at 256; see *Aikens*, supra, at 716; id. at 717–718 (Blackmun, J., joined by Brennan, J., concurring). The possibility of some practical procedure for addressing what *Burdine* calls indirect proof is crucial to the success of most Title VII claims, for the simple reason that employers who discriminate are not likely to announce their discriminatory motive. And yet, under the majority's scheme, a victim of discrimination lacking direct evidence will now be saddled with the tremendous disadvantage of having to confront, not the defined task of proving the employer's stated reasons to be false, but the amorphous requirement of disproving all possible nondiscriminatory reasons that a factfinder might find lurking in the record. In the Court's own words, the plaintiff must "disprove all other reasons suggested, no matter how vaguely, in the record."

While the Court appears to acknowledge that a plaintiff will have the task of disproving even vaguely suggested reasons, and while it recognizes the need for "[c]larity regarding the requisite elements of

---

[9] The foregoing analysis of burdens describes who wins on various combinations of evidence and proof. It may or may not also describe the actual sequence of events at trial. In a bench trial, for example, the parties may be limited in their presentation of evidence until the court has decided whether the plaintiff has made his prima facie showing. But the court also may allow in all the evidence at once. In such a situation, under our decision in *Aikens*, the defendant will have to choose whether it wishes simply to attack the prima facie case or whether it wants to present nondiscriminatory reasons for its actions. If the defendant chooses the former approach, the factfinder will decide at the end of the trial whether the plaintiff has proven his prima facie case. If the defendant takes the latter approach, the only question for the factfinder will be the issue of pretext. United States Postal Service Bd. of Governors v. Aikens, 460 U.S. 711, 715 (1983).

proof," it nonetheless gives conflicting signals about the scope of its holding in this case. In one passage, the Court states that although proof of the falsity of the employer's proffered reasons does not "compe[l] judgment for the plaintiff," such evidence, without more, "will permit the trier of fact to infer the ultimate fact of intentional discrimination." (emphasis omitted). The same view is implicit in the Court's decision to remand this case, keeping Hicks's chance of winning a judgment alive although he has done no more (in addition to proving his prima facie case) than show that the reasons proffered by St. Mary's are unworthy of credence. But other language in the Court's opinion supports a more extreme conclusion, that proof of the falsity of the employer's articulated reasons will not even be sufficient to sustain judgment for the plaintiff. For example, the Court twice states that the plaintiff must show "both that the reason was false, and that discrimination was the real reason." In addition, in summing up its reading of our earlier cases, the Court states that "[I]t is not enough . . . to disbelieve the employer." (emphasis omitted). This "pretext-plus" approach would turn *Burdine* on its head, and it would result in summary judgment for the employer in the many cases where the plaintiff has no evidence beyond that required to prove a prima facie case and to show that the employer's articulated reasons are unworthy of credence. Cf. Carter v. Duncan-Huggins, Ltd., 727 F.2d 1225, 1245 (1984) (Scalia, J., dissenting) ("[I]n order to get to the jury the plaintiff would . . . have to introduce some evidence . . . that the *basis* for [the] discriminatory treatment was race") (emphasis in original). See generally Lanctot, The Defendant Lies and the Plaintiff Loses: The Fallacy of the "Pretext-Plus" Rule in Employment Discrimination Cases, 43 Hastings L.J. 57 (1991) (criticizing the "pretext-plus" approach).

The Court fails to explain, moreover, under either interpretation of its holding, why proof that the employer's articulated reasons are "unpersuasive, or even obviously contrived," falls short. Under *McDonnell Douglas* and *Burdine*, there would be no reason in this situation to question discriminatory intent. The plaintiff has raised an inference of discrimination (though no longer a presumption) through proof of his prima facie case, and as we noted in *Burdine*, this circumstantial proof of discrimination can also be used by the plaintiff to show pretext. Such proof is merely strengthened by showing, through use of further evidence, that the employer's articulated reasons are false, since "common experience" tells us that it is "more likely than not" that the employer who lies is simply trying to cover up the illegality alleged by the plaintiff. *Furnco*, 438 U.S., at 577. Unless *McDonnell Douglas*'s command to structure and limit the case as the employer chooses is to be rendered meaningless, we should not look beyond the employer's lie by assuming the possible existence of other reasons the employer might have proffered without lying. By telling the factfinder to keep digging in cases where the plaintiff's proof of pretext turns on showing the employer's reasons to be unworthy of credence, the majority rejects the very point of the *McDonnell Douglas* rule requiring the scope of the factual inquiry to be limited, albeit in a manner chosen by the employer. What is more, the Court is throwing out the rule for the benefit of employers who have been found to have given false evidence in a court of law. There is simply no justification for favoring these employers by exempting them from responsibility for lies. It may indeed be true that such employers have nondiscriminatory reasons for their actions, but ones so shameful that they wish to conceal them. One can understand human frailty and the natural desire to conceal it, however, without finding in it a justification to dispense with an orderly procedure for getting at "the elusive factual question of intentional discrimination." *Burdine*, 450 U.S., at 255, n.8.

With no justification in the employer's favor, the consequences to actual and potential Title VII litigants stand out sharply. To the extent that workers like Melvin Hicks decide not to sue, given the uncertainties they would face under the majority's scheme, the legislative purpose in adopting Title VII will be frustrated. To the extent such workers nevertheless decide to press forward, the result will likely be wasted time, effort, and money for all concerned. Under the scheme announced today, any conceivable explanation for the employer's actions that might be suggested by the evidence, however unrelated to the employer's articulated reasons, must be addressed by a plaintiff who does not wish to risk losing. Since the Court does not say whether a trial court may limit the introduction of evidence at trial to what is relevant to the employer's articulated reasons, and since the employer can win on the possibility of an unstated reason, the scope of admissible evidence at trial presumably includes any evidence potentially relevant to "the ultimate question" of discrimination, unlimited by the employer's stated reasons. If so, Title VII trials promise to be tedious affairs. But even if, on the contrary, relevant evidence is still somehow to be limited by reference to the employer's reasons, however "vaguely" articulated, the careful plaintiff will have to anticipate all the side issues that might arise even in a more limited evidentiary presentation. Thus, in either case, pretrial discovery will become more extensive and wide-ranging (if the plaintiff can afford it), for a much wider set of facts could prove to be both relevant and important at trial. The majority's scheme, therefore, will promote longer trials and more pre-trial discovery, threatening increased expense and delay in Title VII litigation for both plaintiffs and defendants, and increased burdens on the judiciary. . . .

The enhancement of a Title VII plaintiff's burden wrought by the Court's opinion is exemplified in this case. Melvin Hicks was denied any opportunity, much less a full and fair one, to demonstrate that the supposedly nondiscriminatory explanation for his demotion and termination, the personal animosity of his immediate supervisor, was unworthy of credence. In fact, the District Court did not find that personal animosity (which it failed to recognize might be racially motivated) was the true reason for the actions St. Mary's took; it adduced this reason simply as a possibility in explaining that Hicks had failed to prove "that the crusade [to terminate him] was racially rather than personally motivated." It is hardly surprising that Hicks failed to prove anything about this supposed personal crusade, since St. Mary's never articulated such an explanation for Hicks's discharge, and since the person who allegedly conducted this crusade denied at trial any personal difficulties between himself and Hicks. While the majority may well be troubled about the unfair treatment of Hicks in this instance and thus remands for review of whether the District Court's factual conclusions were clearly erroneous, the majority provides Hicks with no opportunity to produce evidence showing that the District Court's hypothesized explanation, first articulated six months after trial, is unworthy of credence. Whether Melvin Hicks wins or loses on remand, many plaintiffs in a like position will surely lose under the scheme adopted by the Court today, unless they possess both prescience and resources beyond what this Court has previously required Title VII litigants to employ.

Because I see no reason why Title VII interpretation should be driven by concern for employers who are too ashamed to be honest in court, at the expense of victims of discrimination who do not happen to have direct evidence of discriminatory intent, I respectfully dissent.

NOTES ON *ST. MARY'S HONOR CENTER V. HICKS*

1. ***Texas Department of Community Affairs v. Burdine.*** Most of the doctrinal dispute between the majority and the dissent in *St. Mary's Honor Center* concerned the earlier decision in Texas Department of Community Affairs v. Burdine, 450 U.S. 248 (1981). In particular, the opinions disagreed over the interpretation of the following statement from *Burdine* describing the plaintiff's burden of proving pretext:

> The plaintiff retains the burden of persuasion. She now must have the opportunity to demonstrate that the proffered reason was not the true reason for the employment decision. This burden now merges with the ultimate burden of persuading the court that she has been the victim of intentional discrimination. She may succeed in this either directly by persuading the court that a discriminatory reason more likely motivated the employer or indirectly by showing that the employer's proffered explanation is unworthy of credence.

Id. at 256. The majority in *St. Mary's Honor Center* dismisses this statement as dicta, but agrees with the dissent that, if taken literally, it means "that the falsity of the employer's explanation is *alone enough* to compel judgment for the plaintiff" (emphasis in original). Recall, however, that the question in *St. Mary's Honor Center* was whether the judge, sitting without a jury, had to draw an inference of discrimination from the plaintiff's evidence discrediting the defendant's offered reason. This question would be equivalent, in a case tried to a jury, to the question whether a directed verdict had to be granted for the plaintiff. Since the plaintiff has the entire burden of proof on the issue of pretext, both the burden of production and the burden of persuasion, a directed verdict could be granted in her favor only in an exceptional case, in which her evidence was so compelling that the only reasonable inference was that the defendant had engaged in discrimination. Does the quoted passage in *Burdine* really address this question or only the more modest question of how the plaintiff might satisfy her burden of persuasion?

2. **Litigation Strategy.** The underlying issue in *St. Mary's Honor Center* seems to have less to do with the interpretation of prior precedent than the tactical advantage that a defendant gains by offering multiple reasons for making a decision adverse to the plaintiff. As the dissent emphasizes, Hicks himself was faced with an entirely unanticipated reason for the actions taken against him after he had already discredited the "legitimate, nondiscriminatory reasons" first offered by the defendant. This new reason—that his supervisor had a personal grudge against him—was disavowed by the supervisor himself. How likely is an employer consciously to adopt a litigation strategy that requires it to impeach the testimony of its own supervisor? An employer's own interests in presenting a defense on any ground available may diverge from the supervisor's interest in defending his own decisions as soundly based in independently justifiable reasons, allowing him to present himself as a more effective manager than he actually is. These conflicting interests on the defense side often raise problems for the employer's counsel in offering a consistent and persuasive defense of its decisions.

The peculiar nature of the defense offered by St. Mary's Honor Center opens up several grounds for counterattack by the plaintiff. First, personal animosity by a supervisor might not itself constitute a "legitimate, nondiscriminatory reason," since it might be based at least partly on racial prejudice. Hicks's supervisor might have disliked him partly because he was black. Second, in a case tried to a jury, the jurors themselves might be unsympathetic to an employer who allows supervisors to vent their personal animosity on their subordinates. Most jurors, after all, are more likely to be subordinates than supervisors. Third, Hicks and his attorney might have been surprised by this reason offered by the defendant, but the next plaintiff can easily engage in discovery about all the reasons offered, or intended to be offered, by the employer for its decision. A late addition to these reasons at trial can be impeached by the answers to earlier interrogatories or deposition questions, or if the defendant's offered reasons are identified in the pretrial order, excluded entirely from the evidence at trial. And fourth, the defendant's strategy of switching reasons in the middle of the trial always is vulnerable to the argument from the plaintiff that none of the defendant's reasons is convincing. Is *St. Mary's Honor Center* simply a case in which a desperate defendant was lucky to prevail in front of a sympathetic judge?

The dissent raises the possibility that defendants could wear down plaintiffs and deplete the resources available to them by offering multiple reasons at different points in the litigation. Of course, the defendant could, and indeed, in *St. Mary's Honor Center* did, offer multiple reasons initially for its decision. All of them, however, were rejected by the judge before he found personal animosity to be the real reason for Hicks's discharge. Nothing in the dissent would have prohibited an employer from adopting this strategy. Is it nevertheless vulnerable to the same counterattacks as the strategy of offering an entirely new and different reason at trial? Which strategy imposes greater costs on the plaintiff?

3. **The Risk of Perjury.** A leading law review article anticipated and criticized the holding in *St. Mary's Honor Center* as "the defendant lies and the plaintiff loses." Catherine Lanctot, The Defendant Lies and the Plaintiff Loses: The Fallacy of the "Pretext-Plus" Rule in Employment Discrimination Cases, 43 Hastings L.J. 57 (1991). Does this case allow employers to get away with perjury by their supervisors, or at least, with conspicuous inconsistency in the reasons that they offer for their decisions? Even if *St. Mary's Honor Center* doesn't condone perjury, it doesn't punish it either. Are there other mechanisms available to make the defendant pay for the cost of inconsistency?

Regardless of the risk of perjury, *St. Mary's Honor Center* does appear to erode still further the significance of the defendant's rebuttal burden under the structure of proof in *McDonnell Douglas*. Defendants no longer appear to be committed to a single reason, or a single set of reasons, for their decisions, and correspondingly, plaintiffs no longer have a fixed target that they can discredit in order to prove discrimination. This situation leaves plaintiffs back almost where they began before *McDonnell Douglas*, bearing almost the entire burden of uncovering evidence of intentional discrimination. Since that evidence is often hidden—few employers are willing to admit to discrimination—switching to the defendant the burden of producing a "legitimate, nondiscrimination reason" appears to do little to assist the plaintiff in proving the ultimate issue of intentional discrimination.

4. ***Reeves v. Sanderson Plumbing Products, Inc.*** Whether these unfortunate consequences of *St. Mary's Honor Center* would be borne out was the subject of Reeves v. Sanderson Plumbing Products, Inc., 530 U.S. 133 (2000). That case concerned a claim of age discrimination, but it was analyzed under the structure of proof in *McDonnell Douglas*. The reasoning of the decision is therefore fully applicable to claims under Title VII. As the Supreme Court framed the issue:

> This case concerns the kind and amount of evidence necessary to sustain a jury's verdict that an employer unlawfully discriminated on the basis of age. Specifically, we must resolve whether a defendant is entitled to judgment as a matter of law when the plaintiff's case consists exclusively of a prima facie case of discrimination and sufficient evidence for the trier of fact to disbelieve the defendant's legitimate, nondiscriminatory explanation for its action. We must also decide whether the employer was entitled to judgment as a matter of law under the particular circumstances presented here.

The plaintiff, Reeves, was discharged ostensibly for failing to maintain accurate time records for employees under his supervision. He presented evidence discrediting this reason, showing that, on the contrary, his time records were accurate, and evidence of age-based comments by Sanderson's director of manufacturing. The director was involved in the decision to terminate Reeves, but his comments, at least as characterized by the court of appeals, were "stray remarks," not related to the termination decision. Relying on that reason, and on the absence of evidence that other participants in the termination decision were motivated by age discrimination, the court of appeals held that a directed verdict should have been granted for the defendant. The Supreme Court rejected that reasoning.

> [T]he Court of Appeals proceeded from the assumption that a prima facie case of discrimination, combined with sufficient evidence for the trier of fact to disbelieve the defendant's legitimate, nondiscriminatory reason for its decision, is insufficient as a matter of law to sustain a jury's finding of intentional discrimination.
>
> In so reasoning, the Court of Appeals misconceived the evidentiary burden borne by plaintiffs who attempt to prove intentional discrimination through indirect evidence. This much is evident from our decision in *St. Mary's Honor Center*. There we held that the factfinder's rejection of the employer's legitimate, nondiscriminatory reason for its action does not *compel* judgment for the plaintiff. The ultimate question is whether the employer intentionally discriminated, and proof that "the employer's proffered reason is unpersuasive, or even obviously contrived, does not necessarily establish that the plaintiff's proffered reason . . . is correct." In other words, "[i]t is not enough . . . to *dis*believe the employer; the factfinder must *believe* the plaintiff's explanation of intentional discrimination."
>
> In reaching this conclusion, however, we reasoned that it is *permissible* for the trier of fact to infer the ultimate fact of discrimination from the falsity of the employer's explanation. Specifically, we stated:
>
>> "The factfinder's disbelief of the reasons put forward by the defendant (particularly if disbelief is accompanied by a suspicion of mendacity) may, together with the elements of the prima facie case, suffice to show intentional discrimination. Thus, rejection of the defendant's proffered reasons will *permit* the trier of fact to infer the ultimate fact of intentional discrimination." Id. at 511.
>
> Proof that the defendant's explanation is unworthy of credence is simply one form of circumstantial evidence that is probative of intentional discrimination, and it may be quite persuasive. See id. at 517 ("[P]roving the employer's reason false becomes part of (and often considerably assists) the greater enterprise of proving that the real reason was intentional discrimination"). In appropriate circumstances, the trier of fact can reasonably infer from the falsity of the explanation that the employer is dissembling to cover up a discriminatory purpose. Such an inference is consistent with the general principle of evidence law that the factfinder is entitled to

consider a party's dishonesty about a material fact as "affirmative evidence of guilt." Wright v. West, 505 U.S. 277, 296 (1992); see also Wilson v. United States, 162 U.S. 613, 620–621 (1896); 2 J. Wigmore, Evidence § 278(2), p. 133 (J. Chadbourn rev. ed.1979). Moreover, once the employer's justification has been eliminated, discrimination may well be the most likely alternative explanation, especially since the employer is in the best position to put forth the actual reason for its decision. Cf. Furnco Constr. Corp. v. Waters, 438 U.S. 567, 577 (1978) ("[W]hen all legitimate reasons for rejecting an applicant have been eliminated as possible reasons for the employer's actions, it is more likely than not the employer, who we generally assume acts with *some* reason, based his decision on an impermissible consideration"). Thus, a plaintiff's prima facie case, combined with sufficient evidence to find that the employer's asserted justification is false, may permit the trier of fact to conclude that the employer unlawfully discriminated.

This is not to say that such a showing by the plaintiff will *always* be adequate to sustain a jury's finding of liability. Certainly there will be instances where, although the plaintiff has established a prima facie case and set forth sufficient evidence to reject the defendant's explanation, no rational factfinder could conclude that the action was discriminatory. For instance, an employer would be entitled to judgment as a matter of law if the record conclusively revealed some other, nondiscriminatory reason for the employer's decision, or if the plaintiff created only a weak issue of fact as to whether the employer's reason was untrue and there was abundant and uncontroverted independent evidence that no discrimination had occurred. See Aka v. Washington Hospital Center, 156 F.3d, at 1291–1292; see also Fisher v. Vassar College, 114 F.3d, at 1338 ("[I]f the circumstances show that the defendant gave the false explanation to conceal something other than discrimination, the inference of discrimination will be weak or nonexistent"). To hold otherwise would be effectively to insulate an entire category of employment discrimination cases from review under Rule 50, and we have reiterated that trial courts should not "treat discrimination differently from other ultimate questions of fact." *St. Mary's Honor Center*, supra, at 524 (quoting *Aikens*, 460 U.S., at 716).

Whether judgment as a matter of law is appropriate in any particular case will depend on a number of factors. Those include the strength of the plaintiff's prima facie case, the probative value of the proof that the employer's explanation is false, and any other evidence that supports the employer's case and that properly may be considered on a motion for judgment as a matter of law. For purposes of this case, we need not—and could not—resolve all of the circumstances in which such factors would entitle an employer to judgment as a matter of law. It suffices to say that, because a prima facie case and sufficient evidence to reject the employer's

> explanation may permit a finding of liability, the Court of Appeals erred in proceeding from the premise that a plaintiff must always introduce additional, independent evidence of discrimination.

The Supreme Court went on to hold that the plaintiff had presented sufficient evidence to generate an inference of intentional discrimination based on the prima facie case, the evidence discrediting the defendant's offered reason, and the director's role in terminating him to support an inference of discrimination. This holding, and the general analysis in *Sanderson Plumbing*, alleviates some of the concerns raised by *St. Mary's Honor Center*. Where the earlier decision had held that discrediting the defendant's offered reason does not require a judgment for the plaintiff, this decision held that, in combination with other evidence, it may allow a judgment for the plaintiff. This conclusion perhaps is obvious from a careful reading of both opinions. What it obscures is the continued erosion in the significance of the structure of proof in *McDonnell Douglas*.

As the elements in this structure of proof have been progressively refined and articulated, the prospects for reforming employment practices by placing some kind of affirmative obligation upon employers to eliminate discrimination have correspondingly diminished. The initial promise of *McDonnell Douglas* was that employers would document their personnel decisions, and in the process, take steps to assure that those decisions remained free of discrimination. They might also, as in *Furnco Construction*, engage in modest forms of affirmative action in order to reduce their overall exposure to liability. Correspondingly, the plaintiff's burden of proving intentional discrimination would be reduced, making it easier for plaintiffs to prevail in the cases that actually made it to court. With the weakening of the defendant's burden of producing a "legitimate, nondiscriminatory reason," however, all of these hopes have faded. Defendants can meet this burden, or respond to the plaintiff's evidence of pretext, by relying on reasons that can be reconstructed from each plaintiff's individual employment history.

Could a prohibition against discrimination realistically be expected to accomplish anything more? From an employer's perspective, the principal advantage of such a prohibition is its limited scope. It does not tell the employer how to run its business, but only identifies a limited number of factors that cannot be considered in making employment decisions. Does existing law simply recognize the freedom that was preserved to employers by the limited scope of the laws against employment discrimination? Or does it give them too much leeway to hide forms of discrimination that would otherwise result in liability? Recall that the multiple prohibitions in Title VII appear to be targeted at eliminating attempts to evade and conceal discrimination. Have the decisions of the Supreme Court frustrated this purpose of the statute?

5. **Bibliography.** Grafton Bragg, The Work-Rule Doctrine Doesn't Work after *Reeves v. Sanderson Plumbing Products*, 36 Miss. C.L. Rev. 120 (2017); Mark S. Brodin, The Demise of Circumstantial Proof in Employment Discrimination Litigation: *St. Mary's Honor Center v. Hicks*, Pretext, and the "Personality" Excuse, 18 Berk. J. Emp. & Lab. L. 183 (1997); Deborah C.

Malamud, The Last Minuet: Disparate Treatment After *Hicks*, 93 Mich. L. Rev. 2229 (1995); Michael Selmi, Proving Intentional Discrimination: The Reality of Supreme Court Rhetoric, 86 Geo. L.J. 279 (1997); William R. Corbett, An Allegory of the Cave and the Desert Palace, 41 Hous. L. Rev. 1549 (2005); Michael J. Hayes, That Pernicious Pop-Up, the Prima Facie Case, 39 Suffolk U. L. Rev. 343 (2006); Steven J. Kaminshine, Disparate Treatment as a Theory of Discrimination: The Need for a Restatement, Not a Revolution, 2 Stan. J. Civ. Rts. & Civ. Lib. 1 (2005); Martin J. Katz, Unifying Disparate Treatment (Really), 59 Hastings L.J. 643 (2008); Martin J. Katz, Reclaiming *McDonnell Douglas*, 83 Notre Dame L. Rev. 109 (2007); Barrett S. Moore, Shifting the Burden: Genuine Disputes and Employment Discrimination Standards of Proof, 35 U. Ark. Little Rock L. Rev. 113 (2012); Lawrence D. Rosenthal, Motions for Summary Judgment When Employers Offer Multiple Justifications for Adverse Employment Actions: Why the Exceptions Should Swallow the Rule, 2002 Utah L. Rev. 335; Matthew R. Scott & Russell D. Chapman, *Reeves v. Sanderson Plumbing Products*: The Emperor Has No Clothes—Pretext Plus is Alive and Kicking, 37 St. Mary's L.J. 179 (2005); Michael J. Zimmer, The New Discrimination Law: *Price Waterhouse* is Dead, Whither *McDonnell Douglas*?, 53 Emory L.J. 1887 (2004); Symposium, Proof and Pervasiveness: Employment Discrimination in Law and Reality after *Desert Palace, Inc. v. Costa*, 9 Emp. Rts. & Emp. Pol'y J. 427 (2005).

C. AFTER-ACQUIRED EVIDENCE AND MIXED-MOTIVE CASES

McKennon v. Nashville Banner Publishing Co.

513 U.S. 352 (1995).

■ JUSTICE KENNEDY delivered the opinion of the Court.

The question before us is whether an employee discharged in violation of the Age Discrimination in Employment Act of 1967 is barred from all relief when, after her discharge, the employer discovers evidence of wrongdoing that, in any event, would have led to the employee's termination on lawful and legitimate grounds.

I

For some 30 years, petitioner Christine McKennon worked for respondent Nashville Banner Publishing Company. She was discharged, the Banner claimed, as part of a work force reduction plan necessitated by cost considerations. McKennon, who was 62 years old when she lost her job, thought another reason explained her dismissal: her age. She filed suit in the United States District Court for the Middle District of Tennessee, alleging that her discharge violated the Age Discrimination in Employment Act of 1967 (ADEA). The ADEA makes it unlawful for any employer:

> "to discharge any individual or otherwise discriminate against any individual with respect to his compensation, terms, conditions, or privileges of employment, because of such individual's age." 29 U.S.C. § 623(a)(1).

McKennon sought a variety of legal and equitable remedies available under the ADEA, including backpay.

In preparation of the case, the Banner took McKennon's deposition. She testified that, during her final year of employment, she had copied several confidential documents bearing upon the company's financial condition. She had access to these records as secretary to the Banner's comptroller. McKennon took the copies home and showed them to her husband. Her motivation, she averred, was an apprehension she was about to be fired because of her age. When she became concerned about her job, she removed and copied the documents for "insurance" and "protection." A few days after these deposition disclosures, the Banner sent McKennon a letter declaring that removal and copying of the records was in violation of her job responsibilities and advising her (again) that she was terminated. The Banner's letter also recited that had it known of McKennon's misconduct it would have discharged her at once for that reason.

For purposes of summary judgment, the Banner conceded its discrimination against McKennon. The District Court granted summary judgment for the Banner, holding that McKennon's misconduct was grounds for her termination and that neither backpay nor any other remedy was available to her under the ADEA. The United States Court of Appeals for the Sixth Circuit affirmed on the same rationale. We granted certiorari to resolve conflicting views among the Courts of Appeals on the question whether all relief must be denied when an employee has been discharged in violation of the ADEA and the employer later discovers some wrongful conduct that would have led to discharge if it had been discovered earlier. We now reverse.

II

We shall assume, as summary judgment procedures require us to assume, that the sole reason for McKennon's initial discharge was her age, a discharge violative of the ADEA. Our further premise is that the misconduct revealed by the deposition was so grave that McKennon's immediate discharge would have followed its disclosure in any event. The District Court and the Court of Appeals found no basis for contesting that proposition, and for purposes of our review we need not question it here. We do question the legal conclusion reached by those courts that after-acquired evidence of wrongdoing which would have resulted in discharge bars employees from any relief under the ADEA. That ruling is incorrect.

The Court of Appeals considered McKennon's misconduct, in effect, to be supervening grounds for termination. That may be so, but it does not follow, as the Court of Appeals said in citing one of its own earlier cases, that the misconduct renders it "irrelevant whether or not [McKennon] was discriminated against." We conclude that a violation of the ADEA cannot be so altogether disregarded.

The ADEA, enacted in 1967 as part of an ongoing congressional effort to eradicate discrimination in the workplace, reflects a societal condemnation of invidious bias in employment decisions. The ADEA is but part of a wider statutory scheme to protect employees in the workplace nationwide. See Title VII of the Civil Rights Act of 1964, 42 U.S.C. § 2000e et seq. (race, color, sex, national origin, and religion); the Americans with Disabilities Act of 1990, 42 U.S.C. § 12101 et seq. (disability); the National Labor Relations Act, 29 U.S.C. § 158(a) (union activities); the Equal Pay Act of 1963, 29 U. S. C. § 206(d) (sex). The ADEA incorporates some features of both Title VII and the Fair Labor Standards Act, which has led us to describe it as "something of a hybrid." Lorillard v. Pons, 434 U.S. 575, 578 (1978). The substantive, antidiscrimination provisions of the ADEA are modeled upon the prohibitions of Title VII. Its remedial provisions incorporate by reference the provisions of the Fair Labor Standards Act of 1938. 29 U.S.C. § 626(b). When confronted with a violation of the ADEA, a district court is authorized to afford relief by means of reinstatement, backpay, injunctive relief, declaratory judgment, and attorney's fees. In the case of a willful violation of the Act, the ADEA authorizes an award of liquidated damages equal to the backpay award. 29 U.S.C. § 626(b). The Act also gives federal courts the discretion to "grant such legal or equitable relief as may be appropriate to effectuate the purposes of [the Act]."

The ADEA and Title VII share common substantive features and also a common purpose: "the elimination of discrimination in the workplace." Oscar Mayer & Co. v. Evans, 441 U.S. 750, 756 (1979). Congress designed the remedial measures in these statutes to serve as a "spur or catalyst" to cause employers "to self-examine and to self-evaluate their employment practices and to endeavor to eliminate, so far as possible, the last vestiges" of discrimination. Albemarle Paper Co. v. Moody, 422 U.S. 405, 417–418 (1975); see also Franks v. Bowman Transportation Co., 424 U.S. 747, 763 (1976). Deterrence is one object of these statutes. Compensation for injuries caused by the prohibited discrimination is another. The ADEA, in keeping with these purposes, contains a vital element found in both Title VII and the Fair Labor Standards Act: it grants an injured employee a right of action to obtain the authorized relief. 29 U.S.C. § 626(c). The private litigant who seeks redress for his or her injuries vindicates both the deterrence and the compensation objectives of the ADEA. It would not accord with this scheme if after-acquired evidence of wrongdoing that would have resulted in termination operates, in every instance, to bar all relief for an earlier violation of the Act.

The objectives of the ADEA are furthered when even a single employee establishes that an employer has discriminated against him or her. The disclosure through litigation of incidents or practices which violate national policies respecting nondiscrimination in the work force is itself important, for the occurrence of violations may disclose patterns of noncompliance resulting from a misappreciation of the Act's operation or entrenched resistance to its commands, either of which can be of industry-wide significance. The efficacy of its enforcement mechanisms becomes one measure of the success of the Act.

The Court of Appeals in this case relied upon two of its earlier decisions, and the opinion of the Court of Appeals for the Tenth Circuit in Summers v. State Farm Mutual Automobile Ins. Co., 864 F.2d 700 (10th Cir. 1988). Consulting those authorities, it declared that it had "firmly endorsed the principle that after-acquired evidence is a complete bar to any recovery by the former employee where the employer can show it would have fired the employee on the basis of the evidence." Summers, in turn, relied upon our decision in Mt. Healthy City Bd. of Ed. v. Doyle, 429 U.S. 274 (1977), but that decision is inapplicable here.

In *Mt. Healthy* we addressed a mixed-motives case, in which two motives were said to be operative in the employer's decision to fire an employee. One was lawful, the other (an alleged constitutional violation) unlawful. We held that if the lawful reason alone would have sufficed to justify the firing, the employee could not prevail in a suit against the employer. The case was controlled by the difficulty, and what we thought was the lack of necessity, of disentangling the proper motive from the improper one where both played a part in the termination and the former motive would suffice to sustain the employer's action.

That is not the problem confronted here. As we have said, the case comes to us on the express assumption that an unlawful motive was the sole basis for the firing. McKennon's misconduct was not discovered until after she had been fired. The employer could not have been motivated by knowledge it did not have and it cannot now claim that the employee was fired for the nondiscriminatory reason. Mixed-motive cases are inapposite here, except to the important extent they underscore the necessity of determining the employer's motives in ordering the discharge, an essential element in determining whether the employer violated the federal antidiscrimination law. See Price Waterhouse v. Hopkins, 490 U.S. 228, 252 (1989) (plurality opinion) (employer's legitimate reason for discharge in mixed-motive case will not suffice "if that reason did not motivate it at the time of the decision"); id. at 260–261 (White, J., concurring in judgment); id. at 261 (O'Connor, J., concurring in judgment). As we have observed, "proving that the same decision would have been justified . . . is not the same as proving that the same decision would have been made." Id. at 252 (plurality) (internal quotation marks and citations omitted); see also id. at 260–261 (White, J., concurring in judgment).

Our inquiry is not at an end, however, for even though the employer has violated the Act, we must consider how the after-acquired evidence of the employee's wrongdoing bears on the specific remedy to be ordered. Equity's maxim that a suitor who engaged in his own reprehensible conduct in the course of the transaction at issue must be denied equitable relief because of unclean hands, a rule which in conventional formulation operated in limine to bar the suitor from invoking the aid of the equity court, 2 S. Symons, Pomeroy's Equity Jurisprudence § 397, pp. 90–92 (5th ed. 1941), has not been applied where Congress authorizes broad equitable relief to serve important national policies. We have rejected the unclean hands defense "where a private suit serves important public purposes." Perma Life Mufflers, Inc. v. International Parts Corp., 392 U.S. 134, 138 (1968) (Sherman and Clayton Antitrust Acts). That does not mean, however, the employee's own misconduct is irrelevant to all the remedies otherwise available under the statute. The statute controlling this case provides that "the court shall have jurisdiction to grant such legal or equitable relief as may be appropriate to effectuate the purposes of this chapter, including without limitation judgments compelling employment, reinstatement or promotion, or enforcing the liability for [amounts owing to a person as a result of a violation of this chapter]." 29 U.S.C. § 626(b); see also § 216(b). In giving effect to the ADEA, we must recognize the duality between the legitimate interests of the employer and the important claims of the employee who invokes the national employment policy mandated by the Act. The employee's wrongdoing must be taken into account, we conclude, lest the employer's legitimate concerns be ignored. The ADEA, like Title VII, is not a general regulation of the workplace but a law which prohibits discrimination. The statute does not constrain employers from exercising significant other prerogatives and discretions in the course of the hiring, promoting, and discharging of their employees. See Price Waterhouse v. Hopkins, supra, at 239 ("Title VII eliminates certain bases for distinguishing among employees while otherwise preserving employers' freedom of choice"). In determining appropriate remedial action, the employee's wrongdoing becomes relevant not to punish the employee, or out of concern "for the relative moral worth of the parties," Perma Mufflers v. International Parts Corp., supra, at 139, but to take due account of the lawful prerogatives of the employer in the usual course of its business and the corresponding equities that it has arising from the employee's wrongdoing.

The proper boundaries of remedial relief in the general class of cases where, after termination, it is discovered that the employee has engaged in wrongdoing must be addressed by the judicial system in the ordinary course of further decisions, for the factual permutations and the equitable considerations they raise will vary from case to case. We do conclude that here, and as a general rule in cases of this type, neither reinstatement nor front pay is an appropriate remedy. It would be both inequitable and pointless to order the reinstatement of someone the employer would have terminated, and will terminate, in any event and upon lawful grounds.

The proper measure of backpay presents a more difficult problem. Resolution of this question must give proper recognition to the fact that an ADEA violation has occurred which must be deterred and compensated without undue infringement upon the employer's rights and prerogatives. The object of compensation is to restore the employee to the position he or she would have been in absent the discrimination, Franks v. Bowman Transportation Co., 424 U.S. at 764, but that principle is difficult to apply with precision where there is after-acquired evidence of wrongdoing that would have led to termination on legitimate grounds had the employer known about it. Once an employer learns about employee wrongdoing that would lead to a legitimate discharge, we cannot require the employer to ignore the information, even if it is acquired during the course of discovery in a suit against the employer and even if the information might have gone undiscovered absent the suit. The beginning point in the trial court's formulation of a remedy should be calculation of backpay from the date of the unlawful discharge to the date the new information was discovered. In determining the appropriate order for relief, the court can consider taking into further account extraordinary equitable circumstances that affect the legitimate interests of either party. An absolute rule barring any recovery of backpay, however, would undermine the ADEA's objective of forcing employers to consider and examine their motivations, and of penalizing them for employment decisions that spring from age discrimination.

Where an employer seeks to rely upon after-acquired evidence of wrongdoing, it must first establish that the wrongdoing was of such severity that the employee in fact would have been terminated on those grounds alone if the employer had known of it at the time of the discharge. The concern that employers might as a routine matter undertake extensive discovery into an employee's background or performance on the job to resist claims under the Act is not an insubstantial one, but we think the authority of the courts to award attorney's fees, mandated under the statute, 29 U.S.C. §§ 216(b), 626(b), and in appropriate cases to invoke the provisions of Rule 11 of the Federal Rules of Civil Procedure will deter most abuses.

The judgment is reversed, and the case is remanded to the Court of Appeals for the Sixth Circuit for further proceedings consistent with this opinion.

It is so ordered.

NOTES ON *MCKENNON V. NASHVILLE BANNER PUBLISHING CO.*

1. **The Remedy Stage of Litigation.** The opinion in this case draws a sharp distinction between the liability stage of a case—which determines whether the defendant has violated the law—and the remedy stage—which determines the relief that the plaintiff is entitled to. The relevance of after-acquired evidence is limited to the remedy stage, and if accepted by the judge or jury, limits the compensatory relief that the plaintiff is entitled to. It does

not free the defendant from a finding that it has violated the ADEA. (As in *Sanderson Plumbing*, the analysis of this case under the ADEA also applies to cases under Title VII. As a subsequent note in this section discusses, however, the analysis of the related issue of mixed motives might well be different under the two statutes.)

As the term implies, after-acquired evidence is evidence that becomes available to the employer only after it has made a decision adverse to the plaintiff. It is not part of the motivation for its actual decision and, for that reason, does not affect the determination whether the actual decision violated the statute. In *McKennon*, the Supreme Court assumed that the decision to discharge McKennon had already been found to be discriminatory. This case thus begins after both the issue of pretext under *McDonnell Douglas* and the ultimate issue of discrimination have been resolved. As the opinion points out, that finding of discrimination still demands some remedy, in order to deter future violations of the statute and to compensate the plaintiff, if only partially, for the wrong that has been done to her.

The location of this issue in the remedy stage of the case has procedural as well as substantive consequences. As the Supreme Court was careful to point out at the end of its opinion, the burden of proof is upon the employer: "Where an employer seeks to rely upon after-acquired evidence of wrongdoing, it must first establish that the wrongdoing was of such severity that the employee in fact would have been terminated on those grounds alone if the employer had known of it at the time of the discharge." In close cases, where the after-acquired evidence is uncertain or does not clearly support a discharge, the employer will lose. Since a violation of the statute already has been found, putting the risk of loss on the employer makes perfect sense. The violator of the statute, rather than the victim of discrimination, should bear the risk of loss in close cases.

2. **Equitable Limits on Remedies.** The opinion in *McKennon* nevertheless finds that the balance of equities does not always favor the plaintiff. If the defendant makes the necessary showing, the plaintiff loses the right to full compensatory relief. Reinstatement to the job and front pay from the date of judgment until the job becomes available are automatically denied and back pay from the date of discovery of the after-acquired evidence to the date of judgment is presumptively denied. Why should an employer who has engaged in discrimination be relieved of liability to this extent?

An examination of the parties' incentives provides at least a partial answer to this question. The defendant remains subject to other forms of relief: an injunction against future discrimination, back pay between the date of discharge and the date of discovery of the after-acquired evidence, and attorney's fees. These remedies deter employers from violations of the statute, particularly through the award of attorney's fees. The prospect of paying the plaintiff's fees, in addition to its own fees, makes conduct that is likely to violate the statute a risky financial proposition for the employer. If found liable, the employer can, at best, only reduce its liability for back pay, front pay, and perhaps some form of damages. It cannot eliminate its exposure to liability for a monetary recovery entirely. By the same token, an award of attorney's fees provides the plaintiff with the assurance that she will not suffer a net out-of-pocket loss from bringing a lawsuit that results in a finding that the statute has been violated.

Nevertheless, as *McKennon* illustrates, the lawsuit can still cause the plaintiff to suffer a substantial overall financial loss. After all, McKennon herself lost her job. Depending on the condition of the job market, the lawsuit might well appear to her to be a pyrrhic victory. In protecting Nashville Banner from the need to rehire an untrustworthy employee, did the Supreme Court go too far in discouraging lawsuits from plaintiffs in McKennon's position? The lawsuit caused Nashville Banner to take a closer look at her actions as an employee and to find a reason sufficient for discharging her anyway. Could McKennon raise a claim that the employer's inquiry about her use of confidential documents was motivated by her charge of discrimination and so constituted retaliation for participating in proceedings to enforce the statute? Such retaliation constitutes an independent violation of the statute, under § 704(a). As discussed in the next section, such claims often accompany claims of discrimination and independently support an award of relief. Note, however, that on a claim of retaliation, the plaintiff would bear the burden of proof, while the defendant has the burden of proving the sufficiency of after-acquired evidence to justify the plaintiff's discharge.

3. **Mixed-Motive Cases.** The opinion in *McKennon* distinguishes between after-acquired evidence cases and mixed-motive cases. The former involve legitimate reasons that were not available to the employer when it made a decision adverse to the plaintiff; the latter involve legitimate reasons that were available to the employer at that time. This difference in timing leads to a difference in motivation. In after-acquired evidence cases, the employer presumably was motivated entirely by discrimination. In mixed-motive cases, as the term implies, the employer was motivated both by discrimination and by legitimate reasons. Mixed-motive cases therefore present greater problems in disentangling discrimination from legitimate reasons for an employment decision.

The first case to make this attempt was Mt. Healthy City Board of Education v. Doyle, 429 U.S. 274 (1977), which involved a claim of retaliation for the exercise of First Amendment rights. The plaintiff was a public school teacher who had criticized the superintendent of schools in a telephone call to a local radio station, which publicized his remarks. Soon thereafter, the school board refused to renew his contract of employment, in a decision found by the lower courts to be based in "substantial part" on his call to the radio station. The lower courts held that this incident involved protected speech under the First Amendment, but left open the possibility that the teacher's contract was not renewed also for entirely independent reasons. On these facts, the Supreme Court held that the school district could avoid liability only by proving "by a preponderance of the evidence that it would have reached the same decision as to respondent's employment even in the absence of the protected conduct." The burden of proof on the school teacher was only to show that his speech was protected by the First Amendment and that it was a "substantial factor" or a "motivating factor" in the decision not to rehire him.

Very similar reasoning was applied to the claim of sex discrimination under Title VII in Price Waterhouse v. Hopkins, 490 U.S. 228 (1989), as noted in Chapter 1. The plaintiff there was denied a promotion to partner in an accounting firm, partly because some of the existing partners found her behavior not to be sufficiently feminine. Hopkins was told that she was denied a promotion because she should "walk more femininely, talk more femininely, dress more femininely, wear make-up, have her hair styled, and wear jewelry." The Supreme Court found such evidence sufficient to support a finding that "gender played a motivating part" in denying Hopkins the promotion, but that Price Waterhouse could make out a defense by proving, by a preponderance of the evidence, "that it would have made the same decision in the absence of discrimination."[2] Unlike the defense in *Reeves*, this defense goes to the issue of liability, whether the employer violated the statute at all.

This distinction between after-acquired evidence cases and mixed-motive cases, however, was erased by the Civil Rights Act of 1991. This act amended Title VII to define a violation of the statute as requiring the plaintiff only to prove "race, color, religion, sex, or national origin was *a motivating factor* for any employment practice, even though other factors also motivated the practice." § 703(m) (emphasis added). If the plaintiff makes this showing, then the defendant is granted a partial defense, applicable only to compensatory remedies such as reinstatement, back pay, or damages, if it demonstrates that it "would have taken the same action in the absence of the impermissible motivating factor." § 706(g)(2)(B). Declaratory relief, injunctive relief against future discrimination, and attorney's fees can still be awarded to the plaintiff. These provisions firmly locate the issue of mixed motives in the remedy stage of Title VII cases.

Although the decision in *Price Waterhouse* is therefore superseded under Title VII, it may still retain some vitality in claims under other employment discrimination laws, in particular, the ADEA or § 1981. The Civil Rights Act of 1991 made some changes to these other laws, but did not apply the quoted provisions to them directly. This omission by Congress leaves open the inference that it intended the holding in *Price Waterhouse* to continue to apply to mixed-motive cases under other statutes. See, e.g., Miller v. CIGNA Corp., 47 F.3d 586, 597 & n.9 (3d Cir. 1995) (en banc) (applying *Price Waterhouse* under the ADEA).

The distinctive treatment of mixed-motive cases under Title VII was emphasized in Gross v. FBL Financial Services, 557 U.S. 167 (2009). That case is discussed more fully in Chapter 10. It holds that plaintiffs who have claims under the Age Discrimination in Employment Act bear the full burden of proving that consideration of age was the "but for" cause of the action

---

[2] Although the quoted phrases are from the plurality opinion by Justice Brennan, which was joined only by three other justices, Justices White and O'Connor also concurred in the result reached by the plurality. They differed from the plurality's statement of the applicable standards in requiring the plaintiff to prove that sex was a "substantial factor" rather than a "motivating factor" in denying her a promotion.

taken against them. The burden of proof does not shift to the defendant to establish that the same decision would have occurred anyway.

4. "Direct Evidence" Cases. Some courts limited the mixed-motive analysis of *Price Waterhouse* and § 706(g)(2)(B) to cases in which the plaintiff proves discrimination by "direct evidence." E.g., Fernandes v. Costa Bros. Masonry, Inc., 199 F.3d 572, 580–83 (1st Cir. 1999) (citing cases). These courts followed up on the position taken by Justice O'Connor in her separate opinion in *Price Waterhouse*: that the plaintiff must submit "direct evidence that decisionmakers placed substantial negative reliance on an illegitimate criterion in reaching their decision." Thus, on her view, if the plaintiff presents only circumstantial evidence, then he must continue to bear the burden of persuasion, as well as the burden of production, on the issue of pretext under *McDonnell Douglas*. Otherwise the defendant's evidence of a "legitimate, nondiscriminatory reason" would transform every case into a mixed-motive case, in which the burden of persuasion shifted to the defendant.

This attempt to limit the range of mixed-motive cases, however, raises problems of its own, which eventually led the Supreme Court to reject any requirement of proof by "direct evidence." In Desert Palace, Inc. v. Costa, 539 U.S. 90 (2003), the Court held that a jury could properly be instructed that the employer bears the burden of proof on the mixed-motive defense, even if the plaintiff presented only circumstantial evidence of discrimination.

The reasons for this decision begin with the amendments to Title VII made by the Civil Rights Act of 1991. These do not limit the ways in which a plaintiff can prove that race or sex was "a motivating factor" in the disputed employment decision, either by circumstantial or direct evidence. Once that finding is made, then the burden of proof switches to the employer to establish that the plaintiff would have been rejected even in the absence of discrimination. The distinction between direct and circumstantial evidence is not the same as the distinction between mixed-motive and pretext cases. The former is a distinction between kinds of evidence: how the plaintiff attempts to prove a violation of the statute. The latter is a distinction between different kinds of findings. In pretext cases, the court finds discrimination by concluding that the "legitimate, nondiscriminatory reason" offered by the employer is not the real reason for its decision but that race or sex is. In mixed-motive cases, the court finds that both reasons entered into the employer's decision and then must go on to determine whether the employer would have reached the same decision without considering race or sex. Moreover, it is not at all clear how to draw the distinction between direct and circumstantial evidence. In many cases, plaintiffs present both types of evidence, leaving courts that adopted this approach with the question whether to apply a pretext or a mixed-motive analysis to the evidence as a whole.

For all of these reasons, the Supreme Court rejected the "direct evidence" requirement in *Desert Palace*. The Court's precise holding was framed in these terms:

> In order to obtain an instruction under § 2000e–2(m), a plaintiff need only present sufficient evidence for a reasonable jury to conclude, by a preponderance of the evidence, that "race, color, religion, sex, or national origin was a motivating factor for any employment practice."

Does this holding effectively eliminate the distinction between mixed-motive and pretext cases? Although the distinction can still be drawn in the abstract, whenever the plaintiff presents sufficient evidence to get to the jury on the issue of pretext, isn't he or she also entitled to an instruction on mixed motives? Evidence from which a reasonable inference can be drawn that the defendant's offered reason is not the real reason also constitutes evidence that race (or some other prohibited reason) was "a motivating factor" in the disputed decision. When would a plaintiff want to avoid an instruction to this effect, one that requires proof only that race was "a motivating factor" rather than the only factor in the disputed decision?

Of course, if the plaintiff obtains such an instruction under § 703(m), the defendant is entitled to an instruction under § 706(g)(2)(B). Just like the plaintiff, the defendant can obtain such an instruction by presenting evidence from which a reasonable inference to this effect can be drawn. Does this leave the defendant now with too many "bites at the apple"? The defendant can start by offering a "legitimate, nondiscriminatory reason" under *McDonnell Douglas*. If that fails, it can offer an alternative reason to rebut the plaintiff's evidence of pretext under *St. Mary's Honor Center*. And if that fails, the defendant can offer after-acquired evidence under *Reeves* or evidence of mixed motives to limit the compensatory remedies available to the plaintiff. Is it necessary to give the defendant so many opportunities to vindicate its legitimate business reasons for making a personnel decision adverse to the plaintiff? Conversely, would a defendant be well advised to take all these opportunities to make out a defense or would each successive reason that it offered for its decision undermine the reasons previously offered?

The Supreme Court elaborated on proof of causation in the employment context in Staub v. Proctor Hospital, 562 U.S. 411 (2011), a case brought under the Uniformed Services Employment and Reemployment Rights Act (USERRA), by a military reservist who alleged discrimination against him by a private employer because of his military service. The plaintiff was fired based partly on reports by his immediate supervisors, who were hostile to him because of his obligations as a reservist, which required him to miss work. Relying on precedents under Title VII, the Court held that the employer remained liable under USERRA even though the manager who made the ultimate decision relied on information in addition to the discriminatory reports of the supervisors and on his own independent judgment. These factors did not make the manager's decision a "superseding cause" that negated the discriminatory actions of the plaintiff's immediate supervisors. This decision in effect gives considerable scope to the "cat's paw" theory of liability that plaintiff's lawyers frequently use in employment discrimination cases: that the employer remains liable for the discriminatory actions of lower level supervisors and managers who influence the ultimate decisions of those above them in the employer's organizational hierarchy.

5. **Bibliography.** For articles on after-acquired evidence, see William R. Corbett, The "Fall" of *Summers*, the Rise of "Pretext Plus," and the Escalating Subordination of Federal Employment Discrimination Law to Employment at Will: Lessons from *McKennon* and *Hicks*, 30 Ga. L. Rev. 305 (1996); Ann C. McGinley, Reinventing Reality: The Impermissible Intrusion of After-Acquired Evidence in Title VII Litigation, 26 Conn. L. Rev. 145 (1993).

For articles on mixed-motive cases, see Susan Bisom-Rapp, Of Motives and Maleness: A Critical View of Mixed Motive Doctrine in Title VII Sex Discrimination Cases, 1995 Utah L. Rev. 1029 (1995); Alfred W. Blumrosen & Ruth G. Blumrosen, Intentional Job Discrimination—New Tools for the Oldest Problem, 37 U. Mich. J.L. Ref. 681 (2004); Paul J. Gudel, Beyond Causation: The Interpretation of Action and the Mixed Motives Problem in Employment Discrimination Law, 70 Tex. L. Rev. 17 (1991); Matthew R. Scott & Russell D. Chapman, Much Ado About Nothing—Why *Desert Palace* Neither Murdered *McDonnell Douglas* Nor Transformed All Employment Discrimination Cases to Mixed-Motive, 36 St. Mary's L.J. 395 (2005); Sandra F. Sperino, Discrimination Statutes, the Common Law, and Proximate Cause, 2013 U. Ill. L. Rev. 1; Jeffrey A. Van Detta, "Le Roi Est Mort" Redux: Section 703(m), *Costa*, *McDonnell Douglas*, and the Title VII Revolution—A Reply, 52 Drake L. Rev. 427 (2004); Andrew Verstein, the Jurisprudence of Mixed Motives, 127 Yale L.J. ___ (2018); Michael Wells, Three Arguments Against *Mt. Healthy*: Tort Theory, Constitutional Torts, and Freedom of Speech, 51 Mercer L. Rev. 583 (2000); Michael J. Zimmer, The Emerging Uniform Structure of Disparate Treatment Discrimination Litigation, 30 Ga. L. Rev. 563 (1996); Michael J. Zimmer, Leading By Example: An Holistic Approach to Individual Disparate Treatment Law, 11 Kan. J.L. & Pub. Pol'y 177 (2001).

For the treatment of causation in connection and broader issues of what constitutes prohibited discrimination, see Stephen F. Befort & Alison L. Olig, Within the Grasp of the Cat's Paw: Delineating the Scope of Subordinate Bias Liability Under Federal Antidiscrimination Statutes, 60 S.C. L. Rev. 383 (2008); Stephanie Bornstein, Reckless Discrimination, 105 Cal. L. Rev. 1055 (2017); Suzanne B. Goldberg, Discrimination by Comparison, 120 Yale L.J. 728 (2011); Martin J. Katz, The Fundamental Incoherence of Title VII: Making Sense of Causation in Disparate Treatment Law, 94 Geo. L.J. 489 (2006); Minna J. Kotkin, Diversity and Discrimination: A Look at Complex Bias, 50 Wm. & Mary L. Rev. 1439 (2009); Angela Onwuachi Willig, By Any Other Name? On Being "Regarded As" Black, and Why Title VII Should Apply Even if Lakisha and Jamal are White, 2005 Wis. L. Rev. 1283 (2005); Angela Onwuachi-Willig & Mario L. Barnes, Complimentary Discrimination and Complementary Discrimination in Faculty Hiring, 87 Wash. U. L. Rev. 763 (2010); Victor D. Quintanilla & Cheryl R. Kaiser, The Same-Actor Inference of Nondiscrimination: Moral Credentialing and the Psychological and Legal Licensing of Bias, 104 Cal. L. Rev. 14 (2016). Enrique Schaerer, Intragroup Discrimination in the Workplace: The Case for "Race Plus," 45

Harv. C.R.-C.L. L. Rev. 57 (2010); Patrick S. Shin, Discrimination Under a Description, 47 Ga. L. Rev. 1 (2012); Girardeau A. Spann, Good Faith Discrimination, 23 Wm. & Mary Bill Rts. J. 585 (2015); Catherine T. Struve, Shifting Burdens: Discrimination Law Through the Lens of Jury Instructions, 51 B.C. L. Rev. 279 (2010); Charles A. Sullivan, The Phoenix from the Ash: Proving Discrimination by Comparators, 60 Ala. L. Rev. 191 (2009); Kevin Woodson, Derivative Racial Discrimination, 12 Stan. J. C.R. & C.L. 335 (2016); Kimberly A. Yuracko, Trait Discrimination as Race Discrimination: An Argument about Assimilation, 74 Geo. Wash. L. Rev. 365 (2006); Colloquium, Pretext in Peril, 75 Mo. L. Rev. 313 (2010).

D. RETALIATION

University of Texas Southwestern Medical Center v. Nassar

570 U.S. 338 (2013).

■ JUSTICE KENNEDY delivered the opinion of the Court.

When the law grants persons the right to compensation for injury from wrongful conduct, there must be some demonstrated connection, some link, between the injury sustained and the wrong alleged. The requisite relation between prohibited conduct and compensable injury is governed by the principles of causation, a subject most often arising in elaborating the law of torts. This case requires the Court to define those rules in the context of Title VII of the Civil Rights Act of 1964, which provides remedies to employees for injuries related to discriminatory conduct and associated wrongs by employers.

Title VII is central to the federal policy of prohibiting wrongful discrimination in the Nation's workplaces and in all sectors of economic endeavor. This opinion discusses the causation rules for two categories of wrongful employer conduct prohibited by Title VII. The first type is called, for purposes of this opinion, status-based discrimination. The term is used here to refer to basic workplace protection such as prohibitions against employer discrimination on the basis of race, color, religion, sex, or national origin, in hiring, firing, salary structure, promotion and the like. See § 2000e–2(a). The second type of conduct is employer retaliation on account of an employee's having opposed, complained of, or sought remedies for, unlawful workplace discrimination. See § 2000e–3(a).

An employee who alleges status-based discrimination under Title VII need not show that the causal link between injury and wrong is so close that the injury would not have occurred but for the act. So-called but-for causation is not the test. It suffices instead to show that the motive to discriminate was one of the employer's motives, even if the employer also had other, lawful motives that were causative in the employer's decision. This principle is the result of an earlier case from this Court, *Price Waterhouse v. Hopkins,* 490 U.S. 228 (1989), and an ensuing statutory amendment by Congress that codified in part and abrogated in part the holding in *Price Waterhouse,* see §§ 2000e–2(m), 2000e–5(g)(2)(B). The question the Court must answer here is whether that lessened causation standard is applicable to claims of unlawful employer retaliation under § 2000e–3(a).

Although the Court has not addressed the question of the causation showing required to establish liability for a Title VII retaliation claim, it has addressed the issue of causation in general in a case involving employer discrimination under a separate but related statute, the Age Discrimination in Employment Act of 1967 (ADEA), 29 U.S.C. § 623. See *Gross v. FBL Financial Services, Inc.,* 557 U.S. 167 (2009). In *Gross,* the Court concluded that the ADEA requires proof that the prohibited criterion was the but-for cause of the prohibited conduct. The holding and analysis of that decision are instructive here.

I

Petitioner, the University of Texas Southwestern Medical Center (University), is an academic institution within the University of Texas system. The University specializes in medical education for aspiring physicians, health professionals, and scientists. Over the years, the University has affiliated itself with a number of healthcare facilities including, as relevant in this case, Parkland Memorial Hospital (Hospital). As provided in its affiliation agreement with the University, the Hospital permits the University's students to gain clinical experience working in its facilities. The agreement also requires the Hospital to offer empty staff physician posts to the University's faculty members, and, accordingly, most of the staff physician positions at the Hospital are filled by those faculty members.

Respondent is a medical doctor of Middle Eastern descent who specializes in internal medicine and infectious diseases. . . .

In 2004, Dr. Beth Levine was hired as the University's Chief of Infectious Disease Medicine. In that position Levine became respondent's ultimate (though not direct) superior. Respondent alleged that Levine was biased against him on account of his religion and ethnic heritage, a bias manifested by undeserved scrutiny of his billing practices and productivity, as well as comments that " 'Middle Easterners are lazy.' " On different occasions during his employment, respondent met with Dr. Gregory Fitz, the University's Chair of Internal Medicine and Levine's supervisor, to complain about Levine's alleged harassment. Despite obtaining a promotion with Levine's assistance in 2006, respondent continued to believe that she was biased against him. So he tried to arrange to continue working at the Hospital without also being on the University's faculty. After preliminary negotiations with the Hospital suggested this might be possible, respondent resigned his teaching post in July 2006 and sent a letter to Dr. Fitz (among others), in which he stated that the reason for his departure was harassment by Levine. That harassment, he asserted, " 'stems from . . . religious, racial and cultural bias against Arabs and Muslims.' " After reading that letter, Dr. Fitz expressed consternation at respondent's accusations, saying that Levine had been "publicly humiliated by th[e] letter" and that it was "very important that she be publicly exonerated."

Meanwhile, the Hospital had offered respondent a job as a staff physician, as it had indicated it would. On learning of that offer, Dr. Fitz protested to the Hospital, asserting that the offer was inconsistent with the affiliation agreement's requirement that all staff physicians also be members of the University faculty. The Hospital then withdrew its offer.

After exhausting his administrative remedies, respondent filed this Title VII suit in the United States District Court for the Northern District of Texas. He alleged two discrete violations of Title VII. The first was a status-based discrimination claim under § 2000e–2(a). Respondent alleged that Dr. Levine's racially and religiously motivated harassment had resulted in his constructive discharge from the University. Respondent's second claim was that Dr. Fitz's efforts to prevent the Hospital from hiring him were in retaliation for complaining about Dr. Levine's harassment, in violation of § 2000e–3(a). The jury found for respondent on both claims. It awarded him over $400,000 in backpay and more than $3 million in compensatory damages. The District Court later reduced the compensatory damages award to $300,000.

On appeal, the Court of Appeals for the Fifth Circuit affirmed in part and vacated in part. The court first concluded that respondent had submitted insufficient evidence in support of his constructive-discharge claim, so it vacated that portion of the jury's verdict. The court affirmed as to the retaliation finding, however, on the theory that retaliation claims brought under § 2000e–3(a)—like claims of status-based discrimination under § 2000e–2(a)—require only a showing that retaliation was a motivating factor for the adverse employment action, rather than its but-for cause. It further held that the evidence supported a finding that Dr. Fitz was motivated, at least in part, to retaliate against respondent for his complaints against Levine. The Court of Appeals then remanded for a redetermination of damages in light of its decision to vacate the constructive-discharge verdict. . . .

II

A

This case requires the Court to define the proper standard of causation for Title VII retaliation claims. Causation in fact—*i.e.,* proof that the defendant's conduct did in fact cause the plaintiff's injury—is a standard requirement of any tort claim, see Restatement of Torts § 9 (1934) (definition of "legal cause"); § 431, Comment *a* (same); § 279, and Comment *c* (intentional infliction of physical harm); § 280 (other intentional torts); § 281(c) (negligence). This includes federal statutory claims of workplace discrimination. *Hazen Paper Co. v. Biggins,* 507 U.S.

604, 610 (1993) (In intentional-discrimination cases, "liability depends on whether the protected trait" "actually motivated the employer's decision" and "had a determinative influence on the outcome"); *Los Angeles Dept. of Water and Power v. Manhart,* 435 U.S. 702, 711 (1978) (explaining that the "simple test" for determining a discriminatory employment practice is "whether the evidence shows treatment of a person in a manner which but for that person's sex would be different" (internal quotation marks omitted)).

In the usual course, this standard requires the plaintiff to show "that the harm would not have occurred" in the absence of—that is, but for—the defendant's conduct. This, then, is the background against which Congress legislated in enacting Title VII, and these are the default rules it is presumed to have incorporated, absent an indication to the contrary in the statute itself.

B

Since the statute's passage in 1964, it has prohibited employers from discriminating against their employees on any of seven specified criteria. Five of them—race, color, religion, sex, and national origin—are personal characteristics and are set forth in § 2000e–2. (As noted at the outset, discrimination based on these five characteristics is called status-based discrimination in this opinion.) And then there is a point of great import for this case: The two remaining categories of wrongful employer conduct—the employee's opposition to employment discrimination, and the employee's submission of or support for a complaint that alleges employment discrimination—are not wrongs based on personal traits but rather types of protected employee conduct. These latter two categories are covered by a separate, subsequent section of Title VII, § 2000e–3(a).

Under the status-based discrimination provision, it is an "unlawful employment practice" for an employer "to discriminate against any individual . . . because of such individual's race, color, religion, sex, or national origin." § 2000e–2(a). In its 1989 decision in *Price Waterhouse,* the Court sought to explain the causation standard imposed by this language. It addressed in particular what it means for an action to be taken "because of" an individual's race, religion, or nationality. Although no opinion in that case commanded a majority, six Justices did agree that a plaintiff could prevail on a claim of status-based discrimination if he or she could show that one of the prohibited traits was a "motivating" or "substantial" factor in the employer's decision. 490 U.S., at 258 (plurality opinion); *id.,* at 259 (White, J., concurring in judgment); *id.,* at 276 (O'Connor, J., concurring in judgment). If the plaintiff made that showing, the burden of persuasion would shift to the employer, which could escape liability if it could prove that it would have taken the same employment action in the absence of all discriminatory animus. *Id.,* at 258 (plurality opinion); *id.,* at 259–260 (opinion of White, J.); *id.,* at 276–277 (opinion of O'Connor, J.). In other words, the employer had to show that a discriminatory motive was not the but-for cause of the adverse employment action.

Two years later, Congress passed the Civil Rights Act of 1991 (1991 Act), 105 Stat. 1071. This statute (which had many other provisions) codified the burden-shifting and lessened-causation framework of *Price Waterhouse* in part but also rejected it to a substantial degree. The legislation first added a new subsection to the end of § 2000e–2, *i.e.,* Title VII's principal ban on status-based discrimination. See § 107(a), 105 Stat. 1075. The new provision, § 2000e–2(m), states:

> "[A]n unlawful employment practice is established when the complaining party demonstrates that race, color, religion, sex, or national origin was a motivating factor for any employment practice, even though other factors also motivated the practice."

This, of course, is a lessened causation standard. . . .

So, in short, the 1991 Act substituted a new burden-shifting framework for the one endorsed by *Price Waterhouse.* Under that new regime, a plaintiff could obtain declaratory relief, attorney's fees and costs, and some forms of injunctive relief based solely on proof that race, color, religion, sex, or nationality was a motivating factor in the employment action; but the employer's proof that it would still have taken the same employment action would save it from monetary damages and a reinstatement order. See *Gross,* 557 U.S., at 178, n. 5; see also *id.,* at 175, n. 2, 177, n. 3.

After *Price Waterhouse* and the 1991 Act, considerable time elapsed before the Court returned again to the meaning of "because" and the problem of causation. This time it arose in the context of a different, yet similar statute, the ADEA, 29 U.S.C. § 623(a). See *Gross, supra.* Much like the Title VII statute in *Price Waterhouse,* the relevant portion of the ADEA provided that " '[i]t shall be unlawful for an employer . . . to fail or refuse to hire or to discharge any individual or otherwise discriminate against any individual with respect to his compensation, terms, conditions, or privileges of employment, *because of* such individual's age.' " 557 U.S., at 176 (quoting § 623(a)(1); emphasis and ellipsis in original).

Concentrating first and foremost on the meaning of the phrase " '*because of* . . . . age,' " the Court in *Gross* explained that the ordinary meaning of " 'because of' " is " 'by reason of' " or " 'on account of.' " *Id.,* at 176. Thus, the "requirement that an employer took adverse action 'because of' age [meant] that age was the 'reason' that the employer decided to act," or, in other words, that "age was the 'but-for' cause of the employer's adverse decision." 557 U.S., at 176.

In the course of approving this construction, *Gross* declined to adopt the interpretation endorsed by the plurality and concurring opinions in *Price Waterhouse.* Noting that "the ADEA must be 'read . . . the way

Congress wrote it,' " 557 U.S., at 179 (quoting *Meacham v. Knolls Atomic Power Laboratory,* 554 U.S. 84, 102 (2008)), the Court concluded that "the textual differences between Title VII and the ADEA" "prevent[ed] us from applying *Price Waterhouse* . . . to federal age discrimination claims," 557 U.S., at 175, n. 2. In particular, the Court stressed the congressional choice not to add a provision like § 2000e–2(m) to the ADEA despite making numerous other changes to the latter statute in the 1991 Act. *Id.,* at 174–175.

Finally, the Court in *Gross* held that it would not be proper to read *Price Waterhouse* as announcing a rule that applied to both statutes, despite their similar wording and near-contemporaneous enactment. 557 U.S., at 178, n. 5. This different reading was necessary, the Court concluded, because Congress' 1991 amendments to Title VII, including its "careful tailoring of the 'motivating factor' claim" and the substitution of § 2000e–5(g)(2)(B) for *Price Waterhouse* 's full affirmative defense, indicated that the motivating-factor standard was not an organic part of Title VII and thus could not be read into the ADEA. See 557 U.S., at 178, n. 5.

In *Gross,* the Court was careful to restrict its analysis to the statute before it and withhold judgment on the proper resolution of a case, such as this, which arose under Title VII rather than the ADEA. But the particular confines of *Gross* do not deprive it of all persuasive force. Indeed, that opinion holds two insights for the present case. The first is textual and concerns the proper interpretation of the term "because" as it relates to the principles of causation underlying both § 623(a) and § 2000e–3(a). The second is the significance of Congress' structural choices in both Title VII itself and the law's 1991 amendments. These principles do not decide the present case but do inform its analysis, for the issues possess significant parallels.

III

A

As noted, Title VII's antiretaliation provision, which is set forth in § 2000e–3(a), appears in a different section from Title VII's ban on status-based discrimination. The antiretaliation provision states, in relevant part:

> "It shall be an unlawful employment practice for an employer to discriminate against any of his employees . . . because he has opposed any practice made an unlawful practice by this subchapter, or because he has made a charge, testified, assisted, or participated in any manner in an investigation, proceeding, or hearing under this subchapter."

This enactment, like the statute at issue in *Gross,* makes it unlawful for an employer to take adverse employment action against an employee "because" of certain criteria. Cf. 29 U.S.C. § 623(a)(1). Given the lack of any meaningful textual difference between the text in this statute and the one in *Gross,* the proper conclusion here, as in *Gross,* is that Title VII retaliation claims require proof that the desire to retaliate was the but-for cause of the challenged employment action. See *Gross, supra,* at 176.

The principal counterargument offered by respondent and the United States relies on their different understanding of the motivating-factor section, which—on its face—applies only to status discrimination, discrimination on the basis of race, color, religion, sex, and national origin. In substance, they contend that: (1) retaliation is defined by the statute to be an unlawful employment practice; (2) § 2000e–2(m) allows unlawful employment practices to be proved based on a showing that race, color, religion, sex, or national origin was a motivating factor for—and not necessarily the but-for factor in—the challenged employment action; and (3) the Court has, as a matter of course, held that "retaliation for complaining about race discrimination *is* 'discrimination based on race.' "

There are three main flaws in this reading of § 2000e–2(m). The first is that it is inconsistent with the provision's plain language. It must be acknowledged that because Title VII defines "unlawful employment practice" to include retaliation, the question presented by this case would be different if § 2000e–2(m) extended its coverage to all unlawful employment practices. As actually written, however, the text of the motivating-factor provision, while it begins by referring to "unlawful employment practices," then proceeds to address only five of the seven prohibited discriminatory actions—actions based on the employee's status, *i.e.,* race, color, religion, sex, and national origin. This indicates Congress' intent to confine that provision's coverage to only those types of employment practices. The text of § 2000e–2(m) says nothing about retaliation claims. Given this clear language, it would be improper to conclude that what Congress omitted from the statute is nevertheless within its scope.

The second problem with this reading is its inconsistency with the design and structure of the statute as a whole. See *Gross,* 557 U.S., at 175, n. 2, 178, n. 5. Just as Congress' choice of words is presumed to be deliberate, so too are its structural choices. See *id.,* at 177, n. 3. When Congress wrote the motivating-factor provision in 1991, it chose to insert it as a subsection within § 2000e–2, which contains Title VII's ban on status-based discrimination, §§ 2000e–2(a) to (d), (*l*), and says nothing about retaliation. See 1991 Act, § 107(a), 105 Stat. 1075 (directing that "§ 2000e–2 . . . [be] further amended by adding at the end the following new subsection . . . (m)"). The title of the section of the 1991 Act that created § 2000e–2(m)—"Clarifying prohibition against impermissible consideration of race, color, religion, sex, or national origin in employment practices"—also indicates that Congress determined to address only claims of status-based discrimination, not retaliation. See § 107(a), *id.,* at 1075.

What is more, a different portion of the 1991 Act contains an express reference to all unlawful employment actions, thereby reinforcing the conclusion that Congress acted deliberately when it omitted retaliation claims from § 2000e–2(m). See *Arabian American Oil Co.,* 499 U.S., at 256 (congressional amendment of ADEA on a similar subject coupled with congressional failure to amend Title VII weighs against conclusion that the ADEA's standard applies to Title VII); see also *Gross, supra,* at 177, n. 3. The relevant portion of the 1991 Act, § 109(b), allowed certain overseas operations by U.S. employers to engage in "any practice prohibited by section 703 or 704," *i.e.,* § 2000e–2 or § 2000e–3, "if compliance with such section would cause such employer . . . to violate the law of the foreign country in which such workplace is located." 105 Stat. 1077.

If Congress had desired to make the motivating-factor standard applicable to all Title VII claims, it could have used language similar to that which it invoked in § 109. See *Arabian American Oil Co., supra,* at 256. Or, it could have inserted the motivating-factor provision as part of a section that applies to all such claims, such as § 2000e–5, which establishes the rules and remedies for all Title VII enforcement actions. But in writing § 2000e–2(m), Congress did neither of those things, and "[w]e must give effect to Congress' choice." *Gross, supra,* at 177, n. 3.

The third problem with respondent's and the Government's reading of the motivating-factor standard is in its submission that this Court's decisions interpreting federal antidiscrimination law have, as a general matter, treated bans on status-based discrimination as also prohibiting retaliation. In support of this proposition, both respondent and the United States rely upon decisions in which this Court has "read [a] broadly worded civil rights statute . . . as including an antiretaliation remedy." *CBOCS West, Inc. v. Humphries,* 553 U.S. 442, 452–453 (2008). In *CBOCS,* for example, the Court held that 42 U.S.C. § 1981—which declares that all persons "shall have the same right . . . to make and enforce contracts . . . as is enjoyed by white citizens"—prohibits not only racial discrimination but also retaliation against those who oppose it. 553 U.S., at 445. And in Gómez-Pérez v. Potter, 553 U.S. 474 (2008), the Court likewise read a bar on retaliation into the broad wording of the federal-employee provisions of the ADEA. *Id.,* at 479, 487 ("All personnel actions affecting [federal] employees . . . who are at least 40 years of age . . . shall be made free from any discrimination based on age," 29 U.S.C. § 633a(a)); see also *Jackson v. Birmingham Bd. of Ed.,* 544 U.S. 167, 173, 179 (2005) (20 U.S.C. § 1681(a) (Title IX)); *Sullivan v. Little Hunting Park, Inc.,* 396 U.S. 229, 235, n. 3 (1969) (42 U.S.C. § 1982).

These decisions are not controlling here. It is true these cases do state the general proposition that Congress' enactment of a broadly phrased antidiscrimination statute may signal a concomitant intent to ban retaliation against individuals who oppose that discrimination, even where the statute does not refer to retaliation in so many words. What those cases do not support, however, is the quite different rule that every reference to race, color, creed, sex, or nationality in an antidiscrimination statute is to be treated as a synonym for "retaliation." For one thing, § 2000e–2(m) is not itself a substantive bar on discrimination. Rather, it is a rule that establishes the causation standard for proving a violation defined elsewhere in Title VII. The cases cited by respondent and the Government do not address rules of this sort, and those precedents are of limited relevance here.

The approach respondent and the Government suggest is inappropriate in the context of a statute as precise, complex, and exhaustive as Title VII. As noted, the laws at issue in *CBOCS, Jackson,* and *Gómez-Pérez* were broad, general bars on discrimination. In interpreting them the Court concluded that by using capacious language Congress expressed the intent to bar retaliation in addition to status-based discrimination. See *Gómez-Pérez, supra,* at 486–488. In other words, when Congress' treatment of the subject of prohibited discrimination was both broad and brief, its omission of any specific discussion of retaliation was unremarkable.

If Title VII had likewise been phrased in broad and general terms, respondent's argument might have more force. But that is not how Title VII was written, which makes it incorrect to infer that Congress meant anything other than what the text does say on the subject of retaliation. Unlike Title IX, § 1981, § 1982, and the federal-sector provisions of the ADEA, Title VII is a detailed statutory scheme. This statute enumerates specific unlawful employment practices. See §§ 2000e–2(a)(1), (b), (c)(1), (d) (status-based discrimination by employers, employment agencies, labor organizations, and training programs, respectively); § 2000e–2(*l*) (status-based discrimination in employment-related testing); § 2000e–3(a) (retaliation for opposing, or making or supporting a complaint about, unlawful employment actions); § 2000e–3(b) (advertising a preference for applicants of a particular race, color, religion, sex, or national origin). It defines key terms, see § 2000e, and exempts certain types of employers, see § 2000e–1. And it creates an administrative agency with both rulemaking and enforcement authority. See §§ 2000e–5, 2000e–12.

This fundamental difference in statutory structure renders inapposite decisions which treated retaliation as an implicit corollary of status-based discrimination. Text may not be divorced from context. In light of Congress' special care in drawing so precise a statutory scheme, it would be improper to indulge respondent's suggestion that Congress meant to incorporate the default rules that apply only when Congress writes a broad and undifferentiated statute.

Further confirmation of the inapplicability of § 2000e–2(m) to retaliation claims may be found in Congress' approach to the Americans with Disabilities Act of 1990(ADA), 104 Stat. 327. In the ADA Congress provided not just a general prohibition on discrimination "because of [an individual's] disability," but also seven paragraphs of detailed description of the practices that would constitute the prohibited discrimination, see §§ 102(a), (b)(1)–(7), *id.,* at 331–332 (codified at 42 U.S.C. § 12112). And, most pertinent for present purposes, it included an express antiretaliation provision, see § 503(a), 104 Stat. 370 (codified at 42 U.S.C. § 12203). That law, which Congress passed only a year before enacting § 2000e–2(m) and which speaks in clear and direct terms to the question of retaliation, rebuts the claim that Congress must have intended to use the phrase "race, color, religion, sex, or national origin" as the textual equivalent of "retaliation." To the contrary, the ADA shows that when Congress elected to address retaliation as part of a detailed statutory scheme, it did so in clear textual terms. . . .

B

The proper interpretation and implementation of § 2000e–3(a) and its causation standard have central importance to the fair and responsible allocation of resources in the judicial and litigation systems. This is of particular significance because claims of retaliation are being made with ever-increasing frequency. . . .

In sum, Title VII defines the term "unlawful employment practice" as discrimination on the basis of any of seven prohibited criteria: race, color, religion, sex, national origin, opposition to employment discrimination, and submitting or supporting a complaint about employment discrimination. The text of § 2000e–2(m) mentions just the first five of these factors, the status-based ones; and it omits the final two, which deal with retaliation. When it added § 2000e–2(m) to Title VII in 1991, Congress inserted it within the section of the statute that deals only with those same five criteria, not the section that deals with retaliation claims or one of the sections that apply to all claims of unlawful employment practices. And while the Court has inferred a congressional intent to prohibit retaliation when confronted with broadly worded antidiscrimination statutes, Title VII's detailed structure makes that inference inappropriate here. Based on these textual and structural indications, the Court now concludes as follows: Title VII retaliation claims must be proved according to traditional principles of but-for causation, not the lessened causation test stated in § 2000e–2(m). This requires proof that the unlawful retaliation would not have occurred in the absence of the alleged wrongful action or actions of the employer. . . .

V

The text, structure, and history of Title VII demonstrate that a plaintiff making a retaliation claim under § 2000e–3(a) must establish that his or her protected activity was a but-for cause of the alleged adverse action by the employer. The University claims that a fair application of this standard, which is more demanding than the motivating-factor standard adopted by the Court of Appeals, entitles it to judgment as a matter of law. It asks the Court to so hold. That question, however, is better suited to resolution by courts closer to the facts of this case. The judgment of the Court of Appeals for the Fifth Circuit is vacated, and the case is remanded for further proceedings consistent with this opinion.

It is so ordered.

■ JUSTICE GINSBURG, with whom JUSTICE BREYER, JUSTICE SOTOMAYOR, and JUSTICE KAGAN join, dissenting.

Title VII of the Civil Rights Act of 1964, 42 U.S.C. § 2000e *et seq.*, makes it an "unlawful employment practice" to "discriminate against any individual . . . *because of* such individual's race, color, religion, sex, or national origin." § 2000e–2(a) (emphasis added). Backing up that core provision, Title VII also makes it an "unlawful employment practice" to discriminate against any individual " *because* " the individual has complained of, opposed, or participated in a proceeding about, prohibited discrimination. § 2000e–3(a) (emphasis added). This form of discrimination is commonly called "retaliation," although Title VII itself does not use that term. The Court has recognized that effective protection against retaliation, the office of § 2000e–3(a), is essential to securing "a workplace where individuals are not discriminated against because of their racial, ethnic, religious, or gender-based status." *Burlington Northern & S.F.R. Co. v. White,* 548 U.S. 53, 63 (2006). That is so because "fear of retaliation is the leading reason why people stay silent" about the discrimination they have encountered or observed. *Crawford v. Metropolitan Government of Nashville and Davidson Cty.*, 555 U.S. 271, 279 (2009) (internal quotation marks and brackets omitted).

Similarly worded, the ban on discrimination and the ban on retaliation against a discrimination complainant have traveled together: Title VII plaintiffs often raise the two provisions in tandem. Today's decision, however, drives a wedge between the twin safeguards in so-called "mixed-motive" cases. To establish discrimination, all agree, the complaining party need show only that race, color, religion, sex, or national origin was "a motivating factor" in an employer's adverse action; an employer's proof that "other factors also motivated the [action]" will not defeat the discrimination claim. § 2000e–2(m). But a retaliation claim, the Court insists, must meet a stricter standard: The claim will fail unless the complainant shows "but-for" causation, *i.e.,* that the employer would not have taken the adverse employment action but for a design to retaliate.

In so reining in retaliation claims, the Court misapprehends what our decisions teach: Retaliation for complaining about discrimination is tightly bonded to the core prohibition and cannot be disassociated from it. Indeed, this Court has explained again and again that "retaliation in response to a complaint about [proscribed] discrimination *is* discrimination" on the basis of the characteristic Congress sought to immunize against adverse employment action. *Jackson v. Birmingham Bd. of Ed.,* 544 U.S. 167, 179, n. 3 (2005) (emphasis added; internal quotation marks omitted).

The Court shows little regard for the trial judges who will be obliged to charge discrete causation standards when a claim of discrimination "because of," *e.g.*, race is coupled with a claim of discrimination "because" the individual has complained of race discrimination. And jurors will puzzle over the rhyme or reason for the dual standards. Of graver concern, the Court has seized on a provision, § 2000e–2(m), adopted by Congress as part of an endeavor to strengthen Title VII, and turned it into a measure reducing the force of the ban on retaliation. . . .

III

A

The Title VII provision key here, § 2000e–2(m), states that "an unlawful employment practice is established when the complaining party demonstrates that race, color, religion, sex, or national origin was a motivating factor for any employment practice, even though other factors also motivated the practice." Section 2000e–2(m) was enacted as part of the Civil Rights Act of 1991, which amended Title VII, along with other federal antidiscrimination statutes. See 105 Stat. 1071. The amendments were intended to provide "additional protections against unlawful discrimination in employment," *id.*, § 2(3), and to "respon[d] to a number of . . . decisions by [this Court] that sharply cut back on the scope and effectiveness" of antidiscrimination laws, H.R.Rep. No. 102–40, pt. II, pp. 2–4 (1991) (hereinafter House Report Part II).

Among the decisions found inadequately protective was *Price Waterhouse v. Hopkins,* 490 U.S. 228 (1989). . . .

B

There is scant reason to think that, despite Congress' aim to "restore and strengthen . . . laws that ban discrimination in employment," House Report Part II, at 2, Congress meant to exclude retaliation claims from the newly enacted "motivating factor" provision. Section 2000e–2(m) provides that an "unlawful employment practice is established" when the plaintiff shows that a protected characteristic was a factor driving "any employment practice." Title VII, in § 2000e–3(a), explicitly denominates retaliation, like status-based discrimination, an "unlawful employment practice." Because "any employment practice" necessarily encompasses practices prohibited under § 2000e–3(a), § 2000e–2(m), by its plain terms, covers retaliation.

Notably, when it enacted § 2000e–2(m), Congress did not tie the new provision specifically to §§ 2000e–2(a)–(d), which proscribe discrimination "because of" race, color, religion, gender, or national origin. Rather, Congress added an entirely new provision to codify the causation standard, one encompassing "any employment practice." § 2000e–2(m).

Also telling, § 2000e–2(m) is not limited to situations in which *the complainant's* race, color, religion, sex, or national origin motivates the employer's action. In contrast, Title VII's substantive antidiscrimination provisions refer to the protected characteristics of the complaining party. See §§ 2000e–2(a)(1)–(2), (c)(2) (referring to "such individual's" protected characteristics); §§ 2000e–2(b), (c)(1), (d) (referring to "his race, color, religion, sex, or national origin"). Congress thus knew how to limit Title VII's coverage to victims of status-based discrimination when it was so minded. It chose, instead, to bring within § 2000e–2(m) "any employment practice." To cut out retaliation from § 2000e–2(m)'s scope, one must be blind to that choice. . . .

NOTES ON *UNIVERSITY OF TEXAS SOUTHWESTERN MEDICAL CENTER V. NASSAR*

1. **Retaliation Claims Under Title VII.** The prohibition against retaliation in Title VII is twofold: protecting both opposition to unlawful employment practices and participation in enforcement proceedings. § 704(a), 42 U.S.C. § 2000e–3(a). Employees who engage in either form of activity are protected from adverse actions taken by the employer because of their opposition or participation. The rationale for this prohibition is to prevent employers from retaliating against their employees who invoke the procedures for enforcing the statute or who protest in other ways against discriminatory practices. In the absence of such a prohibition, the whole enforcement mechanism for assuring compliance with Title VII would be undermined by the retaliatory action of employers.

Conceptually, retaliation constitutes an additional form of prohibited discrimination: not on the basis of characteristics such as race or sex, but on the basis of activity undertaken to prevent these primary forms of discrimination. Moreover, this form of discrimination often results in an ancillary claim under Title VII, added to the plaintiff's claim of discrimination on other grounds. The plaintiff, for instance, alleges that she was the victim of sex discrimination, and when she complained about it, of retaliation also. This was the pattern in Burlington Northern & Santa Fe Ry. Co. v. White, 548 U.S. 53 (2006), in which the plaintiff originally complained about sexual harassment and then filed a claim under Title VII alleging both sex discrimination and retaliation. Only the latter claim was addressed by the Supreme Court, but the lower courts, as is typical in retaliation cases, also addressed the claim of sex discrimination.

2. **Adapting *McDonnell Douglas*.** The elements of a plaintiff's prima facie case have to be adapted for claims of retaliation to take account of the distinctive issues that these claims raise. An initial issue is whether the plaintiff's conduct is protected at all. In participation cases, this issue usually is easily resolved. Either the plaintiff participated in enforcement proceedings or he did not. (In cases involving other forms of opposition to discriminatory practices, the issue is more complicated, as discussed in the succeeding note.) The plaintiff must also establish that he or she has suffered an adverse employment action, usually in the form of an explicit decision made by the employer to discipline, discharge, or to deny some benefit to the plaintiff. Thus, in the typical case, the only dispute is over the causal connection between the plaintiff's participation and the defendant's decision.

3. **"But for" Causation Under *Nassar*.** The Supreme Court departed in *Nassar* from the standard of causation for other claims under Title VII, rejecting "a motivating factor" in favor of "a but-for" cause. The Court sometimes uses the phrase "the but-for" cause, as in the prior decision in Gross v. FBL Financial Services, Inc., 557 U.S. 167 (2009), which appears in Chapter 8 on age discrimination. Nevertheless, the two phrases appear to be equivalent in the Court's view because both single out the prohibited reason, either retaliation or age, as a necessary condition of the employer's decision adverse to the plaintiff. To go further and identify the prohibited reason as the only necessary condition for the employer's decision does not, on examination, make sense. Many factors are necessary to a decision adverse to the plaintiff, such as the fact that the plaintiff is alive. The Court has used "the" only to emphasize the important role that the prohibited reason must play in the decision.

Requiring proof of "but-for" causation has the practical consequence of placing the entire burden of persuasion upon the plaintiff in mixed-motive cases. To be sure, the defendant still has the burden of production under *McDonnell Douglas* of articulating a "legitimate, nondiscriminatory reason" for the disputed decision, but as we have seen, this burden is very light and easily satisfied. Most cases under *McDonnell Douglas* therefore come down to the issue of "pretext," which in retaliation cases, now means that the employer's offered reason covers up retaliation as a necessary condition of the employer's decision. The plaintiff's burden of proving pretext merges into the issue of "but-for" causation and the plaintiff bears the entire burden of persuasion on this issue. The employer can still submit evidence that it would have made the same decision anyway, but the employer does not bear the burden persuasion at this point. Where the evidence is conflicting and supports reasonable inferences either way on causation, the case must be submitted to the jury (or the judge sitting without a jury). If the evidence is equally balanced on causation, the decision must go against the plaintiff as the party with the entire burden of persuasion.

As a consequence, claims of retaliation under Title VII are more difficult to prove than claims of discrimination on other grounds. The Court reaches this result in *Nassar* primarily on textualist grounds. The Civil Rights Act of 1991 amended Title VII to require proof only of "a motivating factor" for other claims of discrimination but not for retaliation. Section 703(m) enumerates only these other claims, and by implication, excludes claims of retaliation. In response to this argument, Justice Ginsburg contends that the underlying purpose of the 1991 amendments was to alleviate the plaintiff's burden of proving causation. Is it enough for her to appeal to the purpose of the statute to override its explicit terms? Or is her point that effective and coherent interpretation of the statute supports adoption of a single, simple standard of causation?

4. **Opposition to Employment Discrimination.** Where the plaintiff has not participated in enforcement proceedings, but has opposed employment discrimination by other means, she must establish two additional facts: that the particular form of opposition chosen is protected and that it is directed at practices that are, at least, arguably discriminatory.

The first of these issues presents a contrast between the laws against employment discrimination and the laws protecting collective bargaining. Where statutes like Title VII provide administrative and judicial proceedings to enforce the rights of workers, statutes like the National Labor Relations Act (NLRA) establish a structure in which workers can join unions to put economic pressure upon their employers, in the form of strikes and picketing. These devices are essential to the organization of unions and the process of collective bargaining. Accordingly, a substantial body of law has developed on the rights of employees to take unilateral action to protect their right to organize and to bargain with their employer. The forms of protected opposition under Title VII are similar to the rights developed under the NLRA for employees to engage in protected concerted activity. See Craig Robert Senn, Redefining Protected "Opposition" Activity in Employment Retaliation Cases, 37 Cardozo L. Rev. 2035 (2016).

By way of illustration, recall that *McDonnell Douglas* involved a claim of retaliation which, although not addressed by the Supreme Court, was effectively rejected by the Court's holding that the plaintiff's participation in illegal protests constituted a "legitimate, nondiscriminatory reason" for the defendant not to rehire him. It was therefore not a protected form of opposition. By contrast, in Crawford v. Metropolitan Government of Nashville & Davidson County, 555 U.S. 271 (2009), the Supreme Court held that permissible opposition to discriminatory practices included answering questions in the course of an employer's internal investigation. The plaintiff did not need to initiate complaints over discriminatory practices in order to oppose them through the information that she supplied to the employer at the latter's request. The second issue, whether the opposition concerns employment practices that are arguably discriminatory, has been resolved in a manner generally favorable to plaintiffs. There is no need to prove that the disputed practices are, in fact, discriminatory, since that determination would require a degree of expertise that few plaintiffs possess. It is enough that the plaintiff reasonably believed the practice to be discriminatory. See e.g., Berg v. La Crosse Cooler Co., 612 F.2d 1041 (7th Cir. 1980). Whether it actually constitutes discrimination in violation of Title VII can then be left for a judicial decision on a claim for discrimination. For an extension of such reasoning to LGBT cases, see Erin Buzuvis, A Reasonable Belief: In Support of LGBT Plaintiffs' Title VII Retaliation Claims, 91 Denver U.L. Rev. 929 (2014).

5. Further Protection Against Retaliation. Despite *Nassar*, the Supreme Court has expanded the protection from retaliation in other respects. In Burlington Northern & Santa Fe Ry. Co. v. White, 548 UL.S. 53 (2006), the Court held that the retaliation adverse to the plaintiff need not be related to employment or occur at the workplace. It is enough that the employer's actions are "materially adverse to a reasonable employee or job applicant" and that they are "harmful to the point that they could well dissuade a reasonable worker from making or supporting a charge of discrimination." On the facts of the case, such actions arose from a suspension without pay, which the employer later conceded to be erroneous. Even though the employer later awarded the plaintiff back pay, the loss of compensation for over a month was sufficiently harmful to support a jury verdict retaliation.

In Thompson v. North American Stainless, LP, 562 U.S. 170 (2011), the Supreme Court allowed claims for retaliation involving third parties. The plaintiff in this case, Thompson, was the fiancée of an employee, Regalado, who filed a charge of sex discrimination against her employer, for whom Thompson also worked. Thompson alleged that he was fired allegedly in retaliation for Regalado's charge. Although the Court declined to follow earlier dicta allowing anyone who suffered an "injury in fact" to bring a claim under Title VII, it held that Thompson was within the "zone of interests" protected by the statute. In the terms used in § 704(a), he was a "person aggrieved" because Title VII was designed to protect employees like himself from the unlawful acts of their employers and because his discharge was the intended means of retaliating against Regalado.

The trend toward expanding prohibitions against retaliation is also apparent in claims under other statutes. In Kasten v. Saint-Gobain Performance Plastics Corp., 562 U.S. 1 (2011), the Court held that an oral complaint of illegal activity was sufficient to trigger the act's prohibition against retaliation under the Fair Labor Standards Act. That prohibition extended to any employee who "has filed any complaint" of illegal activity under the act, 29 U.S.C. § 215(a)(3), but the Court held that an oral complaint was the functional equivalent, a position supported by agencies that administer the act. No similar issue arises under Title VII because § 704(a) does not use the word "filed." It is sufficient if the plaintiff "opposed" an unlawful practice. Yet *Kasten*, like other cases, is indicative of the expansion of prohibitions against retaliation. See also CBOCS v. Humphries, 553 U.S. 442 (2008), discussed in Chapter 9 of the casebook, on claims of retaliation under 42 U.S.C. § 1981.

6. **Litigation Strategy in Alleging Retaliation.** Plaintiffs can gain several advantages by adding a claim of retaliation, where it is warranted, to an ordinary claim of discrimination. The most obvious is another ground upon which they can recover. It is entirely possible that an employer may prevail on the primary claim of discrimination and yet be found liable for retaliating against the plaintiff for participating in enforcement proceedings or for opposing practices reasonably believed to be discriminatory. Moreover, if the plaintiff prevails on a retaliation claim, he or she can more easily recover punitive damages. Under the general provision governing the recovery of damages under Title VII, punitive damages can be awarded only on a finding that the defendant acted "with malice or with reckless indifference to the federally protected rights of an aggrieved individual." 42 U.S.C. § 1981a(b)(1). Indeed, it is difficult to imagine a case of retaliation in which an inference, if not a finding, of malice or reckless indifference would not follow as a matter of course. And lastly, the evidence used to support a claim of retaliation can provide indirect support for a claim of discrimination, implying, as it does, that the employer has something to hide.

With all these advantages accruing to a plaintiff who adds a claim of retaliation to her lawsuit, how can the employer take steps to protect itself from this increased exposure to liability? Creating internal grievance procedures that employees can resort to before filing a charge of discrimination is one such precaution. As discussed more fully in the chapters concerned with sex discrimination and disability discrimination, an employer who seeks to resolve employee grievances on these grounds obtains certain complete or partial defenses to claims of sexual harassment and claims of failure to reasonably accommodate disabled employees. A related step is to assure nondiscriminatory treatment of employees who have filed charges against the employer or otherwise complained about discriminatory practices. Seemingly routine discipline of employees who are possible victims of discrimination can complicate an employer's defense of any lawsuit that might eventually be filed against it. Wholly apart from decreasing the employer's exposure to liability, do these practices serve the broader purpose of reducing litigation and increasing compliance with Title VII? Would employers adopt these practices even if they were not liable on claims for retaliation?

7. **Bibliography.** Jessica L. Beeler, Turning Title VII's Protection Against Retaliation Into a Never-Fulfilled Promise, 39 Golden Gate U. L. Rev. 141 (2008); Deborah L. Brake, Retaliation in the EEO Office, 50 Tulsa L. Rev. 1 (2014); Deborah L. Brake, Retaliation in an EEO World, 89 Ind. L.J. 115 (2014); Deborah L. Brake, Retaliation, 90 Minn. L. Rev. 18 (2005); Deborah L. Brake, Tortifying Retaliation: Protected Activity at the Intersection of Fault, Duty, and Causation, 75 Ohio St. L.J. 1375 (2014); Troy B. Daniels & Richard A. Bales, Plus at Pretext: Resolving the Split Regarding the Sufficiency of Temporal Proximity Evidence in Title VII Retaliation Cases, 44 Gonz. L. Rev. 493 (2008/09); Matthew W. Green, Jr., What's So Reasonable About Reasonableness? Rejecting a Case Law-Centered Approach to Title VII's Reasonable Belief Doctrine, 62 U. Kan. L. Rev. 759 (2014); Michael Z. Green, Retaliatory Employment Arbitration, 35 Berkeley J. Empl. & Lab. L. 201 (2014); Megan E. Mowrey, Discriminatory Retaliation: Title VII Protection for the Cooperating Employee, 29 Pace L. Rev. 689 (2009); Lawrence D. Rosenthal, To Report or Not to Report: The Case for Eliminating the Objectively Reasonable Requirement for Opposition Activities Under Title VII's Anti-Retaliation Provision, 39 Ariz. St. L.J. 1127 (2007); Craig Robert Senn, Redefining Protected "Opposition" Activity in Employment Retaliation Cases, 37 Cardozo L. Rev. 2035 (2016); Sandra F. Sperino, Retaliation and the Reasonable Person, 67 Fla. L. Rev. 2031 (2015); Ronald Turner, Title VII, the Third-Party Retaliation Issue, and the "Plain Language" Mirage, 5 Ala. C.R. & C.L. L. Rev. 77 (2013); Michael J. Zimmer, Hiding the Statute in Plain View: *University of Texas Southwestern Medical Center v. Nassar*. 14 Nev. L.J. 705 (2014); Michael J. Zimmer, A Pro-Employee Supreme Court? The Retaliation Decisions, 60 S.C. L. Rev. 917 (2009).

CHAPTER 3

CLASS CLAIMS: FROM INTENTIONAL DISCRIMINATION TO DISPARATE IMPACT

A. INTRODUCTION

Class claims are those brought on behalf of a group of employees. These claims usually are defined in procedural terms, which determine whether they are appropriate for certification of a class action under Federal Rule of Civil Procedure 23 or for a "pattern or practice" action brought by the government. These purely procedural issues will be taken up in Chapter 7. The current chapter is concerned with substantive issues: with the elements and defenses to claims that are typically brought on behalf of a class. These issues differ from purely procedural issues in several respects.

First, the cases that are appropriate for class treatment on procedural grounds do not entirely coincide with those in which a class claim is asserted. An individual could bring a claim only on his own behalf even if it could have been brought on behalf of a class. Thus, on the facts of *Teamsters*, covered in Chapter 1, a single African-American city driver could have brought an individual claim of systematic discrimination in hiring, denying him the better-paying job of line driver. He could have used exactly the same evidence as in *Teamsters*, but sought a recovery only for himself. There is no requirement that an individual plaintiff seek certification of a class action even if he could properly do so.

Second, the focus of substantive law is fundamentally different from that of procedural law. It is on the behavior prohibited outside of court and on the evidence to prove it. In procedural law, the focus is on what happens in court, on how claims can be efficiently joined together for litigation, and giving all the parties involved a fair opportunity to be heard.

And third, the scale and significance of class claims necessarily raises questions about the role of Title VII in protecting group rights and, in particular, about the desirability of group remedies in the form of affirmative action. As the opinion in *Teamsters* suggests, the step from using statistical evidence to prove discrimination to using statistics to require affirmative action can appear to be both deceptively short and extremely misleading. Much of the law of class claims, particularly disparate impact claims, is devoted to elucidating the difference between these two different uses of statistical evidence.

B. CLASS CLAIMS OF DISPARATE TREATMENT

Hazelwood School District v. United States

433 U.S. 299 (1977).

■ JUSTICE STEWART delivered the opinion of the Court.

The petitioner Hazelwood School District covers 78 square miles in the northern part of St. Louis County, Mo. In 1973 the Attorney General brought this lawsuit against Hazelwood and various of its officials, alleging that they were engaged in a "pattern or practice" of employment discrimination in violation of Title VII of the Civil Rights Act of 1964. The complaint asked for an injunction requiring Hazelwood to cease its discriminatory practices, to take affirmative steps to obtain qualified Negro faculty members, and to offer employment and give backpay to victims of past illegal discrimination.

Hazelwood was formed from 13 rural school districts between 1949 and 1951 by a process of annexation. By the 1967–1968 school year, 17,550 students were enrolled in the district, of whom only 59 were Negro; the number of Negro pupils increased to 576 of 25,166 in 1972–1973, a total of just over 2%.

From the beginning, Hazelwood followed relatively unstructured procedures in hiring its teachers. Every person requesting an application for a teaching position was sent one, and completed applications were submitted to a central personnel office, where they were kept on file. During the early 1960's the personnel office notified all applicants whenever a teaching position became available, but as the number of applications on file increased in the late 1960's and early 1970's, this practice was no longer considered feasible. The personnel office thus began the practice of selecting anywhere from 3 to 10 applicants for interviews at the school where the vacancy existed. The personnel office did not substantively screen the applicants in determining which of them to send for interviews, other than to ascertain that each applicant, if selected, would be eligible for state certification by the time he began the job. Generally, those who had most recently submitted applications were most likely to be chosen for interviews.

Interviews were conducted by a department chairman, program coordinator, or the principal at the school where the teaching vacancy existed. Although those conducting the interviews did fill out forms rating the applicants in a number of respects, it is undisputed that each school principal possessed virtually unlimited discretion in hiring teachers for his school. The only general guidance given to the principals was to hire the "most competent" person available, and such intangibles as "personality, disposition, appearance, poise, voice, articulation, and ability to deal with people" counted heavily. The principal's choice was routinely honored by Hazelwood's Superintendent and the Board of Education.

In the early 1960's Hazelwood found it necessary to recruit new teachers, and for that purpose members of its staff visited a number of colleges and universities in Missouri and bordering States. All the institutions visited were predominantly white, and Hazelwood did not seriously recruit at either of the two predominantly Negro four-year colleges in Missouri. As a buyer's market began to develop for public school teachers, Hazelwood curtailed its recruiting efforts. For the 1971–1972 school year, 3,127 persons applied for only 234 teaching vacancies; for the 1972–1973 school year, there were 2,373 applications for 282 vacancies. A number of the applicants who were not hired were Negroes.

Hazelwood hired its first Negro teacher in 1969. The number of Negro faculty members gradually increased in successive years: 6 of 957 in the 1970 school year; 16 of 1,107 by the end of the 1972 school year; 22 of 1,231 in the 1973 school year. By comparison, according to 1970 census figures, of more than 19,000 teachers employed in that year in the St. Louis area, 15.4% were Negro. That percentage figure included the St. Louis City School District, which in recent years has followed a policy of attempting to maintain a 50% Negro teaching staff. Apart from that school district, 5.7% of the teachers in the county were Negro in 1970.

Drawing upon these historic facts, the Government mounted its "pattern or practice" attack in the District Court upon four different fronts. It adduced evidence of (1) a history of alleged racially discriminatory practices, (2) statistical disparities in hiring, (3) the standardless and largely subjective hiring procedures, and (4) specific instances of alleged discrimination against 55 unsuccessful Negro applicants for teaching jobs. Hazelwood offered virtually no additional evidence in response, relying instead on evidence introduced by the Government, perceived deficiencies in the Government's case, and its own officially promulgated policy "to hire all teachers on the basis of training, preparation and recommendations, regardless of race, color or creed."

The District Court ruled that the Government had failed to establish a pattern or practice of discrimination. The court was unpersuaded by the alleged history of discrimination, noting that no dual school system had ever existed in Hazelwood. The statistics showing that relatively small numbers of Negroes were employed as teachers were found nonprobative, on the ground that the percentage of Negro pupils in Hazelwood was similarly small. The court found nothing illegal or suspect in the teacher-hiring procedures that Hazelwood had followed. Finally, the court reviewed the evidence in the 55 cases of alleged individual discrimination, and after stating that the burden of proving intentional discrimination was on the Government, it found that this burden had not been sustained in a single instance. Hence, the court entered judgment for the defendants.

The Court of Appeals for the Eighth Circuit reversed. After suggesting that the District Court had assigned inadequate weight to evidence of discriminatory conduct on the part of Hazelwood before the effective date of Title VII, the Court of Appeals rejected the trial court's analysis of the statistical data as resting on an irrelevant comparison of Negro teachers to Negro pupils in Hazelwood. The proper comparison, in the appellate court's view, was one between Negro teachers in Hazelwood and Negro teachers in the relevant labor market area. Selecting St. Louis County and St. Louis City as the relevant area, the Court of Appeals compared the 1970 census figures, showing that 15.4% of teachers in that area were Negro, to the racial composition of Hazelwood's teaching staff. In the 1972–1973 and 1973–1974 school years, only 1.4% and 1.8%, respectively, of Hazelwood's teachers were Negroes. This statistical disparity, particularly when viewed against the background of the teacher-hiring procedures that Hazelwood had followed, was held to constitute a prima facie case of a pattern or practice of racial discrimination.

In addition, the Court of Appeals reasoned that the trial court had erred in failing to measure the 55 instances in which Negro applicants were denied jobs against the four-part standard for establishing a prima facie case of individual discrimination set out in this Court's opinion in McDonnell Douglas Corp. v. Green, 411 U.S. 792, 802. Applying that standard, the appellate court found 16 cases of individual discrimination[10] which "buttressed" the statistical proof. Because Hazelwood had not rebutted the Government's prima facie case of a pattern or practice of racial discrimination, the Court of Appeals directed judgment for the Government and prescribed the remedial order to be entered.

We granted certiorari to consider a substantial question affecting the enforcement of a pervasive federal law.

The petitioners primarily attack the judgment of the Court of Appeals for its reliance on "undifferentiated work force statistics to find an unrebutted prima facie case of employment discrimination."[12] The question they raise, in short, is whether a basic component in the Court of Appeals' finding of a pattern or practice of discrimination—the comparatively small percentage of Negro employees in Hazelwood's teaching staff—was lacking in probative force.

This Court's recent consideration in International Brotherhood of Teamsters v. United States, 431 U.S. 324, of the role of statistics in pattern-or-practice suits under Title VII provides substantial guidance in evaluating the arguments advanced by the petitioners. In that case we

---

[10] The Court of Appeals held that none of the 16 prima facie cases of individual discrimination had been rebutted by the petitioners.

[12] . . . The Government's opening statement in the trial court explained that its evidence was designed to show that the scarcity of Negro teachers at Hazelwood "is the result of purpose" and is attributable to "deliberately continued employment policies." Thus here, as in International Brotherhood of Teamsters v. United States, 431 U.S. 324, "[t]he Government's theory of discrimination was simply that the [employer], in violation of § 703(a) of Title VII, regularly and purposefully treated Negroes . . . less favorably than white persons."

stated that it is the Government's burden to "establish by a preponderance of the evidence that racial discrimination was the (employer's) standard operating procedure—the regular rather than the unusual practice." We also noted that statistics can be an important source of proof in employment discrimination cases, since

> "absent explanation, it is ordinarily to be expected that nondiscriminatory hiring practices will in time result in a work force more or less representative of the racial and ethnic composition of the population in the community from which employees are hired. Evidence of long-lasting and gross disparity between the composition of a work force and that of the general population thus may be significant even though § 703(j) makes clear that Title VII imposes no requirement that a work force mirror the general population." Id. at 340 n.20

Where gross statistical disparities can be shown, they alone may in a proper case constitute prima facie proof of a pattern or practice of discrimination. Teamsters, supra, 431 U.S., at 339.

There can be no doubt, in light of the *Teamsters* case, that the District Court's comparison of Hazelwood's teacher work force to its student population fundamentally misconceived the role of statistics in employment discrimination cases. The Court of Appeals was correct in the view that a proper comparison was between the racial composition of Hazelwood's teaching staff and the racial composition of the qualified public school teacher population in the relevant labor market.[13] See Teamsters, supra, at 337–338, and n.17. The percentage of Negroes on Hazelwood's teaching staff in 1972–1973 was 1.4% and in 1973–1974 it was 1.8%. By contrast, the percentage of qualified Negro teachers in the area was, according to the 1970 census, at least 5.7%.[14] Although these

[13] In *Teamsters*, the comparison between the percentage of Negroes on the employer's work force and the percentage in the general areawide population was highly probative, because the job skill there involved—the ability to drive a truck—is one that many persons possess or can fairly readily acquire. When special qualifications are required to fill particular jobs, comparisons to the general population (rather than to the smaller group of individuals who possess the necessary qualifications) may have little probative value. The comparative statistics introduced by the Government in the District Court, however, were properly limited to public school teachers, and therefore this is not a case like Mayor v. Educational Equality League, 415 U.S. 605, in which the racial-composition comparisons failed to take into account special qualifications for the position in question. Id. at 620–621.

Although the petitioners concede as a general matter the probative force of the comparative work-force statistics, they object to the Court of Appeals' heavy reliance on these data on the ground that applicant-flow data, showing the actual percentage of white and Negro applicants for teaching positions at Hazelwood, would be firmer proof. As we have noted, there was no clear evidence of such statistics. We leave it to the District Court on remand to determine whether competent proof of those data can be adduced. If so, it would, of course, be very relevant. Cf. Dothard v. Rawlinson, 433 U.S., 321, 330.

[14] As is discussed below, the Government contends that a comparative figure of 15.4%, rather than 5.7% is the appropriate one. . . . But even assuming arguendo that the 5.7% figure urged by the petitioners is correct, the disparity between that figure and the percentage of Negroes on Hazelwood's teaching staff would be more than fourfold for the 1972–1973 school year, and threefold for the 1973–1974 school year. A precise method of measuring the significance of such statistical disparities was explained in Castaneda v. Partida, 430 U.S. 482, 496–97 n.17. It involves calculation of the "standard deviation" as a measure of predicted

differences were on their face substantial, the Court of Appeals erred in substituting its judgment for that of the District Court and holding that the Government had conclusively proved its "pattern or practice" lawsuit.

The Court of Appeals totally disregarded the possibility that this prima facie statistical proof in the record might at the trial court level be rebutted by statistics dealing with Hazelwood's hiring after it became subject to Title VII. Racial discrimination by public employers was not made illegal under Title VII until March 24, 1972. A public employer who from that date forward made all its employment decisions in a wholly nondiscriminatory way would not violate Title VII even if it had formerly maintained an all-white work force by purposefully excluding Negroes. For this reason, the Court cautioned in the *Teamsters* opinion that once a prima facie case has been established by statistical work-force disparities, the employer must be given an opportunity to show that "the claimed discriminatory pattern is a product of pre-Act hiring rather than unlawful post-Act discrimination." 431 U.S., at 360.

The record in this case showed that for the 1972–1973 school year, Hazelwood hired 282 new teachers, 10 whom (3.5%) were Negroes; for the following school year it hired 123 new teachers, 5 of whom (4.1%) were Negroes. Over the two-year period, Negroes constituted a total of 15 of the 405 new teachers hired (3.7%). Although the Court of Appeals briefly mentioned these data in reciting the facts, it wholly ignored them in discussing whether the Government had shown a pattern or practice of discrimination. And it gave no consideration at all to the possibility that post-Act data as to the number of Negroes hired compared to the total number of Negro applicants might tell a totally different story.

The difference between these figures may well be important; the disparity between 3.7% (the percentage of Negro teachers hired by Hazelwood in 1972–1973 and 1973–1974) and 5.7% may be sufficiently small to weaken the Government's other proof, while the disparity between 3.7% and 15.4% may be sufficiently large to reinforce it.[17] In

---

fluctuations from the expected value of a sample. Using the 5.7% figure as the basis for calculating the expected value, the expected number of Negroes on the Hazelwood teaching staff would be roughly 63 in 1972–1973 and 70 in 1973–1974. The observed number in those years was 16 and 22, respectively. The difference between the observed and expected values was more than six standard deviations in 1972–1973 and more than five standard deviations in 1973–1974. The Court in *Castaneda* noted that "[a]s a general rule for such large samples, if the difference between the expected value and the observed number is greater than two or three standard deviations," then the hypothesis that teachers were hired without regard to race would be suspect.

[17] Indeed, under the statistical methodology explained in *Castaneda v. Partida*, involving the calculation of the standard deviation as a measure of predicted fluctuations, the difference between using 15.4% and 5.7% as the areawide figure would be significant. If the 15.4% figure is taken as the basis for comparison, the expected number of Negro teachers hired by Hazelwood in 1972–1973 would be 43 (rather than the actual figure of 10) of a total of 282, a difference of more than five standard deviations; the expected number of 1973–1974 would be 19 (rather than the actual figure 5) of a total of 123, a difference of more than three standard deviations. For the two years combined, the difference between the observed number of 15 Negro teachers hired (of a total of 405) would vary from the expected number of 62 by more than six standard deviations. Because a fluctuation of more than two or three standard deviations would undercut the hypothesis that decisions were being made randomly with respect to race, 430 U.S., at 497

determining which of the two figures—or, very possibly, what intermediate figure—provides the most accurate basis for comparison to the hiring figures at Hazelwood, it will be necessary to evaluate such considerations as (i) whether the racially based hiring policies of the St. Louis City School District were in effect as far back as 1970, the year in which the census figures were taken; (ii) to what extent those policies have changed the racial composition of that district's teaching staff from what it would otherwise have been; (iii) to what extent St. Louis' recruitment policies have diverted to the city, teachers who might otherwise have applied to Hazelwood; (iv) to what extent Negro teachers employed by the city would prefer employment in other districts such as Hazelwood; and (v) what the experience in other school districts in St. Louis County indicates about the validity of excluding the City School District from the relevant labor market.

It is thus clear that a determination of the appropriate comparative figures in this case will depend upon further evaluation by the trial court. As this Court admonished in *Teamsters*: "[S]tatistics . . . come in infinite variety. . . . [T]heir usefulness depends on all of the surrounding facts and circumstances." Only the trial court is in a position to make the appropriate determination after further findings. And only after such a determination is made can a foundation be established for deciding whether or not Hazelwood engaged in a pattern or practice of racial discrimination in its employment practices in violation of the law.

We hold, therefore, that the Court of Appeals erred in disregarding the post-Act hiring statistics in the record, and that it should have remanded the case to the District Court for further findings as to the relevant labor market area and for an ultimate determination of whether Hazelwood engaged in a pattern or practice of employment discrimination after March 24, 1972. Accordingly, the judgment is vacated, and the case is remanded to the District Court for further proceedings consistent with this opinion.

It is so ordered.

■ JUSTICE BRENNAN, concurring.

I join the Court's opinion. Similarly to our decision in Dayton Board of Education v. Brinkman, 433 U.S. 406, today's opinion revolves around the relative factfinding roles of district courts and courts of appeals. It

---

n.17, each of these statistical comparisons would reinforce rather than rebut the Government's other proof. If, however, the 5.7% areawide figure is used, the expected number of Negro teachers hired in 1972–1973 would be roughly 16, less than two standard deviations from the observed number of 10; for 1973–1974, the expected value would be roughly seven, less than one standard deviation from the observed value of 5; and for the two years combined, the expected value of 23 would be less than two standard deviations from the observed total of 15. A more precise method of analyzing these statistics confirms the results of the standard deviation analysis. See F. Mosteller, R. Rourke, & G. Thomas, Probability with Statistical Applications 494 (2d ed. 1970).

These observations are not intended to suggest that precise calculations of statistical significance are necessary in employing statistical proof, but merely to highlight the importance of the choice of the relevant labor market area.

should be plain, however, that the liberal substantive standards for establishing a Title VII violation, including the usefulness of statistical proof, are reconfirmed.

In the present case, the District Court had adopted a wholly inappropriate legal standard of discrimination, and therefore did not evaluate the factual record before it in a meaningful way. This remand in effect orders it to do so. It is my understanding, as apparently it is Mr. Justice STEVENS', that the statistical inquiry mentioned by the Court and accompanying text, can be of no help to the Hazelwood School Board in rebutting the Government's evidence of discrimination. Indeed, even if the relative comparison market is found to be 5.7% rather than 15.4% black, the applicable statistical analysis at most will not serve to bolster the Government's case. This obviously is of no aid to Hazelwood in meeting its burden of proof. Nonetheless I think that the remand directed by the Court is appropriate and will allow the parties to address these figures and calculations with greater care and precision. I also agree that given the misapplication of governing legal principles by the District Court, Hazelwood reasonably should be given the opportunity to come forward with more focused and specific applicant-flow data in the hope of answering the Government's prima facie case. If, as presently seems likely, reliable applicant data are found to be lacking, the conclusion reached by my Brother Stevens will inevitably be forthcoming.

■ JUSTICE WHITE, concurring.

I join the Court's opinion . . . but with reservations with respect to the relative neglect of applicant pool data in finding a prima facie case of employment discrimination and heavy reliance on the disparity between the areawide percentage of black public school teachers and the percentage of blacks on Hazelwood's teaching staff. Since the issue is whether Hazelwood discriminated against blacks in hiring after Title VII became applicable to it in 1972, perhaps the Government should have looked initially to Hazelwood's hiring practices in the 1972–1973 and 1973–1974 academic years with respect to the available applicant pool, rather than to history and to comparative work-force statistics from other school districts. Indeed, there is evidence in the record suggesting that Hazelwood, with a black enrollment of only 2%, hired a higher percentage of black applicants than of white applicants for these two years. The Court's opinion, of course, permits Hazelwood to introduce applicant pool data on remand in order to rebut the prima facie case of a discriminatory pattern or practice. This may be the only fair and realistic allocation of the evidence burden, but arguably the United States should have been required to adduce evidence as to the applicant pool before it was entitled to its prima facie presumption. At least it might have been required to present some defensible ground for believing that the racial composition of Hazelwood's applicant pool was roughly the same as that for the school districts in the general area, before relying on comparative work-force data to establish its prima facie case.

■ JUSTICE STEVENS, dissenting.

The basic framework in a pattern-or-practice suit brought by the Government under Title VII of the Civil Rights Act of 1964 is the same as that in any other lawsuit. The plaintiff has the burden of proving a prima facie case; if he does so, the burden of rebutting that case shifts to the defendant. In this case, since neither party complains that any relevant evidence was excluded, our task is to decide (1) whether the Government's evidence established a prima facie case; and (2), if so, whether the remaining evidence is sufficient to carry Hazelwood's burden of rebutting that prima facie case.

I

The first question is clearly answered by the Government's statistical evidence, its historical evidence, and its evidence relating to specific acts of discrimination.

One-third of the teachers hired by Hazelwood resided in the city of St. Louis at the time of their initial employment. As Mr. Justice Clark explained in his opinion for the Court of Appeals, it was therefore appropriate to treat the city, as well as the county, as part of the relevant labor market. In that market, 15% of the teachers were black. In the Hazelwood District at the time of trial less than 2% of the teachers were black. An even more telling statistic is that after Title VII became applicable to it, only 3.7% of the new teachers hired by Hazelwood were black. Proof of these gross disparities was in itself sufficient to make out a prima facie case of discrimination. See International Brotherhood of Teamsters v. United States, 431 U.S. 324, 339 (1977); Castaneda v. Partida, 430 U.S. 482, 494–498.

As a matter of history, Hazelwood employed no black teachers until 1969. Both before and after the 1972 amendment making the statute applicable to public school districts, petitioner used a standardless and largely subjective hiring procedure. Since "relevant aspects of the decisionmaking process had undergone little change," it is proper to infer that the pre-Act policy of preferring white teachers continued to influence Hazelwood's hiring practices.[3]

The inference of discrimination was corroborated by post-Act evidence that Hazelwood had refused to hire 16 qualified black applicants for racial reasons. Taking the Government's evidence as a whole, there can be no doubt about the sufficiency of its prima facie case.

II

Hazelwood "offered virtually no additional evidence in response." It challenges the Government's statistical analysis by claiming that the city of St. Louis should be excluded from the relevant market and pointing

---

[3] Since Hazelwood's hiring before 1972 was so clearly discriminatory, there is some irony in its claim that "Hazelwood continued [after 1972] to select its teachers on the same careful basis that it had relied on before in staffing its growing system."

out that only 5.7% of the teachers in the county (excluding the city) were black. It further argues that the city's policy of trying to maintain a 50% black teaching staff diverted teachers from the county to the city. There are two separate reasons why these arguments are insufficient: they are not supported by the evidence; even if true, they do not overcome the Government's case.

The petitioners offered no evidence concerning wage differentials, commuting problems, or the relative advantages of teaching in an inner-city school as opposed to a suburban school. Without any such evidence in the record, it is difficult to understand why the simple fact that the city was the source of a third of Hazelwood's faculty should not be sufficient to demonstrate that it is a part of the relevant market. The city's policy of attempting to maintain a 50/50 ratio clearly does not undermine that conclusion, particularly when the record reveals no shortage of qualified black applicants in either Hazelwood or other suburban school districts. Surely not all of the 2,000 black teachers employed by the city were unavailable for employment in Hazelwood at the time of their initial hire.

But even if it were proper to exclude the city of St. Louis from the market, the statistical evidence would still tend to prove discrimination. With the city excluded, 5.7% of the teachers in the remaining market were black. On the basis of a random selection, one would therefore expect 5.7% of the 405 teachers hired by Hazelwood in the 1972–1973 and 1973–1974 school years to have been black. But instead of 23 black teachers, Hazelwood hired only 15, less than two-thirds of the expected number. Without the benefit of expert testimony, I would hesitate to infer that the disparity between 23 and 15 is great enough, in itself, to prove discrimination. It is perfectly clear, however, that whatever probative force this disparity has, it tends to prove discrimination and does absolutely nothing in the way of carrying Hazelwood's burden of overcoming the Government's prima facie case.

Absolute precision in the analysis of market data is too much to expect. We may fairly assume that a nondiscriminatory selection process would have resulted in the hiring of somewhere between the 15% suggested by the Government and the 5.7% suggested by petitioners, or perhaps 30 or 40 black teachers, instead of the 15 actually hired. On that assumption, the Court of Appeals' determination that there were 16 individual cases of discriminatory refusal to hire black applicants in the post-1972 period seems remarkably accurate.

In sum, the Government is entitled to prevail on the present record. It proved a prima facie case, which Hazelwood failed to rebut. Why, then, should we burden a busy federal court with another trial? Hazelwood had an opportunity to offer evidence to dispute the 16 examples of racially motivated refusals to hire; but as the Court notes, the Court of Appeals has already "held that none of the 16 prima facie cases of individual discrimination had been rebutted by the petitioners." Hazelwood also had an opportunity to offer any evidence it could muster to show a change in hiring practices or to contradict the fair inference to be drawn from the statistical evidence. Instead, it "offered virtually no additional evidence in response."

Perhaps "a totally different story" might be told by other statistical evidence that was never presented. No lawsuit has ever been tried in which the losing party could not have pointed to a similar possibility. It is always possible to imagine more evidence which could have been offered, but at some point litigation must come to an end.

Rather than depart from well-established rules of procedure, I would affirm the judgment of the Court of Appeals. Since that judgment reflected a correct appraisal of the record, I see no reason to prolong this litigation with a remand neither side requested.

NOTES ON *HAZELWOOD SCHOOL DISTRICT V. UNITED STATES*

1. **Contrast with *Teamsters*.** Because the evidence of discrimination was so clear-cut in *Teamsters*, the Supreme Court felt no need to elaborate on the economic model that applied to the labor market for jobs in the trucking industry. The evidence in *Hazelwood* was not nearly so one-sided, presenting the Court with the first opportunity to discuss the appropriate methods for analyzing statistical evidence to prove employment discrimination. (The Court had previously dealt with the conceptually easier issue of using statistical evidence to determine whether an apparent deviation from the legally mandated random selection of grand jurors established discrimination against Mexican-Americans in Castaneda v. Partida, 430 U.S. 482 (1977).) The discussion in *Hazelwood* did not focus on the mathematical tests for statistical significance, which is just as well, since the Court's brief treatment of this issue in a footnote is, at best, incomplete, and, at worst, inaccurate and misleading. In this respect, the Court's general approach, adapted from *Teamsters*, is a more reliable guide than its application to the facts of the case: "[S]tatistics . . . come in infinite variety. . . . [T]heir usefulness depends on all of the surrounding facts and circumstances."

The Court's elucidation of the surrounding facts and circumstances constitutes the real contribution of the opinion to the analysis of statistical evidence. These facts and circumstances fall under two general headings: the composition of the relevant labor market and the composition of the employer's work force. Only after these elements of the analysis have been appropriately defined can a strictly statistical comparison be made. The proportion of African Americans in the relevant labor market and in the relevant segment of the employer's work force must first be ascertained. Only then can these numbers be compared by strictly statistical means. Moreover, even at that point the analysis is not complete, since the practical significance of any resulting disparity is crucial to drawing an inference of intentional discrimination.

In *Hazelwood*, the Supreme Court itself did not resolve any of these subsidiary issues, but left them for the lower courts on remand. The district court had made the seemingly elementary error of comparing the proportion of African-American students with the proportion of African-American teachers, neglecting an analysis of the labor market entirely. Perhaps the district court was misled by the apparent analogy to school desegregation litigation, in which integration of both students and teachers was necessary to dismantle racially separate school systems.

No such mistake occurred in *Teamsters*. The Supreme Court had felt no need to go into an explicit analysis of the appropriate labor market and employer's work force because the disparities in that case were so large: the "inexorable zero" of minority representation among line drivers all around the country. Yet it is important to note that the same model of analysis was implicitly adopted in *Teamsters* as was explicitly set forth in *Hazelwood*. Both cases compare the proportion of minority group members in the labor market with the proportion hired by the employer in the job in dispute. *Hazelwood* simply refines the terms of this analysis.

2. Defining the Appropriate Labor Market. The essence of a claim of class-wide hiring discrimination is that the employer has hired too few workers of a certain group, such as blacks (in *Teamsters* and *Hazelwood*). To evaluate this claim, one needs to compare the actual percentage of black workers hired to an appropriate benchmark percentage. Determining this benchmark is both essential and difficult. In many employment discrimination cases, the primary issue for the trier of fact is to sort out the conflicting expert opinions concerning the definition of the appropriate labor market and the evidence used to ascertain its racial composition. In *Hazelwood*, the principal dispute was over the geographical scope of the labor market and, in particular, whether it included the city of St. Louis. Other issues of definition were raised by Justice White's argument in his concurring opinion that applicant flow statistics should have been used to ascertain the racial composition of the labor market. In effect, he would have limited the labor market to those who expressed a willingness to be employed in the Hazelwood School District. Still other issues were not contested by the parties, such as the time period over which the labor market should be analyzed (although a similar issue did come up in considering the appropriate definition of the employer's work force). The parties also did not dispute the need for a teacher's certification as a qualification for employment.

Exactly how the job market should be defined, of course, varies from case to case. In theory, the definition is easy enough to state. The labor market for a particular job should contain all those with undisputed qualifications for the position who, over the time period that the job is open, would be willing to accept the job on the terms offered by the employer. All of the difficulties are in determining what this abstract definition means in any concrete case and in finding evidence of the racial composition of the market as so defined. The parties exploit these difficulties according to standardized strategies. The plaintiff seeks to define the labor market so as to increase the proportion of minorities that forms the base line for assessing the defendant's compliance with Title VII. The defendant seeks to do the opposite. Defendants also rely upon the more general strategy of simply discrediting the plaintiff's evidence, arguing that it is insufficient to satisfy the plaintiff's burden of proving discrimination.

So, in *Hazelwood*, the plaintiff sought to include the city of St. Louis within the geographical definition of the labor market and thus to increase the proportion of African-Americans in the labor market from 5.7 percent to 15.4 percent. The plaintiff's objective was to increase the base line by which the defendant's hiring practices were to be judged. Of course, that base line, however it is defined, did not require the defendant to engage in hiring proportional to the composition of the labor market. In section 703(j), Title VII explicitly disclaims any such form of required affirmative action. Yet, the greater the proportion of a minority group in the labor market, the stronger the inference of discrimination from a fixed proportion of that group in the employer's work force. A 15.4 percent benchmark proportion of African-Americans in the labor market would make the small number of African-American teachers in the Hazelwood School District look worse than a 5.7 percent benchmark. Consequently, the school district attempted to define the labor market narrowly, to exclude the African-American teachers in the St. Louis city schools.

Predictable as these motives of the parties are, they do not assist the court in resolving their rival claims. On the record in *Hazelwood*, the Supreme Court found insufficient evidence to resolve even the issue of geographical scope. Yet how plausible is it that the teachers in the inner city schools in St. Louis would not be interested in positions in the suburban school district in Hazelwood? Commuting patterns from the suburbs to the inner city work equally well in the opposite direction, so that teachers who worked in St. Louis, assuming that they lived there also, could just as easily drive to Hazelwood as teachers from other suburban school districts. Does the affirmative action plan of the St. Louis city schools make any difference, as the defendants argued? This plan was designed to encourage the employment of African-American teachers, but would it necessarily exclude all these teachers from the labor market for jobs in the surrounding suburbs? In fact, would any teacher, whether minority or not, rely on an affirmative action plan as the sole basis for choosing a school district in which to work?

While complete exclusion of the teachers in St. Louis would make little sense, it also makes little sense to include all of these teachers in the relevant labor market for the Hazelwood School District. Consider the situation of black (or white) teachers working in St. Louis and living in suburbs on the opposite side of the metropolitan area from Hazelwood. Some of these teachers might be willing to commute to Hazelwood and thus should be included in the relevant labor market. Those teachers who found the magnitude of this commute too daunting, though, should be excluded—unless they might be interested in moving closer to Hazelwood if they could secure a job there. A teacher who was unwilling to commute across the entire metropolitan area to a distant suburban school might well be willing to move closer to Hazelwood if such a job were available. For that matter, a teacher in inner-city Kansas City might prefer to work in a suburban district such as Hazelwood. In other words, there is no easily defined geographic area to which one can look to find the exact pool of workers from which the

Hazelwood School District would be expected to select its teachers. As a general rule, the better the job, the wider the area from which one might expect to receive applications. Applicant pool data can therefore be helpful in establishing the appropriate geographic market or setting the benchmark proportion of minorities, but, as discussed in note 4 below, one must be cautious in relying on applicant data.

3. Defining the Appropriate Work Force. As an initial matter, the plaintiff defines the relevant segment of the employer's work force by identifying the positions in which discrimination is alleged. In *Hazelwood*, the plaintiff alleged discrimination in hiring teachers but not, for instance, in hiring administrators or clerical staff. Only the hiring decisions for this position were at issue. Yet underneath the apparent simplicity of this issue, complications arise because of the need to determine the relevant time period over which hiring decisions were made.

Only certain, fairly recent, employment decisions can be the subject of a timely claim under Title VII. In most cases, the statute of limitations allows courts to consider only decisions that occurred within 300 days before the plaintiff filed a charge with the EEOC. In *Hazelwood*, the situation was a little more complicated, partly because the claim was filed by the United States, not a private individual, and partly because Title VII had only recently been amended, two years before the case was filed, to apply to public employers like the Hazelwood School District. Hence, the plaintiff's claim concerned only discrimination that occurred after the effective date of the amendments. In the generality of cases, however, it is the relatively short statute of limitations, less than one year before filing with the EEOC, that defines the backward limit on claims under Title VII.

Several complications follow from this fact. The most important is that claims of discrimination do not focus on the composition of the employer's work force, even as limited to the jobs in dispute. The employer's overall work force reflects hiring decisions that have occurred over many years, only a few of which fall within the relevant time period. Accordingly, in *Hazelwood*, the Supreme Court did not look to the 1 percent to 2 percent of African-American teachers in the school district's overall work force, but to the 3.7 percent hired over the relevant years of 1972 to 1974.

In the dispute over which of these figures to use, we see the mirror image of the parties' dispute over the composition of the relevant labor market. Just as the plaintiff seeks to *increase* the proportion of minority workers in the labor market to raise the base line from which the defendant is judged, the plaintiff also seeks to *decrease* the proportion of minority workers hired by the defendant to expand the shortfall in minority hiring. The defendant, of course, tries to do the opposite and to reduce the shortfall. So, the plaintiff argued for the 1 percent to 2 percent figures based on the overall work force in *Hazelwood*, while the defendant argued for the 3.7 percent figure based on hiring in the period 1972–1974. Upon analysis, this particular dispute is not difficult to resolve, since Title VII focuses upon employment decisions rather than employment status and only on recent decisions that can be the subject of a timely claim.

Yet the matter cannot rest there because overall work force figures undeniably are relevant to claims of discrimination. Indeed, in *Teamsters*, these were virtually the only figures that the Supreme Court relied on. A close reading of the opinion in *Hazelwood* reveals the way in which such figures become relevant. Evidence of discrimination before 1972, the effective date of Title VII in that case, could not itself establish a violation of the statute. But if the school district's employment practices had not changed, it could furnish evidence of discrimination that continued into the relevant time period. So, too, the overall work force figures, if they reveal a pattern of past discrimination based on unchanged employment practices, constitute evidence of present discrimination.

Who gains by exploiting evidence of past practices? The plaintiff conceivably opens the door to the defendant's argument that it has mended its ways. The defendant, by emphasizing that its discrimination is in the past, apparently concedes that it has already engaged in discrimination. In fact, as a public employer, the Hazelwood School District was already subject to the prohibitions against discrimination in the Fourteenth Amendment long before it became subject to the additional prohibitions in Title VII. Does it make sense for the school district to emphasize its history of discrimination? On the record in *Hazelwood* did it have any other choice?

4. **Available Statistical Evidence.** Because class claims necessarily operate on a larger scale than individual claims, they require both parties to accumulate more evidence in support of their positions. This burden falls particularly heavily on the plaintiff, who bears the initial burden of production and ultimate burden of persuasion to establish liability. Obtaining relevant and reliable statistical evidence usually requires the services of an expert to analyze the raw data that becomes available and often to gather additional evidence tailored to the facts of the particular case.

Establishing the benchmark composition of the labor market usually poses the most severe problem for plaintiffs. Evidence of the employer's work force can be obtained from the defendant itself during discovery and then analyzed as necessary, and even before a case is filed, EEO-1 reports from employers with more than 100 employees are filed annually with the EEOC, and thus can be used by the EEOC in deciding which firms to investigate further. These reports provide a statistical summary of the employer's work force categorized by race, national origin, sex, and similar characteristics, and by broadly defined types of employment, such as managerial, professional, or clerical. 29 C.F.R. § 1602.7. None of this information need be kept or produced by employers in a form that readily supports a claim of discrimination, so that further investigation and analysis almost always is necessary. The source of such further information is known, however, and plaintiffs can readily use discovery devices, such as interrogatories, requests for production, or depositions, to obtain it from the employer.

The employer's own files, of course, yield information about the composition of the labor market, but only in the form of applicant flow statistics. Even these are likely to be sketchy since employers are not required to keep applications for more than one year (unless an investigation commences before the end of that time), 29 C.F.R. § 1602.14; and many inquiries about a job might be so informal (such as a telephone call) that no record of them is ever made at all. Moreover, the crucial information about the race, national origin, or sex of the applicant might not be recorded on the application, or recorded only haphazardly and inaccurately. Other reasons identified by the majority in *Hazelwood* cast doubt on Justice White's suggestion that applicant flow statistics are the preferred means of ascertaining the composition of the labor market. The employer's reputation for engaging in discrimination (or conversely, for engaging in affirmative action) might distort the pool of applicants for jobs with the employer, so that it is not representative of individuals in the labor market generally. Members of minority groups might be discouraged from applying to the employer because of the very hiring practices that are in dispute. On the facts of *Hazelwood*, how strong was such an effect likely to be?

Alternatives to applicant flow statistics require research directly into conditions in the labor market. Fortunately for the plaintiff in *Hazelwood*, the Bureau of the Census had already compiled statistics on teachers in the St. Louis area. These statistics covered the "Standard Metropolitan Statistical Area" or SMSA that included St. Louis and the surrounding suburbs. They also broke down the composition of the teachers by race, furnishing the plaintiff with almost precisely the statistics necessary to establish the composition of the labor market. In many cases, however, such precisely tailored statistics will not be available from an outside source and must be generated, instead, through the plaintiff's own effort and expense. In *Hazelwood*, this would have required the plaintiff to undertake its own survey of teachers in the St. Louis area instead of relying on the survey already conducted by the Census.

Plaintiffs typically are left with a choice: between relying upon generally available statistics, which fit the facts of their own case only approximately, if at all; or relying on studies they commission themselves that fit the facts of their case as closely as possible. They are faced with a trade-off between cost and accuracy, which defendants often exploit by arguing that plaintiffs have not met their burden of proof because they erred too far in the direction of favoring decreased cost over increased accuracy. How wise is it for defendants simply to rely upon inadequacies in the plaintiff's statistical evidence? No such evidence is perfect, if only because predictions about what a nondiscriminatory employer would have done are inherently uncertain. The defendants in both *Teamsters* and *Hazelwood* contented themselves with trying to poke holes in the plaintiff's evidence, leaving them with nothing to fall back on if that evidence was accepted as adequate. Would defendants be wiser to offer their own statistical evidence? Or would this strategy leave them to confront the same trade-off between expense and accuracy that plaintiffs face?

5. The "Prima Facie" Case. Defendants can avoid the pitfalls of submitting their own statistical evidence by arguing that the plaintiff has failed to make out a "prima facie" case. The concept of the "prima facie" case figures prominently in the line of cases beginning with *McDonnell Douglas v. Green*. It also leads to some confusion, as we saw in Chapter 2. The same is true in the analysis of class-wide claims of disparate treatment. Both

Teamsters and *Hazelwood* use the terminology of the "prima facie" case without explaining exactly what it means. An implicit analogy is with individual claims of disparate treatment, in which the plaintiff's success in making out a prima facie case results in shifting the burden of production onto the defendant to offer a legitimate, nondiscriminatory reason for the disputed decision. A similar analogy can be drawn to claims of disparate impact which, as we shall see in the next section, involve a shift of the burden of production and persuasion onto the defendant.

Yet neither *Teamsters* nor *Hazelwood* articulates what either the plaintiff must prove to make out a prima facie case or what the defendant must prove to rebut it. The only conclusion that can be drawn from the Supreme Court's studied silence on this issue is that the plaintiff bears the ordinary burden in civil litigation of producing evidence from which a reasonable inference of intentional discrimination can be drawn and then of persuading the trier of fact actually to draw this inference by finding that discrimination more probably than not occurred. The defendant bears no burden of proof at all, at least as technically defined, either of producing evidence or persuading the trier of fact. Instead, the defendant has the practical burden of presenting evidence that defeats any inference of intentional discrimination, either by showing that it is unreasonable or by showing that, even if it is reasonable, it should not be drawn. Thus, in *Hazelwood*, the only burden on the defendant was to present evidence that would prevent the plaintiff from satisfying its burden of production and persuasion.

Some lower courts have disagreed with this conclusion and have formulated more specific burdens that the defendant must carry in order to defeat a prima facie case of class-wide intentional discrimination. E.g., Segar v. Smith, 738 F.2d 1249, 1268–72 (D.C. Cir. 1984), cert. denied, 471 U.S. 1115 (1985). Others have defined the burdens on both parties only in the most general terms:

> The plaintiffs' prima facie case will thus usually consist of statistical evidence demonstrating substantial disparities in the application of employment actions as to minorities and the unprotected group, buttressed by evidence of general policies or specific instances of discrimination.
>
> If a plaintiff meets this initial burden, the burden then shifts, temporarily to the employer to defeat the prima facie showing of a pattern or practice by demonstrating that the [plaintiffs'] proof is either inaccurate or insignificant.

EEOC v. Sears, Roebuck & Co., 839 F.2d 302, 308 (7th Cir. 1988) (internal quotation marks and citations omitted).

On this view, the only specific burdens that fall upon the parties are not formal requirements of proof, but the practical need to persuade the trier of fact. Thus, in *Sears Roebuck*, the EEOC submitted statistical evidence of massive discrimination against women throughout Sears' operations around the nation, but failed to identify a single instance of discrimination against an individual woman. Although the court recognized that it could have relied entirely on statistical evidence, it found the absence of any anecdotal evidence to be decisive. Sears also presented expert testimony that women were less interested in the commission sales jobs that were dominated by men. As a result, the court concluded that the EEOC had not met its burden of persuasion on the ultimate issue of discrimination. In the words of *Teamsters*, there was no anecdotal evidence that "brought the cold numbers convincingly to life." If the EEOC's claims of systematic, nationwide discrimination were true, some evidence of individual instances of discrimination should have been available. Such evidence, even if not required as a matter of law, was necessary as a practical matter to meet the EEOC's burden of persuading the court that Sears Roebuck had actually engaged in discrimination.

Do these burdens on the plaintiff, both formal and practical, make it too hard for the plaintiff to prove class-wide disparate treatment? The plaintiff must both provide sophisticated statistical evidence of discrimination and convincing evidence of individual instances of discrimination. Moreover, most employers will avoid situations, such as that in *Teamsters*, in which the "inexorable zero" of minority employment is easily proved. Does this argue for an alternative to class claims of disparate treatment in which some of the burden of proof is shifted onto the defendant? The next section of this chapter, on the theory of disparate impact, takes up this question.

NOTES ON STATISTICAL SIGNIFICANCE

We have come this far in the analysis of the statistical evidence in *Hazelwood* without engaging in any technical statistical analysis. That is as it should be, since before turning to the purely mathematical computations one must first develop suitable economic models of the appropriate labor market and the employer's work force and accurate data on the racial composition of each. As statisticians sometimes say of a model that fails accurately to specify the phenomenon under investigation, "garbage in, garbage out." The mathematical tests for statistical significance are only as good as the economic models and data to which they are applied.

Statistics itself is a sophisticated and highly technical branch of mathematics and this brief introductory note can hardly do justice to the subject. In any even moderately complex case, an attorney must work with an expert familiar with the statistical techniques used in labor economics. More often than not, this expert will be an economist, not a statistician, because of the need to analyze statistical evidence using the correct economic models. The attorney's task, unless she becomes an expert herself, is to translate the technical terminology of the economist, including the terminology of statistics, into terms relevant to legal analysis and, equally important, terms understandable by the judge or the jury. Of course, an attorney with some knowledge of the nuances of statistics will have a better understanding of the weaknesses of the opposing statistical evidence and will be more effective in deposing and cross-examining opposing experts. These notes provide a brief introduction to the relevant terminology and basic approach of statistical inference, and to the controversy within the statistics profession over the use of this approach in employment discrimination cases. Perhaps surprisingly, the decision to use certain forms of statistical inference in this context is related to major public policy issues, such as affirmative action and the overall reliability of litigation to enforce the laws against employment discrimination.

1. The Null Hypothesis. Almost all statistical analysis in the social sciences begins with the designation of the "null hypothesis." This is not the hypothesis to be proved, but somewhat paradoxically, the hypothesis to be disproved by the investigation in question. In an employment discrimination case, this status is invariably assigned to the proposition that the defendant has not engaged in discrimination. The statistical evidence then is used to decide whether to reject the null hypothesis.

This double negative approach to proof appears to add unnecessary complexity to statistical inference, but it bears some similarity to the assignment of the burden of proof to the plaintiff, and more importantly, it reflects the genuine complexity of statistical reasoning. Starting with the null hypothesis of "no discrimination" corresponds to assuming the status quo to be no discrimination in the absence of proof to the contrary by the plaintiff. The statistical terminology of rejecting the null hypothesis corresponds to the legal terminology of the plaintiff meeting his burden of proof. Because of the many differences between statistical analysis and legal reasoning, this correspondence is by analogy only. Nevertheless, it explains the assumption, made in virtually all cases, that the null hypothesis is no discrimination. In *Hazelwood*, the Supreme Court made this tacit assumption in testing the statistical significance of the disparity between the representation of African-Americans in the labor market and in the defendant's work force. This disparity is deemed to be statistically significant only if the null hypothesis of "no difference" from the labor market is rejected.

The technical reason why some proposition must be designated as the null hypothesis has to do with the hypothetical nature of statistical reasoning. What tests for statistical significance offer is a prediction of what would happen on some assumed state of the world. The most common tests assume the null hypothesis to be true and ask what the chances are that the existing evidence would have been generated on that assumption. Thus, in *Hazelwood*, the test for statistical significance (described in footnotes 14 and 17) seeks to measure the likelihood that the disparity in representation of African-Americans would have arisen solely by chance in the absence of discrimination. The common sense inference to be drawn is that the smaller this likelihood, the stronger the reasons for concluding that the employer actually engaged in discrimination. In technical terms, the smaller the probability that the disparity resulted solely by chance, the stronger the reasons for rejecting the null hypothesis.

2. The Statistical Test. The basic approach of statistical inference can be illustrated by systematically working through the test that was the foundation of the Supreme Court's more casually described statistical analysis. We begin with the assumption that the benchmark proportion of black teachers in the relevant labor market was 5.7 percent (as opposed to the 15.4 percent figure that the federal government argued for). This benchmark is then to be compared to the observed 3.7 percent of black teachers hired over the relevant time period (15 black teachers among 405 total teachers hired). The Court sought to determine whether the observed proportion of black teachers (3.7 percent) was statistically significantly different from the benchmark proportion (5.7 percent). The implicit statistical model that the Court employed assumed that the selection of black teachers involved 405 independent decisions to select a teacher from a pool where the chance of selecting a black teacher on each occasion was exactly 5.7 percent. Thus, the null hypothesis of "no discrimination" is formalized by stating that, for each teacher hired, the probability that a black teacher would be chosen was 5.7 percent. Of course, just as a perfectly balanced coin with a 50 percent chance of coming up heads will not always register heads exactly half the time, this random selection process will not always yield a work force that is exactly 5.7 percent black. But if the null hypothesis is true, we can compute theoretically the likelihood of observing any particular deviation from the expected value of 5.7 percent.

The Court in *Hazelwood*, writing at a time when computational capabilities were more limited than they are today, did not attempt to calculate the exact probability of observing a 2 percentage-point disparity (or greater) from the 5.7 percent benchmark percentage. Instead, since a large number of teachers were employed, the Court followed a customary practice of relying on an approximation—technically, the normal approximation to the binomial distribution. (The normal distribution yields the familiar bell-shaped curve around an average value. It provides an approximation to the binomial distribution when the number of observations is large.) This approach provides a reasonable estimate because repeated random selection of a group of 405 teachers from a larger pool that was 5.7 percent black would lead to an array of percentages of the black teachers in each group distributed around an average of 5.7 percent in a normal distribution. The percentage of black teachers among all those hired in each group would seldom be exactly 5.7 percent, but it would cluster around 5.7 percent. This normal distribution is completely defined by two parameters: the expected percentage of black teachers hired—given by the benchmark labor market percentage—and the standard deviation around this expected percentage. With those numbers in hand, one can compute a Z-statistic and then consult a Z table indicating the probability that a disparity of the observed magnitude or greater would have occurred by chance if the null hypothesis were in fact true.

In this case, one computes the standard deviation of the proportions for a binomial process in which the number of hires n = 405 and P = .057. This standard deviation is given by the following formula (for sufficiently large n):

Standard Deviation = square root of [(.057)(1—.057)/405] = .0115

With this information we can compute the Z-statistic, which tells us how many standard deviations separate the observed (.037) and the expected (.057) proportions of blacks. In this case:

Z = (.037—.057)/.0115 = −1.74

In other words, the observed percentage of black hires is 1.74 standard deviations below the expected percentage. Looking at a table for the normal distribution (or using the NORMSDIST function in Excel), one sees that the probability of observing a disparity this far or farther from the expected value (in either direction) equals 8.2 percent. Ordinarily, social scientists would conclude that an observed disparity that could occur more than 5 percent of the time by chance is not "statistically significant." Since we just established that the likelihood of observing a disparity of the magnitude seen in *Hazelwood* was 8.2 percent (and thus greater than 5 percent), this disparity would not be deemed to be statistically significant.

Not surprisingly, the same exercise that we just went through would yield a different outcome if we had used the benchmark proportion advocated by the government in *Hazelwood* of 15.4 percent (instead of the 5.7 percent figure urged by the defendant school district). In this event, the standard deviation would equal

Standard Deviation = square root of [(.154)(1—.154)/405] = .0179,

and the Z-statistic would equal:

Z = (.037—.154)/.0179 = –6.54

With this higher benchmark proportion, the disparity between the observed and the expected proportions is greater, and the likelihood that we would observe a disparity of this magnitude by chance is exceedingly small. This disparity would be deemed statistically significant at not only the .05 level but also at the even more exacting .01 level of significance. This exercise reveals the importance of how the labor market is defined and how, more generally, the economic model is specified.

3. Statistical Significance. The concept of statistical significance exercises a perverse fascination over the analysis of statistical evidence, eclipsing other elements in the analysis that often are of equal, if not greater, importance. Technically, it is based on the probability (or "P-value") that an observed (or even greater) disparity would have occurred by chance if the null hypothesis were true. (Note the P-value in *Hazelwood* using the 5.7 percent labor market benchmark was 8.2 percent.) The influence of chance is assumed to be part of the relevant economic model so that, for instance, in *Hazelwood*, the school district was assumed to hire teachers randomly from among those in the labor market. This element of the statistical test embodies a stronger assumption than the simple null hypothesis of no discrimination which, by itself, does not identify any particular method of nondiscriminatory hiring. The assumption of random hiring equates the process of hiring teachers from the labor market to selecting a random sample of teachers from the entire population of those in the labor market.

Putting aside for the moment the plausibility of this assumption, we should note that the Supreme Court addressed the issue of statistical significance not in terms of probabilities or P-values, but in terms of standard deviations. From our calculation of the Z-statistic using a benchmark proportion of 5.7 percent, we in effect established that almost 92 percent of random samples of 405 selections of teachers would have racial compositions ranging from 3.7 percent to 7.7 percent. This follows from the calculation that somewhat over 8 percent of the time, random selection would generate a racial composition that was either less than 3.7 percent or more than 7.7 percent. (Note the probability that the sample proportion will fall inside or outside a specified range must sum to 100 percent.) Samples within a slightly larger band, from 3.45 percent to 7.95 percent, would fall within 1.96 standard deviations of 5.7 percent, and constitute 95 percent of the samples drawn.

Put another way, samples with a racial composition of blacks outside this band (either less than 3.45 percent or greater than 7.95 percent) would constitute only 5 percent of the samples drawn. This 5 percent figure is exactly equivalent to the probability of finding a sample with a racial composition more than 1.96 standard deviations from the racial composition of the labor market. Using our computed Z-statistics from above, we see that the 5.7 percent benchmark yields a Z-statistic of –1.74, which is smaller in absolute value than the 1.96 to achieve statistical significance at the customary .05 level used in the social sciences. But with the 15.4 percent benchmark that the plaintiff advocated in *Hazelwood*, the Z-statistic of –6.91 was substantially higher in absolute value than the 1.96 threshold for statistical significance at the .05 level. The rough rule of thumb that emerges from this exercise is that if the number of standard deviations separating the observed and the benchmark proportions exceeds 2 (that is, the Z-statistic exceeds 2), then the disparity is statistically significant at the conventional .05 level.

4. The Statistical and Public Policy Controversies. The central feature of any test for statistical significance is that one assumes that the null hypothesis is true and then rejects that null hypothesis if the probability that random selection would generate the observed disparity is sufficiently small. As noted, the convention that courts typically adopt is to reject the null hypothesis whenever the calculated probability of occurrence by chance is less than 5 percent. But it is one thing to conclude that the process that generated the observed percentage of black teachers in the Hazelwood School District is unlikely to have been the random binomial process set forth in our null hypothesis. It is another to claim that by establishing a statistically significant disparity, the government has proved that a discriminatory process was operating in the hiring of teachers in that school district. Statisticians are often uncomfortable with this inferential leap for a number of reasons. For a more sustained discussion of these issues, see Paul Meier, Jerome Sacks & Sandy L. Zabell, What Happened in *Hazelwood*: Statistics, Employment Discrimination and the 80% Rule, 1984 Am. B. Found. Res. J. 139.

To understand the gap between what the test establishes and what litigants and courts conclude from it requires a subtle understanding that the analysis offered in *Hazelwood* revealed only the probability of a false positive, or more precisely, a false rejection of the null hypothesis, which is referred to as a "Type I error." The classic illustration of a Type I error is convicting an innocent defendant in a criminal case, where the null hypothesis is one of innocence until proven guilty. Thus, if the null hypothesis of "no discrimination" is in fact true, then our Z-test has generated the probability that we will be making an error in finding the defendant liable. This follows because we used the test to derive the probability that one would observe a disparity of this magnitude or greater *if the null hypothesis were in fact true*. Four basic objections have been raised to the use of this statistical test in the employment discrimination context.

First, the statistical test has told us the probability of observing a disparity of a certain magnitude *if* the hiring process is truly random (call it, the Probability of A given B), but this turns out to be the incorrect conditional probability for purposes of employment discrimination litigation. What the court really wants to know is the reverse conditional probability—specifically, the probability that the process is truly random with respect to race given the evidence of the disparity and other evidence of discrimination (in other words, the Probability of B given A). To illustrate that these are not the same, consider the following conditional probabilities: first, the probability that an individual American gave birth to a child last year given that the individual is female; and second, the probability that an individual is female given that the person is an American who gave birth to a child. The first probability is rather small because there are more than 140 million American females and only about 4 million births last year. The second probability is exactly one since everyone who gave birth is female. This example reveals that one should not confuse the Probability of A given B with the Probability of B given A, and while the statistical test in *Hazelwood* gives us the former, we really want the latter.

Second, even if this test accurately measured Type I errors in favor of the plaintiff, it is still incomplete in that it does not measure the likelihood of "Type II errors," those in favor of the defendant. While the test described above only attempts to identify the likelihood of Type I errors, we are also concerned with Type II errors: erroneous failures to reject the null hypothesis of no discrimination or, in other words, erroneous decisions in favor of the defendant. The mathematics of Type II errors is even more complex than the mathematics of Type I errors, but the intuition can be easily conveyed. The more we insist on a low probability of Type I errors, the harder it will be to establish the existence of discrimination. Just as the high standard of "beyond a reasonable doubt" in the criminal cases reduces the chance of convicting the innocent (Type I errors), it also tends to increase the chance that guilty defendants go free (Type II errors). The same tradeoff applies in discrimination cases. The more we try to minimize the chance of Type I errors—by reducing the likelihood that the observed disparity could have been caused by chance—the more we increase the likelihood of Type II error—by concluding that discrimination is not present when in fact it is. For a more thorough discussion of the complexities in translating the concepts of Type I and Type II errors into the legal analysis of discrimination cases, see David H. Kaye, Apples and Oranges: Confidence Coefficients and the Burden of Persuasion, 73 Cornell L. Rev. 54, 71–73 (1987). Despite the relevance of Type II errors, most of the decided cases follow the lead of opinions like *Hazelwood* and evaluate the statistical evidence only in terms of Type I errors.

Third, it is not clear that the statistical model fits the employment process well enough for the resulting statistical test to be useful. Note that if there is variation in ability across the pool of potential applicants for positions in the Hazelwood School District, which is almost certainly the case, then the chance of selecting a black teacher would probably not be an identical, fixed number for each hiring decision, as the statistical model assumes. Even though all the teachers deemed to be in the labor market are supposed to be "qualified" to perform the central tasks of the job, there must be considerable variation in teacher quality among so large a labor pool. If the variation in teacher quality were uniform across races, then the statistical test would not be severely affected, but if average teacher quality were correlated with race, then the test might be seriously distorted. Specifically, if black teachers had higher average quality than white teachers, then the model would *overstate* the true probability of observing a black shortfall solely by chance, making it unduly difficult to reject the null hypothesis of no discrimination and find the defendant liable. Conversely, if average quality were higher for white teachers, then the statistical model used above might considerably *understate* the likelihood of observing any given disparity solely by making it too easy to reject the null hypothesis. In this scenario, the use of the crude statistical test would understate the likelihood of Type I errors and make it too easy to find the defendant liable.

The government's case against the Hazelwood School District challenged hiring practices in the early 1970s, at a time when a substantial proportion of black teachers in America had been educated in low-quality, segregated Southern schools. Therefore, we might suspect that the implicit assumption of uniform teacher quality aided the government in making its case. One possible consequence of using the approach in *Hazelwood*, then, might be to encourage greater hiring of black teachers to protect against the ability of plaintiffs to bring employment discrimination lawsuits buttressed by numerical evidence of statistically significant shortfalls in black hiring. In other words, reliance on the test in *Hazelwood* under the circumstances of lower average black teacher quality would serve as an implicit policy of affirmative action.

Promoting affirmative action while claiming only to fight employment discrimination has some benefits and some costs. Among the benefits is providing a remedy for the massive and sustained government discrimination in segregated schools that obviously contributed to any shortfall in black teacher quality. On this view, reliance on statistical tests that promote affirmative action might be a less contentious way to advance a necessary policy, because there is far greater political support for prohibitions against discrimination than for racial preferences. Moreover, since one of the costs frequently attributed to affirmative action is the cloud that it casts over minority employees by suggesting that they are less qualified than whites, the reliance on a seemingly objective test of statistical significance might further the goals of affirmative action while reducing any implied stigma from it. On the other hand, resorting to a disguised policy of affirmative action to avoid public opposition can be criticized as anti-democratic. Such an approach might also impose liability and financial loss on employers who have not themselves discriminated, resulting in unfairness toward them and creating the risk of a backlash against the entire structure of civil rights law.

Fourth, even if worker quality is equal across races, the test for statistical significance can be misapplied in another way that statisticians would find objectionable (but which again might to some extent promote affirmative action). The correct approach to using tests for statistical significance proceeds in the following way: after initial concerns over discrimination are raised on other grounds, the statistical test is used to determine if the overall numerical pattern of hiring buttresses the case for discrimination because the observed shortfall in hiring minority employees is unlikely to have been caused by chance. But once statistical tests are freely admitted as evidence of discrimination, there is an opportunity for zealous attorneys (buoyed by the prospect of awards of attorney's fees) to screen for potential defendants by searching for existing shortfalls. Such action undermines the validity of the statistical test, because it no longer tests a pre-existing claim of discrimination based on other evidence. Instead, it is used to select cases based solely on the existence of an ostensibly significant statistical disparity.

To see this point, recall that the statistical test yields the conclusion that if hiring is generated in the manner specified in the null hypothesis, then two propositions are true: first, that discrimination has *not* occurred; and second, that 5 percent of the time, a disparity of more than 1.96 standard deviations from the labor market benchmark would occur. In this event, the first proposition tells us that the plaintiff should not win an employment discrimination lawsuit, but the second proposition exposes thousands of employers to liability based on statistical evidence that shows the opposite of what, by hypothesis, we assume to be true. When the test is used correctly, the chance of falsely concluding that the employer has engaged in discrimination is no more than 5 percent. This represents a judgment that this 5 percent chance of an erroneous judgment against the employer is an acceptable risk, at least in civil litigation. But when the statistical approach is misused, the possibility of error might be substantially greater than 5 percent.

Again, assume the world where the above scenario obtains and both of the above propositions are true. An attorney who pores over numerical data on overall hiring patterns across, say, 1,000 nondiscriminating firms, would find 50 that have disparities that are statistically significant. But the tests we have spoken of are not designed to be run simply on the overall work force of a large company, like Microsoft or General Electric, but on a narrower breakdown of employees, such as sales personnel, or secretaries, or accountants. Again, given the above scenario, there is posited to be no discrimination, but instead of 50 of the firms being sued based on "statistically significant" shortfalls in hiring, the lawyer can multiply that number greatly by looking at a variety of different occupations. Now, instead of 50 nondiscriminating firms subject to claims of discrimination backed up by apparently compelling statistical evidence, there will be some multiple of this number based on the number of different occupations. Assume this caused the number to rise from 50 to 200. But even this occupational breakdown understates the ability of a "number-snooping" attorney to generate evidence of discrimination against posited nondiscriminators. Firms like Wal-Mart and Sears have hundreds or even thousands of stores. At least for those stores that have a work force large enough to generate "statistically significant" shortfalls, the ability to find more evidence of discrimination has been multiplied yet again. It follows that, if claims of discrimination can be asserted solely on the basis of numerical shortfalls, then even in a situation where 1,000 large firms were deemed not to be discriminators, it would be likely that most—perhaps all—of these 1,000 firms would have numerical shortfalls in at least one occupation in at least one of their plants or stores.

For essentially these reasons, at least one scholar has lamented that almost any large employer who has not engaged in discrimination may still be exposed to liability based on statistical evidence of discrimination in some occupational category or store. Kingsley R. Browne, Statistical Proof of Discrimination: Beyond "Damned Lies," 68 Wash. L. Rev. 477 (1993). Yet, if this critique were accurate, then disparities that *favor* women and minorities (which should constitute half the cases involving hiring processes with some random element) would be equally likely to generate litigation. White employees (or those from any disfavored group) would bring claims of reverse discrimination. Why haven't such lawsuits been filed? Is it because statistical evidence alone is not enough to establish liability? If so, how concerned should we be about "number-snooping" attorneys? For a contrary view that examines the headwinds faced by plaintiffs in discrimination cases, see Linda H. Krieger, Rachel K. Best & Lauren B. Edelman. When "Best practices" Win, Employees Lose: Symbolic Compliance and Judicial Inference in Federal Equal Employment Opportunity Cases, 40 Law & Soc. Inquiry 843 (2015).

5. **Practical Significance.** Having said this much about statistical significance, it remains important to keep it in perspective and, in particular, not to confuse it with practical significance. A simple variation on the facts of *Hazelwood* illustrates this point. Suppose that the school district was a much larger employer, so that over the relevant time period, it hired ten times as many teachers, 4,000 instead of 400. The computations for the standard deviation indicate that 95 percent of the samples (now of 4,000 teachers each) would have had a racial composition between 5.0 percent and 6.4 percent. It follows that a sample with a racial composition of 4.9 percent—less than 1 percent from the racial composition of the labor market of 5.7 percent—would have been statistically significant. Would this figure also have been practically significant?

An affirmative answer to this latter question requires further evidence that the school district would discriminate in this fine-grained fashion, hiring African-Americans at a rate somewhat below their representation in the labor market. Perhaps such evidence would be forthcoming, in the form of internal correspondence between school officials or damaging testimony about official hiring policies and quotas. But some such evidence is necessary, like the anecdotal evidence of individual instances of discrimination that "brought the cold numbers convincingly to life" in *Teamsters*. Tests for statistical significance do not, by themselves, answer the question whether the disparity in hiring minorities is large enough to support an inference of intentional discrimination.

This limitation of statistical evidence may assuage the concern that nondiscriminating firms would be too easily found liable for intentional class-wide discrimination only by virtue of statistical evidence. A statistically significant disparity in hiring minorities is necessary, but rarely sufficient, to support such a finding of intentional discrimination. Are defendants, as a practical matter, required to submit statistical evidence of their own? Both Justice Brennan and Justice Stevens pointed out the weakness of the school district's position after it had failed to submit its own evidence for a finding of no discrimination. Does this failure allow the court to give the benefit of the doubt to the plaintiff's evidence, despite its defects?

6. **Misspecified Models.** One such defect in *Hazelwood* was the assumption, underlying the plaintiff's model of the school district's hiring process, that it consisted solely of a random selection of teachers from those available in the labor market. Few, if any, employers hire entirely randomly, even from among all otherwise qualified employees. First, only a few of these employees come to the attention of an employer through inquiries and applications. Second, even among those who do, the employer has every reason to hire those who best fit its own needs. The process of hiring for most employers is random in only a far more limited sense. A variety of factors, other than those explicitly taken into account by the employer or identified explicitly in an economic model, determines who actually is hired.

The existence of such unspecified factors need not be a fatal defect. No models in the social sciences are completely deterministic. The problem lies in the assumption that these unspecified factors operate randomly: that they do not, either separately or together, systematically affect the observed rate of hiring minorities. This is no more than an assumption, and it can be disproved on the facts of any particular case. Some unaccounted factor hidden in the assumed randomness of the hiring process might systematically affect the hiring of minorities. *Hazelwood* only presents the most extreme version of this problem because the role of randomness was assumed to constitute the entire hiring process itself, not to be a residual feature of the process after these factors were taken into account, as it would be in most economic models. The model of hiring in *Hazelwood*, as economists would say, was "misspecified." It should have taken into account other variables that determined who was hired, such as experience, educational achievement, or recommendations. Whether any of these factors were actually considered in the hiring process, either explicitly or implicitly, should have been the subject of further investigation. But the presence of some such factors is a far more plausible assumption than the absence of all of them. One statistical technique for quantifying the effect of such factors is regression analysis, the subject of the case discussed in the following note.

7. ***Bazemore v. Friday.*** In Bazemore v. Friday, 478 U.S. 385 (1986), the Supreme Court considered a claim of discrimination in pay, asserted by a group of black employees who alleged that their pay was set lower than that

of similarly situated white employees. They used a statistical technique, regression analysis, to ascertain the effect of race on pay. A regression analysis determines the effect of various factors—the "independent" or "explanatory" variables in the regression equation—on a particular outcome or result, which is termed the "dependent variable." As this terminology indicates, the regression equation expresses the dependent variable as a function of the independent or explanatory variables. In employment discrimination cases, the dependent variable is a term or condition of employment, like pay, or a decision related to employment, like hiring, firing, or promotion. The independent variables include factors, such as education and experience, that can legitimately affect the dependent variable and a discriminatory factor, such as race, that cannot. If the race variable turned out to be statistically and practically significant, it would support an inference of intentional discrimination. Alternatively, instead of using race as an independent variable, the regression analysis could result in two equations, one for whites and one for blacks, and then allow the inference of discrimination to be drawn from the differences between the equations. Whichever approach is used, the role of the independent variables representing legitimate factors remains the same. They provide a statistical means of comparing the pay of similarly situated employees. In technical terms, these variables allowed a measurement of the correlation between the factors that can legitimately affect pay and actual pay itself. If the regression equation revealed that black employees received less pay than similarly situated white employees, then an inference of discrimination could be drawn against the employer.

The advantage of the more complicated model in *Bazemore* over the simpler model in *Hazelwood* is that it more closely resembles the actual decisionmaking process of the employer. It does not presume that pay is set randomly among otherwise qualified employees. Nevertheless, a more complicated model might be subject to more complicated objections. Because of inevitable limitations in the available evidence and because of theoretical disputes over what factors legitimately affect compensation, a regression analysis cannot feasibly take into account all of the factors that might conceivably affect compensation. In *Bazemore*, the Court recognized that a regression analysis may omit some measurable variables so long as the record as a whole supports an inference of discrimination. The plaintiffs in that case had investigated other economic models and found that one factor omitted from their model, the county where employees worked, did not substantially reduce the difference in pay between black and white employees.

Bazemore does not stand for the proposition that regression analysis is inevitably an appropriate method for analyzing statistical evidence. Whether it is or not depends upon the economic model that provides the context and structure for purely mathematical methods of statistical analysis. In any hard-fought case, the parties will argue over what the appropriately specified economic model is and they will invariably find defects in the model advanced by the opposing side. For this reason, statistical evidence will seldom present an airtight case for either side, regardless of the degree of statistical significance that can be found in it. To quote another saying of statisticians, "the evidence can always be tortured until it confesses." The legal judgment is not whether the plaintiff has presented a perfect case but whether he has presented enough evidence to justify a finding of intentional discrimination. For an alternative to standard regression analysis, see D. James Greiner, Causal Inference in Civil Rights Litigation, 122 Harv. L. Rev. 533 (2008). Greiner argues for a "potential outcome paradigm" that more closely follows the concept of "but for" causation in law and that also is less subject to manipulation than standard regression analysis.

Should the plaintiff's statistical evidence in *Hazelwood* have been given the same benefit of the doubt as the plaintiff's evidence in *Bazemore*? Should a more realistic model of the hiring process have been required of the plaintiff in *Hazelwood*? Does your answer depend upon how much evidence the defendant submitted in rebuttal? The Supreme Court decided in *Hazelwood* that the defendant should be given a second chance to present evidence on remand, an unusual conclusion probably resulting from the district court's general confusion over how to analyze statistical evidence. How should the defendant have taken advantage of this opportunity?

8. Is Statistical Evidence Promoting Better Litigation Outcomes? In thinking about the use of statistical evidence, it is necessary to consider whether this often highly technical evidence is an aid to judges and jurors that promotes accurate litigation outcomes or more often a factor that confuses or misleads the trier of fact. The experience in medical malpractice litigation may offer some insights on this question, not because statistical evidence is particularly important in malpractice cases, but because they are in some respects similar to private class actions under Title VII. Both types of cases are initiated by victims of alleged wrongdoing and are heavily dependent on expert testimony. Extensive research concerning malpractice disputes raises serious concerns about the ability of such litigation to identify and compensate those (and only those) who have been injured through the unlawful conduct of others. Perhaps the most important study of victim-initiated litigation ever undertaken is the Harvard Medical Practice Study, which closely examined 30,121 randomly selected records from hospitals in New York State in 1984, and identified cases in which the patient suffered an adverse effect. They found 1,133 such cases and, based on reviews by a group of physicians, judged that in 280 of them—meaning almost 1 percent of all hospital discharges—the adverse effect was "more probably than not" caused by a doctor's negligence. The study also looked at the number of discharges that resulted in malpractice claims. There were 47 malpractice claims in all, but importantly, only 8 of 280 patients who suffered negligence filed a claim. Only a very small fraction of the patients who suffered negligence filed a claim, while most of the claims (39 of 47) came from the 99 percent of patients who were found *not* to have suffered negligence. A. Russell Localio, et al. Relation Between Malpractice Claims and Adverse Effects due to Negligence, 325 New Eng. J. Med. 245 (1991).

The study also found that there was little relationship between having a meritorious malpractice claim and the probability of success at trial—which may explain why those who actually suffered malpractice sued at such a low rate. The authors closely examined the results of 51 malpractice cases—the 47 identified in the first study and four found in a follow-up study—of which 46 had been closed by the time they wrote up their conclusions. The plaintiffs won 10 of 24 cases that involved no adverse effects, 6 of 13 cases with adverse effects but no negligence, and 5 of 9 cases involving adverse effects due to negligence. These (admittedly small) numbers reveal no significant relationship between the outcome of the case and the occurrence of an adverse effect due to negligence or, for that matter, any adverse effect at all. Factors that did better predicting a plaintiff victory were the presence of a disability and high income on the plaintiff's part, although that was not significant at the 5 percent level. Troyen A. Brennan et al., Relation Between Negligent Adverse Events and the Outcomes of Medical-Malpractice Litigation, 335 New Eng. J. Med. 1963 (1996). Based on this study, the malpractice system does a poor job of making those guilty of negligence pay for their misconduct, and it fails to shield doctors who are not negligent from having to pay damages for meritless claims.

No comparable study has been done on employment discrimination litigation, but it is subject to factors similar to those leading to the high rates of both Type I and Type II errors in malpractice cases: the difficulty victims have in even knowing that they have been injured by the unlawful acts of others, and the biases of a trier of fact who may feel sympathy for a person in difficult straits (even if not because of the defendant's misconduct) or who may share some of the conscious or unconscious biases of the alleged wrongdoers. The evidence that malpractice litigation may be a poor way to compensate victims and improve the quality of health care invites the question whether the rates of Type I and Type II errors are similarly high in employment discrimination cases. If so, this constitutes a major failing of the current system of enforcing antidiscrimination law, which depends almost entirely on privately initiated litigation. On the other hand, if one believes that the system's apparent errors are promoting other desirable social goals, such as affirmative action, then the failure to compensate most victims of discrimination may be acceptable. In the end, our judgment about statistical evidence in employment discrimination cases depends on how its use tips the balance between Type I and Type II errors in light of the societal assessment of the costs of each type of error.

9. **Bibliography.** Several books have addressed the intricacies of statistical inference in litigation. David C. Baldus & James W. Cole, Statistical Proof of Discrimination (1980); David W. Barnes, Statistics as Proof: Fundamentals of Quantitative Evidence (1983); David Barnes & John Conley, Statistical Evidence in Litigation (1986); Statistical Methods in Discrimination Litigation (D. Kaye & M. Aickin eds., 1986). A useful brief summary of the problems posed by statistical evidence is Stephen E. Fienberg et al., Understanding and Evaluating Statistical Evidence in Litigation, 36 Jurimetrics J. 1 (1995), and a more general survey of these problems can be found in Symposium, Statistical Inference in Litigation, 46 Law & Contemp. Probs. 4 (1983).

For treatment of more specific issues, see Amanda Agan & Sonja Starr, Ban the Box, Criminal Records, and Statistical Discrimination: A Field

Experiment, 133. Q. J. Econ. 191 (2018); Ian Ayres, Pervasive Prejudice? Unconventional Evidence of Race and Gender Discrimination (2001); William T. Bielby & Pamela Coukos, "Statistical Dueling" with Unconventional Weapons: What Courts Should Know About Experts in Employment Discrimination Class Actions, 56 Emory L.J. 1563 (2007); Michael O. Finkelstein, The Judicial Reception of Multiple Regression Studies in Race and Sex Discrimination Cases, 80 Colum. L. Rev. 737 (1980); Franklin M. Fisher, Multiple Regression in Legal Proceedings, 80 Colum. L. Rev. 702 (1980); Joseph L. Gastwirth, Statistical Issues Arising in Equal Employment Litigation, 36 Jurimetrics J. 353 (1996); Richard Goldstein, The Comparison of Models in Discrimination Cases, 34 Jurimetrics J. 215 (1994); Joni Hersch & V. Blair Druhan, The Use and Misuse of Econometric Evidence in Employment Discrimination Cases, 71 Wash. & Lee L. Rev. 2365 (2014); David H. Kaye, Improving Legal Statistics, 24 L. & Soc'y Rev. 1255 (1990); David H. Kaye, Statistics for Lawyers and Law for Statistics, 89 Mich. L. Rev. 1520 (1991); Elaine Shoben, Differential Pass-Fail Rates in Employment Testing: Statistical Proof Under Title VII, 91 Harv. L. Rev. 793 (1978); Thomas J. Sugrue & William B. Fairley, A Case of Unexamined Assumptions: The Use and Misuse of the Statistical Analysis of *Castenada/Hazelwood* in Discrimination Litigation, 24 B.C. L. Rev. 925 (1983).

C. CLASS CLAIMS OF DISPARATE IMPACT

Griggs v. Duke Power Co.

401 U.S. 424 (1971).

■ CHIEF JUSTICE BURGER delivered the opinion of the Court.

We granted the writ in this case to resolve the question whether an employer is prohibited by the Civil Rights Act of 1964, Title VII, from requiring a high school education or passing of a standardized general intelligence test as a condition of employment in or transfer to jobs when (a) neither standard is shown to be significantly related to successful job performance, (b) both requirements operate to disqualify Negroes at a substantially higher rate than white applicants, and (c) the jobs in question formerly had been filled only by white employees as part of a longstanding practice of giving preference to whites.

Congress provided, in Title VII of the Civil Rights Act of 1964, for class actions for enforcement of provisions of the Act and this proceeding was brought by a group of incumbent Negro employees against Duke Power Company. All the petitioners are employed at the Company's Dan River Steam Station, a power generating facility located at Draper, North Carolina. At the time this action was instituted, the Company had 95 employees at the Dan River Station, 14 of whom were Negroes; 13 of these are petitioners here.

The District Court found that prior to July 2, 1965, the effective date of the Civil Rights Act of 1964, the Company openly discriminated on the basis of race in the hiring and assigning of employees at its Dan River plant. The plant was organized into five operating departments: (1) Labor, (2) Coal Handling, (3) Operations, (4) Maintenance, and (5) Laboratory and Test. Negroes were employed only in the Labor Department where the highest paying jobs paid less than the lowest paying jobs in the other four "operating" departments in which only whites were employed.[2] Promotions were normally made within each department on the basis of job seniority. Transferees into a department usually began in the lowest position.

In 1955 the Company instituted a policy of requiring a high school education for initial assignment to any department except Labor, and for transfer from the Coal Handling to any "inside" department (Operations, Maintenance, or Laboratory). When the Company abandoned its policy of restricting Negroes to the Labor Department in 1965, completion of high school also was made a prerequisite to transfer from Labor to any other department. From the time the high school requirement was instituted to the time of trial, however, white employees hired before the time of the high school education requirement continued to perform satisfactorily and achieve promotions in the "operating" departments. Findings on this score are not challenged.

The Company added a further requirement for new employees on July 2, 1965, the date on which Title VII became effective. To qualify for placement in any but the Labor Department it became necessary to register satisfactory scores on two professionally prepared aptitude tests, as well as to have a high school education. Completion of high school alone continued to render employees eligible for transfer to the four desirable departments from which Negroes had been excluded if the incumbent had been employed prior to the time of the new requirement. In September 1965, the Company began to permit incumbent employees who lacked a high school education to qualify for transfer from Labor or Coal Handling to an "inside" job by passing two tests—the Wonderlic Personnel Test, which purports to measure general intelligence, and the Bennett Mechanical Comprehension Test. Neither was directed or intended to measure the ability to learn to perform a particular job or category of jobs. The requisite scores used for both initial hiring and transfer approximated the national median for high school graduates.

The District Court had found that while the Company previously followed a policy of overt racial discrimination in a period prior to the Act, such conduct had ceased. The District Court also concluded that Title VII was intended to be prospective only and, consequently, the impact of prior inequities was beyond the reach of corrective action authorized by the Act.

---

[2] A Negro was first assigned to a job in an operating department in August 1966, five months after charges had been filed with the Equal Employment Opportunity Commission. The employee, a high school graduate who had begun in the Labor Department in 1953, was promoted to a job in the Coal Handling Department.

The Court of Appeals was confronted with a question of first impression, as are we, concerning the meaning of Title VII. After careful analysis a majority of that court concluded that a subjective test of the employer's intent should govern, particularly in a close case, and that in this case there was no showing of a discriminatory purpose in the adoption of the diploma and test requirements. On this basis, the Court of Appeals concluded there was no violation of the Act.

The Court of Appeals reversed the District Court in part, rejecting the holding that residual discrimination arising from prior employment practices was insulated from remedial action. The Court of Appeals noted, however, that the District Court was correct in its conclusion that there was no showing of a racial purpose or invidious intent in the adoption of the high school diploma requirement or general intelligence test and that these standards had been applied fairly to whites and Negroes alike. It held that, in the absence of a discriminatory purpose, use of such requirements was permitted by the Act. In so doing, the Court of Appeals rejected the claim that because these two requirements operated to render ineligible a markedly disproportionate number of Negroes, they were unlawful under Title VII unless shown to be job related. We granted the writ on these claims.

The objective of Congress in the enactment of Title VII is plain from the language of the statute. It was to achieve equality of employment opportunities and remove barriers that have operated in the past to favor an identifiable group of white employees over other employees. Under the Act, practices, procedures, or tests neutral on their face, and even neutral in terms of intent, cannot be maintained if they operate to "freeze" the status quo of prior discriminatory employment practices.

The Court of Appeals' opinion, and the partial dissent, agreed that, on the record in the present case, "whites register far better on the Company's alternative requirements" than Negroes.[6] This consequence would appear to be directly traceable to race. Basic intelligence must have the means of articulation to manifest itself fairly in a testing process. Because they are Negroes, petitioners have long received inferior education in segregated schools and this Court expressly recognized these differences in Gaston County v. United States, 395 U.S. 285 (1969). There, because of the inferior education received by Negroes in North Carolina, this Court barred the institution of a literacy test for voter registration on the ground that the test would abridge the right to vote indirectly on account of race. Congress did not intend by Title VII,

---

[6] In North Carolina, 1960 census statistics show that, while 34% of white males had completed high school, only 12% of Negro males had done so. U.S. Bureau of the Census, U.S. Census of Population: 1960, Vol. 1, Characteristics of the Population, pt. 35, Table 47.

Similarly, with respect to standardized tests, the EEOC in one case found that use of a battery of tests, including the Wonderlic and Bennett tests used by the Company in the instant case, resulted in 58% of whites passing the tests, as compared with only 6% of the blacks. Decision of EEOC, CCH Empl. Prac. Guide, para. 17,304.53 (Dec. 2, 1966). See also Decision of EEOC 70–552, CCH Empl. Prac. Guide, para. 6139 (Feb. 19, 1970).

however, to guarantee a job to every person regardless of qualifications. In short, the Act does not command that any person be hired simply because he was formerly the subject of discrimination, or because he is a member of a minority group. Discriminatory preference for any group, minority or majority, is precisely and only what Congress has proscribed. What is required by Congress is the removal of artificial, arbitrary, and unnecessary barriers to employment when the barriers operate invidiously to discriminate on the basis of racial or other impermissible classification.

Congress has now provided that tests or criteria for employment or promotion may not provide equality of opportunity merely in the sense of the fabled offer of milk to the stork and the fox. On the contrary, Congress has now required that the posture and condition of the job-seeker be taken into account. It has—to resort again to the fable—provided that the vessel in which the milk is proffered be one all seekers can use. The Act proscribes not only overt discrimination but also practices that are fair in form, but discriminatory in operation. The touchstone is business necessity. If an employment practice which operates to exclude Negroes cannot be shown to be related to job performance, the practice is prohibited.

On the record before us, neither the high school completion requirement nor the general intelligence test is shown to bear a demonstrable relationship to successful performance of the jobs for which it was used. Both were adopted, as the Court of Appeals noted, without meaningful study of their relationship to job-performance ability. Rather, a vice president of the Company testified, the requirements were instituted on the Company's judgment that they generally would improve the overall quality of the work force.

The evidence, however, shows that employees who have not completed high school or taken the tests have continued to perform satisfactorily and make progress in departments for which the high school and test criteria are now used.[7] The promotion record of present employees who would not be able to meet the new criteria thus suggests the possibility that the requirements may not be needed even for the limited purpose of preserving the avowed policy of advancement within the Company. In the context of this case, it is unnecessary to reach the question whether testing requirements that take into account capability for the next succeeding position or related future promotion might be utilized upon a showing that such long-range requirements fulfill a genuine business need. In the present case the Company has made no such showing.

The Court of Appeals held that the Company had adopted the diploma and test requirements without any "intention to discriminate

[7] For example, between July 2, 1965, and November 14, 1966, the percentage of white employees who were promoted but who were not high school graduates was nearly identical to the percentage of nongraduates in the entire white work force.

against Negro employees." We do not suggest that either the District Court or the Court of Appeals erred in examining the employer's intent; but good intent or absence of discriminatory intent does not redeem employment procedures or testing mechanisms that operate as "built-in headwinds" for minority groups and are unrelated to measuring job capability.

The Company's lack of discriminatory intent is suggested by special efforts to help the undereducated employees through Company financing of two-thirds the cost of tuition for high school training. But Congress directed the thrust of the Act to the *consequences* of employment practices, not simply the motivation. More than that, Congress has placed on the employer the burden of showing that any given requirement must have a manifest relationship to the employment in question.

The facts of this case demonstrate the inadequacy of broad and general testing devices as well as the infirmity of using diplomas or degrees as fixed measures of capability. History is filled with examples of men and women who rendered highly effective performance without the conventional badges of accomplishment in terms of certificates, diplomas, or degrees. Diplomas and tests are useful servants, but Congress has mandated the commonsense proposition that they are not to become masters of reality.

The Company contends that its general intelligence tests are specifically permitted by § 703(h) of the Act. That section authorizes the use of "any professionally developed ability test" that is not "designed, intended *or used* to discriminate because of race. . . ." (Emphasis added.)

The Equal Employment Opportunity Commission, having enforcement responsibility, has issued guidelines interpreting § 703(h) to permit only the use of job-related tests.[9] The administrative interpretation of the Act by the enforcing agency is entitled to great deference. . . . Since the Act and its legislative history support the Commission's construction, this affords good reason to treat the guidelines as expressing the will of Congress.

Section 703(h) was not contained in the House version of the Civil Rights Act but was added in the Senate during extended debate. For a

---

9 EEOC Guidelines on Employment Testing Procedures, issued August 24, 1966, provide:

> "The Commission accordingly interprets 'professionally developed ability test' to mean a test which fairly measures the knowledge or skills required by the particular job or class of jobs which the applicant seeks, or which fairly affords the employer a chance to measure the applicant's ability to perform a particular job or class of jobs. The fact that a test was prepared by an individual or organization claiming expertise in test preparation does not, without more, justify its use within the meaning of Title VII."

The EEOC position has been elaborated in the new Guidelines on Employee Selection Procedures, 29 CFR § 1607 (Aug. 1, 1970). These guidelines demand that employers using tests have available "data demonstrating that the test is predictive of or significantly correlated with important elements of work behavior which comprise or are relevant to the job or jobs for which candidates are being evaluated." Id. at § 1607.4(c).

period, debate revolved around claims that the bill as proposed would prohibit all testing and force employers to hire unqualified persons simply because they were part of a group formerly subject to job discrimination.[10] Proponents of Title VII sought throughout the debate to assure the critics that the Act would have no effect on job-related tests. Senators Case of New Jersey and Clark of Pennsylvania, comanagers of the bill on the Senate floor, issued a memorandum explaining that the proposed Title VII "expressly protects the employer's right to insist that any prospective applicant, Negro or white, *must meet the applicable job qualifications*. Indeed, the very purpose of Title VII is to promote hiring on the basis of job qualifications, rather than on the basis of race or color." 110 Cong. Rec. 7247.[11] (Emphasis added.) Despite these assurances, Senator Tower of Texas introduced an amendment authorizing "professionally developed ability tests." Proponents of Title VII opposed the amendment because, as written, it would permit an employer to give any test, "whether it was a good test or not, so long as it was professionally designed. Discrimination could actually exist under the guise of compliance with the statute." 110 Cong. Rec. 13504 (remarks of Sen. Case).

The amendment was defeated and two days later Senator Tower offered a substitute amendment which was adopted verbatim and is now the testing provision of § 703(h). Speaking for the supporters of Title VII, Senator Humphrey, who had vigorously opposed the first amendment, endorsed the substitute amendment, stating: "Senators on both sides of the aisle who were deeply interested in title VII have examined the text of this amendment and have found it to be in accord with the intent and purpose of that title." The amendment was then adopted.[12] From the sum

---

[10] The congressional discussion was prompted by the decision of a hearing examiner for the Illinois Fair Employment Commission in Myart v. Motorola Co. (The decision is reprinted at 110 Cong. Rec. 5662.) That case suggested that standardized tests on which whites performed better than Negroes could never be used. The decision was taken to mean that such tests could never be justified even if the needs of the business required them. A number of Senators feared that Title VII might produce a similar result. . . .

[11] The Court of Appeals majority, in finding no requirement in Title VII that employment tests be job related, relied in part on a quotation from an earlier Clark-Case interpretative memorandum addressed to the question of the constitutionality of Title VII. The Senators said in that memorandum:

> "There is no requirement in Title VII that employers abandon bona fide qualification tests where, because of differences in background and education, members of some groups are able to perform better on these tests than members of other groups. An employer may set his qualifications as high as he likes, he may test to determine which applicants have these qualifications, and he may hire, assign, and promote on the basis of test performance." 110 Cong. Rec. 7213.

However, nothing there stated conflicts with the later memorandum dealing specifically with the debate over employer testing, 110 Cong. Rec. 7247 (quoted from in the text above), in which Senators Clark and Case explained that tests which measure "applicable job *qualifications*" are permissible under Title VII. In the earlier memorandum Clark and Case assured the Senate that employers were not to be prohibited from using tests that determine qualifications. Certainly a reasonable interpretation of what the Senators meant, in light of the subsequent memorandum directed specifically at employer testing, was that nothing in the Act prevents employers from requiring that applicants be fit for the job.

[12] Senator Tower's original amendment provided in part that a test would be permissible "if . . . in the case of any individual who is seeking employment with such employer, such test is

of the legislative history relevant in this case, the conclusion is inescapable that the EEOC's construction of § 703(h) to require that employment tests be job related comports with congressional intent.

Nothing in the Act precludes the use of testing or measuring procedures; obviously they are useful. What Congress has forbidden is giving these devices and mechanisms controlling force unless they are demonstrably a reasonable measure of job performance. Congress has not commanded that the less qualified be preferred over the better qualified simply because of minority origins. Far from disparaging job qualifications as such, Congress has made such qualifications the controlling factor, so that race, religion, nationality, and sex become irrelevant. What Congress has commanded is that any tests used must measure the person for the job and not the person in the abstract.

The judgment of the Court of Appeals is, as to that portion of the judgment appealed from, reversed.

■ JUSTICE BRENNAN took no part in the consideration or decision of this case.

NOTES ON *GRIGGS V. DUKE POWER CO.*

1. Comparison with Class Claims of Disparate Treatment. In many respects, the evidence of discrimination in *Griggs* was as compelling as the evidence in *Teamsters* and *Hazelwood*. All of the black employees were segregated in the lowest department and all but one remained there, even after explicit segregation ceased. Moreover, as soon as the color bar came down, the testing and education requirements went up, seemingly continuing discrimination by other, less explicit, means. On the evidence available in the case, even without sophisticated statistical analysis, an inference of intentional discrimination could easily have been drawn. Yet it was not, at least by the lower courts, which both found no intentional discrimination.

This conclusion left the Supreme Court with a stark choice: either allow the pattern of continuing exclusion of blacks from all higher-paying jobs or create a new theory of liability that would support the plaintiff's claim of discrimination. The Court took the latter course, in effect relieving the plaintiff of the need to carry the entire burden of proving a violation of Title VII and putting some of the burden on the defendant to justify the practices in dispute. This reallocation of the burden of proof goes to the heart of the theory of disparate impact. Recall that both *Teamsters* and *Hazelwood* spoke of a "prima facie" case that had to be proved by the plaintiff, but that neither case identified precisely what that burden was, apart from the ordinary burden on a plaintiff in civil litigation. Both decisions also spoke of the

designed to determine or predict whether such individual is suitable or trainable with respect to his employment in the particular business or enterprise involved. . . ." This language indicates that Senator Tower's aim was simply to make certain that job-related tests would be permitted. The opposition to the amendment was based on its loose wording which the proponents of Title VII feared would be susceptible of misinterpretation. The final amendment, which was acceptable to all sides, could hardly have required less of a job relation than the first.

defendant's burden of rebuttal, but again, did not identify what that burden was.

Griggs is very different. It makes clear that the plaintiff's burden is not to prove intentional discrimination, but only disparate impact: in the terms used in the opinion, that the test and high school diploma requirements "operate to 'freeze' the status quo of prior discriminatory practices." If the plaintiff carries this burden, then the defendant has the burden of justifying the disputed practices. As one important passage in the opinion put it: "The touchstone is business necessity. If an employment practice which operates to exclude Negroes cannot be shown to be related to job performance, the practice is prohibited." Exactly what these formulations of the burden of proof mean, particularly the defendant's burden of proving business necessity and job relationship, has been the subject of continuing dispute. *Griggs*, however, leaves no doubt that these burdens are not the same as in class claims of disparate treatment.

2. Statutory Basis for the Theory of Disparate Impact. *Griggs* was decided under the original version of Title VII, which contained no provisions specifically addressed to the theory of disparate impact. At most, isolated clauses in the main prohibitions and defenses in the statute obliquely address the issues related to the theory, such as testing. The provisions that now codify the theory of disparate impact were added to the statute only much later, in the Civil Rights Act of 1991, and as we shall see, these provisions perpetuate much of the ambiguity found in the decisions that originally recognized this basis for liability.

In *Griggs* itself, the only statutory provision quoted, or even cited, was the testing clause in section 703(h) (also known as the Tower Amendment by reference to its author, Senator Tower). This clause creates an exception to the main prohibitions in Title VII, allowing the use of "any professionally developed ability test provided that such test, its administration or action upon the results is not designed, intended, or used to discriminate." Is it plausible to base a theory of liability on a provision such as this, which creates an exception to the statute's prohibitions? If the Supreme Court was trying to derive a prohibition against practices with discriminatory effects from a statute addressed mainly to practices with discriminatory intent, why would it rely mainly on a provision limiting liability?

Conceivably, the testing clause was designed simply to clarify the main prohibitions in Title VII, but if so, what do you make of the proviso to the clause? The proviso reasserts liability only for tests "designed, intended, or used to discriminate." The first two of these terms refer explicitly to intentional discrimination and the third, "used to," although emphasized by the Supreme Court, also refers implicitly to intent. A test can be "used to" discriminate only if its use has discrimination as one of its goals. Isn't that the same as intentional discrimination? Is there any other sense of "used to" that could require only proof of discriminatory effects? Even if there is, does it displace the main sense of the term as referring implicitly to intentional discrimination?

Questions such as these apparently led the Supreme Court in later cases to rely on the main prohibitions of Title VII as the statutory basis for the theory of disparate impact. The provision of particular interest was section 703(a)(2), which can be broken down into three parts. This subsection makes it illegal for an employer

> [1] to limit, segregate, or classify his employees or applicants for employment [2] in any way which would deprive or tend to deprive any individual of employment opportunities or otherwise adversely affect his status as an employee, [3] because of such individual's race, color, religion, sex, or national origin.

Decisions such as Connecticut v. Teal, 457 U.S. 440 (1982), have emphasized clause [2], with its use of terms such as "tend to deprive," "employment opportunities," and "otherwise adversely affect his status as an employee." These terms could be interpreted to require only proof of adverse effects rather than discriminatory intent. But is this true only if clause [2] is considered in isolation? Clauses [1] and [3] both appear to import a requirement of intent, clause [1] through the terms "limit, segregate, or classify" and clause [3] through the phrase "because of." Isn't section 703(a)(2) at least ambiguous as between an interpretation requiring proof of discriminatory intent and one requiring only proof of discriminatory effects?

If Congress sought to prohibit neutral practices with discriminatory effects, would it have done so in such ambiguous terms? The codification of the theory of disparate impact in the current version of the statute, in section 703(k), does not leave the issue in doubt. It explicitly refers to an "unlawful employment practice based on disparate impact" and then defines the plaintiff's burden of proving that the defendant uses "a particular employment practice that causes a disparate impact" and the defendant's burden of proving that any such practice "is job related for the position in question and consistent with business necessity." Why wasn't Congress as explicit when Title VII was originally enacted? Was it because the prevalent forms of discrimination at the time were overt and explicit, like the segregation previously practiced by the employer in *Griggs*? Or was it because litigation had not yet focused attention on the need for a theory of liability addressed to neutral practices with adverse effects?

3. **Ambiguity in the Theory of Disparate Impact.** Perhaps because of its uncertain foundations in Title VII as originally enacted, the theory of disparate impact has always suffered from ambiguity. Divergent interpretations of the theory can be traced all the way back to *Griggs*. These concern both the aims and content of the theory, but they all return to a single, central question: Just how different is the theory of disparate impact from liability for intentional discrimination?

The divergent aims of the theory can all be found in the Supreme Court's description of what Title VII prohibits:

> [T]he Act does not command that any person be hired simply because he was formerly the subject of discrimination, or because he is a member of a minority group. Discriminatory preference for any group, minority or majority, is precisely and only what

> Congress has proscribed. What is required by Congress is the removal of artificial, arbitrary, and unnecessary barriers to employment when the barriers operate invidiously to discriminate on the basis of racial or other impermissible classification.

If Congress prohibited only "discriminatory preference," as the Court says, isn't that just another way of saying that it prohibited only intentional discrimination? Or is the Court making the point that the statute's goal was to eliminate all forms of discriminatory preference and that the theory of disparate impact was one means of achieving that goal? If so, why would the theory of disparate impact be necessary as a basis for liability in addition to liability for intentional discrimination? Or does the Court's reference to "the removal of artificial, arbitrary, and unnecessary barriers to employment" invoke a different goal, not just of eliminating intentional discrimination, but of eliminating practices with disparate impact as an end in itself? If this is the ultimate goal of Title VII, however, how can it be reconciled with the Court's position that the statute does not require affirmative action?

Griggs is equally ambiguous on what the plaintiff must do to prove disparate impact and what the defendant must do in rebuttal. On the first issue, the Court does not say much, except to emphasize that the plaintiff need not prove intentional discrimination. Otherwise, the plaintiff's evidence that the defendant acted "to 'freeze' the status quo of prior discriminatory practices" was confined almost entirely to the defendant's own history of prior segregation. Blacks were historically relegated to the lowest department at the power plant and the test and high school diploma requirements kept them there. The only statistics mentioned in the opinion are found in footnote 6 and are limited to general census figures, high school graduation rates in North Carolina, and figures for differential pass rates on the tests in dispute, taken from an unrelated EEOC proceeding. Do these figures provide adequate information about the labor market for higher level jobs at the Duke Power Co.? Was a detailed analysis of the labor market necessary in this case or was it a case, like *Teamsters*, in which the "inexorable zero" spoke for itself?

Griggs goes into greater detail about the defendant's burden of justifying a practice found to have disparate impact, but the details themselves are not quite consistent. The defendant's burden is described in various terms, but the two most significant, "business necessity" and "related to job performance" have already been quoted (in note 1 above). Indeed, these terms have been so widely used that they now appear in the codified version of the theory of disparate impact, in section 703(k). Yet they, too, point in opposite directions, just like other terms used in the opinion. "Business necessity" appears to place a heavy burden upon the defendant, to show that the disputed employment practice is essential to the operation of his business: that he could not do business without it. "Related to job performance" suggests a lighter burden, depending upon the degree of relationship that must be shown. The defendant only needs to show that the disputed practice is related to the job for which it is used to screen applicants.

Look again at the passage from the opinion in which these terms are used. The Supreme Court apparently treats them as if they were synonymous. But are they? Could the Court be using these contrasting terms to identify some intermediate requirement? In the next paragraph in the opinion, the Court refers to "a demonstrable relationship to successful performance of the jobs" for which the selection devices are used and then to "meaningful study of their relationship to job-performance ability." Still later, the Court frames the requirement as proof of "a manifest relationship to the employment in question." None of these standards was met by the Duke Power Co., which submitted only conclusory testimony of a vice president about the company's desire to improve the quality of its work force. Given such weak evidence, did the Court have to formulate precise standards for what the defendant must prove? If not, what weight should be given to the various formulations of the defendant's burden of proof in *Griggs*?

4. ***Albemarle Paper Co. v. Moody.*** In subsequent decisions, the Supreme Court tried to answer these questions and to dispel some of the ambiguity surrounding the theory of disparate impact. This process began in Albemarle Paper Co. v. Moody, 422 U.S. 405 (1975). The record in this case, very much like that in *Griggs*, contained strong evidence of intentional discrimination. The defendant had previously segregated its employees explicitly by race, placing black employees only in low-level jobs. Even after this policy was abandoned when Title VII took effect, almost no black employees progressed to higher-level jobs. Tests and a high school diploma, just as in *Griggs*, were used to limit access to these jobs, and very few black employees could meet these requirements. *Albemarle Paper* differs from *Griggs* mainly in two respects, the first involving a formal matter of how the theory of disparate impact is framed, and the second involving a matter of substance about how it is implemented.

The formal difference concerns the explicit articulation of the parties' burdens of proof. In a brief introductory paragraph, the Court summarized the parties' burdens of proof, seemingly as formulated in *Griggs*, but actually in terms that were both different and more explicit than those used in that case. First, the plaintiff must show "that the tests in question select applicants for hire or promotion in a racial pattern significantly different from that of the pool of applicants." This requirement was implied by, but never explicitly stated in, *Griggs*. If the plaintiff meets that burden, then the defendant must prove "a manifest relationship to the employment in question." This statement selects among one of the several passages in *Griggs* articulating what the defendant must prove. As the following note reveals, *Albemarle Paper* goes into great detail about what this standard means in practice. The opinion then adds a third step to claims of disparate impact in which, if the defendant meets its burden of proof, the plaintiff can prove pretext, defined as a showing "that other tests or selection devices, without a similarly undesirable racial effect, would also serve the employer's legitimate interest in 'efficient and trustworthy workmanship.'" This third step is analogous to the third step in individual claims of intentional discrimination under *McDonnell Douglas*.

The substantive difference of implementation concerned the means by which the defendant met its burden of proof. Unlike *Griggs*, in which the defendant submitted almost no evidence at all to justify the tests and high school diploma requirements in that case, the defendant in *Albemarle Paper* submitted a validation study to justify the tests that it had used. A validation study examines the relationship between good performance on the test and good performance on the job. Validation, insofar as it is required by the theory of disparate impact, imposes the same standards of empirical verification on the defendant as the use of statistical evidence under *Hazelwood* imposes on the plaintiff. The defendant must submit evidence, almost always from an expert in testing or in personnel management, that establishes a connection between the disputed test and the job for which it is used. Right at the outset, the expertise required for validation created problems for the Albemarle Paper Co. It retained an expert who only spent half a day at the plant analyzing the jobs for which the tests were used and setting up the validation procedure. Several specific defects in the validation followed immediately from this lack of professional attention: the jobs for which the tests were used were grouped according to the traditional lines of progression at the plant, rather than similarity of skills; the standards for good performance on the job were simply supervisors' rankings of employees' performance, which were based entirely on subjective evaluations without the benefit of any further standards; and the validation study was performed on employees who currently held the higher-level jobs, who might have improved their performance by learning on the job rather than by having the skills measured by the tests. Wholly apart from these problems of method, the most obvious problem with the validation study concerned its results, which revealed no systematic correlation between good performance on the tests and good performance on the job. In the Court's words, the validation study produced only an "odd patchwork of results."

The defects in this validation study are clear enough, and some of them, such as the lack of professional evaluation of the jobs under consideration and of the standards of good performance, could have been overcome in a more thorough study. What is not so clear is whether the added expenditure entailed in making a more rigorous study would have made any difference in the results obtained or in the ultimate outcome. As with proof of intentional discrimination through statistical evidence, establishing validation through statistical studies invites criticism at many different levels, from the design of the study, to the measures of job performance, to the significance of the reported correlations. It is, for instance, easy enough to criticize the use of supervisors' rankings as a criterion of good performance on the job. It is difficult, however, to imagine a substitute that does not rely at some point on supervisors' rankings to evaluate the performance of jobs that are not utterly routine.

5. **Bibliography.** For articles on the basic justification and derivation of the theory of disparate impact, see Foundations of Indirect Discrimination Law, (Deborah Hellman ed. 2018); Richard H. Fallon Jr., To Each According to His Ability, From None According to His Race: The Concept of Merit in the Law of Antidiscrimination, 60 B.U. L. Rev. 815 (1980); George Rutherglen, Disparate Impact Under Title VII: An Objective Theory of Discrimination, 73 Va. L. Rev. 1297 (1987).

For debate over the origins of the theory of disparate impact and its significance, see Robert Belton, The Crusade for Equality in the Workplace: The *Griggs v. Duke Power* Story (Stephen L. Wasby, ed. 2014); Elizabeth Bartholet, Application of Title VII to Jobs in High Places, 95 Harv. L. Rev. 947 (1982); Earl M. Maltz, Title VII and Upper Level Employment—A Response to Professor Bartholet, 77 Nw. U. L. Rev. 776 (1983); Olatunde C. A. Johnson, The Agency Roots of Disparate Impact, 49 Harv. C.R.-C.L. L. Rev. 125 (2014); Rosemary C. Hunter & Elaine W. Shoben, Disparate Impact Discrimination: American Oddity or Internationally Accepted Concept?, 19 Berkeley J. Emp. & Lab. L. 108 (1998); Noah D. Zatz, Disparate Impact and the Unity of Equality Law, 97 B.U. L. Rev. 1357 (2017). For adaptation of the theory of disparate impact to address discrimination in the digital age, see Pauline T. Kim, Data Driven Discrimination at Work, 58 Wm. & Mary L. Rev. 857 (2017).

Uniform Guidelines on Employee Selection Procedures

INTRODUCTORY NOTE ON THE UNIFORM GUIDELINES

Both *Griggs* and *Albemarle Paper* relied upon versions of the EEOC guidelines on employment tests and both found those guidelines to be "entitled to great deference." The particular defects of the validation study in *Albemarle Paper* reflected a general failure to comply with the detailed guidelines in effect at the time of the decision, but those guidelines generated doubts among employers about whether they could ever succeed in validating a test. Such doubts eventually led to the promulgation of the Uniform Guidelines on Employee Selection Procedures. Another reason was that the earlier guidelines had been promulgated without prior opportunity for public comment. A still further reason was that other federal agencies with jurisdiction over employment practices, such as the Department of Justice and the Department of Labor, had adopted regulations at variance with the EEOC's. Thus the Uniform Guidelines represented an attempt to reform, consolidate, and harmonize federal regulation of employment practices.

For its part, the EEOC undertook this initiative under its power, in common with other federal agencies, to offer its own interpretation of the statutes it was charged with enforcing. The EEOC's authority to promulgate regulations with the force of law is limited by Title VII, in section 713(a), to procedural regulations. Substantive regulations, like the Uniform Guidelines, have only the force that courts are willing to give them as a matter of agency expertise. Despite the "great deference" given the guidelines in *Griggs* and *Albemarle Paper*, other decisions of the Supreme Court have departed from other regulations of the EEOC. General Electric Co., City of v. Gilbert, 429 U.S. 125, 140–45 (1976); City of Los Angeles, Dep't of Water & Power v. Manhart, 435 U.S. 702, 719 n.36 (1978). This variable approach suggests that the degree of deference accorded to the EEOC depends on the regulation at issue. In the notes that follow, try to ascertain which provisions in the Uniform Guidelines concern technical issues uniquely within the competence of the EEOC and which concern questions of statutory interpretation on which the courts usually have the last word.

The fundamental question of statutory interpretation raised by the Uniform Guidelines involves the consequences of imposing a heavy burden of validation upon employers. When faced with the prospect of a costly validation, which might fail as it did in *Albemarle Paper*, employers might adopt two other strategies: first, to abandon tests and similar selection devices that invite claims of disparate impact; or second, to eliminate the disparate impact of such devices through affirmative action. The first strategy would incline employers toward discretionary methods of hiring and promotion, relying entirely on subjective standards of evaluation. Such standards, however, might do more to hide implicit forms of discrimination than bring it out into the open. The second strategy would encourage employers to engage in affirmative action. Yet § 703(j) of Title VII specifically disclaims any interpretation of the statute that would "require" affirmative action. Is there a difference between encouraging employers to engage in affirmative action—by giving employers a means of avoiding liability under the theory of disparate impact—and requiring them to engage in affirmative action—by imposing liability upon them under the same theory if they do not meet their burden of validation? Such questions have preoccupied the Supreme Court throughout its subsequent decisions on the theory of disparate impact. They also influence the weight that is given to the Uniform Guidelines, whose two central provisions appear below:

29 C.F.R. § 1607.4. Information on impact.

A. Records concerning impact. Each user should maintain and have available for inspection records or other information which will disclose the impact which its tests and other selection procedures have upon employment opportunities of persons by identifiable race, sex, or ethnic group as set forth in subparagraph B below in order to determine compliance with these guidelines. Where there are large numbers of applicants and procedures are administered frequently, such information may be retained on a sample basis, provided that the sample is appropriate in terms of the applicant population and adequate in size.

B. Applicable race, sex, and ethnic groups for recordkeeping. The records called for by this section are to be maintained by sex, and the following races and ethnic groups: Blacks (Negroes), American Indians (including Alaskan Natives), Asians (including Pacific Islanders), Hispanic (including persons of Mexican, Puerto Rican, Cuban, Central or South American, or other Spanish origin or culture regardless of race), whites (Caucasians) other than Hispanic, and totals. The race, sex, and ethnic classifications called for by this section are consistent with the Equal Employment Opportunity Standard Form 100, Employer Information Report EEO-1 series of reports. The user should adopt safeguards to insure that the records required by this paragraph are used for appropriate purposes such as determining adverse impact, or (where required) for developing and monitoring affirmative action programs, and that such records are not used improperly. See sections 4E and 17(4), below.

C. Evaluation of selection rates. The "bottom line." If the information called for by sections 4A and B above shows that the total selection process for a job has an adverse impact, the individual components of the selection process should be evaluated for adverse impact. If this information shows that the total selection process does not have an adverse impact, the Federal enforcement agencies, in the exercise of their administrative and prosecutorial discretion, in usual circumstances, will not expect a user to evaluate the individual components for adverse impact, or to validate such individual components, and will not take enforcement action based upon adverse impact, of any component of that process, including the separate parts of a multipart selection procedure or any separate procedure that is used as an alternative method of selection. However, in the following circumstances the Federal enforcement agencies will expect a user to evaluate the individual components for adverse impact and may, where appropriate, take enforcement action with respect to the individual components: (1) where the selection procedure is a significant factor in the continuation of patterns of assignments of incumbent employees caused by prior discriminatory employment practices, (2) where the weight of court decisions or administrative interpretations hold that a specific procedure (such as height or weight requirements or no-arrest records) is not job related in the same or similar circumstances. In unusual circumstances, other than those listed in (1) and (2) above, the Federal enforcement agencies may request a user to evaluate the individual components for adverse impact and may, where appropriate, take enforcement action with respect to the individual component.

D. Adverse impact and the "four-fifths rule." A selection rate for any race, sex, or ethnic group which is less than four-fifths (4/5) (or eighty percent) of the rate for the group with the highest rate will generally be regarded by the Federal enforcement agencies as evidence of adverse impact, while a greater than four-fifths rate will generally not be regarded by Federal enforcement agencies as evidence of adverse impact. Smaller differences in selection rate may nevertheless constitute adverse impact, where they are significant in both statistical and practical terms or where a user's actions have discouraged applicants disproportionately on grounds of race, sex, or ethnic group. Greater differences in selection rate may not constitute adverse impact where the differences are based on small numbers and are not statistically significant, or where special recruiting or other programs cause the pool of minority or female candidates to be atypical of the normal pool of applicants from that group. Where the user's evidence concerning the impact of a selection procedure indicates adverse impact but is based upon numbers which are too small to be reliable, evidence concerning the impact of the procedure over a longer period of time and/or evidence concerning the impact which the selection procedure had when used in the same manner in similar circumstances elsewhere may be considered in determining adverse impact. Where the user has not maintained data on adverse impact as required by the documentation section of applicable guidelines, the Federal enforcement agencies may draw an inference of adverse impact of the selection process from the failure of the user to maintain such data, if the user has an underutilization of a group in the job category, as compared to the group's representation in the relevant labor market or, in the case of jobs filled from within, the applicable work force.

E. Consideration of user's equal employment opportunity posture. In carrying out their obligations, the Federal enforcement agencies will consider the general posture of the user with respect to equal employment opportunity for the job or group of jobs in question. Where a user has adopted an affirmative action program, the Federal enforcement agencies will consider the provisions of that program, including the goals and timetables which the user has adopted and the progress which the user has made in carrying out that program and in meeting the goals and timetables. While such affirmative action programs may in design and execution be race, color, sex, or ethnic conscious, selection procedures under such programs should be based upon the ability or relative ability to do the work.

29 C.F.R. § 1607.5. General standards for validity studies.

A. Acceptable types of validity studies. For the purposes of satisfying these guidelines, users may rely upon criterion-related validity studies, content validity studies or construct validity studies, in accordance with the standards set forth in the technical standards of these guidelines, section 14 below. New strategies for showing the validity of selection procedures will be evaluated as they become accepted by the psychological profession.

B. Criterion-related, content, and construct validity. Evidence of the validity of a test or other selection procedure by a criterion-related validity study should consist of empirical data demonstrating that the selection procedure is predictive of or significantly correlated with important elements of job performance. See section 14B below. Evidence of the validity of a test or other selection procedure by a content validity study should consist of data showing that the content of the selection procedure is representative of important aspects of performance on the job for which the candidates are to be evaluated. See 14C below. Evidence of the validity of a test or other selection procedure through a construct validity study should consist of data showing that the procedure measures the degree to which candidates have identifiable characteristics which have been determined to be important in successful performance in the job for which the candidates are to be evaluated. See section 14D below.

C. Guidelines are consistent with professional standards. The provisions of these guidelines relating to validation of selection procedures are intended to be consistent with generally accepted professional standards for evaluating standardized tests and other selection procedures, such as those described in the Standards for Educational and Psychological Tests prepared by a joint committee of the American Psychological Association, the American Educational Research Association, and the National Council on Measurement in Education (American Psychological Association, Washington, D.C., 1974) (hereinafter "A.P.A. Standards") and standard textbooks and journals in the field of personnel selection.

D. Need for documentation of validity. For any selection procedure which is part of a selection process which has an adverse impact and which selection procedure has an adverse impact, each user should maintain and have available such documentation as is described in section 15 below.

E. Accuracy and standardization. Validity studies should be carried out under conditions which assure insofar as possible the adequacy and accuracy of the research and the report. Selection procedures should be administered and scored under standardized conditions.

F. Caution against selection on basis of knowledge, skills, or ability learned in brief orientation period. In general, users should avoid making employment decisions on the basis of measures of knowledge, skills, or abilities which are normally learned in a brief orientation period, and which have an adverse impact.

G. Method of use of selection procedures. The evidence of both the validity and utility of a selection procedure should support the method the user chooses for operational use of the procedure, if that method of use has a greater adverse impact than another method of use. Evidence which may be sufficient to support the use of a selection procedure on a pass/fail (screening) basis may be insufficient to support the use of the same procedure on a ranking basis under these guidelines. Thus, if a user decides to use a selection procedure on a ranking basis, and that method of use has a greater adverse impact than use on an appropriate pass/fail basis (see section 5H below), the user should have sufficient evidence of validity and utility to support the use on a ranking basis. See sections 3B, 14B(5) and (6), and 14C(8) and (9).

H. Cutoff scores. Where cutoff scores are used, they should normally be set so as to be reasonable and consistent with normal expectations of acceptable proficiency within the work force. Where applicants are ranked on the basis of properly validated selection procedures and those applicants scoring below a higher cutoff score than appropriate in light of such expectations have little or no chance of being selected for employment, the higher cutoff score may be appropriate, but the degree of adverse impact should be considered.

I. Use of selection procedures for higher level jobs. If job progression structures are so established that employees will probably, within a reasonable period of time and in a majority of cases, progress to a higher level, it may be considered that the applicants are being evaluated for a job or jobs at the higher level. However, where job progression is not so nearly automatic, or the time span is such that higher level jobs or employees' potential may be expected to change in significant ways, it should be considered that applicants are being evaluated for a job at or near the entry level. A "reasonable period of time" will vary for different jobs and employment situations but will seldom be more than 5 years. Use of selection procedures to evaluate applicants for a higher level job would not be appropriate:

If the majority of those remaining employed do not progress to the higher level job;

If there is a reason to doubt that the higher level job will continue to require essentially similar skills during the progression period; or

If the selection procedures measure knowledge, skills, or abilities required for advancement which would be expected to develop principally from the training or experience on the job.

J. Interim use of selection procedures. Users may continue the use of a selection procedure which is not at the moment fully supported by the required evidence of validity, provided: (1) The user has available substantial evidence of validity, and (2) the user has in progress, when technically feasible, a study which is designed to produce the additional evidence required by these guidelines within a reasonable time. If such a study is not technically feasible, see section 6B. If the study does not demonstrate validity, this provision of these guidelines for interim use shall not constitute a defense in any action, nor shall it relieve the user of any obligations arising under Federal law.

K. Review of validity studies for currency. Whenever validity has been shown in accord with these guidelines for the use of a particular selection procedure for a job or group of jobs, additional studies need not be performed until such time as the validity study is subject to review as provided in section 3B above. There are no absolutes in the area of determining the currency of a validity study. All circumstances concerning the study, including the validation strategy used, and changes in the relevant labor market and the job should be considered in the determination of when a validity study is outdated.

NOTES ON THE UNIFORM GUIDELINES ON EMPLOYEE SELECTION PROCEDURES

1. **General Principles and Technical Standards.** Of the 18 regulations that comprise the Uniform Guidelines, only two have been excerpted in these materials. They are taken from the largest group of regulations, entitled "General Principles." Two additional regulations, concerning "Technical standards for validity studies," 29 C.F.R. § 1607.14, and "Documentation of Impact and Validity," 29 C.F.R. § 1607.15, are nearly as long as all the other regulations combined. The guidelines also include a "Policy statement on affirmative action," in § 1607.17, and a comprehensive list of defined terms, in § 1607.18.

The General Principles address a variety of different issues, from the scope of the guidelines to cooperative validation studies. On the issue of scope, § 1607.2 makes clear that the guidelines cover all selection procedures, whether tests, educational and experience requirements, or entirely subjective hiring and promotion procedures. This view of the scope of the theory of disparate impact was eventually adopted by the Supreme Court in Watson v. Fort Worth Bank & Trust, 487 U.S. 977, 989–91 (1988).

Sections 1607.4 and 1607.5, excerpted above, contain the most important of the general principles, concerned, respectively, with the two main stages of a disparate impact case: the plaintiff's burden of proving disparate impact and the defendant's burden of proving business necessity and job relationship. Section 1607.4, although it is concerned with an issue on which the plaintiff has the burden of proof, is framed in terms of information on disparate impact that the defendant must maintain. This follows from the fact that the guidelines are addressed to employers and used by the EEOC in the exercise of its enforcement powers under Title VII. The EEOC cannot determine whether to sue an employer or whether to find good cause that the statute has been violated in the absence of information on disparate impact. The detailed provisions of this regulation are postponed to the discussion of proof of disparate impact later in this chapter. Notice, however, that this regulation refers, in § 1607.4E, to the employer's "equal opportunity posture" and, in particular, to "programs of affirmative action." This reference is amplified in other provisions of the Uniform Guidelines, most explicitly in § 1607.6, on circumstances in which validation is not required, and in § 1607.17, on affirmative action. Neither of these provisions clearly endorses affirmative action as a remedy for practices with disparate impact, but they strongly suggest that employers should consider it as an option. Is this lack of clarity justified? Should the regulations have confronted the issue of affirmative action directly? Bear in mind that the EEOC has also promulgated regulations specifically addressing affirmative action, in 29 C.F.R. pt. 1608. How should employers react to the tacit recognition in the Uniform Guidelines that they can avoid liability under the theory of disparate impact by engaging in affirmative action? What risks do they run in creating programs of affirmative action for this reason? In failing to do so?

Section 1607.5 directly concerns the defendant's burden of proof, under the title of "General standards for validity." Together with the elaborate provisions on technical standards and documentation, in § 1607.14 and § 1607.15, this section imposes rigorous requirements for validity studies, covering all of the issues raised by the attempted validation in *Albemarle Paper* and several others in addition. The most general requirement is for professional standards in devising, executing, and documenting validation studies, set forth in § 1607.5C, D, and E. The limited participation of the expert in *Albemarle Paper* and the reliance upon discretionary supervisors' evaluations both violated this general requirement. A necessary preliminary for any such study is an analysis of the jobs for which the test or other selection device is used. This requirement is not spelled out in so many words in § 1607.5, but it is prominently emphasized in the technical standards in § 1607.14A. It is also implicit in the cautions, found in § 1607.5H and I, that cut-off scores and testing for skills in higher-level jobs, other than the one for which the selection device is used, must be specifically addressed in a validation study. Both of these warnings presuppose that an analysis of the job for which a selection device is used reveals minimum levels of performance and the likelihood of progression to higher-level jobs. Again, in *Albemarle Paper*, the grouping of higher-level and lower-level jobs, and the complete absence of any job analysis, violated these requirements. A selection device must also be validated as used, under § 1607.5G, with precautions against measuring skills learned through on-the-job training, under § 1607.5F. Both of these requirements were violated in *Albemarle Paper* by validating the test on incumbent employees, instead of applicants.

In some respects, the Uniform Guidelines relaxed the requirements of validation, by allowing interim use of selection devices, until a validation study could be performed, in § 1607.5J, and by allowing cooperative validation studies, in § 1607.7. The provisions on differential validation, for each different ethnic group, were significantly weakened and reformulated under the heading of "test fairness" in the technical standards in section 1607.14B(8). Despite these changes, are the Uniform Guidelines on the whole favorable to employers? Do they preserve the requirement of rigorous empirical proof established by the earlier guidelines and endorsed in *Albemarle Paper*? Is this interpretation of the requirement of business necessity and job relationship, first formulated by the Supreme Court in *Griggs*, within the special expertise of the EEOC?

2. **Types of Validation.** The complexity of the Uniform Guidelines becomes most apparent in the provisions on different kinds of validation studies: content, criterion, and construct validation. Each of these is recognized as an accepted form of validation in the General Principles, in § 1607.5B, and in the Technical Standards, in § 1607.14B, C, and D. Each of them also must meet the general standards for validity studies. They differ only in the ways that they seek to establish a connection between good performance on a test or other selection device and good performance on the job.

Content validation is the simplest and most intuitively plausible form of validation, but also the most limited in its application. A test is content valid if it is "representative of important aspects of performance on the job for which the candidates are to be evaluated." § 1607.5B. Performing the job itself, in effect, becomes the test for the job. This validation strategy works, however, only if the test contains the most important aspects of the job and those aspects of the job are readily observable. This latter requirement distinguishes content validation from construct validation, which focuses on abilities (or "constructs" in the jargon of psychology) used in performing a job. Content validity focuses only on the observable aspects of a single job. Construct validity looks to abilities that are more generally useful in a variety of jobs.

The limitations of content validity are apparent even in the standard example of a typing test, content valid for the position of typist, but not for any secretarial position involving more complicated duties, such as taking dictation or making appointments. A typing test reveals the limitations of content validity in another way as well. A typing test is easy to administer and results in no mistakes that are costly for the employer. Tests that reproduce more complicated jobs would require more complicated behavior of the applicant, often involving specialized equipment that would be costly to use and risk mistakes that would cause injury or damage. A content valid test for a complicated job amounts to virtually the same thing as a probationary period of employment. Yet few jobs are suitable for employment of applicants routinely on such terms. A probationary police officer, employed without any training, could cause great harm, and not just to effective law enforcement. For this reason, the opportunity to use content validation, although attractive, is necessarily limited.

Criterion validation is the form of validation viewed most sympathetically by the Uniform Guidelines. It is so named because it selects some criterion of performance on the job and then seeks to correlate good performance according to that criterion with good performance on the test or other selection device. It was the form of validation attempted in *Albemarle Paper*, in which a correlation was sought between test scores and supervisors' evaluations. Unlike content validation, the components of the test need not be part of the job itself, and unlike construct validation, the test need not measure abstract abilities used on the job. All that criterion validation seeks is a correlation between performance on the job according to the chosen criterion and performance on the test.

Other criteria of job performance are error rate, output, or customer satisfaction. This last criterion reveals, in common with supervisors' evaluations, that most of the realistic criteria of good performance, especially for complicated jobs, involve an element of subjective judgment. This element of subjectivity leads to questions about uniformity and reliability of evaluations, like those raised in *Albemarle Paper*. These concerns are also raised by the Uniform Guidelines. § 1607.14B(5). Another obstacle that criterion validation must overcome is validating the selection device on the right group of employees, neither incumbents who have learned skills on the job, again as in *Albemarle Paper*, nor unscreened applicants whose mistakes on the job might prove to be too costly, as with content validation. A final hurdle, also well illustrated by *Albemarle Paper*, is finding a correlation that is both practically and statistically significant, as required by § 1607.14B(8). Note that the process of validating this test, like the process of validating the typing test discussed earlier, does not make any appeal to the abstract ability or construct of manual dexterity. Even a test that purported to measure some other construct, for instance, intelligence, would be criterion valid if it was shown to have a statistically significant correlation with good performance on the job according to the specified criteria. This form of validation, even though favored by the Uniform Guidelines, can still prove to be costly and risky for an employer, according to one estimate running into the hundreds of thousands of dollars. Barbara Lindemann Schlei & Paul Grossman, Employment Discrimination Law 113 n.106 (2d ed. 1983).

Employers therefore would like to validate tests for a wide variety of different jobs. Construct validation, by relying upon abstract abilities used in many different jobs, seeks to meet this need. It is, however, the least favored form of validation under the Uniform Guidelines. Construct validation requires a showing that a selection procedure actually measures an abstract ability or construct, such as intelligence or manual dexterity, and that this ability is correlated with good performance on the job. The notorious problems with intelligence tests illustrate the problems posed by construct validation. Any construct like intelligence is difficult to define, precisely because it is so abstract. Intelligence in writing, speaking, or conversation might have no relationship to intelligence in mathematics or computer science and intelligence in any of these fields might have nothing to do with intelligence in management, finance, or customer relations. Moreover, constructs that are difficult to define are also difficult to measure, leading to charges that constructs such as intelligence are measured by tests that purport to find only what the test designers themselves value. To avoid such problems, the Uniform Guidelines impose exacting standards for construct validation, among them, a preliminary requirement that the construct itself have been related to good performance on the job by criterion validation. § 1607.15D(7). This requirement leaves employers better off if they rely directly on criterion validation and eliminate the intermediate step of relying upon a suspect construct. Thus, in *Albemarle Paper*, even though the attempted validation failed, the employer did not appeal to the tests in question as measures of intelligence which was itself correlated with good performance on the job. Only the correlation between performance on the test and on the job was at issue.

None of these forms of validation reduce the burden on the employer, except forms of content validation applicable to the simplest tests for the simplest jobs. These are not, however, the jobs to which most plaintiffs seek access through litigation. If a court determines that a particular job is so complicated that validation under the Uniform Guidelines is not feasible—and most skilled and well-paid jobs fit this description—what is the court likely to do? It cannot insist that the employer abandon all selection procedures. Would it require the employer to abandon all selection procedures with disparate impact? If so, would that be consistent with the statements by supporters of Title VII, quoted in *Griggs*, that "[a]n employer may set his qualifications as high as he likes, he may test to determine which applicants have these qualifications, and he may hire, assign, and promote on the basis of test performance"? Would a court require an employer to keep the disputed test or selection device and engage in affirmative action? If so, would that be consistent with the disclaimer in section 703(j) that Title VII does not require affirmative action?

3. **Pre-employment Testing.** Prof. Mark Kelman argues that the use of general ability job tests may be illegitimate not only because they fail to predict applicants' performance on jobs as currently structured, but also because they violate other norms of nondiscrimination. Mark Kelman, Concepts of Discrimination in "General Ability" Job Testing, 104 Harv. L. Rev. 1158 (1991). According to Kelman, pre-employment tests may suffer from "static," "dynamic," "distributive," or "individual-output-centered" discrimination. Static discrimination involves the type of discrimination most often recognized by courts: a pre-employment test that does not predict how well applicants will perform on the job is illegitimate because it rejects workers who may be just as productive as workers whom the test accepts. Concern over this type of discrimination is what motivates validation studies. Dynamic discrimination, on the other hand, refers to situations in which there is a reasonable correlation between test performance and job performance, but the marginal productivity difference between workers is solely a function of organizational practices that employers can (and in some instances, are legally obligated to) change. For example, women might have a lower test performance and be victims of sexual harassment at work that diminishes their productivity. The test then might appear to predict work

performance reasonably well, but it would not be accurately measuring the traits needed to perform the job in the absence of sexual harassment.

In distributive discrimination, a test may be discriminatory insofar as employers' productivity judgments tend to devalue traits that protected groups possess. For example, a psychological test battery measuring aggression may be statistically valid in the sense that those with higher aggression scores perform better as litigators. The test, however, may still be discriminatory if productivity evaluation is largely a function of employers' illegitimate emphasis on or irrational overvaluation of skills that men typically possess. Finally, individual-output-centered discrimination refers to a situation in which an applicant may perform just as well as any other worker on the job, so long as the employer makes certain accommodations. That is, this conception of discrimination demands that employers ignore input differentials and treat applicants equally if their capacity to produce output is the same.

Except for static discrimination, are the other conceptions of discrimination too radical or too broad to be of use to courts concerned with practical enforceability of legal rules? For example, under the individual-output-centered notion of discrimination, how would an employer facing hundreds of applicants be able to discern what each applicant's full "potential" for output would be without actually hiring her and providing appropriate accommodations? One suggestion that Kelman makes is that we should abandon ex ante testing in favor of ex post screening systems that are based on evaluations of on-the-job performance. What are the problems inherent in demanding that employers rely only on ex-post screening systems? As you read the excerpt later in this chapter from Washington v. Davis, 426 U.S. 229 (1976), consider the legal and policy ramifications of applying some of these conceptions of discrimination to that case and what its outcome might have been if the court had adopted dynamic, distributive, or individual-output-centered conceptions of discrimination.

Kelman also argues that even if we were to reject these broader conceptions of discrimination and adopt only the static discrimination approach, pre-employment testing would still fail to comport with individualistic notions of meritocracy demanded by conservatives who support this form of testing. Kelman submits that even if we were to assume that general ability tests do modestly predict productivity and are not racially biased (because they do not systematically underpredict the performance of a minority group), the use of such tests is still discriminatory because it does not lead to hiring that is strictly based on "merit" (defined as "capacity to do work as well as another"). Kelman argues that when the minority group is a socially identifiable group with a long history of subjugation, such as African-Americans, the social cost of wrongful rejection based on an employment test is much greater because these results strengthen and justify existing notions of exclusion and inferiority. In effect, Kelman takes the individual meritocratic principle on its own terms and tries to show that even a validated test will fail to meet the demands of that principle. Would you have found his arguments more persuasive if he had argued instead that individualistic notions of meritocracy that underlie these tests are themselves fundamentally flawed? Does the preoccupation of the courts and the EEOC (as highlighted below in the excerpt from the Uniform Guidelines on Employee Selection Procedures) with the mechanics of validation studies seem misguided and short-sighted given the deeper flaws with the use of such tests posited by Kelman? For further discussion of pre-employment testing, see John Donohue, Foundations of Employment Discrimination 103–25 (2003).

4. **Bibliography.** Fairness in Employment Testing: Validity Generalizations, Minority Issues, and the General Aptitude Test Battery (J. Hartigan & A. Wigdor eds., 1989); The Black-White Test Score Gap (Christopher Jencks & Meredith Phillips eds., 1998); Alfred W. Blumrosen, The Bottom Line in Equal Employment Guidelines: Administering a Polycentric Problem, 33 Admin. L. Rev. 323 (1981).

Washington v. Davis

426 U.S. 229 (1976).

■ JUSTICE WHITE delivered the opinion of the Court.

This case involves the validity of a qualifying test administered to applicants for positions as police officers in the District of Columbia Metropolitan Police Department. The test was sustained by the District Court but invalidated by the Court of Appeals. We are in agreement with the District Court and hence reverse the judgment of the Court of Appeals.

I

This action began on April 10, 1970, when two Negro police officers filed suit against the then Commissioner of the District of Columbia, the Chief of the District's Metropolitan Police Department, and the Commissioners of the United States Civil Service Commission. An amended complaint, filed December 10, alleged that the promotion policies of the Department were racially discriminatory and sought a declaratory judgment and an injunction. The respondents Harley and Sellers were permitted to intervene, their amended complaint asserting that their applications to become officers in the Department had been rejected, and that the Department's recruiting procedures discriminated on the basis of race against black applicants by a series of practices including, but not limited to, a written personnel test which excluded a disproportionately high number of Negro applicants. These practices were asserted to violate respondents' rights "under the due process clause of the Fifth Amendment to the United States Constitution, under 42 U.S.C. § 1981 and under D.C. Code § 1–320." Defendants answered, and discovery and various other proceedings followed. Respondents then filed a motion for partial summary judgment with respect to the recruiting phase of the case, seeking a declaration that the test administered to those applying to become police officers is "unlawfully discriminatory and thereby in violation of the due process clause of the Fifth

Amendment. . . ." No issue under any statute or regulation was raised by the motion. The District of Columbia defendants, petitioners here, and the federal parties also filed motions for summary judgment with respect to the recruiting aspects of the case, asserting that respondents were entitled to relief on neither constitutional nor statutory grounds. The District Court granted petitioners' and denied respondents' motions.

According to the findings and conclusions of the District Court, to be accepted by the Department and to enter an intensive 17-week training program, the police recruit was required to satisfy certain physical and character standards, to be a high school graduate or its equivalent, and to receive a grade of at least 40 out of 80 on "Test 21," which is "an examination that is used generally throughout the federal service," which "was developed by the Civil Service Commission, not the Police Department," and which was "designed to test verbal ability, vocabulary, reading and comprehension."

The validity of Test 21 was the sole issue before the court on the motions for summary judgment. The District Court noted that there was no claim of "an intentional discrimination or purposeful discriminatory acts" but only a claim that Test 21 bore no relationship to job performance and "has a highly discriminatory impact in screening out black candidates." Respondents' evidence, the District Court said, warranted three conclusions: "(a) The number of black police officers, while substantial, is not proportionate to the population mix of the city. (b) A higher percentage of blacks fail the Test than whites. (c) The Test has not been validated to establish its reliability for measuring subsequent job performance." This showing was deemed sufficient to shift the burden of proof to the defendants in the action, petitioners here; but the court nevertheless concluded that on the undisputed facts respondents were not entitled to relief. The District Court relied on several factors. Since August 1969, 44% of new police force recruits had been black; that figure also represented the proportion of blacks on the total force and was roughly equivalent to 20- to 29-year-old blacks in the 50-mile radius in which the recruiting efforts of the Police Department had been concentrated. It was undisputed that the Department had systematically and affirmatively sought to enroll black officers many of whom passed the test but failed to report for duty. The District Court rejected the assertion that Test 21 was culturally slanted to favor whites and was "satisfied that the undisputable facts prove the test to be reasonably and directly related to the requirements of the police recruit training program and that it is neither so designed nor operates [sic] to discriminate against otherwise qualified blacks." It was thus not necessary to show that Test 21 was not only a useful indicator of training school performance but had also been validated in terms of job performance—"The lack of job performance validation does not defeat the Test, given its direct relationship to recruiting and the valid part it plays in this process." The District Court ultimately concluded that "[t]he proof is wholly lacking that a police officer qualifies on the color of his skin rather than ability" and that the Department "should not be required on this showing to lower standards or to abandon efforts to achieve excellence."

Having lost on both constitutional and statutory issues in the District Court, respondents brought the case to the Court of Appeals claiming that their summary judgment motion, which rested on purely constitutional grounds, should have been granted. The tendered constitutional issue was whether the use of Test 21 invidiously discriminated against Negroes and hence denied them due process of law contrary to the commands of the Fifth Amendment. The Court of Appeals, addressing that issue, announced that it would be guided by Griggs v. Duke Power Co., 401 U.S. 424 (1971), a case involving the interpretation and application of Title VII of the Civil Rights Act of 1964, and held that the statutory standards elucidated in that case were to govern the due process question tendered in this one. The court went on to declare that lack of discriminatory intent in designing and administering Test 21 was irrelevant; the critical fact was rather that a far greater proportion of blacks—four times as many—failed the test than did whites. This disproportionate impact, standing alone and without regard to whether it indicated a discriminatory purpose, was held sufficient to establish a constitutional violation, absent proof by petitioners that the test was an adequate measure of job performance in addition to being an indicator of probable success in the training program, a burden which the court ruled petitioners had failed to discharge. That the Department had made substantial efforts to recruit blacks was held beside the point and the fact that the racial distribution of recent hirings and of the Department itself might be roughly equivalent to the racial makeup of the surrounding community, broadly conceived, was put aside as a "comparison [not] material to this appeal." The Court of Appeals, over a dissent, accordingly reversed the judgment of the District Court and directed that respondents' motion for partial summary judgment be granted. We granted the petition for certiorari filed by the District of Columbia officials.[7]

II

Because the Court of Appeals erroneously applied the legal standards applicable to Title VII cases in resolving the constitutional issue before it, we reverse its judgment in respondents' favor. Although the petition for certiorari did not present this ground for reversal, our Rule 40(1)(d)(2) provides that we "may notice a plain error not presented"; and this is an appropriate occasion to invoke the Rule.

[7] The Civil Service Commissioners, defendants in the District Court, did not petition for writ of certiorari but have filed a brief as respondents. See our Rule 21(4). We shall at times refer to them as the "federal parties."

As the Court of Appeals understood Title VII,[10] employees or applicants proceeding under it need not concern themselves with the employer's possibly discriminatory purpose but instead may focus solely on the racially differential impact of the challenged hiring or promotion practices. This is not the constitutional rule. We have never held that the constitutional standard for adjudicating claims of invidious racial discrimination is identical to the standards applicable under Title VII, and we decline to do so today.

The central purpose of the Equal Protection Clause of the Fourteenth Amendment is the prevention of official conduct discriminating on the basis of race. It is also true that the Due Process Clause of the Fifth Amendment contains an equal protection component prohibiting the United States from invidiously discriminating between individuals or groups. Bolling v. Sharpe, 347 U.S. 497 (1954). But our cases have not embraced the proposition that a law or other official act, without regard to whether it reflects a racially discriminatory purpose, is unconstitutional solely because it has a racially disproportionate impact. . . .

This is not to say that the necessary discriminatory racial purpose must be express or appear on the face of the statute, or that a law's disproportionate impact is irrelevant in cases involving Constitution-based claims of racial discrimination. A statute, otherwise neutral on its face, must not be applied so as invidiously to discriminate on the basis of race. Yick Wo v. Hopkins, 118 U.S. 356 (1886). It is also clear from the cases dealing with racial discrimination in the selection of juries that the systematic exclusion of Negroes is itself such an "unequal application of the law . . . as to show intentional discrimination." Akins v. Texas, 325 U.S. 398, 404 (1945). . . . A prima facie case of discriminatory purpose may be proved as well by the absence of Negroes on a particular jury combined with the failure of the jury commissioners to be informed of eligible Negro jurors in a community, Hill v. Texas, 316 U.S. 400, 404 (1942), or with racially nonneutral selection procedures, Alexander v. Louisiana, 405 U.S. 625 (1972); Avery v. Georgia, 345 U.S. 559 (1953); Whitus v. Georgia, 385 U.S. 545 (1967). With a prima facie case made out, "the burden of proof shifts to the State to rebut the presumption of unconstitutional action by showing that permissible racially neutral

[10] Although Title VII standards have dominated this case, the statute was not applicable to federal employees when the complaint was filed; and although the 1972 amendments extending the Title to reach Government employees were adopted prior to the District Court's judgment, the complaint was not amended to state a claim under that Title, nor did the case thereafter proceed as a Title VII case. Respondents' motion for partial summary judgment, filed after the 1972 amendments, rested solely on constitutional grounds; and the Court of Appeals ruled that the motion should have been granted. At the oral argument before this Court, when respondents' counsel was asked whether "this is just a purely Title VII case as it comes to us from the Court of Appeals without any constitutional overtones," counsel responded: "My trouble honestly with that proposition is the procedural requirements to get into court under Title VII, and this case has not met them."

selection criteria and procedures have produced the monochromatic result." *Alexander*, supra, at 632. . . .

Necessarily, an invidious discriminatory purpose may often be inferred from the totality of the relevant facts, including the fact, if it is true, that the law bears more heavily on one race than another. It is also not infrequently true that the discriminatory impact—in the jury cases for example, the total or seriously disproportionate exclusion of Negroes from jury venires—may for all practical purposes demonstrate unconstitutionality because in various circumstances the discrimination is very difficult to explain on nonracial grounds. Nevertheless, we have not held that a law, neutral on its face and serving ends otherwise within the power of government to pursue, is invalid under the Equal Protection Clause simply because it may affect a greater proportion of one race than of another. Disproportionate impact is not irrelevant, but it is not the sole touchstone of an invidious racial discrimination forbidden by the Constitution. Standing alone, it does not trigger the rule, McLaughlin v. Florida, 379 U.S. 184 (1964), that racial classifications are to be subjected to the strictest scrutiny and are justifiable only by the weightiest of considerations.

There are some indications to the contrary in our cases. In Palmer v. Thompson, 403 U.S. 217 (1971), the city of Jackson, Miss., following a court decree to this effect, desegregated all of its public facilities save five swimming pools which had been operated by the city and which, following the decree, were closed by ordinance pursuant to a determination by the city council that closure was necessary to preserve peace and order and that integrated pools could not be economically operated. Accepting the finding that the pools were closed to avoid violence and economic loss, this Court rejected the argument that the abandonment of this service was inconsistent with the outstanding desegregation decree and that the otherwise seemingly permissible ends served by the ordinance could be impeached by demonstrating that racially invidious motivations had prompted the city council's action. The holding was that the city was not overtly or covertly operating segregated pools and was extending identical treatment to both whites and Negroes. The opinion warned against grounding decision on legislative purpose or motivation, thereby lending support for the proposition that the operative effect of the law rather than its purpose is the paramount factor. But the holding of the case was that the legitimate purposes of the ordinance—to preserve peace and avoid deficits—were not open to impeachment by evidence that the councilmen were actually motivated by racial considerations. Whatever dicta the opinion may contain, the decision did not involve, much less invalidate, a statute or ordinance having neutral purposes but disproportionate racial consequences.

Wright v. Council of City of Emporia, 407 U.S. 451 (1972), also indicates that in proper circumstances, the racial impact of a law, rather than its discriminatory purpose, is the critical factor. That case involved the division of a school district. The issue was whether the division was consistent with an outstanding order of a federal court to desegregate the dual school system found to have existed in the area. The constitutional predicate for the District Court's invalidation of the divided district was "the enforcement until 1969 of racial segregation in a public school system of which Emporia had always been a part." There was thus no need to find "an independent constitutional violation." Citing *Palmer v. Thompson*, we agreed with the District Court that the division of the district had the effect of interfering with the federal decree and should be set aside. . . .

Both before and after *Palmer v. Thompson*, however, various Courts of Appeals have held in several contexts, including public employment, that the substantially disproportionate racial impact of a statute or official practice standing alone and without regard to discriminatory purpose, suffices to prove racial discrimination violating the Equal Protection Clause absent some justification going substantially beyond what would be necessary to validate most other legislative classifications. The cases impressively demonstrate that there is another side to the issue; but, with all due respect, to the extent that those cases rested on or expressed the view that proof of discriminatory racial purpose is unnecessary in making out an equal protection violation, we are in disagreement.

As an initial matter, we have difficulty understanding how a law establishing a racially neutral qualification for employment is nevertheless racially discriminatory and denies "any person . . . equal protection of the laws" simply because a greater proportion of Negroes fail to qualify than members of other racial or ethnic groups. Had respondents, along with all others who had failed Test 21, whether white or black, brought an action claiming that the test denied each of them equal protection of the laws as compared with those who had passed with high enough scores to qualify them as police recruits, it is most unlikely that their challenge would have been sustained. Test 21, which is administered generally to prospective Government employees, concededly seeks to ascertain whether those who take it have acquired a particular level of verbal skill; and it is untenable that the Constitution prevents the Government from seeking modestly to upgrade the communicative abilities of its employees rather than to be satisfied with some lower level of competence, particularly where the job requires special ability to communicate orally and in writing. Respondents, as Negroes, could no more successfully claim that the test denied them equal protection than could white applicants who also failed. The conclusion would not be different in the face of proof that more Negroes than whites had been disqualified by Test 21. That other Negroes also failed to score well would, alone, not demonstrate that respondents individually were being denied equal protection of the laws by the application of an otherwise valid qualifying test being administered to prospective police recruits.

Nor on the facts of the case before us would the disproportionate impact of Test 21 warrant the conclusion that it is a purposeful device to discriminate against Negroes and hence an infringement of the constitutional rights of respondents as well as other black applicants. As we have said, the test is neutral on its face and rationally may be said to serve a purpose the Government is constitutionally empowered to pursue. Even agreeing with the District Court that the differential racial effect of Test 21 called for further inquiry, we think the District Court correctly held that the affirmative efforts of the Metropolitan Police Department to recruit black officers, the changing racial composition of the recruit classes and of the force in general, and the relationship of the test to the training program negated any inference that the Department discriminated on the basis of race or that "a police officer qualifies on the color of his skin rather than ability."

Under Title VII, Congress provided that when hiring and promotion practices disqualifying substantially disproportionate numbers of blacks are challenged, discriminatory purpose need not be proved, and that it is an insufficient response to demonstrate some rational basis for the challenged practices. It is necessary, in addition, that they be "validated" in terms of job performance in any one of several ways, perhaps by ascertaining the minimum skill, ability, or potential necessary for the position at issue and determining whether the qualifying tests are appropriate for the selection of qualified applicants for the job in question.[13] However this process proceeds, it involves a more probing judicial review of, and less deference to, the seemingly reasonable acts of administrators and executives than is appropriate under the Constitution where special racial impact, without discriminatory purpose, is claimed. We are not disposed to adopt this more rigorous standard for the purposes of applying the Fifth and the Fourteenth Amendments in cases such as this.

A rule that a statute designed to serve neutral ends is nevertheless invalid, absent compelling justification, if in practice it benefits or burdens one race more than another would be far reaching and would raise serious questions about, and perhaps invalidate, a whole range of

---

[13] It appears beyond doubt by now that there is no single method for appropriately validating employment tests for their relationship to job performance. Professional standards developed by the American Psychological Association in its Standards for Educational and Psychological Tests and Manuals (1966), accept three basic methods of validation: "empirical" or "criterion" validity (demonstrated by identifying criteria that indicate successful job performance and then correlating test scores and the criteria so identified); "construct" validity (demonstrated by examinations structured to measure the degree to which job applicants have identifiable characteristics that have been determined to be important in successful job performance); and "content" validity (demonstrated by tests whose content closely approximates tasks to be performed on the job by the applicant). These standards have been relied upon by the Equal Employment Opportunity Commission in fashioning its Guidelines on Employee Selection Procedures, 29 CFR pt. 1607 (1975), and have been judicially noted in cases where validation of employment tests has been in issue.

tax, welfare, public service, regulatory, and licensing statutes that may be more burdensome to the poor and to the average black than to the more affluent white.[14]

Given that rule, such consequences would perhaps be likely to follow. However, in our view, extension of the rule beyond those areas where it is already applicable by reason of statute, such as in the field of public employment, should await legislative prescription.

As we have indicated, it was error to direct summary judgment for respondents based on the Fifth Amendment.

III

We also hold that the Court of Appeals should have affirmed the judgment of the District Court granting the motions for summary judgment filed by petitioners and the federal parties. Respondents were entitled to relief on neither constitutional nor statutory grounds.

The submission of the defendants in the District Court was that Test 21 complied with all applicable statutory as well as constitutional requirements; and they appear not to have disputed that under the statutes and regulations governing their conduct standards similar to those obtaining under Title VII had to be satisfied.[15] The District Court also assumed that Title VII standards were to control the case, identified the determinative issue as whether Test 21 was sufficiently job related and proceeded to uphold use of the test because it was "directly related to a determination of whether the applicant possesses sufficient skills requisite to the demands of the curriculum a recruit must master at the police academy." The Court of Appeals reversed because the relationship between Test 21 and training school success, if demonstrated at all, did not satisfy what it deemed to be the crucial requirement of a direct

[14] Goodman, De Facto School Segregation: A Constitutional and Empirical Analysis, 60 Calif. L. Rev. 275, 300 (1972), suggests that disproportionate-impact analysis might invalidate "tests and qualifications for voting, draft deferment, public employment, jury service, and other government-conferred benefits and opportunities . . ., [s]ales taxes, bail schedules, utility rates, bridge tolls, license fees, and other state-imposed charges." It has also been argued that minimum wage and usury laws as well as professional licensing requirements would require major modifications in light of the unequal-impact rule. Silverman, Equal Protection, Economic Legislation, and Racial Discrimination, 25 Vand. L. Rev. 1183 (1972). See also Demsetz, Minorities in the Market Place, 43 N.C. L. Rev. 271 (1965).

[15] In their memorandum supporting their motion for summary judgment, the federal parties argued:

> "In *Griggs,* supra, the Supreme Court set a job relationship standard for the private sector employers which has been a standard for federal employment since the passage of the Civil Service Act in 1883. In that act Congress has mandated that the federal government must use '. . . examinations for testing applicants for appointment . . . which . . . as far as possible relate to matters that fairly test the relative capacity and fitness of the applicants for the appointments sought.' 5 U.S.C. § 3304(a)(1). Defendants contend that they have been following the job related standards of *Griggs,* supra, for the past eighty-eight years by virtue of the enactment of the Civil Service Act which guaranteed open and fair competition for jobs."

They went on to argue that the *Griggs* standard had been satisfied. In granting the motions for summary judgment filed by petitioners and the federal parties, the District Court necessarily decided adversely to respondents the statutory issues expressly or tacitly tendered by the parties.

relationship between performance on Test 21 and performance on the policeman's job.

We agree with petitioners and the federal parties that this was error. The advisability of the police recruit training course informing the recruit about his upcoming job, acquainting him with its demands, and attempting to impart a modicum of required skills seems conceded. It is also apparent to us, as it was to the District Judge, that some minimum verbal and communicative skill would be very useful, if not essential, to satisfactory progress in the training regimen. Based on the evidence before him, the District Judge concluded that Test 21 was directly related to the requirements of the police training program and that a positive relationship between the test and training-course performance was sufficient to validate the former, wholly aside from its possible relationship to actual performance as a police officer. This conclusion of the District Judge that training-program validation may itself be sufficient is supported by regulations of the Civil Service Commission, by the opinion evidence placed before the District Judge, and by the current views of the Civil Service Commissioners who were parties to the case.[16] Nor is the conclusion foreclosed by either *Griggs* or Albemarle Paper Co. v. Moody, 422 U.S. 405 (1975); and it seems to us the much more sensible construction of the job-relatedness requirement.

The District Court's accompanying conclusion that Test 21 was in fact directly related to the requirements of the police training program was supported by a validation study, as well as by other evidence of record;[17] and we are not convinced that this conclusion was erroneous.

---

[16] See note 17 infra. Current instructions of the Civil Service Commission on "Examining, Testing, Standards, and Employment Practices" provide in pertinent part:

"S2–2—Use of applicant appraisal procedures

"a. *Policy*. The Commission's staff develops and uses applicant appraisal procedures to assess the knowledge, skills, and abilities of persons for jobs and not persons in the abstract.

"(1) Appraisal procedures are designed to reflect real, reasonable, and necessary qualifications for effective job behavior.

"(2) An appraisal procedure must, among other requirements, have a demonstrable and rational relationship to important job-related performance objectives identified by management, such as:

"(a) Effective job performance;

"(b) Capability;

"(c) Success in training;

"(d) Reduced turnover; or

"(e) Job satisfaction." 37 Fed. Reg. 21557 (1972).

See also Equal Employment Opportunity Commission Guidelines on Employee Selection Procedures, 29 CFR § 1607.5(b)(3) (1975), discussed in Albemarle Paper Co. v. Moody, 422 U.S., at 430–435.

[17] The record includes a validation study of Test 21's relationship to performance in the recruit training program. The study was made by D. L. Futransky of the Standards Division, Bureau of Policies and Standards, United States Civil Service Commission. Findings of the study included data "supporting the conclusion that Test 21 is effective in selecting trainees who can learn the material that is taught at the Recruit School." Opinion evidence, submitted by qualified experts examining the Futransky study and/or conducting their own research, affirmed the correlation between scores on Test 21 and success in the training program. E.g.,

The federal parties, whose views have somewhat changed since the decision of the Court of Appeals and who still insist that training-program validation is sufficient, now urge a remand to the District Court for the purpose of further inquiry into whether the training-program test scores, which were found to correlate with Test 21 scores, are themselves an appropriate measure of the trainee's mastership of the material taught in the course and whether the training program itself is sufficiently related to actual performance of the police officer's task. We think a remand is inappropriate. The District Court's judgment was warranted by the record before it, and we perceive no good reason to reopen it, particularly since we were informed at oral argument that although Test 21 is still being administered, the training program itself has undergone substantial modification in the course of this litigation. If there are now deficiencies in the recruiting practices under prevailing Title VII standards, those deficiencies are to be directly addressed in accordance with appropriate procedures mandated under that Title.

The judgment of the Court of Appeals accordingly is reversed.

So ordered.

■ JUSTICE STEWART joins Parts I and II of the Court's opinion.

■ JUSTICE STEVENS, concurring.

While I agree with the Court's disposition of this case, I add these comments on the constitutional issue discussed in Part II and the statutory issue discussed in Part III of the Court's opinion.

The requirement of purposeful discrimination is a common thread running through the cases summarized in Part II. These cases include criminal convictions which were set aside because blacks were excluded from the grand jury, a reapportionment case in which political boundaries were obviously influenced to some extent by racial considerations, a school desegregation case, and a case involving the unequal administration of an ordinance purporting to prohibit the operation of laundries in frame buildings. Although it may be proper to use the same language to describe the constitutional claim in each of these contexts, the burden of proving a prima facie case may well involve differing evidentiary considerations. The extent of deference that one pays to the trial court's determination of the factual issue, and indeed, the extent to which one characterizes the intent issue as a question of fact or a question of law, will vary in different contexts.

Affidavit of Dr. Donald J. Schwartz (personnel research psychologist, United States Civil Service Commission) ("It is my opinion . . . that Test 21 has a significant positive correlation with success in the MPD Recruit School for both Blacks and whites and is therefore shown to be job related . . ."); affidavit of Diane E. Wilson (personnel research psychologist, United States Civil Service Commission) ("It is my opinion that there is a direct and rational relationship between the content and difficulty of Test 21 and successful completion of recruit school training"). The Court of Appeals was "willing to assume for purposes of this appeal that appellees have shown that Test 21 is predictive of further progress in Recruit School."

Frequently the most probative evidence of intent will be objective evidence of what actually happened rather than evidence describing the subjective state of mind of the actor. For normally the actor is presumed to have intended the natural consequences of his deeds. This is particularly true in the case of governmental action which is frequently the product of compromise, of collective decisionmaking, and of mixed motivation. It is unrealistic, on the one hand, to require the victim of alleged discrimination to uncover the actual subjective intent of the decisionmaker or, conversely, to invalidate otherwise legitimate action simply because an improper motive affected the deliberation of a participant in the decisional process. A law conscripting clerics should not be invalidated because an atheist voted for it.

My point in making this observation is to suggest that the line between discriminatory purpose and discriminatory impact is not nearly as bright, and perhaps not quite as critical, as the reader of the Court's opinion might assume. I agree, of course, that a constitutional issue does not arise every time some disproportionate impact is shown. On the other hand, when the disproportion is as dramatic as in Gomillion v. Lightfoot, 364 U.S. 339, or Yick Wo v. Hopkins, 118 U.S. 356, it really does not matter whether the standard is phrased in terms of purpose or effect. Therefore, although I accept the statement of the general rule in the Court's opinion, I am not yet prepared to indicate how that standard should be applied in the many cases which have formulated the governing standard in different language.

My agreement with the conclusion reached in Part II of the Court's opinion rests on a ground narrower than the Court describes. I do not rely at all on the evidence of good-faith efforts to recruit black police officers. In my judgment, neither those efforts nor the subjective good faith of the District administration, would save Test 21 if it were otherwise invalid.

There are two reasons why I am convinced that the challenge to Test 21 is insufficient. First, the test serves the neutral and legitimate purpose of requiring all applicants to meet a uniform minimum standard of literacy. Reading ability is manifestly relevant to the police function, there is no evidence that the required passing grade was set at an arbitrarily high level, and there is sufficient disparity among high schools and high school graduates to justify the use of a separate uniform test. Second, the same test is used throughout the federal service. The applicants for employment in the District of Columbia Police Department represent such a small fraction of the total number of persons who have taken the test that their experience is of minimal probative value in assessing the neutrality of the test itself. That evidence, without more, is not sufficient to overcome the presumption that a test which is this widely used by the Federal Government is in fact neutral in its effect as well as its "purpose" as that term is used in constitutional adjudication.

My study of the statutory issue leads me to the same conclusion reached by the Court in Part III of its opinion. Since the Court of Appeals set aside the portion of the District Court's summary judgment granting the defendants' motion, I agree that we cannot ignore the statutory claims even though, as the Court makes clear, there is no Title VII question in this case. The actual statutory holdings are limited to 42 U.S.C. § 1981 and § 1–320 of the District of Columbia Code, to which regulations of the Equal Employment Opportunity Commission have no direct application.

The parties argued the case as though Title VII standards were applicable. In a general way those standards shed light on the issues, but there is sufficient individuality and complexity to that statute, and to the regulations promulgated under it, to make it inappropriate simply to transplant those standards in their entirety into a different statutory scheme having a different history. Moreover, the subject matter of this case—the validity of qualifications for the law enforcement profession—is one in which federal district judges have a greater expertise than in many others. I therefore do not regard this as a case in which the District Court was required to apply Title VII standards as strictly as would be necessary either in other contexts or in litigation actually arising under that statute.

The Court's specific holding on the job-relatedness question contains, I believe, two components. First, as a matter of law, it is permissible for the police department to use a test for the purpose of predicting ability to master a training program even if the test does not otherwise predict ability to perform on the job. I regard this as a reasonable proposition and not inconsistent with the Court's prior holdings, although some of its prior language obviously did not contemplate this precise problem. Second, as a matter of fact, the District Court's finding that there was a correlation between success on the test and success in the training program has sufficient evidentiary support to withstand attack under the "clearly erroneous" standard mandated by Fed. Rule Civ. Proc. 52(a). Whether or not we would have made the same finding of fact, the opinion evidence identified in n.17 of the Court's opinion—and indeed the assumption made by the Court of Appeals quoted therein—is surely adequate to support the finding under the proper standard of appellate review.

On the understanding that nothing which I have said is inconsistent with the Court's reasoning, I join the opinion of the Court except to the extent that it expresses an opinion on the merits of the cases cited ante at n.12.

■ JUSTICE BRENNAN, with whom JUSTICE MARSHALL joins, dissenting.

The Court holds that the job qualification examination (Test 21) given by the District of Columbia Metropolitan Police Department does not unlawfully discriminate on the basis of race under either constitutional or statutory standards.

Initially, it seems to me that the Court should not pass on the statutory questions, because they are not presented by this case. The Court says that respondents' summary judgment motion "rested on purely constitutional grounds," and that "the Court of Appeals erroneously applied the legal standards applicable to Title VII cases in resolving the constitutional issue before it." There is a suggestion, however, that petitioners are entitled to prevail because they met the burden of proof imposed by 5 U.S.C. § 3304. As I understand the opinion, the Court therefore holds that Test 21 is job related under § 3304, but not necessarily under Title VII. But that provision, by the Court's own analysis, is no more in the case than Title VII; respondents' "complaint asserted no claim under § 3304." If it was "plain error" for the Court of Appeals to apply a statutory standard to this case, as the Court asserts, then it is unfortunate that the Court does not recognize that it is also plain error to address the statutory issues in Part III of its opinion.

Nevertheless, although it appears unnecessary to reach the statutory questions, I will accept the Court's conclusion that respondents were entitled to summary judgment if they were correct in their statutory arguments, and I would affirm the Court of Appeals because petitioners have failed to prove that Test 21 satisfies the applicable statutory standards.[1] All parties' arguments and both lower court decisions were based on Title VII standards. In this context, I think it wrong to focus on § 3304 to the exclusion of the Title VII standards, particularly because the Civil Service Commission views the job-relatedness standards of Title VII and § 3304 as identical.

In applying a Title VII test, both the District Court and the Court of Appeals held that respondents had offered sufficient evidence of discriminatory impact to shift to petitioners the burden of proving job-relatedness. The Court does not question these rulings, and the only issue before us is what petitioners were required to show and whether they carried their burden. The Court agrees with the District Court's conclusion that Test 21 was validated by a positive relationship between Test 21 scores and performance in police training courses. This result is based upon the Court's reading of the record, its interpretation of instructions governing testing practices issued by the Civil Service Commission (CSC), and "the current views of the Civil Service Commissioners who were parties to the case." We are also assured that today's result is not foreclosed by Griggs v. Duke Power Co., 401 U.S. 424 (1971), and Albemarle Paper Co. v. Moody, 422 U.S. 405 (1975). Finally, the Court asserts that its conclusion is "the much more sensible

[1] Although I do not intend to address the constitutional questions considered by the Court in Part II of its opinion, I feel constrained to comment upon the propriety of footnote 12. One of the cases "disapproved" therein is presently scheduled for plenary consideration by the Court in the 1976 Term, Metropolitan Housing Development Corp. v. Village of Arlington Heights, 517 F.2d 409 (7th Cir.), cert. granted, 423 U.S. 1030 (1975). If the Court regarded this case only a few months ago as worthy of full briefing and argument, it ought not be effectively reversed merely by its inclusion in a laundry list of lower court decisions.

construction of the job-relatedness requirement." But the CSC instructions cited by the Court do not support the District Court's conclusion. More importantly, the brief filed in this Court by the CSC takes the position that petitioners did not satisfy the burden of proof imposed by the CSC guidelines. It also appears that longstanding regulations of the Equal Employment Opportunity Commission (EEOC)—previously endorsed by this Court—require a result contrary to that reached by the Court. Furthermore, the Court's conclusion is inconsistent with my understanding of the interpretation of Title VII in *Griggs* and *Albemarle*. I do not find this conclusion "much more sensible," and with all respect I suggest that today's decision has the potential of significantly weakening statutory safeguards against discrimination in employment.

I

On October 12, 1972, the CSC issued a supplement to the Federal Personnel Manual containing instructions for compliance with its general regulations concerning employment practices. The provision cited by the Court requires that Test 21 "have a demonstrable and rational relationship to important job-related performance objectives identified by management." "Success in training" is one example of a possible objective. The statistical correlation established by the Futransky validity study was between applicants' scores on Test 21 and recruits' average scores on final examinations given during the police training course. . . .

The CSC's standards thus recognize that Test 21 can be validated by a correlation between Test 21 scores and recruits' averages on training examinations only if (1) the training averages predict job performance or (2) the averages are proved to measure performance in job-related training. There is no proof that the recruits' average is correlated with job performance after completion of training. And although a positive relationship to the recruits' average might be sufficient to validate Test 21 if the average were proved to reflect mastery of material on the training curriculum that was in turn demonstrated to be relevant to job performance, the record is devoid of proof in this regard. First, there is no demonstration by petitioners that the training-course examinations measure comprehension of the training curriculum; indeed, these examinations do not even appear in the record. Furthermore, the Futransky study simply designated an average of 85 on the examination as a "good" performance and assumed that a recruit with such an average learned the material taught in the training course. Without any further proof of the significance of a score of 85, and there is none in the record, I cannot agree that Test 21 is predictive of "success in training."

II

Today's decision is also at odds with EEOC regulations issued pursuant to explicit authorization in Title VII. 42 U.S.C. § 2000e–12(a). Although the dispute in this case is not within the EEOC's jurisdiction, as I noted above, the proper construction of Title VII nevertheless is relevant. Moreover, the 1972 extension of Title VII to public employees gave the same substantive protection to those employees as had previously been accorded in the private sector, Morton v. Mancari, 417 U.S. 535, 546–547 (1974), and it is therefore improper to maintain different standards in the public and private sectors. Chandler v. Roudebush, 425 U.S. 840, 864 (1976).

As with an agency's regulations, the construction of a statute by the agency charged with its administration is entitled to great deference. The deference due the pertinent EEOC regulations is enhanced by the fact that they were neither altered nor disapproved when Congress extensively amended Title VII in 1972. These principles were followed in *Albemarle*—where the Court explicitly endorsed various regulations no fewer than eight times in its opinion, 422 U.S., at 431–436—and *Griggs*, 401 U.S., at 433–434.

The EEOC regulations require that the validity of a job qualification test be proved by "empirical data demonstrating that the test is predictive of or significantly correlated with important elements of work behavior which comprise or are relevant to the job or jobs for which candidates are being evaluated." 29 CFR § 1607.4(c) (1975). This construction of Title VII was approved in *Albemarle*, where we quoted this provision and remarked that "[t]he message of these Guidelines is the same as that of the *Griggs* case." 422 U.S., at 431. The regulations also set forth minimum standards for validation and delineate the criteria that may be used for this purpose.

> "The work behaviors or other criteria of employee adequacy which the test is intended to predict or identify must be fully described; and, additionally, in the case of rating techniques, the appraisal form(s) and instructions to the rater(s) must be included as a part of the validation evidence. Such criteria may include measures other than actual work proficiency, such as training time, supervisory ratings, regularity of attendance and tenure. Whatever criteria are used they must represent major or critical work behaviors as revealed by careful job analyses." 29 CFR § 1607.5(b)(3) (1975).

This provision was also approved in *Albemarle*. 422 U.S., at 432, and n.30.

If we measure the validity of Test 21 by this standard, which I submit we are bound to do, petitioners' proof is deficient in a number of ways similar to those noted above. First, the criterion of final training examination averages does not appear to be "fully described." Although the record contains some general discussion of the training curriculum, the examinations are not in the record, and there is no other evidence completely elucidating the subject matter tested by the training examinations. Without this required description we cannot determine whether the correlation with training examination averages is sufficiently related to petitioners' need to ascertain "job-specific ability." See *Albemarle*, 422 U.S., at 433. Second, the EEOC regulations do not expressly permit validation by correlation to training performance, unlike the CSC instructions. Among the specified criteria the closest to training performance is "training time." All recruits to the Metropolitan Police Department, however, go through the same training course in the same amount of time, including those who experience some difficulty. Third, the final requirement of § 1607.5(b)(3) has not been met. There has been no job analysis establishing the significance of scores on training examinations, nor is there any other type of evidence showing that these scores are of "major or critical" importance.

Accordingly, EEOC regulations that have previously been approved by the Court set forth a construction of Title VII that is distinctly opposed to today's statutory result.

III

The Court also says that its conclusion is not foreclosed by *Griggs* and *Albemarle*, but today's result plainly conflicts with those cases. *Griggs* held that "[i]f an employment practice which operates to exclude Negroes cannot be shown to be *related to job performance*, the practice is prohibited." 401 U.S., at 431 (emphasis added). Once a discriminatory impact is shown, the employer carries the burden of proving that the challenged practice "bear[s] a *demonstrable relationship to successful performance of the jobs* for which it was used." Ibid. (emphasis added). We observed further:

> "Nothing in the Act precludes the use of testing or measuring procedures; obviously they are useful. What Congress has forbidden is giving these devices and mechanisms controlling force unless they are demonstrably a reasonable measure of job performance.... What Congress has commanded is that any tests used must measure the person for the job and not the person in the abstract." Id., at 436.

Albemarle read *Griggs* to require that a discriminatory test be validated through proof "by professionally acceptable methods" that it is " 'predictive of or significantly correlated with *important* elements of work behavior *which comprise or are relevant to the job or jobs* for which candidates are being evaluated.' " 422 U.S., at 431 (emphasis added), quoting 29 CFR § 1607.4(c) (1975). Further, we rejected the employer's attempt to validate a written test by proving that it was related to supervisors' job performance ratings, because there was no demonstration that the ratings accurately reflected job performance. We were unable "to determine whether the criteria *actually* considered were sufficiently related to the [employer's] legitimate interest in job-specific ability to justify a testing system with a racially discriminatory impact." 422 U.S., at 433 (emphasis in original). To me, therefore, these cases read Title VII as requiring proof of a significant relationship to job performance to establish the validity of a discriminatory test. See also

McDonnell Douglas Corp. v. Green, 411 U.S. 792, 802, and n.14 (1973). Petitioners do not maintain that there is a demonstrated correlation between Test 21 scores and job performance. Moreover, their validity study was unable to discern a significant positive relationship between training averages and job performance. Thus, there is no proof of a correlation—either direct or indirect—between Test 21 and performance of the job of being a police officer.

It may well be that in some circumstances, proof of a relationship between a discriminatory qualification test and training performance is an acceptable substitute for establishing a relationship to job performance. But this question is not settled, and it should not be resolved by the minimal analysis in the Court's opinion. Moreover, it is particularly inappropriate to decide the question on this record. "Professionally acceptable methods" apparently recognize validation by proof of a correlation with training performance, rather than job performance, if (1) the training curriculum includes information proved to be important to job performance and (2) the standard used as a measure of training performance is shown to reflect the trainees' mastery of the material included in the training curriculum. See Brief for CSC 24–29; Brief for the Executive Committee of Division 14 of the American Psychological Assn. as Amicus Curiae at 37–43. But no authority, whether professional, administrative, or judicial, has accepted the sufficiency of a correlation with training performance in the absence of such proof. For reasons that I have stated above, the record does not adequately establish either factor. As a result, the Court's conclusion cannot be squared with the focus on job performance in *Griggs* and *Albemarle*, even if this substitute showing is reconcilable with the holdings in those cases. . . .

Accordingly, accepting the Court's assertion that it is necessary to reach the statutory issue, I would hold that petitioners have not met their burden of proof and affirm the judgment of the Court of Appeals.

NOTES ON *WASHINGTON V. DAVIS*

1. **The Constitutional Holding.** *Washington v. Davis* is best known for its constitutional holding: that claims of discrimination in violation of the Fifth Amendment (and by implication, the Fourteenth Amendment) require proof of intentional discrimination; proof of disparate impact, alone, is not enough. The justification for this holding has been much debated, but the motivation for it appears plainly enough in footnote 14. The Supreme Court was concerned about the range of government programs, from housing to taxes, that could be encompassed by claims of disparate impact under the Constitution. The theory of disparate impact under Title VII, by contrast, carries no risk of indefinite expansion. It applies only within the field of employment. And even within that field, another salient difference between constitutional and statutory law operates to limit it further. Congress can overrule or modify decisions applying the theory of disparate impact under

Title VII by legislation amending the statute, whereas it has no such power over constitutional decisions. Judicial decisions adopting the theory as a matter of constitutional law could be altered only through the cumbersome process of constitutional amendment. These reasons, although they do not fully justify the constitutional holding in *Washington v. Davis*, indicate why constitutional claims might be limited to intentional discrimination when statutory claims are not.

Despite this limitation on constitutional claims, statistical evidence of discriminatory effects can still be used to prove intentional discrimination. Both *Teamsters* and *Hazelwood* allowed the use of such evidence to prove class claims of disparate treatment under Title VII and the same reasoning that supported those decisions applies with equal force to similar claims under the Constitution. This principle was explicitly recognized in Village of Arlington Heights v. Metropolitan Housing Development Corp., 429 U.S. 252 (1977). Evidence of disparate impact, so to speak, can be used to prove disparate treatment, but the court must explicitly find discriminatory intent, not just discriminatory effects. Anticipating this result, Justice Stevens suggested in *Washington v. Davis* "that the line between discriminatory purpose and discriminatory impact is not nearly as bright, and perhaps not quite as critical, as the reader of the Court's opinion might assume." Does this explain why the Court rejected the plaintiffs' statutory claim of disparate impact along with their constitutional claim of disparate treatment? If the two claims are not that different, how could one be rejected and the other sustained?

2. The Statutory Holding. While the constitutional holding in *Washington v. Davis* is well known, the statutory holding is obscure. It did not directly concern Title VII because, as counsel for the plaintiffs candidly acknowledged, the procedural prerequisites for bringing a Title VII claim had not been satisfied. Instead, it concerned a claim under a Reconstruction civil rights act, 42 U.S.C. § 1981, and a claim under a statute applicable only to the District of Columbia, the federal equivalent of a municipal ordinance. The latter was the subject of several concessions by the Civil Service Commission, which administered the statute at the time, representing that it was applied and interpreted just like Title VII. Beyond these concessions, however, there was little evidence to support any equivalence between this local law and the far more general provisions of Title VII. In an unusual procedural step, the Supreme Court also reached out to decide these statutory claims, despite the fact that they had not been addressed by the court of appeals, whose decision was limited entirely to the constitutional claim.

All of this might lead to the conclusion that the statutory holding in *Washington v. Davis* has only the most limited significance and hardly any at all for the interpretation of Title VII. Yet, if so, the extended discussion of validation in Part III of the opinion remains inexplicable. The Supreme Court does not usually render opinions on issues of significance only within the District of Columbia, as opposed to the nation as a whole. Instead, the Court went out of its way to address several issues of general significance: the proper methods of validation, the application of a widely used federal civil service test, and the appropriate qualifications for police officers. All of these issues could easily arise in claims properly presented under Title VII.

The Court's specific statutory holding was that the methods of validation enumerated in the EEOC guidelines did not exhaust the available means of justifying a test that has a disparate impact on minorities. The EEOC guidelines then in effect, as in *Albemarle Paper*, were the predecessors of the Uniform Guidelines, but they identified the same three methods of validation: content, criterion, and construct validation. The Court did not rigorously apply any of these methods, but instead endorsed a different method, relating the test to performance in a training program, concluding that "it seems to us the much more sensible construction of the job-relatedness requirement." What justification did the Court have for departing from the guidelines? Or, conversely, what justification did the EEOC have for setting out the exclusive methods of validation? If these methods of validation turn out to be too difficult for employers to meet, why shouldn't courts try to devise alternatives?

3. **Defects in the Validation Study.** As Justice Brennan pointed out in his dissent, the validation study in *Washington v. Davis* has almost as many defects as the validation study in *Albemarle Paper*. While good performance on the verbal ability test was correlated with good performance on the test administered at the end of the training program, the latter test was not correlated with anything at all. It was not correlated with performance in the training program or with performance on the job. The only correlation was between two paper-and-pencil tests, which is not at all remarkable. Both tests involve much the same behavior, of writing answers to questions based on previously acquired skills and knowledge, and little of the actual behavior of police officers on the job. It is possible to believe with the Court "that some minimum verbal and communicative skill would be very useful, if not essential, to satisfactory progress in the training regimen" without believing that it was necessary for satisfactory progress as a police officer. Moreover, all recruits were given the training test until they passed, so that even the police department did not believe that all its recruits had to be able readily to absorb even a minimum of the material in the training program.

If these defects in the validation study were so apparent, why did the Court nevertheless agree with the district court that it was sufficient? Why didn't the Court require some evidence that the test, which measured verbal ability, was related to the job and not just to training for the job? Is it because, as Justice Stevens suggested, judges have a good sense of what is required of police officers and how verbal ability would help them meet these requirements? Does that distinguish this case from *Albemarle Paper*, where the judges could bring no special expertise to analyzing work in a paper mill?

Or is this case distinguishable from *Albemarle Paper* on different grounds, involving the evidence of discrimination by the District of Columbia police department? Was this employer as likely as a mill operator in North Carolina to engage in continued discrimination based on a history of explicit segregation? Was the affirmative action program adopted by the police department relevant to an evaluation of its testing requirement? More generally, does the weakness of the evidence of disparate treatment, which caused the plaintiffs to lose on their constitutional claim, also undercut their statutory claim of disparate impact? If so, is Justice Stevens right that claims of disparate impact are not, in the end, all that different from claims of disparate treatment?

The next two cases examine these questions from the plaintiff's perspective: What constitutes evidence sufficient to prove disparate impact?

4. **Bibliography.** The constitutional holding in *Washington v. Davis* has generated an extensive literature. Paul Brest, The Supreme Court, 1975 Term—Foreword: In Defense of the Antidiscrimination Principle, 90 Harv. L. Rev. 1 (1976); Alan D. Freeman, Legitimizing Racial Discrimination Through Antidiscrimination Law: A Critical Review of Supreme Court Doctrine, 62 Minn. L. Rev. 1049 (1978); Charles Lawrence, The Id, the Ego, and Equal Protection: Reckoning with Unconscious Racism, 39 Stan. L. Rev. 317 (1987); Daniel R. Ortiz, The Myth of Intent in Equal Protection, 42 Stan. L. Rev. 1105 (1989); Richard Primus, Equal Protection and Disparate Impact: Round Three, 117 Harv. L. Rev. 493 (2003); David A. Strauss, Discriminatory Intent and the Taming of *Brown*, 56 U. Chi. L. Rev. 935 (1989).

For articles on the statutory holding, see Craig Haney, Employment Tests and Employment Discrimination: A Dissenting Psychological Opinion, 5 Indus. Rel. L.J. 1 (1982); Barbara Lerner, *Washington v. Davis*: Quantity, Quality and Equality in Employment Testing, 1976 Sup. Ct. Rev. 263; Barbara Lerner, Employment Discrimination: Adverse Impact, Validity, and Equality, 1979 Sup. Ct. Rev. 17.

Dothard v. Rawlinson

433 U.S. 321 (1977).

■ JUSTICE STEWART delivered the opinion of the Court.

Appellee Dianne Rawlinson sought employment with the Alabama Board of Corrections as a prison guard, called in Alabama a "correctional counselor." After her application was rejected, she brought this class suit under Title VII of the Civil Rights Act of 1964 and under 42 U.S.C. § 1983, alleging that she had been denied employment because of her sex in violation of federal law. A three-judge Federal District Court for the Middle District of Alabama decided in her favor. We noted probable jurisdiction of this appeal from the District Court's judgment.

I

At the time she applied for a position as correctional counselor trainee, Rawlinson was a 22-year-old college graduate whose major course of study had been correctional psychology. She was refused employment because she failed to meet the minimum 120-pound weight requirement established by an Alabama statute. The statute also establishes a height minimum of 5 feet 2 inches.

After her application was rejected because of her weight, Rawlinson filed a charge with the Equal Employment Opportunity Commission, and ultimately received a right-to-sue letter. She then filed a complaint in the District Court on behalf of herself and other similarly situated women, challenging the statutory height and weight minima as violative of Title VII and the Equal Protection Clause of the Fourteenth Amendment. A three-judge court was convened. While the suit was pending, the Alabama Board of Corrections adopted Administrative Regulation 204, establishing gender criteria for assigning correctional counselors to maximum-security institutions for "contact positions," that is, positions requiring continual close physical proximity to inmates of the institution. Rawlinson amended her class-action complaint by adding a challenge to Regulation 204 as also violative of Title VII and the Fourteenth Amendment.

Like most correctional facilities in the United States, Alabama's prisons are segregated on the basis of sex. Currently the Alabama Board of Corrections operates four major all-male penitentiaries—Holman Prison, Kilby Corrections Facility, G. K. Fountain Correction Center, and Draper Correctional Center. The Board also operates the Julia Tutwiler Prison for Women, the Frank Lee Youth Center, the Number Four Honor Camp, the State Cattle Ranch, and nine Work Release Centers, one of which is for women. The Julia Tutwiler Prison for Women and the four male penitentiaries are maximum-security institutions. Their inmate living quarters are for the most part large dormitories, with communal showers and toilets that are open to the dormitories and hallways. The Draper and Fountain penitentiaries carry on extensive farming operations, making necessary a large number of strip searches for contraband when prisoners re-enter the prison buildings.

A correctional counselor's primary duty within these institutions is to maintain security and control of the inmates by continually supervising and observing their activities. To be eligible for consideration as a correctional counselor, an applicant must possess a valid Alabama driver's license, have a high school education or its equivalent, be free from physical defects, be between the ages of 20½ years and 45 years at the time of appointment, and fall between the minimum height and weight requirements of 5 feet 2 inches, and 120 pounds, and the maximum of 6 feet 10 inches, and 300 pounds. Appointment is by merit, with a grade assigned each applicant based on experience and education. No written examination is given.

At the time this litigation was in the District Court, the Board of Corrections employed a total of 435 people in various correctional counselor positions, 56 of whom were women. Of those 56 women, 21 were employed at the Julia Tutwiler Prison for Women, 13 were employed in noncontact positions at the four male maximum-security institutions, and the remaining 22 were employed at the other institutions operated by the Alabama Board of Corrections. Because most of Alabama's prisoners are held at the four maximum-security male penitentiaries, 336 of the 435 correctional counselor jobs were in those institutions, a majority of them concededly in the "contact" classification. Thus, even though meeting the statutory height and weight requirements, women applicants could under Regulation 204 compete equally with men for only about 25% of the correctional counselor jobs available in the Alabama prison system.

II

In enacting Title VII, Congress required "the removal of artificial, arbitrary, and unnecessary barriers to employment when the barriers operate invidiously to discriminate on the basis of racial or other impermissible classification." Griggs v. Duke Power Co., 401 U.S. 424, 431. The District Court found that the minimum statutory height and weight requirements that applicants for employment as correctional counselors must meet constitute the sort of arbitrary barrier to equal employment opportunity that Title VII forbids. The appellants assert that the District Court erred both in finding that the height and weight standards discriminate against women, and in its refusal to find that, even if they do, these standards are justified as "job related."

A

The gist of the claim that the statutory height and weight requirements discriminate against women does not involve an assertion of purposeful discriminatory motive. It is asserted, rather, that these facially neutral qualification standards work in fact disproportionately to exclude women from eligibility for employment by the Alabama Board of Corrections. We dealt in *Griggs v. Duke Power Co.*, supra, and Albemarle Paper Co. v. Moody, 422 U.S. 405, with similar allegations that facially neutral employment standards disproportionately excluded Negroes from employment, and those cases guide our approach here.

Those cases make clear that to establish a prima facie case of discrimination, a plaintiff need only show that the facially neutral standards in question select applicants for hire in a significantly discriminatory pattern. Once it is thus shown that the employment standards are discriminatory in effect, the employer must meet "the burden of showing that any given requirement [has] . . . a manifest relationship to the employment in question." Griggs v. Duke Power Co., supra, at 432. If the employer proves that the challenged requirements are job related, the plaintiff may then show that other selection devices without a similar discriminatory effect would also "serve the employer's legitimate interest in 'efficient and trustworthy workmanship.'" Albemarle Paper Co. v. Moody, supra, at 425, quoting McDonnell Douglas Corp. v. Green, 411 U.S. 792, 801.

Although women 14 years of age or older compose 52.75% of the Alabama population and 36.89% of its total labor force, they hold only 12.9% of its correctional counselor positions. In considering the effect of the minimum height and weight standards on this disparity in rate of hiring between the sexes, the District Court found that the 5′2″—

requirement would operate to exclude 33.29% of the women in the United States between the ages of 18–79, while excluding only 1.28% of men between the same ages. The 120-pound weight restriction would exclude 22.29% of the women and 2.35% of the men in this age group. When the height and weight restrictions are combined, Alabama's statutory standards would exclude 41.13% of the female population while excluding less than 1% of the male population.[12] Accordingly, the District Court found that Rawlinson had made out a prima facie case of unlawful sex discrimination.

The appellants argue that a showing of disproportionate impact on women based on generalized national statistics should not suffice to establish a prima facie case. They point in particular to Rawlinson's failure to adduce comparative statistics concerning actual applicants for correctional counselor positions in Alabama. There is no requirement, however, that a statistical showing of disproportionate impact must always be based on analysis of the characteristics of actual applicants. The application process itself might not adequately reflect the actual potential applicant pool, since otherwise qualified people might be discouraged from applying because of a self-recognized inability to meet the very standards challenged as being discriminatory. See Teamsters v. United States, 431 U.S. 324, 365–367. A potential applicant could easily determine her height and weight and conclude that to make an application would be futile. Moreover, reliance on general population demographic data was not misplaced where there was no reason to suppose that physical height and weight characteristics of Alabama men and women differ markedly from those of the national population.

For these reasons, we cannot say that the District Court was wrong in holding that the statutory height and weight standards had a discriminatory impact on women applicants. The plaintiffs in a case such as this are not required to exhaust every possible source of evidence, if the evidence actually presented on its face conspicuously demonstrates a job requirement's grossly discriminatory impact. If the employer discerns fallacies or deficiencies in the data offered by the plaintiff, he is free to adduce countervailing evidence of his own. In this case no such effort was made.

B

We turn, therefore, to the appellants' argument that they have rebutted the prima facie case of discrimination by showing that the

---

[12] Affirmatively stated, approximately 99.76% of the men and 58.87% of the women meet both these physical qualifications. From the separate statistics on height and weight of males it would appear that after adding the two together and allowing for some overlap the result would be to exclude between 2.35% and 3.63% of males from meeting Alabama's statutory height and weight minima. None of the parties has challenged the accuracy of the District Court's computations on this score, however, and the discrepancy is in any event insignificant in light of the gross disparity between the female and male exclusions. Even under revised computations the disparity would greatly exceed the 34% to 12% disparity that served to invalidate the high school diploma requirement in the *Griggs* case. 401 U.S., at 430.

height and weight requirements are job related. These requirements, they say, have a relationship to strength, a sufficient but unspecified amount of which is essential to effective job performance as a correctional counselor. In the District Court, however, the appellants produced no evidence correlating the height and weight requirements with the requisite amount of strength thought essential to good job performance. Indeed, they failed to offer evidence of any kind in specific justification of the statutory standards.[14]

If the job-related quality that the appellants identify is bona fide, their purpose could be achieved by adopting and validating a test for applicants that measures strength directly. Such a test, fairly administered, would fully satisfy the standards of Title VII because it would be one that "measure[s] the person for the job and not the person in the abstract." Griggs v. Duke Power Co., 401 U.S., at 436. But nothing in the present record even approaches such a measurement.

For the reasons we have discussed, the District Court was not in error in holding that Title VII of the Civil Rights Act of 1964, as amended, prohibits application of the statutory height and weight requirements to Rawlinson and the class she represents.

III

[This part of the opinion, upholding the exclusion of women from contact positions as a bona fide occupational qualification, is postponed to Chapter 5 on sex discrimination.]

The judgment is accordingly affirmed in part and reversed in part, and the case is remanded to the District Court for further proceedings consistent with this opinion.

It is so ordered.

■ JUSTICE REHNQUIST, with whom THE CHIEF JUSTICE and JUSTICE BLACKMUN join, concurring in the result and concurring in part.

I agree with, and join, Parts I and III of the Court's opinion in this case and with its judgment. While I also agree with the Court's conclusion in Part II of its opinion, holding that the District Court was "not in error" in holding the statutory height and weight requirements in this case to be invalidated by Title VII, the issues with which that Part deals are bound to arise so frequently that I feel obliged to separately state the reasons for my agreement with its result. I view affirmance of the District

---

[14] In what is perhaps a variation on their constitutional challenge to the validity of Title VII itself, the appellants contend that the establishment of the minimum height and weight standards by statute requires that they be given greater deference than is typically given private employer-established job qualifications. The relevant legislative history of the 1972 amendments extending Title VII to the States as employers does not, however, support such a result. Instead, Congress expressly indicated the intent that the same Title VII principles be applied to governmental and private employers alike. Thus for both private and public employers, "[t]he touchstone is business necessity," *Griggs*, 401 U.S., at 431; a discriminatory employment practice must be shown to be necessary to safe and efficient job performance to survive a Title VII challenge.

Court in this respect as essentially dictated by the peculiarly limited factual and legal justifications offered below by appellants on behalf of the statutory requirements. For that reason, I do not believe—and do not read the Court's opinion as holding—that all or even many of the height and weight requirements imposed by States on applicants for a multitude of law enforcement agency jobs are pretermitted by today's decision.

I agree that the statistics relied upon in this case are sufficient, absent rebuttal, to sustain a finding of a prima facie violation of § 703(a)(2), in that they reveal a significant discrepancy between the numbers of men, as opposed to women, who are automatically disqualified by reason of the height and weight requirements. The fact that these statistics are national figures of height and weight, as opposed to statewide or pool-of-labor-force statistics, does not seem to me to require us to hold that the District Court erred as a matter of law in admitting them into evidence. It is for the District Court, in the first instance, to determine whether these statistics appear sufficiently probative of the ultimate fact in issue—whether a given job qualification requirement has a disparate impact on some group protected by Title VII. In making this determination, such statistics are to be considered in light of all other relevant facts and circumstances. Cf. Teamsters v. United States, 431 U.S. 324, 340 (1977). The statistics relied on here do not suffer from the obvious lack of relevancy of the statistics relied on by the District Court in *Hazelwood School Dist. v. United States*. A reviewing court cannot say as a matter of law that they are irrelevant to the contested issue or so lacking in reliability as to be inadmissible.

If the defendants in a Title VII suit believe there to be any reason to discredit plaintiffs' statistics that does not appear on their face, the opportunity to challenge them is available to the defendants just as in any other lawsuit. They may endeavor to impeach the reliability of the statistical evidence, they may offer rebutting evidence, or they may disparage in arguments or in briefs the probative weight which the plaintiffs' evidence should be accorded. Since I agree with the Court that appellants made virtually no such effort, I also agree with it that the District Court cannot be said to have erred as a matter of law in finding that a prima facie case had been made out in the instant case.

While the District Court's conclusion is by no means required by the proffered evidence, I am unable to conclude that the District Court's finding in that respect was clearly erroneous. In other cases there could be different evidence which could lead a district court to conclude that height and weight are in fact an accurate enough predictor of strength to justify, under all the circumstances, such minima. Should the height and weight requirements be found to advance the job-related qualification of strength sufficiently to rebut the prima facie case, then, under our cases, the burden would shift back to appellee Rawlinson to demonstrate that other tests, without such disparate effect, would also meet that concern. Albemarle Paper Co. v. Moody, 422 U.S. 405, 425 (1975). But, here, the

District Court permissibly concluded that appellants had not shown enough of a nexus even to rebut the inference.

Appellants, in order to rebut the prima facie case under the statute, had the burden placed on them to advance job-related reasons for the qualification. McDonnell Douglas Corp. v. Green, 411 U.S. 792, 802 (1973). This burden could be shouldered by offering evidence or by making legal arguments not dependent on any new evidence. The District Court was confronted, however, with only one suggested job-related reason for the qualification—that of strength. Appellants argued only the job-relatedness of actual physical strength; they did not urge that an equally job-related qualification for prison guards is the appearance of strength. As the Court notes, the primary job of correctional counselor in Alabama prisons "is to maintain security and control of the inmates . . .", a function that I at least would imagine is aided by the psychological impact on prisoners of the presence of tall and heavy guards. If the appearance of strength had been urged upon the District Court here as a reason for the height and weight minima, I think that the District Court would surely have been entitled to reach a different result than it did. For, even if not perfectly correlated, I would think that Title VII would not preclude a State from saying that anyone under 5′2″ or 120 pounds, no matter how strong in fact, does not have a sufficient appearance of strength to be a prison guard.

But once the burden has been placed on the defendant, it is then up to the defendant to articulate the asserted job-related reasons underlying the use of the minima. McDonnell Douglas Corp. v. Green, supra, at 802; Griggs v. Duke Power Co., 401 U.S. 424, 431 (1971); Albemarle Paper Co. v. Moody, supra, at 425. Because of this burden, a reviewing court is not ordinarily justified in relying on arguments in favor of a job qualification that were not first presented to the trial court. . . . As appellants did not even present the "appearance of strength" contention to the District Court as an asserted job-related reason for the qualification requirements, I agree that their burden was not met. The District Court's holding thus did not deal with the question of whether such an assertion could or did rebut appellee Rawlinson's prima facie case.

[JUSTICE MARSHALL, joined by JUSTICE BRENNAN, dissented on the application of the bona fide occupational qualification to contact positions.]

■ JUSTICE WHITE, dissenting.

. . . I have more trouble agreeing that a prima facie case of sex discrimination was made out by statistics showing that the Alabama height and weight requirements would exclude a larger percentage of women in the United States than of men. As in *Hazelwood*, the issue is whether there was discrimination in dealing with actual or potential applicants; but in *Hazelwood* there was at least a colorable argument that the racial composition of the areawide teacher work force was a reasonable proxy for the composition of the relevant applicant pool and hence that a large divergence between the percentage of blacks on the teaching staff and the percentage in the teacher work force raised a fair inference of racial discrimination in dealing with the applicant pool. In *Dothard*, however, I am unwilling to believe that the percentage of women applying or interested in applying for jobs as prison guards in Alabama approximates the percentage of women either in the national or state population. A plaintiff could, of course, show that the composition of the applicant pool was distorted by the exclusion of nonapplicants who did not apply because of the allegedly discriminatory job requirement. But no such showing was made or even attempted here; and although I do not know what the actual fact is, I am not now convinced that a large percentage of the actual women applicants, or of those who are seriously interested in applying, for prison guard positions would fail to satisfy the height and weight requirements. Without a more satisfactory record on this issue, I cannot conclude that appellee Rawlinson has either made out a prima facie case for the invalidity of the restrictions or otherwise proved that she was improperly denied employment as a prison guard. There being no showing of discrimination, I do not reach the question of justification; nor, since she does not meet the threshold requirements for becoming a prison guard, need I deal with the gender-based requirements for contact positions. I dissent from the Court's judgment in *Dothard* insofar as it affirms the judgment of the District Court.

NOTES ON *DOTHARD V. RAWLINSON*

1. **Nature of the Claims.** *Dothard v. Rawlinson* involved claims both of disparate treatment and disparate impact, the first concerned with the explicit exclusion of women from certain jobs, "contact positions," in prisons for men, and the second concerned with height and weight requirements that all applicants, both male and female, had to meet. The first claim, of disparate treatment, is considered in Chapter 5, on sex discrimination. The second claim, of disparate impact, is the subject of the preceding excerpt from the opinion. Ironically enough, the Supreme Court denied the first claim, upholding the explicit exclusion of women from contact positions, but agreed with the second claim, striking down the neutral height and weight requirements.

Nevertheless, the simple relationship between these two parts of the opinion reveals what the plaintiff must prove in order to establish disparate impact. It is, first of all, less than proving intentional discrimination. The plaintiff need not show that the neutral height and weight requirements were a subterfuge for the intentional exclusion of women. The two claims could be treated, as they were in this case, entirely independently of one another. Second, it follows that statistical evidence of disparate impact need not establish so large a disparity that it also proves intentional discrimination. Otherwise, the difference between the two theories of liability would collapse. Plaintiffs would gain nothing by asserting claims of disparate impact if they had to bear the same burden of proof as for claims of disparate treatment. The statistical methods used to evaluate the plaintiff's evidence remain the same for both types of claims, but the result of the statistical analysis does not.

2. Statistical Evidence of Disparate Impact. *Dothard* was decided together with *Hazelwood*. The different results in these cases, the first finding disparate impact and imposing liability upon the defendant, and the second remanding the case for further analysis of the statistical evidence of disparate treatment, supports the difference between these two theories of liability. The Supreme Court could more easily find disparate impact than disparate treatment because the plaintiff's burden of proving disparate impact is less. Yet, as Justice White's dissenting opinion reveals, the methods of analyzing the statistical evidence are the same for both types of claims. In fact, he wrote only a single dissent applicable to both cases.

The analysis of statistical methods follows the same three-step process discussed in the notes following *Hazelwood*. First, the composition of the relevant labor market must be ascertained; second, the composition of the relevant segment of the employer's work force must be determined; and third, any resulting difference between these figures must be analyzed for statistical and practical significance. Judged by these standards, the statistical evidence in *Dothard* suffers from several weaknesses, the most serious of which concerns the use of general population figures.

The Court relied on these figures to determine the proportion of women screened out by application of the height and weight requirements. Yet, as Justice White pointed out, these figures give only the roughest approximation to the proportion of women interested in becoming prison guards. Is it obvious that women are as interested in this job as men? Is there anything in Title VII that requires the assumption that they are? Would it be sexist to assume otherwise? Even if women are as interested as men, does it follow that women who have an interest in the job would have the same overall distribution of height and weight as women in general? Justice White argued that the answers to these questions could be determined only by looking at applicant flow statistics. Do the criticisms of these statistics, made in *Hazelwood*, that they might reflect the effects of the employer's reputation for discrimination, also apply in *Dothard*? Does it make any difference that the employer in this case did not offer any statistical evidence of its own, including applicant flow statistics?

The Court overlooked the defects in the plaintiffs' statistical evidence partly because it revealed such a large disparity in the rate at which women and men were disqualified by the height and weight requirements. Almost half of working age women were excluded by these requirements, but almost no men were excluded. Does this disparity in results make up for defects in method? Perhaps it suggests that the requirements were tailored to the characteristics of men? Are height and weight requirements too closely tied to stereotypes that women are not generally suited for employment outside the home? As in *Griggs* and *Albemarle Paper*, background evidence of intentional discrimination might make up for other defects in the plaintiff's case. If so, does it make claims of disparate impact more dependent on evidence of disparate treatment than they at first appear to be?

3. **The Employer's Evidence of Business Necessity and Job Relationship.** Just as the employer presented no statistical evidence on the issue of disparate impact, it also presented hardly any on the issue of business necessity and job relationship. The employer's evidence was confined to testimony that the height and weight requirements were adopted as a proxy for strength. Is this relationship so implausible that the Court should have dismissed it out of hand? What about Justice Rehnquist's suggestion that height and weight are not a proxy for strength but for the appearance of strength? Is this any more plausible? How would the employer have established that either of these characteristics, strength or the appearance of strength, was related to the position of prison guard?

The very weakness of the employer's evidence on this issue was fatal to its case after the Court found disparate impact. The employer had the burden of proof on business necessity and job relationship and simply failed to present any evidence. Did the absence of evidence on this issue also undermine the defendant's arguments on the issue of disparate impact? Although analytically distinct, the issue of business necessity and job relationship is one component, along with disparate impact, in finding that Title VII has been violated. Doesn't it make it easier for a court to find a violation of Title VII if the defendant offers essentially no justification for the employment practice in dispute?

4. **Proof of Disparate Impact Under the Uniform Guidelines.** The Uniform Guidelines take a simplified approach to proof of disparate impact, reducing each of the three steps in the analysis of statistical evidence from *Hazelwood* to simpler elements. The composition of the labor market is reduced to an analysis of applicant flow statistics. The relevant figures from the employer's work force are the "bottom line" rates at which members of different groups are hired. And the appropriate comparison is according to the "4/5ths rule," resulting in a finding of disparate impact if the plaintiff's group is hired at a rate less than four-fifths of the rate of the most favored group, typically white males. Section 1607.4D acknowledges the need to depart from the "4/5ths rule" when it yields results that are not statistically significant or, conversely, where it neglects statistically significant disparities. Departures from the "bottom line" rule also are recognized, in particular, for tests or qualifications that have previously been found to violate Title VII. For a discussion of the limitations of the 4/5ths rule, see Philip L. Ruth, Philip Bobko & Fred S. Switzer, Jr., Modeling the Behavior of the 4/5ths Rule for Determining Adverse Impact: Reasons for Caution, 91 J. App. Psych. 507 (2006).

These elements all appear in § 1607.4 of the Uniform Guidelines, excerpted from the guidelines earlier in this chapter. As discussed in the notes following this excerpt, these elements are not framed as part of the plaintiff's burden of proof, but as the kind of evidence that employers should maintain on the issue of disparate impact. In this respect, the guidelines offer statements of enforcement policy rather than an interpretation of the substantive requirements of Title VII. This approach appears more explicitly in § 1607.4E, which provides that "[i]n carrying out their obligations, the Federal enforcement agencies will consider the general posture of the user with respect to equal employment opportunity for the job or group of jobs in question." The officially stated purpose of the guidelines is to advise potential defendants of the steps to take to avoid enforcement actions by the EEOC.

Is it realistic to believe that the Uniform Guidelines would be limited to this purpose? Just as they give guidance to employers, don't they also offer guidance to the courts? Just as with the provisions on validation, don't those on disparate impact aspire to some influence on judicial decisions? Otherwise, wouldn't the EEOC and the other federal enforcement agencies be putting themselves in the position of bringing cases they couldn't win?

5. ***Connecticut v. Teal.*** The Supreme Court considered a departure from the "bottom line" rule of the guidelines in Connecticut v. Teal, 457 U.S. 440 (1982). That case concerned a written promotion test with an adverse impact upon black employees. Several of the black employees who failed the test then sued, alleging liability under the theory of disparate impact. The employer then belatedly instituted an affirmative action plan that eliminated the adverse impact of the test by granting a preference to black employees who passed it, resulting in a higher proportion of blacks among those receiving promotions than among those who took the test. The employer relied on the argument that, under the Uniform Guidelines, the "bottom line" promotion rate for blacks showed no disparate impact. The Supreme Court, however, limited the guidelines to their purported effect of controlling enforcement discretion rather than determining any "underlying question of law."

That question led the Court to the main prohibitions in Title VII and, in particular, to § 703(a)(2) and its prohibition against depriving "any individual of employment opportunities." The Court emphasized both the protection of "any individual," presumably referring to the black applicants who failed the test, and the protection of their "employment opportunities," presumably their opportunity to be further considered in the hiring process. On the first point, does the Court's reasoning also extend to white applicants who failed the test? If so, what about the fact that whites as a whole suffered no adverse impact from the test? On the second point, are the plaintiffs' remedies limited simply to an injunction against future use of the test and further consideration of their applications in the hiring process? Do they have any further right to compensatory relief?

6. **The Role of Affirmative Action.** The whole "bottom line" issue arose in *Connecticut v. Teal* because the employer instituted an affirmative action plan after the test was challenged under the theory of disparate impact. Does the late adoption of this plan undermine the employer's claim that it was providing equal opportunities to all applicants for employment? Would a plan adopted earlier, when the test was first used, make any difference under the Court's reasoning?

After *Connecticut v. Teal*, employers plainly have less incentive to adopt affirmative action plans since they no longer can avoid liability under the theory of disparate impact by this means. Can they, however, avoid being sued for this reason? The EEOC seems to think so. Recall the provision in the Uniform Guidelines in § 1607.4E, allowing "the general posture of the user with respect to equal employment opportunity" to be taken into account by the EEOC in making enforcement decisions. Would the same factors weigh as heavily with private plaintiffs? Would an attorney be as likely to advise a private individual to sue if the figures on the employer's overall work force did not reveal any disparate impact? Recall that in *Furnco Construction Co. v. Waters*, discussed in Chapter 2, the plaintiff lost an individual claim of disparate treatment because the employer engaged in a form of belated affirmative action not too different from that in *Connecticut v. Teal*.

Given the controversy over affirmative action, should it carry over into debates over the theory of disparate impact? Was the Court wise to avoid making affirmative action the equivalent of an absolute defense to claims of disparate impact? Or did affirmative action contribute to *Connecticut v. Teal* only in leading the Court to adopt the rhetoric of individual opportunities rather than group rights? These issues were taken up by Congress when it reconsidered the theory of disparate impact in the Civil Rights Act of 1991. This legislation was preceded by the following case, in which the Supreme Court itself reconsidered the theory of disparate impact. Although the Court's decision was substantially modified by Congress, it is necessary to understand what the Court decided in order to understand what Congress did in rejecting parts of that decision and accepting others. The relevant parts of the opinion are excerpted below.

7. **Bibliography.** For articles on the kinds of physical qualifications at issue in *Dothard*, see Ruth Colker, Rank-Order Physical Abilities Selection Devices for Traditionally Male Occupations as Gender-Based Employment Discrimination, 19 U.C. Davis L. Rev. 761 (1986); Hannah A. Furnish, A Path Through the Maze: Disparate Impact and Disparate Treatment Under Title VII of the Civil Rights Act of 1964 After *Beazer* and *Burdine*, 23 B.C. L. Rev. 419 (1982).

For articles on the "bottom line" rule and its significance after *Connecticut v. Teal*, see Alfred W. Blumrosen, The "Bottom Line" After *Connecticut v. Teal*, 8(4) Employee Rel. L.J., 572; Martha Chamallas, Evolving Conceptions of Equality Under Title VII: Disparate Impact Theory and the Demise of the Bottom Line Principle, 31 UCLA L. Rev. 305 (1983).

Wards Cove Packing Co. v. Atonio

490 U.S. 642 (1989).

■ JUSTICE WHITE delivered the opinion of the Court.

[This case involved claims of disparate impact against canneries that operated in the summer in remote locations in Alaska. The jobs at the canneries were divided into two general types: "cannery jobs" on the cannery line, which were unskilled; and "noncannery jobs," which included a variety of positions most of which were skilled. The cannery jobs were filled predominantly by nonwhites, Filipinos hired through a union or Native Alaskans hired in nearby villages, while the noncannery jobs were filled predominantly by whites hired in the off-season at the companies' offices in Washington and Oregon. Almost all the cannery jobs paid less than the noncannery jobs. This case was brought by nonwhites working in cannery jobs who alleged, among other things, that they had been discriminatorily denied positions as noncannery workers. The plaintiffs (respondents) lost in the district court and before a panel of the Ninth Circuit, but prevailed before the Ninth Circuit sitting en banc on their claims of disparate impact. That court held that they could assert claims of disparate impact based on subjective hiring practices, and on remand, a panel of the Ninth Circuit held that they had made out a prima facie case of disparate impact.]

II

In holding that respondents had made out a prima facie case of disparate impact, the Court of Appeals relied solely on respondents' statistics showing a high percentage of nonwhite workers in the cannery jobs and a low percentage of such workers in the noncannery positions. Although statistical proof can alone make out a prima facie case, see Teamsters v. United States, 431 U.S. 324, 339 (1977); Hazelwood School Dist. v. United States, 433 U.S. 299, 307–308 (1977), the Court of Appeals' ruling here misapprehends our precedents and the purposes of Title VII, and we therefore reverse.

"There can be no doubt," as there was when a similar mistaken analysis had been undertaken by the courts below in *Hazelwood*, supra at 308, "that the . . . comparison . . . fundamentally misconceived the role of statistics in employment discrimination cases." The "proper comparison [is] between the racial composition of [the at-issue jobs] and the racial composition of the qualified . . . population in the relevant labor market." It is such a comparison—between the racial composition of the qualified persons in the labor market and the persons holding at-issue jobs—that generally forms the proper basis for the initial inquiry in a disparate-impact case. Alternatively, in cases where such labor market statistics will be difficult if not impossible to ascertain, we have recognized that certain other statistics—such as measures indicating the racial composition of "otherwise-qualified applicants" for at-issue jobs—are equally probative for this purpose. See, e.g., New York City Transit Authority v. Beazer, 440 U.S. 568, 585 (1979).

It is clear to us that the Court of Appeals' acceptance of the comparison between the racial composition of the cannery work force and that of the noncannery work force, as probative of a prima facie case of disparate impact in the selection of the latter group of workers, was flawed for several reasons. Most obviously, with respect to the skilled noncannery jobs at issue here, the cannery work force in no way reflected "the pool of qualified job applicants" or the "qualified population in the labor force." Measuring alleged discrimination in the selection of accountants, managers, boat captains, electricians, doctors, and engineers—and the long list of other "skilled" noncannery positions found to exist by the District Court—by comparing the number of nonwhites occupying these jobs to the number of nonwhites filling cannery worker positions is nonsensical. If the absence of minorities holding such skilled positions is due to a dearth of qualified nonwhite applicants (for reasons that are not petitioners' fault), petitioners' selection methods or employment practices cannot be said to have had a "disparate impact" on nonwhites.

One example illustrates why this must be so. Respondents' own statistics concerning the noncannery work force at one of the canneries at issue here indicate that approximately 17% of the new hires for medical jobs, and 15% of the new hires for officer worker positions, were nonwhite. If it were the case that less than 15 to 17% of these jobs were nonwhite and that nonwhites made up a lower percentage of the relevant qualified labor market, it is hard to see how respondents, without more, cf. Connecticut v. Teal, 457 U.S. 440 (1982), would have made out a prima facie case of disparate impact. Yet, under the Court of Appeals' theory, simply because nonwhites comprise 52% of the cannery workers at the cannery in question, respondents would be successful in establishing a prima facie case of racial discrimination under Title VII.

Such a result cannot be squared with our cases or with the goals behind the statute. The Court of Appeals' theory, at the very least, would mean that any employer who had a segment of his work force that was—for some reason—racially imbalanced, could be haled into court and forced to engage in the expensive and time-consuming task of defending the "business necessity" of the methods used to select the other members of his work force. The only practicable option for many employers would be to adopt racial quotas, insuring that no portion of their work forces deviated in racial composition from the other portions thereof; this is a result that Congress expressly rejected in drafting Title VII. . . . The Court of Appeals' theory would "leave the employer little choice . . . but to engage in a subjective quota system of employment selection. This, of course, is far from the intent of Title VII." Albemarle Paper Co. v. Moody, 422 U.S. 405, 449 (1975) (BLACKMUN, J., concurring in judgment).

The Court of Appeals also erred with respect to the unskilled noncannery positions. Racial imbalance in one segment of an employer's work force does not, without more, establish a prima facie case of disparate impact with respect to the selection of workers for the employer's other positions, even where workers for the different positions may have somewhat fungible skills (as is arguably the case for cannery and unskilled noncannery workers). As long as there are no barriers or practices deterring qualified nonwhites from applying for noncannery positions, if the percentage of selected applicants who are nonwhite is not significantly less than the percentage of qualified applicants who are nonwhite, the employer's selection mechanism probably does not operate with a disparate impact on minorities. Where this is the case, the percentage of nonwhite workers found in other positions in the employer's labor force is irrelevant to the question of a prima facie statistical case of disparate impact. As noted above, a contrary ruling on this point would almost inexorably lead to the use of numerical quotas in the workplace, a result that Congress and this Court have rejected repeatedly in the past.

Moreover, isolating the cannery workers as the potential "labor force" for unskilled noncannery positions is at once both too broad and too narrow in its focus. It is too broad because the vast majority of these cannery workers did not seek jobs in unskilled noncannery positions; there is no showing that many of them would have done so even if none of the arguably "deterring" practices existed. Thus, the pool of cannery workers cannot be used as a surrogate for the class of qualified job applicants because it contains many persons who have not (and would not) be noncannery job applicants. Conversely, if respondents propose to use the cannery workers for comparison purposes because they represent the "qualified labor population" generally, the group is too narrow because there are obviously many qualified persons in the labor market for noncannery jobs who are not cannery workers.

The peculiar facts of this case further illustrate why a comparison between the percentage of nonwhite cannery workers and nonwhite noncannnery workers is an improper basis for making out a claim of disparate impact. Here, the District Court found that nonwhites were "overrepresent[ed]" among cannery workers because petitioners had contracted with a predominantly nonwhite union (Local 37) to fill these positions. . . . As a result, if petitioners (for some permissible reason) ceased using Local 37 as its hiring channel for cannery positions, it appears that the racial stratification between the cannery and noncannery workers might diminish to statistical insignificance. Under the Court of Appeals' approach, therefore, it is possible that with no change whatsoever in their hiring practices for noncannery workers—the jobs at issue in this lawsuit—petitioners could make respondents' prima facie case of disparate impact "disappear." But if there would be no prima facie case of disparate impact in the selection of noncannery workers absent petitioners' use of Local 37 to hire cannery workers, surely petitioners' reliance on the union to fill the cannery jobs not at issue here (and its resulting "overrepresentation" of nonwhites in those positions) does not—standing alone—make out a prima facie case of disparate impact. Yet it is precisely such an ironic result that the Court of Appeals reached below.

Consequently, we reverse the Court of Appeals' ruling that a comparison between the percentage of cannery workers who are nonwhite and the percentage of noncannery workers who are nonwhite makes out a prima facie case of disparate impact. Of course, this leaves unresolved whether the record made in the District Court will support a conclusion that a prima facie case of disparate impact has been established on some basis other than the racial disparity between cannery and noncannery workers. This is an issue that the Court of Appeals or the District Court should address in the first instance.

III

[The Court then instructed the lower courts on how to analyze the issue of disparate impact upon remand, identifying two specific questions to address.]

A

First is the question of causation in a disparate-impact case. The law in this respect was correctly stated by Justice O'Connor's opinion last Term in Watson v. Fort Worth Bank & Trust, 487 U.S., at 994:

> "[W]e note that the plaintiff's burden in establishing a prima facie case goes beyond the need to show that there are statistical disparities in the employer's work force. The plaintiff must begin by identifying the specific employment practice that is challenged. . . . Especially in cases where an employer combines subjective criteria with the use of more rigid standardized rules or tests, the plaintiff is in our view responsible for isolating and identifying the specific employment practices that are allegedly responsible for any observed statistical disparities."

Cf. also id. at 1000 (Blackmun, J., concurring in part and concurring in judgment).

Indeed, even the Court of Appeals—whose decision petitioners assault on this score—noted that "it is . . . essential that the practices identified by the cannery workers be linked causally with the demonstrated adverse impact." Notwithstanding the Court of Appeals' apparent adherence to the proper inquiry, petitioners contend that that court erred by permitting respondents to make out their case by offering "only [one] set of cumulative comparative statistics as evidence of the disparate impact of each and all of [petitioners' hiring] practices."

Our disparate-impact cases have always focused on the impact of particular hiring practices on employment opportunities for minorities. Just as an employer cannot escape liability under Title VII by demonstrating that, "at the bottom line," his work force is racially balanced (where particular hiring practices may operate to deprive minorities of employment opportunities), see Connecticut v. Teal, 457 U.S., at 450, a Title VII plaintiff does not make out a case of disparate impact simply by showing that, "at the bottom line," there is racial imbalance in the work force. As a general matter, a plaintiff must demonstrate that it is the application of a specific or particular employment practice that has created the disparate impact under attack. Such a showing is an integral part of the plaintiff's prima facie case in a disparate-impact suit under Title VII. . . .

Some will complain that this specific causation requirement is unduly burdensome on Title VII plaintiffs. But liberal civil discovery rules give plaintiffs broad access to employers' records in an effort to document their claims. Also, employers falling within the scope of the Uniform Guidelines on Employee Selection Procedures, 29 CFR § 1607.1 et seq. (1988), are required to "maintain . . . records or other information which will disclose the impact which its tests and other selection procedures have upon employment opportunities of persons by identifiable race, sex, or ethnic group[s]." See § 1607.4(A). This includes records concerning "the individual components of the selection process" where there is a significant disparity in the selection rates of whites and nonwhites. See § 1607.4(C). Plaintiffs as a general matter will have the benefit of these tools to meet their burden of showing a causal link between challenged employment practices and racial imbalances in the work force; respondents presumably took full advantage of these opportunities to build their case before the trial in the District Court was held.

Consequently, on remand, the courts below are instructed to require, as part of respondents' prima facie case, a demonstration that specific elements of the petitioners' hiring process have a significantly disparate impact on nonwhites.

B

If, on remand, respondents meet the proof burdens outlined above, and establish a prima facie case of disparate impact with respect to any of petitioners' employment practices, the case will shift to any business justification petitioners offer for their use of these practices. This phase of the disparate-impact case contains two components: first, a consideration of the justifications an employer offers for his use of these practices; and second, the availability of alternative practices to achieve the same business ends, with less racial impact. See, e.g., Albemarle Paper Co. v. Moody, 422 U.S., at 425. We consider these two components in turn.

(1)

Though we have phrased the query differently in different cases, it is generally well established that at the justification stage of such a disparate-impact case, the dispositive issue is whether a challenged practice serves, in a significant way, the legitimate employment goals of the employer. . . . The touchstone of this inquiry is a reasoned review of the employer's justification for his use of the challenged practice. A mere insubstantial justification in this regard will not suffice, because such a low standard of review would permit discrimination to be practiced through the use of spurious, seemingly neutral employment practices. At the same time, though, there is no requirement that the challenged practice be "essential" or "indispensable" to the employer's business for it to pass muster: this degree of scrutiny would be almost impossible for most employers to meet, and would result in a host of evils we have identified above.

In this phase, the employer carries the burden of producing evidence of a business justification for his employment practice. The burden of persuasion, however, remains with the disparate-impact plaintiff. To the extent that the Ninth Circuit held otherwise in its en banc decision in this case, or in the panel's decision on remand—suggesting that the persuasion burden should shift to petitioners once respondents established a prima facie case of disparate impact—its decisions were erroneous. "The ultimate burden of proving that discrimination against a protected group has been caused by a specific employment practice remains with the plaintiff *at all times*." *Watson*, supra, at 997 (O'Connor, J.) (emphasis added). This rule conforms with the usual method for allocating persuasion and production burdens in the federal courts, see Fed. Rule Evid. 301, and more specifically, it conforms to the rule in disparate-treatment cases that the plaintiff bears the burden of disproving an employer's assertion that the adverse employment action or practice was based solely on a legitimate neutral consideration. See Texas Dept. of Community Affairs v. Burdine, 450 U.S. 248, 256–258 (1981). We acknowledge that some of our earlier decisions can be read as suggesting otherwise. See *Watson*, supra, 487 U.S., at 1006–1008 (Blackmun, J., concurring). But to the extent that those cases speak of an employer's "burden of proof" with respect to a legitimate business justification defense, see, e.g., Dothard v. Rawlinson, 433 U.S. 321, 329 (1977), they should have been understood to mean an employer's production—but not persuasion—burden. Cf., e.g., NLRB v. Transportation Management Corp., 462 U.S. 393, 404, n.7 (1983). The persuasion burden here must remain with the plaintiff, for it is he who must prove that it was "because of such individual's race, color," etc., that he was denied a desired employment opportunity. See 42 U.S.C. § 2000e–2(a).

(2)

Finally, if on remand the case reaches this point, and respondents cannot persuade the trier of fact on the question of petitioners' business necessity defense, respondents may still be able to prevail. To do so, respondents will have to persuade the factfinder that "other tests or selection devices, without a similarly undesirable racial effect, would also serve the employer's legitimate [hiring] interest[s]"; by so demonstrating, respondents would prove that "[petitioners were] using [their] tests merely as a 'pretext' for discrimination." *Albemarle Paper Co.*, supra, at 425; see also *Watson*, 487 U.S., at 998 (O'CONNOR, J.); id. at 1005–1006 (Blackmun, J., concurring in part and concurring in judgment). If respondents, having established a prima facie case, come forward with alternatives to petitioners' hiring practices that reduce the racially disparate impact of practices currently being used, and petitioners refuse to adopt these alternatives, such a refusal would belie a claim by petitioners that their incumbent practices are being employed for nondiscriminatory reasons.

Of course, any alternative practices which respondents offer up in this respect must be equally effective as petitioners' chosen hiring procedures in achieving petitioners' legitimate employment goals. Moreover, "factors such as the cost or other burdens of proposed alternative selection devices are relevant in determining whether they would be equally as effective as the challenged practice in serving the employer's legitimate business goals." *Watson*, supra, at 998 (O'Connor, J.). "Courts are generally less competent than employers to restructure business practices," Furnco Construction Corp. v. Waters, 438 U.S. 567, 578 (1978); consequently, the judiciary should proceed with care before mandating that an employer must adopt a plaintiff's alternative selection or hiring practice in response to a Title VII suit. . . .

[The dissenting opinions of Justice Stevens and Justice Blackmun are omitted.]

NOTES ON *WARDS COVE* AND THE CIVIL RIGHTS ACT OF 1991

1. **The Different Holdings in *Wards Cove*.** All three stages in the proof of claims of disparate impact were addressed in *Wards Cove*: the plaintiff's burden of proving adverse impact; the defendant's burden of proving business necessity and job relationship; and the plaintiff's final burden of proving pretext. All three of these stages were also addressed by Congress when it reacted to *Wards Cove* by codifying the theory of disparate impact in the Civil Rights Act of 1991. In doing so, Congress said that it was rejecting the decision in *Wards Cove*, but this is true only with respect to some of the Court's holdings and not others. Congress largely accepted the holding on adverse impact, elaborating upon it in some detail, and Congress clearly rejected only the holding on business necessity and job relationship. Congress did not approve of the holding on pretext, but neither did it make any obvious change in the law. Each of the holdings in *Wards Cove* and each of the provisions of the Civil Rights Act of 1991 addressed to these holdings must be considered separately.

2. **Proof of Disparate Impact.** The Court held that the plaintiffs could not establish disparate impact simply by proving that most minority workers were employed in cannery jobs and few in the better-paying noncannery jobs. The plaintiffs, instead, had to identify a particular hiring practice that resulted in this disparity. Does this holding simply follow from *Connecticut v. Teal*? That case held that the *plaintiff* could choose to attack a particular selection device rather than the entire selection process. This case holds that the *defendant* can insist on the same degree of particularity. Must both parties begin with exactly the same power to choose how to frame the issue of disparate impact? Or is the holding in *Wards Cove* that neither party has any choice in the matter?

Wholly apart from the failure to identify a specific employment practice with disparate impact, the plaintiffs' evidence in *Wards Cove* appears to be defective for a more basic reason: it assumes that the appropriate labor market for noncannery jobs, from which minorities allegedly were excluded, was the same as the market for cannery jobs, in which they were overrepresented. Was there any basis for this assumption? Are the two kinds of jobs sufficiently similar that the labor market for one should be taken to be the labor market for the other? If this assumption is false, doesn't this holding in *Wards Cove* follow directly from the holding in *Hazelwood* on the proper definition of the labor market?

Whatever the larger problems with the plaintiffs' evidence, Congress took the holding in *Wards Cove* to be concerned with specificity and required the plaintiff to "demonstrate that each particular challenged employment practice causes a disparate impact." § 703(k)(1)(B)(i). The only exception to this requirement was for cases in which the elements of a defendant's decision-making process could not be analyzed separately. If the plaintiff could prove this fact, then the entire process could be treated as a single employment practice. Do all these requirements put too great a burden of proof upon the plaintiff: either to identify a specific employment practice, or to prove that one cannot be identified, and then to establish a causal connection between the relevant practice and the disparate impact in the employer's work force? Recall that these burdens come in addition to those required by *Hazelwood* for the proper definition of the labor market and the analysis of statistical evidence generally. Do all these complications deter plaintiffs from bringing claims of disparate impact, effectively insulating employers from justifying disputed employment practices?

3. The Defendant's Burden of Proving Business Necessity and Job Relationship. *Wards Cove* did not define the defendant's burden of proof in terms of business necessity and job relationship. In fact, it took pains to avoid this terminology from earlier cases such as *Griggs*, requiring only "a reasoned review of the employer's justification for his use of the challenged practice." *Wards Cove* also relieved the defendant of the burden of persuasion on this issue, imposing only the burden of production: the burden only of submitting evidence from which a reasonable inference could be drawn in its favor. In both respects, *Wards Cove* followed a plurality of opinion for four justices in an earlier case, Watson v. Fort Worth Bank & Trust, 487 U.S. 977 (1988) (opinion of O'Connor, J.). Since the Supreme Court was evenly divided, four-to-four on this issue in *Watson*, this holding first became law in *Wards Cove*. It did not, however, last long.

A stated purpose of the Civil Rights Act of 1991 was to turn the clock back on this issue to where it was just before *Wards Cove* was decided. Pub. L. No. 102–166, §§ 2(2), 3(2), 105 Stat. 1071 (1991). In particular, Congress returned to the terminology of business necessity and job relationship, requiring the defendant to "demonstrate that the challenged practice is job related for the position in question and consistent with business necessity." § 703(k)(1)(A)(i). Congress also specifically defined "demonstrate" to mean "meets the burden of production and persuasion." § 701(m). Because the issue of the defendant's burden of proof was so controversial, Congress also took the unusual step of defining, by statute, the parts of the legislative history that were relevant to this issue. Pub. L. No. 102–166, §§ 3(2), 105(b), 105 Stat. 1071, 1075 (1991) (referring to an interpretive memorandum that appears at 137 Cong. Rec. S15,276 (daily ed. Oct. 25, 1991), 137 Cong. Rec.

28,623 (permanent ed. 1991)). All of these statutory provisions appear in the Statutory Appendix.

What prompted Congress to take such unusual steps? The predecessor of the Civil Rights Act of 1991, a bill that was vetoed by the first President Bush, was denounced by its opponents as a "quota bill." In what way does codification of the theory of disparate impact involve quotas? Is it because both focus upon the effects of employment practices rather than on discriminatory intent? Or is it because the only practical way for employers to avoid liability under the theory of disparate impact is to engage in affirmative action? Recall that the holding in *Connecticut v. Teal* severed any logical connection between the use of affirmative action plans and rebuttal of claims of disparate impact. This holding, as we have seen, was expanded in *Wards Cove* and then endorsed by Congress in the Civil Rights Act of 1991. Do these developments, concerned with the plaintiff's burden of proof, blunt any charge that the theory of disparate impact promotes affirmative action through the burden of proof that it places on the defendant?

Do the decisions before *Wards Cove* support the need for some additional evidence of discrimination? Those decisions were ambiguous between placing a heavy burden of proof upon the defendant, through the use of the term "business necessity," and placing a light burden upon the defendant, using the language of "job relationship." The Civil Rights Act of 1991 perpetuates this ambiguity by using both terms. The defendant must show "that the challenged practice is job related for the position in question and consistent with business necessity." This provision, along with the authorized legislative history, leaves open exactly how strong the showing of job relationship must be. The term "business necessity," which suggests the need to demonstrate a strong relationship, loses much of its force when considered in context. The challenged practice need only be "consistent with" business necessity—not required by it; the defendant only needs to show that the challenged practice can coexist with the continued operation of the business. The cases that used the term "business necessity" seemed to have the opposite kind of requirement in mind—that the challenged practice is essential to the continued operation of the business. Does a reliance on the exact words that Congress used read too much into this provision? Or does it read too little? Should the previous decisions, before *Wards Cove*, be dispositive on this issue or should the language that Congress has enacted? Is either source of law capable of resolving all of the questions raised by the theory of disparate impact?

4. **The Plaintiff's Burden of Proving Pretext.** On this issue as well, Congress sought to overrule *Wards Cove* and turn the clock back to the law as it existed before that decision. It is not clear, however, that Congress succeeded in doing so, or indeed, whether anything significant was at stake. *Wards Cove* held that in consideration of this case on remand, if the defendants carried their burden of proof, then the plaintiffs could still prevail by proving that an alternative employment practice, with a reduced adverse impact, could have been used instead. Quoting *Albemarle Paper*, the Court held that such evidence would be sufficient to show pretext, adding only that

the courts should defer to the employer's judgment about the effectiveness of different employment practices.

In codifying the theory of disparate impact, Congress meant to reject the latter suggestion, returning to the law as stated in *Albemarle Paper*. But *Albemarle Paper* did not say much at all about proof of pretext and few other decisions do either, since virtually all disparate impact cases are resolved at either of the previous two stages of proof. The only study to have searched for cases resolved on the issue of pretext found only a single one on which this issue was dispositive. Michael Rothschild & Gregory J. Werden, Title VII and the Use of Employment Tests: An Illustration of the Limits of the Judicial Process, 11 J. Leg. Stud. 261, 273 & n.44 (1982). The detailed provisions on proof of pretext, now found in § 703(k)(1)(C), seem to apply in hardly any cases at all.

The only question raised by these provisions, and by this stage of proof in disparate impact cases, is entirely theoretical: Does proof of pretext in this context differ at all from proof of pretext in claims of intentional discrimination? If it does, then what could the differences be? And if it doesn't, what does this tell us about the relationship between claims of disparate impact and disparate treatment? At some level, are they both aimed at the same goal, of uncovering hidden discrimination?

5. Consequences of the Civil Rights Act of 1991. Two scholars who examined the empirical evidence on the question whether the theory of disparate impact in effect requires affirmative action found no evidence that it did so. Ian Ayres & Peter Siegelman, The Q-Word as Red Herring: Why Disparate Impact Liability Does Not Induce Hiring Quotas, 74 Tex. L. Rev. 1485 (1996). For the assertion of the contrary position, see Paul Oyer & Scott Schaefer, Sorting, Quotas, and the Civil Rights Act of 1991: Who Hires When It's Hard to Fire?, 45 J. Law & Econ. 41 (2002). Another scholar has argued that the theory of disparate impact must be made available to white workers on the same terms as minority workers. Otherwise whites would be disfavored and the theory of disparate impact would itself amount to unconstitutional reverse discrimination. Charles A. Sullivan, The World Turned Upside Down?: Disparate Impact Claims by White Males, 98 Nw. U. L. Rev. 1505 (2004). If he is right, would claims of disparate impact always be available by members of some group, whether majority or minority, whenever an employment practice resulted in any significant imbalance in an employer's work force? Or does the theory of disparate impact have to be supplemented by some evidence that the group in question was likely to be the victim of discrimination? If it does, would that rebut any inference that it requires employers to engage in affirmative action or that it amounts to a form of affirmative action itself?

6. Bibliography. For other articles on *Wards Cove* and the Civil Rights Act of 1991, see Kingsley R. Browne, The Civil Rights Act of 1991: A "Quota Bill," A Codification of *Griggs*, a Partial Return to *Wards Cove*, or All of the Above?, 43 Case W. Res. L. Rev. 287 (1993); Paul Burstein & Mark Evan Edwards, The Impact of Employment Discrimination Litigation on Racial Disparity in Earnings: Evidence and Unresolved Issues, 28 Law & Soc'y Rev. 79 (1994); Steven R. Greenberger, A Productivity Approach to Disparate

Impact and the Civil Rights Act of 1991, 72 Or. L. Rev. 253 (1993); Ramona L. Paetzold & Steven L. Willborn, Deconstructing Disparate Impact: A View of the Model Through New Lenses, 74 N.C. L. Rev. 325 (1996); Elaine Shoben, Employee Recruitment by Design or Default: Uncertainty Under Title VII, 47 Ohio St. L.J. 891 (1986); Symposium, The Civil Rights Act of 1991, 54 La. L. Rev. 1459 (1994); Symposium, The Civil Rights Act of 1991: Theory and Practice, 68 Notre Dame L. Rev. 911 (1993); Symposium, The Civil Rights Act of 1991: Unraveling the Controversy, 45 Rutgers L. Rev. 887 (1993).

For recent articles on the theory of disparate impact, see Charles F. Abernathy, Legal Realism and the Failure of the "Effects" Test for Discrimination, 94 Geo. L.J. 267 (2006); Daniel A. Biddle & Patrick M. Nooren, Validity Generalization vs. Title VII: Can Employers Successfully Defend Tests Without Conducting Local Validation Studies?, 57 Lab. L.J. 216 (2006); Matthew E. Blakely, Title VII: Discriminatory Use of Test Scores Watchdog, Evolution of the Regulation over Employment Test Score Usage from 703(h) to 703(*l*), 44 Sw. L. Rev. 27 (2014); Susan D. Carle, A Social Movement History of Title VII Disparate Impact Analysis, 63 Fla. L. Rev. 251 (2011); Alan M. Goldstein & Shoshanah D. Epstein, Personality Testing in Employment: Useful Business Tool or Civil Rights Violation?, 24 Lab. L. 243 (2008); Melissa Hart, Disparate Impact Discrimination: The Limits of Litigation, the Possibilities for Internal Compliance, 33 J.C. & U.L. Rev. 547 (2007); Alexandra Harwin, Title VII Challenges to Employment Discrimination Against Minority Men with Criminal Records, 14 Berkeley J. Afr.-Am. L. & Pol'y 2 (2012); Tammy R. Pettinato, Employment Discrimination Against Ex-Offenders: the Promise and Limits of Title VII Disparate Impact Theory, 98 Marq. L. Rev. 831 (2014); Joseph A. Seiner, Plausibility and Disparate Impact, 64 Hastings L.J. 287 (2013); Lawrence Rosenthal, Saving Disparate Impact, 34 Cardozo L. Rev. 2157 (2013); Michael L. Selmi, Was the Disparate Impact Theory a Mistake?, 53 UCLA L. Rev. 701 (2006); Girardeau A. Spann, Disparate Impact, 98 Geo. L.J. 1133 (2010); Charles A. Sullivan, Disparate Impact: Looking Past the *Desert Palace* Mirage, 47 Wm. & Mary L. Rev. 911 (2005); Amy L. Wax, Disparate Impact Realism, 53 Wm. & Mary L. Rev. 621 (2011).

Ricci v. DeStefano

557 U.S. 557 (2009).

■ JUSTICE KENNEDY delivered the opinion of the Court.

In the fire department of New Haven, Connecticut—as in emergency-service agencies throughout the Nation—firefighters prize their promotion to and within the officer ranks. An agency's officers command respect within the department and in the whole community; and, of course, added responsibilities command increased salary and benefits. Aware of the intense competition for promotions, New Haven, like many cities, relies on objective examinations to identify the best qualified candidates.

In 2003, 118 New Haven firefighters took examinations to qualify for promotion to the rank of lieutenant or captain. Promotion examinations in New Haven (or City) were infrequent, so the stakes were high. The results would determine which firefighters would be considered for promotions during the next two years, and the order in which they would be considered. Many firefighters studied for months, at considerable personal and financial cost.

When the examination results showed that white candidates had outperformed minority candidates, the mayor and other local politicians opened a public debate that turned rancorous. Some firefighters argued the tests should be discarded because the results showed the tests to be discriminatory. They threatened a discrimination lawsuit if the City made promotions based on the tests. Other firefighters said the exams were neutral and fair. And they, in turn, threatened a discrimination lawsuit if the City, relying on the statistical racial disparity, ignored the test results and denied promotions to the candidates who had performed well. In the end the City took the side of those who protested the test results. It threw out the examinations.

Certain white and Hispanic firefighters who likely would have been promoted based on their good test performance sued the City and some of its officials. Theirs is the suit now before us. The suit alleges that, by discarding the test results, the City and the named officials discriminated against the plaintiffs based on their race, in violation of both Title VII of the Civil Rights Act of 1964, 78 Stat. 253, as amended, 42 U.S.C. § 2000e *et seq.*, and the Equal Protection Clause of the Fourteenth Amendment. The City and the officials defended their actions, arguing that if they had certified the results, they could have faced liability under Title VII for adopting a practice that had a disparate impact on the minority firefighters. The District Court granted summary judgment for the defendants, and the Court of Appeals affirmed.

We conclude that race-based action like the City's in this case is impermissible under Title VII unless the employer can demonstrate a strong basis in evidence that, had it not taken the action, it would have been liable under the disparate-impact statute. The respondents, we further determine, cannot meet that threshold standard. As a result, the City's action in discarding the tests was a violation of Title VII. In light of our ruling under the statutes, we need not reach the question whether respondents' actions may have violated the Equal Protection Clause.

I

This litigation comes to us after the parties' cross-motions for summary judgment . . . .

A

When the City of New Haven undertook to fill vacant lieutenant and captain positions in its fire department (Department), the promotion and hiring process was governed by the city charter, in addition to federal and state law. The charter establishes a merit system. That system requires the City to fill vacancies in the classified civil-service ranks with the most qualified individuals, as determined by job-related examinations. After each examination, the New Haven Civil Service Board (CSB) certifies a ranked list of applicants who passed the test. Under the charter's "rule of three," the relevant hiring authority must fill each vacancy by choosing one candidate from the top three scorers on the list. Certified promotional lists remain valid for two years.

The City's contract with the New Haven firefighters' union specifies additional requirements for the promotion process. Under the contract, applicants for lieutenant and captain positions were to be screened using written and oral examinations, with the written exam accounting for 60 percent and the oral exam 40 percent of an applicant's total score. To sit for the examinations, candidates for lieutenant needed 30 months' experience in the Department, a high-school diploma, and certain vocational training courses. Candidates for captain needed one year's service as a lieutenant in the Department, a high-school diploma, and certain vocational training courses.

After reviewing bids from various consultants, the City hired Industrial/Organizational Solutions, Inc. (IOS) to develop and administer the examinations, at a cost to the City of $100,000. IOS is an Illinois company that specializes in designing entry-level and promotional examinations for fire and police departments. In order to fit the examinations to the New Haven Department, IOS began the test-design process by performing job analyses to identify the tasks, knowledge, skills, and abilities that are essential for the lieutenant and captain positions. IOS representatives interviewed incumbent captains and lieutenants and their supervisors. They rode with and observed other on-duty officers. Using information from those interviews and ride-alongs, IOS wrote job-analysis questionnaires and administered them to most of the incumbent battalion chiefs, captains, and lieutenants in the Department. At every stage of the job analyses, IOS, by deliberate choice, oversampled minority firefighters to ensure that the results—which IOS would use to develop the examinations—a would not unintentionally favor white candidates.

With the job-analysis information in hand, IOS developed the written examinations to measure the candidates' job-related knowledge. For each test, IOS compiled a list of training manuals, Department procedures, and other materials to use as sources for the test questions. IOS presented the proposed sources to the New Haven fire chief and assistant fire chief for their approval. Then, using the approved sources, IOS drafted a multiple-choice test for each position. Each test had 100 questions, as required by CSB rules, and was written below a 10th-grade reading level. After IOS prepared the tests, the City opened a 3-month study period. It gave candidates a list that identified the source material for the questions, including the specific chapters from which the questions were taken.

IOS developed the oral examinations as well. These concentrated on job skills and abilities. Using the job-analysis information, IOS wrote hypothetical situations to test incident-command skills, firefighting tactics, interpersonal skills, leadership, and management ability, among other things. Candidates would be presented with these hypotheticals and asked to respond before a panel of three assessors.

IOS assembled a pool of 30 assessors who were superior in rank to the positions being tested. At the City's insistence (because of controversy surrounding previous examinations), all the assessors came from outside Connecticut. IOS submitted the assessors' resumes to City officials for approval. They were battalion chiefs, assistant chiefs, and chiefs from departments of similar sizes to New Haven's throughout the country. Sixty-six percent of the panelists were minorities, and each of the nine three-member assessment panels contained two minority members. IOS trained the panelists for several hours on the day before it administered the examinations, teaching them how to score the candidates' responses consistently using checklists of desired criteria.

Candidates took the examinations in November and December 2003. Seventy-seven candidates completed the lieutenant examination—43 whites, 19 blacks, and 15 Hispanics. Of those, 34 candidates passed—25 whites, 6 blacks, and 3 Hispanics. 554 F. Supp. 2d, at 145. Eight lieutenant positions were vacant at the time of the examination. As the rule of three operated, this meant that the top 10 candidates were eligible for an immediate promotion to lieutenant. All 10 were white. Subsequent vacancies would have allowed at least 3 black candidates to be considered for promotion to lieutenant.

Forty-one candidates completed the captain examination—25 whites, 8 blacks, and 8 Hispanics. Of those, 22 candidates passed—16 whites, 3 blacks, and 3 Hispanics. Seven captain positions were vacant at the time of the examination. Under the rule of three, 9 candidates were eligible for an immediate promotion to captain—7 whites and 2 Hispanics.

B

The City's contract with IOS contemplated that, after the examinations, IOS would prepare a technical report that described the examination processes and methodologies and analyzed the results. But in January 2004, rather than requesting the technical report, City officials, including the City's counsel, Thomas Ude, convened a meeting with IOS Vice President Chad Legel. (Legel was the leader of the IOS team that developed and administered the tests.) Based on the test results, the City officials expressed concern that the tests had discriminated against minority candidates. Legel defended the examinations' validity, stating that any numerical disparity between white and minority candidates was likely due to various external factors and was in line with results of the Department's previous promotional examinations.

Several days after the meeting, Ude sent a letter to the CSB purporting to outline its duties with respect to the examination results. Ude stated that under federal law, "a statistical demonstration of disparate impact," standing alone, "constitutes a sufficiently serious claim of racial discrimination to serve as a predicate for employer-initiated, voluntar[y] remedies—even . . . race-conscious remedies." [The CSB then held meetings over five days to consider whether to certify the test results. The first witnesses were firefighters who had taken the tests.]

Although they did not know whether they had passed or failed, some firefighter-candidates spoke at the first CSB meeting in favor of certifying the test results. Michael Blatchley stated that "[e]very one" of the questions on the written examination "came from the [study] material. . . . [I]f you read the materials and you studied the material, you would have done well on the test." Frank Ricci stated that the test questions were based on the Department's own rules and procedures and on "nationally recognized" materials that represented the "accepted standard[s]" for firefighting. Ricci stated that he had "several learning disabilities," including dyslexia; that he had spent more than $1,000 to purchase the materials and pay his neighbor to read them on tape so he could "give it [his] best shot"; and that he had studied "8 to 13 hours a day to prepare" for the test. "I don't even know if I made it," Ricci told the CSB, "[b]ut the people who passed should be promoted. When your life's on the line, second best may not be good enough."

Other firefighters spoke against certifying the test results. They described the test questions as outdated or not relevant to firefighting practices in New Haven. Gary Tinney stated that source materials "came out of New York. . . . Their makeup of their city and everything is totally different than ours." And they criticized the test materials, a full set of which cost about $500, for being too expensive and too long. [The CSB also considered evidence from the president of the New Haven firefighters' union and representatives of the International Association of Black Professional Firefighters. The Board then invited a representative of IOS to testify.]

At a third meeting, on February 11, Legel addressed the CSB on behalf of IOS. Legel stated that IOS had previously prepared entry-level firefighter examinations for the City but not a promotional examination. He explained that IOS had developed examinations for departments in communities with demographics similar to New Haven's, including Orange County, Florida; Lansing, Michigan; and San Jose, California.

Legel explained the exam-development process to the CSB. He began by describing the job analyses IOS performed of the captain and lieutenant positions—the interviews, ride-alongs, and questionnaires

IOS designed to "generate a list of tasks, knowledge, skills and abilities that are considered essential to performance" of the jobs. He outlined how IOS prepared the written and oral examinations, based on the job-analysis results, to test most heavily those qualities that the results indicated were "critica[l]" or "essentia[l]." And he noted that IOS took the material for each test question directly from the approved source materials. Legel told the CSB that third-party reviewers had scrutinized the examinations to ensure that the written test was drawn from the source material and that the oral test accurately tested real-world situations that captains and lieutenants would face. Legel confirmed that IOS had selected oral-examination panelists so that each three-member assessment panel included one white, one black, and one Hispanic member.

Near the end of his remarks, Legel "implor[ed] anyone that had . . . concerns to review the content of the exam. In my professional opinion, it's facially neutral. There's nothing in those examinations . . . that should cause somebody to think that one group would perform differently than another group."

[The Board also heard from other experts on testing, among them, Christopher Hornick.] Hornick is an industrial/organizational psychologist from Texas who operates a consulting business that "direct[ly]" competes with IOS. Hornick, who had not "stud[ied] the test at length or in detail" and had not "seen the job analysis data," told the CSB that the scores indicated a "relatively high adverse impact." He stated that "[n]ormally, whites outperform ethnic minorities on the majority of standardized testing procedures," but that he was "a little surprised" by the disparity in the candidates' scores—although "[s]ome of it is fairly typical of what we've seen in other areas of the countr[y] and other tests." Hornick stated that the "adverse impact on the written exam was somewhat higher but generally in the range that we've seen professionally."

When asked to explain the New Haven test results, Hornick opined in the telephone conversation that the collective-bargaining agreement's requirement of using written and oral examinations with a 60/40 composite score might account for the statistical disparity. He also stated that "[b]y not having anyone from within the [D]epartment review" the tests before they were administered—a limitation the City had imposed to protect the security of the exam questions—"you inevitably get things in there" that are based on the source materials but are not relevant to New Haven. Hornick suggested that testing candidates at an "assessment center" rather than using written and oral examinations "might serve [the City's] needs better." Hornick stated that assessment centers, where candidates face real-world situations and respond just as they would in the field, allow candidates "to demonstrate how they would address a particular problem as opposed to just verbally saying it or identifying the correct option on a written test."

Hornick made clear that he was "not suggesting that [IOS] somehow created a test that had adverse impacts that it should not have had." He described the IOS examinations as "reasonably good test[s]." He stated that the CSB's best option might be to "certify the list as it exists" and work to change the process for future tests, including by "[r]ewriting the Civil Service Rules." Hornick concluded his telephonic remarks by telling the CSB that "for the future," his company "certainly would like to help you if we can."

The second witness was Vincent Lewis, a fire program specialist for the Department of Homeland Security and a retired fire captain from Michigan. Lewis, who is black, had looked "extensively" at the lieutenant exam and "a little less extensively" at the captain exam. He stated that the candidates "should know that material." In Lewis's view, the "questions were relevant for both exams," and the New Haven candidates had an advantage because the study materials identified the particular book chapters from which the questions were taken. In other departments, by contrast, "you had to know basically the . . . entire book." Lewis concluded that any disparate impact likely was due to a pattern that "usually whites outperform some of the minorities on testing," or that "more whites . . . take the exam."

[A final expert testified that no matter what test the City had administered, it would have revealed "a disparity between blacks and whites, Hispanics and whites," particularly on a written test. After further testimony, the Board voted on a motion to certify the examinations, and because one member was recused, the motion failed by a tie vote of two to two, resulting in a decision not to certify the results.

This decision led the plaintiffs, 17 white firefighters and 1 Hispanic firefighter who passed the examinations, to sue the city and various individual officials. The complaint alleged violations of both the Equal Protection Clause and Title VII. On cross-motions for summary judgment, the defendants argued that they had a good faith belief that the examination, if certified, would have resulted in liability under the theory of disparate impact. The plaintiffs argued that a good faith belief was not a valid defense to a claim of intentional discrimination under Title VII and the Constitution. The district court accepted the defendants' argument and granted summary judgment for them. The court of appeals affirmed in a brief per curiam opinion, with a 7–6 majority of judges denying rehearing en banc.]

This action presents two provisions of Title VII to be interpreted and reconciled, with few, if any, precedents in the courts of appeals discussing the issue. Depending on the resolution of the statutory claim, a fundamental constitutional question could also arise. We found it prudent and appropriate to grant certiorari. We now reverse.

II

Petitioners raise a statutory claim, under the disparate-treatment prohibition of Title VII, and a constitutional claim, under the Equal Protection Clause of the Fourteenth Amendment. A decision for petitioners on their statutory claim would provide the relief sought, so we consider it first.

A

. . .

As enacted in 1964, Title VII's principal nondiscrimination provision held employers liable only for disparate treatment. That section retains its original wording today. It makes it unlawful for an employer "to fail or refuse to hire or to discharge any individual, or otherwise to discriminate against any individual with respect to his compensation, terms, conditions, or privileges of employment, because of such individual's race, color, religion, sex, or national origin." § 2000e–2(a)(1); see also 78 Stat. 255. Disparate-treatment cases present "the most easily understood type of discrimination," *Teamsters* v. *United States*, 431 U.S. 324, 335, n. 15 (1977), and occur where an employer has "treated [a] particular person less favorably than others because of" a protected trait. *Watson* v. *Fort Worth Bank & Trust*, 487 U.S. 977, 985–986 (1988). A disparate-treatment plaintiff must establish "that the defendant had a discriminatory intent or motive" for taking a job-related action. *Id.*, at 986.

The Civil Rights Act of 1964 did not include an express prohibition on policies or practices that produce a disparate impact. But in *Griggs* v. *Duke Power Co.*, 401 U.S. 424 (1971), the Court interpreted the Act to prohibit, in some cases, employers' facially neutral practices that, in fact, are "discriminatory in operation." *Id.*, at 431. The *Griggs* Court stated that the "touchstone" for disparate-impact liability is the lack of "business necessity": "If an employment practice which operates to exclude [minorities] cannot be shown to be related to job performance, the practice is prohibited." *Ibid.;* see also *id.*, at 432 (employer's burden to demonstrate that practice has "a manifest relationship to the employment in question"); *Albemarle Paper Co.* v. *Moody*, 422 U.S. 405, 425 (1975). Under those precedents, if an employer met its burden by showing that its practice was job-related, the plaintiff was required to show a legitimate alternative that would have resulted in less discrimination. *Ibid.* (allowing complaining party to show "that other tests or selection devices, without a similarly undesirable racial effect, would also serve the employer's legitimate interest").

Twenty years after *Griggs*, the Civil Rights Act of 1991, 105 Stat. 1071, was enacted. The Act included a provision codifying the prohibition on disparate-impact discrimination. That provision is now in force along with the disparate-treatment section already noted. Under the disparate-impact statute, a plaintiff establishes a prima facie violation by showing that an employer uses "a particular employment practice that causes a disparate impact on the basis of race, color, religion, sex, or national origin." 42 U.S.C. § 2000e–2(k)(1)(A)(i). An employer may defend against liability by demonstrating that the practice is "job related for the position in question and consistent with business necessity." *Ibid.* Even if the employer meets that burden, however, a plaintiff may still succeed by showing that the employer refuses to adopt an available alternative employment practice that has less disparate impact and serves the employer's legitimate needs. §§ 2000e–2(k)(1)(A)(ii) and (C).

B

Petitioners allege that when the CSB refused to certify the captain and lieutenant exam results based on the race of the successful candidates, it discriminated against them in violation of Title VII's disparate-treatment provision. The City counters that its decision was permissible because the tests "appear[ed] to violate Title VII's disparate-impact provisions."

Our analysis begins with this premise: The City's actions would violate the disparate-treatment prohibition of Title VII absent some valid defense. All the evidence demonstrates that the City chose not to certify the examination results because of the statistical disparity based on race—*i.e.*, how minority candidates had performed when compared to white candidates. As the District Court put it, the City rejected the test results because "too many whites and not enough minorities would be promoted were the lists to be certified." 554 F. Supp. 2d, at 152; see also *ibid.* (respondents' "own arguments . . . show that the City's reasons for advocating non-certification were related to the racial distribution of the results"). Without some other justification, this express, race-based decisionmaking violates Title VII's command that employers cannot take adverse employment actions because of an individual's race. See § 2000e–2(a)(1).

The District Court did not adhere to this principle, however. It held that respondents' "motivation to avoid making promotions based on a test with a racially disparate impact . . . does not, as a matter of law, constitute discriminatory intent." 554 F. Supp. 2d, at 160. And the Government makes a similar argument in this Court. It contends that the "structure of Title VII belies any claim that an employer's intent to comply with Title VII's disparate-impact provisions constitutes prohibited discrimination on the basis of race." Brief for United States as *Amicus Curiae* 11. But both of those statements turn upon the City's objective—avoiding disparate-impact liability—while ignoring the City's conduct in the name of reaching that objective. Whatever the City's ultimate aim—however well intentioned or benevolent it might have seemed—the City made its employment decision because of race. The City rejected the test results solely because the higher scoring candidates were white. The question is not whether that conduct was discriminatory but whether the City had a lawful justification for its race-based action.

We consider, therefore, whether the purpose to avoid disparate-impact liability excuses what otherwise would be prohibited disparate-treatment discrimination. Courts often confront cases in which statutes and principles point in different directions. Our task is to provide guidance to employers and courts for situations when these two prohibitions could be in conflict absent a rule to reconcile them. In providing this guidance our decision must be consistent with the important purpose of Title VII—that the workplace be an environment free of discrimination, where race is not a barrier to opportunity.

With these principles in mind, we turn to the parties' proposed means of reconciling the statutory provisions. Petitioners take a strict approach, arguing that under Title VII, it cannot be permissible for an employer to take race-based adverse employment actions in order to avoid disparate-impact liability—even if the employer knows its practice violates the disparate-impact provision. Petitioners would have us hold that, under Title VII, avoiding unintentional discrimination cannot justify intentional discrimination. That assertion, however, ignores the fact that, by codifying the disparate-impact provision in 1991, Congress has expressly prohibited both types of discrimination. We must interpret the statute to give effect to both provisions where possible. See, *e.g.*, *United States* v. *Atlantic Research Corp.*, 551 U.S. 128, 137 (2007) (rejecting an interpretation that would render a statutory provision "a dead letter"). We cannot accept petitioners' broad and inflexible formulation.

Petitioners next suggest that an employer in fact must be in violation of the disparate-impact provision before it can use compliance as a defense in a disparate-treatment suit. Again, this is overly simplistic and too restrictive of Title VII's purpose. The rule petitioners offer would run counter to what we have recognized as Congress's intent that "voluntary compliance" be "the preferred means of achieving the objectives of Title VII." *Firefighters* v. *Cleveland*, 478 U.S. 501, 515 (1986); see also *Wygant* v. *Jackson Bd. of Ed.*, 476 U.S. 267, 290 (1986) (O'Connor, J., concurring in part and concurring in judgment). Forbidding employers to act unless they know, with certainty, that a practice violates the disparate-impact provision would bring compliance efforts to a near standstill. Even in the limited situations when this restricted standard could be met, employers likely would hesitate before taking voluntary action for fear of later being proven wrong in the course of litigation and then held to account for disparate treatment.

At the opposite end of the spectrum, respondents and the Government assert that an employer's good-faith belief that its actions are necessary to comply with Title VII's disparate-impact provision should be enough to justify race-conscious conduct. But the original, foundational prohibition of Title VII bars employers from taking adverse action "because of . . . race." § 2000e–2(a)(1). And when Congress codified the disparate-impact provision in 1991, it made no exception to disparate-treatment liability for actions taken in a good-faith effort to comply with the new, disparate-impact provision in subsection (k). Allowing employers to violate the disparate-treatment prohibition based on a mere good-faith fear of disparate-impact liability would encourage race-based action at the slightest hint of disparate impact. A minimal standard could cause employers to discard the results of lawful and beneficial promotional examinations even where there is little if any evidence of disparate-impact discrimination. That would amount to a *de facto* quota system, in which a "focus on statistics . . . could put undue pressure on employers to adopt inappropriate prophylactic measures." *Watson*, 487 U.S., at 992 (plurality opinion). Even worse, an employer could discard test results (or other employment practices) with the intent of obtaining the employer's preferred racial balance. That operational principle could not be justified, for Title VII is express in disclaiming any interpretation of its requirements as calling for outright racial balancing. § 2000e–2(j). The purpose of Title VII "is to promote hiring on the basis of job qualifications, rather than on the basis of race or color." *Griggs*, 401 U.S., at 434.

In searching for a standard that strikes a more appropriate balance, we note that this Court has considered cases similar to this one, albeit in the context of the Equal Protection Clause of the Fourteenth Amendment. The Court has held that certain government actions to remedy past racial discrimination-actions that are themselves based on race—are constitutional only where there is a " 'strong basis in evidence' " that the remedial actions were necessary. *Richmond* v. *J. A. Croson Co.*, 488 U.S. 469, 500 (1989) (quoting *Wygant*, *supra*, at 277 (plurality opinion)). This suit does not call on us to consider whether the statutory constraints under Title VII must be parallel in all respects to those under the Constitution. That does not mean the constitutional authorities are irrelevant, however. Our cases discussing constitutional principles can provide helpful guidance in this statutory context. See *Watson*, *supra*, at 993 (plurality opinion).

Writing for a plurality in *Wygant* and announcing the strong-basis-in-evidence standard, Justice Powell recognized the tension between eliminating segregation and discrimination on the one hand and doing away with all governmentally imposed discrimination based on race on the other. 476 U.S., at 277. The plurality stated that those "related constitutional duties are not always harmonious," and that "reconciling them requires . . . employers to act with extraordinary care." *Ibid.* The plurality required a strong basis in evidence because "[e]videntiary support for the conclusion that remedial action is warranted becomes crucial when the remedial program is challenged in court by nonminority employees." *Ibid.* The Court applied the same standard in *Croson*, observing that "an amorphous claim that there has been past discrimination . . . cannot justify the use of an unyielding racial quota." 488 U.S., at 499.

The same interests are at work in the interplay between the disparate-treatment and disparate-impact provisions of Title VII. Congress has imposed liability on employers for unintentional discrimination in order to rid the workplace of "practices that are fair in form, but discriminatory in operation." *Griggs*, *supra*, at 431. But it has also prohibited employers from taking adverse employment actions "because of" race. § 2000e–2(a)(1). Applying the strong-basis-in-evidence standard to Title VII gives effect to both the disparate-treatment and disparate-impact provisions, allowing violations of one in the name of compliance with the other only in certain, narrow circumstances. The standard leaves ample room for employers' voluntary compliance efforts, which are essential to the statutory scheme and to Congress's efforts to eradicate workplace discrimination. See *Firefighters*, *supra,* at 515. And the standard appropriately constrains employers' discretion in making race-based decisions: It limits that discretion to cases in which there is a strong basis in evidence of disparate-impact liability, but it is not so restrictive that it allows employers to act only when there is a provable, actual violation.

Resolving the statutory conflict in this way allows the disparate-impact prohibition to work in a manner that is consistent with other provisions of Title VII, including the prohibition on adjusting employment-related test scores on the basis of race. See § 2000e–2(*l*). Examinations like those administered by the City create legitimate expectations on the part of those who took the tests. As is the case with any promotion exam, some of the firefighters here invested substantial time, money, and personal commitment in preparing for the tests. Employment tests can be an important part of a neutral selection system that safeguards against the very racial animosities Title VII was intended to prevent. Here, however, the firefighters saw their efforts invalidated by the City in sole reliance upon race-based statistics.

If an employer cannot rescore a test based on the candidates' race, § 2000e–2(*l*), then it follows *a fortiori* that it may not take the greater step of discarding the test altogether to achieve a more desirable racial distribution of promotion-eligible candidates—absent a strong basis in evidence that the test was deficient and that discarding the results is necessary to avoid violating the disparate-impact provision. Restricting an employer's ability to discard test results (and thereby discriminate against qualified candidates on the basis of their race) also is in keeping with Title VII's express protection of bona fide promotional examinations. For the foregoing reasons, we adopt the strong-basis-in-evidence standard as a matter of statutory construction to resolve any conflict between the disparate-treatment and disparate-impact provisions of Title VII.

Our statutory holding does not address the constitutionality of the measures taken here in purported compliance with Title VII. We also do not hold that meeting the strong-basis-in-evidence standard would satisfy the Equal Protection Clause in a future case. As we explain below, because respondents have not met their burden under Title VII, we need not decide whether a legitimate fear of disparate impact is ever sufficient to justify discriminatory treatment under the Constitution.

Nor do we question an employer's affirmative efforts to ensure that all groups have a fair opportunity to apply for promotions and to participate in the process by which promotions will be made. But once that process has been established and employers have made clear their selection criteria, they may not then invalidate the test results, thus upsetting an employee's legitimate expectation not to be judged on the basis of race. Doing so, absent a strong basis in evidence of an impermissible disparate impact, amounts to the sort of racial preference that Congress has disclaimed, § 2000e–2(j), and is antithetical to the notion of a workplace where individuals are guaranteed equal opportunity regardless of race.

Title VII does not prohibit an employer from considering, before administering a test or practice, how to design that test or practice in order to provide a fair opportunity for all individuals, regardless of their race. And when, during the test-design stage, an employer invites comments to ensure the test is fair, that process can provide a common ground for open discussions toward that end. We hold only that, under Title VII, before an employer can engage in intentional discrimination for the asserted purpose of avoiding or remedying an unintentional disparate impact, the employer must have a strong basis in evidence to believe it will be subject to disparate-impact liability if it fails to take the race-conscious, discriminatory action.

C

The City argues that, even under the strong-basis-in-evidence standard, its decision to discard the examination results was permissible under Title VII. That is incorrect. Even if respondents were motivated as a subjective matter by a desire to avoid committing disparate-impact discrimination, the record makes clear there is no support for the conclusion that respondents had an objective, strong basis in evidence to find the tests inadequate, with some consequent disparate-impact liability in violation of Title VII.

On this basis, we conclude that petitioners have met their obligation to demonstrate that there is "no genuine issue as to any material fact" and that they are "entitled to judgment as a matter of law." Fed. Rule Civ. Proc. 56(c). On a motion for summary judgment, "facts must be viewed in the light most favorable to the nonmoving party only if there is a 'genuine' dispute as to those facts." *Scott* v. *Harris*, 550 U.S. 372, 380 (2007). "Where the record taken as a whole could not lead a rational trier of fact to find for the nonmoving party, there is no genuine issue for trial." *Matsushita Elec. Industrial Co.* v. *Zenith Radio Corp.*, 475 U.S. 574, 587 (1986) (internal quotation marks omitted). In this Court, the City's only defense is that it acted to comply with Title VII's disparate-impact provision. To succeed on their motion, then, petitioners must demonstrate that there can be no genuine dispute that there was no strong basis in evidence for the City to conclude it would face disparate-impact liability if it certified the examination results. See *Celotex Corp.* v. *Catrett*, 477 U.S. 317, 324 (1986) (where the nonmoving party "will bear the burden of proof at trial on a dispositive issue," the nonmoving party bears the burden of production under Rule 56 to "designate specific facts showing that there is a genuine issue for trial" (internal quotation marks omitted)).

The racial adverse impact here was significant, and petitioners do not dispute that the City was faced with a prima facie case of disparate-impact liability. On the captain exam, the pass rate for white candidates was 64 percent but was 37.5 percent for both black and Hispanic candidates. On the lieutenant exam, the pass rate for white candidates was 58.1 percent; for black candidates, 31.6 percent; and for Hispanic candidates, 20 percent. The pass rates of minorities, which were approximately one-half the pass rates for white candidates, fall well below the 80-percent standard set by the EEOC to implement the disparate-impact provision of Title VII.

Based on how the passing candidates ranked and an application of the "rule of three," certifying the examinations would have meant that the City could not have considered black candidates for any of the then-vacant lieutenant or captain positions.

Based on the degree of adverse impact reflected in the results, respondents were compelled to take a hard look at the examinations to determine whether certifying the results would have had an impermissible disparate impact. The problem for respondents is that a prima facie case of disparate-impact liability—essentially, a threshold showing of a significant statistical disparity, *Connecticut* v. *Teal*, 457 U.S. 440, 446 (1982), and nothing more—is far from a strong basis in evidence that the City would have been liable under Title VII had it certified the results. That is because the City could be liable for disparate-impact discrimination only if the examinations were not job related and consistent with business necessity, or if there existed an equally valid, less-discriminatory alternative that served the City's needs but that the City refused to adopt. § 2000e–2(k)(1)(A), (C). We conclude there is no strong basis in evidence to establish that the test was deficient in either of these respects. We address each of the two points in turn, based on the record developed by the parties through discovery—a record that concentrates in substantial part on the statements various witnesses made to the CSB.

1

There is no genuine dispute that the examinations were job-related and consistent with business necessity. The City's assertions to the contrary are "blatantly contradicted by the record." *Scott*, *supra*, at 380. The CSB heard statements from Chad Legel (the IOS vice president) as well as city officials outlining the detailed steps IOS took to develop and administer the examinations. IOS devised the written examinations, which were the focus of the CSB's inquiry, after painstaking analyses of the captain and lieutenant positions—analyses in which IOS made sure that minorities were overrepresented. And IOS drew the questions from source material approved by the Department. Of the outside witnesses who appeared before the CSB, only one, Vincent Lewis, had reviewed the examinations in any detail, and he was the only one with any firefighting experience. Lewis stated that the "questions were relevant for both exams." The only other witness who had seen any part of the examinations, Christopher Hornick (a competitor of IOS's), criticized the fact that no one within the Department had reviewed the tests—a condition imposed by the City to protect the integrity of the exams in light of past alleged security breaches. But Hornick stated that the exams "appea[r] to be . . . reasonably good" and recommended that the CSB certify the results.

Arguing that the examinations were not job-related, respondents note some candidates' complaints that certain examination questions were contradictory or did not specifically apply to firefighting practices in New Haven. But Legel told the CSB that IOS had addressed those concerns—that it entertained "a handful" of challenges to the validity of particular examination questions, that it "reviewed those challenges and provided feedback [to the City] as to what we thought the best course of action was," and that he could remember at least one question IOS had thrown out ("offer[ing] credit to everybody for that particular question"). For his part, Hornick said he "suspect[ed] that some of the criticisms . . . [leveled] by candidates" were not valid.

The City, moreover, turned a blind eye to evidence that supported the exams' validity. Although the City's contract with IOS contemplated that IOS would prepare a technical report consistent with EEOC guidelines for examination-validity studies, the City made no request for its report. After the January 2004 meeting between Legel and some of the city-official respondents, in which Legel defended the examinations, the City sought no further information from IOS, save its appearance at a CSB meeting to explain how it developed and administered the examinations. IOS stood ready to provide respondents with detailed information to establish the validity of the exams, but respondents did not accept that offer.

2

Respondents also lacked a strong basis in evidence of an equally valid, less-discriminatory testing alternative that the City, by certifying the examination results, would necessarily have refused to adopt. Respondents raise three arguments to the contrary, but each argument fails. First, respondents refer to testimony before the CSB that a different composite-score calculation—weighting the written and oral examination scores 30/70—would have allowed the City to consider two black candidates for then-open lieutenant positions and one black candidate for then-open captain positions. (The City used a 60/40 weighting as required by its contract with the New Haven firefighters' union.) But respondents have produced no evidence to show that the 60/40 weighting was indeed arbitrary. In fact, because that formula was the result of a union-negotiated collective-bargaining agreement, we presume the parties negotiated that weighting for a rational reason. Nor does the record contain any evidence that the 30/70 weighting would be an equally valid way to determine whether candidates possess the proper mix of job knowledge and situational skills to earn promotions. Changing the weighting formula, moreover, could well have violated Title VII's prohibition of altering test scores on the basis of race. See § 2000e–2(*l*). On this record, there is no basis to conclude that a 30/70 weighting was an equally valid alternative the City could have adopted.

Second, respondents argue that the City could have adopted a different interpretation of the "rule of three" that would have produced less discriminatory results. The rule, in the New Haven city charter, requires the City to promote only from "those applicants with the three highest scores" on a promotional examination. New Haven, Conn., Code of Ordinances, Tit. I, Art. XXX, § 160 (1992). A state court has interpreted the charter to prohibit so-called "banding"—the City's previous practice of rounding scores to the nearest whole number and considering all candidates with the same whole-number score as being of one rank. Banding allowed the City to consider three ranks of candidates (with the possibility of multiple candidates filling each rank) for purposes of the rule of three. See *Kelly* v. *New Haven*, No. CV000444614, 2004 WL 114377, *3 (Conn. Super. Ct., Jan. 9, 2004). Respondents claim that employing banding here would have made four black and one Hispanic candidates eligible for then-open lieutenant and captain positions.

A state court's prohibition of banding, as a matter of municipal law under the charter, may not eliminate banding as a valid alternative under Title VII. See 42 U.S.C. § 2000e–7. We need not resolve that point, however. Here, banding was not a valid alternative for this reason: Had the City reviewed the exam results and then adopted banding to make the minority test scores appear higher, it would have violated Title VII's prohibition of adjusting test results on the basis of race. § 2000e–2(*l*); see also *Chicago Firefighters Local 2* v. *Chicago*, 249 F. 3d 649, 656 (CA7 2001) (Posner, J.) ("We have no doubt that if banding were adopted in order to make lower black scores seem higher, it would indeed be . . . forbidden"). As a matter of law, banding was not an alternative available to the City when it was considering whether to certify the examination results.

Third, and finally, respondents refer to statements by Hornick in his telephone interview with the CSB regarding alternatives to the written examinations. Hornick stated his "belie[f]" that an "assessment center process," which would have evaluated candidates' behavior in typical job tasks, "would have demonstrated less adverse impact." But Hornick's brief mention of alternative testing methods, standing alone, does not raise a genuine issue of material fact that assessment centers were available to the City at the time of the examinations and that they would have produced less adverse impact. Other statements to the CSB indicated that the Department could not have used assessment centers for the 2003 examinations. And although respondents later argued to the CSB that Hornick had pushed the City to reject the test results, the truth is that the essence of Hornick's remarks supported its certifying the test results. See *Scott*, 550 U.S., at 380. Hornick stated that adverse impact in standardized testing "has been in existence since the beginning of testing," and that the disparity in New Haven's test results was "somewhat higher but generally in the range that we've seen professionally." He told the CSB he was "not suggesting" that IOS "somehow created a test that had adverse impacts that it should not have had." And he suggested that the CSB should "certify the list as it exists."

Especially when it is noted that the strong-basis-in-evidence standard applies, respondents cannot create a genuine issue of fact based on a few stray (and contradictory) statements in the record. And there is no doubt respondents fall short of the mark by relying entirely on isolated statements by Hornick. Hornick had not "stud[ied] the test at length or in detail." And as he told the CSB, he is a "direct competitor" of IOS's. The remainder of his remarks showed that Hornick's primary concern—somewhat to the frustration of CSB members—was marketing his services for the future, not commenting on the results of the tests the City had already administered. Hornick's hinting had its intended effect: The City has since hired him as a consultant. As for the other outside witnesses who spoke to the CSB, Vincent Lewis (the retired fire captain) thought the CSB should certify the test results. And Janet Helms (the Boston College professor) declined to review the examinations and told the CSB that, as a society, "we need to develop a new way of assessing people." That task was beyond the reach of the CSB, which was concerned with the adequacy of the test results before it.

3

On the record before us, there is no genuine dispute that the City lacked a strong basis in evidence to believe it would face disparate-impact liability if it certified the examination results. In other words, there is no evidence—let alone the required strong basis in evidence—that the tests were flawed because they were not job-related or because other, equally valid and less discriminatory tests were available to the City. Fear of litigation alone cannot justify an employer's reliance on race to the detriment of individuals who passed the examinations and qualified for promotions. The City's discarding the test results was impermissible under Title VII, and summary judgment is appropriate for petitioners on their disparate-treatment claim. . . .

The record in this litigation documents a process that, at the outset, had the potential to produce a testing procedure that was true to the promise of Title VII: No individual should face workplace discrimination based on race. Respondents thought about promotion qualifications and relevant experience in neutral ways. They were careful to ensure broad racial participation in the design of the test itself and its administration. As we have discussed at length, the process was open and fair.

The problem, of course, is that after the tests were completed, the raw racial results became the predominant rationale for the City's refusal to certify the results. The injury arises in part from the high, and justified, expectations of the candidates who had participated in the testing process on the terms the City had established for the promotional process. Many of the candidates had studied for months, at considerable personal and financial expense, and thus the injury caused by the City's reliance on raw racial statistics at the end of the process was all the more severe. Confronted with arguments both for and against certifying the test results—and threats of a lawsuit either way—the City was required to make a difficult inquiry. But its hearings produced no strong evidence of a disparate-impact violation, and the City was not entitled to disregard the tests based solely on the racial disparity in the results.

Our holding today clarifies how Title VII applies to resolve competing expectations under the disparate-treatment and disparate-impact provisions. If, after it certifies the test results, the City faces a disparate-impact suit, then in light of our holding today it should be clear that the City would avoid disparate-impact liability based on the strong basis in evidence that, had it not certified the results, it would have been subject to disparate-treatment liability.

Petitioners are entitled to summary judgment on their Title VII claim, and we therefore need not decide the underlying constitutional question. The judgment of the Court of Appeals is reversed, and the cases are remanded for further proceedings consistent with this opinion.

It is so ordered.

■ JUSTICE SCALIA, concurring.

I join the Court's opinion in full, but write separately to observe that its resolution of this dispute merely postpones the evil day on which the Court will have to confront the question: Whether, or to what extent, are the disparate-impact provisions of Title VII of the Civil Rights Act of 1964 consistent with the Constitution's guarantee of equal protection? The question is not an easy one. See generally Primus, Equal Protection and Disparate Impact: Round Three, 117 Harv. L. Rev. 493 (2003).

The difficulty is this: Whether or not Title VII's disparate-treatment provisions forbid "remedial" race-based actions when a disparate-impact violation would *not* otherwise result—the question resolved by the Court today—it is clear that Title VII not only permits but affirmatively *requires* such actions when a disparate-impact violation *would* otherwise result. But if the Federal Government is prohibited from discriminating on the basis of race, *Bolling* v. *Sharpe*, 347 U.S. 497, 500 (1954), then surely it is also prohibited from enacting laws mandating that third parties—*e.g.*, employers, whether private, State, or municipal-discriminate on the basis of race. See *Buchanan* v. *Warley*, 245 U.S. 60, 78–82 (1917). As the facts of these cases illustrate, Title VII's disparate-impact provisions place a racial thumb on the scales, often requiring employers to evaluate the racial outcomes of their policies, and to make decisions based on (because of) those racial outcomes. That type of racial decisionmaking is, as the Court explains, discriminatory.

To be sure, the disparate-impact laws do not mandate imposition of quotas, but it is not clear why that should provide a safe harbor. Would a private employer not be guilty of unlawful discrimination if he refrained from establishing a racial hiring quota but intentionally designed his hiring practices to achieve the same end? Surely he would. Intentional discrimination is still occurring, just one step up the chain. Government compulsion of such design would therefore seemingly violate equal protection principles. Nor would it matter that Title VII requires consideration of race on a wholesale, rather than retail, level. "[T]he Government must treat citizens as individuals, not as simply components of a racial, religious, sexual or national class." *Miller* v. *Johnson*, 515 U.S. 900, 911 (1995) (internal quotation marks omitted). And of course the purportedly benign motive for the disparate-impact provisions cannot save the statute. See *Adarand Constructors, Inc.* v. *Pena*, 515 U.S. 200, 227 (1995).

It might be possible to defend the law by framing it as simply an evidentiary tool used to identify genuine, intentional discrimination—to "smoke out," as it were, disparate treatment. See Primus, *supra*, at 498–499, 520–521. Disparate impact is sometimes (though not always, see *Watson* v. *Fort Worth Bank & Trust*, 487 U.S. 977, 992 (1988) (plurality opinion)) a signal of something illicit, so a regulator might allow statistical disparities to play some role in the evidentiary process. Cf. *McDonnell Douglas Corp.* v. *Green*, 411 U.S. 792, 802–803 (1973). But arguably the disparate-impact provisions sweep too broadly to be fairly characterized in such a fashion—since they fail to provide an affirmative defense for good-faith (*i.e.*, nonracially motivated) conduct, or perhaps even for good faith plus hiring standards that are entirely reasonable. See *post*, at 15–16, and n. 1 (Ginsburg, J., dissenting) (describing the demanding nature of the "business necessity" defense). This is a question that this Court will have to consider in due course. It is one thing to free plaintiffs from proving an employer's illicit intent, but quite another to preclude the employer from proving that its motives were pure and its actions reasonable.

The Court's resolution of these cases makes it unnecessary to resolve these matters today. But the war between disparate impact and equal protection will be waged sooner or later, and it behooves us to begin thinking about how—and on what terms—to make peace between them.

■ JUSTICE ALITO, with whom JUSTICE SCALIA and JUSTICE THOMAS join, concurring.

I join the Court's opinion in full. I write separately only because the dissent, while claiming that "[t]he Court's recitation of the facts leaves out important parts of the story," provides an incomplete description of the events that led to New Haven's decision to reject the results of its exam. The dissent's omissions are important because, when all of the evidence in the record is taken into account, it is clear that, even if the legal analysis in Parts II and III-A of the dissent were accepted, affirmance of the decision below is untenable.

. . .

II

A

As initially described by the dissent, the process by which the City reached the decision not to accept the test results was open, honest, serious, and deliberative. But even the District Court admitted that "a jury could rationally infer that city officials worked behind the scenes to sabotage the promotional examinations because they knew that, were the exams certified, the Mayor would incur the wrath of [Rev. Boise] Kimber and other influential leaders of New Haven's African-American community." 554 F. Supp. 2d 142, 162 (Conn. 2006), summarily aff'd, 530 F. 3d 87 (CA2 2008) *(per curiam).*

[Justice Alito then recounts in detail the evidence in the record supporting this conclusion.]

C

Taking into account all the evidence in the summary judgment record, a reasonable jury could find the following. Almost as soon as the City disclosed the racial makeup of the list of firefighters who scored the highest on the exam, the City administration was lobbied by an influential community leader to scrap the test results, and the City administration decided on that course of action before making any real assessment of the possibility of a disparate-impact violation. To achieve that end, the City administration concealed its internal decision but worked—as things turned out, successfully—to persuade the CSB that acceptance of the test results would be illegal and would expose the City to disparate-impact liability. But in the event that the CSB was not persuaded, the Mayor, wielding ultimate decisionmaking authority, was prepared to overrule the CSB immediately. Taking this view of the evidence, a reasonable jury could easily find that the City's real reason for scrapping the test results was not a concern about violating the disparate-impact provision of Title VII but a simple desire to please a politically important racial constituency. It is noteworthy that the

Solicitor General—whose position on the principal legal issue in this case is largely aligned with the dissent—concludes that "[n]either the district court nor the court of appeals ... adequately considered whether, viewing the evidence in the light most favorable to petitioners, a genuine issue of material fact remained whether respondents' claimed purpose to comply with Title VII was a pretext for intentional racial discrimination ...." Brief for United States as *Amicus Curiae* 6; see also *id.,* at 32–33.

II

[Justice Alito then comments briefly on Justice Ginsburg's criticism of his analysis in her dissent, concluding as follows:]

The dissent grants that petitioners' situation is "unfortunate" and that they "understandably attract this Court's sympathy." But "sympathy" is not what petitioners have a right to demand. What they have a right to demand is evenhanded enforcement of the law—of Title VII's prohibition against discrimination based on race. And that is what, until today's decision, has been denied them.

■ JUSTICE GINSBURG, with whom JUSTICE STEVENS, JUSTICE SOUTER, and JUSTICE BREYER join, dissenting.

In assessing claims of race discrimination, "[c]ontext matters." *Grutter* v. *Bollinger*, 539 U.S. 306, 327 (2003). In 1972, Congress extended Title VII of the Civil Rights Act of 1964 to cover public employment. At that time, municipal fire departments across the country, including New Haven's, pervasively discriminated against minorities. The extension of Title VII to cover jobs in firefighting effected no overnight change. It took decades of persistent effort, advanced by Title VII litigation, to open firefighting posts to members of racial minorities.

The white firefighters who scored high on New Haven's promotional exams understandably attract this Court's sympathy. But they had no vested right to promotion. Nor have other persons received promotions in preference to them. New Haven maintains that it refused to certify the test results because it believed, for good cause, that it would be vulnerable to a Title VII disparate-impact suit if it relied on those results. The Court today holds that New Haven has not demonstrated "a strong basis in evidence" for its plea. In so holding, the Court pretends that "[t]he City rejected the test results solely because the higher scoring candidates were white." That pretension, essential to the Court's disposition, ignores substantial evidence of multiple flaws in the tests New Haven used. The Court similarly fails to acknowledge the better tests used in other cities, which have yielded less racially skewed outcomes.

By order of this Court, New Haven, a city in which African-Americans and Hispanics account for nearly 60 percent of the population, must today be served—as it was in the days of undisguised discrimination—by a fire department in which members of racial and ethnic minorities are rarely seen in command positions. In arriving at its order, the Court barely acknowledges the pathmarking decision in *Griggs* v. *Duke Power Co.*, 401 U.S. 424 (1971), which explained the centrality of the disparate-impact concept to effective enforcement of Title VII. The Court's order and opinion, I anticipate, will not have staying power.

I

A

The Court's recitation of the facts leaves out important parts of the story. Firefighting is a profession in which the legacy of racial discrimination casts an especially long shadow. In extending Title VII to state and local government employers in 1972, Congress took note of a U.S. Commission on Civil Rights (USCCR) report finding racial discrimination in municipal employment even "more pervasive than in the private sector." H. R. Rep. No. 92–238, p. 17 (1971). According to the report, overt racism was partly to blame, but so too was a failure on the part of municipal employers to apply merit-based employment principles. In making hiring and promotion decisions, public employers often "rel[ied] on criteria unrelated to job performance," including nepotism or political patronage. 118 Cong. Rec. 1817 (1972). Such flawed selection methods served to entrench preexisting racial hierarchies. The USCCR report singled out police and fire departments for having "[b]arriers to equal employment . . . greater . . . than in any other area of State or local government," with African-Americans "hold[ing] almost no positions in the officer ranks." *Ibid.*

The city of New Haven (City) was no exception. In the early 1970's, African-Americans and Hispanics composed 30 percent of New Haven's population, but only 3.6 percent of the City's 502 firefighters. The racial disparity in the officer ranks was even more pronounced: "[O]f the 107 officers in the Department only one was black, and he held the lowest rank above private." *Firebird Soc. of New Haven, Inc.* v. *New Haven Bd. of Fire Comm'rs*, 66 F. R. D. 457, 460 (Conn. 1975).

Following a lawsuit and settlement agreement, see *ibid.*, the City initiated efforts to increase minority representation in the New Haven Fire Department (Department). Those litigation-induced efforts produced some positive change. New Haven's population includes a greater proportion of minorities today than it did in the 1970's: Nearly 40 percent of the City's residents are African-American and more than 20 percent are Hispanic. Among entry-level firefighters, minorities are still underrepresented, but not starkly so. As of 2003, African-Americans and Hispanics constituted 30 percent and 16 percent of the City's firefighters, respectively. In supervisory positions, however, significant disparities remain. Overall, the senior officer ranks (captain and higher) are nine percent African-American and nine percent Hispanic. Only one of the Department's 21 fire captains is African-American. It is against this backdrop of entrenched inequality that the promotion process at issue in this litigation should be assessed.

[Justice Ginsburg then recounted the development and administration of the tests in this case, the testimony at the hearings before the Civil Service Board, and the opinions of the district court and the court of appeals.]

II

[After recounting the development of the theory of disparate impact under Title VII, Justice Ginsburg turned to its relationship to claims of disparate treatment.]

B

Neither Congress' enactments nor this Court's Title VII precedents (including the now-discredited decision in *Wards Cove*) offer even a hint of "conflict" between an employer's obligations under the statute's disparate-treatment and disparate-impact provisions. Standing on an equal footing, these twin pillars of Title VII advance the same objectives: ending workplace discrimination and promoting genuinely equal opportunity. See *McDonnell Douglas Corp.* v. *Green*, 411 U.S. 792, 800 (1973).

Yet the Court today sets at odds the statute's core directives. When an employer changes an employment practice in an effort to comply with Title VII's disparate-impact provision, the Court reasons, it acts "because of race"—something Title VII's disparate-treatment provision, see § 2000e–2(a)(1), generally forbids. This characterization of an employer's compliance-directed action shows little attention to Congress' design or to the *Griggs* line of cases Congress recognized as pathmarking.

"[O]ur task in interpreting separate provisions of a single Act is to give the Act the most harmonious, comprehensive meaning possible in light of the legislative policy and purpose." *Weinberger* v. *Hynson, Westcott & Dunning, Inc.*, 412 U.S. 609, 631–632 (1973) (internal quotation marks omitted). A particular phrase need not "extend to the outer limits of its definitional possibilities" if an incongruity would result. *Dolan* v. *Postal Service*, 546 U.S. 481, 486 (2006). Here, Title VII's disparate-treatment and disparate-impact proscriptions must be read as complementary.

In codifying the *Griggs* and *Albemarle* instructions, Congress declared unambiguously that selection criteria operating to the disadvantage of minority group members can be retained only if justified by business necessity. In keeping with Congress' design, employers who reject such criteria due to reasonable doubts about their reliability can hardly be held to have engaged in discrimination "because of" race. A reasonable endeavor to comply with the law and to ensure that qualified candidates of all races have a fair opportunity to compete is simply not what Congress meant to interdict. I would therefore hold that an employer who jettisons a selection device when its disproportionate racial impact becomes apparent does not violate Title VII's disparate-treatment bar automatically or at all, subject to this key condition: The employer must have good cause to believe the device would not withstand examination for business necessity. . . .

Our precedents defining the contours of Title VII's disparate-treatment prohibition further confirm the absence of any intra-statutory discord. In *Johnson* v. *Transportation Agency, Santa Clara Cty.*, 480 U.S. 616 (1987), we upheld a municipal employer's voluntary affirmative-action plan against a disparate-treatment challenge. Pursuant to the plan, the employer selected a woman for a road-dispatcher position, a job category traditionally regarded as "male." A male applicant who had a slightly higher interview score brought suit under Title VII. This Court rejected his claim and approved the plan, which allowed consideration of gender as "one of numerous factors." *Id.*, at 638. Such consideration, we said, is "fully consistent with Title VII" because plans of that order can aid "in eliminating the vestiges of discrimination in the workplace." *Id.*, at 642.

This litigation does not involve affirmative action. But if the voluntary affirmative action at issue in *Johnson* does not discriminate within the meaning of Title VII, neither does an employer's reasonable effort to comply with Title VII's disparate-impact provision by refraining from action of doubtful consistency with business necessity.

C

To "reconcile" the supposed "conflict" between disparate treatment and disparate impact, the Court offers an enigmatic standard. Employers may attempt to comply with Title VII's disparate-impact provision, the Court declares, only where there is a "strong basis in evidence" documenting the necessity of their action. The Court's standard, drawn from inapposite equal protection precedents, is not elaborated. One is left to wonder what cases would meet the standard and why the Court is so sure this case does not.

1

In construing Title VII, I note preliminarily, equal protection doctrine is of limited utility. The Equal Protection Clause, this Court has held, prohibits only intentional discrimination; it does not have a disparate-impact component. . . .

The cases from which the Court draws its strong-basis-in-evidence standard are particularly inapt; they concern the constitutionality of absolute racial preferences. See *Wygant* v. *Jackson Bd. of Ed.*, 476 U.S. 267, 277 (1986) (plurality opinion) (invalidating a school district's plan to lay off nonminority teachers while retaining minority teachers with less seniority); *Croson*, 488 U.S., at 499–500 (rejecting a set-aside program for minority contractors that operated as "an unyielding racial quota"). An employer's effort to avoid Title VII liability by repudiating a suspect selection method scarcely resembles those cases. Race was not merely a relevant consideration in *Wygant* and *Croson;* it was the decisive factor. Observance of Title VII's disparate-impact provision, in contrast, calls for no racial preference, absolute or otherwise. The very purpose of the provision is to ensure that individuals are hired and promoted based on qualifications manifestly necessary to successful performance of the job in question, qualifications that do not screen out members of any race.[6]

2

. . .

As a result of today's decision, an employer who discards a dubious selection process can anticipate costly disparate-treatment litigation in which its chances for success—even for surviving a summary-judgment motion—are highly problematic. Concern about exposure to disparate-impact liability, however well grounded, is insufficient to insulate an employer from attack. Instead, the employer must make a "strong" showing that (1) its selection method was "not job related and consistent with business necessity," or (2) that it refused to adopt "an equally valid, less-discriminatory alternative." It is hard to see how these requirements differ from demanding that an employer establish "a provable, actual violation" *against itself*. There is indeed a sharp conflict here, but it is not the false one the Court describes between Title VII's core provisions. It is, instead, the discordance of the Court's opinion with the voluntary compliance ideal.

3

The Court's additional justifications for announcing a strong-basis-in-evidence standard are unimpressive. First, discarding the results of tests, the Court suggests, calls for a heightened standard because it "upset[s] an employee's legitimate expectation." This rationale puts the cart before the horse. The legitimacy of an employee's expectation depends on the legitimacy of the selection method. If an employer reasonably concludes that an exam fails to identify the most qualified individuals and needlessly shuts out a segment of the applicant pool, Title VII surely does not compel the employer to hire or promote based on the test, however unreliable it may be. Indeed, the statute's prime objective is to prevent exclusionary practices from "operat[ing] to 'freeze' the status quo." *Griggs*, 401 U.S., at 430.

Second, the Court suggests, anything less than a strong-basis-in-evidence standard risks creating "a *de facto* quota system, in which . . . an employer could discard test results . . . with the intent of obtaining the employer's preferred racial balance." Under a reasonableness standard, however, an employer could not cast aside a selection method based on a

6 Even in Title VII cases involving race-conscious (or gender-conscious) affirmative-action plans, the Court has never proposed a strong-basis-in-evidence standard. In *Johnson* v. *Transportation Agency, Santa Clara Cty.*, 480 U.S. 616 (1987), the Court simply examined the municipal employer's action for reasonableness: "Given the obvious imbalance in the Skilled Craft category, and given the Agency's commitment to eliminating such imbalances, it was plainly not unreasonable for the Agency . . . to consider as one factor the sex of [applicants] in making its decision." *Id.*, at 637. See also *Firefighters* v. *Cleveland*, 478 U.S. 501, 516 (1986) ("Title VII permits employers and unions voluntarily to make use of reasonable race-conscious affirmative action.").

statistical disparity alone. The employer must have good cause to believe that the method screens out qualified applicants and would be difficult to justify as grounded in business necessity. Should an employer repeatedly reject test results, it would be fair, I agree, to infer that the employer is simply seeking a racially balanced outcome and is not genuinely endeavoring to comply with Title VII.

D

The Court stacks the deck further by denying respondents any chance to satisfy the newly announced strong-basis-in-evidence standard. When this Court formulates a new legal rule, the ordinary course is to remand and allow the lower courts to apply the rule in the first instance. See, *e.g.*, *Johnson* v. *California*, 543 U.S. 499, 515 (2005); *Pullman-Standard* v. *Swint*, 456 U.S. 273, 291 (1982). I see no good reason why the Court fails to follow that course in this case. Indeed, the sole basis for the Court's peremptory ruling is the demonstrably false pretension that respondents showed "nothing more" than "a significant statistical disparity."

III

A

Applying what I view as the proper standard to the record thus far made, I would hold that New Haven had ample cause to believe its selection process was flawed and not justified by business necessity. Judged by that standard, petitioners have not shown that New Haven's failure to certify the exam results violated Title VII's disparate-treatment provision.

The City, all agree, "was faced with a prima facie case of disparate-impact liability": The pass rate for minority candidates was half the rate for nonminority candidates, and virtually no minority candidates would have been eligible for promotion had the exam results been certified. Alerted to this stark disparity, the CSB heard expert and lay testimony, presented at public hearings, in an endeavor to ascertain whether the exams were fair and consistent with business necessity. Its investigation revealed grave cause for concern about the exam process itself and the City's failure to consider alternative selection devices.

Chief among the City's problems was the very nature of the tests for promotion. In choosing to use written and oral exams with a 60/40 weighting, the City simply adhered to the union's preference and apparently gave no consideration to whether the weighting was likely to identify the most qualified fire-officer candidates. There is strong reason to think it was not.

Relying heavily on written tests to select fire officers is a questionable practice, to say the least. Successful fire officers, the City's description of the position makes clear, must have the "[a]bility to lead personnel effectively, maintain discipline, promote harmony, exercise sound judgment, and cooperate with other officials." These qualities are not well measured by written tests. Testifying before the CSB, Christopher Hornick, an exam-design expert with more than two decades of relevant experience, was emphatic on this point: Leadership skills, command presence, and the like "could have been identified and evaluated in a much more appropriate way."

Hornick's commonsense observation is mirrored in case law and in Title VII's administrative guidelines. Courts have long criticized written firefighter promotion exams for being "more probative of the test-taker's ability to recall what a particular text stated on a given topic than of his firefighting or supervisory knowledge and abilities." *Vulcan Pioneers, Inc.* v. *New Jersey Dept. of Civil Serv.*, 625 F. Supp. 527, 539 (NJ 1985). A fire officer's job, courts have observed, "involves complex behaviors, good interpersonal skills, the ability to make decisions under tremendous pressure, and a host of other abilities-none of which is easily measured by a written, multiple choice test." *Firefighters Inst. for Racial Equality* v. *St. Louis*, 616 F. 2d 350, 359 (CA8 1980). Interpreting the Uniform Guidelines, EEOC and other federal agencies responsible for enforcing equal opportunity employment laws have similarly recognized that, as measures of "interpersonal relations" or "ability to function under danger (*e.g.*, firefighters)," "[p]encil-and-paper tests . . . generally are not close enough approximations of work behaviors to show content validity." 44 Fed. Reg. 12007 (1979). See also 29 CFR § 1607.15(C)(4).

Given these unfavorable appraisals, it is unsurprising that most municipal employers do not evaluate their fire-officer candidates as New Haven does. Although comprehensive statistics are scarce, a 1996 study found that nearly two-thirds of surveyed municipalities used assessment centers ("simulations of the real world of work") as part of their promotion processes. P. Lowry, A Survey of the Assessment Center Process in the Public Sector, 25 Public Personnel Management 307, 315 (1996). That figure represented a marked increase over the previous decade, see *ibid.*, so the percentage today may well be even higher. Among municipalities still relying in part on written exams, the median weight assigned to them was 30 percent—half the weight given to New Haven's written exam. *Id.*, at 309.

B

Concurring in the Court's opinion, Justice Alito asserts that summary judgment for respondents would be improper even if the City had good cause for its noncertification decision. A reasonable jury, he maintains, could have found that respondents were not actually motivated by concern about disparate-impact litigation, but instead sought only "to placate a politically important [African-American] constituency." As earlier noted, I would not oppose a remand for further proceedings fair to both sides. It is the Court that has chosen to short-circuit this litigation based on its pretension that the City has shown, and can show, nothing more than a statistical disparity. See *supra*, at 24, n. 8, 25. Justice Alito compounds the Court's error.

Offering a truncated synopsis of the many hours of deliberations undertaken by the CSB, Justice Alito finds evidence suggesting that respondents' stated desire to comply with Title VII was insincere, a mere "pretext" for discrimination against white firefighters. In support of his assertion, Justice Alito recounts at length the alleged machinations of Rev. Boise Kimber (a local political activist), Mayor John DeStefano, and certain members of the mayor's staff.

Most of the allegations Justice Alito repeats are drawn from petitioners' statement of facts they deem undisputed, a statement displaying an adversarial zeal not uncommonly found in such presentations. What cannot credibly be denied, however, is that the decision against certification of the exams was made neither by Kimber nor by the mayor and his staff. The relevant decision was made by the CSB, an unelected, politically insulated body. It is striking that Justice Alito's concurrence says hardly a word about the CSB itself, perhaps because there is scant evidence that its motivation was anything other than to comply with Title VII's disparate-impact provision. Notably, petitioners did not even seek to take depositions of the two commissioners who voted against certification. Both submitted uncontested affidavits declaring unequivocally that their votes were "based solely on [their] good faith belief that certification" would have discriminated against minority candidates in violation of federal law.

. . .

This case presents an unfortunate situation, one New Haven might well have avoided had it utilized a better selection process in the first place. But what this case does not present is race-based discrimination in violation of Title VII. I dissent from the Court's judgment, which rests on the false premise that respondents showed "a significant statistical disparity," but "nothing more."

NOTES ON *RICCI V. DESTEFANO*

1. **Constitutional Issues.** In his opinion for the Court, Justice Kennedy insists at several points that this case decides no constitutional questions. It rests entirely on interpretation of Title VII and results in summary judgment against the city for intentional discrimination in violation of the statute. The Court therefore does not need to decide whether the City also violated the Constitution.

Justice Scalia, alone among the justices, would have gone on to reach the constitutional question whether the theory of disparate impact can be reconciled with constitutional restrictions on affirmative action. These restrictions would come into play through the "equal protection component" of the Fifth Amendment's Due Process Clause (discussed more fully in the Notes on *Morton v. Mancari*, in Chapter 4 on Affirmative Action). The constitutional argument would be that the federal government, by imposing liability on employers for neutral practices with discriminatory effects, coerces them into engaging in prohibited forms of affirmative action. As

Justice Scalia recognizes, however, this argument is convincing only if the theory of disparate impact does something more than "smoke out" intentional discrimination.

In addition to avoiding the immediate constitutional questions in *Ricci*, does the Court additionally signal that it would also avoid the questions anticipated by Justice Scalia? It could do so by narrowly interpreting the theory of disparate impact only to shift a light burden onto the defendant to justify practices with a disparate impact. Can the Court take this step by itself? Recall that the Civil Rights Act of 1991 added section 703(k) to Title VII, specifically defining the defendant's burden of proof as demonstrating "that the challenged practice is job related for the position in question and consistent with business necessity."

For articles discussing constitutional challenges to the theory of disparate impact, see Richard Primus, Equal Protection and Disparate Impact: Round Three, 117 Harv. L. Rev. 493 (2003); Charles A. Sullivan, The World Turned Upside Down? Disparate Impact Claims by White Males, 98 Nw. U. L. Rev. 1505 (2004). The first of these articles was cited prominently by Justice Scalia, as well as by Justice Ginsburg in her dissent.

2. **The Influence of Constitutional Decisions.** The standard adopted by the Court for discarding the results of the test based on their adverse impact upon minorities requires "a strong basis in evidence of an impermissible disparate impact." This standard was taken from two earlier opinions, both concerned with the constitutionality of affirmative action plans. These opinions required a "strong basis in evidence" that the plans were necessary to remedy past discrimination. Richmond v. J.A. Croson Co., 488 U.S. 469, 500 (1989) (plurality opinion); Wygant v. Jackson Board of Education, 476 U.S. 267, 277 (1986) (plurality opinion). Both involved public employers, like the City of New Haven in this case, illustrating another way in which constitutional standards can enter into the litigation of employment discrimination claims. Public employers have to comply with the requirements of both Title VII and the Constitution.

The Court stops short of equating the constitutional standards for proof of intentional discrimination under these two different sources of law. This preserves the possibility that even "a strong basis in evidence" might not be enough to justify the City's actions under the Constitution. Again, the Court did not have to reach this issue because it held the City liable under Title VII. Suppose, however, the City had presented a strong basis in evidence for not certifying the test results and therefore made out a defense to a claim of disparate treatment under Title VII. Are there any conceivable circumstances in which it could still be held liable under the Constitution? Or is the Court just immunizing its views of intentional discrimination under the Constitution from congressional revision of the standards for disparate treatment under Title VII?

3. **The Theory of Disparate Impact Under Title VII.** The competing arguments of the plaintiffs and the City in this case both depended upon the City's exposure to liability for disparate impact. The plaintiffs would have relieved the City of liability for disparate treatment toward them only if the

City knew it would have been held liable for disparate impact toward the minority firefighters who failed the test. The Court rejected this stringent standard because it would have interfered with the provisions in Title VII meant to favor voluntary compliance with the statute. Employers would have been reluctant to use any test or selection procedure based on its adverse impact upon minorities. In fact, they might have refused to use any objective test or job qualification for fear that they might be liable to someone.

The Court also rejected the more lenient standard proposed by the City, because it "would amount to a *de facto* quota system, in which a 'focus on statistics . . . could put undue pressure on employers to adopt inappropriate prophylactic measures.'" Quoting Watson v. Fort Worth Bank & Trust Co., 487 U.S. 977, 992 (1988) (plurality opinion). This reference to quotas raises the same constitutional concerns as the Court's reliance on the constitutional decisions in *Croson* and *Wygant*. By quoting *Watson*, it also returns the law on disparate impact to decisions before the Civil Rights Act of 1991. *Watson* was a predecessor to *Wards Cove*, which in turn led to the changes made in the theory of disparate impact by the 1991 Act.

As Justice Ginsburg emphasizes in her dissent, the majority slights developments under Title VII that support a strong version of the theory of disparate impact—one that places a heavier burden upon defendants to justify practices with an adverse impact upon minorities. The majority opinion contains only a short discussion of *Griggs*, *Albemarle Paper*, and the codification of the theory of disparate impact by the 1991 Act. Where the majority opinion does rely upon the 1991 Act, it emphasizes the prohibition in § 703(*l*) on "race norming": adjusting the results of a test to secure greater representation of groups that did poorly on it. Discarding the results of a test because of its disparate impact is worse, in the Court's view, than adjusting scores on the basis of race. The Court also emphasizes the disclaimer in § 703(j) of any form of required affirmative action under Title VII. This approach leads naturally to a weak version of the theory of disparate impact—one that imposes a reduced burden on employers to show job relationship and business necessity. Under a weak version of the theory, employers would be less inclined to engage in affirmative action because they would have a greater prospect of successfully justifying practices with adverse impact.

All of these considerations affect the contours of the defense recognized in *Ricci*. Under a weak version of the theory, employers are less likely to make out "a strong basis in evidence" for concluding that they would be held liable for disparate impact. They would have to establish that the test failed the weakened requirements of job relationship and business necessity, or alternatively, that an equally valid test was available with less adverse impact upon minorities. As a weak version of the theory favors employers sued for disparate impact, it correspondingly disfavors employers in the City's situation, seeking to justify discarding the results of a test because they might be held liable for disparate impact.

4. **Scope and Practical Impact of *Ricci*.** In theory, *Ricci* applies to all employers subject to Title VII, public and private employers alike. Because it does not reach the constitutional issues, the Court rests its holding entirely

on liability for intentional discrimination under Title VII. In theory, the decision is very broad. In practice, however, it may be limited to the peculiar situation in which the City of New Haven placed itself. It gave a test, resulting in an identifiable group of candidates eligible for promotion, and then it took away the opportunity for advancement they had gained. Having identified a group of winners, it took away what they had won because no African-Americans and few Hispanics made it to the winner's circle. All employers will now want to avoid putting themselves in this situation. The question is how they can do so.

At the end of Part IIB of its opinion, the Court suggests that employers can take account of considerations about diversity and representation in their work force. This passage also limits the seeming scope of the decision in this case to discarding the results of a selection process. Employers can take steps to assure equal opportunity for all employees in choosing a selection process, "[b]ut once that process has been established and employers have made clear their selection criteria, they may not then invalidate the test results, thus upsetting an employee's legitimate expectation not to be judged on the basis of race." How much leeway does this passage give employers to stay out of the bind that the City placed itself in? Or does this passage simply indicate how narrow the present decision is, leaving open the possibility of a broader decision in the future?

Interestingly, New Haven relied on a paper and pencil test as the basis for selecting officers in its fire department, while the nearby city of Bridgeport, Connecticut, instead largely relied on "assessment centers" to select its officers. In this latter selection process, applicants are put into simulated situations designed to mimic those they might face in real life and then evaluated on the basis of how well they handle them. While written tests likely provide useful information on one type of intelligence, as well as on the willingness and ability to memorize certain information, the assessment centers are intended to better measure leadership, communications skills, and the ability to effectively deal with emergencies. Of course, such assessments are also more likely to include subjective judgments, which have the potential to mask decisions that are influenced by either racial hostility or affirmative action. In any event, the result is that Bridgeport has a core of fire lieutenants and captains that match the proportions of the city's black and Hispanic population, while New Haven does not. Steven Greenhouse, "For Employers, Ruling Offers Little Guidance on How to Make Their Hiring Fair," N. Y. Times, June 30, 2009, at A13. A likely consequence of the court's decision is that more cities will abandon testing and move to assessment centers as the primary basis to select their fire officers. Consider the likely impact of this shift on the quality of firefighting and the level of racial resentment.

5. **Summary Judgment in *Ricci*.** The narrow holding in *Ricci* concerns summary judgment for the plaintiffs and against the City. The Court first characterizes the decision to discard the test results because of the adverse impact on minorities as a decision based on race. It then allows a limited defense to this form of intentional discrimination if it is necessary to avoid some other form of liability under Title VII. Since the burden of proof is on

the defendant to make out this defense, the defendant must present evidence from which a reasonable inference could be drawn that the elements of the defense have been met. These elements are "a strong basis in evidence" for liability under the theory of disparate impact. Strictly speaking, then, evidence should come into play at two stages in the analysis: first, the evidence presented on summary judgment and the reasonable inferences from it; and second, whether the evidence and reasonable inferences together yield "a strong basis in evidence" for liability. For the sake of simplicity, this two-step process could be condensed into a single requirement that the defendant present "a strong basis in evidence" at summary judgment, but the Court is careful to frame its holding in terms of a "genuine issue as to any material fact": the City failed to raise a genuine issue that it had a strong basis in evidence for rejecting the test results.

The problem with this reasoning, as Justice Ginsburg points out in her dissent, is that it exaggerates the deficiencies in the City's evidence, finding "no evidence—let alone the required strong basis in evidence—that the tests were flawed because they were not job-related or because other, equally valid and less discriminatory tests were available to the City." 129 S.Ct. 2658, 2681. There was considerable evidence, both in the record in this case and from similar cases, that paper-and-pencil tests do not validly measure leadership ability, as the tests in this case purported to do. Leading a group of firefighters is an activity far removed from answering written questions. Even if some minimum of knowledge is necessary for effective leadership, and even if it was measured by tests, it would hardly have justified the City's use of the test to rank order candidates for promotion. The "rule of three" that required the City to consider only the three highest scoring candidates for each open position effectively magnified small differences in test scores that could not easily be proven to reflect job performance.

The City nevertheless invited this reasoning by the Court by insisting that it could rely upon the adverse impact of the tests alone to establish a defense to the plaintiffs' claim. The City accordingly de-emphasized the evidence on the tests' lack of validity. It did not ask the firm that devised the test to conduct a validity study. The experts who did testify on the validity of the tests either emphasized the precautions taken in devising the tests—which supported validity rather than undermining it—or indicated that they were not closely acquainted with the content of the tests or how they were used. Did the City lose the case by not adequately preparing this defense?

Justice Ginsburg, although she strongly disagrees with the majority, also "would not oppose a remand fair to both sides." She objects mainly to the new standards imposed by the majority without giving the City an opportunity to respond to and meet those standards. Yet she also would have vacated the summary judgment granted to the City and remanded for the development of further evidence on its reasons for discarding the test results. By insisting that its good faith alone was enough, and downplaying the evidence of invalidity, the City understandably tried to preserve the summary judgment entered in its favor by the lower courts. Did it also gamble—and lose—on the question whether summary judgment should be entered against it?

Justice Alito emphasizes Justice Ginsburg's willingness to remand the case for the submission of further evidence, but then takes issue with her analysis of the sufficiency of the existing evidence. On this point, however, all the justices seem to agree. Summary judgment for the *defendants* could not be affirmed. The only difference between the majority and the dissenters is over granting summary judgment to the *plaintiffs*. The real disagreement between Justice Alito and Justice Ginsburg concerns a different issue, discussed in the next note.

6. **Evidence of Racial Politics in *Ricci*.** Justice Alito devotes most of his concurring opinion, only part of which is excerpted here, to the evidence of racial politics surrounding the rejection of the test results in this case. A local minister, Rev. Kimber, who was a leader in the African-American community, allegedly put pressure on the City to reject the test results because no African-Americans scored high enough to be eligible for promotion. Justice Ginsburg responds in detail to the evidence recounted by Justice Alito in support of this allegation, again in parts of her opinion only partially excerpted here. In contrast to both opinions, the majority opinion alludes to this issue only in passing, noting that after the test results became known, "the mayor and other local politicians opened a public debate that turned rancorous."

What role should the existence of such a debate have played in the resolution of this case? Firefighters perform an essential public function, dependent upon the support of the entire community. It is entirely predictable—not to mention, democratically valuable—to have a public debate over who holds high positions in the department. Should the racial overtones in such a debate be held against the City of New Haven, in much the same way as prevailing segregation was held against the employers in *Griggs* and *Albemarle Paper*? Is the Court right to be suspicious of local politics or is it an inevitable feature of enforcing antidiscrimination law against public employers? In voting rights cases, the Court has been critical of measures, like race-conscious redistricting, that foster racially identified politics, while it has also recognized the role that race plays in politics and has allowed it so long as it is not the "predominant" factor. Miller v. Johnson, 515 U.S. 900, 916–17 (1995). Does race play the same ambivalent role in the background of *Ricci*? Is that why the majority opinion gives it less prominence than Justice Alito?

7. **The Future of Affirmative Action Under Title VII, or the Past?** As noted earlier, the Court adopts the standard of "a strong basis in evidence" from constitutional decisions on affirmative action. The Court does not rely upon, or even cite, the leading decision on affirmative action under Title VII, United Steelworkers v. Weber, 443 U.S. 193 (1979). This decision is discussed more fully in the next chapter, on affirmative action. Justice Ginsburg cites only *Johnson*, and in footnote 6 of her dissent, endorses its standard for allowing race-conscious decisionmaking under Title VII so long as it is a "reasonable" response to a pre-existing imbalance in the employer's work force. Both *Weber* and *Johnson* represent the most lenient standard that the Court has adopted for affirmative action plans under Title VII. The Court's opinion, by contrast, requires far more than a "reasonable" response

to racial imbalance. Does the Court's neglect of *Weber* and *Johnson* indicate that these cases are now likely to be overruled?

In place of these decisions, the Court relies on opinions from the same era that are more skeptical of affirmative action—the constitutional decisions in *Croson* and *Wygant* and the statutory decision in *Watson* on disparate impact. Does the fact that all these decisions are several decades old indicate that nothing has changed in the debate over affirmative action and its relationship to claims of disparate impact? If the election of President Obama heralded a new era in race relations, why has the Supreme Court confined itself to legal doctrine from the past? Is this characteristic of judicial reliance upon precedent or does it reveal that there is nothing new to be said on these issues?

8. **Bibliography.** For articles on *Ricci* and its implications, see Michelle Adams, Is Integration a Discriminatory Purpose?, 96 Iowa L. Rev. 837 (2011); Mark S. Brodin, *Ricci v. Destefano*: The New Haven Firefighters Case & the Triumph of White Privilege, 20 S. Cal. Rev. L. & Soc. Just. 161 (2011); Cheryl I. Harris & Kimberly West-Faulcon, Reading *Ricci*: Whitening Discrimination, Racing Test Fairness, 58 UCLA L. Rev. 73 (2010); Jennifer S. Hendricks, Contingent Equal Protection: Reaching for Equality after *Ricci* and *PICS*, 16 Mich. J. Gender & L. 397 (2010); Allen R. Kamp, *Ricci v. DeStefano* and Disparate Treatment: How the Case Makes Title VII and the Equal Protection Clause Unworkable, 39 Cap. U. L. Rev. 1 (2011); Marcia L. McCormick, Disparate Impact and Equal Protection after *Ricci v. DeStefano*. 27 Wis. J.L. Gender & Soc'y 100 (2012); Ann C. McGinley, Cognitive Illiberalism, Summary Judgment, and Title VII: An Examination of *Ricci v. DeStefano*, 57 N.Y.L. Sch. L. Rev. 865 (2012/13); Eang L. Ngov, War and Peace Between Title VII's Disparate Impact Provision and the Equal Protection Clause: Battling for A Compelling Interest, 42 Loy. U. Chi. L.J. 1 (2010); Eang L. Ngov, When "The Evil Day" Comes, Will Title VII's Disparate Impact Provision Be Narrowly Tailored to Survive an Equal Protection Clause Challenge?, 60 Am. U. L. Rev. 535 (2011); Helen Norton, The Supreme Court's Post-Racial Turn Towards a Zero-Sum Understanding of Equality, 52 Wm. & Mary L. Rev. 197 (2010); Richard Primus, The Future of Disparate Impact, 108 Mich. L. Rev. 1341 (2010); George Rutherglen, *Ricci v. DeStefano*: Affirmative Action and the Lessons of Adversity, 2009 Sup. Ct. Rev. 83 (2009); Joseph A. Seiner & Benjamin N. Gutman, Does *Ricci* Herald a New Disparate Impact?, 90 B.U. L. Rev. 2181 (2010); Reva B. Siegel, Race-Conscious But Race-Neutral: The Constitutionality of Disparate Impact in the Roberts Court, 66 Ala. L. Rev. 653 (2015); Reva B. Siegal, From Colorblindness to Antibalkanization: An Emerging Ground of Decision in Race Equality Cases, 120 Yale L.J. 1278 (2011); Kerri Lynn Stone, *Ricci* Glitch? The Unexpected Appearance of Transferred Intent in Title VII, 55 Loy. L. Rev. 751 (2009); Charles A. Sullivan, *Ricci v. DeStefano*: End of the Line or Just Another Turn on the Disparate Impact Road?, 104 Nw. U. L. Rev. Colloquy 201 (2009). See also Corey Ciocchetti & John Holcomb, The Frontier of Affirmative Action: Employment Preferences and Diversity in the Private Workplace, 12 U. Pa. J. Bus. Law 283 (2010); Tristin K. Green, Race

and Sex in Organizing Work: "Diversity," Discrimination, and Integration, 59 Emory L.J. 585 (2010).

CHAPTER 4

AFFIRMATIVE ACTION

A. CONSTITUTIONAL STANDARDS

INTRODUCTORY NOTES

1. **Evolution Towards Strict Scrutiny.** Most of the law of affirmative action is constitutional law. Affirmative action plans in higher education, in government contracting, and in public employment have repeatedly been examined by the Supreme Court. Even where affirmative action plans have been challenged under Title VII alone, the Constitution has been visible in the background, influencing the outcome in a variety of different ways: by providing the standards for evaluating any form of government action involving affirmative action; by defining the fundamental concept of discrimination that ultimately determines the permissible forms of affirmative action; and by limiting the justifications that can be offered for any kind of affirmative action plan. The standards for permissible affirmative action under Title VII are, as we shall see, different from but similar to the constitutional standards. How far apart they are as a practical matter remains one of the important open questions in the law of affirmative action. Yet the dominant role of constitutional standards cannot be disputed.

The course of constitutional decisions on this issue has been remarkable, both for its vicissitudes and for its stability. The Supreme Court initially applied a more lenient standard than strict scrutiny to race-conscious affirmative action plans, often in badly split decisions in which no one opinion represented the views of a majority of the Court. These cases focused on affirmative action by the federal government. Metro Broadcasting, Inc. v. FCC, 497 U.S. 547 (1990) (upholding a preference for minority-owned businesses in the award of broadcast licenses by the FCC); Fullilove v. Klutznick, 448 U.S. 448 (1980) (upholding a set-aside for minority-owned contractors in local public works financed with federal funds). They were, however, first narrowed and then overruled in cases involving government contracts, both by the states and by the federal government. City of Richmond v. J.A. Croson Co., 488 U.S. 469 (1989); Adarand Constructors, Inc. v. Pena, 515 U.S. 200, 235–36 (1995) (opinion of O'Connor, J.).[1] It is now clear that all racial classifications by government must meet the same standard of "strict scrutiny" under the Constitution and must be narrowly tailored to serve a compelling government interest.

2. **Strict Scrutiny in Education.** Having adopted a standard of strict scrutiny, the Supreme Court has left unclear exactly how it should be applied. The decisions on affirmative action in education are illustrative. These decisions began with Regents of the University of California v. Bakke,

---

[1] Justice Scalia provided the crucial fifth vote for the decision in *Adarand*. He would have gone further than Justice O'Connor and simply prohibited all government classifications on the basis of race. 515 U.S. at 239 (Scalia, J., concurring in part and concurring in the judgment).

438 U.S. 265 (1978), in which Justice Powell provided the decisive fifth vote. Four justices would have upheld the affirmative action plan at issue in that case, reserving a specified number of places in medical school for designated minorities, and four justices would have struck it down. Justice Powell held that the particular plan at issue was unconstitutional because it considered race in too rigid a fashion, but that a plan that allowed race to be considered as one factor among others would have served a compelling government interest in diversity in higher education. Id. at 291.

Some decades later, his position was eventually adopted by a majority of the Court in Grutter v. Bollinger, 539 U.S. 306 (2003). That case upheld an affirmative action plan by the University of Michigan Law School which, as Justice Powell had recommended in *Bakke*, considered race as only one factor among others in the individual evaluation of each applicant. In her opinion for the Court, Justice O'Connor emphasized a position that she had taken in her plurality opinion in *Adarand Constructors, Inc. v. Pena*, 515 U.S. 200, 237–38 (1995) (opinion of O'Connor, J.): "Strict scrutiny is not 'strict in theory, but fatal in fact.'" Diversity provided a sufficient justification for affirmative action, provided that race was used flexibly in the admissions process, because of the importance of universities and law schools in training the nation's leaders: "In order to cultivate a set of leaders with legitimacy in the eyes of the citizenry, it is necessary that the path to leadership be visibly open to talented and qualified individuals of every race and ethnicity." By contrast, the companion case of Gratz v. Bollinger, 539 U.S. 244 (2003), struck down the affirmative action plan for admissions to the undergraduate college at the University of Michigan. That plan awarded a fixed number of points in the admissions process to applicants from specified minority groups and, because it considered race in this mechanical fashion, was not narrowly tailored to serve a compelling interest in diversity.

A recent decision involving affirmative action in elementary and secondary education suggests that the Court may be taking an increasingly strict approach. In Parents Involved in Community Schools v. Seattle School Dist. No. 1, 551 U.S. 701 (2007), the Court held that school districts in Seattle, Washington, and Louisville, Kentucky, had failed to justify the use of race in student assignments. Race was used to break ties in a limited number of cases in which white students sought to attend schools in which whites were already overrepresented (or black students in schools in which blacks were overrepresented). By a vote of five-to-four, the Court found an insufficient connection between these race-based assignments and any attempt to remedy past discrimination or segregation. The Court also distinguished its prior decisions upholding affirmative action in higher education because those plans were narrowly tailored to achieve diversity. The plans in *Parents Involved*, by contrast, were not narrowly tailored either to achieve diversity or to remedy past discrimination. Justice Kennedy provided the crucial fifth vote in an opinion concurring in the judgment, in which he was somewhat more sympathetic to the aims of affirmative action than Chief Justice Roberts in his opinion for the plurality. Nevertheless, it is clear that a majority of the justices are now taking a more skeptical view of affirmative action, although not yet in cases concerned with higher education or employment.

3. Affirmative Action in Employment. Where the constitutional decisions have concerned employment, they have tended to impose standards similar to those under Title VII. Although the constitutional and statutory standards are framed in different terms, the decisions tend to reach the same results. A representative case is Wygant v. Jackson Board of Education, 476 U.S. 267 (1986), which involved a preference in layoffs, protecting minority employees of a public school district. Teachers ordinarily were laid off in reverse order of seniority, but under the preference, white teachers with greater seniority were laid off instead of minority teachers with lower seniority. The Court held that this preference was unconstitutional, with different justices offering different reasons for this conclusion. Justice Powell found insufficient evidence of past employment discrimination by the school district. He was not persuaded that the preference was justified by the interest in providing role models to minority students or remedying general societal discrimination. He also found that the preference imposed too great a burden upon laid-off white employees, id. at 274–84 (opinion of Powell, J.), a conclusion largely shared by Justice White. Id. at 294–95 (White, J., concurring in the judgment). Justice O'Connor added that the preference was defective because it sought to match the percentage of minority teachers with the percentage of minority students. Id. at 294 (O'Connor, J., concurring in part and concurring in the judgment).

Despite the differing approaches in all these opinions, each reached the conclusion that preferences affecting layoffs required a genuinely compelling justification if, indeed, such preferences were allowed at all. The Court previously had reached almost exactly the same result in a Title VII case, Firefighters Local Union No. 1784 v. Stotts, 467 U.S. 561 (1984). That case concerned a preference in layoffs established through judicial interpretation of a consent decree, which the Court struck down for a variety of different reasons. Some had to do with the consent decree itself, but others concerned detailed provisions of Title VII, including the special protection afforded to seniority systems by § 703(h). No one of these reasons corresponds exactly to the constitutional arguments offered by the various opinions in *Wygant*, but they combine to support the same conclusion: affirmative action cannot be imposed at the expense of laid off employees whose seniority would otherwise allow them to keep their jobs. This same principle finds expression in an opinion, otherwise very favorable to affirmative action, United Steelworkers v. Weber, 443 U.S. 193 (1979), which appears later in this chapter. That case upheld a preference in admission to a training program, overriding admission based entirely on seniority, but it did so with this caveat: "The plan does not require the discharge of white workers and their replacement with new black hirees." Id. at 208.

This principle, protecting the right of incumbent employees to their jobs, illustrates only one aspect of the convergence of constitutional and statutory standards for permissible affirmative action. The cases that follow these notes illustrate others, ironically in the extreme situations in which very weak evidence or very strong evidence is offered in support of an affirmative action plan.

4. **Affirmative Action in Europe.** Some kind words for affirmative action come from a somewhat unlikely source in Richard Posner's discussion of Muslim riots in France:

> Another factor in the recent French riots may be the French refusal to engage in affirmative action. The French are reluctant even to collect statistics on the number of people in France of various ethnicities, their incomes, and their unemployment rates. No effort is made to encourage discrimination in favor of restive minorities (as distinct from women, who are beneficiaries of affirmative action in France) and as a result there are very few African-origin French in prominent positions in commerce, the media, or the government. Affirmative action in the United States took off at approximately the same time as the 1967 and 1968 race riots, and is interpretable (so far as affirmative action for blacks is concerned) as a device for reducing black unemployment, creating opportunities for the ablest blacks to rise, promoting at least the appearance of racial equality, and in all these ways reducing the economic and emotional precipitants of race riots. Of particular importance, affirmative action was used to greatly increase the fraction of police that are black, while the "community policing" movement improved relations between the police and the residents of black communities. French police, traditionally brutal, have by all accounts very bad relations with the inhabitants of the Muslim slums. The French riots are a reminder that affirmative action, although offensive to meritocratic principles, may have redeeming social value in particular historical circumstances.

The French Riots—Posner's Comment, The Becker-Posner Blog on Nov. 13, 2005, http://www.becker-posner-blog.com/archives/2005/11/.

A left-leaning government in Norway recently mandated an aggressive affirmative action requirement to advance women into the upper tiers of business. The new law requires that, within two years of its enactment, women make up 40 percent of the board members of the nation's 519 largest publicly traded private companies. The law succeeded in achieving this goal, but at the cost of concentrating board membership in a select group of women. A study of the law found "that the maximum number of boards that a single director is part of has doubled during our observation period. This has led to the concentration of the benefits associated with prominence to a select few. Moreover, a select group of women have also become the most prominent directors. Since this benefit is only enjoyed by a few directors and associated with a particular sex, the intention of the Norwegian Government in creating a more equal setting can be questioned." Cathrine Seierstad & Tore Opsahl, For the Few Not the Many? The Effects of Affirmative Action on Presence, Prominence, and Social Capital of Women Directors in Norway. 27(1) Scandinavian Journal of Management 44 (2011).

5. **Bibliography.** The literature on affirmative action is vast. For some of the leading articles, collections of essays, and books, see Richard Posner, The *DeFunis* Case and the Constitutionality of Preferential Treatment of Racial Minorities, 1974 Sup. Ct. Rev. 1; Equality and Preferential Treatment (Marshall Cohen, Thomas Nagel & Thomas Scanlon eds., 1977); Discrimination, Affirmative Action, and Equal Opportunity: An Economic and Social Perspective (Walter Block & Michael A. Walker eds., 1982); Preferential Treatment in Employment: Affirmative Action or Reverse Discrimination? (Kenneth C. McGuiness ed., 1977); Reverse Discrimination (Barry R. Gross ed., 1977); Colloquy on the Anticaste Principle and Affirmative Action, 97 Mich. L. Rev. 1296 (1999); Comments and Papers from a Symposium on Affirmative Action and the Law, 1995 Ann. Surv. Am. L. 359; Symposium, Affirmative Action: Diversity of Opinions, 68 U. Colo. L. Rev. 833 (1997); Symposium on Affirmative Action, 43 UCLA L. Rev. 1731 (1996); Robert K. Fullinwider, The Reverse Discrimination Controversy: A Moral and Legal Analysis (1980); Nathan Glazer, Affirmative Discrimination: Ethnic Inequality and Public Policy (1975); Alan H. Goldman, Justice and Reverse Discrimination (1979).

Several, more specific, articles have examined the implications of the Supreme Court's decisions on affirmative action in higher education for employment. Lorin J. Lapidu, Diversity's Divergence: A Post-*Grutter* Examination of Racial Preferences in Employment, 28 W. New Eng. L. Rev. 199 (2006); Jared M. Mellott, The Diversity Rationale for Affirmative Action in Employment After *Grutter*: The Case for Containment, 48 Wm. & Mary L. Rev. 1091 (2006); Stephen M. Rich, What Diversity Contributes to Equal Opportunity, 89 S. Cal. L. Rev. 1011 (2016); Darnell Weeden, Back to the Future: Should *Grutter*'s Diversity Rationale Apply to Faculty Hiring? Is Title VII Implicated?, 26 Berkeley J. Emp. & Lab. L. 511 (2005); Symposium, The Effect of the University of Michigan Cases on Affirmative Action in Employment, 8 Emp. Rts. & Emp. Pol'y J. 127 (2004).

Morton v. Mancari

417 U.S. 535 (1974).

■ JUSTICE BLACKMUN delivered the opinion of the Court.

The Indian Reorganization Act of 1934, also known as the Wheeler-Howard Act, 48 Stat. 984, 25 U.S.C. § 461 et seq., accords an employment preference for qualified Indians in the Bureau of Indian Affairs (BIA or Bureau). Appellees, non-Indian BIA employees, challenged this preference as contrary to the anti-discrimination provisions of the Equal Employment Opportunity Act of 1972, 86 Stat. 103, 42 U.S.C. § 2000e et seq., and as violative of the Due Process Clause of the Fifth Amendment. A three-judge Federal District Court concluded that the Indian preference under the 1934 Act was impliedly repealed by the 1972 Act. We noted probable jurisdiction in order to examine the statutory and constitutional validity of this longstanding Indian preference. 414 U.S. 1142 (1974); 415 U.S. 946 (1974).

I

Section 12 of the Indian Reorganization Act, 48 Stat. 986, 25 U.S.C. § 472, provides:

> "The Secretary of the Interior is directed to establish standards of health, age, character, experience, knowledge, and ability for Indians who may be appointed, without regard to civil-service laws, to the various positions maintained, now or hereafter, by the Indian Office, in the administration of functions or services affecting any Indian tribe. Such qualified Indians shall hereafter have the preference to appointment to vacancies in any such positions."

In June 1972, pursuant to this provision, the Commissioner of Indian Affairs, with the approval of the Secretary of the Interior, issued a directive (Personnel Management Letter No. 72–12) stating that the BIA's policy would be to grant a preference to qualified Indians not only, as before, in the initial hiring stage, but also in the situation where an Indian and a non-Indian, both already employed by the BIA, were competing for a promotion within the Bureau. The record indicates that this policy was implemented immediately.

Shortly thereafter, appellees, who are non-Indian employees of the BIA at Albuquerque, instituted this class action, on behalf of themselves and other non-Indian employees similarly situated, in the United States District Court for the District of New Mexico, claiming that the "so-called 'Indian Preference Statutes,'" were repealed by the 1972 Equal Employment Opportunity Act and deprived them of rights to property without due process of law, in violation of the Fifth Amendment. Named as defendants were the Secretary of the Interior, the Commissioner of Indian Affairs, and the BIA Directors for the Albuquerque and Navajo Area Offices. Appellees claimed that implementation and enforcement of the new preference policy "placed and will continue to place [appellees] at a distinct disadvantage in competing for promotion and training programs with Indian employees, all of which has and will continue to subject the [appellees] to discrimination and deny them equal employment opportunity."

A three-judge court was convened pursuant to 28 U.S.C. § 2282 because the complaint sought to enjoin, as unconstitutional, the enforcement of a federal statute. Appellant Amerind, a nonprofit organization representing Indian employees of the BIA, moved to intervene in support of the preference; this motion was granted by the District Court and Amerind thereafter participated at all stages of the litigation.

After a short trial focusing primarily on how the new policy, in fact, has been implemented, the District Court concluded that the Indian preference was implicitly repealed by § 11 of the Equal Employment Opportunity Act of 1972, Pub. L. 92–261, 86 Stat. 111, 42 U.S.C. § 2000e–

16(a), proscribing discrimination in most federal employment on the basis of race. Having found that Congress repealed the preference, it was unnecessary for the District Court to pass on its constitutionality. The court permanently enjoined appellants "from implementing any policy in the Bureau of Indian Affairs which would hire, promote, or reassign any person in preference to another solely for the reason that such person is an Indian." The execution and enforcement of the judgment of the District Court was stayed by Mr. Justice Marshall on August 16, 1973, pending the disposition of this appeal.

II

The federal policy of according some hiring preference to Indians in the Indian service dates at least as far back as 1834. Since that time, Congress repeatedly has enacted various preferences of the general type here at issue. The purpose of these preferences, as variously expressed in the legislative history, has been to give Indians a greater participation in their own self-government; to further the Government's trust obligation toward the Indian tribes; and to reduce the negative effect of having non-Indians administer matters that affect Indian tribal life.

The preference directly at issue here was enacted as an important part of the sweeping Indian Reorganization Act of 1934. The overriding purpose of that particular Act was to establish machinery whereby Indian tribes would be able to assume a greater degree of self-government, both politically and economically. Congress was seeking to modify the then-existing situation whereby the primarily non-Indian-staffed BIA had plenary control, for all practical purposes, over the lives and destinies of the federally recognized Indian tribes. Initial congressional proposals would have diminished substantially the role of the BIA by turning over to federally chartered self-governing Indian communities many of the functions normally performed by the Bureau. Committee sentiment, however, ran against such a radical change in the role of the BIA. The solution ultimately adopted was to strengthen tribal government while continuing the active role of the BIA, with the understanding that the Bureau would be more responsive to the interests of the people it was created to serve.

One of the primary means by which self-government would be fostered and the Bureau made more responsive was to increase the participation of tribal Indians in the BIA operations. In order to achieve this end, it was recognized that some kind of preference and exemption from otherwise prevailing civil service requirements was necessary. Congressman Howard, the House sponsor, expressed the need for the preference:

> "The Indians have not only been thus deprived of civic rights and powers, but they have been largely deprived of the opportunity to enter the more important positions in the service of the very bureau which manages their affairs. Theoretically, the Indians have the right to qualify for the Federal civil service.

> In actual practice there has been no adequate program of training to qualify Indians to compete in these examinations, especially for technical and higher positions; and even if there were such training, the Indians would have to compete under existing law, on equal terms with multitudes of white applicants. . . . The various services on the Indian reservations are actually local rather than Federal services and are comparable to local municipal and county services, since they are dealing with purely local Indian problems. It should be possible for Indians with the requisite vocational and professional training to enter the service of their own people without the necessity of competing with white applicants for these positions. This bill permits them to do so." 78 Cong. Rec. 11729 (1934).

Congress was well aware that the proposed preference would result in employment disadvantages within the BIA for non-Indians. Not only was this displacement unavoidable if room were to be made for Indians, but it was explicitly determined that gradual replacement of non-Indians with Indians within the Bureau was a desirable feature of the entire program for self-government. Since 1934, the BIA has implemented the preference with a fair degree of success. The percentage of Indians employed in the Bureau rose from 34% in 1934 to 57% in 1972. This reversed the former downward trend, and was due, clearly, to the presence of the 1934 Act. The Commissioner's extension of the preference in 1972 to promotions within the BIA was designed to bring more Indians into positions of responsibility and, in that regard, appears to be a logical extension of the congressional intent.

III

It is against this background that we encounter the first issue in the present case: whether the Indian preference was repealed by the Equal Employment Opportunity Act of 1972. Title VII of the Civil Rights Act of 1964 was the first major piece of federal legislation prohibiting discrimination in *private* employment on the basis of "race, color, religion, sex, or national origin." 42 U.S.C. § 2000e–2(a). Significantly, §§ 701(b) and 703(i) of that Act explicitly exempted from its coverage the preferential employment of Indians by Indian tribes or by industries located on or near Indian reservations. 42 U.S.C. §§ 2000e(b) and 2000e–2(i). This exemption reveals a clear congressional recognition, within the framework of Title VII, of the unique legal status of tribal and reservation-based activities. The Senate sponsor, Senator Humphrey, stated on the floor by way of explanation:

> "This exemption is consistent with the Federal Government's policy of encouraging Indian employment and with the special legal position of Indians." 110 Cong. Rec. 12723 (1964).

The 1964 Act did not specifically outlaw employment discrimination by the Federal Government. Yet the mechanism for enforcing longstanding Executive Orders forbidding Government discrimination had proved ineffective for the most part. In order to remedy this, Congress, by the 1972 Act, amended the 1964 Act and proscribed discrimination in most areas of federal employment. In general, it may be said that the substantive anti-discrimination law embraced in Title VII was carried over and applied to the Federal Government. As stated in the House Report:[21]

> "To correct this entrenched discrimination in the Federal service, it is necessary to insure the effective application of uniform, fair and strongly enforced policies. The present law and the proposed statute do not permit industry and labor organizations to be the judges of their own conduct in the area of employment discrimination. There is no reason why government agencies should not be treated similarly. . . ." H.R. Rep. No. 92–238, on H.R. 1746, pp. 24–25 (1971).

Nowhere in the legislative history of the 1972 Act, however, is there any mention of Indian preference. Appellees assert, and the District Court held, that since the 1972 Act proscribed racial discrimination in Government employment, the Act necessarily, albeit sub silentio, repealed the provision of the 1934 Act that called for the preference in the BIA of one racial group, Indians, over non-Indians:

> "When a conflict such as in this case, is present, the most recent law or Act should apply and the conflicting Preferences passed some 39 years earlier should be impliedly repealed." Brief for Appellees 7.

We disagree. For several reasons we conclude that Congress did not intend to repeal the Indian preference and that the District Court erred in holding that it was repealed.

First: There are the above-mentioned affirmative provisions in the 1964 Act excluding coverage of tribal employment and of preferential treatment by a business or enterprise on or near a reservation. 42 U.S.C. §§ 2000e(b) and 2000e–2(i). These 1964 exemptions as to private employment indicate Congress' recognition of the longstanding federal policy of providing a unique legal status to Indians in matters concerning tribal or "on or near" reservation employment. The exemptions reveal a clear congressional sentiment that an Indian preference in the narrow context of tribal or reservation-related employment did not constitute racial discrimination of the type otherwise proscribed. In extending the

---

[21] The 1964 Act, however, did contain a proviso, expressed in somewhat precatory language: "That it shall be the policy of the United States to insure equal employment opportunities for Federal employees without discrimination because of race, color, religion, sex or national origin." 78 Stat. 254.

This statement of policy was re-enacted as 5 U.S.C. § 7151, 80 Stat. 523 (1966), and the 1964 Act's proviso was repealed, id., at 662.

general anti-discrimination machinery to federal employment in 1972, Congress in no way modified these private employment preferences built into the 1964 Act, and they are still in effect. It would be anomalous to conclude that Congress intended to eliminate the longstanding statutory preferences in BIA employment, as being racially discriminatory, at the very same time it was reaffirming the right of tribal and reservation-related private employers to provide Indian preference. Appellees' assertion that Congress implicitly repealed the preference as racially discriminatory, while retaining the 1964 preferences, attributes to Congress irrationality and arbitrariness, an attribution we do not share.

Second: Three months after Congress passed the 1972 amendments, it enacted two new Indian preference laws. These were part of the Education Amendments of 1972, 86 Stat. 235, 20 U.S.C. §§ 887c(a) and (d), and § 1119a (1970 ed., Supp. II). The new laws explicitly require that Indians be given preference in Government programs for training teachers of Indian children. It is improbable, to say the least, that the same Congress which affirmatively approved and enacted these additional and similar Indian preferences was, at the same time, condemning the BIA preference as racially discriminatory. In the total absence of any manifestation of supportive intent, we are loathe to imply this improbable result.

Third: Indian preferences, for many years, have been treated as exceptions to Executive Orders forbidding Government employment discrimination. The 1972 extension of the Civil Rights Act to Government employment is in large part merely a codification of prior anti-discrimination Executive Orders that had proved ineffective because of inadequate enforcement machinery. There certainly was no indication that the substantive proscription against discrimination was intended to be any broader than that which previously existed. By codifying the existing anti-discrimination provisions, and by providing enforcement machinery for them, there is no reason to presume that Congress affirmatively intended to erase the preferences that previously had co-existed with broad anti-discrimination provisions in Executive Orders.

Fourth: Appellees encounter head-on the "cardinal rule . . . that repeals by implication are not favored." They and the District Court read the congressional silence as effectuating a repeal by implication. There is nothing in the legislative history, however, that indicates affirmatively any congressional intent to repeal the 1934 preference. Indeed, as explained above, there is ample independent evidence that the legislative intent was to the contrary.

This is a prototypical case where an adjudication of repeal by implication is not appropriate. The preference is a longstanding, important component of the Government's Indian program. The anti-discrimination provision, aimed at alleviating minority discrimination in employment, obviously is designed to deal with an entirely different and, indeed, opposite problem. Any perceived conflict is thus more apparent than real.

In the absence of some affirmative showing of an intention to repeal, the only permissible justification for a repeal by implication is when the earlier and later statutes are irreconcilable. Georgia v. Pennsylvania R. Co., 324 U.S. 439, 456–457 (1945). Clearly, this is not the case here. A provision aimed at furthering Indian self-government by according an employment preference within the BIA for qualified members of the governed group can readily co-exist with a general rule prohibiting employment discrimination on the basis of race. Any other conclusion can be reached only by formalistic reasoning that ignores both the history and purposes of the preference and the unique legal relationship between the Federal Government and tribal Indians.

Furthermore, the Indian preference statute is a specific provision applying to a very specific situation. The 1972 Act, on the other hand, is of general application. Where there is no clear intention otherwise, a specific statute will not be controlled or nullified by a general one, regardless of the priority of enactment. . . .

The courts are not at liberty to pick and choose among congressional enactments, and when two statutes are capable of co-existence, it is the duty of the courts, absent a clearly expressed congressional intention to the contrary, to regard each as effective. "When there are two acts upon the same subject, the rule is to give effect to both if possible. . . . The intention of the legislature to repeal 'must be clear and manifest.'" United States v. Borden Co., 308 U.S. 188, 198 (1939). In light of the factors indicating no repeal, we simply cannot conclude that Congress consciously abandoned its policy of furthering Indian self-government when it passed the 1972 amendments.

We therefore hold that the District Court erred in ruling that the Indian preference was repealed by the 1972 Act.

IV

We still must decide whether, as the appellees contend, the preference constitutes invidious racial discrimination in violation of the Due Process Clause of the Fifth Amendment. Bolling v. Sharpe, 347 U.S. 497 (1954). The District Court, while pretermitting this issue, said: "[W]e could well hold that the statute must fail on constitutional grounds."

Resolution of the instant issue turns on the unique legal status of Indian tribes under federal law and upon the plenary power of Congress, based on a history of treaties and the assumption of a "guardian-ward" status, to legislate on behalf of federally recognized Indian tribes. The plenary power of Congress to deal with the special problems of Indians is drawn both explicitly and implicitly from the Constitution itself. Article I, § 8, cl. 3, provides Congress with the power to "regulate Commerce . . . with the Indian Tribes," and thus, to this extent, singles Indians out as a proper subject for separate legislation. Article II, § 2, cl. 2, gives the

President the power, by and with the advice and consent of the Senate, to make treaties. This has often been the source of the Government's power to deal with the Indian tribes. The Court has described the origin and nature of the special relationship:

> "In the exercise of the war and treaty powers, the United States overcame the Indians and took possession of their lands, sometimes by force, leaving them an uneducated, helpless and dependent people, needing protection against the selfishness of others and their own improvidence. Of necessity the United States assumed the duty of furnishing that protection, and with it the authority to do all that was required to perform that obligation and to prepare the Indians to take their place as independent, qualified members of the modern body politic. . . ." Board of County Comm'rs v. Seber, 318 U.S. 705, 715 (1943).

Literally every piece of legislation dealing with Indian tribes and reservations, and certainly all legislation dealing with the BIA, single out for special treatment a constituency of tribal Indians living on or near reservations. If these laws, derived from historical relationships and explicitly designed to help only Indians, were deemed invidious racial discrimination, an entire Title of the United States Code (25 U.S.C.) would be effectively erased and the solemn commitment of the Government toward the Indians would be jeopardized. . . .

It is in this historical and legal context that the constitutional validity of the Indian preference is to be determined. As discussed above, Congress in 1934 determined that proper fulfillment of its trust required turning over to the Indians a greater control of their own destinies. The overly paternalistic approach of prior years had proved both exploitative and destructive of Indian interests. Congress was united in the belief that institutional changes were required. An important part of the Indian Reorganization Act was the preference provision here at issue.

Contrary to the characterization made by appellees, this preference does not constitute "racial discrimination." Indeed, it is not even a "racial" preference.[24] Rather, it is an employment criterion reasonably

[24] The preference is not directed towards a "racial" group consisting of "Indians"; instead, it applies only to members of "federally recognized" tribes. This operates to exclude many individuals who are racially to be classified as "Indians." In this sense, the preference is political rather than racial in nature. The eligibility criteria appear in 44 BIAM 335, 3.1:

> "1. Policy—An Indian has preference in appointment in the Bureau. To be eligible for preference in appointment, promotion, and training, an individual must be one-fourth or more degree Indian blood and be a member of a Federally-recognized tribe. It is the policy for promotional consideration that where two or more candidates who met the established qualification requirements are available for filling a vacancy, if one of them is an Indian, he shall be given preference in filling the vacancy. In accordance with the policy statement approved by the Secretary, the Commissioner may grant exceptions to this policy by approving the selection and appointment of non-Indians, when he considers it in the best interest of the Bureau.
>
> "This program does not restrict the right of management to fill positions by methods other than through promotion. Positions may be filled by transfers, reassignment, reinstatement, or initial appointment." App. 92.

designed to further the cause of Indian self-government and to make the BIA more responsive to the needs of its constituent groups. It is directed to participation by the governed in the governing agency. The preference is similar in kind to the constitutional requirement that a United States Senator, when elected, be "an Inhabitant of that State for which he shall be chosen," Art. I, § 3, cl. 3, or that a member of a city council reside within the city governed by the council. Congress has sought only to enable the BIA to draw more heavily from among the constituent group in staffing its projects, all of which, either directly or indirectly, affect the lives of tribal Indians. The preference, as applied, is granted to Indians not as a discrete racial group, but, rather, as members of quasi-sovereign tribal entities whose lives and activities are governed by the BIA in a unique fashion. See n.24, supra. In the sense that there is no other group of people favored in this manner, the legal status of the BIA is truly sui generis. Furthermore, the preference applies only to employment in the Indian service. The preference does not cover any other Government agency or activity, and we need not consider the obviously more difficult question that would be presented by a blanket exemption for Indians from all civil service examinations. Here, the preference is reasonably and directly related to a legitimate, nonracially based goal. This is the principal characteristic that generally is absent from proscribed forms of racial discrimination.

On numerous occasions this Court specifically has upheld legislation that singles out Indians for particular and special treatment. . . . As long as the special treatment can be tied rationally to the fulfillment of Congress' unique obligation toward the Indians, such legislative judgments will not be disturbed. Here, where the preference is reasonable and rationally designed to further Indian self-government, we cannot say that Congress' classification violates due process.

The judgment of the District Court is reversed and the cases are remanded for further proceedings consistent with this opinion.

It is so ordered.

Judgment reversed and case remanded.

NOTES ON *MORTON V. MANCARI*

1. **Preferences for Native Americans Under Title VII.** Unlike other minorities, Native Americans benefit from provisions in Title VII that explicitly allow affirmative action on their behalf. Section 703(i) allows preferences for the employment of Native Americans on or near Indian reservations, and § 701(b) completely exempts Indian tribes from coverage as employers. Both of these provisions apply only to federally recognized Indian tribes, which, as the regulations in footnote 24 of *Morton v. Mancari* reveal, make membership dependent upon Indian ancestry. The Supreme Court does not characterize this element of the regulations as racially defined, for reasons discussed in the next note, but the effect of the

provisions, as well as the Supreme Court's own opinion, is to permit preferential treatment of Native Americans.

The existence of these provisions reveals the multicultural character of racial and ethnic discrimination, a feature of civil rights law that has become ever more apparent as different minorities have asserted claims to equal treatment. Even though laws like Title VII were passed mainly to redress discrimination against African-Americans, they have always been framed in terms that benefit all racial and ethnic groups. No single group, or even collection of groups, is the sole beneficiary of the laws against discrimination. Contrary to what is sometimes asserted, there are no "protected classes" under Title VII. The ideals of equal treatment protect all individuals alike, regardless of their group affiliations.

Paradoxically, however, the demand for equal treatment can be invoked to justify different treatment of groups, and the individuals affiliated with them, based on the historical circumstances that determine the group's current status. The abstract concept of equality requires the same treatment only of those who are similarly situated and it leaves open the possibility that different racial and ethnic groups are differentially situated. For an argument to this effect, with specific application to Native Americans, see Guido Calabresi, *Bakke* as Pseudo Tragedy, 28 Cath. U. L. Rev. 427 (1979). Regardless of how widely this argument is accepted, it was certainly accepted by Congress in adopting the provisions in Title VII allowing affirmative action in favor of Native Americans.

In *Morton v. Mancari*, the Supreme Court took these provisions one step further, relying on them to imply a further exception to the general prohibition against discrimination by the federal government. The Court also relied on the long history of special federal legislation on behalf of Native Americans. Does this appeal to tradition answer the objection that Title VII was intended as a dramatic break with the traditional treatment of minorities? Or does the Court implicitly assume that past legislation, ostensibly for the benefit of Native Americans, does not constitute the kind of discrimination prohibited by Title VII? Does this assumption just beg the question by presupposing the very form of preferential treatment at issue?

Attempts to generalize the Court's reasoning to affirmative action on behalf of other groups have proved to be far more controversial than affirmative action limited to Native Americans. Is this because this particular form of affirmative action has been endorsed by Congress? Or did Congress endorse it because Native Americans are a relatively small minority, comprising 1.7 percent of the nation's overall population and concentrated in only a handful of states? See U.S. Census Bureau, The American Indian and Alaska Native Population 2010 (Census 2010 Brief Jan. 2012). Do these demographic facts reduce the force of political objections to affirmative action on behalf of Native Americans? Do they reduce the force of the arguments against affirmative action based on principle?

2. Preferences for Native Americans Under the Constitution. The constitutional holding in *Morton v. Mancari* relies, even more so than the statutory holding, on the tradition of special federal legislation on behalf of

Native Americans. This tradition goes as far back as the reference to "Indian Tribes" in the Constitution as quasi-sovereign nations, both in the Commerce Clause and in the Treaty Power. Art. I, § 8, cl. 3; Art. II § 2, cl. 2. The Commerce Clause, in particular, equates commerce "with the Indian Tribes" with commerce among the states and with foreign nations and gives Congress the power to regulate it in the same terms. Does the Commerce Clause, as the Court assumes, also allow Congress to favor Native Americans through federal legislation?

This clause, like the others in Article I, § 8, confers power on Congress without addressing independent constraints upon that power. At least since Bolling v. Sharpe, 347 U.S. 497 (1954), a companion case to Brown v. Board of Education, 347 U.S. 483 (1954), the Fifth Amendment has prohibited racial discrimination by the federal government in the same terms as the Fourteenth Amendment prohibits such discrimination by the states. More recent cases on affirmative action, moreover, have taken the further step of applying the same standards of strict scrutiny to affirmative action both by the federal government and by the states. E.g., Adarand Constructors, Inc. v. Pena, 515 U.S. 200 (1995). By contrast, *Morton v. Mancari* applies only a standard of rational basis review, finding that the preference for Native Americans rationally furthers the aim of Indian self-government. Can this lenient standard be reconciled with the recent cases on affirmative action?

In *Morton v. Mancari*, the Court argues for a lenient standard based on the desperate expedient of characterizing the preference in favor of Native Americans as one based on the quasi-sovereignty of the Indian tribes rather than as one based on race. Can this response survive the Court's candid admission in footnote 24 that membership in a federally recognized tribe depends upon Indian ancestry? If this isn't a racial prerequisite for receiving special treatment, what is? Does the tradition of treating Indian tribes as quasi-sovereign entities eliminate the racial nature of the benefit provided or does it provide a justification for it? If the latter, doesn't the special treatment of Native Americans based on tradition again beg the question, just as much on the constitutional issue in *Morton* as on the statutory issue? How can special treatment of Native Americans in a program of government hiring be justified by special treatment of Indian tribes as an abstract principle of constitutional law? Doesn't the assumption of special treatment have to be justified by a neutral principle that does not simply favor Native Americans at some point?

For a debate over the significance and scope of *Morton v. Mancari*, see Paul Spruhan, A Legal History of Blood Quantum in Federal Indian Law to 1935, 51 S.D. L. Rev. 1 (2006); David Williams, The Borders of the Equal Protection Clause: Indians as Peoples, 38 UCLA L. Rev. 759 (1991); Carole Goldberg-Ambrose, Not " 'Strictly' Racial: A Response to Indians as Peoples," 39 UCLA L. Rev. 169 (1991); David Williams, Sometimes Suspect: A Response to Professor Goldberg-Ambrose, 39 UCLA L. Rev. 191 (1991).

3. Limiting or Extending *Morton v. Mancari*. Whatever the force of the reasoning in *Morton v. Mancari*, it has not been extended beyond preferences for Native Americans. In Rice v. Cayetano, 528 U.S. 495 (2000), the Supreme Court held unconstitutional a racial classification by the state of Hawaii favoring citizens of Hawaiian ancestry in obtaining admission to special schools established by a trust fund for this purpose. The Court specifically distinguished native Hawaiians from members of federally recognized Indian tribes. Id. at 524. Does this limitation on *Morton v. Mancari* make the decision more or less justifiable? Doesn't it just call still more attention to the lenient treatment of affirmative action in favor of Native Americans, in contrast to all other ethnic groups? How much longer can the Supreme Court exempt affirmative action on their behalf from strict scrutiny?

Of course, another way to eliminate the anomaly created by *Morton v. Mancari* is to subject all forms of affirmative action only to rational basis review. This proposal was advanced most forcefully by John Hart Ely in The Constitutionality of Reverse Racial Discrimination, 41 U. Chi. L. Rev. 723 (1974). He argued against heightened judicial review when the majority has acted against its own interests in establishing an affirmative action plan for the benefit of a racial or ethnic minority. On his view, the only scope for judicial review of affirmative action was in determining whether it was genuinely for the benefit of a minority group, rather than a covert attempt to impose disadvantages on another such group, for instance, white ethnic groups usually thought to be part of the majority. Is there any question about the federal government's motive for preferring Native Americans for employment in the Bureau of Indian Affairs?

Sheet Metal Workers' Int'l Association v. EEOC

478 U.S. 421 (1986).

■ JUSTICE BRENNAN announced the judgment of the Court and delivered the opinion of the Court with respect to Parts I, II, III, and VI, and an opinion with respect to Parts IV, V, and VII in which JUSTICE MARSHALL, JUSTICE BLACKMUN, and JUSTICE STEVENS join.

In 1975, petitioners were found guilty of engaging in a pattern and practice of discrimination against black and Hispanic individuals (nonwhites) in violation of Title VII of the Civil Rights Act of 1964, 42 U.S.C. § 2000e et seq., and ordered to end their discriminatory practices, and to admit a certain percentage of nonwhites to union membership by July 1981. In 1982 and again in 1983, petitioners were found guilty of civil contempt for disobeying the District Court's earlier orders. They now challenge the District Court's contempt finding, and also the remedies the court ordered both for the Title VII violation and for contempt. Principally, the issue presented is whether the remedial provision of Title VII, see 42 U.S.C. § 2000e–5(g), empowers a district court to order race-conscious relief that may benefit individuals who are not identified victims of unlawful discrimination.

I

Petitioner Local 28 of the Sheet Metal Workers' International Association (Local 28) represents sheet metal workers employed by contractors in the New York City metropolitan area. Petitioner Local 28

Joint Apprenticeship Committee (JAC) is a management-labor committee which operates a 4-year apprenticeship training program designed to teach sheet metal skills. Apprentices enrolled in the program receive training both from classes and from on-the-job work experience. Upon completing the program, apprentices become journeyman members of Local 28. Successful completion of the program is the principal means of attaining union membership.

In 1964, the New York State Commission for Human Rights determined that petitioners had excluded blacks from the union and the apprenticeship program in violation of state law. The State Commission found, among other things, that Local 28 had never had any black members or apprentices, and that "admission to apprenticeship is conducted largely on a [nepotistic] basis involving sponsorship by incumbent union members," creating an impenetrable barrier for nonwhite applicants. Petitioners were ordered to "cease and desist" their racially discriminatory practices. The New York State Supreme Court affirmed the State Commission's findings, and directed petitioners to implement objective standards for selecting apprentices. State Comm'n for Human Rights v. Farrell, 43 Misc. 2d 958 (1964). . . .

In 1971, the United States initiated this action under Title VII and Executive Order No. 11246, 3 CFR 339 (1964–1965 Comp.) to enjoin petitioners from engaging in a pattern and practice of discrimination against black and Hispanic individuals (nonwhites). The New York City Commission on Human Rights (City) intervened as plaintiff to press claims that petitioners had violated municipal fair employment laws, and had frustrated the City's efforts to increase job opportunities for minorities in the construction industry. United States v. Local 638, Enterprise Assn. of Steam, Hot Water, Hydraulic Sprinkler, Pneumatic Tube, Compressed Air, Ice Machine, Air Conditioning, and General Pipefitters, 347 F. Supp. 164 (S.D.N.Y. 1972). In 1970, the City had adopted a plan requiring contractors on its projects to employ one minority trainee for every four journeyman union members. Local 28 was the only construction local which refused to comply voluntarily with the plan. In early 1974, the City attempted to assign six minority trainees to sheet metal contractors working on municipal construction projects. After Local 28 members stopped work on the projects, the District Court directed the JAC to admit the six trainees into the apprenticeship program, and enjoined Local 28 from causing any work stoppage at the affected job sites. The parties subsequently agreed to a consent order that required the JAC to admit up to 40 minorities into the apprenticeship program by September 1974. The JAC stalled compliance with the consent order, and only completed the indenture process under threat of contempt.

Following a trial in 1975, the District Court concluded that petitioners had violated both Title VII and New York law by discriminating against nonwhite workers in recruitment, selection, training, and admission to the union. EEOC v. Local 638, 401 F. Supp. 467 (S.D.N.Y. 1975). [Over the years, the District Court entered repeated findings of discrimination, injunctions, and citations of contempt.]

The District Court . . . once again adjudicated petitioners guilty of civil contempt. The court ordered petitioners to pay for a computerized recordkeeping system to be maintained by outside consultants, but deferred ruling on additional contempt fines pending submission of the administrator's fund proposal. The court subsequently adopted the administrator's proposed Employment, Training, Education, and Recruitment Fund (Fund) to "be used for the purpose of remedying discrimination." The Fund was used for a variety of purposes. In order to increase the pool of qualified nonwhite applicants for the apprenticeship program, the Fund paid for nonwhite union members to serve as liaisons to vocational and technical schools with sheet metal programs, created part-time and summer sheet metal jobs for qualified nonwhite youths, and extended financial assistance to needy apprentices. The Fund also extended counseling and tutorial services to nonwhite apprentices, giving them the benefits that had traditionally been available to white apprentices from family and friends. Finally, in an effort to maximize employment opportunities for all apprentices, the Fund provided financial support to employers otherwise unable to hire a sufficient number of apprentices, as well as matching funds to attract additional funding for job training programs.

The District Court also entered an Amended Affirmative Action Plan and Order (AAAPO) which modified RAAPO in several respects. AAAPO established a 29.23% minority membership goal to be met by August 31, 1987. The new goal was based on the labor pool in the area covered by the newly expanded union. The court abolished the apprenticeship examination, concluding that "the violations that have occurred in the past have been so egregious that a new approach must be taken to solve the apprentice selection problem." Apprentices were to be selected by a three-member Board, which would select one minority apprentice for each white apprentice indentured. Finally, to prevent petitioners from underutilizing the apprenticeship program, the JAC was required to assign to Local 28 contractors one apprentice for every four journeymen, unless the contractor obtained a written waiver from respondents.

Petitioners appealed the District Court's contempt orders, the Fund order, and the order adopting AAAPO. A divided panel of the Court of Appeals affirmed the District Court's contempt findings, except the finding based on adoption of the older workers' provision. EEOC v. Local 638, 753 F.2d 1172 (1985). The court concluded that "[particularly] in light of the determined resistance by Local 28 to all efforts to integrate its membership, . . . the combination of violations found by [the District Court] amply demonstrates the union's foot-dragging egregious noncompliance . . . and adequately supports [its] findings of civil contempt against both Local 28 and the JAC." Id., at 1183. The court also affirmed the District Court's contempt remedies, including the Fund order, and affirmed AAAPO with two modifications: it set aside the requirement that one minority apprentice be indentured for every white apprentice, and clarified the District Court's orders to allow petitioners to implement objective, nondiscriminatory apprentice selection procedures. The court found the 29.23% nonwhite membership goal to be proper in light of Local 28's "long continued and egregious racial discrimination," Id., at 1186, and because it "will not unnecessarily trammel the rights of any readily ascertainable group of non-minority individuals." Id., at 1187. The court rejected petitioners' argument that the goal violated Title VII or the Constitution. The court also distinguished AAAPO from the race-conscious order invalidated by this Court in Firefighters v. Stotts, 467 U.S. 561 (1984), on three grounds: (1) unlike the order in *Stotts*, AAAPO did not conflict with a bona fide seniority plan; (2) the *Stotts* discussion of § 706(g) of Title VII, 42 U.S.C. § 2000e–5(g), applied only to "make whole" relief and did not address the prospective relief contained in AAAPO and the Fund order; and (3) this case, unlike *Stotts*, involved intentional discrimination. . . .

IV

Petitioners, joined by the EEOC, argue that the membership goal, the Fund order, and other orders which require petitioners to grant membership preferences to nonwhites are expressly prohibited by § 706(g), 42 U.S.C. § 2000e–5(g), which defines the remedies available under Title VII. Petitioners and the EEOC maintain that § 706(g) authorizes a district court to award preferential relief only to the actual victims of unlawful discrimination. They maintain that the membership goal and the Fund violate this provision, since they require petitioners to admit to membership, and otherwise to extend benefits to, black and Hispanic individuals who are not the identified victims of unlawful discrimination. We reject this argument, and hold that § 706(g) does not prohibit a court from ordering, in appropriate circumstances, affirmative race-conscious relief as a remedy for past discrimination. Specifically, we hold that such relief may be appropriate where an employer or a labor union has engaged in persistent or egregious discrimination, or where necessary to dissipate the lingering effects of pervasive discrimination.

A

Section 706(g) states:

> "If the court finds that the respondent has intentionally engaged in or is intentionally engaging in an unlawful employment practice . . ., the court may enjoin the respondent from engaging in such unlawful employment practice, and order such affirmative action as may be appropriate, which may include, but is not limited to, reinstatement or hiring of employees, with or without back pay . . ., or any other equitable relief as the court deems appropriate. . . . No order of the court shall require the admission or reinstatement of an individual as a member of a

union, or the hiring, reinstatement, or promotion of an individual as an employee, or the payment to him of any back pay, if such individual was refused admission, suspended, or expelled, or was refused employment or advancement or was suspended or discharged for any reason other than discrimination of account of race, color, religion, sex, or national origin in violation of . . . this title." 42 U.S.C. § 2000e–5(g).

The language of § 706(g) plainly expresses Congress' intent to vest district courts with broad discretion to award "appropriate" equitable relief to remedy unlawful discrimination. Teamsters v. United States, 431 U.S. 324, 364 (1977); Franks v. Bowman Transportation Co., 424 U.S. 747, 771 (1976); Albemarle Paper Co. v. Moody, 422 U.S. 405, 421 (1975). Nevertheless, petitioners and the EEOC argue that the last sentence of § 706(g) prohibits a court from ordering an employer or labor union to take affirmative steps to eliminate discrimination which might incidentally benefit individuals who are not the actual victims of discrimination. This reading twists the plain language of the statute.

The last sentence of § 706(g) prohibits a court from ordering a union to admit an individual who was "refused admission . . . for any reason other than discrimination." It does not, as petitioners and the EEOC suggest, say that a court may order relief only for the actual victims of past discrimination. The sentence on its face addresses only the situation where a plaintiff demonstrates that a union (or an employer) has engaged in unlawful discrimination, but the union can show that a particular individual would have been refused admission even in the absence of discrimination, for example, because that individual was unqualified. In these circumstances, § 706(g) confirms that a court could not order the union to admit the unqualified individual. . . . In this case, neither the membership goal nor the Fund order required petitioners to admit to membership individuals who had been refused admission for reasons unrelated to discrimination. Thus, we do not read § 706(g) to prohibit a court from ordering the kind of affirmative relief the District Court awarded in this case.

B

The availability of race-conscious affirmative relief under § 706(g) as a remedy for a violation of Title VII also furthers the broad purposes underlying the statute. Congress enacted Title VII based on its determination that racial minorities were subject to pervasive and systematic discrimination in employment. "[I]t was clear to Congress that '[t]he crux of the problem [was] to open employment opportunities for Negroes in occupations which have been traditionally closed to them,' . . . and it was to this problem that Title VII's prohibition against racial discrimination in employment was primarily addressed." Steelworkers v. Weber, 443 U.S. 193, 203 (1979) (quoting 110 Cong. Rec. 6548 (1964) (remarks of Sen. Humphrey)). Title VII was designed "to achieve equality of employment opportunities and remove barriers that have operated in the past to favor an identifiable group of white employees over other employees." Griggs v. Duke Power Co., 401 U.S. 424, 429–430 (1971); see Teamsters, supra, at 364–365; Franks, supra, at 763, 771; Albemarle Paper, supra, at 417–418. In order to foster equal employment opportunities, Congress gave the lower courts broad power under § 706(g) to fashion "the most complete relief possible" to remedy past discrimination. *Franks*, supra, at 770; *Albemarle Paper*, supra, at 418.

In most cases, the court need only order the employer or union to cease engaging in discriminatory practices, and award make-whole relief to the individuals victimized by those practices. In some instances, however, it may be necessary to require the employer or union to take affirmative steps to end discrimination effectively to enforce Title VII. Where an employer or union has engaged in particularly longstanding or egregious discrimination, an injunction simply reiterating Title VII's prohibition against discrimination will often prove useless and will only result in endless enforcement litigation. In such cases, requiring recalcitrant employers or unions to hire and to admit qualified minorities roughly in proportion to the number of qualified minorities in the work force may be the only effective way to ensure the full enjoyment of the rights protected by Title VII. . . .

Further, even where the employer or union formally ceases to engage in discrimination, informal mechanisms may obstruct equal employment opportunities. An employer's reputation for discrimination may discourage minorities from seeking available employment. . . . In these circumstances, affirmative race-conscious relief may be the only means available "to assure equality of employment opportunities and to eliminate those discriminatory practices and devices which have fostered racially stratified job environments to the disadvantage of minority citizens." McDonnell Douglas Corp. v. Green, 411 U.S. 792, 800 (1973); see Teamsters, 431 U.S., at 348. Affirmative action "promptly operates to change the outward and visible signs of yesterday's racial distinctions and thus, to provide an impetus to the process of dismantling the barriers, psychological or otherwise, erected by past practices." NAACP v. Allen, 493 F.2d, at 621.

Finally, a district court may find it necessary to order interim hiring or promotional goals pending the development of nondiscriminatory hiring or promotion procedures. In these cases, the use of numerical goals provides a compromise between two unacceptable alternatives: an outright ban on hiring or promotions, or continued use of a discriminatory selection procedure. . . .

C

Despite the fact that the plain language of § 706(g) and the purposes of Title VII suggest the opposite, petitioners and the EEOC maintain that the legislative history indicates that Congress intended that affirmative relief under § 706(g) benefit only the identified victims of past discrimination. To support this contention, petitioners and the EEOC rely principally on statements made throughout the House and Senate debates to the effect that Title VII would not require employers or labor unions to adopt quotas or preferences that would benefit racial minorities.

Our examination of the legislative history of Title VII convinces us that, when examined in context, the statements relied upon by petitioners and the EEOC do not indicate that Congress intended to limit relief under § 706(g) to that which benefits only the actual victims of unlawful discrimination. Rather, these statements were intended largely to reassure opponents of the bill that it would not require employers or labor unions to use racial quotas or to grant preferential treatment to racial minorities in order to avoid being charged with unlawful discrimination. See Weber, 443 U.S., at 205. The bill's supporters insisted that this would not be the intent and effect of the legislation, and eventually agreed to state this expressly in § 703(j), 42 U.S.C. § 2000e–2(j). Contrary to the arguments made by petitioners and the EEOC, these statements do not suggest that a court may not order preferential relief under § 706(g) when appropriate to remedy past discrimination. Rather, it is clear that the bill's supporters only wished to emphasize that an employer would not violate the statute merely by having a racially imbalanced work force, and, consequently, that a court could not order an employer to adopt racial preferences merely to correct such an imbalance. . . .

To summarize, many opponents of Title VII argued that an employer could be found guilty of discrimination under the statute simply because of a racial imbalance in his work force, and would be compelled to implement racial "quotas" to avoid being charged with liability. Weber, 443 U.S., at 205. At the same time, supporters of the bill insisted that employers would not violate Title VII simply because of racial imbalance, and emphasized that neither the Commission nor the courts could compel employers to adopt quotas solely to facilitate racial balancing. Id., at 207, n.7. The debate concerning what Title VII did and did not require culminated in the adoption of § 703(j), which stated expressly that the statute did not require an employer or labor union to adopt quotas or preferences simply because of a racial imbalance. However, while Congress strongly opposed the use of quotas or preferences merely to maintain racial balance, it gave no intimation as to whether such measures would be acceptable as *remedies* for Title VII violations.

Congress' failure to consider this issue is not surprising, since there was relatively little civil rights litigation prior to the adoption of the 1964 Civil Rights Act. More importantly, the cases that had been litigated had not resulted in the sort of affirmative-action remedies that, as later became apparent, would sometimes be necessary to eliminate effectively the effects of past discrimination. Thus, the use of racial preferences as a *remedy* for past discrimination simply was not an issue at the time Title VII was being considered. Our task then is to determine whether

Congress intended to preclude a district court from ordering affirmative action in appropriate circumstances as a remedy for past discrimination. . . . Our examination of the legislative policy behind Title VII leads us to conclude that Congress did not intend to prohibit a court from exercising its remedial authority in that way.[37] Congress deliberately gave the district courts broad authority under Title VII to fashion the most complete relief possible to eliminate "the last vestiges of an unfortunate and ignominious page in this country's history," Albemarle Paper, 422 U.S., at 418. As we noted above, affirmative race-conscious relief may in some instances be necessary to accomplish this task. In the absence of any indication that Congress intended to limit a district court's remedial authority in a way which would frustrate the court's ability to enforce Title VII's mandate, we decline to fashion such a limitation ourselves. . . .

E

Although we conclude that § 706(g) does not foreclose a district court from instituting some sorts of racial preferences where necessary to remedy past discrimination, we do not mean to suggest that such relief is always proper. While the fashioning of "appropriate" remedies for a particular Title VII violation invokes the "equitable discretion of the district courts," Franks, 424 U.S., at 770, we emphasize that a court's judgment should be guided by sound legal principles. In particular, the court should exercise its discretion with an eye towards Congress' concern that race-conscious affirmative measures not be invoked simply to create a racially balanced work force. In the majority of Title VII cases, the court will not have to impose affirmative action as a remedy for past discrimination, but need only order the employer or union to cease engaging in discriminatory practices and award make-whole relief to the individuals victimized by those practices. However, in some cases, affirmative action may be necessary in order effectively to enforce Title VII. As we noted before, a court may have to resort to race-conscious affirmative action when confronted with an employer or labor union that has engaged in persistent or egregious discrimination. Or such relief may be necessary to dissipate the lingering effects of pervasive discrimination. Whether there might be other circumstances that justify the use of court-ordered affirmative action is a matter that we need not

---

[37] We also reject petitioners' argument that the District Court's remedies contravened § 703(j), since they require petitioners to grant preferential treatment to blacks and Hispanics based on race. Our examination of the legislative history convinces us that § 703(j) was added to Title VII to make clear that an employer or labor union does not engage in "discrimination" simply because of a racial imbalance in its work force or membership, and would not be required to institute preferential quotas to avoid Title VII liability. See Steelworkers v. Weber, 443 U.S. 193, 205, n.5 (1979) ("[Section] 703(j) speaks to substantive liability under Title VII"); Teamsters, 431 U.S., at 339–340, n.20 ("[Section] 703(j) makes clear that Title VII imposes no requirement that a work force mirror the general population"); Franks, 424 U.S., at 758 ("[T]he . . . provisions of § 703 . . . delineat[e] which employment practices are illegal and thereby prohibited and which are not"). We reject the notion that § 703(j) somehow qualifies or proscribes a court's authority to order relief otherwise appropriate under § 706(g) in circumstances where an illegal discriminatory act or practice is established. . . .

decide here. We note only that a court should consider whether affirmative action is necessary to remedy past discrimination in a particular case before imposing such measures, and that the court should also take care to tailor its orders to fit the nature of the violation it seeks to correct. In this case, several factors lead us to conclude that the relief ordered by the District Court was proper.

First, both the District Court and the Court of Appeals agreed that the membership goal and Fund order were necessary to remedy petitioners' pervasive and egregious discrimination. The District Court set the original 29% membership goal upon observing that "[t]he record in both state and federal courts against [petitioners] is replete with instances of their bad faith attempts to prevent or delay affirmative action." The court extended the goal after finding petitioners in contempt for refusing to end their discriminatory practices and failing to comply with various provisions of RAAPO. In affirming the revised membership goal, the Court of Appeals observed that "[this] court has twice recognized Local 28's long continued and egregious racial discrimination . . . and Local 28 has presented no facts to indicate that our earlier observations are no longer apposite." In light of petitioners' long history of "foot-dragging resistance" to court orders, simply enjoining them from once again engaging in discriminatory practices would clearly have been futile. Rather, the District Court properly determined that affirmative race-conscious measures were necessary to put an end to petitioners' discriminatory ways.

Both the membership goal and Fund order were similarly necessary to combat the lingering effects of past discrimination. In light of the District Court's determination that the union's reputation for discrimination operated to discourage nonwhites from even applying for membership, it is unlikely that an injunction would have been sufficient to extend to nonwhites equal opportunities for employment. Rather, because access to admission, membership, training, and employment in the industry had traditionally been obtained through informal contacts with union members, it was necessary for a substantial number of nonwhite workers to become members of the union in order for the effects of discrimination to cease. The Fund, in particular, was designed to insure that nonwhites would receive the kind of assistance that white apprentices and applicants had traditionally received through informal sources. On the facts of this case, the District Court properly determined that affirmative, race-conscious measures were necessary to assure the equal employment opportunities guaranteed by Title VII.

Second, the District Court's flexible application of the membership goal gives strong indication that it is not being used simply to achieve and maintain racial balance, but rather as a benchmark against which the court could gauge petitioners' efforts to remedy past discrimination. The court has twice adjusted the deadline for achieving the goal, and has continually approved of changes in the size of the apprenticeship classes to account for the fact that economic conditions prevented petitioners from meeting their membership targets; there is every reason to believe that both the court and the administrator will continue to accommodate *legitimate* explanations for petitioners' failure to comply with the court's orders. Moreover, the District Court expressly disavowed any reliance on petitioners' failure to meet the goal as a basis for the contempt finding, but instead viewed this failure as symptomatic of petitioners' refusal to comply with various subsidiary provisions of RAAPO. In sum, the District Court has implemented the membership goal as a means by which it can measure petitioners' compliance with its orders, rather than as a strict racial quota.

Third, both the membership goal and the Fund order are temporary measures. Under AAAPO "[p]referential selection of [union members] will end as soon as the percentage of [minority union members] approximates the percentage of [minorities] in the local labor force." Weber, 443 U.S., at 208–209. Similarly, the Fund is scheduled to terminate when petitioners achieve the membership goal, and the court determines that it is no longer needed to remedy past discrimination. The District Court's orders thus operate "as a temporary tool for remedying past discrimination without attempting to 'maintain' a previously achieved balance." Weber, 443 U.S., at 216 (BLACKMUN, J., concurring).

Finally, we think it significant that neither the membership goal nor the Fund order "unnecessarily [trammels] the interests of white employees." Id., at 208; Teamsters, 431 U.S., at 352–353. Petitioners concede that the District Court's orders did not require any member of the union to be laid off, and did not discriminate against *existing* union members. See Weber, supra, at 208. While whites seeking admission into the union may be denied benefits extended to their nonwhite counterparts, the court's orders do not stand as an absolute bar to such individuals; indeed, a majority of new union members have been white. Many provisions of the court's orders are race-neutral (for example, the requirement that the JAC assign one apprentice for every four journeyman workers), and petitioners remain free to adopt the provisions of AAAPO and the Fund order for the benefit of white members and applicants.

V

Petitioners also allege that the membership goal and Fund order contravene the equal protection component of the Due Process Clause of the Fifth Amendment because they deny benefits to white individuals based on race. We have consistently recognized that government bodies constitutionally may adopt racial classifications as a remedy for past discrimination. . . . We have not agreed, however, on the proper test to be applied in analyzing the constitutionality of race-conscious remedial measures. . . . We need not resolve this dispute here, since we conclude that the relief ordered in this case passes even the most rigorous test—it is narrowly tailored to further the Government's compelling interest in remedying past discrimination.

In this case, there is no problem, as there was in *Wygant*, with a proper showing of prior discrimination that would justify the use of remedial racial classifications. Both the District Court and Court of Appeals have repeatedly found petitioners guilty of egregious violations of Title VII, and have determined that affirmative measures were necessary to remedy their racially discriminatory practices. More importantly, the District Court's orders were properly tailored to accomplish this objective. First, the District Court considered the efficacy of alternative remedies, and concluded that, in light of petitioners' long record of resistance to official efforts to end their discriminatory practices, stronger measures were necessary. The court devised the temporary membership goal and the Fund as tools for remedying past discrimination. More importantly, the District Court's orders will have only a marginal impact on the interests of white workers. . . . Again, petitioners concede that the District Court's orders did not disadvantage *existing* union members. While white applicants for union membership may be denied certain benefits available to their nonwhite counterparts, the court's orders do not stand as an absolute bar to the admission of such individuals; again, a majority of those entering the union after entry of the court's orders have been white. We therefore conclude that the District Court's orders do not violate the equal protection safeguards of the Constitution. . . .

Affirmed.

■ JUSTICE POWELL, concurring in part and concurring in the judgment.

. . .

I

Petitioners contend that the Fund order and the membership goal imposed by the District Court and upheld by the Court of Appeals are forbidden by § 706(g) because that provision authorizes an award of preferential relief only to the actual victims of unlawful discrimination. The plain language of Title VII does not clearly support a view that all remedies must be limited to benefiting victims. And although the matter is not entirely free from doubt, I am unpersuaded by petitioners' reliance on the legislative history of Title VII. Rather, in cases involving particularly egregious conduct a district court may fairly conclude that an injunction alone is insufficient to remedy a proven violation of Title VII. This is such a case.

The history of petitioners' contemptuous racial discrimination and their successive attempts to evade all efforts to end that discrimination is well stated in Part I of the Court's opinion. Under these circumstances the District Court acted within the remedial authority granted by § 706(g) in establishing the Fund order and numerical goal at issue in this case. This Court's decision in Firefighters v. Stotts, 467 U.S. 561

(1984), is not to the contrary. There, the question whether Title VII might *ever* authorize a remedy that benefits those who were not victims of discrimination was not before us, although there is language in the opinion suggesting an answer to that question.

II

There remains for consideration the question whether the Fund order and membership goal contravene the equal protection component of the Due Process Clause of the Fifth Amendment because they may deny benefits to white individuals based on race. I have recently reiterated what I believe to be the standard for assessing a constitutional challenge to a racial classification:

> " 'Any preference based on racial or ethnic criteria must necessarily receive a most searching examination to make sure that it does not conflict with constitutional guarantees.' Fullilove v. Klutznick, 448 U.S. 448, 491 (1980) (opinion of BURGER, C.J.). There are two prongs to this examination. First, any racial classification 'must be justified by a compelling governmental interest' Palmore v. Sidoti, 466 U.S. 429, 432 (1984); see Loving v. Virginia, 388 U.S. 1, 11 (1967); cf. Graham v. Richardson, 403 U.S. 365, 375 (1971) (alienage). Second, the means chosen by the State to effectuate its purpose must be 'narrowly tailored to the achievement of that goal.' *Fullilove*, supra, at 480." Wygant v. Jackson Board of Education, 476 U.S. 267, 273–274 (1986).

The finding by the District Court and the Court of Appeals that petitioners have engaged in egregious violations of Title VII establishes, without doubt, a compelling governmental interest sufficient to justify the imposition of a racially classified remedy. It would be difficult to find defendants more determined to discriminate against minorities. My inquiry, therefore, focuses on whether the District Court's remedy is "narrowly tailored," see *Wygant*, supra, at 280, n.6, to the goal of eradicating the discrimination engaged in by petitioners. I believe it is.

The Fund order is supported not only by the governmental interest in eradicating petitioners' discriminatory practices, it also is supported by the societal interest in compliance with the judgments of federal courts. . . . The Fund order was not imposed until *after* petitioners were held in contempt. In requiring the Union to create the Fund, the District Court expressly considered " 'the consequent seriousness of the burden' to the defendants." App. to Pet. for Cert. 156, quoting 330 U.S., at 304. Moreover, the focus of the Fund order was to give minorities opportunities that for years had been available informally only to nonminorities. The burden this imposes on nonminorities is slight. Under these circumstances, I have little difficulty concluding that the Fund order was carefully structured to vindicate the compelling governmental interests present in this case. . . .

The flexible application of the goal requirement in this case demonstrates that it is not a means to achieve racial balance. The contempt order was not imposed for the Union's failure to achieve the goal, but for its failure to take the prescribed steps that would facilitate achieving the goal. Additional flexibility is evidenced by the fact that this goal, originally set to be achieved by 1981, has been twice delayed and is now set for 1987.

It is also important to emphasize that on the record before us, it does not appear that nonminorities will be burdened directly, if at all. Petitioners' counsel conceded at oral argument that imposition of the goal would not require the layoff of nonminority union workers, and that therefore the District Court's order did not disadvantage existing union members. This case is thus distinguishable from *Wygant* where the plurality opinion noted that "layoffs impose the entire burden of achieving racial equality on particular individuals, often resulting in serious disruption of their lives." 476 U.S., at 283. In contrast to the layoff provision in *Wygant*, the goal at issue here is akin to a hiring goal. In *Wygant* the plurality observed:

> "In cases involving valid *hiring* goals, the burden to be borne by individuals is diffused to a considerable extent among society generally. Though hiring goals may burden some innocent individuals, they simply do not impose the same kind of injury that layoffs impose." Id., at 282.

My view that the imposition of flexible goals as a remedy for past discrimination may be permissible under the Constitution is not an endorsement of their indiscriminate use. Nor do I imply that the adoption of such a goal will always pass constitutional muster.

■ JUSTICE O'CONNOR, concurring in part and dissenting in part.

. . . I would reverse the judgment of the Court of Appeals on statutory grounds insofar as the membership "goal" and the Fund order are concerned, and I would not reach petitioners' constitutional claims. I agree with Justice White, however, that the membership "goal" in this case operates as a rigid racial quota that cannot feasibly be met through good-faith efforts by Local 28. In my view, § 703(j), 42 U.S.C. § 2000e–2(j), and § 706(g), 42 U.S.C. § 2000e–5(g), read together, preclude courts from ordering racial quotas such as this. I therefore dissent from the Court's judgment insofar as it affirms the use of these mandatory quotas. . . .

In Steelworkers v. Weber, 443 U.S. 193, 205, n.5 (1979), the Court stated that "Section 703(j) speaks to substantive liability under Title VII." While this is *one* purpose of § 703(j), the Court in *Weber* had no occasion to consider whether it was the *exclusive* purpose. In my view, the words "Nothing contained in this title shall be interpreted to require" plainly make § 703(j) applicable to the interpretation of *any* provision of Title VII, including § 706(g). Therefore, when a court interprets § 706(g) as authorizing it to require an employer to adopt a racial quota, that court contravenes § 703(j) to the extent that the relief imposed as a purported remedy for a violation of Title VII's substantive provisions in fact operates to require racial preferences "on account of [a racial] imbalance." In addition, since § 703(j) by its terms limits the circumstances in which an employer or union may be required to extend "preferential treatment to any individual *or to any group* because of . . . race," the plurality's distinction between make-whole and classwide relief is plainly ruled out insofar as § 703(j) is concerned.

The plurality's restrictive reading of § 703(j) rests largely on its view of the legislative history, which the plurality claims establishes that Congress simply did not consider the use of racial preferences to remedy past discrimination when it enacted Title VII. According to the plurality, the sole focus of concern over racial quotas involved the scope of substantive liability under Title VII: the fear was that employers or unions would be found liable for violating Title VII merely on account of a racial imbalance. This reading of the legislative history ignores authoritative statements—relied on by the Court in *Stotts*, 467 U.S., at 580–582—addressing the relief courts could order, and making plain that racial *quotas*, at least, were not among the permissible remedies for past discrimination. See, e.g., 110 Cong. Rec. 6549 (1964) ("Contrary to the allegations of some opponents of this title, there is nothing in it that will give any power to the Commission or to any court to require hiring, firing, or promotion of employees in order to meet a racial 'quota' or to achieve a certain racial balance") (Sen. Humphrey); id., at 6566 ("[T]itle VII does not permit the ordering of racial quotas in businesses or unions. . . .") (memorandum of Republican House sponsors); id., at 14665 ("Under title VII, not even a court, much less the Commission, could order racial quotas or the hiring, reinstatement, admission to membership or payment of back pay for anyone who is not discriminated against in violation of this title") (statement of Senate sponsors in a bipartisan newsletter delivered to Senators supporting the bill during an attempted filibuster). . . .

To be consistent with § 703(j), a racial hiring or membership goal must be intended to serve merely as a benchmark for measuring compliance with Title VII and eliminating the lingering effects of past discrimination, rather than as a rigid numerical requirement that must unconditionally be met on pain of sanctions. To hold an employer or union to achievement of a particular percentage of minority employment or membership, and to do so regardless of circumstances such as economic conditions or the number of available qualified minority applicants, is to impose an impermissible quota. By contrast, a permissible goal should require only a good-faith effort on the employer's or union's part to come within a range demarcated by the goal itself. . . .

If, as the Court holds, Title VII sometimes allows district courts to employ race-conscious remedies that may result in racially preferential treatment for nonvictims, it does so only where such remedies are truly necessary. In fashioning any such remedy, including racial hiring goals, the court should exercise caution and "take care to tailor its orders to fit the nature of the violation it seeks to correct." As the plurality suggests, goals should generally be temporary measures rather than efforts to maintain a previously achieved racial balance, and should not unnecessarily trammel the interests of nonminority employees. Furthermore, the use of goals is least likely to be consistent with § 703(j) where the adverse effects of any racially preferential treatment attributable to the goals will be "concentrated upon a relatively small, ascertainable group of non-minority persons." EEOC v. Local 638, 753 F.2d 1172, 1186 (CA2 1985). In sum, the creation of racial preferences by courts, even in the more limited form of goals rather than quotas, must be done sparingly and only where manifestly necessary to remedy violations of Title VII if the policy underlying § 703(j) and § 706(g) is to be honored.

In this case, I agree with Justice White that the membership "goal" established by the District Court's successive orders in this case has been administered and will continue to operate "not just [as] a minority membership goal but also [as] a strict racial quota that the union was required to attain." It is important to realize that the membership "goal" ordered by the District Court goes well beyond a requirement, such as the ones the plurality discusses approvingly, that a union "admit qualified minorities roughly in proportion to the number of qualified minorities in the work force." The "goal" here requires that the racial composition of Local 28's entire membership mirror that of the relevant labor pool by August 31, 1987, without regard to variables such as the number of qualified minority applicants available or the number of new apprentices needed. The District Court plainly stated that "[if] the goal is not attained by that date, defendants will face fines that will threaten their very existence." . . .

Whether the unequivocal rejection of racial quotas by the Congress that enacted Title VII is said to be expressed in § 706(g), in § 703(j), or in both, a "remedy" such as this membership quota cannot stand. For similar reasons, I believe that the Fund order, which created benefits for minority apprentices that nonminority apprentices were precluded from enjoying, operated as a form of racial quota. Accordingly, I would reverse the judgment of the Court of Appeals on statutory grounds insofar as the membership "goal" and Fund order are concerned, without reaching petitioners' constitutional claims.

[The dissenting opinions of Justice White and Justice Rehnquist, joined by Chief Justice Burger, are omitted.]

NOTES ON *SHEET METAL WORKERS' INT'L UNION V. EEOC*

1. Constitutional Standards for Judicially Ordered Affirmative Action. If *Morton v. Mancari* presents the weakest possible evidence that can justify affirmative action, *Sheet Metal Workers* presents the strongest. The union in this case had been discriminating against minority workers in violation of state law even before the enactment of Title VII. It had continued to discriminate despite repeated orders to stop by state administrative agencies, state courts, and eventually the federal court in this case. The order before the Supreme Court was not the district court's initial remedy for the union's violations of Title VII, but was eventually imposed as a remedy for failure to comply with earlier orders after a finding of contempt. It is difficult to imagine a stronger record of past discrimination and defiance, both of the law and of attempts to enforce the law. A compelling government interest in remedying past discrimination and preventing future discrimination was more than amply documented in this case.

The problem is with the requirement of "narrow tailoring." As Justice O'Connor points out in her dissent, the affirmative action plan seemingly operated like a quota, specifying the proportion of minorities to be admitted to the union down to the hundredth of a percentage point. Whites were effectively denied membership in the union to make way for African-Americans and Hispanics. The majority, composed of the four justices who joined Justice Brennan's opinion and Justice Powell, tries to get around this problem by interpreting the district court's order more flexibly than a literal reading of its terms would warrant. Is such after-the-fact flexibility, imposed by a higher court on a lower court's ruling, justified by the need to preserve the validity of the district court's order? Or does it simply reflect the power of the Supreme Court to make the district court's order say whatever it wants? What would have been the practical consequences in this case of invalidating the district court's attempt to bring the union into compliance with the law?

Both Justice Brennan and Justice Powell apply the standard of strict scrutiny to the preference ordered here, both with respect to union membership and to funding training for minority workers. Both also limit the scope of judicially ordered preferences to a correspondingly narrow range of cases, involving egregious discrimination that could not be remedied by less drastic means. Both also find the preference narrowly tailored, with minimal and temporary burdens on white employees, for the reasons discussed already. None of these conclusions is surprising, nor do they open the door to widespread use of preferences as a judicially imposed remedy.

What accounts for the reluctance of the majority, even supporters of affirmative action like Justice Brennan, to broadly endorse judicially required affirmative action? Is it the fear of popular resistance to affirmative action imposed externally, without the acquiescence of unions, the employees they represent, and employers? Or is it the absence of any endorsement for such forms of affirmative action by the democratically elected branches of government? A narrow view of *Sheet Metal Workers* takes as paramount the need of the judiciary to assure compliance with its own orders, requiring affirmative action only as a last resort when other measures have failed. A broad view of the decision takes it as only one instance in which this remedy is appropriate, leaving open other circumstances in which it might be ordered. Justice Brennan, in the parts of his plurality opinion concerned with statutory issues, identifies two other such circumstances: when informal mechanisms may obstruct equal employment opportunities (for instance, when an employer has a reputation for discrimination); and when interim goals are necessary "pending the development of nondiscriminatory hiring or promotion procedures." Justice Powell conspicuously failed to adopt this dictum and endorsed only the narrow view of when preferences could be ordered.

A case decided one year later, United States v. Paradise, 480 U.S. 149 (1987), bears out the narrow view. That case involved findings of longstanding racial discrimination by the Alabama State Troopers and upheld a preference for African-Americans in hiring and promotions. The plaintiffs alleged only violations of the Constitution, without bringing any claims under Title VII. Again speaking for a plurality of four justices, Justice Brennan found egregious discrimination to be a sufficient ground for judicially ordered preferences. Id. at 166–71. Justice Stevens concurred in the judgment based on the broad remedial authority of federal courts to remedy constitutional violations. Id. at 189–95. In his opinion, even more explicitly than in the opinions in *Sheet Metal Workers*, the integrity of the judicial process figured in the justification for ordering affirmative action. Defiance of the courts, after they have found a violation of the Constitution, could not be allowed to continue.

2. **Judicially Ordered Affirmative Action Under Title VII.** The statutory issues in *Sheet Metal Workers* were, in many ways, more complicated than the constitutional issues. The majority based its decision primarily on the plenary authority to order equitable relief under § 706(g)(1). This provision broadly authorizes courts to order any steps necessary to remedy violations of Title VII, including, surprisingly, "such affirmative action as may be appropriate." This reference to affirmative action, however, is not taken, even by the majority, to refer to preferential treatment. It refers, instead, to a court's equitable authority to order the defendant to take affirmative steps to remedy past violations of the law, as opposed simply to the negative step of not engaging in further violations in the future. The difficulty with § 706(g)(1) is not with its failure specifically to authorize preferential treatment, but with several other provisions in Title VII that seemingly restrict the authority that it confers.

The most significant of these is § 703(j), which specifically disavows any interpretation of Title VII that purports to require affirmative action. As this section states: "Nothing contained in this title shall be interpreted to require" affirmative action. Section 706(g)(1) plainly appears "in this title" and so apparently comes within the scope of this disclaimer. The majority tries to get around this problem by narrowing the application of § 703(j) to the substantive provisions of Title VII, rather than the remedial provisions like § 706(g)(1). How can this reasoning be squared with the introductory phrase, "Nothing contained in this title," which, on a literal interpretation, encompasses all of Title VII, not just its substantive provisions? In rejecting a literal interpretation of the statute, the Court is plainly giving priority to the broad grant of remedial authority in § 706(g)(1) over the apparent restriction in § 706(j). Does it do so for the same reason that it found the district court's order constitutional: because courts have inherent authority to take all steps necessary to remedy past violations of the law and to prevent future violations? If Congress were to limit this authority, how could it have done so more explicitly than in § 703(j)?

One way would have been to refer explicitly to the remedial authority granted by the statute. This leads to the second restriction on the scope of § 706(g)(1). A further provision in this section, now codified in § 706(g)(2)(A), prevents the award of compensatory relief to any individual who "was refused admission, suspended, or expelled, or was refused employment or advancement or was suspended or discharged for any reason other than discrimination." An earlier decision, Firefighters Local Union No. 1784 v. Stotts, 467 U.S. 561 (1984), discussed in the introductory note to this chapter, stated that this provision confined awards of compensatory relief to victims of discrimination. A defining feature of affirmative action is that it confers benefits on individuals who might not be victims of discrimination and so *Stotts* could be taken to condemn most forms of affirmative action. The majority in *Sheet Metal Workers* could easily distinguish the facts of *Stotts*, which concerned a preference in layoffs preserving the jobs of black workers at the expense of whites. As the majority interpreted the record in *Sheet Metal Workers*, no such effect on whites was present. The language of § 706(g)(1)(A) was more difficult to distinguish because it has a broader scope than the holding in *Stotts*, but it, too, is distinguishable. It appears to address the situation of employees who have somehow disqualified themselves for compensatory relief to which they would otherwise be entitled. As noted in Chapter 2, the further provisions in § 706(g)(2)(B), applicable to mixed-motive cases, address a similar situation.

Nevertheless, the principle of limiting compensatory relief to proven victims of discrimination is an attractive one. Why doesn't it justify limitations on judicial authority to order affirmative action? The majority, of course, recognizes such limitations, finding only a narrow range of cases in which such remedies are appropriate. Does this flexible limitation, as opposed to a clear rule barring this form of relief, better serve the overall purposes of Title VII? Or does it frustrate the attempt of Congress to avoid endorsing any form of affirmative action? The next section examines cases that address these questions over the much wider range of cases in which employers and unions adopt affirmative action plans in the absence of judicial compulsion.

3. **Bibliography.** For a discussion of affirmative action as a judicially ordered or approved remedy for past discrimination, see Harry T. Edwards, Race Discrimination in Employment, What Price Equality?, 1976 U. Ill. L.F. 572; Harry T. Edwards & Barry L. Zaretsky, Preferential Remedies for Employment Discrimination, 74 Mich. L. Rev. 1 (1970); Richard H. Fallon, Jr. & Paul C. Weiler, *Firefighters v. Stotts*: Conflicting Models of Racial Justice, 1984 Sup. Ct. Rev. 1; George Rutherglen & Daniel R. Ortiz, Affirmative Action Under the Constitution and Title VII: From Confusion to Convergence, 35 UCLA. L. Rev. 467 (1988); Eric Schnapper, The Varieties of Numerical Remedies, 39 Stan. L. Rev. 851 (1987); Kathleen M. Sullivan,

Comment—Sins of Discrimination: Last Term's Affirmative Action Cases, 100 Harv. L. Rev. 78 (1986).

For articles on affirmative action in employment generally, see Jerry Kang & Mahzarin Banaji, Fair Measures: A Behavioral Realist Revision of "Affirmative Action," 94 Cal. L. Rev. 1063 (2006); Justin McCrary, The Effect of Court-Ordered Hiring Quotas on the Composition and Quality of Police, 97 Am. Econ. Rev. 318 (2007); Naomi Schoenbaum, The Case for Symmetry in Anti-Discrimination Law, 2017 Wis. L. Rev. 69; Patrick S. Shin, Treatment as an Individual and the Priority of Persons over Groups in Antidiscrimination Law, 12 Duke J. Con. L. & Pol'y 107 (2016); Susan Sturm, The Architecture of Inclusion: Advancing Workplace Equity in Higher Education, 29 Harv. J. L. & Gender 247 (2006); Noah Zatz, Special Treatment Everywhere, Special Treatment Nowhere, 95 B.U. L. Rev. 1155 (2015).

B. AFFIRMATIVE ACTION UNDER TITLE VII

United Steelworkers v. Weber

443 U.S. 193 (1979).

■ JUSTICE BRENNAN delivered the opinion of the Court.

Challenged here is the legality of an affirmative action plan—collectively bargained by an employer and a union—that reserves for black employees 50% of the openings in an in-plant craft-training program until the percentage of black craftworkers in the plant is commensurate with the percentage of blacks in the local labor force. The question for decision is whether Congress, in Title VII of the Civil Rights Act of 1964, 78 Stat., 253, as amended, 42 U.S.C. § 2000e et seq., left employers and unions in the private sector free to take such race-conscious steps to eliminate manifest racial imbalances in traditionally segregated job categories. We hold that Title VII does not prohibit such race-conscious affirmative action plans.

I

In 1974, petitioner United Steelworkers of America (USWA) and petitioner Kaiser Aluminum & Chemical Corp. (Kaiser) entered into a master collective-bargaining agreement covering terms and conditions of employment at 15 Kaiser plants. The agreement contained, inter alia, an affirmative action plan designed to eliminate conspicuous racial imbalances in Kaiser's then almost exclusively white craft-work forces. Black craft-hiring goals were set for each Kaiser plant equal to the percentage of blacks in the respective local labor forces. To enable plants to meet these goals, on-the-job training programs were established to teach unskilled production workers—black and white—the skills necessary to become craftworkers. The plan reserved for black employees 50% of the openings in these newly created in-plant training programs.

This case arose from the operation of the plan at Kaiser's plant in Gramercy, La. Until 1974, Kaiser hired as craftworkers for that plant only persons who had had prior craft experience. Because blacks had long been excluded from craft unions,[1] few were able to present such credentials. As a consequence, prior to 1974 only 1.83% (5 out of 273) of the skilled craftworkers at the Gramercy plant were black, even though the work force in the Gramercy area was approximately 39% black.

Pursuant to the national agreement Kaiser altered its craft-hiring practice in the Gramercy plant. Rather than hiring already trained outsiders, Kaiser established a training program to train its production workers to fill craft openings. Selection of craft trainees was made on the basis of seniority, with the proviso that at least 50% of the new trainees were to be black until the percentage of black skilled craftworkers in the Gramercy plant approximated the percentage of blacks in the local labor force.

During 1974, the first year of the operation of the Kaiser-USWA affirmative action plan, 13 craft trainees were selected from Gramercy's production work force. Of these, seven were black and six white. The most senior black selected into the program had less seniority than several white production workers whose bids for admission were rejected. Thereafter one of those white production workers, respondent Brian Weber (hereafter respondent), instituted this class action in the United States District Court for the Eastern District of Louisiana.

The complaint alleged that the filling of craft trainee positions at the Gramercy plant pursuant to the affirmative action program had resulted in junior black employees' receiving training in preference to senior white employees, thus discriminating against respondent and other similarly situated white employees in violation of §§ 703(a) and (d) of Title VII. The District Court held that the plan violated Title VII, entered a judgment in favor of the plaintiff class, and granted a permanent injunction prohibiting Kaiser and the USWA "from denying plaintiffs, Brian F. Weber and all other members of the class, access to on-the-job training programs on the basis of race." A divided panel of the Court of Appeals for the Fifth Circuit affirmed, holding that all employment preferences based upon race, including those preferences incidental to bona fide affirmative action plans, violated Title VII's prohibition against racial discrimination in employment. We granted certiorari. We reverse.

II

We emphasize at the outset the narrowness of our inquiry. Since the Kaiser-USWA plan does not involve state action, this case does not present an alleged violation of the Equal Protection Clause of the Fourteenth Amendment. Further, since the Kaiser-USWA plan was adopted voluntarily, we are not concerned with what Title VII requires

---

[1] Judicial findings of exclusion from crafts on racial grounds are so numerous as to make such exclusion a proper subject for judicial notice. . . .

or with what a court might order to remedy a past proved violation of the Act. The only question before us is the narrow statutory issue of whether Title VII *forbids* private employers and unions from voluntarily agreeing upon bona fide affirmative action plans that accord racial preferences in the manner and for the purpose provided in the Kaiser-USWA plan. That question was expressly left open in McDonald v. Santa Fe Trail Transp. Co., 427 U.S. 273, 281 n.8 (1976), which held, in a case not involving affirmative action, that Title VII protects whites as well as blacks from certain forms of racial discrimination.

Respondent argues that Congress intended in Title VII to prohibit all race-conscious affirmative action plans. Respondent's argument rests upon a literal interpretation of §§ 703(a) and (d) of the Act. Those sections make it unlawful to "discriminate . . . because of . . . race" in hiring and in the selection of apprentices for training programs. Since, the argument runs, *McDonald v. Santa Fe Trail Transp. Co.,* supra, settled that Title VII forbids discrimination against whites as well as blacks, and since the Kaiser-USWA affirmative action plan operates to discriminate against white employees solely because they are white, it follows that the Kaiser-USWA plan violates Title VII.

Respondent's argument is not without force. But it overlooks the significance of the fact that the Kaiser-USWA plan is an affirmative action plan voluntarily adopted by private parties to eliminate traditional patterns of racial segregation. In this context respondent's reliance upon a literal construction of §§ 703(a) and (d) and upon *McDonald* is misplaced. See *McDonald v. Santa Fe Trail Transp. Co.*, supra, at 281 n.8. It is a "familiar rule that a thing may be within the letter of the statute and yet not within the statute, because not within its spirit nor within the intention of its makers." Holy Trinity Church v. United States, 143 U.S. 457, 459 (1892). The prohibition against racial discrimination in §§ 703(a) and (d) of Title VII must therefore be read against the background of the legislative history of Title VII and the historical context from which the Act arose. . . . Examination of those sources makes clear that an interpretation of the sections that forbade all race-conscious affirmative action would "bring about an end completely at variance with the purpose of the statute" and must be rejected. United States v. Public Utilities Comm'n, 345 U.S. 295, 315 (1953).

Congress' primary concern in enacting the prohibition against racial discrimination in Title VII of the Civil Rights Act of 1964 was with "the plight of the Negro in our economy." 110 Cong. Rec. 6548 (1964) (remarks of Sen. Humphrey). Before 1964, blacks were largely relegated to "unskilled and semi-skilled jobs." Ibid. (remarks of Sen. Humphrey); id., at 7204 (remarks of Sen. Clark); id., at 7379–7380 (remarks of Sen. Kennedy). Because of automation the number of such jobs was rapidly decreasing. See id., at 6548 (remarks of Sen. Humphrey); id., at 7204 (remarks of Sen. Clark). As a consequence, "the relative position of the

Negro worker [was] steadily worsening. In 1947 the nonwhite unemployment rate was only 64 percent higher than the white rate; in 1962 it was 124 percent higher." Id., at 6547 (remarks of Sen. Humphrey). See also id., at 7204 (remarks of Sen. Clark). Congress considered this a serious social problem. As Senator Clark told the Senate:

> "The rate of Negro unemployment has gone up consistently as compared with white unemployment for the past 15 years. This is a social malaise and a social situation which we should not tolerate. That is one of the principal reasons why the bill should pass." Id., at 7220.

Congress feared that the goals of the Civil Rights Act—the integration of blacks into the mainstream of American society—could not be achieved unless this trend were reversed. And Congress recognized that that would not be possible unless blacks were able to secure jobs "which have a future." Id., at 7204 (remarks of Sen. Clark). See also id., at 7379–7380 (remarks of Sen. Kennedy). As Senator Humphrey explained to the Senate:

> "What good does it do a Negro to be able to eat in a fine restaurant if he cannot afford to pay the bill? What good does it do him to be accepted in a hotel that is too expensive for his modest income? How can a Negro child be motivated to take full advantage of integrated educational facilities if he has no hope of getting a job where he can use that education?" Id., at 6547.
>
> "Without a job, one cannot afford public convenience and accommodations. Income from employment may be necessary to further a man's education, or that of his children. If his children have no hope of getting a good job, what will motivate them to take advantage of educational opportunities?" Id., at 6552.

These remarks echoed President Kennedy's original message to Congress upon the introduction of the Civil Rights Act in 1963.

> "There is little value in a Negro's obtaining the right to be admitted to hotels and restaurants if he has no cash in his pocket and no job." 109 Cong. Rec. at 11159.

Accordingly, it was clear to Congress that "[t]he crux of the problem [was] to open employment opportunities for Negroes in occupations which have been traditionally closed to them," 10 Cong. Rec. 6548 (1964) (remarks of Sen. Humphrey), and it was to this problem that Title VII's prohibition against racial discrimination in employment was primarily addressed.

It plainly appears from the House Report accompanying the Civil Rights Act that Congress did not intend wholly to prohibit private and voluntary affirmative action efforts as one method of solving this problem. The Report provides:

> "No bill can or should lay claim to eliminating all of the causes and consequences of racial and other types of discrimination against minorities. There is reason to believe, however, that national leadership provided by the enactment of Federal legislation dealing with the most troublesome problems *will create an atmosphere conducive to voluntary or local resolution of other forms of discrimination*." H.R. Rep. No. 914, 88th Cong., 1st Sess., pt. 1, p. 18 (1963) (Emphasis supplied.)

Given this legislative history, we cannot agree with respondent that Congress intended to prohibit the private sector from taking effective steps to accomplish the goal that Congress designed Title VII to achieve. The very statutory words intended as a spur or catalyst to cause "employers and unions to self-examine and to self-evaluate their employment practices and to endeavor to eliminate, so far as possible, the last vestiges of an unfortunate and ignominious page in this country's history," Albemarle Paper Co. v. Moody, 422 U.S. 405, 418 (1975), cannot be interpreted as an absolute prohibition against all private, voluntary, race-conscious affirmative action efforts to hasten the elimination of such vestiges. It would be ironic indeed if a law triggered by a Nation's concern over centuries of racial injustice and intended to improve the lot of those who had "been excluded from the American dream for so long," 110 Cong. Rec. 6552 (1964) (remarks of Sen. Humphrey), constituted the first legislative prohibition of all voluntary, private, race-conscious efforts to abolish traditional patterns of racial segregation and hierarchy.

Our conclusion is further reinforced by examination of the language and legislative history of § 703(j) of Title VII. Opponents of Title VII raised two related arguments against the bill. First, they argued that the Act would be interpreted to *require* employers with racially imbalanced work forces to grant preferential treatment to racial minorities in order to integrate. Second, they argued that employers with racially imbalanced work forces would grant preferential treatment to racial minorities, even if not required to do so by the Act. See 110 Cong. Rec. 8618–8619 (1964) (remarks of Sen. Sparkman). Had Congress meant to prohibit all race-conscious affirmative action, as respondent urges, it easily could have answered both objections by providing that Title VII would not require or *permit* racially preferential integration efforts. But Congress did not choose such a course. Rather, Congress added § 703(j) which addresses only the first objection. The section provides that nothing contained in Title VII "shall be interpreted to *require* any employer . . . to grant preferential treatment . . . to any group because of the race . . . of such . . . group on account of" a de facto racial imbalance in the employer's work force. The section does not state that "nothing in Title VII shall be interpreted to *permit*" voluntary affirmative efforts to correct racial imbalances. The natural inference is that Congress chose not to forbid all voluntary race-conscious affirmative action.

The reasons for this choice are evident from the legislative record. Title VII could not have been enacted into law without substantial support from legislators in both Houses who traditionally resisted federal regulation of private business. Those legislators demanded as a price for their support that "management prerogatives, and union freedoms . . . be left undisturbed to the greatest extent possible." H.R. Rep. No. 914, 88th Cong., 1st Sess., pt. 2, p. 29 (1963), U.S. Code Cong. & Admin. News 1964, p. 2391. Section 703(j) was proposed by Senator Dirksen to allay any fears that the Act might be interpreted in such a way as to upset this compromise. The section was designed to prevent § 703 of Title VII from being interpreted in such a way as to lead to undue "Federal Government interference with private businesses because of some Federal employee's ideas about racial balance or racial imbalance." 110 Cong. Rec. 14314 (1964) (remarks of Sen. Miller). Clearly, a prohibition against all voluntary, race-conscious, affirmative action efforts would disserve these ends. Such a prohibition would augment the powers of the Federal Government and diminish traditional management prerogatives while at the same time impeding attainment of the ultimate statutory goals. In view of this legislative history and in view of Congress' desire to avoid undue federal regulation of private businesses, use of the word "require" rather than the phrase "require or permit" in § 703(j) fortifies the conclusion that Congress did not intend to limit traditional business freedom to such a degree as to prohibit all voluntary, race-conscious affirmative action.[7]

We therefore hold that Title VII's prohibition in §§ 703(a) and (d) against racial discrimination does not condemn all private, voluntary, race-conscious affirmative action plans.

---

7 Respondent argues that our construction of § 703 conflicts with various remarks in the legislative record. We do not agree. In Senator Humphrey's words, these comments were intended as assurances that Title VII would not allow establishment of systems "to *maintain* racial balance in employment." Id., at 11848 (emphasis added). They were not addressed to temporary, voluntary, affirmative action measures undertaken to eliminate manifest racial imbalance in traditionally segregated job categories. Moreover, the comments referred to by respondent all preceded the adoption of § 703(j), 42 U.S.C. § 2000e–2(j). After § 703(j) was adopted, congressional comments were all to the effect that employers would not be *required* to institute preferential quotas to avoid Title VII liability, see, e.g., 110 Cong. Rec. 12819 (1964) (remarks of Sen. Dirksen); id., at 13079–13080 (remarks of Sen. Clark); id., at 15876 (remarks. of Rep. Lindsay). There was no suggestion after the adoption of § 703(j) that wholly voluntary, race-conscious, affirmative action efforts would in themselves constitute a violation of Title VII. On the contrary, as Representative MacGregor told the House shortly before the final vote on Title VII:

> "Important as the scope and extent of this bill is, it is also vitally important that all Americans understand what this bill does not cover.
>
> "Your mail and mine, your contacts and mine with our constituents, indicates a great degree of misunderstanding about this bill. People complain about . . . preferential treatment or quotas in employment. There is a mistaken belief that Congress is legislating in these areas in this bill. When we drafted this bill we excluded these issues largely because the problems raised by these controversial questions are more properly handled at a governmental level closer to the American people and by communities and individuals themselves." 110 Cong. Rec. 15893 (1964).

III

We need not today define in detail the line of demarcation between permissible and impermissible affirmative action plans. It suffices to hold that the challenged Kaiser-USWA affirmative action plan falls on the permissible side of the line. The purposes of the plan mirror those of the statute. Both were designed to break down old patterns of racial segregation and hierarchy. Both were structured to "open employment opportunities for Negroes in occupations which have been traditionally closed to them." 110 Cong. Rec. 6548 (1964) (remarks of Sen. Humphrey).

At the same time, the plan does not unnecessarily trammel the interests of the white employees. The plan does not require the discharge of white workers and their replacement with new black hirees. Cf. McDonald v. Santa Fe Trail Transp. Co., 427 U.S. 273 (1976). Nor does the plan create an absolute bar to the advancement of white employees; half of those trained in the program will be white. Moreover, the plan is a temporary measure; it is not intended to maintain racial balance, but simply to eliminate a manifest racial imbalance. Preferential selection of craft trainees at the Gramercy plant will end as soon as the percentage of black skilled craftworkers in the Gramercy plant approximates the percentage of blacks in the local labor force. See 415 F. Supp., at 763.

We conclude, therefore, that the adoption of the Kaiser-USWA plan for the Gramercy plant falls within the area of discretion left by Title VII to the private sector voluntarily to adopt affirmative action plans designed to eliminate conspicuous racial imbalance in traditionally segregated job categories. Accordingly, the judgment of the Court of Appeals for the Fifth Circuit is

Reversed.

▪ JUSTICE POWELL and JUSTICE STEVENS took no part in the consideration or decision of these cases.

▪ JUSTICE BLACKMUN, concurring.

While I share some of the misgivings expressed in Mr. Justice Rehnquist's dissent, concerning the extent to which the legislative history of Title VII clearly supports the result the Court reaches today, I believe that additional considerations, practical and equitable, only partially perceived, if perceived at all, by the 88th Congress, support the conclusion reached by the Court today, and I therefore join its opinion as well as its judgment.

I

In his dissent from the decision of the United States Court of Appeals for the Fifth Circuit, Judge Wisdom pointed out that this litigation arises from a practical problem in the administration of Title VII. The broad prohibition against discrimination places the employer and the union on what he accurately described as a "high tightrope without a net beneath them." If Title VII is read literally, on the one hand they face liability for past discrimination against blacks, and on the other they face liability to whites for any voluntary preferences adopted to mitigate the effects of prior discrimination against blacks.

In this litigation, Kaiser denies prior discrimination but concedes that its past hiring practices may be subject to question. Although the labor force in the Gramercy area was proximately 39% black, Kaiser's work force was less than 15% black, and its craftwork force was less than 2% black. Kaiser had made some effort to recruit black painters, carpenters, insulators, and other craftsmen, but it continued to insist that those hired have five years' prior industrial experience, a requirement that arguably was not sufficiently job related to justify under Title VII any discriminatory impact it may have had. . . . The parties dispute the extent to which black craftsmen were available in the local labor market. They agree, however, that after critical reviews from the Office of Federal Contract Compliance, Kaiser and the Steelworkers established the training program in question here and modeled it along the lines of a Title VII consent decree later entered for the steel industry. . . . Yet when they did this, respondent Weber sued, alleging that Title VII prohibited the program because it discriminated against him as a white person and it was not supported by a prior judicial finding of discrimination against blacks.

Respondent Weber's reading of Title VII endorsed by the Court of Appeals, places voluntary compliance with Title VII in profound jeopardy. The only way for the employer and the union to keep their footing on the "tightrope" it creates would be to eschew all forms of voluntary affirmative action. Even a whisper of emphasis on minority recruiting would be forbidden. Because Congress intended to encourage private efforts to come into compliance with Title VII, see Alexander v. Gardner-Denver Co., 415 U.S. 36, 44 (1974), Judge Wisdom concluded that employers and unions who had committed "arguable violations" of Title VII should be free to make reasonable responses without fear of liability to whites. Preferential hiring along the lines of the Kaiser program is a reasonable response for the employer, whether or not a court, on these facts, could order the same step as a remedy. The company is able to avoid identifying victims of past discrimination, and so avoids claims for backpay that would inevitably follow a response limited to such victims. If past victims should be benefited by the program, however, the company mitigates its liability to those persons. Also, to the extent that Title VII liability is predicated on the "disparate effect" of an employer's past hiring practices, the program makes it less likely that such an effect could be demonstrated. Cf. County of Los Angeles v. Davis, 440 U.S. 625, 633–634 (1979) (hiring could moot a past Title VII claim). And the Court has recently held that work-force statistics resulting from private affirmative action were probative of benign intent in a "disparate treatment" case. Furnco Construction Corp. v. Waters, 438 U.S. 567, 579–580 (1978).

The "arguable violation" theory has a number of advantages. It responds to a practical problem in the administration of Title VII not anticipated by Congress. It draws predictability from the outline of present law and closely effectuates the purpose of the Act. Both Kaiser and the United States urge its adoption here. Because I agree that it is the soundest way to approach this case, my preference would be to resolve this litigation by applying it and holding that Kaiser's craft training program meets the requirement that voluntary affirmative action be a reasonable response to an "arguable violation" of Title VII.

II

The Court, however, declines to consider the narrow "arguable violation" approach and adheres instead to an interpretation of Title VII that permits affirmative action by an employer whenever the job category in question is "traditionally segregated." The sources cited suggest that the Court considers a job category to be "traditionally segregated" when there has been a societal history of purposeful exclusion of blacks from the job category, resulting in a persistent disparity between the proportion of blacks in the labor force and the proportion of blacks among those who hold jobs within the category.

"Traditionally segregated job categories," where they exist, sweep far more broadly than the class of "arguable violations" of Title VII. The Court's expansive approach is somewhat disturbing for me because, as Mr. Justice Rehnquist points out, the Congress that passed Title VII probably thought it was adopting a principle of nondiscrimination that would apply to blacks and whites alike. While setting aside that principle can be justified where necessary to advance statutory policy by encouraging reasonable responses as a form of voluntary compliance that mitigates "arguable violations," discarding the principle of nondiscrimination where no countervailing statutory policy exists appears to be at odds with the bargain struck when Title VII was enacted.

A closer look at the problem, however, reveals that in each of the principal ways in which the Court's "traditionally segregated job categories" approach expands on the "arguable violations" theory, still other considerations point in favor of the broad standard adopted by the Court, and make it possible for me to conclude that the Court's reading of the statute is an acceptable one.

A. The first point at which the Court departs from the "arguable violations" approach is that it measures an individual employer's capacity for affirmative action solely in terms of a statistical disparity. The individual employer need not have engaged in discriminatory practices in the past. While, under Title VII, a mere disparity may provide the basis for a prima facie case against an employer, Dothard v. Rawlinson, 433 U.S. 321, 329–331 (1977), it would not conclusively prove a violation of the Act. Teamsters v. United States, 431 U.S. 324, 339–340, n.20 (1977); see § 703(j), 42 U.S.C. § 2000e–2(j). As a practical matter, however, this difference may not be that great. While the "arguable violation" standard is conceptually satisfying, in practice the emphasis would be on "arguable" rather than on "violation." The great difficulty in the District Court was that no one had any incentive to prove that Kaiser had violated the Act. Neither Kaiser nor the Steelworkers wanted to establish a past violation, nor did Weber. The blacks harmed had never sued and so had no established representative. The Equal Employment Opportunity Commission declined to intervene, and cannot be expected to intervene in every case of this nature. To make the "arguable violation" standard work, it would have to be set low enough to permit the employer to prove it without obligating himself to pay a damages award. The inevitable tendency would be to avoid hairsplitting litigation by simply concluding that a mere disparity between the racial composition of the employer's work force and the composition of the qualified local labor force would be an "arguable violation," even though actual liability could not be established on that basis alone. See Note, 57 N.C. L. Rev. 695, 714–719 (1979).

B. The Court also departs from the "arguable violation" approach by permitting an employer to redress discrimination that lies wholly outside the bounds of Title VII. For example, Title VII provides no remedy for pre-Act discrimination. Hazelwood School District v. United States, 433 U.S. 299, 309–310 (1977); yet the purposeful discrimination that creates a "traditionally segregated job category" may have entirely predated the Act. More subtly, in assessing a prima facie case of Title VII liability, the composition of the employer's work force is compared to the composition of the pool of workers who meet valid job qualifications. Hazelwood, 433 U.S., at 308 and n.13; Teamsters v. United States, 431 U.S., at 339–340, and n.20. When a "job category" is traditionally segregated, however, that pool will reflect the effects of segregation, and the Court's approach goes further and permits a comparison with the composition of the labor force as a whole, in which minorities are more heavily represented.

Strong considerations of equity support an interpretation of Title VII that would permit private affirmative action to reach where Title VII itself does not. The bargain struck in 1964 with the passage of Title VII guaranteed equal opportunity for white and black alike, but where Title VII provides no remedy for blacks, it should not be construed to foreclose private affirmative action from supplying relief. It seems unfair for respondent Weber to argue, as he does, that the asserted scarcity of black craftsmen in Louisiana, the product of historic discrimination, makes Kaiser's training program illegal because it ostensibly absolves Kaiser of all Title VII liability. Brief for Respondents 60. Absent compelling evidence of legislative intent, I would not interpret Title VII itself as a means of "locking in" the effects of segregation for which Title VII provides no remedy. Such a construction, as the Court points out, would be "ironic," given the broad remedial purposes of Title VII.

Mr. Justice Rehnquist's dissent, while it focuses more on what Title VII does not require than on what Title VII forbids, cites several passages that appear to express an intent to "lock in" minorities. In mining the legislative history anew, however, the dissent, in my view, fails to take proper account of our prior cases that have given that history a much more limited reading than that adopted by the dissent. For example, in Griggs v. Duke Power Co., 401 U.S. 424, 434–436, and n.11 (1971), the Court refused to give controlling weight to the memorandum of Senators Clark and Case which the dissent now finds so persuasive. And in quoting a statement from that memorandum that an employer would not be "permitted . . . to prefer Negroes for future vacancies," the dissent does not point out that the Court's opinion in Teamsters v. United States, 431 U.S., at 349–351, implies that that language is limited to the protection of established seniority systems. Here, seniority is not in issue because the craft training program is new and does not involve an abrogation of pre-existing seniority rights. In short, the passages marshaled by the dissent are not so compelling as to merit the whip hand over the obvious equity of permitting employers to ameliorate the effects of past discrimination for which Title VII provides no direct relief.

III

I also think it significant that, while the Court's opinion does not foreclose other forms of affirmative action, the Kaiser program it approves is a moderate one. The opinion notes that the program does not afford an absolute preference for blacks, and that it ends when the racial composition of Kaiser's craftwork force matches the racial composition of the local population. It thus operates as a temporary tool for remedying past discrimination without attempting to "maintain" a previously achieved balance. See University of California Regents v. Bakke, 438 U.S. 265, 342 n.17 (1978) (opinion of Brennan, White, Marshall, and Blackmun, JJ.). Because the duration of the program is finite, it perhaps will end even before the "stage of maturity when action along this line is no longer necessary." Id., at 403 (opinion of Blackmun, J.). And if the Court has misperceived the political will, it has the assurance that because the question is statutory Congress may set a different course if it so chooses.

[The dissenting opinion of Chief Justice Burger is omitted.]

■ JUSTICE REHNQUIST, with whom THE CHIEF JUSTICE joins, dissenting.

. . . [B]y a tour de force reminiscent not of jurists such as Hale, Holmes, and Hughes, but of escape artists such as Houdini, the Court eludes clear statutory language, "uncontradicted" legislative history and uniform precedent in concluding that employers are, after all, permitted to consider race in making employment decisions. It may be that one or more of the principal sponsors of Title VII would have preferred to see a provision allowing preferential treatment of minorities written into the bill. Such a provision, however, would have to have been expressly or impliedly excepted from Title VII's explicit prohibition on all racial discrimination in employment. There is no such exception in the Act. And a reading of the legislative debates concerning Title VII, in which proponents and opponents alike uniformly denounced discrimination in favor of, as well as discrimination against, Negroes, demonstrates clearly that any legislator harboring an unspoken desire for such a provision could not possibly have succeeded in enacting it into law. . . .

II

Were Congress to act today specifically to prohibit the type of racial discrimination suffered by Weber, it would be hard pressed to draft language better tailored to the task than that found in § 703(d) of Title VII:

> "It shall be an unlawful employment practice for any employer, labor organization, or joint labor-management committee controlling apprenticeship or other training or retraining, including on-the-job training programs to discriminate against any individual because of his race, color, religion, sex, or national origin in admission to, or employment in, any program established to provide apprenticeship or other training." 42 U.S.C. § 2000e–2(d).

Equally suited to the task would be § 703(a)(2), which makes it unlawful for an employer to classify his employees "in any way which would deprive or tend to deprive any individual of employment opportunities or otherwise adversely affect his status as an employee, because of such individual's race, color, religion, sex, or national origin." 78 Stat. 255, 42 U.S.C. § 2000e–2(a)(2).

Entirely consistent with these two express prohibitions is the language of § 703(j) of Title VII, which provides that the Act is not to be interpreted "to require any employer . . . to grant preferential treatment to any individual or to any group because of the race . . . of such individual or group" to correct a racial imbalance in the employer's work force. 42 U.S.C. § 2000e–2(j). Seizing on the word "require," the Court infers that Congress must have intended to "permit" this type of racial discrimination. Not only is this reading of § 703(j) outlandish in the light of the flat prohibitions of §§ 703(a) and (d), but also, as explained in Part III, it is totally belied by the Act's legislative history.

Quite simply, Kaiser's racially discriminatory admission quota is flatly prohibited by the plain language of Title VII. This normally dispositive fact, however, gives the Court only momentary pause. An "interpretation" of the statute upholding Weber's claim would, according to the Court, " 'bring about an end completely at variance with the purpose of the statute.' " Quoting United States v. Public Utilities Comm'n, 345 U.S. 295, 315 (1953). To support this conclusion, the Court calls upon the "spirit" of the Act, which it divines from passages in Title VII's legislative history indicating that enactment of the statute was prompted by Congress' desire " 'to open employment opportunities for

Negroes in occupations which [had] been traditionally closed to them.' " Quoting 110 Cong. Rec. 6548 (1964) (remarks of Sen. Humphrey). But the legislative history invoked by the Court to avoid the plain language of §§ 703(a) and (d) simply misses the point. To be sure, the reality of employment discrimination against Negroes provided the primary impetus for passage of Title VII. But this fact by no means supports the proposition that Congress intended to leave employers free to discriminate against white persons. In most cases, "[l]egislative history . . . is more vague than the statute we are called upon to interpret." Supra at 320 (Jackson, J., concurring). Here, however, the legislative history of Title VII is as clear as the language of §§ 703(a) and (d), and it irrefutably demonstrates that Congress meant precisely what it said in §§ 703(a) and (d)—that *no* racial discrimination in employment is permissible under Title VII, not even preferential treatment of minorities to correct racial imbalance.

III

In undertaking to review the legislative history of Title VII, I am mindful that the topic hardly makes for light reading, but I am also fearful that nothing short of a thorough examination of the congressional debates will fully expose the magnitude of the Court's misinterpretation of Congress' intent.

A

Introduced on the floor of the House of Representatives on June 20, 1963, the bill—H.R. 7152—that ultimately became the Civil Rights Act of 1964 contained no compulsory provisions directed at private discrimination in employment. The bill was promptly referred to the Committee on the Judiciary, where it was amended to include Title VII. With two exceptions, the bill reported by the House Judiciary Committee contained §§ 703(a) and (d) as they were ultimately enacted. Amendments subsequently adopted on the House floor added § 703's prohibition against sex discrimination and § 703(d)'s coverage of "on-the-job training."

After noting that "[t]he purpose of [Title VII] is to eliminate . . . discrimination in employment based on race, color, religion, or national origin," the Judiciary Committee's Report simply paraphrased the provisions of Title VII without elaboration. H.R. Rep., pt. 1, p. 26, U.S. Code Cong. & Admin. News 1964, p. 2401. In a separate Minority Report, however, opponents of the measure on the Committee advanced a line of attack which was reiterated throughout the debates in both the House and Senate and which ultimately led to passage of § 703(j). Noting that the word "discrimination" was nowhere defined in H.R. 7152, the Minority Report charged that the absence from Title VII of any reference to "racial imbalance" was a "public relations" ruse and that "the administration intends to rely upon its own construction of 'discrimination' as including the lack of racial balance. . . ." H.R. Rep., pt. 1, pp. 67–68, U.S. Code Cong. & Admin. News 1964, p. 2436. To demonstrate how the bill would operate in practice, the Minority Report posited a number of hypothetical employment situations, concluding in each example that the employer "*may be forced to hire according to race,* to 'racially balance' those who work for him *in every job classification* or be in violation of Federal law." Id., at 69 (emphasis in original).

When H.R. 7152 reached the House floor, the opening speech in support of its passage was delivered by Representative Celler, Chairman of the House Judiciary Committee and the Congressman responsible for introducing the legislation. A portion of that speech responded to criticism "seriously misrepresent[ing] what the bill would do and grossly distort[ing] its effects":

> "[T]he charge has been made that the Equal Employment Opportunity Commission to be established by title VII of the bill would have the power to prevent a business from employing and promoting the people it wished, and that a 'Federal inspector' could then order the hiring and promotion only of employees of certain races or religious groups. This description of the bill is entirely wrong. . . .
>
> "Even [a] court could not order that any preference be given to any particular race, religion or other group, but would be limited to ordering an end of discrimination. The statement that a Federal inspector could order the employment and promotion only of members of a specific racial or religious group is therefore patently erroneous. . . .
>
> ". . . The Bill would do no more than prevent . . . employers from discriminating against *or in favor* of workers because of their race, religion, or national origin.
>
> "It is likewise not true that the Equal Employment Opportunity Commission would have power to rectify existing 'racial or religious imbalance' in employment by requiring the hiring of certain people without regard to their qualifications simply because they are of a given race or religion. Only actual discrimination could be stopped." 110 Cong. Rec. 1518 (1964) (emphasis added).

Representative Celler's construction of Title VII was repeated by several other supporters during the House debate.

Thus, the battle lines were drawn early in the legislative struggle over Title VII, with opponents of the measure charging that agencies of the Federal Government such as the Equal Employment Opportunity Commission (EEOC), by interpreting the word "discrimination" to mean the existence of "racial imbalance," would "require" employers to grant preferential treatment to minorities, and supporters responding that the EEOC would be granted no such power and that, indeed, Title VII prohibits discrimination "in favor of workers because of their race." Supporters of H.R. 7152 in the House ultimately prevailed by a vote of

290 to 130, and the measure was sent to the Senate to begin what became the longest debate in that body's history.

B

The Senate debate was broken into three phases: the debate on sending the bill to Committee, the general debate on the bill prior to invocation of cloture, and the debate following cloture.

1

When debate on the motion to refer the bill to Committee opened, opponents of Title VII in the Senate immediately echoed the fears expressed by their counterparts in the House. . . .

Senator Humphrey, perhaps the primary moving force behind H.R. 7152 in the Senate, was the first to state the proponents' understanding of Title VII. Responding to a political advertisement charging that federal agencies were at liberty to interpret the word "discrimination" in Title VII to require racial balance, Senator Humphrey stated: "[T]he meaning of racial or religious discrimination is perfectly clear. . . . [I]t means a distinction in treatment given to different individuals because of their different race, religion, or national origin." Id., at 5423. Stressing that Title VII "does not limit the employer's freedom to hire, fire, promote or demote for any reasons—or no reasons—so long as his action is not based on race," Senator Humphrey further stated that "nothing in the bill would permit any official or court to require any employer or labor union to give preferential treatment to any minority group." Ibid.

After 17 days of debate, the Senate voted to take up the bill directly, without referring it to a committee. Id., at 6455. Consequently, there is no Committee Report in the Senate.

2

Formal debate on the merits of H.R. 7152 began on March 30, 1964. Supporters of the bill in the Senate had made elaborate preparations for this second round. Senator Humphrey, the majority whip, and Senator Kuchel, the minority whip, were selected as the bipartisan floor managers on the entire civil rights bill. Responsibility for explaining and defending each important title of the bill was placed on bipartisan "captains." Senators Clark and Case were selected as the bipartisan captains responsible for Title VII. Vaas, Title VII: Legislative History, 7 B.C. Ind. & Com. L. Rev. 431, 444–445 (1966) (hereinafter Title VII: Legislative History).

In the opening speech of the formal Senate debate on the bill, Senator Humphrey addressed the main concern of Title VII's opponents, advising that not only does Title VII not require use of racial quotas, it does not permit their use. "The truth," stated the floor leader of the bill, "is that this title forbids discriminating against anyone on account of race. This is the simple and complete truth about title VII." 110 Cong. Rec. 6549 (1964). Senator Humphrey continued:

> "Contrary to the allegations of some opponents of this title, there is nothing in it that will give any power to the Commission or to any court to require hiring, firing, or promotion of employees in order to meet a racial 'quota' or to achieve a certain racial balance.
>
> "That bugaboo has been brought up a dozen times; but it is nonexistent. In fact, *the very opposite is true*. Title VII *prohibits discrimination*. In effect, it says that race, religion and national origin are not to be used as the basis for hiring and firing. Title VII is designed to encourage hiring on the basis of ability and qualifications, not race or religion." Ibid. (emphasis added).

At the close of his speech, Senator Humphrey returned briefly to the subject of employment quotas: "It is claimed that the bill would require racial quotas for all hiring, when in fact it provides that race shall not be a basis for making personnel decisions." Id., at 6553.

Senator Kuchel delivered the second major speech in support of H.R. 7152. In addressing the concerns of the opposition, he observed that "[n]othing could be further from the truth" than the charge that "Federal inspectors" would be empowered under Title VII to dictate racial balance and preferential advancement of minorities. Id., at 6563. Senator Kuchel emphasized that seniority rights would in no way be affected by Title VII: "Employers and labor organizations could not discriminate *in favor of or against* a person because of his race, his religion, or his national origin. In such matters . . . the bill now before us . . . is color-blind." Id., at 6564 (emphasis added).

A few days later the Senate's attention focused exclusively on Title VII, as Senators Clark and Case rose to discuss the title of H.R. 7152 on which they shared floor "captain" responsibilities. In an interpretative memorandum submitted jointly to the Senate, Senators Clark and Case took pains to refute the opposition's charge that Title VII would result in preferential treatment of minorities. Their words were clear and unequivocal:

> "There is no requirement in title VII that an employer maintain a racial balance in his work force. On the contrary, any deliberate attempt to maintain a racial balance, whatever such a balance may be, would involve a violation of title VII because maintaining such a balance would require an employer to hire or to refuse to hire on the basis of race. It must be emphasized that discrimination is prohibited as to any individual." Id., at 7213.

Of particular relevance to the instant litigation were their observations regarding seniority rights. As if directing their comments at Brian Weber, the Senators said:

> "Title VII would have no effect on established seniority rights. Its effect is prospective and not retrospective. Thus, for

> example, if a business has been discriminating in the past and as a result has an all-white working force, when the title comes into effect the employer's obligation would be simply to fill future vacancies on a nondiscriminatory basis. He would not be obliged—*or indeed permitted*—to fire whites in order to hire Negroes, *or to prefer Negroes for future vacancies, or, once Negroes are hired, to give them special seniority rights at the expense of the white workers hired earlier*." Id. (emphasis added).

Thus, with virtual clairvoyance the Senate's leading supporters of Title VII anticipated precisely the circumstances of this case and advised their colleagues that the type of minority preference employed by Kaiser would violate Title VII's ban on racial discrimination. To further accentuate the point, Senator Clark introduced another memorandum dealing with common criticisms of the bill, including the charge that racial quotas would be imposed under Title VII. The answer was simple and to the point: "Quotas are themselves discriminatory." Id., at 7218.

Despite these clear statements from the bill's leading and most knowledgeable proponents, the fears of the opponents were not put to rest. Senator Robertson reiterated the view that "discrimination" could be interpreted by a federal "bureaucrat" to require hiring quotas. Id., at 7418–7420. Senators Smathers and Sparkman, while conceding that Title VII does not in so many words require the use of hiring quotas, repeated the opposition's view that employers would be coerced to grant preferential hiring treatment to minorities by agencies of the Federal Government. Senator Williams was quick to respond:

> "Those opposed to H.R. 7152 should realize that to hire a Negro solely because he is a Negro is racial discrimination, just as much as a 'white only' employment policy. Both forms of discrimination are prohibited by title VII of this bill. The language of that title simply states that race is not a qualification for employment. . . . Some people charge that H.R. 7152 favors the Negro, at the expense of the white majority. But how can the language of equality favor one race or one religion over another? Equality can have only one meaning, and that meaning is self-evident to reasonable men. Those who say that equality means favoritism do violence to common sense." Id., at 8921.

Senator Williams concluded his remarks by noting that Title VII's only purpose is "the elimination of racial and religious discrimination in employment." Ibid. On May 25, Senator Humphrey again took the floor to defend the bill against "the well-financed drive by certain opponents to confuse and mislead the American people." Id., at 11846. Turning once again to the issue of preferential treatment, Senator Humphrey remained faithful to the view that he had repeatedly expressed:

> "The title does not provide that any preferential treatment in employment shall be given to Negroes or to any other persons or

groups. It does not provide that any quota systems may be established to maintain racial balance in employment. In fact, *the title would prohibit preferential treatment for any particular group,* and any person, whether or not a member of any minority group would be permitted to file a complaint of discriminatory employment practices." Id., at 11848 (emphasis added).

While the debate in the Senate raged, a bipartisan coalition under the leadership of Senators Dirksen, Mansfield, Humphrey, and Kuchel was working with House leaders and representatives of the Johnson administration on a number of amendments to H.R. 7152 designed to enhance its prospects of passage. The so-called "Dirksen-Mansfield" amendment was introduced on May 26 by Senator Dirksen as a substitute for the entire House-passed bill. The substitute bill, which ultimately became law, left unchanged the basic prohibitory language of §§ 703(a) and (d), as well as the remedial provisions in § 706(g). It added, however, several provisions defining and clarifying the scope of Title VII's substantive prohibitions. One of those clarifying amendments, § 703(j), was specifically directed at the opposition's concerns regarding racial balancing and preferential treatment of minorities, providing in pertinent part: "Nothing contained in [Title VII] shall be interpreted to require any employer . . . to grant preferential treatment to any individual or to any group because of the race . . . of such individual or group on account of" a racial imbalance in the employer's work force. 42 U.S.C. § 2000e–2(j). . . .

Contrary to the Court's analysis, the language of § 703(j) is precisely tailored to the objection voiced time and again by Title VII's opponents. Not once during the 83 days of debate in the Senate did a speaker, proponent or opponent, suggest that the bill would allow employers *voluntarily* to prefer racial minorities over white persons. In light of Title VII's flat prohibition on discrimination "against any individual . . . because of such individual's race," § 703(a), 42 U.S.C. § 2000e–2(a), such a contention would have been, in any event, too preposterous to warrant response. Indeed, speakers on both sides of the issue, as the legislative history makes clear, recognized that Title VII would tolerate no *voluntary* racial preference, whether in favor of blacks or whites. The complaint consistently voiced by the opponents was that Title VII, particularly the word "discrimination," would be *interpreted* by federal agencies such as the EEOC to *require* the correction of racial imbalance through the granting of preferential treatment to minorities. Verbal assurances that Title VII would not require—indeed, would not permit—preferential treatment of blacks having failed, supporters of H.R. 7152 responded by proposing an amendment carefully worded to meet, and put to rest, the opposition's charge. Indeed, unlike §§ 703(a) and (d), which are by their terms directed at entities—e.g., employers, labor unions—whose actions are restricted by Title VII's prohibitions, the language of § 703(j) is specifically directed at entities—federal agencies and courts—charged with the responsibility of interpreting Title VII's provisions.

In light of the background and purpose of § 703(j), the irony of invoking the section to justify the result in this case is obvious. The Court's frequent references to the "voluntary" nature of Kaiser's racially discriminatory admission quota bear no relationship to the facts of this case. Kaiser and the Steelworkers acted under pressure from an agency of the Federal Government, the Office of Federal Contract Compliance, which found that minorities were being "underutilized" at Kaiser's plants. See n.2, supra. That is, Kaiser's work force was racially imbalanced. Bowing to that pressure, Kaiser instituted an admissions quota preferring blacks over whites, thus confirming that the fears of Title VII's opponents were well founded. Today, § 703(j), adopted to allay those fears, is invoked by the Court to uphold imposition of a racial quota under the very circumstances that the section was intended to prevent.

Section 703(j) apparently calmed the fears of most of the opponents; after its introduction, complaints concerning racial balance and preferential treatment died down considerably. Proponents of the bill, however, continued to reassure the opposition that its concerns were unfounded. In a lengthy defense of the entire civil rights bill, Senator Muskie emphasized that the opposition's "torrent of words . . . cannot obscure this basic, simple truth: Every American citizen has the right to equal treatment—not favored treatment, not complete individual equality—just equal treatment." 110 Cong. Rec. 12614 (1964). With particular reference to Title VII, Senator Muskie noted that the measure "seeks to afford to all Americans equal opportunity in employment without discrimination. Not equal pay. Not 'racial balance.' Only equal opportunity." Id., at 12617.

Senator Saltonstall, Chairman of the Republican Conference of Senators participating in the drafting of the Dirksen-Mansfield amendment, spoke at length on the substitute bill. He advised the Senate that the Dirksen-Mansfield substitute, which included § 703(j), "provides no preferential treatment for any group of citizens. In fact, *it specifically prohibits such treatment*." 110 Cong. Rec. 12691 (1964) (emphasis added). . . .

3

On June 10, the Senate, for the second time in its history, imposed cloture on its Members. The limited debate that followed centered on proposed amendments to the Dirksen-Mansfield substitute. Of some 24 proposed amendments, only 5 were adopted.

As the civil rights bill approached its final vote, several supporters rose to urge its passage. Senator Muskie adverted briefly to the issue of preferential treatment: "It has been said that the bill discriminates in favor of the Negro at the expense of the rest of us. It seeks to do nothing more than to lift the Negro from the status of inequality to one of *equality* of treatment." 110 Cong. Rec. 14328 (1964) (emphasis added). Senator Moss, in a speech delivered on the day that the civil rights bill was finally passed, had this to say about quotas:

> "The bill does not accord to any citizen advantage or preference—it does not fix quotas of employment or school population—it does not force personal association. What it does is to prohibit public officials and those who invite the public generally to patronize their businesses or to apply for employment, to utilize the offensive, humiliating, and cruel practice of discrimination on the basis of race. In short, the bill does not accord special consideration; it establishes *equality*." Id. at 14484 (emphasis added).

Later that day, June 19, the issue was put to a vote, and the Dirksen-Mansfield substitute bill was passed.

C

The Act's return engagement in the House was brief. The House Committee on Rules reported the Senate version without amendments on June 30, 1964. By a vote of 289 to 126, the House adopted H. Res. 789, thus agreeing to the Senate's amendments of H.R. 7152.[30] Later that same day, July 2, the President signed the bill and the Civil Rights Act of 1964 became law.

IV

. . . [S]upporters of the civil rights bill drafted and introduced § 703(j). Specifically addressed to the opposition's charge, § 703(j) simply enjoins federal agencies and courts from interpreting Title VII to require an employer to prefer certain racial groups to correct imbalances in his work force. The section says nothing about voluntary preferential treatment of minorities because such racial discrimination is plainly proscribed by §§ 703(a) and (d). Indeed, had Congress intended to except voluntary, race-conscious preferential treatment from the blanket prohibition of racial discrimination in §§ 703(a) and (d), it surely could have drafted language better suited to the task than § 703(j). It knew how. Section 703(i) provides:

> Nothing contained in [Title VII] shall apply to any business or enterprise on or near an Indian reservation with respect to any publicly announced employment practice of such business or enterprise under which a preferential treatment is given to

[30] Only three Congressmen spoke to the issue of racial quotas during the House's debate on the Senate amendments. Representative Lindsay stated: "[W]e wish to emphasize also that this bill does not require quotas, racial balance, or any of the other things that the opponents have been saying about it." 110 Cong. Rec. 15876 (1964). Representative McCulloch echoed this understanding, remarking that "[t]he bill does not permit the Federal Government to require an employer or union to hire or accept for membership a quota of persons from any particular minority group." Id., at 15893. The remarks of Representative MacGregor, quoted by the Court, are singularly unhelpful. He merely noted that by adding § 703(j) to Title VII of the House bill, "[t]he Senate . . . spelled out [the House's] intentions more specifically." 110 Cong. Rec. 15893 (1964).

any individual because he is an Indian living on or near a reservation.

78 Stat. 257, 42 U.S.C. § 2000e–2(i). . . .

NOTES ON *UNITED STEELWORKERS V. WEBER*

1. **The Text of Title VII.** The text of Title VII in some ways posed fewer problems for the decision in *Weber* than the decision in *Sheet Metal Workers*; in some ways, it posed more problems. Section 703(j), as Justice Brennan emphasized in his majority opinion, does not address permitted forms of affirmative action at all, stating only that nothing in Title VII shall be interpreted to "require" affirmative action. The difficulty arises, as Justice Rehnquist points out in his dissent, with the main prohibitions of Title VII, in § 703(a), (c), and (d). These prohibit, respectively, employers, unions, and joint labor-management committees from discriminating on the basis of race, and the first two subsections additionally prohibit classifications on the basis of race. The training program in *Weber*, insofar as it favors black employees, seems to violate all of these prohibitions. This conclusion is seemingly confirmed by § 703(i), which specifically permits affirmative action on behalf of Native Americans, but not on behalf of any other racial minority. A literal interpretation of these provisions would require the affirmative action plan in *Weber* to be struck down.

Justice Brennan departs from a literal interpretation of Title VII by appealing to the underlying purpose of the statute which, in his view, was twofold: first, to achieve a degree of economic equality for minority employees; and second, to do so with a minimum of government interference in management and labor relations. How successful is this attempt to get behind the literal terms of the statute? Does it amount only to the claim that Congress had not fully considered the need for employers to engage in affirmative action in order to increase the opportunities available to minority employees? Or does it attribute to Congress an intent to endorse affirmative action? Do either of these alternatives adequately account for the narrowly restricted exception for affirmative action plans on behalf of Native Americans?

Justice Blackmun, in his concurring opinion, endorses a version of the majority's argument, reasoning that in the absence of affirmative action employers would face a dilemma under the theory of disparate impact. If they did not engage in affirmative action, minority employees could attack neutral practices with an adverse impact on minority employment. But if they did engage in affirmative action, they would be subject to claims of reverse discrimination from white employees. Does this argument give too much weight to the theory of disparate impact? As we saw in Chapter 3, this theory of liability itself is ambiguous between serving as a means of uncovering hidden discrimination and serving as a means of assuring proportional economic opportunities based on the representation of minority groups in the labor market. Which version of the theory of disparate impact does Justice Blackmun endorse?

2. The Legislative History of Title VII. Both the majority and dissenting opinions analyze the passages in the legislative history that support the overall goal of increasing economic opportunities for minorities and of minimizing government interference. Justice Rehnquist emphasizes those passages condemning any form of required affirmative action, as does § 703(j). Several of these passages, particularly by sponsors of Title VII, added that the statute also prohibited even voluntary forms of affirmative action. Most of these statements were made in the Senate where, as we have seen in earlier chapters, parliamentary maneuvers prevented referral of Title VII to committee. A few of these statements were also made in the House of Representatives, but since § 703(j) was added to Title VII in the Senate, that chamber was the place where affirmative action was more frequently discussed.

Does the legislative history resolve the issue in *Weber* one way or the other? Or does it, as Justice Blackmun states, just reveal more about what Title VII doesn't do than what it does do? What about the absence of any statement by any supporter of Title VII that it permitted voluntary forms of affirmative action? Would such a statement have derailed attempts to get Title VII passed, particularly in the Senate, where a two-thirds vote was necessary to end debate? Or does it bear out Justice Blackmun's observation that Congress did not focus upon operational problems that would subsequently appear in enforcing the statute?

3. Regulation of Federal Contractors. In the background of *Weber*, issues of government coercion arose through attempts to regulate Kaiser Aluminum as a federal contractor. Executive Order 11,246 created an elaborate structure for preventing discrimination by federal contractors and, in addition, for requiring them to engage in affirmative action. This executive order, issued by the President on the basis of his statutory authority over federal contracts, prohibits discrimination and requires affirmative action by federal contractors on the basis of race, national origin, sex, and religion. Exec. Order No. 11,246, 3 C.F.R. 339 (1964–65), reprinted as amended in 42 U.S.C. § 2000e note. These obligations are stated in only the most general terms in the executive order itself, but they are spelled out in great detail in the regulations of the Office of Federal Contract Compliance Programs (OFCCP). 41 C.F.R. §§ 60–1.1 et seq. The OFCCP is located in the Department of Labor, an executive agency directly answerable to the President. Accordingly, the nature and degree of affirmative action required by the Executive Order and implementing regulations has always depended upon the enforcement policy of the Executive Branch. See Michael Brody, Congress, the President, and Federal Equal Employment Policymaking: A Problem in Separation of Powers, 60 B.U. L. Rev. 239 (1980); Robert P. Schuwerk, Comment, The Philadelphia Plan: A Study in the Dynamics of Executive Power, 39 U. Chi. L. Rev. 723 (1972); Thomas J. Sugrue, Affirmative Action from Below: Civil Rights, The Building Trades, and the Politic of Racial Equality in the Urban North, 1945–1969, 91 J. Am. Hist. 145 (2004).

The OFCCP regulations apply to all employers who have contracts with the federal government in excess of $10,000, with increased compliance and reporting requirements for employers with 50 or more employees and contracts in excess of $50,000. 41 C.F.R. §§ 60–1.5(a)(1), –1.40(a). Employers in the latter category must prepare written affirmative action plans, containing a "work force analysis," a determination whether any racial or ethnic minority group or women have been "underutilized" by the employer, and "goals and timetables" to remedy any underutilization found. Id. §§ 60–2.11, –2.12. The regulations elaborate on each of these three requirements and add further requirements as well, and compliance is enforced by sanctions, such as administrative decisions of the OFCCP to terminate contracts or to suspend or debar contractors or to bring public actions against contractors to enforce their obligations under the order. Id. §§ 60–1.26, –1.27, –2.13, –2.14, –2.20 to –2.26. Moreover, special provisions apply to employers with federal construction contracts in excess of $10,000, with goals set by the OFCCP for employment of minority groups and women in most major geographical areas. Id. §§ 60–4.1 to –4.9.

Enough has been said to reveal the complexity of the scheme for regulating federal contractors. As a practical matter, the OFCCP reserves the most severe sanctions for the employers found to have engaged in outright discrimination. Most other employers achieve a negotiated settlement in which the employer retains its eligibility for federal contracts by making appropriate changes in its personnel practices to meet the demands of the OFCCP. In *Weber*, the employer and the union anticipated this entire process by agreeing to an affirmative action plan in advance of any formal proceedings by the OFCCP. Their actions, in other words, were taken in the shadow of potential enforcement actions by the OFCCP. Only Justice Rehnquist called attention to this feature of the case. Does it contradict Justice Brennan's assertion that this case involves only voluntary affirmative action? Does it also undercut his claim that this case raises no constitutional question because no government coercion was involved in the adoption of the affirmative action plan? Or were the employer and the union doing nothing more than structuring their personnel practices to avoid any form of liability, whether under the Executive Order or under Title VII?

4. **Effects of Affirmative Action.** Regardless of the precise role that the Executive Order played in *Weber*, a number of empirical studies have documented its effect in reducing discrimination and in increasing the employment opportunities available to minorities. Most of these studies concerned the enforcement of the Executive Order, in combination with Title VII, at the height of the civil rights era in the late 1960s and the 1970s. These studies show that combined enforcement of these federal laws resulted in elimination of the most obvious forms of discrimination and, among federal contractors, resulted in a small, but steady increase in minority employment. John J. Donohue III & James J. Heckman, Continuous Versus Episodic Change: The Impact of Civil Rights Policy on the Economic Status of Blacks, 19 J. Econ. Literature 1603 (1991); James J. Heckman & Brook S. Payner, Determining the Impact of Federal Antidiscrimination Policy on the Economic Status of Blacks: A Study of South Carolina, 79 Am. Econ. Rev. 138 (1989). A more skeptical assessment of the benefits of affirmative action can be found in James P. Smith, Affirmative Action and the Racial Wage

Gap, 83 Am. Econ. Rev. 79 (1993), in which the author argues that longer term economic forces, such as the slowing of black education gains (relative to whites) and the rising wage inequality that affected all low-wage workers, explain the more recent lack of relative black economic progress better than a declining commitment to affirmative action.

For the analysis specifically of affirmative action plans, see Harry Holzer & David Neumark, Assessing Affirmative Action, 38 J. Econ. Lit. 483, 559 (2000) ("affirmative action offers significant redistribution toward women and minorities, with relatively small efficiency consequences"); Jonathan S. Leonard, The Effectiveness of Equal Employment Law and Affirmative Action Regulation, 8 Res. Lab. Econ. 319 (1986); Jonathan S. Leonard, What Promises Are Worth: The Impact of Affirmative Action Goals, 20 Hum. Res. 3 (1985). These studies support the conclusion that affirmative action is a necessary, but hardly sufficient, means of eliminating the consequences of discrimination. They do not, as supporters of affirmative action sometimes suggest, indicate that it immediately results in racial and ethnic balance in all the positions to which it is applied. Nor, as the critics suggest, do these studies conclude that affirmative action imposes substantial burdens on the groups not favored by the particular preferential program. As Holzer and Neumark conclude: "There is virtually no evidence of weaker education qualifications or job performance among females who benefit from affirmative action relative to males, especially within occupational grade." As a remedy for past discrimination, affirmative action is a complement to, rather than a substitute for, vigorous enforcement of the laws directly against employment discrimination.

If this conclusion is accepted, does it furnish another rationale for the decision in *Weber*: that voluntary affirmative action is one of the few means available to employers and unions to assure that they are in compliance with Title VII? Managers concerned that their supervisors might be engaged in discrimination can more easily monitor their personnel decisions through an established affirmative action plan, rather than through detailed inquiry into the existence of discrimination against any particular individual or group. See Note, Rethinking *Weber*: The Business Response to Affirmative Action, 102 Harv. L. Rev. 658 (1989). Does this practical concern with effective compliance overcome the objection of critics that affirmative action is itself a form of discrimination? Or does the answer to this question depend, as *Weber* holds, on the burden that affirmative action plans place on other employees?

5. **The Precedential Force of *Weber*.** Two decisions reaffirmed *Weber* in the 1980's, Johnson v. Transportation Agency, 480 U.S. 616 (1987), and Local No. 93, International Ass'n of Firefighters v. Cleveland, 478 U.S. 501, 514 (1986). None of these decisions—neither *Weber* nor *Johnson* nor *Firefighters*—was cited in the recent decision in Ricci v. DeStefano, 557 U.S. 557 (2009). As discussed in the previous chapter, *Ricci* directly concerned liability for disparate impact, but not far in the background were concerns about affirmative action. It is therefore surprising that none of these prior decisions was cited in that case, raising doubts about their continued force and influence.

In *Johnson*, the Supreme Court applied the standards from *Weber* to an affirmative action plan in favor of women. The key fact in that case concerned the complete absence of women from the entire department into which a single female employee was promoted under the affirmative action plan. The case returned to the "inexorable zero" of no representation at all that figured in the early decision in Teamsters v. United States, 431 U.S. 324 (1977). The decision in *Firefighters* concerned a consent decree, approved by the district court and agreed to by the original parties, the plaintiffs who were a group of black firefighters and the defendant, the city of Cleveland. The firefighters' union had intervened to challenge the consent decree on the ground that it exceeded the district court's remedial authority under Title VII. The Supreme Court rejected this challenge, finding that the affirmative action plan was necessary to remedy manifest imbalance and did not unnecessarily trammel the interest of white employees under the standards of *Weber*. Nevertheless, the Court indicated that the consent decree was binding only on the original parties to the lawsuit, not on the union or on individual firefighters, who could object to the consent decree on other grounds, for instance, under the Constitution because the city of Cleveland was a government employer.

Collateral attack on such grounds was specifically allowed in a subsequent decision, Martin v. Wilks, 490 U.S. 755 (1989). The Court there held that individuals who were neither a party to the underlying action nor in privity with a party were under no duty to intervene to object to a consent decree adopting an affirmative action plan. They could, instead, make their objections in an independent action. This holding was itself later modified, and to some extent superseded, by the Civil Rights Act of 1991. The Act contains elaborate provisions making judgments and consent decrees binding on nonparties with actual notice of the proposed order and an opportunity to object to it, as well as on nonparties whose interests were adequately represented by an existing party. § 703(n), codified as 42 U.S.C. § 2000e–2(n). As this provision recognizes, however, the binding effect of any consent decree is subject to the requirements of due process. At some point, parties who object to a consent decree have a right to be heard. If they did not have any notice of the underlying action and were not adequately represented by an existing party, they have a right to challenge any resulting judgment insofar as it has adverse effects upon them. For articles on these issues, see Andrea Catania & Charles A. Sullivan, Judging Judgments: The 1991 Civil Rights Act and the Lingering Ghost of *Martin v. Wilks*, 57 Brook. L. Rev. 995 (1992); Douglas Laycock, Consent Decrees Without Consent: The Rights of Nonconsenting Third Parties, 1987 U. Chi. Legal F. 103 (1987); George Rutherglen, Procedures and Preferences, Remedies for Employment Discrimination, 5 Rev. Lit. 73 (1986); Marjorie Silver, Fairness and Finality: Third-Party Challenges to Employment Discrimination Consent Decrees After the 1991 Civil Rights Act, 62 Ford. L. Rev. 321 (1993).

6. Statutory and Constitutional Standards for Affirmative Action. The decisions endorsing *Weber*, like *Weber* itself, were treated as if they raised questions solely under Title VII, not under the Constitution. Does this narrow focus on statutory issues account for the persistence of the standards from *Weber*? As we have seen, the constitutional standards for affirmative action are much more demanding, evolving in a series of cases to require strict scrutiny of all government preferences on the basis of race and national origin. These constitutional decisions would not have applied directly to the preference in *Johnson*, which was based on sex and so was subject to the slightly more lenient standard requiring an "exceedingly persuasive" justification in order to be held constitutional. United States v. Virginia, 518 U.S. 515, 531 (1996).

Curiously, even with respect to race, the decisions on affirmative action in higher education offer a lenient interpretation of strict scrutiny, based on a compelling interest in achieving diversity. This is a consistent pattern from Justice Powell's separate opinion in *Bakke* to Justice O'Connor's opinion for the Court in Grutter v. Bollinger, 539 U.S. 306 (2003). The need to achieve diversity does not have as much relevance to employment as to higher education, although some positions in public employment, like those of police officers and teachers, might be better performed by a diverse work force. Justice O'Connor also relies upon a related, but distinct, justification for affirmative action in *Grutter*. In a passage quoted earlier, she emphasizes the desirability of opening higher-level positions to members of all racial and ethnic groups: "In order to cultivate a set of leaders with legitimacy in the eyes of the citizenry, it is necessary that the path to leadership be visibly open to talented and qualified individuals of every race and ethnicity." Reasoning along these lines has far more direct relevance to employment, particularly to promotion cases like *Johnson*, than an appeal to diversity alone. Recognizing this fact, many employers submitted amicus briefs in *Grutter* arguing for the preservation of a range of permissible forms of affirmative action.

The overriding difference between the constitutional and statutory standards is that the latter can be altered by Congress. In *Johnson*, Justice Brennan argued that Congress endorsed the standards in *Weber* by failing to take any action to modify them. Justice Scalia vehemently disagreed on the ground that Congress might have refused to act for any number of other reasons. In fact, where Congress has legislated with respect to affirmative action under Title VII, it has done so either in very narrow terms or in exceedingly ambiguous terms. Section 703(i), allowing preferences for Native Americans, has already been discussed. Three further provisions, added by the Civil Rights Act of 1991, follow the same pattern. One provision, now found in § 703(*l*) prohibits any adjustment in test scores based on race, national origin, sex, or religion. Another provision, found in § 703(n), limits collateral attack on court orders imposing or approving affirmative action plans. A final, uncodified provision, § 116 of the Act, provides that nothing in the amendments made by the Act to Title VII "shall be construed to affect court-ordered remedies, affirmative action, or conciliation agreements, that are in accordance with the law." This Delphic pronouncement suggests that pre-existing forms of affirmative action remain unaffected by the Civil Rights Act of 1991.

7. Bibliography. For articles directly concerned with *Weber*, see Alfred W. Blumrosen, Affirmative Action in Employment After *Weber*, 34 Rutgers

L. Rev. 1 (1981); Harry T. Edwards, Affirmative Action or Reverse Discrimination: The Head and Tail of *Weber*, 13 Creighton L. Rev. 713 (1980); Bernard D. Meltzer, The *Weber* Case: The Judicial Abrogation of the Anti-Discrimination Standard in Employment, 47 U. Chi. L. Rev. 423 (1980); George Schatzki, *United Steelworkers of America v. Weber*: An Exercise in Understandable Indecision, 56 Wash. L. Rev. 51 (1980); Thomas Sowell, *Weber* and *Bakke* and the Presuppositions of "Affirmative Action," 26 Wayne L. Rev. 1309 (1980).

For discussion of affirmative action in employment after *Weber*, see John Skrentny, After Civil Rights: Racial Realism in the New American Workplace (2015); Kingsley R. Browne, Title VII and Diversity, 14 Nev. L.J. 806 (2014); Richard Thompson Ford, Civil Rights 2.0: Encouraging Innovation to Tackle Silicon Valley's Diversity Deficit, 11 Stan. J. C.R. & C.L. 155 (2015); Sophia Z. Lee, A Revolution at War with Itself? Preserving Employment Preferences from *Weber* to *Ricci*, 123 Yale L.J. 2964 (2014); Sandra R. Levitsky, Reasonably Accommodating Race: Lessons from the ADA for Race-Targeted Affirmative Action, 18 L. & Ineq. 85 (2000); Deborah C. Malamud, The Strange Persistence of Affirmative Action under Title VII, 118 W. Va. L. Rev. 1 (2015); Michael Selmi, Testing for Equality: Merit, Efficiency, and the Affirmative Action Debate, 42 UCLA L. Rev. 1251 (1995); Charles A. Sullivan, Circling Back to the Obvious: The Convergence of Traditional and Reverse Discrimination in Title VII Proof, 46 Wm. & Mary L. Rev. 1031 (2004).

For an analysis of the recent constitutional decisions on affirmative action and the significance of diversity as a justification for affirmative action programs, see Devon Carbado, Mitu Gulati & Patrick Shin, The Diversity Feedback Loop, 2014 U. Chi. Legal F. 345; Janine S. Hiller & Stephen P. Ferris, Separating Myth From Reality: An Economic Analysis of Voluntary Affirmative Action Programs, 23 Mem. St. U. L. Rev. 773 (1993); Joel K. Goldstein, Beyond *Bakke: Grutter-Gratz* and the Promise of *Brown*, 48 St. Louis U. L.J. 899 (2004); Samuel Issacharoff, Law and Misdirection in the Debate over Affirmative Action, 2002 U. Chi. Legal F. 11; John C. Jeffries, Jr., *Bakke* Revisited, 2003 Sup. Ct. Rev. 1; Wendy Parker, Recognizing Discrimination: Lessons from White Plaintiffs, 65 Fla. L. Rev. 1871 (2013); David B. Oppenheimer, the Disappearance of Voluntary Affirmative Action from the U.S. Workplace, J. Poverty & Soc'l Justice (2016) at https://policypress.co.uk/journals/journal-of-poverty-and-social-justice; Camille Gear Rich, Affirmative Action in the Era of Elective Race: Racial Commodification and the Promise of the New Functionalism, 102 Geo. L.J. 179 (2013); Peter H. Schuck, Affirmative Action: Past, Present, and Future, 20 Yale L. & Pol'y Rev. 1 (2002). For other articles on the debate over affirmative action as it led up to these decisions, see Carl E. Brody Jr., A Historical Review of Affirmative Action and the Interpretation of Its Legislative Intent by the Supreme Court, 29 Akron L. Rev. 291 (1996); Linda Hamilton Krieger, Civil Rights Perestroika: Intergroup Relations After Affirmative Action, 86 Cal. L. Rev. 1251 (1998); Charles R. Lawrence III & Mari J. Matsuda, We Won't Go Back: Making the Case for Affirmative Action (1997); John E. Morrison, Colorblindness, Individuality, and Merit: An

Analysis of the Rhetoric Against Affirmative Action, 79 Iowa L. Rev. 313 (1994); Jed Rubenfeld, Affirmative Action, 107 Yale L.J. 427 (1997).

CHAPTER 5

SEX DISCRIMINATION UNDER THE EQUAL PAY ACT AND TITLE VII

A. INTRODUCTION

1. **Statutory and Constitutional Developments.** The decision in Price Waterhouse v. Hopkins, 490 U.S. 228 (1989), discussed in Chapter 1, raises many issues of sex discrimination at every level of generality: from the abstract question of why and to what extent it is prohibited to the concrete question of what constitutes evidence of impermissible stereotyping. This chapter takes up these questions in more detail, beginning with an examination of the historical origins of legislation against sex discrimination.

The prohibition against racial discrimination in Title VII came almost a century after the constitutional amendments prohibiting discrimination on the basis of race. Legislative enactment of this prohibition therefore followed in the wake of a considerable body of constitutional jurisprudence concerning the contours of impermissible racial discrimination, albeit only in the context of governmental action. The development of the law of sex discrimination followed the opposite pattern, with Congress enacting statutory prohibitions against sex discrimination before a related body of constitutional jurisprudence could develop.

Title VII is the most important of these statutes, but it was not the first. It was preceded by the Equal Pay Act of 1963, which was enacted by the same Congress that enacted the Civil Rights Act of 1964. In contrast to Title VII, the Equal Pay Act prohibits sex discrimination only in compensation and only when women and men perform equal work. The interpretation and enforcement of both statutes have been complicated by the history of their enactment. The Equal Pay Act was passed only after repeatedly being introduced in Congress in the years after World War II. While it was subject to extended congressional debate and modification, the prohibition against sex discrimination was added to Title VII through an amendment on the floor of the House of Representatives. This amendment was introduced by Representative Howard W. Smith of Virginia, a legislator adamantly opposed to any civil rights legislation. Although he insisted that he genuinely supported the rights of women, his motives in offering this amendment were at best ambiguous. See Carl M. Brauer, Women Activists, Southern Conservatives, and the Prohibition of Sex Discrimination in Title VII of the 1964 Civil Rights Act, 49 J. S. Hist. 37 (1983). Whatever his motives, the absence of any committee consideration of this amendment, either in the House or the Senate, left many questions about its interpretation and enforcement to the courts.

These questions were made all the more difficult because the Supreme Court did not recognize a general constitutional prohibition against sex discrimination until several years after the enactment of Title VII. Reed v. Reed, 404 U.S. 71 (1971). Even this line of decisions became complicated, however, by the simultaneous consideration of the proposed Equal Rights Amendment, which eventually failed to receive the necessary ratification by three-quarters of the states. See Donald L. Mathews & Jane D. Hart, Sex, Gender, and the Politics of the ERA (1990). Partly for this reason, the constitutional prohibition against sex discrimination has never required strict scrutiny of government classifications on the basis of sex. Current doctrine requires an "exceedingly persuasive" justification for such classifications, a seemingly weaker standard of scrutiny. United States v. Virginia, 518 U.S. 515, 531 (1996).

The sequence of constitutional law following statutory law was the reverse of that for racial discrimination, in which constitutional decisions came first. Moreover, the Constitution itself contains only one prohibition explicitly addressed to discrimination on the basis of sex discrimination: the Nineteenth Amendment, which is limited to voting. The statutory prohibitions against sex discrimination are far broader and more explicit than the constitutional prohibitions and they have no pre-existing basis even in constitutional decisions of the Supreme Court. Consequently, they continue to raise persistent questions which have endured to this day: How is the prohibition against sex discrimination related to the prohibition against racial discrimination? Is it narrower, or broader, or simply different? Is the continued existence of sex discrimination as great a problem as continued racial discrimination? Should the conceptions of equality that apply to racial discrimination also apply to sex discrimination? These questions arise most forcefully in interpreting distinctive statutory provisions that apply only to sex discrimination. For recent discussions of these questions, see Serena Mayeri, Reasoning from Race: Feminism, Law, and the Civil Rights Revolution (2011); Kimberly A. Yuracko, The Antidiscrimination Paradox: Why Sex Before Race?, 104 Nw. U. L. Rev. 1 (2010); Nancy Levit, June Carbone & Naomi Cahn, Gender and the Tournament: Reinventing Antidiscrimination Law in an Age of Inequality, 96 Tex. L. Rev. ___ (2018).

2. **Feminist Theory.** These questions of statutory interpretation raise still more profound questions about the role of women in our society, and more generally, about the significance that is or should be attached to sexual differences and gender roles. These questions have led feminists to take a wide range of different positions on the essential significance of biological differences based on sex, the traditional gender roles allocated

on the basis of sex, the power relationships between women and men, the connection between sexual activity and discrimination on the basis of sex, and the feasible strategies for change. An extensive and insightful literature has developed around all of these questions, which have far-reaching implications for the law.

A number of books and collections of articles have explored these implications, among them: Feminism Confronts Homo Economicus: Gender, Law, and Society (Martha Fineman & Terrance Dougherty eds., 2005); Applications of Feminist Legal Theory to Women's Lives: Sex, Violence, Work, and Reproduction (D. Kelly Weisburg ed., 1996); Feminist Legal Theory (Frances E. Olsen ed., 1995); Feminist Legal Theory: Foundations (D. Kelly Weisburg ed., 1993); Deborah L. Rhode, Justice: Sex Discrimination and the Law (1989); Symposium, Sexuality at Work, 29 T. Jefferson L. Rev. 1 (2006); Symposium, Innate Differences: Responses to the Remarks by Lawrence H. Summers, 11 Cardozo Women's L.J. 497 (2005); 2001 Women and the Law Conference: Women as Workers, 24 T. Jefferson L. Rev. 121 (2002); Symposium, The Law of Sex Discrimination, 1999 U. Chi. Legal F. 1; Men, Masculinities, and Law: A Symposium on Multidimensional Masculinities Theory, 13 Nev. L.J. 315 (2013). See also Zachary A. Kramer, The New Sex Discrimination, 63 Duke L.J. 891 (2014).

Feminists have been particularly concerned with the conflict between the obligations of women at home and their obligations at work, an issue that bears directly on whether they actually have the same employment opportunities as men. Joan Williams, Unbending Gender: Why Family and Work Conflict and What To Do About It (2000); Rachel Croson & Uri Gneezy, Gender Differences in Preferences, 47 J. Econ. Lit. 448 (2009); Sylvia A. Law, Women, Work, Welfare, and the Preservation of Patriarchy, 131 U. Pa. L. Rev. 1249 (1983); Justin D. Levinson, Implicit Gender Bias in the Legal Profession: An Empirical Study, 18 Duke J. Gender L. & Pol'y 1 (2010); Ann C. McGinley, Reproducing Gender on Law School Faculties, 2009 B.Y.U. L. Rev. 99 (2009); Gregory S. Parks & Quinnetta M. Robertson, Michelle Obama: A Contemporary Analysis of Race and Gender Discrimination Through the Lens of Title VII, 20 Hastings Women's L.J. 3 (2009); Vicki Schultz, Feminism and Workplace Flexibility, 42 Conn. L. Rev. 1203 (2010); Julie C. Suk, Are Gender Stereotypes Bad for Women? Rethinking Antidiscrimination Law and Work-Family Conflict, 100 Colum. L. Rev. 1 (2010); Joan Williams, Canaries in the Mine: Work/Family Conflict and the Law, 70 Fordham L. Rev. 2221 (2002).

3. Economic Studies. Another series of books and articles has specifically addressed the economic consequences of discrimination on the basis of sex. These works have examined both the progress that women have made in entering the workforce and the obstacles they face in achieving complete equality. Susan Bisom-Rapp & Malcolm Sargeant Lifetime Disadvantage, Discrimination and the Gendered Workforce

(2016); Gender and Family Issues in the Workplace (Francine D. Blau & Ronald G. Ehrenberg eds., 1997); Daphne Spain & Suzanne M. Bianchi, Balancing Act: Motherhood, Marriage, and Employment Among American Women (1996); Claudia Goldin, Understanding the Gender Gap: An Economic History of American Women (1990); Victor R. Fuchs, Women's Quest for Economic Equality (1988); Virginia Valian, Why So Slow? The Advancement of Women (1999); Francine D. Blau, Trends in the Well-Being of American Women, 1970–1995, 36 J. Econ. Lit. 112 (1998); Alfred W. Blumrosen & Ruth G. Blumrosen, First Statistical Report on Intentional Job Discrimination Against Women, 25 Women's Rts. L. Rep. 63 (2003); John J. Donohue III, Prohibiting Sex Discrimination in the Workplace: An Economic Perspective, 56 U. Chi. L. Rev. 1337 (1989); Edward J. McCaffery, Slouching Towards Equality: Gender Discrimination, Market Efficiency, and Social Change, 103 Yale L.J. 595 (1993); Symposium, Minding the Gap: Reflections on the Achievement Gap Between Men and Women in the Workplace in 2013, 8 Fla. Int'l U. L. Rev. 263 (2013).

Claudia Goldin, a prominent labor economist, has offered an informed summary of the development of women's increasing role in the paid economy. The Quiet Revolution that Transformed Women's Employment, Education, and Family, 96 Am. Econ. Rev. 1 (2006). She identifies four phases in the emerging role of women: the first from the late 19th century to the 1920s; the second from 1930 to 1950; the third from the 1950s to the late 1970s; and the fourth from 1970 on. In her view, the first three of these phases are evolutionary, while the fourth is revolutionary, revealed by evidence of women's greater attachment to the workplace, greater identity with their careers, and better ability to make joint decisions with their spouses. She speculates about whether this revolution will continue, but finds no conclusive evidence from the experience of women who recently entered the labor force.

Two issues of particular concern have been unequal pay and occupational segregation of women. See Francine D. Blau & Lawrence M. Kahn, At Home and Abroad, in U.S. Labor Market Performance in International Perspective 228 (2002); Francine D. Blau, Equal Pay in the Office (1977); Women and the Workplace: The Implications of Occupational Segregation (Martha Blaxall & Barbara Reagan eds., 1976); Morley Gunderson, Male-Female Wage Differentials and Policy Responses, 27 J. Econ. Literature 46 (1989); Jessica Pan, Gender Segregation in Occupations: The Role of Tipping and Social Interactions, 33 J. Lab. Econ. 365 (2015); Vicki Schultz & Stephen Petterson, Race, Gender, Work, and Choice: An Empirical Study of the Lack of Interest Defense in Title VII Cases Challenging Job Segregation, 59 U. Chi. L. Rev. 1073 (1992). See also Serena Mayeri, The Strange Career of Jane Crow: Sex Segregation and the Transformation of Anti-Discrimination Discourse, 18 Yale J.L. & Hum. 187 (2006); Ann. C. McGinley, Masculinities at Work, 83 Or. L. Rev. 359 (2004); Kimberly A. Yuracko,

Trait Discrimination as Sex Discrimination: An Argument Against Neutrality, 83 Tex. L. Rev. 167 (2004). These issues are taken up in the first section of this chapter.

B. THE EQUAL PAY ACT

INTRODUCTORY NOTES ON THE EQUAL PAY ACT

1. **Passage of the Equal Pay Act.** The differences between the legal treatment of race discrimination and sex discrimination begin with the way in which the prohibitions against employment discrimination on these grounds were enacted. The prohibitions against sex discrimination began with the Equal Pay Act, 29 U.S.C. § 206(d), which narrowly prohibits only discrimination on the basis of sex and only discrimination in pay. Narrow though it is, the Equal Pay Act was preceded by a series of bills (all of which failed to be enacted) that sought to codify prohibitions against sex discrimination established originally during World War II by the National War Labor Board. The war saw the entry of vast numbers of women into jobs previously reserved for men, but which, because of wartime demand for men in the armed forces, now had to be filled by women. The regulations of the National War Labor Board prohibited discrimination in pay against women who held jobs that were "comparable" to those held by men. It was a prohibition motivated by the desire both to compensate everyone equally who participated in the war effort and to prevent women from losing pay on the ground that the positions they held, by definition, required only "women's work."

When peace returned, the men returned to their jobs and the regulations of the National War Labor Board were dismantled. Not all women, however, returned to the home, and the early 1950s saw the beginning of a gradual, but steady, increase in the participation of women in the labor force. The entry of women into jobs previously held only by men was accompanied by proposals to reinstate the requirement of equal pay from the war years. As the following cases indicate, these proposals initially took the form of equal pay for "comparable" work on the model of the wartime regulations. But because of objections to the breadth of and uncertainty over what constituted "comparable" work, the prohibition in the Equal Pay Act was limited by the condition of "equal" work. Women were entitled to the same pay as men only if they performed "equal" work with men.

2. **Content of the Equal Pay Act.** The narrowness of the Equal Pay Act was assured by several of its provisions. The first of these is implicit in the title of the Act itself. It prohibits only discrimination in pay. Unlike the far broader prohibition against sex discrimination in Title VII, it does not extend to all the terms and conditions of employment. An employer can comply with the Equal Pay Act, but not with Title VII, simply by refusing to employ women in any job in which they would perform equal work with men. Another contrast with Title VII involves the grounds of discrimination addressed by the Equal Pay Act. It is concerned with discrimination only on the basis of sex, not on the basis of race, national origin, or religion.

The limitation of most concern to Congress was the definition of "equal" work and it is reflected in the main prohibition in the Act, which is limited to "equal work on jobs the performance of which requires equal skill, effort, and responsibility, and which are performed under similar working conditions." In addition, this prohibition is subject to four separate exceptions. The first three concern payment according to seniority, merit, or piecework systems, and the fourth is a catch-all exception for "a differential based on any other factor other than sex." The first three of these exceptions also can be found in Title VII, in § 703(h), and they establish a limited analogy between the two statutes. A further prohibition in the Equal Pay Act prevents employers from "leveling down": remedying any inequality in pay by reducing the pay of the higher paid sex.

The limited ambitions of the Equal Pay Act also are reflected in its enactment and codification as an amendment to the Fair Labor Standards Act (FLSA), the federal minimum wage law. The Equal Pay Act was presented to Congress as a modest addition to the main federal statute regulating minimum rates of pay. Because it was enacted as an amendment to the FLSA, the Equal Pay Act is enforced according to the provisions found in that Act. These have taken on a complicated life of their own, discussed in a note later in this chapter, but again, they provide a further contrast with Title VII, which has its own distinctive enforcement provisions. The provisions in the Equal Pay Act and Title VII have been brought into harmony only on the issue of public enforcement actions, which have been consolidated in the EEOC through a presidential reorganization plan not yet reflected in the statutory language of the FLSA.

3. **Goals of the Equal Pay Act.** The Equal Pay Act addresses a large and persistent problem resulting from the entry of women into the labor market: that they regularly receive lower pay than men. Estimates of this wage gap vary, from findings that working women, on average, earn 60 percent of what men earn to findings that they earn up to 90 percent as much. Paul Weiler, The Wages of Sex: The Uses and Limits of Comparable Worth, 99 Harv. L. Rev. 1728, 1779 (1986). The higher figure controls for a variety of variables that have an effect on earnings, from the higher average hours worked by men to the concentration of men in higher paying occupations. Nevertheless, even after all these factors are taken into account, a residual gap remains. Moreover, the factors themselves might well be tainted by sex discrimination, such as preferential selection of men for higher paying jobs. Recent figures indicate that the median weekly earnings of women who work full time are between 77 percent and 83 percent of those for men. Bureau of Labor Statistics, Highlights of Women's Earnings in 2014 at https://www.bls.gov/opub/reports/womens-earnings/archive/highlights-of-womens-earnings-in-2014.pdf (83%); Robert Drago & Claudia Williams, The Gender Wage Gap 2009, Institute for Women's Policy Research (September 2010) (77.0%), available at http://www.iwpr.org/publications/pubs/the-gender-wage-gap–2009.

The Equal Pay Act attempts to eliminate this disparity in pay through a simple legal prohibition against discrimination in that aspect of employment. The cases that follow raise, in one form or another, the question whether this strategy is the correct one: whether a direct attack on discrimination in pay alone is the best way, or even an effective way, of correcting inequalities in pay. The same strategy has not been pursued for discrimination on other grounds. Title VII addresses discrimination in pay on the basis of race, national origin, and religion through the broad prohibitions against any form of discrimination on these grounds. Would this have been the correct approach also to take with discrimination on the basis of sex?

4. **Bibliography.** There have been many economic studies of differences in compensation between women and men. For a recent review and analysis of the literature, see Francine D. Blau & Lawrence M. Kahn, The Gender Wage Gap: Extent, Trends, and Explanations, 55 J. Econ. Literature 789 (2017).

Corning Glass Works v. Brennan

417 U.S. 188 (1974).

■ JUSTICE MARSHALL delivered the opinion of the Court.

These cases arise under the Equal Pay Act of 1963, 29 U.S.C. § 206 (d)(1), which added to § 6 of the Fair Labor Standards Act of 1938 the principle of equal pay for equal work regardless of sex. The principal question posed is whether Corning Glass Works violated the Act by paying a higher base wage to male night shift inspectors than it paid to female inspectors performing the same tasks on the day shift, where the higher wage was paid in addition to a separate night shift differential paid to all employees for night work. In No. 73–29, the Court of Appeals for the Second Circuit, in a case involving several Corning plants in Corning, New York, held that this practice violated the Act. In No. 73–695, the Court of Appeals for the Third Circuit, in a case involving a Corning plant in Wellsboro, Pennsylvania, reached the opposite conclusion. We granted certiorari and consolidated the cases to resolve this unusually direct conflict between two circuits. Finding ourselves in substantial agreement with the analysis of the Second Circuit, we affirm in No. 73–29 and reverse in No. 73–695.

I

Prior to 1925, Corning operated its plants in Wellsboro and Corning only during the day, and all inspection work was performed by women. Between 1925 and 1930, the company began to introduce automatic production equipment which made it desirable to institute a night shift. During this period, however, both New York and Pennsylvania law prohibited women from working at night. As a result, in order to fill inspector positions on the new night shift, the company had to recruit male employees from among its male dayworkers. The male employees so transferred demanded and received wages substantially higher than those paid to women inspectors engaged on the two day shifts. During this same period, however, no plant-wide shift differential existed and male employees working at night, other than inspectors, received the same wages as their day shift counterparts. Thus a situation developed where the night inspectors were all male, the day inspectors all female, and the male inspectors received significantly higher wages.

In 1944, Corning plants at both locations were organized by a labor union and a collective-bargaining agreement was negotiated for all production and maintenance employees. This agreement for the first time established a plant-wide shift differential, but this change did not eliminate the higher base wage paid to male night inspectors. Rather, the shift differential was superimposed on the existing difference in base wages between male night inspectors and female day inspectors.

Prior to June 11, 1964, the effective date of the Equal Pay Act, the law in both Pennsylvania and New York was amended to permit women to work at night. It was not until some time after the effective date of the Act, however, that Corning initiated efforts to eliminate the differential rates for male and female inspectors. Beginning in June 1966, Corning started to open up jobs on the night shift to women. Previously separate male and female seniority lists were consolidated and women became eligible to exercise their seniority, on the same basis as men, to bid for the higher paid night inspection jobs as vacancies occurred.

On January 20, 1969, a new collective-bargaining agreement went into effect, establishing a new "job evaluation" system for setting wage rates. The new agreement abolished for the future the separate base wages for day and night shift inspectors and imposed a uniform base wage for inspectors exceeding the wage rate for the night shift previously in effect. All inspectors hired after January 20, 1969, were to receive the same base wage, whatever their sex or shift. The collective-bargaining agreement further provided, however, for a higher "red circle" rate for employees hired prior to January 20, 1969, when working as inspectors on the night shift. This "red circle" rate served essentially to perpetuate the differential in base wages between day and night inspectors.

The Secretary of Labor brought these cases to enjoin Corning from violating the Equal Pay Act and to collect back wages allegedly due female employees because of past violations. Three distinct questions are presented: (1) Did Corning ever violate the Equal Pay Act by paying male night shift inspectors more than female day shift inspectors? (2) If so, did Corning cure its violation of the Act in 1966 by permitting women to work as night shift inspectors? (3) Finally, if the violation was not remedied in 1966, did Corning cure its violation in 1969 by equalizing day and night inspector wage rates but establishing higher "red circle" rates for existing employees working on the night shift?

II

Congress' purpose in enacting the Equal Pay Act was to remedy what was perceived to be a serious and endemic problem of employment discrimination in private industry—the fact that the wage structure of "many segments of American industry has been based on an ancient but outmoded belief that a man, because of his role in society, should be paid more than a woman even though his duties are the same." S. Rep. No. 176, 88th Cong., 1st Sess., 1 (1963). The solution adopted was quite simple in principle: to require that "equal work will be rewarded by equal wages." Ibid.

The Act's basic structure and operation are similarly straightforward. In order to make out a case under the Act, the Secretary must show that an employer pays different wages to employees of opposite sexes "for equal work on jobs the performance of which requires equal skill, effort, and responsibility, and which are performed under similar working conditions." Although the Act is silent on this point, its legislative history makes plain that the Secretary has the burden of proof on this issue, as both of the courts below recognized.

The Act also establishes four exceptions—three specific and one a general catchall provision—where different payment to employees of opposite sexes "is made pursuant to (i) a seniority system; (ii) a merit system; (iii) a system which measures earnings by quantity or quality of production; or (iv) a differential based on any other factor other than sex." Again, while the Act is silent on this question, its structure and history also suggest that once the Secretary has carried his burden of showing that the employer pays workers of one sex more than workers of the opposite sex for equal work, the burden shifts to the employer to show that the differential is justified under one of the Act's four exceptions. All of the many lower courts that have considered this question have so held, and this view is consistent with the general rule that the application of an exemption under the Fair Labor Standards Act is a matter of affirmative defense on which the employer has the burden of proof.

The contentions of the parties in this case reflect the Act's underlying framework. Corning argues that the Secretary has failed to prove that Corning ever violated the Act because day shift work is not "performed under similar working conditions" as night shift work. The Secretary maintains that day shift and night shift work are performed under "similar working conditions" within the meaning of the Act. Although the Secretary recognizes that higher wages may be paid for night shift work, the Secretary contends that such a shift differential would be based upon a "factor other than sex" within the catchall exception to the Act and that Corning has failed to carry its burden of proof that its higher base wage for male night inspectors was in fact based on any factor other than sex.

The courts below relied in part on conflicting statements in the legislative history having some bearing on this question of statutory construction. The Third Circuit found particularly significant a statement of Congressman Goodell, a sponsor of the Equal Pay bill, who, in the course of explaining the bill on the floor of the House, commented that "standing as opposed to sitting, pleasantness or unpleasantness of surroundings, periodic rest periods, hours of work, *difference in shift*, all would logically fall within the working condition factor." 109 Cong. Rec. 9209 (1963) (emphasis added). The Second Circuit, in contrast, relied on a statement from the House Committee Report which, in describing the broad general exception for differentials "based on any other factor other than sex," stated: "Thus, among other things, shift differentials . . . would also be excluded. . . ." H.R. Rep. No. 309, 88th Cong., 1st Sess., 3 (1963).

We agree with Judge Friendly, however, that in this case a better understanding of the phrase "performed under similar working conditions" can be obtained from a consideration of the way in which Congress arrived at the statutory language than from trying to reconcile or establish preferences between the conflicting interpretations of the Act by individual legislators or the committee reports. As Mr. Justice Frankfurter remarked in an earlier case involving interpretation of the Fair Labor Standards Act, "regard for the specific history of the legislative process that culminated in the Act now before us affords more solid ground for giving it appropriate meaning." United States v. Universal C.I.T. Credit Corp., 344 U.S. 218, 222 (1952).

The most notable feature of the history of the Equal Pay Act is that Congress recognized early in the legislative process that the concept of equal pay for equal work was more readily stated in principle than reduced to statutory language which would be meaningful to employers and workable across the broad range of industries covered by the Act. As originally introduced, the Equal Pay bill required equal pay for "equal work on jobs the performance of which requires equal skills." There were only two exceptions—for differentials "made pursuant to a seniority or merit increase system which does not discriminate on the basis of sex. . . ."

In both the House and Senate committee hearings, witnesses were highly critical of the Act's definition of equal work and of its exemptions. Many noted that most of American industry used formal, systematic job evaluation plans to establish equitable wage structures in their plants. Such systems, as explained coincidentally by a representative of Corning Glass Works who testified at both hearings, took into consideration four separate factors in determining job value—skill, effort, responsibility and working conditions—and each of these four components was further systematically divided into various subcomponents. Under a job evaluation plan, point values are assigned to each of the subcomponents of a given job, resulting in a total point figure representing a relatively objective measure of the job's value.

In comparison to the rather complex job evaluation plans used by industry, the definition of equal work used in the first drafts of the Equal Pay bill was criticized as unduly vague and incomplete. Industry representatives feared that as a result of the bill's definition of equal work, the Secretary of Labor would be cast in the position of second-guessing the validity of a company's job evaluation system. They repeatedly urged that the bill be amended to include an exception for job classification systems, or otherwise to incorporate the language of job evaluation into the bill. Thus Corning's own representative testified:

> "Job evaluation is an accepted and tested method of attaining equity in wage relationship.
>
> "A great part of industry is committed to job evaluation by past practice and by contractual agreement as the basis for wage administration.
>
> " 'Skill' alone, as a criterion, fails to recognize other aspects of the job situation that affect job worth.
>
> "We sincerely hope that this committee in passing legislation to eliminate wage differences based on sex alone, will recognize in its language the general role of job evaluation in establishing equitable rate relationship."

We think it plain that in amending the bill's definition of equal work to its present form, the Congress acted in direct response to these pleas. Spokesmen for the amended bill stated, for example, during the House debates:

> "The concept of equal pay for jobs demanding equal skill has been expanded to require also equal effort, responsibility, and similar working conditions. These factors are the core of all job classification systems. They form a legitimate basis for differentials in pay."

Indeed, the most telling evidence of congressional intent is the fact that the Act's amended definition of equal work incorporated the specific language of the job evaluation plan described at the hearings by Corning's own representative—that is, the concepts of "skill," "effort," "responsibility," and "working conditions."

Congress' intent, as manifested in this history, was to use these terms to incorporate into the new federal Act the well-defined and well-accepted principles of job evaluation so as to ensure that wage differentials based upon bona fide job evaluation plans would be outside the purview of the Act. The House Report emphasized:

> "This language recognizes that there are many factors which may be used to measure the relationships between jobs and which establish a valid basis for a difference in pay. These factors will be found in a majority of the job classification systems. Thus, it is anticipated that a bona fide job classification program that does not discriminate on the basis of sex will serve as a valid defense to a charge of discrimination." H.R. Rep. No. 309, supra, at 3.

It is in this light that the phrase "working conditions" must be understood, for where Congress has used technical words or terms of art, "it [is] proper to explain them by reference to the art or science to which they [are] appropriate." Greenleaf v. Goodrich, 101 U.S. 278, 284 (1880). This principle is particularly salutary where, as here, the legislative history reveals that Congress incorporated words having a special meaning within the field regulated by the statute so as to overcome objections by industry representatives that statutory definitions were vague and incomplete.

While a layman might well assume that time of day worked reflects one aspect of a job's "working conditions," the term has a different and much more specific meaning in the language of industrial relations. As Corning's own representative testified at the hearings, the element of working conditions encompasses two subfactors: "surroundings" and "hazards." "Surroundings" measures the elements, such as toxic chemicals or fumes, regularly encountered by a worker, their intensity, and their frequency. "Hazards" takes into account the physical hazards regularly encountered, their frequency, and the severity of injury they can cause. This definition of "working conditions" is not only manifested in Corning's own job evaluation plans but is also well accepted across a wide range of American industry.

Nowhere in any of these definitions is time of day worked mentioned as a relevant criterion. The fact of the matter is that the concept of "working conditions," as used in the specialized language of job evaluation systems, simply does not encompass shift differentials. Indeed, while Corning now argues that night inspection work is not equal to day inspection work, all of its own job evaluation plans, including the one now in effect, have consistently treated them as equal in all respects, including working conditions. And Corning's Manager of Job Evaluation testified that time of day worked was not considered to be a "working condition." Significantly, it is not the Secretary in this case who is trying to look behind Corning's bona fide job evaluation system to require equal pay for jobs which Corning has historically viewed as unequal work. Rather, it is Corning which asks us to differentiate between jobs which the company itself has always equated. We agree with the Second Circuit that the inspection work at issue in this case, whether performed during the day or night, is "equal work" as that term is defined in the Act.[24]

This does not mean, of course, that there is no room in the Equal Pay Act for nondiscriminatory shift differentials. Work on a steady night shift no doubt has psychological and physiological impacts making it less attractive than work on a day shift. The Act contemplates that a male night worker may receive a higher wage than a female day worker, just

[24] Corning also claimed that the night inspection work was not equal to day shift inspection work because night shift inspectors had to do a certain amount of packing, lifting, and cleaning which was not performed by day shift inspectors. Noting that it is now well settled that jobs need not be identical in every respect before the Equal Pay Act is applicable, the Court of Appeals concluded that the extra work performed by night inspectors was of so little consequence that the jobs remained substantially equal. See also Shultz v. Wheaton Glass Co., 421 F.2d, at 265; Shultz v. American Can Co., 424 F.2d, at 360; Hodgson v. Fairmont Supply Co., 454 F.2d, at 493. The company has not pursued this issue here.

as it contemplates that a male employee with 20 years' seniority can receive a higher wage than a woman with two years' seniority. Factors such as these play a role under the Act's four exceptions—the seniority differential under the specific seniority exception, the shift differential under the catchall exception for differentials "based on any other factor other than sex."

The question remains, however, whether Corning carried its burden of proving that the higher rate paid for night inspection work, until 1966 performed solely by men, was in fact intended to serve as compensation for night work, or rather constituted an added payment based upon sex. We agree that the record amply supports the District Court's conclusion that Corning had not sustained its burden of proof. As its history revealed, "the higher night rate was in large part the product of the generally higher wage level of male workers and the need to compensate them for performing what were regarded as demeaning tasks." The differential in base wages originated at a time when no other night employees received higher pay than corresponding day workers, and it was maintained long after the company instituted a separate plant-wide shift differential which was thought to compensate adequately for the additional burdens of night work. The differential arose simply because men would not work at the low rates paid women inspectors, and it reflected a job market in which Corning could pay women less than men for the same work. That the company took advantage of such a situation may be understandable as a matter of economics, but its differential nevertheless became illegal once Congress enacted into law the principle of equal pay for equal work.

III

We now must consider whether Corning continued to remain in violation of the Act after 1966 when, without changing the base wage rates for day and night inspectors, it began to permit women to bid for jobs on the night shift as vacancies occurred. It is evident that this was more than a token gesture to end discrimination, as turnover in the night shift inspection jobs was rapid. The record in No. 73–29 shows, for example, that during the two-year period after June 1, 1966, the date women were first permitted to bid for night inspection jobs, women took 152 of the 278 openings, and women with very little seniority were able to obtain positions on the night shift. Relying on these facts, the company argues that it ceased discriminating against women in 1966, and was no longer in violation of the Equal Pay Act.

But the issue before us is not whether the company, in some abstract sense, can be said to have treated men the same as women after 1966. Rather, the question is whether the company remedied the specific violation of the Act which the Secretary proved. We agree with the Second Circuit, as well as with all other circuits that have had occasion to consider this issue, that the company could not cure its violation except by equalizing the base wages of female day inspectors with the higher rates paid the night inspectors. This result is implicit in the Act's language, its statement of purpose, and its legislative history. . . .

The judgment in No. 73–29 is affirmed. The judgment in No. 73–695 is reversed and the case remanded to the Court of Appeals for further proceedings consistent with this opinion.

It is so ordered.

[Chief Justice Burger, joined by Justices Blackmun and Rehnquist dissented.]

NOTES ON *CORNING GLASS WORKS V. BRENNAN*

1. **Burdens of Proof Under the Equal Pay Act.** Just as under Title VII, burdens of proof play a crucial role in the application and interpretation of the Equal Pay Act. The elements of the plaintiff's case and the defenses available to the employer determine the outcome of many cases under the Act. *Corning Glass Works* is illustrative. It was decided almost entirely by the allocation to the defendant of the burden of proving that the difference in pay between certain night inspectors (apparently mostly men) and all day inspectors (apparently mostly women) did not have its origins in discrimination. This issue was very murky, requiring an examination of the job structure at Corning Glass going back several decades.

The narrow holding in the case was that the definition of "equal work" in terms of "similar working conditions" did not include the time at which work was performed. Shift differentials instead fell under the catch-all defense of "any other factor other than sex." Why should the technical definition of "equal work," which was designed to protect employers, have caused Corning Glass to lose this case? Is the broad message of the case that employers must accept the bitter with the sweet? That is, Corning Glass, having obtained a technical definition of "equal work" in order to protect its discretion in defining jobs and setting pay, cannot now complain that it has the burden of proof on issues involving similar working conditions as they are ordinarily understood.

Or does the case turn on the belated attempts of Corning Glass to eliminate segregation on the basis of sex by finally allowing women to work as night inspectors in 1966, after Title VII had already prohibited sex discrimination generally in employment? Did pre-existing restrictions preventing women from working at night, which were required by state law, become completely unjustified as soon as Title VII was enacted and the state laws in question were repealed? In any event, Corning Glass did abandon the restrictions. Its only fault was in preserving a differential in pay that, in fact, benefited the women who immediately moved into the position of night inspector. Is the real lesson of this case that employers proceed at their own risk when they do not act quickly enough to abandon outmoded stereotypes about the limited role of women in the economy?

2. **Corrective Action Perpetuating Past Discrimination.** The holding that Corning Glass took the wrong form of corrective action is based on the proviso in the Equal Pay Act, prohibiting any action to "reduce the wage rate

of any employee" in order to correct any unlawful difference in pay. If this proviso is read literally, did Corning Glass violate it in any way? No employee's pay was actually reduced. Only the special differential for night inspectors, over and above the differential for anyone on the night shift, was preserved. Does the Supreme Court misinterpret the proviso by reading it to provide the only means of coming into compliance with the Act? If the Court had let Corning Glass off, would other employers have corrected previous violations of the Act simply by integrating their jobs on the basis of sex, something that Title VII required them to do anyway?

A further complication in the Court's reasoning concerns the need to undertake a detailed history of the job structure at Corning Glass, stretching back well before the Equal Pay Act was enacted. In *Hazelwood School District*, we saw that discriminatory action undertaken before the effective date of Title VII plays only a limited role in establishing liability. It is only evidence of continuing discrimination that can lead to liability. It does not itself constitute an actionable violation of the statute. Is the role of pre-act discrimination any different under the Equal Pay Act? Would *Corning Glass Works* have come out any differently if the pay differential could not be traced to pre-act discrimination? Or was it essential that some violation of the Act occurred after its effective date? As we shall see in Chapter 7, in the discussion of statutes of limitations, claims of discrimination in pay are one of the few in which courts regularly rely on evidence of past violations to support current claims. Indeed, such claims under both the Equal Pay Act and under Title VII receive particularly lenient treatment. Is this because claims of discrimination in pay, as in *Corning Glass Works*, require a detailed analysis of pay scales and their origins? Or is it because a difference in pay that has its origins in the distant past has an immediate and obvious effect on the pay that employees currently receive?

3. **"Substantially" Equal Work.** In the leading case of Shultz v. Wheaton Glass Co., 421 F.2d 259 (3rd Cir. 1970), the Third Circuit held that the plaintiff's burden was only to establish "substantially" equal work, not precisely equal work. According to the court, "Congress in prescribing 'equal' work did not require that the jobs be identical, but only that they must be substantially equal. Any other interpretation would destroy the remedial purposes of the Act." The court concluded that the Act "does not permit artificial classification to prevent inquiry where there exists a difference in pay for substantially equal work." In *Shultz*, the difference in pay left "female selector packers" earning nearly 10 percent% less than "male selector packers," although employees in both positions had the same basic job duties. The only difference between the positions was that "male selector packers" had additional duties comparable to those of "snap up boys," who were paid only slightly more than "female selector packers." The court rejected this difference as insignificant based on a comparison of the rates of pay for all three positions. Do these facts distinguish the requirement of "substantially" equal work from the requirement of "comparable" work rejected by Congress in its deliberations over the Equal Pay Act?

As in *Corning Glass Works*, the holding on this issue was framed in terms of the burden of proof; in *Shultz*, the plaintiff's burden of proving a prima facie violation of the Act. Why does the court conclude that requiring the plaintiff to prove exact identity of jobs "would destroy the remedial purposes of the Act"? Would it make the plaintiff's case all but impossible to prove? Or would it make evasion by employers all too easy to accomplish? Requiring the plaintiff to prove exact identity of jobs would allow the employer to advance any number of after-the-fact justifications without putting on any evidence of its own. Requiring the plaintiff only to prove substantial equality then forces the defendant, as a practical matter, to submit its own evidence on this issue. Recall that even if the plaintiff has the burden of proof on an issue, the defendant has the right to submit its own evidence in rebuttal and almost always does so. Most cases under the Equal Pay Act actually turn on a detailed comparison of the jobs held by women and those held by men.

Or was there an entirely different problem with the employer's justification in *Shultz*: not that it is implausible or that it lacks a basis in evidence, but that the evidence shows it to be based on sex? Could an employer realistically hope to prevail in a sex discrimination case by relying on jobs themselves defined in terms of sex? Would this case have come out differently if the employer had dropped the terms "female selector packer," "male selector packer," and "snap up boy"? Or only if the employer had not explicitly segregated its work force by sex?

4. **Job Segregation and the Equal Pay Act.** The sex-based difference in pay in *Corning Glass Works* arose from a sex-segregated job structure. Originally, only men could work as night inspectors and only women worked as day inspectors. This pattern is typical of the high degree of sex segregation that has persisted over the years throughout the U.S. labor market, despite the steady rise in female labor participation and increasing pressures of egalitarianism. According to Barbara Reskin, an index of segregation across detailed occupational categories was virtually unchanged between 1910 and 1970 (from 69 percent to 67.6 percent). Barbara Reskin, Sex Segregation in the Workplace, 19 Ann. Rev. Soc. 241 (1993). It was not until the 1970s and the 1980s that sex segregation declined noticeably (to 60 percent in 1980). But even in 1990, sex segregation across detailed occupations remained high at 56 percent, dropping only to 52 percent by 2000. Jerry A. Jacobs, Detours on the Road to Equality: Women, Work and Higher Education, 2 Contexts 32 (2003); Maria Charles and David B. Grusky, Occupational Ghettos: The Worldwide Segregation of Women and Men (2004). This means that about 52 percent of the employed women in the U.S. would have to switch to a male-majority occupation in order to achieve equal distribution of men and women among occupations.

The persistence of high levels of sex segregation in employment is a significant cause for concern, given the conclusion of a considerable body of empirical work that sex segregation accounts for much of the gender wage gap. Women's Work, Men's Work: Sex Segregation on the Job (Barbara F. Reskin & Heidi I. Hartmann eds., 1986); Jerry A. Jacobs, Revolving Doors: Sex Segregation and Women's Careers (1989); Trond Petersen & Laurie A. Morgan, Separate and Unequal: Occupation-Establishment Sex Segregation and the Gender Wage Gap, 101 Am. J. Soc. 329 (1995). There is considerable academic debate over whether sex segregation contributes to the gender wage gap as a result of cultural devaluation of "women's work" or because the market is appropriately catering to preferences of men and women by allowing them to sort into different jobs and occupations that can better accommodate life-style choices and utilize different skills and qualifications. Francine D. Blau, Gender Inequality and Wages (2012); Patricia A. Roos & Mary L. Gatta, The Gender Gap in Earnings: Trends, Explanations, and Prospects in Handbook of Gender & Work 95 (Gary N. Powell ed., 1999); Irene Padavic & Barbara Reskin, Women and Men at Work (2002).

Another book argues that modern Western culture strongly discourages women from pursuing their interests in the workforce as aggressively as men do. Linda Babcock & Sara Laschever, Women Don't Ask: The High Cost of Avoiding Negotiation—and Positive Strategies for Change (2003). Catherine Hakim, a sociologist at the London School of Economics, argues that women do not have the same work aspirations as men. Hakim reports that men are three times as likely as women to view themselves as "work-centered." She contends that while women in general want opportunities, they do not want a life dominated by work. According to Hakim, antidiscrimination policy has been premised on the inaccurate belief that both men and women desire similar full-time employment when in fact women simply have different preferences from men, and most would rather spend time with their families than in the office. Catherine Hakim, Work-Lifestyle Choices in the 21st Century: Preference Theory (2000); Catherine Hakim, Models of the Family in Modern Societies: Ideals and Realities (2003).

Hakim's critics contend that she takes an antiquated view of female preferences, which themselves have been shaped by the discriminatory practices of society and the labor market. Reviews of her work have divided particularly over the extent to which preferences are formed before or after women enter the labor market. See Linda Waite, Book Review, 28 Pop. & Develop. Rev. 800 (2002); Heather Joshi, Book Review, 30 Pop. & Develop. Rev. 767 (2004); Jane Elliot, Book Review, Brit. J. Sociology 152 (2002). Some new controlled experiments have been offered to support the view that, on average, male workers seem to have a greater competitive drive than female workers, and that these differences are evident well before entry into the labor market. Uri Gneezy, et al., Performance in Competitive Environments: Gender Differences, 118 Q.J. Econ. 1049 (2003), Uri Gneezy & Aldo Rustichini, Gender and Competition at a Young Age, 94 Am. Econ. Rev. 377 (2004). The authors find that in certain settings, competition between males and females tends to degrade female performance, which might also be a factor encouraging sex segregation in the work force. Does this research suggest that certain ways of structuring the environment might be more effective for male, rather than female, workers and that, accordingly, an employer who allowed practices to remain in place that had this effect might be the subject of a disparate impact claim?

Considered by itself, does the Equal Pay Act encourage job segregation on the basis of sex? Recall that the Act does not cover discrimination in hiring or promotions, so that it leaves employers free to maintain an entirely segregated work force, with women and men performing entirely different jobs. In fact, in the absence of Title VII, doesn't the Equal Pay Act have the perverse effect of discouraging employers from hiring women in jobs traditionally held by men? It is only after they are employed in such positions that they can establish the element of equal work that is essential to a claim under the Act. As Christine Jolls has demonstrated, employees are far more likely to sue for discrimination in pay and in other conditions of employment than they are to sue for discrimination in hiring, creating a systematic disincentive for employers to hire women (and members of minority groups) in jobs that they have not traditionally occupied. This disincentive persisted even after the enactment of Title VII. Christine Jolls, Antidiscrimination and Accommodation, 115 Harv. L. Rev. 642, 693–95 (2001). In the absence of Title VII, however, it would operate without any restrictions on the employer's ability to avoid one kind of discrimination by engaging in another. Does this imply that it was only a matter of time before the narrow prohibition in the Equal Pay Act would lead to the broad prohibition in Title VII? The relationship between these two statutes emerges as the dominant theme in the next two cases.

5. **Title VII and the Equal Pay Act.** The issue of occupational segregation raises the question of how the narrow prohibition in the Equal Pay Act is related to the broad prohibition in Title VII. Only the latter prohibits the employer's division of its work force into sex-based job categories. *Shultz v. Wheaton Glass* nevertheless relies on the employer's violation of Title VII to justify imposing liability also under the Equal Pay Act. As a doctrinal matter, several different maxims of statutory interpretation could be invoked, either to support or to criticize the court's reasoning on this issue. The later statute, Title VII, could be invoked to broaden the scope of the earlier statute, resulting in an expanded interpretation of the Equal Pay Act. Alternatively, the narrower statute, the Equal Pay Act, could be given priority on the precise issue within the scope of its coverage.

The court does not quite endorse the first of these arguments and it entirely neglects the second. The court reasons, instead, that "both statutes serve the same fundamental purpose against discrimination in employment based on sex" and therefore that the Equal Pay Act must be construed so as not to conflict with Title VII. In particular, employers cannot be allowed to rely upon practices, such as sex segregation in employment, that violate Title VII to justify pay differentials under the Equal Pay Act. Is this reasoning sound? Or does its validity depend upon the particular provisions in Title VII that attempt to reconcile the provisions of the two statutes? These provisions, found in § 703(h), are the subject of the next case in this chapter.

6. **Bibliography.** Analysis of the Equal Pay Act itself has been eclipsed by scholarship analyzing its relationship to Title VII. Nevertheless, several early articles analyzed the Act in detail, among them: Caruthers G. Berger, Equal Pay, Equal Employment Opportunity and Equal Enforcement of the Law for Women, 5 Val. U. L. Rev. 326 (1971); Albert H. Ross & Frank V. McDermott, The Equal Pay Act of 1963: A Decade of Enforcement, 16 B.C. Indus. & Com. L. Rev. 1 (1974); Gary Siniscalco, Lauri Damrell & Morain Nabity, The Pay Gap, the Glass Ceiling, and Pay Bias: Moving Forward Fifty

Years After the Equal Pay Act, 29 A.B.A. J. Lab. & Emp. L. 395 (2014); Charles A. Sullivan, The Equal Pay Act of 1963: Making and Breaking a Prima Facie Case, 31 Ark. L. Rev. 545 (1978).

NOTE ON PROCEDURE AND REMEDIES UNDER THE EQUAL PAY ACT

The procedures and remedies under the Equal Pay Act derive from its status as an amendment to the Fair Labor Standards Act (FLSA). The enforcement provisions of the FLSA authorize criminal actions for "willful" violations by employers, but the Act is mainly enforced through civil actions against employers, brought both by private individuals and the EEOC. 29 U.S.C. §§ 215–217. As noted earlier, the statute itself refers to actions brought by the Secretary of Labor, but this enforcement authority has since been transferred by executive order to the EEOC. Reorg. Plan No. 1 of 1978, 3 C.F.R. 321 (1979), reprinted in 5 U.S.C. app. at 719 (2012).

Public actions can be brought either under § 216(c) or under § 217. The difference between the two sections largely concerns the remedies available to the EEOC. Under § 216(c), the EEOC can seek back pay and an equal amount in liquidated damages to be awarded in the discretion of the district court. Under § 217, the EEOC can seek only injunctive relief, which can include an order for back pay but not liquidated damages. E.g., Brennan v. Board of Education, 374 F. Supp. 817 (D.N.J. 1974). These differences in available remedies are not, as a practical matter, significant, since nothing in the statute prohibits the EEOC from suing under both sections in a single action.

Private actions are authorized by § 216(b), but are subject to the priority of public actions. The private plaintiff can sue only if she has not previously accepted relief awarded in a public action and a public action has not yet been filed on her behalf. If a private plaintiff prevails on the merits, she is entitled to back pay and, in the discretion of the district court, an equal amount in liquidated damages. The FLSA itself provides for a complete defense of reliance on written policy, 29 U.S.C. § 259, and a partial defense of good faith, or reasonable belief in compliance with the act, which may reduce liquidated damages in the discretion of the district court. 29 U.S.C. § 260.

Procedures under the FLSA, both in public and in private actions, differ in certain important respects from those under Title VII. The FLSA, unlike Title VII, does not require exhaustion of administrative remedies and claims need only be brought within a specified limitation period: two years for ordinary violations and three years for "willful" violations, where "willful" is defined as a knowing or reckless disregard of the fact that the disputed action is in violation of the law. McLaughlin v. Richland Shoe Co., 486 U.S. 128, 131–35 (1988). The procedure in class actions also contrasts with the procedure under Title VII, which follows the ordinary provisions of Federal Rule of Civil Procedure 23. Private actions under the FLSA can be brought only on behalf of employees who have given their written consent, 29 U.S.C. § 216(b), leading to the additional requirement in class actions that individuals affirmatively "opt in" to the case. See Hoffmann-La Roche Inc. v. Sperling, 493 U.S. 165, 169 (1989) (federal district court has discretion to facilitate notice to class members in ADEA action); LaChapelle v. Owens-Illinois, Inc., 513 F.2d 286 (5th Cir. 1975) (opt-in class action allowed on ADEA claim).

These different procedures and remedies resulted from the history of adoption of the Equal Pay Act as part of the FLSA. Does this history justify the continued separation of these provisions from the corresponding procedures and remedies under Title VII? As Chapter 7 discusses in more detail, the provisions governing those issues under Title VII establish a wholly different structure for administrative and judicial enforcement. Can—or should—two such different schemes coexist within the same field?

C. SEX DISCRIMINATION IN PAY UNDER TITLE VII

County of Washington v. Gunther

452 U.S. 161 (1981).

■ JUSTICE BRENNAN delivered the opinion of the Court.

The question presented is whether § 703(h) of Title VII of the Civil Rights Act of 1964, 42 U.S.C. § 2000e–2(h), restricts Title VII's prohibition of sex-based wage discrimination to claims of equal pay for equal work.

I

This case arises over the payment by petitioner County of Washington, Ore., of substantially lower wages to female guards in the female section of the county jail than it paid to male guards in the male section of the jail.[1] Respondents are four women who were employed to guard female prisoners and to carry out certain other functions in the jail. In January 1974, the county eliminated the female section of the jail, transferred the female prisoners to the jail of a nearby county, and discharged respondents.

Respondents filed suit against petitioners in Federal District Court under Title VII, 42 U.S.C. § 2000e et seq., seeking backpay and other relief. They alleged that they were paid unequal wages for work substantially equal to that performed by male guards, and in the alternative, that part of the pay differential was attributable to intentional sex discrimination. The latter allegation was based on a claim that, because of intentional discrimination, the county set the pay scale for female guards, but not for male guards, at a level lower than that warranted by its own survey of outside markets and the worth of the jobs.

[1] Prior to February 1, 1973, the female guards were paid between $476 and $606 per month, while the male guards were paid between $668 and $853. Effective February 1, 1973, the female guards were paid between $525 and $668, while salaries for male guards ranged from $701 to $940. 20 FEP Cases 788, 789 (Or. 1976).

After trial, the District Court found that the male guards supervised more than 10 times as many prisoners per guard as did the female guards, and that the females devoted much of their time to less valuable clerical duties. It therefore held that respondents' jobs were not substantially equal to those of the male guards, and that respondents were thus not entitled to equal pay. The Court of Appeals affirmed on that issue, and respondents do not seek review of the ruling.

The District Court also dismissed respondents' claim that the discrepancy in pay between the male and female guards was attributable in part to intentional sex discrimination. It held as a matter of law that a sex-based wage discrimination claim cannot be brought under Title VII unless it would satisfy the equal work standard of the Equal Pay Act of 1963, 29 U.S.C. § 206(d). The court therefore permitted no additional evidence on this claim, and made no findings on whether petitioner county's pay scales for female guards resulted from intentional sex discrimination.

The [Ninth Circuit] Court of Appeals reversed, holding that persons alleging sex discrimination "are not precluded from suing under Title VII to protest . . . discriminatory compensation practices" merely because their jobs were not equal to higher paying jobs held by members of the opposite sex. The court remanded to the District Court with instructions to take evidence on respondents' claim that part of the difference between their rate of pay and that of the male guards is attributable to sex discrimination. We granted certiorari and now affirm.

We emphasize at the outset the narrowness of the question before us in this case. Respondents' claim is not based on the controversial concept of "comparable worth," under which plaintiffs might claim increased compensation on the basis of a comparison of the intrinsic worth or difficulty of their job with that of other jobs in the same organization or community. Rather, respondents seek to prove, by direct evidence, that their wages were depressed because of intentional sex discrimination, consisting of setting the wage scale for female guards, but not for male guards, at a level lower than its own survey of outside markets and the worth of the jobs warranted. The narrow question in this case is whether such a claim is precluded by the last sentence of § 703(h) of Title VII, called the "Bennett Amendment."

II

Title VII makes it an unlawful employment practice for an employer "to discriminate against any individual with respect to his compensation, terms, conditions, or privileges of employment, because of such individual's . . . sex. . . ." 42 U.S.C. § 2000e–2(a). The Bennett Amendment to Title VII, however, provides:

> "It shall not be an unlawful employment practice under this subchapter for any employer to differentiate upon the basis of sex in determining the amount of the wages or compensation

> paid or to be paid to employees of such employer if such differentiation is authorized by the provisions of section 206(d) of title 29." 42 U.S.C. § 2000e–2(h).

To discover what practices are exempted from Title VII's prohibitions by the Bennett Amendment, we must turn to § 206(d)—the Equal Pay Act—which provides in relevant part:

> "No employer having employees subject to any provisions of this section shall discriminate, within any establishment in which such employees are employed, between employees on the basis of sex by paying wages to employees in such establishment at a rate less than the rate at which he pays wages to employees of the opposite sex in such establishment for equal work on jobs the performance of which requires equal skill, effort, and responsibility, and which are performed under similar working conditions, except where such payment is made pursuant to (i) a seniority system; (ii) a merit system; (iii) a system which measures earnings by quantity or quality of production; or (iv) a differential based on any other factor other than sex." 29 U.S.C. § 206 (d)(1).

On its face, the Equal Pay Act contains three restrictions pertinent to this case. First, its coverage is limited to those employers subject to the Fair Labor Standards Act. Thus, the Act does not apply, for example, to certain businesses engaged in retail sales, fishing, agriculture, and newspaper publishing. See 29 U.S.C. §§ 203(s), 213(a). Second, the Act is restricted to cases involving "equal work on jobs the performance of which requires equal skill, effort, and responsibility, and which are performed under similar working conditions." 29 U.S.C. § 206(d)(1). Third, the Act's four affirmative defenses exempt any wage differentials attributable to seniority, merit, quantity or quality of production, or "any other factor other than sex." Ibid.

Petitioners argue that the purpose of the Bennett Amendment was to restrict Title VII sex-based wage discrimination claims to those that could also be brought under the Equal Pay Act, and thus that claims not arising from "equal work" are precluded. Respondents, in contrast, argue that the Bennett Amendment was designed merely to incorporate the four affirmative defenses of the Equal Pay Act into Title VII for sex-based wage discrimination claims. Respondents thus contend that claims for sex-based wage discrimination can be brought under Title VII even though no member of the opposite sex holds an equal but higher paying job, provided that the challenged wage rate is not based on seniority, merit, quantity or quality of production, or "any other factor other than sex." The Court of Appeals found respondents' interpretation the "more persuasive." While recognizing that the language and legislative history of the provision are not unambiguous, we conclude that the Court of Appeals was correct.

A

The language of the Bennett Amendment suggests an intention to incorporate only the affirmative defenses of the Equal Pay Act into Title VII. The Amendment bars sex-based wage discrimination claims under Title VII where the pay differential is "authorized" by the Equal Pay Act. Although the word "authorize" sometimes means simply "to permit," it ordinarily denotes affirmative enabling action. Black's Law Dictionary 122 (5th ed. 1979) defines "authorize" as "[to] empower; to give a right or authority to act." Cf. 18 U.S.C. § 1905 (prohibiting the release by federal employees of certain information "to any extent not authorized by law"); 28 U.S.C. § 1343 (1976 ed., Supp. III) (granting district courts jurisdiction over "any civil action authorized by law"). The question, then, is what wage practices have been affirmatively authorized by the Equal Pay Act.

The Equal Pay Act is divided into two parts: a definition of the violation, followed by four affirmative defenses. The first part can hardly be said to "authorize" anything at all: it is purely prohibitory. The second part, however, in essence "authorizes" employers to differentiate in pay on the basis of seniority, merit, quantity or quality of production, or any other factor other than sex, even though such differentiation might otherwise violate the Act. It is to these provisions, therefore, that the Bennett Amendment must refer.

Petitioners argue that this construction of the Bennett Amendment would render it superfluous. See United States v. Menasche, 348 U.S. 528, 538–539 (1955). Petitioners claim that the first three affirmative defenses are simply redundant of the provisions elsewhere in § 703(h) of Title VII that already exempt bona fide seniority and merit systems and systems measuring earnings by quantity or quality of production, and that the fourth defense—"any other factor other than sex"—is implicit in Title VII's general prohibition of sex-based discrimination.

We cannot agree. The Bennett Amendment was offered as a "technical amendment" designed to resolve any potential conflicts between Title VII and the Equal Pay Act. Thus, with respect to the first three defenses, the Bennett Amendment has the effect of guaranteeing that courts and administrative agencies adopt a consistent interpretation of like provisions in both statutes. Otherwise, they might develop inconsistent bodies of case law interpreting two sets of nearly identical language.

More importantly, incorporation of the fourth affirmative defense could have significant consequences for Title VII litigation. Title VII's prohibition of discriminatory employment practices was intended to be broadly inclusive, proscribing "not only overt discrimination but also practices that are fair in form, but discriminatory in operation." Griggs v. Duke Power Co., 401 U.S. 424, 431 (1971). The structure of Title VII litigation, including presumptions, burdens of proof, and defenses, has been designed to reflect this approach. The fourth affirmative defense of the Equal Pay Act, however, was designed differently, to confine the application of the Act to wage differentials attributable to sex discrimination. H.R. Rep. No. 309, 88th Cong., 1st Sess., 3 (1963). Equal Pay Act litigation, therefore, has been structured to permit employers to defend against charges of discrimination where their pay differentials are based on a bona fide use of "other factors other than sex."[11] Under the Equal Pay Act, the courts and administrative agencies are not permitted to "substitute their judgment for the judgment of the employer . . . who [has] established and applied a bona fide job rating system," so long as it does not discriminate on the basis of sex. 109 Cong. Rec. 9209 (1963) (statement of Rep. Goodell, principal exponent of the Act). Although we do not decide in this case how sex-based wage discrimination litigation under Title VII should be structured to accommodate the fourth affirmative defense of the Equal Pay Act, we consider it clear that the Bennett Amendment, under this interpretation, is not rendered superfluous.

We therefore conclude that only differentials attributable to the four affirmative defenses of the Equal Pay Act are "authorized" by that Act within the meaning of § 703(h) of Title VII.

B

The legislative background of the Bennett Amendment is fully consistent with this interpretation.

Title VII was the second bill relating to employment discrimination to be enacted by the 88th Congress. Earlier, the same Congress passed the Equal Pay Act "to remedy what was perceived to be a serious and endemic problem of [sex-based] employment discrimination in private industry," Corning Glass Works v. Brennan, 417 U.S. 188, 195 (1974). Any possible inconsistency between the Equal Pay Act and Title VII did not surface until late in the debate over Title VII in the House of Representatives, because, until then, Title VII extended only to discrimination based on race, color, religion, or national origin, see H.R. Rep. No. 914, 88th Cong., 1st Sess., 10 (1963), while the Equal Pay Act applied only to sex discrimination. Just two days before voting on Title VII, the House of Representatives amended the bill to proscribe sex discrimination, but did not discuss the implications of the overlapping jurisdiction of Title VII, as amended, and the Equal Pay Act. See 110 Cong. Rec. 2577–2584 (1964). The Senate took up consideration of the House version of the Civil Rights bill without reference to any committee.

---

[11] The legislative history of the Equal Pay Act was examined by this Court in Corning Glass Works v. Brennan, 417 U.S. 188, 198–201 (1974). The Court observed that earlier versions of the Equal Pay bill were amended to define equal work and to add the fourth affirmative defense because of a concern that bona fide job-evaluation systems used by American businesses would otherwise be disrupted. Id. at 199–201. This concern is evident in the remarks of many legislators. Representative Griffin, for example, explained that the fourth affirmative defense is a "broad principle," which "makes clear and explicitly states that a differential based on any factor or factors other than sex would not violate this legislation." 109 Cong. Rec. 9203 (1963). . . .

Thus, neither House of Congress had the opportunity to undertake formal analysis of the relation between the two statutes.[12]

Several Senators expressed concern that insufficient attention had been paid to possible inconsistencies between the statutes. See id. at 7217 (statement of Sen. Clark); id. at 13647 (statement of Sen. Bennett). In an attempt to rectify the problem, Senator Bennett proposed his amendment. Id. at 13310. The Senate leadership approved the proposal as a "technical amendment" to the Civil Rights bill, and it was taken up on the floor on June 12, 1964, after cloture had been invoked. The Amendment engendered no controversy, and passed without recorded vote. The entire discussion comprised a few short statements:

> "Mr. Bennett. Mr. President, after many years of yearning by members of the fair sex in this country, and after very careful study by the appropriate committees of Congress, last year Congress passed the so-called Equal Pay Act, which became effective only yesterday.
>
> "By this time, programs have been established for the effective administration of this act. Now, when the civil rights bill is under consideration, in which the word 'sex' has been inserted in many places, I do not believe sufficient attention may have been paid to possible conflicts between the wholesale insertion of the word 'sex' in the bill and in the Equal Pay Act.
>
> "The purpose of my amendment is to provide that in the event of conflicts, the provisions of the Equal Pay Act shall not be nullified.
>
> "I understand that the leadership in charge of the bill have agreed to the amendment as a proper technical correction of the bill. If they will confirm that understand [sic], I shall ask that the amendment be voted on without asking for the yeas and nays.

---

[12] To answer certain objections raised by Senators concerning the House version of the Civil Rights bill, Senator Clark, principal Senate spokesman for Title VII, drafted a memorandum, printed in the Congressional Record. One such objection and answer concerned the relation between Title VII and the Equal Pay Act:

> "Objection: The sex antidiscrimination provisions of the bill duplicate the coverage of the Equal Pay Act of 1963. But more than this, they extend far beyond the scope and coverage of the Equal Pay Act. They do not include the limitations in that act with respect to equal work on jobs requiring equal skills in the same establishments, and thus, cut across different jobs.
>
> "Answer: The Equal Pay Act is a part of the wage hour law, with different coverage and with numerous exemptions unlike title VII. Furthermore, under title VII, jobs can no longer be classified as to sex, except where there is a rational basis for discrimination on the ground of bona fide occupational qualification. The standards in the Equal Pay Act for determining discrimination as to wages, of course, are applicable to the comparable situation under title VII." 110 Cong. Rec. 7217 (1964).

This memorandum constitutes the only formal discussion of the relation between the statutes prior to consideration of the Bennett Amendment. It need not concern us here, because it relates to Title VII before it was amended by the Bennett Amendment. The memorandum obviously has no bearing on the meaning of the terms of the Bennett Amendment itself.

"Mr. Humphrey. The amendment of the Senator from Utah is helpful. I believe it is needed. I thank him for his thoughtfulness. The amendment is fully acceptable.

"Mr. Dirksen. Mr. President, I yield myself 1 minute.

"We were aware of the conflict that might develop, because the Equal Pay Act was an amendment to the Fair Labor Standards Act. The Fair Labor Standards Act carries out certain exceptions.

"All that the pending amendment does is recognize those exceptions, that are carried in the basic act.

"Therefore, this amendment is necessary, in the interest of clarification." Id. at 13647.

As this discussion shows, Senator Bennett proposed the Amendment because of a general concern that insufficient attention had been paid to the relation between the Equal Pay Act and Title VII, rather than because of a *specific* potential conflict between the statutes. His explanation that the Amendment assured that the provisions of the Equal Pay Act "shall not be nullified" in the event of conflict with Title VII may be read as referring to the affirmative defenses of the Act. Indeed, his emphasis on the "technical" nature of the Amendment and his concern for not disrupting the "effective administration" of the Equal Pay Act are more compatible with an interpretation of the Amendment as incorporating the Act's affirmative defenses, as administratively interpreted, than as engrafting all the restrictive features of the Equal Pay Act onto Title VII.

Senator Dirksen's comment that all that the Bennett Amendment does is to "recognize" the exceptions carried in the Fair Labor Standards Act, suggests that the Bennett Amendment was necessary because of the exceptions to coverage in the Fair Labor Standards Act, which made the Equal Pay Act applicable to a narrower class of employers than was Title VII. The Bennett Amendment clarified that the standards of the Equal Pay Act would govern even those wage discrimination cases where only Title VII would otherwise apply. So understood, Senator Dirksen's remarks are not inconsistent with our interpretation.

Although there was no debate on the Bennett Amendment in the House of Representatives when the Senate version of the Act returned for final approval, Representative Celler explained each of the Senate's amendments immediately prior to the vote. He stated that the Bennett Amendment "[provides] that compliance with the Fair Labor Standards Act as amended satisfies the requirement of the title barring discrimination because of sex. . . ." 110 Cong. Rec. 15896 (1964). If taken literally, this explanation would restrict Title VII's coverage of sex discrimination more severely than even petitioners suggest: not only would it confine *wage discrimination claims* to those actionable under the Equal Pay Act, but it would block *all other* sex discrimination claims as well. We can only conclude that Representative Celler's explanation was not intended to be precise, and does not provide a solution to the present problem.

Thus, although the few references by Members of Congress to the Bennett Amendment do not explicitly confirm that its purpose was to incorporate into Title VII the four affirmative defenses of the Equal Pay Act in sex-based wage discrimination cases, they are broadly consistent with such a reading, and do not support an alternative reading.

C

The interpretations of the Bennett Amendment by the agency entrusted with administration of Title VII—the Equal Employment Opportunity Commission—do not provide much guidance in this case. Cf. Griggs v. Duke Power Co., 401 U.S., at 433–434. The Commission's 1965 Guidelines on Discrimination Because of Sex stated that "the standards of 'equal pay for equal work' set forth in the Equal Pay Act for determining what is unlawful discrimination in compensation are applicable to Title VII." 29 CFR § 1604.7(a) (1966). In 1972, the EEOC deleted this portion of the Guideline, see 37 Fed. Reg. 6837 (1972). Although the original Guideline may be read to support petitioners' argument that no claim of sex discrimination in compensation may be brought under Title VII except where the Equal Pay Act's "equal work" standard is met, EEOC practice under this Guideline was considerably less than steadfast.

The restrictive interpretation suggested by the 1965 Guideline was followed in several opinion letters in the following years. During the same period, however, EEOC decisions frequently adopted the opposite position. For example, a reasonable-cause determination issued by the Commission in 1968 stated that "the existence of separate and different wage rate schedules for male employees on the one hand, and female employees on the other doing reasonably comparable work, establishes discriminatory wage rates based solely on the sex of the workers." Harrington v. Picadilly Cafeteria, Case No. AU 7–3–173 (Apr. 25, 1968).

The current Guideline does not purport to explain whether the equal work standard of the Equal Pay Act has any application to Title VII, see 29 CFR § 1604.8 (1980), but the EEOC now supports respondents' position in its capacity as amicus curiae. In light of this history, we feel no hesitation in adopting what seems to us the most persuasive interpretation of the Amendment, in lieu of that once espoused, but not consistently followed, by the Commission.

D

Our interpretation of the Bennett Amendment draws additional support from the remedial purposes of Title VII and the Equal Pay Act. Section 703(a) of Title VII makes it unlawful for an employer "to fail or refuse to hire or to discharge any individual, or *otherwise to discriminate* against any individual with respect to his compensation, terms, conditions, or privileges of employment" because of such individual's sex. 42 U.S.C. § 2000e–2(a) (emphasis added). As Congress itself has indicated, a "broad approach" to the definition of equal employment opportunity is essential to overcoming and undoing the effect of discrimination. S. Rep. No. 867, 88th Cong., 2d Sess., 12 (1964). We must therefore avoid interpretations of Title VII that deprive victims of discrimination of a remedy, without clear congressional mandate.

Under petitioners' reading of the Bennett Amendment, only those sex-based wage discrimination claims that satisfy the "equal work" standard of the Equal Pay Act could be brought under Title VII. In practical terms, this means that a woman who is discriminatorily underpaid could obtain no relief—no matter how egregious the discrimination might be—unless her employer also employed a man in an equal job in the same establishment, at a higher rate of pay. Thus, if an employer hired a woman for a unique position in the company and then admitted that her salary would have been higher had she been male, the woman would be unable to obtain legal redress under petitioners' interpretation. Similarly, if an employer used a transparently sex-biased system for wage determination, women holding jobs not equal to those held by men would be denied the right to prove that the system is a pretext for discrimination. Moreover, to cite an example arising from a recent case, Los Angeles, Dept. of Water & Power v. Manhart, 435 U.S. 702 (1978), if the employer required its female workers to pay more into its pension program than male workers were required to pay, the only women who could bring a Title VII action under petitioners' interpretation would be those who could establish that a man performed equal work: a female auditor thus might have a cause of action while a female secretary might not. Congress surely did not intend the Bennett Amendment to insulate such blatantly discriminatory practices from judicial redress under Title VII.

Moreover, petitioners' interpretation would have other far-reaching consequences. Since it rests on the proposition that any wage differentials not prohibited by the Equal Pay Act are "authorized" by it, petitioners' interpretation would lead to the conclusion that discriminatory compensation by employers not covered by the Fair Labor Standards Act is "authorized"—since not prohibited—by the Equal Pay Act. Thus it would deny Title VII protection against sex-based wage discrimination by those employers not subject to the Fair Labor Standards Act but covered by Title VII. There is no persuasive evidence that Congress intended such a result, and the EEOC has rejected it since at least 1965. See 29 CFR § 1604.7 (1966). Indeed, petitioners themselves apparently acknowledge that Congress intended Title VII's broader coverage to apply to equal pay claims under Title VII, thus impliedly admitting the fallacy in their own argument.

Petitioners' reading is thus flatly inconsistent with our past interpretations of Title VII as "[prohibiting] all practices in whatever form which create inequality in employment opportunity due to discrimination on the basis of race, religion, sex, or national origin." Franks v. Bowman Transportation Co., 424 U.S. 747, 763 (1976). As we said in *Los Angeles, Dept. of Water & Power v. Manhart*, supra, at 707, n.13: "In forbidding employers to discriminate against individuals because of their sex, Congress intended to strike at the *entire spectrum* of disparate treatment of men and women resulting from sex stereotypes." (Emphasis added.) We must therefore reject petitioners' interpretation of the Bennett Amendment.

III

Petitioners argue strenuously that the approach of the Court of Appeals places "the pay structure of virtually every employer and the entire economy . . . at risk and subject to scrutiny by the federal courts." They raise the specter that "Title VII plaintiffs could draw any type of comparison imaginable concerning job duties and pay between any job predominantly performed by women and any job predominantly performed by men." But whatever the merit of petitioners' arguments in other contexts, they are inapplicable here, for claims based on the type of job comparisons petitioners describe are manifestly different from respondents' claim. Respondents contend that the County of Washington evaluated the worth of their jobs; that the county determined that they should be paid approximately 95% as much as the male correctional officers; that it paid them only about 70% as much, while paying the male officers the full evaluated worth of their jobs; and that the failure of the county to pay respondents the full evaluated worth of their jobs can be proved to be attributable to intentional sex discrimination. Thus, respondents' suit does not require a court to make its own subjective assessment of the value of the male and female guard jobs, or to attempt by statistical technique or other method to quantify the effect of sex discrimination on the wage rates.

We do not decide in this case the precise contours of lawsuits challenging sex discrimination in compensation under Title VII. It is sufficient to note that respondents' claims of discriminatory undercompensation are not barred by § 703(h) of Title VII merely because respondents do not perform work equal to that of male jail guards. The judgment of the Court of Appeals is therefore

Affirmed.

■ JUSTICE REHNQUIST, with whom the CHIEF JUSTICE, JUSTICE STEWART, and JUSTICE POWELL join, dissenting.

The Court today holds a plaintiff may state a claim of sex-based wage discrimination under Title VII without even establishing that she has performed "equal or substantially equal work" to that of males as defined in the Equal Pay Act. Because I believe that the legislative history of both the Equal Pay Act of 1963 and Title VII clearly establish that there can be no Title VII claim of sex-based wage discrimination without proof of "equal work," I dissent. . . .

II

The Equal Pay Act

The starting point for any discussion of sex-based wage discrimination claims must be the Equal Pay Act of 1963, enacted as an amendment to the Fair Labor Standards Act of 1938, 29 U.S.C. §§ 201–219. It was there that Congress, after 18 months of careful and exhaustive study, specifically addressed the problem of sex-based wage discrimination. The Equal Pay Act states that employers shall not discriminate on the basis of sex by paying different wages for jobs that require equal skill, effort, and responsibility. In adopting the "equal pay for equal work" formula, Congress carefully considered and ultimately rejected the "equal pay for comparable worth" standard advanced by respondents and several amici. As the legislative history of the Equal Pay Act amply demonstrates, Congress realized that the adoption of the comparable-worth doctrine would ignore the economic realities of supply and demand and would involve both governmental agencies and courts in the impossible task of ascertaining the worth of comparable work, an area in which they have little expertise.

The legislative history of the Equal Pay Act begins in 1962 when Representatives Green and Zelenko introduced two identical bills, H.R. 8898 and H.R. 10226 respectively, representing the Kennedy administration's proposal for equal pay legislation. Both bills stated in pertinent part:

> "SEC. 4. No employer . . . shall discriminate . . . between employees on the basis of sex by paying wages to any employee at a rate less than the rate at which he pays wages to any employee of the opposite sex *for work of comparable character on jobs the performance of which requires comparable skills*, except where such payment is made pursuant to a seniority or merit increase system which does not discriminate on the basis of sex." H.R. 8898, 87th Cong., 1st Sess. (1961); H.R. 10226, 87th Cong., 2d Sess. (1962) (emphasis supplied).

During the extensive hearings on the proposal, the administration strenuously urged that Congress adopt the "comparable" language, noting that the comparability of different jobs could be determined through job evaluation procedures. Hearings on H.R. 8898, H.R. 10226 before the Select Subcommittee on Labor of the House Committee on Education and Labor, 87th Cong., 2d Sess., 16, 27 (1962) (testimony of Secretary of Labor Arthur Goldberg and Assistant Secretary of Labor Esther Peterson). A bill containing the comparable-work formula, then denominated H.R. 11677, was reported out of the House Committee on Education and Labor and reached the full House. Once there, Representative St. George objected to the "comparable work" language of the bill and offered an amendment which limited equal pay claims to those "for equal work on jobs, the performance of which requires equal skills." 108 Cong. Rec. 14767 (1962). As she explained, her purpose was to limit wage discrimination claims to the situation where men and women were paid differently for performing the same job.

> "What we want to do in this bill is to make it exactly what it says. It is called equal pay for equal work in some of the committee hearings. *There is a great difference between the word 'comparable' and the word 'equal.'*
>
> . . .
>
> ". . . *The word 'comparable' opens up great vistas.* It gives tremendous latitude to whoever is to be arbitrator in these disputes." Ibid. (Emphasis supplied.)

Representative Landrum echoed those remarks. He stressed that the St. George amendment would prevent "the trooping around all over the country of employees of the Labor Department harassing business with their various interpretations of the term 'comparable' when 'equal' is capable of the same definition throughout the United States." The administration, represented by Representatives Zelenko and Green, vigorously urged the House to reject the St. George amendment. They observed that the "equal work" standard was narrower than the existing "equal pay for comparable work" language and cited correspondence from Secretary of Labor Goldberg that "comparable is a key word in our proposal." The House, however, rejected that advice and adopted the St. George amendment. When the Senate considered the bill, it too rejected the "comparable work" theory in favor of the "equal work" standard.

Because the Conference Committee failed to report a bill out of Committee, enactment of equal pay legislation was delayed until 1963. Equal pay legislation, containing the St. George amendment, was reintroduced at the beginning of the session. The congressional debate on that legislation leaves no doubt that Congress clearly rejected the entire notion of "comparable worth." For example, Representative Goodell, a cosponsor of the Act, stressed the significance of the change from "comparable work" to "equal work."

> "I think it is important that we have clear legislative history at this point. *Last year when the House changed the word 'comparable' to 'equal' the clear intention was to narrow the whole concept.* We went from 'comparable' to 'equal' meaning that the jobs involved should be virtually identical, that is, that they would be very much alike or closely related to each other.
>
> "We do not expect the Labor Department to go into an establishment and attempt to rate jobs that are not equal. We do not want to hear the Department say, 'Well, they amount to the same thing,' and evaluate them so that they come up to the same skill or point. We expect this to apply only to jobs that are

> substantially identical or equal." 109 Cong. Rec. 9197 (1963) (emphasis supplied).

Representative Frelinghuysen agreed with those remarks.

> "[We] can expect that the administration of the equal pay concept, while fair and effective, will not be excessive nor excessively wide ranging. What we seek to insure, where men and women are doing the same job under the same working conditions[,] that they will receive the same pay. It is not intended that either the Labor Department or individual employees will be equipped with hunting licenses.
>
> . . .
>
> ". . . [*The EPA*] *is not intended to compare unrelated jobs, or jobs that have been historically and normally considered by the industry to be different.*" Id. at 9196 (emphasis supplied).

Thus, the legislative history of the Equal Pay Act clearly reveals that Congress was unwilling to give either the Federal Government or the courts broad authority to determine comparable wage rates. Congress recognized that the adoption of such a theory would ignore economic realities and would result in major restructuring of the American economy. Instead, Congress concluded that governmental intervention to equalize wage differentials was to be undertaken only within one circumstance: when men's and women's jobs were identical or nearly so, hence unarguably of equal worth. It defies common sense to believe that the same Congress—which, after 18 months of hearings and debates, had decided in 1963 upon the extent of federal involvement it desired in the area of wage rate claims—intended *sub silentio* to reject all of this work and to abandon the limitations of the equal work approach just one year later, when it enacted Title VII.

Title VII

Congress enacted the Civil Rights Act of 1964, 42 U.S.C. § 2000a et seq., one year after passing the Equal Pay Act. Title VII prohibits discrimination in employment on the basis of race, color, national origin, religion, and sex. 42 U.S.C. § 2000e–2(a)(1). The question is whether Congress intended to completely turn its back on the "equal work" standard enacted in the Equal Pay Act of 1963 when it adopted Title VII only one year later.

The Court answers that question in the affirmative, concluding that Title VII must be read more broadly than the Equal Pay Act. In so holding, the majority wholly ignores this Court's repeated adherence to the doctrine of *in pari materia*, namely, that "[where] there is no clear intention otherwise, a specific statute will not be controlled or nullified by a general one, regardless of the priority of enactment." Radzanower v. Touche Ross & Co., 426 U.S. 148, 153 (1976), citing Morton v. Mancari, 417 U.S. 535, 550–551 (1974); United States v. United Continental Tuna Corp., 425 U.S. 164, 169 (1976). . . .

When those principles are applied to this case, there can be no doubt that the Equal Pay Act and Title VII should be construed *in pari materia*. The Equal Pay Act is the more specific piece of legislation, dealing solely with sex-based wage discrimination, and was the product of exhaustive congressional study. Title VII, by contrast, is a general antidiscrimination provision, passed with virtually no consideration of the specific problem of sex-based wage discrimination. See General Electric Co. v. Gilbert, 429 U.S. 125, 143 (1976) (the legislative history of the sex discrimination amendment is "notable primarily for its brevity"). Most significantly, there is absolutely nothing in the legislative history of Title VII which reveals an intent by Congress to repeal by implication the provisions of the Equal Pay Act. Quite the contrary, what little legislative history there is on the subject—such as the comments of Senators Clark and Bennett and Representative Celler, and the contemporaneous interpretation of the EEOC—indicates that Congress intended to incorporate the substantive standards of the Equal Pay Act into Title VII so that sex-based wage discrimination claims would be governed by the equal work standard of the Equal Pay Act and by that standard alone. Title VII was first considered by the House, where the prohibition against sex discrimination was added on the House floor. When the bill reached the Senate it bypassed the Senate Committee system and was presented directly to the full Senate. It was there that concern was expressed about the relation of the Title VII sex discrimination ban to the Equal Pay Act. In response to questions by Senator Dirksen, Senator Clark, the floor manager for the bill, prepared a memorandum in which he attempted to put to rest certain objections which he believed to be unfounded. Senator Clark's answer to Senator Dirksen reveals that Senator Clark believed that all cases of wage discrimination under Title VII would be treated under the standards of the Equal Pay Act:

> "*Objection*. The sex antidiscrimination provisions of the bill duplicate the coverage of the Equal Pay Act of 1963. But more than this, they extend far beyond the scope and coverage of the Equal Pay Act. *They do not include the limitations in that act with respect to equal work on jobs requiring equal skills in the same establishments, and thus, cut across different jobs.*
>
> "*Answer*. The Equal Pay Act is a part of the wage hour law, with different coverage and with numerous exemptions unlike title VII. Furthermore, under title VII, jobs can no longer be classified as to sex, except where there is a rational basis for discrimination on the ground of bona fide occupational qualification. *The standards in the Equal Pay Act for determining discrimination as to wages, of course, are applicable to the comparable situation under title VII.*" 110 Cong. Rec. 7217 (1964) (emphasis added).

In this passage, Senator Clark asserted that the sex discrimination provisions of Title VII were necessary, notwithstanding the Equal Pay Act, because (a) the Equal Pay Act had numerous exemptions for various types of businesses, and (b) Title VII covered discrimination in access (e.g., assignment and promotion) to jobs, not just compensation. In addition, Senator Clark made clear that in the compensation area the equal work standard would continue to be the applicable standard. He explained, in answer to Senator Dirksen's concern, that when *different jobs* were at issue, the Equal Pay Act's legal standard—the "equal work" standard—would apply to limit the reach of Title VII. Thus Senator Clark rejected as unfounded the objections that the sex provisions of Title VII were unnecessary on the one hand or extended beyond the equal work standard on the other.

Notwithstanding Senator Clark's explanation, Senator Bennett remained concerned that, absent an explicit cross-reference to the Equal Pay Act, the "wholesale insertion" of the word "sex" in Title VII could nullify the carefully conceived Equal Pay Act standard. Accordingly, he offered, and the Senate accepted, the following amendment to Title VII:

> "It shall not be an unlawful employment practice under this subchapter for any employer to differentiate upon the basis of sex in determining the amount of the wages or compensation paid or to be paid to employees of such employer if such differentiation is authorized by the provisions of [§ 6(d) of the Equal Pay Act]."

Although the language of the Bennett Amendment is ambiguous, the most plausible interpretation of the Amendment is that it incorporates the substantive standard of the Equal Pay Act—the equal pay for equal work standard—into Title VII. A number of considerations support that view. In the first place, that interpretation is wholly consistent with, and in fact confirms, Senator Clark's earlier explanation of Title VII. Second, in the limited time available to Senator Bennett when he offered his amendment—the time for debate having been limited by cloture—he explained the Amendment's purpose.

> "Mr. President, after many years of yearning by members of the fair sex in this country, and after very careful study by the appropriate committees of Congress, last year Congress passed the so-called Equal Pay Act, which became effective only yesterday.
>
> "By this time, programs have been established for the effective administration of this act. Now when the civil rights bill is under consideration, in which the word 'sex' has been inserted in many places, I do not believe sufficient attention may have been paid to possible conflicts between the wholesale insertion of the word 'sex' in the bill and in the Equal Pay Act."

"The purpose of my amendment is to provide that in the event of conflicts, the provisions of the Equal Pay Act shall not be nullified." 110 Cong. Rec. 13647 (1964) (emphasis supplied).

It is obvious that the principal way in which the Equal Pay Act could be "nullified" would be to allow plaintiffs unable to meet the "equal pay for equal work" standard to proceed under Title VII asserting some other theory of wage discrimination, such as "comparable worth." If plaintiffs can proceed under Title VII without showing that they satisfy the "equal work" criterion of the Equal Pay Act, one would expect all plaintiffs to file suit under the "broader" Title VII standard. Such a result would, for all practical purposes, constitute an implied repeal of the equal work standard of the Equal Pay Act and render that Act a nullity. This was precisely the result Congress sought to avert when it adopted the Bennett Amendment, and the result the Court today embraces.

NOTES ON *COUNTY OF WASHINGTON V. GUNTHER*

1. **The Meaning of the Bennett Amendment.** Like the seniority clause in *Teamsters* and the testing clause in *Griggs*, the Bennett Amendment was one of several amendments made on the floor of the Senate in order to assure passage of Title VII. Coincidentally, all of these amendments appear in § 703(h) which became a kind of repository for compromises over the language of the statute. The particular terms of the Bennett Amendment, however, leave the nature of the compromise over equal pay claims unclear. The overall purpose of the amendment is apparent and indisputable: to harmonize the prohibition against sex discrimination in Title VII with the recently passed Equal Pay Act. The difficulty lies in the way in which this attempt to reconcile the two statutes is framed.

The Bennett Amendment allows employers "to differentiate upon the basis of sex" in paying their employees "if such differentiation is authorized" by the Equal Pay Act. Taken literally, the amendment presupposes that the Act at least allows some forms of sex discrimination in pay. But the whole point of the Act was to prohibit all such forms of discrimination. Thus, defense (iv) in the Act specifically allows employers to justify a difference in pay "based on any other factor other than sex," implying that any factor involving sex remains prohibited. Strictly speaking, the Act allows sex discrimination only in practices not covered by the Act at all, such as assignment of employees on the basis of sex. These practices, to the extent that they affect compensation—and, of course, they do—might be thought to permit the related differences in pay. But that interpretation of the Act just raises a further problem with the Bennett Amendment: What does the term "authorized" mean?

The Equal Pay Act does not confer any kind of authority upon employers to engage in any kind of action that they were previously prevented from performing. At most, it permits them to continue to engage in practices that they could have engaged in all along. These practices are permitted, not "authorized" by the Act in the usual sense of the term, only because they fall outside the scope of the act's prohibition against unequal pay for equal work.

The question raised by the Bennett Amendment is which of these exclusions are to count as "authorized" in the peculiar sense used in the amendment. There are three possibilities, which can be taken either singly or in combination, to identify "authorized" forms of sex discrimination in pay.

First, the differences in the coverage of "employers" and "employees" subject to the Equal Pay Act and Title VII might give rise to some differences in pay "authorized" by the Equal Pay Act. The two statutes define covered "employers" and "employees" in different terms, with the Equal Pay Act following, but not entirely duplicating the coverage of the Fair Labor Standards Act (FLSA). See 29 U.S.C. §§ 203, 213, 216–17. Title VII has its own provisions on coverage which might, in certain circumstances, be narrower than those of the Equal Pay Act. See §§ 701, 702. Neither the majority nor the dissent in *County of Washington v. Gunther* adopt this interpretation of "authorized," probably because Congress would have adopted a compromise based on coverage in this sense through amendments to the coverage provisions of Title VII. These already reflect compromises such as exempting employers with fewer than the statutory minimum of 15 employees.

Second, the difference in the defenses available under the two statutes might yield some form of "authorized" discrimination. This is the interpretation adopted by Justice Brennan in the majority opinion, which construes defenses (i) to (iv) in the Equal Pay Act to "authorize" discrimination which is then permitted under Title VII by the Bennett Amendment. Several difficulties with this conclusion are raised by the dissent, which is discussed in the following note.

And third, the prerequisite of equal work under the Equal Pay Act might be thought to "authorize" discrimination in pay in jobs involving unequal work. The Equal Pay Act permits discrimination in these circumstances, but Title VII in the absence of the Bennett Amendment would not. This is the position taken by Justice Rehnquist (as he then was) in his dissent. As he emphasizes, Congress focused on the need to prove "equal work" in order to establish liability under the Equal Pay Act, but it did so only in its deliberations over that act. The debate over the Bennett Amendment did not have a similar focus, or even a very clear reference, to what Congress had debated a year earlier in passing the Equal Pay Act. Was this only a product of the parliamentary maneuverings that were necessary to get Title VII through the Senate? Or does it reflect genuine uncertainty in Congress over the meaning of the two statutes and over how they were to be reconciled?

2. The Majority Opinion. The majority opinion interprets the Bennett Amendment to incorporate defenses (i) to (iv) of the Equal Pay Act as the forms of "authorized" discrimination that are also permitted by Title VII. As the dissenting opinion points out, this interpretation appears to make the Bennett Amendment redundant. Defenses (i) to (iii) permit differences in pay based on seniority systems, merit systems, and piecework systems, all of which are already subject to exceptions found in § 703(h) of Title VII. Defense (iv) is the only defense that is not already found in Title VII, but it is the catch-all defense for "any other factor other than sex." The dissenting opinion claims that defense (iv) simply repeats the main prohibition in Title VII against sex discrimination, bringing out only the negative implication that such a prohibition permits differences in pay on other grounds. Yet if defense (iv) is redundant if it is incorporated in Title VII, isn't it already redundant in the Equal Pay Act? That statute, too, has a prohibition against sex discrimination with the same negative implication.

The majority opinion tries to save some independent meaning for defense (iv) and for the Bennett Amendment by suggesting—although not clearly stating—that these provisions prevent application of the theory of disparate impact to claims of sex discrimination in pay. The majority's reasoning appears to be that neutral means of setting pay that nevertheless have a disparate impact on the basis of sex fall within the literal terms of defense (iv) as "any other factor other than sex." Is this, however, what Congress had in mind in framing this defense? Recall that the theory of disparate impact was not codified in Title VII until the Civil Rights Act of 1991. How likely is it that Congress considered limitations on this theory of liability when it passed the Equal Pay Act in 1963, even before it considered Title VII in 1964? And in Title VII itself as originally enacted, the only provision addressed at all to issues raised by the theory of disparate impact was the testing clause in § 703(h). Wouldn't Congress have considered additional limitations on the theory of disparate impact in that clause rather than in the Bennett Amendment?

3. **The Dissenting Opinion.** Justice Rehnquist forcefully advances the preceding criticisms of the majority opinion, but his position has problems of its own. As he acknowledges toward the end of his opinion, his view would make it difficult—if not impossible—for a plaintiff to prevail in any case in which women and men held entirely different jobs. He still holds out the theoretical hope that a female plaintiff could make out a claim under Title VII by proving that a man who held her job would be paid more than she was, but he concedes that such evidence would be nearly impossible to obtain. This strained hypothetical reveals a more systematic problem with his position. It would allow sex discrimination in pay whenever men and women held jobs that were not substantially equal, reading this limitation on the scope of the Equal Pay Act into the broad prohibition against sex discrimination in Title VII. Does this make sense?

Of course, Congress could have enacted the Bennett Amendment as legislation that does not, considered in isolation, make the best possible adjustment between Title VII and the Equal Pay Act. It still might have passed the provision as a compromise necessary to secure the enactment of Title VII. The Senate debates over the Bennett Amendment and Title VII certainly support this conclusion. Yet all it establishes is that Congress meant to reconcile Title VII with the Equal Pay Act, not what the terms of reconciliation would be. Having failed to be more precise than in the obscure terms of the Bennett Amendment, didn't Congress leave the issue of reconciliation to the courts, if only by default? If so, doesn't that leave the courts free to work out the most sensible basis for reconciling the two statutes?

4. **Claims of Comparable Worth.** The majority opinion carefully distinguishes claims of "comparable worth," based on a judicial evaluation of

the value of jobs held predominantly by women and those held predominantly by men from the claim actually brought by the plaintiffs. This claim was distinctive in two respects: First, the highest paid female guard received less than the lowest paid male guard, reflecting a startling gap in the defendant's pay structure. Second, the defendant's own survey established that the women were paid less than their jobs were worth, supporting the conclusion that the defendant itself recognized the discriminatory nature of its pay structure. The courts themselves did not have to evaluate the relative worth of the admittedly different responsibilities of female and male prison guards, including differences in the number of prisoners supervised.

Comparable worth claims, by contrast, invited courts to make just this comparison and to impose liability under Title VII when women's pay was not comparable to men's based on the relative worth of the jobs predominantly held by each sex. See Paul Weiler, The Wages of Sex: The Uses and Limits of Comparable Worth, 99 Harv. L. Rev. 1728, 1779–94 (1986). Critics of this theory of liability initially denounced it as an attempt to centralize decisions over compensation rather than rely on the decentralized processes of the market, but later critics have focused on the risk that it is self-defeating. Daniel R. Fischell & Edward P. Lazear, Comparable Worth and Discrimination in Labor Markets, 53 U. Chi. L. Rev. 891 (1986). These critics see the concentration of women in lower-paying jobs as the fundamental cause of the gap in pay between women and men. So, far from reducing this form of occupational segregation, according to these critics, claims of comparable worth would enhance it by making the jobs in which women are already concentrated still more attractive to them. Even if men also were attracted to these occupations, the increased supply of workers would decrease the compensation that employers would have to pay to them, eventually causing the levels of compensation in occupations dominated by women to fall.

All laws against employment discrimination interfere with markets in some way. Are claims of comparable worth any more intrusive than claims of discrimination in hiring and promotions? If claims of the latter sort were sufficient to eliminate the pay gap between women and men, why hasn't it disappeared in the decades since Title VII was enacted? Is it significant that claims of race discrimination in pay also have been rare, even though they are not restricted at all by the Bennett Amendment? Did *County of Washington v. Gunther* significantly reduce those restrictions for claims of sex discrimination in pay?

5. ***AFSCME v State of Washington.*** Concerns over comparable worth were at the heart of the Ninth Circuit's decision in AFSCME v. State of Washington, 770 F.2d 1401 (9th Cir. 1985). Judge Kennedy, as he then was, rejected claims of disparate impact and disparate treatment based on the lower pay that the state employees received in jobs predominantly held by women. Those claims depended primarily upon a study that the state itself had commissioned that found a disparity in pay. Although the state enacted legislation to gradually eliminate this disparity over a ten-year period, the plaintiff unions brought this action to have it eliminated immediately. Their

claim of disparate impact failed, however, because the union could not identify a particular employment practice that caused the disparity. So, too, the claim of disparate treatment failed because the state tried to match its pay to prevailing rates paid by other public and private employers. As the court reasoned, "Neither law nor logic deems the free market system a suspect enterprise."

The state's pay study was commissioned by the legislature at the instance of the two plaintiffs in this case, unions that represented many of the state's employees. Recall that a similar pay study was crucial to the decision in favor of the plaintiffs in *County of Washington v. Gunther*. Why doesn't it help the plaintiffs' case here? Is the difference between the single job at issue there—jail guards—and the many jobs at issue in this case? Is the elimination of disparities in pay across a broad range of jobs better accomplished through the legislature or through the courts? Who is in a better position to make the many detailed adjustments in existing pay scales? Would imposing liability under Title VII based on job evaluation studies discourage employers from undertaking such studies in the first place? Or is the court concerned that public employers, like the state in this case, might be caught between the political pressure from public employee unions if they fail to undertake such studies and the legal consequences of a lawsuit by these unions if they do so?

6. Comparable Worth Outside the Courts. Claims of comparable worth did not meet with much success in other cases, which consistently reached the same result as *AFSCME*. See, e.g., American Nurses' Ass'n v. Illinois, 783 F.2d 716 (7th Cir. 1986); Lemons v. City of Denver, 620 F.2d 228 (10th Cir.), cert. denied, 449 U.S. 888 (1980). As the *AFSCME* case also illustrates, however, these claims have met with more success in the political process. Typically, the legislature orders a comprehensive pay study and, if it reveals disparities in pay between men and women, the legislature then enacts programs that gradually eliminate the disparities. The entire process has proved to be both complicated and lengthy, but with results that coincided with a slow but continued narrowing of the pay gap between men and women. See Peggy Kahn, Introduction: Equal Pay for Work of Equal Value in Britain and the USA, in Equal Value/Comparable Worth in the UK and the USA 1–29 (Peggy Kahn & Elizabeth Meehan eds., 1992).

Does transforming the debate from one in the courts over legal liability to one in the legislature over public policy affect the underlying force of the arguments for comparable worth as a remedy for sex discrimination? Comparable worth requires the same interference with the market, whether it is accomplished by the judiciary or by the political branches of government. Is it any more manageable as a remedy when it is undertaken by these other branches of government? Can its implementation be limited through legislation, either by restrictions on its scope or by extending the period for compliance, in ways that cannot easily be achieved through judicial decisions? Or was this strategy already tried and found wanting in the restricted scope of the Equal Pay Act? If this strategy for remedying sex discrimination is minimized or abandoned, what alternative remedies should be used instead?

7. **Bibliography.** Henry J. Aaron & Cameron M. Lougy, The Comparable Worth Controversy (1986); Comparable Worth: Issues and Alternatives (E. Robert Livernash ed., 1980); Mary E. Becker, Comparable Worth in Antidiscrimination Legislation: A Reply to Freed and Polsby, 51 U. Chi. L. Rev. 1112 (1984); Mayer G. Freed & Daniel D. Polsby, Comparable Worth in the Equal Pay Act, 51 U. Chi. L. Rev. 1078 (1984); Stephanie Bornstein, Equal Work, 77 Md. L. Rev. ___ (2018). For consideration of the implications of *AFSCME* and similar cases, see Robert L. Nelson & William P. Bridges, Legalizing Gender Inequality: Courts, Markets and Unequal Pay for Women in America (1999); James T. McKeown, Statistics for Wage Discrimination Cases: Why the Statistical Models Used Cannot Prove or Disprove Sex Discrimination, 67 Ind. L.J. 633 (1992); Symposium, The Gender Gap in Compensation, 82 Geo. L.J. 27 (1993).

D. FORMAL INTERPRETATION OF THE PROHIBITION AGAINST SEX DISCRIMINATION

Department of Water & Power v. Manhart

435 U.S. 702 (1978).

■ JUSTICE STEVENS delivered the opinion of the Court.

As a class, women live longer than men. For this reason, the Los Angeles Department of Water and Power required its female employees to make larger contributions to its pension fund than its male employees. We granted certiorari to decide whether this practice discriminated against individual female employees because of their sex in violation of § 703(a)(1) of the Civil Rights Act of 1964, as amended.

For many years the Department has administered retirement, disability, and death-benefit programs for its employees. Upon retirement each employee is eligible for a monthly retirement benefit computed as a fraction of his or her salary multiplied by years of service. The monthly benefits for men and women of the same age, seniority, and salary are equal. Benefits are funded entirely by contributions from the employees and the Department, augmented by the income earned on those contributions. No private insurance company is involved in the administration or payment of benefits.

Based on a study of mortality tables and its own experience, the Department determined that its 2,000 female employees, on the average, will live a few years longer than its 10,000 male employees. The cost of a pension for the average retired female is greater than for the average male retiree because more monthly payments must be made to the average woman. The Department therefore required female employees to make monthly contributions to the fund which were 14.84% higher than the contributions required of comparable male employees. Because employee contributions were withheld from paychecks, a female employee took home less pay than a male employee earning the same salary.

Since the effective date of the Equal Employment Opportunity Act of 1972, the Department has been an employer within the meaning of Title VII of the Civil Rights Act of 1964. See 42 U.S.C. § 2000e. In 1973, respondents brought this suit in the United States District Court for the Central District of California on behalf of a class of women employed or formerly employed by the Department. They prayed for an injunction and restitution of excess contributions.

While this action was pending, the California Legislature enacted a law prohibiting certain municipal agencies from requiring female employees to make higher pension fund contributions than males. The Department therefore amended its plan, effective January 1, 1975. The current plan draws no distinction, either in contributions or in benefits, on the basis of sex. On a motion for summary judgment, the District Court held that the contribution differential violated § 703(a)(1) and ordered a refund of all excess contributions made before the amendment of the plan. The United States Court of Appeals for the Ninth Circuit affirmed.

The Department and various amici curiae contend that: (1) the differential in take-home pay between men and women was not discrimination within the meaning of § 703(a)(1) because it was offset by a difference in the value of the pension benefits provided to the two classes of employees; (2) the differential was based on a factor "other than sex" within the meaning of the Equal Pay Act of 1963 and was therefore protected by the so-called Bennett Amendment; (3) the rationale of General Electric Co. v. Gilbert, 429 U.S. 125, requires reversal; and (4) in any event, the retroactive monetary recovery is unjustified. We consider these contentions in turn.

I

There are both real and fictional differences between women and men. It is true that the average man is taller than the average woman; it is not true that the average woman driver is more accident prone than the average man. Before the Civil Rights Act of 1964 was enacted, an employer could fashion his personnel policies on the basis of assumptions about the differences between men and women, whether or not the assumptions were valid.

It is now well recognized that employment decisions cannot be predicated on mere "stereotyped" impressions about the characteristics of males or females. Myths and purely habitual assumptions about a woman's inability to perform certain kinds of work are no longer acceptable reasons for refusing to employ qualified individuals, or for paying them less. This case does not, however, involve a fictional difference between men and women. It involves a generalization that the parties accept as unquestionably true: Women, as a class, do live longer than men. The Department treated its women employees differently from its men employees because the two classes are in fact different. It is equally true, however, that all individuals in the respective classes do not share the characteristic that differentiates the average class representatives. Many women do not live as long as the average man and many men outlive the average woman. The question, therefore, is whether the existence or nonexistence of "discrimination" is to be determined by comparison of class characteristics or individual characteristics. A "stereotyped" answer to that question may not be the same as the answer that the language and purpose of the statute command.

The statute makes it unlawful "to discriminate against any *individual* with respect to his compensation, terms, conditions, or privileges of employment, because of such *individual's* race, color, religion, sex, or national origin." 42 U.S.C. § 2000e–2(a)(1) . . . . The statute's focus on the individual is unambiguous. It precludes treatment of individuals as simply components of a racial, religious, sexual, or national class. If height is required for a job, a tall woman may not be refused employment merely because, on the average, women are too short. Even a true generalization about the class is an insufficient reason for disqualifying an individual to whom the generalization does not apply.

That proposition is of critical importance in this case because there is no assurance that any individual woman working for the Department will actually fit the generalization on which the Department's policy is based. Many of those individuals will not live as long as the average man. While they were working, those individuals received smaller paychecks because of their sex, but they will receive no compensating advantage when they retire.

It is true, of course, that while contributions are being collected from the employees, the Department cannot know which individuals will predecease the average woman. Therefore, unless women as a class are assessed an extra charge, they will be subsidized, to some extent, by the class of male employees. It follows, according to the Department, that fairness to its class of male employees justifies the extra assessment against all of its female employees.

But the question of fairness to various classes affected by the statute is essentially a matter of policy for the legislature to address. Congress has decided that classifications based on sex, like those based on national origin or race, are unlawful. Actuarial studies could unquestionably identify differences in life expectancy based on race or national origin, as well as sex.[14] But a statute that was designed to make race irrelevant in

[14] The size of the subsidy involved in this case is open to doubt, because the Department's plan provides for survivors' benefits. Since female spouses of male employees are likely to have greater life expectancies than male spouses of female employees, whatever benefits men lose in "primary" coverage for themselves, they may regain in "secondary" coverage for their wives.

the employment market, see Griggs v. Duke Power Co., 401 U.S. 424, 436, could not reasonably be construed to permit a take-home-pay differential based on a racial classification.

Even if the statutory language were less clear, the basic policy of the statute requires that we focus on fairness to individuals rather than fairness to classes. Practices that classify employees in terms of religion, race, or sex tend to preserve traditional assumptions about groups rather than thoughtful scrutiny of individuals. The generalization involved in this case illustrates the point. Separate mortality tables are easily interpreted as reflecting innate differences between the sexes; but a significant part of the longevity differential may be explained by the social fact that men are heavier smokers than women.

Finally, there is no reason to believe that Congress intended a special definition of discrimination in the context of employee group insurance coverage. It is true that insurance is concerned with events that are individually unpredictable, but that is characteristic of many employment decisions. Individual risks, like individual performance, may not be predicted by resort to classifications proscribed by Title VII. Indeed, the fact that this case involves a group insurance program highlights a basic flaw in the Department's fairness argument. For when insurance risks are grouped, the better risks always subsidize the poorer risks. Healthy persons subsidize medical benefits for the less healthy; unmarried workers subsidize the pensions of married workers; persons who eat, drink, or smoke to excess may subsidize pension benefits for persons whose habits are more temperate. Treating different classes of risks as though they were the same for purposes of group insurance is a common practice that has never been considered inherently unfair. To insure the flabby and the fit as though they were equivalent risks may be more common than treating men and women alike; but nothing more than habit makes one "subsidy" seem less fair than the other.[20]

An employment practice that requires 2,000 individuals to contribute more money into a fund than 10,000 other employees simply because each of them is a woman, rather than a man, is in direct conflict with both the language and the policy of the Act. Such a practice does not pass the simple test of whether the evidence shows "treatment of a person in a manner which but for that person's sex would be different." It

[20] A variation on the Department's fairness theme is the suggestion that a gender-neutral pension plan would itself violate Title VII because of its disproportionately heavy impact on male employees. Cf. Griggs v. Duke Power Co., 401 U.S. 424. This suggestion has no force in the sex discrimination context because each retiree's total pension benefits are ultimately determined by his *actual life span*; any differential in benefits paid to men and women in the aggregate is thus "based on [a] factor other than sex," and consequently immune from challenge under the Equal Pay Act, 29 U.S.C. § 206 (d); cf. n.24, infra. Even under Title VII itself—assuming disparate-impact analysis applies to fringe benefits, cf. Nashville Gas Co. v. Satty, 434 U.S. 136, 144–145—the male employees would not prevail. Even a completely neutral practice will inevitably have *some* disproportionate impact on one group or another. *Griggs* does not imply, and this Court has never held, that discrimination must always be inferred from such consequences.

constitutes discrimination and is unlawful unless exempted by the Equal Pay Act of 1963 or some other affirmative justification.

II

Shortly before the enactment of Title VII in 1964, Senator Bennett proposed an amendment providing that a compensation differential based on sex would not be unlawful if it was authorized by the Equal Pay Act, which had been passed a year earlier. The Equal Pay Act requires employers to pay members of both sexes the same wages for equivalent work, except when the differential is pursuant to one of four specified exceptions. The Department contends that the fourth exception applies here. That exception authorizes a "differential based on any other factor other than sex."

The Department argues that the different contributions exacted from men and women were based on the factor of longevity rather than sex. It is plain, however, that any individual's life expectancy is based on a number of factors, of which sex is only one. The record contains no evidence that any factor other than the employee's sex was taken into account in calculating the 14.84% differential between the respective contributions by men and women. We agree with Judge Duniway's observation that one cannot "say that an actuarial distinction based entirely on sex is 'based on any other factor other than sex.' Sex is exactly what it is based on." 553 F.2d 581, 588 (1976).

We are also unpersuaded by the Department's reliance on a colloquy between Senator Randolph and Senator Humphrey during the debate on the Civil Rights Act of 1964. Commenting on the Bennett Amendment, Senator Humphrey expressed his understanding that it would allow many differences in the treatment of men and women under industrial benefit plans, including earlier retirement options for women. Though he did not address differences in employee contributions based on sex, Senator Humphrey apparently assumed that the 1964 Act would have little, if any, impact on existing pension plans. His statement cannot, however, fairly be made the sole guide to interpreting the Equal Pay Act, which had been adopted a year earlier; and it is the 1963 statute, with its exceptions, on which the Department ultimately relies. We conclude that Senator Humphrey's isolated comment on the Senate floor cannot change the effect of the plain language of the statute itself.

III

The Department argues that reversal is required by General Electric Co. v. Gilbert, 429 U.S. 125. We are satisfied, however, that neither the holding nor the reasoning of *Gilbert* is controlling.

In *Gilbert* the Court held that the exclusion of pregnancy from an employer's disability benefit plan did not constitute sex discrimination within the meaning of Title VII. Relying on the reasoning in Geduldig v. Aiello, 417 U.S. 484, the Court first held that the General Electric plan did not involve "discrimination based upon gender as such." The two groups of potential recipients which that case concerned were pregnant women and nonpregnant persons. " 'While the first group is exclusively female, the second includes members of both sexes.' " 429 U.S., at 135. In contrast, each of the two groups of employees involved in this case is composed entirely and exclusively of members of the same sex. On its face, this plan discriminates on the basis of sex whereas the General Electric plan discriminated on the basis of a special physical disability.

In *Gilbert* the Court did note that the plan as actually administered had provided more favorable benefits to women as a class than to men as a class. This evidence supported the conclusion that not only had plaintiffs failed to establish a prima facie case by proving that the plan was discriminatory on its face, but they had also failed to prove any discriminatory effect.

In this case, however, the Department argues that the absence of a discriminatory effect on women as a class justifies an employment practice which, on its face, discriminated against individual employees because of their sex. But even if the Department's actuarial evidence is sufficient to prevent plaintiffs from establishing a prima facie case on the theory that the effect of the practice on women as a class was discriminatory, that evidence does not defeat the claim that the practice, on its face, discriminated against every individual woman employed by the Department.

In essence, the Department is arguing that the prima facie showing of discrimination based on evidence of different contributions for the respective sexes is rebutted by its demonstration that there is a like difference in the cost of providing benefits for the respective classes. That argument might prevail if Title VII contained a cost-justification defense comparable to the affirmative defense available in a price discrimination suit. But neither Congress nor the courts have recognized such a defense under Title VII.

Although we conclude that the Department's practice violated Title VII, we do not suggest that the statute was intended to revolutionize the insurance and pension industries. All that is at issue today is a requirement that men and women make unequal contributions to an employer-operated pension fund. Nothing in our holding implies that it would be unlawful for an employer to set aside equal retirement contributions for each employee and let each retiree purchase the largest benefit which his or her accumulated contributions could command in the open market. Nor does it call into question the insurance industry practice of considering the composition of an employer's work force in determining the probable cost of a retirement or death benefit plan.[34]

[34] Title VII bans discrimination against an "individual" because of "such individual's" sex. 42 U.S.C. § 2000e–2(a)(1). The Equal Pay Act prohibits discrimination "within any establishment," and discrimination is defined as "paying wages to employees . . . at a rate less than the rate at which [the employer] pays wages to employees of the opposite sex" for equal work. 29 U.S.C. § 206 (d)(1). Neither of these provisions makes it unlawful to determine the

Finally, we recognize that in a case of this kind it may be necessary to take special care in fashioning appropriate relief.

IV

The Department challenges the District Court's award of retroactive relief to the entire class of female employees and retirees. Title VII does not require a district court to grant any retroactive relief. A court that finds unlawful discrimination "may enjoin [the discrimination] . . . and order such affirmative action as may be appropriate, which may include, but is not limited to, reinstatement . . . with or without back pay . . . or any other equitable relief as the court deems appropriate." 42 U.S.C. § 2000e–5(g). To the point of redundancy, the statute stresses that retroactive relief "may" be awarded if it is "appropriate."

In Albemarle Paper Co. v. Moody, 422 U.S. 405, the Court reviewed the scope of a district court's discretion to fashion appropriate remedies for a Title VII violation and concluded that "backpay should be denied only for reasons which, if applied generally, would not frustrate the central statutory purposes of eradicating discrimination throughout the economy and making persons whole for injuries suffered through past discrimination." Applying that standard, the Court ruled that an award of backpay should not be conditioned on a showing of bad faith. But the *Albemarle* Court also held that backpay was not to be awarded automatically in every case.

The *Albemarle* presumption in favor of retroactive liability can seldom be overcome, but it does not make meaningless the district courts' duty to determine that such relief is appropriate. For several reasons, we conclude that the District Court gave insufficient attention to the equitable nature of Title VII remedies. Although we now have no doubt about the application of the statute in this case, we must recognize that conscientious and intelligent administrators of pension funds, who did not have the benefit of the extensive briefs and arguments presented to us, may well have assumed that a program like the Department's was entirely lawful. The courts had been silent on the question, and the administrative agencies had conflicting views. The Department's failure to act more swiftly is a sign, not of its recalcitrance, but of the problem's complexity. As commentators have noted, pension administrators could reasonably have thought it unfair—or even illegal—to make male employees shoulder more than their "actuarial share" of the pension burden. There is no reason to believe that the threat of a backpay award is needed to cause other administrators to amend their practices to conform to this decision.

Nor can we ignore the potential impact which changes in rules affecting insurance and pension plans may have on the economy. Fifty million Americans participate in retirement plans other than Social

---

funding requirements for an establishment's benefit plan by considering the composition of the entire force.

Security. The assets held in trust for these employees are vast and growing—more than $400 billion was reserved for retirement benefits at the end of 1976 and reserves are increasing by almost $50 billion a year. These plans, like other forms of insurance, depend on the accumulation of large sums to cover contingencies. The amounts set aside are determined by a painstaking assessment of the insurer's likely liability. Risks that the insurer foresees will be included in the calculation of liability, and the rates or contributions charged will reflect that calculation. The occurrence of major unforeseen contingencies, however, jeopardizes the insurer's solvency and, ultimately, the insureds' benefits. Drastic changes in the legal rules governing pension and insurance funds, like other unforeseen events, can have this effect. Consequently, the rules that apply to these funds should not be applied retroactively unless the legislature has plainly commanded that result. The EEOC itself has recognized that the administrators of retirement plans must be given time to adjust gradually to Title VII's demands. Courts have also shown sensitivity to the special dangers of retroactive Title VII awards in this field. See Rosen v. Public Serv. Elec. & Gas Co., 328 F. Supp. 454, 466–468 (D.N.J. 1970).

There can be no doubt that the prohibition against sex-differentiated employee contributions represents a marked departure from past practice. Although Title VII was enacted in 1964, this is apparently the first litigation challenging contribution differences based on valid actuarial tables. Retroactive liability could be devastating for a pension fund. The harm would fall in large part on innocent third parties. If, as the courts below apparently contemplated, the plaintiffs' contributions are recovered from the pension fund, the administrators of the fund will be forced to meet unchanged obligations with diminished assets. If the reserve proves inadequate, either the expectations of all retired employees will be disappointed or current employees will be forced to pay not only for their own future security but also for the unanticipated reduction in the contributions of past employees.

Without qualifying the force of the *Albemarle* presumption in favor of retroactive relief, we conclude that it was error to grant such relief in this case. Accordingly, although we agree with the Court of Appeals' analysis of the statute, we vacate its judgment and remand the case for further proceedings consistent with this opinion.

It is so ordered.

[Justice Brennan took no part in this case and Justice Blackmun wrote an opinion concurring in part and concurring in the judgment.]

■ CHIEF JUSTICE BURGER, with whom JUSTICE REHNQUIST joins, concurring in part and dissenting in part.

I join Part IV of the Court's opinion; as to Parts I, II, and III, I dissent.

Gender-based actuarial tables have been in use since at least 1843, and their statistical validity has been repeatedly verified. The vast life insurance, annuity, and pension plan industry is based on these tables. As the Court recognizes, it is a fact that "women, as a class, do live longer than men." It is equally true that employers cannot know in advance when individual members of the classes will die. Yet, if they are to operate economically workable group pension programs, it is only rational to permit them to rely on statistically sound and proved disparities in longevity between men and women. Indeed, it seems to me irrational to assume Congress intended to outlaw use of the fact that, for whatever reasons or combination of reasons, women as a class outlive men.

The Court's conclusion that the language of the civil rights statute is clear, admitting of no advertence to the legislative history, such as there was, is not soundly based. An effect upon pension plans so revolutionary and discriminatory—this time favorable to women at the expense of men—should not be read into the statute without either a clear statement of that intent in the statute, or some reliable indication in the legislative history that this was Congress' purpose. The Court's casual dismissal of Senator Humphrey's apparent assumption that the "Act would have little, if any, impact on existing pension plans," is to dismiss a significant manifestation of what impact on industrial benefit plans was contemplated. It is reasonably clear there was no intention to abrogate an employer's right, in this narrow and limited context, to treat women differently from men in the face of historical reliance on mortality experience statistics.

The reality of differences in human mortality is what mortality experience tables reflect. The difference is the added longevity of women. All the reasons why women statistically outlive men are not clear. But categorizing people on the basis of sex, the one acknowledged immutable difference between men and women, is to take into account all of the unknown reasons, whether biologically or culturally based, or both, which give women a significantly greater life expectancy than men. It is therefore true as the Court says, "that any individual's life expectancy is based on a number of factors, of which sex is only one." But it is not true that by seizing upon the only constant, "measurable" factor, no others were taken into account. All other factors, whether known but variable—or unknown—are the elements which automatically account for the actuarial disparity. And all are accounted for when the constant factor is used as a basis for determining the costs and benefits of a group pension plan.

Here, of course, petitioners are discriminating in take-home pay between men and women. The practice of petitioners, however, falls squarely under the exemption provided by the Equal Pay Act of 1963, 29 U.S.C. § 206(d), incorporated into Title VII by the so-called Bennett Amendment, 78 Stat. 257, now 42 U.S.C. § 2000e–2(h). That exemption tells us that an employer may not discriminate between employees on the basis of sex by paying one sex lesser compensation than the other "except where such payment is made pursuant to . . . a differential based on any other factor other than sex. . . ." The "other factor other than sex" is longevity; sex is the umbrella-constant under which all of the elements leading to differences in longevity are grouped and assimilated, and the only objective feature upon which an employer—or anyone else, including insurance companies—may reliably base a cost differential for the "risk" being insured.

This is in no sense a failure to treat women as "individuals" in violation of the statute, as the Court holds. It is to treat them as individually as it is possible to do in the face of the unknowable length of each individual life. Individually, every woman has the same statistical possibility of outliving men. This is the essence of basing decisions on reliable statistics when individual determinations are infeasible or, as here, impossible.

Of course, women cannot be disqualified from, for example, heavy labor just because the generality of women are thought not as strong as men—a proposition which perhaps may sometime be statistically demonstrable, but will remain individually refutable. When, however, it is impossible to tailor a program such as a pension plan to the individual, nothing should prevent application of reliable statistical facts to the individual, for whom the facts cannot be disproved until long after planning, funding, and operating the program have been undertaken.

I find it anomalous, if not contradictory, that the Court's opinion tells us, in effect, that the holding is not really a barrier to responding to the complaints of men employees, as a group. The Court states that employers may give their employees precisely the same dollar amount and require them to secure their own annuities directly from an insurer, who, of course, is under no compulsion to ignore 135 years of accumulated, recorded longevity experience.

■ JUSTICE MARSHALL, concurring in part and dissenting in part.

I agree that Title VII of the Civil Rights Act of 1964, as amended, forbids petitioners' practice of requiring female employees to make larger contributions to a pension fund than do male employees. I therefore join all of the Court's opinion except Part IV.

I also agree with the Court's statement in Part IV that, once a Title VII violation is found, Albemarle Paper Co. v. Moody, 422 U.S. 405 (1975), establishes a "presumption in favor of retroactive liability" and that this presumption "can seldom be overcome." But I do not agree that the presumption should be deemed overcome in this case, especially since the relief was granted by the District Court in the exercise of its discretion and was upheld by the Court of Appeals. I would affirm the decision below and therefore cannot join Part IV of the Court's opinion or the Court's judgment.

NOTES ON *DEPARTMENT OF WATER & POWER V. MANHART*

1. **Pensions as Compensation.** *Manhart* concerned contributions to a pension established by the employer and partly funded by its own contributions. The remaining contributions, which were in dispute in this case, came from the employees themselves. A pension plan, just like life insurance or medical insurance, is a fringe benefit of employment. To the extent that it is subsidized by the employer, it is a form of deferred compensation, in which employees receive some of their pay through pensions instead of their regular paychecks. The employer in *Manhart* used sex-based actuarial tables that predicted different life expectancies for male and female employees to compute the contributions required from those employees to fund the plan. Not only did these actuarial tables take account of sex, they did so in a way that required higher contributions from women than from men. Why did the employer think that it could engage in such outright sex discrimination?

The employer's justification partly rested on the widespread use of sex-based actuarial tables, in life insurance plans as well as pension plans. But the employer relied on more than common practice. Sex-based actuarial tables were widely used because, it was thought, sex was an accurate predictor of life expectancy. Women, on average, tended to live longer than men and so tended to receive pension benefits over a longer period of time. In the employer's pension plan, women received the same regular payments as similarly situated men, but because of their greater longevity, they received greater total benefits on average than men. The higher contributions required of them (matched also by higher contributions from the employer) were necessary to fund the greater total benefits that they were predicted to receive.

After the fact, of course, individual men and women receive different total benefits, depending on when they died, and some men would, in fact, receive greater total benefits than some women. Before the fact, however, it was impossible to know who would die at what time. And, indeed, the very purpose of a pension plan is to reduce the consequences of such uncertainty. Pension plans protect retired employees from outliving their accumulated assets. As such, pension plans are a form of insurance, in many ways the opposite of life insurance. Pension plans protect employees from living too long—beyond the assets that they have accumulated for retirement—whereas life insurance plans protect individuals from dying too early—before they have been able to provide for their dependents.

One way to frame the fundamental question in *Manhart* is whether pensions should be valued ex post, after the fact, or ex ante, before the fact. The Supreme Court does not endorse an ex post view, perhaps because it looks only to the long term, in which, as the economist J.M. Keynes famously observed, "we are all dead." It is only in the short term, in which risks remain unrealized, that any form of insurance makes sense. It follows that the nature of pensions as a form of insurance supports an ex ante view. Yet the Supreme Court does not endorse this view either, at least insofar as it depends upon sex in making predictions about life expectancy.

2. **Exceptions to Title VII.** Title VII contains several exceptions, either express or implied, to its prohibition against sex discrimination. The first has already been covered in general terms. It is in the Bennett Amendment and incorporates in Title VII the defenses available under the Equal Pay Act. Because pensions are a form of compensation, the pension contributions in *Manhart* fall within the range of employment practices covered by this exception. Yet, as the Supreme Court points out, none of the defenses under the Equal Pay Act permit the use of sex-based actuarial tables. As Judge Duniway recognized in the opinion for the court of appeals, defense (iv), for "any other factor other than sex," is not available. It is impossible to "say that an actuarial distinction based entirely on sex is 'based on any other factor other than sex.' Sex is exactly what it is based on." Isn't it an exaggeration, however, to say that the employer relied only on sex in making predictions of life expectancy? All sex-based actuarial tables also take account of age, in this case, the age at retirement. Does it help the employer's argument that sex is not the only factor that entered into its pension calculations? Or is this a kind of "mixed motive" case in which the employer has essentially conceded that it relied in part on sex? If it is a "mixed motive" case, what would the employer have to show in order to avoid liability for back pay?

Title VII also contains another exception to its prohibition against sex discrimination: for any "bona fide occupational qualification" (or BFOQ) reasonably necessary for a particular job. It is found in § 703(e)(1) and is discussed later in this chapter. Whatever its appropriate scope, as its name indicates, it applies only to qualifications for a job, not to compensation. A related exception, developed almost entirely through judicial interpretation, involves sex-based standards for dress and appearance. It originates in a line of cases from the 1970s that allow employers to impose different standards for men and women in matters such as hair length. E.g., Willingham v. Macon Telegraph Publishing Co., 507 F.2d 1084 (5th Cir. 1975) (en banc). It is an open question exactly how far such standards, based as they are on traditional gender roles, can be taken as conditions of employment, as discussed in Chapter 1 in connection with Jespersen v. Harrah's Operating Co., Inc., 444 F.3d 1104 (9th Cir. 2006) (en banc). But even if this exception is given the broadest possible scope, it has, like the BFOQ, no apparent application to questions of compensation. The same can be said of the judicially implied exception for affirmative action plans. Such plans mainly are justified as a remedy for past discrimination, but it is not apparent how sex-based actuarial tables counteract past discrimination on the basis of sex. See Johnson v. Transportation Agency, 480 U.S. 616 (1987). On the contrary, Chief Justice Burger argued in his dissent in *Manhart* that sex-neutral actuarial tables—not sex-based tables—constituted an unjustifiable form of affirmative action.

The Court considered the possibility of developing still another exception to Title VII based on an analogy to the antitrust laws. This exception would allow sex-based classifications that could be justified on grounds of cost. The Court found no basis for this defense in the statute itself and rejected it on this ground. The opinion in *Manhart* can therefore be summarized in entirely formal terms. The employer used a sex-based classification generally prohibited by Title VII. This classification fell within none of the recognized exceptions to Title VII. It follows that the employer violated the statute.

Although this reasoning is sound within the narrow frame of reference that it presupposes, it neglects the employer's own reason for using sex-based actuarial tables: they predict life expectancy more accurately than actuarial tables that do not take account of sex. This is an argument about more than the employer's own cost in providing pensions. It is an argument about how to treat men and women equally. If women are likely to receive greater benefits from a pension plan, shouldn't they be required to make greater contributions?

3. **Evidence of Sex-Based Differences in Life Expectancy.** The Court casts some doubt on the accuracy of sex-based actuarial tables, finding that any insurance plan results in one group of participants subsidizing another. In a pension plan, the less fit employees, with a lower actual life expectancy, subsidize the more fit employees, with a greater life expectancy. Yet the Court also conceded that sex-based actuarial tables, as compared to other sex-based stereotypes, were accurate. These tables do not assume, for instance, that women are more fit than men. Is the Court just equivocating between the ex post and ex ante perspectives that can be taken on insurance plans? Ex post, after a plan's participants have received all their benefits, some come out ahead and others do not. Ex ante, however, it is impossible to ascertain which beneficiaries will fall in which group. If, for instance, an employer could ascertain the fitness of employees as easily as their sex, then that factor could be taken into account in devising actuarial tables. But isn't fitness far more difficult for an employer to ascertain than sex, let alone to reassess constantly throughout an employee's working life? Doesn't that fact impose practical limits on what factors can actually be taken into account in actuarial tables?

Some authors have argued that sex does not determine life expectancy, at least not in any stable way that could reliably be taken into account in pension and life insurance plans. The sex-based difference in life expectancy, in fact, has proved to be remarkably variable over the last century, as a variety of cultural factors, including gender roles, have changed. See Lea Brilmayer et al., Sex Discrimination in Employer-Sponsored Insurance Plans: A Legal and Demographic Analysis, 47 U. Chi. L. Rev. 505, 539–59 (1980); George J. Benston, The Economics of Gender Discrimination in Employee Fringe Benefits: *Manhart* Revisited, 49 U. Chi. L. Rev. 489 (1982); Lea Brilmayer et al., The Efficient Use of Group Averages as Nondiscrimination: A Rejoinder to Professor Benston, 50 U. Chi. L. Rev. 222 (1983); George Rutherglen, Sexual Equality in Fringe-Benefit Plans, 65 Va. L. Rev. 199 (1979). Because all actuarial tables are based on past experience, the population from which the tables are developed necessarily lives (and dies) earlier than the employees to which the tables apply. If this is so, how can an employer be certain that any actuarial table is accurate? Or should employers only rely upon the greater stability of predictions of overall life expectancy, regardless of sex, than of predictions of life expectancy of men and women considered separately? How far should a court go in resolving such questions?

The Supreme Court was reluctant to go very far at all in *Manhart*. In footnote 34, the Court allows an employer to take account of the proportion of men and women in its work force in determining overall life expectancy. This footnote presumes that a work force composed almost entirely of women will have a life expectancy very similar to that for women alone, with life expectancy decreasing as more men are added to the work force. How does this reasoning fit with the formal approach to interpreting Title VII taken elsewhere in the opinion in *Manhart*? Is the Court permitting sex to be taken into account as a factor in setting compensation, so long as an employer is not too obvious about it? Or is the Court just acknowledging the weight of the evidence supporting the use of sex-based actuarial tables?

4. Scope of the Decision in *Manhart*. The Court imposed other limitations on the holding in *Manhart*. Some are derived from limitations on the coverage of Title VII itself. Thus, the decision does not apply to pension and insurance plans offered independently of any employment relationship. These plans are governed mainly by state law, which can, but seldom actually does, prohibit the use of sex-based distinctions in insurance offered to the general public. Jill Gaulding, Note, Race, Sex, and Genetic Discrimination in Insurance: What's Fair?, 80 Cornell L. Rev. 1646, 1658–64 (1995); see also Robert H. Jerry, II & Kyle B. Mansfield, Justifying Unisex Insurance: Another Perspective, 34 Am. U. L. Rev. 329 (1985); Leah Wortham, Insurance Classification: Too Important to Be Left to the Actuaries, 19 U. Mich. J.L. Ref. 349 (1986). This form of state regulation, whatever its content, exists wholly apart from regulation of the employment relationship under Title VII and many pension and insurance plans remain within the coverage of the statute. The tax advantages of fringe benefit plans make them attractive to both employers and employees. If such plans qualify under the tax laws, employers can deduct the immediate cost of their contributions to fund such plans, while employees can defer any tax on payments from the plans until they retire. By contrast, cash payments to employees, with which they could purchase independently available plans, would be immediately taxed to them as income.

Another limitation on the holding has proved to be more controversial. The Court refused to order back pay to women participating in the plan, denying them restitution of the greater contributions that they had made to the plan. The Court expressed concern over the solvency of pension plans generally, not just the pension plan in this case, if retrospective relief were routinely granted. This limitation on the holding was again invoked in a later case, Arizona Governing Committee v. Norris, 463 U.S. 1073 (1983), where the employer had used sex-based actuarial tables in determining the benefits available to retired employees, as opposed to the contributions in *Manhart*. In both *Norris* and *Manhart*, the refusal to award back pay rested in part on the employer's reasonable reliance on official advice permitting the use of either sex-based or sex-neutral means of predicting longevity. Is allowing a partial defense on this ground consistent with the main holding in these cases that employers cannot take account of sex in setting contributions or benefits from a pension plan? Shouldn't the employer in *Norris* have been on notice from the decision in *Manhart* that it needed to change its pension plan? Or do both decisions simply recognize the difficulty of making the transition from sex-based to sex-neutral means of administering plans that accumulate and disburse billions of dollars over several decades?

E. CLASSIFICATIONS ON THE BASIS OF PREGNANCY

Geduldig v. Aiello

417 U.S. 484 (1974).

■ JUSTICE STEWART delivered the opinion of the Court.

For almost 30 years California has administered a disability insurance system that pays benefits to persons in private employment who are temporarily unable to work because of disability not covered by workmen's compensation. The appellees brought this action to challenge the constitutionality of a provision of the California program that, in defining "disability," excludes from coverage certain disabilities resulting from pregnancy. Because the appellees sought to enjoin the enforcement of this state statute, a three-judge court was convened pursuant to 28 U.S.C. §§ 2281 and 2284. On the appellees' motion for summary judgment, the District Court, by a divided vote, held that this provision of the disability insurance program violates the Equal Protection Clause of the Fourteenth Amendment, and therefore enjoined its continued enforcement. The District Court denied a motion to stay its judgment pending appeal. The appellant thereupon filed a similar motion in this Court, which we granted. We subsequently noted probable jurisdiction of the appeal.

I

California's disability insurance system is funded entirely from contributions deducted from the wages of participating employees. Participation in the program is mandatory unless the employees are protected by a voluntary private plan approved by the State. Each employee is required to contribute one percent of his salary, up to an annual maximum of $85. These contributions are placed in the Unemployment Compensation Disability Fund, which is established and administered as a special trust fund within the state treasury. It is from this Disability Fund that benefits under the program are paid.

An individual is eligible for disability benefits if, during a one-year base period prior to his disability, he has contributed one percent of a minimum income of $300 to the Disability Fund. In the event he suffers a compensable disability, the individual can receive a "weekly benefit amount" of between $25 and $105, depending on the amount he earned during the highest quarter of the base period. Benefits are not paid until the eighth day of disability, unless the employee is hospitalized, in which case benefits commence on the first day of hospitalization. In addition to the "weekly benefit amount," a hospitalized employee is entitled to receive "additional benefits" of $12 per day of hospitalization. "Weekly benefit amounts" for any one disability are payable for 26 weeks so long as the total amount paid does not exceed one-half of the wages received during the base period. "Additional benefits" for any one disability are paid for a maximum of 20 days.

In return for his one-percent contribution to the Disability Fund, the individual employee is insured against the risk of disability stemming from a substantial number of "mental or physical illness[es] and mental or physical injur[ies]." Cal. Unemp. Ins. Code § 2626. It is not every disabling condition, however, that triggers the obligation to pay benefits under the program. As already noted, for example, any disability of less than eight days' duration is not compensable, except when the employee is hospitalized. Conversely, no benefits are payable for any single disability beyond 26 weeks. Further, disability is not compensable if it results from the individual's court commitment as a dipsomaniac, drug addict, or sexual psychopath. Finally, § 2626 of the Unemployment Insurance Code excludes from coverage certain disabilities that are attributable to pregnancy. It is this provision that is at issue in the present case.

Appellant is the Director of the California Department of Human Resources Development. He is responsible for the administration of the State's disability insurance program. Appellees are four women who have paid sufficient amounts into the Disability Fund to be eligible for benefits under the program. Each of the appellees became pregnant and suffered employment disability as a result of her pregnancy. With respect to three of the appellees, Carolyn Aiello, Augustina Armendariz, and Elizabeth Johnson, the disabilities were attributable to abnormal complications encountered during their pregnancies. The fourth, Jacqueline Jaramillo, experienced a normal pregnancy, which was the sole cause of her disability.

At all times relevant to this case, § 2626 of the Unemployment Insurance Code provided:

> "'Disability' or 'disabled' includes both mental or physical illness and mental or physical injury. An individual shall be deemed disabled in any day in which, because of his physical or mental condition, he is unable to perform his regular or customary work. *In no case shall the term 'disability' or 'disabled' include any injury or illness caused by or arising in connection with pregnancy up to the termination of such pregnancy and for a period of 28 days thereafter.*"

(Emphasis added.) Appellant construed and applied the final sentence of this statute to preclude the payment of benefits for any disability resulting from pregnancy. As a result, the appellees were ruled ineligible for disability benefits by reason of this provision, and they sued to enjoin its enforcement. The District Court, finding "that the exclusion of pregnancy-related disabilities is not based upon a classification having a rational and substantial relationship to a legitimate state purpose," held that the exclusion was unconstitutional under the Equal Protection Clause.

Shortly before the District Court's decision in this case, the California Court of Appeal, in a suit brought by a woman who suffered an ectopic pregnancy, held that § 2626 does not bar the payment of benefits on account of disability that results from medical complications arising during pregnancy. Rentzer v. Unemployment Insurance Appeals Board, 32 Cal. App. 3d 604, 108 Cal. Rptr. 336 (1973).

. . . Thus, the issue before the Court on this appeal is whether the California disability insurance program invidiously discriminates against Jaramillo and others similarly situated by not paying insurance benefits for disability that accompanies normal pregnancy and childbirth.

II

It is clear that California intended to establish this benefit system as an insurance program that was to function essentially in accordance with insurance concepts. Since the program was instituted in 1946, it has been totally self-supporting, never drawing on general state revenues to finance disability or hospital benefits. The Disability Fund is wholly supported by the one percent of wages annually contributed by participating employees. At oral argument, counsel for the appellant informed us that in recent years between 90% and 103% of the revenue to the Disability Fund has been paid out in disability and hospital benefits. This history strongly suggests that the one-percent contribution rate, in addition to being easily computable, bears a close and substantial relationship to the level of benefits payable and to the disability risks insured under the program.

Over the years California has demonstrated a strong commitment not to increase the contribution rate above the one-percent level. The State has sought to provide the broadest possible disability protection that would be affordable by all employees, including those with very low incomes. Because any larger percentage or any flat dollar-amount rate of contribution would impose an increasingly regressive levy bearing most heavily upon those with the lowest incomes, the State has resisted any attempt to change the required contribution from the one-percent level. The program is thus structured, in terms of the level of benefits and the risks insured, to maintain the solvency of the Disability Fund at a one-percent annual level of contribution.

In ordering the State to pay benefits for disability accompanying normal pregnancy and delivery, the District Court acknowledged the State's contention "that coverage of these disabilities is so extraordinarily expensive that it would be impossible to maintain a program supported by employee contributions if these disabilities are included." There is considerable disagreement between the parties with respect to how great the increased costs would actually be, but they would clearly be substantial. For purposes of analysis the District Court accepted the State's estimate, which was in excess of $100 million annually, and stated: "It is clear that including these disabilities would not destroy the program. The increased costs could be accommodated quite easily by making reasonable changes in the contribution rate, the maximum benefits allowable, and the other variables affecting the solvency of the program."

Each of these "variables"—the benefit level deemed appropriate to compensate employee disability, the risks selected to be insured under the program, and the contribution rate chosen to maintain the solvency of the program and at the same time to permit low-income employees to participate with minimal personal sacrifice—represents a policy determination by the State. The essential issue in this case is whether the Equal Protection Clause requires such policies to be sacrificed or compromised in order to finance the payment of benefits to those whose disability is attributable to normal pregnancy and delivery.

We cannot agree that the exclusion of this disability from coverage amounts to invidious discrimination under the Equal Protection Clause. California does not discriminate with respect to the persons or groups which are eligible for disability insurance protection under the program. The classification challenged in this case relates to the asserted underinclusiveness of the set of risks that the State has selected to insure. Although California has created a program to insure most risks of employment disability, it has not chosen to insure all such risks, and this decision is reflected in the level of annual contributions exacted from participating employees. This Court has held that, consistently with the Equal Protection Clause, a State "may take one step at a time, addressing itself to the phase of the problem which seems most acute to the legislative mind. . . . The legislature may select one phase of one field and apply a remedy there, neglecting the others. . . ." Williamson v. Lee Optical Inc., 348 U.S. 483, 489 (1955); Jefferson v. Hackney, 406 U.S. 535 (1972). Particularly with respect to social welfare programs, so long as the line drawn by the State is rationally supportable, the courts will not interpose their judgment as to the appropriate stopping point. "The Equal Protection Clause does not require that a State must choose between attacking every aspect of a problem or not attacking the problem at all." Dandridge v. Williams, 397 U.S. 471, 486–487 (1970).

The District Court suggested that moderate alterations in what it regarded as "variables" of the disability insurance program could be made to accommodate the substantial expense required to include normal pregnancy within the program's protection. The same can be said, however, with respect to the other expensive class of disabilities that are excluded from coverage—short-term disabilities. If the Equal Protection Clause were thought to compel disability payments for normal pregnancy, it is hard to perceive why it would not also compel payments for short-term disabilities suffered by participating employees.

It is evident that a totally comprehensive program would be substantially more costly than the present program and would inevitably require state subsidy, a higher rate of employee contribution, a lower scale of benefits for those suffering insured disabilities, or some combination of these measures. There is nothing in the Constitution, however, that requires the State to subordinate or compromise its legitimate interests solely to create a more comprehensive social insurance program than it already has.

The State has a legitimate interest in maintaining the self-supporting nature of its insurance program. Similarly, it has an interest in distributing the available resources in such a way as to keep benefit payments at an adequate level for disabilities that are covered, rather than to cover all disabilities inadequately. Finally, California has a legitimate concern in maintaining the contribution rate at a level that will not unduly burden participating employees, particularly low-income employees who may be most in need of the disability insurance.

These policies provide an objective and wholly noninvidious basis for the State's decision not to create a more comprehensive insurance program than it has. There is no evidence in the record that the selection of the risks insured by the program worked to discriminate against any definable group or class in terms of the aggregate risk protection derived by that group or class from the program.[20] There is no risk from which men are protected and women are not. Likewise, there is no risk from which women are protected and men are not.[21]

The appellee simply contends that, although she has received insurance protection equivalent to that provided all other participating

---

[20] The dissenting opinion to the contrary, this case is thus a far cry from cases like Reed v. Reed, 404 U.S. 71 (1971), and Frontiero v. Richardson, 411 U.S. 677 (1973), involving discrimination based upon gender as such. The California insurance program does not exclude anyone from benefit eligibility because of gender but merely removes one physical condition—pregnancy—from the list of compensable disabilities. While it is true that only women can become pregnant, it does not follow that every legislative classification concerning pregnancy is a sex-based classification like those considered in *Reed*, supra, and *Frontiero*, supra. Normal pregnancy is an objectively identifiable physical condition with unique characteristics. Absent a showing that distinctions involving pregnancy are mere pretexts designed to effect an invidious discrimination against the members of one sex or the other, lawmakers are constitutionally free to include or exclude pregnancy from the coverage of legislation such as this on any reasonable basis, just as with respect to any other physical condition.

The lack of identity between the excluded disability and gender as such under this insurance program becomes clear upon the most cursory analysis. The program divides potential recipients into two groups—pregnant women and nonpregnant persons. While the first group is exclusively female, the second includes members of both sexes. The fiscal and actuarial benefits of the program thus accrue to members of both sexes.

[21] Indeed, the appellant submitted to the District Court data that indicated that both the annual claim rate and the annual claim cost are greater for women than for men. As the District Court acknowledged, "women contribute about 28 percent of the total disability insurance fund and receive back about 38 percent of the fund in benefits." 359 F. Supp. 792, 800. Several amici curiae have represented to the Court that they have had a similar experience under private disability insurance programs.

employees, she has suffered discrimination because she encountered a risk that was outside the program's protection. For the reasons we have stated, we hold that this contention is not a valid one under the Equal Protection Clause of the Fourteenth Amendment.

The stay heretofore issued by the Court is vacated, and the judgment of the District Court is reversed.

■ JUSTICE BRENNAN, with whom JUSTICE DOUGLAS and JUSTICE MARSHALL join, dissenting.

Relying upon Dandridge v. Williams, 397 U.S. 471 (1970), and Jefferson v. Hackney, 406 U.S. 535 (1972), the Court today rejects appellees' equal protection claim and upholds the exclusion of normal-pregnancy-related disabilities from coverage under California's disability insurance program on the ground that the legislative classification rationally promotes the State's legitimate cost-saving interests in "maintaining the self-supporting nature of its insurance program[,] . . . distributing the available resources in such a way as to keep benefit payments at an adequate level for disabilities that are covered, . . . [and] maintaining the contribution rate at a level that will not unduly burden participating employees. . . ." Because I believe that Reed v. Reed, 404 U.S. 71 (1971), and Frontiero v. Richardson, 411 U.S. 677 (1973), mandate a stricter standard of scrutiny which the State's classification fails to satisfy, I respectfully dissent.

California's disability insurance program was enacted to supplement the State's unemployment insurance and workmen's compensation programs by providing benefits to wage earners to cushion the economic effects of income loss and medical expenses resulting from sickness or injury. The legislature's intent in enacting the program was expressed clearly in § 2601 of the Unemployment Insurance Code:

> "The purpose of this part is to compensate in part for the wage loss sustained by individuals unemployed because of sickness or injury and to reduce to a minimum the suffering caused by unemployment resulting therefrom. This part shall be construed liberally in aid of its declared purpose to mitigate the evils and burdens which fall on the unemployed and disabled worker and his family."

To achieve the Act's broad humanitarian goals, the legislature fashioned a pooled-risk disability fund covering all employees at the same rate of contribution, regardless of individual risk. The only requirement that must be satisfied before an employee becomes eligible to receive disability benefits is that the employee must have contributed one percent of a minimum income of $300 during a one-year base period. Cal. Unemp. Ins. Code § 2652. The "basic benefits," varying from $25 to $119 per week, depending upon the employee's base-period earnings, begin on the eighth day of disability or on the first day of hospitalization. §§ 2655, 2627(b), 2802. Benefits are payable for a maximum of 26 weeks, but may not exceed one-half of the employee's total base-period earnings. § 2653. Finally, compensation is paid for virtually all disabling conditions without regard to cost, voluntariness, uniqueness, predictability, or "normalcy" of the disability. Thus, for example, workers are compensated for costly disabilities such as heart attacks, voluntary disabilities such as cosmetic surgery or sterilization, disabilities unique to sex or race such as prostatectomies or sickle-cell anemia, pre-existing conditions inevitably resulting in disability such as degenerative arthritis or cataracts, and "normal" disabilities such as removal of irritating wisdom teeth or other orthodontia.

Despite the Code's broad goals and scope of coverage, compensation is denied for disabilities suffered in connection with a "normal" pregnancy—disabilities suffered only by women. Cal. Unemp. Ins. Code §§ 2626, 2626.2 (Supp. 1974). Disabilities caused by pregnancy, however, like other physically disabling conditions covered by the Code, require medical care, often include hospitalization, anesthesia and surgical procedures, and may involve genuine risk to life. Moreover, the economic effects caused by pregnancy-related disabilities are functionally indistinguishable from the effects caused by any other disability: wages are lost due to a physical inability to work, and medical expenses are incurred for the delivery of the child and for postpartum care. In my view, by singling out for less favorable treatment a gender-linked disability peculiar to women, the State has created a double standard for disability compensation: a limitation is imposed upon the disabilities for which women workers may recover, while men receive full compensation for all disabilities suffered, including those that affect only or primarily their sex, such as prostatectomies, circumcision, hemophilia, and gout. In effect, one set of rules is applied to females and another to males. Such dissimilar treatment of men and women, on the basis of physical characteristics inextricably linked to one sex, inevitably constitutes sex discrimination. . . .

In the past, when a legislative classification has turned on gender, the Court has justifiably applied a standard of judicial scrutiny more strict than that generally accorded economic or social welfare programs. Yet, by its decision today, the Court appears willing to abandon that higher standard of review without satisfactorily explaining what differentiates the gender-based classification employed in this case from those found unconstitutional in *Reed* and *Frontiero*. The Court's decision threatens to return men and women to a time when "traditional" equal protection analysis sustained legislative classifications that treated differently members of a particular sex solely because of their sex.

I cannot join the Court's apparent retreat. I continue to adhere to my view that "classifications based upon sex, like classifications based upon race, alienage, or national origin, are inherently suspect, and must therefore be subjected to strict judicial scrutiny." *Frontiero v. Richardson*, supra, at 688. When, as in this case, the State employs a legislative classification that distinguishes between beneficiaries solely by reference to gender-linked disability risks, "the Court is not . . . free to sustain the statute on the ground that it rationally promotes legitimate governmental interests; rather, such suspect classifications can be sustained only when the State bears the burden of demonstrating that the challenged legislation serves overriding or compelling interests that cannot be achieved either by a more carefully tailored legislative classification or by the use of feasible, less drastic means." Kahn v. Shevin, 416 U.S. 351, 357–358 (1974) (Brennan, J., dissenting).

The State has clearly failed to meet that burden in the present case. The essence of the State's justification for excluding disabilities caused by a normal pregnancy from its disability compensation scheme is that covering such disabilities would be too costly. To be sure, as presently funded, inclusion of normal pregnancies "would be substantially more costly than the present program." The present level of benefits for insured disabilities could not be maintained without increasing the employee contribution rate, raising or lifting the yearly contribution ceiling, or securing state subsidies. But whatever role such monetary considerations may play in traditional equal protection analysis, the State's interest in preserving the fiscal integrity of its disability insurance program simply cannot render the State's use of a suspect classification constitutional. For while "a State has a valid interest in preserving the fiscal integrity of its programs[,] . . . a State may not accomplish such a purpose by invidious distinctions between classes of its citizens. . . . The saving of welfare costs cannot justify an otherwise invidious classification." Shapiro v. Thompson, 394 U.S. 618, 633 (1969). Thus, when a statutory classification is subject to strict judicial scrutiny, the State "must do more than show that denying [benefits to the excluded class] saves money." Memorial Hospital v. Maricopa County, 415 U.S. 250, 263 (1974). . . .

Moreover, California's legitimate interest in fiscal integrity could easily have been achieved through a variety of less drastic, sexually neutral means. As the District Court observed:

> "Even using [the State's] estimate of the cost of expanding the program to include pregnancy-related disabilities, however, it is clear that including these disabilities would not destroy the program. The increased costs could be accommodated quite easily by making reasonable changes in the contribution rate, the maximum benefits allowable, and the other variables affecting the solvency of the program. For example, the entire cost increase estimated by defendant could be met by requiring workers to contribute an additional amount of approximately .364 percent of their salary and increasing the maximum annual contribution to about $119." 359 F. Supp. 792, 798.

I would therefore affirm the judgment of the District Court.

NOTES ON *GEDULDIG V. AIELLO*

1. Discrimination on the Basis of Pregnancy Under the Constitution. *Geduldig v. Aiello* was entirely a constitutional case. It did not involve a claim under Title VII and it did not concern any employment practices, even of a public employer like the state of California. Instead, it concerned a general unemployment insurance program applicable to every employer and employee in the state. State law excluded normal pregnancy as a covered disability and employers themselves played no role in determining the coverage, benefits, or funding of the program. The Supreme Court therefore treated the program as social welfare legislation subject only to constitutional review for a rational basis in serving some legitimate state interest. This lenient standard was easily met by the need to assure that the program was adequately funded from a minimal tax on employees' compensation.

So much of the Court's reasoning cannot be doubted, but the Court's decision presupposes that no stricter standard of constitutional review should have been applied. At the time, the constitutional standard for sex-based classifications remained in doubt. It was not yet clear that the appropriate standard was an intermediate form of scrutiny, stronger than rational basis review but not the strict scrutiny applied to classifications on the basis of race. Instead of addressing this issue, the Court avoided it entirely by holding that classifications on the basis of pregnancy are not classifications on the basis of sex. The reasoning supporting this conclusion, found in footnote 20, distinguishes pregnancy from sex on the ground that some women are not or do not become pregnant. These women can be classified with men, as "nonpregnant persons" who received the full benefit of the unemployment insurance program. Only pregnant women were excluded from the program and only for disability resulting from normal pregnancy.

Must a classification work to the disadvantage of all women in order to discriminate on the basis of sex? Consider an explicit exclusion of all women from the California program. It would have imposed a disadvantage only on working women, but would that have made it legitimate? Is it necessary for a sex-based classification to achieve universal discrimination in order to be discriminatory at all?

Before *Geduldig*, the Court had previously held that a public employer could not force their female employees to take leaves of absence during the later stages of pregnancy, finding such a requirement to be an unconstitutional irrebuttable presumption that pregnancy made women incapable of working. Cleveland Bd. of Educ. v. LaFleur, 414 U.S. 632 (1974). The exclusion of pregnancy benefits in *Geduldig* had the opposite effect, discouraging women from taking leave during pregnancy. The risk emphasized by the employer in *LaFleur* was that pregnant women would be unable to work. The risk in *Geduldig* was that they would take a job only in order to obtain disability leave. In any event, the line of cases imposing heightened scrutiny on irrebuttable presumptions soon came to an end. Weinberger v. Salfi, 422 U.S. 749, 767–85 (1975). But does this line of cases reveal a problem with any presumption that pregnancy must be treated differently from other physical conditions? In particular, does it presume that women are likely to seek employment solely in order to obtain benefits for pregnancy? Supposing that they do, how is this different from men seeking employment in order to obtain medical insurance coverage? For additional discussion on *LaFleur*, see Deborah Dinner, Recovering the LaFleur Doctrine, 22 Yale J.L. & Feminism 343 (2010).

2. **Intentional Discrimination Under the Constitution.** Under the current standard, sex-based classifications must have an "exceedingly persuasive" justification in order to be held constitutional. United States v. Virginia, 518 U.S. 515, 531 (1996). This standard appears to be somewhat stricter than the previously formulated standard: that such classifications "must serve important governmental objectives and must be substantially related to achievement of those objectives." E.g., Craig v. Boren, 429 U.S. 190, 197 (1976). Regardless of exactly what these standards require, they apply only to government action and only to intentional discrimination. In this respect, the heightened scrutiny of sex-based classifications under the Constitution is no different from that of race-based classifications. Both are based on the Fifth and Fourteenth Amendments, which apply only to the federal government and the states, and both are subject to the requirement, previously discussed in Washington v. Davis, 426 U.S. 229 (1976), that the plaintiff prove disparate treatment, not just disparate impact. Heightened scrutiny of sex-based classifications, just as with race-based classifications, presupposes a prior finding that the government has, in fact, taken account of sex.

Although the Supreme Court has been willing to extend heightened scrutiny to government actions explicitly based on sex, it has been reluctant to find that seemingly neutral actions were actually based on sex. The leading case on this issue is Personnel Administrator v. Feeney, 442 U.S. 256 (1979), involving a claim of sex discrimination in awarding a preference in state employment to veterans who served during wartime. The overwhelming majority of such veterans, over 98 percent, were men. Yet the Supreme Court found no intentional discrimination on the basis of sex, reasoning that the preference left a large number of men, who did not have the requisite veteran status, at the same competitive disadvantage as women in obtaining state employment. The Court distinguished between wartime veterans, almost all of whom were men, and nonveterans, composed of all other men and almost all women. Is this distinction any better than the distinction in *Geduldig* between pregnant women and nonpregnant persons? Is there a difference between counting who benefits from a government classification and who is burdened by it? Only the latter have an incentive to object to a government program through the political process. In *Feeney*, this group was composed of both men and women, while in *Geduldig*, it was only women. Does that distinguish these cases? Or is *Geduldig* less justifiable simply because the exclusion in that case was based on sex? By definition, excluding pregnancy from coverage meant that no men were excluded on this ground. By contrast, providing benefits to wartime veterans in *Feeney* meant that many men were excluded from the program and that some women were included in it.

Another ground for distinguishing the cases has to do with veterans' preferences themselves. The plaintiffs could not bring a Title VII claim in *Feeney* because veterans' preferences are explicitly exempted from the coverage of Title VII by § 712. This provision, in turn, reflects the historical exclusion of women from the armed forces or, in more recent years, the limited roles that they have been assigned. These limitations have gradually eased, although the Supreme Court has upheld a restriction on draft registration to men based on the assumption that only men could fill combat positions, Rostker v. Goldberg, 448 U.S. 1306 (1980). That assumption, however, has largely broken down as women have gradually assumed a greater role in the military.

3. **Discrimination on the Basis of Pregnancy Under Title VII.** Despite its basis solely on the Constitution, *Geduldig* exerted an almost immediate influence on decisions under Title VII. The Supreme Court first extended the reasoning and the result in *Geduldig* to the exclusion of pregnancy from a disability plan established by a private employer. Although the employer was not subject to the constitutional prohibition against discrimination, because it did not engage in state action, it was subject to Title VII. The Court nevertheless held that the prohibition against sex discrimination in Title VII should be interpreted in the same way as the constitutional prohibition. General Electric Co. v. Gilbert, 429 U.S. 125 (1976). This holding was later extended to sick leave plans, although with qualifications relating to the disparate impact of penalizing women for taking leave related to pregnancy. Nashville Gas Co. v. Satty, 434 U.S. 136, 143–46 (1977).

Whatever the ultimate scope of these decisions, they were soon superseded by the Pregnancy Discrimination Act, now codified as § 701(k) of Title VII, which rejected any application to Title VII of the reasoning or result in *Geduldig*. Section 701(k) first defined "because of sex" or "on the basis of sex" to include "because of or on the basis of pregnancy, childbirth, or related medical conditions." It then went on to require that pregnant women be "treated the same for all employment-related purposes" as others "similar in their ability or inability to work" and by specifically applying this requirement to "receipt of benefits under fringe benefit programs." The only exception to these provisions was for benefits related to abortion, which employers are required to provide only if the woman's life would be endangered if she carried the pregnancy to term. The implications of the Pregnancy Discrimination Act and, in particular, its rejection of decisions previously interpreting Title VII, are taken up in the following case.

4. **Bibliography.** *Geduldig* presupposes that discrimination on the basis of sex is unconstitutional. For articles on the general nature of the constitutional prohibition against sex discrimination, see Mary Anne Case, Reflections on Constitutionalizing Women's Equality, 90 Cal. L. Rev. 765 (2002); Ruth Bader Ginsburg, Sexual Equality Under the Fourteenth and Equal Rights Amendments, 1979 Wash. U. L.Q. 161; Herma Hill Kay, Models of Equality, 1985 U. Ill. L. Rev. 39; Kathleen M. Sullivan,

Constitutionalizing Women's Equality, 90 Cal. L. Rev. 735 (2002); Symposium, Rawls and the Law, 72 Fordham L. Rev. 1381 (2004).

For an examination of the specific issue of discrimination on the basis of pregnancy, see Deborah Dinner, Strange Bedfellows at Work: Neomaternalism in the Making of Sex Discrimination Law, 91 Wash. U. L. Rev. 453 (2014); Lucinda M. Finley, Transcending Equality Theory: A Way Out of the Maternity and the Workplace Debate, 86 Colum. L. Rev. 1118 (1986); Herma Hill Kay, Equality and Difference: The Case of Pregnancy, 1 Berkeley Women's L.J. 1 (1985); Wendy W. Williams, Equality's Riddle: Pregnancy and the Equal Treatment/Special Treatment Debate, 13 N.Y.U. Rev. L. & Soc. Change 325 (1984–1985).

In addition, a large literature continues to develop on the relationship of childbearing, family responsibilities, and work. Rachel S. Arnow-Richman, Public Law and Private Process: Toward an Incentivized Organizational Justice Model of Equal Employment Quality for Caregivers, 2007 Utah L. Rev. 25; Laura T. Kessler, Keeping Discrimination Theory Front and Center in the Discourse Over Work and Family Conflict, 34 Pepp. L. Rev. 313 (2007); Reva B. Siegel, You've Come a Long Way Baby: Rehnquist's New Approach to Pregnancy Discrimination in *Hibbs*, 58 Stan. L. Rev. 1871 (2006); Joan C. Williams & Stephanie Bornstein, Caregivers in the Courtroom: The Growing Trend of Family Responsibilities Discrimination, 41 U.S.F. L. Rev. 171 (2006).

Newport News Shipbuilding & Dry Dock Co. v. EEOC

462 U.S. 669 (1983).

■ JUSTICE STEVENS delivered the opinion of the Court.

In 1978 Congress decided to overrule our decision in General Electric Co. v. Gilbert, 429 U.S. 125 (1976), by amending Title VII of the Civil Rights Act of 1964 "to prohibit sex discrimination on the basis of pregnancy." On the effective date of the act, petitioner amended its health insurance plan to provide its female employees with hospitalization benefits for pregnancy-related conditions to the same extent as for other medical conditions. The plan continued, however, to provide less favorable pregnancy benefits for spouses of male employees. The question presented is whether the amended plan complies with the amended statute.

Petitioner's plan provides hospitalization and medical-surgical coverage for a defined category of employees and a defined category of dependents. Dependents covered by the plan include employees' spouses, unmarried children between 14 days and 19 years of age, and some older dependent children. Prior to April 29, 1979, the scope of the plan's coverage for eligible dependents was identical to its coverage for employees. All covered males, whether employees or dependents, were treated alike for purposes of hospitalization coverage. All covered females, whether employees or dependents, also were treated alike.

Moreover, with one relevant exception, the coverage for males and females was identical. The exception was a limitation on hospital coverage for pregnancy that did not apply to any other hospital confinement.

After the plan was amended in 1979, it provided the same hospitalization coverage for male and female employees themselves for all medical conditions, but it differentiated between female employees and spouses of male employees in its provision of pregnancy-related benefits. In a booklet describing the plan, petitioner explained the amendment that gave rise to this litigation in this way:

> "B. Effective April 29, 1979, maternity benefits for female employees will be paid the same as any other hospital confinement as described in question 16. This applies only to deliveries beginning on April 29, 1979 and thereafter.
>
> "C. Maternity benefits for the wife of a male employee will continue to be paid as described in part 'A' of this question."

In turn, Part A stated, "The Basic Plan pays up to $500 of the hospital charges and 100% of reasonable and customary for delivery and anesthesiologist charges." As the Court of Appeals observed, "To the extent that the hospital charges in connection with an uncomplicated delivery may exceed $500, therefore, a male employee receives less complete coverage of spousal disabilities than does a female employee."

After the passage of the Pregnancy Discrimination Act, and before the amendment to petitioner's plan became effective, the Equal Opportunity Employment Commission issued "interpretive guidelines" in the form of questions and answers. Two of those questions, numbers 21 and 22, made it clear that the EEOC would consider petitioner's amended plan unlawful. Number 21 read as follows:

> "21. Q. Must an employer provide health insurance coverage for the medical expenses of pregnancy-related conditions of the spouses of male employees? Of the dependents of all employees?
>
> "A. Where an employer provides no coverage for dependents, the employer is not required to institute such coverage. However, if an employer's insurance program covers the medical expenses of spouses of female employees, then it must equally cover the medical expenses of spouses of male employees, including those arising from pregnancy-related conditions.
>
> "But the insurance does not have to cover the pregnancy-related conditions of non-spouse dependents as long as it excludes the pregnancy-related conditions of such non-spouse dependents of male and female employees equally." 44 Fed. Reg. 23807 (Apr. 20, 1979).

On September 20, 1979, one of petitioner's male employees filed a charge with the EEOC alleging that petitioner had unlawfully refused to provide full insurance coverage for his wife's hospitalization caused by pregnancy; a month later the United Steelworkers filed a similar charge on behalf of other individuals. Petitioner then commenced an action in the United States District Court for the Eastern District of Virginia, challenging the Commission's guidelines and seeking both declaratory and injunctive relief. The complaint named the EEOC, the male employee, and the United Steelworkers of America as defendants. Later the EEOC filed a civil action against petitioner alleging discrimination on the basis of sex against male employees in the company's provision of hospitalization benefits. Concluding that the benefits of the new Act extended only to female employees, and not to spouses of male employees, the District Court held that petitioner's plan was lawful and enjoined enforcement of the EEOC guidelines relating to pregnancy benefits for employees' spouses. It also dismissed the EEOC's complaint. The two cases were consolidated on appeal.

A divided panel of the United States Court of Appeals for the Fourth Circuit reversed, reasoning that since "the company's health insurance plan contains a distinction based on pregnancy that results in less complete medical coverage for male employees with spouses than for female employees with spouses, it is impermissible under the statute." After rehearing the case en banc, the court reaffirmed the conclusion of the panel over the dissent of three judges who believed the statute was intended to protect female employees "in their ability or inability to work," and not to protect spouses of male employees. Because the important question presented by the case had been decided differently by the United States Court of Appeals for the Ninth Circuit, EEOC v. Lockheed Missiles and Space Co., 680 F.2d 1243 (9th Cir. 1982), we granted certiorari.

Ultimately the question we must decide is whether petitioner has discriminated against its male employees with respect to their compensation, terms, conditions, or privileges of employment because of *their* sex within the meaning of § 703(a)(1) of Title VII. Although the Pregnancy Discrimination Act has clarified the meaning of certain terms in this section, neither that Act nor the underlying statute contains a definition of the word "discriminate." In order to decide whether petitioner's plan discriminates against male employees because of their sex, we must therefore go beyond the bare statutory language. Accordingly, we shall consider whether Congress, by enacting the Pregnancy Discrimination Act, not only overturned the specific holding in *General Electric v. Gilbert*, supra, but also rejected the test of discrimination employed by the Court in that case. We believe it did. Under the proper test petitioner's plan is unlawful, because the protection it affords to married male employees is less comprehensive than the protection it affords to married female employees.

I

At issue in *General Electric v. Gilbert* was the legality of a disability plan that provided the company's employees with weekly compensation during periods of disability resulting from nonoccupational causes. Because the plan excluded disabilities arising from pregnancy, the District Court and the Court of Appeals concluded that it discriminated against female employees because of their sex. This Court reversed.

After noting that Title VII does not define the term "discrimination," the Court applied an analysis derived from cases construing the Equal Protection Clause of the Fourteenth Amendment to the Constitution. The *Gilbert* opinion quoted at length from a footnote in Geduldig v. Aiello, 417 U.S. 484 (1974), a case which had upheld the constitutionality of excluding pregnancy coverage under California's disability insurance plan. "Since it is a finding of sex-based discrimination that must trigger, in a case such as this, the finding of an unlawful employment practice under § 703(a)(1)," the Court added, "*Geduldig* is precisely in point in its holding that an exclusion of pregnancy from a disability-benefits plan providing general coverage is not a gender-based discrimination at all.". . . .

When Congress amended Title VII in 1978, it unambiguously expressed its disapproval of both the holding and the reasoning of the Court in the *Gilbert* decision. It incorporated a new subsection in the "definitions" applicable "[f]or the purposes of this subchapter." 42 U.S.C. § 2000e–2. The first clause of the Act states, quite simply: "The terms 'because of sex' or 'on the basis of sex' include, but are not limited to, because of or on the basis of pregnancy, childbirth, or related medical conditions." § 2000e–(k). The House Report stated, "It is the Committee's view that the dissenting Justices correctly interpreted the Act." Similarly, the Senate Report quoted passages from the two dissenting opinions, stating that they "correctly express both the principle and the meaning of title VII." Proponents of the bill repeatedly emphasized that the Supreme Court had erroneously interpreted Congressional intent and that amending legislation was necessary to reestablish the principles of Title VII law as they had been understood prior to the *Gilbert* decision. Many of them expressly agreed with the views of the dissenting Justices.

As petitioner argues, congressional discussion focused on the needs of female members of the work force rather than spouses of male employees. This does not create a "negative inference" limiting the scope of the Act to the specific problem that motivated its enactment. See United States v. Turkette, 452 U.S. 576, 591 (1981). Cf. McDonald v. Santa Fe Trail Transp. Co., 427 U.S. 273, 285–296 (1976). Congress apparently assumed that existing plans that included benefits for dependents typically provided no less pregnancy-related coverage for the wives of male employees than they did for female employees. When the question of differential coverage for dependents was addressed in the Senate Report, the Committee indicated that it should be resolved "on the basis of existing title VII principles."[20] The legislative context makes it clear that Congress was not thereby referring to the view of Title VII reflected in this Court's *Gilbert* opinion. Proponents of the legislation stressed throughout the debates that Congress had always intended to protect *all* individuals from sex discrimination in employment—including but not limited to pregnant women workers. Against this background we review the terms of the amended statute to decide whether petitioner has unlawfully discriminated against its male employees.

II

Section 703(a) makes it an unlawful employment practice for an employer to "discriminate against any individual with respect to his compensation, terms, conditions, or privileges of employment, because of such individual's race, color, religion, sex, or national origin. . . ." 42 U.S.C. § 2000e–2(a) (1976). Health insurance and other fringe benefits are "compensation, terms, conditions, or privileges of employment." Male as well as female employees are protected against discrimination. Thus, if a private employer were to provide complete health insurance coverage for the dependents of its female employees, and no coverage at all for the dependents of its male employees, it would violate Title VII. Such a practice would not pass the simple test of Title VII discrimination that we enunciated in Los Angeles, Department of Water & Power v. Manhart, 435 U.S. 702, 711 (1978), for it would treat a male employee with dependents "in a manner which but for that person's sex would be different." The same result would be reached even if the magnitude of the

---

[20] "Questions were raised in the committee's deliberations regarding how this bill would affect medical coverage for dependents of employees, as opposed to employees themselves. In this context it must be remembered that the basic purpose of this bill is to protect women employees, it does not alter the basic principles of title VII law as regards sex discrimination. Rather, this legislation clarifies the definition of sex discrimination for title VII purposes. Therefore the question in regard to dependents' benefits would be determined on the basis of existing title VII principles." Leg. Hist. at 42–43; S. Rep. No. 95–331, p. 6 (1977).

This statement does not imply that the new statutory definition has no applicability; it merely acknowledges that the new definition does not itself resolve the question.

The dissent quotes extensive excerpts from an exchange on the Senate floor between Senators Hatch and Williams. Taken in context, this colloquy clearly deals only with the second clause of the bill, and Senator Williams, the principal sponsor of the legislation, addressed only the bill's effect on income maintenance plans. Leg. Hist. at 80. Senator Williams first stated, in response to Senator Hatch, "With regard to more maintenance plans for pregnancy-related disabilities, I do not see how this language could be misunderstood." Upon further inquiry from Senator Hatch, he replied, "If there is any ambiguity, with regard to income maintenance plans, I cannot see it." At the end of the same response, he stated, "It is narrowly drawn and would not give any employee the right to obtain income maintenance as a result of the pregnancy of someone who is not an employee." These comments, which clearly limited the scope of Senator Williams' responses, are omitted from the dissent's lengthy quotation.

Other omitted portions of the colloquy make clear that it was logical to discuss the pregnancies of employees' spouses in connection with income maintenance plans. Senator Hatch asked, "what about the status of a woman coworker who is not pregnant but rides with a pregnant woman and cannot get to work once the pregnant female commences her maternity leave or the employed mother who stays home to nurse her pregnant daughter?" The reference to spouses of male employees must be understood in light of these hypothetical questions; it seems to address the situation in which a male employee wishes to take time off from work because his wife is pregnant.

discrimination were smaller. For example, a plan that provided complete hospitalization coverage for the spouses of female employees but did not cover spouses of male employees when they had broken bones would violate Title VII by discriminating against male employees.

Petitioner's practice is just as unlawful. Its plan provides limited pregnancy-related benefits for employees' wives, and affords more extensive coverage for employees' spouses for all other medical conditions requiring hospitalization. Thus the husbands of female employees receive a specified level of hospitalization coverage for all conditions; the wives of male employees receive such coverage except for pregnancy-related conditions. Although *Gilbert* concluded that an otherwise inclusive plan that singled out pregnancy-related benefits for exclusion was nondiscriminatory on its face, because only women can become pregnant, Congress has unequivocally rejected that reasoning. The 1978 Act makes clear that it is discriminatory to treat pregnancy-related conditions less favorably than other medical conditions. Thus petitioner's plan unlawfully gives married male employees a benefit package for their dependents that is less inclusive than the dependency coverage provided to married female employees.

There is no merit to petitioner's argument that the prohibitions of Title VII do not extend to discrimination against pregnant spouses because the statute applies only to discrimination in employment. A two-step analysis demonstrates the fallacy in this contention. The Pregnancy Discrimination Act has now made clear that, for all Title VII purposes, discrimination based on a woman's pregnancy is, on its face, discrimination because of her sex. And since the sex of the spouse is always the opposite of the sex of the employee, it follows inexorably that discrimination against female spouses in the provision of fringe benefits is also discrimination against male employees. Cf. Wengler v. Druggists Mutual Ins. Co., 446 U.S. 142, 147 (1980). By making clear that an employer could not discriminate on the basis of an employee's pregnancy, Congress did not erase the original prohibition against discrimination on the basis of an employee's sex.

In short, Congress' rejection of the premises of *General Electric v. Gilbert* forecloses any claim that an insurance program excluding pregnancy coverage for female beneficiaries and providing complete coverage to similarly situated male beneficiaries does not discriminate on the basis of sex. Petitioner's plan is the mirror image of the plan at issue in *Gilbert*. The limitation in this case violates Title VII by discriminating against male employees.[26]

---

[26] Because the 1978 Act expressly states that exclusion of pregnancy coverage is gender-based discrimination on its face, it eliminates any need to consider the average monetary value of the plan's coverage to male and female employees. Cf. *Gilbert*, 429 U.S., at 137–140.

The cost of providing complete health insurance coverage for the dependents of male employees, including pregnant wives, might exceed the cost of providing such coverage for the dependents of female employees. But although that type of cost differential may properly be analyzed in passing on the constitutionality of a State's health insurance plan, see *Geduldig v.*

The judgment of the Court of Appeals is affirmed.

■ JUSTICE REHNQUIST, with whom JUSTICE POWELL joins, dissenting.

In General Electric Co. v. Gilbert, 429 U.S. 125 (1976), we held that an exclusion of pregnancy from a disability-benefits plan is not discrimination "because of [an] individual's . . . sex" within the meaning of Title VII of the Civil Rights Act of 1964, § 703(a)(1), 78 Stat. 255, 42 U.S.C. § 2000e–2(a)(1). In our view, therefore, Title VII was not violated by an employer's disability plan that provided all employees with non-occupational sickness and accident benefits, but excluded from the plan's coverage disabilities arising from pregnancy. Under our decision in *Gilbert*, petitioner's otherwise inclusive benefits plan that excludes pregnancy benefits for a male employee's spouse clearly would not violate Title VII. For a different result to obtain, *Gilbert* would have to be judicially overruled by this Court or Congress would have to legislatively overrule our decision in its entirety by amending Title VII.

Today, the Court purports to find the latter by relying on the Pregnancy Discrimination Act of 1978, Pub. L. 95–555, 92 Stat. 2076, 42 U.S.C. § 2000e(k), a statute that plainly speaks only of female employees affected by pregnancy and says nothing about spouses of male employees. Congress, of course, was free to legislatively overrule *Gilbert* in whole or in part, and there is no question but what the Pregnancy Discrimination Act manifests congressional dissatisfaction with the result we reached in *Gilbert*. But I think the Court reads far more into the Pregnancy Discrimination Act than Congress put there, and that therefore it is the Court, and not Congress, which is now overruling *Gilbert*.

In a case presenting a relatively simple question of statutory construction, the Court pays virtually no attention to the language of the Pregnancy Discrimination Act or the legislative history pertaining to that language. The Act provides in relevant part:

> "The terms 'because of sex' or 'on the basis of sex' include, but are not limited to, because of or on the basis of pregnancy, childbirth, or related medical conditions; and women affected by pregnancy, childbirth, or related medical conditions shall be treated the same for all employment-related purposes, including receipt of benefits under fringe benefit programs, as other persons not so affected but similar in their ability or inability to work. . . ."

The Court recognizes that this provision is merely definitional and that "[u]ltimately the question we must decide is whether petitioner has discriminated against its male employees . . . because of their sex within the meaning of § 703(a)(1)" of Title VII. Section 703(a)(1) provides in part:

Aiello, supra, no such justification is recognized under Title VII once discrimination has been shown. *Manhart*, supra, 435 U.S., at 716–717; 29 CFR § 1604.9(e) (1982) ("It shall not be a defense under Title VII to a charge of sex discrimination in benefits that the cost of such benefits is greater with respect to one sex than the other.")

> "It shall be an unlawful employment practice for an employer . . . to fail or refuse to hire or to discharge any individual, or otherwise to discriminate against any individual with respect to his compensation, terms, conditions, or privileges of employment, because of such individual's race, color, religion, sex, or national origin. . . ."

It is undisputed that in § 703(a)(1) the word "individual" refers to an employee or applicant for employment. As modified by the first clause of the definitional provision of the Pregnancy Discrimination Act, the proscription in § 703(a)(1) is for discrimination "against any individual . . . *because of such individual's* . . . *pregnancy*, childbirth, or related medical conditions." This can only be read as referring to the pregnancy of an *employee*.

That this result was not inadvertent on the part of Congress is made very evident by the second clause of the Act, language that the Court essentially ignores in its opinion. When Congress in this clause further explained the proscription it was creating by saying that "women affected by pregnancy . . . shall be treated the same . . . as other persons not so affected but *similar in their ability or inability to work*" it could only have been referring to *female employees*. The Court of Appeals below stands alone in thinking otherwise.

The Court concedes that this is a correct reading of the second clause. Then in an apparent effort to escape the impact of this provision, the Court asserts that "[t]he meaning of the first clause is not limited by the specific language in the second clause." I do not disagree. But this conclusion does not help the Court, for as explained above, when the definitional provision of the first clause is inserted in § 703(a)(1), it says the very same thing: the proscription added to Title VII applies only to female employees.

The plain language of the Pregnancy Discrimination Act leaves little room for the Court's conclusion that the Act was intended to extend beyond female employees. The Court concedes that "congressional discussion focused on the needs of female members of the work force rather than spouses of male employees." In fact, the singular focus of discussion on the problems of the *pregnant worker* is striking. . . .

Under our decision in *General Electric Co. v. Gilbert*, petitioner's exclusion of pregnancy benefits for male employee's spouses would not violate Title VII. Since nothing in the Pregnancy Discrimination Act even arguably reaches beyond female employees affected by pregnancy, *Gilbert* requires that we reverse the Court of Appeals. Because the Court concludes otherwise, I dissent.

NOTES ON *NEWPORT NEWS SHIPBUILDING & DRY DOCK CO. V. EEOC*

1. **The Formal Interpretation of Sex Discrimination Under Title VII.** *Newport News* presents the paradox of men successfully asserting a claim of discrimination on the basis of pregnancy. Their spouses did not receive the full coverage that the spouses of female employees received. Does the paradox that men can demand equal treatment on a ground typically available only to women reveal a weakness or a strength of the Supreme Court's interpretation of Title VII? On the facts of *Newport News*, do pregnancy benefits for the wives of male employees reinforce support for traditional gender roles in which the wife stays at home and the husband works? Or does this case demonstrate that even members of the dominant group can benefit from prohibitions against discrimination?

The employer apparently excluded pregnancy benefits for the wives of male employees out of concern for costs. As a shipbuilding company, it probably employed far more men than women and granting pregnancy benefits only to female employees was much less costly than extending the full range of such benefits to the wives of male employees. The Supreme Court makes clear that the employer could limit the benefits paid to the spouses of all employees, whether male or female, in order to limit the costs of its medical plan. Is cutting benefits a feasible approach to this problem or would it lead to objections from the employees' union and discontent among the employees themselves? Would cutting benefits have violated the prohibition in the Equal Pay Act against "leveling down" to achieve equal pay? Through the Bennett Amendment, does this prohibition apply to Title VII?

As in *Manhart*, the Court does not rely at all on the cost of extending full benefits for pregnancy to the wives of male employees. Does this simply follow from the fact that Congress has decreed that classifications on the basis of pregnancy are to be treated just like classifications on the basis of sex? Does the holding in *Manhart* then require the employer to justify any such classification on grounds different from or in addition to cost?

2. **The Effect of the Pregnancy Discrimination Act.** The majority takes a deferential approach to the Pregnancy Discrimination Act, refusing to rely on the earlier decisions criticized in the legislative history of the Act and, according to the majority, at least, repudiated by the terms of the Act. The dissent takes a different and narrower approach, reading the Act with the general prohibitions in Title VII to prohibit discrimination based only on the *employee's* pregnancy. As a literal matter of plugging the definitional provisions of § 701(k) into the prohibitions in § 703(a), the dissent has a point, doesn't it? The latter prohibits only discrimination "because of *such individual's*" sex, referring to the individual who is employed or seeks employment.

Are the literal terms of the statute all there is to the differences between the Supreme Court and Congress? Congress's evident disapproval of the Court's earlier decisions does not appear to leave much room for classifications on the basis of pregnancy that cannot be justified under some other exception, such as the BFOQ, under Title VII. Did Congress reject the entire approach taken in the earlier cases or only the narrow results, concerned with fringe benefits that went directly to female employees?

In any event, the reduced medical coverage received by male employees depends upon their sex because only they had wives who received reduced coverage for pregnancy. Does this make the outcome in this case depend upon the availability of marriage only to heterosexual couples? If same-sex marriage had been possible at the time, then some male employees would have had male spouses who did not receive reduced coverage. And, conversely, some female employees would have had female spouses who did receive reduced coverage. Would the existence of same-sex marriage have eliminated the sex-based discrimination against male employees found by the Court in this case? Should the outcome of this case depend upon controversial developments in the law of marriage and gay rights?

3. The Family Medical Leave Act. A consistent theme in the legislative history of the Pregnancy Discrimination Act concerns the difference between the disability of employees and the disability of their dependents. As noted earlier, employers remained free to cover the former without at all covering the latter. They could, in particular, provide paid leave to their employees to recover from their own disabilities, without giving them paid leave to take care of the disabilities (or other needs) of their dependents. These comments were motivated, in part, by the limitations of a prohibition against discrimination. It requires only equality of benefits between male and female employees. It does not require benefits at any particular level. Just as employers could provide no medical benefits for dependents, they could also provide no coverage for their employees. Employers remain free to set the level of benefits wherever they like, so long as they treat all their employees equally.

In this respect, Title VII contrasts dramatically with legislation that requires some minimal level of benefits. At the federal level, the foremost example of such legislation is the Family and Medical Leave Act, 29 U.S.C. §§ 2601–2619 (2000), requiring employers with 50 or more employees to provide up to 12 weeks of unpaid leave per year to employees to care for immediate family members. Even a requirement of unpaid leave can impose costs on employers that cannot be minimized below a certain level. The comments in the debates over the Pregnancy Discrimination Act express concern over the greater costs of paid leave to care for family members. Such leave would be available in a far wider range of situations and at far greater cost to employers than leave granted to employees only to take care of their own disabilities.

But just as the cost of such leave is greater for employers, the benefit it confers on employees is larger too. This benefit, it is widely assumed, would be particularly valuable for female employees, who traditionally have been primarily responsible for caring for children and other family members. Paid leave would allow them to fulfill their family responsibilities without sacrificing their careers. Arguments along these lines have led to the passage of legislation in some states, notably California, requiring employers above a certain size to provide paid leave at a proportion of the employee's full compensation. Cal. Gov't Code §§ 12945.1, 12945.2, 19702.3 (Supp. 2003).

An earlier version of the California legislation, requiring employers to grant unpaid leave to pregnant employees, was upheld by the Supreme Court in California Federal Savings & Loan Ass'n v. Guerra, 479 U.S. 272 (1987). The Court reasoned that this law was not preempted by the Pregnancy Discrimination Act because it served the same basic purpose of increasing the employment opportunities of women, and although it required leave to be made available only to pregnant employees, it did not prevent employers from extending similar benefits to all employees. The law was therefore consistent with Title VII. (It was not challenged under the Equal Protection Clause apparently because, under *Geduldig*, classifications on the basis of pregnancy do not constitute discrimination on the basis of sex.)

The decision in *California Federal* illustrates both the advantages and the disadvantages of the formal approach to interpreting the prohibition against sex discrimination. The advantage lies in the limited demands that this approach makes, in this case, on states that seek to promote sexual equality by other means. More generally, the formal interpretation of Title VII places limited demands on courts, which can simply examine an employer's practices to determine if they take account of sex, and on employers themselves, who remain free to adopt a wide range of neutral employment practices. The disadvantages arise from the failure of the formal approach to take account of the effects of employment practices, either the costs to employers or the benefits to employees. See, for example, evidence that paid maternal leave discourages employers from hiring female workers of child-bearing age. Natasha Sarin, The Impact of Paid Leave on Female Employment Outcomes (November 29, 2016) at https://papers.ssrn.com/sol3/papers.cfm?abstract_id=2877015; Nikolay Angelov, Per Johansson & Erica Lindahl, Is the Persistent Gender Gap in Income and Wages Due to Unequal Family Responsibilities?, 34 J. Lab. Econ. 545 (2016); The narrow focus on formal differences in Title VII simplifies judicial decisions, as in *Manhart* and *Newport News*, but it neglects the wider economic and social context in which claims of sex discrimination arise. These are reflected in laws like the Family and Medical Leave Act and in the exceptions to the prohibition against sex discrimination in Title VII, foremost among them the bona fide occupational qualification on the basis of sex.

4. **Bibliography.** For articles on the Family and Medical Leave Act, see Stephanie Bornstein, The Law of Gender Stereotyping and the Work-Family Conflicts of Men, 63 Hastings L.J. 1297 (2012); Stephanie Bornstein, Work, Family, and Discrimination at the Bottom of the Ladder, 19 Geo. J. on Poverty L. & Pol'y 1 (2012); Rona K. Kitchen, Missing the Mark: How FMLA's Bonding Leave Fails Mothers, 31 Hofstra Lab. & Emp. L.J. 303 (2014); Gillian Lester, In Defense of Paid Family Leave, 28 Harv. Women's L.J. 1 (2005); Michael Selmi, Family Leave and the Gender Wage Gap, 78 N.C. L. Rev. 707 (2000); Nicole Buonocore Porter, Finding a Fix for the FMLA: A New Perspective, a New Solution, 31 Hofstra Lab. & Emp. L.J. 327 (2014); Symposium, The Family and Medical Leave Act of 1993: Ten Years of Experience, 15 Wash. U. J.L. & Pol'y 1 (2004); Symposium, Litigating the

Glass Ceiling and the Maternal Wall: Using Stereotyping and Cognitive Bias Evidence to Prove Gender Discrimination, 7 Emp. Rts. & Emp. Pol'y J. 253 (2003).

For articles on the more general issue of the relationship between family responsibilities and work, see Rachel S. Arnow-Richman, Accommodation Subverted: The Future of Work/Family Initiatives in a "Me, Inc." World, 12 Tex. J. Women & L. 345 (2003); Stephanie Bornstein, The Law of Gender Stereotyping and the Work Family Conflicts of Men, 63 Hastings L.J., Vol. 1297 (2012); Stephanie Bornstein, Work, Family, and Discrimination at the Bottom of the Ladder, 19 Geo. J. Pov. L. & Pol'y 1 (2012); Stephanie Bornstein, Joan C. Williams & Genevieve Renard Painter, Discrimination Against Mothers Is the Strongest Form of Workplace Gender Discrimination: Lessons from US Caregiver Discrimination Law, 28 Int'l J. Comp. & Lab. L. & Indus. Rel. 45 (2012); Naomi R. Cahn & Michael L. Selmi, Caretaking and the Contradictions of Contemporary Policy, 55 Me. L. Rev. 289 (2003); Ruth Colker, Pregnancy, Parenting, and Capitalism, 58 Ohio St. L.J. 61 (1997); Keith Cunningham-Parmeter, Men at Work, Fathers at Home: Uncovering the Masculine Face of Caregiver Discrimination, 24 Colum. J. Gender & L. 253 (2013); Martha Albertson Fineman, Fatherhood, Feminism and Family Law, 32 McGeorge L. Rev. 1031 (2001); Joanna L. Grossman & Gillian Thomas, Making Pregnancy Work: Overcoming the Pregnancy Discrimination Act's Capacity-Based Model, 21 Yale J.L. & Feminism 15 (2009); Joanna L. Grossman, Pregnancy, Work, and the Promise of Equal Citizenship, 98 Geo. L.J. 567 (2010); Julie C. Suk, Work-Family Conflict and the Pipeline to Power: Lessons from the European Gender Quotas, 2012 Mich. St. L. Rev. 1797; Joan C. Williams & Nancy Segal, Beyond the Maternal Wall: Relief for Family Caregivers Who are Discriminated Against on the Job, 26 Harv. Women's L.J. 77 (2003); Symposium, Gender, Work & Family Project Inaugural Feminist Legal Theory Lecture, 8 Am. U. J. Gender Soc. Pol'y & L. 1 (2000); Symposium, Still Hostile After All These Years: Gender, Work & Family Revisited, 44 Vill. L. Rev. 297 (1999). See also Rachel S. Arnow-Richman, Incenting Flexibility: The Relationship Between Public Law and Voluntary Action in Enhancing Work/Life Balance, 42 Conn. L. Rev. 1081 (2010).

Young v. United Parcel Service, Inc.

135 S. Ct. 1338 (2015).

■ JUSTICE BREYER delivered the opinion of the Court.

The Pregnancy Discrimination Act makes clear that Title VII's prohibition against sex discrimination applies to discrimination based on pregnancy. It also says that employers must treat "women affected by pregnancy . . . the same for all employment-related purposes . . . as other persons not so affected but similar in their ability or inability to work." 42 U.S.C. § 2000e(k). We must decide how this latter provision applies in the context of an employer's policy that accommodates many, but not all, workers with nonpregnancy-related disabilities.

In our view, the Act requires courts to consider the extent to which an employer's policy treats pregnant workers less favorably than it treats nonpregnant workers similar in their ability or inability to work. And here—as in all cases in which an individual plaintiff seeks to show disparate treatment through indirect evidence—it requires courts to consider any legitimate, nondiscriminatory, nonpretextual justification for these differences in treatment. Ultimately the court must determine whether the nature of the employer's policy and the way in which it burdens pregnant women shows that the employer has engaged in intentional discrimination. *McDonnell Douglas Corp. v. Green*, 411 U.S. 792, 802 (1973). The Court of Appeals here affirmed a grant of summary judgment in favor of the employer. Given our view of the law, we must vacate that court's judgment.

I

A

We begin with a summary of the facts. The petitioner, Peggy Young, worked as a part-time driver for the respondent, United Parcel Service (UPS). Her responsibilities included pickup and delivery of packages that had arrived by air carrier the previous night. In 2006, after suffering several miscarriages, she became pregnant. Her doctor told her that she should not lift more than 20 pounds during the first 20 weeks of her pregnancy or more than 10 pounds thereafter. UPS required drivers like Young to be able to lift parcels weighing up to 70 pounds (and up to 150 pounds with assistance). UPS told Young she could not work while under a lifting restriction. Young consequently stayed home without pay during most of the time she was pregnant and eventually lost her employee medical coverage.

Young subsequently brought this federal lawsuit. We focus here on her claim that UPS acted unlawfully in refusing to accommodate her pregnancy-related lifting restriction. Young said that her co-workers were willing to help her with heavy packages. She also said that UPS accommodated other drivers who were "similar in their . . . inability to work." She accordingly concluded that UPS must accommodate her as well.

UPS responded that the "other persons" whom it had accommodated were (1) drivers who had become disabled on the job, (2) those who had lost their Department of Transportation (DOT) certifications, and (3) those who suffered from a disability covered by the Americans with Disabilities Act of 1990 (ADA). UPS said that, since Young did not fall within any of those categories, it had not discriminated against Young on the basis of pregnancy but had treated her just as it treated all "other" relevant "persons." . . .

C

[In opposition to UPS's motion for summary judgment, Young submitted evidence that UPS accommodated other drivers who could not meet its lifting requirements, in particular, those who were entitled to an accommodation under the ADA, who were "unable to perform their normal work assignments due to an on-the-job injury," or who had lost their certification as truck drivers from the Department of Transportation. She also submitted evidence that her manager determined that she was not qualified for a temporary alternative work assignment. The district court nevertheless granted UPS's motion for summary judgment, concluding that Young could not prove intentional discrimination by either direct or circumstantial evidence. On appeal, the Fourth Circuit affirmed, reasoning that "UPS has crafted a pregnancy-blind policy" that is "at least facially a 'neutral and legitimate business practice,' and not evidence of UPS's discriminatory animus toward pregnant workers."]

D

We note that statutory changes made after the time of Young's pregnancy may limit the future significance of our interpretation of the Act. In 2008, Congress expanded the definition of "disability" under the ADA to make clear that "physical or mental impairment[s] that substantially limi[t]" an individual's ability to lift, stand, or bend are ADA-covered disabilities. ADA Amendments Act of 2008, 122 Stat. 3555, codified at 42 U.S.C. §§ 12102(1)–(2). As interpreted by the EEOC, the new statutory definition requires employers to accommodate employees whose temporary lifting restrictions originate off the job. See 29 CFR pt. 1630, App., § 1630.2(j)(1)(ix). We express no view on these statutory and regulatory changes.

II

The parties disagree about the interpretation of the Pregnancy Discrimination Act's second clause. As we have said, the Act's first clause specifies that discrimination " 'because of sex' " includes discrimination "because of . . . pregnancy." But the meaning of the second clause is less clear; it adds: "[W]omen affected by pregnancy, childbirth, or related medical conditions shall be treated the same for all employment-related purposes . . . as other persons not so affected but similar in their ability or inability to work." 42 U.S.C. § 2000e(k) (emphasis added). Does this clause mean that courts must compare workers only in respect to the work limitations that they suffer? Does it mean that courts must ignore all other similarities or differences between pregnant and nonpregnant workers? Or does it mean that courts, when deciding who the relevant "other persons" are, may consider other similarities and differences as well? If so, which ones?

The differences between these possible interpretations come to the fore when a court, as here, must consider a workplace policy that distinguishes between pregnant and nonpregnant workers in light of characteristics not related to pregnancy. Young poses the problem directly in her reply brief when she says that the Act requires giving "the same accommodations to an employee with a pregnancy-related work limitation as it would give that employee if her work limitation stemmed from a different cause but had a similar effect on her inability to work." Suppose the employer would not give "that [pregnant] employee" the "same accommodations" as another employee, but the employer's reason for the difference in treatment is that the pregnant worker falls within a facially neutral category (for example, individuals with off-the-job injuries). What is a court then to do?

The parties propose very different answers to this question. Young and the United States believe that the second clause of the Pregnancy Discrimination Act "requires an employer to provide the same accommodations to workplace disabilities caused by pregnancy that it provides to workplace disabilities that have other causes but have a similar effect on the ability to work." In other words, Young contends that the second clause means that whenever "an employer accommodates only a subset of workers with disabling conditions," a court should find a Title VII violation if "pregnant workers who are similar in the ability to work" do not "receive the same [accommodation] even if still other non-pregnant workers do not receive accommodations."

UPS takes an almost polar opposite view. It contends that the second clause does no more than define sex discrimination to include pregnancy discrimination. Under this view, courts would compare the accommodations an employer provides to pregnant women with the accommodations it provides to others within a facially neutral category (such as those with off-the-job injuries) to determine whether the employer has violated Title VII.

A

We cannot accept either of these interpretations. Young asks us to interpret the second clause broadly and, in her view, literally. As just noted, she argues that, as long as "an employer accommodates only a subset of workers with disabling conditions," "pregnant workers who are similar in the ability to work [must] receive the same treatment even if still other nonpregnant workers do not receive accommodations." She adds that, because the record here contains "evidence that pregnant and nonpregnant workers were not treated the same," that is the end of the matter, she must win; there is no need to refer to *McDonnell Douglas*.

The problem with Young's approach is that it proves too much. It seems to say that the statute grants pregnant workers a "most-favored-nation" status. As long as an employer provides one or two workers with an accommodation—say, those with particularly hazardous jobs, or those whose workplace presence is particularly needed, or those who have worked at the company for many years, or those who are over the age of 55—then it must provide similar accommodations to all pregnant workers (with comparable physical limitations), irrespective of the nature of their jobs, the employer's need to keep them working, their ages, or any other criteria. . . .

We agree with UPS to this extent: We doubt that Congress intended to grant pregnant workers an unconditional most-favored-nation status. The language of the statute does not require that unqualified reading. The second clause, when referring to nonpregnant persons with similar disabilities, uses the open-ended term "other persons." It does not say that the employer must treat pregnant employees the "same" as "any other persons" (who are similar in their ability or inability to work), nor does it otherwise specify which other persons Congress had in mind.

Moreover, disparate-treatment law normally permits an employer to implement policies that are not intended to harm members of a protected class, even if their implementation sometimes harms those members, as long as the employer has a legitimate, nondiscriminatory, nonpretextual reason for doing so. There is no reason to believe Congress intended its language in the Pregnancy Discrimination Act to embody a significant deviation from this approach. Indeed, the relevant House Report specifies that the Act "reflect[s] no new legislative mandate." H.R. Rep. No. 95–948, pp. 3–4 (1978), 1978 U.S.C.C.A.N. 4749, 4751. And the Senate Report states that the Act was designed to "reestablis[h] the law as it was understood prior to" this Court's decision in *General Electric Co. v. Gilbert*, 429 U.S. 125 (1976). S. Rep. No. 95–331, p. 8 (1978). . . .

C

. . . UPS says that the second clause simply defines sex discrimination to include pregnancy discrimination. But that cannot be so.

The first clause accomplishes that objective when it expressly amends Title VII's definitional provision to make clear that Title VII's words "because of sex" and "on the basis of sex" "include, but are not limited to, because of or on the basis of pregnancy, childbirth, or related medical conditions." 42 U.S.C. § 2000e(k). We have long held that " 'a statute ought, upon the whole, to be so construed that, if it can be prevented, no clause' " is rendered " 'superfluous, void, or insignificant.' " *TRW Inc. v. Andrews*, 534 U.S. 19, 31 (2001) (quoting *Duncan v. Walker*, 533 U.S. 167, 174 (2001)). But that is what UPS' interpretation of the second clause would do.

The dissent, basically accepting UPS' interpretation, says that the second clause is not "superfluous" because it adds "clarity." (internal quotation marks omitted). It makes "plain," the dissent adds, that unlawful discrimination "includes disfavoring pregnant women relative to other workers of similar inability to work." Perhaps we fail to understand. *McDonnell Douglas* itself makes clear that courts normally consider how a plaintiff was treated relative to other "persons of [the plaintiff's] qualifications" (which here include disabilities). 411 U.S., at 802. If the second clause of the Act did not exist, we would still say that an employer who disfavored pregnant women relative to other workers of similar ability or inability to work had engaged in pregnancy discrimination. In a word, there is no need for the "clarification" that the dissent suggests the second sentence provides.

Moreover, the interpretation espoused by UPS and the dissent would fail to carry out an important congressional objective. As we have noted, Congress' "unambiguou[s]" intent in passing the Act was to overturn "both the holding and the reasoning of the Court in the *Gilbert* decision." *Newport News Shipbuilding & Dry Dock Co. v. EEOC*, 462 U.S. 669, 678 (1983); see also post, at 1364 (recognizing that "the object of the Pregnancy Discrimination Act is to displace this Court's conclusion in [*Gilbert*]"). In *Gilbert*, the Court considered a company plan that provided "nonoccupational sickness and accident benefits to all employees" without providing "disability-benefit payments for any absence due to pregnancy." 429 U.S., at 128. The Court held that the plan did not violate Title VII; it did not discriminate on the basis of sex because there was "no risk from which men are protected and women are not." *Id.*, at 138 (internal quotation marks omitted). Although pregnancy is "confined to women," the majority believed it was not "comparable in all other respects to [the] diseases or disabilities" that the plan covered. *Id.*, at 136. Specifically, the majority explained that pregnancy "is not a 'disease' at all," nor is it necessarily a result of accident. *Ibid.* Neither did the majority see the distinction the plan drew as "a subterfuge" or a "pretext" for engaging in gender-based discrimination. *Ibid.* In short, the *Gilbert* majority reasoned in part just as the dissent reasons here. The employer did "not distinguish between pregnant women and others of similar ability or inability because of pregnancy." It distinguished between them on a neutral ground—i.e., it accommodated only sicknesses and accidents, and pregnancy was neither of those. See 429 U.S., at 136.

Simply including pregnancy among Title VII's protected traits (i.e., accepting UPS' interpretation) would not overturn *Gilbert* in full—in particular, it would not respond to *Gilbert's* determination that an employer can treat pregnancy less favorably than diseases or disabilities resulting in a similar inability to work. As we explained in *California Fed. Sav. & Loan Assn. v. Guerra*, 479 U.S. 272 (1987), "the first clause of the [Act] reflects Congress' disapproval of the reasoning in *Gilbert*" by "adding pregnancy to the definition of sex discrimination prohibited by Title VII." *Id.*, at 284. But the second clause was intended to do more than that—it "was intended to overrule the holding in *Gilbert* and to illustrate how discrimination against pregnancy is to be remedied." *Id.*, at 285. The dissent's view, like that of UPS', ignores this precedent.

III

The statute lends itself to an interpretation other than those that the parties advocate and that the dissent sets forth. Our interpretation minimizes the problems we have discussed, responds directly to Gilbert, and is consistent with longstanding interpretations of Title VII.

In our view, an individual pregnant worker who seeks to show disparate treatment through indirect evidence may do so through application of the *McDonnell Douglas* framework. That framework requires a plaintiff to make out a prima facie case of discrimination. But it is "not intended to be an inflexible rule." *Furnco Constr. Corp. v. Waters*, 438 U.S. 567, 575 (1978). Rather, an individual plaintiff may establish a prima facie case by "showing actions taken by the employer from which one can infer, if such actions remain unexplained, that it is more likely than not that such actions were based on a discriminatory criterion illegal under" Title VII. *Id.*, at 576, (internal quotation marks omitted). The burden of making this showing is "not onerous." *Texas Dep't of Community Affairs v. Burdine*, 450 U.S. 248, 253 (1981). In particular, making this showing is not as burdensome as succeeding on "an ultimate finding of fact as to" a discriminatory employment action. *Furnco*, supra, at 576. Neither does it require the plaintiff to show that those whom the employer favored and those whom the employer disfavored were similar in all but the protected ways.

Thus, a plaintiff alleging that the denial of an accommodation constituted disparate treatment under the Pregnancy Discrimination Act's second clause may make out a prima facie case by showing, as in *McDonnell Douglas*, that she belongs to the protected class, that she sought accommodation, that the employer did not accommodate her, and that the employer did accommodate others "similar in their ability or inability to work."

The employer may then seek to justify its refusal to accommodate the plaintiff by relying on "legitimate, nondiscriminatory" reasons for denying her accommodation. 411 U.S., at 802. But, consistent with the Act's basic objective, that reason normally cannot consist simply of a claim that it is more expensive or less convenient to add pregnant women to the category of those ("similar in their ability or inability to work") whom the employer accommodates. After all, the employer in *Gilbert* could in all likelihood have made just such a claim.

If the employer offers an apparently "legitimate, nondiscriminatory" reason for its actions, the plaintiff may in turn show that the employer's proffered reasons are in fact pretextual. We believe that the plaintiff may reach a jury on this issue by providing sufficient evidence that the employer's policies impose a significant burden on pregnant workers, and that the employer's "legitimate, nondiscriminatory" reasons are not sufficiently strong to justify the burden, but rather—when considered along with the burden imposed—give rise to an inference of intentional discrimination.

The plaintiff can create a genuine issue of material fact as to whether a significant burden exists by providing evidence that the employer accommodates a large percentage of nonpregnant workers while failing to accommodate a large percentage of pregnant workers. Here, for example, if the facts are as Young says they are, she can show that UPS accommodates most nonpregnant employees with lifting limitations while categorically failing to accommodate pregnant employees with lifting limitations. Young might also add that the fact that UPS has multiple policies that accommodate nonpregnant employees with lifting restrictions suggests that its reasons for failing to accommodate pregnant employees with lifting restrictions are not sufficiently strong—to the point that a jury could find that its reasons for failing to accommodate pregnant employees give rise to an inference of intentional discrimination.

This approach, though limited to the Pregnancy Discrimination Act context, is consistent with our longstanding rule that a plaintiff can use circumstantial proof to rebut an employer's apparently legitimate, nondiscriminatory reasons for treating individuals within a protected class differently than those outside the protected class. See *Burdine*, supra, at 255, n. 10. In particular, it is hardly anomalous (as the dissent makes it out to be) that a plaintiff may rebut an employer's proffered justifications by showing how a policy operates in practice. In *McDonnell Douglas* itself, we noted that an employer's "general policy and practice with respect to minority employment"—including "statistics as to" that policy and practice—could be evidence of pretext. 411 U.S., at 804–805. Moreover, the continued focus on whether the plaintiff has introduced sufficient evidence to give rise to an inference of intentional discrimination avoids confusing the disparate-treatment and disparate-impact doctrines.

Our interpretation of the Act is also, unlike the dissent's, consistent with Congress' intent to overrule *Gilbert's* reasoning and result. The dissent says that "[i]f a pregnant woman is denied an accommodation under a policy that does not discriminate against pregnancy, she has been 'treated the same' as everyone else." This logic would have found no problem with the employer plan in *Gilbert*, which "denied an accommodation" to pregnant women on the same basis as it denied accommodations to other employees—i.e., it accommodated only sicknesses and accidents, and pregnancy was neither of those. In arguing to the contrary, the dissent's discussion of *Gilbert* relies exclusively on the opinions of the dissenting Justices in that case. But Congress' intent in passing the Act was to overrule the *Gilbert* majority opinion, which viewed the employer's disability plan as denying coverage to pregnant employees on a neutral basis.

IV

Under this interpretation of the Act, the judgment of the Fourth Circuit must be vacated. A party is entitled to summary judgment if there is "no genuine dispute as to any material fact and the movant is entitled to judgment as a matter of law." Fed. Rule Civ. Proc. 56(a). We have already outlined the evidence Young introduced. See Part I-C, supra. Viewing the record in the light most favorable to Young, there is a genuine dispute as to whether UPS provided more favorable treatment to at least some employees whose situation cannot reasonably be distinguished from Young's. In other words, Young created a genuine dispute of material fact as to the fourth prong of the *McDonnell Douglas* analysis.

Young also introduced evidence that UPS had three separate accommodation policies (on-the-job, ADA, DOT). Taken together, Young argued, these policies significantly burdened pregnant women. See App. 504 (shop steward's testimony that "the only light duty requested [due to physical] restrictions that became an issue" at UPS "were with women who were pregnant"). The Fourth Circuit did not consider the combined effects of these policies, nor did it consider the strength of UPS' justifications for each when combined. That is, why, when the employer accommodated so many, could it not accommodate pregnant women as well?

We do not determine whether Young created a genuine issue of material fact as to whether UPS' reasons for having treated Young less favorably than it treated these other nonpregnant employees were pretextual. We leave a final determination of that question for the Fourth Circuit to make on remand, in light of the interpretation of the Pregnancy Discrimination Act that we have set out above. . . .

■ JUSTICE ALITO, concurring in the judgment.

As originally enacted, Title VII of the Civil Rights Act of 1964, 42 U.S.C. § 2000e–2(a)(1), made it an unlawful employment practice to discriminate "because of [an] individual's . . . sex" but made no mention of discrimination because of pregnancy. In *General Elec. Co. v. Gilbert*, 429 U.S. 125, 135–140 (1976), this Court held that Title VII did not reach pregnancy discrimination. Congress responded by enacting the Pregnancy Discrimination Act (PDA), which added subsection (k) to a definitional provision, § 2000e. Subsection (k) contains two clauses. The first is straightforward; the second is not. . . .

III

I understand petitioner in this case to assert claims under both the first and second clauses of § 2000e(k). With respect to her claim under the first clause, I agree with the Court that the information in the summary judgment record is sufficient (albeit barely) to take the question to the trier of fact.

I believe that the judgment of the Court of Appeals with respect to petitioner's claim under the second clause must also be vacated. Petitioner sought to be excused during her pregnancy from the lifting requirements that were among her tasks as a driver. Under the policy that United Parcel Service claims to have had in force at the time in question, drivers who were physically unable to perform the tasks required by that position fell into three groups.

First, some drivers were reassigned to less physically demanding positions. Included in this group were (a) those who were unable to work as drivers due to an injury incurred on the job, (b) those drivers who were unable to work as drivers due to a disability as defined by the Americans

With Disabilities Act of 1990 (ADA), and (c) those drivers who, as the result of a medical condition or injury, lost the Department of Transportation (DOT) certification needed to work in that capacity.

The second group of drivers consisted of those who were not pregnant and were denied transfer to a light-duty job. Drivers who were injured off the job fell into this category. The third group was made up of pregnant drivers like petitioner.

It is obvious that respondent had a neutral reason for providing an accommodation when that was required by the ADA. Respondent also had neutral grounds for providing special accommodations for employees who were injured on the job. If these employees had not been permitted to work at all, it appears that they would have been eligible for workers' compensation benefits.

The accommodations that are provided to drivers who lost their DOT certifications, however, are another matter. A driver may lose DOT certification for a variety of reasons, including medical conditions or injuries incurred off the job that impair the driver's ability to operate a motor vehicle. Such drivers may then be transferred to jobs that do not require physical tasks incompatible with their illness or injury. It does not appear that respondent has provided any plausible justification for treating these drivers more favorably than drivers who were pregnant. . . .

For these reasons, it is not at all clear that respondent had any neutral business ground for treating pregnant drivers less favorably than at least some of its nonpregnant drivers who were reassigned to other jobs that they were physically capable of performing. I therefore agree with the Court that the decision of the Court of Appeals with respect to petitioner's claim under the second clause of the PDA must be vacated, and the case must be remanded for further proceedings with respect to that claim.

■ JUSTICE SCALIA, with whom JUSTICE KENNEDY and JUSTICE THOMAS join, dissenting.

Faced with two conceivable readings of the Pregnancy Discrimination Act, the Court chooses neither. It crafts instead a new law that is splendidly unconnected with the text and even the legislative history of the Act. To "treat" pregnant workers "the same . . . as other persons," we are told, means refraining from adopting policies that impose "significant burden[s]" upon pregnant women without "sufficiently strong" justifications. *Ante*, at 1354. Where do the "significant burden" and "sufficiently strong justification" requirements come from? Inventiveness posing as scholarship—which gives us an interpretation that is as dubious in principle as it is senseless in practice.

I

. . . Young and the Court leave behind the part of the law defining pregnancy discrimination as sex discrimination, and turn to the part requiring that "women affected by pregnancy . . . be treated the same . . . as other persons not so affected but similar in their ability or inability to work." § 2000e(k). The most natural way to understand the same-treatment clause is that an employer may not distinguish between pregnant women and others of similar ability or inability because of pregnancy. Here, that means pregnant women are entitled to accommodations on the same terms as other workers with disabling conditions. If a pregnant woman is denied an accommodation under a policy that does not discriminate against pregnancy, she has been "treated the same" as everyone else. UPS's accommodation for drivers who lose their certifications illustrates the point. A pregnant woman who loses her certification gets the benefit, just like any other worker who loses his. And a pregnant woman who keeps her certification does not get the benefit, again just like any other worker who keeps his. That certainly sounds like treating pregnant women and others the same.

There is, however, another way to understand "treated the same," at least looking at that phrase on its own. One could read it to mean that an employer may not distinguish at all between pregnant women and others of similar ability. Here, that would mean pregnant women are entitled, not to accommodations on the same terms as others, but to the same accommodations as others, no matter the differences (other than pregnancy) between them. UPS's accommodation for decertified drivers illustrates this usage too. There is a sense in which a pregnant woman denied an accommodation (because she kept her certification) has not been treated the same as an injured man granted an accommodation (because he lost his certification). He got the accommodation and she did not.

Of these two readings, only the first makes sense in the context of Title VII. The point of Title VII's bans on discrimination is to prohibit employers from treating one worker differently from another because of a protected trait. It is not to prohibit employers from treating workers differently for reasons that have nothing to do with protected traits. See *Texas Dept. of Community Affairs v. Burdine*, 450 U.S. 248, 259 (1981). Against that backdrop, a requirement that pregnant women and other workers be treated the same is sensibly read to forbid distinctions that discriminate against pregnancy, not all distinctions whatsoever.

Prohibiting employers from making any distinctions between pregnant workers and others of similar ability would elevate pregnant workers to most favored employees. If Boeing offered chauffeurs to injured directors, it would have to offer chauffeurs to pregnant mechanics. And if Disney paid pensions to workers who can no longer work because of old age, it would have to pay pensions to workers who can no longer work because of childbirth. It is implausible that Title VII, which elsewhere creates guarantees of equal treatment, here alone creates a guarantee of favored treatment.

Let it not be overlooked, moreover, that the thrust of the Pregnancy Discrimination Act is that pregnancy discrimination is sex discrimination. Instead of creating a freestanding ban on pregnancy discrimination, the Act makes plain that the existing ban on sex discrimination reaches discrimination because of pregnancy. Reading the same-treatment clause to give pregnant women special protection unavailable to other women would clash with this central theme of the Act, because it would mean that pregnancy discrimination differs from sex discrimination after all.

All things considered, then, the right reading of the same-treatment clause prohibits practices that discriminate against pregnant women relative to workers of similar ability or inability. It does not prohibit denying pregnant women accommodations, or any other benefit for that matter, on the basis of an evenhanded policy.

II

The Court agrees that the same-treatment clause is not a most-favored-employee law, but at the same time refuses to adopt the reading I propose—which is the only other reading the clause could conceivably bear. . . .

[The dissenting opinion of JUSTICE KENNEDY is omitted.]

NOTES ON *YOUNG V. UNITED PARCEL SERVICE, INC.*

1. **What Was Decided.** This case might be more notable for the positions that the Court rejected than for the position that it accepted. The Court refused to adopt the positions put forward by both the plaintiff and the defendant. The plaintiff argued for imposing liability upon any employer who treated any of its employees "similar in their ability or inability to work" better than pregnant employees. The defendant argued that it should be relieved of liability whenever it had a neutral reason, unrelated to sex or pregnancy, for treating the two groups of employees differently. The Court instead decided that liability depended upon the structure of shifting burdens of production under *McDonnell Douglas*. According to the Court, the plaintiff can reach the jury on the issue of pretext "by providing sufficient evidence that the employer's policies impose a significant burden on pregnant workers, and that the employer's 'legitimate, nondiscriminatory' reasons are not sufficiently strong to justify the burden, but rather—when considered along with the burden impose—give rise to an inference of intentional discrimination."

Neither of the parties, in the Court's view, offered a persuasive interpretation of the second clause of § 701(k), requiring pregnant workers to be treated "the same for all employment-related purposes . . . as other persons not so affected but similar in their ability or inability to work." The plaintiff tried to transform the open-ended statutory phrase, "other persons," into the more definite phrase, "any person." The former allowed a range of comparisons and a variety of reasons for treating workers differently, while the latter required pregnant workers always to receive to the most favorable treatment accorded to other workers. The Court rejected the requirement that pregnant workers receive such "most favored nation" status. The Court also rejected the defendant's suggestion, adopted by Justice Scalia in dissent, that the second clause of § 701(k) simply clarifies the application of the first clause, which defines "sex discrimination" to include "discrimination because of or on the basis of pregnancy, childbirth, or related medical conditions." On that view, the second clause just makes clear how this general definition applies to disabilities related to pregnancy. That interpretation, according to the Court, failed to give enough independent content to the second clause, which should be interpreted in its view to import some version of an effects test into § 701(k).

2. Reasonable Accommodation Under the Americans with Disabilities Act. Disabilities related to pregnancy could be covered under the Americans with Disabilities Act (ADA), although this case did not raise the issue for two related reasons. First, pregnancy itself is not a disability, at least as the EEOC has interpreted the ADA. It is not a disability because it is not the result of a physiological disorder. 29 C.F.R. § 1630.2(h). On the contrary, infertility is a disability since, under the current terms of the statute, it is a substantial impairment of "reproductive functions." § 3(1), (2)(B). Second, as the Court points out, the ADA was amended after this case arose, expanding the definition of covered disabilities. These now include substantial impairments of "standing, lifting, bending." § 3(1), (2)(A). Hence if this case arose today, the plaintiff could claim coverage on this basis. It would make no difference that the impairments arose from pregnancy. The plaintiff could then a claim a right to reasonable accommodation of those disabilities under the ADA, as elaborated further in Chapter 11.C. of the casebook.

Moreover, the EEOC has substantial rulemaking authority under the ADA and has defined covered disabilities to include temporary impairments of these functions. § 506; 29 C.F.R. § 1630.2(j)(1)(ix). The regulatory authority of the EEOC under the ADA now stands in marked contrast with its limited authority to interpret Title VII. The Court, in fact, refused to defer to the EEOC's interpretation of § 701(k) in *Young*, partly because it departed from previous interpretations and partly because it was offered in support of the plaintiff's position after this litigation had commenced. The effect of its regulations under the ADA would receive far more deference under the standards of *Chevron, U.S.A., Inc. v. Natural Resources Defense Council, Inc.*, 467 U.S. 837 (1984). That difference reinforces the contrast between this case under Title VII and any later case brought under the ADA.

It also casts further doubt on the significance of this decision. If the gravamen of any subsequent claim lies under the ADA, with its explicit duty of reasonable accommodation, then the Court's intricate analysis of intentional discrimination under § 701(k) would seem to make relatively little difference. Does this decision amount to a holding action until the effect of the subsequent amendments to the ADA can be fully appreciated?

3. Treatment of Other Workers. The defendant in this case gave accommodations to three other categories of workers who resembled the plaintiff in their inability to work: those who had a right to accommodations under the ADA; those who had been injured on the job; and those who had been disqualified by the Department of Transportation (DOT) from continuing to work as truck drivers. The Court leaves the effect of all three accommodations to be considered on remand. Justice Alito, in his opinion concurring in the judgment, finds the first two categories of workers not to be comparable to the plaintiff, while the dissent finds all three categories to reveal the defendant's neutral reasons for not accommodating the plaintiff.

The difference between these positions reveals again how narrow the Court's decision is. Everything depends upon the effect of particular accommodations made by the employer to other workers. Accommodations under the ADA perhaps can be discounted, because all employers covered by that statute have to make those accommodations. The same might be true of accommodations for employees injured on the job, as Justice Alito points out, because virtually all such employees could file worker's compensation claims that might be costly for the employer to insure against. That leaves the third category of workers who were disqualified by the DOT, for reasons including injuries and conditions acquired outside of employment. Justice Alito found no apparent justification for accommodating these employees, but not accommodating pregnant workers. He left that question, as did the Court, for consideration on remand.

In that posture, the lower courts would consider whether there was sufficient evidence to get the case past summary judgment, and if similar evidence were presented at trial, to a jury for its consideration. Even if those courts rule for the plaintiff, their decision would not stand for anything more than the sufficiency of the evidence on the record in this case. Is the Court's holding any broader than that? Or is it typical of decisions under the *McDonnell Douglas* structure of proof in which most cases come down to a fact-specific determination whether the employer's offered reason is really just a pretext for discrimination?

4. **Arguments of the Dissent.** From the beginning of his dissent, Justice Scalia castigates the opinion of the Court as essentially unprincipled: "[f]aced with two conceivable readings of the Pregnancy Discrimination Act, the Court chooses neither. It crafts instead a new law that is splendidly unconnected with the text and even the legislative history of the Act." Of course, much as he disapproves of the Court's position, he finds the plaintiff's position equally unacceptable because "[p]rohibiting employers from making any distinctions between pregnant workers and others of similar ability would elevate pregnant workers to most favored employees." Instead of either of these alternatives, he would adopt the defendant's position and allow employers to make any distinction between pregnant workers and other workers that did not take account of either sex or pregnancy.

Is his concern about judicial overreaching justified in light of the Court's extraordinarily narrow holding? The jury, literally, is still out on whether the plaintiff has made a persuasive showing of pretext on the facts of this case. Is there any reason to suppose that juries would show more sympathy for pregnant workers than for the employees accommodated by the defendant under its current policy? Other employers, of course, may take the cautionary lesson from *Young* that they should limit the accommodations that they make to other workers, or alternatively, extend the same accommodations to pregnant workers. Would that be such a bad outcome?

Is Justice Scalia's complaint not with the result of the decision but with the way in which it was reached? Does he regard it as judicial meddling with the text of the Pregnancy Discrimination Act? Yet the second clause of the Act invites precisely the inquiry that the Court undertakes. Is it enough for Justice Scalia to contend that it only performs a clarifying function and that it otherwise repeats the prohibition against discrimination in the first clause of the act? That position leaves him giving a purely formal interpretation to the phrase "other persons not so affected but similar in their ability or inability to work." On his view, an employer could offer neutral reasons that would be entirely permissible for accommodating other workers "similar in their ability or inability to work" but not pregnant workers. Does that interpretation really result in equal treatment regardless of pregnancy?

5. **Bibliography.** Sheerine Alemzadeh, Claiming Disability, Reclaiming Pregnancy: A Critical Analysis of the ADA's Pregnancy Exclusion, 27 Wis. J.L. Gender & Soc'y 1 (2012); Deborah L. Brake. The Shifting Sands of Employment Discrimination: From Unjustified Impact to Disparate Treatment in Pregnancy and Pay, 105 Geo. L.J. 559 (2017); William R. Corbett, *United Parcel Service, Inc.*: *McDonnell Douglas* to the Rescue?, 92 Wash. U. L. Rev. 1683 (2015); Lara Grow, Pregnancy Discrimination in the Wake of *Young v. UPS*,19 U. Pa. J.L. & Soc. Change 133 (2016); Thelma L. Harmon, *Young v. United Parcel Services, Inc.*: The Equal Treatment Fallacy, 20 J. Gender Race & Just. 97 (2017); Michael Harper, Distinguishing Disparate Treatment from Disparate Impact; Confusion on the Court, 96 B.U.L. Rev. 543 (2016); L. Camille Hebert, Disparate Impact and Pregnancy: Title VII's Other Accommodation Requirement, 24 Am. U. J. Gender Soc. Pol'y & L. 107 (2015); Samuel Issacharoff & Elyse Rosenblum, Women and the Workplace: Accommodating the Demands of Pregnancy, 94 Colum. L. Rev. 2154 (1994); Candace Saari Kovacic-Fleischer, Litigating Against Employment Penalties for Pregnancy, Breastfeeding and Childcare, 44 Vill. L. Rev. 355 (1999); Rubeena Sachdev, How to Protect Pregnancy in the Workplace, 50 U.S.F. L. Rev. 333 (2016); Deborah A. Widiss. The Interaction of the Pregnancy Discrimination Act and the Americans with Disabilities Act after *Young v. UPS*, 50 U.C. Davis L. Rev. 1423 (2017); Mary Ziegler, Choice at Work: *Young v. United Parcel Service*, Pregnancy Discrimination, and Reproductive Liberty, 93 Denv. L. Rev. 219 (2015).

F. BONA FIDE OCCUPATIONAL QUALIFICATIONS ON THE BASIS OF SEX

Dothard v. Rawlinson

433 U.S. 321 (1977).

■ JUSTICE STEWART delivered the opinion of the Court.

Appellee Dianne Rawlinson sought employment with the Alabama Board of Corrections as a prison guard, called in Alabama a "correctional counselor." After her application was rejected, she brought this class suit under Title VII of the Civil Rights Act of 1964 and under 42 U.S.C. § 1983, alleging that she had been denied employment because of her sex in violation of federal law. A three-judge Federal District Court for the Middle District of Alabama decided in her favor. We noted probable jurisdiction of this appeal from the District Court's judgment. . . .

III

Unlike the statutory height and weight requirements, Regulation 204 explicitly discriminates against women on the basis of their sex. In defense of this overt discrimination, the appellants rely on § 703(e) of Title VII, 42 U.S.C. § 2000e–2(e), which permits sex-based discrimination "in those certain instances where . . . sex . . . is a bona fide occupational qualification reasonably necessary to the normal operation of that particular business or enterprise."

The District Court rejected the bona-fide-occupational-qualification (BFOQ) defense, relying on the virtually uniform view of the federal courts that § 703(e) provides only the narrowest of exceptions to the general rule requiring equality of employment opportunities. This view has been variously formulated. In Diaz v. Pan American World Airways, 442 F.2d 385, 388, the Court of Appeals for the Fifth Circuit held that "discrimination based on sex is valid only when the *essence* of the business operation would be undermined by not hiring members of one sex exclusively." (Emphasis in original.) In an earlier case, Weeks v. Southern Bell Tel. & Tel. Co., 408 F.2d 228, 235, the same court said that an employer could rely on the BFOQ exception only by proving "that he had reasonable cause to believe, that is, a factual basis for believing, that all or substantially all women would be unable to perform safely and efficiently the duties of the job involved." See also Phillips v. Martin Marietta Corp., 400 U.S. 542. But whatever the verbal formulation, the federal courts have agreed that it is impermissible under Title VII to refuse to hire an individual woman or man on the basis of stereotyped characterizations of the sexes, and the District Court in the present case held in effect that Regulation 204 is based on just such stereotypical assumptions.

We are persuaded—by the restrictive language of § 703(e), the relevant legislative history, and the consistent interpretation of the Equal Employment Opportunity Commission—that the BFOQ exception was in fact meant to be an extremely narrow exception to the general prohibition of discrimination on the basis of sex. In the particular factual circumstances of this case, however, we conclude that the District Court erred in rejecting the State's contention that Regulation 204 falls within the narrow ambit of the BFOQ exception.

The environment in Alabama's penitentiaries is a peculiarly inhospitable one for human beings of whatever sex. Indeed, a Federal District Court has held that the conditions of confinement in the prisons of the State, characterized by "rampant violence" and a "jungle atmosphere," are constitutionally intolerable. Pugh v. Locke, 406 F. Supp. 318, 325 (M.D. Ala.). The record in the present case shows that because of inadequate staff and facilities, no attempt is made in the four maximum-security male penitentiaries to classify or segregate inmates according to their offense or level of dangerousness—a procedure that, according to expert testimony, is essential to effective penological administration. Consequently, the estimated 20% of the male prisoners who are sex offenders are scattered throughout the penitentiaries' dormitory facilities.

In this environment of violence and disorganization, it would be an oversimplification to characterize Regulation 204 as an exercise in "romantic paternalism." Cf. Frontiero v. Richardson, 411 U.S. 677, 684. In the usual case, the argument that a particular job is too dangerous for women may appropriately be met by the rejoinder that it is the purpose of Title VII to allow the individual woman to make that choice for herself. More is at stake in this case, however, than an individual woman's decision to weigh and accept the risks of employment in a "contact" position in a maximum-security male prison.

The essence of a correctional counselor's job is to maintain prison security. A woman's relative ability to maintain order in a male, maximum-security, unclassified penitentiary of the type Alabama now runs could be directly reduced by her womanhood. There is a basis in fact for expecting that sex offenders who have criminally assaulted women in the past would be moved to do so again if access to women were established within the prison. There would also be a real risk that other inmates, deprived of a normal heterosexual environment, would assault women guards because they were women.[22] In a prison system where violence is the order of the day, where inmate access to guards is facilitated by dormitory living arrangements, where every institution is understaffed, and where a substantial portion of the inmate population is composed of sex offenders mixed at random with other prisoners, there are few visible deterrents to inmate assaults on women custodians.

Appellee Rawlinson's own expert testified that dormitory housing for aggressive inmates poses a greater security problem than single-cell lockups, and further testified that it would be unwise to use women as guards in a prison where even 10% of the inmates had been convicted of sex crimes and were not segregated from the other prisoners.[23] The likelihood that inmates would assault a woman because she was a woman would pose a real threat not only to the victim of the assault but

---

[22] The record contains evidence of an attack on a female clerical worker in an Alabama prison, and of an incident involving a woman student who was taken hostage during a visit to one of the maximum-security institutions.

[23] Alabama's penitentiaries are evidently not typical. Appellee Rawlinson's two experts testified that in a normal, relatively stable maximum-security prison—characterized by control over the inmates, reasonable living conditions, and segregation of dangerous offenders—women guards could be used effectively and beneficially. Similarly, an amicus brief filed by the State of California attests to that State's success in using women guards in all-male penitentiaries.

also to the basic control of the penitentiary and protection of its inmates and the other security personnel. The employee's very womanhood would thus directly undermine her capacity to provide the security that is the essence of a correctional counselor's responsibility.

There was substantial testimony from experts on both sides of this litigation that the use of women as guards in "contact" positions under the existing conditions in Alabama maximum-security male penitentiaries would pose a substantial security problem, directly linked to the sex of the prison guard. On the basis of that evidence, we conclude that the District Court was in error in ruling that being male is not a bona fide occupational qualification for the job of correctional counselor in a "contact" position in an Alabama male maximum-security penitentiary.

■ JUSTICE MARSHALL, with whom JUSTICE BRENNAN joins, concurring in part and dissenting in part.

I agree entirely with the Court's analysis of Alabama's height and weight requirements for prison guards, and with its finding that these restrictions discriminate on the basis of sex in violation of Title VII. Accordingly, I join Parts I and II of the Court's opinion. I also agree with much of the Court's general discussion in Part III of the bona-fide-occupational-qualification exception contained in § 703(e) of Title VII. The Court is unquestionably correct when it holds "that the BFOQ exception was in fact meant to be an extremely narrow exception to the general prohibition of discrimination on the basis of sex." I must, however, respectfully disagree with the Court's application of the BFOQ exception in this case.

The Court properly rejects two proffered justifications for denying women jobs as prison guards. It is simply irrelevant here that a guard's occupation is dangerous and that some women might be unable to protect themselves adequately. Those themes permeate the testimony of the state officials below, but as the Court holds, "the argument that a particular job is too dangerous for women" is refuted by the "purpose of Title VII to allow the individual woman to make that choice for herself." Some women, like some men, undoubtedly are not qualified and do not wish to serve as prison guards, but that does not justify the exclusion of all women from this employment opportunity. Thus, "[in] the usual case," the Court's interpretation of the BFOQ exception would mandate hiring qualified women for guard jobs in maximum-security institutions. The highly successful experiences of other States allowing such job opportunities, see briefs for the States of California and Washington as amici curiae, confirm that absolute disqualification of women is not, in the words of Title VII, "reasonably necessary to the normal operation" of a maximum-security prison.

What would otherwise be considered unlawful discrimination against women is justified by the Court, however, on the basis of the "barbaric and inhumane" conditions in Alabama prisons, conditions so bad that state officials have conceded that they violate the Constitution. See Pugh v. Locke, 406 F. Supp. 318, 329, 331 (M.D. Ala. 1976). To me, this analysis sounds distressingly like saying two wrongs make a right. It is refuted by the plain words of § 703(e). The statute requires that a BFOQ be "reasonably necessary to the normal operation of that particular business or enterprise." But no governmental "business" may operate "normally" in violation of the Constitution. Every action of government is constrained by constitutional limitations. While those limits may be violated more frequently than we would wish, no one disputes that the "normal operation" of all government functions takes place within them. A prison system operating in blatant violation of the Eighth Amendment is an exception that should be remedied with all possible speed, as Judge Johnson's comprehensive order in *Pugh v. Locke*, supra, is designed to do. In the meantime, the existence of such violations should not be legitimatized by calling them "normal." Nor should the Court accept them as justifying conduct that would otherwise violate a statute intended to remedy age-old discrimination.

The Court's error in statutory construction is less objectionable, however, than the attitude it displays toward women. Though the Court recognizes that possible harm to women guards is an unacceptable reason for disqualifying women, it relies instead on an equally speculative threat to prison discipline supposedly generated by the sexuality of female guards. There is simply no evidence in the record to show that women guards would create any danger to security in Alabama prisons significantly greater than that which already exists. All of the dangers—with one exception discussed below—are inherent in a prison setting, whatever the gender of the guards.

The Court first sees women guards as a threat to security because "there are few visible deterrents to inmate assaults on women custodians." In fact, any prison guard is constantly subject to the threat of attack by inmates, and "invisible" deterrents are the guard's only real protection. No prison guard relies primarily on his or her ability to ward off an inmate attack to maintain order. Guards are typically unarmed and sheer numbers of inmates could overcome the normal complement. Rather, like all other law enforcement officers, prison guards must rely primarily on the moral authority of their office and the threat of future punishment for miscreants. As one expert testified below, common sense, fairness, and mental and emotional stability are the qualities a guard needs to cope with the dangers of the job. Well qualified and properly trained women, no less than men, have these psychological weapons at their disposal.

The particular severity of discipline problems in the Alabama maximum-security prisons is also no justification for the discrimination sanctioned by the Court. The District Court found in *Pugh v. Locke*, supra, that guards "must spend all their time attempting to maintain control or to protect themselves." If male guards face an impossible situation, it is difficult to see how women could make the problem worse, unless one relies on precisely the type of generalized bias against women that the Court agrees Title VII was intended to outlaw. For example, much of the testimony of appellants' witnesses ignores individual differences among members of each sex and reads like "ancient canards about the proper role of women." Phillips v. Martin Marietta Corp., 400 U.S., at 545. The witnesses claimed that women guards are not strict disciplinarians; that they are physically less capable of protecting themselves and subduing unruly inmates; that inmates take advantage of them as they did their mothers, while male guards are strong father figures who easily maintain discipline, and so on. Yet the record shows that the presence of women guards has not led to a single incident amounting to a serious breach of security in any Alabama institution. And, in any event, "[g]uards rarely enter the cell blocks and dormitories," Pugh v. Locke, 406 F. Supp., at 325, where the danger of inmate attacks is the greatest.

It appears that the real disqualifying factor in the Court's view is "[t]he employee's very womanhood." The Court refers to the large number of sex offenders in Alabama prisons, and to "[the] likelihood that inmates would assault a woman because she was a woman." In short, the fundamental justification for the decision is that women as guards will generate sexual assaults. With all respect, this rationale regrettably perpetuates one of the most insidious of the old myths about women—that women, wittingly or not, are seductive sexual objects. The effect of the decision, made I am sure with the best of intentions, is to punish women because their very presence might provoke sexual assaults. It is women who are made to pay the price in lost job opportunities for the threat of depraved conduct by prison inmates. Once again, "[t]he pedestal upon which women have been placed has . . ., upon closer inspection, been revealed as a cage." Sail'er Inn, Inc. v. Kirby, 485 P.2d 529, 541 (Ca. 1971). It is particularly ironic that the case is erected here in response to feared misbehavior by imprisoned criminals.

The Court points to no evidence in the record to support the asserted "likelihood that inmates would assault a woman because she was a woman." Perhaps the Court relies upon common sense, or "innate recognition." But the danger in this emotionally laden context is that common sense will be used to mask the " 'romantic paternalism' " and persisting discriminatory attitudes that the Court properly eschews. To me, the only matter of innate recognition is that the incidence of sexually motivated attacks on guards will be minute compared to the "likelihood that inmates will assault" a *guard* because he or she is a *guard*.

The proper response to inevitable attacks on both female and male guards is not to limit the employment opportunities of law-abiding women who wish to contribute to their community, but to take swift and sure punitive action against the inmate offenders. Presumably, one of the goals of the Alabama prison system is the eradication of inmates' antisocial behavior patterns so that prisoners will be able to live one day in free society. Sex offenders can begin this process by learning to relate to women guards in a socially acceptable manner. To deprive women of job opportunities because of the threatened behavior of convicted criminals is to turn our social priorities upside down.[5]

Although I do not countenance the sex discrimination condoned by the majority, it is fortunate that the Court's decision is carefully limited to the facts before it. I trust the lower courts will recognize that the decision was impelled by the shockingly inhuman conditions in Alabama prisons, and thus that the "extremely narrow [BFOQ] exception" recognized here will not be allowed "to swallow the rule" against sex discrimination. See Phillips v. Martin Marietta Corp., 400 U.S., at 545. Expansion of today's decision beyond its narrow factual basis would erect a serious roadblock to economic equality for women.

NOTES ON *DOTHARD V. RAWLINSON*

1. **The Exclusion from Contact Positions.** This excerpt from *Dothard v. Rawlinson* concerns only the explicit exclusion of women from contact positions in prisons for men. Since the great majority of prisoners were male, most of the contact positions were in the prisons for men. The practical effect of excluding women from these positions was therefore even more damaging than the height and weight requirements, struck down for their disparate impact upon women (as discussed in Chapter 3). The Supreme Court nevertheless upheld this exclusion because of the threat of sexual assault on female prison guards based on their "very womanhood."

Can this reasoning be defended at all on the paternalistic grounds of protecting women from risks in the work place? Even if it could, isn't it unrealistic to suppose that the threat of sexual assault in prisons is confined to women? Reports of homosexual assaults on male prisoners are commonplace. Is the risk to women necessarily any greater? The Court is careful to avoid reliance on the threats to the women alone, referring instead to the general threat of disruption to the prison's operation. How different is this reasoning from overtly paternalistic reasoning? Any threat to an individual prison guard while on duty could compromise the security of the prison. Perhaps for this reason, the Court also refers to the generally

[5] The appellants argue that restrictions on employment of women are also justified by consideration of inmates' privacy. It is strange indeed to hear state officials who have for years been violating the most basic principles of human decency in the operation of their prisons suddenly become concerned about inmate privacy. It is stranger still that these same officials allow women guards in contact positions in a number of nonmaximum-security institutions, but strive to protect inmates' privacy in the prisons where personal freedom is most severely restricted. I have no doubt on this record that appellants' professed concern is nothing but a feeble excuse for discrimination.

As the District Court suggested, it may well be possible, once a constitutionally adequate staff is available, to rearrange work assignments so that legitimate privacy concerns are respected without denying jobs to women. Finally, if women guards behave in a professional manner at all times, they will engender reciprocal respect from inmates, who will recognize that their privacy is being invaded no more than if a woman doctor examines them. The suggestion implicit in the privacy argument that such behavior is unlikely on either side is an insult to the professionalism of guards and the dignity of inmates.

precarious security and deteriorating conditions in the Alabama prisons, suggesting a kind of "clear and present danger" analysis. The BFOQ can be invoked as an exception to Title VII's general prohibition against sex discrimination only in truly exceptional cases. Does this reasoning narrow the significance of this case almost to the vanishing point?

2. **Scope of the BFOQ.** The Court offered several different formulations of the BFOQ, but endorsed none of them as a definitive test. Two widely quoted tests from the Fifth Circuit do not seem to add much to the terms of the BFOQ in § 703(e) itself, that sex as a qualification for the job is "reasonably necessary to that particular business or enterprise." One test makes the BFOQ available only when "the *essence* of the business operation would be undermined by not hiring members of one sex exclusively." Diaz v. Pan Am. World Airways, 442 F.2d 385, 388 (5th Cir.), cert. denied, 404 U.S. 950 (1971). The other requires the employer to prove "that he had reasonable cause to believe, that is, a factual basis for believing, that all or substantially all women would be unable to perform safely and efficiently the duties of the job involved." Weeks v. Southern Bell Telephone & Telegraph Co., 408 F.2d 228, 235 (5th Cir. 1969). Both of these presuppose the answer to difficult questions, the first about what constitutes "the *essence* of the business operation" and the second about what constitutes a sufficient "factual basis for believing" that women could not perform the job. The employer's answers to these questions presumably are not dispositive, but if not, how is the court to go about answering them? It is less acquainted than the employer with the needs of its business and, while it is expert in evaluating factual evidence, the underlying questions about the scope of the BFOQ appear to be less empirical than normative. In what circumstances should women (or men) be excluded from a particular job?

The Supreme Court hinted at how difficult these questions are by confining itself simply to the observation that the BFOQ "provides only the narrowest of exceptions to the general rule requiring equality of employment opportunities." In doing so, did the Court ignore the congressional judgment that the prohibition against sex discrimination, unlike the prohibition against race discrimination, had to be subject to exceptions? Or was the Court more concerned that exceptions to the prohibition against sex discrimination, unless narrowly construed, might swallow the rule? Does the narrowness of the BFOQ allow the courts to avoid much of the controversy surrounding changing views about appropriate gender roles by presuming that the complete exclusion of one sex or the other from an entire line of employment is hardly ever allowed? On this view, employers must come up with a very good reason to justify any such exclusion. Is this any different from the constitutional standard requiring an "exceedingly persuasive" justification for any sex-based classification by government? See United States v. Virginia, 518 U.S. 515, 531 (1996).

3. **Privacy and the BFOQ.** Subsequent cases have vindicated the Supreme Court's judgment that the BFOQ represents "only the narrowest of exceptions," even in cases involving prison guards. See, e.g., United States v. Gregory, 818 F.2d 1114, 1117–18 (4th Cir. 1987). Nevertheless, recent decisions have granted a degree of deference to prison authorities in making

the decision whether guards must be of the same sex as the inmates they guard. Everson v. Michigan Dep't of Corrections, 391 F.3d 737, 750 (6th Cir. 2004); Torres v. Wisconsin Dep't of Health & Soc. Servs., 859 F.2d 1523 (7th Cir. 1988) (en banc), cert. denied, 489 U.S. 1017, 1082 (1989) (empirical studies and other forms of objective evidence not required). These cases have also involved arguments that limiting guards to a single sex was necessary to safeguard the inmates' privacy. Such arguments have been raised by the inmates themselves in support of constitutional claims that their right to privacy was violated by comprehensive surveillance and contact from guards of the opposite sex. Bonitz v. Fair, 804 F.2d 164 (1st Cir. 1986); Forts v. Ward, 621 F.2d 1210 (2d Cir. 1980). For an account of the increased employment of women in corrections. Brenda V. Smith & Melissa C. Loomis, After *Dothard*: Female Correctional Workers and the Challenge to Employment Law, 8 Fla. Int'l U.L. Rev. 469 (2013)

Outside of prisons, the courts have applied the BFOQ mainly to cases involving privacy to justify sex-based exclusions from particular jobs. E.g., Fesel v. Masonic Home of Delaware, Inc., 447 F.Supp. 1346 (D. Del. 1978), aff'd, 591 F.2d 1334 (3d Cir. 1979) (per curiam) (nurse at retirement home); Jennings v. New York State Office of Mental Health, 786 F.Supp. 376 (S.D.N.Y.), aff'd, 977 F.2d 731 (2d Cir. 1992) (per curiam) (personal care of mentally ill). And even in such cases, employers have not always succeeded in establishing a BFOQ. See Olsen v. Marriott Int'l, Inc., 75 F. Supp. 2d 1052, 1070–75 (D. Ariz. 1999) (no BFOQ for massage therapist). For discussions of these issues, see Jillian B. Berman, Defining the "Essence of the Business": An Analysis of Title VII's Privacy BFOQ After *Johnson Controls*, 67 U. Chi. L. Rev. 749 (2000); Rebecca Jurado, The Essence of Her Womanhood: Defining the Privacy Rights of Women Prisoners and the Employment Rights of Women Guards, 7 Am. U. J. Gender & L. 1 (1999); Sharon M. McGowan, The Bona Fide Body: Title VII's Last Bastion of Intentional Sex Discrimination, 12 Colum. J. Gender & L. 77 (2003).

4. **Explicitly Sexualized Jobs.** Jobs in the entertainment industry that involve explicitly sexualized conduct, such as pornographic modeling and acting, "exotic dancing," and prostitution (where it is legal), have raised obvious questions about the scope of the BFOQ. On the one hand, the whole point of these jobs is that they are performed by women, or less frequently, men. On the other, they also exploit the most extreme stereotypes of sexually objectified women. For analysis of the conflicting arguments for applying the BFOQ see Naomi Schoenbaum, The Law of Intimate Work, 90 Wash. L. Rev. 1167 (2015); Naomi Schoenbaum, Gender and the Sharing Economy, 43 Fordham Urb. L.J. 1023 (2016); Sarkar, Intimate Employment, 39 Harv. J.L. & Gender 429 (2016); Lu-in Wang, When the Customer is King: Employment Discrimination as Customer Service, 23 Va. J. Soc. Pol'y & L. 249 (2016); Lua K. Yuille, Sex in the Sexy Workplace, 9 Nw. J.L. & Soc'l Pol'y 88 (2013); Kimberly A. Yuracko, Private Nurses and Playboy Bunnies: Explaining Permissible Sex Discrimination, 92 Cal. L. Rev. 147 (2004).

Less sensational aspects of employment, such as those involving dress or appearance, raise similar issues about the extent of sexually differentiated conduct in the workplace. See Noa Ben-Asher, The Two Laws of Sex

Stereotyping, 57 B. C. L. Rev. 1187 (2016); Katharine T. Bartlett, Only Girls Wear Barrettes: Dress and Appearance Standards, Community Norms, and Workplace Identity, 92 Mich. L. Rev. 2541 (1994); Anita Bernstein, What's Wrong with Stereotyping?, 55 Ariz. L. Rev. 655 (2013); David B. Cruz, Disestablishing Sex and Gender, 90 Cal. L. Rev. 997 (2002); Katherine M. Franke, The Central Mistake of Sex Discrimination Law: The Disaggregation of Sex From Gender, 144 U. Pa. L. Rev. 1 (1995); Karl E. Klare, Power/Dressing: Regulation of Employee Appearance, 26 New Eng. L. Rev. 1395 (1992); Ernest F. Lidge, III, Law Firm Employment Discrimination in Case Assignments at the Client's Insistence: A Bona Fide Occupational Qualification?, 38 Conn. L. Rev. 159 (2005); Kimberly A. Yuracko, Soul of a Woman: The Sex Stereotyping Prohibition at Work, 161 U. Pa. L. Rev. 757 (2013).

At the opposite extreme from explicitly sexualized conduct, religious practices also raise questions about the scope of the BFOQ for sex (wholly apart from the BFOQ for religion itself allowing an exception to the prohibition against discrimination on that ground). See Gila Stopler, Countenancing the Oppression of Women: How Liberals Tolerate Religious and Cultural Practices That Discriminate Against Women, 12 Colum. J. Gender & L. 154 (2003).

United Automobile Workers v. Johnson Controls

499 U.S. 187 (1991).

■ JUSTICE BLACKMUN delivered the opinion of the Court.

In this case we are concerned with an employer's gender-based fetal-protection policy. May an employer exclude a fertile female employee from certain jobs because of its concern for the health of the fetus the woman might conceive?

I

Respondent Johnson Controls, Inc., manufactures batteries. In the manufacturing process, the element lead is a primary ingredient. Occupational exposure to lead entails health risks, including the risk of harm to any fetus carried by a female employee.

Before the Civil Rights Act of 1964 became law, Johnson Controls did not employ any woman in a battery-manufacturing job. In June 1977, however, it announced its first official policy concerning its employment of women in lead-exposure work:

> "[P]rotection of the health of the unborn child is the immediate and direct responsibility of the prospective parents. While the medical profession and the company can support them in the exercise of this responsibility, it cannot assume it for them without simultaneously infringing their rights as persons. . . .
>
> ". . . Since not all women who can become mothers wish to become mothers (or will become mothers), it would appear to be

illegal discrimination to treat all who are capable of pregnancy as though they will become pregnant."

Consistent with that view, Johnson Controls "stopped short of excluding women capable of bearing children from lead exposure," but emphasized that a woman who expected to have a child should not choose a job in which she would have such exposure. The company also required a woman who wished to be considered for employment to sign a statement that she had been advised of the risk of having a child while she was exposed to lead. The statement informed the woman that although there was evidence "that women exposed to lead have a higher rate of abortion," this evidence was "not as clear . . . as the relationship between cigarette smoking and cancer," but that it was, "medically speaking, just good sense not to run that risk if you want children and do not want to expose the unborn child to risk, however small. . . ."

Five years later, in 1982, Johnson Controls shifted from a policy of warning to a policy of exclusion. Between 1979 and 1983, eight employees became pregnant while maintaining blood lead levels in excess of 30 micrograms per deciliter. This appeared to be the critical level noted by the Occupational Health and Safety Administration (OSHA) for a worker who was planning to have a family. See 29 CFR § 1910.1025 (1989). The company responded by announcing a broad exclusion of women from jobs that exposed them to lead:

> "[I]t is [Johnson Controls'] policy that women who are pregnant or who are capable of bearing children will not be placed into jobs involving lead exposure or which could expose them to lead through the exercise of job bidding, bumping, transfer or promotion rights."

The policy defined "women . . . capable of bearing children" as "all women except those whose inability to bear children is medically documented." It further stated that an unacceptable work station was one where, "over the past year," an employee had recorded a blood lead level of more than 30 micrograms per deciliter or the work site had yielded an air sample containing a lead level in excess of 30 micrograms per cubic meter.

II

In April 1984, petitioners filed in the United States District Court for the Eastern District of Wisconsin a class action challenging Johnson Controls' fetal-protection policy as sex discrimination that violated Title VII of the Civil Rights Act of 1964. Among the individual plaintiffs were petitioners Mary Craig, who had chosen to be sterilized in order to avoid losing her job, Elsie Nason, a 50-year-old divorcee, who had suffered a loss in compensation when she was transferred out of a job where she was exposed to lead, and Donald Penney, who had been denied a request for a leave of absence for the purpose of lowering his lead level because he intended to become a father. Upon stipulation of the parties, the

District Court certified a class consisting of "all past, present and future production and maintenance employees" in United Auto Workers bargaining units at nine of Johnson Controls' plants "who have been and continue to be affected by [the employer's] Fetal Protection Policy implemented in 1982."

The District Court granted summary judgment for defendant-respondent Johnson Controls. Applying a three-part business necessity defense derived from fetal-protection cases in the Courts of Appeals for the Fourth and Eleventh Circuits, the District Court concluded that while "there is a disagreement among the experts regarding the effect of lead on the fetus," the hazard to the fetus through exposure to lead was established by "a considerable body of opinion"; that although "expert opinion has been provided which holds that lead also affects the reproductive abilities of men and women . . . [and] that these effects are as great as the effects of exposure of the fetus . . . a great body of experts are of the opinion that the fetus is more vulnerable to levels of lead that would not affect adults"; and that petitioners had "failed to establish that there is an acceptable alternative policy which would protect the fetus." The court stated that, in view of this disposition of the business necessity defense, it did not "have to undertake a bona fide occupational qualification's (BFOQ) analysis."

The Court of Appeals for the Seventh Circuit, sitting en banc, affirmed the summary judgment by a 7-to-4 vote. The majority held that the proper standard for evaluating the fetal-protection policy was the defense of business necessity; that Johnson Controls was entitled to summary judgment under that defense; and that even if the proper standard was a BFOQ, Johnson Controls still was entitled to summary judgment. . . .

III

The bias in Johnson Controls' policy is obvious. Fertile men, but not fertile women, are given a choice as to whether they wish to risk their reproductive health for a particular job. Section 703(a) of the Civil Rights Act of 1964 prohibits sex-based classifications in terms and conditions of employment, in hiring and discharging decisions, and in other employment decisions that adversely affect an employee's status. Respondent's fetal-protection policy explicitly discriminates against women on the basis of their sex. The policy excludes women with childbearing capacity from lead-exposed jobs and so creates a facial classification based on gender. Respondent assumes as much in its brief before this Court.

Nevertheless, the Court of Appeals assumed, as did the two appellate courts who already had confronted the issue, that sex-specific fetal-protection policies do not involve facial discrimination. *Hayes*, 726 F.2d, at 1547; *Wright*, 697 F.2d, at 1190. These courts analyzed the policies as though they were facially neutral, and had only a discriminatory effect upon the employment opportunities of women.

Consequently, the courts looked to see if each employer in question had established that its policy was justified as a business necessity. The business necessity standard is more lenient for the employer than the statutory BFOQ defense. The Court of Appeals here went one step further and invoked the burden-shifting framework set forth in Wards Cove Packing Co. v. Atonio, 490 U.S. 642 (1989), thus requiring petitioners to bear the burden of persuasion on all questions. The court assumed that because the asserted reason for the sex-based exclusion (protecting women's unconceived offspring) was ostensibly benign, the policy was not sex-based discrimination. That assumption, however, was incorrect.

First, Johnson Controls' policy classifies on the basis of gender and childbearing capacity, rather than fertility alone. Respondent does not seek to protect the unconceived children of all its employees. Despite evidence in the record about the debilitating effect of lead exposure on the male reproductive system, Johnson Controls is concerned only with the harms that may befall the unborn offspring of its female employees. Accordingly, it appears that Johnson Controls would have lost in the Eleventh Circuit under *Hayes* because its policy does not "effectively and equally protect the offspring of all employees." This Court faced a conceptually similar situation in Phillips v. Martin Marietta Corp., 400 U.S. 542 (1971), and found sex discrimination because the policy established "one hiring policy for women and another for men—each having pre-school-age children." Johnson Controls' policy is facially discriminatory because it requires only a female employee to produce proof that she is not capable of reproducing.

Our conclusion is bolstered by the Pregnancy Discrimination Act of 1978 (PDA), 92 Stat. 2076, 42 U.S.C. § 2000e(k), in which Congress explicitly provided that, for purposes of Title VII, discrimination "on the basis of sex" includes discrimination "because of or on the basis of pregnancy, childbirth, or related medical conditions." "The Pregnancy Discrimination Act has now made clear that, for all Title VII purposes, discrimination based on a woman's pregnancy is, on its face, discrimination because of her sex." Newport News Shipbuilding & Dry Dock Co. v. EEOC, 462 U.S. 669, 684 (1983). In its use of the words "capable of bearing children" in the 1982 policy statement as the criterion for exclusion, Johnson Controls explicitly classifies on the basis of potential for pregnancy. Under the PDA, such a classification must be regarded, for Title VII purposes, in the same light as explicit sex discrimination. Respondent has chosen to treat all its female employees as potentially pregnant; that choice evinces discrimination on the basis of sex.

We concluded above that Johnson Controls' policy is not neutral because it does not apply to the reproductive capacity of the company's male employees in the same way as it applies to that of the females. Moreover, the absence of a malevolent motive does not convert a facially discriminatory policy into a neutral policy with a discriminatory effect. Whether an employment practice involves disparate treatment through explicit facial discrimination does not depend on why the employer discriminates but rather on the explicit terms of the discrimination. In *Martin Marietta*, supra, the motives underlying the employers' express exclusion of women did not alter the intentionally discriminatory character of the policy. Nor did the arguably benign motives lead to consideration of a business necessity defense. The question in that case was whether the discrimination in question could be justified under § 703(e) as a BFOQ. The beneficence of an employer's purpose does not undermine the conclusion that an explicit gender-based policy is sex discrimination under § 703(a) and thus may be defended only as a BFOQ.

The enforcement policy of the Equal Employment Opportunity Commission accords with this conclusion. On January 24, 1990, the EEOC issued a Policy Guidance in the light of the Seventh Circuit's decision in the present case. The document noted: "For the plaintiff to bear the burden of proof in a case in which there is direct evidence of a facially discriminatory policy is wholly inconsistent with settled Title VII law." The Commission concluded: "We now think BFOQ is the better approach."

In sum, Johnson Controls' policy "does not pass the simple test of whether the evidence shows 'treatment of a person in a manner which but for that person's sex would be different.' " Los Angeles Dept. of Water & Power v. Manhart, 435 U.S. 702, 711 (1978), quoting Developments in the Law, Employment Discrimination and Title VII of the Civil Rights Act of 1964, 84 Harv. L. Rev. 1109, 1170 (1971). We hold that Johnson Controls' fetal-protection policy is sex discrimination forbidden under Title VII unless respondent can establish that sex is a "bona fide occupational qualification."

IV

Under § 703(e)(1) of Title VII, an employer may discriminate on the basis of "religion, sex, or national origin in those certain instances where religion, sex, or national origin is a bona fide occupational qualification reasonably necessary to the normal operation of that particular business or enterprise." 42 U.S.C. § 2000e–2(e)(1). We therefore turn to the question whether Johnson Controls' fetal-protection policy is one of those "certain instances" that come within the BFOQ exception.

The BFOQ defense is written narrowly, and this Court has read it narrowly. See, e.g., Dothard v. Rawlinson, 433 U.S. 321, 332–337 (1977); Trans World Airlines, Inc. v. Thurston, 469 U.S. 111, 122–125 (1985). We have read the BFOQ language of § 4(f) of the Age Discrimination in Employment Act of 1967 (ADEA), 81 Stat. 603, as amended, 29 U.S.C. § 623(f)(1), which tracks the BFOQ provision in Title VII, just as narrowly. See Western Air Lines, Inc. v. Criswell, 472 U.S. 400 (1985). Our emphasis on the restrictive scope of the BFOQ defense is grounded on both the language and the legislative history of § 703.

The wording of the BFOQ defense contains several terms of restriction that indicate that the exception reaches only special situations. The statute thus limits the situations in which discrimination is permissible to "certain instances" where sex discrimination is "reasonably necessary" to the "normal operation" of the "particular" business. Each one of these terms—certain, normal, particular—prevents the use of general subjective standards and favors an objective, verifiable requirement. But the most telling term is "occupational"; this indicates that these objective, verifiable requirements must concern job-related skills and aptitudes.

Justice White defines "occupational" as meaning related to a job. According to him, any discriminatory requirement imposed by an employer is "job-related" simply because the employer has chosen to make the requirement a condition of employment. In effect, he argues that sterility may be an occupational qualification for women because Johnson Controls has chosen to require it. This reading of "occupational" renders the word mere surplusage. "Qualification" by itself would encompass an employer's idiosyncratic requirements. By modifying "qualification" with "occupational," Congress narrowed the term to qualifications that affect an employee's ability to do the job.

Johnson Controls argues that its fetal-protection policy falls within the so-called safety exception to the BFOQ. Our cases have stressed that discrimination on the basis of sex because of safety concerns is allowed only in narrow circumstances. In *Dothard v. Rawlinson*, this Court indicated that danger to a woman herself does not justify discrimination. We there allowed the employer to hire only male guards in contact areas of maximum-security male penitentiaries only because more was at stake than the "individual woman's decision to weigh and accept the risks of employment." We found sex to be a BFOQ inasmuch as the employment of a female guard would create real risks of safety to others if violence broke out because the guard was a woman. Sex discrimination was tolerated because sex was related to the guard's ability to do the job—maintaining prison security. We also required in *Dothard* a high correlation between sex and ability to perform job functions and refused to allow employers to use sex as a proxy for strength although it might be a fairly accurate one.

Similarly, some courts have approved airlines' layoffs of pregnant flight attendants at different points during the first five months of pregnancy on the ground that the employer's policy was necessary to ensure the safety of passengers. . . . In two of these cases, the courts pointedly indicated that fetal, as opposed to passenger, safety was best left to the mother. . . .

We considered safety to third parties in *Western Airlines, Inc. v. Criswell*, supra, in the context of the ADEA. We focused upon "the nature of the flight engineer's tasks," and the "actual capabilities of persons over age 60" in relation to those tasks. Our safety concerns were not independent of the individual's ability to perform the assigned tasks, but rather involved the possibility that, because of age-connected debility, a flight engineer might not properly assist the pilot, and might thereby cause a safety emergency. Furthermore, although we considered the safety of third parties in *Dothard* and *Criswell*, those third parties were indispensable to the particular business at issue. In *Dothard*, the third parties were the inmates; in *Criswell*, the third parties were the passengers on the plane. We stressed that in order to qualify as a BFOQ, a job qualification must relate to the "essence," *Dothard*, 433 U.S., at 333, or to the "central mission of the employer's business," *Criswell*, 472 U.S., at 413.

Justice White ignores the "essence of the business" test and so concludes that "the safety to fetuses in carrying out the duties of battery manufacturing is as much a legitimate concern as is safety to third parties in guarding prisons (*Dothard*) or flying airplanes (*Criswell*)." By limiting his discussion to cost and safety concerns and rejecting the "essence of the business" test that our case law has established, he seeks to expand what is now the narrow BFOQ defense. Third-party safety considerations properly entered into the BFOQ analysis in *Dothard* and *Criswell* because they went to the core of the employee's job performance. Moreover, that performance involved the central purpose of the enterprise. *Dothard*, 433 U.S., at 335 ("The essence of a correctional counselor's job is to maintain prison security"); *Criswell*, 472 U.S., at 413 (the central mission of the airline's business was the safe transportation of its passengers). Justice White attempts to transform this case into one of customer safety. The unconceived fetuses of Johnson Controls' female employees, however, are neither customers nor third parties whose safety is essential to the business of battery manufacturing. No one can disregard the possibility of injury to future children; the BFOQ, however, is not so broad that it transforms this deep social concern into an essential aspect of battery making.

Our case law, therefore, makes clear that the safety exception is limited to instances in which sex or pregnancy actually interferes with the employee's ability to perform the job. This approach is consistent with the language of the BFOQ provision itself, for it suggests that permissible distinctions based on sex must relate to ability to perform the duties of the job. Johnson Controls suggests, however, that we expand the exception to allow fetal-protection policies that mandate particular standards for pregnant or fertile women. We decline to do so. Such an expansion contradicts not only the language of the BFOQ and the narrowness of its exception but the plain language and history of the Pregnancy Discrimination Act.

The PDA's amendment to Title VII contains a BFOQ standard of its own: unless pregnant employees differ from others "in their ability or inability to work," they must be "treated the same" as other employees "for all employment-related purposes." 42 U.S.C. § 2000e(k). This language clearly sets forth Congress' remedy for discrimination on the basis of pregnancy and potential pregnancy. Women who are either pregnant or potentially pregnant must be treated like others "similar in their ability . . . to work." In other words, women as capable of doing their jobs as their male counterparts may not be forced to choose between having a child and having a job.

Justice White asserts that the PDA did not alter the BFOQ defense. Justice White arrives at this conclusion by ignoring the second clause of the Act which states that "women affected by pregnancy, childbirth, or related medical conditions shall be treated the same for all employment-related purposes . . . as other persons not so affected but similar in their ability or inability to work." 42 U.S.C. § 2000e(k). Until this day, every Member of this Court had acknowledged that "the second clause [of the PDA] could not be clearer: it mandates that pregnant employees 'shall be treated the same for all employment-related purposes' as nonpregnant employees similarly situated with respect to their ability or inability to work." California Federal S. & L. Assn. v. Guerra, 479 U.S. 272, 297 (1987) (White, J., dissenting). Justice White now seeks to read the second clause out of the Act. . . .

V

We have no difficulty concluding that Johnson Controls cannot establish a BFOQ. Fertile women, as far as appears in the record, participate in the manufacture of batteries as efficiently as anyone else. Johnson Controls' professed moral and ethical concerns about the welfare of the next generation do not suffice to establish a BFOQ of female sterility. Decisions about the welfare of future children must be left to the parents who conceive, bear, support, and raise them rather than to the employers who hire those parents. Congress has mandated this choice through Title VII, as amended by the Pregnancy Discrimination Act. Johnson Controls has attempted to exclude women because of their reproductive capacity. Title VII and the PDA simply do not allow a woman's dismissal because of her failure to submit to sterilization.

Nor can concerns about the welfare of the next generation be considered a part of the "essence" of Johnson Controls' business. Judge Easterbrook in this case pertinently observed: "It is word play to say that 'the job' at Johnson [Controls] is to make batteries without risk to fetuses in the same way 'the job' at Western Air Lines is to fly planes without crashing." 886 F.2d, at 913.

Johnson Controls argues that it must exclude all fertile women because it is impossible to tell which women will become pregnant while working with lead. This argument is somewhat academic in light of our conclusion that the company may not exclude fertile women at all; it perhaps is worth noting, however, that Johnson Controls has shown no "factual basis for believing that all or substantially all women would be unable to perform safely and efficiently the duties of the job involved." Weeks v. Southern Bell Tel. & Tel. Co., 408 F.2d 228, 235 (CA5 1969), quoted with approval in Dothard, 433 U.S., at 333. Even on this sparse record, it is apparent that Johnson Controls is concerned about only a small minority of women. Of the eight pregnancies reported among the female employees, it has not been shown that any of the babies have birth defects or other abnormalities. The record does not reveal the birth rate for Johnson Controls' female workers but national statistics show that approximately nine percent of all fertile women become pregnant each year. The birthrate drops to two percent for blue collar workers over age 30. Johnson Controls' fear of prenatal injury, no matter how sincere, does not begin to show that substantially all of its fertile women employees are incapable of doing their jobs.

VI

A word about tort liability and the increased cost of fertile women in the workplace is perhaps necessary. One of the dissenting judges in this case expressed concern about an employer's tort liability and concluded that liability for a potential injury to a fetus is a social cost that Title VII does not require a company to ignore. It is correct to say that Title VII does not prevent the employer from having a conscience. The statute, however, does prevent sex-specific fetal-protection policies. These two aspects of Title VII do not conflict.

More than 40 States currently recognize a right to recover for a prenatal injury based either on negligence or on wrongful death. . . . According to Johnson Controls, however, the company complies with the lead standard developed by OSHA and warns its female employees about the damaging effects of lead. It is worth noting that OSHA gave the problem of lead lengthy consideration and concluded that "there is no basis whatsoever for the claim that women of childbearing age should be excluded from the workplace in order to protect the fetus or the course of pregnancy." 43 Fed. Reg. 52952, 52966 (1978). Instead, OSHA established a series of mandatory protections which, taken together, "should effectively minimize any risk to the fetus and newborn child." Id. at 52966. See 29 CFR § 1910.125(k)(ii) (1989). Without negligence, it would be difficult for a court to find liability on the part of the employer. If, under general tort principles, Title VII bans sex-specific fetal-protection policies, the employer fully informs the woman of the risk, and the employer has not acted negligently, the basis for holding an employer liable seems remote at best.

Although the issue is not before us, the concurrence observes that "it is far from clear that compliance with Title VII will preempt state tort liability." . . .

If state tort law furthers discrimination in the workplace and prevents employers from hiring women who are capable of manufacturing the product as efficiently as men, then it will impede the accomplishment of Congress' goals in enacting Title VII. Because Johnson Controls has not argued that it faces any costs from tort liability, not to mention crippling ones, the pre-emption question is not before us.

We therefore say no more than that the concurrence's speculation appears unfounded as well as premature.

The tort-liability argument reduces to two equally unpersuasive propositions. First, Johnson Controls attempts to solve the problem of reproductive health hazards by resorting to an exclusionary policy. Title VII plainly forbids illegal sex discrimination as a method of diverting attention from an employer's obligation to police the workplace. Second, the spectre of an award of damages reflects a fear that hiring fertile women will cost more. The extra cost of employing members of one sex, however, does not provide an affirmative Title VII defense for a discriminatory refusal to hire members of that gender. See *Manhart*, 435 U.S., at 716–718, and n.32. Indeed, in passing the PDA, Congress considered at length the considerable cost of providing equal treatment of pregnancy and related conditions, but made the "decision to forbid special treatment of pregnancy despite the social costs associated therewith." Arizona Governing Committee v. Norris, 463 U.S. 1073, 1084, n.14 (1983) (opinion of Marshall, J.). See Price Waterhouse v. Hopkins, 490 U.S. 228 (1989).

We, of course, are not presented with, nor do we decide, a case in which costs would be so prohibitive as to threaten the survival of the employer's business. We merely reiterate our prior holdings that the incremental cost of hiring women cannot justify discriminating against them.

VII

. . .

It is no more appropriate for the courts than it is for individual employers to decide whether a woman's reproductive role is more important to herself and her family than her economic role. Congress has left this choice to the woman as hers to make.

The judgment of the Court of Appeals is reversed and the case is remanded for further proceedings consistent with this opinion.

It is so ordered.

■ JUSTICE WHITE, with whom the CHIEF JUSTICE and JUSTICE KENNEDY join, concurring in part and concurring in the judgment.

The Court properly holds that Johnson Controls' fetal protection policy overtly discriminates against women, and thus is prohibited by Title VII unless it falls within the bona fide occupational qualification (BFOQ) exception, set forth at 42 U.S.C. § 2000e–2(e). The Court erroneously holds, however, that the BFOQ defense is so narrow that it could never justify a sex-specific fetal protection policy. I nevertheless concur in the judgment of reversal because on the record before us summary judgment in favor of Johnson Controls was improperly entered by the District Court and affirmed by the Court of Appeals.

I

In evaluating the scope of the BFOQ defense, the proper starting point is the language of the statute. . . . Title VII forbids discrimination on the basis of sex, except "in those certain instances where . . . sex . . . is a bona fide occupational qualification reasonably necessary to the normal operation of that particular business or enterprise." 42 U.S.C. § 2000e–2(e)(1). For the fetal protection policy involved in this case to be a BFOQ, therefore, the policy must be "reasonably necessary" to the "normal operation" of making batteries, which is Johnson Controls' "particular business." Although that is a difficult standard to satisfy, nothing in the statute's language indicates that it could *never* support a sex-specific fetal protection policy.[1]

On the contrary, a fetal protection policy would be justified under the terms of the statute if, for example, an employer could show that exclusion of women from certain jobs was reasonably necessary to avoid substantial tort liability. Common sense tells us that it is part of the normal operation of business concerns to avoid causing injury to third parties, as well as to employees, if for no other reason than to avoid tort liability and its substantial costs. This possibility of tort liability is not hypothetical; every State currently allows children born alive to recover in tort for prenatal injuries caused by third parties, see W. Keeton, D. Dobbs, R. Keeton, & D. Owen, Prosser and Keeton on Law of Torts § 55 p.368 (5th ed. 1984), and an increasing number of courts have recognized a right to recover even for prenatal injuries caused by torts committed prior to conception, see 3 F. Harper, F. James, & O. Gray, Law of Torts § 18.3, pp. 677–678, n.15 (2d ed. 1986).

The Court dismisses the possibility of tort liability by no more than speculating that if "Title VII bans sex-specific fetal-protection policies, the employer fully informs the woman of the risk, and the employer has not acted negligently, the basis for holding an employer liable seems remote at best." Such speculation will be small comfort to employers. First, it is far from clear that compliance with Title VII will pre-empt state tort liability, and the Court offers no support for that proposition. Second, although warnings may preclude claims by injured *employees*, they will not preclude claims by injured children because the general rule is that parents cannot waive causes of action on behalf of their children, and the parents' negligence will not be imputed to the children. Finally, although state tort liability for prenatal injuries generally requires negligence, it will be difficult for employers to determine in advance what

---

1 The Court's heavy reliance on the word "occupational" in the BFOQ statute, is unpersuasive. *Any* requirement for employment can be said to be an occupational qualification, since "occupational" merely means related to a job. See Webster's Third New International Dictionary 1560 (1976). Thus, Johnson Controls' requirement that employees engaged in battery manufacturing be either male or non-fertile clearly is an "occupational qualification." The issue, of course, is whether that qualification is "reasonably necessary to the normal operation" of Johnson Controls' business. It is telling that the Court offers no case support, either from this Court or the lower Federal Courts, for its interpretation of the word "occupational."

will constitute negligence. Compliance with OSHA standards, for example, has been held not to be a defense to state tort or criminal liability. . . . Moreover, it is possible that employers will be held strictly liable, if, for example, their manufacturing process is considered "abnormally dangerous." See Restatement (Second) of Torts § 869, comment b (1979). . . .

Dothard and *Criswell* make clear that avoidance of substantial safety risks to third parties is *inherently* part of both an employee's ability to perform a job and an employer's "normal operation" of its business. Indeed, in both cases, the Court approved the statement in Weeks v. Southern Bell Telephone & Telegraph Co., 408 F.2d 228 (5th Cir. 1969), that an employer could establish a BFOQ defense by showing that "all or substantially all women would be unable to perform *safely and efficiently* the duties of the job involved." Id. at 235. . . . The Court's statement in this case that "the safety exception is limited to instances in which sex or pregnancy actually interferes with the employee's ability to perform the job," therefore adds no support to its conclusion that a fetal protection policy could never be justified as a BFOQ. On the facts of this case, for example, protecting fetal safety while carrying out the duties of battery manufacturing is as much a legitimate concern as is safety to third parties in guarding prisons (*Dothard*) or flying airplanes (*Criswell*).

Dothard and *Criswell* also confirm that costs are relevant in determining whether a discriminatory policy is reasonably necessary for the normal operation of a business. In *Dothard*, the safety problem that justified exclusion of women from the prison guard positions was largely a result of inadequate staff and facilities. See 433 U.S., at 335. If the cost of employing women could not be considered, the employer there should have been required to hire more staff and restructure the prison environment rather than exclude women. Similarly, in *Criswell* the airline could have been required to hire more pilots and install expensive monitoring devices rather than discriminate against older employees. The BFOQ statute, however, reflects "Congress' unwillingness to require employers to change the very nature of their operations." Price Waterhouse v. Hopkins, 490 U.S. 228, 242 (1989) (plurality opinion).

The Pregnancy Discrimination Act (PDA), 42 U.S.C. § 2000e(k), contrary to the Court's assertion, did not restrict the scope of the BFOQ defense. The PDA was only an amendment to the "Definitions" section of Title VII, 42 U.S.C. § 2000e, and did not purport to eliminate or alter the BFOQ defense. Rather, it merely clarified Title VII to make it clear that pregnancy and related conditions are included within Title VII's antidiscrimination provisions. As we have already recognized, "the purpose of the PDA was simply to make the treatment of pregnancy consistent with general Title VII principles." Arizona Governing Committee for Tax Deferred Annuity and Deferred Compensation Plans v. Norris, 463 U.S. 1073, 1085, n.14 (1983). . . .

In enacting the BFOQ standard, "Congress did not ignore the public interest in safety." *Criswell*, supra, at 419. The Court's narrow interpretation of the BFOQ defense in this case, however, means that an employer cannot exclude even *pregnant* women from an environment highly toxic to their fetuses. It is foolish to think that Congress intended such a result, and neither the language of the BFOQ exception nor our cases requires it.

II

Despite my disagreement with the Court concerning the scope of the BFOQ defense, I concur in reversing the Court of Appeals because that court erred in affirming the District Court's grant of summary judgment in favor of Johnson Controls. First, the Court of Appeals erred in failing to consider the level of risk-avoidance that was part of Johnson Controls' "normal operation." Although the court did conclude that there was a "substantial risk" to fetuses from lead exposure in fertile women, 886 F.2d 871, 879–883, 898 (CA7 1989), it merely meant that there was a high risk that some fetal injury would occur absent a fetal protection policy. That analysis, of course, fails to address the *extent* of fetal injury that is likely to occur. If the fetal protection policy insists on a risk-avoidance level substantially higher than other risk levels tolerated by Johnson Controls such as risks to employees and consumers, the policy should not constitute a BFOQ.

Second, even without more information about the normal level of risk at Johnson Controls, the fetal protection policy at issue here reaches too far. This is evident both in its presumption that, absent medical documentation to the contrary, all women are fertile regardless of their age, see Id. at 876, n.8, and in its exclusion of presumptively fertile women from positions that might result in a promotion to a position involving high lead exposure, Id. at 877. There has been no showing that either of those aspects of the policy is reasonably necessary to ensure safe and efficient operation of Johnson Controls' battery-manufacturing business. Of course, these infirmities in the company's policy do not warrant invalidating the entire fetal protection program.

Third, it should be recalled that until 1982 Johnson Controls operated without an exclusionary policy, and it has not identified any grounds for believing that its current policy is reasonably necessary to its normal operations. Although it is now more aware of some of the dangers of lead exposure, Id. at 899, it has not shown that the risks of fetal harm or the costs associated with it have substantially increased. Cf. *Manhart*, 435 U.S., at 716, n.30, in which we rejected a BFOQ defense because the employer had operated prior to the discrimination with no significant adverse effects.

Finally, the Court of Appeals failed to consider properly petitioners' evidence of harm to offspring caused by lead exposure in males. The court considered that evidence only in its discussion of the business necessity standard, in which it focused on whether *petitioners* had met their burden of proof. The burden of proving that a discriminatory qualification is a BFOQ, however, rests with the employer. . . . Thus, the court should have analyzed whether the evidence was sufficient for petitioners to survive summary judgment in light of *respondent's* burden of proof to establish a BFOQ. Moreover, the court should not have discounted the evidence as "speculative" merely because it was based on animal studies. We have approved the use of animal studies to assess risks, see Industrial Union Dept. v. American Petroleum Institute, 448 U.S. 607, 657, n.64 (1980), and OSHA uses animal studies in establishing its lead control regulations, see United Steelworkers of America, AFL-CIO-CLC v. Marshall, 208 U.S. App. D.C. 60, 128, 647 F.2d 1189, 1257, n.97 (1980), cert. denied, 453 U.S. 913 (1981). It seems clear that if the Court of Appeals had properly analyzed that evidence, it would have concluded that summary judgment against petitioners was not appropriate because there was a dispute over a material issue of fact.

As Judge Posner observed below:

> "The issue of the legality of fetal protection is as novel and difficult as it is contentious and the most sensible way to approach it at this early stage is on a case-by-case basis, involving careful examination of the facts as developed by the full adversary process of a trial. The record in this case is too sparse. The district judge jumped the gun. By affirming on this scanty basis we may be encouraging incautious employers to adopt fetal protection policies that could endanger the jobs of millions of women for minor gains in fetal safety and health.
>
> "But although the defendant did not present enough evidence to warrant the grant of summary judgment in its favor, there is no ground for barring it from presenting additional evidence at trial. Therefore it would be equally precipitate for us to direct the entry of judgment in the plaintiffs' favor. . . ."

■ JUSTICE SCALIA, concurring in the judgment.

I generally agree with the Court's analysis, but have some reservations, several of which bear mention. . . .

[T]he Court points out that "Johnson Controls has shown no factual basis for believing that all or substantially all women would be unable to perform safely . . . the duties of the job involved," (internal quotations omitted). In my view, this is not only "somewhat academic in light of our conclusion that the company may not exclude fertile women at all," it is entirely irrelevant. By reason of the Pregnancy Discrimination Act, it would not matter if all pregnant women placed their children at risk in taking these jobs, just as it does not matter if no men do so. As Judge Easterbrook put it in his dissent below, "Title VII gives parents the power to make occupational decisions affecting their families. A legislative forum is available to those who believe that such decisions should be made elsewhere." International Union, UAW v. Johnson Controls, Inc., 886 F.2d 871, 915 (7th Cir. 1989) (Easterbrook, J., dissenting). . . .

NOTES ON *UNITED AUTOMOBILE WORKERS V. JOHNSON CONTROLS*

1. **Scope of the BFOQ.** *Dothard* recognized that the BFOQ was "only the narrowest of exceptions," but nevertheless found that its terms were met on the basis of weak evidence of the risks to female prison guards. *Johnson Controls* endorses the narrowness of the BFOQ and takes it a step further, explicitly placing the burden of proof upon the employer to make out the defense and finding that it was not met by the defendant's evidence of the risks to women from exposure to lead. The Court rejects both the relevance and the validity of the scientific evidence of the risk to the fetus from the mother's exposure to lead. Justice Blackmun, for the majority, concludes that the employer "may not exclude fertile women at all," but offers the opinion that even if it could, it has shown "no factual basis" for doing so. Justice Scalia agrees with the majority's conclusion, but finds the presence or absence of a factual basis for excluding women "entirely irrelevant." Only Justice White would remand the case for additional evidence on the level of risk, and even he interprets the BFOQ to set "a difficult standard to satisfy."

What accounts for the different result in *Johnson Controls* as compared with *Dothard*? The jobs at issue in *Dothard* were narrowly defined. Excluding women from positions as prison guards in men's prisons would not have greatly reduced the opportunities for employment open to women. The jobs at issue in *Johnson Controls* were potentially far more numerous, depending upon the showing required to support a BFOQ. On a minimal showing, any job involving exposure to toxic chemicals might have been closed to women. Certainly the employer took only the most minimal steps to narrow its policy of excluding women, allowing only women who could prove that they were sterile to take jobs involving exposure to lead. Would approval of this policy have led to a privately imposed version of "protective legislation," historically used to limit the jobs available to women to protect them from abuse?

Would a narrower policy, supported by stronger evidence, have solved all the problems that the employer faced? Such a policy would have affected fewer jobs, but its permissible scope would still have remained uncertain, depending on the number of jobs affected and the degree of evidence required. Is there any value to employers in establishing a strong presumption that almost all jobs are open to women and that few can be closed based on the BFOQ? Does the Court's discussion of the preemptive effect of Title VII on state tort law help to answer this question?

2. **Implications of the Pregnancy Discrimination Act.** Both Justice Blackmun for the majority and Justice Scalia in his separate opinion rely heavily upon the Pregnancy Discrimination Act. Both opinions interpret the Act, following *Newport News*, to express a general presumption against the use of classifications on the basis of pregnancy and related medical conditions. As Justice White points out in his separate opinion, however, the

first clause in the Act only added a definitional provision to Title VII. It did not prohibit all classifications on the basis of pregnancy. It only made classifications on the basis of pregnancy equivalent to classifications on the basis of sex. The BFOQ exception therefore applies equally to classifications on either basis.

Yet the Court concludes that the Pregnancy Discrimination Act prevents any showing of risk to the fetus sufficient to support a BFOQ. The majority opinion emphasizes the terms of the BFOQ itself, and in particular, the reference to "occupational qualification." It also emphasizes the second clause in § 701(k), requiring all pregnant women to be treated the same as other employees based on "their ability or inability to work." Any risk to the fetus has nothing to do with the work of making batteries because the fetus neither participates in the process of manufacture nor uses the batteries produced. Does this reasoning justify the Court in rejecting the relevance of any evidence, no matter how strong, that exposure to lead would pose risks to the fetus?

Note that all the opinions agree, however, in distinguishing the BFOQ from proof of job relationship and business necessity under the theory of disparate impact. The latter constitutes a defense only to claims that a neutral employment practice has a disparate impact upon women. The BFOQ, by contrast, applies only to practices that explicitly discriminate on the basis of sex. Because of the Pregnancy Discrimination Act, all classifications on the basis of pregnancy are treated like classifications on the basis of sex. Does it follow that any defense available to justify a classification on the basis of pregnancy requires a stronger showing than the defense necessary to justify a neutral practice with disparate impact?

3. **The Relevance of the Abortion Decisions.** Justice Scalia endorses the Court's reasoning that the Pregnancy Discrimination Act makes evidence of risks irrelevant, yet he writes a separate opinion concurring only in the judgment. Why doesn't he join in Justice Blackmun's opinion for the Court? Consider the following passage from the conclusion of Justice Blackmun's opinion:

> It is no more appropriate for the courts than it is for individual employers to decide whether a woman's reproductive role is more important to herself and her family than her economic role. Congress has left this choice to the woman as hers to make.

Is this reasoning more concerned with the scope of the BFOQ under Title VII or with the scope of the right to reproductive freedom under the Constitution? Congress did not address the reproductive role of women in the BFOQ, which speaks only of "bona fide occupational qualifications reasonably necessary to the normal operation of that particular business or enterprise." Nor did Congress address issues of reproductive freedom in the Pregnancy Discrimination Act, which contains an exception for "health benefits for abortion." Justice Blackmun, of course, wrote the opinion in Roe v. Wade, 410 U.S. 113 (1973), and Justice Scalia has been an outspoken critic of that decision. Planned Parenthood of Southeastern Pennsylvania v. Casey, 505 U.S. 833, 979 (1992) (Scalia, J., concurring in the judgment in part and dissenting in part). Given the controversy over the abortion decisions, should the Court have relied upon reasoning that presupposes that those decisions were correct? Does it make a difference that *Johnson Controls* was a statutory case rather than a constitutional case?

4. **Bibliography.** Much was written about the issue in *Johnson Controls*, both before and after the decision. Almost all of the commentary is favorable to the result ultimately reached by the Supreme Court, although different authors give different weight to the medical evidence of reproductive hazards (both to men and to women), the economic incentives of women in the workplace, and the conceptions of equality that justify prohibitions against sex discrimination. Mary Becker, From *Muller v. Oregon* to Fetal Vulnerability Policies, 53 U. Chi. L. Rev. 1219 (1986); Mary Becker, Reproductive Hazards, After *Johnson Controls*, 31 Hous. L. Rev. 43 (1994); Jillian B. Berman, Defining the "Essence of the Business": An Analysis of Title VII's Privacy BFOQ After *Johnson Controls*, 67 U. Chi. L. Rev. 749 (2000); Emily Busse, Getting Beyond Discrimination: A Regulatory Solution to the Problem of Fetal Hazards in the Workplace, 95 Yale L.J. 577 (1986); Hannah A. Furnish, Prenatal Exposure to Fetally Toxic Work Environments: The Dilemma of the 1978 Pregnancy Amendment to Title VII of the Civil Rights Act of 1964, 66 Iowa L. Rev. 63 (1980); Wendy W. Williams, Firing the Woman to Protect the Fetus: The Reconciliation of Fetal Protection Policies with Employment Opportunity Goals Under Title VII, 69 Geo. L.J. 641 (1981).

G. SEXUAL HARASSMENT

Meritor Savings Bank, FSB v. Vinson

477 U.S. 57 (1986).

■ JUSTICE REHNQUIST delivered the opinion of the Court.

This case presents important questions concerning claims of workplace "sexual harassment" brought under Title VII of the Civil Rights Act of 1964.

I

In 1974, respondent Mechelle Vinson met Sidney Taylor, a vice president of what is now petitioner Meritor Savings Bank (bank) and manager of one of its branch offices. When respondent asked whether she might obtain employment at the bank, Taylor gave her an application, which she completed and returned the next day; later that same day Taylor called her to say that she had been hired. With Taylor as her supervisor, respondent started as a teller-trainee, and thereafter was promoted to teller, head teller, and assistant branch manager. She worked at the same branch for four years, and it is undisputed that her advancement there was based on merit alone. In September 1978, respondent notified Taylor that she was taking sick leave for an indefinite period. On November 1, 1978, the bank discharged her for excessive use of that leave.

Respondent brought this action against Taylor and the bank, claiming that during her four years at the bank she had "constantly been subjected to sexual harassment" by Taylor in violation of Title VII. She sought injunctive relief, compensatory and punitive damages against Taylor and the bank, and attorney's fees.

At the 11-day bench trial, the parties presented conflicting testimony about Taylor's behavior during respondent's employment. Respondent testified that during her probationary period as a teller-trainee, Taylor treated her in a fatherly way and made no sexual advances. Shortly thereafter, however, he invited her out to dinner and, during the course of the meal, suggested that they go to a motel to have sexual relations. At first she refused, but out of what she described as fear of losing her job she eventually agreed. According to respondent, Taylor thereafter made repeated demands upon her for sexual favors, usually at the branch, both during and after business hours; she estimated that over the next several years she had intercourse with him some 40 or 50 times. In addition, respondent testified that Taylor fondled her in front of other employees, followed her into the women's restroom when she went there alone, exposed himself to her, and even forcibly raped her on several occasions. These activities ceased after 1977, respondent stated, when she started going with a steady boyfriend.

Respondent also testified that Taylor touched and fondled other women employees of the bank, and she attempted to call witnesses to support this charge. But while some supporting testimony apparently was admitted without objection, the District Court did not allow her "to present wholesale evidence of a pattern and practice relating to sexual advances to other female employees in her case in chief, but advised her that she might well be able to present such evidence in rebuttal to the defendants' cases." Respondent did not offer such evidence in rebuttal. Finally, respondent testified that because she was afraid of Taylor she never reported his harassment to any of his supervisors and never attempted to use the bank's complaint procedure.

Taylor denied respondent's allegations of sexual activity, testifying that he never fondled her, never made suggestive remarks to her, never engaged in sexual intercourse with her, and never asked her to do so. He contended instead that respondent made her accusations in response to a business-related dispute. The bank also denied respondent's allegations and asserted that any sexual harassment by Taylor was unknown to the bank and engaged in without its consent or approval.

The District Court denied relief, but did not resolve the conflicting testimony about the existence of a sexual relationship between respondent and Taylor. It found instead that

> "[i]f [respondent] and Taylor did engage in an intimate or sexual relationship during the time of [respondent's] employment with [the bank], that relationship was a voluntary one having

nothing to do with her continued employment at [the bank] or her advancement or promotions at that institution."

The court ultimately found that respondent "was not the victim of sexual harassment and was not the victim of sexual discrimination" while employed at the bank.

Although it concluded that respondent had not proved a violation of Title VII, the District Court nevertheless went on to address the bank's liability. After noting the bank's express policy against discrimination, and finding that neither respondent nor any other employee had ever lodged a complaint about sexual harassment by Taylor, the court ultimately concluded that "the bank was without notice and cannot be held liable for the alleged actions of Taylor."

The Court of Appeals for the District of Columbia Circuit reversed. Relying on its earlier holding in Bundy v. Jackson, 641 F.2d 934 (D.C. Cir. 1981), decided after the trial in this case, the court stated that a violation of Title VII may be predicated on either of two types of sexual harassment: harassment that involves the conditioning of concrete employment benefits on sexual favors, and harassment that, while not affecting economic benefits, creates a hostile or offensive working environment. . . .

II

Title VII of the Civil Rights Act of 1964 makes it "an unlawful employment practice for an employer . . . to discriminate against any individual with respect to his compensation, terms, conditions, or privileges of employment, because of such individual's race, color, religion, sex, or national origin." 42 U.S.C. § 2000e–2(a)(1). The prohibition against discrimination based on sex was added to Title VII at the last minute on the floor of the House of Representatives. 110 Cong. Rec. 2577–2584 (1964). The principal argument in opposition to the amendment was that "sex discrimination" was sufficiently different from other types of discrimination that it ought to receive separate legislative treatment. . . . This argument was defeated, the bill quickly passed as amended, and we are left with little legislative history to guide us in interpreting the Act's prohibition against discrimination based on "sex."

Respondent argues, and the Court of Appeals held, that unwelcome sexual advances that create an offensive or hostile working environment violate Title VII. Without question, when a supervisor sexually harasses a subordinate because of the subordinate's sex, that supervisor "discriminate[s]" on the basis of sex. Petitioner apparently does not challenge this proposition. It contends instead that in prohibiting discrimination with respect to "compensation, terms, conditions, or privileges" of employment, Congress was concerned with what petitioner describes as "tangible loss" of "an economic character," not "purely psychological aspects of the workplace environment." In support of this claim petitioner observes that in both the legislative history of Title VII and this Court's Title VII decisions, the focus has been on tangible, economic barriers erected by discrimination.

We reject petitioner's view. First, the language of Title VII is not limited to "economic" or "tangible" discrimination. The phrase "terms, conditions, or privileges of employment" evinces a congressional intent " 'to strike at the entire spectrum of disparate treatment of men and women' " in employment. Los Angeles Dept. of Water and Power v. Manhart, 435 U.S. 702, 707, n.13 (1978), quoting Sprogis v. United Air Lines, Inc., 444 F.2d 1194, 1198 (7th Cir. 1971). Petitioner has pointed to nothing in the Act to suggest that Congress contemplated the limitation urged here.

Second, in 1980 the EEOC issued Guidelines specifying that "sexual harassment," as there defined, is a form of sex discrimination prohibited by Title VII. As an "administrative interpretation of the Act by the enforcing agency," Griggs v. Duke Power Co., 401 U.S. 424, 433–434 (1971), these Guidelines, " 'while not controlling upon the courts by reason of their authority, do constitute a body of experience and informed judgment to which courts and litigants may properly resort for guidance,' " General Electric Co. v. Gilbert, 429 U.S. 125, 141–142 (1976), quoting Skidmore v. Swift & Co., 323 U.S. 134, 140 (1944). The EEOC Guidelines fully support the view that harassment leading to noneconomic injury can violate Title VII.

In defining "sexual harassment," the Guidelines first describe the kinds of workplace conduct that may be actionable under Title VII. These include "[u]nwelcome sexual advances, requests for sexual favors, and other verbal or physical conduct of a sexual nature." 29 CFR § 1604.11(a) (1985). Relevant to the charges at issue in this case, the Guidelines provide that such sexual misconduct constitutes prohibited "sexual harassment," whether or not it is directly linked to the grant or denial of an economic quid pro quo, where "such conduct has the purpose or effect of unreasonably interfering with an individual's work performance or creating an intimidating, hostile, or offensive working environment." § 1604.11(a)(3).

In concluding that so-called "hostile environment" (i.e., non quid pro quo) harassment violates Title VII, the EEOC drew upon a substantial body of judicial decisions and EEOC precedent holding that Title VII affords employees the right to work in an environment free from discriminatory intimidation, ridicule, and insult. See generally 45 Fed. Reg. 74676 (1980). Rogers v. EEOC, 454 F.2d 234 (5th Cir. 1971), cert. denied, 406 U.S. 957 (1972), was apparently the first case to recognize a cause of action based upon a discriminatory work environment. In *Rogers*, the Court of Appeals for the Fifth Circuit held that a Hispanic complainant could establish a Title VII violation by demonstrating that her employer created an offensive work environment for employees by giving discriminatory service to its Hispanic clientele. The court explained that an employee's protections under Title VII extend beyond the economic aspects of employment:

> "[T]he phrase 'terms, conditions or privileges of employment' in [Title VII] is an expansive concept which sweeps within its protective ambit the practice of creating a working environment heavily charged with ethnic or racial discrimination. . . . One can readily envision working environments so heavily polluted with discrimination as to destroy completely the emotional and psychological stability of minority group workers. . . ." 454 F.2d, at 238.

Courts applied this principle to harassment based on race, . . . religion, . . . and national origin. . . . Nothing in Title VII suggests that a hostile environment based on discriminatory *sexual* harassment should not be likewise prohibited. The Guidelines thus appropriately drew from, and were fully consistent with, the existing case law.

Since the Guidelines were issued, courts have uniformly held, and we agree, that a plaintiff may establish a violation of Title VII by proving that discrimination based on sex has created a hostile or abusive work environment. As the Court of Appeals for the Eleventh Circuit wrote in Henson v. Dundee, 682 F.2d 897, 902 (11th Cir. 1982):

> "Sexual harassment which creates a hostile or offensive environment for members of one sex is every bit the arbitrary barrier to sexual equality at the workplace that racial harassment is to racial equality. Surely, a requirement that a man or woman run a gauntlet of sexual abuse in return for the privilege of being allowed to work and make a living can be as demeaning and disconcerting as the harshest of racial epithets. . . ."

Of course, as the courts in both *Rogers* and *Henson* recognized, not all workplace conduct that may be described as "harassment" affects a "term, condition, or privilege" of employment within the meaning of Title VII. . . . For sexual harassment to be actionable, it must be sufficiently severe or pervasive "to alter the conditions of [the victim's] employment and create an abusive working environment." Respondent's allegations in this case—which include not only pervasive harassment but also criminal conduct of the most serious nature—are plainly sufficient to state a claim for "hostile environment" sexual harassment.

The question remains, however, whether the District Court's ultimate finding that respondent "was not the victim of sexual harassment" effectively disposed of respondent's claim. The Court of Appeals recognized, we think correctly, that this ultimate finding was likely based on one or both of two erroneous views of the law. First, the District Court apparently believed that a claim for sexual harassment will not lie absent an *economic* effect on the complainant's employment. See 23 FEP Cases at 43 ("It is without question that sexual harassment of female employees in which they are asked or required to submit to sexual demands as *a condition to obtain employment or to maintain employment or to obtain promotions* falls within protection of Title VII") (emphasis added). Since it appears that the District Court made its findings without ever considering the "hostile environment" theory of sexual harassment, the Court of Appeals' decision to remand was correct.

Second, the District Court's conclusion that no actionable harassment occurred might have rested on its earlier "finding" that "[if] [respondent] and Taylor did engage in an intimate or sexual relationship . . ., that relationship was a voluntary one." But the fact that sex-related conduct was "voluntary," in the sense that the complainant was not forced to participate against her will, is not a defense to a sexual harassment suit brought under Title VII. The gravamen of any sexual harassment claim is that the alleged sexual advances were "unwelcome." 29 CFR § 1604.11(a) (1985). While the question whether particular conduct was indeed unwelcome presents difficult problems of proof and turns largely on credibility determinations committed to the trier of fact, the District Court in this case erroneously focused on the "voluntariness" of respondent's participation in the claimed sexual episodes. The correct inquiry is whether respondent by her conduct indicated that the alleged sexual advances were unwelcome, not whether her actual participation in sexual intercourse was voluntary.

Petitioner contends that even if this case must be remanded to the District Court, the Court of Appeals erred in one of the terms of its remand. Specifically, the Court of Appeals stated that testimony about respondent's "dress and personal fantasies," which the District Court apparently admitted into evidence, "had no place in this litigation." The apparent ground for this conclusion was that respondent's voluntariness *vel non* in submitting to Taylor's advances was immaterial to her sexual harassment claim. While "voluntariness" in the sense of consent is not a defense to such a claim, it does not follow that a complainant's sexually provocative speech or dress is irrelevant as a matter of law in determining whether he or she found particular sexual advances unwelcome. To the contrary, such evidence is obviously relevant. The EEOC Guidelines emphasize that the trier of fact must determine the existence of sexual harassment in light of "the record as a whole" and "the totality of circumstances, such as the nature of the sexual advances and the context in which the alleged incidents occurred." 29 CFR § 1604.11(b) (1985). Respondent's claim that any marginal relevance of the evidence in question was outweighed by the potential for unfair prejudice is the sort of argument properly addressed to the District Court. In this case the District Court concluded that the evidence should be admitted, and the Court of Appeals' contrary conclusion was based upon the erroneous, categorical view that testimony about provocative dress and publicly expressed sexual fantasies "had no place in this litigation." While the District Court must carefully weigh the applicable considerations in deciding whether to admit evidence of this kind, there is no per se rule against its admissibility.

III

Although the District Court concluded that respondent had not proved a violation of Title VII, it nevertheless went on to consider the question of the bank's liability. Finding that "the bank was without notice" of Taylor's alleged conduct, and that notice to Taylor was not the equivalent of notice to the bank, the court concluded that the bank therefore could not be held liable for Taylor's alleged actions. The Court of Appeals took the opposite view, holding that an employer is strictly liable for a hostile environment created by a supervisor's sexual advances, even though the employer neither knew nor reasonably could have known of the alleged misconduct. The court held that a supervisor, whether or not he possesses the authority to hire, fire, or promote, is necessarily an "agent" of his employer for all Title VII purposes, since "even the appearance" of such authority may enable him to impose himself on his subordinates. . . .

This debate over the appropriate standard for employer liability has a rather abstract quality about it given the state of the record in this case. We do not know at this stage whether Taylor made any sexual advances toward respondent at all, let alone whether those advances were unwelcome, whether they were sufficiently pervasive to constitute a condition of employment, or whether they were "so pervasive and so long continuing . . . that the employer must have become conscious of [them]," Taylor v. Jones, 653 F.2d 1193, 1197–1199 (8th Cir. 1981) (holding employer liable for racially hostile working environment based on constructive knowledge).

We therefore decline the parties' invitation to issue a definitive rule on employer liability, but we do agree with the EEOC that Congress wanted courts to look to agency principles for guidance in this area. While such common-law principles may not be transferable in all their particulars to Title VII, Congress' decision to define "employer" to include any "agent" of an employer, 42 U.S.C. § 2000e(b), surely evinces an intent to place some limits on the acts of employees for which employers under Title VII are to be held responsible. For this reason, we hold that the Court of Appeals erred in concluding that employers are always automatically liable for sexual harassment by their supervisors. See generally Restatement (Second) of Agency §§ 219–237 (1958). For the same reason, absence of notice to an employer does not necessarily insulate that employer from liability.

Finally, we reject petitioner's view that the mere existence of a grievance procedure and a policy against discrimination, coupled with respondent's failure to invoke that procedure, must insulate petitioner from liability. While those facts are plainly relevant, the situation before us demonstrates why they are not necessarily dispositive. Petitioner's general nondiscrimination policy did not address sexual harassment in particular, and thus did not alert employees to their employer's interest in correcting that form of discrimination. Moreover, the bank's grievance procedure apparently required an employee to complain first to her supervisor, in this case Taylor. Since Taylor was the alleged perpetrator, it is not altogether surprising that respondent failed to invoke the procedure and report her grievance to him. Petitioner's contention that respondent's failure should insulate it from liability might be substantially stronger if its procedures were better calculated to encourage victims of harassment to come forward.

IV

In sum, we hold that a claim of "hostile environment" sex discrimination is actionable under Title VII, that the District Court's findings were insufficient to dispose of respondent's hostile environment claim, and that the District Court did not err in admitting testimony about respondent's sexually provocative speech and dress. As to employer liability, we conclude that the Court of Appeals was wrong to entirely disregard agency principles and impose absolute liability on employers for the acts of their supervisors, regardless of the circumstances of a particular case.

Accordingly, the judgment of the Court of Appeals reversing the judgment of the District Court is affirmed, and the case is remanded for further proceedings consistent with this opinion.

It is so ordered.

■ JUSTICE STEVENS, concurring.

Because I do not see any inconsistency between the two opinions, and because I believe the question of statutory construction that Justice Marshall has answered is fairly presented by the record, I join both the Court's opinion and Justice Marshall's opinion.

■ JUSTICE MARSHALL, with whom JUSTICE BRENNAN, JUSTICE BLACKMUN, and JUSTICE STEVENS join, concurring in the judgment.

I fully agree with the Court's conclusion that workplace sexual harassment is illegal, and violates Title VII. Part III of the Court's opinion, however, leaves open the circumstances in which an employer is responsible under Title VII for such conduct. Because I believe that question to be properly before us, I write separately.

The issue the Court declines to resolve is addressed in the EEOC Guidelines on Discrimination Because of Sex, which are entitled to great deference. . . . The Guidelines explain:

> "Applying general Title VII principles, an employer . . . is responsible for its acts and those of its agents and supervisory employees with respect to sexual harassment regardless of whether the specific acts complained of were authorized or even forbidden by the employer and regardless of whether the employer knew or should have known of their occurrence. The

> Commission will examine the circumstances of the particular employment relationship and the job [functions] performed by the individual in determining whether an individual acts in either a supervisory or agency capacity.
>
> "With respect to conduct between fellow employees, an employer is responsible for acts of sexual harassment in the workplace where the employer (or its agents or supervisory employees) knows or should have known of the conduct, unless it can show that it took immediate and appropriate corrective action." 29 CFR §§ 1604.11(c), (d) (1985).

The Commission, in issuing the Guidelines, explained that its rule was "in keeping with the general standard of employer liability with respect to agents and supervisory employees. . . . [T]he Commission and the courts have held for years that an employer is liable if a supervisor or an agent violates the Title VII, regardless of knowledge or any other mitigating factor." 45 Fed. Reg. 74676 (1980). I would adopt the standard set out by the Commission.

An employer can act only through individual supervisors and employees; discrimination is rarely carried out pursuant to a formal vote of a corporation's board of directors. Although an employer may sometimes adopt companywide discriminatory policies violative of Title VII, acts that may constitute Title VII violations are generally effected through the actions of individuals, and often an individual may take such a step even in defiance of company policy. Nonetheless, Title VII remedies, such as reinstatement and backpay, generally run against the employer as an entity. The question thus arises as to the circumstances under which an employer will be held liable under Title VII for the acts of its employees.

The answer supplied by general Title VII law, like that supplied by federal labor law, is that the act of a supervisory employee or agent is imputed to the employer. Thus, for example, when a supervisor discriminatorily fires or refuses to promote a black employee, that act is, without more, considered the act of the employer. The courts do not stop to consider whether the employer otherwise had "notice" of the action, or even whether the supervisor had actual authority to act as he did. . . . Following that approach, every Court of Appeals that has considered the issue has held that sexual harassment by supervisory personnel is automatically imputed to the employer when the harassment results in tangible job detriment to the subordinate employee. . . .

NOTES ON *MERITOR SAVINGS BANK, FSB V. VINSON*

1. **What Was Decided.** *Meritor Savings Bank* addressed two broad questions, but resolved only the first of them: What constitutes sexual harassment actionable under Title VII? As an initial matter, the Court held that the plaintiff need not allege that the harassing conduct was so severe that she was forced into sexual activity against her will. It is sufficient if the

harassing conduct was "unwelcome." The Court's main holding was that the plaintiff could assert a "hostile environment" claim under Title VII. The plaintiff need only allege that she was subjected to sexual harassment that was "sufficiently severe or pervasive to alter the conditions of [the victim's] employment and create an abusive working environment." (Internal quotation marks omitted.) The plaintiff need not allege "quid pro quo" sexual harassment, in which the grant or denial of economic benefits is conditioned upon the plaintiff's submission to sexual advances. Both forms of sexual harassment are prohibited by Title VII, but in hostile environment cases, the plaintiff need not establish any connection between the harassment and concrete economic benefits, such as a raise or promotion.

The second question, discussed by the Court but not entirely resolved, was the circumstances under which an employer can be held liable for sexual harassment of its employees. This question arises in any case in which the harassing employee cannot be immediately identified with the employer. Sexual harassment committed by a sole proprietor or by the president or other high official of an organizational employer can easily be attributed to the employer itself. Harassment by other individuals raises a question under the coverage provisions of Title VII, which apply only to an "employer" as defined by the statute (generally, a public employer or a private employer with 15 or more employees), or to "any agent" of an employer. The Court resolved this question only to the extent of rejecting two per se rules, one imposing vicarious liability upon employers for all forms of harassment by their supervisors and one relieving employers entirely of liability in the absence of notice of the harassing conduct. The Court left the law on this question to be developed according to common law principles.

Both what constitutes sexual harassment under Title VII and when an employer can be held liable for sexual harassment are questions that have been addressed in cases after *Meritor Savings Bank*.

2. *Harris v. Forklift Systems, Inc.* In Harris v. Forklift Systems, Inc., 510 U.S. 17 (1993), the plaintiff alleged that the president of Forklift Systems had engaged in various forms of sexual harassment. The case therefore presented no question of vicarious liability of the employer. The only question was whether the acts alleged were "sufficiently severe or pervasive to alter the conditions of the victim's employment and create an abusive working environment." As the Court described the facts:

> The Magistrate found that, throughout Harris' time at Forklift, Hardy [the employer's president] often insulted her because of her gender and often made her the target of unwanted sexual innuendoes. Hardy told Harris on several occasions, in the presence of other employees, "You're a woman, what do you know" and "We need a man as the rental manager"; at least once, he told her she was "a dumb ass woman." Again in front of others, he suggested that the two of them "go to the Holiday Inn to negotiate [Harris'] raise." Hardy occasionally asked Harris and other female employees to get coins from his front pants pocket. He threw objects on the ground in front of Harris and other women, and asked them

to pick the objects up. He made sexual innuendoes about Harris' and other women's clothing.

In mid August 1987, Harris complained to Hardy about his conduct. Hardy said he was surprised that Harris was offended, claimed he was only joking, and apologized. He also promised he would stop, and based on this assurance Harris stayed on the job. But in early September, Hardy began anew: While Harris was arranging a deal with one of Forklift's customers, he asked her, again in front of other employees, "What did you do, promise the guy . . . some [sex] Saturday night?" On October 1, Harris collected her paycheck and quit.

Based on these facts, the District Court found no sexual harassment because Hardy's comments, although offensive were not "so severe as to be expected to seriously affect [Harris'] psychological well being." The Court of Appeals affirmed. Justice O'Connor, writing for a unanimous Court, reversed, reasoning as follows:

[The standard from *Meritor Savings Bank*], which we reaffirm today, takes a middle path between making actionable any conduct that is merely offensive and requiring the conduct to cause a tangible psychological injury. As we pointed out in *Meritor*, "mere utterance of an . . . epithet which engenders offensive feelings in an employee," ibid. (internal quotation marks omitted) does not sufficiently affect the conditions of employment to implicate Title VII. Conduct that is not severe or pervasive enough to create an objectively hostile or abusive work environment, an environment that a reasonable person would find hostile or abusive, is beyond Title VII's purview. Likewise, if the victim does not subjectively perceive the environment to be abusive, the conduct has not actually altered the conditions of the victim's employment, and there is no Title VII violation.

But Title VII comes into play before the harassing conduct leads to a nervous breakdown. A discriminatorily abusive work environment, even one that does not seriously affect employees' psychological well being, can and often will detract from employees' job performance, discourage employees from remaining on the job, or keep them from advancing in their careers. Moreover, even without regard to these tangible effects, the very fact that the discriminatory conduct was so severe or pervasive that it created a work environment abusive to employees because of their race, gender, religion, or national origin offends Title VII's broad rule of workplace equality. The appalling conduct alleged in *Meritor*, and the reference in that case to environments "so heavily polluted with discrimination as to destroy completely the emotional and psychological stability of minority group workers," merely present some especially egregious examples of harassment. They do not mark the boundary of what is actionable.

> We therefore believe the District Court erred in relying on whether the conduct "seriously affect[ed] plaintiff's psychological well being" or led her to "suffe[r] injury." Such an inquiry may needlessly focus the factfinder's attention on concrete psychological harm, an element Title VII does not require. Certainly Title VII bars conduct that would seriously affect a reasonable person's psychological well being, but the statute is not limited to such conduct. So long as the environment would reasonably be perceived, and is perceived, as hostile or abusive, *Meritor*, supra, 477 U.S. at 67, there is no need for it also to be psychologically injurious.
>
> This is not, and by its nature cannot be, a mathematically precise test. . . . But we can say that whether an environment is "hostile" or "abusive" can be determined only by looking at all the circumstances. These may include the frequency of the discriminatory conduct; its severity; whether it is physically threatening or humiliating, or a mere offensive utterance; and whether it unreasonably interferes with an employee's work performance. The effect on the employee's psychological well being is, of course, relevant to determining whether the plaintiff actually found the environment abusive. But while psychological harm, like any other relevant factor, may be taken into account, no single factor is required.

Justice Scalia filed a brief concurring opinion, pointing out the lack of clarity in the standard for liability: " 'Abusive' (or 'hostile,' which in this context I take to mean the same thing) does not seem to me a very clear standard, and I do not think clarity is at all increased by adding the adverb 'objectively' or by appealing to a 'reasonable person's' notion of what the vague word means." Justice Ginsburg also filed a short concurring opinion emphasizing that, apart from the BFOQ, "Title VII declares discriminatory practices based on race, gender, religion, or national origin equally unlawful."

For articles on the general implications of *Meritor* and *Harris*, see Cheryl L. Anderson, "Thinking Within the Box": How Proof Models are Used to Limit the Scope of Sexual Harassment Law, 19 Hofstra Lab. & Emp. L.J. 125 (2001); Wendy N. Hess, Workplace Rumors About Women's Sexual Promiscuity as Gender-Based Insults Under Title VII, 31 A.B.A. J. Lab. & Emp. L. 447 (2016); Wendy N. Hess, Slut-Shaming in the Workplace: Sexual Rumors & Hostile Environment Claims, 40 N.Y.U. Rev. L. & Soc. Change 581 (2016); Richard C. Sorenson et al., Solving the Chronic Problem of Sexual Harassment in the Workplace: An Empirical Study of Factors Affecting Employee Perceptions and Consequences of Sexual Harassment, 34 Cal. W. L. Rev. 457 (1998).

3. The Meaning of "Severe or Pervasive." In *Meritor Savings Bank*, the Court had no need to articulate the precise content of the standard for hostile environment sexual harassment. The conduct there was so extreme that it satisfied any plausible standard of severity. *Harris v. Forklift Systems* was different. The Court deliberately set the standard somewhere between conduct that is "merely offensive" and conduct causing "a tangible psychological injury." See Eugene Volokh, What Speech Does "Hostile Work Environment" Harassment Law Restrict?, 85 Geo. L.J. 627 (1997).

Consider, first, the risks of setting the standard for establishing liability too low. Would it transform Title VII into a code of etiquette in the work place, imposing liability simply for bad manners? From the perspective of employees, it would deter them from engaging in casual discussion whenever there was any risk of offending members of the opposite sex. For employers, it would impose onerous burdens of policing the way in which individual employees interact with one another. Or, alternatively, it might discourage employers from mixing male and female employees together, possibly leading to a decrease in the employment opportunities of women instead of the increase that Title VII was intended to foster.

For discussion of these issues, see Judith J. Jamison, License to Harass Women: Requiring Hostile Environment Sexual Harassment to Be "Severe or Pervasive" Discriminates Among "Terms and Conditions" of Employment, 62 Md. L. Rev. 85 (2003); Beth A. Quinn, The Paradox of Complaining: Law, Humor, and Harassment in the Everyday Work World, 25 Law & Soc. Inquiry 1151 (2000); Anita Bernstein, Treating Sexual Harassment with Respect, 111 Harv. L. Rev. 445 (1997); Henry L. Chambers, Jr., (Un)Welcome Conduct and the Sexually Hostile Environment, 53 Ala. L. Rev. 733 (2002); Nancy Ehrenreich, Pluralist Myths and Powerless Men: The Ideology of Reasonableness in Sexual Harassment Law, 99 Yale L.J. 1177 (1990).

4. **Reasonable Person or Reasonable Woman (or Man)?** Related to the question of how high the standard for establishing sexual harassment should be set is the question whether it should be framed in sex-specific terms, and in particular, in terms of a "reasonable woman" if the plaintiff is a woman. Without explicitly addressing this question, all of the opinions in *Harris* use the sex-neutral phrase "reasonable person," rather than sex-specific phrases such as "reasonable woman" or "reasonable man." Does the Supreme Court's choice of a sex-neutral phrase lay this issue to rest? Assuming that the jury is instructed to determine whether a "reasonable person" would find the alleged harassment to be severe or pervasive, would it necessarily take into account the sex of the plaintiff in actually applying this standard? How could it avoid doing so?

In a departure from the Supreme Court's neutral terminology, the Ninth Circuit has used the "reasonable woman" standard to assess the effects on women of abusive conduct directed at employees of both sexes. In EEOC v. National Education Association, 422 F.3d 840 (9th Cir. 2005), three women working for the defendant labor union, the National Education Association (NEA), claimed that it had created a sex-based hostile work environment because their supervisor frequently "screamed" profanities at female employees, with little or no provocation, and acted in a menacing manner. Although the behavior had no sexual dimension, and the supervisor seemed to act similarly towards male employees, the impact on the men seemed to be far less negative than it was for the women, some of whom became fearful and even resigned from their jobs. The district court dismissed the claim because there was no sexual dimension to the supervisor's behavior or no animus against women on his part, but the Ninth Circuit reversed, holding that the plaintiffs had adequately pleaded a claim of sex discrimination: "There is no legal requirement that hostile acts be overtly sex- or gender-specific in content, whether marked by language, by sex or gender stereotypes, or by sexual overtures." Because the plaintiffs responded more negatively to the behavior than men, as reasonable women would, the supervisor's conduct was deemed to treat women differently, even if, in fact, the supervisor treated men and women identically. The court found that the only important inquiry was into the effect of the behavior, both subjectively and objectively. The women's complaints convinced the court they suffered greater subjective harm than did the men, in effect subjecting the employer to liability for behavior that is not discriminatory in intent. Does this case essentially involve a claim for disparate impact? If so, how would it fit with the requirements for proof of sexual harassment?

Several commentators have discussed the significance of the Supreme Court's use of the "reasonable person" standard. Kathryn Abrams, The New Jurisprudence of Sexual Harassment, 83 Cornell L. Rev. 1169 (1998); Anita Bernstein, Treating Sexual Harassment with Respect, 111 Harv. L. Rev. 446 (1997); Jeremy A. Blumenthal, The Reasonable Woman Standard: A Meta-Analytic Review of Gender Differences in Perceptions of Sexual Harassment, 22 L. & Hum. Behav. 33 (1998); Kingsley R. Browne, An Evolutionary Perspective on Sexual Harassment: Seeking Roots in Biology Rather than Ideology, 8 J. Contemp. Issues 5 (1997); Katherine M. Franke, What's Wrong With Sexual Harassment?, 49 Stan. L. Rev. 691 (1997); Elissa L. Perry, Carol T. Kulik & Anne C. Bourhis, The Reasonable Woman Standard: Effects on Sexual Harassment Court Decisions, 28 L. & Hum. Behav. 9 (2004); Stephanie M. Wildman, Ending Male Privilege Beyond the Reasonable Woman, 98 Mich. L. Rev. 1797 (2000).

5. Constitutional Limits. Constitutional arguments that the prohibition against sexual harassment goes too far most naturally take the form of an assertion of the right to privacy: that what employees do or say to other employees at work is their own business, or at most the business also of their employer. But because places of employment are open to so many people, from co-employees to members of the public, it is difficult to find a strong constitutionally protected interest in individual privacy in the workplace. Critics of the law of sexual harassment have therefore turned to the First Amendment, arguing that it results in a government-imposed regime of employer censorship. Kingsley R. Browne, Title VII as Censorship: Hostile-Environment Harassment and the First Amendment, 52 Ohio St. L.J. 481 (1991); Eugene Volokh, Comment, Freedom of Speech and Workplace Harassment, 39 UCLA L. Rev. 1791 (1992). Is it a sufficient reply to this argument that the requirement that the harassment be "severe or pervasive" eliminates most problems of censorship? Employees who would express themselves through harassment in the workplace can either choose more moderate means of expression or engage in harassing speech in some other forum. The victims of harassment have no such choice, short of quitting and looking for a new job. For discussion of this issue and a comprehensive analysis of the public nature of the workplace, see Cynthia Estlund, Working

Together: How Workplace Bonds Strengthen a Diverse Democracy (2003); Cynthia Estlund, Freedom of Speech in the Workplace and the Problem of Discriminatory Harassment, 75 Tex. L. Rev. 687 (1997).

The argument that the law of sexual harassment violates the First Amendment has led to a lively debate in the academic literature. See J.M. Balkin, Free Speech and Hostile Environments, 99 Colum. L. Rev. 2295 (1999); David E. Bernstein, Defending the First Amendment From Antidiscrimination Laws, 82 N.C. L. Rev. 223 (2003); Kingsley R. Browne, Zero Tolerance for the First Amendment: Title VII's Regulation of Employee Speech, 27 Ohio N.U. L. Rev. 563 (2001); Deborah Epstein, Can a "Dumb Ass Woman" Achieve Equality in the Workplace? Running the Gauntlet of Hostile Environment Harassing Speech, 84 Geo. L.J. 399 (1996); Richard H. Fallon, Jr., Sexual Harassment, Content Neutrality, and the First Amendment Dog That Didn't Bark, 1994 Sup. Ct. Rev. 1 (1994); Nadine Strossen, Regulating Workplace Sexual Harassment and Upholding the First Amendment—Avoiding a Collision, 37 Vill. L. Rev. 757 (1992); Nadine Strossen, The Tensions Between Regulating Workplace Harassment and the First Amendment: No Trump, 71 Chi.-Kent L. Rev. 701 (1995).

6. Evidence of the Plaintiff's Behavior. Related to the question of what constitutes sexual harassment is the evidentiary question of how it can be proved and, in particular, what kind of evidence is admissible on the question whether the allegedly harassing conduct was unwelcome to the plaintiff. After the decision in *Meritor Savings Bank*, the Federal Rules of Evidence were amended to make evidence of the plaintiff's sexual history inadmissible in most circumstances. This "rape shield" rule, originating in concerns about protecting complaining witnesses in rape cases from intrusive cross-examination, also applies in civil litigation, including sexual harassment cases. It provides as follows:

> **Federal Rule of Evidence 412. Sex-Offense Cases: The Victim**
>
> **(a) Prohibited Uses.** The following evidence is not admissible in a civil or criminal proceeding involving alleged sexual misconduct:
>
> (1) evidence offered to prove that a victim engaged in other sexual behavior; or
>
> (2) evidence offered to prove a victim's sexual predisposition.
>
> **(b) Exceptions.** . . .
>
> (2) Civil Cases. In a civil case, the court may admit evidence offered to prove a victim's sexual behavior or sexual predisposition if its probative value substantially outweighs the danger of harm to any victim and of unfair prejudice to any party. The court may admit evidence of a victim's reputation only if the victim has placed it in controversy.

This rule also requires a written motion 14 days before trial to obtain admission of such evidence and stipulates that any hearing on admissibility be held in camera, with the records of the hearing and all related papers maintained under seal. After passage of this rule, how much is left of the discussion in *Meritor Savings Bank* of the evidence of the plaintiff's behavior that can be used to prove that she acquiesced in the allegedly harassing conduct? Does the rule make any difference to the plaintiff's burden of proving that the conduct was unwelcome? Does it make it any easier for the plaintiff to meet this burden?

7. **Bibliography.** For books and collections of essays on the law of sexual harassment, see Directions in Sexual Harassment Law (Catharine A. MacKinnon and Reva B. Siegel eds., 2004); Theresa M. Beiner, Gender Myths v. Working Realities: Using Social Science to Reformulate Sexual Harassment Law (2005); Mane Hajdin, The Law of Sexual Harassment: A Critique (2002); Barbara Lindemann & David D. Kadue, Sexual Harassment in Employment Law (1992 & Supp. 1999); Jeffry Minso, Questions of Conduct: Sexual Harassment, Citizenship, Government (1993); Titus E. Aaron & Judith Isaksen, Sexual Harassment in the Workplace: A Guide to the Law and a Research Overview for Employers and Employees (1993); Symposium, Global Perspectives on Workplace Harassment Law, 8 Emp. Rts. & Emp. Pol'y J. 151 (2004); Colloquy on Sexual Harassment, 83 Cornell L. Rev. 1169 (1998); Special Project, Current Issues in Sexual Harassment Law, 48 Vand. L. Rev. 1009 (1995); Symposium, Biology and Sexual Aggression: Part I, 39 Jurimetrics 113 (1999); Symposium, Strengthening Title VII: 1997–1998 Sexual Harassment Jurisprudence, 7 Wm. & Mary Bill Rts. J. 671 (1999); Symposium, Balancing the Equities: The Evolving Law of Sexual Harassment, 34 Wake Forest L. Rev. 1 (1999).

For general articles surveying the field of sexual harassment, see Elizabeth Anderson, Recent Thinking About Sexual Harassment: A Review Essay, 34 Phil. & Pub. Aff. 284 (2006); Mary Anne Franks, Sexual Harassment 2.0, 71 Md. L. Rev. 655 (2012); Ann Juliano & Stewart J. Schwab, The Sweep of Sexual Harassment Cases, 86 Cornell L. Rev. 548 (2001); Catherine A. MacKinnon, Directions in Sexual Harassment Law, 31 Nova L. Rev. 225 (2007); Ann C. McGinley, Harassment of Sex(y) Workers: Applying Title VII to Sexualized Industries, 18 Yale J.L. & Feminism 65 (2006); Vicki Schultz, Sex and Work, 18 Yale J.L. & Feminism 223 (2006); Rebecca K. Lee, The Organization as a Gendered Entity: A Response to Professor Schultz's "The Sanitized Workplace," 15 Colum. J. Gender & L. 609 (2006). See also Henry L. Chambers, Jr., A Unifying Theory of Sex Discrimination, 34 Ga. L. Rev. 1591 (2000); Jennifer Ann Drobac, Sex and the Workplace: Consenting Adolescents and a Conflict of Laws, 79 Wash. L. Rev. 471 (2004); L. Camille Hebert, The Disparate Impact of Sexual Harassment: Does Motive Matter?, 53 U. Kan. L. Rev. 341 (2004); Joni Hersch & Beverly Moran, He Said, She Said, Let's Hear What the Data Say: Sexual Harassment in the Media, Courts, EEOC, and Social Science, 101 Ky. L.J. 753 (2012–2013); Lua Kamal Yuille, Liberating Sexual Harassment Law, 22 Mich. J. Gender & L. 345 (2015); Noah D. Zatz, Managing the Macaw: Third-Party Harassers, Accommodation, and the Disaggregation of Discriminatory Intent, 109 Colum. L. Rev. 1357 (2009); Symposium, The Law of Workplace Bullying, 32 Comp. Lab. L. & Pol'y J. 1 (2010).

For empirical evidence on the extent of sexual harassment, see Heather Antecol & Deborah Cobb-Clark, The Changing Nature of Employment-Related Sexual Harassment: Evidence From the U.S. Federal Government,

1978–1994, 57 Ind. & Lab. Rel. Rev. 443 (2004); J. Mitchell Pickerill, Robert A. Jackson & Meredith Newman, Changing Perceptions of Sexual Harassment in the Federal Workforce, 1987–94, 28 Law & Pol'y 368 (2006); Catherine M. Sharkey, Dissecting Damages: An Empirical Exploration of Sexual Harassment Awards, 3 J. Empirical Legal Stud. 1 (2006).

Oncale v. Sundowner Offshore Services, Inc.

523 U.S. 75 (1998).

■ JUSTICE SCALIA delivered the opinion of the Court.

This case presents the question whether workplace harassment can violate Title VII's prohibition against "discriminat[ion] . . . because of . . . sex," 42 U.S.C. § 2000e–2(a)(1), when the harasser and the harassed employee are of the same sex.

I

The District Court having granted summary judgment for respondent, we must assume the facts to be as alleged by petitioner Joseph Oncale. The precise details are irrelevant to the legal point we must decide, and in the interest of both brevity and dignity we shall describe them only generally. In late October 1991, Oncale was working for respondent Sundowner Offshore Services on a Chevron U.S.A., Inc., oil platform in the Gulf of Mexico. He was employed as a roustabout on an eight-man crew which included respondents John Lyons, Danny Pippen, and Brandon Johnson. Lyons, the crane operator, and Pippen, the driller, had supervisory authority. On several occasions, Oncale was forcibly subjected to sex-related, humiliating actions against him by Lyons, Pippen and Johnson in the presence of the rest of the crew. Pippen and Lyons also physically assaulted Oncale in a sexual manner, and Lyons threatened him with rape.

Oncale's complaints to supervisory personnel produced no remedial action; in fact, the company's Safety Compliance Clerk, Valent Hohen, told Oncale that Lyons and Pippen "picked [on] him all the time too," and called him a name suggesting homosexuality. Oncale eventually quit—asking that his pink slip reflect that he "voluntarily left due to sexual harassment and verbal abuse." When asked at his deposition why he left Sundowner, Oncale stated "I felt that if I didn't leave my job, that I would be raped or forced to have sex."

Oncale filed a complaint against Sundowner in the United States District Court for the Eastern District of Louisiana, alleging that he was discriminated against in his employment because of his sex. Relying on the Fifth Circuit's decision in Garcia v. Elf Atochem North America, 28 F.3d 446, 451–452 (5th Cir. 1994), the district court held that "Mr. Oncale, a male, has no cause of action under Title VII for harassment by male co-workers." On appeal, a panel of the Fifth Circuit concluded that *Garcia* was binding Circuit precedent, and affirmed. We granted certiorari.

II

Title VII of the Civil Rights Act of 1964 provides, in relevant part, that "[i]t shall be an unlawful employment practice for an employer . . . to discriminate against any individual with respect to his compensation, terms, conditions, or privileges of employment, because of such individual's race, color, religion, sex, or national origin." 42 U.S.C. § 2000e–2(a)(1). We have held that this not only covers "terms" and "conditions" in the narrow contractual sense, but "evinces a congressional intent to strike at the entire spectrum of disparate treatment of men and women in employment." Meritor Savings Bank, FSB v. Vinson, 477 U.S. 57, 64 (1986) (citations and internal quotation marks omitted). "When the workplace is permeated with discriminatory intimidation, ridicule, and insult that is sufficiently severe or pervasive to alter the conditions of the victim's employment and create an abusive working environment, Title VII is violated." Harris v. Forklift Systems, Inc., 510 U.S. 17, 21 (1993) (citations and internal quotation marks omitted).

Title VII's prohibition of discrimination "because of . . . sex" protects men as well as women, Newport News Shipbuilding & Dry Dock Co. v. EEOC, 462 U.S. 669, 682 (1983), and in the related context of racial discrimination in the workplace we have rejected any conclusive presumption that an employer will not discriminate against members of his own race. "Because of the many facets of human motivation, it would be unwise to presume as a matter of law that human beings of one definable group will not discriminate against other members of that group." Castaneda v. Partida, 430 U.S. 482, 499 (1977). See also Id. at 514 n. 6 (Powell, J., joined by Burger, C.J., and REHNQUIST, J., dissenting). In Johnson v. Transportation Agency, Santa Clara Cty., 480 U.S. 616 (1987), a male employee claimed that his employer discriminated against him because of his sex when it preferred a female employee for promotion. Although we ultimately rejected the claim on other grounds, we did not consider it significant that the supervisor who made that decision was also a man. If our precedents leave any doubt on the question, we hold today that nothing in Title VII necessarily bars a claim of discrimination "because of . . . sex" merely because the plaintiff and the defendant (or the person charged with acting on behalf of the defendant) are of the same sex.

Courts have had little trouble with that principle in cases like *Johnson*, where an employee claims to have been passed over for a job or promotion. But when the issue arises in the context of a "hostile environment" sexual harassment claim, the state and federal courts have taken a bewildering variety of stances. Some, like the Fifth Circuit in this case, have held that same-sex sexual harassment claims are never cognizable under Title VII. See also, e.g., Goluszek v. H.P. Smith, 697 F. Supp. 1452 (N.D. Ill. 1988). Other decisions say that such claims are actionable only if the plaintiff can prove that the harasser is homosexual (and thus presumably motivated by sexual desire). Compare McWilliams

v. Fairfax County Board of Supervisors, 72 F.3d 1191 (4th Cir. 1996), with Wrightson v. Pizza Hut of America, 99 F.3d 138 (4th Cir. 1996). Still others suggest that workplace harassment that is sexual in content is always actionable, regardless of the harasser's sex, sexual orientation, or motivations. See Doe v. Belleville, 119 F.3d 563 (7th Cir. 1997).

We see no justification in the statutory language or our precedents for a categorical rule excluding same-sex harassment claims from the coverage of Title VII. As some courts have observed, male-on-male sexual harassment in the workplace was assuredly not the principal evil Congress was concerned with when it enacted Title VII. But statutory prohibitions often go beyond the principal evil to cover reasonably comparable evils, and it is ultimately the provisions of our laws rather than the principal concerns of our legislators by which we are governed. Title VII prohibits "discriminat[ion] . . . because of . . . sex" in the "terms" or "conditions" of employment. Our holding that this includes sexual harassment must extend to sexual harassment of any kind that meets the statutory requirements.

Respondents and their amici contend that recognizing liability for same-sex harassment will transform Title VII into a general civility code for the American workplace. But that risk is no greater for same-sex than for opposite-sex harassment, and is adequately met by careful attention to the requirements of the statute. Title VII does not prohibit all verbal or physical harassment in the workplace; it is directed only at "*discriminat[ion]* . . . because of . . . sex." We have never held that workplace harassment, even harassment between men and women, is automatically discrimination because of sex merely because the words used have sexual content or connotations. "The critical issue, Title VII's text indicates, is whether members of one sex are exposed to disadvantageous terms or conditions of employment to which members of the other sex are not exposed." *Harris*, supra, at 25 (GINSBURG, J., concurring).

Courts and juries have found the inference of discrimination easy to draw in most male-female sexual harassment situations, because the challenged conduct typically involves explicit or implicit proposals of sexual activity; it is reasonable to assume those proposals would not have been made to someone of the same sex. The same chain of inference would be available to a plaintiff alleging same-sex harassment, if there were credible evidence that the harasser was homosexual. But harassing conduct need not be motivated by sexual desire to support an inference of discrimination on the basis of sex. A trier of fact might reasonably find such discrimination, for example, if a female victim is harassed in such sex-specific and derogatory terms by another woman as to make it clear that the harasser is motivated by general hostility to the presence of women in the workplace. A same-sex harassment plaintiff may also, of course, offer direct comparative evidence about how the alleged harasser treated members of both sexes in a mixed-sex workplace. Whatever evidentiary route the plaintiff chooses to follow, he or she must always prove that the conduct at issue was not merely tinged with offensive sexual connotations, but actually constituted "*discrimina[tion]* . . . because of . . . sex."

And there is another requirement that prevents Title VII from expanding into a general civility code: As we emphasized in *Meritor* and *Harris*, the statute does not reach genuine but innocuous differences in the ways men and women routinely interact with members of the same sex and of the opposite sex. The prohibition of harassment on the basis of sex requires neither asexuality nor androgyny in the workplace; it forbids only behavior so objectively offensive as to alter the "conditions" of the victim's employment. "Conduct that is not severe or pervasive enough to create an objectively hostile or abusive work environment—an environment that a reasonable person would find hostile or abusive—is beyond Title VII's purview." *Harris*, 510 U.S., at 21, citing *Meritor*, 477 U.S., at 67. We have always regarded that requirement as crucial, and as sufficient to ensure that courts and juries do not mistake ordinary socializing in the workplace—such as male-on-male horseplay or intersexual flirtation—for discriminatory "conditions of employment."

We have emphasized, moreover, that the objective severity of harassment should be judged from the perspective of a reasonable person in the plaintiff's position, considering "all the circumstances." *Harris*, supra, at 23. In same-sex (as in all) harassment cases, that inquiry requires careful consideration of the social context in which particular behavior occurs and is experienced by its target. A professional football player's working environment is not severely or pervasively abusive, for example, if the coach smacks him on the buttocks as he heads onto the field—even if the same behavior would reasonably be experienced as abusive by the coach's secretary (male or female) back at the office. The real social impact of workplace behavior often depends on a constellation of surrounding circumstances, expectations, and relationships which are not fully captured by a simple recitation of the words used or the physical acts performed. Common sense, and an appropriate sensitivity to social context, will enable courts and juries to distinguish between simple teasing or roughhousing among members of the same sex, and conduct which a reasonable person in the plaintiff's position would find severely hostile or abusive.

III

Because we conclude that sex discrimination consisting of same-sex sexual harassment is actionable under Title VII, the judgment of the Court of Appeals for the Fifth Circuit is reversed, and the case is remanded for further proceedings consistent with this opinion.

It is so ordered.

■ JUSTICE THOMAS, concurring.

I concur because the Court stresses that in every sexual harassment case, the plaintiff must plead and ultimately prove Title VII's statutory requirement that there be discrimination "because of . . . sex."

NOTES ON *ONCALE V. SUNDOWNER OFFSHORE SERVICES, INC.*

1. **What Is Sexual About Sexual Harassment?** A persistent question about the foundations of the law of sexual harassment has been why it is prohibited at all by Title VII. If it is sex-based only in the sense that it involves sexual conduct, then it seems to fall wholly outside the coverage of the statute, which is concerned only with discrimination on the specified grounds of race, national origin, sex, and religion. If, on the other hand, it is sex-based only because it is directed at women, then claims of sexual harassment violate the evenhanded policy of the statute, not to protect any one group to the exclusion of others, but to prohibit discrimination against all groups. Even if the gravamen of sexual harassment claims is framed more neutrally, to prohibit harassment of men by women as well as the reverse, such claims would still be confined almost entirely to harassment of women. Instances of sexual harassment of men by women have proved to be relatively rare.

Oncale has laid all of these concerns to rest, first, by recognizing a claim of same-sex sexual harassment, and second, by recognizing that no aspect of the harassment need involve sexual conduct. As the Court said:

> [H]arassing conduct need not be motivated by sexual desire to support an inference of discrimination on the basis of sex. A trier of fact might reasonably find such discrimination, for example, if a female victim is harassed in such sex-specific and derogatory terms by another woman as to make it clear that the harasser is motivated by general hostility to the presence of women in the workplace.

Why did it take so long for these issues to be resolved? Is it the predominance of cases of men harassing women? Or is it the typically sexual nature of the comments or actions involved in male harassment of women? The opinion in *Meritor Savings Bank* should have dispensed with any need to prove sexual conduct, since it reviewed cases developing the law of sexual harassment by analogy to claims of racial harassment, which need not involve any sexual element at all.

Professor Vicki Schultz was the first to raise these questions. See Vicki Schultz, Reconceptualizing Sexual Harassment, 107 Yale L.J. 1683 (1998). In this article, she argued that courts focused too much on harassment related to sexual conduct, preventing plaintiffs from establishing harassment through conduct that is simply hostile to women in the workplace. Professor Schultz also offered an answer to the basic theoretical question of why Title VII prohibits sexual harassment at all. It does not establish a code of sexual behavior, in the workplace or anywhere else. Instead, she argued, the law of sexual harassment should serve the central purpose of the statute: "to enable everyone, regardless of their identities as men or women, or their personae as masculine or feminine, to pursue their chosen endeavors on equal, empowering terms." In a more recent article, she has elaborated on these arguments, even to the extent of expressing sympathy with the usually conservative criticism that sexual harassment law raises questions under the First Amendment. Vicki Schultz, The Sanitized Workplace, 112 Yale L.J. 2061 (2003). She argued that imposing liability on employers for sexual harassment based on sexual activity leads to overenforcement: to employers prohibiting all forms of sexual activity by their employees. Is this a consequence of the rules defining what constitutes sexual harassment or the rules governing the vicarious liability of employers? For another view of these questions, see Martin J. Katz, Reconsidering Attraction in Sexual Harassment, 79 Ind. L.J. 101 (2004).

Having resolved those questions, however, the opinion in *Oncale* has raised others in their place. The most puzzling is the "equal opportunity" harasser: a supervisor or co-employee who harasses both men and women equally. Immediately following the passage quoted above, the Court adds the following:

> A same-sex harassment plaintiff may also, of course, offer direct comparative evidence about how the alleged harasser treated members of both sexes in a mixed-sex workplace. Whatever evidentiary route the plaintiff chooses to follow, he or she must always prove that the conduct at issue was not merely tinged with offensive sexual connotations, but actually constituted "*discrimina[tion]* . . . because of . . . sex."

Does this passage insulate the "equal opportunity" harasser from liability? What if the harassment differs, as it usually does, depending upon the sex of the victim? Does it remain permissible to subject men and women to harassment that involves the same "tangible employment actions" or that is equally "severe or pervasive"? Doesn't this get the law exactly backwards, giving employers incentives to tolerate more rather than less harassment?

The Court relies heavily on decisions prohibiting other forms of reverse discrimination. On this view, *Oncale* is analogous to cases such as McDonald v. Santa Fe Trail Transportation Co., 427 U.S. 273 (1976), discussed more fully in Chapter 9, which held that whites could also sue for racial discrimination. Is same-sex sexual harassment exactly analogous? In particular, would a decision excluding this form of discrimination from the coverage of Title VII raise the same constitutional questions as excluding reverse racial discrimination?

2. Discrimination on the Basis of Sexual Orientation. Only recently has Title VII been interpreted to prohibit discrimination on the basis of sexual orientation. See Hively v. Ivy Tech Community College of Indiana, 853 F.3d 339 (7th Cir. 2017), which appears as a principal case in Chapter 6. Earlier decisions had uniformly rejected this interpretation of the statute. E.g., DeSantis v. Pacific Telephone & Telegraph Co., 608 F.2d 327 (9th Cir. 1979). And, in fact, bills to amend Title VII to prohibit discrimination on the basis of sexual orientation have been introduced in Congress, but have not yet been enacted. See Equality Act, S. 1006, 115th Cong. (2017); Equality Act, H.R. 2282, 115th Cong. (2017).

The changed interpretation of Title VII followed a seesawing course of constitutional decisions that finally resulted in the protection of gay sex from criminal prohibitions and the recognition of gay marriage despite state and federal laws to the contrary. Lawrence v. Texas, 539 U.S. 558 (2003); United States v. Windsor, 133 S. Ct. 2675 (2013); Obergefell v. Hodges, 135 S. Ct. 2584 (2015). These decisions, like others in constitutional law, have exercised a profound influence on interpretation of Title VII, altering its scope and coverage in ways that cannot be immediately appreciated. *Oncale* itself stops well short of recognizing any form of protection from harassment on the basis of sexual preference under Title VII. The closest the Court comes is to allow that the sexual preference of the harassing supervisor or employee, but not of the victim, might be relevant to a claim of same-sex sexual harassment. But if one form of evidence is relevant, how could the other be excluded? And, in practice, won't it prove to be difficult, if not impossible, to distinguish harassment based on the victim's sex from harassment based on the victim's sexual orientation? If a man is a victim of harassment because he is gay, isn't he also a victim of harassment because he is a man? Would extending the holding in *Oncale* to homosexual harassment amount to a sweeping change in the law? Does the practical effect of any such extension have to be distinguished from its theoretical implications?

3. **Bibliography.** The scholarly analysis of *Oncale* has concentrated on its implications for proof of sexual harassment generally and for harassment on the basis of sexual orientation in particular. See Mary Coombs, Title VII and Homosexual Harassment After *Oncale*: Was It a Victory?, 6 Duke J. Gender L. & Pol'y 113 (1999); Andrew Koppelman, Why Discrimination Against Lesbians and Gay Men is Sex Discrimination, 69 N.Y.U. L. Rev. 197 (1994); Zachary A. Kramer, Heterosexuality and Title VII, 103 Nw. U. L. Rev. 205 (2009); Zachary A. Kramer, The Ultimate Gender Stereotype: Equalizing Gender-Conforming and Gender-Nonconforming Homosexuals Under Title VII, 2004 U. Ill. L. Rev. 465; David S. Schwartz, When is Sex Because of Sex? The Causation Problem in Sexual Harassment Law, 150 U. Pa. L. Rev. 1697 (2002); Ronald Turner, Title VII and the Inequality-Enhancing Effects of the Bisexual and Equal Opportunity Harasser Defenses, 7 U. Pa. J. Lab. & Emp. L. 341 (2005); Steven L. Willborn, Taking Discrimination Seriously: *Oncale* and the Fate of Exceptionalism in Sexual Harassment Law, 7 Wm. & Mary Bill Rts. J. 677 (1999); David C. Yamada, The Phenomenon of "Workplace Bullying" and the Need for Status-Blind Hostile Work Environment Protection, 88 Geo. L.J. 475 (2000).

Burlington Industries, Inc. v. Ellerth

524 U.S. 742 (1998).

■ JUSTICE KENNEDY delivered the opinion of the Court.

We decide whether, under Title VII of the Civil Rights Act of 1964, an employee who refuses the unwelcome and threatening sexual advances of a supervisor, yet suffers no adverse, tangible job consequences, can recover against the employer without showing the employer is negligent or otherwise at fault for the supervisor's actions.

I

Summary judgment was granted for the employer, so we must take the facts alleged by the employee to be true. United States v. Diebold, Inc., 369 U.S. 654, 655 (1962) (*per curiam*). The employer is Burlington Industries, the petitioner. The employee is Kimberly Ellerth, the respondent. From March 1993 until May 1994, Ellerth worked as a salesperson in one of Burlington's divisions in Chicago, Illinois. During her employment, she alleges, she was subjected to constant sexual harassment by her supervisor, one Ted Slowik.

In the hierarchy of Burlington's management structure, Slowik was a mid-level manager. Burlington has eight divisions, employing more than 22,000 people in some 50 plants around the United States. Slowik was a vice president in one of five business units within one of the divisions. He had authority to make hiring and promotion decisions subject to the approval of his supervisor, who signed the paperwork. According to Slowik's supervisor, his position was "not considered an upper-level management position," and he was "not amongst the decision-making or policy-making hierarchy." Slowik was not Ellerth's immediate supervisor. Ellerth worked in a two-person office in Chicago, and she answered to her office colleague, who in turn answered to Slowik in New York.

Against a background of repeated boorish and offensive remarks and gestures which Slowik allegedly made, Ellerth places particular emphasis on three alleged incidents where Slowik's comments could be construed as threats to deny her tangible job benefits. In the summer of 1993, while on a business trip, Slowik invited Ellerth to the hotel lounge, an invitation Ellerth felt compelled to accept because Slowik was her boss. When Ellerth gave no encouragement to remarks Slowik made about her breasts, he told her to "loosen up" and warned, "you know, Kim, I could make your life very hard or very easy at Burlington."

In March 1994, when Ellerth was being considered for a promotion, Slowik expressed reservations during the promotion interview because she was not "loose enough." The comment was followed by his reaching over and rubbing her knee. Ellerth did receive the promotion; but when Slowik called to announce it, he told Ellerth, "you're gonna be out there with men who work in factories, and they certainly like women with pretty butts/legs."

In May 1994, Ellerth called Slowik, asking permission to insert a customer's logo into a fabric sample. Slowik responded, "I don't have time for you right now, Kim—unless you want to tell me what you're wearing." Ellerth told Slowik she had to go and ended the call. A day or two later, Ellerth called Slowik to ask permission again. This time he denied her request, but added something along the lines of, "are you wearing shorter skirts yet, Kim, because it would make your job a whole heck of a lot easier."

A short time later, Ellerth's immediate supervisor cautioned her about returning telephone calls to customers in a prompt fashion. In response, Ellerth quit. She faxed a letter giving reasons unrelated to the alleged sexual harassment we have described. About three weeks later, however, she sent a letter explaining she quit because of Slowik's behavior.

During her tenure at Burlington, Ellerth did not inform anyone in authority about Slowik's conduct, despite knowing Burlington had a policy against sexual harassment. In fact, she chose not to inform her immediate supervisor (not Slowik) because " 'it would be his duty as my supervisor to report any incidents of sexual harassment.' " On one occasion, she told Slowik a comment he made was inappropriate.

In October 1994, after receiving a right-to-sue letter from the Equal Employment Opportunity Commission (EEOC), Ellerth filed suit in the United States District Court for the Northern District of Illinois, alleging Burlington engaged in sexual harassment and forced her constructive discharge, in violation of Title VII. The District Court granted summary judgment to Burlington. The Court found Slowik's behavior, as described by Ellerth, severe and pervasive enough to create a hostile work environment, but found Burlington neither knew nor should have known about the conduct. There was no triable issue of fact on the latter point, and the Court noted Ellerth had not used Burlington's internal complaint procedures. Although Ellerth's claim was framed as a hostile work environment complaint, the District Court observed there was a quid pro quo 'component' to the hostile environment. Proceeding from the premise that an employer faces vicarious liability for quid pro quo harassment, the District Court thought it necessary to apply a negligence standard because the quid pro quo merely contributed to the hostile work environment. The District Court also dismissed Ellerth's constructive discharge claim.

The Court of Appeals en banc reversed in a decision which produced eight separate opinions and no consensus for a controlling rationale. The judges were able to agree on the problem they confronted. Vicarious liability, not failure to comply with a duty of care, was the essence of Ellerth's case against Burlington on appeal. The judges seemed to agree Ellerth could recover if Slowik's unfulfilled threats to deny her tangible job benefits was sufficient to impose vicarious liability on Burlington. Jansen v. Packaging Corp. of America, 123 F.3d 490, 494 (7th Cir. 1997) (per curiam). With the exception of Judges Coffey and Easterbrook, the judges also agreed Ellerth's claim could be categorized as one of quid pro quo harassment, even though she had received the promotion and had suffered no other tangible retaliation.

The consensus disintegrated on the standard for an employer's liability for such a claim. Six judges, Judges Flaum, Cummings, Bauer,

Evans, Rovner, and Diane P. Wood, agreed the proper standard was vicarious liability, and so Ellerth could recover even though Burlington was not negligent. They had different reasons for the conclusion. According to Judges Flaum, Cummings, Bauer, and Evans, whether a claim involves a quid pro quo determines whether vicarious liability applies; and they in turn defined quid pro quo to include a supervisor's threat to inflict a tangible job injury whether or not it was completed. Judges Wood and Rovner interpreted agency principles to impose vicarious liability on employers for most claims of supervisor sexual harassment, even absent a quid pro quo.

Although Judge Easterbrook did not think Ellerth had stated a quid pro quo claim, he would have followed the law of the controlling State to determine the employer's liability, and by this standard, the employer would be liable here. In contrast, Judge Kanne said Ellerth had stated a quid pro quo claim, but negligence was the appropriate standard of liability when the quid pro quo involved threats only.

Chief Judge Posner, joined by Judge Manion, disagreed. He asserted Ellerth could not recover against Burlington despite having stated a quid pro quo claim. According to Chief Judge Posner, an employer is subject to vicarious liability for "act[s] that significantly alter the terms or conditions of employment," or "company act[s]." In the emergent terminology, an unfulfilled quid pro quo is a mere threat to do a company act rather than the act itself, and in these circumstances, an employer can be found liable for its negligence only. Chief Judge Posner also found Ellerth failed to create a triable issue of fact as to Burlington's negligence.

Judge Coffey rejected all of the above approaches because he favored a uniform standard of negligence in almost all sexual harassment cases.

The disagreement revealed in the careful opinions of the judges of the Court of Appeals reflects the fact that Congress has left it to the courts to determine controlling agency law principles in a new and difficult area of federal law. We granted certiorari to assist in defining the relevant standards of employer liability. 522 U.S. 1086 (1998).

II

At the outset, we assume an important proposition yet to be established before a trier of fact. It is a premise assumed as well, in explicit or implicit terms, in the various opinions by the judges of the Court of Appeals. The premise is: a trier of fact could find in Slowik's remarks numerous threats to retaliate against Ellerth if she denied some sexual liberties. The threats, however, were not carried out or fulfilled. Cases based on threats which are carried out are referred to often as quid pro quo cases, as distinct from bothersome attentions or sexual remarks that are sufficiently severe or pervasive to create a hostile work environment. The terms quid pro quo and hostile work environment are helpful, perhaps, in making a rough demarcation between cases in which threats are carried out and those where they are not or are absent altogether, but beyond this are of limited utility.

Section 703(a) of Title VII forbids

"an employer—

"(1) to fail or refuse to hire or to discharge any individual, or otherwise to discriminate against any individual with respect to his compensation, terms, conditions or privileges of employment, because of such individual's . . . sex." 42 U.S.C. § 2000e–2(a)(1).

"Quid pro quo" and "hostile work environment" do not appear in the statutory text. The terms appeared first in the academic literature, see C. MacKinnon, Sexual Harassment of Working Women (1979); found their way into decisions of the Courts of Appeals, see, e.g., Henson v. Dundee, 682 F.2d 897, 909 (11th Cir. 1982); and were mentioned in this Court's decision in Meritor Savings Bank, FSB v. Vinson, 477 U.S. 57 (1986). See generally E. Scalia, The Strange Career of Quid Pro Quo Sexual Harassment, 21 Harv. J.L. & Pub. Policy 307 (1998).

In *Meritor*, the terms served a specific and limited purpose. There we considered whether the conduct in question constituted discrimination in the terms or conditions of employment in violation of Title VII. We assumed, and with adequate reason, that if an employer demanded sexual favors from an employee in return for a job benefit, discrimination with respect to terms or conditions of employment was explicit. Less obvious was whether an employer's sexually demeaning behavior altered terms or conditions of employment in violation of Title VII. We distinguished between quid pro quo claims and hostile environment claims and said both were cognizable under Title VII, though the latter requires harassment that is severe or pervasive. The principal significance of the distinction is to instruct that Title VII is violated by either explicit or constructive alterations in the terms or conditions of employment and to explain the latter must be severe or pervasive. The distinction was not discussed for its bearing upon an employer's liability for an employee's discrimination. On this question *Meritor* held, with no further specifics, that agency principles controlled.

Nevertheless, as use of the terms grew in the wake of *Meritor*, they acquired their own significance. The standard of employer responsibility turned on which type of harassment occurred. If the plaintiff established a quid pro quo claim, the Courts of Appeals held, the employer was subject to vicarious liability. See Davis v. Sioux City, 115 F.3d 1365, 1367 (CA8 1997); Nichols v. Frank, 42 F.3d 503, 513–514 (9th Cir. 1994); Bouton v. BMW of North America, Inc., 29 F.3d 103, 106–107 (3rd Cir. 1994); Sauers v. Salt Lake County, 1 F.3d 1122, 1127 (10th Cir. 1993); Kauffman v. Allied Signal, Inc., 970 F.2d 178, 185–186 (6th Cir.), cert. denied, 506 U.S. 1041 (1992); Steele v. Offshore Shipbuilding, Inc., 867 F.2d 1311, 1316 (11th Cir. 1989). The rule encouraged Title VII plaintiffs to state their claims as quid pro quo claims, which in turn put expansive pressure on the definition. The equivalence of the quid pro quo label and vicarious liability is illustrated by this case. The question presented on certiorari is whether Ellerth can state a claim of quid pro quo harassment, but the issue of real concern to the parties is whether Burlington has vicarious liability for Slowik's alleged misconduct, rather than liability limited to its own negligence. The question presented for certiorari asks:

> "Whether a claim of quid pro quo sexual harassment may be stated under Title VII . . . where the plaintiff employee has neither submitted to the sexual advances of the alleged harasser nor suffered any tangible effects on the compensation, terms, conditions or privileges of employment as a consequence of a refusal to submit to those advances?"

We do not suggest the terms quid pro quo and hostile work environment are irrelevant to Title VII litigation. To the extent they illustrate the distinction between cases involving a threat which is carried out and offensive conduct in general, the terms are relevant when there is a threshold question whether a plaintiff can prove discrimination in violation of Title VII. When a plaintiff proves that a tangible employment action resulted from a refusal to submit to a supervisor's sexual demands, he or she establishes that the employment decision itself constitutes a change in the terms and conditions of employment that is actionable under Title VII. For any sexual harassment preceding the employment decision to be actionable, however, the conduct must be severe or pervasive. Because Ellerth's claim involves only unfulfilled threats, it should be categorized as a hostile work environment claim which requires a showing of severe or pervasive conduct. See Oncale v. Sundowner Offshore Services, Inc., 523 U.S. 75, 81 (1998); Harris v. Forklift Systems, Inc., 510 U.S. 17, 21 (1993). For purposes of this case, we accept the District Court's finding that the alleged conduct was severe or pervasive. The case before us involves numerous alleged threats, and we express no opinion as to whether a single unfulfilled threat is sufficient to constitute discrimination in the terms or conditions of employment.

When we assume discrimination can be proved, however, the factors we discuss below, and not the categories quid pro quo and hostile work environment, will be controlling on the issue of vicarious liability. That is the question we must resolve.

III

We must decide, then, whether an employer has vicarious liability when a supervisor creates a hostile work environment by making explicit threats to alter a subordinate's terms or conditions of employment, based on sex, but does not fulfill the threat. We turn to principles of agency law, for the term "employer" is defined under Title VII to include "agents." 42 U.S.C. § 2000e(b); see *Meritor*, supra, at 72. In express terms, Congress has directed federal courts to interpret Title VII based on agency principles. Given such an explicit instruction, we conclude a uniform and predictable standard must be established as a matter of federal law. We rely "on the general common law of agency, rather than on the law of any particular State, to give meaning to these terms." Community for Creative Non-Violence v. Reid, 490 U.S. 730, 740 (1989). The resulting federal rule, based on a body of case law developed over time, is statutory interpretation pursuant to congressional direction. This is not federal common law in "the strictest sense, i.e., a rule of decision that amounts, not simply to an interpretation of a federal statute . . ., but, rather, to the judicial 'creation' of a special federal rule of decision." Atherton v. FDIC, 519 U.S. 213, 218 (1997). State court decisions, applying state employment discrimination law, may be instructive in applying general agency principles, but, it is interesting to note, in many cases their determinations of employer liability under state law rely in large part on federal court decisions under Title VII. E.g., Arizona v. Schallock, 941 P.2d 1275, 1284 (Ariz. 1997); Lehmann v. Toys 'R' Us, Inc., 626 A. 2d 445, 463 (N.J. 1993); Thompson v. Berta Enterprises, Inc., 864 P. 2d 983, 986–988 (Wash. App. 1994).

As *Meritor* acknowledged, the Restatement (Second) of Agency (1957) (hereinafter Restatement), is a useful beginning point for a discussion of general agency principles. Since our decision in *Meritor*, federal courts have explored agency principles, and we find useful instruction in their decisions, noting that "common-law principles may not be transferable in all their particulars to Title VII." The EEOC has issued Guidelines governing sexual harassment claims under Title VII, but they provide little guidance on the issue of employer liability for supervisor harassment. See 29 CFR § 1604.11(c) (1997) (vicarious liability for supervisor harassment turns on "the particular employment relationship and the job functions performed by the individual").

A

Section 219(1) of the Restatement sets out a central principle of agency law:

> "A master is subject to liability for the torts of his servants committed while acting in the scope of their employment."

An employer may be liable for both negligent and intentional torts committed by an employee within the scope of his or her employment. Sexual harassment under Title VII presupposes intentional conduct. While early decisions absolved employers of liability for the intentional torts of their employees, the law now imposes liability where the employee's "purpose, however misguided, is wholly or in part to further the master's business." W. Keeton, D. Dobbs, R. Keeton, & D. Owen, Prosser and Keeton on Law of Torts § 70, p. 505 (5th ed. 1984) (hereinafter Prosser and Keeton on Torts). In applying scope of employment principles to intentional torts, however, it is accepted that "it is less likely that a willful tort will properly be held to be in the course of employment and that the liability of the master for such torts will naturally be more limited." F. Mechem, Outlines of the Law of Agency § 394, p. 266 (P. Mechem 4th ed., 1952). The Restatement defines conduct, including an intentional tort, to be within the scope of employment when "actuated, at least in part, by a purpose to serve the [employer]," even if it is forbidden by the employer. Restatement §§ 228(1)(c), 230. For example, when a salesperson lies to a customer to make a sale, the tortious conduct is within the scope of employment because it benefits the employer by increasing sales, even though it may violate the employer's policies. See Prosser and Keeton on Torts § 70, at 505–506.

As Courts of Appeals have recognized, a supervisor acting out of gender-based animus or a desire to fulfill sexual urges may not be actuated by a purpose to serve the employer. See, e.g., Harrison v. Eddy Potash, Inc., 112 F.3d 1437, 1444 (10th Cir. 1997), cert. pending, No. 97–232; Torres v. Pisano, 116 F.3d 625, 634, n.10 (2nd Cir. 1997). But see Kauffman v. Allied Signal, Inc., 970 F.2d, at 184–185 (holding harassing supervisor acted within scope of employment, but employer was not liable because of its quick and effective remediation). The harassing supervisor often acts for personal motives, motives unrelated and even antithetical to the objectives of the employer. Cf. *Mechem*, supra, § 368 ("[f]or the time being [the supervisor] is conspicuously and unmistakably seeking a personal end"); see also Restatement § 235, Illustration 2 (tort committed while "[a]cting purely from personal ill will" not within the scope of employment); § 235, Illustration 3 (tort committed in retaliation for failing to pay the employee a bribe not within the scope of employment). There are instances, of course, where a supervisor engages in unlawful discrimination with the purpose, mistaken or otherwise, to serve the employer. E.g., Sims v. Montgomery County Comm'n, 766 F. Supp. 1052, 1075 (M.D. Ala. 1990) (supervisor acting in scope of employment where employer has a policy of discouraging women from seeking advancement and "sexual harassment was simply a way of furthering that policy").

The concept of scope of employment has not always been construed to require a motive to serve the employer. E.g., Ira S. Bushey & Sons, Inc. v. United States, 398 F.2d 167, 172 (2nd Cir. 1968). Federal courts have nonetheless found similar limitations on employer liability when applying the agency laws of the States under the Federal Tort Claims Act, which makes the Federal Government liable for torts committed by employees within the scope of employment. 28 U.S.C. § 1346(b); see, e.g., Jamison v. Wiley, 14 F.3d 222, 237 (4th Cir. 1994) (supervisor's unfair criticism of subordinate's work in retaliation for rejecting his sexual advances not within scope of employment); Wood v. United States, 995 F.2d 1122, 1123 (1st Cir. 1993) (Breyer, C. J.) (sexual harassment amounting to assault and battery "clearly outside the scope of employment"); see also 2 L. Jayson & R. Longstreth, Handling Federal Tort Claims § 9.07 [4], p. 9–211 (1998).

The general rule is that sexual harassment by a supervisor is not conduct within the scope of employment.

B

Scope of employment does not define the only basis for employer liability under agency principles. In limited circumstances, agency principles impose liability on employers even where employees commit torts outside the scope of employment. The principles are set forth in the much-cited § 219(2) of the Restatement:

> "(2) A master is not subject to liability for the torts of his servants acting outside the scope of their employment, unless:
>
> > "(a) the master intended the conduct or the consequences, or
> >
> > "(b) the master was negligent or reckless, or
> >
> > "(c) the conduct violated a non-delegable duty of the master, or
> >
> > "(d) the servant purported to act or to speak on behalf of the principal and there was reliance upon apparent authority, or he was aided in accomplishing the tort by the existence of the agency relation."

See also § 219, Comment e (Section 219(2) "enumerates the situations in which a master may be liable for torts of servants acting solely for their own purposes and hence not in the scope of employment").

Subsection (a) addresses direct liability, where the employer acts with tortious intent, and indirect liability, where the agent's high rank in the company makes him or her the employer's *alter ego*. None of the parties contend Slowik's rank imputes liability under this principle. There is no contention, furthermore, that a nondelegable duty is involved. See § 219(2)(c). So, for our purposes here, subsections (a) and (c) can be put aside.

Subsections (b) and (d) are possible grounds for imposing employer liability on account of a supervisor's acts and must be considered. Under subsection (b), an employer is liable when the tort is attributable to the employer's own negligence. Thus, although a supervisor's sexual harassment is outside the scope of employment because the conduct was for personal motives, an employer can be liable, nonetheless, where its own negligence is a cause of the harassment. An employer is negligent with respect to sexual harassment if it knew or should have known about the conduct and failed to stop it. Negligence sets a minimum standard for employer liability under Title VII; but Ellerth seeks to invoke the more stringent standard of vicarious liability.

Subsection 219(2)(d) concerns vicarious liability for intentional torts committed by an employee when the employee uses apparent authority (the apparent authority standard), or when the employee "was aided in accomplishing the tort by the existence of the agency relation" (the aided in the agency relation standard). As other federal decisions have done in discussing vicarious liability for supervisor harassment, e.g., Henson v. Dundee, 682 F. 2d 897, 909 (11th Cir. 1982), we begin with § 219(2)(d).

C

As a general rule, apparent authority is relevant where the agent purports to exercise a power which he or she does not have, as distinct from where the agent threatens to misuse actual power. Compare Restatement § 6 (defining "power") with § 8 (defining "apparent authority"). In the usual case, a supervisor's harassment involves misuse of actual power, not the false impression of its existence. Apparent authority analysis therefore is inappropriate in this context. If, in the unusual case, it is alleged there is a false impression that the actor was a supervisor, when he in fact was not, the victim's mistaken conclusion must be a reasonable one. Restatement § 8, Comment c ("Apparent authority exists only to the extent it is reasonable for the third person dealing with the agent to believe that the agent is authorized"). When a party seeks to impose vicarious liability based on an agent's misuse of delegated authority, the Restatement's aided in the agency relation rule, rather than the apparent authority rule, appears to be the appropriate form of analysis.

D

We turn to the aided in the agency relation standard. In a sense, most workplace tortfeasors are aided in accomplishing their tortious objective by the existence of the agency relation: Proximity and regular contact may afford a captive pool of potential victims. See Gary v. Long, 59 F.3d 1391, 1397 (D.C. Cir. 1995). Were this to satisfy the aided in the agency relation standard, an employer would be subject to vicarious liability not only for all supervisor harassment, but also for all co-worker harassment, a result enforced by neither the EEOC nor any court of appeals to have considered the issue. See, e.g., Blankenship v. Parke Care Centers, Inc., 123 F.3d 868, 872 (6th Cir. 1997), cert. denied, 522 U.S. 1110 (1998) (sex discrimination); McKenzie v. Illinois Dept. of Transp., 92 F.3d 473, 480 (7th Cir. 1996) (sex discrimination); Daniels v. Essex Group, Inc., 937 F.2d 1264, 1273 (7th Cir. 1991) (race discrimination); see also 29 CFR 1604.11(d) (1997) ("knows or should have known" standard of liability for cases of harassment between "fellow employees"). The aided in the agency relation standard, therefore, requires the existence of something more than the employment relation itself.

At the outset, we can identify a class of cases where, beyond question, more than the mere existence of the employment relation aids in commission of the harassment: when a supervisor takes a tangible employment action against the subordinate. Every Federal Court of Appeals to have considered the question has found vicarious liability when a discriminatory act results in a tangible employment action. See, e.g., Sauers v. Salt Lake County, 1 F.3d 1122, 1127 (10th Cir. 1993) (" 'If the plaintiff can show that she suffered an economic injury from her supervisor's actions, the employer becomes strictly liable without any further showing . . .' "). In *Meritor*, we acknowledged this consensus. See 477 U.S., at 70–71 ("[T]he courts have consistently held employers liable for the discriminatory discharges of employees by supervisory personnel, whether or not the employer knew, or should have known, or approved of the supervisor's actions"). Although few courts have elaborated how agency principles support this rule, we think it reflects a correct application of the aided in the agency relation standard.

In the context of this case, a tangible employment action would have taken the form of a denial of a raise or a promotion. The concept of a tangible employment action appears in numerous cases in the Courts of Appeals discussing claims involving race, age, and national origin discrimination, as well as sex discrimination. Without endorsing the specific results of those decisions, we think it prudent to import the concept of a tangible employment action for resolution of the vicarious liability issue we consider here. A tangible employment action constitutes a significant change in employment status, such as hiring, firing, failing to promote, reassignment with significantly different responsibilities, or a decision causing a significant change in benefits. Compare Crady v. Liberty Nat. Bank & Trust Co. of Ind., 993 F.2d 132, 136 (7th Cir. 1993) ("A materially adverse change might be indicated by a termination of employment, a demotion evidenced by a decrease in wage or salary, a less distinguished title, a material loss of benefits, significantly diminished material responsibilities, or other indices that might be unique to a particular situation"), with Flaherty v. Gas Research Institute, 31 F.3d 451, 456 (7th Cir. 1994) (a "bruised ego" is not enough); Kocsis v. Multi-Care Management, Inc., 97 F.3d 876, 887 (6th Cir. 1996) (demotion without change in pay, benefits, duties, or prestige insufficient) and Harlston v. McDonnell Douglas Corp., 37 F.3d 379, 382 (8th Cir. 1994) (reassignment to more inconvenient job insufficient).

When a supervisor makes a tangible employment decision, there is assurance the injury could not have been inflicted absent the agency relation. A tangible employment action in most cases inflicts direct economic harm. As a general proposition, only a supervisor, or other person acting with the authority of the company, can cause this sort of injury. A co-worker can break a co-worker's arm as easily as a supervisor, and anyone who has regular contact with an employee can inflict psychological injuries by his or her offensive conduct. See Gary, 59 F.3d, at 1397; Henson, 682 F.2d, at 910; Barnes v. Costle, 561 F.2d 983, 996 (D.C. Cir. 1977) (MacKinnon, J., concurring). But one co-worker (absent some elaborate scheme) cannot dock another's pay, nor can one co-worker demote another. Tangible employment actions fall within the special province of the supervisor. The supervisor has been empowered by the company as a distinct class of agent to make economic decisions affecting other employees under his or her control.

Tangible employment actions are the means by which the supervisor brings the official power of the enterprise to bear on subordinates. A tangible employment decision requires an official act of the enterprise, a company act. The decision in most cases is documented in official company records, and may be subject to review by higher level supervisors. E.g., Shager v. Upjohn Co., 913 F.2d 398, 405 (7th Cir. 1990) (noting that the supervisor did not fire plaintiff; rather, the Career Path Committee did, but the employer was still liable because the Committee functioned as the supervisor's "cat's-paw"). The supervisor often must obtain the imprimatur of the enterprise and use its internal processes. See Kotcher v. Rosa & Sullivan Appliance Center, Inc., 957 F.2d 59, 62 (2nd Cir. 1992) ("From the perspective of the employee, the supervisor and the employer merge into a single entity").

For these reasons, a tangible employment action taken by the supervisor becomes for Title VII purposes the act of the employer. Whatever the exact contours of the aided in the agency relation standard, its requirements will always be met when a supervisor takes a tangible employment action against a subordinate. In that instance, it would be implausible to interpret agency principles to allow an employer to escape liability, as *Meritor* itself appeared to acknowledge.

Whether the agency relation aids in commission of supervisor harassment which does not culminate in a tangible employment action is less obvious. Application of the standard is made difficult by its malleable terminology, which can be read to either expand or limit liability in the context of supervisor harassment. On the one hand, a supervisor's power and authority invests his or her harassing conduct with a particular threatening character, and in this sense, a supervisor always is aided by the agency relation. See *Meritor*, 477 U.S., at 77 (Marshall, J., concurring in judgment) ("[I]t is precisely because the supervisor is understood to be clothed with the employer's authority that he is able to impose unwelcome sexual conduct on subordinates"). On the other hand, there are acts of harassment a supervisor might commit which might be the same acts a co-employee would commit, and there may be some circumstances where the supervisor's status makes little difference.

It is this tension which, we think, has caused so much confusion among the Courts of Appeals which have sought to apply the aided in the agency relation standard to Title VII cases. The aided in the agency relation standard, however, is a developing feature of agency law, and we hesitate to render a definitive explanation of our understanding of the standard in an area where other important considerations must affect our judgment. In particular, we are bound by our holding in *Meritor* that agency principles constrain the imposition of vicarious liability in cases of supervisory harassment. See *Meritor*, supra, at 72 ("Congress' decision to define 'employer' to include any 'agent' of an employer, 42 U.S.C.

§ 2000e(b), surely evinces an intent to place some limits on the acts of employees for which employers under Title VII are to be held responsible"). Congress has not altered *Meritor*'s rule even though it has made significant amendments to Title VII in the interim. See Illinois Brick Co. v. Illinois, 431 U.S. 720, 736 (1977) ("[W]e must bear in mind that considerations of *stare decisis* weigh heavily in the area of statutory construction, where Congress is free to change this Court's interpretation of its legislation").

Although *Meritor* suggested the limitation on employer liability stemmed from agency principles, the Court acknowledged other considerations might be relevant as well. See, 477 U.S., at 72 ("common-law principles may not be transferable in all their particulars to Title VII"). For example, Title VII is designed to encourage the creation of antiharassment policies and effective grievance mechanisms. Were employer liability to depend in part on an employer's effort to create such procedures, it would effect Congress' intention to promote conciliation rather than litigation in the Title VII context, see EEOC v. Shell Oil Co., 466 U.S. 54, 77 (1984), and the EEOC's policy of encouraging the development of grievance procedures. See 29 CFR § 1604.11(f) (1997); EEOC Policy Guidance on Sexual Harassment, 8 BNA FEP Manual 405:6699 (Mar. 19, 1990). To the extent limiting employer liability could encourage employees to report harassing conduct before it becomes severe or pervasive, it would also serve Title VII's deterrent purpose. See McKennon v. Nashville Banner Publishing Co., 513 U.S. 352, 358 (1995). As we have observed, Title VII borrows from tort law the avoidable consequences doctrine, see Ford Motor Co. v. EEOC, 458 U.S. 219, 231, n.15 (1982), and the considerations which animate that doctrine would also support the limitation of employer liability in certain circumstances.

In order to accommodate the agency principles of vicarious liability for harm caused by misuse of supervisory authority, as well as Title VII's equally basic policies of encouraging forethought by employers and saving action by objecting employees, we adopt the following holding in this case and in *Faragher v. Boca Raton*, also decided today. An employer is subject to vicarious liability to a victimized employee for an actionable hostile environment created by a supervisor with immediate (or successively higher) authority over the employee. When no tangible employment action is taken, a defending employer may raise an affirmative defense to liability or damages, subject to proof by a preponderance of the evidence, see Fed. Rule Civ. Proc. 8(c). The defense comprises two necessary elements: (a) that the employer exercised reasonable care to prevent and correct promptly any sexually harassing behavior, and (b) that the plaintiff employee unreasonably failed to take advantage of any preventive or corrective opportunities provided by the employer or to avoid harm otherwise. While proof that an employer had promulgated an anti-harassment policy with complaint procedure is not necessary in every instance as a matter of law, the need for a stated policy suitable to the employment circumstances may appropriately be addressed in any case when litigating the first element of the defense. And while proof that an employee failed to fulfill the corresponding obligation of reasonable care to avoid harm is not limited to showing any unreasonable failure to use any complaint procedure provided by the employer, a demonstration of such failure will normally suffice to satisfy the employer's burden under the second element of the defense. No affirmative defense is available, however, when the supervisor's harassment culminates in a tangible employment action, such as discharge, demotion, or undesirable reassignment.

IV

Relying on existing case law which held out the promise of vicarious liability for all quid pro quo claims, Ellerth focused all her attention in the Court of Appeals on proving her claim fit within that category. Given our explanation that the labels quid pro quo and hostile work environment are not controlling for purposes of establishing employer liability, Ellerth should have an adequate opportunity to prove she has a claim for which Burlington is liable.

Although Ellerth has not alleged she suffered a tangible employment action at the hands of Slowik, which would deprive Burlington of the availability of the affirmative defense, this is not dispositive. In light of our decision, Burlington is still subject to vicarious liability for Slowik's activity, but Burlington should have an opportunity to assert and prove the affirmative defense to liability.

For these reasons, we will affirm the judgment of the Court of Appeals, reversing the grant of summary judgment against Ellerth. On remand, the District Court will have the opportunity to decide whether it would be appropriate to allow Ellerth to amend her pleading or supplement her discovery.

The judgment of the Court of Appeals is affirmed.

It is so ordered.

■ JUSTICE GINSBURG, concurring in the judgment.

I agree with the Court's ruling that "the labels quid pro quo and hostile work environment are not controlling for purposes of establishing employer liability." I also subscribe to the Court's statement of the rule governing employer liability, which is substantively identical to the rule the Court adopts in *Faragher v. Boca Raton*.

■ JUSTICE THOMAS, with whom JUSTICE SCALIA joins, dissenting.

The Court today manufactures a rule that employers are vicariously liable if supervisors create a sexually hostile work environment, subject to an affirmative defense that the Court barely attempts to define. This rule applies even if the employer has a policy against sexual harassment, the employee knows about that policy, and the employee never informs anyone in a position of authority about the supervisor's conduct. As a result, employer liability under Title VII is judged by different standards depending upon whether a sexually or racially hostile work environment is alleged. The standard of employer liability should be the same in both instances: An employer should be liable if, and only if, the plaintiff proves that the employer was negligent in permitting the supervisor's conduct to occur. . . .

NOTES ON *BURLINGTON INDUSTRIES, INC. V. ELLERTH*

1. ***Faragher v. City of Boca Raton.*** The Supreme Court decided *Burlington Industries* with a companion case, Faragher v. City of Boca Raton, 524 U.S. 775 (1998), which elaborated on the first of the two elements of the defense available to employers in hostile environment cases. The plaintiffs in *Faragher* were two female lifeguards who worked at a location far removed from the headquarters of the city parks and recreation department, for which they worked. The plaintiffs alleged that their supervisors at this location, Terry and Silverman, created a hostile environment by repeatedly engaging in uninvited and offensive touching, by making lewd remarks, and by speaking of women in offensive terms. The facts found by the lower courts bore out these allegations, but the court of appeals held that the city could not be held liable for the supervisors' conduct. After elaborating on the justification for the defense recognized in *Burlington Industries* and after summarizing the elements of the defense, the Court analyzed its application in the following terms:

> Applying these rules here, we believe that the judgment of the Court of Appeals must be reversed. The District Court found that the degree of hostility in the work environment rose to the actionable level and was attributable to Silverman and Terry. It is undisputed that these supervisors "were granted virtually unchecked authority" over their subordinates, "directly controll[ing] and supervis[ing] all aspects of [Faragher's] day-to-day activities." 111 F.3d, at 1544 (Barkett, J., dissenting in part and concurring in part). It is also clear that Faragher and her colleagues were "completely isolated from the City's higher management." Ibid. The City did not seek review of these findings.
>
> While the City would have an opportunity to raise an affirmative defense if there were any serious prospect of its presenting one, it appears from the record that any such avenue is closed. The District Court found that the City had entirely failed to disseminate its policy against sexual harassment among the beach employees and that its officials made no attempt to keep track of the conduct of supervisors like Terry and Silverman. The record also makes clear that the City's policy did not include any assurance that the harassing supervisors could be bypassed in registering complaints. Under such circumstances, we hold as a matter of law that the City could not be found to have exercised reasonable care to prevent the supervisors' harassing conduct. Unlike the employer of a small workforce, who might expect that sufficient care to prevent tortious behavior could be exercised

> informally, those responsible for city operations could not reasonably have thought that precautions against hostile environments in any one of many departments in far-flung locations could be effective without communicating some formal policy against harassment, with a sensible complaint procedure.

Note that the Supreme Court held the city liable despite the fact that the plaintiffs had not complained of the supervisors' conduct to the management of the parks and recreation department at headquarters. The terms of the defense recognized in *Burlington Industries* require the employer to establish both elements of the defense: both "(a) that the employer exercised reasonable care to prevent and correct promptly any sexually harassing behavior, and (b) that the plaintiff employee unreasonably failed to take advantage of any preventive or corrective opportunities provided by the employer or to avoid harm otherwise." The employer in *Faragher* had failed to satisfy the first element of the defense, and so the plaintiffs' failure to satisfy the second was irrelevant.

The converse situation could also result in liability for the employer. If the plaintiffs satisfy the second element of the defense, by complaining of sexual harassment, the defendant will be held liable even if it satisfied the first element by having a policy against sexual harassment in place and acting promptly on their complaint. The defense consists of two elements, both of which must be met. So, for instance, on the facts of *Meritor Savings Bank*, if the supervisor had committed only one act of harassment, but it was severe enough to create a hostile environment, and the employee had filed a prompt complaint, the employer would still be liable for the single act of harassment. Does this result make sense? Or does it demonstrate that the employer's liability in these circumstances would be limited? What if the single act of harassment were, as was alleged of some of the acts in *Meritor Savings Bank*, a sexual assault? One court refused to hold an employer liable for a single act of harassment if it had acted promptly to remedy it. McCurdy v. Arkansas State Police, 375 F.3d 762, cert. denied, 543 U.S. 1121 (2005).

2. **Direct and Indirect Liability.** *Burlington Industries* and *Faragher* focus upon the vicarious liability of employers for sexual harassment. In examining the standards for vicarious liability, it is important not to lose sight of the cases in which employers are directly or indirectly liable. In these cases, the defense recognized in *Burlington Industries* is not available to the employer, so that the scope of direct and indirect liability can be quite important as a practical matter.

Cases of direct liability are likely to be confined to sexual harassment by the sole proprietor of a business that does not take the corporate or partnership form. Most employers that take the form of legally recognized organizations have a strong interest, especially after *Burlington Industries* and *Faragher*, in declaring that they are opposed to all forms of sexual harassment. Cases of "indirect liability" are likely to be more common, involving sexual harassment by high officials in the employer's organization, such as the president of the corporate employer in *Harris v. Forklift Systems*. "Indirect liability" is the term used by the Restatement (Second) of Agency and, according to *Burlington Industries*, it imposes vicarious liability upon the employer "where the agent's high rank in the company makes him or her the employer's alter ego." The plaintiff in *Burlington Industries* did not argue that the harassing supervisor's rank was high enough to impose liability on the employer on this ground. Is the question just one of degree, how high the harassing supervisor is in the employer's management hierarchy? Or is there a qualitative difference between supervisors for whom the employer can invoke a defense and those for whom it cannot?

3. **Tangible Employment Actions.** The defense also is limited by the kind of harassment that occurred. It applies only to "hostile environment" claims, which are defined negatively as all forms of harassment not involving "tangible employment actions." The latter, in turn, are defined by example: they constitute "a significant change in employment status, such as hiring, firing, failing to promote, reassignment with significantly different responsibilities, or a decision causing a significant change in benefits." Note that one of these examples more closely resembles an omission rather than an action, consisting of "failing to promote." In the same vein, *Burlington Industries* also includes "denial of a raise" in the possible tangible employment actions on the facts of that case. Yet the case holds that a threat by a supervisor that involves a tangible employment action, but does not culminate in one, does not itself constitute a tangible employment action. Such threats could have been found on the facts in *Burlington Industries*, but the Court held that the newly recognized defense was nevertheless available to the employer. What happens if a supervisor threatens an employee with a tangible employment action and, for that reason, she succumbs to his advances? Is the case still one that involves only a hostile environment? One court has interpreted a tangible employment action to include such cases. Holly D. v. California Institute of Technology, 339 F.3d 1158 (9th Cir. 2003).

In a subsequent case, Pennsylvania State Police v. Suders, 542 U.S. 129 (2004), the Supreme Court addressed the question, left open in *Burlington Industries*, whether a constructive discharge amounted to a tangible employment action. A constructive discharge occurs when the terms and conditions of the plaintiff's employment force her to quit. On the one hand, a constructive discharge might constitute a tangible employment action because the employer's actions ultimately resulted in the plaintiff's loss of employment. On the other hand, the decision actually to quit was made by the plaintiff. The Court decided that the nature of a constructive discharge depended upon the nature of the underlying discrimination. If the plaintiff was forced to quit because of a tangible employment action, such as a cut in pay, then constructive discharge also was a tangible employment action. Otherwise, it was not.

For an analysis of what constitutes a tangible employment action, see Susan Grover, After *Ellerth*: The Tangible Employment Action in Sexual Harassment Analysis, 35 U. Mich. J.L. Reform 809 (2002); Kelly Collins Woodford & Harry A. Rissetto, Tangible Employment Action: What Did the Supreme Court Really Mean in *Faragher* and *Ellerth*?, 19 Lab. L. 63 (2003).

4. **Who Qualifies as a Supervisor?** The Supreme Court addressed this question in Vance v. Ball State University, 133 S. Ct. 2434 (2013), concluding

"that an employees is a 'supervisor' for purposes of vicarious liability under Title VII if he or she is empowered by the employer to take tangible employment actions against the victim . . . ." Simply the power to direct how the employee should perform the job, without the power to take tangible economic action against the employee, does not make a co-employee into a supervisor. This result has virtue of simplicity, aligning the status of supervisor with the rules governing harassment involving tangible employment action. As Justice Ginsburg pointed out in dissent, however, it narrows the definition of "supervisor" beyond the common understanding of employees who are subject to the day-to-day direction of other employees. Would an employee subject to such direction be more or less vulnerable to sexual harassment in this situation than they would be to harassment by a genuinely equal employee? If so, shouldn't the employer be held to a standard of liability that is stricter simply than negligence?

5. **Individual Liability for Sexual Harassment.** The law, as it has evolved under Title VII, makes only the employer liable for violations of the statute. The strong trend in the lower court decisions is to impose no liability at all upon individual supervisors and employees under Title VII. E.g., Sheridan v. E.I. DuPont de Nemours, 100 F.3d 1061, 1077–78 (3d Cir. 1996); Spencer v. Ripley County State Bank, 123 F.3d 690 (8th Cir. 1997). These decisions have reasoned, in an argument neither accepted nor rejected by the Supreme Court, that Congress meant to insulate individual employees from liability when it imposed limits on the liability of employers for damages in the Civil Rights Act of 1991. If small employers are subject to lower caps on liability than larger employers (as discussed in the following note), and if private employers with fewer than 15 employees are not covered at all by Title VII, then according to this argument, individual employees should not be liable at all. Is this argument strong enough to overcome the literal terms of Title VII defining a covered employer in § 701(b) to include both any employer with 15 or more employees engaged in commerce and "any agent of such a person"?

6. **Economic Theories of Vicarious Liability.** All the issues concerning liability and defenses affect the incentives of the employer and its employees to comply with the requirements of Title VII, as well as the litigation strategy of the victim of alleged harassment. The economic theory of the principal-agent relationship is well developed and focuses on the monitoring and bonding costs to guarantee that the employee's actions are in the employer's interests. Sanford J. Grossman & Oliver D. Hart, An Analysis of the Principal-Agent Problem, 51 Econometrica 7 (1983); see also David E.M. Sappington, Incentives in Principal-Agent Relationships, 5 J. Econ. Persp. 45 (1991); William D. White, Information and the Control of Agents, 18 J. Econ. Behav. & Org. 111 (1992). Monitoring costs are those expended to supervise the agent directly and bonding costs are those expended indirectly to reduce the risk of agent misconduct. In the context of sexual harassment, monitoring costs would be those incurred by watching over managers (or other employees) to make sure that they did not engage in sexual harassment. Bonding costs would involve steps taken to prevent situations

in which harassment might arise, for instance, by forbidding closed-door meetings between a manager and an employee of the opposite sex.

In most employment discrimination cases, the true employer is a corporate entity owned by shareholders, and the managers of the firm are actually employees who will have different interests from the owners. If there is a market penalty—in the form of reduced profits—resulting from discrimination on the part of managers, the owners will pay it and will presumably take steps to reduce this loss through either monitoring or bonding mechanisms. But since these mechanisms of control are themselves costly, the owners of a firm will not find it profitable to eliminate all discrimination by their managers. In the language of economics, even in a competitive market, discrimination will not be entirely eliminated because there is a privately "optimal" level of discrimination for the corporate employer that is greater than zero. This provides another rationale for adding a legal penalty to the market sanction, since it would provide a further incentive for the firm to reduce discrimination by its managers toward the legally desired goal of zero discrimination.

A detailed analysis of vicarious liability, with specific application to claims of sexual harassment, has been offered by Professor Alan O. Sykes, who reaches the same general conclusion as the Supreme Court: that vicarious liability should more readily be imposed for the acts of supervisors rather than co-employees. Alan O. Sykes, The Boundaries of Vicarious Liability: An Economic Analysis of the Scope of Employment Rule and Related Legal Doctrines, 101 Harv. L. Rev. 563 (1988); see also Alan O. Sykes, The Economics of Vicarious Liability, 93 Yale L.J. 1231 (1984). However, he would impose such liability for all forms of sexual harassment by supervisors, not just those involving tangible employment actions. For criticism of Professor Sykes's position, see J. Hoult Verkerke, Notice Liability in Employment Discrimination Law, 81 Va. L. Rev. 273 (1995). Professor Verkerke argues that liability should be imposed on employers only when they have received notice, in some form, that supervisors or co-employees have engaged in discrimination. He would apply this principle to all forms of discrimination, not just sexual or racial harassment, on the ground that it would improve both detection of discrimination and compliance with Title VII.

The defense recognized in *Burlington Industries* directly encourages monitoring by the employer to prevent sexual harassment or, if it occurs, to promptly remedy it. Such steps can be expensive for the employer, particularly if they involve the alienation or loss of an employee erroneously accused of misconduct. The defense neglects bonding as an alternative strategy to prevent harassment, but the emphasis that *Burlington Industries* places upon remedies for harassment presupposes that harassing employees can lose their jobs, along with their accumulated benefits, if they are found guilty. Their future at the company depends upon good behavior. Yet bonding in this form does not relieve the employer of the cost of monitoring to make sure that their employees have not engaged in harassment.

The nightmare scenario for an employer who receives a complaint of sexual harassment is illustrated by Cotran v. Rollins Hudig Hall Intern.,

Inc., 948 P.2d 412 (Cal. 1998). In that case, two workers complained of harassment by a senior vice-president of Rollins. The women signed sworn affidavits setting forth that the vice-president "had exposed himself and masturbated in their presence more than once; both also accused plaintiff of making repeated obscene telephone calls to them at home." After an extensive investigation by the firm, which involved interviewing 21 individuals who had worked with the vice-president, the president of the company accepted the conclusion of the firm's manager for EEO compliance that the harassment had occurred, and fired the vice-president. The terminated vice-president then sued the employer for wrongful discharge on an implied contract theory that the firm would only fire him for "good cause." A jury specifically found that the alleged harassment had not occurred and awarded the vice-president $1.78 million in damages. The California Supreme Court reversed, saying that had the vice-president had an explicit contractual right not to be discharged absent good cause, the verdict would have stood, but because there was only an implied contract, the correct legal standard did not turn on whether or not the harassment actually occurred but on whether the firm had acted reasonably after a full, fair, and impartial investigation. Employers dread having to choose between competing versions of events and then facing costly litigation and possible punitive damages in a lawsuit brought by the party they refused to believe. As *Cotran* illustrates, the effectiveness of a bonding approach that tries to discourage workers from engaging in discriminatory or harassing conduct by threatening to fire them is jeopardized when the alleged harassers can turn around and sue the company for wrongful discharge.

The Court's analysis in *Burlington Industries* also fails to take account of the incentives that plaintiffs have to complain of harassment and to bring suit. *Burlington Industries* imposes upon the plaintiff the burden of discovering and reporting harassment, but only in cases involving a hostile environment. The Court assumes that in these cases the plaintiff can more easily monitor the actions of the harassing employee than the employer, while the employer is better able to monitor cases involving a tangible employment action. Is there any reason to believe that the latter form of harassment is more easily discovered by the employer? What if the plaintiff in *Burlington Industries* had actually been denied a promotion because of her failure to submit to advances by her supervisors? Would those advances have been more readily apparent to an employer? More generally, do employers closely monitor all of the many tangible employment actions taken by their supervisors to assure that these actions are not motivated by ulterior purposes? How could they?

At this point in the Court's analysis, considerations of litigation strategy seem to predominate over the comparative advantage of either the employer or the employee to prevent harassment. If plaintiffs were required to take reasonable steps to report harassment involving tangible employment actions, and if employers had a defense if they did not, then any claim of employment discrimination would seemingly be subject to the same requirements. Cases not involving harassment at all, but wholly independent forms of discrimination, would be subject to exactly the same defense recognized in *Burlington Industries*. What effect would pervasive recognition of this defense have on the incentives of plaintiffs to sue? On the complexity and uncertainty of employment discrimination claims?

7. **Damages Under Title VII.** The stakes in winning or losing a claim of sexual harassment increased dramatically with the passage of the Civil Rights Act of 1991. As originally enacted, Title VII provided only for the recovery of equitable relief. It did not provide for the recovery of damages. Equitable relief was nevertheless broadly extended beyond the typical equitable remedy of an injunction, to include various explicitly compensatory remedies, such as orders for hiring, promotions, and reinstatement; awards of back pay and fringe benefits; and even awards of "front pay" for loss of future earnings. See § 706(g). A separate provision also authorized the award of attorney's fees. § 706(k). The absence of an award of damages was not thought to be a major defect in the statute, and from the plaintiff's perspective, it was advantageous in some respects. In the early years after passage of Title VII, black plaintiffs alleging racial discrimination did not have to present their claims to juries composed mainly, or even entirely, of whites.

The developments under a Reconstruction statute, 42 U.S.C. § 1981, gradually changed this perception. As discussed more fully in Chapter 9 plaintiffs asserting claims of racial discrimination under that statute could obtain the full array of appropriate remedies, including damages as well as equitable relief. This development left plaintiffs who asserted claims of sex discrimination under Title VII in a worse position than plaintiffs under section 1981. The Civil Rights Act of 1991 alleviated this disadvantage, but not entirely. The Act added a new section to the code, somewhat confusingly numbered § 1981a, to augment the remedies available to plaintiffs with claims under Title VII. If plaintiffs under Title VII establish a claim of intentional discrimination, like sexual harassment, then they may recover damages under the terms of § 1981a. These terms generally limit awards of punitive damages, of damages for future pecuniary losses, and of damages for all nonpecuniary losses to various amounts ranging from $50,000 for employers with up to 100 employees to $300,000 for employers with more than 500 employees.

Despite these limits, plaintiffs in sexual harassment cases now have a far larger potential recovery available to them, one that does not depend on losing their job and recovering back pay, and one that can be submitted to a jury to determine whether damages for emotional distress can be awarded. With this increase in potential awards to the plaintiff, the plaintiff's attorney also could seek an increase in attorney's fees, either awarded directly from the defendant or as part of a contingent fee contract with the plaintiff. This prospect of increased fees made these claims far more valuable to the plaintiffs' bar, giving them an incentive to bring more such claims and to prosecute them more forcefully. Does this development argue for or against the new defense recognized in *Burlington Industries*? Or does it just indicate that both plaintiffs and defendants now search for every possible advantage in this kind of litigation and, in the process, make the law more complicated?

8. **Bibliography.** For scholarly commentary on *Burlington Industries* and *Faragher*, see Samuel R. Bagenstos, Formalism and Employer Liability Under Title VII, 2014 U. Chi. Leg. Forum No. 1; Michael C. Harper, Answering the Title VII Agency Question: A Policy Basis for *Faragher* and *Ellerth*, and J.H. Verkerke, The Triumph of Formalism in the Supreme Court's Recent Employer Liability Decisions, both in Proceedings of N.Y.U. Fifty-First Annual National Conference on Labor: Sexual Harassment in the Workplace (S. Estreicher ed., 1999); Michael C. Harper, Employer Liability for Harassment Under Title VII: A Functional Rationale for *Faragher* and *Ellerth*, 36 San Diego L. Rev. 41 (1999); Donald P. Harris, Daniel B. Garrie & Matthew J. Armstrong, Sexual Harassment: Limiting the Affirmative Defense in the Digital Workplace, 39 U. Mich. J.L. Reform 73 (2005); Justine Tinkler, Skylar Gremillion & Kira Arthurs, Perceptions of Legitimacy: The Sex of the Legal Messenger and Reactions to Sexual Harassment Training, 40 Law & Soc. Inquiry 152 (2015). See also Juan Carlos Bisso & Albert H. Choi, Optimal Agency Contracts: The Effect of Vicarious Liability and Judicial Error, 28 Int'l Rev. L. & Econ. 166 (2008).

CHAPTER 6

OTHER GROUNDS OF DISCRIMINATION AND COVERAGE

A. INTRODUCTION

This chapter considers an array of different issues, all united by a common theme. These issues are, in one way or another, related to and dependent upon developments and legal doctrine in other areas of law. The significance of these issues derives from the way they amplify or qualify the prohibitions against discrimination found elsewhere in Title VII. Thus discrimination on the basis of national origin or religion adds a dimension to discrimination on the basis of race, reflecting the often uncertain overlap among these different grounds of discrimination. So, too, issues of coverage reveal just how far Congress, the courts, and society as a whole are willing to carry the prohibitions against discrimination into different forms of employment. The practical significance of these issues also is not to be slighted, since grounds of discrimination and forms of employment not covered by Title VII entirely deprive the plaintiff of any claim under the statute. The plaintiff is then forced to consider other statutes that cover her claim or to recast her claim in terms that are covered by Title VII.

This chapter addresses these issues in illustrative rather than exhaustive terms. The aim is not to analyze all the various ways in which such issues might arise but to demonstrate how they are connected to fundamental concerns expressed in other areas of law.

B. NATIONAL ORIGIN

Espinoza v. Farah Manufacturing Co.

414 U.S. 86 (1973).

■ JUSTICE MARSHALL delivered the opinion of the Court.

This case involves interpretation of the phrase "national origin" in Title VII of the Civil Rights Act of 1964. Petitioner Cecilia Espinoza is a lawfully admitted resident alien who was born in and remains a citizen of Mexico. She resides in San Antonio, Texas, with her husband, Rudolfo Espinoza, a United States citizen. In July 1969, Mrs. Espinoza sought employment as a seamstress at the San Antonio division of respondent Farah Manufacturing Co. Her employment application was rejected on the basis of a longstanding company policy against the employment of aliens. After exhausting their administrative remedies with the Equal Employment Opportunity Commission, petitioners commenced this suit in the District Court alleging that respondent had discriminated against Mrs. Espinoza because of her "national origin" in violation of § 703 of Title VII. The District Court granted petitioners' motion for summary judgment, holding that a refusal to hire because of lack of citizenship constitutes discrimination on the basis of "national origin." The Court of Appeals reversed, concluding that the statutory phrase "national origin" did not embrace citizenship. We granted the writ to resolve this question of statutory construction and now affirm.

Section 703 makes it "an unlawful employment practice for an employer . . . to fail or refuse to hire . . . any individual . . . because of such individual's race, color, religion, sex, or national origin." Certainly the plain language of the statute supports the result reached by the Court of Appeals. The term "national origin" on its face refers to the country where a person was born, or, more broadly, the country from which his or her ancestors came.

The statute's legislative history, though quite meager in this respect, fully supports this construction. The only direct definition given the phrase "national origin" is the following remark made on the floor of the House of Representatives by Congressman Roosevelt, Chairman of the House Subcommittee which reported the bill: "It means the country from which you or your forebears came. . . . You may come from Poland, Czechoslovakia, England, France, or any other country." 110 Cong. Rec. 2549 (1964). We also note that an earlier version of § 703 had referred to discrimination because of "race, color, religion, national origin, or ancestry." H.R. 7152, 88th Cong., 1st Sess., § 804, Oct. 2, 1963 (Comm. print). . . . The deletion of the word "ancestry" from the final version was not intended as a material change, see, H.R. Rep. No. 914, 88th Cong., 1st Sess. 87 (1963), suggesting that the terms "national origin" and "ancestry" were considered synonymous.

There are other compelling reasons to believe that Congress did not intend the term "national origin" to embrace citizenship requirements. Since 1914, the Federal Government itself, through Civil Service Commission regulations, has engaged in what amounts to discrimination against aliens by denying them the right to enter competitive examination for federal employment. Exec. Order No. 1997, H.R. Doc. No. 1258, 63d Cong., 3d Sess. 118 (1914); see 5 U.S.C. § 3301; 5 CFR § 338.101 (1972). But it has never been suggested that the citizenship requirement for federal employment constitutes discrimination because of national origin, even though since 1943, various Executive Orders have expressly prohibited discrimination on the basis of national origin in Federal Government employment. See, e.g., Exec. Order No. 9346, 3 CFR 1280 (Cum. Supp. 1938–1943); Exec. Order No. 11478, 3 CFR 446 (1970).

Moreover, § 701(b) of Title VII, in language closely paralleling § 703, makes it "the policy of the United States to insure equal employment opportunities for Federal employees without discrimination because of . . . national origin. . . ." The legislative history of that section reveals no mention of any intent on Congress' part to reverse the longstanding practice of requiring federal employees to be United States citizens. To the contrary, there is every indication that no such reversal was intended. Congress itself has on several occasions since 1964 enacted statutes barring aliens from federal employment. The Treasury, Postal Service, and General Government Appropriation Act, 1973, for example, provides that "no part of any appropriation contained in this or any other act shall be used to pay the compensation of any officer or employee of the Government of the United States . . . unless such person (1) is a citizen of the United States."

To interpret the term "national origin" to embrace citizenship requirements would require us to conclude that Congress itself has repeatedly flouted its own declaration of policy. This Court cannot lightly find such a breach of faith. See Bate Refrigerating Co. v. Sulzberger, 157 U.S. 1, 38 (1895). So far as federal employment is concerned, we think it plain that Congress has assumed that the ban on national origin discrimination in § 701(b) did not affect the historical practice of requiring citizenship as a condition of employment. See First National Bank in St. Louis v. Missouri, 263 U.S. 640, 658 (1924). And there is no reason to believe Congress intended the term "national origin" in § 703 to have any broader scope. Cf. King v. Smith, 392 U.S. 309, 330–331 (1968). Petitioners have suggested that the statutes and regulations discriminating against noncitizens in federal employment are unconstitutional under the Due Process Clause of the Fifth Amendment. We need not address that question here, for the issue presented in this case is not whether Congress has the power to discriminate against aliens in federal employment, but rather, whether Congress intended to prohibit such discrimination in private employment. Suffice it to say that we cannot conclude Congress would at once continue the practice of requiring citizenship as a condition of federal employment and, at the same time, prevent private employers from doing likewise. Interpreting § 703 as petitioners suggest would achieve the rather bizarre result of preventing Farah from insisting on United States citizenship as a condition of employment while the very agency charged with enforcement of Title VII would itself be required by Congress to place such a condition on its own personnel.

The District Court drew primary support for its holding from an interpretative guideline issued by the Equal Employment Opportunity Commission which provides:

> "Because discrimination on the basis of citizenship has the effect of discriminating on the basis of national origin, a lawfully immigrated alien who is domiciled or residing in this country

may not be discriminated against on the basis of his citizenship. . . ." 29 CFR § 1606.1(d) (1972).

Like the Court of Appeals, we have no occasion here to question the general validity of this guideline insofar as it can be read as an expression of the Commission's belief that there may be many situations where discrimination on the basis of citizenship would have the effect of discriminating on the basis of national origin. In some instances, for example, a citizenship requirement might be but one part of a wider scheme of unlawful national origin discrimination. In other cases, an employer might use a citizenship test as a pretext to disguise what is in fact national origin discrimination. Certainly Title VII prohibits discrimination on the basis of citizenship whenever it has the purpose or effect of discriminating on the basis of national origin. "The Act proscribes not only overt discrimination but also practices that are fair in form, but discriminatory in operation." Griggs v. Duke Power Co., 401 U.S. 424, 431 (1971).

It is equally clear, however, that these principles lend no support to petitioners in this case. There is no indication in the record that Farah's policy against employment of aliens had the purpose or effect of discriminating against persons of Mexican national origin. It is conceded that Farah accepts employees of Mexican origin, provided the individual concerned has become an American citizen. Indeed, the District Court found that persons of Mexican ancestry make up more than 96% of the employees at the company's San Antonio division, and 97% of those doing the work for which Mrs. Espinoza applied. While statistics such as these do not automatically shield an employer from a charge of unlawful discrimination, the plain fact of the matter is that Farah does not discriminate against persons of Mexican national origin with respect to employment in the job Mrs. Espinoza sought. She was denied employment, not because of the country of her origin, but because she had not yet achieved United States citizenship. In fact, the record shows that the worker hired in place of Mrs. Espinoza was a citizen with a Spanish surname.

The Commission's guideline may have significance for a wide range of situations, but not for a case such as this where its very premise that discrimination on the basis of citizenship has the effect of discrimination on the basis of national origin is not borne out. It is also significant to note that the Commission itself once held a different view as to the meaning of the phrase "national origin." When first confronted with the question, the Commission, through its General Counsel, said: " 'National origin' refers to the country from which the individual or his forebears came . . ., not to whether or not he is a United States citizen. . . ." EEOC General Counsel's Opinion Letter, 1 CCH Employment Prac. Guide 1220.20 (1967). The Commission's more recent interpretation of the statute in the guideline relied on by the District Court is no doubt entitled to great deference, . . . but that deference must have limits where, as here, application of the guideline would be inconsistent with an obvious congressional intent not to reach the employment practice in question. Courts need not defer to an administrative construction of a statute where there are "compelling indications that it is wrong." Red Lion Broadcasting Co. v. FCC, 395 U.S. 367, 381 (1969). . . .

Finally, petitioners seek to draw support from the fact that Title VII protects all individuals from unlawful discrimination, whether or not they are citizens of the United States. We agree that aliens are protected from discrimination under the Act. That result may be derived not only from the use of the term "any individual" in § 703, but also as a negative inference from the exemption in § 702, which provides that Title VII "shall not apply to an employer with respect to the employment of aliens outside any State. . . ." 42 U.S.C. § 2000e–1. Title VII was clearly intended to apply with respect to the employment of aliens inside any State.

The question posed in the present case, however, is not whether aliens are protected from illegal discrimination under the Act, but what kinds of discrimination the Act makes illegal. Certainly it would be unlawful for an employer to discriminate against aliens because of race, color, religion, sex, or national origin—for example, by hiring aliens of Anglo Saxon background but refusing to hire those of Mexican or Spanish ancestry. Aliens are protected from illegal discrimination under the Act, but nothing in the Act makes it illegal to discriminate on the basis of citizenship or alienage.

We agree with the Court of Appeals that neither the language of the Act, nor its history, nor the specific facts of this case indicate that respondent has engaged in unlawful discrimination because of national origin.

Affirmed.

■ JUSTICE DOUGLAS, dissenting.

It is odd that the Court which holds that a State may not bar an alien from the practice of law or deny employment to aliens can read a federal statute that prohibits discrimination in employment on account of "national origin" so as to permit discrimination against aliens.

Alienage results from one condition only: being born outside the United States. Those born within the country are citizens from birth. It could not be more clear that Farah's policy of excluding aliens is de facto a policy of preferring those who were born in this country. Therefore the construction placed upon the "national origin" provision is inconsistent with the construction this Court has placed upon the same Act's protections for persons denied employment on account of race or sex.

In connection with racial discrimination we have said that the Act prohibits "practices, procedures, or tests neutral on their face, and even neutral in terms of intent," if they create "artificial, arbitrary, and unnecessary barriers to employment when the barriers operate invidiously to discriminate on the basis of racial *or other impermissible classification.*" Griggs v. Duke Power Co., 401 U.S. 424, 430–431 (1971) (emphasis added). There we found that the employer could not use test or diploma requirements which on their face were racially neutral, when in fact those requirements had a de facto discriminatory result and the employer was unable to justify them as related to job performance. The tests involved in *Griggs* did not eliminate all blacks seeking employment, just as the citizenship requirement here does not eliminate all applicants of foreign origin. Respondent here explicitly conceded that the citizenship requirement is imposed without regard to the alien's qualifications for the job.

These petitioners against whom discrimination is charged are Chicanos. But whether brown, yellow, black, or white, the thrust of the Act is clear: alienage is no barrier to employment here. *Griggs*, as I understood it until today, extends its protective principles to all, not to blacks alone. Our cases on sex discrimination under the Act yield the same result as *Griggs*. . . .

The construction placed upon the statute in the majority opinion is an extraordinary departure from prior cases, and it is opposed by the Equal Employment Opportunity Commission, the agency provided by law with the responsibility of enforcing the Act's protections. The Commission takes the only permissible position: that discrimination on the basis of alienage always has the effect of discrimination on the basis of national origin. Refusing to hire an individual because he is an alien "is discrimination based on birth outside the United States and is thus discrimination based on national origin in violation of Title VII." Brief for Commission as *Amicus Curiae*. The Commission's interpretation of the statute is entitled to great weight.

There is no legislative history to cast doubt on this construction. Indeed, any other construction flies in the face of the underlying congressional policy of removing "artificial, arbitrary, and unnecessary barrier(s) to employment." McDonnell Douglas Corp. v. Green, 411 U.S. 792, 806 (1973).

Mrs. Espinoza is a permanent resident alien, married to an American citizen, and her children will be native born American citizens. But that first generation has the greatest adjustments to make to their new country. Their unfamiliarity with America makes them the most vulnerable to exploitation and discriminatory treatment. They, of course, have the same obligation as American citizens to pay taxes, and they are subject to the draft on the same basis. But they have never received equal treatment in the job market. Writing of the immigrants of the late 1800's, Oscar Handlin has said:

> "For want of alternatives, the immigrants took the lowest places in the ranks of industry. They suffered in consequence from the poor pay and miserable working conditions characteristic of the sweat shops and the homework in the garment trades and in

cigar making. But they were undoubtedly better off than the Irish and Germans of the 1840's for whom there had been no place at all." The Newcomers 24 (1959).

The majority decides today that in passing sweeping legislation guaranteeing equal job opportunities, the Congress intended to help only the immigrant's children, excluding those "for whom there (is) no place at all." I cannot impute that niggardly an intent to Congress.

NOTES ON *ESPINOZA V. FARAH MANUFACTURING CO.*

1. **Relationship of National Origin to Alien Status.** The immediate issue in *Espinoza* arose from the overlap between national origin and alien status. Because all persons born within the territorial boundaries of the United States are citizens under the Fourteenth Amendment, all noncitizens necessarily have a foreign national origin. It follows, as Justice Douglas emphasizes in his dissent, that claims of discrimination against aliens also involve discrimination on the basis of national origin. Yet the legal treatment of these two grounds of discrimination is strikingly different, both under the Constitution and under Title VII and other statutes.

Under the Constitution, discrimination on the basis of national origin has been treated virtually the same as discrimination on the basis of race. The modern case establishing strict scrutiny for racial classifications, in fact, concerned discrimination on the basis of national origin. In Korematsu v. United States, 323 U.S. 214 (1944), the Supreme Court upheld a military order excluding Japanese-Americans, but no other Asians, from the West Coast. The Court declared that "all legal restrictions which curtail the civil rights of a single racial group are immediately suspect." This decision is notorious for the lax manner in which strict scrutiny was applied, based on little real evidence of the threat that Japanese-Americans posed to the war effort. Many have doubted whether the exacting requirements of strict scrutiny were satisfied, but not the way the standard itself was framed or the assumed equivalence of national origin with race. Subsequent decisions have continued to take this same general approach as, for instance, in cases reviewing the constitutionality of affirmative action plans on the basis of both race and national origin. E.g., Grutter v. Bollinger, 539 U.S. 306 (2003); Gratz v. Bollinger, 539 U.S. 244 (2003).

Classifications on the basis of alienage, by contrast, have been treated according to varying constitutional standards, depending on whether the disputed classification was established by state or federal law and on how closely it involves the attributes of citizenship. In general, the states cannot discriminate against aliens, except in areas that "go to the heart of representative government," such as school teachers and police. Cabell v. Chavez-Salido, 454 U.S. 432 (1982). Other occupations, such as lawyers and notaries, must be open to lawfully admitted aliens. Bernal v. Fainter, 467 U.S. 216 (1984). State classifications on the basis of alienage must satisfy a standard that approximates strict scrutiny. Such classifications by the federal government, on the other hand, need only satisfy a standard that approximates to rational basis. The federal government has plenary authority to classify on the basis of alienage as part of its constitutional power to "establish an uniform Rule of Naturalization," as upheld, for instance, in Mathews v. Diaz, 426 U.S. 67 (1976).

Congress has exercised this power by comprehensively regulating the status and actions of aliens in this country in the Immigration and Naturalization Act. This act has been amended to address certain limited forms of discrimination against aliens. The amending statute, the Immigration Reform and Control Act of 1986, contained two complicated prohibitions against employment discrimination. Pub. L. No. 99–603, 100 Stat. 3359 (1986), codified as amended at 8 U.S.C. § 1324b(a)(2)(A)–(B). The first was designed mainly to protect aliens who were lawfully in this country and had the right to work here despite their status as aliens. It extends, however, to any "protected individual," which includes citizens and several technically defined categories of aliens, and it prohibits any form of discrimination on the basis of "citizenship status." The second prohibition is against discrimination on the basis of national origin, but only by employers who are not covered by Title VII because they have fewer than 15 employees. Both prohibitions in the amended act apply only to employers who have at least four employees.

Espinoza was decided before this legislation was enacted, but the opinion relies upon other legislation specifically concerned with employment of aliens by the federal government. Does the existence of this comprehensive body of federal law inevitably affect the interpretation of Title VII? Does it require the term "national origin" to be construed in Title VII so as to avoid a conflict with other federal laws? Note that the immigration laws protect aliens from discrimination on this basis only if they are lawfully in the country and are entitled to work. Even if Title VII were amended to prohibit discrimination on the basis of alienage, wouldn't it have to contain a similar limitation?

2. Theories of Liability in *Espinoza*. The plaintiffs in *Espinoza*, although they were aliens, were nevertheless protected from discrimination on the basis of national origin. They fell within the definition of any "individual" protected from discrimination on the grounds covered by Title VII. Alienage, as the Court held, was not one of those covered grounds. Why couldn't the plaintiffs have made out a case of discrimination on the basis of their Hispanic national origin? As we have seen, in cases from *Teamsters* onwards, the same theories of liability that can be used to prove racial discrimination can also be used to prove discrimination on the basis of national origin. Unlike *Teamsters*, however, the "inexorable zero" does not apply to the employment of Hispanics in this case, but to the employment of every other ethnic group. Over 96 percent of Farah Manufacturing's employees were Hispanic.

Does this overrepresentation of Hispanics raise a problem of reverse discrimination? Or is it a characteristic feature of hiring among ethnic minorities and recent immigrants? Recruitment by word-of-mouth in closely knit communities has a cumulative effect, resulting in a concentration of employees from specific ethnic groups. One case that illustrates this tendency is EEOC v. Chicago Miniature Lamp Works, 947 F.2d 292 (7th Cir.

1991), where the court rejected claims of discrimination against blacks because of the nearly exclusive hiring of Hispanics and Asians by the employer. The workers who were hired were referred through a word-of-mouth network that favored recent immigrants because the employer did not require entry-level employees to be fluent in English. Are such practices desirable, because they integrate recent immigrants into the job market, or undesirable, because they exclude other groups from employment? Why shouldn't a class-wide theory of liability, either of disparate treatment or disparate impact, have applied in this case?

3. **Relationship of National Origin to Race.** Conceptually, national origin is a broader and more easily defined category than race. As we have seen, constitutional law treats the two concepts as virtually interchangeable. Upon examination, however, the concept of race lacks any independent significance. Attempts to base it on genetic variation fall into dubious theories of racial purity that have no scientific basis. Genetic variation within the conventionally defined races is greater than genetic variation among them. There is, for example, more genetic variation likely to be found among whites than between whites as a group and blacks as a group. Moreover, as the concept is usually invoked, race has as many cultural as physical components, as revealed, for instance, by the traditional classification of individuals of mixed race as belonging entirely to one race or another. Drawing fine distinctions between different races bears a disturbing similarity to Nazi laws, and those of other racist regimes, identifying specific groups for "ethnic cleansing." Thus, in an opinion early in his career, Justice Stevens compared the distinctions drawn in an affirmative action plan, defining who would benefit from it, to the racial laws in Nazi Germany. Fullilove v. Klutznick, 448 U.S. 448, 533–35 & n.5 (1980) (Stevens, J., dissenting).

In the abstract, it is easy to find cases in which a distinction between broader and narrower group affiliation can be drawn, but it is misleading to characterize such distinctions as between race and national origin. A person of Japanese ancestry, for instance, might suffer discrimination based on racial status as an Asian or discrimination based on Japanese national origin. Claims of discrimination on either of these grounds would have to be supported by different evidence that varies, for instance, with the treatment of Asians from other nations. All that these examples establish, however, is that particular individuals have multiple affiliations and that discrimination on the basis of any of them might be illegal. It is obviously possible to draw these distinctions, but not at all obvious that they should be drawn, causing discrimination on one ground to be treated differently from discrimination on the other. See generally Juan F. Perea, Ethnicity and Prejudice: Reevaluating "National Origin" Discrimination Under Title VII, 35 Wm. & Mary L. Rev. 805 (1994).

4. **Color as an Independent Basis for Discrimination.** The main prohibitions in Title VII include "color" as an independent form of prohibited discrimination, along with race and national origin. Did Congress include "color" in this list just out of concern about attempts at evasion? In its absence, would employers have said they discriminated on the basis of skin

color rather than on the basis of race or national origin? The presence of all three forms of prohibited discrimination suggests that the distinctions among them are not as important as the similarities, in particular, in the way in which they have been used to stigmatize and subordinate members of minority groups. Given the emphasis on pretext in cases such as McDonnell Douglas Corp. v. Green, 411 U.S. 792 (1973), color would not appear to be a plausible legitimate, nondiscriminatory reason for alleged discrimination on other grounds. Even in the absence of an explicit prohibition on this ground, employers could not invoke skin color as the justification for a disputed employment decision.

With the enactment of a separate prohibition, on the other hand, Title VII addresses discrimination within minority groups, for instance, the widely perceived discrimination against darker-skinned African-Americans. See Taunya Lovell Banks, Colorism Among South Asians: Title VII and Skin-Tone Discrimination, 14 Wash. U. Global L. Rev. 665 (2015); Ronald Turner, The Color Complex: Intraracial Discrimination in the Workplace, 46 Lab. L.J. 678 (1995); Joni Hersch, Skin Tone Effects Among African Americans: Perceptions and Reality, 96 Am. Econ. Rev. 251 (2006). Is significance of the prohibition confined to such cases? For an argument that it is not, but instead serves the broader and more fundamental purpose of attacking all privileges associated with lighter skin color, see Trina Jones, Shades of Brown: The Law of Skin Color, 49 Duke L.J. 1487 (2000); Cynthia E. Nance, Colorable Claims: The Continuing Significance of Color Under Title VII 40 Years After Its Passage, 26 Berkeley J. Emp. & Lab. L. 435 (2005).

The separate prohibition against discrimination on the basis of color raises further questions about the exact nature of race as a legal construct. For articles addressed to this subject and to the nature of racial discrimination generally, see Bradley A. Areheart, Intersectionality and Identity: Revisiting a Wrinkle in Title VII, 17 Geo. Mason U. Civ. Rts. J. 199 (2006); Pat K. Chew, Freeing Racial Harassment from the Sexual Harassment Model, 85 Or. L. Rev. 615 (2006); Pat K. Chew & Robert E. Kelley, Unwrapping Racial Harassment Law, 27 Berkeley J. Emp. & Lab. L. 49 (2006); N. Jeremi Duru, Fielding a Team for the Fans: The Societal Consequences and Title VII Implications of Race-Considered Roster Construction in Professional Sports, 84 Wash. U. L. Rev. 375 (2006); Sharona Hoffman, Is There a Place for "Race" as a Legal Concept?, 36 Ariz. St. L.J. 1093 (2004); Harry J. Holzer, Steven Raphael & Michael A. Stoll, Perceived Criminality, Criminal Background Checks, and the Racial Hiring Practices of Employers, 49 J.L. & Econ. 451 (2006); Russell K. Robinson, Casting and Caste-ing: Reconciling Artistic Freedom and Antidiscrimination Norms, 95 Cal. L. Rev. 1 (2007).

5. **The BFOQ for National Origin.** The BFOQ for national origin, just like the BFOQ for sex, squarely raises the issue whether to distinguish between different grounds of discrimination. The BFOQ for national origin is available only when national origin is "a bona fide occupational qualification reasonably necessary to the normal operation of that particular business or enterprise." § 703(e)(1)The BFOQ creates a narrow exception to discrimination on this ground (in addition to sex and religion), but not to the

prohibition against discrimination on the basis of race or color. The omission of a BFOQ on these grounds reflects a deliberate congressional decision to prohibit all racial classifications in employment. It also creates the anomaly that some classifications on the basis of national origin are permissible, while similar classifications on the basis of race are not. In constitutional law, as noted earlier, the two forms of discrimination have been regarded as equivalent.

As a matter of legal doctrine, the anomaly created by the BFOQ for national origin has been almost entirely eliminated by decisions giving it an exceedingly narrow interpretation. The Supreme Court has never upheld a BFOQ for national origin, only suggesting in dictum that the BFOQ might justify a requirement that executives of a subsidiary of a Japanese corporation be of Japanese origin. Sumitomo Shoji America, Inc. v. Avagliano, 457 U.S. 176, 189 n.19 (1982). This decision also raises the further question of the relationship between Title VII and "treaties of freedom and navigation" that allow foreign corporations in the United States to give preferential treatment to citizens of their own country. To the extent that discrimination in favor of foreign citizens also constitutes discrimination on the basis of national origin, the treaty might allow conduct prohibited by Title VII, raising the question whether the treaty would supersede the statute. See MacNamara v. Korean Air Lines, 863 F.2d 1135, 1138–41 (3d Cir. 1988), cert. denied, 493 U.S. 944 (1989) (treaty provision that employers may select managers based on citizenship does not conflict with Title VII, but would conflict with and preempt Title VII if it resulted in a disparate impact on the basis of race or national origin). For further analysis of this issue, see Michael Braswell & Stephen L. Poe, Employment Discrimination and FCN Treaties: Are Foreign Companies Exempt From Title VII?, 44 Lab. L.J. 27 (1993).

6. **Bibliography.** A number of articles analyze the relationship between discrimination on the basis of national origin and immigration, as well as the nature of national origin generally. Devon Carbado, Yellow by Law, 97 Cal. L. Rev. 633 (2009); Christine N. Cimini, Ask, Don't Tell: Ethical Issues Surrounding Undocumented Workers' Status in Employment Litigation, 61 Stan. L. Rev. 355 (2008); Keith Cunningham-Parmeter, Redefining the Rights of Undocumented Workers, 58 Am. U. L. Rev. 1361 (2009); Kevin R. Johnson, The End of "Civil Rights" as We Know It? Immigration and Civil Rights in the New Millennium, 49 UCLA L. Rev. 1481 (2002); Kathleen Kim, The Trafficked Worker as Private Attorney General: A Model for Enforcing the Civil Rights of Undocumented Workers, 2009 U. Chi. Legal F. 247; Stephen Lee, Private Immigration Screening in the Workplace, 61 Stan. L. Rev. 1103 (2009); Leticia M. Saucedo, The Employer Preference for the Subservient Worker and the Making of the Brown Collar Workplace, 67 Ohio St. L.J. 961 (2006); Camille Gear Rich, Elective Race: Recognizing Race Discrimination in the Era of Racial Self-Identification, 102 Geo. L.J. 1501 (2014); Leticia M. Saucedo, Intersectionality, Multidimensionality, Latino Immigrant Workers, and Title VII, 67 SMU L. Rev. 257 (2014); Leticia M. Saucedo, National Origin, Immigrants, and the Workplace: The Employment Cases in *Latinos and the Law* and the Advocate's Perspective, 12 Harv.

Latino L. Rev. 53 (2009); Craig R. Senn, Proposing a Uniform Remedial Approach for Undocumented Workers Under Federal Employment Discrimination Law, 77 Ford. L. Rev. 113 (2008); Symposium, LatCrit: Latinas/os and Law, 85 Cal. L. Rev. 1087 (1997) and 10 La Raza L.J. 1 (1998); Symposium, Work, Migration & Identity, 27 N.C. J. Int'l L. & Com. Reg. 389 (2002).

For an argument for retaining the priority of racial discrimination, see Roy L. Brooks & Kirsten Widner, In Defense of the Black/White Binary: Reclaiming a Tradition of Civil Rights Scholarship, 12 Berkeley J. Afr.-Am. L. & Pol'y 107 (2010).

Garcia v. Spun Steak Co.

998 F.2d 1480 (9th Cir. 1993).

■ O'SCANNLAIN, CIRCUIT JUDGE:

We are called upon to decide whether an employer violates Title VII of the Civil Rights Act of 1964 in requiring its bilingual workers to speak only English while working on the job.

I

Spun Steak Company ("Spun Steak") is a California corporation that produces poultry and meat products in South San Francisco for wholesale distribution. Spun Steak employs thirty-three workers, twenty-four of whom are Spanish-speaking. Virtually all of the Spanish-speaking employees are Hispanic. While two employees speak no English, the others have varying degrees of proficiency in English. Spun Steak has never required job applicants to speak or to understand English as a condition of employment.

Approximately two-thirds of Spun Steak's employees are production line workers or otherwise involved in the production process. Appellees Garcia and Buitrago are production line workers; they stand before a conveyor belt, remove poultry or other meat products from the belt and place the product into cases or trays for resale. Their work is done individually. Both Garcia and Buitrago are fully bilingual, speaking both English and Spanish.

Appellee Local 115, United Food and Commercial Workers International Union, AFL-CIO ("Local 115"), is the collective bargaining agent representing the employees at Spun Steak.

Prior to September 1990, these Spun Steak employees spoke Spanish freely to their co-workers during work hours. After receiving complaints that some workers were using their bilingual capabilities to harass and to insult other workers in a language they could not understand, Spun Steak began to investigate the possibility of requiring its employees to speak only English in the workplace. Specifically, Spun Steak received complaints that Garcia and Buitrago made derogatory, racist comments in Spanish about two co-workers, one of whom is African-American and the other Chinese-American.

The company's president, Kenneth Bertelson, concluded that an English-only rule would promote racial harmony in the workplace. In addition, he concluded that the English-only rule would enhance worker safety because some employees who did not understand Spanish claimed that the use of Spanish distracted them while they were operating machinery, and would enhance product quality because the U.S.D.A. inspector in the plant spoke only English and thus could not understand if a product-related concern was raised in Spanish. Accordingly, the following rule was adopted:

> "[I]t is hereafter the policy of this Company that only English will be spoken in connection with work. During lunch, breaks, and employee's own time, they are obviously free to speak Spanish if they wish. However, we urge all of you not to use your fluency in Spanish in a fashion which may lead other employees to suffer humiliation."

In addition to the English-only policy, Spun Steak adopted a rule forbidding offensive racial, sexual, or personal remarks of any kind.

It is unclear from the record whether Spun Steak strictly enforced the English-only rule. According to the plaintiffs-appellees, some workers continued to speak Spanish without incident. Spun Steak issued written exceptions to the policy allowing its clean-up crew to speak Spanish, allowing its foreman to speak Spanish, and authorizing certain workers to speak Spanish to the foreman at the foreman's discretion. One of the two employees who speak only Spanish is a member of the clean-up crew and thus is unaffected by the policy.

In November 1990, Garcia and Buitrago received warning letters for speaking Spanish during working hours. For approximately two months thereafter, they were not permitted to work next to each other. Local 115 protested the English-only policy and requested that it be rescinded but to no avail.

On May 6, 1991, Garcia, Buitrago, and Local 115 filed charges of discrimination against Spun Steak with the U.S. Equal Employment Opportunity Commission ("EEOC"). The EEOC conducted an investigation and determined that "there is reasonable cause to believe [Spun Steak] violated Title VII of the Civil Rights Act of 1964, as amended, with respect to its adoption of an English-only rule and with respect to retaliation when [Garcia, Buitrago, and Local 115] complained."

Garcia, Buitrago, and Local 115, on behalf of all Spanish-speaking employees of Spun Steak, (collectively, "the Spanish-speaking employees") filed suit, alleging that the English-only policy violated Title VII. On September 6, 1991, the parties filed cross-motions for summary judgment. The district court denied Spun Steak's motion and granted the

Spanish-speaking employees' motion for summary judgment, concluding that the English-only policy disparately impacted Hispanic workers without sufficient business justification, and thus violated Title VII. Spun Steak filed this timely appeal and the EEOC filed a brief *amicus curiae* and participated in oral argument. The Spanish-speaking employees do not contend that Spun Steak intentionally discriminated against them in enacting the English-only policy. Rather, they contend that the policy had a discriminatory impact on them because it imposes a burdensome term or condition of employment exclusively upon Hispanic workers and denies them a privilege of employment that non-Spanish-speaking workers enjoy. . . .

B

To make out a prima facie case of discriminatory impact, a plaintiff must identify a specific, seemingly neutral practice or policy that has a significantly adverse impact on persons of a protected class. Connecticut v. Teal, 457 U.S. 440, 446 (1982). If the prima facie case is established, the burden shifts to the employer to "demonstrate that the challenged practice is job related for the position in question and consistent with business necessity." 42 U.S.C. § 2000e–2(k)(1)(A) In this case, the district court granted summary judgment in favor of the Spanish-speaking employees, concluding that, as a matter of law, the employees had made out the prima facie case and the justifications offered by the employer were inadequate.

1

We first consider whether the Spanish-speaking employees have made out the prima facie case. "[T]he requirements of a prima facie disparate impact case are in some respects more exacting than those of a disparate treatment case." Spaulding v. University of Washington, 740 F.2d 686, 705 (9th Cir.) (citation omitted), cert. denied, 469 U.S. 1036 (1984). In the disparate treatment context, a plaintiff can make out a prima facie case merely by presenting evidence sufficient to give rise to an inference of discrimination. McDonnell Douglas Corp. v. Green, 411 U.S. 792, 802–06 (1973). In a disparate impact case, by contrast, plaintiffs must do more than merely raise an inference of discrimination before the burden shifts; they "must actually prove the discriminatory impact at issue." Rose v. Wells Fargo & Co., 902 F.2d 1417, 1421 (9th Cir. 1990). In the typical disparate impact case, in which the plaintiff argues that a selection criterion excludes protected applicants from jobs or promotions, the plaintiff proves discriminatory impact by showing statistical disparities between the number of protected class members in the qualified applicant group and those in the relevant segment of the workforce. Wards Cove Packing Co. v. Atonio, 490 U.S. 642, 650 (1989). While such statistics are often difficult to compile, whether the protected group has been disadvantaged turns on quantifiable data. When the alleged disparate impact is on the conditions, terms, or privileges of employment, however, determining whether the protected group has been adversely affected may depend on subjective factors not easily quantified. The fact that the alleged effects are subjective, however, does not relieve the plaintiff of the burden of proving disparate impact. The plaintiff may not merely assert that the policy has harmed members of the group to which he or she belongs. Instead, the plaintiff must prove the existence of adverse effects of the policy, must prove that the impact of the policy is on terms, conditions, or privileges of employment of the protected class, must prove that the adverse effects are significant, and must prove that the employee population in general is not affected by the policy to the same degree.

It is beyond dispute that, in this case, if the English-only policy causes any adverse effects, those effects will be suffered disproportionately by those of Hispanic origin. The vast majority of those workers at Spun Steak who speak a language other than English—and virtually all those employees for whom English is not a first language—are Hispanic. It is of no consequence that not all Hispanic employees of Spun Steak speak Spanish; nor is it relevant that some non-Hispanic workers may speak Spanish. If the adverse effects are proved, it is enough under Title VII that Hispanics are disproportionately impacted.

The crux of the dispute between Spun Steak and the Spanish-speaking employees, however, is not over whether Hispanic workers will disproportionately bear any adverse effects of the policy; rather, the dispute centers on whether the policy causes any adverse effects at all, and if it does, whether the effects are significant. The Spanish-speaking employees argue that the policy adversely affects them in the following ways: (1) it denies them the ability to express their cultural heritage on the job; (2) it denies them a privilege of employment that is enjoyed by monolingual speakers of English; and (3) it creates an atmosphere of inferiority, isolation, and intimidation. We discuss each of these contentions in turn.

a

The employees argue that denying them the ability to speak Spanish on the job denies them the right to cultural expression. It cannot be gainsaid that an individual's primary language can be an important link to his ethnic culture and identity. Title VII, however, does not protect the ability of workers to express their cultural heritage at the workplace. Title VII is concerned only with disparities in the treatment of workers; it does not confer substantive privileges. See, e.g., Garcia v. Gloor, 618 F.2d 264, 269 (5th Cir.1980), cert. denied, 449 U.S. 1113 (1981). It is axiomatic that an employee must often sacrifice individual self-expression during working hours. Just as a private employer is not required to allow other types of self-expression, there is nothing in Title VII which requires an employer to allow employees to express their cultural identity. . .

ii

We do not foreclose the prospect that in some circumstances English-only rules can exacerbate existing tensions, or, when combined with other discriminatory behavior, contribute to an overall environment of discrimination. Likewise, we can envision a case in which such rules are enforced in such a draconian manner that the enforcement itself amounts to harassment. In evaluating such a claim, however, a court must look to the totality of the circumstances in the particular factual context in which the claim arises.

In holding that the enactment of an English-only while working policy does not inexorably lead to an abusive environment for those whose primary language is not English, we reach a conclusion opposite to the EEOC's longstanding position. The EEOC Guidelines provide that an employee meets the prima facie case in a disparate impact cause of action merely by proving the existence of the English-only policy. See 29 C.F.R. § 1606.7(a) & (b) (1991). Under the EEOC's scheme, an employer must always provide a business justification for such a rule. Id. The EEOC enacted this scheme in part because of its conclusion that English-only rules may "create an atmosphere of inferiority, isolation and intimidation based on national origin which could result in a discriminatory working environment." 29 C.F.R. § 1606.7(a).

We do not reject the English-only rule Guideline lightly. We recognize that "as an administrative interpretation of the Act by the enforcing agency, these Guidelines . . . constitute a body of experience and informed judgment to which courts and litigants may properly resort for guidance." Meritor Sav. Bank, 477 U.S. at 65 (internal quotations and citations omitted). But we are not bound by the Guidelines. See Espinoza v. Farah Mfg. Co., Inc., 414 U.S. 86, 94 (1973). We will not defer to "an administrative construction of a statute where there are 'compelling indications that it is wrong.' " Id.

We have been impressed by Judge Rubin's pre-Guidelines analysis for the Fifth Circuit in *Garcia*, which we follow today. Garcia, 618 F.2d 264. Nothing in the plain language of section 703(a)(1) supports EEOC's English-only rule Guideline. "Title VII could not have been enacted into law without substantial support from legislators in both Houses who traditionally resisted federal regulation of private business." United Steelworkers of America, AFL-CIO v. Weber, 443 U.S. 193 (1979). "Those legislators demanded as a price for their support that," id., management prerogatives, and union freedoms are to be left undisturbed to the greatest extent possible. Internal affairs of employers and labor organizations must not be interfered with except to the limited extent that correction is required in discrimination practices. Statement of William M. McCulloch, et al., H.R. Rep. No. 914, 88 Cong., 2d Sess. (1964), (quoted in part in *Steelworkers*, 443 U.S. at 206). It is clear that Congress intended a balance to be struck in preventing discrimination and preserving the independence of the employer. In striking that balance, the Supreme Court has held that a plaintiff in a disparate impact case must prove the alleged discriminatory effect before the burden shifts to the employer. The EEOC Guideline at issue here contravenes that policy by presuming that an English-only policy has a disparate impact in the absence of proof. We are not aware of, nor has counsel shown us, anything in the legislative history to Title VII that indicates that English-only policies are to be presumed discriminatory. Indeed, nowhere in the legislative history is there a discussion of English-only policies at all.

2

Because the bilingual employees have failed to make out a prima facie case, we need not consider the business justifications offered for the policy as applied to them. On remand, if Local 115 is able to make out a prima facie case with regard to employees with limited proficiency in English, the district court could then consider any business justification offered by Spun Steak.

IV

In sum, we conclude that the bilingual employees have not made out a prima facie case and that Spun Steak has not violated Title VII in adopting an English-only rule as to them. Thus, we reverse the grant of summary judgment in favor of Garcia, Buitrago, and Local 115 to the extent it represents the bilingual employees, and remand with instructions to grant summary judgment in favor of Spun Steak on their claims. A genuine issue of material fact exists as to whether there are one or more employees represented by Local 115 with limited proficiency in English who were adversely impacted by the policy. As to such employee or employees, we reverse the grant of summary judgment in favor of Local 115, and remand for further proceedings.

REVERSED and REMANDED.

■ BOOCHEVER, CIRCUIT JUDGE, dissenting in part:

I agree with most of the majority's carefully crafted opinion. I dissent, however, from the majority's rejection of the EEOC guidelines. The guidelines provide that an employee establishes a prima facie case in a disparate impact claim by proving the existence of an English-only policy, thereby shifting the burden to the employer to show a business necessity for the rule. See 29 C.F.R. § 1606.7(b) (1991) ("An employer may have a rule requiring that employees speak only in English at certain times where the employer can show that the rule is justified by business necessity."). I would defer to the Commission's expertise in construing the Act, by virtue of which it concluded that English-only rules may "create an atmosphere of inferiority, isolation and intimidation based on national origin which could result in a discriminatory working environment." Id. § 1606.7(a).

As the majority indicates, proof of such an effect of English-only rules requires analysis of subjective factors. It is hard to envision how the burden of proving such an effect would be met other than by conclusory self-serving statements of the Spanish-speaking employees or possibly by expert testimony of psychologists. The difficulty of meeting such a burden may well have been one of the reasons for the promulgation of the guideline. On the other hand, it should not be difficult for an employer to give specific reasons for the policy, such as the safety reasons advanced in this case. . . .

NOTES ON *GARCIA V. SPUN STEAK CO.*

1. **The Nature of Language Claims.** Especially among recent immigrants, use of a foreign language often accompanies a distinctive national origin. It is part of the cultural heritage that, together with ancestry, determines national origin. For this reason also, national origin and religion often overlap, leading to a coincidence between claims of discrimination on these grounds. Discrimination against Jews, for instance, could be on both grounds, and other ethnic minorities also are associated with a particular religion. The broad range of cultural practices correlated with, or perhaps even definitionally part of, national origin raise doctrinal questions under Title VII about the nature of claims concerned with these practices.

In *Garcia v. Spun Steak*, the plaintiffs asserted a claim only of disparate impact, not disparate treatment. Could they have asserted a claim of disparate treatment, based on the close association of speaking Spanish with Hispanic national origin? The EEOC guidelines characterized their claim as one of disparate impact, but gave it the benefit of a presumption of adverse impact without any statistical showing of adverse effects. Does this amount to treating the claim like one of intentional discrimination? Or is the crucial difference the defense of job relationship and business necessity available to a claim of disparate impact, but not one of disparate treatment? Do the cultural practices associated with national origin require this degree of flexibility in the legal standards applied to them?

2. **The Employer's Interests.** An unsettling feature of the claims in *Garcia v. Spun Steak* is that the employer's English-only rule was established only after complaints that Hispanic employees harassed and insulted other employees in Spanish. This fact created a kind of "unclean hands" background to the plaintiffs' claim, perhaps inclining the court towards sympathetic treatment of an employer seeking to manage a multicultural work force. Should these efforts by employers be discouraged or encouraged by Title VII?

These incidents also reveal the broader reasons an employer might have for establishing an English-only rule. Monitoring the behavior of employees who speak a foreign language is much more difficult than monitoring their behavior if they speak English. If the employer does not have supervisors who are fluent in the employees' language, it may be at a loss to figure out what they are saying, and therefore doing, in the work place. The court in *Garcia v. Spun Steak* never discusses this problem because it finds no disparate impact on Hispanic employees. The dissent, following the presumption of adverse impact in the EEOC guidelines, would place the burden of proof on the employer on this issue.

How difficult would it be for the employer to demonstrate job relationship and business necessity based on the need effectively to monitor the behavior of its employees? Does the answer to this question depend upon the breadth of the English-only rule? The rule in *Garcia v. Spun Steak* applied only during working time, leaving employees free to speak Spanish during their breaks. Is this rule tailored closely enough to the employer's interest in monitoring its employees? Or does the employer have to make some additional showing, like the risk of harassment or the possibility of alienating customers who do not speak Spanish, in order to make out a defense?

3. The Remaining Scope of Claims Against English-Only Rules. The court leaves open the possibility that the plaintiffs might prevail on behalf of employees with "limited proficiency in English." The adverse impact of the English-only rule on such employees is obvious, but so too, is the employer's defense. If employees are not fluent in English, the employer's ability to communicate with them necessarily is diminished, again in the absence of supervisors fluent in the employees' language. The same is true of fellow employees, customers, suppliers, and other individuals that an employee must deal with. Couldn't employers justifiably claim that the cost of making employees fluent in English should not be forced upon them?

But if this is true, what scope is left for claims against English-only rules? Has the court in *Garcia v. Spun Steak* turned the EEOC's presumption against such rules on its head, creating a presumption that they are valid? Does this result strike the right balance between recognizing the cultural practices associated with national origin and the interests of employers in efficient operations?

4. Bibliography. Christopher David Ruiz Cameron, How the Garcia Cousins Lost Their Accents: Understanding the Language of Title VII Decisions Approving English-Only Rules as the Product of Racial Dualism, Latino Invisibility, and Legal Indeterminacy, 85 Cal. L. Rev. 1347 (1997) (1998); Drucilla Cornell & William W. Bratton, Deadweight Costs and Intrinsic Wrongs of Nativism: Economics, Freedom, and Legal Suppression of Spanish, 84 Cornell L. Rev. 595 (1999); Cristinia M. Rodriguez, Language Diversity in the Workplace, 100 Nw. U. L. Rev. 1689 (2006); Juliet Stumpf, English-Only Cases: Litigating the Diverse Workplace, 34 A.B.A. Emp. & Lab. L. 6 (2006); Julie C. Suk, Economic Opportunities and the Protection of Minority Languages, 1 L. Ethics & Hum. Rts. 134 (2007).

C. RELIGIOUS DISCRIMINATION

Trans World Airlines v. Hardison

432 U.S. 63 (1977).

■ JUSTICE WHITE delivered the opinion of the Court.

Section 703(a)(1) of the Civil Rights Act of 1964, Title VII, makes it an unlawful employment practice for an employer to discriminate against an employee or a prospective employee on the basis of his or her religion. At the time of the events involved here, a guideline of the Equal Employment Opportunity Commission (EEOC), 29 CFR § 1605.1(b) (1968), required, as the Act itself now does, 42 U.S.C. § 2000e(j), that an employer, short of "undue hardship," make "reasonable accommodations" to the religious needs of its employees. The issue in this case is the extent of the employer's obligation under Title VII to accommodate an employee whose religious beliefs prohibit him from working on Saturdays.

I

We summarize briefly the facts found by the District Court.

Petitioner Trans World Airlines (TWA) operates a large maintenance and overhaul base in Kansas City, Mo. On June 5, 1967, respondent Larry G. Hardison was hired by TWA to work as a clerk in the Stores Department at its Kansas City base. Because of its essential role in the Kansas City operation, the Stores Department must operate 24 hours per day, 365 days per year, and whenever an employee's job in that department is not filled, an employee must be shifted from another department, or a supervisor must cover the job, even if the work in other areas may suffer.

Hardison, like other employees at the Kansas City base, was subject to a seniority system contained in a collective bargaining agreement that TWA maintains with petitioner International Association of Machinists and Aerospace Workers (IAM). The seniority system is implemented by the union steward through a system of bidding by employees for particular shift assignments as they become available. The most senior employees have first choice for job and shift assignments, and the most junior employees are required to work when the union steward is unable to find enough people willing to work at a particular time or in a particular job to fill TWA's needs.

In the spring of 1968 Hardison began to study the religion known as the Worldwide Church of God. One of the tenets of that religion is that one must observe the Sabbath by refraining from performing any work from sunset on Friday until sunset on Saturday. The religion also proscribes work on certain specified religious holidays.

When Hardison informed Everett Kussman, the manager of the Stores Department, of his religious conviction regarding observance of the Sabbath, Kussman agreed that the union steward should seek a job swap for Hardison or a change of days off; that Hardison would have his religious holidays off whenever possible if Hardison agreed to work the traditional holidays when asked; and that Kussman would try to find Hardison another job that would be more compatible with his religious beliefs. The problem was temporarily solved when Hardison transferred to the 11 p.m.–7 a.m. shift. Working this shift permitted Hardison to observe his Sabbath.

The problem soon reappeared when Hardison bid for and received a transfer from Building 1, where he had been employed, to Building 2, where he would work the day shift. The two buildings had entirely separate seniority lists; and while in Building 1 Hardison had sufficient seniority to observe the Sabbath regularly, he was second from the bottom on the Building 2 seniority list.

In Building 2 Hardison was asked to work Saturdays when a fellow employee went on vacation. TWA agreed to permit the union to seek a change of work assignments for Hardison, but the union was not willing to violate the seniority provisions set out in the collective bargaining contract, and Hardison had insufficient seniority to bid for a shift having Saturdays off.

A proposal that Hardison work only four days a week was rejected by the company. Hardison's job was essential, and on weekends he was the only available person on his shift to perform it. To leave the position empty would have impaired supply shop functions, which were critical to airline operations; to fill Hardison's position with a supervisor or an employee from another area would simply have undermanned another operation; and to employ someone not regularly assigned to work Saturdays would have required TWA to pay premium wages.

When an accommodation was not reached, Hardison refused to report for work on Saturdays. A transfer to the twilight shift proved unavailing since that schedule still required Hardison to work past sundown on Fridays. After a hearing, Hardison was discharged on grounds of insubordination for refusing to work during his designated shift.

Hardison, having first invoked the administrative remedy provided by Title VII, brought this action for injunctive relief in the United States District Court against TWA and IAM, claiming that his discharge by TWA constituted religious discrimination in violation of Title VII, 42 U.S.C. § 2000e–2(a)(1). He also charged that the union had discriminated against him by failing to represent him adequately in his dispute with TWA and by depriving him of his right to exercise his religious beliefs. Hardison's claim of religious discrimination rested on 1967 EEOC guidelines requiring employers "to make reasonable accommodations to the religious needs of employees" whenever such accommodation would not work an "undue hardship," 29 CFR § 1605.1 (1968), and on similar language adopted by Congress in the 1972 amendments to Title VII, 42 U.S.C. § 2000e(j).

After a bench trial, the District Court ruled in favor of the defendants. Turning first to the claim against the union, the District Court ruled that although the 1967 EEOC guidelines were applicable to unions, the union's duty to accommodate Hardison's belief did not require it to ignore its seniority system as Hardison appeared to claim. As for Hardison's claim against TWA, the District Court rejected at the outset TWA's contention that requiring it in any way to accommodate the religious needs of its employees would constitute an unconstitutional establishment of religion. As the District Court construed the Act, however, TWA had satisfied its "reasonable accommodations" obligation, and any further accommodation would have worked an undue hardship on the company.

The Court of Appeals for the Eighth Circuit reversed the judgment for TWA. It agreed with the District Court's constitutional ruling, but held that TWA had not satisfied its duty to accommodate. Because it did not appear that Hardison had attacked directly the judgment in favor of the union, the Court of Appeals affirmed that judgment without ruling on its substantive merits.

In separate petitions for certiorari TWA and IAM contended that adequate steps had been taken to accommodate Hardison's religious observances and that to construe the statute to require further efforts at accommodation would create an establishment of religion contrary to the First Amendment of the Constitution. TWA also contended that the Court of Appeals improperly ignored the District Court's findings of fact.

We granted both petitions for certiorari. Because we agree with petitioners that their conduct was not a violation of Title VII, we need not reach the other questions presented. . . .

The prohibition against religious discrimination soon raised the question of whether it was impermissible under § 703(a)(1) to discharge or refuse to hire a person who for religious reasons refused to work during the employer's normal workweek. In 1966 an EEOC guideline dealing with this problem declared that an employer had an obligation under the statute "to accommodate to the reasonable religious needs of employees . . . where such accommodation can be made without serious inconvenience to the conduct of the business." 29 CFR § 1605.1 (1967).

In 1967 the EEOC amended its guidelines to require employers "to make reasonable accommodations to the religious needs of employees and prospective employees where such accommodations can be made without undue hardship on the conduct of the employer's business." 29 CFR § 1605.1 (1968). The EEOC did not suggest what sort of accommodations are "reasonable" or when hardship to an employer becomes "undue."

This question—the extent of the required accommodation—remained unsettled when this Court, in Dewey v. Reynolds Metals Co., 402 U.S. 689 (1971), affirmed by an equally divided Court the Sixth

Circuit's decision in 429 F.2d 324 (1970). The discharge of an employee who for religious reasons had refused to work on Sundays was there held by the Court of Appeals not to be an unlawful employment practice because the manner in which the employer allocated Sunday work assignments was discriminatory in neither its purpose nor effect; and consistent with the 1967 EEOC guidelines, the employer had made a reasonable accommodation of the employee's beliefs by giving him the opportunity to secure a replacement for his Sunday work.

In part "to resolve by legislation" some of the issues raised in Dewey, 118 Cong. Rec. 706 (1972) (remarks of Sen. Randolph), Congress included the following definition of religion in its 1972 amendments to Title VII:

> "The term 'religion' includes all aspects of religious observance and practice, as well as belief, unless an employer demonstrates that he is unable to reasonably accommodate to an employee's or prospective employee's religious observance or practice without undue hardship on the conduct of the employer's business." § 701(j).

The intent and effect of this definition was to make it an unlawful employment practice under § 703(a)(1) for an employer not to make reasonable accommodations, short of undue hardship, for the religious practices of his employees and prospective employees. But like the EEOC guidelines, the statute provides no guidance for determining the degree of accommodation that is required of an employer. The brief legislative history of § 701(j) is likewise of little assistance in this regard. The proponent of the measure, Senator Jennings Randolph, expressed his general desire "to assure that freedom from religious discrimination in the employment of workers is for all time guaranteed by law," 118 Cong. Rec. 705 (1972), but he made no attempt to define the precise circumstances under which the "reasonable accommodation" requirement would be applied.

In brief, the employer's statutory obligation to make reasonable accommodation for the religious observances of its employees, short of incurring an undue hardship, is clear, but the reach of that obligation has never been spelled out by Congress or by EEOC guidelines. With this in mind, we turn to a consideration of whether TWA has met its obligation under Title VII to accommodate the religious observances of its employees.

III

The Court of Appeals held that TWA had not made reasonable efforts to accommodate Hardison's religious needs under the 1967 EEOC guidelines in effect at the time the relevant events occurred. In its view, TWA had rejected three reasonable alternatives, any one of which would have satisfied its obligation without undue hardship. First, within the framework of the seniority system, TWA could have permitted Hardison to work a four day week, utilizing in his place a supervisor or another worker on duty elsewhere. That this would have caused other shop functions to suffer was insufficient to amount to undue hardship in the opinion of the Court of Appeals. Second according to the Court of Appeals, also within the bounds of the collective bargaining contract the company could have filled Hardison's Saturday shift from other available personnel competent to do the job, of which the court said there were at least 200. That this would have involved premium overtime pay was not deemed an undue hardship. Third, TWA could have arranged a "swap between Hardison and another employee either for another shift or for the Sabbath days." In response to the assertion that this would have involved a breach of the seniority provisions of the contract, the court noted that it had not been settled in the courts whether the required statutory accommodation to religious needs stopped short of transgressing seniority rules, but found it unnecessary to decide the issue because, as the Court of Appeals saw the record, TWA had not sought, and the union had therefore not declined to entertain, a possible variance from the seniority provisions of the collective bargaining agreement. The company had simply left the entire matter to the union steward who the Court of Appeals said "likewise did nothing."

We disagree with the Court of Appeals in all relevant respects. It is our view that TWA made reasonable efforts to accommodate and that each of the Court of Appeals' suggested alternatives would have been an undue hardship within the meaning of the statute as construed by the EEOC guidelines.

A

It might be inferred from the Court of Appeals' opinion and from the brief of the EEOC in this Court that TWA's efforts to accommodate were no more than negligible. The findings of the District Court, supported by the record, are to the contrary. In summarizing its more detailed findings, the District Court observed:

> "TWA established as a matter of fact that it did take appropriate action to accommodate as required by Title VII. It held several meetings with plaintiff at which it attempted to find a solution to plaintiff's problems. It did accommodate plaintiff's observance of his special religious holidays. It authorized the union steward to search for someone who would swap shifts, which apparently was normal procedure."

It is also true that TWA itself attempted without success to find Hardison another job. The District Court's view was that TWA had done all that could reasonably be expected within the bounds of the seniority system.

The Court of Appeals observed, however, that the possibility of a variance from the seniority system was never really posed to the union. This is contrary to the District Court's findings and to the record. The District Court found that when TWA first learned of Hardison's religious observances in April 1968, it agreed to permit the union's steward to seek a swap of shifts or days off but that "the steward reported that he was unable to work out scheduling changes and that he understood that no one was willing to swap days with plaintiff." Later, in March 1969, at a meeting held just two days before Hardison first failed to report for his Saturday shift, TWA again "offered to accommodate plaintiff's religious observance by agreeing to any trade of shifts or change of sections that plaintiff and the union could work out.... Any shift or change was impossible within the seniority framework and the union was not willing to violate the seniority provisions set out in the contract to make a shift or change." As the record shows, Hardison himself testified that Kussman was willing, but the union was not, to work out a shift or job trade with another employee.

We shall say more about the seniority system, but at this juncture it appears to us that the system itself represented a significant accommodation to the needs, both religious and secular, of all of TWA's employees. As will become apparent, the seniority system represents a neutral way of minimizing the number of occasions when an employee must work on a day that he would prefer to have off. Additionally, recognizing that weekend work schedules are the least popular, the company made further accommodation by reducing its work force to a bare minimum on those days.

B

We are also convinced, contrary to the Court of Appeals, that TWA itself cannot be faulted for having failed to work out a shift or job swap for Hardison. Both the union and TWA had agreed to the seniority system; the union was unwilling to entertain a variance over the objections of men senior to Hardison; and for TWA to have arranged unilaterally for a swap would have amounted to a breach of the collective bargaining agreement.

(1)

Hardison and the EEOC insist that the statutory obligation to accommodate religious needs takes precedence over both the collective bargaining contract and the seniority rights of TWA's other employees. We agree that neither a collective bargaining contract nor a seniority system may be employed to violate the statute, but we do not believe that the duty to accommodate requires TWA to take steps inconsistent with the otherwise valid agreement. Collective bargaining, aimed at effecting workable and enforceable agreements between management and labor, lies at the core of our national labor policy, and seniority provisions are universally included in these contracts. Without a clear and express indication from Congress, we cannot agree with Hardison and the EEOC that an agreed upon seniority system must give way when necessary to accommodate religious observances. The issue is important and warrants some discussion.

Any employer who, like TWA, conducts an around-the-clock operation is presented with the choice of allocating work schedules either in accordance with the preferences of its employees or by involuntary assignment. Insofar as the varying shift preferences of its employees complement each other, TWA could meet its manpower needs through voluntary work scheduling. In the present case, for example, Hardison's supervisor foresaw little difficulty in giving Hardison his religious holidays off since they fell on days that most other employees preferred to work, while Hardison was willing to work on the traditional holidays that most other employees preferred to have off.

Whenever there are not enough employees who choose to work a particular shift, however, some employees must be assigned to that shift even though it is not their first choice. Such was evidently the case with regard to Saturday work; even though TWA cut back its weekend work force to a skeleton crew, not enough employees chose those days off to staff the Stores Department through voluntary scheduling. In these circumstances, TWA and IAM agreed to give first preference to employees who had worked in a particular department the longest.

Had TWA nevertheless circumvented the seniority system by relieving Hardison of Saturday work and ordering a senior employee to replace him, it would have denied the latter his shift preference so that Hardison could be given his. The senior employee would also have been deprived of his contractual rights under the collective bargaining agreement.

It was essential to TWA's business to require Saturday and Sunday work from at least a few employees even though most employees preferred those days off. Allocating the burdens of weekend work was a matter for collective bargaining. In considering criteria to govern this allocation, TWA and the union had two alternatives: adopt a neutral system, such as seniority, a lottery, or rotating shifts; or allocate days off in accordance with the religious needs of its employees. TWA would have had to adopt the latter in order to assure Hardison and others like him of getting the days off necessary for strict observance of their religion, but it could have done so only at the expense of others who had strong, but perhaps nonreligious, reasons for not working on weekends. There were no volunteers to relieve Hardison on Saturdays, and to give Hardison Saturdays off, TWA would have had to deprive another employee of his shift preference at least in part because he did not adhere to a religion that observed the Saturday Sabbath.

Title VII does not contemplate such unequal treatment. The repeated, unequivocal emphasis of both the language and the legislative history of Title VII is on eliminating discrimination in employment, and such discrimination is proscribed when it is directed against majorities as well as minorities. Indeed, the foundation of Hardison's claim is that TWA and IAM engaged in religious discrimination in violation of 703(a)(1) when they failed to arrange for him to have Saturdays off. It would be anomalous to conclude that by "reasonable accommodation" Congress meant that an employer must deny the shift and job preference of some employees, as well as deprive them of their contractual rights, in order to accommodate or prefer the religious needs of others, and we conclude that Title VII does not require an employer to go that far.

(2)

Our conclusion is supported by the fact that seniority systems are afforded special treatment under Title VII itself. Section 703(h) provides in pertinent part:

> "Notwithstanding any other provision of this subchapter, it shall not be an unlawful employment practice for an employer to apply different standards of compensation, or different terms, conditions, or privileges of employment pursuant to a bona fide seniority or merit system . . . provided that such differences are not the result of an intention to discriminate because of race, color, religion, sex, or national origin."

"[T]he unmistakable purpose of § 703(h) was to make clear that the routine application of a bona fide seniority system would not be unlawful under Title VII." Teamsters v. United States, 431 U.S. 324, 352 (1977). See also United Air Lines, Inc. v. Evans, 431 U.S. 553 (1977). Section 703(h) is "a definitional provision; as with the other provisions of § 703, subsection (h) delineates which employment practices are illegal and thereby prohibited and which are not." Franks v. Bowman Transportation Co., 424 U.S. 747, 758 (1976). Thus, absent a discriminatory purpose, the operation of a seniority system cannot be an unlawful employment practice even if the system has some discriminatory consequences.

There has been no suggestion of discriminatory intent in this case. "The seniority system was not designed with the intention to discriminate against religion nor did it act to lock members of any religion into a pattern wherein their freedom to exercise their religion was limited. It was coincidental that in plaintiff's case the seniority system acted to compound his problems in exercising his religion." 375 F. Supp. at 883. The Court of Appeals' conclusion that TWA was not limited by the terms of its seniority system was in substance nothing more than a ruling that operation of the seniority system was itself an unlawful employment practice even though no discriminatory purpose had been shown. That ruling is plainly inconsistent with the dictates of § 703(h), both on its face and as interpreted in the recent decisions of this Court.

As we have said, TWA was not required by Title VII to carve out a special exception to its seniority system in order to help Hardison to meet his religious obligations.

C

The Court of Appeals also suggested that TWA could have permitted Hardison to work a four day week if necessary in order to avoid working on his Sabbath. Recognizing that this might have left TWA short handed on the one shift each week that Hardison did not work, the court still concluded that TWA would suffer no undue hardship if it were required to replace Hardison either with supervisory personnel or with qualified personnel from other departments. Alternatively, the Court of Appeals suggested that TWA could have replaced Hardison on his Saturday shift with other available employees through the payment of premium wages. Both of these alternatives would involve costs to TWA, either in the form of lost efficiency in other jobs or higher wages.

To require TWA to bear more than a de minimis cost in order to give Hardison Saturdays off is an undue hardship. Like abandonment of the seniority system, to require TWA to bear additional costs when no such costs are incurred to give other employees the days off that they want would involve unequal treatment of employees on the basis of their religion. By suggesting that TWA should incur certain costs in order to give Hardison Saturdays off the Court of Appeals would in effect require TWA to finance an additional Saturday off and then to choose the employee who will enjoy it on the basis of his religious beliefs. While incurring extra costs to secure a replacement for Hardison might remove the necessity of compelling another employee to work involuntarily in Hardison's place, it would not change the fact that the privilege of having Saturdays off would be allocated according to religious beliefs.

As we have seen, the paramount concern of Congress in enacting Title VII was the elimination of discrimination in employment. In the absence of clear statutory language or legislative history to the contrary, we will not readily construe the statute to require an employer to discriminate against some employees in order to enable others to observe their Sabbath.

Reversed.

■ JUSTICE MARSHALL, with whom JUSTICE BRENNAN joins, dissenting.

One of the most intractable problems arising under Title VII has been whether an employer is guilty of religious discrimination when he discharges an employee (or refuses to hire a job applicant) because of the employee's religious practices. Particularly troublesome has been the plight of adherents to minority faiths who do not observe the holy days on which most businesses are closed—Sundays, Christmas, and Easter—but who need time off for their own days of religious observance. The Equal Employment Opportunity Commission has grappled with this problem in two sets of regulations, and in a long line of decisions. Initially the Commission concluded that an employer was "free under Title VII to establish a normal workweek . . . generally applicable to all employees," and that an employee could not "demand any alteration in [his work schedule] to accommodate his religious needs." 29 CFR §§ 1605.1(a)(3), (b)(3) (1967). Eventually, however, the Commission changed its view and decided that employers must reasonably accommodate such requested schedule changes except where "undue hardship" would result—for example, "where the employee's needed work cannot be performed by another employee of substantially similar qualifications during the period of absence." 29 CFR § 1605.1(b) (1976). In amending Title VII in 1972 Congress confronted the same problem, and adopted the second position of the EEOC. Both before and after the 1972 amendment the lower courts have considered at length the circumstances in which employers must accommodate the religious practices of employees, reaching what the Court correctly describes as conflicting results. And on two occasions this Court has attempted to provide guidance to the lower courts, only to find ourselves evenly divided. Parker Seal Co. v. Cummins, 429 U.S. 65 (1976); Dewey v. Reynolds Metals Co., 402 U.S. 689 (1971).

Today's decision deals a fatal blow to all efforts under Title VII to accommodate work requirements to religious practices. The Court holds, in essence, that although the EEOC regulations and the Act state that an employer must make reasonable adjustments in his work demands to take account of religious observances, the regulation and Act do not really mean what they say. An employer, the Court concludes, need not grant even the most minor special privilege to religious observers to enable them to follow their faith. As a question of social policy, this result is deeply troubling, for a society that truly values religious pluralism cannot compel adherents of minority religions to make the cruel choice of surrendering their religion or their job. And as a matter of law today's result is intolerable, for the Court adopts the very position that Congress expressly rejected in 1972, as if we were free to disregard congressional choices that a majority of this Court thinks unwise. I therefore dissent.

I

With respect to each of the proposed accommodations to respondent Hardison's religious observances that the Court discusses, it ultimately notes that the accommodation would have required "unequal treatment" in favor of the religious observer. That is quite true. But if an accommodation can be rejected simply because it involves preferential treatment, then the regulation and the statute, while brimming with "sound and fury," ultimately "signif[y] nothing."

The accommodation issue by definition arises only when a neutral rule of general applicability conflicts with the religious practices of a particular employee. In some of the reported cases, the rule in question has governed work attire; in other cases it has required attendance at some religious function; in still other instances, it has compelled membership in a union; and in the largest class of cases, it has concerned work schedules. What all these cases have in common is an employee who could comply with the rule only by violating what the employee views as a religious commandment. In each instance, the question is whether the employee is to be exempt from the rule's demands. To do so will always result in a privilege being "allocated according to religious beliefs," unless the employer gratuitously decides to repeal the rule in toto. What the statute says, in plain words, is that such allocations are required unless "undue hardship" would result.

The point is perhaps best made by considering a not altogether hypothetical example. See CCH EEOC Decisions (1973) ¶ 6180. Assume that an employer requires all employees to wear a particular type of hat at work in order to make the employees readily identifiable to customers. Such a rule obviously does not, on its face, violate Title VII, and an employee who altered the uniform for reasons of taste could be discharged. But a very different question would be posed by the discharge of an employee who, for religious reasons, insisted on wearing over her hair a tightly fitted scarf which was visible through the hat. In such a case the employer could accommodate this religious practice without undue hardship or any hardship at all. Yet as I understand the Court's analysis—and nothing in the Court's response is to the contrary—the accommodation would not be required because it would afford the privilege of wearing scarfs to a select few based on their religious beliefs. The employee thus would have to give up either the religious practice or the job. This, I submit, makes a mockery of the statute.

In reaching this result, the Court seems almost oblivious of the legislative history of the 1972 amendments to Title VII which is briefly recounted in the Court's opinion. That history is far more instructive than the Court allows. After the EEOC promulgated its second set of guidelines requiring reasonable accommodations unless undue hardship would result, at least two courts issued decisions questioning, whether the guidelines were consistent with Title VII. Dewey v. Reynolds Metals Co., 429 F.2d 324 (6th Cir. 1970), aff'd by equally divided Court, 402 U.S. 689 (1971); Riley v. Bendix Corp., 330 F. Supp. 583 (M.D. Fla. 1971), rev'd, 464 F.2d 1113 (5th Cir. 1972). These courts reasoned, in language strikingly similar to today's decision, that to excuse religious observers from neutral work rules would "discriminate against ... other employees" and "constitute unequal administration of the collective bargaining agreement." Dewey v. Reynolds Metals Co., supra, at 330. They therefore refused to equate "religious discrimination with failure to accommodate." 429 F.2d at 335. When Congress was reviewing Title VII in 1972, Senator Jennings Randolph informed the Congress of these decisions which, he said, had "clouded" the meaning of religious discrimination. 118 Cong. Rec. 706 (1972). He introduced an amendment, tracking the language of the EEOC regulation, to make clear that Title VII requires religious accommodation, even though unequal treatment would result. The primary purpose of the amendment, he explained, was to protect Saturday Sabbatarians like himself from employers who refuse "to hire or to continue in employment employees whose religious practices rigidly require them to abstain from work in the nature of hire on particular days." Id. at 705. His amendment was unanimously approved by the Senate on a roll call vote, id. at 731, and was accepted by the Conference Committee, H.R. Rep. No. 92–899, p.15 (1972); S. Rep.

No. 92–681, p.15 (1972), whose report was approved by both Houses, 118 Cong. Rec. 7169, 7573 (1972). Yet the Court today, in rejecting any accommodation that involves preferential treatment, follows the *Dewey* decision in direct contravention of congressional intent.

The Court's interpretation of the statute, by effectively nullifying it, has the singular advantage of making consideration of petitioner's constitutional challenge unnecessary. The Court does not even rationalize its construction on this ground, however, nor could it, since "resort to an alternative construction to avoid deciding a constitutional question is appropriate only when such a course is 'fairly possible' or when the statute provides a 'fair alternative' construction." Swain v. Pressley, 430 U.S. 372, 378 n.11 (1977). Moreover, while important constitutional questions would be posed by interpreting the law to compel employers (or fellow employees) to incur substantial costs to aid the religious observer, not all accommodations are costly, and the constitutionality of the statute is not placed in serious doubt simply because it sometimes requires an exemption from a work rule. Indeed, this Court has repeatedly found no Establishment Clause problems in exempting religious observers from state imposed duties, . . . even when the exemption was in no way compelled by the Free Exercise Clause. . . . If the State does not establish religion over nonreligion by excusing religious practitioners from obligations owed the State, I do not see how the State can be said to establish religion by requiring employers to do the same with respect to obligations owed the employer. Thus, I think it beyond dispute that the Act does and, consistently with the First Amendment, can require employers to grant privileges to religious observers as part of the accommodation process. . . .

NOTES ON *TRANS WORLD AIRLINES V. HARDISON*

1. Religious Discrimination Under Title VII. The prohibition against religious discrimination under Title VII is subject to several exceptions, qualifications, and elaborations. These provisions reflect the need to depart from the straightforward command not to discriminate as it developed in the law of racial discrimination and to modify it to take account of the distinctive features of religion. The "colorblind" perspective applied to race has no counterpart in a "religion-blind" perspective on religious discrimination. Most of the complications in the law of religious discrimination reflect the special status of religion under the Establishment Clause and the Free Exercise Clause of the First Amendment, which greatly limit the permissible forms of government regulation of religion.

Thus, several provisions restrict the scope of the prohibition against religious discrimination. Like sex and national origin, religion is subject to the BFOQ for bona fide occupational qualifications based on religion that are "reasonably necessary to the normal operation of that particular business or enterprise." § 703(e)(1). This version of the BFOQ applies most directly to religious organizations and schools as in, for instance, the hiring of ministers and religious teachers. These employers, however, can also take advantage of a further exception for religious organizations and schools insofar as they employ "individuals of a particular religion to perform work connected with the carrying on" of their activities. § 702. Another, seemingly redundant, exception applies only to religious schools. § 703(e)(2). All of these exceptions apply only to discrimination on the basis of religion, but as the next case illustrates, a further exception allows religious organizations freedom to discriminate on other grounds in employing ministers.

The provision at issue in *Hardison*, the duty of employers to accommodate religious practices, goes in the opposite direction, expanding rather than contracting the prohibition against discrimination. In this respect, it raises issues similar to those in *Garcia v. Spun Steak*, expanding the prohibition against discrimination on one ground to include related social practices. As the opinions in *Hardison* make clear, the addition of § 701(j) to Title VII was meant to expand the negative prohibition against considering religion to include an affirmative duty to accommodate religious practices. This affirmative duty, however, was subject to two important qualifications: first, it was only "to reasonably accommodate" religious practices; and second, it applied only when it did not cause "undue hardship on the conduct of the employer's business." As *Hardison* illustrates, these qualifications greatly narrowed the scope of the duty itself.

2. Proposed Accommodations in *Hardison*. The plaintiff proposed three possible accommodations in *Hardison*: first, that the employer go shorthanded on his shift, substituting a supervisor or manager if necessary to take his place; second, that the employer pay premium wages to another regular employee to take his place; and third, that a higher-seniority employee be forced to switch shifts with him, contrary to the collective bargaining agreement. The Court dismisses the first two alternatives on the ground that they imposed "more than a de minimis cost" on the employer and therefore amounted to undue hardship. The Court rejects the third alternative on two distinct grounds, partly because it would contradict the protection afforded to seniority by § 703(h) and partly because it would result in unequal treatment of other employees, imposing burdens on them because of their religious practices. Their practices, presumably, were different from Hardison's and did not require them to observe the Sabbath as he did.

As the Supreme Court has subsequently made clear, an employer is under no obligation to accept an employee's proposed accommodations. Ansonia Bd. of Educ. v. Philbrook, 479 U.S. 60 (1986). Yet the employer must offer its own reasonable accommodation or its reasons for rejecting any accommodation at all. The most fundamental reason offered in *Hardison* was the last, invoking as it does the rights of other employees to be free from religious discrimination. This reason is all the more powerful on the facts of *Hardison* itself because the plaintiff seems to have brought all his problems on himself through his own actions. It was his decision to transfer from Building 1 where he had high seniority, and could obtain shifts consistent with his observance of the Sabbath, to Building 2, where he had low seniority.

Yet the general interpretation of "undue hardship" established by the Court does not allude to any of these factors and relies, instead, only on the cost to the employer. The duty of reasonable accommodation does not require the employer to undertake any "more than a de minimis cost." How are these different concerns related? Are the rights of other employees to equal treatment based on their religion more or less important than the employer's interest in efficient operation of its business? Could the two be connected because the burden imposed on other employees could always be transformed into a cost imposed on the employer simply by finding someone to do the job at premium wages? Is the Court's ultimate concern, then, that the employer might be forced to subsidize the plaintiff's religious observances through the duty of reasonable accommodation? Did the Court seek to avoid the constitutional questions raised by such a subsidy through a narrow construction of the duty of reasonable accommodation?

3. Constitutional Considerations and Employer Interests. Subsequent constitutional decisions have clarified and reinforced the doubts implicit in the opinion in *Hardison* about a broad construction of the duty of reasonable accommodation. In Estate of Thornton v. Caldor, Inc., 472 U.S. 703 (1985), the Court held unconstitutional a state statute that gave employees an absolute right to refuse to work on the Sabbath of their choice. The Court held that this statute violated the Establishment Clause because it conferred a benefit only on employees who observed the Sabbath and because it allowed for no exceptions, unlike the duty of reasonable accommodation under Title VII.

Another decision involved a federal statute, the Religious Freedom Restoration Act of 1993 (RFRA). 107 Stat. 1488, codified as 42 U.S.C. §§ 2000bb to 2000bb–4 (1994). This Act was intended to expand upon protection afforded to religious practices by decisions of the Supreme Court under the First Amendment. In those decisions, the Court required only strict neutrality toward religion, neither favoring nor disfavoring it. RFRA prohibited the states and the federal government from imposing any substantial burden upon the exercise of religion, even by neutral rules of general application, unless it was accomplished by the least restrictive means available to serve a compelling government interest. When the constitutionality of RFRA was subsequently considered by the Supreme Court, however, the statute was held unconstitutional insofar as it applied to state programs (as opposed to self-regulation by the Federal Government of its own programs). City of Boerne v. Flores, 521 U.S. 507, 529–36 (1997). According to the Court, RFRA exceeded the power of Congress to enforce constitutional rights under the Fourteenth Amendment and, instead, sought to redefine those rights contrary to the Court's own prior decisions. Legislative protection of religious freedom, according to the Court, could only operate within the narrow area defined by the Free Exercise and Establishment Clauses of the First Amendment. See Sidney A. Rosenzweig, Comment, Restoring Religious Freedom to the Workplace: Title VII, RFRA and Religious Accommodation, 144 U. Pa. L. Rev. 2513 (1996).

As applied to Title VII, these decisions confirm the result in *Hardison*, even though the element of government action and government coercion is more subtle under Title VII than under RFRA. The First Amendment applies only to attempts by government to curtail religious freedom. Actions by private employers do not, by themselves, violate the First Amendment. The requirements imposed by Title VII, however, do involve government action in coercing private employers and, for that reason, are subject to the First Amendment. To the extent that these requirements involve affirmative duties, like the duty of reasonable accommodation, they raise questions about government support for religion under the Establishment Clause. Thus the employer's interests in managing the workplace coincide with the constitutionally protected interests of the employer and employees alike in remaining free from government coercion on matters related to religion.

Does this line of reasoning fully explain the test in *Hardison* for undue hardship, based on "a more than de minimis cost"? Was the Court concerned with the costs actually imposed on employers by the duty of reasonable accommodation or with the costs that might be imposed in the future? Was the Court worried about the consequences of too close a judicial inquiry into the costs of different religious practices, with the danger of intrusive judicial regulation of religion in the workplace? Or was this caution excessive, giving too little protection to religious minorities, as Justice Marshall argued in his dissent?

4. **The Affirmative Nature of the Duty to Accommodate.** Prohibitions against discrimination usually are cast in entirely negative terms, as a duty not to take race, national origin, sex, or religion into account in making employment decisions. The duty to accommodate is different. It requires employers to pay attention to religion and to make exceptions to otherwise neutral policies and rules to protect some aspects of religious observance. Conceptually, the duty to accommodate requires employers to do more than simply not discriminate.

Whether the duty to accommodate is that different from a duty not to discriminate in its impact on employers may be doubted, as Christine Jolls has argued. Accommodation Mandates, 53 Stan. L. Rev. 223 (2000). She points out that ordinary prohibitions against discrimination require employers to deviate from what they take to be the most efficient way to run their business, incurring costs in the process. The costs of complying with an affirmative duty to accommodate are no different from the employer's perspective. Her article mainly concerns the duty to accommodate disabilities, imposed under the Rehabilitation Act and the Americans with Disabilities Act, discussed more fully in Chapter 11. Nevertheless, the duty to accommodate under those statutes was adopted, nearly verbatim, from the duty to accommodate religious practices under Title VII, and her argument could apply equally well to religion as to disabilities.

Despite this similarity in costs of compliance, do affirmative duties still give rise to a lingering suspicion, greater than for negative duties, of undue government interference in private activity? Most cases find that the employer either has no duty to accommodate or that it has satisfied whatever duty it had. See, e.g., Virts v. Consolidated Freightways Corp., 285 F.3d 508, 517–21 (6th Cir. 2002) (no duty to relieve employee of overnight trucking runs with female employees based on his religious beliefs); Anderson v. U.S.F. Logistics (IMC), Inc., 274 F.3d 470, 475–77 (7th Cir. 2001) (no duty to allow employee to make religious comments to customers); Bruff v. North

Mississippi Health Services, Inc., 244 F.3d 495, 499–503 (5th Cir. 2001) (no duty to allow counselor to refuse to advise clients on homosexual and extra-marital relationships). These outcomes are only to be expected given the broad definition of undue hardship established in *Hardison*. Yet, wholly apart from constitutional concerns, this skepticism about the duty of reasonable accommodation may reflect the open-ended burdens that affirmative obligations may impose upon employers. As we shall see, the duty of reasonable accommodation under the Americans with Disabilities Act has also been narrowly construed, although it obviously raises no questions under the religion clauses of the First Amendment.

5. ***EEOC v. Abercrombie & Fitch Stores, Inc.*** Does an employee or applicant for employment need to inform the employer of the need for an accommodation in order to establish a claim for religious discrimination? The Supreme Court answered "no" in EEOC v. Abercrombie & Fitch Stores, Inc., 135 S. Ct. 2028 (2015). In that case, the EEOC alleged that the employer refused to hire an applicant because she wore a headscarf as required by her Muslim faith. The employer allegedly found that the headscarf violated its "Look Policy" for its stores. These allegations in the Courts were sufficient because "[a]n employer may not make an applicant's religious practice, confirmed or otherwise, a factor in employment decisions."

Is this rule needed to prevent employers from circumventing the accommodation requirement by pre-emptively refusing to employ applicants who might request an accommodation? For discussions of this question, see Jeffrey M. Hirsch, *EEOC v. Abercrombie & Fitch Stores, Inc.*: Mistakes, Same-Sex Marriage, and Unintended Consequences, 94 Tex. L. Rev. 95 (2015)

6. **Bibliography.** Keith S. Blair, Better Disabled Than Devout? Why Title VII Has Failed to Provide Adequate Accommodations Against Workplace Religious Discrimination, 63 Ark. L. Rev. 515 (2010); Roberto L. Corrada, Toward an Integrated Disparate Treatment and Accommodation Framework for Title VII Religion Cases, 77 U. Cin. L. Rev. 1411 (2009); Dallan F. Flake, Religious Discrimination Based on Employer Misperception, 2016 Wis. L. Rev. 87; Robert J. Friedman, Religious Discrimination in the Workplace: The Persistent Polarized Struggle, 11 Transactions: Tenn. J. Bus. L. 143 (2010); Kent Greenawalt, Title VII and Religious Liberty, 33 Loy. U. Chi. L.J. 1 (2001); Debbie N. Kaminer, Religious Accommodation in the Workplace: Why Federal Courts Fail to Provide Meaningful Protection of Religious Employees, 20 Tex. Rev. L. & Pol. 107 (2015); Debbie N. Kaminer, Title VII's Failure to Provide Meaningful and Consistent Protection of Religious Employees: Proposals for an Amendment, 21 Berkeley J. Emp. & Lab. L. 575 (2000); Craig W. Mandell, Tough Pill to Swallow: Whether Catholic Institutions Are Obligated Under Title VII to Cover Their Employees' Prescription Contraceptives, 8 U. Md. L.J. Race, Religion, Gender & Class 199 (2008); Michael D. Moberly, Bad News for Those Proclaiming the Good News? The Employer's Ambiguous Duty to Accommodate Religious Proselytizing, 42 Santa Clara L. Rev. 1 (2001); Nantiya Ruan, Accommodating Respectful Religious Expression in the Workplace, 92 Marq. L. Rev. 1 (2008); William W. Van Alstyne, Religion in the Workplace: A

Report on the Layers of Relevant Law in the United States, 30 Comp. Lab. L. & Pol'y J. 627 (2009); Eugene Volokh, Freedom of Speech, Religious Harassment Law, and Religious Accommodation Law, 33 Loy. U. Chi. L.J. 57 (2001); Deborah M. Weiss, The Impossibility of Agnostic Discrimination Law, 2011 Utah L. Rev. 1677; Symposium, Religious Accommodation in the Age of Civil Rights, 38 Harv. J.L. & Gender 1 (2015); Symposium, Religious Accommodation in the Age of Civil Rights, 88 S. Cal. L. Rev. 453 (2015); Symposium, Religious Accommodation in the Age of Civil Rights, 9 Harv. L. & Pol'y Rev. 1 (2015); Symposium, The New Face of Discrimination: "Muslim" in America, 2 Duke F. L. & Soc. Change 1 (2010).

Hosanna-Tabor Evangelical Lutheran Church and School v. EEOC

565 U.S. 171 (2012).

■ CHIEF JUSTICE ROBERTS delivered the opinion of the Court.

Certain employment discrimination laws authorize employees who have been wrongfully terminated to sue their employers for reinstatement and damages. The question presented is whether the Establishment and Free Exercise Clauses of the First Amendment bar such an action when the employer is a religious group and the employee is one of the group's ministers.

I

A

Petitioner Hosanna-Tabor Evangelical Lutheran Church and School is a member congregation of the Lutheran Church-Missouri Synod, the second largest Lutheran denomination in America. Hosanna-Tabor operated a small school in Redford, Michigan, offering a "Christ-centered education" to students in kindergarten through eighth grade.

The Synod classifies teachers into two categories: "called" and "lay." "Called" teachers are regarded as having been called to their vocation by God through a congregation. To be eligible to receive a call from a congregation, a teacher must satisfy certain academic requirements. One way of doing so is by completing a "colloquy" program at a Lutheran college or university. The program requires candidates to take eight courses of theological study, obtain the endorsement of their local Synod district, and pass an oral examination by a faculty committee. A teacher who meets these requirements may be called by a congregation. Once called, a teacher receives the formal title "Minister of Religion, Commissioned." A commissioned minister serves for an open-ended term; at Hosanna-Tabor, a call could be rescinded only for cause and by a supermajority vote of the congregation.

"Lay" or "contract" teachers, by contrast, are not required to be trained by the Synod or even to be Lutheran. At Hosanna-Tabor, they were appointed by the school board, without a vote of the congregation, to one-year renewable terms. Although teachers at the school generally performed the same duties regardless of whether they were lay or called, lay teachers were hired only when called teachers were unavailable.

Respondent Cheryl Perich was first employed by Hosanna-Tabor as a lay teacher in 1999. After Perich completed her colloquy later that school year, Hosanna-Tabor asked her to become a called teacher. Perich accepted the call and received a "diploma of vocation" designating her a commissioned minister.

Perich taught kindergarten during her first four years at Hosanna-Tabor and fourth grade during the 2003–2004 school year. She taught math, language arts, social studies, science, gym, art, and music. She also taught a religion class four days a week, led the students in prayer and devotional exercises each day, and attended a weekly school-wide chapel service. Perich led the chapel service herself about twice a year.

Perich became ill in June 2004 with what was eventually diagnosed as narcolepsy. Symptoms included sudden and deep sleeps from which she could not be roused. Because of her illness, Perich began the 2004–2005 school year on disability leave. On January 27, 2005, however, Perich notified the school principal, Stacey Hoeft, that she would be able to report to work the following month. Hoeft responded that the school had already contracted with a lay teacher to fill Perich's position for the remainder of the school year. Hoeft also expressed concern that Perich was not yet ready to return to the classroom.

On January 30, Hosanna-Tabor held a meeting of its congregation at which school administrators stated that Perich was unlikely to be physically capable of returning to work that school year or the next. The congregation voted to offer Perich a "peaceful release" from her call, whereby the congregation would pay a portion of her health insurance premiums in exchange for her resignation as a called teacher. Id., at 178, 186. Perich refused to resign and produced a note from her doctor stating that she would be able to return to work on February 22. The school board urged Perich to reconsider, informing her that the school no longer had a position for her, but Perich stood by her decision not to resign.

On the morning of February 22—the first day she was medically cleared to return to work—Perich presented herself at the school. Hoeft asked her to leave but she would not do so until she obtained written documentation that she had reported to work. Later that afternoon, Hoeft called Perich at home and told her that she would likely be fired. Perich responded that she had spoken with an attorney and intended to assert her legal rights.

Following a school board meeting that evening, board chairman Scott Salo sent Perich a letter stating that Hosanna-Tabor was reviewing the process for rescinding her call in light of her "regrettable" actions. Salo subsequently followed up with a letter advising Perich that the congregation would consider whether to rescind her call at its next meeting. As grounds for termination, the letter cited Perich's "insubordination and disruptive behavior" on February 22, as well as the damage she had done to her "working relationship" with the school by "threatening to take legal action." The congregation voted to rescind Perich's call on April 10, and Hosanna-Tabor sent her a letter of termination the next day.

B

Perich filed a charge with the Equal Employment Opportunity Commission, alleging that her employment had been terminated in violation of the Americans with Disabilities Act. The ADA prohibits an employer from discriminating against a qualified individual on the basis of disability. § 12112(a). It also prohibits an employer from retaliating "against any individual because such individual has opposed any act or practice made unlawful by [the ADA] or because such individual made a charge, testified, assisted, or participated in any manner in an investigation, proceeding, or hearing under [the ADA]." § 12203(a). [None of the defenses specifically for religious organizations under the ADA apply to claims of retaliation.]

The EEOC brought suit against Hosanna-Tabor, alleging that Perich had been fired in retaliation for threatening to file an ADA lawsuit. Perich intervened in the litigation, claiming unlawful retaliation under both the ADA and the Michigan Persons with Disabilities Civil Rights Act, Mich. Comp. Laws § 37.1602(a) (1979). The EEOC and Perich sought Perich's reinstatement to her former position (or frontpay in lieu thereof), along with backpay, compensatory and punitive damages, attorney's fees, and other injunctive relief.

Hosanna-Tabor moved for summary judgment. Invoking what is known as the "ministerial exception," the Church argued that the suit was barred by the First Amendment because the claims at issue concerned the employment relationship between a religious institution and one of its ministers. According to the Church, Perich was a minister, and she had been fired for a religious reason—namely, that her threat to sue the Church violated the Synod's belief that Christians should resolve their disputes internally.

The District Court agreed that the suit was barred by the ministerial exception and granted summary judgment in Hosanna-Tabor's favor. . . .

The Court of Appeals for the Sixth Circuit vacated and remanded, directing the District Court to proceed to the merits of Perich's retaliation claims. The Court of Appeals recognized the existence of a ministerial exception barring certain employment discrimination claims against religious institutions—an exception "rooted in the First Amendment's guarantees of religious freedom." The court concluded, however, that Perich did not qualify as a "minister" under the exception, noting in particular that her duties as a called teacher were identical to her duties as a lay teacher. Judge White concurred. She viewed the question whether Perich qualified as a minister to be closer than did the majority, but agreed that the "fact that the duties of the contract teachers are the same as the duties of the called teachers is telling." . . .

II

The First Amendment provides, in part, that "Congress shall make no law respecting an establishment of religion, or prohibiting the free exercise thereof." We have said that these two Clauses "often exert conflicting pressures," Cutter v. Wilkinson, 544 U.S. 709 (2005), and that there can be "internal tension . . . between the Establishment Clause and the Free Exercise Clause," Tilton v. Richardson, 403 U.S. 672, 677 (1971) (plurality opinion). Not so here. Both Religion Clauses bar the government from interfering with the decision of a religious group to fire one of its ministers.

[The Court then recounted the history of adoption and interpretation of the Religion Clauses.]

C

Until today, we have not had occasion to consider whether this freedom of a religious organization to select its ministers is implicated by a suit alleging discrimination in employment. The Courts of Appeals, in contrast, have had extensive experience with this issue. Since the passage of Title VII of the Civil Rights Act of 1964, and other employment discrimination laws, the Courts of Appeals have uniformly recognized the existence of a "ministerial exception," grounded in the First Amendment, that precludes application of such legislation to claims concerning the employment relationship between a religious institution and its ministers.

We agree that there is such a ministerial exception. The members of a religious group put their faith in the hands of their ministers. Requiring a church to accept or retain an unwanted minister, or punishing a church for failing to do so, intrudes upon more than a mere employment decision. Such action interferes with the internal governance of the church, depriving the church of control over the selection of those who will personify its beliefs. By imposing an unwanted minister, the state infringes the Free Exercise Clause, which protects a religious group's right to shape its own faith and mission through its appointments. According the state the power to determine which individuals will minister to the faithful also violates the Establishment Clause, which prohibits government involvement in such ecclesiastical decisions.

The EEOC and Perich acknowledge that employment discrimination laws would be unconstitutional as applied to religious groups in certain circumstances. They grant, for example, that it would violate the First Amendment for courts to apply such laws to compel the ordination of women by the Catholic Church or by an Orthodox Jewish seminary. According to the EEOC and Perich, religious organizations could successfully defend against employment discrimination claims in those circumstances by invoking the constitutional right to freedom of association—a right "implicit" in the First Amendment. Roberts v. United States Jaycees, 468 U.S. 609, 622 (1984). The EEOC and Perich thus see no need—and no basis—for a special rule for ministers grounded in the Religion Clauses themselves.

We find this position untenable. The right to freedom of association is a right enjoyed by religious and secular groups alike. It follows under the EEOC's and Perich's view that the First Amendment analysis should be the same, whether the association in question is the Lutheran Church, a labor union, or a social club. That result is hard to square with the text of the First Amendment itself, which gives special solicitude to the rights of religious organizations. We cannot accept the remarkable view that the Religion Clauses have nothing to say about a religious organization's freedom to select its own ministers.

The EEOC and Perich also contend that our decision in Employment Div., Dept. of Human Resources of Ore. v. Smith, 494 U.S. 872 (1990), precludes recognition of a ministerial exception. In *Smith*, two members of the Native American Church were denied state unemployment benefits after it was determined that they had been fired from their jobs for ingesting peyote, a crime under Oregon law. We held that this did not violate the Free Exercise Clause, even though the peyote had been ingested for sacramental purposes, because the "right of free exercise does not relieve an individual of the obligation to comply with a valid and neutral law of general applicability on the ground that the law proscribes (or prescribes) conduct that his religion prescribes (or proscribes)." Id., at 879 (internal quotation marks omitted).

It is true that the ADA's prohibition on retaliation, like Oregon's prohibition on peyote use, is a valid and neutral law of general applicability. But a church's selection of its ministers is unlike an individual's ingestion of peyote. *Smith* involved government regulation of only outward physical acts. The present case, in contrast, concerns government interference with an internal church decision that affects the faith and mission of the church itself. See id., at 877 (distinguishing the government's regulation of "physical acts" from its "lend[ing] its power to one or the other side in controversies over religious authority or dogma"). The contention that *Smith* forecloses recognition of a ministerial exception rooted in the Religion Clauses has no merit.

III

Having concluded that there is a ministerial exception grounded in the Religion Clauses of the First Amendment, we consider whether the exception applies in this case. We hold that it does.

Every Court of Appeals to have considered the question has concluded that the ministerial exception is not limited to the head of a religious congregation, and we agree. We are reluctant, however, to adopt a rigid formula for deciding when an employee qualifies as a minister. It is enough for us to conclude, in this our first case involving the ministerial exception, that the exception covers Perich, given all the circumstances of her employment.

To begin with, Hosanna-Tabor held Perich out as a minister, with a role distinct from that of most of its members. When Hosanna-Tabor extended her a call, it issued her a "diploma of vocation" according her the title "Minister of Religion, Commissioned." She was tasked with performing that office "according to the Word of God and the confessional standards of the Evangelical Lutheran Church as drawn from the Sacred Scriptures." The congregation prayed that God "bless [her] ministrations to the glory of His holy name, [and] the building of His church." In a supplement to the diploma, the congregation undertook to periodically review Perich's "skills of ministry" and "ministerial responsibilities," and to provide for her "continuing education as a professional person in the ministry of the Gospel."

Perich's title as a minister reflected a significant degree of religious training followed by a formal process of commissioning. To be eligible to become a commissioned minister, Perich had to complete eight college-level courses in subjects including biblical interpretation, church doctrine, and the ministry of the Lutheran teacher. She also had to obtain the endorsement of her local Synod district by submitting a petition that contained her academic transcripts, letters of recommendation, personal statement, and written answers to various ministry-related questions. Finally, she had to pass an oral examination by a faculty committee at a Lutheran college. It took Perich six years to fulfill these requirements. And when she eventually did, she was commissioned as a minister only upon election by the congregation, which recognized God's call to her to teach. At that point, her call could be rescinded only upon a supermajority vote of the congregation—a protection designed to allow her to "preach the Word of God boldly." Brief for Lutheran Church-Missouri Synod as Amicus Curiae 15.

Perich held herself out as a minister of the Church by accepting the formal call to religious service, according to its terms. She did so in other ways as well. For example, she claimed a special housing allowance on her taxes that was available only to employees earning their compensation " 'in the exercise of the ministry.' " ("If you are not conducting activities 'in the exercise of the ministry,' you cannot take advantage of the parsonage or housing allowance exclusion" (quoting Lutheran Church-Missouri Synod Brochure on Whether the IRS Considers Employees as a Minister) (2007)). In a form she submitted to the Synod following her termination, Perich again indicated that she regarded herself as a minister at Hosanna-Tabor, stating: "I feel that God is leading me to serve in the teaching ministry. . . . I am anxious to be in the teaching ministry again soon."

Perich's job duties reflected a role in conveying the Church's message and carrying out its mission. Hosanna-Tabor expressly charged her with "lead[ing] others toward Christian maturity" and "teach[ing] faithfully the Word of God, the Sacred Scriptures, in its truth and purity and as set forth in all the symbolical books of the Evangelical Lutheran Church." In fulfilling these responsibilities, Perich taught her students religion four days a week, and led them in prayer three times a day. Once a week, she took her students to a school-wide chapel service, and—about twice a year—she took her turn leading it, choosing the liturgy, selecting the hymns, and delivering a short message based on verses from the Bible. During her last year of teaching, Perich also led her fourth graders in a brief devotional exercise each morning. As a source of religious instruction, Perich performed an important role in transmitting the Lutheran faith to the next generation.

In light of these considerations—the formal title given Perich by the Church, the substance reflected in that title, her own use of that title, and the important religious functions she performed for the Church—we conclude that Perich was a minister covered by the ministerial exception. . . .

Perich no longer seeks reinstatement, having abandoned that relief before this Court. But that is immaterial. Perich continues to seek frontpay in lieu of reinstatement, backpay, compensatory and punitive damages, and attorney's fees. An award of such relief would operate as a penalty on the Church for terminating an unwanted minister, and would be no less prohibited by the First Amendment than an order overturning the termination. Such relief would depend on a determination that Hosanna-Tabor was wrong to have relieved Perich of her position, and it is precisely such a ruling that is barred by the ministerial exception.

The EEOC and Perich suggest that Hosanna-Tabor's asserted religious reason for firing Perich—that she violated the Synod's commitment to internal dispute resolution—was pretextual. That suggestion misses the point of the ministerial exception. The purpose of the exception is not to safeguard a church's decision to fire a minister only when it is made for a religious reason. The exception instead ensures that the authority to select and control who will minister to the faithful—a matter "strictly ecclesiastical," Kedroff v. Saint Nicholas Cathedral of Russian Orthodox Church in North America, 344 U.S. 94, 119 (1952) — is the church's alone.[4]

IV

The EEOC and Perich foresee a parade of horribles that will follow our recognition of a ministerial exception to employment discrimination

---

[4] A conflict has arisen in the Courts of Appeals over whether the ministerial exception is a jurisdictional bar or a defense on the merits. We conclude that the exception operates as an affirmative defense to an otherwise cognizable claim, not a jurisdictional bar. That is because the issue presented by the exception is "whether the allegations the plaintiff makes entitle him to relief," not whether the court has "power to hear [the] case." Morrison v. National Australia Bank Ltd., 130 S. Ct. 2869, 2877 (2010) (internal quotation marks omitted). District courts have power to consider ADA claims in cases of this sort, and to decide whether the claim can proceed or is instead barred by the ministerial exception.

suits. According to the EEOC and Perich, such an exception could protect religious organizations from liability for retaliating against employees for reporting criminal misconduct or for testifying before a grand jury or in a criminal trial. What is more, the EEOC contends, the logic of the exception would confer on religious employers "unfettered discretion" to violate employment laws by, for example, hiring children or aliens not authorized to work in the United States.

Hosanna-Tabor responds that the ministerial exception would not in any way bar criminal prosecutions for interfering with law enforcement investigations or other proceedings. Nor, according to the Church, would the exception bar government enforcement of general laws restricting eligibility for employment, because the exception applies only to suits by or on behalf of ministers themselves. Hosanna-Tabor also notes that the ministerial exception has been around in the lower courts for 40 years, see McClure v. Salvation Army, 460 F.2d 553, 558 (C.A.5 1972), and has not given rise to the dire consequences predicted by the EEOC and Perich.

The case before us is an employment discrimination suit brought on behalf of a minister, challenging her church's decision to fire her. Today we hold only that the ministerial exception bars such a suit. We express no view on whether the exception bars other types of suits, including actions by employees alleging breach of contract or tortious conduct by their religious employers. There will be time enough to address the applicability of the exception to other circumstances if and when they arise.

The interest of society in the enforcement of employment discrimination statutes is undoubtedly important. But so too is the interest of religious groups in choosing who will preach their beliefs, teach their faith, and carry out their mission. When a minister who has been fired sues her church alleging that her termination was discriminatory, the First Amendment has struck the balance for us. The church must be free to choose those who will guide it on its way.

The judgment of the Court of Appeals for the Sixth Circuit is reversed. It is so ordered.

■ JUSTICE THOMAS, concurring.

I join the Court's opinion. I write separately to note that, in my view, the Religion Clauses require civil courts to apply the ministerial exception and to defer to a religious organization's good-faith understanding of who qualifies as its minister.

. . .

■ JUSTICE ALITO, with whom JUSTICE KAGAN joins, concurring.

I join the Court's opinion, but I write separately to clarify my understanding of the significance of formal ordination and designation as a "minister" in determining whether an "employee" of a religious group falls within the so-called "ministerial" exception. The term "minister" is commonly used by many Protestant denominations to refer to members of their clergy, but the term is rarely if ever used in this way by Catholics, Jews, Muslims, Hindus, or Buddhists. In addition, the concept of ordination as understood by most Christian churches and by Judaism has no clear counterpart in some Christian denominations and some other religions. Because virtually every religion in the world is represented in the population of the United States, it would be a mistake if the term "minister" or the concept of ordination were viewed as central to the important issue of religious autonomy that is presented in cases like this one. Instead, courts should focus on the function performed by persons who work for religious bodies.

The First Amendment protects the freedom of religious groups to engage in certain key religious activities, including the conducting of worship services and other religious ceremonies and rituals, as well as the critical process of communicating the faith. Accordingly, religious groups must be free to choose the personnel who are essential to the performance of these functions.

The "ministerial" exception should be tailored to this purpose. It should apply to any "employee" who leads a religious organization, conducts worship services or important religious ceremonies or rituals, or serves as a messenger or teacher of its faith. If a religious group believes that the ability of such an employee to perform these key functions has been compromised, then the constitutional guarantee of religious freedom protects the group's right to remove the employee from his or her position. . . .

NOTES ON *HOSANNA-TABOR EVANGELICAL LUTHERAN CHURCH AND SCHOOL V. EEOC*

1. **Statutory Exceptions for Religious Employers.** *Hosanna-Tabor* arose under the Americans with Disabilities Act, which has exceptions for religious discrimination by religious organizations. § 103(d), 42 U.S.C. § 12113(d). These apply, however, only to disability discrimination claims under Title I of the ADA, not to retaliation claims under Title V. In *Hosanna-Tabor*, the Supreme Court therefore had to reach the constitutional question whether Perich was a minister exempt from the ADA regardless of the limited scope of the statutory exceptions.

Almost exactly the same question would have arisen under Title VII, whose statutory exceptions for religious organizations also fail to reach claims of retaliation. §§ 702, 703(e), 42 U.S.C. §§ 2000e–1, –2(e). Section 702 creates an exception for religious organizations, including schools, "with respect to the employment of individuals of a particular religion to perform work connected" to the organization's activities. Somewhat redundantly, section 703(e)(2) creates a similar exception just for religious schools. Section 703(e)(1) provides that the BFOQ also applies "in those certain instances where religion, sex, or national origin is a bona fide occupational qualification reasonably necessary to the normal operation of that particular business or enterprise."

Together with the duty to accommodate religious practices, these exceptions reveal how influential religious groups have been in protecting their interests, either in limiting the prohibition against religious discrimination or in expanding it beyond religious beliefs and affiliation. Recognition of a ministerial exception goes still further, as *Hosanna-Tabor* illustrates, to create an exception for discrimination on grounds other than religion. (The BFOQ also has this effect, but as discussed in Chapter 5, it has received a narrow interpretation under Title VII.)

The Supreme Court emphasizes at the end of its opinion that the ministerial exception applies to any "employment discrimination suit brought on behalf of a minister." Nevertheless the constitutional exception resembles the statutory exceptions in important respects. It protects religious organizations as potential defendants to employment discrimination claims. It depends upon the same solicitude for the independence of religious organizations and for the separation of church and state. And although the constitutional exception goes further—because it is framed in categorical terms dependent only upon the plaintiff's status as a minister—it does so only to avoid intrusive inquiries into the decisions and operations of religious organizations. All of these factors figure in the constitutional justification for the ministerial exception.

2. Recognition of a Ministerial Exception. *Hosanna-Tabor* starts by establishing the major premise that there is a ministerial exception and then proceeds to the minor premise that the teacher in this case was a minister. The major premise had been unanimously accepted, as the Supreme Court notes, by every court of appeals to address the issue. In recognizing the ministerial exception, the decision broke no new ground, although the Court rejected the EEOC's attempt to recast the exception entirely in terms of freedom of association rather than freedom of religion. Instead of following the EEOC's approach, which would have narrowed the exception considerably, the Court based the exception on the Religion Clauses of the First Amendment, both the Free Exercise Clause and the Establishment Clause. The exception, on the Court's view, was necessary to protect free exercise by guaranteeing the autonomy of religious organizations in selecting their leaders and to prevent establishment by avoiding government entanglement in religious aspects of the selection process. Together, both clauses supported a wide immunity for religious organizations in hiring, firing, and employing ministers.

The scope of the ministerial exception presented more problems for the Court, and to lower courts, which had repeatedly addressed the application of the exception to teachers in religious schools. At one extreme, the exception plainly covers priests, rabbis, mullahs, and others who lead a religion or congregation, while at the opposite extreme, it plainly fails to cover employees who provide ordinary services, such as maintenance or accounting. Teachers, like Perich, hold positions in the disputed middle ground between these extremes. On the one hand, Perich had been "called" to the ministry by the Lutheran church and she gave religious instruction in her classes. On the other hand, she engaged in no more religious instruction than would a teacher in the Hosanna-Tabor school who had not been "called." And many teachers in other religious schools teach only secular subjects and engage in no religious instruction at all. Partly because of the diversity of these employment situations, the Court declined "to adopt a rigid formula for deciding when an employee qualifies as a minister." Instead, the Court found four factors decisive in identifying Perich as a minister: "the formal title given Perich by the Church, the substance reflected in that title, her own use of that title, and the important religious functions she performed for the Church."

The concurring opinions in *Hosanna-Tabor* would have given greater scope to the exception. Justice Thomas would have deferred "to a religious organization's good-faith understanding of who qualifies as a minister," presumably making the good-faith conferral of the title "minister" a sufficient condition for the exception. He does not, however, say it is a necessary condition, a point emphasized by the concurrence of Justice Alito, joined by Justice Kagan. They would have applied the exception whenever an individual, regardless of title, "leads a religious organization, conducts worship service or important religious ceremonies or rituals, or serves as a messenger or teacher of its faith." Justice Alito emphasized the absence of officially appointed ministers in a range of religions. All the concurring justices, however, joined in the opinion of the Court, making it a unanimous decision.

The Court's reliance upon multiple factors in applying the exception raises the question of what to do in doubtful cases. Would the exception have applied if Perich had not been "called" to the ministry? If she had taught fewer religious subjects in her courses? If the religious school was not affiliated with a particular religion? More generally, how should courts resolve close cases after *Hosanna-Tabor*? As a matter of formal doctrine, the Court places the burden of proof on the defendant to prove the exception as an affirmative defense. Yet in its discussion of the issue of pretext, the Court indicates that religious organizations might receive the benefit of the doubt. The Court reasons that the ministerial exception is necessary precisely in order to foreclose inquiry into whether the justification for terminating the plaintiff (usually based on religion in some way, as in *Hosanna-Tabor*) was the real justification or just a pretext for discrimination. If the Constitution requires courts to avoid an analysis of pretext (and the related issue of mixed motives), does it also require them to avoid a close inquiry into whether an employee is a minister?

3. Other Remedies Against Religious Organizations. The EEOC raised the specter of systematic deterrence of whistleblowers if claims for retaliation, like Perich's, were barred by the ministerial exception. Church scandals, particularly those involving abuse of children, formed the background for this argument. The Court responded to it in several ways: by reserving the application of general laws to religious organizations (apart from those creating liability for employment discrimination); by also reserving the availability of individual tort and contract claims; and by noting the widespread recognition of the ministerial exception in the lower courts. The first two qualifications apparently rely upon the need for uniform enforcement of general criminal and regulatory laws, and the third point notes the apparent absence of efforts by religious organizations to exploit the exception to hide otherwise illegal activity. How persuasive are these attempts to limit the consequences of the decision?

By confirming the existence of the ministerial exception and then by giving it a seemingly broad interpretation, the Court has necessarily increased the visibility and legitimacy of the exception. Religious organizations are now more likely to invoke it and more likely to succeed in doing so. Can the Court disclaim the predictable consequences of its decision? When the government and private plaintiffs bring other claims against religious organizations, the same principles of religious freedom can be invoked as in *Hosanna-Tabor* to support defenses and other limitations on liability. Reserving those issues for another day does not counteract the implications of the decision, especially as they extend outside the precise holding in this case.

The decision also necessarily leaves employees like Perich without any civil remedy for the discrimination against them. Does that allow religious organizations to act with impunity in disregard of the law, knowing that they can retaliate against any whistleblower who is classified as a minister? Or are religious organizations subject to other pressures that lead them to conform to the law, including enforcement of laws of general application? Suppose, for instance, that the disability discrimination against Perich had been clearly established (an issue never resolved in this case). Would the Hosanna-Tabor Lutheran Church have willingly subjected itself to public criticism for blatant discrimination against individuals with disabilities? Across a wide range of discrimination claims, religious organizations want to avoid the charge of hypocrisy in failing to practice what they preach. Do such forms of public criticism, and the resulting harm to reputation, deter religious organizations from making too much of the ministerial exception? Do alternatives other than individual claims for employment discrimination constitute generally adequate remedies, even if they leave individual employees without relief?

As discussed in Chapter 7, on procedures for enforcing Title VII, many employees in purely secular positions must arbitrate their claims pursuant to contractual arbitration clauses. Some denominations, such as the branch of the Lutheran church involved in *Hosanna-Tabor,* have well-developed grievance procedures for ministers. Other churches, of course, might not, but among those that do, employees subject to the ministerial exception fare no worse than employees subject to an arbitration clause. Both kinds of employees can raise any claim before the arbitrator that they could in court under Title VII. Does this fact make the ministerial exception a less significant departure from the ordinary rules of employment discrimination law than it first appears to be? Or does it just accentuate the plight of ministers who have no access to adequate grievance procedures?

4. **Bibliography.** For comments on *Hosanna Tabor*, see Ashutosh Bhagwat, Religious Associations: *Hosanna-Tabor* and the Instrumental Value of Religious Groups, 92 Wash. U. L. Rev. 71 (2014); Caroline M.

Corbin, The Irony of *Hosanna-Tabor Evangelical Lutheran Church and School v. EEOC*, 106 Nw. U. L. Rev. 951 (2012); Douglas Laycock, *Hosanna-Tabor* and the Ministerial Exception, 35 Harv. J.L. & Pub. Pol'y 839 (2012); Christopher C. Lund, Free Exercise Reconceived: The Logic and Limits of *Hosanna-Tabor*, 108 Nw. U. L. Rev. 1183 (2014); Michael W. McConnell, Reflections on *Hosanna-Tabor*, 35 Harv. J.L. & Pub. Pol'y 821 (2012); Peter J. Smith & Robert W. Tuttle, Civil Procedure and the Ministerial Exception, 86 Fordham L. Rev. 1847 (2017); Mark Strasser, *Hosanna-Tabor*, the Ministerial Exception, and Judicial Compliance, 6 Elon L. Rev. 151 (2014); Ioanna Tourkochoriti, Revisiting *Hosanna-Tabor v. EEOC*: The Road Not Taken, 49 Tulsa L. Rev. 47 (2013); Ioanna Tourkochoriti, Revisiting *Hosanna Tabor v. E.E.O.C.*: The Road Not Taken, 49 Tulsa L. Rev. 49 (2013).

Religious discrimination in the workplace has raised a range of other issues discussed in the law review literature, from religious harassment to the employment practices of religious organizations. Carl H. Esbeck, When Accommodations for Religion Violate the Establishment Clause: Regularizing the Supreme Court's Analysis, 110 W. Va. L. Rev. 357 (2007); Leslie C. Griffin, The Sins of *Hosanna-Tabor*, 88 Ind. L.J. 981 (2013); Douglas Laycock, Church Autonomy Revisited, 7 Geo. J.L. & Pub. Pol'y 253 (2009); Ira C. Lupu & Robert W. Tuttle, Courts, Clergy, and Congregations: Disputes Between Religious Institutions and Their Leaders, 7 Geo. J.L. & Pub. Pol'y 119 (2009); Christopher C. Lund, In Defense of the Ministerial Exception, 90 N.C. L. Rev. 1 (2011); Stephanie N. Phillips, A Text-Based Interpretation of Title VII's Religious-Employer Exemption, 20 Tex. Rev. L. & Pol. 295 (2016); Nantiya Ruan, The Justices Find Religion: Why the Supreme Court Ought to Expand Religious Accommodation Rights, 92 Marq. L. Rev. 1 (2008).

D. SEXUAL ORIENTATION AND GENDER IDENTITY

Following the trend in a majority of states and many municipalities, Congress considered legislation to extend many of the prohibitions in Title VII to discrimination on the basis of sexual orientation and gender identity. This legislation was introduced previously in Congress on numerous occasions. In the 112th Congress, the version of the bill with the widest support, H.R. 1397 and S. 811, 112th Cong., was entitled "The Employment Non-Discrimination Act" or ENDA for short. (A subsequent bill with similar provisions was introduced in the 115th under the title of "The Equality Act" as S. 1006 and H.R. 2282.) The key provisions of ENDA are as follows:

SEC. 3. DEFINITIONS.

(a)(6) GENDER IDENTITY—The term "gender identity" means the gender-related identity, appearance, or mannerisms or other gender-related characteristics of an individual, with or without regard to the individual's designated sex at birth.

. . .

(7) SEXUAL ORIENTATION—The term "sexual orientation" means homosexuality, heterosexuality, or bisexuality.

SEC. 4. EMPLOYMENT DISCRIMINATION PROHIBITED.

(a) Employer Practices—It shall be an unlawful employment practice for an employer—

(1) to fail or refuse to hire or to discharge any individual, or otherwise discriminate against any individual with respect to the compensation, terms, conditions, or privileges of employment of the individual, because of such individual's actual or perceived sexual orientation or gender identity; or

(2) to limit, segregate, or classify the employees or applicants for employment of the employer in any way that would deprive or tend to deprive any individual of employment or otherwise adversely affect the status of the individual as an employee, because of such individual's actual or perceived sexual orientation or gender identity.

(b) Employment Agency Practices—It shall be an unlawful employment practice for an employment agency to fail or refuse to refer for employment, or otherwise to discriminate against, any individual because of the actual or perceived sexual orientation or gender identity of the individual or to classify or refer for employment any individual on the basis of the actual or perceived sexual orientation or gender identity of the individual.

(c) Labor Organization Practices—It shall be an unlawful employment practice for a labor organization—

(1) to exclude or to expel from its membership, or otherwise to discriminate against, any individual because of the actual or perceived sexual orientation or gender identity of the individual;

(2) to limit, segregate, or classify its membership or applicants for membership, or to classify or fail or refuse to refer for employment any individual, in any way that would deprive or tend to deprive any individual of employment, or would limit such employment or otherwise adversely affect the status of the individual as an employee or as an applicant for employment because of such individual's actual or perceived sexual orientation or gender identity; or

(3) to cause or attempt to cause an employer to discriminate against an individual in violation of this section.

(d) Training Programs—It shall be an unlawful employment practice for any employer, labor organization, or joint labor-management committee controlling apprenticeship or other training or retraining, including on-the-job training programs, to discriminate against any individual because of the actual or perceived sexual orientation or gender identity of the individual in admission to, or employment in, any program established to provide apprenticeship or other training.

(e) Association—An unlawful employment practice described in any of subsections (a) through (d) shall be considered to include an action described in that subsection, taken against an individual based on the actual or perceived sexual orientation or gender identity of a person with whom the individual associates or has associated.

(f) No Preferential Treatment or Quotas—Nothing in this Act shall be construed or interpreted to require or permit—

(1) any covered entity to grant preferential treatment to any individual or to any group because of the actual or perceived sexual orientation or gender identity of such individual or group on account of an imbalance which may exist with respect to the total number or percentage of persons of any actual or perceived sexual orientation or gender identity employed by any employer, referred or classified for employment by any employment agency or labor organization, admitted to membership or classified by any labor organization, or admitted to, or employed in, any apprenticeship or other training program, in comparison with the total number or percentage of persons of such actual or perceived sexual orientation or gender identity in any community, State, section, or other area, or in the available work force in any community, State, section, or other area; or

(2) the adoption or implementation by a covered entity of a quota on the basis of actual or perceived sexual orientation or gender identity.

(g) Disparate Impact—Only disparate treatment claims may be brought under this Act.

SEC. 6. EXEMPTION FOR RELIGIOUS ORGANIZATIONS.

This Act shall not apply to a corporation, association, educational institution, or society that is exempt from the religious discrimination provisions of title VII of the Civil Rights Acts of 1964 pursuant to section 702(a) or 703(e)(2) of such Act (42 U.S.C. 2000e–1(a); 2000e–2(e)(2)).

SEC. 7. NONAPPLICATION TO MEMBERS OF THE ARMED FORCES; VETERANS' PREFERENCES.

(a) Armed Forces—

(1) EMPLOYMENT—In this Act, the term "employment" does not apply to the relationship between the United States and members of the Armed Forces.

(2) ARMED FORCES—In paragraph (1) the term "Armed Forces" means the Army, Navy, Air Force, Marine Corps, and Coast Guard.

(b) Veterans' Preferences—This title does not repeal or modify any Federal, State, territorial, or local law creating a special right or preference concerning employment for a veteran.

NOTES ON ENDA

1. **Coverage and Terms.** Note that ENDA prohibits both discrimination on the basis of "sexual orientation"—a matter of preference for sexual partners—and "gender identity"—a matter of social role with or without regard to biologically identifiable sex. The first basis for prohibited discrimination is aimed mainly at discrimination against gays, lesbians, and bisexuals, but it covers discrimination also against people who are heterosexual. A similar point applies to the second basis for prohibited discrimination. It is aimed mainly at individuals who are transgender or transvestite, but it applies to anyone who takes on a gender role "with or without regard to the individual's designated sex at birth." Like the existing prohibitions in Title VII, ENDA has universal coverage. There is no "protected class" of individuals who alone obtain the benefit of the statute.

ENDA also follows Title VII in the structure of its prohibitions and exceptions, adopting them nearly verbatim from the earlier statute. The exceptions nevertheless are narrower than those under Title VII, being available only for religious employers and for the armed forces. There is, for instance, no BFOQ allowed for gender identity or sexual orientation. Perhaps as the legislation makes its way through Congress, additional exceptions might be added to the statute, but in its present form, its prohibitions are more absolute than those under Title VII. Along these lines, no form of affirmative action is either required or permitted under the statute.

2. **Constitutional Law.** The immediate predecessor of ENDA was state and local legislation against discrimination, which often has broader prohibitions extending to additional grounds than those covered by federal law. It also followed constitutional decisions of the Supreme Court, principally Lawrence v. Texas, 539 U.S. 558 (2003), recognizing a right to engage in gay sex but not a right to avoid discrimination. The Court held that the states had no legitimate interest in criminalizing homosexual conduct between consenting adults, overruling a prior decision to the contrary. Bowers v. Hardwick, 478 U.S. 186 (1986). The Court relied on the Due Process Clause, stopping well short of a holding under the Equal Protection Clause that all classifications on the basis of sexual orientation were suspect and subject to strict scrutiny. As applied to employment, this holding does not reach private employers at all, because they do not engage in state action within the scope of the Fourteenth Amendment. It does extend to government employers, but it may leave them free to discriminate on the basis of sexual orientation, so long as the government stops short of making homosexual conduct criminal. *Lawrence* does support the broader trend evident in the decisions requiring recognition of gay marriage. Obergefell v. Hodges, 135 S. Ct. 2584 (2015); United States v. Windsor, 133 S. Ct. 2675 (2013). These constitutional developments, and the related statutory issues, deserve extended treatment in their own right and whole books have been devoted to them. For a comprehensive survey of the literature, see William N. Eskridge, Nan D. Hunter & Courtney G. Joslin, Sexuality, Gender, and the Law (4th ed. 2018). These brief notes simply indicate how such

developments are likely to affect federal prohibitions against employment discrimination.

3. **Bibliography.** For articles on ENDA and its relationship to other federal laws, see Jennifer S. Hendricks, Instead of ENDA, A Course Correction for Title VII, Nw. U. L. Rev. Colloquy (2008); Edward J. Reeves & Lainie D. Decker, Before ENDA: Sexual Orientation and Gender Identity Protections in the Workplace Under Federal Law, 20 Law & Sexuality 61 (2011); Alex Reed, Abandoning ENDA, 51 Harv. J. on Legis. 277 (2014); Jill D. Weinberg, Gender Nonconformity: An Analysis of Perceived Sexual Orientation and Gender Identity Protection Under the Employment Non-Discrimination Act, 44 USF L. Rev. 1 (2009).

For articles on the general issues raised by ENDA, see Jessica A. Clarke, Inferring Desire, 63 Duke L.J. 525 (2013); Zachary A. Kramer, Heterosexuality and Title VII, 103 Nw. U. L. Rev. 205 (2009); Ann C. McGinley, Reconsidering Legal Regulation of Race, Sex and Sexual Orientation, 50 Tulsa L. Rev. 341 (2015); Ann C. McGinley, Erasing Boundaries: Masculinities, Sexual Minorities, and Employment Discrimination, 43 U. Mich. J. L. Reform 713 (2010); Ann E. Tweedy & Karen Yescavage, Employment Discrimination Against Bisexuals: An Empirical Study, 21 Wm. & Mary J. Women & L. 699 (2015); Michael T. Zugelder. Toward Equal Rights for LGBT Employees: Legal and Managerial Implications for Employers, 43 Ohio N.U. L. Rev. 193(2017); Symposium, Sexuality & Gender Law: Assessing the Field, Envisioning the Future, 57 UCLA L. Rev. 1129 (2010).

For articles on discrimination on the basis of transgender and gender identity, see David B. Cruz, Transgender Rights after *Obergefell*, 84 UMKC L. Rev. 693–705 (2016); Chai Feldblum, Law, Policies in Practice and Social Norms: Coverage of Transgender Discrimination under Sex Discrimination Law, 14 J. L. Soc'y 1–27 (2013); Ilana Gelfman, Because of Intersex: Intersexuality, Title VII, and the Reality of Discrimination "Because of . . . [Perceived] Sex," 34 N.Y.U. Rev. L. & Soc. Change 55 (2010); L. Camille Hebert, Transforming Transsexual and Transgender Rights, 15 Wm. & Mary J. Women & L. 535 (2009); Katie Koch & Richard Bales, Transgender Employment Discrimination, 17 UCLA Women's L.J. 243 (2008); S. Elizabeth Malloy, What Best to Protect Transsexuals from Discrimination: Using Current Legislation or Adopting a New Judicial Framework, 32 Women's Rts. L. Rep. 283 (2011); Shannon Price Minter, "Deja Vu All Over Again": The Recourse to Biology by Opponents of Transgender Equality, 95 N.C. L. Rev. 1161 (2017); Shawn D. Twing & Timothy C. Williams, Title VII's Transgender Trajectory: An Analysis of Whether Transgender People Are A Protected Class Under the Term "Sex" and Practical Implications of Inclusion, 15 Tex. J. on C.L. & C.R. 173 (2010); Symposium, Transgender Issues and the Law, 8 Seattle J. for Soc. Just. 445 (2010); Symposium, Beyond the Binary: What Can Feminists Learn from Intersex and Transgender Jurisprudence, 17 Mich. J. Gender & L. 13 (2010); Symposium. Transcending Barriers: Strategies for Change in Transgender Rights, 35 Harv. J.L. & Gender 357 (2012).

Hively v. Ivy Tech Community College of Indiana

853 F.3d 339 (7th Cir. 2017) (en banc).

■ WOOD, CHIEF JUDGE.

Title VII of the Civil Rights Act of 1964 makes it unlawful for employers subject to the Act to discriminate on the basis of a person's "race, color, religion, sex, or national origin . . . ." 42 U.S.C. § 2000e–2(a). For many years, the courts of appeals of this country understood the prohibition against sex discrimination to exclude discrimination on the basis of a person's sexual orientation. The Supreme Court, however, has never spoken to that question. In this case, we have been asked to take a fresh look at our position in light of developments at the Supreme Court extending over two decades. We have done so, and we conclude today that discrimination on the basis of sexual orientation is a form of sex discrimination. We therefore reverse the district court's judgment dismissing Kimberly Hively's suit against Ivy Tech Community College and remand for further proceedings.

I

Hively is openly lesbian. She began teaching as a part-time, adjunct professor at Ivy Tech Community College's South Bend campus in 2000. Hoping to improve her lot, she applied for at least six full-time positions between 2009 and 2014. These efforts were unsuccessful; worse yet, in July 2014 her part-time contract was not renewed. Believing that Ivy Tech was spurning her because of her sexual orientation, she filed a pro se charge with the Equal Employment Opportunity Commission on December 13, 2013. [She then sued in federal court and when her complaint was dismissed for failure to state a claim, she appealed. A panel of the Seventh Circuit affirmed based on pre-existing precedent in that circuit. Consideration en banc followed.]

II

A

. . . Ivy Tech sets great store on the fact that Congress has frequently considered amending Title VII to add the words "sexual orientation" to the list of prohibited characteristics, yet it has never done so. Many of our sister circuits have also noted this fact. In our view, however, it is simply too difficult to draw a reliable inference from these truncated legislative initiatives to rest our opinion on them. The goalposts have been moving over the years, as the Supreme Court has shed more light on the scope of the language that already is in the statute: no sex discrimination.

The dissent makes much of the fact that Congresses acting more than thirty years after the passage of Title VII made use of the term "sexual orientation" to prohibit discrimination or violence on that basis in statutes such as the Violence Against Women Act and the federal Hate Crimes Act. But this gets us no closer to answering the question at hand, for Congress may certainly choose to use both a belt and suspenders to achieve its objectives, and the fact that "sex" and "sexual orientation" discrimination may overlap in later statutes is of no help in determining whether sexual orientation discrimination is discrimination on the basis of sex for the purposes of Title VII. See, e.g., McEvoy v. IEI Barge Servs., Inc., 622 F.3d 671, 677 (7th Cir. 2010) ("Congress may choose a belt-and-suspenders approach to promote its policy objectives . . . .").

Moreover, the agency most closely associated with this law, the Equal Employment Opportunity Commission, in 2015 announced that it now takes the position that Title VII's prohibition against sex discrimination encompasses discrimination on the basis of sexual orientation. See Baldwin v. Foxx, EEOC Appeal No. 0120133080, 2015 WL 4397641 (July 15, 2015). Our point here is not that we have a duty to defer to the EEOC's position. We assume for present purposes that no such duty exists. But the Commission's position may have caused some in Congress to think that legislation is needed to carve sexual orientation out of the statute, not to put it in. In the end, we have no idea what inference to draw from congressional inaction or later enactments, because there is no way of knowing what explains each individual member's votes, much less what explains the failure of the body as a whole to change this 1964 statute.

Our interpretive task is guided instead by the Supreme Court's approach in the closely related case of *Oncale*, where it had this to say as it addressed the question whether Title VII covers sexual harassment inflicted by a man on a male victim:

> We see no justification in the statutory language or our precedents for a categorical rule excluding same-sex harassment claims from the coverage of Title VII. As some courts have observed, male-on-male sexual harassment in the workplace was assuredly not the principal evil Congress was concerned with when it enacted Title VII. But statutory prohibitions often go beyond the principal evil to cover reasonably comparable evils, and it is ultimately the provisions of our laws rather than the principal concerns of our legislators by which we are governed. Title VII prohibits "discriminat[ion] . . . because of . . . sex" in the "terms" or "conditions" of employment. Our holding that this includes sexual harassment must extend to sexual harassment of any kind that meets the statutory requirements.

523 U.S. at 79–80. The Court could not have been clearer: the fact that the enacting Congress may not have anticipated a particular application of the law cannot stand in the way of the provisions of the law that are on the books. . . .

B

Hively offers two approaches in support of her contention that "sex discrimination" includes discrimination on the basis of sexual orientation. The first relies on the tried-and-true comparative method in which we attempt to isolate the significance of the plaintiff's sex to the employer's decision: has she described a situation in which, holding all other things constant and changing only her sex, she would have been treated the same way? The second relies on the Loving v. Virginia, 388 U.S. 1 (1967), line of cases, which she argues protect her right to associate intimately with a person of the same sex. Although the analysis differs somewhat, both avenues end up in the same place: sex discrimination.

1

It is critical, in applying the comparative method, to be sure that only the variable of the plaintiff's sex is allowed to change. The fundamental question is not whether a lesbian is being treated better or worse than gay men, bisexuals, or transsexuals, because such a comparison shifts too many pieces at once. Framing the question that way swaps the critical characteristic (here, sex) for both the complainant and the comparator and thus obscures the key point—whether the complainant's protected characteristic played a role in the adverse employment decision. The counterfactual we must use is a situation in which Hively is a man, but everything else stays the same: in particular, the sex or gender of the partner.

Hively alleges that if she had been a man married to a woman (or living with a woman, or dating a woman) and everything else had stayed the same, Ivy Tech would not have refused to promote her and would not have fired her. (We take the facts in the light most favorable to her, because we are here on a Rule 12(b)(6) dismissal; naturally nothing we say will prevent Ivy Tech from contesting these points in later proceedings.) This describes paradigmatic sex discrimination. To use the phrase from Ulane, Ivy Tech is disadvantaging her *because she is a woman*. Nothing in the complaint hints that Ivy Tech has an anti-marriage policy that extends to heterosexual relationships, or for that matter even an anti-partnership policy that is gender-neutral.

Viewed through the lens of the gender non-conformity line of cases, Hively represents the ultimate case of failure to conform to the female stereotype (at least as understood in a place such as modern America, which views heterosexuality as the norm and other forms of sexuality as exceptional): she is not heterosexual. Our panel described the line between a gender nonconformity claim and one based on sexual orientation as gossamer-thin; we conclude that it does not exist at all. Hively's claim is no different from the claims brought by women who were rejected for jobs in traditionally male workplaces, such as fire departments, construction, and policing. The employers in those cases were policing the boundaries of what jobs or behaviors they found acceptable for a woman (or in some cases, for a man).

This was the critical point that the Supreme Court was making in *Price Waterhouse v. Hopkins*. The four justices in the plurality and the two justices concurring in the judgment recognized that Hopkins had alleged that her employer was discriminating only against women who behaved in what the employer viewed as too "masculine" a way—no makeup, no jewelry, no fashion sense. And even before *Hopkins*, courts had found sex discrimination in situations where women were resisting stereotypical roles. As far back as 1971, the Supreme Court held that Title VII does not permit an employer to refuse to hire women with pre-school-age children, but not men. Phillips v. Martin Marietta Corp., 400 U.S. 542 (1971). Around the same time, this court held that Title VII "strike[s] at the entire spectrum of disparate treatment of men and women resulting from sex stereotypes," Sprogis v. United Air Lines, Inc., 444 F.2d 1194, 1198 (7th Cir. 1971), and struck down a rule requiring only the female employees to be unmarried. In both those instances, the employer's rule did not affect every woman in the workforce. Just so here: a policy that discriminates on the basis of sexual orientation does not affect every woman, or every man, but it is based on assumptions about the proper behavior for someone of a given sex. The discriminatory behavior does not exist without taking the victim's biological sex (either as observed at birth or as modified, in the case of transsexuals) into account. Any discomfort, disapproval, or job decision based on the fact that the complainant—woman or man—dresses differently, speaks differently, or dates or marries a same-sex partner, is a reaction purely and simply based on sex. That means that it falls within Title VII's prohibition against sex discrimination, if it affects employment in one of the specified ways.

The virtue of looking at comparators and paying heed to gender non-conformity is that this process sheds light on the interpretive question raised by Hively's case: is sexual-orientation discrimination a form of sex discrimination, given the way in which the Supreme Court has interpreted the word "sex" in the statute? The dissent criticizes us for not trying to rule out sexual-orientation discrimination by controlling for it in our comparator example and for not placing any weight on the fact that if someone had asked Ivy Tech what its reasons were at the time of the discriminatory conduct, it probably would have said "sexual orientation," not "sex." We assume that this is true, but this thought experiment does not answer the question before us—instead, it begs that question. It commits the logical fallacy of assuming the conclusion it sets out to prove. It makes no sense to control for or rule out discrimination on the basis of sexual orientation if the question before us is whether that type of discrimination is nothing more or less than a form of sex discrimination. Repeating that the two are different, as the dissent does at numerous points, also does not advance the analysis.

2

As we noted earlier, Hively also has argued that action based on sexual orientation is sex discrimination under the associational theory. It is now accepted that a person who is discriminated against because of the protected characteristic of one with whom she associates is actually being disadvantaged because of her own traits. This line of cases began with *Loving*, in which the Supreme Court held that "restricting the freedom to marry solely because of racial classifications violates the central meaning of the Equal Protection Clause." 388 U.S. at 12. The Court rejected the argument that miscegenation statutes do not violate equal protection because they "punish equally both the white and the Negro participants in an interracial marriage." Id. at 8. When dealing with a statute containing racial classifications, it wrote, "the fact of equal application does not immunize the statute from the very heavy burden of justification" required by the Fourteenth Amendment for lines drawn by race. Id. at 9. . . .

The fact that we now accept this analysis tells us nothing, however, about the world in 1967, when *Loving* reached the Supreme Court. The dissent implies that we are adopting an anachronistic view of Title VII, enacted just three years before *Loving*, but it is the dissent's understanding of *Loving* and the miscegenation laws that is an anachronism. Thanks to *Loving* and the later cases we mentioned, society understands now that such laws are (and always were) inherently racist. But as of 1967 (and thus as of 1964), Virginia and 15 other states had anti-miscegenation laws on the books. *Loving*, 388 U.S. at 6. These laws were long defended and understood as non-discriminatory because the legal obstacle affected both partners. The Court in *Loving* recognized that equal application of a law that prohibited conduct only between members of different races did not save it. Changing the race of one partner made a difference in determining the legality of the conduct, and so the law rested on "distinctions drawn according to race," which were unjustifiable and racially discriminatory. *Loving*, 388 U.S. at 11. So too, here. If we were to change the sex of one partner in a lesbian relationship, the outcome would be different. This reveals that the discrimination rests on distinctions drawn according to sex.

The dissent would instead have us compare the treatment of men who are attracted to members of the male sex with the treatment of women who are attracted to members of the female sex, and ask whether an employer treats the men differently from the women. But even setting to one side the logical fallacy involved, *Loving* shows why this fails. In the context of interracial relationships, we could just as easily hold constant a variable such as "sexual or romantic attraction to persons of a different race" and ask whether an employer treated persons of different races who shared that propensity the same. That is precisely the rule that Loving rejected, and so too must we, in the context of sexual associations. . . .

III

Today's decision must be understood against the backdrop of the Supreme Court's decisions, not only in the field of employment discrimination, but also in the area of broader discrimination on the basis of sexual orientation. We already have discussed the employment cases, especially *Hopkins* and *Oncale*. The latter line of cases began with Romer v. Evans, 517 U.S. 620 (1996), in which the Court held that a provision of the Colorado Constitution forbidding any organ of government in the state from taking action designed to protect "homosexual, lesbian, or bisexual" persons, id. at 624, violated the federal Equal Protection Clause. *Romer* was followed by Lawrence v. Texas, 539 U.S. 558 (2003), in which the Court found that a Texas statute criminalizing homosexual intimacy between consenting adults violated the liberty provision of the Due Process Clause. Next came United States v. Windsor, 133 S.Ct. 2675 (2013), which addressed the constitutionality of the part of the Defense of Marriage Act (DOMA) that excluded a same-sex partner from the definition of "spouse" in other federal statutes. The Court held that this part of DOMA "violate[d] basic due process and equal protection principles applicable to the Federal Government." Id. at 2693. Finally, the Court's decision in Obergefell v. Hodges, 135 S.Ct. 2584 (2015), held that the right to marry is a fundamental liberty right, protected by the Due Process and Equal Protection Clauses of the Fourteenth Amendment. 135 S.Ct. at 2604. The Court wrote that "[i]t is now clear that the challenged laws burden the liberty of same-sex couples, and it must be further acknowledged that they abridge central precepts of equality." Id. . . .

. . . The judgment of the district court is REVERSED and the case is REMANDED for further proceedings.

■ POSNER, CIRCUIT JUDGE, concurring.

I agree that we should reverse, and I join the majority opinion, but I wish to explore an alternative approach that may be more straightforward. . . .

[I]nterpretation can mean giving a fresh meaning to a statement (which can be a statement found in a constitutional or statutory text)—a meaning that infuses the statement with vitality and significance today. An example of this . . . form of interpretation—the form that in my mind is most clearly applicable to the present case—is the Sherman Antitrust Act, enacted in 1890, long before there was a sophisticated understanding of the economics of monopoly and competition. Times have changed; and for more than thirty years the Act has been interpreted in conformity to the modern, not the nineteenth-century, understanding of the relevant economics. The Act has thus been updated by, or in the name of, judicial interpretation—the form of interpretation that consists of making old law satisfy modern needs and understandings. And a common form of interpretation it is, despite its flouting "original meaning." Statutes and constitutional provisions frequently are interpreted on the basis of present need and present understanding rather than original meaning—constitutional provisions even more frequently, because most of them are older than most statutes.

Title VII of the Civil Rights Act of 1964, now more than half a century old, invites an interpretation that will update it to the present, a present that differs markedly from the era in which the Act was enacted. But I need to emphasize that this . . . form of interpretation—call it judicial interpretive updating—presupposes a lengthy interval between enactment and (re)interpretation. A statute when passed has an understood meaning; it takes years, often many years, for a shift in the political and cultural environment to change the understanding of the statute. . . .

It is well-nigh certain that homosexuality, male or female, did not figure in the minds of the legislators who enacted Title VII. I had graduated from law school two years before the law was enacted. Had I been asked then whether I had ever met a male homosexual, I would have answered: probably not; had I been asked whether I had ever met a lesbian I would have answered "only in the pages of À la recherche du temps perdu." Homosexuality was almost invisible in the 1960s. It became visible in the 1980s as a consequence of the AIDS epidemic; today it is regarded by a large swathe of the American population as normal. But what is certain is that the word "sex" in Title VII had no immediate reference to homosexuality; many years would elapse before it could be understood to include homosexuality.

A diehard "originalist" would argue that what was believed in 1964 defines the scope of the statute for as long as the statutory text remains unchanged, and therefore until changed by Congress's amending or replacing the statute. But as I noted earlier, statutory and constitutional provisions frequently are interpreted on the basis of present need and understanding rather than original meaning. Think for example of Justice Scalia's decisive fifth vote to hold that burning the American flag as a political protest is protected by the free-speech clause of the First Amendment, provided that it's your flag and is not burned in circumstances in which the fire might spread. Texas v. Johnson, 491 U.S. 397 (1989); United States v. Eichman, 496 U.S. 310 (1990). Burning a flag is not speech in the usual sense and there is no indication that the framers or ratifiers of the First Amendment thought that the word "speech" in the amendment embraced flag burning or other nonverbal methods of communicating. . . .

The most tenable and straightforward ground for deciding in favor of Hively is that while in 1964 sex discrimination meant discrimination against men or women as such and not against subsets of men or women such as effeminate men or mannish women, the concept of sex discrimination has since broadened in light of the recognition, which barely existed in 1964, that there are significant numbers of both men and women who have a sexual orientation that sets them apart from the heterosexual members of their genetic sex (male or female), and that while they constitute a minority their sexual orientation is not evil and does not threaten our society. Title VII in terms forbids only sex discrimination, but we now understand discrimination against homosexual men and women to be a form of sex discrimination; and to paraphrase Holmes, "We must consider what this country has become in deciding what that [statute] has reserved."

The majority opinion states that Congress in 1964 "may not have realized or understood the full scope of the words it chose." This could be understood to imply that the statute forbade discrimination against homosexuals but the framers and ratifiers of the statute were not smart enough to realize that. I would prefer to say that theirs was the then-current understanding of the key word—sex. "Sex" in 1964 meant gender, not sexual orientation. What the framers and ratifiers understandably didn't understand was how attitudes toward homosexuals would change in the following half century. They shouldn't be blamed for that failure of foresight. We understand the words of Title VII differently not because we're smarter than the statute's framers and ratifiers but because we live in a different era, a different culture. Congress in the 1960s did not foresee the sexual revolution of the 2000s. What our court announced in Doe v. City of Belleville, 119 F.3d 563, 572 (7th Cir. 1997), is what Congress had declared in 1964: "the traditional notion of 'sex.' "

I would prefer to see us acknowledge openly that today we, who are judges rather than members of Congress, are imposing on a half-century-old statute a meaning of "sex discrimination" that the Congress that enacted it would not have accepted. This is something courts do fairly frequently to avoid statutory obsolescence and concomitantly to avoid placing the entire burden of updating old statutes on the legislative branch. We should not leave the impression that we are merely the obedient servants of the 88th Congress (1963–1965), carrying out their wishes. We are not. We are taking advantage of what the last half century has taught.

[Judge Flaum, joined by Judge Ripple, concurred in Parts I and II of the majority opinion. He emphasized that "discrimination against an employee on the basis of their homosexuality is necessarily, in part, discrimination based on their sex" just as discrimination based on an interracial relationship is in part based on race.]

■ SYKES, CIRCUIT JUDGE, with whom BAUER and KANNE, CIRCUIT JUDGES, join, dissenting.

Any case heard by the full court is important. This one is momentous. All the more reason to pay careful attention to the limits on the court's role. The question before the en banc court is one of statutory interpretation. The majority deploys a judge-empowering, common-law decision method that leaves a great deal of room for judicial discretion. So does Judge Posner in his concurrence. Neither is faithful to the statutory text, read fairly, as a reasonable person would have understood it when it was adopted. The result is a statutory amendment courtesy of unelected judges. Judge Posner admits this; he embraces and argues for this conception of judicial power. The majority does not, preferring instead to smuggle in the statutory amendment under cover of an aggressive reading of loosely related Supreme Court precedents. Either way, the result is the same: the circumvention of the legislative process by which the people govern themselves.

Respect for the constraints imposed on the judiciary by a system of written law must begin with fidelity to the traditional first principle of statutory interpretation: When a statute supplies the rule of decision, our role is to give effect to the enacted text, interpreting the statutory language as a reasonable person would have understood it at the time of enactment. We are not authorized to infuse the text with a new or unconventional meaning or to update it to respond to changed social, economic, or political conditions.

In a handful of statutory contexts, Congress has vested the federal courts with authority to consider and make new rules of law in the common-law way. The Sherman Act is the archetype of the so-called "common-law statutes," but there are very few of these and Title VII is not one of them. Nw. Airlines, Inc. v. Transp. Workers Union of Am., AFL-CIO, 451 U.S. 77, 95–97 (1981); id. at 98 n.42. So our role is interpretive only; we lack the discretion to ascribe to Title VII a meaning it did not bear at its inception. Sitting en banc permits us to overturn our own precedents, but in a statutory case, we do not sit as a common-law court free to engage in "judicial interpretive updating," as Judge Posner calls it, or to do the same thing by pressing hard on tenuously related Supreme Court opinions, as the majority does.

NOTES ON *HIVELY V. IVY TECH COMMUNITY COLLEGE OF INDIANA*

1. **The Constitutional Right to Gay Marriage.** The trend in favor of prohibitions against discrimination on the basis of sexual orientation gained momentum when the Supreme Court extended the constitutional prohibition against discrimination on the basis of sexual orientation in United States v. Windsor, 133 S.Ct. 2675 (2013). Although the case did not concern employment, it invalidated a federal statute that discriminated against same-sex couples who were married under state law. The Court held unconstitutional a section of the Defense of Marriage Act (DOMA) that required the federal government to ignore such marriages, even when they were entirely valid under state law. The Court reasoned that marriage was primarily a concern of the states and that the only reason DOMA refused to recognize same-sex marriages was hostility to gays and lesbians. The Court concluded its discussion in the following sweeping terms:

> The class to which DOMA directs its restrictions and restraints are those persons who are joined in same-sex marriages made lawful by the State. DOMA singles out a class of persons deemed by a State entitled to recognition and protection to enhance

> their own liberty. It imposes a disability on the class by refusing to acknowledge a status the State finds to be dignified and proper. DOMA instructs all federal officials, and indeed all persons with whom same-sex couples interact, including their own children, that their marriage is less worthy than the marriages of others. The federal statute is invalid, for no legitimate purpose overcomes the purpose and effect to disparage and to injure those whom the State, by its marriage laws, sought to protect in personhood and dignity. By seeking to displace this protection and treating those persons as living in marriages less respected than others, the federal statute is in violation of the Fifth Amendment. This opinion and its holding are confined to those lawful marriages.

This reasoning led the Supreme Court two years later to hold that same-sex couples had a right to marry under the Due Process and Equal Protection Clauses. Obergefell v. Hodges, 135 S.Ct. 2584 (2015). Because the decision emphasized that "the right to marry is a fundamental right inherent in the liberty of the person," it has no immediate implications for discrimination on the basis of sexual orientation in other spheres, such as employment. The decisions nevertheless will lend support to claims of discrimination on this ground in government employment, which constitutes state action covered by the Fifth and Fourteenth Amendments.

The Court also mentioned discrimination on a completely different ground, based on religion against those who have beliefs inconsistent with same-sex marriage. The Court cautioned that their religious practices were not to be compromised by its decision requiring government to allow such marriages:

> Finally, it must be emphasized that religions, and those who adhere to religious doctrines, may continue to advocate with utmost, sincere conviction that, by divine precepts, same-sex marriage should not be condoned. The First Amendment ensures that religious organizations and persons are given proper protection as they seek to teach the principles that are so fulfilling and so central to their lives and faiths, and to their own deep aspirations to continue the family structure they have long revered. The same is true of those who oppose same-sex marriage for other reasons. In turn, those who believe allowing same-sex marriage is proper or indeed essential, whether as a matter of religious conviction or secular belief, may engage those who disagree with their view in an open and searching debate. The Constitution, however, does not permit the State to bar same-sex couples from marriage on the same terms as accorded to couples of the opposite sex.

2. **The Failure of ENDA.** As noted earlier, bills regularly have been proposed in Congress to amend Title VII to prohibit discrimination on the basis of sexual orientation and gender identity. What effect should the repeated failure of ENDA to gain enactment have on interpretation of Title VII?

Decisions like *Hively v. Ivy Tech* discount the failure of ENDA and then rely upon a formal interpretation of Title VII to prohibit discrimination on the basis of sexual orientation. Do they extend the formal interpretation to its logical limit—or beyond it? Discrimination against someone because they are attracted to members of the same sex does take into account their sex. Men attracted to men are treated differently than women attracted to men.

A similar argument could be made for protection of people who were identified as one sex at birth and now identify with another sex. If an employer establishes special rules for such people, and those rules work to their disadvantage, the employer has taken account of sex in violation of Title VII. And indeed, the recent versions of ENDA also have protected against discrimination on the basis of gender identity.

Should the courts wait for Congress to enact some form of ENDA? Or should they rely on the canon of construction that congressional inaction has, by definition, no operative force? Does the argument come down to the fact that the people who would be protected by ENDA already have waited long enough?

3. **The Dispute over Transgender Bathroom Access.** Title IX of the Education Amendments Act of 1972 prohibits sex discrimination in education programs that receive federal funds, which effectively reaches almost all aspects of education. Disputes have arisen over whether Title IX requires schools to grant students who have or who are now undergoing gender reassignment the access to the bathrooms and locker rooms of their preferred gender.

In interpreting Title IX, and Title VII as well, the Obama Administration equated discrimination on the basis of gender identity with discrimination on the basis of sex, in positions taken by both the Department of Justice and the EEOC. Lusardi v. McHough, EEOC Appeal No. 0120133395, 2015 WL 1607756 (Apr. 1, 2015); Memorandum from the Attorney General, Treatment of Transgender Employment Discrimination Claims Under Title VII of the Civil Rights Act of 1964 to U.S. Attorneys (Dec. 15, 2014), https://www.justice.gov/file/188671/ download. The Trump Administration, through its Justice Department, has rejected this interpretation of Title VII. Brief for the United States as Amicus Curiae, Zarda v. Altitude Express, Inc., 855 F.3d 76 (2d Cir. 2017) (No. 15–3775) (2d Cir. July 26, 2017). The Trump Administration has also rescinded the Obama Administration's interpretation of Title IX. Dep't of Justice, Dear Colleague Letter from Sandra Battle, Acting Ass't Sec. for Civil Rights, U.S. Dep't of Educ. & T.E. Wheeler, II, Acting Ass't Att'y General for Civil Rights, U.S. Dep't of Justice (Feb. 22, 2017), https://www2.ed.gov/about/offices/list/ocr/letters/colleague–201702–title–ix.pdf. Do these changes in executive interpretation of the statutes indicate that Congress should amend Title IX and Title VII to resolve these questions? Or does the high profile that these questions have now acquired make it unlikely that Congress could pass any such amendments?

4. **Bibliography.** For a selection of recent articles on discrimination on the basis of sexual orientation and gender identity under Title VII, see

Kimberly A. Yuracko, Gender Nonconformity and the Law (2016); Gender Identity and Sexual Orientation Discrimination in the Workplace: A Practical Guide (Christine M. Duffy & Denise M. Visconti eds., 2014); Leora F. Eisenstadt, Fluid Identify Discrimination, 52 Am. Bus. L.J. 789 (2015); Stephen F. Befort & Michael J. Vargas, Same-Sex Marriage and Title VII, 56 Santa Clara L. Rev. 207 (2016); Jessica A. Clarke, Frontiers of Sex Discrimination Law, 115 Mich. L. Rev. 809 (2017); Linda B. Dwoskin et al., It's Not Your Parents' Definition of "Sex" Anymore, 42 Empl. Rel. L.J. 3 (2017); William N. Eskridge, Jr., Title VII's Statutory History and the Sex Discrimination Argument for LGBT Workplace Protections, 127 Yale. L.J. 322 (2017); Zachary A. Kramer, The New Sex Discrimination, 63 Duke L.J. 891 (2014); Keith Cunningham-Parmeter, Marriage Equality, Workplace Inequality: The Next Gay Rights Battle, 67 Fla. L. Rev. 1099 (2015); Naomi Schoenbaum, Heteronormativity in Employment Discrimination Law, 56 Washburn L.J. 245 (2017).

E. ANCILLARY PROHIBITIONS

Like any other comprehensive regulatory statute, Title VII contains ancillary prohibitions to safeguard its enforcement and to assure compliance with its main prohibitions. The most significant of these covers retaliation for opposing discriminatory practices or for participating in enforcement proceedings. These provisions, found in § 704(a), have already been discussed in Chapter 2 in connection with individual claims of intentional discrimination. Claims of retaliation often accompany and amplify claims of discrimination on other grounds. As such, they play an important role in the enforcement of Title VII.

Another ancillary prohibition plays a more symbolic role and seldom actually leads to litigation. Section 704(b) prohibits discrimination in advertising. Because it regulates the press, it was initially thought to raise questions under the First Amendment, but these were soon resolved, based on the principle that, if the underlying activity is prohibited, so is advertising to engage in that activity. See, e.g., Pittsburgh Press Co. v. Pittsburgh Commission on Human Relations, 413 U.S. 376 (1973). Hence, "help wanted male" and "help wanted female" advertisements, which were common before Title VII took effect, have entirely disappeared through the operation of this provision. For this reason also, claims of discrimination in advertising have been rare. The success of the provision has made enforcement actions unnecessary.

In any event, claims based solely on discriminatory advertising face a further obstacle based on the plaintiff's standing, both as a doctrinal and as a practical matter. The only individuals who could bring such claims are those who were deterred from applying for a job by the discriminatory ad in question. Yet these individuals may have difficulty proving that they suffered actual harm if they did not actually attempt to apply for the job or if they accepted employment elsewhere. If the former, they have a straightforward claim of discrimination in hiring. If the latter, they are not likely to take the trouble to sue in any event. For all these reasons, the prohibition against discriminatory advertising plays a role mainly in the background of other claims of discrimination. No employer would want to be faced with its own discriminatory advertising in a case alleging discrimination in hiring or promotions.

F. COVERAGE

Questions of coverage under Title VII arise in four different dimensions: who can be a plaintiff; who can be a defendant; what grounds of discrimination are covered; and what actions sufficiently related to employment are covered. On the plaintiff side, the answer is that the statute covers "any individual." § 703(a)–(d). On the defendant side, it mainly covers any employer with 15 or more employees in an industry "affecting commerce." § 701(a). As the following notes point out this simple answer is both too broad and too narrow and technical questions complicate the analysis. As for covered grounds of discrimination, we have seen in this chapter and earlier ones that the statute covers discrimination on the basis of race, national origin, color, sex, religion, and possibly sexual orientation and gender identity. It also prohibits retaliation. As for covered practices, we first saw this issue with respect to retaliation, but it also comes up with cases involving fringe benefits. These notes begin with the intricacies of the definition of covered employers and then proceed to covered employment practices.

1. **Covered Defendants.** The main provisions on coverage apply Title VII to all employers with 15 or more employees in an industry affecting commerce; all labor organizations in an industry affecting commerce; and all employment agencies that regularly provide employment to statutorily defined employers. § 701(b)–(e). For decisions on who counts as an employee and how to determine whether the employer meets the threshold of 15 employees, see Clackamas Gastroenterology Associates v. Wells, 538 U.S. 440 (2003); Walters v. Metropolitan Education Enterprises, Inc., 519 U.S. 202 (1997).

The limit on the size of employers, together with provisions in the Civil Rights Act of 1991 limiting liability for damages based on the size of the employer, has led most of the circuits to hold that individual agents of an employer are not covered by the statute at all. E.g., Tomka v. Seiler Corp., 66 F.3d 1295 (2d Cir. 1995); Miller v. Maxwell's International Inc., 991 F.2d 583 (9th Cir. 1993), cert. denied, 510 U.S. 1109 (1994).

The provisions on coverage also include state and local governments within the definition of "employer," but exclude the United States and related entities, Indian tribes, and some private membership clubs. § 701(a)–(b). There are, however, special provisions for coverage of the United States and related entities, although these provisions themselves exclude some parts of the Federal Government, such as the armed services. These provisions, to the extent that they cover the United States, result in special procedures for enforcement of claims on behalf of federal employees. §§ 717(a), 717b, 42 U.S.C. §§ 2000e–16(a), 16b. Special provisions also apply to claims by employees of Congress. 2 U.S.C. §§ 1301, 1311. And others apply to claims by state employees appointed to serve elected officials. § 717c, 42 U.S.C. § 2000e–16c.

A further question of coverage, increasingly important in this age of international trade, concerns employment overseas: whether Title VII covers employees who work outside the United States. This question of coverage was first resolved by the Supreme Court against application of Title VII. EEOC v. Arabian American Oil Co., 499 U.S. 244 (1991). That decision, however, was superseded by the Civil Rights Act of 1991, which extended coverage to American citizens employed overseas by American employers and corporations controlled by such employers, subject to a defense that compliance with Title VII would violate the law of the country of employment. §§ 701(f), 702(b).

Some courts had doubted whether a federal court had jurisdiction over a claim against a defendant outside the coverage of Title VII, by analogy to the limits on the legislative jurisdiction of Congress under the Commerce Clause. In Arbaugh v. Y & H Corp., 546 U.S. 500 (2006), the Supreme Court laid such doubts to rest, holding that the limitation on coverage of Title VII to private employers with at least 15 employees was not jurisdictional. This limitation did not affect the subject-matter jurisdiction of a federal court considering a Title VII claim and so an objection that the defendant was not covered could be waived if not asserted in a timely manner.

2. Covered Employment Practices. The adverse effect suffered by a plaintiff must bear a significant relationship to employment to gain coverage under Title VII. In retaliation cases, the plaintiff must show "that a reasonable employee would have found the challenged action materially adverse, which in this context means it well might have dissuaded a reasonable worker from making or supporting a charge of discrimination." Burlington Northern & Santa Fe Ry. Co. v. White, 549 U.S. 53, 68 (2006) (internal quotation marks and citations omitted). In fringe benefit cases, like Los Angeles Department of Water & Power v. Manhart, 435 U.S. 702 (1978), the statute covers any denial of benefits to employees on a discriminatory basis. Another case that elaborates on the benefits that trigger coverage of the statute is Hishon v. King & Spaulding, 467 U.S. 69 (1984). The Court there held that Title VII covered discriminatory denial of promotion to partnership, reasoning that a covered benefit "need only be a term, condition, or privilege of employment" and that it was "of no consequence that employment as an associate necessarily ends when an associate becomes partner." In a concurring opinion, Justice Powell emphasized that the relationship of partners among themselves was different from an employment relationship and so was not covered by Title VII. Like the Court, Justice Powell also rejected the argument that coverage under Title VII undermined rights of expression or association because the employer had voluntarily assumed the obligation to consider associates for partnership. The same sets of issues, with the same result, came up in Price Waterhouse v. Hopkins, 490 U.S. 228 (1989), considered in Chapter 1. Between them, don't these cases make clear that any benefit provided in connection with employment is covered by Title VII?

3. **The Role of Freedom of Association.** The only basis for restricting the otherwise broad coverage of Title VII comes from the constitutional protection of free expression and association. Subsequent decisions have recognized claims of freedom of association, but mainly with respect to the expression of political or moral views. Boy Scouts of America v. Dale, 530 U.S. 640, 653–61 (2000); New York State Club Association v. New York, 487 U.S. 1, 10–15 (1988). Organizations with commercial interests and objectives have not succeeded in advancing such claims, although more often because they were not genuinely private. Instead, they were open to the general public, excluding only individuals from specified groups. Board of Directors of Rotary International v. Rotary Club of Duarte, 481 U.S. 537, 544–49 (1987); Roberts v. United States Jaycees, 468 U.S. 609, 617–29 (1984).

Could partnerships and other business organizations plausibly advance claims of freedom of association? Recall that these organizations are creatures of state law and so have no right to exist protected by the Constitution. If they can be created and regulated by the states, why can't they be subject to prohibitions against discrimination in their operation? To the extent that Title VII itself protects rights of expression and association, it does so indirectly by regulating the size of covered employers. Small employers, as an earlier note indicated, are entirely exempt from coverage of the statute.

4. **Bibliography.** Theresa M. Beiner, Do Reindeer Games Count as Terms, Conditions or Privileges of Employment Under Title VII?, 37 B.C. L. Rev. 643 (1996); Nancy E. Dowd, The Test of Employee Status: Economic Realities and Title VII, 26 Wm. & Mary L. Rev. 75 (1984); Orly Lobel, The Gig Economy & The Future of Employment and Labor Law, 51 U.S.F. L. Rev. 51 (2017); Ann C. McGinley, Discrimination in Our Midst: Law Schools' Potential Liability for Employment Practices, 14 UCLA Women's L.J. 1 (2005); Ann C. McGinley, Functionality or Formalism? Partners and Shareholders as "Employees" Under the Anti-Discrimination Laws, 57 SMU L. Rev. 3 (2004); Christine N. O'Brien & Stephanie Greene, Employee Threshold on Federal Antidiscrimination Statutes: A Matter of the Merits, 95 Ky. L.J. 429 (2006–07); Lawrence D. Rosenthal, No Good Deed Goes Unpunished: The Lack of Protection for Volunteers Under Federal Anti-Discrimination Statutes, 2016 BYU L. Rev. 117; Rebecca H. White, De Minimis Discrimination, 47 Emory L.J. 1121 (1998).

CHAPTER 7

PROCEDURES UNDER TITLE VII

A. INTRODUCTION

1. **Procedural Structure for Enforcing Title VII.** Title VII is enforced according to a complex set of procedures and remedies that seek to implement a variety of different, and sometimes conflicting, principles. These principles have deeply influenced the procedural requirements that plaintiffs must meet in order to recover under the statute and the nature of the remedies available. The basic compromise needed to secure passage of the Civil Rights Act of 1964 concerned the choice between judicial and administrative enforcement of the statute. Congress opted for enforcement through the courts, rather than through an administrative agency such as the National Labor Relations Board (NLRB), with the power to issue cease-and-desist orders. Employers had grown wary of the NLRB as a large and powerful administrative agency that protected the rights of employees to engage in collective bargaining, and they feared that the Equal Employment Opportunity Commission (EEOC) would enforce the rights of employees under Title VII in the same manner.

Both when Title VII was originally enacted and when it was significantly amended in the Equal Employment Opportunity Act of 1972, opponents of administrative enforcement succeeded in limiting the role of the EEOC. The EEOC possesses authority to adjudicate claims of discrimination only by federal employees. The claims of all other employees can be adjudicated only by a court, and the role of the EEOC is limited to the preliminary stages of investigating charges of discrimination, attempting to resolve them through mediation, and deciding whether to sue in its own name.

In Mach Mining, LLC v. EEOC, 135 S. Ct. 1645 (2015), the Supreme Court held that the EEOC's alleged failure to conduct conciliation was subject to judicial review. Review, however, was limited to the following basic requirements: "the EEOC must inform the employer about the specific allegation in the charge," including "both what the employer has done and which employees (or what class of employees) have suffered as a result"; and "the EEOC must try to engage the employer in some form of discussion (whether written or oral), so as to give the employer an opportunity to remedy the allegedly discriminatory practice." The need for judicial review followed from the basic principle that any agency action was subject to review for compliance with statutory requirements, while the review was limited to preserve the EEOC's discretion in the conciliation process.

On a related matter, the Supreme Court held that a district court's decision on enforcement of a subpoena issued by the EEOC should be reviewed on appeal only for "abuse of discretion." McLane Co. v. EEOC, 137 S. Ct. 1159 (2017). Such decisions typically involve case-specific determinations whether the evidence sought is relevant to the charge pending before the EEOC or whether production of the evidence would be unduly burdensome. The EEOC thus retains some role in enforcing the statute, although less than the role of the NLRB in enforcing the laws on collective bargaining. Exhaustion of administrative procedures remains a prerequisite for any form of litigation under Title VII. Private individuals first must file a charge with the EEOC, and only after they receive a "right-to-sue" letter, usually after a period of at least 180 days, can they sue in court. § 706(b), (f)(1), 42 U.S.C. § 2000e–5(b), (f)(1). Such a letter will be issued only if the charge of discrimination has not been settled through a conciliation agreement and has not been made the subject of a public enforcement action. Although few such actions are brought, the EEOC has the authority to sue private employers, and the Department of Justice can sue public employers in the form of state and local government. Federal employees are subject to entirely separate procedures that allow them to choose between adjudication by the EEOC or adjudication in court. §§ 717(b), (c), 717b, 42 U.S.C. §§ 2000e–16(b), (c), –16b. The EEOC also adjudicates claims by state employees appointed to serve elected officials. § 717c, 42 U.S.C. § 2000e–16c.

This divided system of enforcement is made more complex by provisions requiring exhaustion of administrative procedures at the state and local level. In states and localities that have such procedures—and most now do—the charging party must first give state and local agencies an opportunity to resolve his or her claim. This period of exclusive state or local jurisdiction lasts only for 60 days, § 706(c), (d), 42 U.S.C. § 2000e–5(c), (d), but it raises questions about complying with the applicable time limit for filing charges with the EEOC. These questions are taken up in the first section of this chapter.

The provisions for exhaustion of administrative remedies, as well as for public actions to enforce Title VII, serve several different purposes: promoting the expeditious resolution of claims; encouraging state and local participation in enforcement efforts; and reserving important cases for litigation by the federal government. All of these purposes are worthwhile, but each of them adds to the complexity of the procedures for enforcing Title VII. A question to keep in mind throughout this chapter is whether these procedures have become too complex. In seeking to serve so many different purposes, have they served any of them effectively? In particular, have they given victims of discrimination a fair opportunity to present their claims and to obtain appropriate relief?

2. The Role of Procedures and Remedies. Enforcement provisions can serve a variety of different goals. The least controversial are stated at the highest level of abstraction. Thus, the Federal Rules of Civil Procedure are designed "to secure the just, speedy, and inexpensive determination of every action." Fed. R. Civ. P. 1. Moreover, back pay can be denied under Title VII "only for reasons which, if applied generally would not frustrate the central statutory purposes of eradicating discrimination throughout the economy and making persons whole for injuries suffered through past discrimination." Albemarle Paper Co. v. Moody, 422 U.S. 405, 421 (1975). Only when these broad generalizations are reduced to specific rules or decisions does the complexity of mixing different procedural and remedial goals become apparent. The combination of administrative and judicial enforcement of Title VII, mentioned earlier, illustrates just how easily seemingly compatible goals can end up competing with one another.

These goals cannot be reconciled simply by characterizing them all as substantive goals endorsed by Congress. As the cases discussed in earlier chapters reveal, such goals may be unclear, contradictory, and subject to continuing controversy. Protecting the seniority rights of incumbent employees, for instance, collides with the interest in making victims of discrimination whole for the wrongs that they have suffered. This issue, raised as a matter of substantive law in Chapter 1, reappears as an issue of remedies in Chapter 8. As we saw in the excerpt from International Brotherhood of Teamsters v. United States, 431 U.S. 324 (1977), seniority systems receive special protection under Title VII through an exemption from liability under the theory of disparate impact. Another excerpt from *Teamsters* describes the equitable limitations upon the awards of seniority as a form of relief for past discrimination.

This line of cases reveals a further source of conflict among the various goals implicated in any enforcement scheme. Procedural and remedial principles tend to take on a life of their own, supporting goals entirely independent of the substantive aims that the statute seeks to achieve. This tendency is most apparent with respect to procedural goals, such as assuring a fair opportunity to be heard, which often come at the expense of efficient enforcement of the law. If both parties have a right to be fully heard, the proceedings often must be prolonged simply to give the losing party its day in court. Remedial principles are no less independent, raising issues such as the right to jury trial, discussed in the preceding note, or the duty of a plaintiff to mitigate damages by seeking alternative forms of employment. Neither of these principles can be derived from the purely substantive provisions of Title VII, let alone the overriding goal of preventing discrimination. Instead, all of these various goals must be reconciled and compromised with one another. How existing law attempts to achieve this result, and whether it is successful in creating an enforcement scheme that is both effective and acceptable, are the fundamental questions raised in this chapter.

3. **Bibliography.** The division of enforcement authority between state and local agencies, the EEOC, and the courts has raised a variety of issues, from technical questions of procedure to basic questions of policy. See Zachary D. Clopton, Redundant Public-Private Enforcement, 69 Vand. L. Rev. 285 (2016); Michael Z. Green, Proposing a New Paradigm for EEOC Enforcement After 35 Years: Outsourcing Charge Processing by Mandatory Mediation, 105 Dick. L. Rev. 305 (2001); Robert A. Kearney, Who's "In Charge" at the EEOC?, 50 Drake L. Rev. 1 (2001); Pauline T. Kim, Addressing Systemic Discrimination: Public Enforcement and the Role of the EEOC, 95 B.U. L. Rev. 1133 (2015); Margaret H. Lemos, The Consequences of Congress's Choice of Delegate: Judicial and Agency Interpretations of Title VII, 63 Vand. L. Rev. 363 (2010); Natiya Ruan, Facilitating Wage Theft: How Courts Use Procedural Rules to Undermine Substantive Rights of Low-Wage Workers, 63 Vand. L. Rev. 727 (2010); Michael Selmi, The Value of the EEOC: Reexamining the Agency's Role in Employment Discrimination Law, 57 Ohio St. L.J. 1 (1996); Margo Schlanger & Pauline Kim, The Equal Employment Opportunity Commission and Structural Reform of the American Workplace, 91 Wash. U. L. Rev. 1519 (2014); Julie C. Suk, Procedural Path Dependence: Discrimination and the Civil-Criminal Divide, 85 Wash. U. L. Rev. 1315 (2008); Lisa M. Durham Taylor, Untangling the Web Spun by Title VII's Referral and Deferral Scheme, 59 Cath. U. L. Rev. 427 (2010) Elinor A. Swanson, A Textualist Approach to Title VII: Aggrieved Individuals May Bypass the EEOC, 32 Hofstra Lab. & Emp. L.J. 345 (2015).

B. STATUTE OF LIMITATIONS

United Air Lines, Inc. v. Evans

431 U.S. 553 (1977).

■ JUSTICE STEVENS delivered the opinion of the Court.

Respondent was employed by United Air Lines as a flight attendant from November 1966 to February 1968. She was rehired in February 1972. Assuming, as she alleges, that her separation from employment in 1968 violated Title VII of the Civil Rights Act of 1964, the question now presented is whether the employer is committing a second violation of Title VII by refusing to credit her with seniority for any period prior to February 1972.

Respondent filed charges with the Equal Employment Opportunity Commission in February 1973 alleging that United discriminated and continues to discriminate against her because she is a female. After receiving a letter granting her the right to sue, she commenced this action in the United States District Court for the Northern District of

Illinois. Because the District Court dismissed her complaint, the facts which she has alleged are taken as true. They may be simply stated.

During respondent's initial period of employment, United maintained a policy of refusing to allow its female flight attendants to be married. When she married in 1968, she was therefore forced to resign. Although it was subsequently decided that such a resignation violated Title VII, Sprogis v. United Air Lines, 444 F.2d 1194 (CA7 1971), cert. denied, 404 U.S. 991, respondent was not a party to that case and did not initiate any proceedings of her own in 1968 by filing a charge with the EEOC within 90 days of her separation.[3] A claim based on that discriminatory act is therefore barred.

In November 1968, United entered into a new collective-bargaining agreement which ended the pre-existing "no marriage" rule and provided for the reinstatement of certain flight attendants who had been terminated pursuant to that rule. Respondent was not covered by that agreement. On several occasions she unsuccessfully sought reinstatement; on February 16, 1972, she was hired as a new employee. Although her personnel file carried the same number as it did in 1968, for seniority purposes she has been treated as though she had no prior service with United. She has not alleged that any other rehired employees were given credit for prior service with United, or that United's administration of the seniority system has violated the collective-bargaining agreement covering her employment.

Informal requests to credit her with pre-1972 seniority having been denied, respondent commenced this action. The District Court dismissed the complaint, holding that the failure to file a charge within 90 days of her separation in 1968 caused respondent's claim to be time barred and foreclosed any relief under Title VII.

A divided panel of the Court of Appeals initially affirmed; then, after our decision in Franks v. Bowman Transportation Co., 424 U.S. 747, the panel granted respondent's petition for rehearing and unanimously reversed. We granted certiorari and now hold that the complaint was properly dismissed.

Respondent recognizes that it is now too late to obtain relief based on an unlawful employment practice which occurred in 1968. She contends, however, that United is guilty of a present, continuing violation of Title VII and therefore that her claim is timely.[9] She advances two

---

[3] Section 706(d), 78 Stat. 260, 42 U.S.C. § 2000e–5(e), then provided in part: "A charge under subsection (a) shall be filed within ninety days after the alleged unlawful employment practice occurred. . . ." The 1972 amendments to Title VII added a new subsection (a) to § 706. Consequently, subsection (d) was redesignated as subsection (e). At the same time it was amended to enlarge the limitations period to 180 days. See 86 Stat. 105, 42 U.S.C. § 2000e–5(e).

[9] Respondent cannot rely for jurisdiction on the single act of failing to assign her seniority credit for her prior service at the time she was rehired, for she filed her discrimination charge with the Equal Employment Opportunity Commission on February 21, 1973, more than one year after she was rehired on February 16, 1972. The applicable time limit in February 1972, was 90 days; effective March 24, 1972, this time was extended to 180 days, see n. 3, supra.

reasons for holding that United's seniority system illegally discriminates against her: First, she is treated less favorably than males who were hired after her termination in 1968 and prior to her re-employment in 1972; second, the seniority system gives present effect to the past illegal act and therefore perpetuates the consequences of forbidden discrimination. Neither argument persuades us that United is presently violating the statute.

It is true that some male employees with less total service than respondent have more seniority than she. But this disparity is not a consequence of their sex, or of her sex. For females hired between 1968 and 1972 also acquired the same preference over respondent as males hired during that period. Moreover, both male and female employees who had service prior to February 1968, who resigned or were terminated for a nondiscriminatory reason (or for an unchallenged discriminatory reason), and who were later re-employed, also were treated as new employees receiving no seniority credit for their prior service. Nothing alleged in the complaint indicates that United's seniority system treats existing female employees differently from existing male employees, or that the failure to credit prior service differentiates in any way between prior service by males and prior service by females. Respondent has failed to allege that United's seniority system differentiates between similarly situated males and females on the basis of sex.

Respondent is correct in pointing out that the seniority system gives present effect to a past act of discrimination. But United was entitled to treat that past act as lawful after respondent failed to file a charge of discrimination within the 90 days then allowed by § 706(d). A discriminatory act which is not made the basis for a timely charge is the legal equivalent of a discriminatory act which occurred before the statute was passed. It may constitute relevant background evidence in a proceeding in which the status of a current practice is at issue, but separately considered, it is merely an unfortunate event in history which has no present legal consequences.

Respondent emphasizes the fact that she has alleged a continuing violation. United's seniority system does indeed have a continuing impact on her pay and fringe benefits. But the emphasis should not be placed on mere continuity; the critical question is whether any present violation exists. She has not alleged that the system discriminates against former female employees or that it treats former employees who were discharged for a discriminatory reason any differently from former employees who resigned or were discharged for a nondiscriminatory reason. In short, the system is neutral in its operation.[10]

---

[10] This case does not involve any claim by respondent that United's seniority system deterred her from asserting any right granted by Title VII. It does not present the question raised in the so-called departmental seniority cases. See, e. g., Quarles v. Philip Morris, Inc., 279 F. Supp. 505 (ED Va. 1968).

Our decision in *Franks v. Bowman Transportation Co.*, supra, does not control this case. In *Franks* we held that retroactive seniority was an appropriate remedy to be awarded under § 706(g) of Title VII once an illegal discriminatory act or practice had been proved. When that case reached this Court, the issues relating to the timeliness of the charge and the violation of Title VII had already been decided; we dealt only with a question of remedy. In contrast, in the case now before us we do not reach any remedy issue because respondent did not file a timely charge based on her 1968 separation and she has not alleged facts establishing a violation since she was rehired in 1972.[13]

The difference between a remedy issue and a violation issue is highlighted by the analysis of § 703(h) of Title VII in *Franks*. As we held in that case, by its terms that section does not bar the award of retroactive seniority after a violation has been proved. Rather, § 703(h) "delineates which employment practices are illegal and thereby prohibited and which are not."

That section expressly provides that it shall not be an unlawful employment practice to apply different terms of employment pursuant to a bona fide seniority system, provided that any disparity is not the result of intentional discrimination. Since respondent does not attack the bona fides of United's seniority system, and since she makes no charge that the system is intentionally designed to discriminate because of race, color, religion, sex, or national origin, § 703(h) provides an additional ground for rejecting her claim. The Court of Appeals read § 703(h) as intended to bar an attack on a seniority system based on the consequences of discriminatory acts which occurred prior to the effective date of Title VII in 1965, but having no application to such attacks based on acts occurring after 1965. This reading of § 703(h) is too narrow. The statute does not foreclose attacks on the current operation of seniority systems which are subject to challenge as discriminatory. But such a challenge to a neutral system may not be predicated on the mere fact that a past event which has no present legal significance has affected the calculation of seniority credit, even if the past event might at one time have justified a valid claim against the employer. A contrary view would substitute a claim for seniority credit for almost every claim which is barred by limitations. Such a result would contravene the mandate of § 703(h).

The judgment of the Court of Appeals is reversed. It is so ordered.

■ JUSTICE MARSHALL, with whom JUSTICE BRENNAN joins, dissenting.

But for her sex, respondent Carolyn Evans presently would enjoy all of the seniority rights that she seeks through this litigation. Petitioner

[13] At the time she was rehired in 1972, respondent had no greater right to a job than any other applicant for employment with United. Since she was in fact treated like any other applicant when she was rehired, the employer did not violate Title VII in 1972. And if the employer did not violate Title VII in 1972 by refusing to credit respondent with back seniority, its continued adherence to that policy cannot be illegal.

United Air Lines has denied her those rights pursuant to a policy that perpetuates past discrimination by awarding the choicest jobs to those possessing a credential married women were unlawfully prevented from acquiring: continuous tenure with United. While the complaint respondent filed in the District Court was perhaps inartfully drawn, it adequately draws into question this policy of United's.

For the reasons stated in the Court's opinion and in my separate opinion in Teamsters v. United States, 431 U.S. 324, 378, I think it indisputable that, absent § 703(h), the seniority system at issue here would constitute an "unlawful employment practice" under Title VII. And for the reasons developed at length in my separate opinion in *Teamsters*, I believe § 703(h) does not immunize seniority systems that perpetuate post-Act discrimination.

The only remaining question is whether Ms. Evans' complaint is barred by the applicable statute of limitations. Her cause of action accrued, if at all, at the time her seniority was recomputed after she was rehired. Although she apparently failed to file a charge with the EEOC within 180 days after her seniority was determined, Title VII recognizes that certain violations, once commenced, are continuing in nature. In these instances, discriminatees can file charges at any time up to 180 days after the violation ceases. (They can, however, receive back pay only for the two years preceding the filing of charges with the Equal Employment Opportunity Commission. 42 U.S.C. § 2000e–5(g).) In the instant case, the violation treating respondent as a new employee even though she was wrongfully forced to resign is continuing to this day. Respondent's charge therefore was not time barred, and the Court of Appeals judgment reinstating her complaint should be affirmed.

NOTES ON *UNITED AIR LINES, INC. V. EVANS*

1. Statutes of Limitations Under Title VII. The time limits for filing claims under Title VII correspond to the three stages of presenting a claim under enforcement: first, resorting to state or local administrative remedies, if there are any; second, exhausting administrative remedies before the EEOC; and third, filing a claim in court. The last two time limits were specified by Title VII itself and, as noted in *Evans*, were lengthened by amendments to Title VII in the Equal Employment Opportunity Act of 1972.

The time limits for resorting to state and local administrative agencies, by contrast, are set by state or local law. These time limits were not at issue in *Evans* because, at the time, Illinois did not have an agency that enforced laws against employment discrimination. Virtually all states now do, however. In the rare case in which there is no state or local agency, a charge must be filed with the EEOC by or on behalf of the plaintiff within 180 days of the alleged discrimination. In the typical case, in which there is a state or local agency, the charge must be filed within 300 days of the date of the alleged discrimination or within 30 days of notice of termination of state or local proceedings, whichever occurs first. § 706(e)(1), 42 U.S.C. § 2000e–

5(e)(1). The 30-day time limit has not proved to be very significant, since relatively few charges are resolved by state agencies before the expiration of the 300-day time limit, and most of those are subject to agreements with the EEOC by which they are automatically referred to the EEOC upon termination of state or local proceedings.

Thus the 300-day limitation period has proved to be the most significant issue in litigation under Title VII. It is longer than the 180-day limitation currently applied in the absence of a state or local agency in order to give the plaintiff a longer time to resort to remedies made available by state or local law. Where such remedies are available, the EEOC must defer action on a charge for 60 days after filing with the state or local agency, or until termination of state or local proceedings, to give the state or local agency an opportunity to resolve the charge without federal interference. § 706(c), (d), 42 U.S.C. § 2000e–5(c), (d). The interaction of this deferral period with the 300-day limitation period was one of the subjects eventually simplified through the joint efforts of the EEOC and the Supreme Court. It is enough to note now that the deferral period, as originally interpreted by the Supreme Court, effectively required the plaintiff to file a charge with the EEOC at some period earlier than 300 days from the date of the alleged discrimination, usually 60 days earlier, so that the deferral period could be satisfied before a charge was timely filed with the EEOC. Mohasco Corp. v. Silver, 447 U.S. 807 (1980).

Even after satisfying the limitation period for filing with the EEOC, the plaintiff must also satisfy the limitation period for filing in court. Title VII specifies a time limit only for private actions. Public actions, by the EEOC or the Department of Justice, need only satisfy the equitable doctrine of laches. Occidental Life Insurance Co. v. EEOC, 432 U.S. 355 (1977). This doctrine bars an action only if the plaintiff has delayed unreasonably to the defendant's detriment in bringing a claim. Public actions still must be supported by a timely charge, which can be filed either by a private individual or by an EEOC commissioner. § 706(b), 42 U.S.C. § 2000e–5(b). But if this requirement is satisfied, the EEOC or the Department of Justice need only file a public action within a reasonable time.

If no public action is filed, and the plaintiff has not entered into a conciliation agreement settling the charge of discrimination, a "right-to-sue letter" is sent to the plaintiff. The plaintiff must then file suit within 90 days of receipt of the right-to-sue letter. § 706(f)(1), 42 U.S.C. § 2000e–5(f)(1). This letter advises the plaintiff that the EEOC has completed its investigation and its efforts at conciliation and that no public action has been filed. The plaintiff can also request a right-to-sue letter after the EEOC has considered his charge, § 706(c), 42 U.S.C. § 2000e–5(c); and he can sue even if the EEOC dismisses his charge or finds no reasonable cause to support it. McDonnell Douglas Corp. v. Green, 411 U.S. 792, 798–800 (1973). The only circumstances in which a plaintiff is barred from suing by administrative action is when a conciliation agreement has been reached with the plaintiff's consent, effectively settling the claim of discrimination, or when the EEOC or the Department of Justice sues instead, leaving the plaintiff only with a right to intervene in the public action.

Applying the 90-day limitation period is relatively straightforward. It begins to run from the plaintiff's receipt of the right-to-sue letter and it is satisfied by filing a complaint in court within 90 days thereafter. In federal court, where most Title VII claims are brought, an action "is commenced by filing a complaint with the court." Fed. R. Civ. P. 3. Because both the date when the 90-day limitation period begins to run and the date when it is satisfied are easily determined, it has not given rise to nearly as much litigation as the limitation period for filing charges with the EEOC. As *Evans* illustrates, it is this limitation period that has most frequently defeated claims under Title VII.

2. **Why Are the Limitation Periods So Short?** All of the time limits under Title VII are short. Even the longest—the 300-day limitation period for filing charges with the EEOC after resorting to state or local administrative agencies—is still shorter than a year. As the Supreme Court remarked in *Mohasco*, "Congress carefully prescribed a series of deadlines measured by numbers of days—rather than months or years." Indeed, these limitation periods are so short that some courts held that they were jurisdictional, presumably on the model of time limits for filing appeals or for seeking review of actions by administrative agencies. The Supreme Court eventually reached the opposite conclusion and treated these limitation periods just like other statutes of limitations, subject to waiver, tolling, and estoppel. Zipes v. Trans World Airlines, Inc., 455 U.S. 385, 392–98 (1982). Yet the reasons that Congress adopted such short limitation periods remain uncertain.

The justifications most commonly offered for statutes of limitations invoke both procedural and substantive policies. The procedural policy favors resolution of claims based on fresh evidence: testimony and documents that have not been lost or compromised through the passage of time. This policy is often framed in terms of avoiding litigation based on "stale evidence." The substantive policy favors repose: settling the parties' legal relations so that they act free of the risk that past disputes become the subject of future litigation. This policy usually favors defendants, and therefore supports shorter limitation periods, because it seeks to eliminate the uncertainty faced by potential defendants acting under the shadow of legal liability. Another policy, which combines procedural and substantive elements, also has been offered for the short limitation periods in Title VII. It is that meritorious claims are likely to be filed sooner rather than later, either because the plaintiff has better evidence supporting the claim or a more genuine belief that it is meritorious. See *Mohasco*, 447 U.S. at 820. This policy presupposes that instances of employment discrimination can be quickly detected and promptly remedied and that plaintiffs with meritorious claims are more likely to act quickly to obtain relief than plaintiffs whose claims are doubtful.

Which of these reasons justifies the decision in *Evans*? Was her claim barred because it was based on unreliable evidence? By the time she sued, it was clear that employers could not impose no-marriage rules only upon women (or in jobs, like that of flight cabin attendant, predominantly held by women). Does the need to protect the employer from liability to previously discharged plaintiffs, like Evans, alone justify barring her otherwise meritorious claim? In the terms used in the debates over Title VII, should she be penalized because she did not recognize her claim to be meritorious in the period immediately after she was discharged? At that time, judges were divided on the question whether no-marriage policies in this situation constituted sex discrimination, let alone whether they were justified as bona fide occupational qualifications. See Sprogis v. United Air Lines, Inc., 444 F.2d 1194, 1198 (7th Cir. 1971) (holding such policies to be discriminatory over the dissent of then Judge Stevens). A short limitation period designed to favor meritorious claims in fact operates to disfavor novel claims, as a discharge claim originally would have been for Evans. What justification can be offered for exempting employers from liability on such claims? See JoAnn Lach, A Liability Loophole for the Undeserving? Timeliness in Title VII Challenges After *United Airlines v. Evans*, 3 Indus. Rel. L.J. 72 (1979).

Of course, a statute of limitations does not generally permit an inquiry into the purposes behind it. It is applied as a rule, in an all-or-nothing fashion based on a definite time limit. In this respect, it contrasts with the equitable doctrine of laches which requires equitable claims to be filed only within a reasonable period. In adopting short statutes of limitations in Title VII, Congress sharply defined their character as rules. If the plaintiff has not satisfied these rules, down to the day as noted in *Mohasco*, the plaintiff's claim is barred.

3. **The "Continuing Violation" Theory.** Against the short and rigid limitation periods established by Title VII, the continuing violation theory stands as an exception. It allows a claim based on conduct that occurred outside the limitation period, like the claim in *Evans*, to be brought in circumstances in which it would otherwise be barred. In particular, if the same conduct continued, in some sense, within the limitation period, a claim based on earlier conduct can also go forward. The plaintiff's discharge in *Evans*, and even her rehiring without seniority, occurred outside the limitation period, counting back from the date a charge was filed with the EEOC. These claims therefore ordinarily would be barred because they could no longer be the subject of a timely charge. Only the defendant's continuing denial of seniority to her occurred within the limitation period. This claim could be asserted in a timely fashion, and if the continuing violation theory were available, it would also revive the plaintiff's earlier claims.

The Court denied that any such revival was possible. In its view, an earlier discriminatory act can support a charge based on a later act, but not the other way around:

> A discriminatory act which is not made the basis for a timely charge is the legal equivalent of a discriminatory act which occurred before the statute was passed. It may constitute relevant background evidence in a proceeding in which the status of a current practice is at issue, but separately considered, it is merely an unfortunate event in history which has no present legal consequences.

On the facts of *Evans*, the plaintiff could not bring a timely claim based on her earlier discharge or on her rehiring without seniority. These claims were barred by the time she filed her charge with the EEOC. Nor could these acts form the basis for a claim that the seniority system operated in a discriminatory fashion, since these acts had "no present legal consequences." The plaintiff could have brought a timely claim independently against the seniority system, arguing that it was discriminatory wholly apart from these prior acts, but she brought no such claim, as the Court pointed out in footnote 10.

The effect of the seniority system will be considered in the next note, but the Court's basic position is clear enough: The continuing violation theory is fundamentally inconsistent with the statute of limitations as it normally operates. The continuing consequences of a wrongful act, which can last indefinitely into the future, cannot be used to revive a claim that is otherwise barred. Otherwise, the plaintiff could postpone filing a claim indefinitely, so long as she continued to suffer the consequences of the wrongful act. The statute of limitations begins to run from the date of the alleged wrongful act, not from the date of the latest consequences that it has for the plaintiff. A new wrongful act, within the appropriate limitations period, is necessary to support a timely claim. That claim, however, is distinct from any claim based on an earlier act, outside the limitation period.

Is there any objection to this reasoning, at least in the terms in which it is framed? Does it presuppose that there is a hard-and-fast distinction between a wrongful act and its consequences? In *Evans*, the plaintiff was discharged under the no-marriage policy years before she filed a charge with the EEOC. This discrete act can be easily distinguished from the consequences that followed from it. Suppose, however, that when she reapplied for employment, she was denied a job because her employer had kept the no-marriage policy in effect. She could, at that time, have filed a timely charge based on this new act of discrimination. If she had, would she have been able to obtain relief for her prior discriminatory discharge? If not, what relief could she have obtained instead? Would your answer to either of those questions change if she had not reapplied for employment because her application would have been futile? In these circumstances, she could claim that she was deterred from applying for re-employment by the employer's discriminatory policy. International Brotherhood of Teamsters v. United States, 431 U.S. 324, 367–71 (1977). If she made such a claim, could she have obtained the same relief as if she had filed a timely claim based on her original discharge? Or is that act still "merely an unfortunate event in history which has no present legal consequences," as the Supreme Court says in *Evans*?

4. **Seniority and the Statute of Limitations.** Seniority blurs the distinction between prior wrongful acts and their consequences. The very purpose of a seniority system is to make an individual's prior employment history relevant to current decisions about her terms and conditions of employment. In *Evans*, the plaintiff's rate of pay, vacation and other fringe benefits, and protection from layoff all depended on her seniority. But her seniority was permanently diminished by her discharge under the no-marriage policy, which deprived her of any seniority at all when she was

eventually rehired. The consequences of this past act affected current employment decisions.

If the plaintiff had been laid off, not for lack of seniority, but only because she had previously been discharged under the no-marriage policy, she would have had a claim of discrimination based on this decision. It explicitly relied on a prior discriminatory act to impose new disadvantages upon her. Yet if she had been treated exactly the same way because she had less seniority than employees hired after she was originally discharged, she could not bring any claim of discrimination. Does this difference in outcome make any sense at all?

As we saw in the discussion of *Teamsters* in Chapter 1, seniority systems receive special protection under Title VII. Even if a seniority system perpetuates the effects of past discrimination, as it did on the facts of *Evans*, it remains permissible under § 703(h). This protection does not follow as a matter of logic, but as one of the compromises necessary to secure the enactment of the statute. Union support for Title VII was conditioned upon protection of the seniority rights of union members.

Apart from the consequences of her prior discharge, Evans asserted no claim that her employer's seniority system operated in a discriminatory fashion. Such a claim would have failed under *Teamsters*, and a claim that her prior discharge was discriminatory would have failed under the statute of limitations. Because it could no longer be the subject of a timely charge, it was, according to the Court, "the legal equivalent of a discriminatory act which occurred before the statute was passed." She was therefore in the same position as the plaintiffs in *Teamsters*, who relied on discrimination before the effective date of Title VII to support their claims that the seniority system continued to discriminate afterwards.

Does the special protection of seniority systems limit the holding of *Evans* to claims based on denial of seniority? Most of the opinion relies on general arguments about the ordinary operation of statutes of limitations, recounted in the previous note. Does the Court's discussion of seniority systems limit the scope of those arguments? Or does it only elucidate the distinction between a wrong act and its consequences? These issues are taken up in the next principal case.

Claims that a seniority system itself is discriminatory—independently of any other wrongful act—were addressed subsequently by both the Court and Congress. The Court first narrowly limited the time period during which such claims could be brought. In Lorance v. AT & T Technologies, Inc., 490 U.S. 900 (1989), the Court held that the statute of limitations begins to run on a claim against a facially neutral seniority system when the system was first established. This decision was superseded, however, by the Civil Rights Act of 1991, which amended Title VII to provide that the limitation period began to run from any of three events: when the seniority system was adopted, when the plaintiff became subject to the seniority system, or when the plaintiff was injured by the application of the seniority system. § 706(e)(2), 42 U.S.C. § 2000e–5(e)(2). This provision allows the plaintiff to choose from the latest of these events to determine when the limitation period begins to run. Does this provision expand the scope of the continuing violation theory contrary to *Evans*? Would it have made any difference on the facts of *Evans* itself?

5. **Bibliography.** Thelma A. Crivens, The Continuing Violation Theory and Systemic Discrimination: In Search of a Judicial Standard for Timely Filing, 41 Vand. L. Rev. 1171 (1988); Charles C. Jackson & John H. Matheson, The Continuing Violation Theory and the Concept of Jurisdiction in Title VII Suits, 67 Geo. L.J. 811 (1979); Douglas Laycock, Continuing Violations, Disparate Impact in Compensation and Other Title VII Issues, 49 L. & Contemp. Prob. 53 (1986); Elad Peled, Rethinking the Continuing Violation Doctrine: The Application of Statutes of Limitations to Continuing Tort Claims, 41 Ohio Northern U. L. Rev. 343 (2015).

National Railroad Passenger Corp. v. Morgan

536 U.S. 101 (2002).

■ JUSTICE THOMAS delivered the opinion of the Court.

Respondent Abner Morgan, Jr., sued petitioner National Railroad Passenger Corporation (Amtrak) under Title VII of the Civil Rights Act of 1964, as amended, 42 U.S.C. § 2000e et seq., alleging that he had been subjected to discrete discriminatory and retaliatory acts and had experienced a racially hostile work environment throughout his employment. Section 2000e–5(e)(1) requires that a Title VII plaintiff file a charge with the Equal Employment Opportunity Commission (EEOC) either 180 or 300 days "after the alleged unlawful employment practice occurred." We consider whether, and under what circumstances, a Title VII plaintiff may file suit on events that fall outside this statutory time period.

The United States Court of Appeals for the Ninth Circuit held that a plaintiff may sue on claims that would ordinarily be time barred so long as they either are "sufficiently related" to incidents that fall within the statutory period or are part of a systematic policy or practice of discrimination that took place, at least in part, within the limitations period. We reverse in part and affirm in part. We hold that the statute precludes recovery for discrete acts of discrimination or retaliation that occur outside the statutory time period. We also hold that consideration of the entire scope of a hostile work environment claim, including behavior alleged outside the statutory time period, is permissible for the purposes of assessing liability, so long as any act contributing to that hostile environment takes place within the statutory time period. The application of equitable doctrines, however, may either limit or toll the time period within which an employee must file a charge.

I

On February 27, 1995, Abner J. Morgan, Jr., a black male, filed a charge of discrimination and retaliation against Amtrak with the EEOC and cross-filed with the California Department of Fair Employment and

Housing. Morgan alleged that during the time period that he worked for Amtrak he was "consistently harassed and disciplined more harshly than other employees on account of his race." The EEOC issued a "Notice of Right to Sue" on July 3, 1996, and Morgan filed this lawsuit on October 2, 1996. While some of the allegedly discriminatory acts about which Morgan complained occurred within 300 days of the time that he filed his charge with the EEOC, many took place prior to that time period. Amtrak filed a motion, arguing, among other things, that it was entitled to summary judgment on all incidents that occurred more than 300 days before the filing of Morgan's EEOC charge. The District Court granted summary judgment in part to Amtrak, holding that the company could not be liable for conduct occurring before May 3, 1994, because that conduct fell outside of the 300-day filing period. The court employed a test established by the United States Court of Appeals for the Seventh Circuit in Galloway v. General Motors Service Parts Operations, 78 F.3d 1164 (C.A.7 1996): A "plaintiff may not base [the] suit on conduct that occurred outside the statute of limitations unless it would have been unreasonable to expect the plaintiff to sue before the statute ran on that conduct, as in a case in which the conduct could constitute, or be recognized, as actionable harassment only in the light of events that occurred later, within the period of the statute of limitations." Id., at 1167. The District Court held that "because Morgan believed that he was being discriminated against at the time that all of these acts occurred, it would not be unreasonable to expect that Morgan should have filed an EEOC charge on these acts before the limitations period on these claims ran."

Morgan appealed. The United States Court of Appeals for the Ninth Circuit reversed, relying on its previous articulation of the continuing violation doctrine, which "allows courts to consider conduct that would ordinarily be time barred 'as long as the untimely incidents represent an ongoing unlawful employment practice.'" 232 F.3d 1008, 1014 (C.A.9 2000) (quoting Anderson v. Reno, 190 F.3d 930, 936 (C.A.9 1999)). . . .

We granted certiorari and now reverse in part and affirm in part.

II

. . . Title 42 U.S.C. § 2000e–5(e)(1) is a charge filing provision that "specifies with precision" the prerequisites that a plaintiff must satisfy before filing suit. Alexander v. Gardner-Denver Co., 415 U.S. 36, 47 (1974). An individual must file a charge within the statutory time period and serve notice upon the person against whom the charge is made. In a State that has an entity with the authority to grant or seek relief with respect to the alleged unlawful practice, an employee who initially files a grievance with that agency must file the charge with the EEOC within 300 days of the employment practice; in all other States, the charge must be filed within 180 days. A claim is time barred if it is not filed within these time limits.

For our purposes, the critical sentence of the charge filing provision is: "A charge under this section shall be filed within one hundred and eighty days after the alleged unlawful employment practice occurred." § 2000e–5(e)(1) (emphasis added). The operative terms are "shall," "after . . . occurred," and "unlawful employment practice." "[S]hall" makes the act of filing a charge within the specified time period mandatory. See, e.g., Lexecon Inc. v. Milberg Weiss Bershad Hynes & Lerach, 523 U.S. 26, 35 (1998) ("the mandatory 'shall,' . . . normally creates an obligation impervious to judicial discretion"). "[O]ccurred" means that the practice took place or happened in the past. The requirement, therefore, that the charge be filed "after" the practice "occurred" tells us that a litigant has up to 180 or 300 days after the unlawful practice happened to file a charge with the EEOC.

The critical questions, then, are: What constitutes an "unlawful employment practice" and when has that practice "occurred"? Our task is to answer these questions for both discrete discriminatory acts and hostile work environment claims. The answer varies with the practice.

A

We take the easier question first. A discrete retaliatory or discriminatory act "occurred" on the day that it "happened." A party, therefore, must file a charge within either 180 or 300 days of the date of the act or lose the ability to recover for it. . . .

We have repeatedly interpreted the term "practice" to apply to a discrete act or single "occurrence," even when it has a connection to other acts. For example, in Electrical Workers v. Robbins & Myers, Inc., 429 U.S. 229, 234 (1976), an employee asserted that his complaint was timely filed because the date "the alleged unlawful employment practice occurred" was the date after the conclusion of a grievance arbitration procedure, rather than the earlier date of his discharge. The discharge, he contended, was "tentative" and "nonfinal" until the grievance and arbitration procedure ended. Not so, the Court concluded, because the discriminatory act occurred on the date of discharge—the date that the parties understood the termination to be final. Similarly, in Bazemore v. Friday, 478 U.S. 385 (1986) (per curiam), a pattern-or-practice case, when considering a discriminatory salary structure, the Court noted that although the salary discrimination began prior to the date that the act was actionable under Title VII, "each week's paycheck that deliver less to a black than to a similarly situated white is a wrong actionable under Title VII. . . ."

This Court has also held that discrete acts that fall within the statutory time period do not make timely acts that fall outside the time period. In United Air Lines, Inc. v. Evans, 431 U.S. 553 (1977), United forced Evans to resign after she married because of its policy against married female flight attendants. Although Evans failed to file a timely charge following her initial separation, she nonetheless claimed that United was guilty of a present, continuing violation of Title VII because its seniority system failed to give her credit for her prior service once she was re-hired. The Court disagreed, concluding that "United was entitled to treat [Evans' resignation] as lawful after [she] failed to file a charge of discrimination within the" charge filing period then allowed by the statute. At the same time, however, the Court noted that "it may constitute relevant background evidence in a proceeding in which the status of a current practice is at issue." The emphasis, however, "should not be placed on mere continuity" but on "whether any present violation exist[ed]." (Emphasis in original.)

In Delaware State College v. Ricks, 449 U.S. 250 (1980), the Court evaluated the timeliness of an EEOC complaint filed by a professor who argued that he had been denied academic tenure because of his national origin. Following the decision to deny tenure, the employer offered him a " 'terminal' " contract to teach an additional year. Claiming, in effect, a " 'continuing violation,' " the professor argued that the time period did not begin to run until his actual termination. The Court rejected this argument: "Mere continuity of employment, without more, is insufficient to prolong the life of a cause of action for employment discrimination." In order for the time period to commence with the discharge, "he should have identified the alleged discriminatory acts that continued until, or occurred at the time of, the actual termination of his employment." He could not use a termination that fell within the limitations period to pull in the time-barred discriminatory act. Nor could a time-barred act justify filing a charge concerning a termination that was not independently discriminatory.

We derive several principles from these cases. First, discrete discriminatory acts are not actionable if time barred, even when they are related to acts alleged in timely filed charges. Each discrete discriminatory act starts a new clock for filing charges alleging that act. The charge, therefore, must be filed within the 180- or 300-day time period after the discrete discriminatory act occurred. The existence of past acts and the employee's prior knowledge of their occurrence, however, does not bar employees from filing charges about related discrete acts so long as the acts are independently discriminatory and charges addressing those acts are themselves timely filed. Nor does the statute bar an employee from using the prior acts as background evidence in support of a timely claim.

As we have held, however, this time period for filing a charge is subject to equitable doctrines such as tolling or estoppel. See Zipes v. Trans World Airlines, Inc., 455 U.S. 385, 393 (1982) ("We hold that filing a timely charge of discrimination with the EEOC is not a jurisdictional prerequisite to suit in federal court, but a requirement that, like a statute of limitations, is subject to waiver, estoppel, and equitable tolling"). Courts may evaluate whether it would be proper to apply such doctrines, although they are to be applied sparingly. See Baldwin County Welcome Center v. Brown, 466 U.S. 147, 152 (1984) (per curiam). ("Procedural requirements established by Congress for gaining access to the federal courts are not to be disregarded by courts out of a vague sympathy for particular litigants").

The Court of Appeals applied the continuing violations doctrine to what it termed "serial violations," holding that so long as one act falls within the charge filing period, discriminatory and retaliatory acts that are plausibly or sufficiently related to that act may also be considered for the purposes of liability. With respect to this holding, therefore, we reverse.

Discrete acts such as termination, failure to promote, denial of transfer, or refusal to hire are easy to identify. Each incident of discrimination and each retaliatory adverse employment decision constitutes a separate actionable "unlawful employment practice." Morgan can only file a charge to cover discrete acts that "occurred" within the appropriate time period. While Morgan alleged that he suffered from numerous discriminatory and retaliatory acts from the date that he was hired through March 3, 1995, the date that he was fired, only incidents that took place within the timely filing period are actionable. Because Morgan first filed his charge with an appropriate state agency, only those acts that occurred 300 days before February 27, 1995, the day that Morgan filed his charge, are actionable. During that time period, Morgan contends that he was wrongfully suspended and charged with a violation of Amtrak's "Rule L" for insubordination while failing to complete work assigned to him, denied training, and falsely accused of threatening a manager. All prior discrete discriminatory acts are untimely filed and no longer actionable.

B

Hostile environment claims are different in kind from discrete acts. Their very nature involves repeated conduct. See 1 B. Lindemann & P. Grossman, Employment Discrimination Law 348–349 (3d ed. 1996) (hereinafter Lindemann) ("The repeated nature of the harassment or its intensity constitutes evidence that management knew or should have known of its existence"). The "unlawful employment practice" therefore cannot be said to occur on any particular day. It occurs over a series of days or perhaps years and, in direct contrast to discrete acts, a single act of harassment may not be actionable on its own. See Harris v. Forklift Systems, Inc., 510 U.S. 17, 21 (1993) ("As we pointed out in Meritor [Savings Bank, FSB v. Vinson, 477 U.S. 57, 67 (1986),] 'mere utterance of an . . . epithet which engenders offensive feelings in a[n] employee,' (internal quotation marks omitted) does not sufficiently affect the conditions of employment to implicate Title VII"). Such claims are based on the cumulative effect of individual acts.

"We have repeatedly made clear that although [Title VII] mentions specific employment decisions with immediate consequences, the scope of the prohibition 'is not limited to "economic" or tangible" discrimination," ' Harris, 510 U.S., at 21 (quoting Meritor Savings Bank,

FSB v. Vinson, 477 U.S. at 64, and that it covers more than 'terms' and 'conditions' in the narrow contractual sense.") Faragher v. Boca Raton, 524 U.S. 775, 786 (1998) (quoting Oncale v. Sundowner Offshore Services, Inc., 523 U.S. 75, 78 (1998)). As the Court stated in Harris, "the phrase 'terms, conditions, or privileges of employment' [of 42 U.S.C. § 2000e–2(a)(1)] evinces a congressional intent 'to strike at the entire spectrum of disparate treatment of men and women' in employment, which includes requiring people to work in a discriminatorily hostile or abusive environment." 510 U.S., at 21. "Workplace conduct is not measured in isolation . . ." Clark County School Dist. v. Breeden, 532 U.S. 268, 270 (2001) (per curiam). Thus, "when the workplace is permeated with 'discriminatory intimidation, ridicule, and insult,' that is 'sufficiently severe or pervasive to alter the conditions of the victim's employment and create an abusive working environment,' Title VII is violated." Harris, 510 U.S., at 21 (internal citations omitted).

In determining whether an actionable hostile work environment claim exists, we look to "all the circumstances," including "the frequency of the discriminatory conduct; its severity; whether it is physically threatening or humiliating, or a mere offensive utterance; and whether it unreasonably interferes with an employee's work performance." Id., at 23. To assess whether a court may, for the purposes of determining liability, review all such conduct, including those acts that occur outside the filing period, we again look to the statute. It provides that a charge must be filed within 180 or 300 days "after the alleged unlawful employment practice occurred." A hostile work environment claim is comprised of a series of separate acts that collectively constitute one "unlawful employment practice." 42 U.S.C. § 2000e–5(e)(1). The timely filing provision only requires that a Title VII plaintiff file a charge within a certain number of days after the unlawful practice happened. It does not matter, for purposes of the statute, that some of the component acts of the hostile work environment fall outside the statutory time period. Provided that an act contributing to the claim occurs within the filing period, the entire time period of the hostile environment may be considered by a court for the purposes of determining liability.

That act need not, however, be the last act. As long as the employer has engaged in enough activity to make out an actionable hostile environment claim, an unlawful employment practice has "occurred," even if it is still occurring. Subsequent events, however, may still be part of the one hostile work environment claim and a charge may be filed at a later date and still encompass the whole.

It is precisely because the entire hostile work environment encompasses a single unlawful employment practice that we do not hold, as have some of the Circuits, that the plaintiff may not base a suit on individual acts that occurred outside the statute of limitations unless it would have been unreasonable to expect the plaintiff to sue before the statute ran on such conduct. The statute does not separate individual acts that are part of the hostile environment claim from the whole for the purposes of timely filing and liability. And the statute does not contain a requirement that the employee file a charge prior to 180 or 300 days "after" the single unlawful practice "occurred." Given, therefore, that the incidents comprising a hostile work environment are part of one unlawful employment practice, the employer may be liable for all acts that are part of this single claim. In order for the charge to be timely, the employee need only file a charge within 180 or 300 days of any act that is part of the hostile work environment.

The following scenarios illustrate our point: (1) Acts on days 1–400 create a hostile work environment. The employee files the charge on day 401. Can the employee recover for that part of the hostile work environment that occurred in the first 100 days? (2) Acts contribute to a hostile environment on days 1–100 and on day 401, but there are no acts between days 101–400. Can the act occurring on day 401 pull the other acts in for the purposes of liability? In truth, all other things being equal, there is little difference between the two scenarios as a hostile environment constitutes one "unlawful employment practice" and it does not matter whether nothing occurred within the intervening 301 days so long as each act is part of the whole. Nor, if sufficient activity occurred by day 100 to make out a claim, does it matter that the employee knows on that day that an actionable claim happened; on day 401 all incidents are still part of the same claim. On the other hand, if an act on day 401 had no relation to the acts between days 1–100, or for some other reason, such as certain intervening action by the employer, was no longer part of the same hostile environment claim, then the employee cannot recover for the previous acts, at least not by reference to the day 401 act.

Our conclusion with respect to the incidents that may be considered for the purposes of liability is reinforced by the fact that the statute in no way bars a plaintiff from recovering damages for that portion of the hostile environment that falls outside the period for filing a timely charge. Morgan correctly notes that the timeliness requirement does not dictate the amount of recoverable damages. It is but one in a series of provisions requiring that the parties take action within specified time periods, see, e.g., §§ 2000e–5(b), (c), (d), none of which function as specific limitations on damages.

Explicit limitations on damages are found elsewhere in the statute. Section 1981a(b)(3), for example, details specific limitations on compensatory and punitive damages. Likewise, § 2000e–5(g)(1) allows for recovery of back pay liability for up to two years prior to the filing of the charge. If Congress intended to limit liability to conduct occurring in the period within which the party must file the charge, it seems unlikely that Congress would have allowed recovery for two years of back pay. And the fact that Congress expressly limited the amount of recoverable damages elsewhere to a particular time period indicates that the timely filing provision was not meant to serve as a specific limitation either on damages or the conduct that may be considered for the purposes of one actionable hostile work environment claim. . . .

Simply put, § 2000e–5(e)(1) is a provision specifying when a charge is timely filed and only has the consequence of limiting liability because filing a timely charge is a prerequisite to having an actionable claim. A court's task is to determine whether the acts about which an employee complains are part of the same actionable hostile work environment practice, and if so, whether any act falls within the statutory time period.

With respect to Morgan's hostile environment claim, the Court of Appeals concluded that "the pre-and post-limitations period incidents involve the same type of employment actions, occurred relatively frequently, and were perpetrated by the same managers." To support his claims of a hostile environment, Morgan presented evidence from a number of other employees that managers made racial jokes, performed racially derogatory acts, made negative comments regarding the capacity of blacks to be supervisors, and used various racial epithets. Although many of the acts upon which his claim depends occurred outside the 300 day filing period, we cannot say that they are not part of the same actionable hostile environment claim. On this point, we affirm.

C

Our holding does not leave employers defenseless against employees who bring hostile work environment claims that extend over long periods of time. Employers have recourse when a plaintiff unreasonably delays filing a charge. As noted in Zipes v. Trans World Airlines, Inc., 455 U.S. 385 (1982), the filing period is not a jurisdictional prerequisite to filing a Title VII suit. Rather, it is a requirement subject to waiver, estoppel, and equitable tolling "when equity so requires." These equitable doctrines allow us to honor Title VII's remedial purpose "without negating the particular purpose of the filing requirement, to give prompt notice to the employer."

This Court previously noted that despite the procedural protections of the statute "a defendant in a Title VII enforcement action might still be significantly handicapped in making his defense because of an inordinate EEOC delay in filing the action after exhausting its conciliation efforts." Occidental Life Ins. Co. of Cal. v. EEOC, 432 U.S. 355, 373 (1977). The same is true when the delay is caused by the employee, rather than by the EEOC. Cf. Albemarle Paper Co. v. Moody, 422 U.S. 405, 424 (1975) ("party may not be 'entitled' to relief if its conduct of the cause has improperly and substantially prejudiced the other party"). In such cases, the federal courts have the discretionary power to "to locate 'a just result' in light of the circumstances peculiar to the case."

In addition to other equitable defenses, therefore, an employer may raise a laches defense, which bars a plaintiff from maintaining a suit if he unreasonably delays in filing a suit and as a result harms the defendant. This defense " 'requires proof of (1) lack of diligence by the party against whom the defense is asserted, and (2) prejudice to the party asserting the defense.' " Kansas v. Colorado, 514 U.S. 673, 687 (1995) (quoting Costello v. United States, 365 U.S. 265, 282 (1961)). We do not address questions here such as "how—and how much—prejudice must be shown" or "what consequences follow if laches is established." 2 Lindemann 1496–1500. We observe only that employers may raise various defenses in the face of unreasonable and prejudicial delay.

III

We conclude that a Title VII plaintiff raising claims of discrete discriminatory or retaliatory acts must file his charge within the appropriate time period—180 or 300 days—set forth in 42 U.S.C. § 2000e–5(e)(1). A charge alleging a hostile work environment claim, however, will not be time barred so long as all acts which constitute the claim are part of the same unlawful employment practice and at least one act falls within the time period. Neither holding, however, precludes a court from applying equitable doctrines that may toll or limit the time period.

For the foregoing reasons, the Court of Appeals' judgment is affirmed in part and reversed in part, and the case is remanded for further proceedings consistent with this opinion.

It is so ordered.

[Justice O'Connor filed an opinion dissenting in part, on the ground that the time limits under Title VII should apply to "all types of Title VII suits, including those based on a claim that a plaintiff has been subjected to a hostile work environment."]

NOTES ON *NATIONAL RAILROAD PASSENGER CORP. V. MORGAN*

1. **Discrete Versus Continuous Acts.** Just as *Evans* distinguishes between discriminatory acts and their effects, *Morgan* distinguishes between discrete acts and continuous acts. Only discrete acts that occurred within the limitation period—within either 180 or 300 days of filing with the EEOC—can be the subject of a timely claim. Discrete acts include "termination, failure to promote, denial of transfer, or refusal to hire." These acts are easy to identify and each independently supports a claim of discrimination. Continuous acts, like hostile environment claims, necessarily extend over a period of time and do not accrue until a series of acts becomes "severe or pervasive." These claims can be brought if one element of the alleged harassment occurs within the limitation period. Moreover, the remedies available to the plaintiff extend over the entire course of conduct, even the part that lies outside the limitation period.

Does this distinction depend upon the evidence available to the plaintiff or upon the essential nature of the illegal conduct? Much discriminatory activity is hidden from the plaintiff's view, as we have repeatedly seen, by various forms of pretext or otherwise inadequate justifications offered by the employer. In general, however, the limitation period begins to run when the plaintiff discovers that he has suffered an adverse employment decision, not when he discovers that it is or might be discriminatory. Thus, in a case involving denial of tenure, the limitation period begins to run when the decision to deny tenure is made and communicated to the plaintiff. Delaware State College v. Ricks, 449 U.S. 250, 259 (1980). Conversely, the limitation begins to run on a claims for constructive discharge when the plaintiff notifies the employer of the decisions to quit. Green v. Brennan, 136 S. Ct. 1769 (2016). Only rarely does conduct of the defendant alone stop the limitation period from running, and statements by the employer's managers and officers denying that there has been discrimination almost never are sufficient to do so. See, e.g., Bishop v. Gainer, 272 F.3d 1009, 1014–15 (7th Cir. 2001) (rejecting tolling and equitable estoppel on this ground). A continuing violation can therefore be found only when the adverse effects of a series of acts only gradually become apparent to the plaintiff.

In hostile environment claims, it is the degree of adversity from a series of acts that may only become apparent over a period of time. Does the Court apply the continuing violation theory to such claims to prevent the plaintiff from being caught in a bind: between filing a claim too early and filing it too late? It would be too early if there were not enough evidence of severe or pervasive hostility to support the claim on the merits. It would be too late if the statute of limitations had run on most of the conduct giving rise to the claim. The Court avoids this dilemma by finding all of the harassment actionable if any of it occurs within the limitation period. Are any other claims of discrimination similar in their cumulative nature? A claim of disparate impact might arise gradually, as a test administered over a period of time or as a selection procedure is used repeatedly and its adverse impact upon a particular minority group becomes apparent. Does *Morgan* rule out the continuing violation theory in any case involving failure to promote or refusal to hire? Is that because the harm to the individual plaintiff is apparent as soon as the decision is communicated to him? If the plaintiff alleges disparate impact, isn't he in the same position as the plaintiff in a hostile environment case, knowing that he has suffered some harm but awaiting further evidence to determine if it is the kind of harm prohibited by Title VII?

2. **Time Limits for the Award of Back Pay.** A logical extension of the reasoning in *Evans* and *Morgan* is that available remedies extend back only as far as the actionable discrimination. Claims based on earlier acts are barred by the statute of limitations and do not support any award of relief at all, while claims based on later acts can only support relief for later harms caused by those acts. As *Morgan* notes, however, a provision on remedies allows the award of back pay up for as long as two years before a charge is filed with the EEOC. § 706(g)(1), 42 U.S.C. § 2000e–5(g)(1). This provision does not dispense with the need for the plaintiff to file a timely charge, which must be based on some discriminatory act that occurs within the limitation. But if such a charge is filed, the provision raises the possibility of awards of back pay that extend back before the limitation period. The two-year limit

on back pay is over twice as long as the limitation on filing with the EEOC, which is, at most, 300 days.

This provision originated in the Equal Employment Opportunity Act of 1972 and was added to Title VII at the instance of employers, who originally proposed a two-year limit going back from the date that a claim was filed in court. At the time, charges could remain for years under consideration by the EEOC, so that a two-year limit on back pay from the date of filing in court protected employers from liability for back pay that accrued during delays in the administrative process. In Congress, however, this proposal was changed to its current form, where the two-year limit runs back from the date of filing with the EEOC. See S. Rep. No. 92–681, at 18–19 (1972). The current provision is no longer favorable to employers, but the opposite. It extends their liability for back pay beyond what would ordinarily be provided by the statute of limitations.

This ironic turn of events has left the courts with the task of reconciling the two-year limit on back pay with the shorter limitation periods for filing with the EEOC. *Morgan* suggests two different ways to reconcile these time limits: first, by applying the two-year limit on back pay only to claims of continuing violations; or second, by distinguishing between limits on remedies and those on filing. The first approach is implied by the Court's discussion of this issue only in connection with its argument for treating hostile environment claims as continuing violations. If the Court meant the limitation to apply to discrete acts of discrimination, it would have raised this issue earlier in its opinion. The second, broader, approach is based on what the Court actually says: "If Congress intended to limit liability to conduct occurring in the period within which the party must file the charge, it seems unlikely that Congress would have allowed recovery for two years of back pay." Does this language open up the possibility that a series of discrete acts, some of which extend into the limitation period, can support recovery outside it? For instance, a claim of discrimination in pay can, as we saw in the previous note, easily involve payments within the limitation period, making the charge of discrimination timely. Nevertheless, the same claim can also involve payments that occurred earlier, supporting remedies within the two-year time limit. If this interpretation is accepted, does it create another version of the continuing violation theory, applicable to the question of remedies of alone?

3. ***Ledbetter v. Goodyear Tire & Rubber Co.*** In *Morgan*, the Supreme Court cited Bazemore v. Friday, 478 U.S. 385 (1986) (per curiam), as an example of a case in which repeated discriminatory acts do not amount to a continuing violation. Nevertheless, the claim in that case, for discrimination in pay, could be the subject of a timely charge because the payments extended into the limitation period and the discrimination was renewed with each payment. A far more controversial pay case came before the Supreme Court in Ledbetter v. Goodyear Tire & Rubber Co., Inc., 550 U.S. 618 (2007), in which the plaintiff claimed that she had systematically received lower raises than men, most of which occurred outside the limitation period. The Court held that she could recover only for instances of lower pay that both occurred within the limitation period and were accompanied by

discrimination within that period. Unlike *Bazemore*, the plaintiff was not a victim of discrimination that automatically renewed with each payment. As *Ledbetter* reasoned, claims of discrimination in pay under Title VII involve discrete acts, which must each be the subject of a timely charge. See Nicole C. Leet, *Ledbetter v. Goodyear Tire*: Past Discrimination and the Fallacy of the Paycheck Accrual Theory, 31 Am. J. Trial Advoc. 215 (2007).

A counterexample to this principle might be found in cases such as Corning Glass Works v. Brennan, 417 U.S. 188 (1974), which appears in the material on the Equal Pay Act in Chapter 5. That case turned entirely on the origins of a shift differential for night inspectors used to attract men to this position in the 1920s. Because it was a claim under the Equal Pay Act, it was also subject to more lenient treatment under the applicable statute of limitations, allowing claims for discrimination based on pay decisions made well outside it. All that was necessary was that women received unequal pay within the limitation period. This is, in any event how *Corning Glass Works* has been interpreted by the lower federal courts. See, e.g., Pollis v. New School for Social Research, 132 F.3d 115, 119 (2d Cir. 1997). The special treatment of claims under the Equal Pay Act was recognized by the Supreme Court in *Ledbetter*, but distinguished from the treatment of claims under Title VII. The grounds for the distinction were the absence of any requirement under the Equal Pay Act that the plaintiff file a charge with the EEOC or that the plaintiff prove intentional discrimination. Are these grounds persuasive? Should it matter whether a statute of limitations applies to filing a charge with the EEOC rather than, as under the Equal Pay Act, filing directly in court? Doesn't the Equal Pay Act also require evidence of intentional discrimination in the form of proof that men and women are paid differently for doing jobs of "equal skill, effort, and responsibility, and which are performed under similar working conditions"? 29 U.S.C. § 206(d)(1).

4. **Logic Versus Practicality in *Ledbetter*.** At one level, the reasoning of *Ledbetter* is irrefutable. If decisions about pay are discrete acts, then the statute of limitations begins to run as soon as the decision is made. Subsequently issued paychecks are then simply the consequences of a past discrete act. It follows that paychecks issued within the limitation period do not revive claims based on a decision made before the limitation period that were not themselves the subject of a timely claim. That decision is, in the words of *United Air Lines, Inc. v. Evans*, merely "a past event which has no present legal consequences."

This argument depends upon the premise that the decision to set pay is a discrete act independent of the later payments to the employee. The majority in *Ledbetter* assimilates decisions about pay to other discrete acts identified in *Morgan*, such as discrimination in hiring, firing, or promotions. These acts all have in common the feature that once the decision is made, the plaintiff has a claim that can be the subject of an actionable charge of discrimination. Claims of hostile environment discrimination, by contrast, might take some time to develop. The paychecks subsequently received by the plaintiff then determine only the amount of damages that are recoverable, not the existence of discrimination. This reasoning from the nature of the plaintiff's claim certainly provides a tenable basis for the majority's characterization of decisions about pay as discrete acts.

The dissent in *Ledbetter* disagreed less over the logic of the majority's analysis than over its practical implications for the plaintiff, who learns of any discrimination in pay long after the limitation period for filing with the EEOC has expired. In many workplaces, she will not have ready access to information about how her pay was set or what her co-workers' pay is. Unlike a discharge decision, she would not immediately be put on notice that she has suffered the adverse consequences of not being paid as much as she deserved as a matter of equal treatment. Consequently, she might well lose her claim even before she knows she has it.

Arrayed against these practical concerns on the plaintiff's side are the practical concerns of the defendant about litigation, as in *Corning Glass Works*, that focus on compensation decisions long in the past. The defendant might have lost all its records about how the plaintiff's pay was set, and the supervisors and managers who made those decisions might have departed. Meanwhile, the defendant's potential liability would continue to mount as the plaintiff continued to receive allegedly discriminatory pay. How serious are these concerns if the plaintiff has the burden of proof on the issue of discrimination? Under Title VII, it is the plaintiff, not the defendant, who suffers most from lost or inaccessible evidence, causing her to fail to meet her burden of production and resulting in summary judgment or judgment as a matter of law against her. If the plaintiff is willing to take the risk of litigation with uncertain sources of proof and the risk of a dismissal, why should the defendant get the benefit of an added defense under the statute of limitations?

5. **The Lilly Ledbetter Fair Pay Act.** The decision in *Ledbetter* elicited a firestorm of controversy, resulting in the passage of the Lilly Ledbetter Fair Pay Act early in 2009. The Act specifically disapproves of *Ledbetter*, following the pattern set by other recent civil rights legislation, such as the Civil Rights Act of 1991 and the Americans with Disabilities Act Amendments Act of 2008. The Act amends § 706(e) of Title VII (and analogous provisions in other employment discrimination statutes) to provide that "an unlawful employment practice occurs, with respect to discrimination in compensation in violation of this title, when a discriminatory compensation decision or other practice is adopted, when an individual becomes subject to a discriminatory compensation decision or other practice, or when an individual is affected by application of a discriminatory compensation decision or other practice, including each time wages, benefits, or other compensation is paid, resulting in whole or in part from such a decision or other practice." S. 181 § 3, 111th Cong., 1st Sess. (2009). The full text of the Act appears in the Statutory Appendix, mainly as an amendment to § 706 (but also as to the corresponding provisions in the other laws against employment discrimination).

The Act is modeled on the provisions in § 706(e)(2) that govern the statute of limitations for seniority claims. The limitation period begins to run from the latest of three dates: when a decision or practice is made or adopted; when the plaintiff becomes subject to it; or whenever the plaintiff is affected by it, "including each time wages, benefits, or other compensation is paid." Although this new provision applies only to claims "with respect to discrimination in compensation," the claim need not result from a "compensation decision," but may result from any "other practice." Presumably this language does not cover a claim of discriminatory discharge, for which the plaintiff seeks back pay only as a remedy. In such a case, the plaintiff receives no further paycheck from which the limitation can begin to run. But does this language apply to any case in which the plaintiff continues to receive a paycheck, but claims that her pay was reduced for a discriminatory reason? Does it, for instance, apply to a claim that the plaintiff's pay was reduced because of a discriminatory demotion? If so, the Act essentially repeals the statute of limitations as to any such claim, leaving only the two-year time period for back pay awards in § 706(g)(1) as a restriction on remedies.

The effective date of the Act goes back to May 28, 2007, the day before *Ledbetter* was decided, making it applicable to all cases "that are pending on or after that date." § 6. The Act accordingly would have changed the outcome in *Ledbetter* itself, assuming that the judgment against Ledbetter could have been re-opened after the Act was passed. Even retroactive legislation cannot, however, re-open final judgments reached by the judiciary, under the constitutional doctrine of separation of powers. Plaut v. Spendthrift Farm, Inc., 514 U.S. 211 (1995). The new Act therefore applies to all cases pending on or after May 28, 2007, and still pending after the Act was passed. By giving the Act retroactive effect, Congress demonstrated how strongly it disagreed with the decision in *Ledbetter*.

This reaction to *Ledbetter* was widely shared. Justice Ginsburg, who authored the dissent in *Ledbetter*, took the unusual step of advocating the need for legislation to overrule the decision at a keynote address to the Alaska bar in 2008. See 32 Alaska Bar Rag., Apr.–June 2008 at 1. The decision also was widely criticized in the law review literature. See Jason R. Bent, What the Lilly Ledbetter Fair Pay Act Doesn't Do: "Discrete Acts" and the Future of Pattern or Practice Litigation, 33 Rutgers L. Rec. 31 (2009); Deborah L. Brake & Joanna L. Grossman, The Failure of Title VII as a Rights-Claiming System, 86 N.C. L. Rev. 859 (2008); Katherine A. Eidmann, *Ledbetter* in Congress: The Limits of a Narrow Legislative Override, 117 Yale L.J. 971 (2008); Paula A. Monopoli, In a Different Voice: Lessons from Ledbetter, 34 J.C. & U.L. 555 (2008); Charles A. Sullivan, Raising the Dead?: The Lilly Ledbetter Fair Pay Act, 84 Tul. L. Rev. 499 (2010); Jonathon Wright, Note, The Problematic Application of Title VII's Limitations Period in the Pay Discrimination Context: *Ledbetter v. Goodyear*, the Ledbetter Fair Pay Act, and an Argument for a Modified Balancing Test, 42 Ind. L. Rev. 503 (2009).

OTHER REQUIREMENTS FOR FILING A TIMELY CHARGE WITH THE EEOC

1. **Filing with State or Local Agencies.** As noted in the introduction to this chapter, Title VII requires that the plaintiff file with state or local agencies before filing with the EEOC. If such agencies are available, the

plaintiff is entitled to a longer limitation period for filing with the EEOC, generally 300 days rather than 180 days. The interaction between procedures before the state or local agency and those before the EEOC raises a number of complex questions, most of them resolved in favor of simplifying the procedural obstacles faced by plaintiffs, many of them unrepresented by counsel before an action has been filed.

The first question is whether the plaintiff must file with the state or local agency in the time limit established by state law. Ascertaining the correct limitation period under state law and its interaction with the limitation period under Title VII itself could become a very complicated issue, depending on the length of the state limitation period and whether it suspended the relevant limitation period under Title VII. This question could arise in many cases, under different variations depending upon state law, and if state law were decisive, it might cut off the plaintiff's claim at its inception because of failure to comply with state time limits. Perhaps for this reason, the Supreme Court decided that failure to comply with a state or local limitation period did not affect the plaintiff's ability to bring a claim under federal law. Oscar Mayer & Co. v. Evans, 441 U.S. 750 (1979). Although this case concerned a claim under the Age Discrimination in Employment Act (ADEA), the Court interpreted language in that statute taken verbatim from Title VII. That provision requires only "the filing of a written and signed statement of the facts upon which the proceeding is based" in order to commence proceedings under state or local law. § 706(c), 42 U.S.C. § 2000e–5(c). The Court held that this provision did not require compliance with the state or local limitation period in order to exhaust state or local administrative remedies before filing a claim under Title VII. Complying with these limitation periods, of course, still remains necessary if the plaintiff seeks to pursue a claim under state or local law. The Supreme Court did nothing to disturb the ordinary operation of such time limits on claims under state or local law.

A second question concerns the effect of the plaintiff's filing with the EEOC before filing with the state or local agency. Title VII seems to bar any premature filing with the EEOC by providing that no such filing can be made "before the expiration of sixty days after proceedings have been commenced under State or local law, unless such proceedings have been earlier terminated." § 706(c), 42 U.S.C. § 2000e–5(c). In Love v. Pullman Co., 404 U.S. 522 (1972), however, the Supreme Court upheld regulations of the EEOC that relieved the plaintiff of the need to file a charge initially with a state or local agency to which deferral was necessary. Under these regulations, the plaintiff could initially file a charge with the EEOC, which would then refer it to the state or local agency in order to satisfy the 60-day deferral period. During that period, the state or local agency had exclusive jurisdiction, and upon its expiration, the charge could then automatically be revived in the EEOC.

A third question concerns the interaction between this deferral period and the limitation period for filing with the EEOC. Both of these periods are themselves subdivided into two components. The deferral period lasts either for 60 days or until termination of state or local proceedings, whichever occurs earlier. § 706(c), 42 U.S.C. § 2000e–5(c). The limitation period for filing with the EEOC when such proceedings are available is either 300 days or 30 days from notice of termination of state or local proceedings, again whichever occurs earlier. The interaction of all these time limits was first considered in Mohasco Corp. v. Silver, 447 U.S. 807 (1980). Emphasizing the short limitation periods established by Title VII, the Supreme Court held that a charge could be effectively filed with the EEOC only after the deferral period had expired. It followed that a charge actually filed with the EEOC and referred to a state or local agency under *Love v. Pullman Co.* would be effectively filed with the EEOC only after it was revived by the EEOC when the deferral period expired.

This rule posed no problem for charges filed with the EEOC more than 300 days after the alleged discrimination, since such charges were untimely regardless of the deferral period. Nor did it pose any problem for charges filed with the EEOC within 240 days of the alleged discrimination, since these charges were effectively filed with the EEOC no more than 60 days later but still within the 300-day limitation period. The problem with *Mohasco* was with charges filed with the EEOC more than 240 but within 300 days of the alleged discrimination. These charges were timely only if the state or local proceedings terminated in less than 60 days—since the deferral period would also terminate at that time, permitting the charge to be effectively filed with the EEOC before the 300-day limitation period ran. Hence *Mohasco* established what the dissent in that case called the "240-day maybe" rule. 447 U.S. at 834 n.6 (Blackmun, J., dissenting). A plaintiff could safely take advantage of the automatic deferral procedure established by the EEOC only by filing a charge within 240 days of the alleged discrimination. Any later filing was untimely unless it was within 300 days of the alleged discrimination and state or local proceedings terminated within that period as well. As the dissent pointed out, the "240-day maybe" rule did not appear anywhere in the statute and could not have been easily deduced by anyone who was not well versed in the procedures under Title VII. Yet the whole point of automatic deferral under *Love v. Pullman Co.* was to assist lay people, who might not yet be represented by counsel, in complying with the various time limits under Title VII.

2. ***EEOC v. Commercial Office Products Co.*** The Supreme Court considered the effect of all these prior attempts to simplify the procedure for filing claims with the EEOC in EEOC v. Commercial Office Products Co., 486 U.S. 107 (1988). In response to *Mohasco*, the EEOC entered into "worksharing agreements" that tried to circumvent the "240-day maybe" rule created by the decision and effectively implement the 300-day

limitation period found in the statute. The EEOC entered into worksharing agreements with state and local agencies that provided for an automatic waiver of the deferral period for all charges initially filed with the EEOC. These agreements were augmented by an EEOC regulation providing that all charges filed with the EEOC within 300 days of the alleged discrimination were considered to be timely. See 29 C.F.R. § 1601.13(a)(4)(ii).

The Supreme Court upheld the EEOC's authority in a case in which the plaintiff initially filed a charge 290 days after the alleged discrimination. The EEOC then deferred it to the state agency which, pursuant to the worksharing agreement, automatically terminated its consideration of the charge 10 days later, causing the deferral period to end (because it ends upon termination of state proceedings) and reviving the charge with the EEOC within 300 days (causing it to be effectively filed with the EEOC within the 300-day limitation period). When the EEOC finished considering the charge, the state agency reserved the right to reactivate it itself. This last feature of the worksharing agreement prompted an argument by the defendant that the state agency had not really terminated its consideration of the charge and so the deferral period had not ended within the 300-day limitation period. The Supreme Court rejected this argument and concluded that this arrangement was well within the authority granted to the EEOC by Title VII:

> The deferral provisions of § 706 were enacted as part of a compromise forged during the course of one of the longest filibusters in the Senate's history. The bill that had passed the House provided for "deferral" to state and local enforcement efforts only in the sense that it directed the EEOC to enter into agreements with state agencies providing for the suspension of federal enforcement in certain circumstances. See H.R. 7152, 88th Cong., 2d Sess., § 708, 110 Cong. Rec. 2511–2512 (1964). The House bill further directed the EEOC to rescind any agreement with a state agency if the EEOC determined that the agency was no longer effectively exercising its power to combat discrimination. In the Senate, this bill met with strenuous opposition on the ground that it placed the EEOC in the position of monitoring state enforcement efforts, granting States exclusive jurisdiction over local discrimination claims only upon the EEOC's determination that state efforts were effective. See, e.g., id. at 6449 (remarks of Sen. Dirksen). The bill's opponents voiced their concerns against the backdrop of the federal-state civil rights conflicts of the early 1960's, which no doubt intensified their fear of "the steady and deeper intrusion of the Federal power." See id. at 8193 (remarks of Sen. Dirksen). These concerns were resolved by the "Dirksen-Mansfield substitute,"

which proposed the 60-day deferral period now in § 706(c) of the Act. See 110 Cong. Rec. at 11926–11935.

The proponents of the Dirksen-Mansfield substitute identified two goals of the deferral provisions, both of which fully support the EEOC's conclusion that States may, if they choose, waive the 60-day deferral period but retain jurisdiction over discrimination charges by entering into worksharing agreements with the EEOC. First, the proponents of the substitute deferral provisions explained that the 60-day deferral period was meant to give States a "reasonable opportunity to act under State law before the commencement of any Federal proceedings." (remarks of Sen. Humphrey). Nothing in the waiver provisions of the worksharing agreements impinges on the opportunity of the States to have an exclusive 60-day period for processing a discrimination charge. The waiver of that opportunity in specified instances is a voluntary choice made through individually negotiated agreements, not an imposition by the Federal Government. Indeed, eight worksharing States and the District of Columbia filed a brief as amici in this case, explaining their satisfaction with the operation of the waiver provisions of the worksharing agreements: "By clarifying primary responsibility for different categories of charges, worksharing agreements benefit both the EEOC and the states." Moreover, most worksharing agreements are flexible, permitting States to express interest in cases ordinarily waived under the agreement and to call upon the EEOC to refrain from assuming jurisdiction in such cases. See, e.g., Worksharing Agreement Between CCRD and EEOC.

In contrast, respondent's argument that States should not be permitted to waive the deferral period because its creation reflected a congressional preference for state as opposed to federal enforcement is entirely at odds with the voluntarism stressed by the proponents of deferral. Congress clearly foresaw the possibility that States might decline to take advantage of the opportunity for enforcement afforded them by the deferral provisions. It therefore gave the EEOC the authority and responsibility to act when a State is "unable or unwilling" to provide relief. 110 Cong. Rec. 12725 (1964) (remarks of Sen. Humphrey). This Court, too, has recognized that Congress envisioned federal intervention when "States decline, for whatever reason, to take advantage of [their] opportunities" to settle grievances in "a voluntary and localized manner." Oscar Mayer & Co. v. Evans, 441 U.S. at 761. As counsel for the EEOC explained, deferral was meant to work as "a carrot, but not a stick," affording States an opportunity to act, but not penalizing their failure to do so other than by authorizing federal intervention. The waiver provisions of worksharing agreements are fully consistent with this goal.

In addition to providing States with an opportunity to forestall federal intervention, the deferral provisions were meant to promote "time economy and the expeditious handling of cases." 110 Cong. Rec. 9790 (1964) (remarks of Sen. Dirksen). Respondent's proposed interpretation of § 706(c), adopted by the Court of Appeals, is irreconcilable with this purpose because it would result in extraordinary inefficiency without furthering any other goal of the Act. The EEOC would be required to wait 60 days before processing its share of discrimination claims under a worksharing agreement, even though both the EEOC and the relevant state or local agency agree that the State or locality will take no action during that period. Or, in an effort to avoid this pointless 60-day delay, state and local agencies could abandon their worksharing agreements with the EEOC and attempt to initially process all charges during the 60-day deferral period, a solution suggested by respondent. Such a solution would create an enormous backlog of discrimination charges in States and localities, preventing them from securing for their citizens the quick attention to discrimination claims afforded under worksharing agreements. Or, in another scenario proposed by respondent, state or local agencies could rewrite their worksharing agreements with the EEOC to provide for "termination" of state or local proceedings in accordance with respondent's definition of that term—complete relinquishment of jurisdiction. This solution would prevent a pointless 60-day delay, but it would also preclude a State's reactivation of a discrimination charge upon the conclusion of federal proceedings.[5] Requiring that States completely relinquish authority over claims in order to avoid needless delay turns on its head the dual purposes of the deferral provisions: deference to the States and efficient processing of claims. As the amici States observe, such a requirement "frustrates the congressional intent to ensure state and local agencies the opportunity to employ their expertise to resolve discrimination complaints."

In a separate holding, the Court also went on to make clear that the plaintiff was under no obligation to file a charge with the state agency that was timely under state law, recognizing that its prior holding in

[5] Reactivation of state proceedings after the conclusion of federal proceedings serves the useful function of permitting States to enforce their discrimination laws when these laws are more protective than Title VII. For example, Title VII does not give the EEOC jurisdiction to enforce the Act against employers of fewer than 15 employees or against bona fide private membership clubs. § 701(b), 42 U.S.C. § 2000e(b). Each year, the CCRD reactivates four to five charges in which the EEOC has determined after investigation that it lacks jurisdiction. Brief for Colorado et al. as Amici Curiae 7.

Oscar Mayer applied equally to claims under Title VII as under the ADEA.

3. **Rulemaking Authority of the EEOC.** The dissent in *Commercial Office Products* addressed only the first holding in the case, essentially viewing the worksharing agreements and regulations established by the EEOC to be beyond its authority: to be an attempt to subvert the deferral and limitation periods established by Congress and to undermine the Court's earlier decision in *Mohasco.* The dissent, of course, is correct in assuming that the EEOC would lose in any direct confrontation with Congress or the Supreme Court: Congress because it could amend the statute to supersede the EEOC's interpretation of it; the Court because it could find the EEOC's interpretation to be contrary to the unambiguous terms of the statute in its present form. The real questions in *Commercial Office Products*, however, were somewhat different: first, whether the EEOC's actions were authorized by Congress, and second, whether they were consistent with the Court's own interpretation of Title VII.

Congress conferred two forms of authority on the EEOC to coordinate its procedures with those of state and local agencies. The EEOC has general authority "to issue, amend, or rescind suitable procedural regulations to carry out the provisions of [Title VII]." § 713(a), 42 U.S.C. § 2000e–12(a). It also has specific authority to "cooperate with State and local agencies charged with the administration of State fair employment practices laws" and to "enter into written agreements with such State or local agencies" on processing charges. § 709(b), 42 U.S.C. § 2000e–8(b). These provisions do not authorize the Commission to alter the time limits under Title VII, but they do give it the power to change how these time limits are implemented and satisfied.

The Supreme Court's own prior decisions recognized the EEOC's authority to assist plaintiffs in meeting the administrative prerequisites to filing suit. In particular, in *Love v. Pullman*, the Court approved the Commission's regulations on automatic deferral to state and local agencies because they avoided technicalities that were "particularly inappropriate in a statutory scheme in which laymen, unassisted by trained lawyers, initiate the process." The Court also emphasized that the interests of state and local agencies in exclusive jurisdiction during the deferral period were fully served by the regulations. The regulation facilitated rather than frustrated the process of deferral. The same overall goal of simplification, subject to the interests of state and local agencies, was also furthered by the worksharing agreements in *Commercial Office Products.*

Judged by the reasons for them, these agreements fell well within the authority conferred upon the EEOC. It was their effect on the limitation period for filing with the EEOC that was controversial. Did the worksharing agreements effectively lengthen the limitation period to the detriment of the defendant, prejudicing its interests and depriving it of a defense that would otherwise be available? In order to answer this question, it is necessary to consider the three interrelated goals served by the statute of limitations under Title VII: preventing litigation of claims on stale evidence, protecting the defendant's interest in repose, and screening out weak claims. Are any of these goals compromised by the worksharing agreements approved in *Commercial Office Products*? Does it make a difference that these agreements, although they resulted in a waiver of the deferral period by state or local agencies, allowed such agencies to reconsider the plaintiff's charge after the EEOC had concluded its proceedings? Or is that a matter of state or local law that does not affect the plaintiff's claim under Title VII?

4. **Other Filing Requirements Under Title VII.** The contents of a filing with a state or local agency, with the EEOC, or with a court can also raise issues of timeliness. If the filing is inadequate, the limitation period continues to run and the plaintiff's attempt to cure a defective filing with a later submission may itself be untimely. Both Congress and the Court, however, have been lenient in specifying the requirements for a sufficient filing. The content of administrative charges has been defined particularly loosely. State and local charges, as we have seen, need only contain "a written and signed statement of the facts upon which the proceeding is based." § 706(c), 42 U.S.C. § 2000e–5(c). The EEOC has imposed more detailed requirements for charges filed directly under Title VII, but it has allowed a charge to be filed if it contains "a written statement sufficiently precise to identify the parties, and to describe generally the action or practices complained of." 29 C.F.R. §§ 1601.9, 1601.12. Amendments to cure defects in the charge, or to add related allegations of discrimination, can be made later and will relate back to the date of original filing. This latter provision in the regulations was upheld by the Supreme Court in Edelman v. Lynchburg College, 535 U.S. 106 (2002). Even charges filed by an EEOC commissioner need not meet exacting requirements and can be framed in the broadest possible terms. EEOC v. Shell Oil Co., 466 U.S. 54 (1984).

In a recent case arising under the ADEA, the Supreme Court considered precisely how detailed a charge must be. In Federal Express Corporation v. Holowecki, 552 U.S. 389 (2008), the plaintiff had not filled out a "Charge of Discrimination" form provided by the EEOC, but instead only an "Intake Questionnaire," supplemented by a six-page affidavit detailing her accusations against her employer and ending with a request that the EEOC "force Federal Express to end their age discrimination." In finding this filing to be sufficient, the Court adopted an objective intent standard for viewing employee filings, holding that "if a filing is to be deemed a charge it must be reasonably construed as a request for the agency to take remedial action to protect the employee's rights or otherwise settle a dispute between the employer and the employee." The Court also held that the filing could constitute a charge even if the EEOC did not immediately consider it to be one. Since many filings with the

EEOC are pro se, the Court declined to "make the definition of charge dependent upon a condition subsequent over which the parties have no control." The dissenters objected to the Court's loose definition of a charge as merely a "request for action" and expressed concerns about employer notice if even the EEOC cannot determine, ex ante, whether a particular document is intended as a charge of discrimination or merely an employee inquiry.

Complaints filed in court must meet somewhat stricter standards, if only because pleadings must now meet the standard of "plausibility" from Ashcroft v. Iqbal, 556 U.S. 662 (2009). And even before *Iqbal*, a complaint was found inadequate because it consisted simply of the plaintiff's right-to-sue letter. Baldwin County Welcome Center v. Brown, 466 U.S. 147 (1984).

Although most Title VII claims are filed in federal court, jurisdiction over them is concurrent and they can also be filed in state court. Yellow Freight System, Inc. v. Donnelly, 494 U.S. 820 (1990).

5. **The Effect of Filing Other Claims.** In general, the plaintiff's resort to other remedies for employment discrimination does not affect the timeliness of his claim under Title VII. Resort to remedies available through state or local administrative agencies is required, but only in order to satisfy the 60-day deferral period of exclusive state or local jurisdiction. Resort to other remedies does not affect the limitation periods under Title VII at all. Thus, the availability of remedies through a collective bargaining agreement does not prevent these limitation periods from running, Electrical Workers v. Robbins & Myers, Inc., 429 U.S. 229 (1976), and asserting a claim under another civil rights law does not do so either. See Johnson v. Railway Express Agency, 421 U.S. 454 (1975). Only the pendency of a class action covering the plaintiff's claim tolls the running of the limitation periods under Title VII, for the same reason that it does so for any claim. The plaintiff's membership in the class, while the class action is pending, allows him to rely upon the class action as the sole vehicle for obtaining relief. Crown, Cork & Seal Co. v. Parker, 462 U.S. 345 (1983).

6. ***AT&T Corp. v. Hulteen.*** The Supreme Court continued to recognize limits on the theory of continuing violations even after the Lilly Ledbetter Fair Pay Act in AT&T Corp v. Hulteen, 556 U.S. 701 (2009). This case, somewhat like *United Air Lines v. Evans*, involved the present effect of past discriminatory practices. The practice in question was the denial of pregnancy benefits before the effective date of the Pregnancy Discrimination Act, which was entirely permissible under prevailing decisions of the Supreme Court at the time. The denial, however, reduced the plaintiffs' current pension benefits. The Court held that this effect was insulated from challenge under Title VII for several interrelated reasons: the Pregnancy Discrimination Act was not retroactive; pension benefits were determined according to a neutral seniority system under § 703(h); and the special limitation period for challenging the operation

of a seniority system in § 703(e)(2) did not apply. The Lilly Ledbetter Fair Pay Act also was inapplicable because both the initial denial of pregnancy benefits and the seniority system were entirely lawful, so that there was no initial, illegal decrease in compensation.

7. ***Lewis v. City of Chicago.*** In the latest in the series of cases on when a violation of Title VII occurs, the Supreme Court held that claims arising from the use of an employment test were timely insofar as they alleged liability for disparate impact. *Lewis v. City of Chicago*, 560 U.S. 205 (2010). A class of black applicants for positions in the Chicago Fire Department passed a written test for hiring in the department. They did not, however, score high enough to be in the top tier of applicants who received priority in hiring. The test was administered and they received notice of the test results more than 300 days before they filed a charge with the EEOC. They were accordingly passed over for hiring and jobs were given to those in the top tier of applicants in the course of rounds of hiring decisions, most of which occurred within 300 days of the filing of their charge. The question before the Supreme Court was whether the 300-day limitation period began to run when the test results were announced or whether it ran from every use of the test results, including those within the limitation period. Reasoning from the text of § 703(k)(1)(A)(i), the Court reached the following conclusion:

> Thus, a plaintiff establishes a prima facie disparate-impact claim by showing that the employer "*uses* a particular employment practice that causes a disparate impact" on one of the prohibited bases. *Ibid.* (emphasis added). Petitioners' claim satisfies that requirement. Title VII does not define "employment practice," but we think it clear that the term encompasses the conduct of which petitioners complain: the exclusion of passing applicants who scored below [the cutoff for highest tier] when selecting those who would advance. The City "use[d]" that practice in each round of selection. Although the City had adopted the eligibility list (embodying the score cutoffs) earlier and announced its intention to draw from that list, it made use of the practice of excluding those who scored [below the cutoff for the highest tier] each time it filled a new class of firefighters. Petitioners alleged that this exclusion caused a disparate impact. Whether they adequately proved that is not before us. What matters is that their allegations, based on the City's actual implementation of its policy, stated a cognizable claim.

Note that this reasoning makes the application of the statute of limitations depend upon the nature of the plaintiffs' claim. If they had alleged class-wide intentional discrimination in devising the test, their claim would have accrued outside the limitation period, when the test was administered. Does this result make sense? It is, in any event, similar to the result in *National Railroad Passenger Corp. v. Morgan*, 536

U.S. 101 (2002), which carefully distinguished among different claims of sexual harassment and how they determined when the statute of limitations began to run. Is this approach simply a matter of logic: that the statute of limitations necessarily runs from the date of the alleged violation of the statute, which is defined by the elements specified in the statute itself? Or does *City of Chicago* also treat claims for disparate impact in the same lenient way as the Lilly Ledbetter Fair Pay Act, which starts the limitation running whenever a plaintiff "is affected by application of a discriminatory compensation decision"? See § 706(e)(3). Recall that that statute was passed because of concern that plaintiffs might not obtain earlier effective notice that they were subject to discriminatory pay decisions. Which should be decisive: the elements of the plaintiff's claim or the notice that the plaintiff has that a claim has accrued?

C. LITIGATION AND ALTERNATIVES TO IT

INTRODUCTORY NOTE

Individual private actions are the principal means of enforcing Title VII. They do not, however, raise distinctive procedural issues except when they might be displaced by other means of enforcement. These other means are, respectively, class actions brought by other private individuals; public actions brought by the EEOC or the Department of Justice; and arbitration established through individual contracts or collective bargaining. The first two of these alternatives expand the scope and significance of a judicial action; the third replaces it with a form of private dispute resolution.

1. **Class Actions and Public Actions.** The choice among these alternatives raises fundamental issues about the proper means of enforcing Title VII. Should it concentrate on public law litigation, raising issues of general significance applicable to a large number of employees? Many of the influential cases decided early in the history of Title VII had this emphasis, including prominent class actions and public actions, as in Albemarle Paper Co. v. Moody, 422 U.S. 405 (1975), and International Brotherhood of Teamsters v. United States, 431 U.S. 324 (1977). These cases focused on changing the law and changing institutions, rather than adjudicating only the rights of individual plaintiffs and defendants. On one influential view, litigation on such a large scale more closely resembles administrative rulemaking rather than traditional lawsuits in the common law system. Abram Chayes, The Role of the Judge in Public Law Litigation, 89 Harv. L. Rev. 1281 (1976). Not all litigation under Title VII has taken this form, however, even in the early years after enactment of Title VII. Many decisions in individual cases also addressed questions left open by the terms of Title VII itself. Nevertheless, the proportion of class actions and public actions peaked in the first decade or so of enforcing Title VII. The general approach was aptly summarized by the maxim: "Racial discrimination is by definition class discrimination. . . ." Oatis v. Crown Zellerbach Corp., 398 F.2d 496, 499 (5th Cir. 1968).

The trend exemplified by this maxim was abruptly curtailed in the late 1970s, when individual actions became the predominant means of enforcement. This change coincided with the increasing proportion of claims alleging discrimination in termination from employment rather than in hiring. John J. Donohue & Peter Siegelman, The Changing Nature of Employment Discrimination Litigation, 43 Stan. L. Rev. 983, 1016–21 (1991). It also coincided with restrictions imposed on the certification of class actions, such as those discussed in the next principal case, and on more complicated rules on proof of class-wide discrimination, as discussed in Chapter 3. These developments made it harder for individual plaintiffs both to obtain certification of class actions and, once obtained, to prevail on the merits of class-wide claims.

2. **Arbitration.** A still more recent development involves the attempt, overwhelmingly by employers, to displace litigation entirely with private means of alternative dispute resolution. As discussed later in this chapter, the Supreme Court has found no federal policy against arbitration of employment discrimination claims. This method of dispute resolution presupposes an agreement to arbitrate binding on both parties and consistent with the requirements of state law. Additional restrictions apply to judicial enforcement of any arbitration award that is ultimately rendered. If all of those conditions are met, however, litigation is effectively transferred from a public to a private forum, with attendant advantages and disadvantages. Much like settlement, arbitration allows the parties to avoid the formality and cost of litigation, and it also gives them greater control over who decides their dispute. Again like settlement, however, it prevents public deliberation over the plaintiff's claim and a resolution of it with precedential effect. See Owen Fiss, Comment, Against Settlement, 93 Yale L.J. 1073 (1984). Arbitration of employment discrimination claims raises the further problem of an imbalance in bargaining power. Such claims are not subject to waiver, at least in advance of litigation, because they concern mandatory terms of employment: terms designed to redress the outcome of bargaining that occurs in an ordinary contractual relationship. If the right to be free of discrimination cannot be waived directly—by contracting to allow discrimination—then it cannot be waived indirectly—by contracting for arbitration on terms unduly favorable to the employer. Objections along these lines seek to preserve individual litigation as the best means of preserving individual rights.

3. **Bibliography.** For articles discussing the overall structure for administering and enforcing laws against employment discrimination, see Richard Abel, Civil Rights and Wrongs, 38 Loy. L.A. L. Rev. 1421 (2005); Jody D. Armour, Toward a Tort-Based Theory of Civil Rights, Civil Liberties, and Racial Justice, 38 Loy. L.A. L. Rev. 1469 (2005); and Julie C. Suk, Antidiscrimination Law in the Administrative State, 2006 U. Ill. L. Rev. 405.

On litigation generally under Title VII, see Employment Discrimination Litigation: Behavioral, Quantitative, and Legal Perspectives (Frank J. Landy ed., 2005); Kevin M. Clermont & Stewart J. Schwab, Employment Discrimination Plaintiffs in Federal Court: From Bad to Worse?, 3 Harv. L. & Pol'y Rev. 103 (2009); Jessica Fink, Unintended Consequences: How

Antidiscrimination Litigation Increases Group Bias in Employer-Defendants, 38 N.M. L. Rev. 333 (2008); David A. Green, Friend or Foe: The Supreme Court's "Plausible Claim" Standard Provides Another Barrier for Plaintiffs in Employment Discrimination, 39 S.U. L. Rev. 1 (2011); Scott A. Moss, Fighting Discrimination While Fighting Litigation: A Tale of Two Supreme Courts, 76 Fordham L. Rev. 981 (2007); Laura B. Nielsen, Robert L. Nelson & Ryon Lancaster, Individual Justice or Collective Legal Mobilization? Employment Discrimination Litigation in the Post Civil Rights United States, 7 J. Empirical Legal Stud. 175 (2010); Deborah L. Rhode, Litigating Discrimination: Lessons from the Front Lines, 20 J.L. & Pol'y 325 (2012); Elizabeth M. Schneider, The Changing Shape of Federal Civil Pretrial Practice: The Disparate Impact on Civil Rights and Employment Discrimination Cases, 158 U. Pa. L. Rev. 517 (2010); Joseph A. Seiner, The Trouble with *Twombly*: A Proposed Pleading Standard for Employment Discrimination Cases, 2009 U. Ill. L. Rev. 1011 (2009); Michael J. Zimmer, Title VII's Last Hurrah: Can Discrimination Be Plausibly Pled?, 2013 U. Chi. Leg. Forum; Symposium, How Do Discrimination Cases Fare in Court?, 7 Emp. Rts. & Emp. Pol'y J. 533 (2004); Symposium, Employment Discrimination Remedies: The Shape of Lawsuits, the Shape of the Law, 12 Emp. Rts. & Empl. Pol'y J. 297 (2008).

For articles on settlement and waiver of Title VII claims, see Vivian Berger, Michael O. Finkelstein & Kenneth Cheung, Summary Judgment Benchmarks for Settling Employment Discrimination Lawsuits, 23 Hofstra Lab. & Emp. L.J. 45 (2005); Robert Frankhouser, The Enforceability of Pre-Dispute Jury Waiver Agreements in Employment Discrimination Cases, 8 Duq. Bus. L.J. 55 (2006); Andrea Giampetro-Meyer, Standing in the Gap: A Profile of Employment Discrimination Plaintiffs, 27 Berkeley J. Emp. & Lab. L. 431 (2006); Minna J. Kotkin, Invisible Settlements, Invisible Discrimination, 84 N.C. L. Rev. 927 (2006); Minna J. Kotkin, Outing Outcomes: An Empirical Study of Confidential Employment Discrimination Settlements, 64 Wash. & Lee L. Rev. 111 (2007); E. Patrick McDermott & Danny Ervin, The Influence of Procedural and Distributive Variables on Settlement Rates in Employment Discrimination Mediation, 2005 J. Disp. Resol. 45; Daniel P. O'Gorman, A State of Disarray: The "Knowing and Voluntary" Standard for Releasing Claims Under Title VII of the Civil Rights Act of 1964, 8 U. Pa. J. Lab. & Emp. L. 73 (2005); Craig R. Senn, Knowing and Voluntary Waivers of Federal Employment Claims: Replacing the Totality of Circumstances Test with a "Waiver Certainty" Test, 58 Fla. L. Rev. 305 (2006).

1. CLASS ACTIONS

Federal Rule of Civil Procedure 23(a) and (b)

Class Actions

(a) Prerequisites. One or more members of a class may sue or be sued as representative parties on behalf of all only if:

(1) the class is so numerous that joinder of all members is impracticable;

(2) there are questions of law or fact common to the class;

(3) the claims or defenses of the representative parties are typical of the claims or defenses of the class; and

(4) the representative parties will fairly and adequately protect the interests of the class.

(b) Types of Class Actions. A class action may be maintained if Rule 23(a) is satisfied and if:

(1) prosecuting separate actions by or against individual class members would create a risk of

(A) inconsistent or varying adjudications with respect to individual class members that would establish incompatible standards of conduct for the party opposing the class, or

(B) adjudications with respect to individual class members that, as a practical matter, would be dispositive of the interests of the other members not parties to the individual adjudications or would substantially impair or impede their ability to protect their interests; or

(2) the party opposing the class has acted or refused to act on grounds generally applicable to the class, so that final injunctive relief or corresponding declaratory relief is appropriate respecting the class as a whole; or

(3) the court finds that the questions of law or fact common to class members predominate over any questions affecting only individual members, and that a class action is superior to other available methods for fairly and efficiently adjudicating of the controversy. The matters pertinent to the findings include:

(A) the class members' interests in individually controlling the prosecution or defense of separate actions;

(B) the extent and nature of any litigation concerning the controversy already begun by or against class members;

(C) the desirability or undesirability of concentrating the litigation of the claims in the particular forum; and

(D) the difficulties likely to be encountered in managing a class action.

General Telephone Co. v. Falcon

457 U.S. 147 (1982).

■ JUSTICE STEVENS delivered the opinion of the Court.

The question presented is whether respondent Falcon, who complained that petitioner did not promote him because he is a Mexican-

American, was properly permitted to maintain a class action on behalf of Mexican-American applicants for employment whom petitioner did not hire.

I

In 1969 petitioner initiated a special recruitment and training program for minorities. Through that program, respondent Falcon was hired in July 1969 as a groundman, and within a year he was twice promoted, first to lineman and then to lineman-in-charge. He subsequently refused a promotion to installer-repairman. In October 1972 he applied for the job of field inspector; his application was denied even though the promotion was granted several white employees with less seniority.

Falcon thereupon filed a charge with the Equal Employment Opportunity Commission stating his belief that he had been passed over for promotion because of his national origin and that petitioner's promotion policy operated against Mexican-Americans as a class. Falcon v. General Telephone Co. of Southwest, 626 F.2d 369, 372, n.2 (CA5 1980). In due course he received a right-to-sue letter from the Commission and, in April 1975, he commenced this action under Title VII of the Civil Rights Act of 1964, 78 Stat. 253, as amended, 42 U.S.C. § 2000e et seq., in the United States District Court for the Northern District of Texas. His complaint alleged that petitioner maintained "a policy, practice, custom, or usage of: (a) discriminating against [Mexican-Americans] because of national origin and with respect to compensation, terms, conditions, and privileges of employment, and (b) . . . subjecting [Mexican-Americans] to continuous employment discrimination." Respondent claimed that as a result of this policy whites with less qualification and experience and lower evaluation scores than respondent had been promoted more rapidly. The complaint contained no factual allegations concerning petitioner's hiring practices.

Respondent brought the action "on his own behalf and on behalf of other persons similarly situated, pursuant to Rule 23(b)(2) of the Federal Rules of Civil Procedure." The class identified in the complaint was "composed of Mexican-American persons who are employed, or who might be employed, by GENERAL TELEPHONE COMPANY at its place of business located in Irving, Texas, who have been and who continue to be or might be adversely affected by the practices complained of herein."

. . . Without conducting an evidentiary hearing, the District Court certified a class including Mexican-American employees and Mexican-American applicants for employment who had not been hired.

Following trial of the liability issues, the District Court entered separate findings of fact and conclusions of law with respect first to respondent and then to the class. The District Court found that petitioner had not discriminated against respondent in hiring, but that it did discriminate against him in its promotion practices. The court reached converse conclusions about the class, finding no discrimination in promotion practices, but concluding that petitioner had discriminated against Mexican-Americans at its Irving facility in its hiring practices.

Both parties appealed. The Court of Appeals rejected respondent's contention that the class should have encompassed all of petitioner's operations in Texas, New Mexico, Oklahoma, and Arkansas. On the other hand, the court also rejected petitioner's argument that the class had been defined too broadly. For, under the Fifth Circuit's across-the-board rule, it is permissible for "an employee complaining of one employment practice to represent another complaining of another practice, if the plaintiff and the members of the class suffer from essentially the same injury. In this case, all of the claims are based on discrimination because of national origin." The court relied on Payne v. Travenol Laboratories, Inc., 565 F.2d 895 (1978), cert. denied, 439 U.S. 835, in which the Fifth Circuit stated:

> "Plaintiffs' action is an 'across the board' attack on unequal employment practices alleged to have been committed by Travenol pursuant to a policy of racial discrimination. As parties who have allegedly been aggrieved by some of those discriminatory practices, plaintiffs have demonstrated a sufficient nexus to enable them to represent other class members suffering from different practices motivated by the same policies." 565 F.2d, at 900, quoted in 626 F.2d, at 375.

. . . With the merits of both respondent's promotion claim and the class hiring claims remaining open for reconsideration in the District Court on remand, we granted certiorari to decide whether the class action was properly maintained on behalf of both employees who were denied promotion and applicants who were denied employment.

II

The class-action device was designed as "an exception to the usual rule that litigation is conducted by and on behalf of the individual named parties only." Califano v. Yamasaki, 442 U.S. 682, 700–701. Class relief is "peculiarly appropriate" when the "issues involved are common to the class as a whole" and when they "turn on questions of law applicable in the same manner to each member of the class." For in such cases, "the class-action device saves the resources of both the courts and the parties by permitting an issue potentially affecting every [class member] to be litigated in an economical fashion under Rule 23." *Ibid.*

Title VII of the Civil Rights Act of 1964, as amended, authorizes the Equal Employment Opportunity Commission to sue in its own name to secure relief for individuals aggrieved by discriminatory practices forbidden by the Act. See 42 U.S.C. § 2000e–5(f)(1). In exercising this enforcement power, the Commission may seek relief for groups of employees or applicants for employment without complying with the strictures of Rule 23. General Telephone Co. of Northwest v. EEOC, 446

U.S. 318. Title VII, however, contains no special authorization for class suits maintained by private parties. An individual litigant seeking to maintain a class action under Title VII must meet "the prerequisites of numerosity, commonality, typicality, and adequacy of representation" specified in Rule 23(a). These requirements effectively "limit the class claims to those fairly encompassed by the named plaintiff's claims."

We have repeatedly held that "a class representative must be part of the class and 'possess the same interest and suffer the same injury' as the class members." East Texas Motor Freight System Inc. v. Rodriguez, 431 U.S. 395 (quoting Schlesinger v. Reservists Committee to Stop the War, 418 U.S. 208) In *East Texas Motor Freight*, a Title VII action brought by three Mexican-American city drivers, the Fifth Circuit certified a class consisting of the trucking company's black and Mexican-American city drivers allegedly denied on racial or ethnic grounds transfers to more desirable line-driver jobs. We held that the Court of Appeals had "plainly erred in declaring a class action." Because at the time the class was certified it was clear that the named plaintiffs were not qualified for line-driver positions, "they could have suffered no injury as a result of the allegedly discriminatory practices, and they were, therefore, simply not eligible to represent a class of persons who did allegedly suffer injury."

Our holding in *East Texas Motor Freight* was limited; we noted that "a different case would be presented if the District Court had certified a class and only later had it appeared that the named plaintiffs were not class members or were otherwise inappropriate class representatives." We also recognized the theory behind the Fifth Circuit's across-the-board rule, noting our awareness "that suits alleging racial or ethnic discrimination are often by their very nature class suits, involving classwide wrongs," and that "[c]ommon questions of law or fact are typically present." In the same breath, however, we reiterated that "careful attention to the requirements of Fed. Rule Civ. Proc. 23 remains nonetheless indispensable" and that the "mere fact that a complaint alleges racial or ethnic discrimination does not in itself ensure that the party who has brought the lawsuit will be an adequate representative of those who may have been the real victims of that discrimination."

We cannot disagree with the proposition underlying the across-the-board rule—that racial discrimination is by definition class discrimination. But the allegation that such discrimination has occurred neither determines whether a class action may be maintained in accordance with Rule 23 nor defines the class that may be certified. Conceptually, there is a wide gap between (a) an individual's claim that he has been denied a promotion on discriminatory grounds, and his otherwise unsupported allegation that the company has a policy of discrimination, and (b) the existence of a class of persons who have suffered the same injury as that individual, such that the individual's claim and the class claims will share common questions of law or fact and that the individual's claim will be typical of the class claims.[13] For respondent to bridge that gap, he must prove much more than the validity of his own claim. Even though evidence that he was passed over for promotion when several less deserving whites were advanced may support the conclusion that respondent was denied the promotion because of his national origin, such evidence would not necessarily justify the additional inferences (1) that this discriminatory treatment is typical of petitioner's promotion practices, (2) that petitioner's promotion practices are motivated by a policy of ethnic discrimination that pervades petitioner's Irving division, or (3) that this policy of ethnic discrimination is reflected in petitioner's other employment practices, such as hiring, in the same way it is manifested in the promotion practices. These additional inferences demonstrate the tenuous character of any presumption that the class claims are "fairly encompassed" within respondent's claim.

Respondent's complaint provided an insufficient basis for concluding that the adjudication of his claim of discrimination in promotion would require the decision of any common question concerning the failure of petitioner to hire more Mexican-Americans. Without any specific presentation identifying the questions of law or fact that were common to the claims of respondent and of the members of the class he sought to represent, it was error for the District Court to presume that respondent's claim was typical of other claims against petitioner by Mexican-American employees and applicants. If one allegation of specific discriminatory treatment were sufficient to support an across-the-board attack, every Title VII case would be a potential company-wide class action. We find nothing in the statute to indicate that Congress intended to authorize such a wholesale expansion of class-action litigation.[15]

---

[13] The commonality and typicality requirements of Rule 23(a) tend to merge. Both serve as guideposts for determining whether under the particular circumstances maintenance of a class action is economical and whether the named plaintiff's claim and the class claims are so interrelated that the interests of the class members will be fairly and adequately protected in their absence. Those requirements therefore also tend to merge with the adequacy-of-representation requirement, although the latter requirement also raises concerns about the competency of class counsel and conflicts of interest. In this case, we need not address petitioner's argument that there is a conflict of interest between respondent and the class of rejected applicants because an enlargement of the pool of Mexican-American employees will decrease respondent's chances for promotion. See General Telephone Co. of Northwest v. EEOC, 446 U.S. 318, 331 ("In employment discrimination litigation, conflicts might arise, for example, between employees and applicants who were denied employment and who will, if granted relief, compete with employees for fringe benefits or seniority. Under Rule 23, the same plaintiff could not represent these classes"); see also East Texas Motor Freight System Inc. v. Rodriguez, 431 U.S. 395, 404–405.

[15] If petitioner used a biased testing procedure to evaluate both applicants for employment and incumbent employees, a class action on behalf of every applicant or employee who might have been prejudiced by the test clearly would satisfy the commonality and typicality requirements of Rule 23(a). Significant proof that an employer operated under a general policy of discrimination conceivably could justify a class of both applicants and employees if the discrimination manifested itself in hiring and promotion practices in the same general fashion, such as through entirely subjective decisionmaking processes. In this regard it is noteworthy that Title VII prohibits discriminatory employment practices, not an abstract policy of discrimination. The mere fact that an aggrieved private plaintiff is a member of an identifiable

The trial of this class action followed a predictable course. Instead of raising common questions of law or fact, respondent's evidentiary approaches to the individual and class claims were entirely different. He attempted to sustain his individual claim by proving intentional discrimination. He tried to prove the class claims through statistical evidence of disparate impact. Ironically, the District Court rejected the class claim of promotion discrimination, which conceptually might have borne a closer typicality and commonality relationship with respondent's individual claim, but sustained the class claim of hiring discrimination. As the District Court's bifurcated findings on liability demonstrate, the individual and class claims might as well have been tried separately. It is clear that the maintenance of respondent's action as a class action did not advance "the efficiency and economy of litigation which is a principal purpose of the procedure." American Pipe & Construction Co. v. Utah, 414 U.S. 538, 553.

We do not, of course, judge the propriety of a class certification by hindsight. The District Court's error in this case, and the error inherent in the across-the-board rule, is the failure to evaluate carefully the legitimacy of the named plaintiff's plea that he is a proper class representative under Rule 23(a). As we noted in Coopers & Lybrand v. Livesay, 437 U.S. 463, "the class determination generally involves considerations that are 'enmeshed in the factual and legal issues comprising the plaintiff's cause of action.'" Id., at 469 (quoting Mercantile Nat. Bank v. Langdeau, 371 U.S. 555, 558). Sometimes the issues are plain enough from the pleadings to determine whether the interests of the absent parties are fairly encompassed within the named plaintiff's claim, and sometimes it may be necessary for the court to probe behind the pleadings before coming to rest on the certification question. Even after a certification order is entered, the judge remains free to modify it in the light of subsequent developments in the litigation. For such an order, particularly during the period before any notice is sent to members of the class, "is inherently tentative." This flexibility enhances the usefulness of the class-action device; actual, not presumed, conformance with Rule 23(a) remains, however, indispensable.

III

The need to carefully apply the requirements of Rule 23(a) to Title VII class actions was noticed by a member of the Fifth Circuit panel that announced the across-the-board rule. In a specially concurring opinion in Johnson v. Georgia Highway Express, Inc., 417 F.2d, at 1125–1127, Judge Godbold emphasized the need for "more precise pleadings," for "without reasonable specificity the court cannot define the class, cannot determine whether the representation is adequate, and the employer does not know how to defend." He termed as "most significant" the potential unfairness to the class members bound by the judgment if the

class of persons of the same race or national origin is insufficient to establish his standing to litigate on their behalf all possible claims of discrimination against a common employer.

framing of the class is overbroad. And he pointed out the error of the "tacit assumption" underlying the across-the-board rule that "all will be well for surely the plaintiff will win and manna will fall on all members of the class." With the same concerns in mind, we reiterate today that a Title VII class action, like any other class action, may only be certified if the trial court is satisfied, after a rigorous analysis, that the prerequisites of Rule 23(a) have been satisfied.

The judgment of the Court of Appeals affirming the certification order is reversed, and the case is remanded for further proceedings consistent with this opinion.

It is so ordered.

■ CHIEF JUSTICE BURGER, concurring in part and dissenting in part.

I agree with the Court's decision insofar as it states the general principles which apply in determining whether a class should be certified in this case under Rule 23. However, in my view it is not necessary to remand for further proceedings since it is entirely clear on this record that no class should have been certified in this case. I would simply reverse the Court of Appeals and remand with instructions to dismiss the class claim.

NOTES ON *GENERAL TELEPHONE CO. V. FALCON*

1. **Class Actions Generally.** Several different rationales have been offered for class actions as a procedural device, but all of them depend, in one way or another, upon the economies of scale generated by consolidating a large number of similar claims in a single action. Most frequently, the efficiency gained in this manner works to the benefit of plaintiffs, reducing their cost of recovering on their individual claims and, in the extreme, allowing claims to be brought that would otherwise be too small to be pursued individually. Even apart from compensating plaintiffs for the harm they have suffered, class actions also increase the deterrent effect of litigation on the defendant by increasing both the magnitude and the likelihood of any remedies awarded against him. Some of the benefits from increased efficiency also reach the defendant, although a class action seldom is welcomed by a party who only faces the prospect of increased exposure to liability. Nevertheless, in some cases, defendants actively seek or acquiesce in certification of class actions in order to obtain a complete resolution of all the claims against them.

The provisions of Federal Rule 23, only some of which are excerpted before the opinion in *Falcon*, seek to serve these purposes through provisions addressed to three different issues: first, how to achieve the basic goal of efficiency in litigation; second, how to assure fair treatment of all the parties, especially absent class members and the defendant; and third, how to manage the class action. Provisions on all these issues can be found throughout Rule 23, but those focused on efficiency are concentrated in prerequisites for certification in Rule 23(a) and (b). A class action can be certified only when the benefits from consolidating a number of claims outweigh the costs of a single, large lawsuit. These subsections also address issues of fairness, for instance, through the requirement of adequate representation of class members in subdivision (a)(4) and notice to class members in subdivisions (c)(2) and (c)(3). The latter provisions also raise issues of management of class actions, which have received detailed treatment in recent amendments to Rule 23, mainly in Rule 23(e), (f), (g), and (h). These provisions deal with such issues as settlement, appointment of class counsel, attorney's fees, and appeals, elaborating on the broad authority previously granted to courts to manage class actions under Rule 23(d).

2. **Class Claims of Discrimination.** *Falcon* accepts the proposition that "racial discrimination is by definition class discrimination," but rejects it as a basis for any presumption in favor of certifying Title VII class actions. Following up on the earlier decision in East Texas Motor Freight System, Inc. v. Rodriguez, 431 U.S. 395 (1977), the Court closely examines the nature of the plaintiff's claim and the evidence supporting it to determine whether it raises issues sufficiently similar to those of the class that the plaintiff purports to represent. The plaintiff in *Falcon* asserted an individual claim of intentional discrimination on his own behalf and a claim of disparate impact on behalf of the class. In the Court's view, these claims were not sufficiently similar to justify certification of a class action. Is that because of the differences in substantive law governing these two types of claims, one invoking the line of decisions beginning with McDonnell Douglas v. Green, 411 U.S. 792 (1973), and the other the line of decisions beginning with Griggs v. Duke Power Co., 401 U.S. 424 (1971)? Would certification have been appropriate if the plaintiff had also asserted the claim of disparate impact on his own behalf? What if he had used evidence of disparate impact from the class claim to prove pretext in the individual claim?

The Court relies in part on the different disposition of his individual claim and his claim in the district court. He lost on his individual claim but won on the class claim. The initial decision to certify a class, however, must be made before the district court rules on the merits and, indeed, "at an early practicable time" under Rule 23(c)(1)(A). Does that mean that the district court must undertake a preliminary examination of the merits in order to determine whether to certify a class? The Supreme Court disapproved of this practice in Eisen v. Carlisle & Jacquelin, 417 U.S. 156 (1974), but isn't an inquiry into the nature of the plaintiff's evidence, if not its sufficiency on the merits, still necessary? How else can a court determine the similarity between the plaintiff's individual claims and the class claims? For further examination of these issues, see George Rutherglen, Title VII Class Actions, 47 U. Chi. L. Rev. 688 (1980).

In the first decade of enforcing Title VII, the substantive law governing class claims of discrimination developed along with the increasing prevalence of class actions. Actions asserted on behalf of a class supported the creation of class-wide theories of liability. Otherwise, the common issues among different class members could not be efficiently resolved in a single proceeding. These procedural arguments for certification were, in turn, reinforced by class-wide theories of liability once these were recognized as a matter of substantive law. Such class claims, either of disparate treatment or disparate impact, generated common issues that were most efficiently adjudicated in a single action. Thus, statistical evidence of discrimination and the business justification offered by the employer usually raised identical issues for all class members subject to the same allegedly discriminatory practices. The synergistic effect of class actions and class claims, however, depends on what claims the plaintiff actually asserts and the evidence supporting them. Purely individual claims, like that asserted in *Falcon*, do not support certification and may, in fact, defeat it. The plaintiff's interest in pursuing his own claim may make him an inadequate representative of the class on entirely distinct claims.

3. **Remedies in Class Actions.** The issue of remedies, examined later in this chapter, exhibits the same interaction between substantive law and procedure. On the one hand, the remedies available under Title VII have influenced the design of class actions, resulting in "bifurcation" of the proceedings into two parts: a first stage in which issues common to the class are resolved, typically liability and general injunctive relief; and a second stage devoted to individual issues, mostly of compensatory relief in the form of back pay, remedial seniority, and damages. On the other hand, the tensions inherent in class representation become all the more apparent at the remedy stage, particularly insofar as it involves the award of attorney's fees. The class attorney, who usually controls the litigation on behalf of the class, has an interest in maximizing her recovery of fees. Class members, however, have exactly the opposite interest, in minimizing the cost of litigation to themselves and, in particular, in avoiding any reduction in their recovery because of an award of fees to the class attorney.

The incipient conflict of interest between class members and the class attorney has been thoroughly explored in the literature on class actions and on attorney's fees. How to align the interests of clients and their attorneys, especially on the issue of attorney's fees, is a perennial problem. The very persistence of this issue, however, reveals that class actions are not always an appropriate vehicle to vindicate the public interest. In the field of mass torts, plaintiffs' personal injury lawyers have often profited handsomely from class actions that they control. Their self-interest in pursuing these cases does not imply, of course, that they do so at the expense of their clients' interests or contrary to the public interest. What it does imply is that the contrast between class actions and individual actions is not nearly as sharp as it sometimes appears to be. Just as individual actions can establish important propositions of law, class actions can be confined to the immediate interests of the parties. Do these considerations argue for a greater judicial role in class actions than in individual actions, specifically in order to protect absent class members from conflicts of interest with their attorney? Or would this expansion of the judicial role compromise the impartiality of judges in deciding the merits of the case? Is a cautious approach to certifying class actions, like that taken in *Falcon*, a better way to avoid such conflicts of interest?

4. **Bibliography.** Brooke D. Coleman & Elizabeth G. Porter, Reinvigorating Commonality: Gender & Class Actions, 92 N.Y.U. L. Rev. 895

(2017); Suzette Malveaux, The Modern Class Action Rule: Its Civil Rights Roots and Relevance Today, 66 Kan. L. Rev. 325 (2017); George Rutherglen, Notice, Scope, and Preclusion in Title VII Class Actions, 69 Va. L. Rev. 11 (1983); Michael Selmi, The Price of Discrimination: The Nature of Class Action Employment Discrimination Litigation and Its Effects, 81 Tex. L. Rev. 1249 (2003); Steven L. Willborn, Personal Stake, Rule 23, and The Employment Discrimination Class Action, 22 B.C. L. Rev. 1 (1980).

Wal-Mart Stores, Inc. v. Dukes

564 U.S. 338 (2011).

■ JUSTICE SCALIA delivered the opinion of the Court.

We are presented with one of the most expansive class actions ever. The District Court and the Court of Appeals approved the certification of a class comprising about one and a half million plaintiffs, current and former female employees of petitioner Wal-Mart who allege that the discretion exercised by their local supervisors over pay and promotion matters violates Title VII by discriminating against women. In addition to injunctive and declaratory relief, the plaintiffs seek an award of backpay. We consider whether the certification of the plaintiff class was consistent with Federal Rules of Civil Procedure 23(a) and (b)(2).

I

A

Petitioner Wal-Mart is the Nation's largest private employer. It operates four types of retail stores throughout the country: Discount Stores, Supercenters, Neighborhood Markets, and Sam's Clubs. Those stores are divided into seven nationwide divisions, which in turn comprise 41 regions of 80 to 85 stores apiece. Each store has between 40 and 53 separate departments and 80 to 500 staff positions. In all, Wal-Mart operates approximately 3,400 stores and employs more than one million people.

Pay and promotion decisions at Wal-Mart are generally committed to local managers' broad discretion, which is exercised "in a largely subjective manner." 222 F.R.D. 137, 145 (ND Cal. 2004). Local store managers may increase the wages of hourly employees (within limits) with only limited corporate oversight. As for salaried employees, such as store managers and their deputies, higher corporate authorities have discretion to set their pay within preestablished ranges.

Promotions work in a similar fashion. Wal-Mart permits store managers to apply their own subjective criteria when selecting candidates as "support managers," which is the first step on the path to management. Admission to Wal-Mart's management training program, however, does require that a candidate meet certain objective criteria, including an above-average performance rating, at least one year's tenure in the applicant's current position, and a willingness to relocate.

But except for those requirements, regional and district managers have discretion to use their own judgment when selecting candidates for management training. Promotion to higher office—*e.g.*, assistant manager, co-manager, or store manager—is similarly at the discretion of the employee's superiors after prescribed objective factors are satisfied.

B

The named plaintiffs in this lawsuit, representing the 1.5 million members of the certified class, are three current or former Wal-Mart employees who allege that the company discriminated against them on the basis of their sex by denying them equal pay or promotions, in violation of Title VII of the Civil Rights Act of 1964.

Betty Dukes began working at a Pittsburgh, California, Wal-Mart in 1994. She started as a cashier, but later sought and received a promotion to customer service manager. After a series of disciplinary violations, however, Dukes was demoted back to cashier and then to greeter. Dukes concedes she violated company policy, but contends that the disciplinary actions were in fact retaliation for invoking internal complaint procedures and that male employees have not been disciplined for similar infractions. Dukes also claims two male greeters in the Pittsburgh store are paid more than she is.

Christine Kwapnoski has worked at Sam's Club stores in Missouri and California for most of her adult life. She has held a number of positions, including a supervisory position. She claims that a male manager yelled at her frequently and screamed at female employees, but not at men. The manager in question "told her to 'doll up,' to wear some makeup, and to dress a little better."

The final named plaintiff, Edith Arana, worked at a Wal-Mart store in Duarte, California, from 1995 to 2001. In 2000, she approached the store manager on more than one occasion about management training, but was brushed off. Arana concluded she was being denied opportunity for advancement because of her sex. She initiated internal complaint procedures, whereupon she was told to apply directly to the district manager if she thought her store manager was being unfair. Arana, however, decided against that and never applied for management training again. In 2001, she was fired for failure to comply with Wal-Mart's timekeeping policy.

These plaintiffs, respondents here, do not allege that Wal-Mart has any express corporate policy against the advancement of women. Rather, they claim that their local managers' discretion over pay and promotions is exercised disproportionately in favor of men, leading to an unlawful disparate impact on female employees, see 42 U.S.C. § 2000e–2(k). And, respondents say, because Wal-Mart is aware of this effect, its refusal to cabin its managers' authority amounts to disparate treatment, see § 2000e–2(a). Their complaint seeks injunctive and declaratory relief, punitive damages, and backpay. It does not ask for compensatory damages.

Importantly for our purposes, respondents claim that the discrimination to which they have been subjected is common to *all* Wal-Mart's female employees. The basic theory of their case is that a strong and uniform "corporate culture" permits bias against women to infect, perhaps subconsciously, the discretionary decisionmaking of each one of Wal-Mart's thousands of managers—thereby making every woman at the company the victim of one common discriminatory practice. Respondents therefore wish to litigate the Title VII claims of all female employees at Wal-Mart's stores in a nationwide class action.

C

Class certification is governed by Federal Rule of Civil Procedure 23. [After quoting the provisions of the rule, the Court noted that the applicability of Rules 23(b)(1) and 23(b)(3) "to the plaintiff class is not before us."]

Invoking these provisions, respondents moved the District Court to certify a plaintiff class consisting of "[a]ll women employed at any Wal-Mart domestic retail store at any time since December 26, 1998, who have been or may be subjected to Wal-Mart's challenged pay and management track promotions policies and practices." As evidence that there were indeed "questions of law or fact common to" all the women of Wal-Mart, as Rule 23(a)(2) requires, respondents relied chiefly on three forms of proof: statistical evidence about pay and promotion disparities between men and women at the company, anecdotal reports of discrimination from about 120 of Wal-Mart's female employees, and the testimony of a sociologist, Dr. William Bielby, who conducted a "social framework analysis" of Wal-Mart's "culture" and personnel practices, and concluded that the company was "vulnerable" to gender discrimination. 603 F.3d 571, 601 (9th Cir. 2010) (en banc).

Wal-Mart unsuccessfully moved to strike much of this evidence. It also offered its own countervailing statistical and other proof in an effort to defeat Rule 23(a)'s requirements of commonality, typicality, and adequate representation. Wal-Mart further contended that respondents' monetary claims for backpay could not be certified under Rule 23(b)(2), first because that Rule refers only to injunctive and declaratory relief, and second because the backpay claims could not be manageably tried as a class without depriving Wal-Mart of its right to present certain statutory defenses. With one limitation not relevant here, the District Court granted respondents' motion and certified their proposed class.

D

A divided en banc Court of Appeals substantially affirmed the District Court's certification order. The majority concluded that respondents' evidence of commonality was sufficient to "raise the common question whether Wal-Mart's female employees nationwide were subjected to a single set of corporate policies (not merely a number of independent discriminatory acts) that may have worked to unlawfully discriminate against them in violation of Title VII." It also agreed with the District Court that the named plaintiffs' claims were sufficiently typical of the class as a whole to satisfy Rule 23(a)(3), and that they could serve as adequate class representatives, see Rule 23(a)(4). With respect to the Rule 23(b)(2) question, the Ninth Circuit held that respondents' backpay claims could be certified as part of a (b)(2) class because they did not "predominat[e]" over the requests for declaratory and injunctive relief, meaning they were not "superior in strength, influence, or authority" to the nonmonetary claims.

Finally, the Court of Appeals determined that the action could be manageably tried as a class action because the District Court could adopt the approach the Ninth Circuit approved in Hilao v. Estate of Marcos, 103 F.3d 767, 782–787 (1996). There compensatory damages for some 9,541 class members were calculated by selecting 137 claims at random, referring those claims to a special master for valuation, and then extrapolating the validity and value of the untested claims from the sample set. The Court of Appeals "s[aw] no reason why a similar procedure to that used in *Hilao* could not be employed in this case." It would allow Wal-Mart "to present individual defenses in the randomly selected 'sample cases,' thus revealing the approximate percentage of class members whose unequal pay or nonpromotion was due to something other than gender discrimination."

We granted certiorari.

II

The class action is "an exception to the usual rule that litigation is conducted by and on behalf of the individual named parties only." Califano v. Yamasaki, 442 U.S. 682, 700–701 (1979). In order to justify a departure from that rule, "a class representative must be part of the class and 'possess the same interest and suffer the same injury' as the class members." East Tex. Motor Freight System, Inc. v. Rodriguez, 431 U.S. 395, 403 (1977) (quoting Schlesinger v. Reservists Comm. to Stop the War, 418 U.S. 208, 216 (1974)). Rule 23(a) ensures that the named plaintiffs are appropriate representatives of the class whose claims they wish to litigate. The Rule's four requirements—numerosity, commonality, typicality, and adequate representation—"effectively 'limit the class claims to those fairly encompassed by the named plaintiff's claims.'" General Telephone Co. of Southwest v. Falcon, 457 U.S. 147, 156 (1982) (quoting General Telephone Co. of Northwest v. EEOC, 446 U.S. 318, 330 (1980)).

A

The crux of this case is commonality—the rule requiring a plaintiff to show that "there are questions of law or fact common to the class." Rule

23(a)(2).[5] That language is easy to misread, since "[a]ny competently crafted class complaint literally raises common 'questions.'" Nagareda, Class Certification in the Age of Aggregate Proof, 84 N.Y.U. L. Rev. 97, 131–132 (2009). For example: Do all of us plaintiffs indeed work for Wal-Mart? Do our managers have discretion over pay? Is that an unlawful employment practice? What remedies should we get? Reciting these questions is not sufficient to obtain class certification. Commonality requires the plaintiff to demonstrate that the class members "have suffered the same injury," *Falcon, supra,* at 157. This does not mean merely that they have all suffered a violation of the same provision of law. Title VII, for example, can be violated in many ways—by intentional discrimination, or by hiring and promotion criteria that result in disparate impact, and by the use of these practices on the part of many different superiors in a single company. Quite obviously, the mere claim by employees of the same company that they have suffered a Title VII injury, or even a disparate-impact Title VII injury, gives no cause to believe that all their claims can productively be litigated at once. Their claims must depend upon a common contention—for example, the assertion of discriminatory bias on the part of the same supervisor. That common contention, moreover, must be of such a nature that it is capable of classwide resolution—which means that determination of its truth or falsity will resolve an issue that is central to the validity of each one of the claims in one stroke.

> What matters to class certification . . . is not the raising of common "questions"—even in droves—but, rather the capacity of a classwide proceeding to generate common *answers* apt to drive the resolution of the litigation. Dissimilarities within the proposed class are what have the potential to impede the generation of common answers. Nagareda, *supra,* at 132.

Rule 23 does not set forth a mere pleading standard. A party seeking class certification must affirmatively demonstrate his compliance with the Rule—that is, he must be prepared to prove that there are *in fact* sufficiently numerous parties, common questions of law or fact, etc. We recognized in *Falcon* that "sometimes it may be necessary for the court to probe behind the pleadings before coming to rest on the certification question," 457 U.S., at 160, and that certification is proper only if "the trial court is satisfied, after a rigorous analysis, that the prerequisites of Rule 23(a) have been satisfied," *id.,* at 161; see *id.,* at 160 ("[A]ctual, not

[5] We have previously stated in this context that "[t]he commonality and typicality requirements of Rule 23(a) tend to merge. Both serve as guideposts for determining whether under the particular circumstances maintenance of a class action is economical and whether the named plaintiff's claim and the class claims are so interrelated that the interests of the class members will be fairly and adequately protected in their absence. Those requirements therefore also tend to merge with the adequacy-of-representation requirement, although the latter requirement also raises concerns about the competency of class counsel and conflicts of interest." General Telephone Co. of Southwest v. Falcon, 457 U.S. 147, 157–158, n.13 (1982). In light of our disposition of the commonality question, however, it is unnecessary to resolve whether respondents have satisfied the typicality and adequate-representation requirements of Rule 23(a).

presumed, conformance with Rule 23(a) remains . . . indispensable"). Frequently that "rigorous analysis" will entail some overlap with the merits of the plaintiff's underlying claim. That cannot be helped. " '[T]he class determination generally involves considerations that are enmeshed in the factual and legal issues comprising the plaintiff's cause of action.' " *Falcon, supra*, at 160 (quoting Coopers & Lybrand v. Livesay, 437 U.S. 463, 469 (1978); some internal quotation marks omitted).[6] Nor is there anything unusual about that consequence: The necessity of touching aspects of the merits in order to resolve preliminary matters, *e.g.*, jurisdiction and venue, is a familiar feature of litigation. See Szabo v. Bridgeport Machines, Inc., 249 F.3d 672, 676–677 (7th Cir. 2001) (Easterbrook, J.).

In this case, proof of commonality necessarily overlaps with respondents' merits contention that Wal-Mart engages in a *pattern or practice* of discrimination. That is so because, in resolving an individual's Title VII claim, the crux of the inquiry is "the reason for a particular employment decision," Cooper v. Federal Reserve Bank of Richmond, 467 U.S. 867, 876 (1984). Here respondents wish to sue about literally millions of employment decisions at once. Without some glue holding the alleged *reasons* for all those decisions together, it will be impossible to say that examination of all the class members' claims for relief will produce a common answer to the crucial question *why was I disfavored*.

B

This Court's opinion in *Falcon* describes how the commonality issue must be approached. There an employee who claimed that he was deliberately denied a promotion on account of race obtained certification of a class comprising all employees wrongfully denied promotions and all applicants wrongfully denied jobs. 457 U.S., at 152. We rejected that composite class for lack of commonality and typicality, explaining:

> Conceptually, there is a wide gap between (a) an individual's claim that he has been denied a promotion [or higher pay] on discriminatory grounds, and his otherwise unsupported allegation that the company has a policy of discrimination, and (b) the existence of a class of persons who have suffered the same injury as that individual, such that the individual's claim and the class claim will share common questions of law or fact and

[6] A statement in one of our prior cases, Eisen v. Carlisle & Jacquelin, 417 U.S. 156, 177 (1974), is sometimes mistakenly cited to the contrary: "We find nothing in either the language or history of Rule 23 that gives a court any authority to conduct a preliminary inquiry into the merits of a suit in order to determine whether it may be maintained as a class action." But in that case, the judge had conducted a preliminary inquiry into the merits of a suit, not in order to determine the propriety of certification under Rules 23(a) and (b) (he had already done that, see *id.*, at 165), but in order to shift the cost of notice required by Rule 23(c)(2) from the plaintiff to the defendants. To the extent the quoted statement goes beyond the permissibility of a merits inquiry for any other pretrial purpose, it is the purest dictum and is contradicted by our other cases. . . .

that the individual's claim will be typical of the class claims. *Id.*, at 157–158.

Falcon suggested two ways in which that conceptual gap might be bridged. First, if the employer "used a biased testing procedure to evaluate both applicants for employment and incumbent employees, a class action on behalf of every applicant or employee who might have been prejudiced by the test clearly would satisfy the commonality and typicality requirements of Rule 23(a)." *Id.*, at 159, n.15. Second, "[s]ignificant proof that an employer operated under a general policy of discrimination conceivably could justify a class of both applicants and employees if the discrimination manifested itself in hiring and promotion practices in the same general fashion, such as through entirely subjective decisionmaking processes." *Ibid.* We think that statement precisely describes respondents' burden in this case. The first manner of bridging the gap obviously has no application here; Wal-Mart has no testing procedure or other companywide evaluation method that can be charged with bias. The whole point of permitting discretionary decisionmaking is to avoid evaluating employees under a common standard.

The second manner of bridging the gap requires "significant proof" that Wal-Mart "operated under a general policy of discrimination." That is entirely absent here. Wal-Mart's announced policy forbids sex discrimination, and as the District Court recognized the company imposes penalties for denials of equal employment opportunity. The only evidence of a "general policy of discrimination" respondents produced was the testimony of Dr. William Bielby, their sociological expert. Relying on "social framework" analysis, Bielby testified that Wal-Mart has a "strong corporate culture," that makes it " 'vulnerable' " to "gender bias." 222 F.R.D. at 152. He could not, however, "determine with any specificity how regularly stereotypes play a meaningful role in employment decisions at Wal-Mart. At his deposition . . . Dr. Bielby conceded that he could not calculate whether 0.5 percent or 95 percent of the employment decisions at Wal-Mart might be determined by stereotyped thinking." The parties dispute whether Bielby's testimony even met the standards for the admission of expert testimony under Federal Rule of Civil Procedure 702 and our *Daubert* case, see Daubert v. Merrell Dow Pharmaceuticals, Inc., 509 U.S. 579 (1993).[8] The District Court concluded that *Daubert* did not apply to expert testimony at the certification stage of class-action

[8] Bielby's conclusions in this case have elicited criticism from the very scholars on whose conclusions he relies for his social-framework analysis. See Monahan, Walker, & Mitchell, Contextual Evidence of Gender Discrimination: The Ascendance of "Social Frameworks," 94 Va. L. Rev. 1715, 1747 (2008) ("[Bielby's] research into conditions and behavior at Wal-Mart did not meet the standards expected of social scientific research into stereotyping and discrimination"); *id.*, at 1745, 1747 ("[A] social framework necessarily contains only general statements about reliable patterns of relations among variables . . . and goes no further. . . . Dr. Bielby claimed to present a social framework, but he testified about social facts specific to Wal-Mart"); *id.*, at 1747–1748 ("Dr. Bielby's report provides no verifiable method for measuring and testing any of the variables that were crucial to his conclusions and reflects nothing more than Dr. Bielby's 'expert judgment' about how general stereotyping research applied to all managers across all of Wal-Mart's stores nationwide for the multi-year class period").

proceedings. We doubt that is so, but even if properly considered, Bielby's testimony does nothing to advance respondents' case. "[W]hether 0.5 percent or 95 percent of the employment decisions at Wal-Mart might be determined by stereotyped thinking" is the essential question on which respondents' theory of commonality depends. If Bielby admittedly has no answer to that question, we can safely disregard what he has to say. It is worlds away from "significant proof" that Wal-Mart "operated under a general policy of discrimination."

C

The only corporate policy that the plaintiffs' evidence convincingly establishes is Wal-Mart's "policy" of *allowing discretion* by local supervisors over employment matters. On its face, of course, that is just the opposite of a uniform employment practice that would provide the commonality needed for a class action; it is a policy *against having* uniform employment practices. It is also a very common and presumptively reasonable way of doing business—one that we have said "should itself raise no inference of discriminatory conduct," Watson v. Fort Worth Bank & Trust, 487 U.S. 977, 990 (1988).

To be sure, we have recognized that, "in appropriate cases," giving discretion to lower-level supervisors can be the basis of Title VII liability under a disparate-impact theory—since "an employer's undisciplined system of subjective decisionmaking [can have] precisely the same effects as a system pervaded by impermissible intentional discrimination." *Id.*, at 990–991. But the recognition that this type of Title VII claim "can" exist does not lead to the conclusion that every employee in a company using a system of discretion has such a claim in common. To the contrary, left to their own devices most managers in any corporation—and surely most managers in a corporation that forbids sex discrimination—would select sex-neutral, performance-based criteria for hiring and promotion that produce no actionable disparity at all. Others may choose to reward various attributes that produce disparate impact—such as scores on general aptitude tests or educational achievements, see Griggs v. Duke Power Co., 401 U.S. 424, 431–432 (1971). And still other managers may be guilty of intentional discrimination that produces a sex-based disparity. In such a company, demonstrating the invalidity of one manager's use of discretion will do nothing to demonstrate the invalidity of another's. A party seeking to certify a nationwide class will be unable to show that all the employees' Title VII claims will in fact depend on the answers to common questions.

Respondents have not identified a common mode of exercising discretion that pervades the entire company—aside from their reliance on Dr. Bielby's social frameworks analysis that we have rejected. In a company of Wal-Mart's size and geographical scope, it is quite unbelievable that all managers would exercise their discretion in a common way without some common direction. Respondents attempt to make that showing by means of statistical and anecdotal evidence, but their evidence falls well short.

The statistical evidence consists primarily of regression analyses performed by Dr. Richard Drogin, a statistician, and Dr. Marc Bendick, a labor economist. Drogin conducted his analysis region-by-region, comparing the number of women promoted into management positions with the percentage of women in the available pool of hourly workers. After considering regional and national data, Drogin concluded that "there are statistically significant disparities between men and women at Wal-Mart . . . [and] these disparities . . . can be explained only by gender discrimination." 603 F.3d, at 604 (internal quotation marks omitted). Bendick compared work-force data from Wal-Mart and competitive retailers and concluded that Wal-Mart "promotes a lower percentage of women than its competitors."

Even if they are taken at face value, these studies are insufficient to establish that respondents' theory can be proved on a classwide basis. In *Falcon*, we held that one named plaintiff's experience of discrimination was insufficient to infer that "discriminatory treatment is typical of [the employer's employment] practices." 457 U.S., at 158. A similar failure of inference arises here. As Judge Ikuta observed in her dissent, "[i]nformation about disparities at the regional and national level does not establish the existence of disparities at individual stores, let alone raise the inference that a company-wide policy of discrimination is implemented by discretionary decisions at the store and district level." 603 F.3d, at 637. A regional pay disparity, for example, may be attributable to only a small set of Wal-Mart stores, and cannot by itself establish the uniform, store-by-store disparity upon which the plaintiffs' theory of commonality depends.

There is another, more fundamental, respect in which respondents' statistical proof fails. Even if it established (as it does not) a pay or promotion pattern that differs from the nationwide figures or the regional figures in *all* of Wal-Mart's 3,400 stores, that would still not demonstrate that commonality of issue exists. Some managers will claim that the availability of women, or qualified women, or interested women, in their stores' area does not mirror the national or regional statistics. And almost all of them will claim to have been applying some sex-neutral, performance-based criteria—whose nature and effects will differ from store to store. In the landmark case of ours which held that giving discretion to lower-level supervisors can be the basis of Title VII liability under a disparate-impact theory, the plurality opinion *conditioned* that holding on the corollary that merely proving that the discretionary system has produced a racial or sexual disparity *is not enough.* "[T]he plaintiff must begin by identifying the specific employment practice that is challenged." *Watson*, 487 U.S., at 994; accord, Wards Cove Packing Co. v. Atonio, 490 U.S. 642, 656 (1989) (approving that statement), superseded by statute on other grounds, 42 U.S.C. § 2000e–2(k). That is all the more necessary when a class of plaintiffs is sought to be certified. Other than the bare existence of delegated discretion, respondents have identified no "specific employment practice"—much less one that ties all their 1.5 million claims together. Merely showing that Wal-Mart's policy of discretion has produced an overall sex-based disparity does not suffice.

Respondents' anecdotal evidence suffers from the same defects, and in addition is too weak to raise any inference that all the individual, discretionary personnel decisions are discriminatory. [R]espondents filed some 120 affidavits reporting experiences of discrimination—about 1 for every 12,500 class members—relating to only some 235 out of Wal-Mart's 3,400 stores. 603 F.3d, at 634 (Ikuta, J., dissenting). More than half of these reports are concentrated in only six States (Alabama, California, Florida, Missouri, Texas, and Wisconsin); half of all States have only one or two anecdotes; and 14 States have no anecdotes about Wal-Mart's operations at all. *Id.*, at 634–635, and n.10. Even if every single one of these accounts is true, that would not demonstrate that the entire company "operate[s] under a general policy of discrimination," *Falcon*, *supra*, at 159, n.15, which is what respondents must show to certify a companywide class.

The dissent misunderstands the nature of the foregoing analysis. It criticizes our focus on the dissimilarities between the putative class members on the ground that we have "blend[ed]" Rule 23(a)(2)'s commonality requirement with Rule 23(b)(3)'s inquiry into whether common questions "predominate" over individual ones. That is not so. We quite agree that for purposes of Rule 23(a)(2) " '[e]ven a single [common] question' " will do, *post*, at 10, n.9 (quoting Nagareda, The Preexistence Principle and the Structure of the Class Action, 103 Colum. L. Rev. 149, 176, n.110 (2003)). We consider dissimilarities not in order to determine (as Rule 23(b)(3) requires) whether common questions *predominate*, but in order to determine (as Rule 23(a)(2) requires) whether there *is* "[e]ven a single [common] question." And there is not here. Because respondents provide no convincing proof of a companywide discriminatory pay and promotion policy, we have concluded that they have not established the existence of any common question.

In sum, we agree with Chief Judge Kozinski that the members of the class:

> "[H]eld a multitude of different jobs, at different levels of Wal-Mart's hierarchy, for variable lengths of time, in 3,400 stores, sprinkled across 50 states, with a kaleidoscope of supervisors (male and female), subject to a variety of regional policies that all differed. . . . Some thrived while others did poorly. They have little in common but their sex and this lawsuit." 603 F.3d, at 652 (dissenting opinion).

III

We also conclude that respondents' claims for backpay were improperly certified under Federal Rule of Civil Procedure 23(b)(2). Our opinion in Ticor Title Ins. Co. v. Brown, 511 U.S. 117, 121 (1994) (per curiam) expressed serious doubt about whether claims for monetary relief may be certified under that provision. We now hold that they may not, at least where (as here) the monetary relief is not incidental to the injunctive or declaratory relief.

A

Rule 23(b)(2) allows class treatment when "the party opposing the class has acted or refused to act on grounds that apply generally to the class, so that final injunctive relief or corresponding declaratory relief is appropriate respecting the class as a whole." One possible reading of this provision is that it applies *only* to requests for such injunctive or declaratory relief and does not authorize the class certification of monetary claims at all. We need not reach that broader question in this case, because we think that, at a minimum, claims for *individualized* relief (like the backpay at issue here) do not satisfy the Rule. The key to the (b)(2) class is "the indivisible nature of the injunctive or declaratory remedy warranted—the notion that the conduct is such that it can be enjoined or declared unlawful only as to all of the class members or as to none of them." Nagareda, 84 N.Y.U. L. Rev., at 132. In other words, Rule 23(b)(2) applies only when a single injunction or declaratory judgment would provide relief to each member of the class. It does not authorize class certification when each individual class member would be entitled to a *different* injunction or declaratory judgment against the defendant. Similarly, it does not authorize class certification when each class member would be entitled to an individualized award of monetary damages. . . .

Permitting the combination of individualized and classwide relief in a (b)(2) class is also inconsistent with the structure of Rule 23(b). Classes certified under (b)(1) and (b)(2) share the most traditional justifications for class treatment—that individual adjudications would be impossible or unworkable, as in a (b)(1) class, or that the relief sought must perforce affect the entire class at once, as in a (b)(2) class. For that reason these are also mandatory classes: The Rule provides no opportunity for (b)(1) or (b)(2) class members to opt out, and does not even oblige the District Court to afford them notice of the action. Rule 23(b)(3), by contrast, is an "adventuresome innovation" of the 1966 amendments, Amchem Products, Inc. v. Windsor, 521 U.S. 591, 614 (internal quotation marks omitted), framed for situations "in which 'class-action treatment is not as clearly called for'," *id.,* at 615 (quoting Advisory Committee's Notes, 28 U.S.C. App., p. 697 (1994 ed.)). It allows class certification in a much wider set of circumstances but with greater procedural protections. Its only prerequisites are that "the questions of law or fact common to class members predominate over any questions affecting only individual members, and that a class action is superior to other available methods for fairly and efficiently adjudicating the controversy." Rule 23(b)(3). And unlike (b)(1) and (b)(2) classes, the (b)(3) class is not mandatory; class members are entitled to receive "the best notice that is practicable under the circumstances" and to withdraw from the class at their option. See Rule 23(c)(2)(B).

Given that structure, we think it clear that individualized monetary claims belong in Rule 23(b)(3). The procedural protections attending the (b)(3) class—predominance, superiority, mandatory notice, and the right to opt out—are missing from (b)(2) not because the Rule considers them unnecessary, but because it considers them unnecessary *to a (b)(2) class.* When a class seeks an indivisible injunction benefitting all its members at once, there is no reason to undertake a case-specific inquiry into whether class issues predominate or whether class action is a superior method of adjudicating the dispute. Predominance and superiority are self-evident. But with respect to each class member's individualized claim for money, that is not so—which is precisely why (b)(3) requires the judge to make findings about predominance and superiority before allowing the class. Similarly, (b)(2) does not require that class members be given notice and opt-out rights, presumably because it is thought (rightly or wrongly) that notice has no purpose when the class is mandatory, and that depriving people of their right to sue in this manner complies with the Due Process Clause. In the context of a class action predominantly for money damages we have held that absence of notice and opt-out violates due process. See Phillips Petroleum Co. v. Shutts, 472 U.S. 797, 812 (1985). While we have never held that to be so where the monetary claims do not predominate, the serious possibility that it may be so provides an additional reason not to read Rule 23(b)(2) to include the monetary claims here.

B

Against that conclusion, respondents argue that their claims for backpay were appropriately certified as part of a class under Rule 23(b)(2) because those claims do not "predominate" over their requests for injunctive and declaratory relief. They rely upon the Advisory Committee's statement that Rule 23(b)(2) "does not extend to cases in which the appropriate final relief relates *exclusively or predominantly* to money damages." 39 F.R.D. 69, 102 (1966) (emphasis added). The negative implication, they argue, is that it *does* extend to cases in which the appropriate final relief relates only partially and nonpredominantly to money damages. Of course it is the Rule itself, not the Advisory Committee's description of it, that governs. And a mere negative inference does not in our view suffice to establish a disposition that has no basis in the Rule's text, and that does obvious violence to the Rule's structural features. The mere "predominance" of a proper (b)(2) injunctive claim does nothing to justify elimination of Rule 23(b)(3)'s procedural protections: It neither establishes the superiority of *class* adjudication over *individual* adjudication nor cures the notice and opt-out problems. We fail to see why the Rule should be read to nullify these protections whenever a plaintiff class, at its option, combines its monetary claims with a request—even a "predominating request"—for an injunction. . . .

Finally, respondents argue that their backpay claims are appropriate for a (b)(2) class action because a backpay award is equitable in nature. The latter may be true, but it is irrelevant. The Rule does not speak of "equitable" remedies generally but of injunctions and declaratory judgments. As Title VII itself makes pellucidly clear, backpay is neither. See 42 U.S.C. § 2000e–5(g)(2)(B)(i) and (ii) (distinguishing between declaratory and injunctive relief and the payment of "backpay," see § 2000e–5(g)(2)(A)).

C

. . .

Contrary to the Ninth Circuit's view, Wal-Mart is entitled to individualized determinations of each employee's eligibility for backpay. Title VII includes a detailed remedial scheme. If a plaintiff prevails in showing that an employer has discriminated against him in violation of the statute, the court "may enjoin the respondent from engaging in such unlawful employment practice, and order such affirmative action as may be appropriate, [including] reinstatement or hiring of employees, with or without backpay . . . or any other equitable relief as the court deems appropriate." § 2000e–5(g)(1). But if the employer can show that it took an adverse employment action against an employee for any reason other than discrimination, the court cannot order the "hiring, reinstatement, or promotion of an individual as an employee, or the payment to him of any backpay." § 2000e–5(g)(2)(A).

We have established a procedure for trying pattern-or-practice cases that gives effect to these statutory requirements. When the plaintiff seeks individual relief such as reinstatement or backpay after establishing a pattern or practice of discrimination, "a district court must usually conduct additional proceedings . . . to determine the scope of individual relief." Teamsters v. United States, 431 U.S. 324, 361 (1977). At this phase, the burden of proof will shift to the company, but it will have the right to raise any individual affirmative defenses it may have, and to "demonstrate that the individual applicant was denied an employment opportunity for lawful reasons." *Id.,* at 362.

The Court of Appeals believed that it was possible to replace such proceedings with Trial by Formula. A sample set of the class members would be selected, as to whom liability for sex discrimination and the backpay owing as a result would be determined in depositions supervised by a master. The percentage of claims determined to be valid would then be applied to the entire remaining class, and the number of (presumptively) valid claims thus derived would be multiplied by the average backpay award in the sample set to arrive at the entire class recovery—without further individualized proceedings. 603 F.3d, at 625–627. We disapprove that novel project. Because the Rules Enabling Act forbids interpreting Rule 23 to "abridge, enlarge or modify any substantive right," 28 U.S.C. § 2072(b); see Ortiz v. Fibreboard Corp., 527 U.S. 815, 845 (1999), a class cannot be certified on the premise that Wal-Mart will not be entitled to litigate its statutory defenses to individual claims. And because the necessity of that litigation will prevent backpay from being "incidental" to the classwide injunction, respondents' class could not be certified even assuming, *arguendo*, that "incidental" monetary relief can be awarded to a 23(b)(2) class.

The judgment of the Court of Appeals is

Reversed.

■ JUSTICE GINSBURG, with whom JUSTICE BREYER, JUSTICE SOTOMAYOR, and JUSTICE KAGAN join, concurring in part and dissenting in part.

The class in this case, I agree with the Court, should not have been certified under Federal Rule of Civil Procedure 23(b)(2). The plaintiffs, alleging discrimination in violation of Title VII, 42 U.S.C. § 2000e *et seq.*, seek monetary relief that is not merely incidental to any injunctive or declaratory relief that might be available. A putative class of this type may be certifiable under Rule 23(b)(3), if the plaintiffs show that common class questions "predominate" over issues affecting individuals—*e.g.*, qualification for, and the amount of, backpay or compensatory damages—and that a class action is "superior" to other modes of adjudication.

Whether the class the plaintiffs describe meets the specific requirements of Rule 23(b)(3) is not before the Court, and I would reserve that matter for consideration and decision on remand. The Court, however, disqualifies the class at the starting gate, holding that the plaintiffs cannot cross the "commonality" line set by Rule 23(a)(2). In so ruling, the Court imports into the Rule 23(a) determination concerns properly addressed in a Rule 23(b)(3) assessment.

I

A

Rule 23(a)(2) establishes a preliminary requirement for maintaining a class action: "[T]here are questions of law or fact common to the class." The Rule "does not require that all questions of law or fact raised in the litigation be common," 1 H. Newberg & A. Conte, Newberg on Class Actions § 3.10, pp. 3–48 to 3–49 (3d ed. 1992); indeed, "[e]ven a single question of law or fact common to the members of the class will satisfy the commonality requirement," Nagareda, The Preexistence Principle and the Structure of the Class Action, 103 Colum. L. Rev. 149, 176, n.110 (2003). See Advisory Committee's 1937 Notes on Fed. Rule Civ. Proc. 23, 28 U.S.C. App., p. 138 (citing with approval cases in which "there was only a question of law or fact common to" the class members). . . .

B

The District Court, recognizing that "one significant issue common to the class may be sufficient to warrant certification," found that the plaintiffs easily met that test. Absent an error of law or an abuse of discretion, an appellate tribunal has no warrant to upset the District Court's finding of commonality. See Califano v. Yamasaki, 442 U.S. 682, 703 (1979) ("[M]ost issues arising under Rule 23 . . . [are] committed in the first instance to the discretion of the district court.").

The District Court certified a class of "[a]ll women employed at any Wal-Mart domestic retail store at any time since December 26, 1998." The named plaintiffs, led by Betty Dukes, propose to litigate, on behalf of the class, allegations that Wal-Mart discriminates on the basis of gender in pay and promotions. They allege that the company "[r]eli[es] on gender stereotypes in making employment decisions such as . . . promotion[s] [and] pay." Wal-Mart permits those prejudices to infect personnel decisions, the plaintiffs contend, by leaving pay and promotions in the hands of "a nearly all male managerial workforce" using "arbitrary and subjective criteria." Further alleged barriers to the advancement of female employees include the company's requirement, "as a condition of promotion to management jobs, that employees be willing to relocate." Absent instruction otherwise, there is a risk that managers will act on the familiar assumption that women, because of their services to husband and children, are less mobile than men. See Dept. of Labor, Federal Glass Ceiling Commission, Good for Business: Making Full Use of the Nation's Human Capital 151 (1995).

Women fill 70 percent of the hourly jobs in the retailer's stores but make up only "33 percent of management employees." 222 F.R.D., at 146. "[T]he higher one looks in the organization the lower the percentage of women." *Id.*, at 155. The plaintiffs' "largely uncontested descriptive statistics" also show that women working in the company's stores "are paid less than men in every region" and "that the salary gap widens over time even for men and women hired into the same jobs at the same time." *Ibid.*; cf. Ledbetter v. Goodyear Tire & Rubber Co., 550 U.S. 618, 643 (2007) (Ginsburg, J., dissenting).

The District Court identified "systems for . . . promoting in-store employees" that were "sufficiently similar across regions and stores" to conclude that "the manner in which these systems affect the class raises issues that are common to all class members." The selection of employees for promotion to in-store management "is fairly characterized as a 'tap on the shoulder' process," in which managers have discretion about whose shoulders to tap. Vacancies are not regularly posted; from among those employees satisfying minimum qualifications, managers choose whom to promote on the basis of their own subjective impressions.

Wal-Mart's compensation policies also operate uniformly across stores, the District Court found. The retailer leaves open a $2 band for every position's hourly pay rate. Wal-Mart provides no standards or criteria for setting wages within that band, and thus does nothing to counter unconscious bias on the part of supervisors.

Wal-Mart's supervisors do not make their discretionary decisions in a vacuum. The District Court reviewed means Wal-Mart used to maintain a "carefully constructed . . . corporate culture," such as frequent meetings to reinforce the common way of thinking, regular transfers of managers between stores to ensure uniformity throughout the company, monitoring of stores "on a close and constant basis," and "Wal-Mart TV," "broadcas[t] . . . into all stores."

The plaintiffs' evidence, including class members' tales of their own experiences, suggests that gender bias suffused Wal-Mart's company culture. Among illustrations, senior management often refer to female associates as "little Janie Qs." Plaintiffs' Motion for Class Certification. One manager told an employee that "[m]en are here to make a career and women aren't." 222 F.R.D., at 166. A committee of female Wal-Mart executives concluded that "[s]tereotypes limit the opportunities offered to women." Plaintiffs' Motion for Class Certification.

Finally, the plaintiffs presented an expert's appraisal to show that the pay and promotions disparities at Wal-Mart "can be explained only by gender discrimination and not by . . . neutral variables." Using regression analyses, their expert, Richard Drogin, controlled for factors including, *inter alia*, job performance, length of time with the company, and the store where an employee worked. *Id.*, at 159.[5] The results, the District Court found, were sufficient to raise an "inference of discrimination."

C

The District Court's identification of a common question, whether Wal-Mart's pay and promotions policies gave rise to unlawful discrimination, was hardly infirm. The practice of delegating to supervisors large discretion to make personnel decisions, uncontrolled by formal standards, has long been known to have the potential to produce disparate effects. Managers, like all humankind, may be prey to biases of which they are unaware.[6] The risk of discrimination is heightened when

[5] The Court asserts that Drogin showed only average differences at the "regional and national level" between male and female employees. In fact, his regression analyses showed there were disparities *within* stores. The majority's contention to the contrary reflects only an arcane disagreement about statistical method—which the District Court resolved in the plaintiffs' favor. Appellate review is no occasion to disturb a trial court's handling of factual disputes of this order.

[6] An example vividly illustrates how subjective decisionmaking can be a vehicle for discrimination. Performing in symphony orchestras was long a male preserve. Goldin and Rouse, Orchestrating Impartiality: The Impact of "Blind" Auditions on Female Musicians, 90 Am. Econ. Rev. 715, 715–716 (2000). In the 1970's orchestras began hiring musicians through auditions open to all comers. *Id.*, at 716. Reviewers were to judge applicants solely on their musical abilities, yet subconscious bias led some reviewers to disfavor women. Orchestras that permitted reviewers to see the applicants hired far fewer female musicians than orchestras that conducted blind auditions, in which candidates played behind opaque screens. *Id.*, at 738.

those managers are predominantly of one sex, and are steeped in a corporate culture that perpetuates gender stereotypes.

The plaintiffs' allegations resemble those in one of the prototypical cases in this area, Leisner v. New York Tel. Co., 358 F. Supp. 359, 364–365 (S.D.N.Y. 1973). In deciding on promotions, supervisors in that case were to start with objective measures; but ultimately, they were to "look at the individual as a total individual." *Id.,* at 365 (internal quotation marks omitted). The final question they were to ask and answer: "Is this person going to be successful in our business?" *Ibid.* (internal quotation marks omitted). It is hardly surprising that for many managers, the ideal candidate was someone with characteristics similar to their own.

We have held that "discretionary employment practices" can give rise to Title VII claims, not only when such practices are motivated by discriminatory intent but also when they produce discriminatory results. See Watson v. Fort Worth Bank & Trust, 487 U.S. 977, 988, 991 (1988). But see *ante*, at 17 ("[P]roving that [a] discretionary system has produced a . . . disparity *is not enough.*"). In *Watson*, as here, an employer had given its managers large authority over promotions. An employee sued the bank under Title VII, alleging that the "discretionary promotion system" caused a discriminatory effect based on race. 487 U.S., at 984 (internal quotation marks omitted). Four different supervisors had declined, on separate occasions, to promote the employee. *Id.,* at 982. Their reasons were subjective and unknown. The employer, we noted "had not developed precise and formal criteria for evaluating candidates"; "[i]t relied instead on the subjective judgment of supervisors." *Ibid.*

Aware of "the problem of subconscious stereotypes and prejudices," we held that the employer's "undisciplined system of subjective decisionmaking" was an "employment practic[e]" that "may be analyzed under the disparate impact approach." *Id.,* at 990–991. See also Wards Cove Packing Co. v. Atonio, 490 U.S. 642, 657 (1989) (recognizing "the use of 'subjective decision making'" as an "employment practic[e]" subject to disparate-impact attack).

The plaintiffs' allegations state claims of gender discrimination in the form of biased decisionmaking in both pay and promotions. The evidence reviewed by the District Court adequately demonstrated that resolving those claims would necessitate examination of particular policies and practices alleged to affect, adversely and globally, women employed at Wal-Mart's stores. Rule 23(a)(2), setting a necessary but not a sufficient criterion for class-action certification, demands nothing further.

II

A

The Court gives no credence to the key dispute common to the class: whether Wal-Mart's discretionary pay and promotion policies are discriminatory. "What matters," the Court asserts, "is not the raising of common 'questions,'" but whether there are "[d]issimilarities within the proposed class" that "have the potential to impede the generation of common answers."

The Court blends Rule 23(a)(2)'s threshold criterion with the more demanding criteria of Rule 23(b)(3), and thereby elevates the (a)(2) inquiry so that it is no longer "easily satisfied," 5 J. Moore et al., Moore's Federal Practice § 23.23[2], p. 23–72 (3d ed. 2011). Rule 23(b)(3) certification requires, in addition to the four 23(a) findings, determinations that "questions of law or fact common to class members predominate over any questions affecting only individual members" and that "a class action is superior to other available methods for . . . adjudicating the controversy."

The Court's emphasis on differences between class members mimics the Rule 23(b)(3) inquiry into whether common questions "predominate" over individual issues. And by asking whether the individual differences "impede" common adjudication, *ante*, at 10 (internal quotation marks omitted), the Court duplicates 23(b)(3)'s question whether "a class action is superior" to other modes of adjudication. Indeed, Professor Nagareda, whose "dissimilarities" inquiry the Court endorses, developed his position in the context of Rule 23(b)(3). See 84 N.Y.U. L. Rev., at 131 (Rule 23(b)(3) requires "some decisive degree of similarity across the proposed class" because it "speaks of common 'questions' that 'predominate' over individual ones"). "The Rule 23(b)(3) predominance inquiry" is meant to "tes[t] whether proposed classes are sufficiently cohesive to warrant adjudication by representation." Amchem Products, Inc. v. Windsor, 521 U.S. 591, 623 (1997). If courts must conduct a "dissimilarities" analysis at the Rule 23(a)(2) stage, no mission remains for Rule 23(b)(3).

Because Rule 23(a) is also a prerequisite for Rule 23(b)(1) and Rule 23(b)(2) classes, the Court's "dissimilarities" position is far reaching. Individual differences should not bar a Rule 23(b)(1) or Rule 23(b)(2) class, so long as the Rule 23(a) threshold is met. See *Amchem Products*, 521 U.S., at 623, n.19 (Rule 23(b)(1)(B) "does not have a predominance requirement"); *Yamasaki*, 442 U.S., at 701 (Rule 23(b)(2) action in which the Court noted that "[i]t is unlikely that differences in the factual background of each claim will affect the outcome of the legal issue"). For example, in Franks v. Bowman Transp. Co., 424 U.S. 747 (1976), a Rule 23(b)(2) class of African-American truckdrivers complained that the defendant had discriminatorily refused to hire black applicants. We recognized that the "qualification[s] and performance" of individual class members might vary. *Id.,* at 772 (internal quotation marks omitted). "Generalizations concerning such individually applicable evidence," we cautioned, "cannot serve as a justification for the denial of [injunctive] relief to the entire class." *Ibid.*

B

The "dissimilarities" approach leads the Court to train its attention on what distinguishes individual class members, rather than on what unites them. Given the lack of standards for pay and promotions, the majority says, "demonstrating the invalidity of one manager's use of discretion will do nothing to demonstrate the invalidity of another's."

Wal-Mart's delegation of discretion over pay and promotions is a policy uniform throughout all stores. The very nature of discretion is that people will exercise it in various ways. A system of delegated discretion, *Watson* held, is a practice actionable under Title VII when it produces discriminatory outcomes. 487 U.S., at 990–991. A finding that Wal-Mart's pay and promotions practices in fact violate the law would be the first step in the usual order of proof for plaintiffs seeking individual remedies for company-wide discrimination. Teamsters v. United States, 431 U.S. 324, 359 (1977); see Albemarle Paper Co. v. Moody, 422 U.S. 405, 415–423 (1975). That each individual employee's unique circumstances will ultimately determine whether she is entitled to backpay or damages, § 2000e–5(g)(2)(A) (barring backpay if a plaintiff "was refused . . . advancement . . . for any reason other than discrimination"), should not factor into the Rule 23(a)(2) determination.

The Court errs in importing a "dissimilarities" notion suited to Rule 23(b)(3) into the Rule 23(a) commonality inquiry. I therefore cannot join Part II of the Court's opinion.

NOTES ON *WAL-MART STORES, INC. V. DUKES*

1. **What Was Decided.** The Supreme Court unanimously reversed certification of the class under subdivision (b)(2) of Rule 23, and by a vote of five to four, also reversed eligibility for certification of any class action at all for failure to satisfy the requirement of commonality under subdivision (a)(2). The unanimous holding would have left open for consideration on remand whether the class could be certified as a class action for monetary relief under subdivision (b)(3), a question not reached either by Justice Scalia writing for the Court or Justice Ginsburg writing for four justices. The five-to-four holding precluded the possibility of certification under (b)(3) because "questions of law or fact common to the class" are among the prerequisites listed in subdivision (a) for certification of a class under (b)(1), (b)(2), or (b)(3). This disputed holding reaches further than the unanimous holding, both on the facts of the case and in the general law of class actions. On the facts of the case, it prevents certification of any class on remand, and in general, it reinforces commonality as a barrier to certification of all kinds of class actions, not just those concerned with employment discrimination. Commentary on the decision has therefore focused on this holding, so much so that Justice Ginsburg's opinion often is characterized simply as a dissent, when in fact she agrees with the majority that the class could not be certified under (b)(2).

This unanimous holding is important in its own right, particularly in employment discrimination class actions, in which the plaintiffs typically seek backpay and damages, in addition to classwide injunctive relief. From now on, any action in which backpay and damages are more than "incidental"—and perhaps in any case in which they are present at all—must be certified under subdivision (b)(3). This makes a difference for three reasons: class actions are harder to certify under (b)(3) than under (b)(2); class members are entitled to individual notice under (b)(3) but not under (b)(2); and they also have the right to opt out under (b)(3) but not under (b)(2). Class actions can be certified under (b)(3) only if common questions "predominate over any questions affecting only individual class members." As Justice Ginsburg emphasizes this "predominance" requirement is much stricter than the requirement of "commonality" under (a)(2). In addition, the requirement of individual notice under (b)(3) can result in significant expense in maintaining a class action, and in a case as large as *Wal-Mart*, with over a million class members, these expenses can be prohibitive. The related right of individual plaintiffs to opt out from (b)(3) class actions creates difficulties in managing the action and can erode the base of class members for which the plaintiffs' attorneys can obtain relief, and any corresponding award of attorney's fees.

The obvious alternative to certification of employment discrimination class actions under (b)(3) now appears to be to assert only claims for classwide injunctive or declaratory relief and obtain certification under (b)(2). That prospect leaves the class members to fend for themselves in seeking individual relief in the form of backpay and damages, which they might not find to be large enough to justify the cost of an individual lawsuit. It also leaves the plaintiffs' attorneys with a drastically reduced prospect of an award of attorney's fees, which depend mainly upon the extent of the relief obtained for the class. Plaintiffs' attorneys undoubtedly would find it easier to obtain certification of a stripped down class action limited to injunctive relief under (b)(2), but they would also find any recovery on behalf of the class (and for themselves) to be stripped down as well. The "money," so to speak, is in monetary recoveries.

2. **The Difference Between the Majority and the "Dissent."** Justice Scalia, speaking for the five justices in the majority, also holds that the requirement of commonality in (a)(2) was not met. Justice Ginsburg, speaking for four justices, would have deferred to the district court's finding that it was met. This disagreement goes to both the content of the requirement of commonality and the sufficiency of the evidence presented by the plaintiffs in this case. This note addresses the issue of content and the next the sufficiency of the evidence.

On the issue of content, Justice Scalia quotes the late Professor Richard Nagareda for the proposition that the crucial inquiry is "the capacity of a classwide proceeding to generate common *answers* apt to drive the resolution of the litigation." Class-wide questions do not matter unless they are likely to lead to class-wide answers. Finding that they are likely to do so requires an inquiry that goes beyond the pleadings to the factual basis provided by the plaintiffs, a basis that it is itself intertwined with the merits. In an important footnote, note 6, Justice Scalia restricts the implications of the important decision in *Eisen v. Carlisle & Jacquelin*, 417 U.S. 156 (1974), which disapproved of an inquiry into the merits as a preliminary to certification of a class. That holding, Justice Scalia now makes clear, goes only to a preliminary finding that the plaintiffs' claims are meritorious, not to an examination of the merits of the claim insofar as they reveal whether the requirements of Rule 23 have been satisfied. He emphasizes that "rigorous analysis" of the issue of commonality "will entail some overlap with the merits of the plaintiff's underlying claim."

Justice Ginsburg does not deny the need for an examination of the merits insofar as the merits bear on the requirements of the rule, but she would defer to the district court's assessment of these issues in the absence of "an error of law or an abuse of discretion." She also argues that the majority mistakenly imported into the determination of commonality under (a)(2) the requirements of predominance under (b)(3). She argues, based on considerable lower court precedent, that the existence of common questions of law and fact under (a)(2) should be an easy requirement to meet, whereas the predominance of common questions under (b)(3) involves the kind of "rigorous analysis" that the majority engages in.

A surprising consequence of her argument is that, on remand, she doesn't really disagree that much with Justice Scalia, at least if her reasoning is taken literally. Since the Court was unanimous on the need to certify this case under (b)(3), Justice Ginsburg would thus remand for consideration of that issue so long as it contained claims for monetary relief. But (b)(3), of course, includes the predominance requirement that she accuses Justice Scalia of smuggling into (a)(2). On remand, however, the question of predominance would be squarely presented on any view of the rule, and at that point, she could no longer object to the "rigorous analysis" that Justice Scalia engages in. Although neither Justice Scalia nor Justice Ginsburg directly addresses the question whether the requirements of (b)(3) were satisfied, Justice Ginsburg only succeeds in postponing a closer look at the evidence that the majority finds wanting. Perhaps, however, she might evaluate this evidence differently, as discussed in the next note.

3. **Evidence of Common Questions.** For the majority, Justice Scalia finds no evidence of common questions at all, while Justice Ginsburg finds evidence of pervasive gender bias in the subjective decisions made by Wal-Mart's supervisors. Both opinions rely on the same body of evidence submitted by the plaintiffs, which had three main components: anecdotal evidence of particular instances of discrimination; a regression analysis on the low rates at which women were promoted; and a sociological analysis showing a corporate culture vulnerable to gender bias.

All three sources of evidence were, according to Justice Scalia, inadequate to overcome the fact that the only common practice challenged by the plaintiffs was "Wal-Mart's 'policy' of *allowing discretion* by local supervisors over employment matters." For him, this was "a policy *against having* uniform employment practices," which could generate common questions of law or fact only with " 'significant proof' that Wal-Mart 'operated under a general policy of discrimination.' " (All italics in original.) According to Justice Scalia, the anecdotal evidence concerned too many supervisors, in too many different stores, making too many different decisions to generate any inference of common practices. It consisted of affidavits of 120 instances of discrimination scattered over 3,400 stores. The regression analysis was also inadequate on his view. It showed, at most, the low rate at which women were promoted in different regions in which Wal-Mart operated, but it failed to identify any common feature of these promotion decisions that caused this discrepancy. And the sociological analysis could not identify the effect of sex-based stereotyping with any precision at all, whether it affected "0.5 percent or 95 percent of the employment decisions at Wal-Mart."

Justice Ginsburg, as we have seen, started off with a weaker standard for showing commonality and greater discretion according to the district court. She then reached the opposite conclusion by looking at the same evidence as the majority. She was more persuaded by the anecdotal evidence, which in her view did not have to identify instances of discrimination in proportion to the scope of the class. She agreed with the district court that the regression analysis was "sufficient to raise an 'inference of discrimination.'" And without specifically examining the evidence of the plaintiff's sociological study, she found evidence of implicit bias in earlier sex discrimination cases and in other studies, and in particular, in one on discrimination in orchestra auditions, cited in note 6 of her opinion.

The majority and the separate opinion seem to differ less in the detailed analysis of the evidence than they do in their overall attitude towards it. Justice Scalia searches for evidence of a discriminatory policy and finds none. Justice Ginsburg looks for a reason to upset the findings of the district court and also finds none. Who is right? The case certainly looks very different depending upon whether a general policy of discrimination must be proved by the plaintiffs or disproved by the defendant. It also looks very different depending upon assumptions about the prevalence of the particular kind of discrimination alleged. Did Justice Scalia go too far in presuming that Wal-Mart's supervisors made subjective decisions free from pervasive forms of gender bias? Or did he just give Wal-Mart the equivalent of a presumption of innocence in civil proceedings and force the plaintiffs to make some showing of a common policy of discrimination? Conversely, did Justice Ginsburg make the opposite mistake of assuming that Wal-Mart's supervisors, who were mostly male, engaged in gender bias in the absence of sufficient proof? Or did she simply recognize the presence of hidden forms of sex discrimination widely acknowledged to exist in our society?

This difference in attitude also goes to the merits of the case, which still remains separate from the issue of certification, even after Justice Scalia's clarifying footnote on the implications of *Eisen*. Simply as a matter of timing, certification must be decided at "an early practicable time" under Rule 23(c)(1)(A), well before any decision on the merits. For the majority, Justice Scalia apparently sought to avoid any prejudgment that Wal-Mart had engaged in discrimination, and for that reason, he closely evaluated the plaintiffs' evidence on the existence of a general policy of discrimination. Justice Ginsburg did not go so far as to presume that Wal-Mart had engaged in discrimination, but she seemed to be worried that if a class were not certified, Wal-Mart's liability for its general policies on promotions would never be litigated. No individual class member would have the incentive or the resources to fully investigate the overall effect of Wal-Mart's promotion policies. Without aggregating the class members' claims into a single action, the basis of those claims in pervasive implicit discrimination would remain unexamined. As Justice Ginsburg observed in her opinion: "The practice of delegating to supervisors large discretion to make personnel decisions, uncontrolled by formal standards, has long been known to have the potential to produce disparate effects." She reasoned from this background evidence of implicit bias to the sufficiency of the evidence of a common policy presented by the plaintiffs. In doing so, just like Justice Scalia, she would not presume to be prejudging the merits of the case. That still leaves the question, who is right—Justice Scalia in requiring more proof from the plaintiffs, or Justice Ginsburg in finding enough already present.

4. **The Relevance of Substantive Law Under Title VII.** For all the disagreement between them over the evidence, Justice Scalia and Justice Ginsburg expressed few differences over the basic principles governing liability and remedies under Title VII. To begin with, the unanimous holding on the need for certification of monetary claims under (b)(3) depended upon a shared understanding on of how and when individual monetary relief would be awarded after a classwide finding of liability. The Court relied upon previous decisions, notably Teamsters v. United States, 431 U.S. 324, 361 (1977), for the defendant's right to raise defenses to the award of individual relief, such as those enumerated in Title VII in 42 U.S.C. § 2000e–5(g)(2)(A), showing that the employee was not entitled to the position sought. Once this right is conferred on the defendant as a matter of substantive law, the Court doubted whether it could be taken away consistently with the Due Process Clause or the Rules Enabling Act. The former entitles the defendant (and the plaintiff class members as well) to an individualized hearing on this issue and the latter prevents any interpretation of Rule 23 that would "abridge, enlarge, or modify any substantive right." § 2000e–5(g). Interpretation of the rule cannot take away rights granted by superior sources of law.

On the question of commonality, greater disagreement might be expected over the relevant substantive standards under Title VII, but the opinions confine their difference mainly to the sufficiency of the evidence, discussed in the previous note. They do not differ much, if at all, over the content of the standards themselves and, in particular, those imposing liability for the disparate impact of subjective employment practices. Justice Scalia and Justice Ginsburg agree that plaintiffs do not need to prove intentional discrimination, but can simply prove the discriminatory effects of such practices. Where they part company is over how specific the plaintiffs' evidence must be. Justice Scalia emphasizes the requirement, now codified in 42 U.S.C. § 2000e–2(k)(1)(B), that plaintiffs tie the discriminatory effects in most cases to a specific employment practice. For him, allowing discretionary decisions by local supervisors in a company as large as Wal-Mart does not constitute a sufficiently specific practice. For Justice Ginsburg, apparently it does, although she does not directly address the question of how specific the disputed employment practice must be. Suppose that she is right that, at least at the certification stage, the plaintiffs have sufficiently identified a practice by referring to the subjective nature of Wal-Mart's promotion decisions. Has she then only postponed to the merits the question whether a more specific practice must be identified as the cause of the lower promotion rate for women? Do the plaintiffs then have to make the showing required by Justice Scalia at the certification stage, attributing the lower promotion rate for women to some general feature of the many promotion decisions made by Wal-Mart's many managers? Would it be enough for the plaintiffs on the merits simply to repeat that all the supervisors' decisions were subjective? Justice Ginsburg apparently would fill this gap in the plaintiff's case by referring to the possibility of implicit bias: "Managers, like all humankind, may be prey to biases of which they are unaware." Is this enough?

5. **Implications of the Decision.** The decision in *Wal-Mart* provoked great dismay among civil rights supporters and advocates for class action plaintiffs generally, and a sense of relief and triumph by employers and other prospective class action defendants. The decision has led some observers to foresee the "death of class actions," especially when coupled with recent decisions such as *AT&T Mobility LLC v. Concepcion*, 563 U.S. 333 (2011), restricting class actions in claims covered by arbitration agreements. When other recent decisions are taken into account, however, reports of the demise of class actions demise might prove to be greatly exaggerated. For instance, the decision in *Erica P. John Fund, Inc. v. Halliburton Co.*, 563 U.S. 804 (2011), allowed a securities class action to proceed based on a presumption of classwide reliance arising from the fact that the securities in question had been traded on a public exchange. Class actions, at least in this area of law, appear to be alive and well.

The gloomy forecast for the future of class actions comes mainly from the five-to-four holding on commonality, which is often laid to "ideological" divisions on the Supreme Court. That holding foreclosed any attempt to certify a class action against Wal-Mart at all, either under (b)(3) for monetary relief, or under (b)(2) for injunctive relief alone. For reasons already discussed, this prospect was limited in any event, by the higher standards for certification and the diminished likelihood that the claims for monetary relief would be jettisoned to bring the case under (b)(2). Yet, like most decisions of the Supreme Court, *Wal-Mart* has implications that extend far beyond the result in that particular case. The majority opinion was designed to guide the lower federal courts in deciding the many class actions that come before them. In this respect, the restrictive consequences of the decision for employment discrimination class actions are undeniable and general.

Thirty years ago, in *Falcon v. General Telephone Co.*, 457 U.S. 147 (1982), and *East Texas Motor Freight System, Inc. v. Rodriguez*, 431 U.S. 395 (1977), the Supreme Court also restricted employment discrimination class actions, limiting "across-the-board" class actions, alleging discrimination throughout an employer's personnel practices no matter how varied. These decisions were followed by a precipitous drop in employment discrimination class actions. See John J. Donohue III and Peter Siegelman, The Changing

Nature of Employment Discrimination Litigation, 43 Stan. L. Rev. 983, 1019–21 (1991). The decision in *Wal-Mart* might well have the same result, with even greater consequences for class actions in other fields, returning the law back to where it was in the early 1980's. But how bad is this result? The decisions, at least on employment discrimination, from that era have been accepted as a fundamental part of civil rights, and they were handed down by a Supreme Court regarded as decidedly more liberal than the one today. If *Wal-Mart* takes the law back to what it was at the end of the Civil Rights Era, why should that be regarded as a step backwards for civil rights? Do civil rights advocates fear that *Wal-Mart* discards the progress in enforcing employment discrimination claims that has been made over the intervening decades? Or is it that *Wal-Mart* doesn't take the law back to a period more sympathetic to civil rights, but ahead to one that will be increasingly unsympathetic?

Suppose such pessimism is justified. Should the plaintiffs' lawyers in *Wal-Mart* have taken the risk of an adverse decision and its consequences into account in deciding to bring such a large class action? In retrospect, they did not obtain a single vote from the Supreme Court on the propriety of certifying the class under (b)(2), and having lost the case on that ground, they were then left vulnerable to the restrictive interpretation of commonality under (a)(2). Before the decision came down, could they have realistically hoped that five justices would rule in their favor? If not, did they pin their hopes for success on the possibility that the Court might not have granted certiorari to review the case? The Supreme Court only accepted the case for review after decisions in favor of the plaintiffs by the district court and by the Ninth Circuit, the latter first by a panel of three judges and then by the court en banc. The en banc decision, to be sure, was closely divided, by a vote of six to five, greatly enhancing the chances that the Supreme Court would grant certiorari.

But even before that point, the case had attracted considerable publicity both because of the size of the class and the prominence of Wal-Mart as the nation's largest retailer. Why did the plaintiffs' lawyers expand the size of the class to nationwide proportions, resulting in an increased probability of review and reversal by the Supreme Court? Could they have limited the class to employees from a particular state or region, or otherwise limited its scope? Was their theory of liability, based on the pervasive effect of implicit bias in subjective decisionmaking, one that had to be pursued throughout the company or not at all? Or were they dazzled by the prospect of a large judgment against a major corporation, creating a landmark decision of national significance? Such a decision would, of course, have also generated attorney's fees in proportion to the size of the class. Did the plaintiffs' lawyers unduly discount the risk that they would get a landmark decision—which they did—but not the one they wanted?

6. **Bibliography.** For articles on the lower court decisions in *Wal-Mart*, particularly on the use of evidence of implicit bias to support class certification, see Richard Thompson Ford, Discounting Discrimination: *Dukes v. Wal-Mart* Proves That Yesterday's Civil Rights Laws Can't Keep Up With Today's Economy, 5 Harv. L. & Pol'y Rev. 69 (2011); Melissa Hart

& Paul M. Secunda, Essay, A Matter of Context: Social Framework Evidence in Employment Discrimination Class Actions, 78 Fordham L. Rev. 37 (2009); Suzette Malveaux, Class Actions at the Crossroads: An Answer to *Wal-Mart v. Dukes*, 5 Harv. L. & Pol'y Rev. 375 (2011); John Monahan, Laurens Walker & Gregory Mitchell, The Limits of Social Framework Evidence, 8 L. Probability & Risk 307 (2009); Lesley Wexler, Wal-Mart Matters, 46 Wake Forest L. Rev. 95 (2011). For the standards for certification, see the article prominently cited in both opinions, Richard Nagareda, Class Certification in the Age of Aggregate Proof, 84 N.Y.U. L. Rev. 97 (2009).

Commentary on the Supreme Court's decision in *Wal-Mart* has been predominantly negative. See Steven Greenberger. Justice Scalia and the Demise of the Employment Class Action, 21 Emp.Rts. & Emp. Pol'y J. 75 (2017); Michael Harper, Class-Based Adjudication of Title VII Claims in the Age of the Roberts Court, 96 B.U. L. Rev. 1099 (2015); Katherine E. Lamm, Work in Progress: Civil Rights Class Actions after *Wal-Mart v. Dukes*, 50 Harv. C.R.-C.L. L. Rev. 153 (2015); Angela D. Morrison, Duke-ing Out Pattern or Practice after *Wal-Mart*: The EEOC as Fist, 63 Am. U. L. Rev. 87 (2013); Ramona L. Paetzold & W. Steven Rholes, *Wal-Mart v. Dukes*: Justice Scalia and Systemic Disparate Treatment Theory, 21 Emp. Rts. & Emp. Pol'y J. 115 (2017); Elizabeth M. Schneider & Nancy Gertner, "Only Procedural": Thoughts on the Substantive Law Dimensions of Preliminary Procedural Decisions in Employment Discrimination Cases, 57 N.Y. L. Sch. L. Rev. 767 (2012–13); Cindy A. Schipani & Terry M. Dworkin, Class Action Litigation After *Dukes*: In Search of a Remedy for Gender Discrimination in Employment, 46 U. Mich. J.L. Reform 1249 (2013); Michael Selmi, Employment Discrimination Class Actions After *Wal-Mart v. Dukes*, 48 Akron. L. Rev. 803 (2015); Deborah M. Weiss, A Grudging Defense of *Wal-Mart v. Dukes*, 24 Yale J.L. & Feminism 119 (2012); Symposium, Class Actions, 88 Notre Dame L. Rev. 557 (2012); Symposium, Class Action Rollback? *Wal-Mart v. Dukes* and the Future of Class Action Litigation, 62 DePaul L. Rev. 653 (2013).

2. PUBLIC ACTIONS

As originally enacted, Title VII conferred no authority to sue upon the EEOC. Public actions could be brought only by the Department of Justice. This original allocation of authority survives only with respect to actions against state and local government, which are thought to raise sensitive issues of federalism that require the oversight of the Attorney General. Public actions against private employers are now brought by the EEOC. § 706(f), 42 U.S.C. § 2000e–5(f). The statute also provides for public actions alleging a "pattern or practice" of discrimination. § 707(a), 42 U.S.C. § 2000e–6(a). The literal terms of this provision refer only to actions by the Attorney General, but an executive order subsequently allocated authority to bring these actions in the same manner as other public actions, giving the EEOC the power to sue private employers. Reorg. Plan No. 1 of 1978, § 5, 3 C.F.R. 321 (1979), reprinted in 5 U.S.C. app. at 719 (2012).

"Pattern or practice" actions are not clearly distinguished from other public actions under Title VII although, as the name implies, these actions involve an allegation of a pattern or practice of discrimination. Nevertheless, public actions under § 706 can also be brought on behalf of a group of employees, without being certified as a class action. General Telephone Co. v. EEOC, 446 U.S. 318 (1980). The difference between ordinary actions under § 706 and "pattern or practice" actions under § 707 appears to be mainly one of degree. The EEOC or the Department of Justice is more likely to bring an action under § 707 if it attacks employment practices of general scope and significance. In addition, the grant of authority to bring such actions reflects a congressional judgment that public actions are especially necessary in such cases. The same judgment is reflected in the provision authorizing the EEOC or the Department of Justice to intervene in private actions. This step requires certification that the case is of general public importance. § 706(f)(1), codified as 42 U.S.C. § 2000e–5(f)(1).

Although the EEOC and the Department of Justice have broad authority to bring public actions, they exercise this authority in relatively few cases. The EEOC's 2017 Annual Report lists 201 actions in which the commission participated on the merits, either by bringing its own action, intervening in a private action, or enforcing a settlement agreement. By contrast, the EEOC received over 84,000 charges of discrimination filed with it directly or referred to it from state and local agencies. Thus less than 0.3 percent of charges filed with the EEOC resulted in public actions under Title VII. See Stephanie Bornstein, Rights in Recession: Toward Administrative Antidiscrimination Law, 33 Yale Law & Pol'y Rev. 119 (2014); Michael Selmi, Public vs. Private Enforcement of Civil Rights: The Case of Housing and Employment, 45 UCLA L. Rev. 1401 (1998).

Another role for the Federal government in litigation, of course, is as a defendant in claims brought by federal employees. As noted earlier, these actions are subject to their own specialized procedures, requiring exhaustion of administrative remedies in the employee's own agency and compliance with a variety of specific time limits. § 717(c), 42 U.S.C. § 2000e–16(c); 29 C.F.R. §§ 1614.105(a), .106(b), .408. Uniquely in these cases, the EEOC acts in an adjudicatory capacity. Reorganization Plan No. 1 of 1978, § 3, 3 C.F.R. 321 (1979), reprinted in 5 U.S.C. app. at 719 (2012). The federal employee, however, has the option to bring an action in which her claim is considered de novo by the court. Chandler v. Roudebush, 425 U.S. 840 (1976). Title VII provides the exclusive remedy for employment discrimination for employees within its coverage (which does not, for instance, extend to uniformed members of the armed services). Brown v. General Services Administration, 425 U.S. 820, 828–29 (1976); see FDIC v. Meyer, 510 U.S. 471, 483–86 (1994).

3. ARBITRATION

Gilmer v. Interstate/Johnson Lane Corp.

500 U.S. 20 (1991).

■ JUSTICE WHITE delivered the opinion of the Court.

The question presented in this case is whether a claim under the Age Discrimination in Employment Act of 1967 (ADEA), as amended, 29 U.S.C. §§ 621 et seq., can be subjected to compulsory arbitration pursuant to an arbitration agreement in a securities registration application. The Court of Appeals held that it could, 895 F.2d 195 (CA4 1990), and we affirm.

I

Respondent Interstate/Johnson Lane Corporation (Interstate) hired petitioner Robert Gilmer as a Manager of Financial Services in May 1981. As required by his employment, Gilmer registered as a securities representative with several stock exchanges, including the New York Stock Exchange (NYSE). His registration application, entitled "Uniform Application for Securities Industry Registration or Transfer," provided, among other things, that Gilmer "agree[d] to arbitrate any dispute, claim or controversy" arising between him and Interstate "that is required to be arbitrated under the rules, constitutions or by-laws of the organizations with which I register." Of relevance to this case, NYSE Rule 347 provides for arbitration of "[a]ny controversy between a registered representative and any member or member organization arising out of the employment or termination of employment of such registered representative."

Interstate terminated Gilmer's employment in 1987, at which time Gilmer was 62 years of age. After first filing an age discrimination charge with the Equal Employment Opportunity Commission (EEOC), Gilmer subsequently brought suit in the United States District Court for the Western District of North Carolina, alleging that Interstate had discharged him because of his age, in violation of the ADEA. In response to Gilmer's complaint, Interstate filed in the District Court a motion to compel arbitration of the ADEA claim. In its motion, Interstate relied upon the arbitration agreement in Gilmer's registration application, as well as the Federal Arbitration Act (FAA), 9 U.S.C. § 1 et seq. The District Court denied Interstate's motion, based on this Court's decision in Alexander v. Gardner-Denver Co., 415 U.S. 36 (1974), and because it concluded that "Congress intended to protect ADEA claimants from the waiver of a judicial forum." The United States Court of Appeals for the Fourth Circuit reversed, finding "nothing in the text, legislative history, or underlying purposes of the ADEA indicating a congressional intent to preclude enforcement of arbitration agreements." 895 F.2d, at 197. We granted certiorari to resolve a conflict among the Courts of Appeals regarding the arbitrability of ADEA claims.

II

The FAA was originally enacted in 1925, and then reenacted and codified in 1947 as Title 9 of the United States Code. Its purpose was to reverse the longstanding judicial hostility to arbitration agreements that had existed at English common law and had been adopted by American courts, and to place arbitration agreements upon the same footing as other contracts. Dean Witter Reynolds, Inc. v. Byrd, 470 U.S. 213, 219–220, and n.6 (1985); Scherk v. Alberto-Culver Co., 417 U.S. 506, 510, n.4 (1974). Its primary substantive provision states that "[a] written provision in any maritime transaction or a contract evidencing a transaction involving commerce to settle by arbitration a controversy thereafter arising out of such contract or transaction . . . shall be valid, irrevocable, and enforceable, save upon such grounds as exist at law or in equity for the revocation of any contract." 9 U.S.C. § 2. The FAA also provides for stays of proceedings in federal district courts when an issue in the proceeding is referable to arbitration, § 3, and for orders compelling arbitration when one party has failed, neglected, or refused to comply with an arbitration agreement, § 4. These provisions manifest a "liberal federal policy favoring arbitration agreements." Moses H. Cone Memorial Hospital v. Mercury Construction Corp., 460 U.S. 1, 24 (1983).[2]

It is by now clear that statutory claims may be the subject of an arbitration agreement, enforceable pursuant to the FAA. Indeed, in recent years we have held enforceable arbitration agreements relating to claims arising under the Sherman Act, 15 U.S.C. §§ 1–7; § 10(b) of the Securities Exchange Act of 1934, 15 U.S.C. § 78j(b); the civil provisions of the Racketeer Influenced and Corrupt Organizations Act (RICO), 18 U.S.C. § 1961 et seq.; and § 12(2) of the Securities Act of 1933, 15 U.S.C. § 77l(2). See Mitsubishi Motors Corp. v. Soler Chrysler-Plymouth, Inc., 473 U.S. 614 (1985); Shearson/American Express Inc. v. McMahon, 482 U.S. 220 (1987); Rodriguez de Quijas v. Shearson/American Express, Inc., 490 U.S. 477 (1989). In these cases we recognized that "[b]y agreeing to arbitrate a statutory claim, a party does not forgo the substantive rights afforded by the statute; it only submits to their resolution in an arbitral, rather than a judicial, forum." Mitsubishi, 473 U.S., at 628.

Although all statutory claims may not be appropriate for arbitration, "[h]aving made the bargain to arbitrate, the party should be held to it

[2] Section 1 of the FAA provides that "nothing herein contained shall apply to contracts of employment of seamen, railroad employees, or any other class of workers engaged in foreign or interstate commerce." 9 U.S.C. § 1. Several amici curiae in support of Gilmer argue that that section excludes from the coverage of the FAA all "contracts of employment." Gilmer, however, did not raise the issue in the courts below, it was not addressed there, and it was not among the questions presented in the petition for certiorari. In any event, it would be inappropriate to address the scope of the § 1 exclusion because the arbitration clause being enforced here is not contained in a contract of employment. The FAA requires that the arbitration clause being enforced be in writing. See 9 U.S.C. §§ 2, 3. The record before us does not show, and the parties do not contend, that Gilmer's employment agreement with Interstate contained a written arbitration clause. Rather, the arbitration clause at issue is in Gilmer's securities registration application, which is a contract with the securities exchanges, not with Interstate. . . . Consequently, we leave for another day the issue raised by amici curiae.

unless Congress itself has evinced an intention to preclude a waiver of judicial remedies for the statutory rights at issue." Ibid. In this regard, we note that the burden is on Gilmer to show that Congress intended to preclude a waiver of a judicial forum for ADEA claims. If such an intention exists, it will be discoverable in the text of the ADEA, its legislative history, or an "inherent conflict" between arbitration and the ADEA's underlying purposes. Throughout such an inquiry, it should be kept in mind that "questions of arbitrability must be addressed with a healthy regard for the federal policy favoring arbitration." Moses H. Cone, supra, 460 U.S., at 24.

III

Gilmer concedes that nothing in the text of the ADEA or its legislative history explicitly precludes arbitration. He argues, however, that compulsory arbitration of ADEA claims pursuant to arbitration agreements would be inconsistent with the statutory framework and purposes of the ADEA. Like the Court of Appeals, we disagree.

A

Congress enacted the ADEA in 1967 "to promote employment of older persons based on their ability rather than age; to prohibit arbitrary age discrimination in employment; [and] to help employers and workers find ways of meeting problems arising from the impact of age on employment." 29 U.S.C. § 621(b). To achieve those goals, the ADEA, among other things, makes it unlawful for an employer "to fail or refuse to hire or to discharge any individual or otherwise discriminate against any individual with respect to his compensation, terms, conditions, or privileges of employment, because of such individual's age." § 623(a)(1). This proscription is enforced both by private suits and by the EEOC. In order for an aggrieved individual to bring suit under the ADEA, he or she must first file a charge with the EEOC and then wait at least 60 days. § 626(d). An individual's right to sue is extinguished, however, if the EEOC institutes an action against the employer. § 626(c)(1). Before the EEOC can bring such an action, though, it must "attempt to eliminate the discriminatory practice or practices alleged, and to effect voluntary compliance with the requirements of this chapter through informal methods of conciliation, conference, and persuasion." § 626(b); see also 29 CFR § 1626.15.

As Gilmer contends, the ADEA is designed not only to address individual grievances, but also to further important social policies. See, e.g., EEOC v. Wyoming, 460 U.S. 226, 231 (1983). We do not perceive any inherent inconsistency between those policies, however, and enforcing agreements to arbitrate age discrimination claims. It is true that arbitration focuses on specific disputes between the parties involved. The same can be said, however, of judicial resolution of claims. Both of these dispute resolution mechanisms nevertheless also can further broader social purposes. The Sherman Act, the Securities Exchange Act of 1934, RICO, and the Securities Act of 1933 all are designed to advance important public policies, but, as noted above, claims under those statutes are appropriate for arbitration. "[S]o long as the prospective litigant effectively may vindicate [his or her] statutory cause of action in the arbitral forum, the statute will continue to serve both its remedial and deterrent function." Mitsubishi, supra, 473 U.S., at 637.

We also are unpersuaded by the argument that arbitration will undermine the role of the EEOC in enforcing the ADEA. An individual ADEA claimant subject to an arbitration agreement will still be free to file a charge with the EEOC, even though the claimant is not able to institute a private judicial action. Indeed, Gilmer filed a charge with the EEOC in this case. In any event, the EEOC's role in combating age discrimination is not dependent on the filing of a charge; the agency may receive information concerning alleged violations of the ADEA "from any source," and it has independent authority to investigate age discrimination. See 29 CFR §§ 1626.4, 1626.13. Moreover, nothing in the ADEA indicates that Congress intended that the EEOC be involved in all employment disputes. Such disputes can be settled, for example, without any EEOC involvement. See, e.g., Coventry v. United States Steel Corp., 856 F.2d 514, 522 (CA3 1988); Moore v. McGraw Edison Co., 804 F.2d 1026, 1033 (CA8 1986); Runyan v. National Cash Register Corp., 787 F.2d 1039, 1045 (CA6), cert. denied, 479 U.S. 850 (1986). Finally, the mere involvement of an administrative agency in the enforcement of a statute is not sufficient to preclude arbitration. For example, the Securities Exchange Commission is heavily involved in the enforcement of the Securities Exchange Act of 1934 and the Securities Act of 1933, but we have held that claims under both of those statutes may be subject to compulsory arbitration. See Shearson/American Express, Inc. v. McMahon, 482 U.S. 220 (1987); Rodriguez de Quijas v. Shearson/American Express, Inc., 490 U.S. 477 (1989).

Gilmer also argues that compulsory arbitration is improper because it deprives claimants of the judicial forum provided for by the ADEA. Congress, however, did not explicitly preclude arbitration or other nonjudicial resolution of claims, even in its recent amendments to the ADEA. "[I]f Congress intended the substantive protection afforded [by the ADEA] to include protection against waiver of the right to a judicial forum, that intention will be deducible from text or legislative history." Mitsubishi, 473 U.S., at 628. Moreover, Gilmer's argument ignores the ADEA's flexible approach to resolution of claims. The EEOC, for example, is directed to pursue "informal methods of conciliation, conference, and persuasion," 29 U.S.C. § 626(b), which suggests that out-of-court dispute resolution, such as arbitration, is consistent with the statutory scheme established by Congress. In addition, arbitration is consistent with Congress' grant of concurrent jurisdiction over ADEA claims to state and federal courts, see 29 U.S.C. § 626(c)(1) (allowing suits to be brought "in any court of competent jurisdiction"), because arbitration agreements, "like the provision for concurrent jurisdiction, serve to advance the objective of allowing [claimants] a broader right to select the forum for resolving disputes, whether it be judicial or otherwise." Rodriguez de Quijas, supra, at 483.

B

In arguing that arbitration is inconsistent with the ADEA, Gilmer also raises a host of challenges to the adequacy of arbitration procedures. Initially, we note that in our recent arbitration cases we have already rejected most of these arguments as insufficient to preclude arbitration of statutory claims. Such generalized attacks on arbitration "res[t] on suspicion of arbitration as a method of weakening the protections afforded in the substantive law to would-be complainants," and as such, they are "far out of step with our current strong endorsement of the federal statutes favoring this method of resolving disputes." Rodriguez de Quijas, supra, at 481. Consequently, we address these arguments only briefly.

Gilmer first speculates that arbitration panels will be biased. However, "[w]e decline to indulge the presumption that the parties and arbitral body conducting a proceeding will be unable or unwilling to retain competent, conscientious and impartial arbitrators." Mitsubishi, supra, 473 U.S., at 634. In any event, we note that the NYSE arbitration rules, which are applicable to the dispute in this case, provide protections against biased panels. The rules require, for example, that the parties be informed of the employment histories of the arbitrators, and that they be allowed to make further inquiries into the arbitrators' backgrounds. See 2 CCH New York Stock Exchange Guide ¶ 2608, p. 4314 (Rule 608) (1991) (hereinafter 2 N.Y.S.E. Guide). In addition, each party is allowed one peremptory challenge and unlimited challenges for cause. Id., ¶ 2609, at 4315 (Rule 609). Moreover, the arbitrators are required to disclose "any circumstances which might preclude [them] from rendering an objective and impartial determination." Id., ¶ 2610, at 4315 (Rule 610). The FAA also protects against bias, by providing that courts may overturn arbitration decisions "[w]here there was evident partiality or corruption in the arbitrators." 9 U.S.C. § 10(b). There has been no showing in this case that those provisions are inadequate to guard against potential bias.

Gilmer also complains that the discovery allowed in arbitration is more limited than in the federal courts, which he contends will make it difficult to prove discrimination. It is unlikely, however, that age discrimination claims require more extensive discovery than other claims that we have found to be arbitrable, such as RICO and antitrust claims. Moreover, there has been no showing in this case that the NYSE discovery provisions, which allow for document production, information requests, depositions, and subpoenas, see 2 N.Y.S.E. Guide ¶ 2619, pp. 4318–4320 (Rule 619); Securities and Exchange Commission Order Approving Proposed Rule Changes by New York Stock Exchange, Inc., Nat. Assn. of Securities Dealers, Inc., and the American Stock Exchange, Inc., Relating to the Arbitration Process and the Use of Predispute

Arbitration Clauses, 54 Fed. Reg. 21144, 21149–21151 (1989), will prove insufficient to allow ADEA claimants such as Gilmer a fair opportunity to present their claims. Although those procedures might not be as extensive as in the federal courts, by agreeing to arbitrate, a party "trades the procedures and opportunity for review of the courtroom for the simplicity, informality, and expedition of arbitration." Mitsubishi, supra, at 628. Indeed, an important counterweight to the reduced discovery in NYSE arbitration is that arbitrators are not bound by the rules of evidence. See 2 N.Y.S.E. Guide ¶ 2620, p. 4320 (Rule 620).

A further alleged deficiency of arbitration is that arbitrators often will not issue written opinions, resulting, Gilmer contends, in a lack of public knowledge of employers' discriminatory policies, an inability to obtain effective appellate review, and a stifling of the development of the law. The NYSE rules, however, do require that all arbitration awards be in writing, and that the awards contain the names of the parties, a summary of the issues in controversy, and a description of the award issued. See id., ¶ 2627(a), (e), at 4321 (Rules 627(a), (e)). In addition, the award decisions are made available to the public. See id., ¶ 2627(f), at 4322 (Rule 627(f)). Furthermore, judicial decisions addressing ADEA claims will continue to be issued because it is unlikely that all or even most ADEA claimants will be subject to arbitration agreements. Finally, Gilmer's concerns apply equally to settlements of ADEA claims, which, as noted above, are clearly allowed.[4]

It is also argued that arbitration procedures cannot adequately further the purposes of the ADEA because they do not provide for broad equitable relief and class actions. As the court below noted, however, arbitrators do have the power to fashion equitable relief. 895 F.2d, at 199–200. Indeed, the NYSE rules applicable here do not restrict the types of relief an arbitrator may award, but merely refer to "damages and/or other relief." 2 N.Y.S.E. Guide ¶ 2627(e), p. 4321 (Rule 627(e)). The NYSE rules also provide for collective proceedings. Id., ¶ 2612(d), at 4317 (Rule 612(d)). But "even if the arbitration could not go forward as a class action or class relief could not be granted by the arbitrator, the fact that the [ADEA] provides for the possibility of bringing a collective action does not mean that individual attempts at conciliation were intended to be barred." Nicholson v. CPC Int'l Inc., 877 F.2d 221, 241 (CA3 1989) (Becker, J., dissenting). Finally, it should be remembered that arbitration agreements will not preclude the EEOC from bringing actions seeking class-wide and equitable relief.

C

An additional reason advanced by Gilmer for refusing to enforce arbitration agreements relating to ADEA claims is his contention that

---

[4] Gilmer also contends that judicial review of arbitration decisions is too limited. We have stated, however, that "although judicial scrutiny of arbitration awards necessarily is limited, such review is sufficient to ensure that arbitrators comply with the requirements of the statute" at issue. Shearson/American Express, Inc. v. McMahon, 482 U.S. 220, 232 (1987).

there often will be unequal bargaining power between employers and employees. Mere inequality in bargaining power, however, is not a sufficient reason to hold that arbitration agreements are never enforceable in the employment context. Relationships between securities dealers and investors, for example, may involve unequal bargaining power, but we nevertheless held in *Rodriguez de Quijas* and *McMahon* that agreements to arbitrate in that context are enforceable. See 490 U.S., at 484; 482 U.S., at 230. As discussed above, the FAA's purpose was to place arbitration agreements on the same footing as other contracts. Thus, arbitration agreements are enforceable "save upon such grounds as exist at law or in equity for the revocation of any contract." 9 U.S.C. § 2. "Of course, courts should remain attuned to well-supported claims that the agreement to arbitrate resulted from the sort of fraud or overwhelming economic power that would provide grounds 'for the revocation of any contract.'" Mitsubishi, 473 U.S., at 627. There is no indication in this case, however, that Gilmer, an experienced businessman, was coerced or defrauded into agreeing to the arbitration clause in his registration application. As with the claimed procedural inadequacies discussed above, this claim of unequal bargaining power is best left for resolution in specific cases.

IV

In addition to the arguments discussed above, Gilmer vigorously asserts that our decision in Alexander v. Gardner-Denver Co., 415 U.S. 36 (1974), and its progeny—Barrentine v. Arkansas-Best Freight System, Inc., 450 U.S. 728 (1981), and McDonald v. West Branch, 466 U.S. 284 (1984)—preclude arbitration of employment discrimination claims. Gilmer's reliance on these cases, however, is misplaced.

In *Gardner-Denver*, the issue was whether a discharged employee whose grievance had been arbitrated pursuant to an arbitration clause in a collective-bargaining agreement was precluded from subsequently bringing a Title VII action based upon the conduct that was the subject of the grievance. In holding that the employee was not foreclosed from bringing the Title VII claim, we stressed that an employee's contractual rights under a collective-bargaining agreement are distinct from the employee's statutory Title VII rights:

> "In submitting his grievance to arbitration, an employee seeks to vindicate his contractual right under a collective-bargaining agreement. By contrast, in filing a lawsuit under Title VII, an employee asserts independent statutory rights accorded by Congress. The distinctly separate nature of these contractual and statutory rights is not vitiated merely because both were violated as a result of the same factual occurrence." 415 U.S., at 49–50.

We also noted that a labor arbitrator has authority only to resolve questions of contractual rights. The arbitrator's "task is to effectuate the intent of the parties" and he or she does not have the "general authority to invoke public laws that conflict with the bargain between the parties." By contrast, "in instituting an action under Title VII, the employee is not seeking review of the arbitrator's decision. Rather, he is asserting a statutory right independent of the arbitration process." We further expressed concern that in collective-bargaining arbitration "the interests of the individual employee may be subordinated to the collective interests of all employees in the bargaining unit."[5]

Barrentine and *McDonald* similarly involved the issue whether arbitration under a collective-bargaining agreement precluded a subsequent statutory claim. In holding that the statutory claims there were not precluded, we noted, as in *Gardner-Denver*, the difference between contractual rights under a collective-bargaining agreement and individual statutory rights, the potential disparity in interests between a union and an employee, and the limited authority and power of labor arbitrators.

There are several important distinctions between the *Gardner-Denver* line of cases and the case before us. First, those cases did not involve the issue of the enforceability of an agreement to arbitrate statutory claims. Rather, they involved the quite different issue whether arbitration of contract-based claims precluded subsequent judicial resolution of statutory claims. Since the employees there had not agreed to arbitrate their statutory claims, and the labor arbitrators were not authorized to resolve such claims, the arbitration in those cases understandably was held not to preclude subsequent statutory actions. Second, because the arbitration in those cases occurred in the context of a collective-bargaining agreement, the claimants there were represented by their unions in the arbitration proceedings. An important concern therefore was the tension between collective representation and individual statutory rights, a concern not applicable to the present case. Finally, those cases were not decided under the FAA, which, as discussed above, reflects a "liberal federal policy favoring arbitration agreements." Mitsubishi, 473 U.S., at 625. Therefore, those cases provide no basis for refusing to enforce Gilmer's agreement to arbitrate his ADEA claim.

V

We conclude that Gilmer has not met his burden of showing that Congress, in enacting the ADEA, intended to preclude arbitration of claims under that Act. Accordingly, the judgment of the Court of Appeals is

Affirmed.

---

[5] The Court in Alexander v. Gardner-Denver Co., 415 U.S. 36 (1974), also expressed the view that arbitration was inferior to the judicial process for resolving statutory claims. That "mistrust of the arbitral process," however, has been undermined by our recent arbitration decisions. McMahon, 482 U.S., at 231–232. "[W]e are well past the time when judicial suspicion of the desirability of arbitration and of the competence of arbitral tribunals inhibited the development of arbitration as an alternative means of dispute resolution." Mitsubishi Motors Corp. v. Soler Chrysler-Plymouth, Inc., 473 U.S. 614, 626–627 (1985).

■ JUSTICE STEVENS, with whom JUSTICE MARSHALL joins, dissenting.

Section 1 of the Federal Arbitration Act (FAA) states:

> "[N]othing herein contained shall apply to contracts of employment of seamen, railroad employees, or any other class of workers engaged in foreign or interstate commerce." 9 U.S.C. § 1.

The Court today, in holding that the FAA compels enforcement of arbitration clauses even when claims of age discrimination are at issue, skirts the antecedent question whether the coverage of the Act even extends to arbitration clauses contained in employment contracts, regardless of the subject matter of the claim at issue. In my opinion, arbitration clauses contained in employment agreements are specifically exempt from coverage of the FAA, and for that reason respondent Interstate/Johnson Lane Corporation cannot, pursuant to the FAA, compel petitioner to submit his claims arising under the Age Discrimination in Employment Act of 1967 (ADEA), 29 U.S.C. § 621 et seq., to binding arbitration. . . .

II

The Court, declining to reach the issue for the reason that petitioner never raised it below, nevertheless concludes that "it would be inappropriate to address the scope of the § 1 exclusion because the arbitration clause being enforced here is not contained in a contract of employment. . . . Rather, the arbitration clause at issue is in Gilmer's securities registration application, which is a contract with the securities exchanges, not with Interstate." In my opinion the Court too narrowly construes the scope of the exclusion contained in § 1 of the FAA.

There is little dispute that the primary concern animating the FAA was the perceived need by the business community to overturn the common-law rule that denied specific enforcement of agreements to arbitrate in contracts between business entities. The Act was drafted by a committee of the American Bar Association (ABA), acting upon instructions from the ABA to consider and report upon "the further extension of the principle of commercial arbitration." Report of the Forty-third Annual Meeting of the ABA, 45 A.B.A. Rep. 75 (1920). At the Senate Judiciary Subcommittee hearings on the proposed bill, the chairman of the ABA committee responsible for drafting the bill assured the Senators that the bill "is not intended [to] be an act referring to labor disputes, at all. It is purely an act to give the merchants the right or the privilege of sitting down and agreeing with each other as to what their damages are, if they want to do it. Now that is all there is in this." Hearing on S. 4213 and S. 4214 before a Subcommittee of the Senate Committee on the Judiciary, 67th Cong., 4th Sess., 9 (1923). At the same hearing, Senator Walsh stated:

> "The trouble about the matter is that a great many of these contracts that are entered into are really not [voluntary] things

> at all. Take an insurance policy; there is a blank in it. You can take that or you can leave it. The agent has no power at all to decide it. Either you can make that contract or you can not make any contract. It is the same with a good many contracts of employment. A man says, 'These are our terms. All right, take it or leave it.' Well, there is nothing for the man to do except to sign it; and then he surrenders his right to have his case tried by the court, and has to have it tried before a tribunal in which he has no confidence at all." Ibid.

Given that the FAA specifically was intended to exclude arbitration agreements between employees and employers, I see no reason to limit this exclusion from coverage to arbitration clauses contained in agreements entitled "Contract of Employment." In this case, the parties conceded at oral argument that Gilmer had no "contract of employment" as such with respondent. Gilmer was, however, required as a condition of his employment to become a registered representative of several stock exchanges, including the New York Stock Exchange (NYSE). Just because his agreement to arbitrate any "dispute, claim or controversy" with his employer that arose out of the employment relationship was contained in his application for registration before the NYSE rather than in a specific contract of employment with his employer, I do not think that Gilmer can be compelled pursuant to the FAA to arbitrate his employment-related dispute. Rather, in my opinion the exclusion in § 1 should be interpreted to cover any agreements by the employee to arbitrate disputes with the employer arising out of the employment relationship, particularly where such agreements to arbitrate are conditions of employment.

My reading of the scope of the exclusion contained in § 1 is supported by early judicial interpretations of the FAA. As of 1956, three Courts of Appeals had held that the FAA's exclusion of "contracts of employment" referred not only to individual contracts of employment, but also to collective-bargaining agreements. See Lincoln Mills of Ala. v. Textile Workers Union of America, 230 F.2d 81 (CA5 1956), rev'd, 353 U.S. 448 (1957); United Electrical, Radio & Machine Workers of America v. Miller Metal Products, Inc., 215 F.2d 221 (CA4 1954); Amalgamated Assn. of Street Electric R. and Motor Coach Employees of America v. Pennsylvania Greyhound Lines, Inc., 192 F.2d 310 (CA3 1951). Indeed, the application of the FAA's exclusionary clause to arbitration provisions in collective-bargaining agreements was one of the issues raised in the petition for certiorari and briefed at great length in Lincoln Mills and its companion cases, Goodall-Sanford, Inc. v. Textile Workers, 353 U.S. 550 (1957), and General Electric Co. v. Electrical Workers, 353 U.S. 547 (1957). Although the Court decided the enforceability of the arbitration provisions in the collective-bargaining agreements by reference to § 301 of the Labor Management Relations Act, 1947, 29 U.S.C. § 185, it did not reject the Courts of Appeals' holdings that the arbitration provisions would not otherwise be enforceable pursuant to the FAA since they were specifically excluded under § 1. In dissent, Justice Frankfurter perceived a

> "rejection, though not explicit, of the availability of the Federal Arbitration Act to enforce arbitration clauses in collective-bargaining agreements in the silent treatment given that Act by the Court's opinion. If an Act that authorizes the federal courts to enforce arbitration provisions in contracts generally, but specifically denies authority to decree that remedy for 'contracts of employment,' were available, the Court would hardly spin such power out of the empty darkness of § 301. I would make this rejection explicit, recognizing that when Congress passed legislation to enable arbitration agreements to be enforced by the federal courts, it saw fit to exclude this remedy with respect to labor contracts." Textile Workers v. Lincoln Mills, 353 U.S., at 466.

III

Not only would I find that the FAA does not apply to employment-related disputes between employers and employees in general, but also I would hold that compulsory arbitration conflicts with the congressional purpose animating the ADEA, in particular. As this Court previously has noted, authorizing the courts to issue broad injunctive relief is the cornerstone to eliminating discrimination in society. Albemarle Paper Co. v. Moody, 422 U.S. 405, 415 (1975). The ADEA, like Title VII of the Civil Rights Act of 1964, authorizes courts to award broad, class-based injunctive relief to achieve the purposes of the Act. 29 U.S.C. § 626(b). Because commercial arbitration is typically limited to a specific dispute between the particular parties and because the available remedies in arbitral forums generally do not provide for class-wide injunctive relief, see Shell, ERISA and Other Federal Employment Statutes: When is Commercial Arbitration an "Adequate Substitute" for the Courts?, 68 Tex. L. Rev. 509, 568 (1990), I would conclude that an essential purpose of the ADEA is frustrated by compulsory arbitration of employment discrimination claims. Moreover, as Chief Justice Burger explained:

> "Plainly, it would not comport with the congressional objectives behind a statute seeking to enforce civil rights protected by Title VII to allow the very forces that had practiced discrimination to contract away the right to enforce civil rights in the courts. For federal courts to defer to arbitral decisions reached by the same combination of forces that had long perpetuated invidious discrimination would have made the foxes guardians of the chickens." Barrentine v. Arkansas-Best Freight System, Inc., 450 U.S. 728, 750 (1981) (dissenting opinion).

In my opinion the same concerns expressed by Chief Justice Burger with regard to compulsory arbitration of Title VII claims may be said of claims arising under the ADEA. The Court's holding today clearly eviscerates the important role played by an independent judiciary in eradicating employment discrimination.

IV

When the FAA was passed in 1925, I doubt that any legislator who voted for it expected it to apply to statutory claims, to form contracts between parties of unequal bargaining power, or to the arbitration of disputes arising out of the employment relationship. In recent years, however, the Court "has effectively rewritten the statute," and abandoned its earlier view that statutory claims were not appropriate subjects for arbitration. See Mitsubishi Motors v. Soler Chrysler-Plymouth, Inc., 473 U.S. 614, 646–651 (1985) (STEVENS, J., dissenting). Although I remain persuaded that it erred in doing so, the Court has also put to one side any concern about the inequality of bargaining power between an entire industry, on the one hand, and an individual customer or employee, on the other. Until today, however, the Court has not read § 2 of the FAA as broadly encompassing disputes arising out of the employment relationship. I believe this additional extension of the FAA is erroneous. Accordingly, I respectfully dissent.

NOTES ON *GILMER V. INTERSTATE/JOHNSON LANE CORP.*

1. **Trends in Arbitration.** In *Gilmer*, the Court takes great care to distinguish its earlier decision in Alexander v. Gardner-Denver Co., 415 U.S. 36 (1974). That case concerned the most prevalent form of arbitration as it was first used to resolve labor issues. Collective bargaining agreements negotiated between employers and unions typically established grievance procedures and arbitration as the preferred means of resolving disputes raised by covered employees. Control over this method of dispute resolution remained entirely with the union, which could decide to pursue or to abandon an employee's grievance at any stage in the process. Just as the union controlled negotiation of the collective bargaining agreement, it also controlled the process by which the agreement was interpreted and applied. By contrast, arbitration under an individual contract remained under the control of the employee, at least in theory.

The advantages of individual arbitration depend upon those of individual contracts of employment. This form of employment has grown, even if only by default, as the extent of union representation has declined, particularly of employees in the private sector. Unions now represent fewer employees and can significantly influence the terms and conditions of employment only in a narrow range of industries and geographical areas. This long-term decline in union representation has been accompanied by the growth in statutes, like Title VII, that directly regulate the employment relationship, generally in mandatory terms that cannot be waived by agreement. Arbitration effects a partial waiver of the protection of these statutes by altering the means by which they are enforced. Unions cannot waive the rights of individual employees to sue under Title VII because, among other reasons, the employees might sue the union itself. Whether employees can make such a waiver, either at the suggestion of the employer or of the union, is the question decided in *Gilmer*.

Several decisions before *Gilmer* had rejected the argument that arbitration was against public policy under statutes outside the field of employment discrimination law. As the opinion makes clear, the Court had accepted the efficacy of arbitration in enforcing other individual rights, such as those under the federal securities laws. These decisions were part of a trend, fully as significant as the decline in union representation, that favored mechanisms for "alternative dispute resolution" over the usual methods of litigation. In *Gilmer*, the Court considered the confluence of these two trends: whether the policies favoring arbitration could be implemented through arbitration under individual agreements. The Court found no objection to arbitration based on the nature of the plaintiff's claim, asserted under the Age Discrimination in Employment Act (ADEA). The ADEA's provisions for private actions are, in all relevant respects, identical to those under Title VII. The public policy of preventing discrimination also is the same. Hence the decision in *Gilmer* has been taken to determine the arbitrability of claims of discrimination generally. Does resolving such claims through arbitration create a risk of further discrimination in the process of arbitration itself? Or does it compromise in some other way the enforcement of discrimination claims?

2. Contractual Constraints on Arbitration. Since *Gilmer*, the Supreme Court has confirmed both the policy favoring arbitration and its limits in the law of contract. The lower courts have also imposed additional limits, either under state contract law or as a matter of federal law. Although these decisions address a variety of specific doctrinal issues and reach different outcomes, they all concern the same fundamental issue: whether imbalances in bargaining power between employers and employees restrict the enforceability of agreements to arbitrate. This issue in many ways is the mirror image of the issue concerning arbitration under collective bargaining agreements. Under such agreements the equivalence of bargaining power between employers and unions was accepted. Either they actually negotiated on equal terms or they did so on terms that could not be questioned under the National Labor Relations Act. Individual employees were not bound by this bargaining process, with respect to their claims of employment discrimination, only because they were not parties to it. Individual employees, however, are parties to their own contracts of employment and accordingly are bound by them. What they lack is the negotiating leverage that a union has through its status as the representative of all the employees in a bargaining unit. Accordingly, individual contracts of employment might provide for arbitration on terms systematically favorable to the employer. The crucial issue is not so much over the nature of claims of discrimination, decided in *Gilmer*, but the nature of individual contracts of employment.

This issue came up when the Court considered a question left open in *Gilmer*: whether the Federal Arbitration Act extended generally to arbitration under contracts of employment or whether it was subject to a broad exclusion for all contracts in industries affecting interstate commerce. In Circuit City Stores, Inc. v. Adams, 532 U.S. 105 (2001), the Court held that § 1 of the Federal Arbitration Act created only a narrow exception to the broad principle favoring arbitration under the Act. Section 1 excludes from the Act's coverage "contracts of employment of seamen, railroad employees, or any other class of workers engaged in foreign or interstate commerce." 9 U.S.C. § 1. The Court construed this provision to apply only to workers engaged in foreign or interstate transportation, rather than the much larger class of workers engaged in industries affecting interstate commerce. Although *Circuit City* involved a claim under a state law against employment discrimination, the Court's reasoning applies to virtually all claims of employment discrimination, confirming that *Gilmer* does not apply only to claims under the ADEA.

The contractual origins of arbitration, however, limit its application in other ways and, in particular, to claims brought by the EEOC. In EEOC v. Waffle House, Inc., 534 U.S. 279 (2002), the Court held that the EEOC was not precluded from bringing a claim under the Americans with Disabilities Act on behalf of an individual employee who had entered into an arbitration agreement with his employer. The EEOC's authority to sue was conferred by Title VII and was not dependent on any claim by the employee, whose rights were limited to intervention once the EEOC filed its own action. The agreement between the employer and the employee therefore was not binding on the EEOC. As the Court said, the Federal Arbitration Act "does not mention enforcement by public agencies; it ensures the enforceability of private agreements to arbitrate, but otherwise does not purport to place any restriction on a nonparty's choice of a judicial forum."

The contractual origins of arbitration raise issues under state law as well, since almost all forms of employment outside the Federal government are governed by the state law of contract. The two notable exceptions are collective bargaining agreements, which contain arbitration provisions usually governed by federal law, and employment with the Federal government, which has its own system of civil service regulation and special procedures under Title VII. The state law of contract contains well-known restrictions on the enforceability of contracts of adhesion and unconscionable contracts. The California Supreme Court has taken the lead in applying these restrictions to arbitration of employment disputes, holding that arbitration had to be bilateral, applying equally to claims of the employer as well as the employee. Armendariz v. Foundation Health Psychcare Services, Inc., 24 Cal.4th 83, 6 P.3d 669, 99 Cal.Rptr.2d 745 (2000). The court also applied a variety of additional requirements as a matter of public policy to allow the substitution of arbitration for otherwise nonwaivable judicial remedies. These include neutrality of the arbitrator, a written arbitration decision allowing minimal judicial review, adequate discovery, recovery of damages available under applicable substantive law, and limits on the costs of arbitration and attorney's fees imposed on the employee.

3. ***14 Penn Plaza LLC v. Pyett.*** The Supreme Court took the reasoning of *Gilmer* a long step further in *14 Penn Plaza LLC v. Pyett*, 556 U.S. 247 (2009), extending arbitration of employment discrimination claims from individual contracts to collective bargaining agreements. The plaintiffs in this case were subject to a collective bargaining agreement that explicitly

provided for arbitration of all employment discrimination claims, including those brought under federal and state law. The Court held that this provision prevented them from asserting their claims under the ADEA directly in federal court. As the Court said, "The *Gilmer* Court's interpretation of the ADEA fully applies in the collective-bargaining context. Nothing in the law suggests a distinction between the status of arbitration agreements signed by an individual employee and those agreed to by a union representative. This Court has required only that an agreement to arbitrate statutory antidiscrimination claims be 'explicitly stated' in the collective-bargaining agreement. Wright v. Universal Maritime Service Corp., 525 U.S. 70, 80 (1998)." This conclusion, the Court reasoned, was fully supported by the National Labor Relations Act, which authorized the union to enter into collective bargaining agreements binding on the plaintiff, and by the ADEA, which did nothing to detract from the union's authority to agree to arbitration.

Unlike *Gilmer*, the opinion in this case does not take care to preserve much, if anything at all, of the prior decision in *Alexander v. Gardner-Denver*. The Court distinguishes that case almost to the vanishing point, interpreting it to apply only to collective bargaining agreements that do not explicitly authorize arbitration of legal claims. Any arbitration clause, like the one in this case, which explicitly referred to claims under the ADEA, requires the employee to take such claims to arbitration. The holding in *Gardner-Denver*, by contrast, concerned the separate question whether arbitration of purely contractual claims also precluded litigation over statutory claims.

The only potentially limiting feature of the *Penn Plaza* decision, pointed out by Justice Souter in his dissent, is that the Court did not reach the question whether the union could cut off the plaintiffs' access to arbitration. The evidence was conflicting on this issue. The union requested arbitration on the plaintiffs' behalf but then declined to participate further in the arbitration process. Some evidence indicated that the union would have allowed the plaintiffs' claims to go to arbitration, instead of blocking them as most unions can do with respect to purely contractual claims. The Court, in any event, did not resolve this question.

The Court also frankly acknowledged the continued trend in favor of arbitration, recognizing that "the *Gardner-Denver* line of cases included broad dicta that was highly critical of the use of arbitration for the vindication of statutory antidiscrimination rights. That skepticism, however, rested on a misconceived view of arbitration that this Court has since abandoned." The four dissenting justices disputed this conclusion, arguing that *Gardner-Denver* was an established precedent and that any departure from it should be initiated by Congress.

For articles on *Penn Plaza* and related issues, see Steven C. Bennett, Arbitration of Employment Discrimination Claims: Impact of the *Pyett* Decision on Collective Bargaining, 42 Tex. Tech. L. Rev. 23 (2009); Marsha Berzon, "A General Theory of the Collective Bargaining Agreement" at 35, 30 Berkeley J. Emp. & Lab. L. 526 (2009); Sarah Rudolph Cole, "Let the Grand Experiment Begin: *Pyett* Authorizes Arbitration of Unionized Employees' Statutory Discrimination Claims", 14 Lewis & Clark L. Rev. 861

(2010); Susan K. Hippensteele, Revisiting the Promise of Mediation for Employment Discrimination Claims, 9 Pepp. Disp. Resol. L J. 211 (2009).

4. ***Rent-A-Center West Inc. v. Jackson.*** In yet another sign of the increased deference to arbitration, the Supreme Court held that the issue of arbitrability itself could be decided by the arbitrator in some circumstances. In particular, in *Rent-A-Center West Inc. v. Jackson*, 561 U.S. 63 (2010), the Court held that the issue of unconscionability had to be decided by the arbitrator under an agreement that "clearly and unmistakably" assigned the issue to the arbitrator and there was no specific claim that assigning this issue to the arbitrator was itself unconscionable. The plaintiff had challenged the agreement as a whole as unconscionable but that was not sufficient, in the Court's view, to challenge the specific assignment of the issue to the arbitrator. This highly technical distinction forces parties who seek to prevent arbitration entirely to cast their objection in specific terms that can be adjudicated by a court. Under section 2 of the Federal Arbitration Act (FAA), 9 U.S.C. § 2, these are limited to "such grounds as exist at law or in equity for the revocation of any contract."

5. ***AT&T Mobility LLC v. Concepcion.*** The two prominent alternatives to individual litigation—arbitration and class actions—came together in AT&T Mobility LLC v. Concepcion, 563 U.S. 333 (2011). That case concerned arbitration under a consumer contract that required claims to be brought to arbitration in an individual capacity, not as class claims. This restriction was struck down as unconscionable under California law, but that provision of state law was itself struck down under section 2 of the FAA because it operated to disfavor arbitration over litigation as a method of resolving disputes. Accordingly, California law was preempted by the FAA and the limitation in the arbitration clause to individual claims was upheld.

Could this decision be extended from consumer contracts under state law to employment contracts under federal law? *AT&T Mobility* does not, of its own force, apply to claims governed by federal law, such as Title VII, which are not subject to a preemption analysis. The inquiry, instead, would be how to reconcile Title VII with the FAA. But since the Court has already upheld compulsory arbitration of Title VII claims, it go on to uphold contractual limits on arbitration to individual claims. It would be only a small step to move from *Gilmer* and *AT&T Mobility* to the conclusion that contracts of employment can dispense with class actions entirely: first, by requiring arbitration instead of litigation, and second, by requiring only individual arbitration. The Court has not yet taken this step, but it soon may as employment contracts are modified to take advantage of the decision in *AT&T Mobility*.

The federal circuit courts have also recognized the need to impose such restrictions as a matter of public policy, relying both on the Federal Arbitration Act and the federal laws against employment discrimination. These decisions, however, have reached varying conclusions about the degree of protection necessary. Before the decision of the California Supreme Court in *Armendariz*, the D.C. Circuit imposed many of the same restrictions on arbitration in Cole v. Burns International Security Services, 105 F.3d 1465 (D.C. Cir. 1997). In addition, the court also held that the employee could not be required to bear any part of the costs of arbitration. In a conflicting decision, however, the Fourth Circuit has rejected any per se rule against allocating any costs to the employee and has evaluated the overall fairness of arbitration provisions, and particularly the allocation of costs, on a case-by-case basis. Bradford v. Rockwell Semiconductor Systems, Inc., 238 F.3d 549 (4th Cir. 2001). Yet another circuit has held that the Federal Arbitration Act preempts any stricter requirement imposed by state law on valid arbitration agreements that are covered by the Act. Oblix, Inc. v. Winiecki, 374 F.3d 488 (7th Cir. 2004). For a survey of decisions on these issues, see Kenneth D. Schwartz, After *Circuit City*, Are There Any Limits on Enforcing Arbitration Agreements?, 27 Emp. Rel. L.J., Sept., at 5; Martin M. Malin, Privatizing Justice—But by How Much? Questions *Gilmer* Did Not Answer, 16 Ohio St. J. on Disp. Resol. 589 (2001).

6. **Cases After *Concepcion*.** The Supreme Court further explored issues of class arbitration in two recent cases. In the first, Oxford Health Plans LLC v. Sutter, 133 S. Ct. 2064 (2013), the Court held that an arbitrator could conduct class-wide arbitration pursuant to an arbitration clause that did not explicitly authorize class-wide procedures. The arbitrator nevertheless interpreted the agreement to express "the parties' intent that class action arbitration can be maintained." That interpretation, even if erroneous, did not constitute grounds for overturning the arbitrator's award. According to the Court, "Only if the arbitrator acts outside the scope of his contractually delegated authority—issuing an award that simply reflects his own notices of economic justice rather than drawing its essence from the contract—may a court overturn his determination." (Citations, internal quotation marks, and brackets omitted.)

In the second case, American Express Co. v. Italian Colors Restaurant, 133 S. Ct. 2304 (2013), the Court considered arbitration pursuant to an agreement that expressly denied any "right or authority for any Claims to be arbitrated on a class action basis." The claims in that case were for violation of the federal antitrust laws and those claims, according to the plaintiffs, could not feasibly be brought in individualized proceedings. They accordingly brought a class action in federal court. The Court held that a class action could not be maintained because the Federal Arbitration Act required arbitration according to the terms of the parties' agreement. According to the Court, "No contrary congressional command requires us to reject the waiver of class arbitration here." And, in particular, "the antitrust laws do not guarantee an affordable procedural path to the vindication of every claim." The Court also held that the parties' agreement did not prevent effective vindication of the plaintiffs' federal statutory rights because it did not constitute a prospective waiver of their claims.

7. **The Promise and Perils of Arbitration.** Title VII was originally proposed as a statute, like the National Labor Relations Act, that would be enforced primarily through administrative decisions. When the EEOC was denied the general authority to adjudicate claims under Title VII, it was given the power instead to investigate and mediate disputes over discrimination. Its authority to sue only came later and, as discussed earlier, has been exercised in relatively few cases. Through the process of legislative

compromise, Title VII has always favored alternative means of dispute resolution. Indeed, the EEOC currently is engaged in a National Mediation Program in which private employers agree to assist in the resolution of claims against them.

The promise of arbitration is that it will assist in resolving claims of discrimination through a process acceptable to the parties that reduces both the cost that they must bear and the number of cases that courts would otherwise decide. Arbitration is a consensual process analogous to settlement but usually established by agreement before any dispute has arisen. Arbitration can also be used as a means of resolving existing claims when it is created as part of the settlement itself. In both situations, however, it represents a process that has been chosen by the parties. It is also a less formal process than litigation and therefore less expensive, although as its procedures become more elaborate, as some cases require, it also becomes more expensive. To the extent that arbitration diverts cases from the ordinary course of litigation, it also saves the judicial system from the cost of additional litigation. Nevertheless, this benefit, too, is dependent on avoiding collateral litigation over orders compelling arbitration or enforcing arbitration awards.

The risks of arbitration represent the opposite side of the coin from the benefits. It is a consensual process only if employees actually agree to it. To the extent that they are confronted with a take-it-or-leave-it contract of adhesion, and agree only formally to arbitration, their acceptance of the process and its results may be problematic. A number of articles have discussed this threshold issue of voluntariness. Joseph R. Grodin, Arbitration of Employment Discrimination Claims: Doctrine and Policy in the Wake of *Gilmer*, 14 Hofstra Lab. L.J. 1 (1996); Karen Halverson, Arbitration and the Civil Rights Act of 1991, 67 U. Cin. L. Rev. 445 (1999); Sharona Hoffman, Mandatory Arbitration: Alternative Dispute Resolution or Coercive Dispute Suppression?, 17 Berkeley J. Emp. & Lab. L. 131 (1996); Ronald Turner, Employment Discrimination, Labor and Employment Arbitration, and the Case Against Union Waiver of the Individual Worker's Statutory Right to a Judicial Forum, 49 Emory L.J. 135 (2000); Stephen J. Ware, Employment Arbitration and Voluntary Consent, 25 Hofstra L. Rev. 83 (1996).

Nevertheless, the absence of actual bargaining over an arbitration clause has not, by itself, led courts to hold it invalid, and they have, instead, imposed the restrictions on arbitration discussed in the previous note. These restrictions are motivated almost entirely by concerns that the benefits of arbitration accrue to the employer and that the costs are borne mainly by the employee. The costs at issue include more than the out-of-pocket expense of arbitration itself; they include the systematic disadvantages imposed upon employees who seek to pursue their claims of discrimination. Arbitration clauses may provide for only limited discovery and limited remedies and give the employer disproportionate influence over the selection of arbitrators. Do judicial decisions invalidating such provisions adequately protect employees who have lost their right to go to court? Does the very existence of these provisions discourage employees from pursuing their claims in the first place? See Katherine Van Wezel Stone, Mandatory Arbitration of Individual Employment Rights: The Yellow Dog Contract of the 1990s, 73 Denv. U. L. Rev. 1017 (1996).

Recall that most claims of discrimination involve issues of credibility. The employee asserts, for instance, that race was the reason that he was discharged or disciplined, while the employer asserts a legitimate, nondiscriminatory reason for taking this action. Routine cases involving individual claims of intentional discrimination are not too different from those traditionally handled by labor arbitrators under collective bargaining agreements. Such cases do not require the time and expense of litigation and the expertise of a federal judge. Many decisions, in the decades since Title VII was enacted, have developed the meaning and application of the statute to a variety of different situations. Is there any reason to expect that diligent and impartial arbitrators will apply settled law less accurately than federal judges? Or is it necessary to preserve litigation as a vehicle for developing new law for new situations? More generally, is it necessary to maintain litigation as an alternative to arbitration in order to assure the integrity of the arbitration process?

8. **Bibliography.** The arbitration of employment discrimination has been controversial since the statute was first enacted. The early decisions and articles concentrated on arbitration of claims under collective bargaining agreements. See, e.g., Bernard D. Meltzer, Labor Arbitration and Discrimination: The Parties' Process and the Public's Purposes, 43 U. Chi. L. Rev. 724 (1976). The decision in *Gilmer* led to a revival of the debate over arbitration of discrimination claims, with a focus on individual agreements to arbitrate claims of discrimination. See Alexander J.S. Colvin, An Empirical Study of Employment Arbitration: Case Outcomes and Processes, 8 J. Empirical Legal Stud. 1 (2011); Kenneth F. Dunham, Great *Gilmer*'s Ghost: The Haunting Tale of the Role of Employment Arbitration in the Disappearance of Statutory Rights in Employment Cases, 29 Am. J. Trial Advoc. 303 (2005); David Horton & Andrea C. Chandrasekher, Employment Arbitration After the Revolution, 65 DePaul L. Rev. 457 (2016); Martin H. Malin, The Three Phases of the Supreme Court's Arbitration Jurisprudence: Empowering the Already-Empowered, 17 Nev. L.J. 23 (2016); Daniel Markovits, Arbitration's Arbitrage: Social Solidarity at the Nexus of Adjudication and Contract, 59 DePaul L. Rev. 431 (2010); Stephen Plass, Private Dispute Resolution and the Future of Institutional Workplace Discrimination, 54 How. L.J. 45 (2010); Theodore J. St. Antoine, Mandatory Employment Arbitration: Keeping It Fair, Keeping It Lawful, 60 Case W. Res. L. Rev. 629 (2010); Theodore J. St. Antoine, Essay, Labor and Employment Arbitration Today: Mid-Life Crisis or New Golden Age?, 32 Ohio St. J. on Disp. Resol. 1 (2017); Jean R. Sternlight, Disarming Employees: How American Employers Are Using Mandatory Arbitration to Deprive Workers of Legal Protection, 80 Brook. L. Rev. 1309 (2015); Randall Thomas, Erin O'Hara & Kenneth Martin, Arbitration Clauses in CEO Employment Contracts: An Empirical and Theoretical Analysis, 63 Vand. L. Rev. 959 (2010); Symposium, Beyond the FAA: Arbitration, Procedure, Practice, and Policy in Historical Perspective, 2016 J. Disp. Resol. 1;

Symposium, Forced Arbitration in the Workplace, 35 Berkeley J. Emp. & Lab. L. 1 (2014); Symposium, Arbitration, Transparency, and Privatization, 124 Yale L.J. 2804 (2015); Symposium, *Gilmer v. Interstate/Johnson Lane Corporation*: Ten Years After, 16 Ohio St. J. on Disp. Resol. 463 (2001).

CHAPTER 8

REMEDIES

INTRODUCTORY NOTE

The compromise over procedural provisions in Title VII, taking most adjudication away from the EEOC and giving it to the courts, also affected the statute's remedial provisions. As originally enacted, Title VII provided only for the award of equitable relief: injunctions, back pay, and the award of attorney's fees. § 706(g), (k), 42 U.S.C. § 2000e–5(g), (k). Damages could not be awarded and back pay, as computed by the court, represented the only form of monetary relief. This restriction on remedies followed the pattern of remedies awarded by administrative agencies and, in particular, the National Labor Relations Board.

This restriction also served the further purpose of 3avoiding any right to jury trial under Title VII. Supporters of the statute feared that juries, particularly in the South, would act to nullify claims of discrimination by members of minority groups. They accordingly tried to devise a system of remedies that did not trigger the right to jury trial in federal court under the Seventh Amendment. The remedies awarded by administrative agencies, which were also made without any right to jury trial, were a readily available model for the equitable remedies provided originally by Title VII. The provision for attorney's fees, which has no counterpart in most agency proceedings, was added in recognition of the cost to private plaintiffs in taking cases to court rather than submitting them to an administrative agency for prosecution and enforcement.

With the passage of time, and with the experience under other civil rights statutes, the threat of jury nullification appeared to diminish, and the advantages of awarding damages became more apparent. Under two statutes enacted during Reconstruction, 42 U.S.C. §§ 1981, 1983, plaintiffs from minority groups could obtain damages for racial discrimination. They could sue private employers under § 1981 for racial discrimination in contracting, and they could sue state and local officials under § 1983 for racial discrimination in violation of the Constitution. As claims under these statutes became more common, victims of other forms of discrimination, particularly discrimination on the basis of sex, sought the same array of remedies, including damages. In the Civil Rights Act of 1991, they obtained the right to recover, although subject to caps depending on the size of the employer. 42 U.S.C. § 1981a(a), (b). See Lynn Zehrt, Twenty Years of Compromise: How the Caps on Damages in the Civil Rights Act of 1991 Codified Sex Discrimination, 5 Yale J.L. & Feminism 249 (2014). This Act also recognized that any award of damages had to be accompanied by the right to jury trial. 42 U.S.C. § 1981a(c).

The extension of damages to claims under Title VII has had a profound effect on the litigation of claims of employment discrimination. As noted in Chapter 4, claims of sexual harassment have been transformed as the recovery of damages for emotional distress has become available. So, too, the magnitude of recovery on behalf of any particular plaintiff has also increased, making the plaintiff's case more closely resemble one for personal injury than a civil rights action for injunctive relief. Plaintiffs' attorneys have accordingly evaluated cases, and decided whether to take them, more on the model of tort lawyers compensated through contingent fees than as public interest lawyers seeking to change the law. For an early account of these changes in the pattern of employment discrimination litigation, see John J. Donohue III & Peter Siegelman, The Changing Nature of Employment Discrimination Litigation, 43 Stan. L. Rev. 983 (1991); Laura B. Nielsen, Robert L. Nelson & Ryon Lancaster, Individual Justice or Collective Legal Mobilization? Employment Discrimination in the Post Civil Rights United States, 7 J. Empirical Legal Stud. 175 (2010).

A. EQUITABLE REMEDIES

Albemarle Paper Co. v. Moody

422 U.S. 405 (1975).

■ JUSTICE STEWART delivered the opinion of the Court.

[This case involved both issues of substantive law and remedies. In the part of the opinion excerpted in Chapter 3, the Supreme Court held the defendant liable under the theory of disparate impact for tests and educational requirements with an adverse impact upon blacks. The part of the opinion excerpted here concerns the defendant's liability for back pay and injunctive relief.

[The plaintiffs in this case had initially sought only injunctive relief and had "assured the court that the suit involved no claim for any monetary awards on a class basis, but in June 1970, after several years of discovery, the respondents moved to add a class demand for back pay." After considering this issue at trial, the district court denied back pay, reasoning as follows:

> In the instant case there was no evidence of bad faith non-compliance with the Act. It appears that the company as early as 1964 began active recruitment of blacks for its Maintenance Apprentice Program. Certain lines of progression were merged on its own initiative, and as judicial decisions expanded the then existing interpretations of the Act, the defendants took steps to correct the abuses without delay. . . .
>
> In addition, an award of back pay is an equitable remedy. . . . The plaintiffs' claim for back pay was filed nearly five years after the institution of this action. It was not prayed for in the pleadings. Although neither party can be charged with deliberate dilatory tactics in bringing this cause to trial, it is apparent that the defendants would be substantially prejudiced by the granting of such affirmative relief. The defendants might

have chosen to exercise unusual zeal in having this court determine their rights at an earlier date had they known that back pay would be at issue.

[The court of appeals, however, disagreed and ordered an award of back pay despite any showing that the defendant acted in good faith:

> Because of the compensatory nature of a back pay award and the strong congressional policy embodied in Title VII, a district court must exercise its discretion as to back pay in the same manner it must exercise discretion as to attorney fees under Title II of the Civil Rights Act. . . . Thus, a plaintiff or a complaining class who is successful in obtaining an injunction under Title VII of the Act should ordinarily be awarded back pay unless special circumstances would render such an award unjust. Newman v. Piggie Park Enterprises, 390 U.S. 400, . . . (1968). (Footnote omitted.)]

II

Whether a particular member of the plaintiff class should have been awarded any back pay and, if so, how much, are questions not involved in this review. The equities of individual cases were never reached. Though at least some of the members of the plaintiff class obviously suffered a loss of wage opportunities on account of Albemarle's unlawfully discriminatory system of job seniority, the District Court decided that no back pay should be awarded to anyone in the class. The court declined to make such an award on two stated grounds: the lack of "evidence of bad faith non-compliance with the Act," and the fact that "the defendants would be substantially prejudiced" by an award of back pay that was demanded contrary to an earlier representation and late in the progress of the litigation. Relying directly on Newman v. Piggie Park Enterprises, 390 U.S. 400 (1968), the Court of Appeals reversed, holding that back pay could be denied only in "special circumstances." The petitioners argue that the Court of Appeals was in error—that a district court has virtually unfettered discretion to award or deny back pay, and that there was no abuse of that discretion here.[8]

---

[8] The petitioners also contend that no back pay can be awarded to those unnamed parties in the plaintiff class who have not themselves filed charges with the EEOC. We reject this contention. The Courts of Appeals that have confronted the issue are unanimous in recognizing that back pay may be awarded on a class basis under Title VII without exhaustion of administrative procedures by the unnamed class members. . . . The Congress plainly ratified this construction of the Act in the course of enacting the Equal Employment Opportunity Act of 1972, Pub. L. 92–261, 86 Stat. 103. The House of Representatives passed a bill, H.R. 1746, 92d Cong., 1st Sess., that would have barred, in § 3(e), an award of back pay to any individual who "neither filed a charge [with the EEOC] nor was named in a charge or amendment thereto." But the Senate Committee on Labor and Public Welfare recommended, instead, the re-enactment of the back pay provision without such a limitation, and cited with approval several cases holding that back pay was awardable to class members who had not personally filed, nor been named in, charges to the EEOC. S. Rep. No. 92–415, p. 27 (1971). See also 118 Cong. Rec. 4942 (1972). The Senate passed a bill without the House's limitation, id. at 4944, and the Conference Committee adopted the Senate position. A Section-by-Section Analysis of the Conference Committee's resolution notes that "[a] provision limiting class actions was contained in the

Piggie Park Enterprises, supra, is not directly in point. The Court held there that attorneys' fees should "ordinarily" be awarded—i.e., in all but "special circumstances"—to plaintiffs successful in obtaining injunctions against discrimination in public accommodations, under Title II of the Civil Rights Act of 1964. While the Act appears to leave Title II fee awards to the district court's discretion, 42 U.S.C. § 2000a–3(b), the court determined that the great public interest in having injunctive actions brought could be vindicated only if successful plaintiffs, acting as "private attorneys general," were awarded attorneys' fees in all but very unusual circumstances. There is, of course, an equally strong public interest in having injunctive actions brought under Title VII, to eradicate discriminatory employment practices. But this interest can be vindicated by applying the *Piggie Park* standard to the attorneys' fees provision of Title VII, 42 U.S.C. § 2000e–5(k), see Northcross v. Memphis Board of Education, 412 U.S. 427, 428 (1973). For guidance as to the granting and denial of back pay, one must, therefore, look elsewhere.

The petitioners contend that the statutory scheme provides no guidance, beyond indicating that back pay awards are within the District Court's discretion. We disagree. It is true that back pay is not an automatic or mandatory remedy; like all other remedies under the Act, it is one which the courts "may" invoke. The scheme implicitly recognizes that there may be cases calling for one remedy but not another, and—owing to the structure of the federal judiciary—these choices are, of course, left in the first instance to the district courts. However, such discretionary choices are not left to a court's "inclination, but to its judgment; and its judgment is to be guided by sound legal principles." United States v. Burr, 25 F. Cas. 30, 35 (No. 14,692d) (CC Va. 1807) (Marshall, C.J.). The power to award back pay was bestowed by Congress, as part of a complex legislative design directed at a historic evil of national proportions. A court must exercise this power "in light of the large objectives of the Act," Hecht Co. v. Bowles, 321 U.S. 321, 331 (1944). That the court's discretion is equitable in nature, see Curtis v. Loether, 415 U.S. 189, 197 (1974), hardly means that it is unfettered by meaningful standards or shielded from thorough appellate review. In Mitchell v. DeMario Jewelry, 361 U.S. 288, 292 (1960), this Court held, in the face of a silent statute, that district courts enjoyed the "historic power of equity" to award lost wages to workmen unlawfully discriminated against under § 17 of the Fair Labor Standards Act of 1938, 52 Stat. 1069, as amended, 29 U.S.C. § 217 (1958 ed.). The Court simultaneously noted that "the statutory purposes [leave] little room for the exercise of discretion not to order reimbursement."

It is true that "[e]quity eschews mechanical rules . . . [and] depends on flexibility." Holmberg v. Armbrecht, 327 U.S. 392, 396 (1946). But when Congress invokes the Chancellor's conscience to further

House bill and specifically rejected by the Conference Committee," id. at 7168, 7565. The Conference Committee bill was accepted by both Chambers. Id. at 7170, 7573.

transcendent legislative purposes, what is required is the principled application of standards consistent with those purposes and not "equity [which] varies like the Chancellor's foot." Important national goals would be frustrated by a regime of discretion that "produce[d] different results for breaches of duty in situations that cannot be differentiated in policy." Moragne v. States Marine Lines, 398 U.S. 375, 405 (1970).

The District Court's decision must therefore be measured against the purposes which inform Title VII. As the Court observed in Griggs v. Duke Power Co., 401 U.S. at 429–430, the primary objective was a prophylactic one:

> "It was to achieve equality of employment opportunities and remove barriers that have operated in the past to favor an identifiable group of white employees over other employees."

Back pay has an obvious connection with this purpose. If employers faced only the prospect of an injunctive order, they would have little incentive to shun practices of dubious legality. It is the reasonably certain prospect of a back pay award that "provide[s] the spur or catalyst which causes employers and unions to self-examine and to self-evaluate their employment practices and to endeavor to eliminate, so far as possible, the last vestiges of an unfortunate and ignominious page in this country's history." United States v. N.L. Industries, Inc., 479 F.2d 354, 379 (8th Cir. 1973).

It is also the purpose of Title VII to make persons whole for injuries suffered on account of unlawful employment discrimination. This is shown by the very fact that Congress took care to arm the courts with full equitable powers. For it is the historic purpose of equity to "secur[e] complete justice," Brown v. Swann, 10 Pet. 497, 503 (1836); see also Porter v. Warner Holding Co., 328 U.S. 395, 397–398 (1946). "[W]here federally protected rights have been invaded, it has been the rule from the beginning that courts will be alert to adjust their remedies so as to grant the necessary relief." Bell v. Hood, 327 U.S. 678, 684 (1946). Title VII deals with legal injuries of an economic character occasioned by racial or other antiminority discrimination. The terms "complete justice" and "necessary relief" have acquired a clear meaning in such circumstances. Where racial discrimination is concerned, "the [district] court has not merely the power but the duty to render a decree which will so far as possible eliminate the discriminatory effects of the past as well as bar like discrimination in the future." Louisiana v. United States, 380 U.S. 145, 154 (1965). And where a legal injury is of an economic character,

> "[t]he general rule is, that when a wrong has been done, and the law gives a remedy, the compensation shall be equal to the injury. The latter is the standard by which the former is to be measured. The injured party is to be placed, as near as may be, in the situation he would have occupied if the wrong had not been committed." Wicker v. Hoppock, 6 Wall. 94, 99 (1867).

The "make whole" purpose of Title VII is made evident by the legislative history. The back pay provision was expressly modeled on the back pay provision of the National Labor Relations Act.[11] Under that Act, "[m]aking the workers whole for losses suffered on account of an unfair labor practice is part of the vindication of the public policy which the Board enforces." Phelps Dodge Corp. v. NLRB, 313 U.S. 177, 197 (1941). We may assume that Congress was aware that the Board, since its inception, has awarded back pay as a matter of course—not randomly or in the exercise of a standardless discretion, and not merely where employer violations are peculiarly deliberate, egregious, or inexcusable.[12] Furthermore, in passing the Equal Employment Opportunity Act of 1972, Congress considered several bills to limit the judicial power to award back pay. These limiting efforts were rejected, and the back pay provision was re-enacted substantially in its original form. A Section-by-Section Analysis introduced by Senator Williams to accompany the Conference Committee Report on the 1972 Act strongly reaffirmed the "make whole" purpose of Title VII:

> "The provisions of this subsection are intended to give the courts wide discretion exercising their equitable powers to fashion the most complete relief possible. In dealing with the present section 706(g) the courts have stressed that the scope of relief under that section of the Act is intended to make the victims of unlawful discrimination whole, and that the attainment of this objective rests not only upon the elimination of the particular unlawful employment practice complained of, but also requires that persons aggrieved by the consequences and effects of the unlawful employment practice be, so far as possible, restored to

---

[11] Section 10(c) of the NLRA, 49 Stat. 454, as amended, 29 U.S.C. § 160(c), provides that when the Labor Board has found that a person has committed an "unfair labor practice," the Board "shall issue" an order "requiring such person to cease and desist from such unfair labor practice, and to take such affirmative action including reinstatement of employees with or without back pay, as will effectuate the policies of this subchapter." The back pay provision of Title VII provides that when the court has found "an unlawful employment practice," it "may enjoin" the practice "and order such affirmative action as may be appropriate, which may include, but is not limited to, reinstatement or hiring of employees, with or without back pay. . . ." 42 U.S.C. § 2000e–5(g). The framers of Title VII stated that they were using the NLRA provision as a model. 110 Cong. Rec. 6549 (1964) (remarks of Sen. Humphrey); id. at 7214 (interpretative memorandum by Sens. Clark and Case). In early versions of the Title VII provision on remedies, it was stated that a court "may" issue injunctions, but "shall" order appropriate affirmative action. This anomaly was removed by Substitute Amendment No. 656, 110 Cong. Rec. 12814, 12819 (1964). The framers regarded this as merely a "minor language change," id. at 12723–12724 (remarks of Sen. Humphrey). We can find here no intent to back away from the NLRA model or to denigrate in any way the status of back pay relief.

[12] "The finding of an unfair labor practice and discriminatory discharge is presumptive proof that some back pay is owed by the employer," NLRB v. Mastro Plastics Corp., 354 F. 2d 170, 178 (CA2 1965). While the back pay decision rests in the NLRB's discretion, and not with the courts, NLRB v. Rutter-Rex Mfg. Co., 396 U.S. 258, 263 (1969), the Board has from its inception pursued "a practically uniform policy with respect to these orders requiring affirmative action." NLRB, First Annual Report 124 (1936). "[I]n all but a few cases involving discriminatory discharges, discriminatory refusals to employ or reinstate, or discriminatory demotions in violation of section 8(3), the Board has ordered the employer to offer reinstatement to the employee discriminated against and to make whole such employee for any loss of pay that he has suffered by reason of the discrimination." NLRB, Second Annual Report 148 (1937).

a position where they would have been were it not for the unlawful discrimination." 118 Cong. Rec. 7168 (1972).

As this makes clear, Congress' purpose in vesting a variety of "discretionary" powers in the courts was not to limit appellate review of trial courts, or to invite inconsistency and caprice, but rather to make possible the "fashion[ing] [of] the most complete relief possible."

It follows that, given a finding of unlawful discrimination, back pay should be denied only for reasons which, if applied generally, would not frustrate the central statutory purposes of eradicating discrimination throughout the economy and making persons whole for injuries suffered through past discrimination.[14] The courts of appeals must maintain a consistent and principled application of the back pay provision, consonant with the twin statutory objectives, while at the same time recognizing that the trial court will often have the keener appreciation of those facts and circumstances peculiar to particular cases.

The District Court's stated grounds for denying back pay in this case must be tested against these standards. The first ground was that Albemarle's breach of Title VII had not been in "bad faith." This is not a sufficient reason for denying back pay. Where an employer has shown bad faith—by maintaining a practice which he knew to be illegal or of highly questionable legality—he can make no claims whatsoever on the Chancellor's conscience. But, under Title VII, the mere absence of bad faith simply opens the door to equity; it does not depress the scales in the employer's favor. If back pay were awardable only upon a showing of bad faith, the remedy would become a punishment for moral turpitude, rather than a compensation for workers' injuries. This would read the "make whole" purpose right out of Title VII, for a worker's injury is no less real simply because his employer did not inflict it in "bad faith." Title VII is not concerned with the employer's "good intent or absence of discriminatory intent" for "Congress directed the thrust of the Act to the consequences of employment practices, not simply the motivation." Griggs v. Duke Power Co., 401 U.S. at 432. To condition the awarding of back pay on a showing of "bad faith" would be to open an enormous chasm between injunctive and back pay relief under Title VII. There is nothing on the face of the statute or in its legislative history that justifies the creation of drastic and categorical distinctions between those two remedies.

The District Court also grounded its denial of back pay on the fact that the respondents initially disclaimed any interest in back pay, first asserting their claim five years after the complaint was filed. The court concluded that the petitioners had been "prejudiced" by this conduct. The Court of Appeals reversed on the ground "that the broad aims of Title VII require that the issue of back pay be fully developed and determined even

---

[14] It is necessary, therefore, that if a district court does decline to award back pay, it carefully articulate its reasons.

though it was not raised until the post-trial stage of litigation," 474 F.2d at 141. It is true that Title VII contains no legal bar to raising back pay claims after the complaint for injunctive relief has been filed, or indeed after a trial on that complaint has been had. Furthermore, Fed. Rule Civ. Proc. 54(c) directs that

> "every final judgment shall grant the relief to which the party in whose favor it is rendered is entitled, even if the party has not demanded such relief in his pleadings."

But a party may not be "entitled" to relief if its conduct of the cause has improperly and substantially prejudiced the other party. The respondents here were not merely tardy, but also inconsistent, in demanding back pay. To deny back pay because a particular cause has been prosecuted in an eccentric fashion, prejudicial to the other party, does not offend the broad purposes of Title VII. This is not to say, however, that the District Court's ruling was necessarily correct. Whether the petitioners were in fact prejudiced, and whether the respondents' trial conduct was excusable, are questions that will be open to review by the Court of Appeals, if the District Court, on remand, decides again to decline to make any award of back pay. But the standard of review will be the familiar one of whether the District Court was "clearly erroneous" in its factual findings and whether it "abused" its traditional discretion to locate "a just result" in light of the circumstances peculiar to the case, Langnes v. Green, 282 U.S. 531, 541 (1931). On these issues of procedural regularity and prejudice, the "broad aims of Title VII" provide no ready solution. . . .

[The concurring opinion of JUSTICE MARSHALL and the opinion of JUSTICE BLACKMUN concurring in the judgment are omitted.]

■ JUSTICE REHNQUIST, concurring.

I join the opinion of the Court. The manner in which 42 U.S.C. § 2000e–5(g) is construed has important consequences not only as to the circumstances under which back pay may be awarded, but also as to the method by which any such award is to be determined.

To the extent that an award of back pay were to be analogized to an award of damages, such an award upon proper proof would follow virtually as a matter of course from a finding that an employer had unlawfully discriminated contrary to the provisions of Title VII of the Civil Rights Act of 1964, 78 Stat. 253, as amended by the Equal Employment Opportunity Act of 1972, 86 Stat. 103, 42 U.S.C. § 2000e et seq. Plaintiffs would be entitled to the benefit of the rule enunciated in Bigelow v. RKO Radio Pictures, 327 U.S. 251, 265 (1946):

> " 'The constant tendency of the courts is to find some way in which damages can be awarded where a wrong has been done. Difficulty of ascertainment is no longer confused with right of recovery' for a proven invasion of the plaintiff's rights. Story Parchment Co. v. Paterson Co., [282 U.S. 555,] 565."

But precisely to the extent that an award of back pay is thought to flow as a matter of course from a finding of wrongdoing, and thereby becomes virtually indistinguishable from an award for damages, the question (not raised by any of the parties, and therefore quite properly not discussed in the Court's opinion), of whether either side may demand a jury trial under the Seventh Amendment becomes critical. We said in Curtis v. Loether, 415 U.S. 189, 197 (1974), in explaining the difference between the provision for damages under § 812 of the Civil Rights Act of 1968, 82 Stat. 88, 42 U.S.C. § 3612, and the authorization for the award of back pay which we treat here:

> "In Title VII cases, also, the courts have relied on the fact that the decision whether to award back pay is committed to the discretion of the trial judge. There is no comparable discretion here: if a plaintiff proves unlawful discrimination and actual damages, he is entitled to judgment for that amount.... Whatever may be the merit of the 'equitable' characterization in Title VII cases, there is surely no basis for characterizing the award of compensatory and punitive damages here as equitable relief." (Footnote omitted.)

In *Curtis*, supra, the Court further quoted the description of the Seventh Amendment in Mr. Justice Story's opinion for this Court in Parsons v. Bedford, 3 Pet. 433, 447 (1830), to the effect that:

> "In a just sense, the amendment then may well be construed to embrace all suits which are not of equity and admiralty jurisdiction, whatever may be the peculiar form which they may assume to settle legal rights."

To the extent, then, that the District Court retains substantial discretion as to whether or not to award back pay notwithstanding a finding of unlawful discrimination, the nature of the jurisdiction which the court exercises is equitable, and under our cases neither party may demand a jury trial. To the extent that discretion is replaced by awards which follow as a matter of course from a finding of wrongdoing, the action of the court in making such awards could not be fairly characterized as equitable in character, and would quite arguably be subject to the provisions of the Seventh Amendment.

Thus I believe that the broad latitude which the Court's opinion reposes in the district courts in the decision as to whether back pay shall be awarded is not only consistent with the statute, but is supported by policy considerations which would favor the more expeditious disposition which may be made of numerous claims on behalf of frequently large classes by a court sitting without a jury. As the Court states, the back pay remedy provided by Title VII is modeled on the remedial provisions of the NLRA. This Court spoke to the breadth of the latter provision in Phelps Dodge Corp. v. NLRB, 313 U.S. 177, 198 (1941), when it said:

> "[W]e must avoid the rigidities of an either-or rule. The remedy of back pay, it must be remembered, is entrusted to the Board's discretion; it is not mechanically compelled by the Act. And in applying its authority over back pay orders, the Board has not used stereotyped formulas but has availed itself of the freedom given it by Congress to attain just results in diverse, complicated situations."

I agree, nonetheless, with the Court that the District Court should not have denied back pay in this litigation simply on the ground that Albemarle's breach of Title VII had not been in "bad faith." Good faith is a necessary condition for obtaining equitable consideration, but in view of the narrower "good faith" defense created by statute, 42 U.S.C. § 2000e–12(b), it is not for this Court to expand such a defense beyond those situations to which Congress had made it applicable. I do not read the Court's opinion to say, however, that the facts upon which the District Court based its conclusion, would not have supported a finding that the conduct of Albemarle was reasonable under the circumstances as well as being simply in good faith. Nor do I read the Court's opinion to say that such a combination of factors might not, in appropriate circumstances, be an adequate basis for denial of back pay. . . .

A cursory canvass of the decisions of the District Courts and Courts of Appeals which confront these problems much more often than we do suggests that the most frequently recurring problem in this area is the difficulty of ascertaining a sufficient causal connection between the employer's conduct properly found to have been in violation of the statute and an ascertainable amount of back pay lost by a particular claimant as a result of that conduct. United States v. St. Louis-S.F.R. Co., 464 F. 2d 301, 311 (CA8 1972), cert. denied, 409 U.S. 1116 (1973). The Court of Appeals for the Eighth Circuit aptly described the difficulty of fashioning an award of back pay in the circumstances before it, and upheld the District Court's refusal to award back pay, in Norman v. Missouri P.R. Co., 497 F.2d 594, 597 (1974), cert. denied, 420 U.S. 908 (1975):

> "No standard could determine the right to back pay itself nor the date from which to compute any right to back pay. Courts that have found back pay awards to be appropriate remedies in Title VII actions have generally recognized that such awards should be limited to actual damages. . . ."

As the Court recognizes, another factor presented here which is relevant to the District Court's exercise of discretion is the possible detrimental reliance of petitioners on prior representations of respondents that they were not seeking classwide back pay. In 1966 respondents in replying to a motion for summary judgment expressly represented to the District Court that they had no interest in classwide back pay:

> "It is important to understand the exact nature of the class relief being sought by plaintiffs. No money damages are sought for any member of the class not before the court. . . .
>
> ". . . [T]he matter of specific individual relief for other class members is not before this Court."

Five years later, respondents reversed their position and asserted a claim for classwide back pay. Petitioners have argued here and below that they reasonably relied to their detriment on respondents' statement in numerous ways including an interim sale of the mill at a price which did not take into account the ruinous liability with which the new owners are now faced, failure to investigate and prepare defenses to individual back pay claims which are now nine years old, and failure to speed resolution of this lawsuit. This conduct by the respondents presents factual and legal questions to be resolved in the first instance by the District Court, reviewable only on whether its factual findings are "clearly erroneous" and whether its ultimate conclusion is an "abuse of discretion" under all the circumstances of this case. In the same manner that the good faith of an employer may not be viewed in isolation as precluding back pay under any and all circumstances, the excusable nature of respondents' conduct, if found excusable, will not necessarily preclude denial of a back pay award if petitioners are found to have substantially and justifiably relied on respondents' prior representations.

If the award of back pay is indeed governed by equitable considerations, and not simply a thinly disguised form of damages, factors such as these and others, which may argue in favor of or against the equities of either plaintiff or defendants, must be open for consideration by the District Court. It, like the NLRB, must avail itself "of the freedom given it by Congress to attain just results in diverse, complicated situations." Phelps Dodge Corp. v. NLRB, 313 U.S. at 198.

■ CHIEF JUSTICE BURGER, concurring in part and dissenting in part.

. . . With respect to the back pay issue, it must be emphasized that Albemarle was not held liable for practicing overt racial discrimination. It is undisputed that it voluntarily discontinued such practices prior to the effective date of Title VII and that the statute does not—and could not—apply to acts occurring before its passage. The basis of Albemarle's liability was that its seniority system perpetuated the effects of past discrimination and, as the District Court pointed out, the law regarding an employer's obligation to cure such effects was unclear for a considerable period of time. Moreover, the District Court's finding that Albemarle did not act in bad faith was not simply a determination that it thought its seniority system was legal but, rather, a finding that both prior to and after the filing of this lawsuit it took steps to integrate minorities into its labor force and to promptly fulfill its obligations under the law as it developed.

In light of this background, the Court's suggestion that the District Court "conditioned" awards of back pay upon a showing of bad faith is incorrect. Moreover, the District Court's findings on this point cannot be disregarded as irrelevant. As the Court's opinion notes, one of Congress' major purposes in giving district courts discretion to award back pay in Title VII actions was to encourage employers and unions "to self-examine and to self-evaluate their employment practices and to endeavor to eliminate, so far as possible, the last vestiges of an unfortunate and ignominious page in this country's history." By the same token, if employers are to be assessed back pay even where they have attempted in good faith to conform to the law, they will have little incentive to eliminate marginal practices until bound by a court judgment. Plainly, then, the District Court's findings relate to "reasons which, if applied generally, would not frustrate the central statutory purposes. . . ." Because respondents waited five years before changing their original position disclaiming back pay and belatedly seeking it, thus suggesting that a desire to be "made whole" was not a major reason for their pursuit of this litigation, I cannot say that the District Court abused its discretion by denying that remedy. . . .

NOTES ON *ALBEMARLE PAPER CO. V. MOODY*

1. **Equitable Remedies Under Title VII.** The analysis of remedies in *Albemarle Paper* begins with the provisions in § 706(g) derived from the National Labor Relations Act. The original proposal for Title VII sought to confer enforcement authority on the EEOC in much the same terms as the enforcement authority of the National Labor Relations Board (NLRB), including nearly identical authority to issue cease-and-desist orders for both preventive and compensatory relief. Those orders could be enforced by actions brought by the EEOC, which effectively converted them into injunctions. When the EEOC lost its authority to enforce Title VII directly, the power to issue the same remedies was conferred on the courts. Judicial authority to grant equitable relief likewise extended to prospective injunctions, prohibiting discrimination in the future, and to compensatory remedies, such as back pay.

As originally enacted, the remedial provisions in Title VII solved three problems. First, they satisfied the objections of legislators opposed to creating a powerful administrative agency like the NLRB. The EEOC was limited to investigating and mediating charges of discrimination, and through later amendments, it obtained the power to sue. The power to adjudicate claims and to issue remedies was given to the courts. Second, the authority given to the courts included the same range of remedies as the NLRB had used to enforce employees' rights to obtain union representation and to engage in collective bargaining. Congress had some assurance that the remedies devised to protect one set of rights related to employment would also prove to be adequate to protect another. And third, the model of enforcement through the NLRB finessed the question of the right to jury trial once a case made its way to court. Supporters of Title VII, when it was originally enacted, were concerned that a right to jury trial would result in widespread nullification of its provisions, particularly in the South. The absence of any right to jury trial in proceedings before an administrative agency provided the model for equitable remedies, issued by a judge sitting without a jury, when enforcement authority was transferred to the courts.

As the opinion in *Albemarle Paper* emphasizes, judicial authority was further expanded in the amendments made to Title VII by the Equal Employment Opportunity Act of 1972. First, Congress explicitly allowed charges to be filed "by or on behalf of a person aggrieved," implying that class actions could be brought on the basis of such charges, without any further need for absent class members to exhaust administrative remedies themselves. § 706(b), 42 U.S.C. § 2000e–5(b). And second, Congress further broadened judicial power to issue "any other equitable relief as the court deems appropriate." § 706(g)(1), 42 U.S.C. § 2000e–5(g)(1). Thus the authority of courts to issue compensatory relief, like the back pay at issue in *Albemarle Paper*, was at least as broad as the power of the NLRB to issue the same remedy.

2. Remedial Goals and Principles. The general standards for awarding remedies under Title VII are easy to state but difficult to apply. The congressional conference committee that approved the amendments to § 706, 42 U.S.C. § 2000e–5 directed courts to afford "the most complete relief possible," but it stated an abstract ideal rather than a definite guideline. Even the more specific standard articulated in *Albemarle Paper* leaves many issues unresolved. That standard allows a court to deny back pay "only for reasons which, if applied generally, would not frustrate the central statutory purposes of eradicating discrimination throughout the economy and making persons whole for injuries suffered through past discrimination." Stated affirmatively, there is a presumption in favor of awarding back pay to identified victims of discrimination. It can be denied only on a specific showing that it is not necessary to further the deterrent and compensatory purposes of Title VII.

Back pay serves the entirely instrumental purpose of implementing the substantive goals of Title VII: deterring future violations of the statute and compensating for past violations. An award of back pay discourages future violations of the statute by forcing employers to pay twice for work that is only done once. The employer must pay both the employee hired for the job and the victim of discrimination who was wrongly denied the job. Faced with this potential double expense, employers will try to avoid engaging in future discrimination. If back pay were an entirely successful deterrent, it would lead to the goal of "eradicating discrimination throughout the economy." So, too, if back pay perfectly served its compensatory purpose, it would restore to victims of discrimination everything that they had lost. It would put them in the same situation as if no discrimination had occurred. Both as deterrent and as compensation, back pay would lead to the ultimate goal of creating a society free of employment discrimination and its consequences.

Of course, this goal is highly idealized. No remedy is perfect, either as a deterrent or as compensation. For a variety of different reasons, victims of discrimination may not bring meritorious claims, or if they do, they may not recover on them. Potential plaintiffs may find it more to their advantage to seek another job than to sue an employer who has already rejected them. Or, if they decide to sue, their claims may be barred by the statute of limitations, or they may have insufficient evidence to prevail on the merits. These defects in the enforcement process are obvious and are hardly unique to Title VII. Yet they are obscured by the reference to an ideal of deterrence and compensation in determining whether an award of back pay—or indeed, any remedy under Title VII—should be granted. Remedies do not simply or transparently serve the same goals as the substantive law. See Daryl J. Levinson, Rights Essentialism and Remedial Equilibration, 99 Colum. L. Rev. 857 (1999).

Equitable remedies under Title VII are subject to two overriding restrictions: first, they are within the discretion of the trial judge; and second, they must be fair to all the parties involved. These restrictions are connected. Trial judges are given discretion in order to assure that all parties are treated fairly. In *Albemarle Paper*, this allocation of authority to the judge allows the Supreme Court to set forth broad principles of idealized remedies and then to leave to trial judges the task of applying those principles to the messy reality of actual cases. Thus, even on the facts of *Albemarle Paper*, the Court leaves two crucial issues to be determined by the federal district court: first, whether the plaintiffs' delay in seeking an award of back pay put the defendant at an unfair disadvantage; and second, as discussed in the excerpt from this opinion in Chapter 3, how to frame an appropriate injunction in light of the changed structure of the defendant's operations. Isn't it apparent that granting both forms of relief, in some form or other, would further the deterrent and compensatory purposes of Title VII? An award of back pay would impose costs on the employer for past violations of Title VII and an injunction would prevent future violations. The victims of discrimination could obtain full compensation only by receiving an award of back pay. If granting relief would achieve these objectives, on what grounds could the district court deny it? The principal arguments for denying relief concern fairness to the employer, raising issues entirely independent of the effectiveness of the proposed remedies. If taking account of fairness to the employer would compromise the effectiveness of the remedies in this case, would it do so in the general run of cases? Does the answer depend on how unusual the particular employer's situation is?

3. **Judicial Discretion, Statutory Interpretation, and the Right to Jury Trial.** Title VII requires some measure of discretion to be conferred on the trial judge, since it provides that "the court may enjoin" the defendant and "order such affirmative action as may be appropriate," including back pay and "any other equitable relief as the court deems appropriate." § 706(g)(1), 42 U.S.C. § 2000e–5(g)(1). All these terms give the trial judge wide latitude to determine what relief should be granted. Yet the Supreme Court takes much of it away by insisting that back pay can only be denied for a limited number of reasons. The standard articulated by the Court does not go quite as far as requiring awards of back pay in all but exceptional cases, but it comes close. Where does the Court itself obtain the authority to limit the trial judge's discretion? And having limited it to a great extent

already, why doesn't the Court limit the trial judge's discretion further and require an award of back pay in all but exceptional cases?

The references in Title VII to the power of "the court" to award equitable relief seemingly exclude the power of the jury to do so. The phrase "the court" could be taken comprehensively to refer to both the trial judge and the jury, but the further references to injunctions and other forms of equitable relief invoke the practice of the courts of equity, in which cases were tried only to a judge. The fear of jury nullification, already mentioned, led Congress to eliminate the jury from any role in enforcing Title VII as originally enacted. Congress could accomplish this goal only by limiting remedies to those traditionally awarded by a court of equity. Those remedies, such as an injunction, typically are more complicated than the award of damages made by a jury in an action at law. Such remedies therefore require the expertise and discretion of a judge in determining whether they should be awarded and, if so, in what form.

Does the statutory grant of discretion to the trial judge also exclude any role for appellate courts in formulating standards for granting equitable relief? The traditions of equity jurisprudence, although they favored broad principles of fairness, also involved detailed rules about the remedies appropriate in different situations. The decision to grant or deny equitable relief, although it involved the exercise of judicial discretion, was nevertheless subject to appellate review for "abuse of discretion." Because the relief ultimately awarded determined the outcome of litigation, the terms of what amounted to abuse were broadly construed and the trial judge's discretion correspondingly narrowed. See Henry J. Friendly, Some Indiscretion About Discretion, 31 Emory L.J. 747 (1982). Do the remedial provisions in Title VII alter the balance of power between trial courts and appellate courts? If Congress meant to deprive the Supreme Court of power to frame standards for equitable relief, how would it have done so?

Under the standard articulated in *Albemarle Paper*, trial judges still retain a degree of discretion in determining whether to award back pay and, if so, in what amount. As then-Justice Rehnquist pointed out in his dissent, any less flexible standard would have raised questions about the right to jury trial. If back pay were awarded according to the same rules as damages, it would have been converted into a remedy at common law administered by a jury. In cases in federal court, the Seventh Amendment would have guaranteed the parties a right to jury trial. Preserving the trial judge's discretion was necessary to avoid this result. As discussed in the next section of this chapter, the right to jury trial now comes with claims for damages under 42 U.S.C. § 1981a, but this provision was added to the statute long after *Albemarle Paper*. As a practical matter, however, does the standard in *Albemarle Paper* leave the trial judge with any real discretion? Is it realistic to conclude that trial judges would only deny back pay in exceptional cases? If so, how is the standard adopted by the Court different from the one it rejected, based on the award of attorney's fees in all but exceptional cases? Both of these standards determine whether an award of back pay can be denied entirely. If an award is granted, how much discretion does the trial judge have over the amount of the award?

4. **Statutory Restrictions on Awards of Back Pay.** The remedial provisions of Title VII impose their own restrictions on the award of back pay. Some of these have been discussed in Chapter 2, in connection with the remedy phase of mixed-motive cases. Some plaintiffs are not entitled to any compensatory relief at all. Under § 706(g)(2)(A), 42 U.S.C. § 2000e–5(g)(2)(A), plaintiffs who were not victims of discrimination because they were rejected for an entirely legitimate reason are not entitled to such relief. Under the companion provision in § 706(g)(2)(B), 42 U.S.C. § 2000e–5(g)(2)(B), plaintiffs who were victims of mixed-motive discrimination also are denied such relief. The latter were victims of discrimination, in the sense that they suffered from a decision motivated by race or some other prohibited factor. But if the defendant proves that they would have suffered the same adverse decision for an entirely legitimate reason, they have not suffered any tangible economic loss from the discrimination against them.

Among plaintiffs who are entitled to an award of back pay, a duty to mitigate their loss requires any award to them to be reduced by amounts that they have earned or could have earned with reasonable diligence. § 706(g)(1), 42 U.S.C. § 2000e–5(g)(1). As noted earlier in this chapter in the discussion of time limits under Title VII, any award of back pay is also limited to a period of no more than two years before the plaintiff's charge was filed with the EEOC. Id. The Supreme Court also has elaborated on the duty to mitigate by terminating any liability for back pay as of the date that the employer offers to give the plaintiff the job in dispute, subject only to limited conditions. Ford Motor Co. v. EEOC, 458 U.S. 219 (1982).

Do these added rules about the award of back pay support the liberal standard adopted in *Albemarle Paper*? Do they indicate that the issue is not entirely a matter within the trial judge's discretion?

5. **Bibliography.** Howard C. Eglit, Damages Mitigation Doctrine in the Statutory Anti-discrimination Context: Mitigating Its Negative Impact, 69 U. Cin. L. Rev. 7 (2000); Susan K. Grebeldinger, The Role of Workplace Hostility in Determining Prospective Remedies for Employment Discrimination: A Call for Greater Judicial Discretion in Awarding Front Pay, 1996 U. Ill. L. Rev. 319; Mark S. Kende, Deconstructing Constructive Discharge: The Misapplication of Constructive Discharge Standards in Employment Discrimination Remedies, 71 Notre Dame L. Rev. 39 (1995).

NOTES ON REMEDIAL SENIORITY

1. ***Franks v. Bowman Transportation Co.*** The Supreme Court soon applied the standards for awards of back pay under *Albemarle Paper* to awards of "rightful place" seniority in Franks v. Bowman Transportation Co., 424 U.S. 747 (1976). These involved relief to proven victims, which granted them seniority that they would have had in the absence of discrimination. Such relief was generally understood to give full relief to an applicant for employment only when a position became open in the job he sought. "Rightful place" seniority could not be used to remove an incumbent employee entirely from his job, but it became available when a job opened up. The Court framed

the proper approach in terms of a presumption in favor of relief, tempered by the equitable discretion of the trial judge. The Court reasoned as follows:

> Last Term's Albemarle Paper Co. v. Moody, 422 U.S. 405 (1975), consistently with the congressional plan, held that one of the central purposes of Title VII is "to make persons whole for injuries suffered on account of unlawful employment discrimination." To effectuate this "make whole" objective, Congress in § 706(g) vested broad equitable discretion in the federal courts to "order such affirmative action as may be appropriate, which may include, but is not limited to, reinstatement or hiring of employees, with or without back pay . . ., or any other equitable relief as the court deems appropriate." The legislative history supporting the 1972 amendments of § 706(g) of Title VII affirms the breadth of this discretion. "The provisions of [§ 706(g)] are intended to give the courts wide discretion exercising their equitable powers to fashion the most complete relief possible. . . . [T]he Act is intended to make the victims of unlawful employment discrimination whole, and . . . the attainment of this objective . . . requires that persons aggrieved by the consequences and effects of the unlawful employment practice be, so far as possible, restored to a position where they would have been were it not for the unlawful discrimination." Section-by-Section Analysis of H.R. 1746, accompanying the Equal Employment Opportunity Act of 1972—Conference Report, 118 Cong. Rec. 7166, 7168 (1972). This is emphatic confirmation that federal courts are empowered to fashion such relief as the particular circumstances of a case may require to effect restitution, making whole insofar as possible the victims of racial discrimination in hiring. Adequate relief may well be denied in the absence of a seniority remedy slotting the victim in that position in the seniority system that would have been his had he been hired at the time of his application. It can hardly be questioned that ordinarily such relief will be necessary to achieve the "make-whole" purposes of the Act.
>
> Seniority systems and the entitlements conferred by credits earned thereunder are of vast and increasing importance in the economic employment system of this Nation. S. Slichter, J. Healy, & E. Livernash, The Impact of Collective Bargaining on Management 104–115 (1960). Seniority principles are increasingly used to allocate entitlements to scarce benefits among competing employees ("competitive status" seniority) and to compute noncompetitive benefits earned under the contract of employment ("benefit" seniority). We have already said about "competitive status" seniority that it "has become of overriding importance, and one of its major functions is to determine who gets or who keeps an available job." Humphrey v. Moore, 375 U.S. 335, 346–347 (1964). . . .
>
> We are not to be understood as holding that an award of seniority status is requisite in all circumstances. The fashioning of

> appropriate remedies invokes the sound equitable discretion of the district courts. . . .

2. ***International Brotherhood of Teamsters v. United States.*** The Supreme Court followed up on the opinion in *Franks* in yet another aspect of International Brotherhood of Teamsters v. United States, 431 U.S. 324 (1977). In the parts of the opinion excerpted in Chapter 1, the Supreme Court held that the defendants had discriminated against blacks and Hispanics in hiring and transfers to line-driver jobs, but that they had not discriminated in establishing separate lines of seniority for line-driver and city-driver jobs. In the parts of the opinion that follow, the Court applied the holding in *Franks* to the award of remedial seniority to victims of discrimination that occurred after the effective date of Title VII.

> Because the company discriminated both before and after the enactment of Title VII, the seniority system is said to have operated to perpetuate the effects of both pre- and post-Act discrimination. Post-Act discriminatees, however, may obtain full "make whole" relief, including retroactive seniority under *Franks v. Bowman*, supra, without attacking the legality of the seniority system as applied to them. *Franks* made clear and the union acknowledges that retroactive seniority may be awarded as relief from an employer's discriminatory hiring and assignment policies even if the seniority system agreement itself makes no provision for such relief. 424 U.S., at 778–779. Here the Government has proved that the company engaged in a post-Act pattern of discriminatory hiring, assignment, transfer, and promotion policies. Any Negro or Spanish-surnamed American injured by those policies may receive all appropriate relief as a direct remedy for this discrimination. . . .
>
> Although not all class actions will necessarily follow the *Franks* model, the nature of a pattern-or-practice suit brings it squarely within our holding in *Franks*. The plaintiff in a pattern-or-practice action is the Government, and its initial burden is to demonstrate that unlawful discrimination has been a regular procedure or policy followed by an employer or group of employers. At the initial, "liability" stage of a pattern-or-practice suit the Government is not required to offer evidence that each person for whom it will ultimately seek relief was a victim of the employer's discriminatory policy. Its burden is to establish a prima facie case that such a policy existed. The burden then shifts to the employer to defeat the prima facie showing of a pattern or practice by demonstrating that the Government's proof is either inaccurate or insignificant. An employer might show, for example, that the claimed discriminatory pattern is a product of pre-Act hiring rather than unlawful post-Act discrimination, or that during the period it is alleged to have pursued a discriminatory policy it made too few employment decisions to justify the inference that it had engaged in a regular practice of discrimination.
>
> If an employer fails to rebut the inference that arises from the Government's prima facie case, a trial court may then conclude that

a violation has occurred and determine the appropriate remedy. Without any further evidence from the Government, a court's finding of a pattern or practice justifies an award of prospective relief. Such relief might take the form of an injunctive order against continuation of the discriminatory practice, an order that the employer keep records of its future employment decisions and file periodic reports with the court, or any other order "necessary to ensure the full enjoyment of the rights" protected by Title VII.

When the Government seeks individual relief for the victims of the discriminatory practice, a district court must usually conduct additional proceedings after the liability phase of the trial to determine the scope of individual relief. . . .

The proof of the pattern or practice supports an inference that any particular employment decision, during the period in which the discriminatory policy was in force, was made in pursuit of that policy. The Government need only show that an alleged individual discriminatee unsuccessfully applied for a job and therefore was a potential victim of the proved discrimination. As in *Franks*, the burden then rests on the employer to demonstrate that the individual applicant was denied an employment opportunity for lawful reasons. . . .

The question whether seniority relief may be awarded to nonapplicants was left open by our decision in *Franks*, since the class at issue in that case was limited to "identifiable applicants who were denied employment . . . after the effective date . . . of Title VII." We now decide that an incumbent employee's failure to apply for a job is not an inexorable bar to an award of retroactive seniority. Individual nonapplicants must be given an opportunity to undertake their difficult task of proving that they should be treated as applicants and therefore are presumptively entitled to relief accordingly.

To conclude that a person's failure to submit an application for a job does not inevitably and forever foreclose his entitlement to seniority relief under Title VII is a far cry, however, from holding that nonapplicants are always entitled to such relief. A nonapplicant must show that he was a potential victim of unlawful discrimination. Because he is necessarily claiming that he was deterred from applying for the job by the employer's discriminatory practices, his is the not always easy burden of proving that he would have applied for the job had it not been for those practices. Cf. Mt. Healthy City Board of Education v. Doyle, 429 U.S. 274. When this burden is met, the nonapplicant is in a position analogous to that of an applicant and is entitled to the presumption discussed [earlier]. . . .

The task remaining for the District Court on remand will not be a simple one. Initially, the court will have to make a substantial number of individual determinations in deciding which of the

> minority employees were actual victims of the company's discriminatory practices. After the victims have been identified, the court must, as nearly as possible, " 'recreate the conditions and relationships that would have been had there been no' " unlawful discrimination. Franks, 424 U.S. at 773 n.32. This process of recreating the past will necessarily involve a degree of approximation and imprecision. Because the class of victims may include some who did not apply for line-driver jobs as well as those who did, and because more than one minority employee may have been denied each line-driver vacancy, the court will be required to balance the equities of each minority employee's situation in allocating the limited number of vacancies that were discriminatorily refused to class members. . . .
>
> Although not directly controlled by the Act, the extent to which the legitimate expectations of nonvictim employees should determine when victims are restored to their rightful place is limited by basic principles of equity. In devising and implementing remedies under Title VII, no less than in formulating any equitable decree, a court must draw on the "qualities of mercy and practicality [that] have made equity the instrument for nice adjustment and reconciliation between the public interest and private needs as well as between competing private claims." Hecht v. Bowles, 321 U.S. 321, 329–330. . . . Especially when immediate implementation of an equitable remedy threatens to impinge upon the expectations of innocent parties, the courts must "look to the practical realities and necessities inescapably involved in reconciling competing interests," in order to determine the "special blend of what is necessary, what is fair, and what is workable." Lemon v. Kurtzman, 411 U.S. 192, 200–201 (opinion of Burger, C.J.). . . .

3. **The Interests of Other Employees.** The Court concludes its opinion in *Teamsters* by considering the interests of other employees, not necessarily white employees but employees who are not entitled to an award of remedial seniority. The need to award remedial seniority to individual plaintiffs, while at the same time taking account of its effects on other employees, inevitably complicates any attempt to devise fully adequate compensatory relief. As the Court notes, remedial seniority comes in two forms: benefit seniority, which determines fringe benefits, such as pension benefits or vacation time, that are simply a form of in-kind compensation offered by the employer; and competitive seniority, which determines rights with respect to other employees, such as for assignments, promotions, or to avoid layoffs. Simply awarding plaintiffs the seniority they would have obtained in the absence of discrimination does not take account of the differences between these two kinds of seniority.

Benefit seniority can be treated just like back pay because, essentially, it is a form of compensation paid to employees in benefits rather than in cash. The full cost of benefit seniority is borne by the employer. Awards of this form of seniority can be easily subsumed under the standard for awards of back pay from *Albemarle Paper*. Both forms of relief involve compensation solely at the expense of the employer.

Awards of competitive seniority are an entirely different matter. They do not involve a substitute for compensation in cash, but the means to obtain or protect a job in competition with other employees, whose own seniority falls relative to the plaintiffs who receive such awards. The interests of these employees disrupt the mutually reinforcing relationship between deterring future violations of Title VII and compensating for past violations. Awarding competitive seniority has little deterrent effect upon employers who bear none of its costs. Yet such awards are necessary to fully compensate the victims of past discrimination. Indeed, to the extent that awarding such relief antagonizes other employees, it impairs the likelihood of future compliance with Title VII by leading them to pressure the employer to preserve the seniority rights that they have previously obtained.

Despite this tension between the goals of deterrence and compensation, the opinion in *Franks* nevertheless applies the same standard from *Albemarle Paper* for awards of back pay to all forms of remedial seniority. Does the opinion in *Teamsters* depart from the equivalence of all these forms of relief by insisting on the trial court's equitable discretion to adjust the interests of all the parties affected by its decree? Note that even the opinion in *Franks* recognizes the need to take the interests of other employees into account. The form of "rightful place" seniority that it endorses does not result in immediate placement of victims of discrimination in the jobs that they would have held in the absence of discrimination. Instead, they can move into those positions only when a vacancy develops in the department to which they previously applied.

4. **The Special Protection of Seniority.** In the excerpt from *Teamsters* in Chapter 1, the Court emphasized that § 703(h) conferred special protection upon seniority systems, immunizing them from attack under the theory of disparate impact. In this excerpt from *Teamsters*, and in *Franks*, the Court made clear that § 703(h) does not prevent the award of remedial seniority, whether in benefit or competitive form. Yet the Court also acknowledges that the purpose underlying § 703(h)—protecting the interests of existing employees in relying on their own seniority rights—should be taken into account in the trial judge's exercise of equitable discretion. How could the Court transform this statutory provision from a rule protecting seniority systems into just one factor affecting the formulation of relief?

The text of § 703(h) offers one answer to that question. The protection of seniority systems literally extends only to the question whether the seniority system itself violates Title VII. It does not extend to the remedies appropriate for other violations of Title VII, like the refusal to hire or promote minority workers as line drivers. This purely textual approach does not explain, however, how protection of seniority rights remains one factor in devising appropriate remedies. It does so only if § 703(h) declares a congressional policy of protecting seniority rights that either requires deference from the courts or coincides with equitable considerations that courts would otherwise take into account. Which of the following makes more sense: for a court to frame remedies consistent with the policies served by the substantive provisions of Title VII, or to do so contrary to those policies?

5. **Seniority and Affirmative Action.** In a separate opinion in *Franks*, Justice Powell relied on the policy underlying § 703(j), as well as the policy underlying § 703(h), to protect incumbent employees. He analogized an award of competitive seniority to affirmative action, which cannot be required as a matter of substantive law under § 703(j). He recognized that this analogy is not perfect, principally because awards of competitive seniority benefit proven victims of discrimination, whereas affirmative action plans typically benefit nonvictims. Nevertheless, the burden of both forms of relief falls on employees who have not themselves violated Title VII.

How accurate is the characterization of other employees as innocent of illegal discrimination? As the majority opinion in *Franks* pointed out, current line drivers have benefited from the exclusion of minority employees from this position by facing less competition in obtaining their jobs and receiving higher seniority than they would otherwise have had. Moreover, the union that represented them at least acquiesced in the employer's discriminatory practices. Even if these employees themselves are innocent of discrimination, they still are beneficiaries of the employer's and the union's discrimination. What is unfair about reducing them to the "rightful place" that they would have occupied in the absence of discrimination?

Despite the limited analogy between awards of competitive seniority and affirmative action, the Supreme Court has placed significant limits on any form of affirmative action that adversely affects seniority rights. As discussed in Chapter 4, these limits fall under the general requirement that an affirmative action plan "not unnecessarily trammel the interests of the white employees." United Steelworkers v. Weber, 443 U.S. 193, 208 (1979). In particular, an affirmative action plan cannot "require the discharge of white workers and their replacement with new black hirees." Id.; see Firefighters Local Union No. 1784 v. Stotts, 467 U.S. 561 (1984); Wygant v. Jackson Board of Education, 476 U.S. 267 (1986).

6. **Class Claims and Individual Relief.** Both *Franks* and *Teamsters* involved class claims of discrimination, the first as a class action by a private plaintiff and the second as a pattern-or-practice action by the Federal government. In administering these cases, the district courts had to divide the proceedings into those concerned with the class and those concerned with individuals. This process of "bifurcation" approximates, but does not coincide with, the division of a case into two stages, to determine liability and then remedies. As *Teamsters* points out, a case brought on behalf of a class involves class-wide issues of both liability and remedies: whether the defendant has engaged in a general practice of discrimination applicable to the class and, if so, whether an injunction or declaratory judgment should be issued to remedy this practice. The latter step takes the court into the remedy phase of the case. After that point, however, it is necessary to determine entitlement to compensatory relief on an individual basis.

In the individual stage of the case, involving individual compensatory relief, the burden of proof shifts to the defendant, much as it does in purely individual cases. Because a violation of the statute has already been found, individual class members only have to prove that they were subject to the defendant's illegal discriminatory practice. The defendant must then prove that they would have been rejected for an entirely legitimate reason, the same as that used in mixed-motive cases under § 706(g)(2)(B), 42 U.S.C. § 2000e–5(g)(2)(B).

Most individual class members have applied for the position in question, but some may not have. As *Franks* held, all applicants are entitled to compensatory relief whether or not they are employees. The individual claimants in *Teamsters* were all employees, but only some of them had applied for jobs as line drivers. The others claimed that they were deterred from applying for the job by the employer's discriminatory practices. The Court held that a nonapplicant in this situation was entitled to relief if he met "the not always easy burden of proving that he would have applied for the job had it not been for those practices." Why does the Court emphasize the difficulty of meeting this burden of proof? How would the Court have dealt with nonapplicants who were not even employees?

7. **"The Quagmire of Hypothetical Judgment."** No one of the issues involved in framing compensatory relief creates much difficulty by itself. Individual victims of discrimination can be identified. The amount that they would have earned in the positions in question can be computed, as can the amount that they earned in the position that they were given instead. If they held no job at all, an amount that they could have earned with reasonable diligence can be approximated. Awards of benefit and competitive seniority can be ascertained in similar fashion. For an entire class of plaintiffs, this process can be generalized from an individual plaintiff to a group. As these steps multiply, however, the overall degree of uncertainty multiplies as well.

The issue of "front pay" provides a good example of how speculative awards of relief can become. Front pay differs from back pay only in its relationship to the date of judgment. Back pay is computed from the date of the court's award back to the date of the discrimination suffered by the plaintiff. Front pay is computed forward from the date of judgment to the date that the plaintiff obtains the position that he or she was discriminatorily denied. Awards of "rightful place" seniority create the possibility of a gap between the date of judgment and the date, sometime later, when the plaintiff can actually exercise the seniority that he or she has received. During this interim period, the plaintiff is entitled to an award of front pay. Plaintiffs also are entitled to awards of front pay if they cannot be reinstated in a position with the employer. Courts, however, review awards of front pay to assure that they are not unduly speculative, and judges often reduce them for that reason. E.g., McKnight v. General Motors Corp., 973 F.2d 1366, 1372 (7th Cir. 1992).

The speculative nature of front pay awards is hardly unique among remedies for employment discrimination. The fundamental goals of deterrence and compensation require the court to recreate a world without discrimination and its consequences. Speculation is essential to this enterprise. Although it may yield fairly accurate conclusions for a single plaintiff over a limited period of time, these conclusions become increasingly unreliable as the scope of the defendant's illegal conduct expands. In a class action, it is necessary to award relief to a large number of plaintiffs over a longer period of time and to consider the expanding effects of these awards on other employees as well. It is impossible to turn the clock back and ascertain what would have happened to an entire class of employees if the employer had never engaged in discrimination. This is "the quagmire of hypothetical judgment" recognized in Pettway v. American Cast Iron Pipe Co., 494 F.2d 211, 260 (5th Cir. 1974). To take just a simple example, what should the court do if several minority city drivers, each otherwise qualified for the position, were excluded from consideration for a single opening as a line driver? Should only one of these plaintiffs obtain relief? If not, should they each receive a fraction of the relief that would be awarded to a single plaintiff? How should the court select among them to determine who gets the opportunity to fill the next opening as a city driver? For a detailed analysis of the approximations necessary in such cases, see Biondo v. City of Chicago, 382 F.3d 680 (7th Cir. 2004).

The inevitable compromises needed to answer such questions lead courts to encourage negotiation and settlement of remedial questions. Is this the best way to bring complicated litigation over individual rights to a conclusion? Or does it lead the parties to greater acceptance of the judgment eventually rendered? In the absence of precise, judicially ordered remedies for proven acts of discrimination, employers and unions have turned to alternative remedies that can be adopted without litigation. Is this what caused the Supreme Court to endorse privately initiated forms of affirmative action in *Weber* and the cases that followed it?

8. **Bibliography.** For articles generally discussing remedies available under Title VII, see Harry T. Edwards, Race Discrimination in Employment: What Price Equality?, 1976 U. Ill. L.F. 572; John L. Lettes, Note, Irreparable Injury: Improper Standard for Preliminary Injunctive Relief in EEOC Cases?, 38 Stan. L. Rev. 1163 (1986); Note, Tenure and Partnership as Title VII Remedies, 94 Harv. L. Rev. 457 (1980).

B. DAMAGES

INTRODUCTORY NOTES ON THE CIVIL RIGHTS ACT OF 1991

1. **Damages Under the Civil Rights Act of 1991.** The addition of damages to the remedies available under Title VII resulted from developments under 42 U.S.C. § 1981. This statute was enacted during Reconstruction and has had a complex history, recounted in Chapter 9, culminating in amendments made by the Civil Rights Act of 1991. These amendments had a twofold purpose: first, to codify earlier interpretations of § 1981 that recognized it as a general remedy for intentional racial discrimination; and second, to extend similar remedies to victims of discrimination on other grounds. The first purpose concerned the very broad scope of § 1981, extending to intentional racial discrimination in all kinds of contracts, whether public or private, and in all aspects of contracting, from formation to performance. The Civil Rights Act of 1991 amended the statute to make this very broad coverage clear. As applied to contracts of

employment, the availability of a claim under § 1981 means that plaintiffs claiming intentional discrimination on the basis of race or national origin can recover damages, a remedy not available under Title VII as originally enacted.

The second purpose of the 1991 amendments was to extend this remedy to other plaintiffs claiming intentional discrimination on the basis of sex or religion (under Title VII) or disability (under the Rehabilitation Act or the Americans with Disabilities Act). Congress did so by enacting a provision modeled on § 1981 and now codified as § 1981a. The remedies created by § 1981a, however, are not freestanding claims of discrimination brought under an entirely independent statute, like § 1981 itself. These remedies require a finding of intentional discrimination under either Title VII or the disabilities laws. § 1981a(a)(1). Proof of disparate impact alone is not enough and, to avoid duplicative recoveries, awards of damages are restricted in other ways as well. The plaintiff must not be able to obtain relief under § 1981; any award of damages is exclusive of back pay and similar relief; and no award of punitive damages may be recovered against a government employer. § 1981a(a)(1), (b). The damage remedy under § 1981a is also subject to caps, depending on the size of the employer, with an upper limit of $300,000 for employers with more than 500 employees. § 1981a(b)(3). Consistent with established law under the Seventh Amendment, the statute also explicitly recognizes a right to jury trial. § 1981a(c).

2. **The Tort Model of Litigation.** Although the damage remedy created by the Civil Rights Act of 1991 had its roots in another statute and in equalizing remedies among victims of different forms of discrimination, it took Title VII in another direction as well. It made litigation over employment discrimination much closer to ordinary personal injury cases. All plaintiffs under Title VII could now obtain recovery for noneconomic losses such as emotional distress and for punitive damages. The prospect of greater recovery by the plaintiffs also increased the fees that could be received by their attorneys. Such fees generally depend on the recovery obtained by the plaintiff and, in this respect, they closely resemble the fees obtained by plaintiffs' attorneys in personal injury cases. As discussed later in this chapter, attorney's fees are either awarded under Title VII or collected under a contingent fee contract that makes the plaintiffs' success on the merits the principal determinant of the fees obtained by their attorneys. The newly available damages under § 1981a makes claims involving noneconomic loss, such as those for sexual harassment, far more valuable to plaintiffs and thus to their attorneys. By the same token, the exposure of employers to liability is correspondingly increased.

For all those reasons, plaintiffs now have much the same incentives to litigate or to settle as their counterparts in personal injury litigation. They—or, more realistically, their attorneys—will decide to pursue a case only if the present value of any recovery, discounted by the risk of losing, exceeds the cost of pursuing a case further into litigation. These risks are substantial since the ultimate success rate of employment discrimination plaintiffs is lower than that of most other civil litigants. Kevin M. Clermont & Stewart J. Schwab, Employment Discrimination Plaintiffs in Federal Court: From

Bad to Worse?, 3 Harv. J.L. & Pol'y 3 (2009); Kevin M. Clermont & Stewart J. Schwab, How Employment Discrimination Plaintiffs Fare in Federal Court, 1 J. Empirical Leg. Stud. 429 (2004); David Benjamin Oppenheimer, Verdicts Matter: An Empirical Study of California Employment Discrimination and Wrongful Discharge Jury Verdicts Reveals Low Success Rates for Women and Minorities, 37 U.C. Davis L. Rev. 511 (2003); Symposium, Empirical Studies: How Do Discrimination Cases Fare in Court?, 7 Emp. Rts. & Emp. Pol'y J. 533 (2004). The availability of contingent fees to compensate plaintiff's counsel further strengthens the incentives for settlement. Under a contingent fee contract, it is the plaintiff's attorney who bears most of the initial costs in pursuing a claim, as well as the risk that those costs will not be compensated. It is also the attorney who is in the best position to assess the plaintiff's prospects for success and therefore the value of the plaintiff's claim. Attorneys are far more likely to pursue litigation of cases with a higher probability of success and higher potential recovery than those that are riskier and of lower value. These incentives reinforce the tendency of employment discrimination cases to involve discharges, and generally discharges from better paying jobs. John J. Donohue III & Peter Siegelman, The Changing Nature of Employment Discrimination Litigation, 43 Stan. L. Rev. 983 (1991). Does this tendency work to open jobs to previously disfavored groups or only to preserve the jobs that they have obtained by other means?

3. **Bibliography.** Martha Chamallas, Discrimination and Outrage: The Migration from Civil Rights to Tort Law, 48 Wm. & Mary L. Rev. 2115 (2007); Martha Chamallas, Shifting Sands of Federalism: Civil Rights and Tort Claims in the Employment Context, 41 Wake Forest L. Rev. 697 (2006); Rebecca E. Hollander-Blumoff & Matthew T. Bodie, The Effects of Jury Ignorance About Damage Caps: The Case of the 1991 Civil Rights Act, 90 Iowa L. Rev. 1361 (2005); Paul M. Seconda, A Public Interest Model for Applying Lost Chance Theory to Probabilistic Injuries in Employment Discrimination Cases, 2005 Wis. L. Rev. 747; Sandra F. Sperino, Discrimination Law: The New Franken-Tort, 65 DePaul L. Rev. 721 (2016); Charles A. Sullivan, Tortifying Employment Discrimination, 92 B.U. L. Rev. 1431 (2012); Symposium, Torts and Civil Rights Law: Migration and Conflict, 75 Ohio St. L.J. 1021 (2014).

Kolstad v. American Dental Association

527 U.S. 526 (1999).

■ JUSTICE O'CONNOR delivered the opinion of the Court.

Under the terms of the Civil Rights Act of 1991 (1991 Act), punitive damages are available in claims under Title VII of the Civil Rights Act of 1964 and the Americans with Disabilities Act of 1990. Punitive damages are limited, however, to cases in which the employer has engaged in intentional discrimination and has done so "with malice or with reckless indifference to the federally protected rights of an aggrieved individual." Rev. Stat. § 1977, as amended, 42 U.S.C. § 1981a(b)(1). We here consider the circumstances under which punitive damages may be awarded in an action under Title VII.

I

A

In September 1992, Jack O'Donnell announced that he would be retiring as the Director of Legislation and Legislative Policy and Director of the Council on Government Affairs and Federal Dental Services for respondent, American Dental Association (respondent or Association). Petitioner, Carole Kolstad, was employed with O'Donnell in respondent's Washington, D. C., office, where she was serving as respondent's Director of Federal Agency Relations. When she learned of O'Donnell's retirement, she expressed an interest in filling his position. Also interested in replacing O'Donnell was Tom Spangler, another employee in respondent's Washington office. At this time, Spangler was serving as the Association's Legislative Counsel, a position that involved him in respondent's legislative lobbying efforts. Both petitioner and Spangler had worked directly with O'Donnell, and both had received "distinguished" performance ratings by the acting head of the Washington office, Leonard Wheat.

Both petitioner and Spangler formally applied for O'Donnell's position, and Wheat requested that Dr. William Allen, then serving as respondent's Executive Director in the Association's Chicago office, make the ultimate promotion decision. After interviewing both petitioner and Spangler, Wheat recommended that Allen select Spangler for O'Donnell's post. Allen notified petitioner in December 1992 that he had, in fact, selected Spangler to serve as O'Donnell's replacement. Petitioner's challenge to this employment decision forms the basis of the instant action.

B

After first exhausting her avenues for relief before the Equal Employment Opportunity Commission, petitioner filed suit against the Association in Federal District Court, alleging that respondent's decision to promote Spangler was an act of employment discrimination proscribed under Title VII. In petitioner's view, the entire selection process was a sham. Counsel for petitioner urged the jury to conclude that Allen's stated reasons for selecting Spangler were pretext for gender discrimination, and that Spangler had been chosen for the position before the formal selection process began. Among the evidence offered in support of this view, there was testimony to the effect that Allen modified the description of O'Donnell's post to track aspects of the job description used to hire Spangler. In petitioner's view, this "preselection" procedure suggested an intent by the Association to discriminate on the basis of sex. Petitioner also introduced testimony at trial that Wheat told sexually offensive jokes and that he had referred to certain prominent professional women in derogatory terms. Moreover, Wheat allegedly refused to meet with petitioner for several weeks regarding her interest in O'Donnell's position. Petitioner testified, in fact, that she had historically experienced difficulty gaining access to meet with Wheat. Allen, for his part, testified that he conducted informal meetings regarding O'Donnell's position with both petitioner and Spangler, although petitioner stated that Allen did not discuss the position with her.

The District Court denied petitioner's request for a jury instruction on punitive damages. [This decision was first reversed by a panel of the D.C. Circuit, which rejected the employer's argument that punitive damages are available under Title VII only in " 'extraordinarily egregious cases.' " The panel held that a jury should consider the award of punitive damages in most cases in which it could reasonably find intentional discrimination. On rehearing en banc, however, the D.C. Circuit concluded that, "before the question of punitive damages can go to the jury, the evidence of the defendant's culpability must exceed what is needed to show intentional discrimination," and in particular, that the plaintiff must submit evidence that the defendant engaged in some "egregious" misconduct. The Supreme Court then granted certiorari to resolve a conflict among the circuits.]

II

A

Prior to 1991, only equitable relief, primarily back pay, was available to prevailing Title VII plaintiffs; the statute provided no authority for an award of punitive or compensatory damages. See Landgraf v. USI Film Products, 511 U.S. 244, 252–253 (1994). With the passage of the 1991 Act, Congress provided for additional remedies, including punitive damages, for certain classes of Title VII and ADA violations.

The 1991 Act limits compensatory and punitive damages awards, however, to cases of "intentional discrimination"—that is, cases that do not rely on the "disparate impact" theory of discrimination. 42 U.S.C. § 1981a(a)(1). Section 1981a(b)(1) further qualifies the availability of punitive awards:

> "A complaining party may recover punitive damages under this section against a respondent (other than a government, government agency or political subdivision) if the complaining party demonstrates that the respondent engaged in a discriminatory practice or discriminatory practices *with malice or with reckless indifference to the federally protected rights of an aggrieved individual.*" (Emphasis added.)

The very structure of § 1981a suggests a congressional intent to authorize punitive awards in only a subset of cases involving intentional discrimination. Section 1981a(a)(1) limits compensatory and punitive awards to instances of intentional discrimination, while § 1981a(b)(1) requires plaintiffs to make an additional "demonstrat[ion]" of their eligibility for punitive damages. Congress plainly sought to impose two standards of liability—one for establishing a right to compensatory damages and another, higher standard that a plaintiff must satisfy to qualify for a punitive award.

The Court of Appeals sought to give life to this two-tiered structure by limiting punitive awards to cases involving intentional discrimination of an "egregious" nature. We credit the en banc majority's effort to effectuate congressional intent, but, in the end, we reject its conclusion that eligibility for punitive damages can only be described in terms of an employer's "egregious" misconduct. The terms "malice" and "reckless" ultimately focus on the actor's state of mind. See, e.g., Black's Law Dictionary 956–957, 1270 (6th ed. 1990); see also W. Keeton, D. Dobbs, R. Keeton, & D. Owen, Prosser and Keeton, Law of Torts 212–214 (5th ed. 1984) (defining "willful," "wanton," and "reckless"). While egregious misconduct is evidence of the requisite mental state, § 1981a does not limit plaintiffs to this form of evidence, and the section does not require a showing of egregious or outrageous discrimination independent of the employer's state of mind. Nor does the statute's structure imply an independent role for "egregiousness" in the face of congressional silence. On the contrary, the view that § 1981a provides for punitive awards based solely on an employer's state of mind is consistent with the 1991 Act's distinction between equitable and compensatory relief. Intent determines which remedies are open to a plaintiff here as well; compensatory awards are available only where the employer has engaged in "*intentional* discrimination." § 1981a(a)(1) (emphasis added).

Moreover, § 1981a's focus on the employer's state of mind gives some effect to Congress' apparent intent to narrow the class of cases for which punitive awards are available to a subset of those involving intentional discrimination. The employer must act with "malice or with reckless indifference *to [the plaintiff's] federally protected rights.*" § 1981a(b)(1) (emphasis added). The terms "malice" or "reckless indifference" pertain to the employer's knowledge that it may be acting in violation of federal law, not its awareness that it is engaging in discrimination.

We gain an understanding of the meaning of the terms "malice" and "reckless indifference," as used in § 1981a, from this Court's decision in Smith v. Wade, 461 U.S. 30 (1983). The parties, as well as both the en banc majority and dissent, recognize that Congress looked to the Court's decision in *Smith* in adopting this language in § 1981a. Employing language similar to what later appeared in § 1981a, the Court concluded in *Smith* that "a jury may be permitted to assess punitive damages in an action under § 1983 when the defendant's conduct is shown to be motivated by evil motive or intent, or when it involves reckless or callous indifference to the federally protected rights of others." While the *Smith* Court determined that it was unnecessary to show actual malice to qualify for a punitive award, its intent standard, at a minimum, required recklessness in its subjective form. The Court referred to a "subjective consciousness" of a risk of injury or illegality and a " 'criminal indifference to civil obligations.'" Id., at 37, n. 6, 41 (quoting Philadelphia, W. & B.R. Co. v. Quigley, 21 How. 202, 214 (1859)). The Court thus compared the recklessness standard to the requirement that defendants act with " 'knowledge of falsity or reckless disregard for the truth' " before punitive awards are available in defamation actions, Smith, supra, at 50 (quoting Gertz v. Robert Welch, Inc., 418 U.S. 323, 349 (1974)), a subjective standard, Harte-Hanks Communications, Inc. v. Connaughton, 491 U.S. 657 (1989). Applying this standard in the context of § 1981a, an employer must at least discriminate in the face of a perceived risk that its actions will violate federal law to be liable in punitive damages.

There will be circumstances where intentional discrimination does not give rise to punitive damages liability under this standard. In some instances, the employer may simply be unaware of the relevant federal prohibition. There will be cases, moreover, in which the employer discriminates with the distinct belief that its discrimination is lawful. The underlying theory of discrimination may be novel or otherwise poorly recognized, or an employer may reasonably believe that its discrimination satisfies a bona fide occupational qualification defense or other statutory exception to liability. See, e.g., 42 U.S.C. § 2000e–2(e)(1) (setting out Title VII defense "where religion, sex, or national origin is a bona fide occupational qualification"); see also § 12113 (setting out defenses under ADA). In Hazen Paper Co. v. Biggins, 507 U.S. 604, 616 (1993), we thus observed that, in light of statutory defenses and other exceptions permitting age-based decisionmaking, an employer may knowingly rely on age to make employment decisions without recklessly violating the Age Discrimination in Employment Act of 1967 (ADEA). Accordingly, we determined that limiting liquidated damages under the ADEA to cases where the employer "knew or showed reckless disregard for the matter of whether its conduct was prohibited by the statute," without an additional showing of outrageous conduct, was sufficient to give effect to the ADEA's two-tiered liability scheme. . . .

B

The inquiry does not end with a showing of the requisite "malice or . . . reckless indifference" on the part of certain individuals, however. 42 U.S.C. § 1981a(b)(1). The plaintiff must impute liability for punitive damages to respondent. . . .

We have observed that, "[i]n express terms, Congress has directed federal courts to interpret Title VII based on agency principles." Burlington Industries, Inc. v. Ellerth, 524 U.S. 742, 754 (1998); see also Meritor Savings Bank, FSB v. Vinson, 477 U.S. 57, 72 (1986) (noting that, in interpreting Title VII, "Congress wanted courts to look to agency principles for guidance"). Observing the limits on liability that these principles impose is especially important when interpreting the 1991 Act. In promulgating the Act, Congress conspicuously left intact the "limits of employer liability" established in *Meritor*. Faragher v. Boca Raton, 524

U.S. 775, 804, n.4 (1998); see also Burlington Industries, Inc., supra, at 763–764 ("[W]e are bound by our holding in *Meritor* that agency principles constrain the imposition of vicarious liability in cases of supervisory harassment").

. . . The common law as codified in the Restatement (Second) of Agency (1957), provides a useful starting point for defining this general common law. See Burlington Industries, Inc., supra, at 755 ("[T]he Restatement . . . is a useful beginning point for a discussion of general agency principles"); see also Meritor, supra, at 72. The Restatement of Agency places strict limits on the extent to which an agent's misconduct may be imputed to the principal for purposes of awarding punitive damages:

> "Punitive damages can properly be awarded against a master or other principal because of an act by an agent if, but only if:
>
> > "(a) the principal authorized the doing and the manner of the act, or
> >
> > "(b) the agent was unfit and the principal was reckless in employing him, or
> >
> > "(c) the agent was employed in a managerial capacity and was acting in the scope of employment, or
> >
> > "(d) the principal or a managerial agent of the principal ratified or approved the act."
>
> Restatement (Second) of Agency, supra, § 217 C. See also Restatement (Second) of Torts § 909 (same).

The Restatement, for example, provides that the principal may be liable for punitive damages if it authorizes or ratifies the agent's tortious act, or if it acts recklessly in employing the malfeasing agent. The Restatement also contemplates liability for punitive awards where an employee serving in a "managerial capacity" committed the wrong while "acting in the scope of employment." Restatement (Second) of Agency, supra, § 217 C; see also Restatement (Second) of Torts, supra, § 909 (same). "Unfortunately, no good definition of what constitutes a 'managerial capacity' has been found," 2 Ghiardi, supra, § 24.05, at 14, and determining whether an employee meets this description requires a fact-intensive inquiry, id., § 24.05; 1 L. Schlueter & K. Redden, Punitive Damages, § 4.4(B)(2)(a), p. 182 (3d ed. 1995). "In making this determination, the court should review the type of authority that the employer has given to the employee, the amount of discretion that the employee has in what is done and how it is accomplished." Id., § 4.4(B)(2)(a), at 181. Suffice it to say here that the examples provided in the Restatement of Torts suggest that an employee must be "important," but perhaps need not be the employer's "top management, officers, or directors," to be acting "in a managerial capacity." Ibid.

Additional questions arise from the meaning of the "scope of employment" requirement. The Restatement of Agency provides that even intentional torts are within the scope of an agent's employment if the conduct is "the kind [the employee] is employed to perform," "occurs substantially within the authorized time and space limits," and "is actuated, at least in part, by a purpose to serve the" employer. Restatement (Second) of Agency, supra, § 228(1), at 504. According to the Restatement, so long as these rules are satisfied, an employee may be said to act within the scope of employment even if the employee engages in acts "specifically forbidden" by the employer and uses "forbidden means of accomplishing results." Id., § 230, at 511. On this view, even an employer who makes every effort to comply with Title VII would be held liable for the discriminatory acts of agents acting in a "managerial capacity."

Holding employers liable for punitive damages when they engage in good faith efforts to comply with Title VII, however, is in some tension with the very principles underlying common law limitations on vicarious liability for punitive damages—that it is "improper ordinarily to award punitive damages against one who himself is personally innocent and therefore liable only vicariously." Restatement (Second) of Torts, supra, § 909, at 468, Comment b. Where an employer has undertaken such good faith efforts at Title VII compliance, it "demonstrat[es] that it never acted in reckless disregard of federally protected rights." 139 F.3d, at 974 (Tatel, J., dissenting).

Applying the Restatement of Agency's "scope of employment" rule in the Title VII punitive damages context, moreover, would reduce the incentive for employers to implement antidiscrimination programs. . . .

In light of the perverse incentives that the Restatement's "scope of employment" rules create, we are compelled to modify these principles to avoid undermining the objectives underlying Title VII. Recognizing Title VII as an effort to promote prevention as well as remediation, and observing the very principles underlying the Restatements' strict limits on vicarious liability for punitive damages, we agree that, in the punitive damages context, an employer may not be vicariously liable for the discriminatory employment decisions of managerial agents where these decisions are contrary to the employer's "good-faith efforts to comply with Title VII." 139 F.3d, at 974 (Tatel, J., dissenting). As the dissent recognized, "[g]iving punitive damages protection to employers who make good-faith efforts to prevent discrimination in the workplace accomplishes" Title VII's objective of "motivat[ing] employers to detect and deter Title VII violations."

We have concluded that an employer's conduct need not be independently "egregious" to satisfy § 1981a's requirements for a punitive damages award, although evidence of egregious misconduct may be used to meet the plaintiff's burden of proof. We leave for remand the question whether petitioner can identify facts sufficient to support an inference that the requisite mental state can be imputed to respondent. . . .

It is so ordered.

■ CHIEF JUSTICE REHNQUIST, with whom JUSTICE THOMAS joins, concurring in part and dissenting in part.

For the reasons stated by Judge Randolph in his concurring opinion in the Court of Appeals, I would hold that Congress' two-tiered scheme of Title VII monetary liability implies that there is an egregiousness requirement that reserves punitive damages only for the worst cases of intentional discrimination. See 139 F.3d 958, 970 (C.A.D.C.1998). Since the Court has determined otherwise, however, I join that portion of Part II-B of the Court's opinion holding that principles of agency law place a significant limitation, and in many foreseeable cases a complete bar, on employer liability for punitive damages.

■ JUSTICE STEVENS, with whom JUSTICE SOUTER, JUSTICE GINSBURG, and JUSTICE BREYER join, concurring in part and dissenting in part.

The Court properly rejects the Court of Appeals' holding that defendants in Title VII actions must engage in "egregious" misconduct before a jury may be permitted to consider a request for punitive damages. Accordingly, I join Parts I and II-A of its opinion. I write separately, however, because I strongly disagree with the Court's decision to volunteer commentary on an issue that the parties have not briefed and that the facts of this case do not present. I would simply remand for a trial on punitive damages. . . .

NOTES ON *KOLSTAD V. AMERICAN DENTAL ASSOCIATION*

1. **Standards for Awarding Punitive Damages.** In *Kolstad*, the Supreme Court tried to impose limits on punitive damages as one especially open-ended form of liability. The standard set forth in § 1981a(b)(1) requires proof that the defendant acted "with malice or with reckless indifference to the federally protected rights of an aggrieved individual." As interpreted by the Court, this standard conforms to those for recovery of punitive damages under other civil rights laws, requiring proof that the defendant acted "in the face of a perceived risk that its actions will violate federal law." In the case of organizational defendants acting through their managerial agents—as most employers do—the Court adds a significant qualification: that the defendant is relieved of liability if the agent acted "contrary to the defendant's good-faith efforts to comply with Title VII." Does this amount to proof of bad faith or to proof of the absence of good faith? Who has the burden of proof on this issue, the plaintiff or the defendant?

The standard rationale for awarding punitive damages is to increase deterrence. Because of imperfect enforcement of the law, some employers who engage in discrimination escape liability entirely. If compensatory damages have been set at a level that would generate the appropriate level of deterrence in a world of perfect enforcement, then the introduction of enforcement error means that discriminators will not be adequately deterred by the threat of liability for employment discrimination. If only half of those who have been victimized by discrimination complain and ultimately recover, then one can think of the ratio of compensated victims to all victims, which in this stylized example equals one-half, as representing the "enforcement error." The existence of enforcement error leads to inadequate deterrence and, thus, to more discrimination. But note that the use of a punitive multiplier can correct this departure from the optimal overall level of damage awards. The solution is that one can award punitive damages that in effect multiply compensatory damages by the inverse of the likely enforcement error. Using the numbers given above, this would lead to a doubling of liability for every discriminator who was actually caught. See A. Mitchell Polinsky & Steven Shavell, Punitive Damages: An Economic Analysis, 111 Harv. L. Rev. 870 (1998). Even if the probability of being held liable does not go up, the loss resulting from a finding of liability does, resulting in an increase in the total exposure to damages faced by other prospective defendants.

Is *Kolstad* consistent with this rationale for punitive damages? Wouldn't such damages have to be imposed far more frequently in order to make up for the deficiencies in the process of detecting and remedying illegal discrimination? Note that one complexity of the Polinsky-Shavell scheme is that it requires the trier of fact to make a judgment of how likely the litigant was to escape liability. The greater that likelihood, the greater the punitive damages. But this might mean that the most flagrant and egregious discriminators would be subject to the smallest punitive multiplier since they would be most likely to be caught. Thus, the economic theory of punitive damages might lead to exactly the opposite outcome as a system that awarded punitive damages only in the case of egregious misconduct. Are there other expenses of litigation that also impose costs on defendants, thereby increasing the effective penalty that they must pay and increasing the deterrent effect of any finding of liability?

Although the Court did not require proof of "egregious misconduct," it did limit awards of punitive damages to exceptional cases. It did so out of concern for fairness to employers who were themselves "innocent" of any discrimination. Does this reasoning neglect or minimize the fact that the employer has already been held liable for violating Title VII? Can the employer in *Kolstad* be analogized to the white employees whose seniority was threatened in *Franks* and *Teamsters*? In imposing limits on punitive damages, is the Court seeking to impose the optimal level of deterrence against discrimination, or is it invoking an independent principle that limits relief? Can that principle be articulated in more definite terms than simply as fairness?

2. **Vicarious Liability.** Like the cases on vicarious liability for sexual harassment, *Kolstad* relies heavily on common law standards, as summarized in the Restatement (Second) of Agency (1957), to determine vicarious liability for punitive damages. Is this simply a coincidence or does it reflect a fundamental connection between these two issues? As noted earlier, the availability of damages greatly increased the likely recovery on claims of sexual harassment. Unlike a case involving a discharge or refusal

to hire, a claim of sexual harassment may involve little in the way of direct economic loss and liability for back pay. The plaintiff's recovery often consists mainly of damages for emotional distress and punitive damages. Moreover, such damages can usually be recovered only from the employer. Individual supervisors and managers either cannot be held liable at all under Title VII, or even if they can, they do not have the assets sufficient to pay a substantial judgment. As discussed in Chapter 4 in the section on sexual harassment, many lower court cases have found that individual managers and supervisors cannot be sued at all under Title VII. Litigation over both sexual harassment and punitive damages naturally focuses on the vicarious liability of employers.

The application of common law reasoning to the award of punitive damages reinforces the similarities between tort claims and Title VII claims. Does the Restatement's formulation of common law standards strike the right balance for Title VII? All that an employer needs to do to be relieved of liability is to establish "good-faith efforts to comply with Title VII." Recall that for claims of sexual harassment, an employer has no defense if the plaintiff suffered a tangible employment action, making it strictly liable; and even where a defense is available, the employer has to show that it took reasonable steps to prevent such harassment and that the plaintiff unreasonably failed to take advantage of them. Why not impose a similar standard of reasonable care for relieving the employer of liability for punitive damages? Is the difference that punitive damages, by themselves, serve no compensatory purpose? A heightened standard of care imposed upon employers would obviously increase deterrence. Why isn't that alone sufficient?

In tort law generally, courts have become suspicious of awards of punitive damages, not because they are ineffective deterrents, but because they are too effective. Claims for punitive damages can be manipulated and exaggerated by plaintiffs' lawyers who specialize in presenting such claims to sympathetic juries. The Supreme Court itself has stepped into this dispute by imposing restrictions under the Due Process Clause on awards of punitive damages. In State Farm Mutual Automobile Insurance Co. v. Campbell, 538 U.S. 408, 424 (2003), the Court endorsed a presumptive rule that "single-digits are more likely to comport with due process." Are restrictions such as these designed to protect employers who already are liable for punitive damages in some amount? Or are they addressed more broadly to the effect of such awards on employers? Recall that an employer can be held liable for punitive damages only if it has already been found to have violated Title VII and that it has done so through intentional discrimination. Why should the courts be concerned with fairness to employers who already have passed these thresholds for liability?

3. **Insurance.** Another consequence of the growing resemblance between employment discrimination cases and ordinary tort cases is the increasing significance of liability insurance. The availability of damages and other forms of monetary relief has led employers to seek insurance covering liability for employment discrimination. Insurance law, however, generally prohibits insurance for intentional torts as against public policy, raising a

question whether claims of employment discrimination are insurable at all. Yet many claims against employers do not involve any policies on their part explicitly allowing or encouraging discrimination. David Benjamin Oppenheimer, Negligent Discrimination, 141 U. Pa. L. Rev. 899 (1993); Marc R. Poirier, Is Cognitive Bias at Work a Dangerous Condition on Land?, 7 Emp. Rts. & Emp. Pol'y J. 459 (2003); Amy L. Wax, Discrimination as Accident, 74 Ind. L.J. 1129 (1999).

For articles examining the availability of insurance in these circumstances, see Richard A. Bales & Julie McGhaghy, Insuring Title VII Violations, 27 S. Ill. U. L.J. 71 (2002); Francis J. Mootz III, Insurance Coverage of Employment Discrimination Claims, 52 U. Miami L. Rev. 1 (1997); George L. Priest, Insurance and Punitive Damages, 40 Ala. L. Rev. 1009 (1989); Steven L. Willborn, Insurance, Public Policy and Employment Discrimination, 66 Minn. L. Rev. 1003 (1982); Sean W. Gallagher, Note, The Public Policy Exclusion and Insurance for Intentional Discrimination, 92 Mich. L. Rev. 1256 (1994); Symposium, Employment Practices Liability Insurance and the Changing American Workplace, 21 W. New Eng. L. Rev. 245 (1999).

4. **Bibliography.** The debate over punitive damages has been vigorous and wide-ranging. Only a sample of the relevant articles can be provided in a brief note. Robert D. Cooter, Punitive Damages for Deterrence: When and How Much?, 40 Ala. L. Rev. 1143 (1989); Stephen Daniels & Joanne Martin, Myth and Reality in Punitive Damages, 75 Minn. L. Rev. 1 (1990); Theodore Eisenberg et al., The Predictability of Punitive Damages, 26 J. Legal Stud. 623 (1997); Thomas C. Galligan, Jr., Augmented Awards: The Efficient Evolution of Punitive Damages, 51 La. L. Rev. 3 (1990); David G. Owen, A Punitive Damages Overview: Functions, Problems and Reform, 39 Vill. L. Rev. 363 (1994); Jason S. Johnston, Punitive Liability: A New Paradigm of Efficiency in Tort Law, 87 Colum. L. Rev. 1385 (1987); Michael Rustad & Thomas Koenig, The Historical Continuity of Punitive Damages Awards: Reforming the Tort Reformers, 42 Am. U. L. Rev. 1269 (1993); Symposium, Punitive Damages, 56 S. Cal. L. Rev. 1 (1982). See also James D. Ghiardi & John J. Kircher, Punitive Damages: Law and Practice (1996).

For articles specifically concerned with punitive damages under Title VII, see Judith J. Johnson, A Standard for Punitive Damages Under Title VII, 46 Fla. L. Rev. 521 (1994); Judith J. Johnson, A Uniform Standard for Exemplary Damages in Employment Discrimination Cases, 33 U. Rich. L. Rev. 41 (1999); David C. Searle, Note, Keeping the "Civil" in Civil Litigation: The Need for a Punitive Damage-Actual Damage Link in Title VII Cases, 51 Duke L.J. 1683 (2002); Joseph A. Seiner, Punitive Damages, Due Process, and Employment Discrimination, 97 Iowa L. Rev. 473 (2012); Joseph A. Seiner, The Failure of Punitive Damages in Employment Discrimination Cases: A Call for Change, 50 Wm. & Mary L. Rev. 735 (2008). For a discussion of the related issue of damages for emotional distress, see Lewis R. Hagood, Claims of Mental and Emotional Damages in Employment Discrimination Cases, 29 U. Mem. L. Rev. 577 (1999); Brian Owsley, Survivorship Claims Under Employment Discrimination Statutes, 69 Miss. L.J. 423 (1999).

C. ATTORNEY'S FEES

Christiansburg Garment Co. v. EEOC

434 U.S. 412 (1978).

■ JUSTICE STEWART delivered the opinion of the Court.

Section 706(k) of Title VII of the Civil Rights Act of 1964 provides:

> "In any action or proceeding under this title the court, in its discretion, may allow the prevailing party . . . a reasonable attorney's fee. . . ."

The question in this case is under what circumstances an attorney's fee should be allowed when the defendant is the prevailing party in a Title VII action—a question about which the federal courts have expressed divergent views.

I

Two years after Rosa Helm had filed a Title VII charge of racial discrimination against the petitioner Christiansburg Garment Co. (company), the Equal Employment Opportunity Commission notified her that its conciliation efforts had failed and that she had the right to sue the company in federal court. She did not do so. Almost two years later, in 1972, Congress enacted amendments to Title VII. Section 14 of these amendments authorized the Commission to sue in its own name to prosecute "charges pending with the Commission" on the effective date of the amendments. Proceeding under this section, the Commission sued the company, alleging that it had engaged in unlawful employment practices in violation of the amended Act. The company moved for summary judgment on the ground, inter alia, that the Rosa Helm charge had not been "pending" before the Commission when the 1972 amendments took effect. The District Court agreed and granted summary judgment in favor of the company.

The company then petitioned for the allowance of attorney's fees against the Commission pursuant to § 706(k) of Title VII. Finding that "the Commission's action in bringing the suit cannot be characterized as unreasonable or meritless," the District Court concluded that "an award of attorney's fees to petitioner is not justified in this case." A divided Court of Appeals affirmed, and we granted certiorari to consider an important question of federal law.

II

It is the general rule in the United States that in the absence of legislation providing otherwise, litigants must pay their own attorney's fees. Alyeska Pipeline Co. v. Wilderness Society, 421 U.S. 240. Congress has provided only limited exceptions to this rule "under selected statutes granting or protecting various federal rights." Some of these statutes make fee awards mandatory for prevailing plaintiffs; others make awards permissive but limit them to certain parties, usually prevailing plaintiffs. But many of the statutes are more flexible, authorizing the award of attorney's fees to either plaintiffs or defendants, and entrusting the effectuation of the statutory policy to the discretion of the district courts. Section 706(k) of Title VII of the Civil Rights Act of 1964 falls into this last category, providing as it does that a district court may in its discretion allow an attorney's fee to the prevailing party.

In Newman v. Piggie Park Enterprises, 390 U.S. 400, the Court considered a substantially identical statute authorizing the award of attorney's fees under Title II of the Civil Rights Act of 1964. In that case the plaintiffs had prevailed, and the Court of Appeals had held that they should be awarded their attorney's fees "only to the extent that the respondents' defenses had been advanced 'for purposes of delay and not in good faith.' " We ruled that this "subjective standard" did not properly effectuate the purposes of the counsel-fee provision of Title II. Relying primarily on the intent of Congress to cast a Title II plaintiff in the role of "a 'private attorney general,' vindicating a policy that Congress considered of the highest priority," we held that a prevailing plaintiff under Title II "should ordinarily recover an attorney's fee unless special circumstances would render such an award unjust." We noted in passing that if the objective of Congress had been to permit the award of attorney's fees only against defendants who had acted in bad faith, "no new statutory provision would have been necessary," since even the American common-law rule allows the award of attorney's fees in those exceptional circumstances.

In Albemarle Paper Co. v. Moody, 422 U.S. 405, the Court made clear that the *Piggie Park* standard of awarding attorney's fees to a successful plaintiff is equally applicable in an action under Title VII of the Civil Rights Act. It can thus be taken as established, as the parties in this case both acknowledge, that under § 706(k) of Title VII a prevailing plaintiff ordinarily is to be awarded attorney's fees in all but special circumstances.

III

The question in the case before us is what standard should inform a district court's discretion in deciding whether to award attorney's fees to a successful defendant in a Title VII action. Not surprisingly, the parties in addressing the question in their briefs and oral arguments have taken almost diametrically opposite positions.

The company contends that the *Piggie Park* criterion for a successful plaintiff should apply equally as a guide to the award of attorney's fees to a successful defendant. Its submission, in short, is that every prevailing defendant in a Title VII action should receive an allowance of attorney's fees "unless special circumstances would render such an award unjust." The respondent Commission, by contrast, argues that the prevailing defendant should receive an award of attorney's fees only when it is found that the plaintiff's action was brought in bad faith. We have concluded that neither of these positions is correct.

A

Relying on what it terms "the plain meaning of the statute," the company argues that the language of § 706(k) admits of only one interpretation: "A prevailing defendant is entitled to an award of attorney's fees on the same basis as a prevailing plaintiff." But the permissive and discretionary language of the statute does not even invite, let alone require, such a mechanical construction. The terms of § 706(k) provide no indication whatever of the circumstances under which either a plaintiff or a defendant should be entitled to attorney's fees. And a moment's reflection reveals that there are at least two strong equitable considerations counseling an attorney's fee award to a prevailing Title VII plaintiff that are wholly absent in the case of a prevailing Title VII defendant.

First, as emphasized so forcefully in *Piggie Park*, the plaintiff is the chosen instrument of Congress to vindicate "a policy that Congress considered of the highest priority." Second, when a district court awards counsel fees to a prevailing plaintiff, it is awarding them against a violator of federal law. As the Court of Appeals clearly perceived, "these policy considerations which support the award of fees to a prevailing plaintiff are not present in the case of a prevailing defendant." 550 F.2d at 951. A successful defendant seeking counsel fees under § 706(k) must rely on quite different equitable considerations.

But if the company's position is untenable, the Commission's argument also misses the mark. It seems clear, in short, that in enacting § 706(k) Congress did not intend to permit the award of attorney's fees to a prevailing defendant only in a situation where the plaintiff was motivated by bad faith in bringing the action. As pointed out in *Piggie Park*, if that had been the intent of Congress, no statutory provision would have been necessary, for it has long been established that even under the American common-law rule attorney's fees may be awarded against a party who has proceeded in bad faith.

Furthermore, while it was certainly the policy of Congress that Title VII plaintiffs should vindicate "a policy that Congress considered of the highest priority," Piggie Park, 390 U.S. at 402, it is equally certain that Congress entrusted the ultimate effectuation of that policy to the adversary judicial process, Occidental Life Ins. Co. v. EEOC, 432 U.S. 355. A fair adversary process presupposes both a vigorous prosecution and a vigorous defense. It cannot be lightly assumed that in enacting § 706(k), Congress intended to distort that process by giving the private plaintiff substantial incentives to sue, while foreclosing to the defendant the possibility of recovering his expenses in resisting even a groundless action unless he can show that it was brought in bad faith.

B

The sparse legislative history of § 706(k) reveals little more than the barest outlines of a proper accommodation of the competing considerations we have discussed. The only specific reference to § 706(k) in the legislative debates indicates that the fee provision was included to "make it easier for a plaintiff of limited means to bring a meritorious suit." During the Senate floor discussions of the almost identical attorney's fee provision of Title II, however, several Senators explained that its allowance of awards to defendants would serve "to deter the bringing of lawsuits without foundation," "to discourage frivolous suits," and "to diminish the likelihood of unjustified suits being brought." If anything can be gleaned from these fragments of legislative history, it is that while Congress wanted to clear the way for suits to be brought under the Act, it also wanted to protect defendants from burdensome litigation having no legal or factual basis. The Court of Appeals for the District of Columbia Circuit seems to have drawn the maximum significance from the Senate debates when it concluded:

> "[From these debates] two purposes for § 706(k) emerge. First, Congress desired to 'make it easier for a plaintiff of limited means to bring a meritorious suit'. . . . But second, and equally important, Congress intended to 'deter the bringing of lawsuits without foundation' by providing that the 'prevailing party'—be it plaintiff or defendant—could obtain legal fees." Grubbs v. Butz, 548 F.2d 973, 975.

The first federal appellate court to consider what criteria should govern the award of attorney's fees to a prevailing Title VII defendant was the Court of Appeals for the Third Circuit in United States Steel Corp. v. United States, 519 F.2d 359. There a District Court had denied a fee award to a defendant that had successfully resisted a Commission demand for documents, the court finding that the Commission's action had not been " 'unfounded, meritless, frivolous or vexatiously brought.' " The Court of Appeals concluded that the District Court had not abused its discretion in denying the award. A similar standard was adopted by the Court of Appeals for the Second Circuit in Carrion v. Yeshiva University, 535 F.2d 722. In upholding an attorney's fee award to a successful defendant, that court stated that such awards should be permitted "not routinely, not simply because he succeeds, but only where the action brought is found to be unreasonable, frivolous, meritless or vexatious." Id. at 727.

To the extent that abstract words can deal with concrete cases, we think that the concept embodied in the language adopted by these two Courts of Appeals is correct. We would qualify their words only by pointing out that the term "meritless" is to be understood as meaning groundless or without foundation, rather than simply that the plaintiff has ultimately lost his case, and that the term "vexatious" in no way implies that the plaintiff's subjective bad faith is a necessary prerequisite to a fee award against him. In sum, a district court may in its discretion award attorney's fees to a prevailing defendant in a Title VII case upon a finding that the plaintiff's action was frivolous, unreasonable, or without foundation, even though not brought in subjective bad faith.

In applying these criteria, it is important that a district court resist the understandable temptation to engage in post hoc reasoning by concluding that, because a plaintiff did not ultimately prevail, his action must have been unreasonable or without foundation. This kind of hindsight logic could discourage all but the most airtight claims, for seldom can a prospective plaintiff be sure of ultimate success. No matter how honest one's belief that he has been the victim of discrimination, no matter how meritorious one's claim may appear at the outset, the course of litigation is rarely predictable. Decisive facts may not emerge until discovery or trial. The law may change or clarify in the midst of litigation. Even when the law or the facts appear questionable or unfavorable at the outset, a party may have an entirely reasonable ground for bringing suit.

That § 706(k) allows fee awards only to prevailing private plaintiffs should assure that this statutory provision will not in itself operate as an incentive to the bringing of claims that have little chance of success. To take the further step of assessing attorney's fees against plaintiffs simply because they do not finally prevail would substantially add to the risks inhering in most litigation and would undercut the efforts of Congress to promote the vigorous enforcement of the provisions of Title VII. Hence, a plaintiff should not be assessed his opponent's attorney's fees unless a court finds that his claim was frivolous, unreasonable, or groundless, or that the plaintiff continued to litigate after it clearly became so. And, needless to say, if a plaintiff is found to have brought or continued such a claim in bad faith, there will be an even stronger basis for charging him with the attorney's fees incurred by the defense.

IV

In denying attorney's fees to the company in this case, the District Court focused on the standards we have discussed. The court found that "the Commission's action in bringing the suit could not be characterized as unreasonable or meritless" because "the basis upon which petitioner prevailed was an issue of first impression requiring judicial resolution" and because the "Commission's statutory interpretation of § 14 of the 1972 amendments was not frivolous." The court thus exercised its discretion squarely within the permissible bounds of § 706(k). Accordingly, the judgment of the Court of Appeals upholding the decision of the District Court is affirmed.

It is so ordered.

NOTES ON *CHRISTIANSBURG GARMENT CO. V. EEOC*

1. Attorney's Fees in Civil Rights Cases. *Christiansburg Garment* was decided against the background of the "American rule": the rule requiring both parties in civil litigation, whether or not they prevail, to pay their own attorney's fees. The only costs that are routinely shifted in American litigation are fees for filing, service of process, transcripts, copies, and witnesses, and even these are narrowly defined to exclude most expenses connected with discovery. See 28 U.S.C. § 1920. This contrasts with the "British rule," which requires losers to pay winners' fees up to a reasonable limit. Under the American rule, fees can be shifted only in exceptional cases, most of them defined by statute. In civil rights cases, however, the exception has swallowed the rule, at least with respect to the plaintiff's attorney's fees. As the Court states in *Christiansburg Garment*, prevailing plaintiffs are entitled to an award of attorney's fees "unless special circumstances would render such an award unjust." The same rule has been carried over to all civil rights actions by 42 U.S.C. § 1988. See Hensley v. Eckerhart, 461 U.S. 424, 433 n.7 (1983).

The rule favoring awards of attorney's fees to prevailing plaintiffs is even stronger than the rule favoring awards of back pay. Recall that in *Albemarle Paper*, the Court rejected an "exceptional circumstances" rule for awards of back pay. Why should awards of attorney's fees receive more favorable treatment? Do awards of attorney's fees serve the goals of deterrence and compensation as effectively as awards of back pay? If plaintiffs could not recover their attorney's fees, they would face the risk of significantly reduced recoveries, even in cases in which they prevailed. Their attorney's fees would have to be subtracted from any award of back pay or damages to determine their net recovery from the litigation. Are awards of attorney's fees necessary to assure that compensatory remedies are really fully compensatory? As a matter of deterring illegal conduct, awards of attorney's fees to prevailing plaintiffs increase defendants' overall exposure to liability. Even defendants who are not held liable cannot be certain at earlier stages in the litigation that they will eventually prevail. They have to face the risk of a greater loss because they might have to pay the plaintiff's attorney's fees. In this respect, does an award of attorney's fees to prevailing plaintiffs function like an award of punitive damages: increasing the penalty paid by any defendant who is eventually held liable and deterring other prospective defendants from violating the statute in the first place?

2. **Awards of Attorney's Fees to Prevailing Defendants.** The holding in *Christiansburg Garment* specifically concerned the different standards for awarding attorney's fees to plaintiffs and to defendants. Whereas prevailing plaintiffs almost always are entitled to an award of attorney's fees, prevailing defendants almost never are. Defendants can recover attorney's fees "only where the action brought is found to be unreasonable, frivolous, meritless or vexatious." The language of § 706(k), 42 U.S.C. § 2000e–5(k), however, authorizes an award of attorney's fees to a "prevailing party," regardless of the party's status as a plaintiff or defendant. How can the Supreme Court depart from this evenhanded statutory language to impose standards that are so much more favorable to prevailing plaintiffs than to prevailing defendants?

The Court relies on the plaintiff's role in enforcing the congressional policy against discrimination and the defendant's status, after a finding of liability, as a violator of federal law. These reasons apply only to cases in which a plaintiff, not a defendant, has prevailed. Do they presuppose an entirely ex post perspective on the litigation, after its outcome on the merits is known? What effect do awards of attorney's fees have on the parties' incentives ex ante, while the outcome on the merits is still uncertain? The one-sided standards for awarding attorney's fees inevitably have a one-sided effect on the parties' incentives, increasing the expected value of any judgment for the plaintiff and decreasing the expected value of any judgment for the defendant (assuming, as seems likely, that judges and juries do not have some overall target award in mind and lower the measure of damages if they know that attorney's fees will later be added). Plaintiffs (and their attorneys) therefore have greater incentives to bring weaker cases, and defendants (and their attorneys) have greater incentives to settle these cases on terms favorably to plaintiffs. Does it make sense to encourage plaintiffs to bring such cases?

Most plaintiffs have limited resources available from which to finance a lawsuit. Many no longer have a job and therefore are deprived of their principal source of income. For this reason, they usually turn to their attorneys to bear the principal expense and risk of litigation, through either of two devices. Plaintiffs can compensate their attorneys either through the award of attorney's fees, in which the attorney accepts the risk of no award if the plaintiff loses on the merits; or plaintiffs can enter into an explicit contingent fee agreement with their attorneys, which, as a contractual matter, achieves much the same allocation of risk. These means of shifting the risk of litigation from plaintiffs to their attorneys, however, would not work if prevailing defendants were routinely awarded attorney's fees. Of course, with two-way fee shifting, as under the British rule, the plaintiff's attorney might promise herself to pay the attorney's fees of a prevailing defendant in return for some larger fee award when the plaintiff prevails, but the parties are not always free to craft whatever private agreement they want when it comes to fee awards. See John J. Donohue, Opting for the British Rule, Or If Posner and Shavell Can't Remember the Coase Theorem, Who Will?, 104 Harv. L. Rev. 1093 (1991). Ethical rules prevent attorneys from providing financial assistance to the client except in narrowly defined circumstances, not including satisfaction of any judgment against the client. Model Rules of Prof'l Conduct r. 1.8(e), (i) (Am. Bar Ass'n 1983). The risk of fees awarded to the defendant would remain on the plaintiffs, forcing them to consider liability for thousands of dollars in attorney's fees if they lost on the merits. Is *Christiansburg Garment* based less on the need to encourage plaintiffs to sue under Title VII than to avoid discouraging them from suing? Does this consideration justify the Court's one-sided interpretation of § 706(k)?

3. **Administering Awards of Attorney's Fees.** Unlike *Christiansburg Garment*, most of the decisions on awards of attorney's fees concern application, rather than formulation, of the standards governing such awards. Two issues stand out: First, when is a plaintiff a "prevailing party" entitled to an award of fees? And second, how large is the amount of fees to which the plaintiff is entitled? Both of these issues have been addressed

under a variety of different fee-shifting statutes that, with only a few exceptions, have been interpreted like the fee-shifting provisions in Title VII.

The first issue arises in cases in which the plaintiff obtains a judgment that the defendant has acted illegally but receives no significant judicially ordered relief. Thus, in Hewitt v. Helms, 482 U.S. 755 (1987), the plaintiffs obtained an opinion that state prison officials had acted in violation of the Constitution but that they were immune from liability for damages, the only relief that the plaintiffs sought. Despite the fact that the prison officials revised their regulations to conform to the opinion, the plaintiffs were not prevailing parties entitled to an award of attorney's fees. Id. at 759–64. Other cases have denied an award of attorney's fees when the plaintiff's claim became moot before a declaratory judgment was entered in her favor, Rhodes v. Stewart, 488 U.S. 1 (1988), and in which the plaintiff obtained only nominal damages of one dollar. Farrar v. Hobby, 506 U.S. 103 (1992). The general rule is that a plaintiff is entitled to an award of attorney's fees when litigation results in a "material alteration of the legal relationship of the parties." Texas State Teachers Association v. Garland Independent School District, 489 U.S. 782, 792–93 (1989).

This rule might not apply with full force to claims under Title VII because of a provision in the Civil Rights Act of 1991. This provision, discussed in Chapter 2 in connection with mixed-motive cases, explicitly authorizes an award of attorney's fees upon a finding that Title VII has been violated, even if no monetary relief or other compensatory relief is awarded to the plaintiff. § 706(g)(2)(B), codified at 42 U.S.C. § 2000e–5(g)(2)(B). Nevertheless, in the absence of an award of injunctive relief that confers a significant benefit upon the plaintiff or upon others similarly situated, it is difficult to conclude that they have obtained more than nominal relief.

The leading decision on the second issue, computing the amount of a fee award, is Hensley v. Eckerhart, 461 U.S. 424 (1983). It requires the court first to compute the "lodestar" fee: the number of hours reasonably expended, multiplied by a reasonable hourly rate. The reasonable hours expended include time spent on any claim on which the plaintiff prevailed and on any related claim. They also include time spent in administrative proceedings under Title VII, New York Gaslight Club, Inc. v. Carey, 447 U.S. 54 (1980), and the hours reasonably expended by paralegals and law clerks. Missouri v. Jenkins, 491 U.S. 274, 284–89 (1989).[1]

After computing the lodestar, the court then adjusts this figure up or down to take account of other factors, chief among them the results obtained by the plaintiff. If the plaintiff has been only partially successful, the lodestar figure must be reduced so that it reflects only hours reasonably expended on claims on which the plaintiff prevailed or on related claims that contributed to the successful claims. Conversely, if the plaintiff has been exceptionally successful, the lodestar figure may be enhanced. Other factors may also be taken into account in adjusting the lodestar figure up or down, but only to

[1] Awards of costs can also include fees for experts, essentially treating other professionals like attorneys for claims under Title VII and under §§ 1981 and 1981a. § 706(k), 42 U.S.C. § 2000e–5(k); 42 U.S.C. § 1988.

the extent that they are not already reflected in the lodestar figure itself. This last qualification is important, since it has been interpreted in subsequent decisions to eliminate virtually all upward adjustments of the lodestar. City of Burlington v. Dague, 505 U.S. 557 (1992).

The importance of the relief obtained by the plaintiff can hardly be overstated. It determines the threshold issue of whether any fees can be awarded at all, and it also largely determines the amount of fees awarded. Even when the Supreme Court has departed from a test of strict proportionality between the relief obtained and the fees awarded, it has done so only in narrowly defined circumstances. In City of Riverside v. Rivera, 477 U.S. 561 (1986), a divided Supreme Court affirmed an award of $245,000 in attorney's fees to plaintiffs who had recovered a total of $33,000 against police officers arising from an illegal search and arrest. For a plurality of four justices, Justice Brennan concluded that the district court's findings were sufficient to support the lodestar figure as a reasonable fee award. Justice Powell concurred in the judgment on the ground that the district court's detailed findings of fact justified the fee award, but he expressed "serious doubts as to the fairness of the fees awarded in this case." Id. at 586 (Powell, J., concurring in the judgment). Only the elaborate documentation of the fee award, supported by the public interest in preventing police misconduct, justified a fee award greatly in excess of the plaintiffs' own recovery.

As *City of Riverside* also illustrates, fee awards are calculated independently of contingent fee contracts, even though both methods of compensating attorneys depend on the plaintiff's success on the merits. The fees awarded exceeded any damages obtained by the plaintiffs and therefore any award based on a proportion of those damages. This conclusion was confirmed in Blanchard v. Bergeron, 489 U.S. 87 (1989), which concerned an explicit contingent fee contract. The Court held that this contract did not limit the amount that could be awarded under the lodestar method. Another decision has established the converse conclusion: that fees payable under a contingent fee contract are not limited by the amount of a lodestar award. In Venegas v. Mitchell, 495 U.S. 82 (1990), the Court held that an attorney could recover a contingent fee directly from his client to the extent that it exceeded the amount awarded under the lodestar method. Note that under this decision attorneys can enter into contingent fee agreements that allow them to receive a proportion of any settlement obtained early in the litigation, even if they have expended very few hours that could reasonably be compensated under the lodestar method. Does this practice further reinforce the resemblance between Title VII cases and tort cases? Or does the plaintiff's success on the merits as a determinant of fee awards already accomplish this result?

4. **Bibliography.** Attorney's fees constitute a subject unto themselves. Numerous articles address such questions as when they should be awarded, how they are calculated, and the incentive effects they have on the parties and on their attorneys. A good general source is Symposium, Attorney's Fees, 47 Law & Contemp. Prob. 347 (1984). See also Samuel R. Berger, Court Awarded Attorney's Fees: What is "Reasonable"?, 126 U. Pa. L. Rev. 281 (1977); Jeffrey S. Brand, The Second Front in the Fight for Civil Rights: The

Supreme Court, Congress, and Statutory Fees, 69 Tex. L. Rev. 291 (1990); Robert A. Diamond, The Firestorm Over Attorney Fees Awards, 69 A.B.A. J. 1420 (1983); Brian T. Fitzpatrick, An Empirical Study of Class Action Settlements and Their Fee Awards, 7 J. Empirical Legal Stud. 811 (2010); John Leubsdorf, The Contingency Factor in Attorney Fee Awards, 90 Yale L.J. 473 (1981); Thomas D. Rowe, Jr., The Legal Theory of Attorney Fee Shifting: A Critical Overview, 1982 Duke L.J. 651; Thomas D. Rowe, Jr., The Supreme Court on Attorney Fee Awards, 1985 and 1986 Terms: Economics, Ethics, and Ex Ante Analysis, 1 Geo. J. Legal Ethics 621 (1988); Stewart J. Schwab & Theodore Eisenberg, Explaining Constitutional Tort Litigation: The Influence of the Attorney Fees Statutes and the Government as Defendant, 73 Cornell L. Rev. 719 (1988); Charles Silver, Unloading the Lodestar: Toward a New Fee Award Procedure, 70 Tex. L. Rev. 865 (1992).

NOTE ON THE TAX TREATMENT OF REMEDIES

The Internal Revenue Code exempts only certain recoveries, mainly for damages received "on account of personal physical injuries or physical sickness," from income and therefore from the income tax. 26 U.S.C. § 104(a)(2); United States v. Burke, 504 U.S. 229 (1992); Commissioner v. Schleier, 515 U.S. 323 (1995). Recoveries for back pay, front pay, emotional distress, and punitive damages, and any interest on these amounts, are not excluded from income. Recovery of attorney's fees are also included in the plaintiff's income, on the ground that the award of fees first goes to the plaintiff and only later to the plaintiff's attorney. Including any of these amounts in income, without offsetting deductions, necessarily reduces the plaintiff's net recovery in after-tax dollars. All taxpayers face a similar reduction in their net income, but plaintiffs face a further reduction if their recovery is concentrated in a single taxable year. Unless payment of a judgment or settlement is spread over several taxable years, it is taxed at a higher marginal rate and, for a sufficiently large recovery, triggers application of the alternative minimum tax (AMT).

The first of these consequences, bunching income in a single taxable year, can be counteracted by "grossing up" the plaintiff's recovery for any amounts included in income. Following the principle of making the plaintiff whole, this technique works backward from the net income after taxes that the plaintiff would have received in the absence of discrimination. This amount is then augmented by an additional recovery that would be sufficient to pay the taxes attributable to the plaintiff's entire, grossed-up recovery. When this recovery is then taxed, the plaintiff is left with the same after-tax income as he would have received in the absence of discrimination. This technique requires some approximation, as do all attempts to devise remedies based on what would have happened in the absence of discrimination. The contentious issue, on which the circuits are divided, is whether the defendant can be required to pay a grossed-up recovery. Compare Sears v. Atchison, Topeka & Santa Fe Railway Co., 749 F.2d 1451 (10th Cir. 1984) (granting grossed-up recovery), with Dashnaw v. Pena, 12 F.3d 1112 (D.C. Cir. 1994) (denying grossed-up recovery).

The second consequence, the effect of the AMT, comes into play only if attorney's fees are included in the plaintiff's income. If they are, they will usually cause the plaintiff's income to rise above the threshold for application of the AMT, a complex set of provisions that impose a higher tax rate and allow fewer deductions to individuals with high annual income. Among the deductions disallowed are those that would ordinarily apply to the plaintiff's payment of attorney's fees. However, Congress alleviated this problem in discrimination cases, including those brought under the principal federal laws against employment discrimination, by a provision in the American Jobs Creation Act of 2004, 118 Stat. 1418 (2004), amending 26 U.S.C. § 62(20). This provision amended the definition of adjusted gross income to exclude any attorney's fees and court costs awarded or expended in connection with such cases, up to the amount of any judgment or settlement included in gross income. Because this exclusion applies to adjusted gross income, it is not affected by the operation of the AMT. However, in consolidated cases that arose before the effective date of this legislation, the Supreme Court held that contingent fees are not deductible from adjusted gross income and so remain taxable to the plaintiff under the AMT. Commissioner v. Banks, 543 U.S. 426 (2005).

Several articles have explored the intricacies of the tax treatment of recoveries under Title VII and the civil rights law. See Mary L. Heen, An Alternative Approach to the Taxation of Employment Discrimination Recoveries Under Federal Civil Rights Statutes: Income From Human Capital, Realization, and Nonrecognition, 72 N.C. L. Rev. 549 (1994); Shawn A. Johnson & Thomas Roney, "Make Whole": The Need for Gross-Ups in Employment Discrimination Cases, 17 Hous. Bus. & Tax L.J. 31 (2016); Gregg D. Polsky & Stephen F. Befort, Employment Discrimination Remedies and Tax Gross Ups, 90 Iowa L. Rev. 67 (2004); Mark J. Wolff, Sex, Race, and Age: Double Discrimination in Torts and Taxes, 78 Wash. U. L.Q. 1341 (2000); Laura Sager & Stephen Cohen, Discrimination Against Damages for Unlawful Discrimination: The Supreme Court, Congress, and the Income Tax, 35 Harv. J. Legis. 447 (1998); Tim Canney, Comment, Tax Gross-Ups: A Practical Guide to Arguing and Calculating Awards for Adverse Tax Consequences in Discrimination Suits, 59 Cath. U. L. Rev. 1111 (2010).

CHAPTER 9

SECTION 1981 AND OTHER RECONSTRUCTION CIVIL RIGHTS ACTS

A. SECTION 1981

INTRODUCTORY NOTES ON THE HISTORY OF SECTION 1981

1. **Enactment of Section 1981.** Section 1981 was first enacted in the Civil Rights Act of 1866 and re-enacted with some modifications several times since. It is now codified with its companion statute, § 1982, in 42 U.S.C. §§ 1981, 1982. Both statutes raise crucial questions about their intended scope, and, in particular, their applicability to private discrimination or only discrimination involving action by the government. The answer to this question depends upon the origins of §§ 1981 and 1982, which begin in § 1 of the Civil Rights Act of 1866. This section provided as follows:

> *Be it enacted by the Senate and House of Representatives of the United States of America in Congress assembled*, That all persons born in the United States and not subject to any foreign power, . . . are hereby declared to be citizens of the United States; and such citizens, of every race and color, without regard to any previous condition of slavery or involuntary servitude, . . . shall have the same right, in every State and Territory in the United States, to make and enforce contracts, to sue, be parties, and give evidence, to inherit, purchase, lease, sell, hold, and convey real and personal property, and to full and equal benefit of all laws and proceedings for the security of person and property, as is enjoyed by white citizens, and shall be subject to like punishment, pains, and penalties, and to none other, any law, statute, ordinance, regulation, or custom, to the contrary notwithstanding.

In a subsequent codification, this section was split in two, with § 1981 covering most of the rights protected by the 1866 Act and § 1982 covering only the rights related to property. Both sections prohibit racial discrimination with respect to those rights through the guarantee that all persons (under § 1981) or all citizens (under § 1982) shall have the same rights as are "enjoyed by white citizens."

The 1866 Act was passed under congressional authority to enforce the Thirteenth Amendment and to protect the status of the newly freed slaves as individuals with the full capacity of white citizens. The Thirteenth Amendment is unusual among constitutional provisions because it applies to private action as well as to government action, prohibiting slavery in all its forms, whether established by legislation or by private arrangement. The authority of Congress to enforce the Amendment is correspondingly broad, also extending to private forms of involuntary servitude and perpetuation of the "badges and incidents of slavery." Civil Rights Cases, 109 U.S. 3, 20 (1883). Unlike the Fourteenth Amendment, the Thirteenth Amendment contains no restriction on its coverage limiting it to state action. The entire history of §§ 1981 and 1982 turns on the question whether it contains a similar limitation.

Despite the broad power granted to Congress to enforce the Thirteenth Amendment, doubts soon arose about the constitutionality of the 1866 Act, in particular, whether it went beyond eliminating slavery and its immediate consequences to granting general civil rights to the newly freed slaves. Partly for this reason, parts of the Act were incorporated in the Fourteenth Amendment, and the Act as a whole was re-enacted after ratification of that amendment. Although the amendment conferred additional power upon Congress, this power was limited, like the rights granted by the amendment itself, to state action. The Equal Protection and Due Process Clauses protect only against infringement by the states and those acting on their behalf. Legislation to enforce these clauses is correspondingly limited, as the Supreme Court has long recognized. See Civil Rights Cases, 109 U.S. at 18–19; United States v. Morrison, 529 U.S. 598, 621–22 (2000). The fundamental question about the scope of §§ 1981 and 1982 is whether these provisions are subject to the same limitation: whether they apply only to state action because they were re-enacted under the Fourteenth Amendment or whether they also apply to private action because they were initially enacted under the Thirteenth Amendment.

2. *Jones v. Alfred H. Mayer Co.* For almost a century, the interpretation of §§ 1981 and 1982 based on the Fourteenth Amendment prevailed. Claims that might have been brought under these statutes were brought under the Fourteenth Amendment instead, with the statutory claims added only as another ground for recovery for violation of the same rights. Whatever rights were granted by these statutes were also protected by the Fourteenth Amendment, and the statutes themselves had no independent significance.

All of this changed dramatically with the Supreme Court's decision in Jones v. Alfred H. Mayer Co., 392 U.S. 409 (1968). That case concerned a claim under § 1982 of racial discrimination by a private developer. The Court's holding was twofold: first, that the reference to the rights "to inherit, purchase, lease, sell, hold, and convey real and personal property" in § 1982 protected against private discrimination as well as government discrimination; and second, that Congress had the power under the Thirteenth Amendment to enact this prohibition on private discrimination in order to eliminate "the badges and incidents of slavery."

The first holding involved a detailed analysis of the structure of the 1866 Act and its legislative history. Certain provisions in the statute, concerned with its effect on state law and on its enforcement against state officers, were clearly limited to state action. Yet statements by sponsors of the Act emphasized the pervasive discrimination suffered by the newly freed slaves, both from other private individuals and from state officials. The majority concluded from these statements that Congress sought to prohibit all forms of discrimination and that the provisions limited to government action did not affect the scope of the rights granted by § 1982. The dissent reached the opposite conclusion based on the narrow focus of Congress on abuses by state officials, both in the text of the statute and in other passages in the legislative history.

The second holding on congressional power was less controversial because the Supreme Court had already upheld the power of Congress to enact modern civil rights statutes, like Title VII, under the Commerce Clause. The Court found earlier decisions limiting congressional power to enforce the Thirteenth Amendment to be "academic" in light of these decisions. Jones v. Mayer, 392 U.S. at 441 n.78. Whether or not this argument is valid—the existence of congressional power under one clause does not usually justify its expansion under another—this argument does recognize the changed background against which *Jones v. Mayer* was decided. Section 1981 was passed when there was no previous federal legislation prohibiting private discrimination on the basis of race. *Jones v. Mayer* was decided after the passage of Title VII, and other provisions of the Civil Rights Act of 1964, all of which prohibited racial discrimination in a wide range of private commercial transactions. By the time the decision was handed down, Congress had also passed the Civil Rights Act of 1968, 42 U.S.C. §§ 3601–19, which prohibited the very form of discrimination alleged in *Jones v. Mayer* itself. How did this recent legislation, establishing broad prohibitions against private discrimination, affect the significance of the decision in *Jones v. Mayer*? Did it make the decision more acceptable because it was less significant? Did it make the decision more justifiable?

3. Scholarly Assessment of *Jones v. Mayer*. The initial scholarly reaction to *Jones v. Mayer* was critical, particularly of the reasoning in the Court's opinion. Gerhard Casper in *Jones v. Mayer*: Clio, Bemused and Confused Muse, 1968 Sup. Ct. Rev. 89, called the Court's treatment of the history "creation by authoritative revelation" and concluded that "[t]he Civil Rights Act, interpreted historically, does not address itself to the problem [of fair housing]." Id. at 100, 122. And in his History of the Supreme Court of the United States: Reconstruction and Reunion, 1864–88, Part One 1117–1260 (1971), Charles Fairman was even more critical, noting that his "critique has been carried no further than was needed to disembarrass the field of history."

Other scholars have been more favorable to the decision. For a response to Fairman, see Sanford Levinson, Book Review, 26 Stan. L. Rev. 461, 482–83 (1974). Another scholar concluded, after an extensive examination of the legislative record, that "[w]hile statements from the congressional debates may be cited to support both sides of the question, on balance the legislative history clearly justifies the Court's application of the act to private land developers." Robert L. Kohl, The Civil Rights Act of 1866, Its Hour Come Round at Last: *Jones v. Alfred H. Mayer Co.*, 55 Va. L. Rev. 272, 299 (1969). For a similar assessment, see Robert J. Kaczorowski, Revolutionary Constitutionalism in the Era of the Civil War and Reconstruction, 61 N.Y.U. L. Rev. 863 (1986). And for a recent summary of the entire debate, see George

Rutherglen, The Improbable History of Section 1981: Clio Still Bemused and Confused, 2003 Sup. Ct. Rev. 303.

4. **The Significance of *Jones v. Mayer*.** A broad interpretation of § 1982 to reach private discrimination, by itself, would hardly matter to claims of employment discrimination. These do not concern the property rights protected by that statute. Because of the common origins of § 1981 and § 1982, however, the broad interpretation of § 1982 in *Jones v. Mayer* carried over immediately into § 1981. Moreover, § 1981 itself is a much broader statute, covering all forms of contracts which, in our market economy, embrace almost all aspects of commercial and business life.

To be sure, Title VII already prohibited most forms of racial discrimination in employment covered by § 1981, with the significant exception of employers with fewer than 15 employees. See § 701(b), 42 U.S.C. § 2000e(b). The attraction of § 1981 to plaintiffs and their lawyers was in the enhanced remedies that it made available. At the time, Title VII provided only for equitable relief, which could take the monetary form of awards of back pay, but did not include damages. Section 1981, in contrast, provided for an award of damages, including damages for emotional distress related to discrimination, and therefore significantly enhanced the recovery available to plaintiffs.

The implications of *Jones v. Mayer* were not lost on plaintiffs' lawyers, who soon asserted claims under § 1981, apart from or in addition to those under Title VII. Their argument that § 1981 covered private discrimination to the same extent as § 1982 was quickly accepted by the lower federal courts and it was adopted with only cursory examination by the Supreme Court in Johnson v. Railway Express Agency, Inc., 421 U.S. 454 (1975), a case that appears later in this chapter. But just as the breadth of § 1981 led plaintiffs to rely upon it, concerns that it was too broad led to decisions that continued to question its scope. This chapter takes up those decisions and their consequences.

5. **Bibliography.** For additional articles on the history and significance of § 1981, see Alexander Tsesis, The Thirteenth Amendment and American Freedom: A Legal History (2004); The Promises of Liberty: The History and Contemporary Relevance of the Thirteenth Amendment (Alexander Tsesis ed., 2010); Jack M. Balkin, The Reconstruction Power, 85 N.Y.U. L. Rev. 1801 (2010); Karen Blum, Section 1981 Revisited: Looking Beyond *Runyon* and *Patterson*, 32 How. L.J. 1 (1989); Roy L. Brooks, Use of the Civil Rights Acts of 1866 and 1871 to Redress Employment Discrimination, 62 Cornell L. Rev. 258 (1977); William M. Carter, The Thirteenth Amendment and Constitutional Change, 38 N.Y.U. Rev. L. & Soc. Change 583 (2014); Theodore Eisenberg & Stewart Schwab, Comment, The Importance of Section 1981, 73 Cornell L. Rev. 596 (1988); James Gray Pope, Contract, Race, and Freedom of Labor in the Constitutional Law of "Involuntary Servitude," 119 Yale L.J. 1474 (2010); Barry Sullivan, Historical Reconstruction, Reconstruction History, and the Proper Scope of Section 1981, 98 Yale L.J. 541 (1989); Alexander Tsesis, Furthering American Freedom: Civil Rights & the Thirteenth Amendment, 45 B.C. L. Rev. 307 (2004).

For articles on the general power of Congress to enforce the Thirteenth and Fourteenth Amendments, see William M. Carter, Jr., Race, Rights, and the Thirteenth Amendment: Defining the Badges and Incidents of Slavery, 40 UC Davis L. Rev. 1311 (2007); Robert J. Kaczorowski, Congress's Power to Enforce Fourteenth Amendment Rights: Lessons from Federal Remedies the Framers Enacted, 42 Harv. J. Legis. 187 (2005); Alexander Tsesis, A Civil Rights Approach: Achieving Revolutionary Abolitionism Through the Thirteenth Amendment, 39 U.C. Davis L. Rev. 1773 (2006).

McDonald v. Santa Fe Trail Transportation Co.

427 U.S. 273 (1976).

■ JUSTICE MARSHALL delivered the opinion of the Court.

Petitioners, L.N. McDonald and Raymond L. Laird, brought this action in the United States District Court for the Southern District of Texas seeking relief against Santa Fe Trail Transportation Co. (Santa Fe) and International Brotherhood of Teamsters Local 988 (Local 988), which represented Santa Fe's Houston employees, for alleged violations of the Civil Rights Act of 1866, 42 U.S.C. § 1981, and of Title VII of the Civil Rights Act of 1964, 42 U.S.C. § 2000e et seq., in connection with their discharge from Santa Fe's employment. The District Court dismissed the complaint on the pleadings. The Court of Appeals for the Fifth Circuit affirmed. In determining whether the decisions of these courts were correct, we must decide, first, whether a complaint alleging that white employees charged with misappropriating property from their employer were dismissed from employment, while a black employee similarly charged was not dismissed, states a claim under Title VII. Second, we must decide whether § 1981, which provides that "[a]ll persons . . . shall have the same right . . . to make and enforce contracts . . . as is enjoyed by white citizens . . ." affords protection from racial discrimination in private employment to white persons as well as nonwhites. . . .

II

Title VII of the Civil Rights Act of 1964 prohibits the discharge of "any individual" because of "such individual's race," § 703(a)(1), 42 U.S.C. § 2000e–2(a)(1). Its terms are not limited to discrimination against members of any particular race. Thus, although we were not there confronted with racial discrimination against whites, we described the Act in Griggs v. Duke Power Co., 401 U.S. 424, 431 (1971), as prohibiting "[d]iscriminatory preference for *any* [racial] group, *minority* or *majority*" (emphasis added).[6] Similarly the EEOC, whose interpretations are

---

[6] Our discussion in McDonnell Douglas Corp. v. Green, 411 U.S. 792, 802 (1973), of the means by which a Title VII litigant might make out a prima facie case of racial discrimination is not contrary. There we said that a complainant could establish a prima facie case by showing: "(i) that he belongs to a racial minority; (ii) that he applied and was qualified for a job for which the employer was seeking applicants; (iii) that, despite his qualifications, he was rejected; and

entitled to great deference, id. at 433–434, has consistently interpreted Title VII to proscribe racial discrimination in private employment against whites on the same terms as racial discrimination against nonwhites, holding that to proceed otherwise would

> "constitute a derogation of the Commission's Congressional mandate to eliminate all practices which operate to disadvantage the employment opportunities of any group protected by Title VII, including Caucasians." EEOC Decision No. 74–31, 7 FEP 1326, 1328 (1973).

This conclusion is in accord with uncontradicted legislative history to the effect that Title VII was intended to "cover white men and white women and all Americans," 110 Cong. Rec. 2578 (1964) (remarks of Rep. Celler), and create an "obligation not to discriminate against whites," Id. at 7218 (memorandum of Sen. Clark). See also id. at 7213 (memorandum of Sens. Clark and Case); id. at 8912 (remarks of Sen. Williams). We therefore hold today that Title VII prohibits racial discrimination against the white petitioners in this case upon the same standards as would be applicable were they Negroes and Jackson white.[8]

[The remainder of the Court's discussion of Title VII is omitted.]

III

Title 42 U.S.C. § 1981 provides in pertinent part: "All persons within the jurisdiction of the United States shall have the same right in every State and Territory to make and enforce contracts . . . as is enjoyed by white citizens. . . ." We have previously held, where discrimination against Negroes was in question, that § 1981 affords a federal remedy against discrimination in private employment on the basis of race, and respondents do not contend otherwise. . . . The question here is whether § 1981 prohibits racial discrimination in private employment against whites as well as nonwhites.

(iv) that, after his rejection, the position remained open and the employer continued to seek applicants from persons of complainant's qualifications."

> As we particularly noted, however, this "specification . . . of the prima facie proof required . . . is not necessarily applicable in every respect to differing factual situations." Id. at 802 n.13. Requirement (i) of this sample pattern of proof was set out only to demonstrate how the racial character of the discrimination could be established in the most common sort of case, and not as an indication of any substantive limitation of Title VII's prohibition of racial discrimination.

[8] Local 988 explicitly concedes that it makes no difference that petitioners are white and Jackson Negro, rather than the other way around. Santa Fe, while conceding that "across-the-board discrimination in favor of minorities could never be condoned consistent with Title VII," contends nevertheless that "such discrimination . . . in isolated cases which cannot reasonably be said to burden whites as a class unduly," such as is alleged here, "may be acceptable." We cannot agree. There is no exception in the terms of the Act for isolated cases; on the contrary, "Title VII tolerates *no* racial discrimination, subtle or otherwise." McDonnell Douglas Corp. v. Green, supra, 411 U.S., at 801 (emphasis added).

Santa Fe disclaims that the actions challenged here were any part of an affirmative action program, and we emphasize that we do not consider here the permissibility of such a program, whether judicially required or otherwise prompted.

While neither of the courts below elaborated its reasons for not applying § 1981 to racial discrimination against white persons, respondents suggest two lines of argument to support that judgment. First, they argue that by operation of the phrase "as is enjoyed by white citizens," § 1981 unambiguously limits itself to the protection of nonwhite persons against racial discrimination. Second, they contend that such a reading is consistent with the legislative history of the provision, which derives its operative language from § 1 of the Civil Rights Act of 1866, Act of Apr. 9, 1866, c. 31, § 1, 14 Stat. 27. . . . The 1866 statute, they assert, was concerned predominantly with assuring specified civil rights to the former Negro slaves freed by virtue of the Thirteenth Amendment, and not at all with protecting the corresponding civil rights of white persons.

We find neither argument persuasive. Rather, our examination of the language and history of § 1981 convinces us that § 1981 is applicable to racial discrimination in private employment against white persons.

First, we cannot accept the view that the terms of § 1981 exclude its application to racial discrimination against white persons. On the contrary, the statute explicitly applies to "*all* persons" (emphasis added), including white persons. See, e.g., United States v. Wong Kim Ark, 169 U.S. 649, 675–676 (1898). While a mechanical reading of the phrase "as is enjoyed by white citizens" would seem to lend support to respondents' reading of the statute, we have previously described this phrase simply as emphasizing "the racial character of the rights being protected," Georgia v. Rachel, 384 U.S. 780, 791 (1966). In any event, whatever ambiguity there may be in the language of § 1981 is clarified by an examination of the legislative history of § 1981's language as it was originally forged in the Civil Rights Act of 1866. . . . It is to this subject that we now turn.

The bill ultimately enacted as the Civil Rights Act of 1866 was introduced by Senator Trumbull of Illinois as a "bill . . . to protect *all* persons in the United States in their civil rights . . ." (emphasis added), and was initially described by him as applying to "every race and color." Cong. Globe, 39th Cong., 1st Sess., 211 (1866) (hereinafter Cong. Globe). Consistent with the views of its draftsman,[17] and the prevailing view in the Congress as to the reach of its powers under the enforcement section of the Thirteenth Amendment, the terms of the bill prohibited any racial discrimination in the making and enforcement of contracts against whites as well as nonwhites. Its first section provided:

> "[T]here shall be no discrimination in civil rights or immunities among the inhabitants of any State or Territory of the United States on account of race, color, or previous condition

[17] Cf. Cong. Globe 474:

"I take it that any statute which is not equal to all, and which deprives any citizen of civil rights which are secured to other citizens, is an unjust encroachment upon his liberty; and is, in fact, a badge of servitude which, by the Constitution, is prohibited."

of slavery; but the inhabitants of every race and color, without regard to any previous condition of slavery or involuntary servitude, . . . shall have the same right to make and enforce contracts, to sue, be parties, and give evidence, to inherit, purchase, lease, sell, hold, and convey real and personal property, and to full and equal benefit of all laws and proceedings for the security of person and property, and shall be subject to like punishment, pains, and penalties, and to none other, any law, statute, ordinance, regulation, or custom, to the contrary notwithstanding." Id. at 211.[19]

While it is, of course, true that the immediate impetus for the bill was the necessity for further relief of the constitutionally emancipated former Negro slaves, the general discussion of the scope of the bill did not circumscribe its broad language to that limited goal. On the contrary, the bill was routinely viewed, by its opponents and supporters alike, as applying to the civil rights of whites as well as nonwhites.[20] The point was most directly focused on in the closing debate in the Senate. During that debate, in response to the argument of Senator Davis of Kentucky that by providing for the punishment of racial discrimination in its enforcement section, § 2, the bill extended to Negroes a protection never afforded whites, Senator Trumbull said:

"Sir, *this bill applies to white men as well as black men.* It declares that all persons in the United States shall be entitled to the same civil rights, the right to the fruit of their own labor, the right to make contracts, the right to buy and sell, and enjoy liberty and happiness; and that is abominable and iniquitous

---

[19] The bill's concern with equal protection of civil rights for whites as well as nonwhites is also expressed in its § 4, which referred, as introduced, Cong. Globe 211, and enacted, 14 Stat. 28, to "protection to all persons in their constitutional rights of equality before the law, without distinction of race or color." The same concern is reflected in the evolution of an amendment offered by Senator Trumbull to provide, at the beginning of § 1: "That all persons of African descent born in the United States are hereby declared to be citizens of the United States. . . ." Cong. Globe 474. The amendment, accepted in principle, was itself amended to replace "all persons of African descent born in the United States" with "all persons born in the United States and not subject to any foreign power, excluding Indians not taxed," 14 Stat. 27. This provision was ultimately superseded by § 1 of the Fourteenth Amendment.

The congressional design to protect individuals of all races is further emphasized by re-enactment of the 1866 Act as part of the Enforcement Act of 1870, following ratification of the Fourteenth Amendment.

[20] See, e.g., Cong. Globe 504 (remarks of Sen. Howard, a supporter: "[The bill] simply gives to persons who are of different races or colors the same civil rights"); id. at 505 (remarks of Sen. Johnson, an opponent: "[T]he white as well as the black is included in this first section . . ."); id. at 601 (remarks of Sen. Hendricks, an opponent: "[The bill] provides, in the first place, that the civil rights of *all* men, without regard to color, shall be equal)." (Emphasis added.)

Respondents reasonably assert that references to the bill's placing Negroes' and whites' civil rights "upon precisely the same footing," Id. at 604 (remarks of Sen. Cowan, an opponent), and similar remarks might be read consistently either with the position that the measure was solely for relief of nonwhites, or with the position that it applies to protect whites as well. Respondents are unable, however, to summon any congressional debate from any stage in the bill's consideration to *contradict* the plain language of the bill as introduced and the explicit statements of Senator Trumbull, and others, that the bill, as introduced, did comprehend the prohibition of antiwhite discrimination.

> and unconstitutional! Could anything be more monstrous or more abominable than for a member of the Senate to rise in his place and denounce with such epithets as these a bill, the only object of which is to secure equal rights to all the citizens of the country, *a bill that protects a white man just as much as a black man*? With what consistency and with what face can a Senator in his place here say to the Senate and the country that this is a bill for the benefit of black men exclusively when there is no such distinction in it, and when *the very object of the bill is to break down all discrimination between black men and white men*?" Id. at 599 (emphasis supplied).

So advised, the Senate passed the bill shortly thereafter.

It is clear, thus, that the bill, as it passed the Senate, was not limited in scope to discrimination against nonwhites. Accordingly, respondents pitch their legislative history argument largely upon the House's amendment of the Senate bill to add the "as is enjoyed by white citizens" phrase. But the statutory history is equally clear that that phrase was not intended to have the effect of eliminating from the bill the prohibition of racial discrimination against whites.

Representative Wilson of Iowa, Chairman of the Judiciary Committee and the bill's floor manager in the House, proposed the addition of the quoted phrase immediately upon the introduction of the bill. The change was offered explicitly to technically "perfect" the bill, and was accepted as such without objection or debate.

That Wilson's amendment was viewed simply as a technical adjustment without substantive effect is corroborated by the structure of the bill as it then stood. Even as amended the bill still provided that "there shall be no discrimination in civil rights or immunities among citizens of the United States in any State or Territory of the United States on account of race, color, or previous condition of slavery." To read Wilson's amendment as excluding white persons from the particularly enumerated civil rights guarantees of the Act would contradict this more general language; and we would be unwilling to conclude, without further evidence, that in adopting the amendment without debate or discussion, the House so regarded it.

Moreover, Representative Wilson's initial elaboration on the meaning of Senator Trumbull's bill, which immediately followed his securing passage of the foregoing amendment, fortifies our view that the amended bill was intended to protect whites as well as nonwhites. As Wilson described it, the purpose of the measure was to provide "for the equality of citizens . . . in the enjoyment of 'civil rights and immunities.'" Then, speaking in particular of "immunities" as "'freedom or exemption from obligation,'" he made clear that the bill "secures to citizens of the United States equality in the exemptions of the law. . . . Whatever exemptions there may be shall apply to all citizens alike. One race shall not be more favored in this respect than another."[23] Finally, in later dialogue Wilson made quite clear that the purpose of his amendment was not to affect the Act's protection of white persons. Rather, he stated, "the reason for offering [the amendment] was this: it was thought by some persons that unless these qualifying words were incorporated in the bill, those rights might be extended to all citizens, whether male or female, majors or minors." Cong. Globe, App. 157. Thus, the purpose of the amendment was simply "to emphasize the racial character of the rights being protected," Georgia v. Rachel, 384 U.S., at 791, not to limit its application to nonwhite persons.

The Senate debate on the House version of the bill likewise emphasizes that Representative Wilson's amendment was not viewed as limiting the bill's prohibition of racial discrimination against white persons. Senator Trumbull, still managing the bill on the floor of the Senate, was asked whether there was not an inconsistency between the application of the bill to all "citizens of every race and color" and the statement that they shall have "the same right to make and enforce contracts . . . *as is enjoyed by white persons*," (emphasis supplied) and it was suggested that the emphasized words were superfluous. Cong. Globe 1413. Senator Trumbull responded in agreement with the view that the words were merely "superfluous. I do not think they alter the bill. . . . [A]nd as in the opinion of the [Senate Judiciary] [C]ommittee which examined this matter they did not alter the meaning of the bill, the committee thought proper to recommend a concurrence. . . ."

Finally, after the Senate's acquiescence in the House version of the bill, and the subsequent veto by President Johnson,[26] the debate in both the Senate and the House again reflected the proponents' views that the bill did not favor nonwhites. Senator Trumbull once more rejected the view that the bill "discriminates in favor of colored persons," and in a similar vein, Representative Lawrence observed in the House that its "broad and comprehensive philanthropy which regards all men in their civil rights as equal before the law, is not made for any . . . race or color . . . but . . . will, if it become[s] a law, protect every citizen. . . ." On these

[23] Wilson also urged that the bill should pass

> "to protect our citizens, from the highest to the lowest, from the whitest to the blackest, in the enjoyment of the great fundamental rights which belong to all men." Cong. Globe 1118.

Wilson's view that the Act applied equally to protect all races was echoed by other supporters of the bill in the House, as it had been in the Senate. See, e.g., the remarks of Representative Shellabarger:

> "Its whole effect is to require that whatever rights as to each of those enumerated civil . . . matters the States may confer upon one race or color of the citizens shall be held by all races in equality. Your State may deprive women of the right to sue or contract or testify, and children from doing the same. But if you do so, or do not so as to one race, you shall treat the other likewise. . . . It secures—not to all citizens, but to all races as races who are citizens—equality of protection in those enumerated civil rights which the States may deem proper to confer upon any races." Id. at 1293.

[26] In his veto message, President Johnson recognized that the bill attempted to fix "a perfect equality of the white and black races." Cong. Globe 1679.

notes, both Houses passed the bill by the prescribed margins, and the veto was overridden.

This cumulative evidence of congressional intent makes clear, we think, that the 1866 statute, designed to protect the "same right . . . to make and enforce contracts" of "citizens of every race and color" was not understood or intended to be reduced by Representative Wilson's amendment, or any other provision, to the protection solely of nonwhites. Rather, the Act was meant, by its broad terms, to proscribe discrimination in the making or enforcement of contracts against, or in favor of, any race. Unlikely as it might have appeared in 1866 that white citizens would encounter substantial racial discrimination of the sort proscribed under the Act, the statutory structure and legislative history persuade us that the 39th Congress was intent upon establishing in the federal law a broader principle than would have been necessary simply to meet the particular and immediate plight of the newly freed Negro slaves. And while the statutory language has been somewhat streamlined in re-enactment and codification, there is no indication that § 1981 is intended to provide any less than the Congress enacted in 1866 regarding racial discrimination against white persons. . . . Thus, we conclude that the District Court erred in dismissing petitioners' claims under § 1981 on the ground that the protections of that provision are unavailable to white persons.

The judgment of the Court of Appeals for the Fifth Circuit is reversed, and the case is remanded for further proceedings consistent with this opinion. So ordered.

[JUSTICE WHITE dissented, joined by JUSTICE REHNQUIST, on the ground that § 1981 was not codified in a form that applied to private discrimination, as opposed to government discrimination.]

NOTES ON *MCDONALD V. SANTA FE TRAIL TRANSPORTATION CO.*

1. **The Same Right "As Is Enjoyed by White Citizens."** Section 1981 confers on "all persons" the same right to make and enforce contracts "as is enjoyed by white citizens." This formulation presupposes that "white citizens" had rights that other individuals did not possess. In particular, the newly freed slaves had been victimized by a variety of different forms of discrimination, including the passage of "Black Codes" in several of the southern states, which sought to deny them almost all of the rights of citizenship. In passing the Civil Rights Act of 1866, Congress adopted the strategy of raising everyone to the level of "white citizens."

McDonald raises a question about the extent of the rights granted to white citizens: What rights did those citizens have that were extended to all citizens? The plaintiffs in *McDonald* were not asserting the pre-existing rights of white citizens that § 1981 extended to all individuals. Whatever those rights were, they did not include the right to a continued contract of employment. The common law recognized only the right to enter into a contract with a willing party, not the right to force that party into the contract. Nor did the common law recognize the right to enter into contracts free of discrimination. If that right existed, it was only because it was created by § 1981. Yet, as the defendants argued, the measure of the rights protected by § 1981 was the pre-existing rights of white citizens.

The Supreme Court responds to this argument by relying on § 1981's protection of "all persons" from discrimination. But this argument leaves open precisely what "all persons" were protected from. Was it discrimination generally or discrimination only as compared to "white citizens"? At this point, the Court relies on passages in the legislative history minimizing the significance of the quoted phrase, concluding that it was only a way of referring to "the racial character of the rights being protected." Is this persuasive? Doesn't this observation neglect the role of this phrase in setting the baseline for defining all the rights conferred by the statute? Rewriting the statute in terms of discrimination would have changed it from one affirmatively conferring rights—such as "to make and enforce contracts"—to one commanding that those rights not be denied on the basis of race. The nature of the rights protected would have been left wholly unspecified.

A further reason for using "white citizens" as the baseline for identifying those rights appears in a passing reference in the Court's opinion to the concerns of some legislators that § 1981 would expand the rights of women and children. In the absence of this reference, the statute would give "all persons" the right to make and enforce contracts, despite limitations on the capacity of women then to enter into contracts and children, even now, to do so. Doesn't this passage suggest that the statute was mainly concerned with the capacity to enter into contracts, not with the ability actually to find a party willing to enter into them? If so, doesn't it raise questions about the private nature of the rights protected by § 1981, since the capacity to contract is conferred by the state?

2. **Reasons for a Colorblind Interpretation of § 1981.** The preceding questions go to the underlying soundness of the decision in *Jones v. Mayer*. The most plausible justification for allowing whites to sue under § 1981, based on the text of the statute, is to narrowly interpret the rights granted by that statute to the legal capacity normally possessed by white citizens. Yet the opinion in *McDonald* expresses no doubts about the continued validity of *Jones v. Mayer*. As we shall see, subsequent decisions of the Supreme Court were more skeptical. *McDonald* avoids such doubts by shifting the argument from the rights conferred by the statute to the general principle against discrimination.

This approach has some support in the text of the statute, in its coverage of "all persons" although, as we have seen, that provision itself leaves open what rights "all persons" possess. Some statements in the legislative history by supporters of the Civil Rights Act of 1866 amplify the universal coverage of the statute into the general principle against discrimination: that "all persons" are protected from discrimination in all forms. This principle is familiar today, with the passage of statutes like Title VII. And, indeed, in the first part of its opinion, the Court held that Title VII itself prohibits discrimination against whites. A statute that protects everyone from discrimination has more popular political appeal and generates more legislative support than a statute that confers a special benefit only on a single racial minority. The majority of citizens themselves can see that they benefit from general legislation against discrimination.

This argument might not have been as familiar and persuasive at the outset of Reconstruction, when Congress had just begun the task of passing major civil rights legislation, as it is today after decades of enforcement of laws against discrimination. Nevertheless, no purely historical question of the actual intent of Congress was presented in *McDonald*. The question was how to interpret § 1981 in the late twentieth century, not in the nineteenth. Severe, if not insuperable, constitutional problems would have been raised by any interpretation of the statute that refused to recognize the claims of white plaintiffs. These were unknown when the statute was first enacted, even before the ratification of the Fourteenth Amendment. Moreover, any such limiting interpretation of the statute would have appeared to be quixotic given the claims available to whites under Title VII. If Congress has already protected whites from discrimination in Title VII, why deny them the same protection in § 1981?

3. **Discrimination on the Basis of National Origin.** Two cases, Saint Francis College v. Al-Khazraji, 481 U.S. 604 (1987), and Shaare Tefila Congregation v. Cobb, 481 U.S. 615 (1987), held that plaintiffs could sue under §§ 1981 and 1982 for discrimination on the basis of national origin. These cases involved discrimination, respectively, against Arabs and Jews. The Supreme Court's reasoning in both cases depended upon historical conceptions of race that were current when the Civil Rights Act of 1866 was passed.

In *Saint Francis College*, for instance, the Court quoted at length from dictionaries and encyclopedias of the day and reached the following conclusion:

> These dictionary and encyclopedic sources are somewhat diverse, but it is clear that they do not support the claim that for the purposes of § 1981, Arabs, Englishmen, Germans and certain other ethnic groups are to be considered a single race. We would expect the legislative history of § 1981, which the Court held in *Runyon v. McCrary* had its source in the Civil Rights Act of 1866 as well as the Voting Rights Act of 1870, to reflect this common understanding, which it surely does. The debates are replete with references to the Scandinavian races, as well as the Chinese, Latin, Spanish, and Anglo-Saxon races. Jews, Mexicans, and Mongolians were similarly categorized. . . .
>
> Based on the history of § 1981, we have little trouble in concluding that Congress intended to protect from discrimination identifiable classes of persons who are subjected to intentional discrimination solely because of their ancestry or ethnic characteristics. Such discrimination is racial discrimination that Congress intended § 1981 to forbid, whether or not it would be classified as racial in terms of modern scientific theory. The Court of Appeals was thus quite right in holding that § 1981, "at a

> minimum," reaches discrimination against an individual "because he or she is genetically part of an ethnically and physiognomically distinctive subgrouping of homo sapiens." It is clear from our holding, however, that a distinctive physiognomy is not essential to qualify for § 1981 protection. If respondent on remand can prove that he was subjected to intentional discrimination based on the fact that he was born an Arab, rather than solely on the place or nation or his origin, or his religion, he will have made out a case under § 1981.

The Court relied upon exactly the same reasoning in *Shaare Tefila*, framing the question presented in the following terms:

> As *St. Francis* makes clear, the question before us is not whether Jews are considered to be a separate race by today's standards, but whether, at the time § 1982 was adopted, Jews constituted a group of people that Congress intended to protect. It is evident from the legislative history of the section reviewed in *Saint Francis College*, a review that we need not repeat here, that Jews and Arabs were among the peoples then considered to be distinct races and hence within the protection of the statute. Jews are not foreclosed from stating a cause of action against other members of what today is considered to be part of the Caucasian race.

The Court's reliance on contemporary views of race when §§ 1981 and 1982 were first enacted has some appeal. In interpreting an old statute, it is necessary to appreciate the historical and cultural context in which it was passed. But does the Court carry this concern too far? What if the contemporary views of race excluded Arabs and Jews from the category of discrimination prohibited by these statutes? Would the Court have reached the same result? Recall from Chapter 6 that national origin is treated nearly the same as race under the Constitution and Title VII. Given the current interpretation of these sources of federal law, would it have made sense to exclude claims based on national origin from the coverage of §§ 1981 and 1982? See Eileen R. Kaufman & Martin A. Schwartz, Civil Rights in Transition: Sections 1981 and 1982 Cover Discrimination on the Basis of Ancestry and Ethnicity, 4 Touro L. Rev. 183 (1988); Sarah Khanghahi, Thirty Years after *Al-Khazraji*: Revisiting Employment Discrimination Under Section 1981, 64 UCLA L. Rev. 794 (2017).

Johnson v. Railway Express Agency, Inc.

421 U.S. 454 (1975).

■ JUSTICE BLACKMUN delivered the opinion of the Court.

This case presents the issue whether the timely filing of a charge of employment discrimination with the Equal Employment Opportunity Commission (EEOC), pursuant to § 706 of Title VII of the Civil Rights Act of 1964 tolls the running of the period of limitation applicable to an action based on the same facts, instituted under 42 U.S.C. § 1981.

I

Petitioner, Willie Johnson, Jr., is a Negro. He started to work for respondent Railway Express Agency, Inc., now, by change of name, REA Express, Inc. (REA), in Memphis, Tenn., in the spring of 1964 as an express handler. On May 31, 1967, while still employed by REA, but now as a driver rather than as a handler, petitioner, with others, timely filed with the EEOC a charge that REA was discriminating against its Negro employees with respect to seniority rules and job assignments. He also charged the respondent unions, Brotherhood of Railway Clerks Tri-State Local and Brotherhood of Railway Clerks Lily of the Valley Local, with maintaining racially segregated memberships (white and Negro respectively). Three weeks later, on June 20 REA terminated petitioner's employment. Petitioner then amended his charge to include an allegation that he had been discharged because of his race.

The EEOC issued its "Final Investigation Report" on December 22, 1967. The report generally supported petitioner's claims of racial discrimination. It was not until more than two years later, however, on March 31, 1970, that the Commission rendered its decision finding reasonable cause to believe petitioner's charges. And 9½ more months went by before the EEOC, on January 15, 1971, pursuant to 42 U.S.C. § 2000e–5(e) as it then read, gave petitioner notice of his right to institute a Title VII civil action against the respondents within 30 days.

The District Court dismissed the § 1981 claims as barred by Tennessee's one-year statute of limitations. Tenn. Code Ann. § 28–304 (Supp. 1974). Petitioner's remaining claims were dismissed on other grounds.

In his appeal to the United States Court of Appeals for the Sixth Circuit, petitioner, with respect to his § 1981 claims, argued that the running of the one-year period of limitation was suspended during the pendency of his timely filed administrative complaint with the EEOC under Title VII. The Court of Appeals rejected this argument.... Because of an apparent conflict between that ruling, and language and holdings in cases from other Circuits, we granted certiorari restricted to the limitation issue.

II

A

Title VII of the Civil Rights Act of 1964 was enacted "to assure equality of employment opportunities by eliminating those practices and devices that discriminate on the basis of race, color, religion, sex, or national origin." Alexander v. Gardner-Denver Co., 415 U.S. 36, 44 (1974). It creates statutory rights against invidious discrimination in employment and establishes a comprehensive scheme for the vindication of those rights.

Anyone aggrieved by employment discrimination may lodge a charge with the EEOC. That Commission is vested with the "authority to investigate individual charges of discrimination, to promote voluntary compliance with the requirements of Title VII, and to institute civil actions against employers or unions named in a discrimination charge." 415 U.S. at 44. Thus, the Commission itself may institute a civil action. . . . If, however, the EEOC is not successful in obtaining "voluntary compliance" and, for one reason or another, chooses not to sue on the claimant's behalf, the claimant, after the passage of 180 days, may demand a right-to-sue letter and institute the Title VII action himself without waiting for the completion of the conciliation procedures. . . . Some District Courts have ruled that neither compensatory nor punitive damages may be awarded in the Title VII suit.

Despite Title VII's range and its design as a comprehensive solution for the problem of invidious discrimination in employment, the aggrieved individual clearly is not deprived of other remedies he possesses and is not limited to Title VII in his search for relief. "[T]he legislative history of Title VII manifests a congressional intent to allow an individual to pursue independently his rights under both Title VII and other applicable state and federal statutes." Alexander v. Gardner-Denver Co., 415 U.S. at 48. In particular, Congress noted "that the remedies available to the individual under Title VII are co-extensive with the individual's right to sue under the provisions of § 1981, and that the two procedures augment each other and are not mutually exclusive." H.R. Rep. No. 92–238, p.19 (1971), U.S. Code Cong. & Admin. News, 1972 at 2137, 2154. Later, in considering the Equal Employment Opportunity Act of 1972, the Senate rejected an amendment that would have deprived a claimant of any right to sue under § 1981. 118 Cong. Rec. 3371–3373 (1972).

B

Title 42 U.S.C. § 1981, being the present codification of § 16 of the century-old Civil Rights Act of 1870, on the other hand, on its face relates primarily to racial discrimination in the making and enforcement of contracts. Although this Court has not specifically so held, it is well settled among the federal Courts of Appeals—and we now join them—that § 1981 affords a federal remedy against discrimination in private employment on the basis of race. An individual who establishes a cause of action under § 1981 is entitled to both equitable and legal relief, including compensatory and, under certain circumstances, punitive damages. . . . And a back pay award under § 1981 is not restricted to the two years specified for back pay recovery under Title VII.

III

Petitioner, and the United States as amicus curiae, concede, as they must, the independence of the avenues of relief respectively available under Title VII and the older § 1981. See Jones v. Alfred H. Mayer Co., 392 U.S. 409, 416. Further, it has been noted that the filing of a Title VII charge and resort to Title VII's administrative machinery are not prerequisites for the institution of a § 1981 action. . . .

We are satisfied, also, that Congress did not expect that a § 1981 court action usually would be resorted to only upon completion of Title VII procedures and the Commission's efforts to obtain voluntary compliance. Conciliation and persuasion through the administrative process, to be sure, often constitute a desirable approach to settlement of disputes based on sensitive and emotional charges of invidious employment discrimination. We recognize, too, that the filing of a lawsuit might tend to deter efforts at conciliation, that lack of success in the legal action could weaken the Commission's efforts to induce voluntary compliance, and that a suit is privately oriented and narrow, rather than broad, in application, as successful conciliation tends to be. But these are the natural effects of the choice Congress has made available to the claimant by its conferring upon him independent administrative and judicial remedies. The choice is a valuable one. Under some circumstances, the administrative route may be highly preferred over the litigatory; under others the reverse may be true. We are disinclined, in the face of congressional emphasis upon the existence and independence of the two remedies, to infer any positive preference for one over the other, without a more definite expression in the legislation Congress has enacted, as, for example, a proscription of a § 1981 action while an EEOC claim is pending.

We generally conclude, therefore, that the remedies available under Title VII and under § 1981, although related, and although directed to most of the same ends, are separate, distinct, and independent. With this base established, we turn to the limitation issue.

IV

A

Since there is no specifically stated or otherwise relevant federal statute of limitations for a cause of action under § 1981, the controlling period would ordinarily be the most appropriate one provided by state law. . . . For purposes of this case, the one-year limitation period in Tenn. Code Ann. § 28–304 (Supp. 1974) clearly and specifically has application. . . . The cause of action asserted by petitioner accrued if at all, not later than June 20, 1967, the date of his discharge. Therefore, in the absence of some circumstance that suspended the running of the limitation period, petitioner's cause of action under § 1981 was time barred after June 20, 1968, over 2½ years before petitioner filed his complaint. . . .

C

Although state law is our primary guide in this area, it is not, to be sure, our exclusive guide. As the Court noted in Auto Workers v. Hoosier Corp., 383 U.S., at 706–707, considerations of state law may be displaced where their application would be inconsistent with the federal policy underlying the cause of action under consideration. Petitioner argues that a failure to toll the limitation period in this case will conflict seriously with the broad remedial and humane purposes of Title VII. Specifically, he urges that Title VII embodies a strong federal policy in support of conciliation and voluntary compliance as a means of achieving the statutory mandate of equal employment opportunity. He suggests that failure to toll the statute on a § 1981 claim during the pendency of an administrative complaint in the EEOC would force a plaintiff into premature and expensive litigation that would destroy all chances for administrative conciliation and voluntary compliance.

We have noted this possibility above and, indeed, it is conceivable, and perhaps almost to be expected, that failure to toll will have the effect of pressing a civil rights complainant who values his § 1981 claim into court before the EEOC has completed its administrative proceeding. One answer to this, although perhaps not a highly satisfactory one, is that the plaintiff in his § 1981 suit may ask the court to stay proceedings until the administrative efforts at conciliation and voluntary compliance have been completed. But the fundamental answer to petitioner's argument lies in the fact—presumably a happy one for the civil rights claimant—that Congress clearly has retained § 1981 as a remedy against private employment discrimination separate from and independent of the more elaborate and time-consuming procedures of Title VII. Petitioner freely concedes that he could have filed his § 1981 action at any time after his cause of action accrued; in fact, we understand him to claim an unfettered right so to do. Thus, in a very real sense, petitioner has slept on his § 1981 rights. The fact that his slumber may have been induced by faith in the adequacy of his Title VII remedy is of little relevance inasmuch as the two remedies are truly independent. Moreover, since petitioner's Title VII court action now also appears to be time barred because of the peculiar procedural history of this case, petitioner, in effect, would have us extend the § 1981 cause of action well beyond the life of even his Title VII cause of action. We find no policy reason that excuses petitioner's failure to take the minimal steps necessary to preserve each claim independently. . . .

The judgment of the Court of Appeals is affirmed. It is so ordered.

■ JUSTICE MARSHALL, with whom JUSTICE DOUGLAS and JUSTICE BRENNAN join, concurring in part and dissenting in part.

In recognizing that Congress intended to supply aggrieved employees with independent but related avenues of relief under Title VII of the Civil Rights Act of 1964 and § 16 of the Civil Rights Act of 1870, 42 U.S.C. § 1981, the Court emphasizes the importance of a full arsenal of weapons to combat unlawful employment discrimination in the private as well as the public sector. The majority stands on firm ground in recognizing that both remedies are available to victims of discriminatory practices. Accordingly, I concur in Parts I–III of the Court's opinion.

But, the Court stumbles in its analysis of the relation between the two statutes on the tolling question. The majority concludes that the filing of a Title VII charge with the Equal Employment Opportunity

Commission (EEOC) does not toll the applicable statute of limitations. It relies exclusively on state law for the period and effect of the limitation and discounts the importance of the federal policies of conciliation and avoidance of unnecessary litigation in this area. The majority recognizes these policies but concludes that tolling the statute of limitations for a § 1981 suit during the pendency of Title VII proceedings is not an appropriate means of furthering them. I disagree. The congressional purpose of discouraging premature judicial intervention and the absence of any real risk of reviving stale claims suggest the propriety of tolling here. On balance, I view the failure to apply the tolling principle as undermining the foundation of Title VII and frustrating the congressional policy of providing alternative remedies. I must, therefore, dissent from Parts IV and V of the opinion. . . .

NOTES ON *JOHNSON V. RAILWAY EXPRESS AGENCY, INC.*

1. Section 1981 as an Independent Remedy for Employment Discrimination. In *Johnson*, the Supreme Court simply accepts as valid the lower court decisions holding that § 1981 provides a remedy against private employers. As noted earlier, the reasoning of *Jones v. Mayer* concerning claims for discrimination with respect to property under § 1982 seemed to apply directly to claims for discrimination in contracting under § 1981. Most of the opinion in *Johnson* was devoted to the question of the procedures and remedies available under this statute as compared to Title VII.

The Court's answer was that § 1981 provided an independent remedy for employment discrimination with its own distinctive procedures and remedies. The remedies available under § 1981 are broadly defined in another statute dating from Reconstruction, 42 U.S.C. § 1988. These remedies include the standard array of injunctions and damages, and through an amendment to § 1988 in the twentieth century, attorney's fees. The availability of damages for claims under § 1981 carries with it the right to jury trial. Neither this right, nor the right to damages were originally available under Title VII, but were later extended to claims of intentional discrimination under that statute by the Civil Rights Act of 1991, a development discussed more extensively in the next set of notes. Since § 1981 itself does not contain any provisions addressed to these issues, most of them have been resolved by judicial decisions.

As *Johnson* holds, the limitation period for claims under § 1981 is determined and applied independently of claims under Title VII. Exactly what the appropriate limitation period is, however, has become a complicated question. For claims involving discrimination in hiring, or any new employment contract, it is the period "borrowed" from state law for personal injury claims. See Goodman v. Lukens Steel Co., 482 U.S. 656 (1987); Burnett v. Grattan, 468 U.S. 42 (1984). The state statute of limitations does not apply of its own force, but as in *Johnson*, it is "borrowed" to fill a gap in federal law and is interpreted according to federal principles. A new federal catch-all statute of limitations, 28 U.S.C. § 1658, has tried to fill this gap in another way. This statute creates a four-year limitation period for claims under federal statutes enacted after 1990 if those statutes do not themselves contain a limitation period. In Jones v. R.R. Donnelley & Sons Co., 541 U.S. 369 (2004), the Supreme Court held that this new limitation period applies to claims under § 1981(b) for "performance, modification, and termination of contracts" that were not recognized before this provision was added to the statute by the Civil Rights Act of 1991. For purposes of the new statute of limitations, these claims under § 1981(b) arise under a federal statute enacted after 1990.

2. **Prohibited Discrimination Under § 1981.** Although the procedures and remedies under § 1981 are independent of those under Title VII, the substantive prohibitions tend to be based on the same legal doctrine, although limited to intentional discrimination on the basis of race and national origin. Section 1981 does not cover discrimination on the basis of sex or religion and it does not cover claims of disparate impact. The only respect in which § 1981 is broader than Title VII is in its coverage of employers with fewer than 15 employees. Such employers are not embraced within the statutory definition of "employer" in Title VII, but § 1981, because it covers all forms of contracting, also covers those involving small employers.

3. ***General Building Contractors v. Pennsylvania.*** The decision refusing to apply the theory of disparate impact to § 1981, General Building Contractors Association, Inc. v. Pennsylvania, 458 U.S. 375 (1982), revived doubts about the extension of that statute to private discrimination. Justice Rehnquist, writing for the Court, analyzed the issue as follows:

> In determining whether § 1981 reaches practices that merely result in a disproportionate impact on a particular class, or instead is limited to conduct motivated by a discriminatory purpose, we must be mindful of the "events and passions of the time" in which the law was forged. . . . The principal object of the legislation was to eradicate the Black Codes, laws enacted by Southern legislatures imposing a range of civil disabilities on freedmen. Most of these laws embodied express racial classifications and although others, such as those penalizing vagrancy, were facially neutral, Congress plainly perceived all of them as consciously conceived methods of resurrecting the incidents of slavery.

He continued:

> Of course, this Court has found in the legislative history of the 1866 act evidence that Congress sought to accomplish more than the destruction of state-imposed civil disabilities and discriminatory punishments. We have held that both § 1981 and § 1982 " 'prohibit all racial discrimination, whether or not under color of law, with respect to the rights enumerated therein.' " Jones v. Alfred H. Mayer Co., 392 U.S. 409, 436 (1968). See Runyon v. McCrary, 427 U.S. 160, 168 (1976). Nevertheless, the fact that the prohibitions of § 1981 encompass private as well as governmental action does not suggest that the statute reaches more than purposeful discrimination, whether public or private. Indeed, the

> relevant opinions are hostile to such an implication. Thus, although we held in *Jones* that § 1982 reaches private action, we explained that § 1 of the 1866 act " 'was meant to prohibit *all racially motivated* deprivations of the rights enumerated in the statute.' ". . . .
>
> The immediate evils with which the 39th Congress was concerned simply did not include practices that were "neutral on their face, and even neutral in terms of intent," Griggs v. Duke Power Co., 401 U.S. 424, 430 (1971), but that had the incidental effect of disadvantaging blacks to a greater degree than whites. Congress instead acted to protect the freedmen from intentional discrimination. . . . The supporters of the bill repeatedly emphasized that the legislation was designed to eradicate blatant deprivations of civil rights, clearly fashioned with the purpose of oppressing the former slaves. To infer that Congress sought to accomplish more than this would require stronger evidence in the legislative record than we have been able to discern.

Finally, he observed:

> Our conclusion that § 1981 reaches only purposeful discrimination is supported by one final observation about its legislative history. As noted earlier, the origins of the law can be traced to both the Civil Rights Act of 1866 and the Enforcement Act of 1870. Both of these laws, in turn, were legislative cousins of the 14th Amendment. The 1866 act represented Congress' first attempt to ensure equal rights for the freedmen following the formal abolition of slavery effected by the 13th Amendment. As such, it constituted an initial blueprint of the 14th Amendment, which Congress proposed in part as a means of " 'incorporat[ing] the guaranties of the Civil Rights Act of 1866 in the organic law of the land.' " Hurd v. Hodge, 334 U.S. 24, 32 (1948). The 1870 act, which contained the language that now appears in § 1981, was enacted as a means of enforcing the recently ratified amendment. In light of the close connection between these acts and the amendment, it would be incongruous to construe the principal object of their successor, § 1981, in a manner markedly different from that of the amendment itself.
>
> With respect to the latter, "official action will not be held unconstitutional solely because it results in a racially disproportionate impact," Village of Arlington Heights v. Metropolitan Housing Dev. Corp., 429 U.S. 252, 264–65 (1977). "[E]ven if a neutral law has a disproportionately adverse impact upon a racial minority, it is unconstitutional under the equal protection clause only if that impact can be traced to a discriminatory purpose." Personnel Administrator of Mass. v. Feeney, 442 U.S. 256, 272 (1979). See Washington v. Davis, 426 U.S. 229 (1976). The same Congress that proposed the 14th Amendment also passed the Civil Rights Act of 1866, and the ratification of that amendment paved the way for the Enforcement

> Act of 1870. These measures were all products of the same milieu and were directed against the same evils. Although Congress might have charted a different course in enacting the predecessors to § 1981 than it did in proposing the 14th Amendment, we have found no convincing evidence that it did so.
>
> We conclude, therefore, that § 1981, like the equal protection clause, can be violated only by purposeful discrimination.

Justice Stevens concurred in the judgment, emphasizing that *Jones v. Mayer* and the application of § 1981 to private discrimination remained good law, but that limiting § 1981 to intentional discrimination better reflected the intention of the Congress that first enacted it.

Justice Marshall, joined by Justice Brennan, vigorously dissented from this narrow interpretation of § 1981, summarizing his position in the following terms:

> The plain language [of § 1981] does not contain or suggest an intent requirement. A violation of § 1981 is not expressly conditioned on the motivation or intent of any person. The language focuses on the effects of discrimination on the protected class, and not on the intent of the person engaging in discriminatory conduct. Nothing in the statutory language implies that a right denied because of sheer insensitivity, or a pattern of conduct that disproportionately burdens the protected class of persons, is entitled to any less protection than one denied because of racial animus.

4. **Bibliography.** For additional articles on § 1981 as a remedy for employment discrimination, see Joanna L. Grossman, Making a Federal Case Out of It: Section 1981 and At-Will Employment, 67 Brook. L. Rev. 329 (2001); Harry Hutchinson, The Collision of Employment-At-Will, Section 1981 & *Gonzales*: Discharge, Consent and Contract Sufficiency, 3 U. Pa. J. Lab. & Emp. L. 207 (2001); Michael Reiss, Requiem for an "Independent Remedy": The Civil Rights Acts of 1866 and 1871 as Remedies for Employment Discrimination, 50 S. Cal. L. Rev. 961 (1977).

NOTES ON THE CONTINUED VALIDITY OF *JONES V. MAYER* AND THE CIVIL RIGHTS ACT OF 1991

In *General Building Contractors*, the Court interpreted § 1981 to apply only to claims of intentional discrimination, not to claims of disparate impact. Apparently, the Court's doubts about a broad interpretation of the statute in one respect—coverage of private discrimination—led it to adopt a narrow interpretation of the statute in another respect—coverage only of intentional discrimination. The same strategy was pursued less successfully in two other cases, one resulting in a dissent and another in a decision that was soon superseded by the Civil Rights Act of 1991.

1. ***Runyon v. McCrary.*** In Runyon v. McCrary, 427 U.S. 160 (1976), the Supreme Court considered a claim that segregation of private schools violated § 1981 because it denied African-American students and their

parents the right to contract for a private education. The Court upheld this claim based on *Jones v. Mayer* and the decisions, like *Johnson v. Railway Express*, applying its reasoning to § 1981. Justices Powell and Stevens both filed concurring opinions expressing doubts about whether *Jones v. Mayer* was correctly decided as an initial matter, but concluding that it remained binding precedent. Justice Stevens, in particular, offered this observation:

> The policy of the nation as formulated by the Congress in recent years has moved constantly in the direction of eliminating racial segregation in all sectors of society. This Court has given a sympathetic and liberal construction to such legislation. For the Court now to overrule *Jones* would be a significant step backwards, with effects that would not have arisen from a correct decision in the first instance. Such a step would be so clearly contrary to my understanding of the mores of today that I think the Court is entirely correct in adhering to *Jones*.

Justice White dissented, expressly doubting the validity of *Jones v. Mayer*, but distinguishing it from cases involving discrimination in contracting based on details of the enactment, re-enactment, and codification of §§ 1981 and 1982. His complex argument can be summarized in the following terms. Both §§ 1981 and 1982 were first enacted in the Civil Rights Act of 1866 in the exercise of congressional power to enforce the Thirteenth Amendment, which prohibits private as well as public discrimination. Both were then re-enacted in the Enforcement Act of 1870 under the power of Congress to enforce the Fourteenth Amendment, which applies only to state action. When both statutes were later codified, in the Revised Statutes of 1874, § 1981 was codified in its Fourteenth Amendment form, and so applied only to state action, while § 1982 was codified in its Thirteenth Amendment form, applying to private action. The form in which § 1982 was codified justified the decision in *Jones v. Mayer*, but only as applied to that section and not to § 1981.

This argument perhaps is too contrived to be wholly convincing, depending as it does on details of codification that are not generally appreciated, even by experts in civil rights law. It does, however, raise more general questions about the role of historical inquiry and detailed examination of the text of § 1981 in determining its current scope. As we have seen, Justice Rehnquist successfully relied on a similar approach in *General Building Contractors*.

2. *Patterson v. McLean Credit Union*. These arguments also met with some success in Patterson v. McLean Credit Union, 491 U.S. 164 (1989). In that case, the Supreme Court specifically requested reargument on the question whether *Runyon v. McCrary* was correctly decided. The Court, again relying on the precedential force of *Jones v. Mayer*, eventually held that it was. Nevertheless, the Court took the occasion to further narrow the scope of § 1981. The plaintiff in *Patterson* alleged that she had been the victim of racial harassment, refused a promotion, and eventually discharged. The Court held that her claim of racial harassment did not fall within the literal terms of § 1981 because it did not involve the "right to make and enforce contracts," but only aspects of the performance of an existing contract.

Justice Kennedy, writing for the Court, reasoned that claims of racial harassment involved "postformation conduct by the employer relating to the terms and conditions of continuing employment." The plaintiff's claims of racial harassment were not actionable under § 1981.[1] Instead, she was required to resort to Title VII, which explicitly covers discrimination with respect to "compensation, terms, conditions, or privileges of employment." Moreover, interpretation of § 1981 to cover such claims would "undermine the detailed and well-crafted procedures for conciliation and resolution of title VII claims." Justice Kennedy recognized that there was, after *Runyon*, "some necessary overlap" between § 1981 and Title VII. "We should be reluctant, however, to read an earlier statute broadly where the result is to circumvent the detailed remedial scheme constructed in a later statute."

Justice Brennan, joined by Justices Marshall, Blackmun, and Stevens, dissented from this holding on the ground that "the language of § 1981 is quite naturally read as extending to cover postformation conduct that demonstrates that the contract was not really made on equal terms at all." Harassment, in his view, was actionable under § 1981 "if it demonstrates that the employer has in fact imposed discriminatory terms and hence has not allowed blacks to make a contract on an equal basis."

3. Questions About the Interpretation of § 1981. As the preceding opinions illustrate, disputes over the interpretation of § 1981 involve a wide range of different arguments: from the text of the statute, to its complicated legislative history, to the role of stare decisis, and to a comparison with modern statutes like Title VII. These disparate arguments resist synthesis into a coherent whole. In the end, however, they must result in an interpretation of the statute that allows it to be effectively enforced. Once the decision has been made to impose liability for private discrimination, shouldn't that liability be determined in the simplest and most efficient manner possible? Doesn't that argue for an interpretation of the statute freed from as many of the technicalities and historical restrictions as the legislative record permits? The Civil Rights Act of 1991 sought to resolve these questions by requiring a broad interpretation of the statute, but as the next note discusses in more detail, it has not succeeded in putting these questions entirely to rest.

4. The Civil Rights Act of 1991. The Civil Rights Act of 1991 had three consequences for the interpretation of § 1981. First, it added a new subsection (b) to the statute that explicitly superseded the decision in *Patterson*. That provision now makes clear that "the term 'make and enforce contracts' includes the making, performance, modification, and termination of contracts, and the enjoyment of all benefits, privileges, terms, and conditions of the contractual relationship." Section 1981 now extends to all aspects of the contractual relationship.

[1] Nor, for that matter, were her claims of discrimination in promotion or discharge, although the defendant did not raise the issue whether these claims were covered by § 1981.

Second, the Act added a new subsection (c) that endorsed the interpretation of *Jones v. Mayer* as applied to § 1981. This provision now states that the rights granted by § 1981 are now "protected against impairment by nongovernmental discrimination and impairment under color of State law." Curiously, this provision codifies *Jones v. Mayer* only for § 1981, not for § 1982, the statute with which the decision was specifically concerned.

Third, as discussed in Chapter 7, the Act extended the damage remedy available under § 1981 to claims under Title VII (as well as those under the Rehabilitation Act and the Americans with Disabilities Act). These provisions, now found in an entirely new section, 42 U.S.C. § 1981a, provided a limited damage remedy for victims of discrimination who did not have claims under § 1981. The latter claims still must be brought under § 1981 itself, but they provide the plaintiff with the advantage of an unlimited damage remedy. The new damage remedy under § 1981a is capped at $300,000 or lesser amounts depending upon the size of the employer.

For the moment, these amendments have put to rest doubts about the coverage of § 1981. Yet the very breadth of its coverage, extending to all contractual relationships, still raises questions about whether it might go too far, and in particular, invade associational and privacy rights protected by the Constitution. This point was first raised by Justice Powell in his concurring opinion in Runyon v. McCrary, 427 U.S. 160, 187–89 (1976), and it has been given renewed force by more recent decisions. A representative case is Boy Scouts of America v. Dale, 530 U.S. 640, 653–61 (2000), holding that a state law prohibiting discrimination on the basis of sexual orientation could not be applied to an organization that had moral and political objections to gay membership. Would the same be true of the application of § 1981 to an organization that had a specific racial or ethnic identity?

5. ***Domino's Pizza, Inc. v. McDonald.*** In a recent case, the Supreme Court has indicated that the Civil Rights Act of 1991 did not do away with all restrictions on the scope of § 1981. In Domino's Pizza, Inc. v. McDonald, 546 U.S. 470 (2006), the Court held that an individual could not bring a claim based on a contract with a corporation. The individual in question was the sole shareholder and president of the corporation and he alleged that Domino's Pizza had breached a contract with the corporation because he was black. The corporation had subsequently gone into bankruptcy, and the trustee in bankruptcy had settled the corporation's contract claim against Domino's Pizza for $45,000, but had not pursued a claim under § 1981. In these circumstances, the Court held that the sole shareholder and president could not pursue a claim either. Relying on a literal reading of the statute, the Court imposed the following restriction on its scope:

> We have never retreated from what should be obvious from reading the text of the statute: Section 1981 offers relief when racial discrimination blocks the creation of a contractual relationship, as well as when racial discrimination impairs an existing contractual relationship, so long as the plaintiff has or would have rights under the existing or proposed contractual relationship.

Because the individual plaintiff had no rights under the contract, he also had none under § 1981. Would this reasoning require a different result if the plaintiff were a third-party beneficiary of the contract with the corporation? The Court left this question open, id. at 474–76 n.3, as it did the question whether a corporation could itself sue for racial discrimination under § 1981. Id. at 473 n.1. On the latter question, the Court noted only that the lower courts had held that a corporation could sue. Id.

6. ***CBOCS v. Humphries.*** In another recent case, the Supreme Court has recognized claims of retaliation under § 1981, relying upon a "well-embedded interpretation" of the statute. CBOCS v. Humphries, 553 U.S. 442 (2008). The plaintiff in that case alleged that he had been dismissed because of his race and because he had complained about racial discrimination against another employee. Addressing only the second of these claims, the Court held that claims of retaliation had been recognized under § 1982, the companion statute to § 1981, in Sullivan v. Little Hunting Park, Inc., 396 U.S. 229 (1969). These two statutes are construed similarly because they share a common origin in the Civil Rights Act of 1866. Although an intervening decision cast doubt on the application of § 1981 to claims of discrimination in the course of employment, Patterson v. McLean Credit Union, 491 U.S. 164 (1989), that decision was superseded by the Civil Rights Act of 1991. That act added subsection (b) to § 1981, which provides for coverage of discrimination in "the making, performance, modification, and termination of contracts, and the enjoyment of all benefits, privileges, terms, and conditions of the contractual relationship." The Court took this statutory language to reinstate the law as it existed before *Patterson* and to cover claims of retaliation that arose in the course of the employment relationship. Justices Thomas and Scalia dissented on the ground that the literal terms of § 1981 still do not contain an explicit prohibition against retaliation, as does Title VII.

7. **Bibliography.** The breadth of § 1981 raises the question why other civil rights acts are so narrow, in particular, in failing to address discrimination by customers in any systematic way. For analysis of this issue, see Katherine T. Bartlett & G. Mitu Gulati, Why Do We Allow Customer Discrimination?, 102 Iowa L. Rev. 223 (2016); Dallan F. Flake, Employer Liability for Nonemployee Discrimination, 58 B.C. L. Rev. 1169 (2017); Naomi Schoenbaum, Gender and the Sharing Economy, 43 Fordham Urb. L.J. 1023 (2016); Lu-in Wang, When the Customer is King: Employment Discrimination as Customer Service, 23 Va. J. Soc. Pol'y & L. 249 (2016).

For discussion of the continued validity of *Jones v. Mayer* and its application to § 1981, see Robert J. Kaczorowski, The Enforcement Provisions of the Civil Rights Act of 1866: A Legislative History in Light of *Runyon v. McCrary,* 98 Yale L.J. 565 (1989); Allan H. Macurdy, Classical Nostalgia: Racism, Contract Ideology, and Formalist Legal Reasoning in *Patterson v. McLean Credit Union*, 18 N.Y.U. Rev. L. & Soc. Change 987 (1990–91); Ronald D. Rotunda, *Runyon v. McCrary* and the Mosaic of State Action, 67 Wash. U. L.Q. 47 (1989); Martin A. Schwartz and Eileen Kaufman, Addendum: Civil Rights In Jeopardy, 4 Touro L. Rev. 245 (1988);

Symposium: *Patterson v. McLean,* 87 Mich. L. Rev. 1 (1988) (containing a series of articles focusing on the stare decisis issue).

B. SECTIONS 1983 AND 1985(3)

NOTES ON § 1983

1. **Scope of § 1983.** Section 1983 is the most general of the federal civil rights statutes, creating a claim for the deprivation of any federal rights "under color of any statute, ordinance, regulation, custom, or usage of any State." It was enacted as § 1 of the Civil Rights Act of 1871 and it is now codified in 42 U.S.C. § 1983. Most claims under § 1983 allege violation of federal constitutional rights and, in the field of employment discrimination, rights against intentional discrimination on the basis of race, national origin, sex, religion, and in some cases, alien status.

The scope of claims under § 1983 depends upon the scope of the underlying constitutional right. Thus claims for discrimination on the basis of race admit limited exceptions for those racial classifications that serve a compelling government interest, an important qualification, for instance, in the law of affirmative action. See Grutter v. Bollinger, 539 U.S. 306 (2003). So, too, classifications on the basis of sex are allowed if they have an "exceedingly persuasive justification." United States v. Virginia, 518 U.S. 515, 531 (1996). The rights of aliens are more complicated. Under the Fourteenth Amendment, the states cannot discriminate against aliens except in positions bound up with the operation of the states as government entities, such as police or teachers. Ambach v. Norwick, 441 U.S. 68 (1979); Foley v. Connelie, 435 U.S. 291 (1978). By contrast, it prohibits discrimination in essentially clerical positions, such as a notary public. Bernal v. Fainter, 467 U.S. 216 (1984). This presupposes, however, that aliens have a right to work in the United States under the federal immigration statutes. See Mathews v. Diaz, 426 U.S. 67 (1976) (upholding federal statutory regulation of aliens).

All of these constitutional prohibitions against discrimination are subject to two further important restrictions. First, the Constitution prohibits only intentional discrimination, not discrimination under the theory of disparate impact. This proposition was established by Washington v. Davis, 426 U.S. 229, 238–39 (1976), a principal case discussed in Chapter 3. Second, almost all constitutional rights apply only against government action and § 1983 itself requires proof of action under color of state law. Unlike § 1981, § 1983 applies only to state action and therefore only to state employment and state laws and other official actions regulating employment. Private employers are outside the scope of § 1983.

2. **Immunities, Defenses, and Remedies Under § 1983.** A complicated network of rules surrounds the remedies available under § 1983 and the defendants from whom these remedies can be sought. The states themselves and "arms of the state" are not defendants subject to liability under § 1983, partly for reasons related to the text and legislative history of the statute and partly because of the immunity of states from suit under the Eleventh

Amendment. See, e.g., Quern v. Jordan, 440 U.S. 332, 338 (1979). Municipal corporations and other forms of government, however, can be sued under § 1983, on the ground that they are legal entities separate from the state. Liability can be imposed upon them, however, only for actions taken to implement official policy or custom. City of St. Louis v. Praprotnik, 485 U.S. 112, 128 (1988); Owen v. City of Independence, 445 U.S. 622, 657 (1980). The actions of a local official within the scope of her employment do not impose liability upon a city under the doctrine of respondeat superior, as the next principal case emphasizes.

Claims can be brought more readily against state and local officials, but the relief available against them depends upon the capacity in which they are sued. In their official capacity, these individuals can be sued only for the award of attorney's fees, but in their personal capacity, they can be sued for both damages and injunctive or declaratory relief. Hafer v. Melo, 502 U.S. 21 (1991). Damages and other forms of monetary relief, however, can be obtained only by overcoming a defense of official immunity, either absolute or qualified. Scheuer v. Rhodes, 416 U.S. 232 (1974).

All of these doctrinal restrictions make it far more difficult to obtain monetary relief from a state or local government employer, or from an appropriate government official, under § 1983 than under Title VII. Where § 1983 makes the identification of the proper defendant and the appropriate form of relief a difficult and complex issue, Title VII simply allows the employer to be sued directly. Any impediment imposed by the Eleventh Amendment has been overcome by the legislation explicitly abrogating that immunity, as Congress has done under Title VII by using its power to enforce the Fourteenth Amendment. See Fitzpatrick v. Bitzer, 427 U.S. 445 (1976). The only qualification to the direct liability of employers under Title VII has nothing to do with the Eleventh Amendment, but with defenses available to claims of sexual harassment, analyzed in Chapter 4.

3. **Statute of Limitations.** Claims under § 1983, like those under § 1981, do not require exhaustion of administrative remedies. The plaintiff can proceed directly to court and must do so, as under § 1981, within the statute of limitations under state law for tort claims for personal injury. Wilson v. Garcia, 471 U.S. 261 (1985). The next case takes up other, more complicated, relationships between § 1983 and § 1981.

Jett v. Dallas Independent School District

491 U.S. 701 (1989).

■ JUSTICE O'CONNOR delivered the opinion of the Court.

The question before us in these cases is whether 42 U.S.C. § 1981 provides an independent federal cause of action for damages against local governmental entities, and whether that cause of action is broader than the damage remedy available under 42 U.S.C. § 1983, such that a municipality may be held liable for its employees' violations of § 1981 under a theory of respondeat superior.

I

Petitioner Norman Jett, a white male, was employed by respondent Dallas Independent School District (DISD) as a teacher, athletic director, and head football coach at South Oak Cliff High School (South Oak) until his reassignment to another DISD school in 1983. Petitioner was hired by the DISD in 1957, was assigned to assistant coaching duties at South Oak in 1962, and was promoted to athletic director and head football coach of South Oak in 1970. During petitioner's lengthy tenure at South Oak, the racial composition of the school changed from predominantly white to predominantly black. In 1975, the DISD assigned Dr. Fredrick Todd, a black, as principal of South Oak. Petitioner and Todd clashed repeatedly over school policies, and in particular over petitioner's handling of the school's football program. These conflicts came to a head following a November 19, 1982, football game between South Oak and the predominantly white Plano High School. Todd objected to petitioner's comparison of the South Oak team with professional teams before the match, and to the fact that petitioner entered the official's locker room after South Oak lost the game and told two black officials that he would never allow black officials to work another South Oak game. Todd also objected to petitioner's statements, reported in a local newspaper, to the effect that the majority of South Oak players could not meet proposed NCAA academic requirements for collegiate athletes.

On March 15, 1983, Todd informed petitioner that he intended to recommend that petitioner be relieved of his duties as athletic director and head football coach at South Oak. On March 17, 1983, Todd sent a letter to John Kincaide, the director of athletics for DISD, recommending that petitioner be removed based on poor leadership and planning skills and petitioner's comportment before and after the Plano game. Petitioner subsequently met with John Santillo, director of personnel for DISD, who suggested that petitioner should transfer schools because any remaining professional relationship with Principal Todd had been shattered. Petitioner then met with Linus Wright, the superintendent of the DISD. At this meeting, petitioner informed Superintendent Wright that he believed that Todd's criticisms of his performance as head coach were unfounded and that in fact Todd was motivated by racial animus and wished to replace petitioner with a black head coach. Superintendent Wright suggested that the difficulties between Todd and petitioner might preclude petitioner from remaining in his coaching position at South Oak, but assured petitioner that another position in the DISD would be secured for him.

On March 25, 1983, Superintendent Wright met with Kincaide, Santillo, Todd and two other DISD officials to determine whether petitioner should remain at South Oak. After the meeting, Superintendent Wright officially affirmed Todd's recommendation to remove petitioner from his duties as coach and athletic director at South Oak. Wright indicated that he felt compelled to follow the recommendation of the school principal. Soon after this meeting, petitioner was informed by Santillo that effective August 4, 1983, he was reassigned as a teacher at the DISD Business Magnet School, a position that did not include any coaching duties. Petitioner's attendance and performance at the Business Magnet School were poor, and on May 5, 1983, Santillo wrote petitioner indicating that he was being placed on "unassigned personnel budget" and being reassigned to a temporary position in the DISD security department. Upon receiving Santillo's letter, petitioner filed this lawsuit in the District Court for Northern District of Texas. The DISD subsequently offered petitioner a position as a teacher and freshman football and track coach at Jefferson High School. Petitioner did not accept this assignment, and on August 19, 1983, he sent his formal letter of resignation to the DISD.

Petitioner brought this action against the DISD and Principal Todd in his personal and official capacities, under 42 U.S.C. §§ 1981 and 1983, alleging due process, First Amendment, and equal protection violations. Petitioner's due process claim alleged that he had a constitutionally protected property interest in his coaching position at South Oak, of which he was deprived without due process of law. Petitioner's First Amendment claim was based on the allegation that his removal and subsequent transfer were actions taken in retaliation for his statements to the press regarding the sports program at South Oak. His equal protection and § 1981 causes of action were based on the allegation that his removal from the athletic director and head coaching positions at South Oak was motivated by the fact that he was white, and that Principal Todd, and through him the DISD, were responsible for the racially discriminatory diminution in his employment status. Petitioner also claimed that his resignation was in fact the product of racial harassment and retaliation for the exercise of his first amendment rights and thus amounted to a constructive discharge. These claims were tried to a jury, which found for petitioner on all counts. The jury awarded petitioner $650,000 against the DISD, $150,000 against Principal Todd and the DISD jointly and severally, and $50,000 in punitive damages against Todd in his personal capacity.

[On defendants' motion for judgment notwithstanding the verdict and for a new trial, the district court found the damage award against the DISD excessive and ordered a remittitur of $200,000. The punitive damage award against Principal Todd was also set aside and he settled the remaining claims against him and did not participate further in the action. The jury's verdict was otherwise upheld by the district court but that judgment was reversed and remanded in part by the court of appeals. That court found that insufficient evidence to support a finding of municipal liability under section 1983 and that section 1981 did not provide an independent basis for imposing municipal liability under the theory of respondeat superior.]

II

A

[Justice O'Connor began her opinion by assuming, without deciding that the plaintiff's rights under § 1981 had been violated. She then entered into a lengthy examination of the legislative history of § 1981 and related civil rights statutes originally proposed in 1865 and ultimately enacted over President Johnson's veto in 1866. She then concluded:]

Several points relevant to our present inquiry emerge from the history surrounding the adoption of the Civil Rights Act of 1866. First, nowhere did the Act provide for an express damages remedy for violation of the provisions [that became § 1981.] Second, no original federal jurisdiction was created by the 1866 Act which could support a federal damages remedy against state actors. Finally, the penal provision [now 18 U.S.C. § 242], the only provision explicitly directed at state officials, was, in Senator Trumbull's words, designed to punish the "person who, under the color of the law, does the act," not "the community where the custom prevails." Cong. Globe, 39th Cong., 1st Sess., 1758 (1866). . . .

B

What is now § 1983 was enacted as § 1 of "An Act to Enforce the Provisions of the Fourteenth Amendment to the Constitution of the United States and For other Purposes," Act of April 20, 1871. The immediate impetus for the bill was evidence of widespread acts of violence perpetrated against the freedmen and loyal white citizens by groups such as the Ku Klux Klan. On March 23, 1871, President Grant sent a message to Congress indicating that the Klan's reign of terror in the Southern states had "render[ed] life and property insecure," and that "the power to correct these evils [was] beyond the control of state authorities." Cong. Globe, 42nd Cong., 1st Sess., 244 (1871). A special joint committee consisting of 10 distinguished Republicans, five from each House of Congress, was formed in response to President Grant's call for legislation, and drafted the bill that became what is now known as the Ku Klux Klan Act of 1871. As enacted, sections 2 through 6 of the bill specifically addressed the problem of the private acts of violence perpetrated by groups like the Klan.

Unlike the rest of the bill, § 1 is not specifically addressed to the activities of the Klan. As passed by the 42nd Congress, § 1 provided . . .

> "That any person who, under color of any law, statute, ordinance, regulation, custom, or usage of any State, shall subject, or cause to be subjected, any person within the jurisdiction of the United States to the deprivation of any rights, privileges, or immunities secured by the Constitution of the United States, shall, any such law, statute, ordinance, regulation, custom, or usage of the State to the contrary notwithstanding, be liable to the party injured in any action at

> law, suit in equity, or other proper proceeding for redress; such proceeding to be prosecuted in the several district or circuit courts of the United States, with and subject to the same rights of appeal, review upon error, and other remedies provided in like cases in such courts. . . ."

Three points are immediately clear from the face of the Act itself. First, unlike any portion of the 1866 Act, this statute explicitly ordained that any "person" acting under color of state law or custom who was responsible for a deprivation of constitutional rights would "be liable to the party injured in any action at law." Thus, "the 1871 Act was designed to expose state and local officials to a new form of liability." Newport v. Fact Concerts, Inc., 453 U.S. 247, 259 (1981). Second, the 1871 Act explicitly provided original federal jurisdiction for prosecution of these civil actions against state actors. See Will v. Michigan Dept. of State Police, 491 U.S. 58, 66 (1989) ("[A] principle purpose behind the enactment of § 1983 was to provide a federal forum for civil rights claims"). Third, the first section of the 1871 Act was explicitly modeled on § 2 of the 1866 Act, and was seen by both opponents and proponents as amending and enhancing the protections of the 1866 Act by providing a new civil remedy for its enforcement against state actors. See Chapman v. Houston Welfare Rights Org., 441 U.S. 600, 610–11, n.25 (1979) ("Section 1 of the [1871] Act generated the least concern; it merely added civil remedies to the criminal penalties imposed by the 1866 Civil Rights Act").

Even a cursory glance at the House and Senate debates on the 1871 Act makes these three points clear. In introducing the bill to the House, Representative Shellabarger, who served on the joint committee which drafted the bill, stated:

> "The model for it will be found in the second section of the act of April 9, 1866, known as the 'civil rights act.' That section provides a criminal proceeding in identically the same case as this one provides a civil remedy for, except that the deprivation under color of state law must, under the civil rights act, have been on account of race, color or former slavery." Cong. Globe, 42 Cong., 1st Sess., App. 68 (1871).

Representative Shellabarger added that § 1 provided a civil remedy "on the same state of facts" as § 2 of the Civil Rights Act of 1866. Obviously Representative Shellabarger's introduction of § 1 of the bill to his colleagues would have been altogether different if he had been of the view that the 39th Congress, of which he had been a member, had *already* created a *broader* federal damages remedy against state actors in 1866. The view that § 1 of the 1871 Act was an amendment of or supplement to the 1866 Act designed to create new civil remedy against state actors was echoed throughout the debates in the House. . . .

The final aspect of the history behind the adoption of present day § 1983 relevant to the question before us is the rejection by the 42nd

Congress of the Sherman amendment, which specifically proposed the imposition of a form of vicarious liability on municipal governments. [Justice O'Connor then reviewed the legislative history supporting the Court's prior decision in Monell v. New York City Dept. of Social Services, 436 U.S. 658 (1978), holding that municipalities could not be held liable under § 1983 based on a theory of respondeat superior, but only upon a showing of policy or custom resulting in the denial of federal rights. This decision depended heavily on the rejection of the Sherman amendment in the debates over Civil Rights Act of 1871.]

The strong adverse reaction to the Sherman amendment, and continued references to its complete novelty in the law of the United States, make it difficult to entertain petitioner's contention that the 1866 Act had already created a form of vicarious liability against municipal governments. Equally important is the basis for opposition. As we noted in *Monell,* a large number of those who objected to the principle of vicarious liability embodied in the Sherman amendment were of the view that Congress did not have the power to assign the duty to enforce federal law to state instrumentalities by making them liable for the constitutional violations of others. [Prior] decisions of this Court lent direct support to the constitutional arguments of the opponents. . . . In *Monell,* we concluded that it was this constitutional objection which was the driving force behind the eventual rejection of the Sherman amendment. . . .

III

We think the history of the 1866 Act and the 1871 Act recounted above indicates that Congress intended that the explicit remedial provisions of § 1983 be controlling in the context of damages actions brought against state actors alleging violation of the rights declared in § 1981. That we have read § 1 of the 1866 Act to reach private action and have implied a damages remedy to effectuate the declaration of rights contained in that provision does not authorize us to do so in the context of the "state action" portion of § 1981, where Congress has established its own remedial scheme. In the context of the application of § 1981 and § 1982 to private actors, we "had little choice but to hold that aggrieved individuals could enforce this prohibition, *for there existed no other remedy to address such violations of the statute.*" Cannon v. University of Chicago, 441 U.S. 677, 728 (1979) (White, J., dissenting) (emphasis added). That is manifestly not the case here, and whatever the limits of the judicial power to imply or create remedies, it has long been the law that such power should not be exercised in the face of an express decision by Congress concerning the scope of remedies available under a particular statute. See National Railroad Passenger Corp. v. National Assn. of Railroad Passengers, 414 U.S. 453, 458 (1974) ("A frequently stated principle of statutory construction is that when legislation expressly provides a particular remedy or remedies, courts should not expand the coverage of the statute to subsume other remedies"). . . .

Our conclusion that the express cause of action for damages created by § 1983 constitutes the exclusive federal remedy for violation of the rights guaranteed in § 1981 by state governmental units finds support in our decision in Brown v. GSA, 425 U.S. 820 (1976). In *Brown,* we dealt with the interaction of § 1981 and the provisions of § 717 of title VII, 42 U.S.C. § 2000e–16, which proscribe discrimination in federal employment and establish an administrative and judicial enforcement scheme. The petitioner in *Brown* had been passed over for federal promotion on two occasions, and after the second occasion he filed a complaint with his agency alleging that he was denied promotion because of his race. The agency's Director of Civil Rights concluded after investigation that race had not entered into the promotional process, and informed Brown by letter of his right under § 717(c) to bring an action in federal district court within 30 days of the agency's final decision. Forty-two days later Brown filed suit in federal court, alleging violations of both title VII and § 1981. The lower courts dismissed Brown's complaint as untimely under § 717(c), and this Court affirmed, holding that § 717 of title VII constituted the exclusive remedy for allegations of racial discrimination in federal employment.

The Court began its analysis by noting that "Congress simply failed explicitly to describe § 717's position in the constellation of antidiscrimination law." We noted that in 1972, when Congress extended the strictures of title VII to federal employment, the availability of an implied damages remedy under § 1981 for employment discrimination was not yet clear. The Court found that this perception on the part of Congress, "seems to indicate that the congressional intent in 1972 was to create an exclusive, pre-emptive administrative and judicial scheme for the redress of federal employment discrimination." The Court bolstered its holding by invoking the general principle that "a precisely drawn, detailed statute pre-empts more general remedies."

In *Brown,* as here, while Congress has not definitively spoken as to the relationship of § 1981 and § 1983, there is very strong evidence that the 42nd Congress which enacted the precursor of § 1983 thought that it was enacting the first, and at that time the only, federal damages remedy for the violation of federal constitutional and statutory rights by state governmental actors. The historical evidence surrounding the revision of 1874 further indicates that Congress thought that the declaration of rights in § 1981 would be enforced against state actors through the remedial provisions of § 1983. That remedial scheme embodies certain limitations on the liability of local governmental entities based on federalism concerns which had very real constitutional underpinnings for the Reconstruction Congresses. As petitioner here would have it, the careful balance drawn by the 42nd Congress between local autonomy and fiscal integrity and the vindication of federal rights could be completely upset by an artifice of pleading.

[The Court then remanded the case to the court of appeals to determine which officials of the school district had final policymaking authority sufficient to bind the school district for purposes of imposing liability directly upon it.]

It is so ordered.

[The concurring opinion of Justice Scalia is omitted.]

■ JUSTICE BRENNAN, with whom JUSTICE MARSHALL, JUSTICE BLACKMUN, and JUSTICE STEVENS join, dissenting.

. . .

Because I would conclude that § 1981 itself affords a cause of action in damages on the basis of governmental conduct violating its terms, and because I would conclude that such an action may be predicated on a theory of respondeat superior, I dissent. . . .

[The separate dissent of JUSTICE STEVENS is omitted.]

NOTES ON *JETT V. DALLAS INDEPENDENT SCHOOL DISTRICT*

1. **Liability Under the Doctrine of Respondeat Superior.** In *Jett*, the Supreme Court made the remedies available under § 1981 subject to the same complex defenses and immunities under § 1983. As a consequence, the plaintiff's claim against the local school district required proof that some authorized official had taken action against him pursuant to the district's policy or custom. That issue was left for consideration on remand. It is considerably more difficult than proving, as would a plaintiff under Title VII, that the relevant officials acted within the scope of their own employment, which is virtually always the case when they make a disputed employment decision.

The plaintiff's claim against the principal in his individual capacity was settled, but that claim depended on overcoming his immunity, in this case, for actions reasonably believed to be nondiscriminatory. As the Court also noted, the recovery of punitive damages against this defendant was overturned, on the ground that he did not personally have the malice or reckless indifference to the rights of the plaintiff to support such an award.

2. **Claims Against Government Employers.** *Jett* makes recovery of damages and other forms of monetary relief under § 1981 follow the legal doctrine under § 1983, but only for claims against government employers. Private employers and public employers sued under Title VII remain subject to the same forms of direct liability generally available under that statute. What accounts for this difference in treatment?

The Court's reasons take it through a detailed analysis of the intertwined legislative history of §§ 1981 and 1983. Similar historical analysis figured in the cases interpreting § 1981 alone, excerpted earlier in this chapter. In addition to this reasoning, the Court also relies on a case under Title VII, Brown v. GSA, 425 U.S. 820 (1976), holding that the special provisions of that statute governing claims by federal employees provide them with their exclusive remedy for employment discrimination. The general principle suggested by this case is that federal employees, unlike private employees, can take advantage of only a single remedial scheme, rather than multiple remedies, for employment discrimination.

In the first place, state and local government employees can still assert claims under Title VII. What is the point of restricting their remedies under § 1981 if they can still obtain plenary relief under Title VII? To be sure, they must satisfy the procedures for filing a Title VII claim, as required by *Johnson*, but these requirements pose no obstacle to plaintiffs who act in a timely fashion. Moreover, the analogy to federal employees is far from perfect, since Title VII authorizes them to receive all "appropriate remedies, including reinstatement or hiring of employees with or without back pay, as will effectuate the policies of this section" against discrimination. § 717(b). No complex set of defenses and immunities limits the remedies available to federal employees. Why apply such limitations to claims by state and local government employees under § 1981? Are the historical reasons offered by the Court sufficient to justify this outcome?

3. **Effect of the Civil Rights Act of 1991.** *Jett* was decided before the Civil Rights Act of 1991. That act codified a broad interpretation of § 1981 as applied to private employers and, in particular, superseded the restrictive interpretation of the statute in *Patterson*. What effect, if any, should it have on *Jett*? The rights granted by § 1981 are now "protected against impairment by nongovernmental discrimination and impairment under color of State law." Does this provision require exactly the same remedies to be available to private and public employees? Or does the fact that Congress overruled restrictive decisions like *Patterson*, but not decisions such as *Jett*, mean that *Jett* remains good law?

NOTES ON § 1985(3)

1. **Scope of § 1985(3).** Section 1985(3), like § 1983, was enacted as part of the Civil Rights Act of 1871 and is now codified in 42 U.S.C. § 1985(3). This section prohibits conspiracies to deny federal rights to equal treatment. It was aimed at the Ku Klux Klan and consequently gave the informal name to the 1871 Act as the "Ku Klux Klan Act." Section 1985(3) has only limited application to employment cases. The statute was interpreted in Griffin v. Breckenridge, 403 U.S. 88, 102 (1971), to reach purely private conspiracies involving "class-based, invidiously discriminatory animus." This last phrase closely follows the constitutional prohibition against government reliance upon "suspect classifications," and the scope of § 1985(3) has accordingly been limited to discrimination against groups defined in those terms. Thus, nonunion workers are not among the groups protected by the statute. United Brotherhood of Carpenters, Local 610 v. Scott, 463 U.S. 825, 835 (1983). A further limitation on § 1985(3) also follows from this limitation. The "class-based, invidiously discriminatory animus" may result in the deprivation of rights that overlap with those protected by Title VII, but the rights themselves must be derived from other sources of law, such as the Constitution. Section 1985(3) cannot be used to enforce rights granted solely by Title VII, which must be enforced according to the remedial scheme in

Title VII itself. Great American Federal Savings & Loan Association v. Novotny, 442 U.S. 366 (1979).

2. **Bibliography.** Taunya L. Banks, The Scope of Section 1985(3) in Light of *Great American Federal Savings and Loan Association v. Novotny*: Too Little Too Late?, 9 Hastings Const. L.Q. 579 (1982); Neil H. Cogan, Section 1985(3)'s Restructuring of Equality: An Essay on Texts, History, Progress, and Cynicism, 39 Rutgers L. Rev. 515 (1987); Ken Gormley, Private Conspiracies and the Constitution: A Modern Vision of 42 U.S.C. § 1985(3), 64 Tex. L. Rev. 527 (1985); Janis L. McDonald, Starting from Scratch: A Revisionist View of 42 U.S.C. § 1985(3) and Class-Based Animus, 19 Conn. L. Rev. 471 (1987); Steven F. Shatz, The Second Death of 42 U.S.C. § 1985(3): The Use and Misuse of History in Statutory Interpretation, 27 B.C. L. Rev. 911 (1986); John V. White, Vindicating Rights in a Federal System: Rediscovering 42 U.S.C. § 1985(3)'s Equality Right, 69 Temp. L. Rev. 145 (1996); Marl Fockele, Comment, A Construction of Section 1985(c) in Light of Its Original Purpose, 46 U. Chi. L. Rev. 402 (1979).

CHAPTER 10

THE AGE DISCRIMINATION IN EMPLOYMENT ACT

A. INTRODUCTION

Unlike discrimination on the basis of race, national origin, sex, and religion, discrimination on the basis of age does not receive heightened scrutiny under the Constitution. The leading case on this issue is Massachusetts Bd. of Retirement v. Murgia, 427 U.S. 307, 312–14 (1976) (per curiam), involving a claim that mandatory retirement of uniformed police officers at the age of 50 violated the Equal Protection Clause. As the Court reasoned, age does not define a suspect class. "Instead, it marks a stage that each of us will reach if we live out our normal span." In terms of political influence, older individuals do not constitute a "discrete and insular minority," but a powerful interest group, capable of protecting itself in the democratic process. Classifications on the basis of age accordingly are subject only to review for a rational relationship to a legitimate government interest, a standard confirmed in a later case upholding a mandatory retirement age for foreign service officers. Vance v. Bradley, 440 U.S. 93 (1979).

These constitutional decisions are not, within their own sphere, problematic. The political influence of older individuals has been borne out by the passage and expansion of programs such as Social Security and Medicare. These decisions do raise questions, however, about the justification for laws like the Age Discrimination in Employment Act (ADEA). Are they based on the same rationale as the prohibitions against race or sex discrimination? Or must an entirely different rationale be developed for them? If the latter, does it make sense to model the provisions of the ADEA, as many of them are modeled, on those of Title VII? Or should an entirely different approach be taken to discrimination on the basis of age? One indication, although perhaps a minor one, that the ADEA is different from Title VII is that it doesn't protect everyone from age discrimination, but only individuals who are at least 40 years old. 29 U.S.C. § 631(a). The young are not protected at all from discrimination on the basis of age.

The ADEA, itself, resulted partly from the influence of older workers as a political group. In Title VII as originally enacted, the Secretary of Labor was directed to prepare a report on discrimination against older workers. This report, The Older American Worker: Age Discrimination in Employment (1965), resulted in the passage of the ADEA two years later. The ADEA, however, hardly stands alone among statutes offering special protection for seniors. Social Security Act and Medicare have already been mentioned, and even within the field of employment law, the Employment Retirement Income Security Act (codified in 29 U.S.C. § 1001 et seq., and scattered sections of 5, 18, and 26 U.S.C.) protects the pension rights of current and retired workers. Just as the Constitution provides little protection against discrimination on the basis of age, it also creates scarcely any obstacles to affirmative action through special legislation in favor of older individuals. These alternative means of protecting older workers all raise the question, pursued in the cases that follow, of the role of the general prohibitions against age discrimination found in the ADEA.

B. DISPARATE TREATMENT

O'Connor v. Consolidated Coin Caterers Corp.

517 U.S. 308 (1996).

■ JUSTICE SCALIA delivered the opinion of the Court.

This case presents the question whether a plaintiff alleging that he was discharged in violation of the Age Discrimination in Employment Act of 1967 must show that he was replaced by someone outside the age group protected by the ADEA to make out a prima facie case under the framework established by McDonnell Douglas Corp. v. Green, 411 U.S. 792 (1973).

Petitioner James O'Connor was employed by respondent Consolidated Coin Caterers Corporation from 1978 until August 10, 1990, when, at age 56, he was fired. Claiming that he had been dismissed because of his age in violation of the ADEA, petitioner brought suit in the United States District Court for the Western District of North Carolina. After discovery, the District Court granted respondent's motion for summary judgment, and petitioner appealed. The Court of Appeals for the Fourth Circuit stated that petitioner could establish a prima facie case under *McDonnell Douglas* only if he could prove that (1) he was in the age group protected by the ADEA; (2) he was discharged or demoted; (3) at the time of his discharge or demotion, he was performing his job at a level that met his employer's legitimate expectations; and (4) following his discharge or demotion, he was replaced by someone of comparable qualifications outside the protected class. Since petitioner's replacement was 40 years old, the Court of Appeals concluded that the last element of the prima facie case had not been made out. Finding that petitioner's claim could not survive a motion for summary judgment without benefit of the *McDonnell Douglas* presumption (i.e., "under the ordinary standards of proof used in civil cases"), the Court of Appeals affirmed the judgment of dismissal. We granted O'Connor's petition for certiorari.

In *McDonnell Douglas*, we "established an allocation of the burden of production and an order for the presentation of proof in Title VII discriminatory-treatment cases." St. Mary's Honor Center v. Hicks, 509

U.S. 502, 506 (1993). We held that a plaintiff alleging racial discrimination in violation of Title VII of the Civil Rights Act of 1964, 42 U.S.C. § 2000e et seq., could establish a prima facie case by showing "(i) that he belongs to a racial minority; (ii) that he applied and was qualified for a job for which the employer was seeking applicants; (iii) that, despite his qualifications, he was rejected; and (iv) that, after his rejection, the position remained open and the employer continued to seek applicants from persons of [the] complainant's qualifications." McDonnell Douglas, 411 U.S., at 802. Once the plaintiff has met this initial burden, the burden of production shifts to the employer "to articulate some legitimate, nondiscriminatory reason for the employee's rejection." If the trier of fact finds that the elements of the prima facie case are supported by a preponderance of the evidence and the employer remains silent, the court must enter judgment for the plaintiff. *St. Mary's Honor Center*, supra, at 509–510, and n.3; Texas Dept. of Community Affairs v. Burdine, 450 U.S. 248, 254 (1981).

In assessing claims of age discrimination brought under the ADEA, the Fourth Circuit, like others, has applied some variant of the basic evidentiary framework set forth in *McDonnell Douglas*. We have never had occasion to decide whether that application of the Title VII rule to the ADEA context is correct, but since the parties do not contest that point, we shall assume it. Cf. *St. Mary's Honor Center*, supra, at 506, n. 1 (assuming that "the *McDonnell Douglas* framework is fully applicable to racial-discrimination-in-employment claims under 42 U.S.C. § 1983"). On that assumption, the question presented for our determination is what elements must be shown in an ADEA case to establish the prima facie case that triggers the employer's burden of production.

As the very name "prima facie case" suggests, there must be at least a logical connection between each element of the prima facie case and the illegal discrimination for which it establishes a "legally mandatory, rebuttable presumption," *Burdine*, supra, at 254, n.7. The element of replacement by someone under 40 fails this requirement. The discrimination prohibited by the ADEA is discrimination "because of [an] individual's age," 29 U.S.C. § 623(a)(1), though the prohibition is "limited to individuals who are at least 40 years of age," § 631(a). This language does not ban discrimination against employees because they are aged 40 or older; it bans discrimination against employees because of their age, but limits the protected class to those who are 40 or older. The fact that one person in the protected class has lost out to another person in the protected class is thus irrelevant, so long as he has lost out *because of his age*. Or to put the point more concretely, there can be no greater inference of *age* discrimination (as opposed to "40 or over" discrimination) when a 40 year-old is replaced by a 39 year-old than when a 56 year-old is replaced by a 40 year-old. Because it lacks probative value, the fact that an ADEA plaintiff was replaced by someone outside the protected class is not a proper element of the *McDonnell Douglas* prima facie case.

Perhaps some courts have been induced to adopt the principle urged by respondent in order to avoid creating a prima facie case on the basis of very thin evidence—for example, the replacement of a 68 year-old by a 65 year-old. While the respondent's principle theoretically permits such thin evidence (consider the example above of a 40 year-old replaced by a 39 year-old), as a practical matter it will rarely do so, since the vast majority of age-discrimination claims come from older employees. In our view, however, the proper solution to the problem lies not in making an utterly irrelevant factor an element of the prima facie case, but rather in recognizing that the prima facie case requires "*evidence adequate to create an inference that an employment decision was based on a[n] [illegal] discriminatory criterion*. . . ." Teamsters v. United States, 431 U.S. 324, 358 (1977) (emphasis added). In the age-discrimination context, such an inference can not be drawn from the replacement of one worker with another worker insignificantly younger. Because the ADEA prohibits discrimination on the basis of age and not class membership, the fact that a replacement is substantially younger than the plaintiff is a far more reliable indicator of age discrimination than is the fact that the plaintiff was replaced by someone outside the protected class.

The judgment of the Fourth Circuit is reversed, and the case is remanded for proceedings consistent with this opinion.

It is so ordered.

NOTES ON *O'CONNOR V. CONSOLIDATED COIN CATERERS CORP.*

1. **Origins and Purpose of the ADEA.** As recounted earlier, the ADEA developed directly out of Title VII, with much of the language transferred directly from the earlier statute to the later one. The only systematic departure from Title VII in the ADEA concerns the procedures for enforcement and remedies, which were modeled on the Equal Pay Act. The procedural provisions have since been amended to more closely resemble those under Title VII, but the remedial provisions continue to follow the Equal Pay Act.

Like Title VII, the ADEA was intended to increase the employment opportunities of older workers, with a particular emphasis on discrimination in hiring. The Secretary of Labor's report that led to the passage of the ADEA documented this problem at some length. See U.S. Dep't of Labor, The Older American Worker: Age Discrimination in Employment 5–20 (1965). According to the available evidence, this problem has continued to this day. Older workers who have lost their jobs have encountered great difficulty in getting rehired by another employer. See Sewin Chan & Ann H. Stevens, Job Loss and Employment Patterns of Older Workers, 19 J. Lab. Econ. 484 (2001). Most of the claims under the ADEA, however, have alleged discrimination in the termination of older workers. This is the opposite side of the coin from discrimination in hiring. Older workers who continue to hold jobs that they have had for a number of years do not need to seek work elsewhere. The plaintiff in *O'Connor* is typical of employees who bring claims under the ADEA. They sue only because they have lost their jobs.

2. **The "Protected Class" Under the ADEA.** The ADEA, as noted earlier, does not protect everyone. It protects only individuals who are at least 40 years old. Where Title VII protects "any individual," regardless of race, national origin, color, sex, or religion, the ADEA protects the old and middle-aged, but not the young. In a recent case, the Supreme Court has made clear that, even within the "protected class," the ADEA does not protect younger workers from discrimination in favor of older workers. General Dynamics Land Systems, Inc. v. Cline, 540 U.S. 581 (2004). The ADEA only protects workers at least 40 years old from discrimination because they are too old. *O'Connor* concerns the opposite situation: when the plaintiff is replaced by a younger worker who is also within the protected class.

The Court holds that the plaintiff still has a claim under the ADEA, relying on the common sense observation that age discrimination is a matter of degree, not of kind. Whether age discrimination has occurred depends, in part, on the gap between the plaintiff's age and the age of his replacement. Framed in these abstract terms, the holding in *O'Connor* hardly seems controversial or even, apart from the contrary decision of the lower court, worthy of the Supreme Court's consideration. But as with other issues under the ADEA, what seems clear in the abstract can become difficult in any concrete case.

If all ADEA cases are not to be left to the jury, at some point the gap in age must become so small that it warrants summary judgment for the employer. It is, however, difficult to ascertain when this point, at which a matter of degree does become a question of kind, has been reached. The Court carefully avoids any resolution of this question. Does this cautious approach necessarily leave more cases to be resolved by the jury? Or does it, as in much of the litigation over individual claims of disparate treatment under Title VII, just leave the issue for the lower federal courts?

3. **Title VII Doctrine in ADEA Cases.** It comes as no surprise that, in trying to work out such questions, the lower federal courts have turned to doctrine developed under Title VII, and in particular, the structure of proof articulated in *McDonnell Douglas*, which has been adapted to fit the discharge decisions most frequently challenged under the ADEA. *O'Connor* does not quite endorse the same approach, assuming but not deciding that the structure of proof under *McDonnell Douglas* applies to claims under the ADEA.

The wording of the ADEA, taken almost verbatim in its substantive provisions from Title VII, certainly invites this approach. By enacting the same language in both statutes, Congress seemingly intended that it should receive the same interpretation. The reasons for and desirability of this nearly identical language nevertheless remain elusive. On the one hand, simple economy of scale in transferring proven language from one statute to another reduces the difficulty and uncertainty in establishing a new regulatory regime. On the other hand, the differences between different grounds of discrimination and the distinctive problems that they raise become blurred by the similarity in language. The ADEA takes account of such differences mainly through exceptions allowing various forms of age discrimination, but even some of these, such as the bona fide occupational qualification (or BFOQ) for age, have been taken over from Title VII. Both tendencies, towards convergence and separation, have shaped the development of the ADEA. Only with the Civil Rights Act of 1991, as we shall see in the next section, have significant differences appeared between the text of the ADEA and Title VII and in the interpretive approach taken to each.

Wholly apart from the advantages of using pre-existing statutory language, whether real or only apparent, structural features of the concept of discrimination also have forced the ADEA and Title VII to be interpreted and applied in the same fashion. In order to prove discrimination, a plaintiff must submit evidence that a prohibited factor entered into the disputed decision, either as "motivating factor" under Title VII or as a "but for cause" under the ADEA. The employer's most likely response, under any statutory scheme, is to invoke a "legitimate, nondiscriminatory reason" for its decision. To this extent, reliance upon a structure of proof that resembles *McDonnell Douglas* appears to be inevitable. Indeed, the ADEA itself appears to recognize as much by creating an explicit defense "based on reasonable factors other than age" and for discipline or discharge "for good cause." 29 U.S.C. § 623(f)(1), (3). These provisions appear to anticipate the whole approach taken to individual claims of disparate treatment under Title VII. If they did not, however, what alternative would be available?

4. **Bibliography.** For analysis of the effects of laws against age discrimination, see David Neumark, Ian Burn & Patrick Button, Is It Harder for Older Workers to Find Jobs? New and Improved Evidence from a Field Experiment, 126 J. Pol. Econ. ___ (2018); David Neumark & Patrick Button, Did Age Discrimination Protections Help Older Workers Weather the Great Recession?" 33 J. Pol'y Analysis & Mgmnt. 566 (2014).

For general discussions of age discrimination, see Judith D. Fischer, Public Policy and the Tyranny of the Bottom Line in the Termination of Older Workers, 53 S.C. L. Rev. 211 (2002); D. Aaron Lacy, You Are Not Quite As Old As You Think: Making the Case for Reverse Age Discrimination Under the ADEA, 26 Berkeley J. Emp. & Lab. L. 363 (2005); Michael A. McCann, Legality of Age Restrictions in the NBA and the NFL, 56 Case W. Res. L. Rev. 731 (2006); Amy L. Schuchman, The Special Problem of the "Younger Older Worker": Reverse Age Discrimination and the ADEA, 65 U. Pitt. L. Rev. 339 (2004); Sandra F. Sperino, The Sky Remains Intact: Why Allowing Subgroup Evidence is Consistent with the Age Discrimination in Employment Act, 90 Marq. L. Rev. 227 (2006); David B. Wilkins, Partner, Shmartner! *EEOC v. Sidley Austin Brown & Wood*, 120 Harv. L. Rev. 1264 (2007); Michael J. Zimmer, Chaos or Coherence: Individual Disparate Treatment Discrimination and the ADEA, 51 Mercer L. Rev. 693 (2000).

Gross v. FBL Financial Services, Inc.

557 U.S. 167 (2009).

■ JUSTICE THOMAS delivered the opinion of the Court.

The question presented by the petitioner in this case is whether a plaintiff must present direct evidence of age discrimination in order to obtain a mixed-motives jury instruction in a suit brought under the Age Discrimination in Employment Act of 1967 (ADEA). Because we hold that such a jury instruction is never proper in an ADEA case, we vacate the decision below.

I

Petitioner Jack Gross began working for respondent FBL Financial Group, Inc. (FBL), in 1971. As of 2001, Gross held the position of claims administration director. But in 2003, when he was 54 years old, Gross was reassigned to the position of claims project coordinator. At that same time, FBL transferred many of Gross' job responsibilities to a newly created position-claims administration manager. That position was given to Lisa Kneeskern, who had previously been supervised by Gross and who was then in her early forties. Although Gross (in his new position) and Kneeskern received the same compensation, Gross considered the reassignment a demotion because of FBL's reallocation of his former job responsibilities to Kneeskern.

In April 2004, Gross filed suit in District Court, alleging that his reassignment to the position of claims project coordinator violated the ADEA, which makes it unlawful for an employer to take adverse action against an employee "because of such individual's age." 29 U.S.C. § 623(a). The case proceeded to trial, where Gross introduced evidence suggesting that his reassignment was based at least in part on his age. FBL defended its decision on the grounds that Gross' reassignment was part of a corporate restructuring and that Gross' new position was better suited to his skills.

At the close of trial, and over FBL's objections, the District Court instructed the jury that it must return a verdict for Gross if he proved, by a preponderance of the evidence, that FBL "demoted [him] to claims projec[t] coordinator" and that his "age was a motivating factor" in FBL's decision to demote him. The jury was further instructed that Gross' age would qualify as a " 'motivating factor,' if [it] played a part or a role in [FBL]'s decision to demote [him]." The jury was also instructed regarding FBL's burden of proof. According to the District Court, the "verdict must be for [FBL] . . . if it has been proved by the preponderance of the evidence that [FBL] would have demoted [Gross] regardless of his age." The jury returned a verdict for Gross, awarding him $46,945 in lost compensation.

FBL challenged the jury instructions on appeal. The United States Court of Appeals for the Eighth Circuit reversed and remanded for a new trial, holding that the jury had been incorrectly instructed under the standard established in Price Waterhouse v. Hopkins, 490 U.S. 228 (1989). In *Price Waterhouse*, this Court addressed the proper allocation of the burden of persuasion in cases brought under Title VII of the Civil Rights Act of 1964, when an employee alleges that he suffered an adverse employment action because of both permissible and impermissible considerations—i.e., a "mixed-motives" case. 490 U.S., at 232, 244–247 (plurality opinion). The *Price Waterhouse* decision was splintered. . . . Six Justices ultimately agreed that if a Title VII plaintiff shows that discrimination was a "motivating" or a " 'substantial' " factor in the employer's action, the burden of persuasion should shift to the employer to show that it would have taken the same action regardless of that impermissible consideration. . . .

II

. . .

A

Petitioner relies on this Court's decisions construing Title VII for his interpretation of the ADEA. Because Title VII is materially different with respect to the relevant burden of persuasion, however, these decisions do not control our construction of the ADEA.

In *Price Waterhouse*, a plurality of the Court and two Justices concurring in the judgment determined that once a "plaintiff in a Title VII case proves that [the plaintiff's membership in a protected class] played a motivating part in an employment decision, the defendant may avoid a finding of liability only by proving by a preponderance of the evidence that it would have made the same decision even if it had not taken [that factor] into account." 490 U.S., at 258; see also id., at 259–260 (opinion of White, J.); id., at 276 (opinion of O'Connor, J.). But as we explained in Desert Palace, Inc. v. Costa, 539 U.S. 90, 94–95 (2003), Congress has since amended Title VII by explicitly authorizing discrimination claims in which an improper consideration was "a motivating factor" for an adverse employment decision. See 42 U.S.C. § 2000e–2(m) (providing that "an unlawful employment practice is established when the complaining party demonstrates that race, color, religion, sex, or national origin was a motivating factor for any employment practice, even though other factors also motivated the practice" (emphasis added)); § 2000e–5(g)(2)(B) (restricting the remedies available to plaintiffs proving violations of § 2000e–2(m)).

This Court has never held that this burden-shifting framework applies to ADEA claims. And, we decline to do so now. When conducting statutory interpretation, we "must be careful not to apply rules applicable under one statute to a different statute without careful and critical examination." Federal Express Corp. v. Holowecki, 552 U.S. 389, 393 (2008). Unlike Title VII, the ADEA's text does not provide that a plaintiff may establish discrimination by showing that age was simply a motivating factor. Moreover, Congress neglected to add such a provision to the ADEA when it amended Title VII to add §§ 2000e–2(m) and 2000e–5(g)(2)(B), even though it contemporaneously amended the ADEA in several ways, see Civil Rights Act of 1991, § 115, 105 Stat. 1079; id., § 302, at 1088.

We cannot ignore Congress' decision to amend Title VII's relevant provisions but not make similar changes to the ADEA. When Congress amends one statutory provision but not another, it is presumed to have acted intentionally. See EEOC v. Arabian American Oil Co., 499 U.S. 244, 256 (1991). Furthermore, as the Court has explained, "negative implications raised by disparate provisions are strongest" when the provisions were "considered simultaneously when the language raising the implication was inserted." Lindh v. Murphy, 521 U.S. 320, 330, 117 S.Ct. 2059, 138 L.Ed.2d 481 (1997). As a result, the Court's interpretation of the ADEA is not governed by Title VII decisions such as *Desert Palace* and *Price Waterhouse*.

Our inquiry therefore must focus on the text of the ADEA to decide whether it authorizes a mixed-motives age discrimination claim. It does not. "Statutory construction must begin with the language employed by Congress and the assumption that the ordinary meaning of that language accurately expresses the legislative purpose." Engine Mfrs. Assn. v. South Coast Air Quality Management Dist., 541 U.S. 246, 252 (2004) (internal quotation marks omitted). The ADEA provides, in relevant part, that "[i]t shall be unlawful for an employer . . . to fail or refuse to hire or to discharge any individual or otherwise discriminate against any individual with respect to his compensation, terms, conditions, or privileges of employment, because of such individual's age." 29 U.S.C. § 623(a)(1) (emphasis added).

The words "because of" mean "by reason of: on account of." 1 Webster's Third New International Dictionary 194 (1966); see also 1 Oxford English Dictionary 746 (1933) (defining "because of" to mean "By reason of, on account of"(italics in original)); The Random House Dictionary of the English Language 132 (1966) (defining "because" to mean "by reason; on account"). Thus, the ordinary meaning of the ADEA's requirement that an employer took adverse action "because of" age is that age was the "reason" that the employer decided to act. See Hazen Paper Co. v. Biggins, 507 U.S. 604, 610 (1993) (explaining that the claim "cannot succeed unless the employee's protected trait actually played a role in [the employer's decisionmaking] process and had a determinative influence on the outcome"(emphasis added)). To establish a disparate-treatment claim under the plain language of the ADEA, therefore, a plaintiff must prove that age was the "but-for" cause of the employer's adverse decision. See Bridge v. Phoenix Bond & Indemnity Co., 553 U.S. 639, 653–54 (2008) (recognizing that the phrase, "by reason of," requires at least a showing of "but for" causation (internal quotation marks omitted)); Safeco Ins. Co. of America v. Burr, 551 U.S. 47, 63–64, and n. 14 (2007) (observing that "[i]n common talk, the phrase 'based on' indicates a but-for causal relationship and thus a necessary logical condition" and that the statutory phrase, "based on," has the same meaning as the phrase, "because of" (internal quotation marks omitted)); cf. W. Keeton, D. Dobbs, R. Keeton, & D. Owen, Prosser and Keeton on Law of Torts 265 (5th ed. 1984) ("An act or omission is not regarded as a cause of an event if the particular event would have occurred without it").

It follows, then, that under § 623(a)(1), the plaintiff retains the burden of persuasion to establish that age was the "but-for" cause of the employer's adverse action. Indeed, we have previously held that the burden is allocated in this manner in ADEA cases. See Kentucky Retirement Systems v. EEOC, 554 U.S. 135, 139–43, 148–50 (2008); Reeves v. Sanderson Plumbing Products, Inc., 530 U.S. 133, 141, 143 (2000). And nothing in the statute's text indicates that Congress has carved out an exception to that rule for a subset of ADEA cases. Where the statutory text is "silent on the allocation of the burden of persuasion," we "begin with the ordinary default rule that plaintiffs bear the risk of failing to prove their claims." Schaffer v. Weast, 546 U.S. 49, 56 (2005); see also Meacham v. Knolls Atomic Power Laboratory, 554 U.S. 84, 92 (2008) ("Absent some reason to believe that Congress intended otherwise, . . . we will conclude that the burden of persuasion lies where it usually falls, upon the party seeking relief" (internal quotation marks omitted)). We have no warrant to depart from the general rule in this setting.

Hence, the burden of persuasion necessary to establish employer liability is the same in alleged mixed-motives cases as in any other ADEA disparate-treatment action. A plaintiff must prove by a preponderance of the evidence (which may be direct or circumstantial), that age was the "but-for" cause of the challenged employer decision. See Reeves, supra, at 141–143, 147.

III

Finally, we reject petitioner's contention that our interpretation of the ADEA is controlled by *Price Waterhouse*, which initially established that the burden of persuasion shifted in alleged mixed-motives Title VII claims. In any event, it is far from clear that the Court would have the same approach were it to consider the question today in the first instance. Cf. 14 Penn Plaza LLC v. Pyett, 556 U.S. 247, 270 (2009) (declining to "introduc[e] a qualification into the ADEA that is not found in its text"); Meacham, supra, at 102 (explaining that the ADEA must be "read . . . the way Congress wrote it").

Whatever the deficiencies of *Price Waterhouse* in retrospect, it has become evident in the years since that case was decided that its burden-shifting framework is difficult to apply. For example, in cases tried to a jury, courts have found it particularly difficult to craft an instruction to explain its burden-shifting framework. See, e.g., Tyler v. Bethlehem Steel Corp., 958 F.2d 1176, 1179 (C.A.2 1992) (referring to "the murky water of shifting burdens in discrimination cases"); Visser v. Packer Engineering Associates, Inc., 924 F.2d 655, 661 (C.A.7 1991) (en banc)

(Flaum, J., dissenting) ("The difficulty judges have in formulating [burden-shifting] instructions and jurors have in applying them can be seen in the fact that jury verdicts in ADEA cases are supplanted by judgments notwithstanding the verdict or reversed on appeal more frequently than jury verdicts generally"). Thus, even if *Price Waterhouse* was doctrinally sound, the problems associated with its application have eliminated any perceivable benefit to extending its framework to ADEA claims.

IV

We hold that a plaintiff bringing a disparate-treatment claim pursuant to the ADEA must prove, by a preponderance of the evidence, that age was the "but-for" cause of the challenged adverse employment action. The burden of persuasion does not shift to the employer to show that it would have taken the action regardless of age, even when a plaintiff has produced some evidence that age was one motivating factor in that decision. Accordingly, we vacate the judgment of the Court of Appeals and remand the case for further proceedings consistent with this opinion.

It is so ordered.

■ JUSTICE STEVENS, with whom JUSTICE SOUTER, JUSTICE GINSBURG, and JUSTICE BREYER join, dissenting.

The Age Discrimination in Employment Act of 1967 (ADEA), makes it unlawful for an employer to discriminate against any employee "because of" that individual's age, § 623(a). The most natural reading of this statutory text prohibits adverse employment actions motivated in whole or in part by the age of the employee. The "but-for" causation standard endorsed by the Court today was advanced in Justice KENNEDY's dissenting opinion in Price Waterhouse v. Hopkins, 490 U.S. 228, 279 (1989), a case construing identical language in Title VII of the Civil Rights Act of 1964, 42 U.S.C. § 2000e–2(a)(1). Not only did the Court reject the but-for standard in that case, but so too did Congress when it amended Title VII in 1991. Given this unambiguous history, it is particularly inappropriate for the Court, on its own initiative, to adopt an interpretation of the causation requirement in the ADEA that differs from the established reading of Title VII. I disagree not only with the Court's interpretation of the statute, but also with its decision to engage in unnecessary lawmaking. I would simply answer the question presented by the certiorari petition and hold that a plaintiff need not present direct evidence of age discrimination to obtain a mixed-motives instruction. . . .

■ JUSTICE BREYER, with whom JUSTICE SOUTER, JUSTICE GINSBURG join, dissenting.

I agree with Justice Stevens that mixed-motive instructions are appropriate in the Age Discrimination in Employment Act context. And I join his opinion. The Court rejects this conclusion on the ground that the words "because of" require a plaintiff to prove that age was the "but-for" cause of his employer's adverse employment action. But the majority does not explain why this is so. The words "because of" do not inherently require a showing of "but-for" causation, and I see no reason to read them to require such a showing. . . .

NOTES ON *GROSS V. FBL FINANCIAL SERVICES, INC.*

1. **The Relationship Between the ADEA and the Civil Rights Act of 1991.** In *Gross*, the Court refused to follow the allocation of the burden proof under the Civil Rights Act of 1991, a holding from which no justice dissented. The 1991 Act amended Title VII to change the burden of proof in mixed-motive cases under Title VII, rejecting the approach to this issue in *Price Waterhouse*. As discussed more fully in Chapter 2, the 1991 Act requires a Title VII plaintiff only to prove that race, for instance, was "a motivating factor" in the disputed employment decision. Once that showing is made, the liability phase of the case is over, but the defendant has a defense to compensatory relief. In order to make out the defense, the defendant has to prove that it would have made the same decision regardless of race, an issue on which the defendant has the entire burden of proof. The 1991 Act made no similar change in the ADEA, although it did amend the ADEA in other respects.

More controversial was the Court's refusal to apply *Price Waterhouse* to the ADEA. It suggested both that the law under Title VII that predated the 1991 Act did not generally carry over to the ADEA and that *Price Waterhouse* itself was wrong. The Court repeated its previous reservations about whether even *McDonnell Douglas* applied to claims under the ADEA, noting that earlier decisions had only assumed, but had not decided, that it did so. At greater length, however, the Court discussed the defects in *Price Waterhouse* itself. In that case, several separate opinions yielded the holding that the plaintiff had the burden under Title VII of proving that race was a "substantial" or "motivating" factor, but that the defendant had a defense on the issue of liability. Again, however, as under the 1991 Act, the defendant had the entire burden of proof on this issue. (But in contrast to the 1991 Act, a defendant who prevailed on the defense was not liable at all, for any form of relief.)

The Court found *Price Waterhouse* to be inconsistent with the main prohibitions in the ADEA: "Thus, the ordinary meaning of the ADEA's requirement that an employer took adverse action 'because of' age is that age was the 'reason' that the employer decided to act." The term "because of," according to the Court, meant that age was not only *a* reason for the employer's decision but that it was *the* reason. The Court then applied the default rule that the plaintiff has the burden of proving every element of a statutory violation unless the statute otherwise provides. It followed that the plaintiff under the ADEA (as well as under the original version of Title VII) had to prove that age was a "but for" cause of the employer's decision. The Court also noted that the complexity of jury instructions under *Price Waterhouse* had given rise to confusion in mixed-motive cases.

Justice Stevens dissented, mainly on the ground that the first part of the Court's holding, on the application of the 1991 Act, was inconsistent with its second, on the application of *Price Waterhouse*. If the 1991 Act did not change the interpretation of the main prohibition in the ADEA, then it left it identical to the interpretation of the original prohibition in Title VII, which uses the same "because of" language. The interpretation of Title VII before the 1991 Act, however, was governed by *Price Waterhouse*. Does this reasoning offer a full account of the history of enactment of Title VII, originally passed in 1964, and the ADEA, enacted in 1967? *Price Waterhouse*, after all, was not decided until 1989, well after the passage of both statutes. Or is Justice Stevens making a point about what Congress understood the law to be in 1991, when it changed the burden of proof in mixed-motive cases under Title VII, but not under the ADEA? It presumed that prevailing law would continue to apply to the ADEA. As he points out in his dissent, the opinion in *Smith v. City of Jackson*, 544 U.S. 228 (2005), offers exactly this reasoning in interpreting the theory of disparate impact under the ADEA. This decision can be found in the next section of this chapter.

2. **Is Age Different?** The fundamental question raised by *Gross* is whether age discrimination can be analyzed in the same way as discrimination on the basis of race or sex. The ADEA itself presupposes a high degree of similarity between these forms of discrimination by adopting much of the language of Title VII in defining the main prohibitions in the statute, as well as important exceptions, such as the BFOQ for age. See 29 U.S.C. § 623(a)–(f). As we have seen in Chapter 2, decisions on such common issues as the burden of proving individual claims of intentional discrimination also are interchangeable between the two statutes. See, e.g., McKennon v. Nashville Banner Publishing Co., 513 U.S. 352 (1995). Does the doctrinal similarity between the ADEA and Title VII foreclose any consideration of the distinctive nature of age discrimination?

Several scholars have argued that it does not because of the nature of interest groups that support legislation like the ADEA and the identity of the individuals most likely to sue under the statute. Large and powerful organizations, such as the AARP (formerly known as the "American Association of Retired Persons"), regularly lobby for legislation protective of older individuals. From programs that confer special benefits on the elderly, such as Social Security and Medicare, to general prohibitions against discrimination, like the ADEA, these organizations assure that their constituency has a prominent role in the political process. The influence of such organizations has led some to argue that older individuals have fought for and procured an unjustified reallocation of wealth. See Samuel Issacharoff & Erica Worth Harris, Is Age Discrimination Really Age Discrimination?: The ADEA's Unnatural Solution, 72 N.Y.U. L. Rev. 780 (1997).

At the level of individual lawsuits, the ADEA extends its protection to anyone at least 40 years old, whether or not they are a member of any otherwise disfavored group. Furthermore, employees who actually file suit under the ADEA are predominantly white males who hold relatively high status and high-paying jobs. See George Rutherglen, From Race to Age: The

Expanding Scope of Employment Discrimination Law, 24 J. Legal Stud. 491 (1995). Workers who are performing more demanding physical labor are more likely to quit, either voluntarily or because they become disabled and file for disability. Men in highly paid executive positions, though, do not face the physical pressures to leave their employment even as their abilities decline, so they are more likely to try to remain past the point when their employers wish to retain them and thus are more likely to be plaintiffs in age discrimination cases. These are hardly the powerless minorities protected by other laws against discrimination.

Are arguments at this level of generality addressed more to questions of policy, suitable for Congress in considering whether to repeal or amend the ADEA, or to questions of interpretation, suitable for the courts in interpreting the Act? The absence of a strong constitutional prohibition against age discrimination has contradictory implications for this question. On the one hand, it implies that the extent of any such prohibition is a matter for Congress rather than the courts. On the other hand, it also suggests that age discrimination is a less pressing problem than discrimination on other grounds. If this lack of priority is generally accepted, can the courts avoid taking it into account in enforcing the ADEA? Or does any such tendency simply read too much into the absence of a constitutional prohibition against age discrimination?

3. Legitimate Reasons Correlated with Age. A distinctive feature of age discrimination cases involves the close relationship between age discrimination and reliance on factors correlated with age. Pay, for instance, often increases with seniority on the job and therefore with age. In a dissenting opinion, later adopted by the Seventh Circuit, Judge Frank Easterbrook explored this question. Metz v. Transit Mix, Inc., 828 F.2d 1202, 1211 (7th Cir. 1987) (Easterbrook, J., dissenting), (adopted in Anderson v. Baxter Healthcare Corp., 13 F.3d 1120, 1125–26 (7th Cir. 1994)). Judge Easterbrook began his dissenting opinion from the premise that age and ability are correlated, and then reasoned as follows:

> . . . For many years employees add to their skills and as a result do better work; eventually the tables turn, as mental and motor skills slip away. This proceeds at different paces for different people; the ADEA ensures that employers examine each employee's actual performance rather than the average performance of a group defined by age. No one doubts, however, that an employer may discharge an employee, of any age, who no longer performs the job with acceptable skill. But one could say about performance on the job exactly what my colleagues say about wages: a test based on performance hurts the old relative to the young. Does it follow that this adverse impact makes inquiry into performance impermissible? The customary response is that no one is protected by the ADEA unless qualified for the job. An older employee whose skills have diminished is not qualified. Yet there are degrees of skill; an employee is not "qualified" one day and "unqualified" the next. In business the question is not "is Jones qualified?" but "can Jones do the job well enough to cover his wage?" A welder good

> enough to work on simple sheet metal at $10 per hour may be unqualified for a welding job, paying $30 per hour, in a nuclear plant or on a bridge where lives depend on the quality of the joint and other, better welders compete for the position. There is no "qualified welder" in the abstract, and there is no "qualified manager of a cement plant" either. To say that someone is "qualified" to manage the Knox plant is to say that he can handle the manufacture and sale of concrete well enough that he adds to the value of the enterprise at least the cost of his salary. If he cannot do this, he is unqualified for the particular job at the particular time. It is therefore not possible to divorce the ability to do a job from the wage demanded. If the ADEA allows employers to make decisions based on performance—surely it does, even though performance is systematically related to age—then it also allows employers to make decisions based on the interaction of performance and wage. If the wage is too high for the performance, the employer may act.

Judge Easterbrook went on to reject arguments that either the general prohibition against age discrimination in the ADEA, or cases on disparate impact under Title VII, prohibit such practices. Turning to the legislative history of the ADEA, he found the following:

> Little of the history is pertinent. None of the committee reports discusses the extent to which employers may take salary into account in making decisions. To the extent the legislative history addresses the subject, it suggests that employers may consider the costs of hiring older employees—and § 4(f)(2), 29 U.S.C. § 623(f)(2), writes into the statute the permission to use age as a ground of decision when costs so dictate. Section 4(f)(2) provides that employers may use age in, for example, designing insurance plans: term life insurance costs much more for 65-year-old employees than for 25-year-old employees, and § 4(f)(2) permits employers to consider that in designing packages of benefits. Senator Javits's additional statement in the Senate Report, S. Rep. 90–723, 90th Cong., 1st Sess. 14 (1967), applauds § 4(f)(2) on the ground that without it "employers might actually have been discouraged from hiring older employees because of the increased costs involved in providing certain types of benefits to them."
>
> The assumption behind § 4(f)(2) is that without an explicit privilege to use age in the design of welfare and pension plans, the higher costs of fringe benefits for older persons would be a legitimate reason not to employ them. . . .
>
> The structure of the Act accords with its history. Section 4(a) parallels Title VII in some respects but is different in others. One striking difference is § 4(f)(1), which says that "reasonable factors other than age" may be the basis of decision—implying strongly that the employer may use a ground of decision that is not age, even if it varies with age. What else could be the purpose of this language? Surely it does not mean simply that "only age

discrimination is age discrimination." "The prohibition and the exception appear identical. The sentence is incomprehensible unless the prohibition forbids disparate treatment and the exception authorizes disparate impact." Douglas Laycock, Continuing Violations, Disparate Impact in Compensation, and Other Title VII Issues, 49 L. & Contemp. Prob. 53, 55 (Aut.1986) (referring to the identical structure of the Equal Pay Act of 1963). In Washington County v. Gunther, 452 U.S. 161, 170–71 (1981), the Court concluded that the "factor other than sex" language in the Equal Pay Act has independent significance. See also Los Angeles v. Manhart, 435 U.S. 702, 710–11 n. 20, 713 n. 24 (1978), holding the "factor other than sex" exception to the Equal Pay Act precludes reliance on disparate impact analysis. Should not the parallel structure of the ADEA, enacted four years later, yield the same result? There are other differences between Title VII and the ADEA. For example, § 4(f)(2) allows age to be used explicitly. Then there is § 4(f)(3), stating that an employer may discharge anyone for "cause"—another clause missing from Title VII. "Cause," like "qualified," is a continuous rather than dichotomous variable; not being productive enough to cover your wage is "cause."

A growing literature on education, training, employment, and other aspects of human capital suggests that there may be times when employers will pay wages that do not represent the employees' marginal products. For example, while receiving firm-specific training the employee may receive a wage exceeding his product; this is how the firm finances the training (for which the employee will not pay, because it has no use outside the firm). Later the firm will recoup its investment by paying less than the marginal product. See Becker, Human Capital 26–37, 216–23. Other firms that give their employees access to trade secrets or put them in positions of trust may try to cement the employees' loyalty (or honesty) with "golden handcuffs"—wages in excess of the employees' marginal product, a form of special compensation the employee forfeits if he leaves the firm. E.g., Gary S. Becker & George J. Stigler, Law Enforcement, Malfeasance, and Compensation of Enforcers, 3 J. Legal Studies 1 (1974). Still other firms may pay employees slightly less than their marginal product early in their careers, knowing that as each employee's productivity declines at the end of his career, the firm will be paying more than marginal product (thus paying the employee his due over the life cycle). This gives employees strong reasons to stick with their firms and be more productive throughout their careers, which in turn yields society the benefit of everyone's abilities. Edward P. Lazear, Agency, Earnings Profiles, Productivity and Hours Restrictions, 71 Am. Econ. Rev. 606 (1981); Robert Hutchens, Delayed Payment Contracts and a Firm's Propensity to Hire Older Workers, 4 J. Labor Econ. 439 (1986). But cf. Peter Kuhn, Wages, Effort, and Incentive Compatibility in Life-Cycle Employment Contracts, 4 J. Labor Econ. 28 (1986).

> Whenever the age-wage profile of a class of employees includes a period of compensation at more than marginal product, the firm may be inclined to behave opportunistically—to fire the employee as soon as his current productivity no longer covers his current wage. A firm's desire to attract new employees will curtail this opportunism, to the extent new hires learn of the firm's reputation (or depend on a union to police the firm's behavior). When the firm encounters economic trouble or for some other reason plans to shrink, it need not worry about scaring away bright new employees; it is out of that market. The distressed or shrinking firm may try to dispose of higher paid, older employees, cheating them out of the high compensation at the end of their careers. A disparate impact approach under the ADEA might help to curtail this opportunism. . . .

4. **The Life-Cycle Theory of Earnings.** As the excerpts from his opinion reveal, Judge Easterbrook relies upon the "life-cycle theory of earnings" to provide a rationale and a guide for interpreting the ADEA. This theory offers a justification for prohibitions against age discrimination distinct from those against discrimination on the basis of race or sex. The life-cycle theory seeks to explain variations in earnings by age as a form of postponed compensation that provides optimal incentives both for workers to remain on the job and to continue to work hard and for firms to invest in workers by giving them on-the-job training. The implicit contract between workers and employers that underlies the life-cycle theory can be understood by dividing the average employee's career into three stages. In the first stage, compensation paid to the employee exceeds her productivity because she receives additional compensation in the form of on-the-job training. During this phase, the employer would be harmed if the worker left since the employer is paying more for the worker than the employer receives in output. The employer is willing to make this up-front investment in the worker because, during the second stage, the relationship between compensation and productivity is reversed. The employee's productivity now exceeds her compensation, even if that compensation has been increased through promotions and seniority. During this period, the employer makes money on her work. But, of course, paying the worker less than she is worth creates an instability. She may decide to leave or not to work as hard. To avoid this outcome, the employer promises that in the third stage, as the worker ages and slows down on the job, the relationship between compensation and productivity will again reverse and the employer will again pay the employee more than the employer receives in worker output. This provides the worker with an attractive incentive to work hard during the years of peak productivity, since the worker knows that, with increasing age, her productivity will fall but her compensation will stay high or even continue to increase. If the implied contract is working properly, the worker should leave the firm at the point where compensation and productivity are equally balanced over the worker's entire career. But once the worker's productivity falls below her salary, the employer then has an incentive to discharge her before she has been fully compensated for her productivity over her entire career. Laws against age

discrimination can then be used to prevent such opportunistic behavior by employers.

Nevertheless, it is not clear that the ADEA is necessary or optimal in dealing with issues of age and employment, as the life-cycle theory might at first suggest. First, while the life-cycle theory is premised on an implied contract, there is nothing that prevents workers from entering explicit contracts to protect the rights of both workers and employers during the early days of worker training and the final period of declining productivity. Presumably, at least some employees can protect themselves from exploitation by negotiating for pension benefits or other contractual provisions that protect them from discharge late in their careers. Legislation, like ERISA, that protects pension benefits reinforces these contractual means of preventing employer opportunism. The ADEA also recognizes the ability of highly paid employees to protect themselves, by exempting certain executives over the age of 65 from coverage. 29 U.S.C. § 631(c).

But a second problem with the ADEA, if it is designed to address the complex issues posed by the life-cycle theory, is of even more concern. As noted, the life-cycle theory presupposes that, at some point, the worker's total lifetime contributions to productivity will exactly equal the lifetime compensation she has received. At that point, the employer should be free to discharge her. Otherwise, the aging worker is actually taking advantage of the employer by breaching the implied contract to leave when the point of balance is reached. The ADEA originally permitted mandatory retirement, both because it did not cover individuals over the age of 65 and through a provision that explicitly allowed mandatory retirement. These provisions, however, have since been deleted from the statute which, in its current form, has neither an age ceiling on coverage nor provisions allowing mandatory retirement. §§ 631(a); 623(f)(2)(A). The only substitute for them that plausibly serves the same function is the set of provisions for voluntary early retirement. These return to an explicit contractual basis, but one with a default rule that favors the employee, as the basis for terminating the employment relationship. § 623(f)(2)(B). In general, the ADEA makes it harder to fire workers when they have reached the point of appropriate termination under the life-cycle theory. The Act also makes it more difficult to retain such workers while simply paying them according to their diminished productivity. The result is that, because of the law, employers are pushed to keep some workers they don't want and pay them more than they are worth.

5. The ADEA and Claims for Wrongful Discharge. Instead of narrowing the scope of the ADEA, as the life-cycle theory of earnings indicates, the scope of its protection could be broadened, to protect all workers from wrongful discharge. This form of protection currently is available to employees only under state law or through civil service laws, collective bargaining agreements, or other special forms of employment. Although the grounds for claiming wrongful discharge vary according to these different sources of law, most allow a more extensive inquiry than the ADEA into the reasons offered by the employer to justify a disputed discharge decision. Strictly speaking, under the ADEA, the only inquiry is whether age entered into the employer's decision-making process, not whether any other reasons the employer might have had for discharging the employee were valid. Under the law of wrongful discharge, these reasons can be re-examined, more or less extensively depending upon the legal regime that protects the employee's job. E.g., McCoy v. WGN Continental Broad. Co., 957 F.2d 368, 370–73 (7th Cir. 1992); Hanchey v. Energas Co., 925 F.2d 96, 98 (5th Cir. 1990); Lucas v. Dover Corp., Norris Div., 857 F.2d 1397, 1403–04 (10th Cir. 1988).

While this difference is clear in theory, it loses much of its clarity in practice. As with claims of disparate treatment under Title VII, the "legitimate, nondiscriminatory reason" offered by the employer becomes more persuasive as the reasons themselves have more merit on their own. The question whether these reasons have been used as a pretext for discrimination often blurs imperceptibly into the question whether the reasons themselves are valid. The juries that typically hear ADEA cases are especially likely to fall into this tendency. If so, it is worth asking how different the ADEA really is, in practice, from the law of wrongful discharge. Indeed, the proliferation of prohibited grounds of discrimination gradually transforms the question of what an employer cannot do into what an employer can properly do. The law of discrimination, instead of forming a limit on the employer's otherwise broad discretion, becomes a series of commands that leaves that discretion substantially eroded. The ADEA raises this question in particularly acute form, since it protects all workers who are at least 40 years old. They are, among the class of workers who lose their jobs involuntarily, those most likely to raise claims of wrongful discharge, often in the same action as a claim under the ADEA.

For a critical account of how claims of wrongful discharge might operate to freeze the status quo by protecting the jobs of incumbent employees at the expense of new applicants for employment, see Julie C. Suk, Discrimination at Will: Job Security Protections and Equal Employment Opportunity in Conflict, 60 Stan. L. Rev. 73 (2007). Professor Suk argues that the experience in France shows that greater protection of incumbent employees results in fewer opportunities for new entrants into the job market, particularly members of previously excluded minorities.

6. **Early Retirement.** As already noted, the ADEA permits voluntary early retirement plans, which generally favor employees who have not yet reached normal retirement age. Pension plans can make such classifications on the basis of age only if they are cost-justified according to EEOC regulations or if they are part of "a voluntary early retirement incentive plan consistent with the relevant purpose or purposes of [the ADEA]." 29 U.S.C. § 623(f)(2). Unlike the employer in *Hazen Paper*, employers can use voluntary early retirement plans to encourage employees to leave their jobs only at the cost of granting them vested pension rights, often in excess of those payable under the employer's standard pension plan.

Another provision also restricts bargains between employers and their employees, in this case over waiver of their claims under the ADEA. § 626(f). Such waivers, of course, figure prominently in the settlement of ADEA claims. All waivers must be for additional consideration, apart from benefits to which the employee is already entitled, and must allow the employee to consider the agreement over a specified waiting period. Failure to observe the requisite waiting period can result in the employee revoking the waiver even without tendering back the benefits received for it. See Oubre v. Entergy Operations, Inc., 522 U.S. 422, 428 (1998). Further restrictions apply to waivers "in connection with an exit incentive or other employment termination program offered to a group of employees." 29 U.S.C. § 626(f)(1)(H). This last provision obviously includes early retirement plans.

The details of these provisions are exceedingly complex, as are the provisions that govern retirement plans generally. See § 623(i), (k), (*l*). These provisions pose the basic question of policy whether special provisions targeted on the benefits particularly needed by older workers are a preferred means of protecting them rather than a general prohibition against discrimination on the basis of age. For discussion of waivers of rights by older workers, see Michael C. Harper, Age-Based Exit Incentives, Coercion, and the Prospective Waiver of ADEA Rights: The Failure of the Older Workers Benefit Protection Act, 79 Va. L. Rev. 1271 (1993); Gary Minda, Opportunistic Downsizing of Aging Workers: The 1990s Version of Age and Pension Discrimination in Employment, 48 Hastings L.J. 511 (1997).

7. **Bibliography.** For general discussions of the nature of age discrimination, see Howard C. Eglit, Age Discrimination (2d ed. 1994); Richard A. Posner, Aging and Old Age (1995); Howard Eglit, Age Bias in the American Workplace—An Overview, 3 J. Int'l Aging L. & Pol'y 99 (2009); Christine Jolls, Hands-Tying and the Age Discrimination in Employment Act, 74 Tex. L. Rev. 1813 (1996); Nina A. Kohn, Rethinking the Constitutionality of Age Discrimination: A Challenge to a Decades-Old Consensus, 44 U.C. Davis L. Rev. 213 (2010); Symposium, Aging in the US: The Next Civil Rights Movement?, 21 Temp. Pol. & Civ. Rts. L. Rev. 303 (2012); Symposium, Age Discrimination, 32 Hastings L.J. 1093 (1981); Symposium, The Aging American Workforce: Thirty Years Under the Age Discrimination in Employment Act, 31 U. Rich. L. Rev. 579 (1997).

For articles on *Gross* and related developments under the ADEA, see Michael Foreman, *Gross v. FBL Financial Services*—Oh So Gross!, 40 U. Mem. L. Rev. 681 (2010); Michael C. Harper, The Causation Standard in Federal Employment Law: *Gross v. FBL Financial Services, Inc.*, and the Unfulfilled Promise of the Civil Rights Act of 1991, 58 Buff. L. Rev. 69 (2010); Judith J. Johnson, Reasonable Factors Other Than Age: The Emerging Specter of Ageist Stereotypes, 33 Seattle U. L. Rev. 49 (2009); Martin J. Katz, Gross Disunity, 114 Penn St. L. Rev. 857 (2010); Allan G. King, "Two or Three Standard Deviations" from What? How *Gross v. FBL Financial Services* Changes the Statistical Benchmark in ADEA Collective Actions, 37 Employee Rel. L.J. 17 (Summer 2011); Bran Noonan, The Impact of *Gross v. FBL Financial Services, Inc.* and the Meaning of the But-or Requirement, 43 Suffolk U. L. Rev. 921 (2010); Julie C. Suk, Discrimination at Will: Job Security Protections and Equal Employment Opportunity in Conflict, 60 Stan. L. Rev. 73 (2007).

See also Leslie P. Francis & Anita Silvers, Bringing Age Discrimination and Disability Discrimination Together: Too Few Intersections, Too Many

Interstices, 11 Marq. Elder's Advisor 139 (2009); Joanna Lahey, State Age Protection Laws and the Age Discrimination in Employment Act, 51 J.L. & Econ. 433 (2008).

C. DISPARATE IMPACT

INTRODUCTORY NOTES ON DISPARATE IMPACT UNDER THE ADEA

1. ***Hazen Paper Co. v. Biggins.*** The Supreme Court first discussed claims of disparate treatment and disparate impact under the ADEA in Hazen Paper Co. v. Biggins, 507 U.S. 604 (1993). The plaintiff in that case alleged that he had been discharged because his pension was about to vest, asserting claims both under the ADEA and under the Employment Retirement Income Security Act (ERISA), 29 U.S.C. § 1140. The Supreme Court addressed only the ADEA claim, holding that the plaintiff had not proved disparate treatment solely by evidence that his pension was about to vest. According to the Court, the vesting of a pension could not serve as a "proxy" for age discrimination.

A basic premise of the decision in *Hazen Paper* was that a claim under ERISA, in and of itself, does not generate a claim under the ADEA. A claim under ERISA resembles one under the ADEA in that it identifies a prohibited ground for the employer's decision. It is, however, narrower than a claim under the ADEA because the prohibited ground is much more narrowly specified. It does not concern age, but solely the denial of the right to pension benefits. Beneath this simple doctrinal difference in the two claims lies a fundamental difference in the policy of the statutes. The ADEA protects older workers on the model of discrimination against other groups. ERISA protects them by taking account of their special needs for income after retirement. It follows that a violation of one statute does not necessarily result in a violation of the other. This was particularly true on the facts of *Hazen Paper*, where the pension would have vested after only a relatively short period, ten years of employment. This short period might have led the Court to find no inference of disparate treatment under the ADEA. The longer the period of vesting, the stronger the inference that proximity to vesting does play such a role. Would the Court have reached the same result if the period of vesting were 30 years? The opinion leaves this issue unsettled. It does, however, allow a range of other evidence to establish that age also played a role in the decision to discharge the plaintiff.

In *Hazen Paper*, the Supreme Court also went out of its way to express doubt about the existence of any claim of disparate impact under the ADEA. The original text of the ADEA and Title VII would not have supported this suggestion, since the same language that led to the decisions recognizing the theory of disparate impact under Title VII also appears in the ADEA. All of this changed with the Civil Rights Act of 1991, which codified the theory of disparate impact under Title VII but not under the ADEA, even though the Act also made other changes in the latter statute. See generally Howard Eglit, The Age Discrimination in Employment Act, Title VII, and the Civil Rights Act of 1991: Three Acts and a Dog That Didn't Bark, 39 Wayne L. Rev. 1093, 1127–50 (1993).

2. **Implications of *Hazen Paper*.** The difference between the ADEA and Title VII, as both were amended by the Civil Rights Act of 1991, led to a conflict among the circuits on the application of the theory of disparate impact to claims under the ADEA. See, e.g., Adams v. Florida Power Corp., 255 F.3d 1322, 1324–25 (11th Cir. 2001), cert. dismissed as improvidently granted, 535 U.S. 228 (2002) (finding no claim of disparate impact under the ADEA and citing conflicting decisions from other circuits). Other decisions questioned the probative value of statistical evidence in ADEA cases, extending the doubts expressed in *Hazen Paper* to class claims of disparate treatment as well. Moore v. McGraw Edison Co., 804 F.2d 1026, 1031 (8th Cir. 1986).

Whether or not these doubts were justified depends less on doctrinal formulations of the standard of proof under the ADEA than on the underlying purposes that the statute serves. Is it designed, like Title VII, to provide opportunities to workers who have historically been denied employment? Or, because most older workers already successfully have held jobs, usually with the employer they are now suing, does the ADEA only protect them when their careers are drawing to a close? The broader purpose of opening up job opportunities requires a strong version of the theory of disparate impact to make sure that neutral employment practices are not used as obstacles to continue to exclude workers from employment. The narrower purpose requires only a weaker version of the theory, or reliance entirely upon claims of disparate treatment, to assure that neutral practices are not used as a pretext for discrimination. In the next principal case, the Supreme Court resolved these questions.

3. **Bibliography.** For discussion of *Hazen Paper* and its implications, see Robert J. Gregory, There is Life in That Old (I Mean, More "Senior") Dog Yet: The Age-Proxy Theory After *Hazen Paper Co. v. Biggins*, 11 Hofstra Lab. L.J. 391 (1994); Judith J. Johnson, Semantic Cover for Age Discrimination: Twilight of the ADEA, 42 Wayne L. Rev. 1 (1995); Carla J. Rozycki & Patricia A. Bronte, A Game of Numbers: ADEA Compliance and Litigation, 18 Lab. Law. 203 (2002).

Smith v. City of Jackson

544 U.S. 228 (2005).

■ JUSTICE STEVENS announced the judgment of the Court and delivered the opinion of the Court with respect to Parts I, II, and IV, and an opinion with respect to Part III, in which JUSTICE SOUTER, JUSTICE GINSBURG, and JUSTICE BREYER join.

Petitioners, police and public safety officers employed by the city of Jackson, Mississippi (hereinafter City), contend that salary increases received in 1999 violated the Age Discrimination in Employment Act of 1967 because they were less generous to officers over the age of 40 than to younger officers. Their suit raises the question whether the "disparate-impact" theory of recovery announced in Griggs v. Duke Power Co., 401

U.S. 424 (1971), for cases brought under Title VII of the Civil Rights Act of 1964, is cognizable under the ADEA. . . .

I

On October 1, 1998, the City adopted a pay plan granting raises to all City employees. The stated purpose of the plan was to "attract and retain qualified people, provide incentive for performance, maintain competitiveness with other public sector agencies and ensure equitable compensation to all employees regardless of age, sex, race and/or disability." On May 1, 1999, a revision of the plan, which was motivated, at least in part, by the City's desire to bring the starting salaries of police officers up to the regional average, granted raises to all police officers and police dispatchers. Those who had less than five years of tenure received proportionately greater raises when compared to their former pay than those with more seniority. Although some officers over the age of 40 had less than five years of service, most of the older officers had more.

Petitioners are a group of older officers who filed suit under the ADEA claiming both that the City deliberately discriminated against them because of their age (the "disparate-treatment" claim) and that they were "adversely affected" by the plan because of their age (the "disparate impact" claim). The District Court granted summary judgment to the City on both claims. The Court of Appeals held that the ruling on the former claim was premature because petitioners were entitled to further discovery on the issue of intent, but it affirmed the dismissal of the disparate impact claim. Over one judge's dissent, the majority concluded that disparate impact claims are categorically unavailable under the ADEA. Both the majority and the dissent assumed that the facts alleged by petitioners would entitle them to relief under the reasoning of *Griggs*.

We granted the officers' petition for certiorari, 541 U.S. 958 (2004), and now hold that the ADEA does authorize recovery in "disparate impact" cases comparable to *Griggs*. Because, however, we conclude that petitioners have not set forth a valid disparate impact claim, we affirm.

II

During the deliberations that preceded the enactment of the Civil Rights Act of 1964, Congress considered and rejected proposed amendments that would have included older workers among the classes protected from employment discrimination. Congress did, however, request the Secretary of Labor to "make a full and complete study of the factors which might tend to result in discrimination in employment because of age and of the consequences of such discrimination on the economy and individuals affected." § 715, 78 Stat. 265. The Secretary's report, submitted in response to Congress' request, noted that there was little discrimination arising from dislike or intolerance of older people, but that "arbitrary" discrimination did result from certain age limits. Report of the Secretary of Labor, The Older American Worker: Age Discrimination in Employment 22 (June 1965), reprinted in U.S. Equal

Employment Opportunity Commission, Legislative History of the Age Discrimination in Employment Act (1981) (hereinafter Wirtz Report). Moreover, the report observed that discriminatory effects resulted from "[i]nstitutional arrangements that indirectly restrict the employment of older workers." Id., at 15.

In response to that report Congress directed the Secretary to propose remedial legislation, see Fair Labor Standards Amendments of 1966, Pub.L. 89–601, § 606, 80 Stat. 845, and then acted favorably on his proposal. As enacted in 1967, § 4(a)(2) of the ADEA, now codified as 29 U.S.C. § 623(a)(2), provided that it shall be unlawful for an employer "to limit, segregate, or classify his employees in any way which would deprive or tend to deprive any individual of employment opportunities or otherwise adversely affect his status as an employee, because of such individual's age. . . ." 81 Stat. 603. Except for substitution of the word "age" for the words "race, color, religion, sex, or national origin," the language of that provision in the ADEA is identical to that found in § 703(a)(2) of the Civil Rights Act of 1964 (Title VII). Other provisions of the ADEA also parallel the earlier statute. Unlike Title VII, however, § 4(f)(1) of the ADEA, contains language that significantly narrows its coverage by permitting any "otherwise prohibited" action "where the differentiation is based on reasonable factors other than age" (hereinafter RFOA provision).

III

In determining whether the ADEA authorizes disparate-impact claims, we begin with the premise that when Congress uses the same language in two statutes having similar purposes, particularly when one is enacted shortly after the other, it is appropriate to presume that Congress intended that text to have the same meaning in both statutes. We have consistently applied that presumption to language in the ADEA that was "derived in haec verba from Title VII." Lorillard v. Pons, 434 U.S. 575 (1978). Our unanimous interpretation of § 703(a)(2) of the Title VII in *Griggs* is therefore a precedent of compelling importance.

In *Griggs*, a case decided four years after the enactment of the ADEA, we considered whether § 703 of Title VII prohibited an employer "from requiring a high school education or passing of a standardized general intelligence test as a condition of employment in or transfer to jobs when (a) neither standard is shown to be significantly related to successful job performance, (b) both requirements operate to disqualify Negroes at a substantially higher rate than white applicants, and (c) the jobs in question formerly had been filled only by white employees as part of a longstanding practice of giving preference to whites." 401 U.S., at 425–426. Accepting the Court of Appeals' conclusion that the employer had adopted the diploma and test requirements without any intent to discriminate, we held that good faith "does not redeem employment procedures or testing mechanisms that operate as 'built-in headwinds' for minority groups and are unrelated to measuring job capability." Id., at 432.

We explained that Congress had "directed the thrust of the Act to the *consequences* of employment practices, not simply the motivation." Ibid. We relied on the fact that history is "filled with examples of men and women who rendered highly effective performance without the conventional badges of accomplishment in terms of certificates, diplomas, or degrees. Diplomas and tests are useful servants, but Congress has mandated the commonsense proposition that they are not to become masters of reality." Id., at 433. And we noted that the Equal Employment Opportunity Commission (EEOC), which had enforcement responsibility, had issued guidelines that accorded with our view. Id., at 433–434. We thus squarely held that § 703(a)(2) of Title VII did not require a showing of discriminatory intent.[1]

While our opinion in *Griggs* relied primarily on the purposes of the Act, buttressed by the fact that the EEOC had endorsed the same view, we have subsequently noted that our holding represented the better reading of the statutory text as well. See Watson v. Fort Worth Bank & Trust, 487 U.S. 977, 991 (1988). Neither § 703(a)(2) nor the comparable language in the ADEA simply prohibits actions that "limit, segregate, or classify" persons; rather the language prohibits such actions that "deprive any individual of employment opportunities or *otherwise adversely affect* his status as an employee, because of such individual's" race or age. . . . Thus the text focuses on the *effects* of the action on the employee rather than the motivation for the action of the employer.[2]

[1] The congressional purposes on which we relied in *Griggs* have a striking parallel to two important points made in the Wirtz Report. Just as the *Griggs* opinion ruled out discrimination based on racial animus as a problem in that case, the Wirtz Report concluded that there was no significant discrimination of that kind so far as older workers are concerned. Wirtz Report 23. And just as *Griggs* recognized that the high school diploma requirement, which was unrelated to job performance, had an unfair impact on African-Americans who had received inferior educational opportunities in segregated schools, 401 U.S., at 430, the Wirtz Report identified the identical obstacle to the employment of older workers. "Any formal employment standard which requires, for example, a high school diploma will obviously work against the employment of many older workers—unfairly if, despite his limited schooling, an older worker's years of experience have given him the relevant equivalent of a high school education." Wirtz Report 21. Thus, just as the statutory text is identical, there is a remarkable similarity between the congressional goals we cited in *Griggs* and those present in the Wirtz Report.

[2] In reaching a contrary conclusion, Justice O'CONNOR ignores key textual differences between § 4(a)(1), which does not encompass disparate impact liability, and § 4(a)(2). Section (a)(1) makes it unlawful for an employer "to fail or refuse to hire . . . *any individual* . . . because of *such individual's* age." (Emphasis added.) The focus of the section is on the employer's actions with respect to the targeted individual. Paragraph (a)(2), however, makes it unlawful for an employer "to limit . . . his *employees* in any way that would deprive or tend to deprive *any individual* of employment opportunities or otherwise adversely affect his status as an employee, because of *such individual's* age." (Emphasis added.) Unlike in paragraph (a)(2), there is thus an incongruity between the employer's actions—which are focused on his employees generally—and the individual employee who adversely suffers because of those actions. Thus, an employer who classifies his employees without respect to age may still be liable under the terms of this paragraph if such classification adversely affects the employee because of that employee's age the very definition of disparate impact. Justice O'CONNOR is therefore quite wrong to suggest that the textual differences between the two paragraphs are unimportant.

Griggs, which interpreted the identical text at issue here, thus strongly suggests that a disparate impact theory should be cognizable under the ADEA. Indeed, for over two decades after our decision in *Griggs*, the Courts of Appeals uniformly interpreted the ADEA as authorizing recovery on a "disparate-impact" theory in appropriate cases. It was only after our decision in Hazen Paper Co. v. Biggins, 507 U.S. 604 (1993), that some of those courts concluded that the ADEA did not authorize a disparate-impact theory of liability. Our opinion in *Hazen Paper*, however, did not address or comment on the issue we decide today. . . .

The Court of Appeals' categorical rejection of disparate-impact liability, like Justice O'CONNOR's, rested primarily on the RFOA provision and the majority's analysis of legislative history. As we have already explained, we think the history of the enactment of the ADEA, with particular reference to the Wirtz Report, supports the pre-*Hazen Paper* consensus concerning disparate impact liability. And *Hazen Paper* itself contains the response to the concern over the RFOA provision.

The RFOA provision provides that it shall not be unlawful for an employer "to take any action otherwise prohibited under subsectio[n] (a) . . . where the differentiation is based on reasonable factors other than age discrimination. . . ." In most disparate treatment cases, if an employer in fact acted on a factor other than age, the action would not be prohibited under subsection (a) in the first place. In those disparate treatment cases, such as in *Hazen Paper* itself, the RFOA provision is simply unnecessary to avoid liability under the ADEA, since there was no prohibited action in the first place. The RFOA provision is not, as Justice O'CONNOR suggests, a "safe harbor from liability," (emphasis deleted), since there would be no liability under § 4(a).

In disparate impact cases, however, the allegedly "otherwise prohibited" activity is not based on age. It is, accordingly, in cases involving disparate impact claims that the RFOA provision plays its principal role by precluding liability if the adverse impact was attributable to a nonage factor that was "reasonable." Rather than support an argument that disparate impact is unavailable under the ADEA, the RFOA provision actually supports the contrary conclusion.

Finally, we note that both the Department of Labor, which initially drafted the legislation, and the EEOC, which is the agency charged by Congress with responsibility for implementing the statute, 29 U.S.C. § 628, have consistently interpreted the ADEA to authorize relief on a disparate impact theory. The initial regulations, while not mentioning disparate impact by name, nevertheless permitted such claims if the employer relied on a factor that was not related to age. 29 CFR § 860.103(f)(1)(i) (1970) (barring physical fitness requirements that were not "reasonably necessary for the specific work to be performed"). See also § 1625.7 (2004) (setting forth the standards for a disparate-impact claim).

The text of the statute, as interpreted in *Griggs*, the RFOA provision, and the EEOC regulations all support petitioners' view. We therefore conclude that it was error for the Court of Appeals to hold that the disparate impact theory of liability is categorically unavailable under the ADEA.

IV

Two textual differences between the ADEA and Title VII make it clear that even though both statutes authorize recovery on a disparate impact theory, the scope of disparate impact liability under ADEA is narrower than under Title VII. The first is the RFOA provision, which we have already identified. The second is the amendment to Title VII contained in the Civil Rights Act of 1991, 105 Stat. 1071. One of the purposes of that amendment was to modify the Court's holding in Wards Cove Packing Co. v. Atonio, 490 U.S. 642 (1989), a case in which we narrowly construed the employer's exposure to liability on a disparate impact theory. See Civil Rights Act of 1991, § 2, 105 Stat. 1071. While the relevant 1991 amendments expanded the coverage of Title VII, they did not amend the ADEA or speak to the subject of age discrimination. Hence, *Wards Cove*'s pre-1991 interpretation of Title VII's identical language remains applicable to the ADEA.

Congress' decision to limit the coverage of the ADEA by including the RFOA provision is consistent with the fact that age, unlike race or other classifications protected by Title VII, not uncommonly has relevance to an individual's capacity to engage in certain types of employment. To be sure, Congress recognized that this is not always the case, and that society may perceive those differences to be larger or more consequential than they are in fact. However, as Secretary Wirtz noted in his report, "certain circumstances . . . unquestionably affect older workers more strongly, as a group, than they do younger workers." Wirtz Report 28. Thus, it is not surprising that certain employment criteria that are routinely used may be reasonable despite their adverse impact on older workers as a group. Moreover, intentional discrimination on the basis of age has not occurred at the same levels as discrimination against those protected by Title VII. While the ADEA reflects Congress' intent to give older workers employment opportunities whenever possible, the RFOA provision reflects this historical difference.

Turning to the case before us, we initially note that petitioners have done little more than point out that the pay plan at issue is relatively less generous to older workers than to younger workers. They have not identified any specific test, requirement, or practice within the pay plan that has an adverse impact on older workers. As we held in *Wards Cove*, it is not enough to simply allege that there is a disparate impact on workers, or point to a generalized policy that leads to such an impact. Rather, the employee is " 'responsible for isolating and identifying the *specific* employment practices that are allegedly responsible for any observed statistical disparities.' " 490 U.S., at 656 (emphasis added) (quoting *Watson*, 487 U.S., at 994). Petitioners have failed to do so. Their failure to identify the specific practice being challenged is the sort of omission that could "result in employers being potentially liable for 'the myriad of innocent causes that may lead to statistical imbalances. . . .' " 490 U.S., at 657. In this case not only did petitioners thus err by failing to identify the relevant practice, but it is also clear from the record that the City's plan was based on reasonable factors other than age.

The plan divided each of five basic positions—police officer, master police officer, police sergeant, police lieutenant, and deputy police chief—into a series of steps and half-steps. The wage for each range was based on a survey of comparable communities in the Southeast. Employees were then assigned a step (or half-step) within their position that corresponded to the lowest step that would still give the individual a 2% raise. Most of the officers were in the three lowest ranks; in each of those ranks there were officers under age 40 and officers over 40. In none did their age affect their compensation. The few officers in the two highest ranks are all over 40. Their raises, though higher in dollar amount than the raises given to junior officers, represented a smaller percentage of their salaries, which of course are higher than the salaries paid to their juniors. They are members of the class complaining of the "disparate impact" of the award.

Petitioners' evidence established two principal facts: First, almost two thirds (66.2%) of the officers under 40 received raises of more than 10% while less than half (45.3%) of those over 40 did. Second, the average percentage increase for the entire class of officers with less than five years of tenure was somewhat higher than the percentage for those with more seniority. Because older officers tended to occupy more senior positions, on average they received smaller increases when measured as a percentage of their salary. The basic explanation for the differential was the City's perceived need to raise the salaries of junior officers to make them competitive with comparable positions in the market.

Thus, the disparate impact is attributable to the City's decision to give raises based on seniority and position. Reliance on seniority and rank is unquestionably reasonable given the City's goal of raising employees' salaries to match those in surrounding communities. In sum, we hold that the City's decision to grant a larger raise to lower echelon employees for the purpose of bringing salaries in line with that of surrounding police forces was a decision based on a "reasonable factor other than age" that responded to the City's legitimate goal of retaining police officers. Cf. MacPherson v. University of Montevallo, 922 F.2d 766, 772 (C.A.11 1991).

While there may have been other reasonable ways for the City to achieve its goals, the one selected was not unreasonable. Unlike the business necessity test, which asks whether there are other ways for the employer to achieve its goals that do not result in a disparate impact on a protected class, the reasonableness inquiry includes no such requirement.

Accordingly, while we do not agree with the Court of Appeals' holding that that the disparate-impact theory of recovery is never available under the ADEA, we affirm its judgment.

It is so ordered.

THE CHIEF JUSTICE took no part in the decision of this case.

■ JUSTICE SCALIA, concurring in part and concurring in the judgment.

I concur in the judgment of the Court, and join all except Part III of its opinion. As to that Part, I agree with all of the Court's reasoning, but would find it a basis, not for independent determination of the disparate impact question, but for deferral to the reasonable views of the Equal Employment Opportunity Commission (EEOC or Commission) pursuant to Chevron U.S.A. Inc. v. Natural Resources Defense Council, Inc., 467 U.S. 837 (1984). See General Dynamics Land Systems, Inc. v. Cline, 540 U.S. 581, 601–602 (2004) (SCALIA, J., dissenting).

This is an absolutely classic case for deference to agency interpretation. The Age Discrimination in Employment Act of 1967 (ADEA), 29 U.S.C. § 621 et seq., confers upon the EEOC authority to issue "such rules and regulations as it may consider necessary or appropriate for carrying out the" ADEA. § 628. Pursuant to this authority, the EEOC promulgated, after notice and comment rulemaking, see 46 Fed.Reg. 47724, 47727 (1981), a regulation that reads as follows:

> "When an employment practice, including a test, is claimed as a basis for different treatment of employees or applicants for employment on the grounds that it is a 'factor other than' age, and such a practice has an adverse impact on individuals within the protected age group, it can only be justified as a business necessity." 29 CFR § 1625.7(d) (2004).

The statement of the EEOC which accompanied publication of the agency's final interpretation of the ADEA said the following regarding this regulation: "Paragraph (d) of § 1625.7 has been rewritten to make it clear that employment criteria that are age neutral on their face but which nevertheless have a disparate impact on members of the protected age group must be justified as a business necessity. See Laugesen v. Anaconda Co., 510 F.2d 307 (6th Cir.1975); Griggs v. Duke Power Co., 401 U.S. 424 (1971)." 46 Fed.Reg., at 47725. The regulation affirmed, moreover, what had been the longstanding position of the Department of Labor, the agency that previously administered the ADEA, see 29 CFR § 860.103(f)(1)(i) (1970). And finally, the Commission has appeared in numerous cases in the lower courts, both as a party and as amicus curiae, to defend the position that the ADEA authorizes disparate impact claims. Even under the unduly constrained standards of agency deference recited in United States v. Mead Corp., 533 U.S. 218 (2001), the EEOC's reasonable view that the ADEA authorizes disparate impact claims is deserving of deference. Id., at 229–231, and n. 12. A fortiori, it is entitled to deference under the pre-*Mead* formulation of *Chevron*, to which I continue to adhere. See 533 U.S., at 256–257 (Scalia, J., dissenting). . . .

The EEOC has express authority to promulgate rules and regulations interpreting the ADEA. It has exercised that authority to recognize disparate-impact claims. And, for the reasons given by the plurality opinion, its position is eminently reasonable. In my view, that is sufficient to resolve this case.

■ JUSTICE O'CONNOR, with whom JUSTICE KENNEDY and JUSTICE THOMAS join, concurring in the judgment.

"Disparate treatment . . . captures the essence of what Congress sought to prohibit in the [Age Discrimination in Employment Act of 1967 (ADEA), 29 U.S.C. § 621 et seq.] It is the very essence of age discrimination for an older employee to be fired because the employer believes that productivity and competence decline with old age." Hazen Paper Co. v. Biggins, 507 U.S. 604, 610 (1993). In the nearly four decades since the ADEA's enactment, however, we have never read the statute to impose liability upon an employer without proof of discriminatory intent. See ibid.; Markham v. Geller, 451 U.S. 945 (1981) (Rehnquist, J., dissenting from denial of certiorari). I decline to join the Court in doing so today.

I would instead affirm the judgment below on the ground that disparate impact claims are not cognizable under the ADEA. The ADEA's text, legislative history, and purposes together make clear that Congress did not intend the statute to authorize such claims. Moreover, the significant differences between the ADEA and Title VII of the Civil Rights Act of 1964 counsel against transposing to the former our construction of the latter in Griggs v. Duke Power Co., 401 U.S. 424 (1971). Finally, the agencies charged with administering the ADEA have never authoritatively construed the statute's prohibitory language to impose disparate impact liability. Thus, on the precise question of statutory interpretation now before us, there is no reasoned agency reading of the text to which we might defer. . . .

III

The plurality and Justice Scalia offer two principal arguments in favor of their reading of the statute: that the relevant provision of the ADEA should be read in pari materia with the parallel provision of Title VII, and that we should give interpretive weight or deference to agency statements relating to disparate impact liability. I find neither argument persuasive.

A

The language of the ADEA's prohibitory provisions was modeled on, and is nearly identical to, parallel provisions in Title VII. Because *Griggs*, supra, held that Title VII's § 703(a)(2) permits disparate impact claims, the plurality concludes that we should read § 4(a)(2) of the ADEA similarly.

Obviously, this argument would be a great deal more convincing had *Griggs* been decided before the ADEA was enacted. In that case, we could safely assume that Congress had notice (and therefore intended) that the language at issue here would be read to authorize disparate impact claims. But *Griggs* was decided four years after the ADEA's enactment, and there is no reason to suppose that Congress in 1967 could have foreseen the interpretation of Title VII that was to come. See Fogerty v. Fantasy, Inc., 510 U.S. 517, 523, n. 9 (1994). . . .

B

The plurality asserts that the agencies charged with the ADEA's administration "have consistently interpreted the [statute] to authorize relief on a disparate impact theory." In support of this claim, the plurality describes a 1968 interpretive bulletin issued by the Department of Labor as "permitt[ing]" disparate impact claims. Ibid. (citing 29 CFR § 860.103(f)(1)(i) (1970)). And the plurality cites, without comment, an Equal Employment Opportunity Commission (EEOC) policy statement construing the RFOA provision. It is unclear what interpretive value the plurality means to assign to these agency statements. But Justice SCALIA, at least, thinks that the EEOC statement is entitled to deference under Chevron U.S.A. Inc. v. Natural Resources Defense Council, Inc., 467 U.S. 837 (1984), and that "that is sufficient to resolve this case." I disagree and, for the reasons that follow, would give no weight to the statements in question.

The 1968 Labor Department bulletin to which the plurality alludes was intended to "provide 'a practical guide to employers and employees as to how the office representing the public interest in its enforcement will seek to apply it.' " 29 CFR § 860.1 (1970) (quoting Skidmore v. Swift & Co., 323 U.S. 134, 138 (1944)). In discussing the RFOA provision, the bulletin states that "physical fitness requirements" and "[e]valuation factors such as quantity or quality of production, or educational level" can qualify as reasonable nonage factors, so long as they have a valid relationship to job qualifications and are uniformly applied. §§ 860.103(f)(1), (2). But the bulletin does not construe the ADEA's prohibitory provisions, nor does it state or imply that § 4(a) authorizes disparate impact claims. Rather, it establishes "a nonexclusive objective test for employers to use in determining whether they could be certain of qualifying for the" RFOA exemption. Public Employees Retirement System of Ohio v. Betts, 492 U.S. 158, 172 (1989) (discussing 1968 bulletin's interpretation of the § 4(f)(2) exemption). Moreover, the very same bulletin states unequivocally that "[t]he clear purpose [of the ADEA] is to insure that age, within the limits prescribed by the Act, is not *a determining factor in making any decision* regarding the hiring, dismissal, promotion or any other term condition or privilege of employment of an individual." § 860.103(c) (emphasis added). That language is all about discriminatory intent.

The EEOC statement cited by the plurality and relied upon by Justice Scalia is equally unhelpful. This "interpretative rule or policy statement," promulgated in 1981, superseded the 1968 Labor Department bulletin after responsibility for enforcing the ADEA was transferred from Labor to the EEOC. See 46 Fed. Reg. 47724 (1981). It states, in relevant part:

> "[W]hen an employment practice, including a test, is claimed as a basis for different treatment of employees or applicants for employment on the grounds that it is a 'factor other than' age, and such a practice has an adverse impact on individuals within the protected age group, it can only be justified as a business necessity." 29 CFR § 1625.7(d) (2004).

Like the 1968 bulletin it replaces, this statement merely spells out the agency's view, for purposes of its enforcement policy, of what an employer must do to be certain of gaining the safety of the RFOA haven. It says nothing about whether disparate impact claims are authorized by the ADEA. . . .

IV

Although I would not read the ADEA to authorize disparate impact claims, I agree with the Court that, if such claims are allowed, they are strictly circumscribed by the RFOA exemption. That exemption requires only that the challenged employment practice be based on a "reasonable" nonage factor—that is, one that is rationally related to some legitimate business objective. I also agree with the Court that, if disparate impact claims are to be permitted under the ADEA, they are governed by the standards set forth in our decision in Wards Cove Packing Co. v. Atonio, 490 U.S. 642 (1989). That means, as the Court holds that "a plaintiff must demonstrate that it is the application of a *specific or particular employment practice* that has *created* the disparate impact under attack," Wards Cove, supra, at 657 (emphasis added). It also means that once the employer has produced evidence that its action was based on a reasonable nonage factor, the plaintiff bears the burden of disproving this assertion. See Wards Cove, supra, at 659–660. Even if petitioners' disparate impact claim were cognizable under the ADEA, that claim clearly would fail in light of these requirements.

NOTES ON *SMITH V. CITY OF JACKSON*

1. **What Was Decided.** In *City of Jackson*, the Supreme Court decided the question left open in *Hazen Paper*: whether claims based on the theory of disparate impact could be asserted under the ADEA. The Court held that these claims could be asserted, but only under a weaker version of the theory of disparate impact, one less favorable to plaintiffs, than the one currently available under Title VII. While the Court was closely divided on making the

theory available at all under the ADEA, it was unanimous in making the theory available only in this weaker version.

Four justices joined in Part III of Justice Stevens' opinion, which supported application of the theory of disparate impact based on interpretation of the ADEA alone. Justice Scalia reached the same conclusion based on EEOC regulations, deferring to them as a reasonable interpretation of ambiguous statutory provisions. Thus a majority of justices (five of eight because Chief Justice Rehnquist did not participate) agreed that liability could be imposed under the ADEA based on the theory of disparate impact.

In Part IV of his opinion, Justice Stevens concluded that a weaker version of the theory of disparate impact applied to claims under the ADEA, relying on Wards Cove Packing Co. v. Atonio, 490 U.S. 642 (1989), a decision under Title VII that was superseded by the Civil Rights Act of 1991. Five justices joined unconditionally in this part of his opinion, and the remaining three justices did so conditionally, only on the assumption that the theory of disparate impact was available under the ADEA. Justice O'Connor took this position in Part IV of her separate opinion, after arguing in the earlier parts against applying the theory of disparate impact at all under the ADEA.

2. **The Statutory Basis for the Theory of Disparate Impact.** Justice Stevens adopts the theory of disparate impact as it existed under Title VII following *Wards Cove* but before it was codified by the Civil Rights Act of 1991. That Act amended Title VII by adding § 703(k), 42 U.S.C. § 2000e–2(k), but made no corresponding change to the ADEA. In effect, Justice Stevens turns the clock back before 1991 and examines the language common to both statutes at that time. He finds the source of the theory of disparate impact in the provision making it illegal for an employer "to limit, segregate or classify his employees in any way which would deprive or tend to deprive any individual of employment opportunities or otherwise adversely affect his status as an employee" because of race, color, religion, sex, or national origin (in Title VII) and age (in the ADEA). § 703(a)(2), 42 U.S.C. § 2000e–2(a)(2); 29 U.S.C. § 623(a)(2). This "(a)(2)" provision formed the basis for the theory of disparate impact under Title VII, as it was originally recognized in Griggs v. Duke Power Co., 401 U.S. 424 (1971), and as it was subsequently elaborated in decisions like Connecticut v. Teal, 457 U.S. 440 (1982), both discussed in detail in Chapter 3. In Part III of his opinion, on behalf of a plurality of justices, Justice Stevens accepts the straightforward argument that the (a)(2) provision in the ADEA has exactly the same meaning as the (a)(2) provision in Title VII.

This provision, however, makes no direct reference to "disparate impact," in marked contrast to the provision that eventually codified the theory of disparate impact in § 703(k) of Title VII. The (a)(2) provision refers only obliquely to liability for discriminatory effects, rather than discriminatory intent, through phrases such as "tend to deprive" and "otherwise adversely affect." Relying on this language for the textual basis of the theory of disparate impact raises anew all the questions about the source of the theory before it was codified. Moreover, as Justice O'Connor points out in her separate opinion, these questions were not yet resolved—or even clearly raised—when Congress enacted the ADEA in 1967. The Supreme Court did not decide *Griggs* until 1971 and Congress could hardly have foreseen that decision when it enacted the (a)(2) provision in the ADEA in 1967. In what sense, then, could Congress have intended to create liability for discriminatory effects under the ADEA?

Even if Congress did not explicitly address this issue in enacting the ADEA, is there still an argument for interpreting the Act in pari materia with Title VII—for interpreting identical language in statutes on the same subject in the same way? Recall that several of the leading decisions on individual claims of disparate treatment, like McKennon v. Nashville Banner Pub. Co., 513 U.S. 352 (1995), discussed in Chapter 2, arose under the ADEA, yet were decided based on principles developed under Title VII. If the same provisions in both statutes have the same implications for these claims, why shouldn't they also have the same implications for claims of disparate impact?

3. **Differences Between the ADEA and Title VII.** The holding in *City of Jackson* is that the theory of disparate impact under the ADEA is not quite the same as it is under Title VII. Writing for the Court in Part IV of his opinion, Justice Stevens cites two statutory provisions for this difference: first, the "reasonable factor other than age" (RFOA) defense in the ADEA, 29 U.S.C. § 623(f)(1); and second, the codification of the theory of disparate impact in § 703(k) of Title VII.

The RFOA appears in the same subsection of the ADEA as the "bona fide occupational qualification" (BFOQ) defense on the basis of age. Unlike the BFOQ, however, the RFOA has no counterpart in Title VII and, before *City of Jackson*, had been largely neglected by the Supreme Court. Is it plausible to suppose that, almost 40 years after it was enacted in the ADEA, the significance of this provision has finally been discovered? As discussed in the preceding note, Congress itself did not know of decisions like *Griggs* and did not refer to the theory of disparate impact when it enacted the ADEA. How could Congress have intended the RFOA to serve as a restriction on a theory of liability that it was not aware of? At most, doesn't the presence of this provision in the ADEA, but not in Title VII, imply only that Congress intended some difference in the interpretation of the two statutes?

The codification of the theory of disparate impact in Title VII relies on an inference in the opposite direction: from a provision in Title VII but not in the ADEA. In the Civil Rights Act of 1991, Congress generally disapproved of the interpretation of the theory of disparate impact offered in *Wards Cove*, but it enacted a curative amendment only for Title VII. The Act amended the ADEA in other respects, but not in this one. For this reason, Justice Stevens finds *Wards Cove* still to be good law for the ADEA, even if it isn't for Title VII. Is he right to follow *Wards Cove* despite its rejection by Congress? Notice that his opinion turns the clock back to the moment before passage of the Civil Rights Act of 1991 for interpretation of the ADEA, while Congress itself turned the clock back to the moment before the decision in *Wards Cove* for interpretation of Title VII. Does this retrospective interpretation of either statute make sense, particularly since each interpretation refers to a different moment in the past? Wouldn't it be better to focus on what congressional policy is and how it can be effectively enforced now?

Following this approach, couldn't the differences in language between the ADEA and Title VII simply reflect congressional recognition of the differences between age discrimination and discrimination on other grounds? Justice Stevens comes close to this conclusion when, relying on the report that formed the basis for the ADEA, he states that "it is not surprising that certain employment criteria that are routinely used may be reasonable despite their adverse impact on older workers as a group." Shouldn't the Court as a whole have given greater emphasis to this principle than to the intricacies of past interpretations of the statutory language at different times? On the particular facts of *City of Jackson*, the only way in which the older workers suffered from the raises in this case was that they received smaller percentage increases than younger workers, although they received larger increases in absolute terms. Under the life-cycle theory of earnings, the older workers were not subject to any opportunistic exploitation. They only received raises that were not quite as large as they otherwise would have been. Shouldn't an employer be able to adjust the relationship between salary and seniority to meet the competition from other employers for younger employees?

The Court's reasoning also relies upon another weakness in the plaintiffs' case: that they did not identify any specific employment practice within the city's pay structure that resulted in the disparate impact. Note that even under the theory of disparate impact as codified in Title VII, the plaintiffs would have retained this burden unless they could demonstrate that "the elements of the respondent's decisionmaking process are not capable of separation for analysis." § 703(k)(1)(B)(i), 42 U.S.C. § 2000e–2(k)(1)(B)(i). Apart from the pay raise plan itself, they did not identify any such discrete practice. The City of Jackson's burden therefore was only to justify this plan. Again, even under Title VII as amended, such a justification might well have been made out. The defendants' burden would only have been to prove that the plan was "consistent with business necessity," not required by it. § 703(k)(1)(A)(i), 42 U.S.C. § 2000e–2(k)(1)(A)(i). Moreover, contrary to what Justice Stevens implies at the end of his opinion, the city would not have borne the entire burden of proving that it could have adopted an alternative employment practice with less adverse impact on older workers. Under Title VII, the burden of proof on this issue would have been on the plaintiffs, at least to some extent. § 703(k)(1)(A)(ii), 42 U.S.C. § 2000e–2(k)(1)(A)(ii). See the Notes on *Wards Cove* and the Civil Rights Act of 1991 in Chapter 3.

Thus, on the facts of *City of Jackson*, the difference between applying the two versions of the theory of disparate impact—under *Wards Cove* or under the Civil Rights Act of 1991—remains elusive. Does this uncertainty undermine the Court's attempt to distinguish sharply between disparate impact claims under the ADEA and those under Title VII? Or does the Court have to make this distinction in order to reach its ultimate decision upholding summary judgment for the defendants?

4. **The Role of EEOC Regulations.** Justice Scalia provides the crucial fifth vote for recognizing the theory of disparate impact under the ADEA. Although he relies immediately upon EEOC regulations to this effect, his position depends upon a difference in the authority granted to the EEOC to interpret the ADEA and Title VII. Under the ADEA, the EEOC has authority to issue "such rules and regulations as it may consider necessary or appropriate for carrying out" the Act. 29 U.S.C. § 628. Under Title VII, by contrast, its authority is limited to issuing "suitable procedural regulations." § 713(a), 42 U.S.C. § 2000e–12(a). Consequently, the EEOC regulations on the substantive provisions of Title VII have received varying levels of deference. See Notes on the Uniform Guidelines on Employee Selection Procedures in Chapter 3.

Justice Scalia gives a higher level of deference to the EEOC regulations under the ADEA, as a reasonable interpretation of ambiguous statutory provisions by an agency authorized to do so, following the doctrine of Chevron U.S.A., Inc. v. Natural Resources Defense Council, Inc., 467 U.S. 837 (1984). Justice Stevens does not go so far as to give the regulations *Chevron* deference, although in Part III of his opinion, he does rely upon them as a persuasive interpretation of the statute. Only Justice O'Connor would ignore the regulations entirely, offering a variety of reasons, the most fundamental of which appears to be that they do not provide a reasonable interpretation of the statute. They state that practices with a disparate impact "can only be justified as a business necessity," while the justices in the majority reject any requirement that the defendant prove business necessity under the RFOA.

Which of these positions on agency discretion to recognize the theory of disparate impact is most persuasive? Adopting a theory of liability, especially one moving from discriminatory intent to discriminatory effects, usually has been accomplished by congressional enactment or judicial decision, not by agency regulation. If Title VII had never been interpreted to support claims for disparate impact, could the EEOC nevertheless have created such claims by regulation under the ADEA? Or does the existence of decisions like *Griggs* go to the issue whether the EEOC's interpretation of the ADEA was "reasonable" under *Chevron*? Although she does not quite say so, Justice O'Connor apparently would find the EEOC's regulations unreasonable in this respect also because she disagrees fundamentally with the majority over the relevance of decisions under Title VII to liability for discriminatory effects under the ADEA.

If, contrary to her view, the EEOC was reasonable in following decisions under Title VII, does that make the EEOC's requirement of proof of "business necessity" also reasonable? Recall that this phrase itself had received varying interpretations under Title VII. As discussed in the preceding note, Justice Stevens exaggerates the difference between proof of a reasonable factor other than age and proof of business necessity. Do the EEOC regulations necessarily contradict the Court's understanding of the defendant's burden of proof under the ADEA? Justice Scalia apparently thinks that the two can be reconciled, since he endorses both the regulations and this part of Justice Stevens' opinion. Does that put him in the awkward position of giving complete deference to the EEOC's regulations, but only half the time—only insofar as they refer to "disparate impact," but not insofar as they refer to "business necessity"? Note that he does not himself endorse decisions like *Griggs* that form the basis for the EEOC's regulations. Is that because these decisions indirectly encourage various forms of affirmative action, to which he is strongly opposed? Do the EEOC regulations allow Justice Scalia to avoid this issue?

5. ***Meacham v. Knolls Atomic Power Laboratory, Inc.*** The defense of a "reasonable factor other than age" (RFOA) received a slightly different interpretation in Meacham v. Knolls Atomic Power Laboratory, Inc., 552 U.S. 1162 (2008) than in *City of Jackson*, making clear that it switched the burden of proof, both production and persuasion, to the defendant. The Court based its holding on the text and structure of the ADEA, which clearly distinguished between prohibitions and defenses. Since the RFOA was found in the same subsection of the statute as the BFOQ, 29 U.S.C. § 623(f), it had to be treated in the same way, as an affirmative defense on which the defendant bears the entire burden of proof. Accordingly, claims of disparate impact under the ADEA had to be treated differently, to that extent, from claims of disparate impact under *Wards Cove*.

The Court confined its holding to disparate impact cases, but concurring opinions, by Justices Scalia and Thomas, assumed that the same reasoning applied to claims of disparate treatment: that the defendant also bears the entire burden of proof on the RFOA defense in disparate treatment cases as well. Some passages in the majority's opinion cast doubt upon this assumption, especially the following, concerning *City of Jackson* insofar as it applied the RFOA to employer activities with a disparate impact on older employees:

> We emphasized that these were the kinds of employer activities, "otherwise prohibited" by § 623(a)(2), that were mainly what the statute meant to test against the RFOA condition: because "[i]n disparate-impact cases . . . the allegedly 'otherwise prohibited' activity is not based on age," it is "in cases involving disparate-impact claims that the RFOA provision plays its principal role by precluding liability if the adverse impact was attributable to a nonage factor that was 'reasonable.' "

Only in disparate impact cases is there much room to find some factor other than age to justify the employer's decision. In disparate treatment cases, the principal question is whether the employer's decision is based on age.

It is possible, however, that the RFOA could still apply in something like the "mixed-motive" cases under Title VII: where the plaintiff has established that the employer's decision was based on age, but the employer can show another reason for its decision. The majority would certainly limit the RFOA defense to employment practices that are "otherwise prohibited," as the literal terms of § 623(a) require. The defense is available only when the plaintiff has already established that the disputed employment practice would otherwise be prohibited: that the defendant would be found to have violated the statute in the absence of the RFOA. On this interpretation of the

RFOA, it does not undermine the application of *McDonnell Douglas* to ADEA cases. The plaintiff still has the burden of persuasion on the issue of pretext. The burden of persuasion switches to the defendant, just as it does in mixed-motive cases under Title VII, only after pretext has been found. In an ADEA case, the defendant could then show that its decision was based on a "reasonable factor other than age."

6. ***Kentucky Retirement Systems v. EEOC.*** In a case decided the same day as *Meacham*, the Supreme Court extended the analysis of *Hazen Paper Co. v. Biggins*. In Kentucky Retirement Systems v. EEOC, 554 U.S. 135 (2008), a retired state employee received lower pension benefits because he was over age 55 when he became disabled and retired. Employees who became disabled before age 55 would, in his circumstances, have received greater retirement benefits. The EEOC therefore brought a claim on his behalf alleging that he suffered a loss of retirement benefits based on age. The Supreme Court ultimately rejected this claim, finding that he received lower pension benefits because of his pension status rather than his age.

The Kentucky retirement system employed a complicated formula to determine the retirement benefits of employees who became disabled before they became eligible for retirement at age 55. These employees sometimes received greater benefits, sometimes lesser benefits, than employees who became disabled and retired after age 55.

7. **Bibliography.** For articles on claims of disparate impact under the ADEA, see Aida M. Alaka, Corporate Reorganizations, Job Layoffs, and Age Discrimination: Has *Smith v. City of Jackson* Substantially Expanded the Rights of Older Workers Under the ADEA?, 70 Alb. L. Rev. 143 (2006); Ethan S. Burger & Douglas R. Richmond The Future of Law School Faculty Hiring in Light of *Smith v. City of Jackson*, 13 Va. J. Soc. Pol'y & L. 1 (2005); Debra Burke, ADEA Disparate Impact Discrimination: A Pyrrhic Victory?, 9 U.C. Davis Bus. L.J. 47 (2008); Carla J. Rozycki & Emma J. Sullivan, Employees Bringing Disparate-Impact Claims Under the ADEA Continue to Face an Uphill Battle Despite the Supreme Court's Decision in *Smith v. City of Jackson* and *Meacham v. Knolls Atomic Power Laboratory*, 26 A.B.A. J. Lab. & Emp. L. 1 (2010); Ann M. Tracey & Norma Skoog, Is Business Judgment a Catch-22 for ADEA Plaintiffs? The Impact of *Smith v. City of Jackson* on Future ADEA Employment Litigation, 33 U. Dayton L. Rev. 231 (2008); Kenneth R. Davis, Age Discrimination and Disparate Impact: A New Look at an Age-Old Problem, 70 Brook. L. Rev. 361 (2004/2005); Ann Marie Huffman & Norma Skoog, Is Business Judgment a Catch-22 for ADEA Plaintiffs? The Impact of *Smith v. City of Jackson* on Future ADEA Employment Litigation, 33 U. Dayton L. Rev. 231 (2008); Judith J. Johnson, Rehabilitate the Age Discrimination in Employment Act: Resuscitate the "Reasonable Factors Other Than Age" Defense and the Disparate Impact Theory, 55 Hastings L.J. 1399 (2004); Mack A. Player, Proof of Disparate Treatment Under the Age Discrimination in Employment Act: Variations on a Title VII Theme, 17 Ga. L. Rev. 621 (1983); George Rutherglen, Disparate Impact, Discrimination, and the Essentially Contested Concept of Equality, 74 Fordham L. Rev. 2313 (2006); Sandra F. Sperino, Disparate Impact or

Negative Impact? The Future of Non-Intentional Discrimination Claims Brought by the Elderly, 13 Elder L.J. 339 (2005).

D. BONA FIDE OCCUPATIONAL QUALIFICATIONS

Western Air Lines v. Criswell

472 U.S. 400 (1985).

■ JUSTICE STEVENS delivered the opinion of the Court.

The petitioner, Western Air Lines, Inc., requires that its flight engineers retire at age 60. Although the Age Discrimination in Employment Act of 1967 (ADEA), 29 U.S.C. §§ 621–634, generally prohibits mandatory retirement before age 70, the Act provides an exception "where age is a bona fide occupational qualification [BFOQ] reasonably necessary to the normal operation of the particular business." A jury concluded that Western's mandatory retirement rule did not qualify as a BFOQ even though it purportedly was adopted for safety reasons. The question here is whether the jury was properly instructed on the elements of the BFOQ defense.

I

In its commercial airline operations, Western operates a variety of aircraft, including the Boeing 727 and the McDonnell-Douglas DC-10. These aircraft require three crew members in the cockpit: a captain, a first officer, and a flight engineer. "The 'captain' is the pilot and controls the aircraft. He is responsible for all phases of its operation. The 'first officer' is the copilot and assists the captain. The 'flight engineer' usually monitors a side-facing instrument panel. He does not operate the flight controls unless the captain and the first officer become incapacitated." Trans World Airlines, Inc. v. Thurston, 469 U.S. 111, 114 (1985).

A regulation of the Federal Aviation Administration (FAA) prohibits any person from serving as a pilot or first officer on a commercial flight "if that person has reached his 60th birthday." 14 CFR § 121.383(c) (1985). The FAA has justified the retention of mandatory retirement for pilots on the theory that "incapacitating medical events" and "adverse psychological, emotional, and physical changes" occur as a consequence of aging. "The inability to detect or predict with precision an individual's risk of sudden or subtle incapacitation, in the face of known age-related risks, counsels against relaxation of the rule." 49 Fed. Reg. 14695 (1984). See also 24 Fed. Reg. 9776 (1959).

At the same time, the FAA has refused to establish a mandatory retirement age for flight engineers. "While a flight engineer has important duties which contribute to the safe operation of the airplane, he or she may not assume the responsibilities of the pilot in command." 49 Fed. Reg. at 14694. Moreover, available statistics establish that flight engineers have rarely been a contributing cause or factor in commercial aircraft "accidents" or "incidents."

In 1978, respondents Criswell and Starley were captains operating DC-10s for Western. Both men celebrated their 60th birthdays in July 1978. Under the collective-bargaining agreement in effect between Western and the union, cockpit crew members could obtain open positions by bidding in order of seniority. In order to avoid mandatory retirement under the FAA's under-age-60 rule for pilots, Criswell and Starley applied for reassignment as flight engineers. Western denied both requests, ostensibly on the ground that both employees were members of the company's retirement plan which required all crew members to retire at age 60. For the same reason, respondent Ron, a career flight engineer, was also retired in 1978 after his 60th birthday.

Mandatory retirement provisions similar to those contained in Western's pension plan had previously been upheld under the ADEA. United Air Lines, Inc. v. McMann, 434 U.S. 192 (1977). As originally enacted in 1967, the Act provided an exception to its general proscription of age discrimination for any actions undertaken "to observe the terms of a . . . bona fide employee benefit plan such as a retirement, pension, or insurance plan, which is not a subterfuge to evade the purposes of this Act." In April 1978, however, Congress amended the statute to prohibit employee benefit plans from requiring the involuntary retirement of any employee because of age.

Criswell, Starley, and Ron brought this action against Western contending that the under-age-60 qualification for the position of flight engineer violated the ADEA. In the District Court, Western defended, in part, on the theory that the age-60 rule is a BFOQ "reasonably necessary" to the safe operation of the airline. All parties submitted evidence concerning the nature of the flight engineer's tasks, the physiological and psychological traits required to perform them, and the availability of those traits among persons over age 60.

As the District Court summarized, the evidence at trial established that the flight engineer's "normal duties are less critical to the safety of flight than those of a pilot." The flight engineer, however, does have critical functions in emergency situations and, of course, might cause considerable disruption in the event of his own medical emergency.

The actual capabilities of persons over age 60, and the ability to detect disease or a precipitous decline in their faculties, were the subject of conflicting medical testimony. Western's expert witness, a former FAA Deputy Federal Air Surgeon, was especially concerned about the possibility of a "cardiovascular event" such as a heart attack. He testified that "with advancing age the likelihood of onset of disease increases and that in persons over age 60 it could not be predicted whether and when such diseases would occur."

The plaintiffs' experts, on the other hand, testified that physiological deterioration is caused by disease, not aging, and that "it was feasible to determine on the basis of individual medical examinations whether flight deck crew members, including those over age 60, were physically qualified to continue to fly." These conclusions were corroborated by the nonmedical evidence:

> "The record also reveals that both the FAA and the airlines have been able to deal with the health problems of pilots on an individualized basis. Pilots who have been grounded because of alcoholism or cardiovascular disease have been recertified by the FAA and allowed to resume flying. Pilots who were unable to pass the necessary examination to maintain their FAA first class medical certificates, but who continued to qualify for second class medical certificates were allowed to 'downgrade' from pilot to [flight engineer]. There is nothing in the record to indicate that these flight deck crew members are physically better able to perform their duties than flight engineers over age 60 who have not experienced such events or that they are less likely to become incapacitated."

Moreover, several large commercial airlines have flight engineers over age 60 "flying the line" without any reduction in their safety record.

The jury was instructed that the "BFOQ defense is available only if it is reasonably necessary to the normal operation or essence of defendant's business." The jury was informed that "the essence of Western's business is the safe transportation of their passengers." The jury was also instructed:

> "One method by which defendant Western may establish a BFOQ in this case is to prove:
>
> "(1) That in 1978, when these plaintiffs were retired, it was highly impractical for Western to deal with each second officer over age 60 on an individualized basis to determine his particular ability to perform his job safely; and
>
> "(2) That some second officers over age 60 possess traits of a physiological, psychological or other nature which preclude safe and efficient job performance that cannot be ascertained by means other than knowing their age.
>
> "In evaluating the practicability to defendant Western of dealing with second officers over age 60 on an individualized basis, with respect to the medical testimony, you should consider the state of the medical art as it existed in July 1978."

The jury rendered a verdict for the plaintiffs, and awarded damages. After trial, the District Court granted equitable relief, explaining in a written opinion why it found no merit in Western's BFOQ defense to the mandatory retirement rule.

On appeal, Western made various arguments attacking the verdict and judgment below, but the Court of Appeals affirmed in all respects. In particular, the Court of Appeals rejected Western's contention that the instruction on the BFOQ defense was insufficiently deferential to the airline's legitimate concern for the safety of its passengers. We granted certiorari to consider the merits of this question.

II

Throughout the legislative history of the ADEA, one empirical fact is repeatedly emphasized: the process of psychological and physiological degeneration caused by aging varies with each individual. "The basic research in the field of aging has established that there is a wide range of individual physical ability regardless of age." As a result, many older American workers perform at levels equal or superior to their younger colleagues.

In 1965, the Secretary of Labor reported to Congress that despite these well-established medical facts there "is persistent and widespread use of age limits in hiring that in a great many cases can be attributed only to arbitrary discrimination against older workers on the basis of age and regardless of ability." Two years later, the President recommended that Congress enact legislation to abolish arbitrary age limits on hiring. Such limits, the President declared, have a devastating effect on the dignity of the individual and result in a staggering loss of human resources vital to the national economy.

After further study, Congress responded with the enactment of the ADEA. The preamble declares that the purpose of the ADEA is "to promote employment of older persons based on their ability rather than age [and] to prohibit arbitrary age discrimination in employment." 29 U.S.C. § 621(b). Section 4(a)(1) makes it "unlawful for an employer . . . to fail or refuse to hire or to discharge any individual or otherwise discriminate against any individual with respect to his compensation, terms, conditions, or privileges of employment, because of such individual's age." 29 U.S.C. § 623(a)(1). This proscription presently applies to all persons between the ages of 40 and 70. 29 U.S.C. § 631(a).

The legislative history of the 1978 Amendments to the ADEA makes quite clear that the policies and substantive provisions of the Act apply with especial force in the case of mandatory retirement provisions. The House Committee on Education and Labor reported:

> "Increasingly, it is being recognized that mandatory retirement based solely upon age is arbitrary and that chronological age alone is a poor indicator of ability to perform a job. Mandatory retirement does not take into consideration actual differing abilities and capacities. Such forced retirement can cause hardships for older persons through loss of roles and loss of income. Those older persons who wish to be re-employed

> have a much more difficult time finding a new job than younger persons.
>
> "Society, as a whole, suffers from mandatory retirement as well. As a result of mandatory retirement, skills and experience are lost from the work force resulting in reduced GNP. Such practices also add a burden to Government income maintenance programs such as social security."

In the 1978 Amendments, Congress narrowed an exception to the ADEA which had previously authorized involuntary retirement under limited circumstances.

In both 1967 and 1978, however, Congress recognized that classifications based on age, like classifications based on religion, sex, or national origin, may sometimes serve as a necessary proxy for neutral employment qualifications essential to the employer's business. The diverse employment situations in various industries, however, forced Congress to adopt a "case-by-case basis . . . as the underlying rule in the administration of the legislation." H.R. Rep. No. 805, 90th Cong., 1st Sess., 7 (1967). Congress offered only general guidance on when an age classification might be permissible by borrowing a concept and statutory language from Title VII of the Civil Rights Act of 1964 and providing that such a classification is lawful "where age is a bona fide occupational qualification reasonably necessary to the normal operation of the particular business." 29 U.S.C. § 623(f)(1).

Shortly after the passage of the Act, the Secretary of Labor, who was at that time charged with its enforcement, adopted regulations declaring that the BFOQ exception to the ADEA has only "limited scope and application" and "must be construed narrowly." 29 CFR § 860.102(b) (1984). The Equal Employment Opportunity Commission (EEOC) adopted the same narrow construction of the BFOQ exception after it was assigned authority for enforcing the statute. 29 CFR § 1625.6 (1984). The restrictive language of the statute and the consistent interpretation of the administrative agencies charged with enforcing the statute convince us that, like its Title VII counterpart, the BFOQ exception "was in fact meant to be an extremely narrow exception to the general prohibition" of age discrimination contained in the ADEA. Dothard v. Rawlinson, 433 U.S. 321, 334 (1977).

III

In Usery v. Tamiami Trail Tours, Inc., 531 F.2d 224 (5th Cir. 1976), the Court of Appeals for the Fifth Circuit was called upon to evaluate the merits of a BFOQ defense to a claim of age discrimination. Tamiami Trail Tours, Inc., had a policy of refusing to hire persons over age 40 as intercity bus drivers. At trial, the bus company introduced testimony supporting its theory that the hiring policy was a BFOQ based upon safety considerations—the need to employ persons who have a low risk of accidents. In evaluating this contention, the Court of Appeals drew on its Title VII precedents, and concluded that two inquiries were relevant.

First, the court recognized that some job qualifications may be so peripheral to the central mission of the employer's business that no age discrimination can be "reasonably necessary to the normal operation of the particular business." 29 U.S.C. § 623(f)(1). The bus company justified the age qualification for hiring its drivers on safety considerations, but the court concluded that this claim was to be evaluated under an objective standard:

> "[T]he job qualifications which the employer invokes to justify his discrimination must be *reasonably necessary* to the essence of his business—here, the *safe* transportation of bus passengers from one point to another. The greater the safety factor, measured by the likelihood of harm and the probable severity of that harm in case of an accident, the more stringent may be the job qualifications designed to insure safe driving." 531 F.2d, at 236.

This inquiry "adjusts to the safety factor" by ensuring that the employer's restrictive job qualifications are "reasonably necessary" to further the overriding interest in public safety. In *Tamiami*, the court noted that no one had seriously challenged the bus company's safety justification for hiring drivers with a low risk of having accidents.

Second, the court recognized that the ADEA requires that age qualifications be something more than "convenient" or "reasonable"; they must be "reasonably necessary . . . to the particular business," and this is only so when the employer is compelled to rely on age as a proxy for the safety-related job qualifications validated in the first inquiry. This showing could be made in two ways. The employer could establish that it " 'had reasonable cause to believe, that is, a factual basis for believing, that all or substantially all [persons over the age qualifications] would be unable to perform safely and efficiently the duties of the job involved.' " In *Tamiami*, the employer did not seek to justify its hiring qualification under this standard.

Alternatively, the employer could establish that age was a legitimate proxy for the safety-related job qualifications by proving that it is " 'impossible or highly impractical' " to deal with the older employees on an individualized basis. "One method by which the employer can carry this burden is to establish that some members of the discriminated-against class possess a trait precluding safe and efficient job performance that cannot be ascertained by means other than knowledge of the applicant's membership in the class." In *Tamiami*, the medical evidence on this point was conflicting, but the District Court had found that individual examinations could not determine which individuals over the age of 40 would be unable to operate the buses safely. The Court of Appeals found that this finding of fact was not "clearly erroneous," and affirmed the District Court's judgment for the bus company on the BFOQ defense.

Congress, in considering the 1978 Amendments, implicitly endorsed the two-part inquiry identified by the Fifth Circuit in the *Tamiami* case. The Senate Committee Report expressed concern that the amendment prohibiting mandatory retirement in accordance with pension plans might imply that mandatory retirement could not be a BFOQ:

> "For example, in certain types of particularly arduous law enforcement activity, there may be a factual basis for believing that substantially all employees above a specified age would be unable to continue to perform safely and efficiently the duties of their particular jobs, and it may be impossible or impractical to determine through medical examinations, periodic reviews of current job performance and other objective tests the employees' capacity or ability to continue to perform the jobs safely and efficiently.
>
> "Accordingly, the committee adopted an amendment to make it clear that where these two conditions are satisfied and where such a bona fide occupational qualification has therefore been established, an employer may lawfully require mandatory retirement at that specified age." S. Rep. No. 95–493, pp. 10–11 (1977), Legislative History 443–444.

The amendment was adopted by the Senate, but deleted by the Conference Committee because it "neither added to nor worked any change upon present law." H.R. Conf. Rep. No. 95–950, p. 7 (1978), Legislative History 518.

Every Court of Appeals that has confronted a BFOQ defense based on safety considerations has analyzed the problem consistently with the *Tamiami* standard. An EEOC regulation embraces the same criteria. Considering the narrow language of the BFOQ exception, the parallel treatment of such questions under Title VII, and the uniform application of the standard by the federal courts, the EEOC, and Congress, we conclude that this two-part inquiry properly identifies the relevant considerations for resolving a BFOQ defense to an age-based qualification purportedly justified by considerations of safety.

IV

In the trial court, Western preserved an objection to any instruction in the *Tamiami* mold, claiming that "any instruction pertaining to the statutory phrase 'reasonably necessary to the normal operation of [defendant's] business' . . . is irrelevant to and confusing for the deliberations of the jury." Western proposed an instruction that would have allowed it to succeed on the BFOQ defense by proving that "in 1978, when these plaintiffs were retired, there existed a *rational basis* in fact for defendant to believe that use of [flight engineers] over age 60 on its DC-10 airliners would increase the likelihood of risk to its passengers."

The proposed instruction went on to note that the jury might rely on the FAA's age-60 rule for pilots to establish a BFOQ under this standard "without considering any other evidence." It also noted that the medical evidence submitted by the parties might provide a "rational basis in fact."

On appeal, Western defended its proposed instruction, and the Court of Appeals soundly rejected it. In this Court, Western slightly changes its course. The airline now acknowledges that the *Tamiami* standard identifies the relevant general inquiries that must be made in evaluating the BFOQ defense. However, Western claims that in several respects the instructions given below were insufficiently protective of public safety. Western urges that we interpret or modify the *Tamiami* standard to weigh these concerns in the balance.

Reasonably Necessary Job Qualifications

Western relied on two different kinds of job qualifications to justify its mandatory retirement policy. First, it argued that flight engineers should have a low risk of incapacitation or psychological and physiological deterioration. At this vague level of analysis respondents have not seriously disputed—nor could they—that the qualification of good health for a vital crew member is reasonably necessary to the essence of the airline's operations. Instead, they have argued that age is not a necessary proxy for that qualification.

On a more specific level, Western argues that flight engineers must meet the same stringent qualifications as pilots, and that it was therefore quite logical to extend to flight engineers the FAA's age-60 retirement rule for pilots. Although the FAA's rule for pilots, adopted for safety reasons, is relevant evidence in the airline's BFOQ defense, it is not to be accorded conclusive weight. The extent to which the rule is probative varies with the weight of the evidence supporting its safety rationale and "the congruity between the . . . occupations at issue." In this case, the evidence clearly established that the FAA, Western, and other airlines all recognized that the qualifications for a flight engineer were less rigorous than those required for a pilot.

In the absence of persuasive evidence supporting its position, Western nevertheless argues that the jury should have been instructed to defer to "Western's selection of job qualifications for the position of [flight engineer] that are reasonable in light of the safety risks." This proposal is plainly at odds with Congress' decision, in adopting the ADEA, to subject such management decisions to a test of objective justification in a court of law. The BFOQ standard adopted in the statute is one of "reasonable necessity," not reasonableness.

In adopting that standard, Congress did not ignore the public interest in safety. That interest is adequately reflected in instructions that track the language of the statute. When an employer establishes that a job qualification has been carefully formulated to respond to documented concerns for public safety, it will not be overly burdensome to persuade a trier of fact that the qualification is "reasonably necessary" to safe operation of the business. The uncertainty implicit in the concept of managing safety risks always makes it "reasonably necessary" to err on the side of caution in a close case. The employer cannot be expected to establish the risk of an airline accident "to a certainty, for certainty would require running the risk until a tragic accident would prove that the judgment was sound." Usery v. Tamiami Trail Tours, Inc., 531 F.2d, at 238. When the employer's argument has a credible basis in the record, it is difficult to believe that a jury of laypersons—many of whom no doubt have flown or could expect to fly on commercial air carriers—would not defer in a close case to the airline's judgment. Since the instructions in this case would not have prevented the airline from raising this contention to the jury in closing argument, we are satisfied that the verdict is a consequence of a defect in Western's proof rather than a defect in the trial court's instructions.

Western's Statutory Safety Obligation

The instructions defined the essence of Western's business as "the safe transportation of their passengers." Western complains that this instruction was defective because it failed to inform the jury that an airline must conduct its operations "with the highest possible degree of safety."[31]

Jury instructions, of course, "may not be judged in artificial isolation," but must be judged in the "context of the overall charge" and the circumstances of the case. See Cupp v. Naughten, 414 U.S. 141, 147 (1973). In this case, the instructions characterized safe transportation as the "essence" of Western's business and specifically referred to the importance of "safe and efficient job performance" by flight engineers. Moreover, in closing argument counsel pointed out that because "safety is the essence of Western's business," the airline strives for "the highest degree possible of safety." Viewing the record as a whole, we are satisfied that the jury's attention was adequately focused on the importance of safety to the operation of Western's business. . . .

Age as a Proxy for Job Qualifications

Western contended below that the ADEA only requires that the employer establish "a rational basis in fact" for believing that identification of those persons lacking suitable qualifications cannot occur on an individualized basis. This "rational basis in fact" standard would have been tantamount to an instruction to return a verdict in the defendant's favor. Because that standard conveys a meaning that is

---

[31] This standard is set forth in the Federal Aviation Act, which provides, in part:

"In prescribing standards, rules, and regulations, and in issuing certificates under this subchapter, the Secretary of Transportation shall give full consideration to the duty resting upon air carriers to perform their services with the *highest possible degree of safety* in the public interest. . . ." 49 U.S.C. App. § 1421(b) (emphasis added).

significantly different from that conveyed by the statutory phrase "reasonably necessary," it was correctly rejected by the trial court.

Western argues that a "rational basis" standard should be adopted because medical disputes can never be proved "to a certainty" and because juries should not be permitted "to resolve bona fide conflicts among medical experts respecting the adequacy of individualized testing." The jury, however, need not be convinced beyond all doubt that medical testing is impossible, but only that the proposition is true "on a preponderance of the evidence." Moreover, Western's attack on the wisdom of assigning the resolution of complex questions to 12 laypersons is inconsistent with the structure of the ADEA. Congress expressly decided that problems involving age discrimination in employment should be resolved on a "case-by-case basis" by proof to a jury.

The "rational basis" standard is also inconsistent with the preference for individual evaluation expressed in the language and legislative history of the ADEA. Under the Act, employers are to evaluate employees between the ages of 40 and 70 on their merits and not their age. In the BFOQ defense, Congress provided a limited exception to this general principle, but required that employers validate any discrimination as "reasonably necessary to the normal operation of the particular business." It might well be "rational" to require mandatory retirement at *any* age less than 70, but that result would not comply with Congress' direction that employers must justify the rationale for the age chosen. Unless an employer can establish a substantial basis for believing that all or nearly all employees above an age lack the qualifications required for the position, the age selected for mandatory retirement less than 70 must be an age at which it is highly impractical for the employer to insure by individual testing that its employees will have the necessary qualifications for the job.

Western argues that its lenient standard is necessary because "where qualified experts disagree as to whether persons over a certain age can be dealt with on an individual basis, an employer must be allowed to resolve that controversy in a conservative manner." This argument incorrectly assumes that all expert opinion is entitled to equal weight, and virtually ignores the function of the trier of fact in evaluating conflicting testimony. In this case, the jury may well have attached little weight to the testimony of Western's expert witness. A rule that would require the jury to defer to the judgment of any expert witness testifying for the employer, no matter how unpersuasive, would allow some employers to give free reign to the stereotype of older workers that Congress decried in the legislative history of the ADEA.

When an employee covered by the Act is able to point to reputable businesses in the same industry that choose to eschew reliance on mandatory retirement earlier than age 70, when the employer itself relies on individualized testing in similar circumstances, and when the administrative agency with primary responsibility for maintaining airline safety has determined that individualized testing is not impractical for the relevant position, the employer's attempt to justify its decision on the basis of the contrary opinion of experts—solicited for the purposes of litigation—is hardly convincing on any objective standard short of complete deference. Even in cases involving public safety, the ADEA plainly does not permit the trier of fact to give complete deference to the employer's decision.

The judgment of the Court of Appeals is affirmed.

■ JUSTICE POWELL took no part in the decision of this case.

NOTES ON *WESTERN AIR LINES V. CRISWELL*

1. **FAA Regulations.** The parties in *Criswell* did not dispute the validity of the FAA regulations requiring captains and co-captains to retire at age 60. And, indeed, these regulations were subsequently upheld by the D.C. Circuit in a decision finding that they were not "arbitrary and capricious" under the Administrative Procedure Act because they were sufficiently related to airline safety. Professional Pilots Federation v. FAA, 118 F.3d 758, 766–67 (D.C. Cir. 1997), cert. denied, 523 U.S. 1117 (1998). This decision also found that the regulations fell outside the scope of the ADEA because they were not issued in the FAA's capacity as an employer. Id. at 763.

Does the assumption, and later the holding, that these regulations are valid overshadow the actual decision in *Criswell*? If the most important positions in the cockpit are subject to mandatory retirement, isn't the mandatory retirement of flight engineers a relatively minor issue? With the increasing use of computers in modern airliners the position of flight engineer has been gradually phased out. With regard to policy under the ADEA, what justifies the age-based stereotype that pilots over the age of 60 pose a greater risk to airline safety than pilots under that age? Is it the nature of the disabilities that they might suffer or the nature of the risk if they do suffer a disability that makes this case distinctive?

In the Fair Treatment for Experienced Pilots Act, Congress raised the age limit for pilots and co-pilots to fly on commercial airlines from 60 to 65. Pilots and co-pilots over the age of 60 still must fly with one under that age. 49 U.S.C. § 44729.

2. **Standards for the BFOQ.** *Criswell* endorses standards for the BFOQ drawn equally from sex discrimination cases under Title VII and lower court decisions under the ADEA. Does this mixture of authority, concerned with discrimination on different grounds, make sense? From the Title VII decision in *Dothard*, the Court takes the principle that the BFOQ is extremely narrow. From decisions under the ADEA, particularly the Fifth Circuit's decision in *Usery v. Tamiami Trails*, the Court takes the standards for instructing the jury on the BFOQ. These standards require that the essence of the business involve an age-based classification, either because of the risk entailed by employment of older workers or because age is the only available proxy for eliminating this risk.

Do these standards apply in the same way to classifications on the basis of sex and those on the basis of age? Sex, for virtually all individuals, is sharply defined in biological terms. Age is a matter of degree and age-based classifications can therefore be set at different levels with different degrees of justification. Would *Criswell* have been decided the same way if the mandatory retirement age for flight engineers was set at age 65? Age 70? No such adjustments in sex-based classifications are possible. Should that make a difference in the standards for applying the BFOQ to each form of discrimination?

Assuming that the standards are nearly the same, how often are they likely to be satisfied? If, as the Court suggests, the answer is "hardly ever," what role does that leave for the BFOQ in adjusting the ADEA's general prohibition against discrimination to the distinctive features of aging? Is the Court's decision itself of limited significance because the policy at issue involved mandatory retirement, an issue on which Congress has specifically legislated through amendments to the ADEA, eventually almost completely prohibiting this practice? Would the Court's decision be different if a policy against hiring flight engineers over the age of 60 were at stake?

In fact, the Court takes care to avoid resolving the application of the BFOQ itself, leaving this issue for decision by the jury. We have already seen that the standards for finding discrimination under the ADEA leave many close questions for the jury. Does the right to jury trial under the ADEA, conferred by § 625(c), leave the Court any choice? Even if it doesn't, was Congress wise to allow the jury, and in fact, different juries in different cases, to determine the actual scope of the BFOQ? How is an employer likely to react to the inherent uncertainty of jury verdicts, which it must contend with in any case in which the application of the BFOQ is subject to reasonable disagreement? Does this uncertainty increase or decrease the practical scope of this exception to the ADEA?

3. ***Trans World Airlines, Inc. v. Thurston.*** A companion case to *Criswell*, Trans World Airlines, Inc. v. Thurston, 469 U.S. 111 (1985), also considered age restrictions related to flight engineers, not to the position itself but to transfers to the position by captains and co-captains who no longer satisfied the age requirements for those positions. The employer allowed captains and co-captains not disqualified by age from serving in those positions greater rights to transfer to the position of flight engineer than captains and co-captains who were disqualified by age. This constituted an age-based classification that the employer sought to justify either as a BFOQ or as part of its seniority system. The Supreme Court rejected both arguments, in the following terms:

> TWA's discriminatory transfer policy is not permissible under § 4(f)(1) because age is not a BFOQ for the "particular" position of flight engineer. It is necessary to recognize that the airline has two age-based policies: (i) captains are not allowed to serve in that capacity after reaching the age of 60; and (ii) age-disqualified captains are not given the transfer privileges afforded captains disqualified for other reasons. The first policy, which precludes individuals from serving as captains, is not challenged by

respondents. The second practice does not operate to exclude protected individuals from the position of captain; rather it prevents qualified 60-year-olds from working as flight engineers. Thus, it is the "particular" job of flight engineer from which the respondents were excluded by the discriminatory transfer policy. Because age under 60 is not a BFOQ for the position of flight engineer, the age-based discrimination at issue in this case cannot be justified by § 4(f)(1). . . .

TWA also contends that its discriminatory transfer policy is lawful under the Act because it is part of a "bona fide seniority system." 29 U.S.C. § 623(f)(2). The Court of Appeals held that the airline's retirement policy is not mandated by the negotiated seniority plan. We need not address this finding; any seniority system that includes the challenged practice is not "bona fide" under the statute. The Act provides that a seniority system may not "require or permit" the involuntary retirement of a protected individual because of his age. Ibid. Although the FAA "age 60 rule" may have caused respondents' retirement, TWA's seniority plan certainly "permitted" it within the meaning of the ADEA. Ibid. Moreover, because captains disqualified for reasons other than age are allowed to "bump" less senior flight engineers, the mandatory retirement was age based. Therefore, the "bona fide seniority system" defense is unavailable to the petitioners.

Thurston stands for the proposition that the existence of the BFOQ depends on the job that the plaintiff is seeking, rather than the job that the plaintiff has left. This proposition appears to be so obvious that it is surprising that the employer challenged it, particularly in litigation that went all the way to the Supreme Court. How could the lawyers for the employer have made such an obvious mistake in thinking that the BFOQ applied to the transfer policy that they had negotiated with the union? Or did this issue simply get lost in a complicated deal that sought to satisfy the conflicting interests of captains and co-captains on the one hand, and flight engineers on the other? After *Thurston*, do these negotiations have to begin all over again? The union that represented all of these employees, the Airline Pilots Association, in fact, was sued along with the employer and was a strong advocate of the compromise that it had worked out among its members. What role could counsel for the employer take in responding to the union's position?

4. **Other Exceptions to the ADEA.** In addition to the BFOQ, the ADEA also contains a number of other exceptions and exclusions from coverage. Several of these have already been discussed, such as the general exception for "reasonable factors other than age"; 29 U.S.C. § 623(f)(1); the exception for seniority systems, carried over from Title VII, § 623(f)(2)(A); the special provisions governing early retirement and pension plans, § 623(f)(2), (i), (k), (*l*); and the exclusion from coverage of certain executives over the age of 65, § 631(c). There is also an exemption for certain public officials and members of their staffs, § 630(f); and a narrowly defined class of employees exempted by regulation of the EEOC. § 628; 29 C.F.R. § 1627.16.

Two different occupations, firefighters and law enforcement officers, and tenured professors at colleges and universities, have been subject to changing statutory provisions. The original exceptions for those occupations allowed employers to impose maximum ages of employment, or what is virtually the same thing, ages of mandatory retirement. Those exceptions expired at the end of 1993, only to be reinstated later in a different form. States and localities can now set a maximum age for employment of firefighters and law enforcement officers, as well as an age for mandatory retirement. 29 U.S.C. § 623(j). Colleges and universities cannot impose mandatory retirement upon tenured professors, but they can increase the incentives for early retirement. § 623(m).

5. **Bibliography.** Robert L. Fischman, Note, The BFOQ Defense in ADEA Suits: The Scope of "Duties of the Job," 85 Mich. L. Rev. 330 (1986); Note, The Cost of Growing Old: Business Necessity and the Age Discrimination in Employment Act, 88 Yale L.J. 565 (1979).

E. PROCEDURES AND REMEDIES

The ADEA is enforced according to a combination of procedures and remedies taken both from Title VII and the Fair Labor Standards Act (FLSA). This otherwise inexplicable combination of statutory provisions arises from the use of the procedures and remedies under the FLSA to enforce the Equal Pay Act. Accordingly, the ADEA borrows most of the remedial provisions of the FLSA, but through a series of amendments, it's purely procedural provisions, particularly time limits for filing claims, have come to closely resemble those under Title VII. The end result is a system of procedures and remedies that is better explained by its history than by its logic.

1. **Public and Private Actions.** The ADEA allocates enforcement authority between public and private actions according to the provisions of the FLSA, with one exception. See 29 U.S.C. § 626(b). The FLSA authorizes public actions by the Secretary of Labor, but by executive order, authority to enforce the ADEA (like the Equal Pay Act) has been transferred to the EEOC. Reorganization Plan No. 1 of 1978, 5 U.S.C. app. at 719 (2012). Actions by the EEOC need not be preceded by exhaustion of state administrative remedies or by filing a charge with the EEOC, but they must be preceded by attempted conciliation. 29 U.S.C. § 626(b). Public actions can preempt private actions if they are filed earlier, but private individuals have a right to intervene in public actions on their behalf. § 216(b), (c).

2. **Statutes of Limitations.** As under Title VII, private actions under the ADEA must be preceded by filing a charge with the EEOC, followed by a waiting period to allow the EEOC to attempt conciliation. § 626(d). In states that do not have an agency that enforces a state law against employment discrimination on the basis of age, the charge must be filed with the EEOC within 180 days of the alleged discrimination. § 626(d)(1). In states that do have an appropriate agency, the charge must be filed

with the EEOC within 300 days of the alleged discrimination or 30 days of notice of termination of state proceedings, whichever is earlier. § 626(d)(2).

The limitation periods for filing actions under the ADEA originally were the same as those under the Equal Pay Act and the FLSA, but when the EEOC experienced delays in processing charges, many individual plaintiffs lost their claims under these limitations. Congress responded, first by extending the limitation periods for such delayed claims, and then by changing the limitation period so that it was the same under the ADEA as under Title VII. Individuals must now file an action in court within 90 days of receiving a right-to-sue letter. § 626(e). The effect of this amendment is to relieve the EEOC of any explicit limitation period for filing its actions, apparently subject only to the same doctrine of laches that applies to EEOC actions under Title VII. Occidental Life Ins. Co. v. EEOC, 432 U.S. 355, 358–66, 372–73 (1977).

Again like Title VII, the ADEA creates special procedures for claims by federal employees with their own separate time limits. These procedures allow federal employees to choose between pursuing their claims administratively before the EEOC or going directly to court. 29 U.S.C. § 633a(a). In the former alternative, the EEOC adjudicates their claim, just as it does claims of federal employees under Title VII. In the latter alternative, the Act specifically authorizes actions in federal court for "such legal or equitable relief as will effectuate the purposes of this chapter." § 633a(c). The special provisions of the ADEA that apply to claims by federal employees, 29 U.S.C. § 633a, also cover claims of retaliation, as the Supreme Court held in Gómez-Pérez v. Potter, 553 U.S. 474 (2008). Although § 633a literally prohibits only "discrimination based on age," the Court held that it also covers claims of retaliation, based on longstanding interpretation of analogous civil rights statutes, 42 U.S.C. § 1982, and Title IX of the Education Amendments of 1970, codified at 20 U.S.C. § 1681 et seq.

3. **Remedies.** Remedies for other employees under the ADEA again are the same as those under the Equal Pay Act and the FLSA, with the qualification that liquidated damages, in an amount equal to actual damages, are payable only for "willful violations" and that the court is authorized to grant "such legal or equitable relief as may be appropriate to effectuate the purposes of this chapter." These damage remedies led Congress explicitly to grant parties a right to jury trial under the Act. 29 U.S.C. § 626(b). The right to jury trial, while not controversial in most cases, has caused a conflict among the circuits over who decides to make awards of front pay. Some circuits hold that this is an equitable issue to be determined wholly by the judge, e.g., Dominic v. Consolidated Edison Co., 822 F.2d 1249, 1258 (2d Cir. 1987), while others hold that the judge should make an initial determination whether front pay should be awarded and, if so, the jury should decide the amount of the award. E.g., Roush v. KFC Nat'l Mgt. Co., 10 F.3d 392, 398 & n.10 (6th Cir. 1993);

Maxfield v. Sinclair Int'l, 766 F.2d 788, 796 (3d Cir. 1985), cert. denied, 474 U.S. 1057 (1986).

A far more contentious issue over remedies under the ADEA concerns the standard for awarding "liquidated damages," which effectively double the damages recoverable by the plaintiff. In Trans World Airlines v. Thurston, 469 U.S. 111 (1985), the Supreme Court considered this issue after finding that the defendant had violated the ADEA. The Court held that "willful violations," justifying the award of liquidated damages, were available only if " 'the employer . . . knew or showed reckless disregard for the matter of whether its conduct was prohibited by the ADEA.' " Id. at 128–29 (quoting Air Line Pilots Ass'n v. Trans World Airlines, 713 F.2d 940, 956 (2d Cir. 1983)). The Court interpreted this standard to be substantially the same as the standard for determining willfulness under the provision for criminal penalties in the FLSA. Id. at 125–26. On the record before it, the Court held that the employer had not acted willfully because it had sought the advice of counsel and had negotiated with the union representing its employees to bring its collective bargaining agreement into compliance with the Act. The Court later reaffirmed this holding in Hazen Paper v. Biggins, 507 U.S. 604 (1993); and in another case, the Court made clear that this standard requires more than simply unreasonable conduct by the defendant. McLaughlin v. Richland Shoe Co., 486 U.S. 128, 135 & n.13 (1988).

One further complication applies to claims by state employees who cannot, in their own actions, obtain damages from states that have refused to waive their immunity under the Eleventh Amendment. In Kimel v. Florida Board of Regents, 528 U.S. 62 (2000), the Supreme Court held that the ADEA could not be enforced against the states or their instrumentalities through the award of damages. As the Court was careful to point out, however, a prior decision had held that Congress had properly exercised its powers under the Commerce Clause in applying the ADEA to the states. EEOC v. Wyoming, 460 U.S. 226 (1983). Thus, the substantive provisions of the ADEA remain binding upon the states, although enforcement depends upon a range of subsidiary issues developed in the decisions under the Eleventh Amendment. It does not, for instance, forbid claims by individuals for injunctive relief against state officers or claims for damages brought by the EEOC on behalf of individual employees. For a discussion of this case and its implications for employment discrimination law, see Robert C. Post & Reva B. Siegel, Equal Protection by Law: Federal Antidiscrimination Legislation After *Morrison* and *Kimel*, 110 Yale L.J. 441 (2000).

4. **Bibliography.** A number of articles have addressed a range of specific issues involving procedures and remedies under the ADEA. Janet M. Bowermaster, Two (Federal) Wrongs Make a (State) Right: State Class-Action Procedures as an Alternative to the Opt-In Class-Action Provisions of the ADEA, 25 U. Mich. J.L. Reform 7 (1991); David

C. Miller, Alone in Its Field: Judicial Trend to Hold That the ADEA Preempts Section 1983 in Age Discrimination in Employment Claims, 29 Stetson L. Rev. 573 (2000).

CHAPTER 11

DISABILITIES

A. INTRODUCTION

The coverage of the statutes prohibiting discrimination on the basis of disability is large and growing. In the 2010 census, almost 57 million Americans, about 19 percent of the population, were identified as disabled, and over half reported that they were severely disabled. U.S. Census Bureau, Nearly 1 in 5 People Have a Disability in the U.S., Census Bureau Reports: Report Released to Coincide with the 22nd Anniversary of the ADA (July 25, 2012) https://www.census.gov/newsroom/releases/archives/miscellaneous/cb12-134.html. Individuals with a disability constitute one of the largest numerical minorities in the country, if not an actual majority under the broad definition of "disability" now codified in the Americans with Disabilities Act. Like age, however, disability does not constitute a suspect classification in constitutional law. Classifications on the basis of disability, like those on the basis of age, are subject to judicial review only for a rational relationship to a legitimate government interest. City of Cleburne v. Cleburne Living Center, 473 U.S. 432, 442–47 (1985). Consequently, individuals with disabilities depend almost entirely on statutory law for protection from discrimination. The two principal federal statutes protecting disabled individuals are the Rehabilitation Act of 1973, 29 U.S.C. § 700 et seq., and the Americans with Disabilities Act of 1990, 42 U.S.C. § 12101 et seq. (ADA). This chapter begins by summarizing the major provisions and innovations of these two statutes. It then considers the experience gained from litigation under these statutes and the reaction of Congress in recent amending legislation, the Americans with Disabilities Act Amendments Act of 2008, Pub. L. No. 110–325, 122 Stat. 3553. This last act significantly expanded the coverage of the ADA, superseding or modifying several decisions of the Supreme Court interpreting the ADA.

1. The Rehabilitation Act. The Rehabilitation Act reveals both the influence and the limitations of constitutional law as a model for proscribing discrimination on the basis of disability. The Act as a whole emphasized government programs to provide vocational training and employment for individuals with disabilities. The Act's prohibitions against discrimination were added only to assure that these individuals were not excluded from other publicly funded activities. These prohibitions apply to federal employment, participation in federally funded programs, and employment by federal contractors. §§ 501, 503, 504, 29 U.S.C. §§ 791, 793, 794. These provisions were modeled on previously adopted prohibitions against discrimination on the basis of race. The Fifth Amendment directly prohibits racial discrimination by the federal government, a prohibition which was expanded to recipients of federal funds by Title VI of the Civil Rights Act of 1964, 42 U.S.C. § 2000d et seq., and to federal contractors by Executive Order 11,246, reprinted in 42 U.S.C. § 2000e. The Rehabilitation Act represents a further expansion upon this prohibition by applying it to disabilities. Because the Constitution itself does not require strict scrutiny of classifications on the basis of disability, any prohibition on this basis must be accomplished by statute.

By the same token, however, Congress can adopt special programs for the disabled without any risk of engaging in unconstitutional forms of affirmative action. Programs to benefit individuals with disabilities need only have a rational relationship to a legitimate government interest, as they invariably do if they attempt to compensate for the adverse effects of having a disability. All of the provisions for training and employment in the Rehabilitation Act have this goal, as do a number of other statutes uniquely designed for the benefit of individuals with disabilities. Thus, the Individuals with Disabilities Education Act of 1975, 20 U.S.C. § 1400 et seq., requires state primary and secondary schools to provide special education programs for children with disabilities, and the Social Security Disability Insurance Program, 42 U.S.C. § 423(d), provides cash benefits to individuals with a disability so severe that it prevents them from working. This model of government assistance goes beyond prohibiting discrimination to requiring or providing for various forms of affirmative action. In doing so, however, it is necessary to define the class of individuals who can benefit from such programs. Such definitions, in turn, limit the scope of the prohibitions against discrimination contained in statutes like the Rehabilitation Act.

The definition of covered individuals under the Rehabilitation Act has been a source of continuing litigation, both under that act and under the ADA, which adopted the same basic definition of covered disabilities: "a physical or mental impairment that substantially limits one or more major life activities of such individual." § 3(1)(A), 42 U.S.C. § 12102(1)(A). The ADA added coverage based on having "a record of such an impairment" or "being regarded as having such an impairment," § 3(1)(B), (C), 42 U.S.C. § 12102(1)(B), (C), making the nature of the "impairment" still the crucial question for coverage under either statute. The Supreme Court has handed down several decisions on this question, all discussed in the first section of this chapter. The more recent decisions have tended to restrict coverage, seemingly out of concern that the benefits conferred by the statutes would otherwise be spread too broadly. If individuals with only minimal deficiencies in physical or mental ability were covered, then they would be protected from any form of discrimination attributed to those deficiencies. Perhaps this concern resulted from a stereotypical view of disabilities as inherently severe, assimilating the wide range of disabilities to a few salient examples, such as blindness or paralysis. Alternatively, it might have resulted from the nature of the affirmative duties imposed by the legislation. In any event, concerns over coverage were dramatically increased by the ADA, which expanded upon the coverage of the Rehabilitation Act in several other ways as well.

2. The Americans with Disabilities Act. The ADA abandoned the requirement in the Rehabilitation Act of federal involvement as a condition of coverage. Title I of the ADA, which is modeled on Title VII, covers all employers with 15 or more employees in industries affecting commerce. § 101(5), 42 U.S.C. § 12111(5). In separate titles, the ADA also covers public services and public accommodations, the latter in the sense of businesses open to the general public, including those operated by private firms. All of these titles prohibit discrimination, but they also impose affirmative obligations: in employment, to make reasonable accommodations for otherwise qualified individuals with disabilities; and in public services and public accommodations, to modify facilities so that they are accessible to the disabled. The ADA also elaborated on the prohibitions in the Rehabilitation Act, making more explicit exactly what those prohibitions required. In Title I, this process resulted in a prohibition that included the duty of reasonable accommodation as part of the definition of discrimination. Failure to make a reasonable accommodation constitutes a form of prohibited discrimination. This provision continues the dual emphasis, found in different provisions of the Rehabilitation Act, on both preventing discrimination and requiring affirmative action. In most situations, employers cannot take the disabilities of their employees into account, but in making reasonable accommodations, they must also engage in an individualized form of affirmative action, taking account of an employee's disabilities in order to compensate for it.

The tension between these two duties has given rise to considerable litigation, mainly under the ADA. As a purely conceptual matter, it is difficult to subsume the duty of reasonable accommodation into the duty to avoid discrimination. What the first requires, the second seems to forbid. As we have seen, similar difficulties arose under Title VII and the Constitution in the general debate over affirmative action and in the more specific disputes over the duty to accommodate religious practices. The latter was limited by constitutional concerns about favoring some religions over others under the Establishment Clause. Despite the absence of analogous constitutional concerns about favoring individuals with disabilities, the provisions on accommodating religious practices under Title VII formed the textual basis for the duty of reasonable accommodation under the ADA. Creating such a duty makes some practical sense under the ADA because it is difficult to distinguish discrimination against individuals with disabilities based on the stigma attached to many disabilities from discrimination based on the deficiencies in performance resulting from these disabilities. In the absence of the duty of reasonable accommodation, an employer charged with discriminating against the disabled could always assert that he took account, not of the fact of disability, but of its consequences for performing the job. Whether this practical argument is sufficient to justify the duty of reasonable accommodation and to reconcile it with the prohibition against discrimination remains an open question.

This question animates decisions under both the Rehabilitation Act and the ADA, but it is the more specific provisions of the ADA that have taken a dominant role in determining the rights of individuals with disabilities. Decisions under the Rehabilitation Act remain relevant to interpretation of the ADA because the ADA specifically states that it confers at least as much protection on individuals with disabilities as the Rehabilitation Act. § 501(a), 42 U.S.C. § 12201(a). Accordingly, this chapter considers cases under both statutes. For detailed accounts of the legislative history of the ADA and its relationship to the Rehabilitation Act, see Robert L. Burgdorf Jr., The Americans with Disabilities Act: Analysis and Implications of a Second-Generation Civil Rights Statute, 26 Harv. C.R.-C.L. L. Rev. 413 (1991); Ruth Colker, The ADA's Journey Through Congress, 39 Wake Forest L. Rev. 1 (2004).

So, too, decisions under Title VII remain relevant to the ADA, particularly in interpreting provisions framed in identical terms in each statute. Thus the ADA, like Title VII, explicitly prohibits practices with a disparate impact on the basis of disability. § 102(b)(6), (7), 42 U.S.C. § 12112(b)(6), (7). In Raytheon v. Hernandez, 540 U.S. 44 (2003), the Supreme Court recognized that the distinction between claims of disparate impact and claims of disparate treatment is the same under both statutes. Because the plaintiff in that case had not properly raised a claim of disparate impact under the ADA, the Court held that his claim had to be analyzed under the ordinary standards for proving disparate treatment under McDonnell Douglas v. Green, 411 U.S. 792 (1973).

3. The ADA Amendments Act of 2008. If the principal doctrinal innovation of the Rehabilitation Act and the ADA was applying the duty of reasonable accommodation to disability, the principal source of litigation under both statutes concerned the preliminary question of coverage: whether the plaintiff met the statutory requirements of an individual with a "disability." In a series of decisions, the Supreme Court eventually took a restrictive view of coverage, narrowly defining the impairments that constituted a covered "disability": "a physical or mental impairment that substantially limits one or more of the major life activities of such individual." § 3(1)(A), 42 U.S.C. § 12102(1)(A). These decisions also limited coverage on the alternative grounds of having "a record of such an impairment" and "being regarded as having such an impairment." § 3(1)(B), (C), 42 U.S.C. § 12102(1)(B), (C). Only certain actual impairments counted under the main definition, and they also determined what counted as "such an impairment" under the alternative definitions. Any actual impairment must meet two requirements: first, having a substantial effect; second, on a major life activity. If the effect was insubstantial or the affected activity was not a major life activity, then the impairment was not an actual disability. Hence the plaintiffs in Sutton v. United Air Lines, Inc., 527 U.S. 471 (1999), who suffered from poor eyesight that could be corrected by ordinary eyeglasses, did not have an actual disability because their eyesight, as corrected, did not substantially limit a majority life activity. Nor were they "regarded as" having a disability since the employer did not regard their eyesight as having a substantial effect on a major life activity. It followed that the employer could refuse to hire them based on their poor eyesight. The decision in *Sutton* is reproduced in the first section of this chapter, and its reasoning discussed in more detail there. The important point for now is that the decision denied the plaintiffs any claim at all under the statute, even if the employer regarded poor eyesight as an impairment that disqualified them for the job.

The ADA Amendments Act of 2008 (ADAAA) rejected that reasoning by liberalizing the requirements for coverage. It did so in three ways: first, by reducing the effects that the plaintiff's impairment needed to have; second, by expanding the list of major life activities that could be affected; and third, by expanding the impairments that could be "regarded as" disabilities. § 3(2), (3), (4), 42 U.S.C. § 12102(2), (3), (4). These amendments, like those to Title VII in the Civil Rights Act of 1991, were mainly reactive: superseding prior decisions of the Supreme Court and turning the clock back to the law as it existed before those decisions. The amendments explicitly disapproved of the reasoning in restrictive decisions like *Sutton* and changed them by adding detailed provisions to the ADA. Curiously enough, however, the precise holding in *Sutton* on vision problems that could be corrected by ordinary eyeglasses was preserved. Such problems are not an actual disability (although they might be "regarded as" one.) The general approach of the decision was rejected but not its narrow result.

The ADAAA continues a trend, apparent throughout employment discrimination law, of Congress rejecting narrow interpretations of the laws against employment discrimination and expanding coverage to reach new plaintiffs and new claims. This tendency makes the law more complicated because it requires an understanding both of what the courts have previously held and what Congress has done to reject, accept, or modify their decisions. The law accordingly becomes more technical and specialized, not readily understood by individuals, employers, or lawyers outside the field. What are the offsetting benefits of such an intricate dialogue between the judicial and legislative branches? Does it reinforce or undermine public support for laws like the ADA?

4. **Discrimination and Reasonable Accommodation.** By codifying the duty of reasonable accommodation, the ADA prompted a major theoretical debate over the extent to which this duty constituted a genuine innovation in employment discrimination law. In a series of articles, Professor Samuel R. Bagenstos has argued that the ADA sought

to eliminate the same forms of stigmatic discrimination against the disabled that had previously been suffered by minority groups. More recently, however, he has questioned the effectiveness of relying solely upon this model of discrimination to the exclusion of one based on social welfare. Only the latter, in his view, is capable of removing the structural barriers to employment faced by many individuals with disabilities. See Samuel R. Bagenstos, The Future of Disability Law, 114 Yale L.J. 1 (2004); Samuel R. Bagenstos, "Rational Discrimination," Accommodation, and the Politics of (Disability) Civil Rights, 89 Va. L. Rev. 825 (2003); Samuel R. Bagenstos, The Americans with Disabilities Act as Welfare Reform, 44 Wm. & Mary L. Rev. 921 (2003); Samuel R. Bagenstos, Essay, The Americans with Disabilities Act as Risk Regulation, 101 Colum. L. Rev. 1479 (2001); Samuel R. Bagenstos, Subordination, Stigma, and "Disability," 86 Va. L. Rev. 397 (2000); Samuel R. Bagenstos & Margo Schlanger, Hedonic Damages, Hedonic Adaptation, and Disability, 60 Vand. L. Rev. 745 (2007).

Arguing from an economic perspective, Professor Christine Jolls contends that the difference between required accommodation and prohibited discrimination is, at most, a matter of degree, since all forms of regulation impose burdens upon employers to comply with the law. Christine Jolls, Accommodation Mandates, 53 Stan. L. Rev. 223 (2000); Christine Jolls, Commentary, Antidiscrimination and Accommodation, 115 Harv. L. Rev. 642 (2001). See also Nicole B. Porter, The New ADA Backlash, 82 Tenn. L. Rev. 1 (2014); John J. Donohue III, Understanding the Reasons for and Impact of Legislatively Mandated Benefits for Selected Workers, 53 Stan. L. Rev. 897 (2001); Mary Crossley, Reasonable Accommodation as Part and Parcel of the Antidiscrimination Project, 35 Rutgers L.J. 861 (2004); Christopher L. Griffin, Jr., Explaining ADA Employment Discrimination Charges Over the Business Cycle, 84 U. Cin. L. Rev. 737 (2016); Michael Ashley Stein, Same Struggle, Different Difference: ADA Accommodations as Antidiscrimination, 153 U. Pa. L. Rev. 579 (2004); Symposium, Disability Law, Equality, and Difference: American Disability Law and the Civil Rights Model, 55 Ala. L. Rev. 923 (2004).

Others have argued, by contrast, that the duty of reasonable accommodation more closely resembles an individualized form of affirmative action. Pamela S. Karlan & George Rutherglen, Disabilities, Discrimination, and Reasonable Accommodation, 46 Duke L.J. 1 (1996); J.H. Verkerke, Disaggregating Antidiscrimination and Accommodation, 44 Wm. & Mary L. Rev. 1385 (2003); Samuel Issacharoff & Justin Nelson, Discrimination with a Difference: Can Employment Discrimination Law Accommodate the Americans with Disabilities Act?, 79 N.C. L. Rev. 308 (2001).

This position, in turn, has led to comparisons of the duty of reasonable accommodation with other forms of affirmative obligations in pursuit of redistributive goals. See Ruth Colker, Hypercapitalism:

Affirmative Protections for People with Disabilities, Illness and Parenting Responsibilities Under United States Law, 9 Yale J.L. & Feminism 213 (1997); Elizabeth A. Pendo, Substantially Limited Justice? The Possibilities and Limits of a New Rawlsian Analysis of Disability-Based Discrimination, 77 St. John's L. Rev. 225 (2003); Mark S. Stein, Rawls on Redistribution to the Disabled, 6 Geo. Mason L. Rev. 997 (1998); Mark C. Weber, Exile and the Kingdom: Integration, Harassment, and the Americans with Disabilities Act, 63 Md. L. Rev. 162 (2004); Mark C. Weber, Beyond the Americans with Disabilities Act: A National Employment Policy for People with Disabilities, 46 Buff. L. Rev. 123 (1998).

5. **Effects of the ADA.** Related to this theoretical debate has been a debate over empirical evidence showing that plaintiffs in disability discrimination cases have an extraordinarily low success rate in litigation, prevailing in less than 10 percent of the cases that they bring. See Ruth O'Brien, Crippled Justice: The History of Modern Disability Policy in the Workplace (2001); Stephen F. Befort & Holly L. Thomas, The ADA in Turmoil: Judicial Dissonance, the Supreme Court's Response, and the Future of Disability Discrimination Law, 78 Or. L. Rev. 27 (1999); Peter Blanck et al., Employment of People with Disabilities: Twenty-Five Years Back and Ahead, 25 Law & Ineq. 323 (2007); Ruth Colker, The Americans with Disabilities Act: A Windfall for Defendants, 34 Harv. C.R.-C.L. L. Rev. 99 (1999); Charles B. Craver, The Judicial Disabling of the Employment Discrimination Provisions of the Americans with Disabilities Act, 18 Lab. Law. 417 (2003); Michael Ashley Stein, Empirical Implications of Title I, 85 Iowa L. Rev. 1671 (2000); Michael Ashley Stein, Disability, Employment Policy, and the Supreme Court, 55 Stan. L. Rev. 607 (2002); Michelle A. Travis, Leveling the Playing Field or Stacking the Deck? The "Unfair Advantage" Critique of Perceived Disability Claims, 78 N.C. L. Rev. 901 (2000); Jeffrey A. Van Detta & Dan R. Gallipeau, Judges and Juries: Why Are So Many ADA Plaintiffs Losing Summary Judgment Motions, and Would They Fare Better Before a Jury? A Response to Professor Colker, 19 Rev. Litig. 505 (2000); Symposium, Backlash Against the ADA: Interdisciplinary Perspectives and Implications for Social Justice Strategies, 21 Berkeley J. Emp. & Lab. L. 1 (2000).

Because of data inadequacies and difficulties in the definition and classification of "disability," there is some debate over the *extent* of changes in the employment rate of disabled persons since the enactment of the ADA. Richard V. Burkhauser et al., Self-Reported Work-Limitation Data: What They Can and Cannot Tell Us, 39 Demography 541 (2002); Douglas Kruse & Lisa Schur, Employment of People with Disabilities Following the ADA, 42 Indus. Rel. 31 (2003); Susan Schwochau & Peter Blanck, Does the ADA Disable the Disabled?—More Comments, 42 Indus. Rel. 67 (2003). There is, however, a broad consensus that disabled persons have experienced a steady decline in employment throughout the

1990s, whereas the employment rate of nondisabled persons has remained constant (for men) or has increased (for women) during the same period. Empirical research on the question whether the decline in employment of disabled persons can be attributed to the enactment of the ADA has produced mixed findings. Some studies have relied on econometric analysis of national labor market data to link falling employment rates for the disabled with the temporal adoption of the ADA. Thomas DeLeire, The Wage and Employment Effects of the Americans with Disabilities Act, 35 J. Hum. Resources 693 (2000); Daron Acemoglu & Joshua Angrist, Consequences of Employment Protection? The Case of the Americans with Disabilities Act, 109 J. Pol. Econ. 915 (2001). While these studies of the overall impact of the ADA are not able to identify what aspect of the ADA would generate this disemployment effect, their general surmise is that the accommodation mandates of the ADA make it costly for firms to employ people with disabilities, leading to a decline in employment. Samuel R. Bagenstos, Review Essay, Has the Americans with Disabilities Act Reduced Employment for People with Disabilities?, 25 Berkeley J. Emp. & Lab. L. 827 (2004).

An important recent article does develop a strategy for establishing the separate influences of the antidiscrimination and reasonable accommodation components of the ADA by analyzing the impact of the national law across states that had previously adopted neither, one, or both of these elements. Christine Jolls & J.J. Prescott, Disaggregating Employment Protection: The Case of Disability Discrimination, (Harvard Pub. Law, Working Paper No. 106), https://papers.ssrn.com/papers.cfm?abstactid=580741.123. (2005). Jolls and Prescott offer a mixed assessment about the prior speculation: "We find strong evidence that the immediate post-enactment employment effects of the ADA are attributable to its requirement of reasonable accommodations for disabled employees rather than to its potential imposition of firing costs for such employees. Moreover, the pattern of the ADA's effects across states suggests, contrary to widely-discussed prior findings based on national-level data, that declining disabled employment after the immediate post-ADA period may reflect other factors rather than the ADA itself." For another study raising questions about this conclusion, but finding an effect on the wages of individuals with disabilities, see John J. Donohue III et al., Assessing Post-ADA Employment: Some Econometric Evidence and Policy Considerations, 8 J. Empirical Legal Stud. 477 (2011).

A number of studies have explored factors other than the ADA in order to explain the declining rates of employment among disabled persons. Some researchers trace the decline to expansion of disability benefits in the 1980s and 1990s, which may have induced or at least facilitated the withdrawal of people with disabilities from the labor market, independent of any effects of the ADA. John Bound & Timothy Waidmann, Accounting for Recent Declines in Employment Rates among

Working-Aged Men and Women with Disabilities, 37 J. Hum. Resources 231 (2002); Andrew J. Houtenville & Richard V. Burkhauser, Cornell Univ.: Sch. of Labor Relations, Did the Employment of People with Disabilities Decline in the 1990s, and Was the ADA Responsible? (2004), www.edl.cornell.edu/publicationds/RB EmpDecline.pdf. Others point to such factors as increased educational opportunities, pre-existing employment trends among the disabled, increased severity of impairments, and other changes in the social environment. Christine Jolls, Identifying the Effects of the Americans with Disabilities Act Using State Law Variation: Preliminary Evidence on Educational Participation Effects, 94 Am. Econ. Rev. 447 (2004); Kathleen Beegle & Wendy A. Stock, The Labor Market Effects of Disability Discrimination Laws, 38 J. Hum. Resources 806 (2003); Douglas Kruse & Lisa Schur, Does the Definition Affect the Outcome? Employment Trends Under Alternative Measures of Disability, in The Decline in Employment of People with Disabilities: A Policy Puzzle 279 (David C. Stapleton & Richard V. Burkhauser eds., 2003). For an empirical analysis of the ADA's possible impact on labor market outcomes other than the employment rate, see Julie L. Hotchkiss, The Labor Market Experience of Workers with Disabilities: The ADA and Beyond (2003). For a useful discussion of indicators that can be used to assess the achievement of various goals embodied in the ADA, see Frederick C. Collignon, Is the ADA Successful? Indicators for Tracking Gains, 549 Annals Am. Acad. Pol. & Soc. Sci. 129 (1997).

Professor Peter D. Blanck has also examined the empirical evidence on the effects of the ADA in a series of books and articles that are less pessimistic about the impact of the legislation than many of the studies cited above. Peter D. Blanck, The Americans with Disabilities Act and the Emerging Workforce: Employment of People with Mental Retardation (David Braddock ed., 1998); Employment, Disability, and the Americans with Disabilities Act: Issues in Law, Public Policy, and Research (Peter D. Blanck ed., 2000); Peter D. Blanck, Employment Integration, Economic Opportunity, and the Americans with Disabilities Act: Empirical Studies from 1990–1993, 79 Iowa L. Rev. 853 (1994); Peter D. Blanck & Walter Olson, The Unintended Consequences of the Americans with Disabilities Act, 85 Iowa L. Rev. 1811 (2000); Susan Schwochau & Peter D. Blanck, The Economics of the Americans with Disabilities Act, Part III: Does the ADA Disable the Disabled?, 21 Berkeley J. Emp. & Lab. L. 271 (2000); Susan Schwochau & Peter D. Blanck, Does the ADA Disable the Disabled?—More Comments, 42 Indus. Rel. 67 (2003); Peter D. Blanck, Helen A. Schartz & Kevin M. Schartz, Labor Force Participation and Income of Individuals with Disabilities in Sheltered and Competitive Employment: Cross-Sectional and Longitudinal Analyses of Seven States During the 1980s and 1990s, 44 Wm. & Mary L. Rev. 1029 (2003). He concludes generally that reports of the ineffectiveness of the ADA have been much exaggerated based on narrow and inadequate empirical studies.

6. **Bibliography.** In addition, numerous books and collections of articles have addressed the overall scope and purpose of the Rehabilitation Act and the ADA, among them: Robert L. Burgdorf, Jr., Disability Discrimination in Employment Law (1995); Ruth Colker & Paul D. Grossman, The Law of Disability Discrimination (8th ed. 2013); Brian J. Doyle, Disability, Discrimination, and Equal Opportunities: A Comparative Study of the Employment Rights of Disabled Persons (1995); Martha C. Nussbaum, Frontiers of Justice: Disability, Nationality, Species Membership (2006); Joseph P. Shapiro, No Pity: People with Disabilities Forging a New Civil Rights Movement (1993); Mark S. Stein, Distributive Justice and Disability: Utilitarianism Against Egalitarianism (2006); Symposium, Employment Discrimination and the Americans with Disabilities Act at 25 Years, 63 Drake L. Rev. 739 (2015); Symposium, The ADA at 25: The Continued Inequality of Americans with Disabilities, 13 U. St. Thomas L.J. 1 (2016); Symposium on Disability Discrimination and Law, 17 Employee Rts. & Emp. Pol'y J. 1 (2013); Symposium, The Americans with Disabilities Act at 155—Past, Present, & Future, 75 Miss. L.J. 917 (2006); Symposium, Disability, 116 Ethics 153 (2005).

For separate articles on disability discrimination, see Bradley A. Areheart, When Disability Isn't "Just Right": The Entrenchment of the Medical Model of Disability and the *Goldilocks* Dilemma, 83 Ind. L.J. 181 (2008); Ruth Colker, Anti-Subordination Above All: A Disability Perspective, 82 Notre Dame L. Rev. 1415 (2007); Elizabeth F. Emens, Framing Disability, 2012 U. Ill. L. Rev. 1383; Michael Ashley Stein, Disability Human Rights, 95 Cal. L. Rev. 75 (2007); Michael Evan Waterstone, Disability Constitutional Law, 63 Emory L.J. 527 (2014).

Several articles have also examined the history and development of the ADA. Peter D. Blanck, Americans with Disabilities and Their Civil Rights: Past, Present, and Future, 66 U. Pitt. L. Rev. 687 (2005); Ruth Colker, The Disability Pendulum: The First Decade of the Americans with Disabilities Act (2005); Michael Evan Waterstone, The Untold Story of the Rest of the Americans with Disabilities Act, 58 Vand. L. Rev. 1807 (2005).

For a timely book analyzing the history of the disability rights movement and the tension between different aims within the movement, see Samuel R. Bagenstos, Law and the Contradictions of the Disability Rights Movement (2009). For other general discussions of disability rights, see Kevin J. Coco, Beyond the Price Tag: An Economic Analysis of Title III of the Americans with Disabilities Act, 20 Kan. J.L. & Pub. Pol'y 58 (2010); Ruth Colker, When Is Separate Unequal? A Disability Perspective (2009); Jeannette Cox, Disability Stigma and Intraclass Discrimination, 62 Fla. L. Rev. 429 (2010); Wendy F. Hensel, The Disability Dilemma: A Skeptical Bench & Bar, 69 U. Pitt. L. Rev. 637 (2008); Michael L. Perlin, "Simplify You, Classify You": Stigma, Stereotypes and Civil Rights in Disability Classification Systems, 25 Ga.

St. U. L. Rev. 607 (2009); Ani B. Satz, Disability, Vulnerability, and the Limits of Antidiscrimination, 83 Wash. L. Rev. 513 (2008); Michelle A. Travis, Impairment as Protected Status: A New Universality for Disability Rights, 46 Ga. L. Rev. 937 (2012); Michelle A. Travis, Lashing Back at the ADA Backlash: How the Americans with Disabilities Act Benefits Americans Without Disabilities, 76 Tenn. L. Rev. 311 (2009); Mark C. Weber, The Common Law of Disability Discrimination, 2012 Utah L. Rev. 429; Mark C. Weber, Disability Rights, Disability Discrimination, and Social Insurance, 25 Ga. St. U. L. Rev. 575 (2009); David A. Weisbach, Toward a New Approach to Disability Law, 2009 U. Chi. Legal F. 47.

For articles on disability rights in particular occupations, see Carrie Griffin Basas, Indulgent Employment? Careers in the Arts for People with Disabilities, 40 Rutgers L.J. 613 (2009); Carrie Griffin Basas, The New Boys: Women With Disabilities and the Legal Profession, 25 Berkeley J. Gender L. & Just. 32 (2010); Robert F. Moore, The Interaction Between the Americans with Disabilities Act and Drug and Alcohol Addiction in Sports, 16 Sports Law. J. 231 (2009); Symposium: Lawyers and Disabilities, 69 U. Pitt. L. Rev. 389 (2008).

B. COVERED DISABILITIES

NOTES ON THE DEFINITION AND SIGNIFICANCE OF COVERED DISABILITIES

1. **Statutory Definitions.** Both the Rehabilitation Act and the ADA contain the same three-part definition of covered disabilities:

> The term "disability" means with respect to an individual—
>
> (A) a physical or mental impairment that substantially limits one or more major life activities of such individual;
>
> (B) a record of such an impairment; or
>
> (C) being regarded as having such an impairment.

§ 3(1), 42 U.S.C. § 12102(1). The Rehabilitation Act contains the same definition by cross-reference to the ADA, although originally it relied upon language nearly identical to subdivision (A) above. See § 7(9)(B), 29 U.S.C. § 706(9)(B). The ADA's definition applies to all three of its separate titles, so that the next principal case, concerned with discrimination in public accommodations under Title III, also applies to discrimination in employment under Title I.

Having a disability, however, is not enough to gain protection from employment discrimination. Title I imposes additional requirements for coverage which themselves are intertwined with the substantive prohibitions of the statute. Only a "qualified individual" is protected from employment discrimination. Such an individual is one "who, with or without reasonable accommodation, can perform the essential functions of the employment position that such individual holds or desires." § 101(8), 42

U.S.C. § 12111(8). The term "reasonable accommodation" is then defined in a separate subsection. § 101(9), 42 U.S.C. § 12111(9). It follows, as a definitional matter, that any plaintiff who succeeds in establishing coverage also succeeds in establishing many of the elements of a claim on the merits. A plaintiff who proves that she is a "qualified individual" and that she was denied a job because of her disability has established a claim under the ADA, subject to limited defenses.

2. The Significance of Coverage. As a matter of litigation strategy, the significance of coverage is obvious. It is a crucial preliminary issue that results either in a decision for the defendant if the plaintiff is not covered, or if the plaintiff is covered, requires an examination of the merits and available defenses. Because issues of coverage overlap with those on the merits, however, the distinction between these issues is not as clear as it initially appears to be, resulting in practical problems in allocating the burden of proof. Plaintiffs generally have the burden of proof on coverage and on proving discrimination, but defendants have the burden of proof on issues such as whether a proposed accommodation causes an undue hardship or whether the plaintiff poses a direct threat in the work place. All these issues overlap to some degree and can be difficult to distinguish from one another. Moreover, as the next case illustrates, the consequences of finding coverage often depend upon the issues left open on the merits.

At the level of legal policy, the issue of which disabilities are covered under the ADA determines who benefits from the statute. This issue does not exist under Title VII or § 1981, where the statute covers "any individual" or "all persons," or under the ADEA, which covers everyone who is at least 40 years old. Coverage of disabilities is a more complicated issue, one that raises fundamental questions about the severity of impairments necessary to obtain special treatment and the extent of the special treatment that should be made available. The affirmative obligations created by virtually every statute concerned with disabilities—whether in the form of payments, medical care, education and training, or reasonable accommodation—impose practical constraints on who may benefit from such obligations. If coverage provided by these statutes is spread too widely, the benefits that they confer are likely to be spread too thin. There is a practical need to define a genuine "protected class" under statutes like the Rehabilitation Act and the ADA.

3. Exceptions to Coverage. Both the Rehabilitation Act and the ADA contain exceptions to coverage for conditions that Congress found to be morally reprehensible, such as current illegal use of drugs; current use of alcohol by an alcoholic; homosexuality and bisexuality; transvestitism, transsexualism, and similar conditions; compulsive gambling, kleptomania, and pyromania. § 7(20)(C), (E), (F), 29 U.S.C. § 705(20)(C), (E), (F); §§ 104, 509, 511, 512, 42 U.S.C. §§ 12114, 12208, 12210, 12211. Several of these exceptions are narrowly defined, especially those involving drugs and alcohol, in order to allow recovering addicts and alcoholics to continue to benefit from coverage so long as they do not relapse into substance abuse. Another exception under the Rehabilitation Act is for contagious diseases and infections, but only if they pose a direct threat to other individuals. § 7(20)(D), 29 U.S.C. § 705(20)(D). This exception was generalized into a defense in the ADA for any condition that causes a direct threat. § 103(b), 42 U.S.C. § 12113(b). Because these exceptions are technically complex, none of them should be invoked without consulting the precise terms in which they are framed. Moreover, those concerned with sexual practices might well be restricted further or invalidated because they are inconsistent with the constitutional prohibition against discrimination based on sexual orientation. See Obergefell v. Hodges, 135 S. Ct. 2584 (2015); Lawrence v. Texas, 539 U.S. 558 (2003). For an analysis of some the issues surrounding these exceptions to coverage, see Paul E. Starkman, Answering the Tough Questions About Alcoholism and Substance Abuse Under the ADA and FMLA, 25 Employee Rel. L.J., Spring 2000, at 43.

4. **Bibliography.** As noted earlier, and as discussed in more detail in the next section of this chapter, the coverage of the ADA was greatly enlarged by the ADA Amendments Act of 2008 (ADAAA). For discussions of the general effect of the ADAAA, see Cheryl L. Anderson, Ideological Dissonance, Disability Backlash, and the ADA Amendments Act, 55 Wayne L. Rev. 1267 (2009); Kevin Barry, Brian East & Marcy Karin, Pleading Disability After the ADAAA, 31 Hofstra Lab. & Emp. L.J. 1 (2013); Stephen F. Befort, An Empirical Examination of Case Outcomes Under the ADA Amendments Act, 70 Wash. & Lee L. Rev. 2027 (2013); Teressa L. Elliott, The Path to the Americans with Disabilities Act Amendments Act: U.S. Supreme Court Cases, Congressional Intent, and Substantial Change, 48 Gonz. L. Rev. 395 (2012/13); Amelia M. Joiner, The ADAAA: Opening the Floodgates, 47 San Diego L. Rev. 331 (2010); Jeffrey Douglas Jones, Enfeebling the ADA: The ADA Amendments Act of 2008, 62 Okla. L. Rev. 667 (2010); Charles E. Mitchell, Assessing the Impact of the Americans with Disabilities Amendments Act of 2008: An Analysis of Litigation Efforts under Title I of the Act, 43 Empl. Rel. L.J. 36 (2017); Nicole B. Porter, Special Treatment Stigma After the ADA Amendments Act, 43 Pepp. L. Rev. 213 (2016); Michelle A. Travis, Disqualifying Universality Under the Americans with Disabilities Act Amendments Act, 2015 Mich. St. L. Rev. 1689.

For more specific issues of coverage, see Blake R. Bertagna, The Internet—Disability or Distraction? An Analysis of Whether "Internet Addiction" Can Qualify as a Disability Under the Americans with Disabilities Act, 25 Hofstra Lab. & Emp. L.J. 419 (2008); Susan D. Carle, Analyzing Social Impairments Under Title I of the Americans with Disabilities Act, 50 U.C. Davis L. Rev. 1109 (2017); Doron Dorfman, Re-Claiming Disability: Identity, Procedural Justice, and the Disability Determination Process, 42 Law & Soc. Inquiry 195 (2017); Jeannette Cox, "Corrective" Surgery and the Americans with Disabilities Act, 46 San Diego L. Rev. 113 (2009); Sharona Hoffman, Corrective Justice and Title I of the ADA, 52 Am. U. L. Rev. 1213 (2003); James A. Inman & Sandra L. Inman, Fibromyalgia and the Americans with Disabilities Act: Overcoming Hurdles for Successful Litigation, 13 Mich. St. U. J. Med. & L. 39 (2009); Dale Larson, Unconsciously Regarded as Disabled: Implicit Bias and the Regarded-As Prong of the Americans with Disabilities Act, 56 UCLA L. Rev. 451 (2008); Paul A. Race & Seth M. Dornier, ADA Amendments Act of 2008: The Effect on Employers and Educators, 46 Willamette L. Rev. 357 (2009); Maya

Sabatello, Who's Got Parental Rights? The Intersection Between Infertility, Reproductive Technologies, and Disability Rights Law, 6 J. Health & Biomedical L. 227 (2010); Ani B. Satz, Fragmented Lives: Disability Discrimination and the Role of "Environment-Framing," 68 Wash. & Lee L. Rev. 187 (2011); Joseph A. Seiner, Pleading Disability, 51 B.C. L. Rev. 95 (2010); Craig R. Senn, Perception over Reality: Extending the ADA's Concept of "Regarded As" Protection Under Federal Employment Discrimination Law, 36 Fla. St. U. L. Rev. 827 (2009); Michael Waterstone, Returning Veterans and Disability Law, 85 Notre Dame L. Rev. 1081 (2010).

Toyota Motor Manufacturing, Kentucky, Inc. v. Williams

534 U.S. 184 (2002).

■ JUSTICE O'CONNOR delivered the opinion of the Court.

Under the Americans with Disabilities Act of 1990, a physical impairment that "substantially limits one or more . . . major life activities" is a "disability." 42 U.S.C. § 12102(2)(A). Respondent, claiming to be disabled because of her carpal tunnel syndrome and other related impairments, sued petitioner, her former employer, for failing to provide her with a reasonable accommodation as required by the ADA. See § 12112(b)(5)(A). The District Court granted summary judgment to petitioner, finding that respondent's impairments did not substantially limit any of her major life activities. The Court of Appeals for the Sixth Circuit reversed, finding that the impairments substantially limited respondent in the major life activity of performing manual tasks, and therefore granting partial summary judgment to respondent on the issue of whether she was disabled under the ADA. We conclude that the Court of Appeals did not apply the proper standard in making this determination because it analyzed only a limited class of manual tasks and failed to ask whether respondent's impairments prevented or restricted her from performing tasks that are of central importance to most people's daily lives.

I

Respondent began working at petitioner's automobile manufacturing plant in Georgetown, Kentucky, in August 1990. She was soon placed on an engine fabrication assembly line, where her duties included work with pneumatic tools. Use of these tools eventually caused pain in respondent's hands, wrists, and arms. She sought treatment at petitioner's in-house medical service, where she was diagnosed with bilateral carpal tunnel syndrome and bilateral tendonitis. Respondent consulted a personal physician who placed her on permanent work restrictions that precluded her from lifting more than 20 pounds or from "frequently lifting or carrying . . . objects weighing up to 10 pounds," engaging in "constant repetitive . . . flexion or extension of [her] wrists or elbows," performing "overhead work," or using "vibratory or pneumatic tools."

In light of these restrictions, for the next two years petitioner assigned respondent to various modified duty jobs. Nonetheless, respondent missed some work for medical leave, and eventually filed a claim under the Kentucky Workers' Compensation Act. Ky. Rev. Stat. Ann. 342.0011 et seq. The parties settled this claim, and respondent returned to work. She was unsatisfied by petitioner's efforts to accommodate her work restrictions, however, and responded by bringing an action in the United States District Court for the Eastern District of Kentucky alleging that petitioner had violated the ADA by refusing to accommodate her disability. That suit was also settled, and as part of the settlement, respondent returned to work in December 1993.

Upon her return, petitioner placed respondent on a team in Quality Control Inspection Operations (QCIO). QCIO is responsible for four tasks: (1) "assembly paint"; (2) "paint second inspection"; (3) "shell body audit"; and (4) "ED surface repair." Respondent was initially placed on a team that performed only the first two of these tasks, and for a couple of years, she rotated on a weekly basis between them. In assembly paint, respondent visually inspected painted cars moving slowly down a conveyor. She scanned for scratches, dents, chips, or any other flaws that may have occurred during the assembly or painting process, at a rate of one car every 54 seconds. When respondent began working in assembly paint, inspection team members were required to open and shut the doors, trunk, and/or hood of each passing car. Sometime during respondent's tenure, however, the position was modified to include only visual inspection with few or no manual tasks. Paint second inspection required team members to use their hands to wipe each painted car with a glove as it moved along a conveyor. The parties agree that respondent was physically capable of performing both of these jobs and that her performance was satisfactory.

During the fall of 1996, petitioner announced that it wanted QCIO employees to be able to rotate through all four of the QCIO processes. Respondent therefore received training for the shell body audit job, in which team members apply a highlight oil to the hood, fender, doors, rear quarter panel, and trunk of passing cars at a rate of approximately one car per minute. The highlight oil has the viscosity of salad oil, and employees spread it on cars with a sponge attached to a block of wood. After they wipe each car with the oil, the employees visually inspect it for flaws. Wiping the cars required respondent to hold her hands and arms up around shoulder height for several hours at a time.

A short while after the shell body audit job was added to respondent's rotations, she began to experience pain in her neck and shoulders. Respondent again sought care at petitioner's in-house medical service, where she was diagnosed with myotendonitis bilateral periscapular, an inflammation of the muscles and tendons around both of her shoulder blades; myotendonitis and myositis bilateral forearms with nerve compression causing median nerve irritation; and thoracic outlet compression, a condition that causes pain in the nerves that lead to the upper extremities. Respondent requested that petitioner accommodate her medical conditions by allowing her to return to doing only her original two jobs in QCIO, which respondent claimed she could still perform without difficulty.

The parties disagree about what happened next. According to respondent, petitioner refused her request and forced her to continue working in the shell body audit job, which caused her even greater physical injury. According to petitioner, respondent simply began missing work on a regular basis. Regardless, it is clear that on December 6, 1996, the last day respondent worked at petitioner's plant, she was placed under a no-work-of-any-kind restriction by her treating physicians. On January 27, 1997, respondent received a letter from petitioner that terminated her employment, citing her poor attendance record.

Respondent filed a charge of disability discrimination with the Equal Employment Opportunity Commission (EEOC). After receiving a right to sue letter, respondent filed suit against petitioner in the United States District Court for the Eastern District of Kentucky. Her complaint alleged that petitioner had violated the ADA and the Kentucky Civil Rights Act, Ky. Rev. Stat. Ann. § 344.010 et seq., by failing to reasonably accommodate her disability and by terminating her employment. Respondent later amended her complaint to also allege a violation of the Family and Medical Leave Act of 1993 (FMLA).

Respondent based her claim that she was "disabled" under the ADA on the ground that her physical impairments substantially limited her in (1) manual tasks; (2) housework; (3) gardening; (4) playing with her children; (5) lifting; and (6) working, all of which, she argued, constituted major life activities under the Act. Respondent also argued, in the alternative, that she was disabled under the ADA because she had a record of a substantially limiting impairment and because she was regarded as having such an impairment. See 42 U.S.C. §§ 12102(2)(B)–(C).

After petitioner filed a motion for summary judgment and respondent filed a motion for partial summary judgment on her disability claims, the District Court granted summary judgment to petitioner. The court found that respondent had not been disabled, as defined by the ADA, at the time of petitioner's alleged refusal to accommodate her, and that she had therefore not been covered by the Act's protections or by the Kentucky Civil Rights Act, which is construed consistently with the ADA. The District Court held that respondent had suffered from a physical impairment, but that the impairment did not qualify as a disability because it had not "substantially limit[ed]" any "major life activit[y]," 42 U.S.C. § 12102(2)(A). The court rejected respondent's arguments that gardening, doing housework, and playing with children are major life activities. Although the court agreed that performing manual tasks, lifting, and working are major life activities, it found the evidence insufficient to demonstrate that respondent had been substantially limited in lifting or working. The court found respondent's claim that she was substantially limited in performing manual tasks to be "irretrievably contradicted by [respondent's] continual insistence that she could perform the tasks in assembly [paint] and paint [second] inspection without difficulty." The court also found no evidence that respondent had had a record of a substantially limiting impairment, or that petitioner had regarded her as having such an impairment.

The District Court also rejected respondent's claim that her termination violated the ADA and the Kentucky Civil Rights Act. The court found that even if it assumed that respondent was disabled at the time of her termination, she was not a "qualified individual with a disability," 42 U.S.C. § 12111(8), because, at that time, her physicians had restricted her from performing work of any kind. Finally, the court found that respondent's FMLA claim failed, because she had not presented evidence that she had suffered any damages available under the FMLA.

Respondent appealed all but the gardening, housework, and playing-with-children rulings. The Court of Appeals for the Sixth Circuit reversed the District Court's ruling on whether respondent was disabled at the time she sought an accommodation, but affirmed the District Court's rulings on respondent's FMLA and wrongful termination claims. 224 F.3d 840 (2000). The Court of Appeals held that in order for respondent to demonstrate that she was disabled due to a substantial limitation in the ability to perform manual tasks at the time of her accommodation request, she had to "show that her manual disability involve a 'class' of manual activities affecting the ability to perform tasks at work." Id., at 843. Respondent satisfied this test, according to the Court of Appeals, because her ailments "prevent her from doing the tasks associated with certain types of manual assembly line jobs, manual product handling jobs and manual building trade jobs (painting, plumbing, roofing, etc.) that require the gripping of tools and repetitive work with hands and arms extended at or above shoulder levels for extended periods of time." Ibid. In reaching this conclusion, the court disregarded evidence that respondent could "tend to her personal hygiene [and] carry out personal or household chores," finding that such evidence "does not affect a determination that her impairment substantially limit her ability to perform the range of manual tasks associated with an assembly line job," ibid. Because the Court of Appeals concluded that respondent had been substantially limited in performing manual tasks and, for that reason, was entitled to partial summary judgment on the issue of whether she was disabled under the Act, it found that it did not need to determine whether respondent had been substantially limited in the major life activities of lifting or working, ibid., or whether she had had a "record of" a disability or had been "regarded as" disabled, id., at 844.

We granted certiorari to consider the proper standard for assessing whether an individual is substantially limited in performing manual tasks. We now reverse the Court of Appeals' decision to grant partial summary judgment to respondent on the issue of whether she was substantially limited in performing manual tasks at the time she sought an accommodation. We express no opinion on the working, lifting, or other arguments for disability status that were preserved below but which were not ruled upon by the Court of Appeals.

II

The ADA requires covered entities, including private employers, to provide "reasonable accommodations to the known physical or mental limitations of an otherwise qualified individual with a disability who is an applicant or employee, unless such covered entity can demonstrate that the accommodation would impose an undue hardship." 42 U.S.C. § 12112(b)(5)(A); see also § 12111(2) ("The term 'covered entity' means an employer, employment agency, labor organization, or joint labor-management committee"). The Act defines a "qualified individual with a disability" as "an individual with a disability who, with or without reasonable accommodation, can perform the essential functions of the employment position that such individual holds or desires." § 12111(8). In turn, a "disability" is:

> "(A) a physical or mental impairment that substantially limits one or more of the major life activities of such individual;
>
> "(B) a record of such an impairment; or
>
> "(C) being regarded as having such an impairment." § 12102(2).

There are two potential sources of guidance for interpreting the terms of this definition—the regulations interpreting the Rehabilitation Act of 1973, 87 Stat. 361, as amended, 29 U.S.C. § 706(8)(B), and the EEOC regulations interpreting the ADA. Congress drew the ADA's definition of disability almost verbatim from the definition of "handicapped individual" in the Rehabilitation Act, § 706(8)(B), and Congress' repetition of a well-established term generally implies that Congress intended the term to be construed in accordance with pre-existing regulatory interpretations. Bragdon v. Abbott, 524 U.S. 624, 631 (1998); FDIC v. Philadelphia Gear Corp., 476 U.S. 426, 437–438 (1986); ICC v. Parker, 326 U.S. 60, 65 (1945). As we explained in *Bragdon v. Abbott*, Congress did more in the ADA than suggest this construction; it adopted a specific statutory provision directing as follows:

> "Except as otherwise provided in this chapter, nothing in this chapter shall be construed to apply a lesser standard than the standards applied under title V of the Rehabilitation Act of 1973 (29 U.S.C. § 790 et seq.) or the regulations issued by Federal agencies pursuant to such title." 42 U.S.C. § 12201(a).

The persuasive authority of the EEOC regulations is less clear. As we have previously noted, see Sutton v. United Air Lines, Inc., 527 U.S. 471, 479 (1999), no agency has been given authority to issue regulations interpreting the term "disability" in the ADA. Nonetheless, the EEOC has done so. See 29 CFR §§ 1630.2(g)–(j). Because both parties accept the EEOC regulations as reasonable, we assume without deciding that they are, and we have no occasion to decide what level of deference, if any, they are due. See Sutton v. United Air Lines, Inc., supra, at 480; Albertson's, Inc. v. Kirkingburg, 527 U.S. 555, 563, n.10 (1999).

To qualify as disabled under subsection (A) of the ADA's definition of disability, a claimant must initially prove that he or she has a physical or mental impairment. See 42 U.S.C. § 12102(2)(A). The Rehabilitation Act regulations issued by the Department of Health, Education, and Welfare (HEW) in 1977, which appear without change in the current regulations issued by the Department of Health and Human Services, define "physical impairment," the type of impairment relevant to this case, to mean "any physiological disorder or condition, cosmetic disfigurement, or anatomical loss affecting one or more of the following body systems: neurological; musculoskeletal; special sense organs; respiratory, including speech organs; cardiovascular; reproductive, digestive, genito-urinary; hemic and lymphatic; skin; and endocrine." 45 CFR § 84.3(j)(2)(i). The HEW regulations are of particular significance because at the time they were issued, HEW was the agency responsible for coordinating the implementation and enforcement of § 504 of the Rehabilitation Act, 29 U.S.C. § 794, which prohibits discrimination against individuals with disabilities by recipients of federal financial assistance. Bragdon v. Abbott, supra, at 632 (citing Consolidated Rail Corporation v. Darrone, 465 U.S. 624, 634 (1984)).

Merely having an impairment does not make one disabled for purposes of the ADA. Claimants also need to demonstrate that the impairment limits a major life activity. See 42 U.S.C. § 12102(2)(A). The HEW Rehabilitation Act regulations provide a list of examples of "major life activities" that includes "walking, seeing, hearing," and, as relevant here, "performing manual tasks." 45 CFR § 84.3(j)(2)(ii).

To qualify as disabled, a claimant must further show that the limitation on the major life activity is "substantial." 42 U.S.C. § 12102(2)(A). Unlike "physical impairment" and "major life activities," the HEW regulations do not define the term "substantially limits." See Nondiscrimination on the Basis of Handicap in Programs and Activities Receiving or Benefiting from Federal Financial Assistance, 42 Fed. Reg. 22676, 22685 (1977) (stating HEW's position that a definition of "substantially limits" was not possible at that time). The EEOC, therefore, has created its own definition for purposes of the ADA. According to the EEOC regulations, "substantially limit" means "unable to perform a major life activity that the average person in the general population can perform"; or "significantly restricted as to the condition, manner or duration under which an individual can perform a particular major life activity as compared to the condition, manner, or duration under which the average person in the general population can perform that same major life activity." 29 CFR § 1630.2(j). In determining whether an individual is substantially limited in a major life activity, the regulations instruct that the following factors should be considered: "the nature and severity of the impairment; the duration or expected duration of the impairment; and the permanent or long-term impact, or the expected permanent or long-term impact of or resulting from the impairment." §§ 1630.2(j)(2)(i)–(iii).

III

The question presented by this case is whether the Sixth Circuit properly determined that respondent was disabled under subsection (A) of the ADA's disability definition at the time that she sought an accommodation from petitioner. 42 U.S.C. § 12102(2)(A). The parties do not dispute that respondent's medical conditions, which include carpal tunnel syndrome, myotendonitis, and thoracic outlet compression, amount to physical impairments. The relevant question, therefore, is whether the Sixth Circuit correctly analyzed whether these impairments substantially limited respondent in the major life activity of performing manual tasks. Answering this requires us to address an issue about which the EEOC regulations are silent: what a plaintiff must demonstrate to establish a substantial limitation in the specific major life activity of performing manual tasks.

Our consideration of this issue is guided first and foremost by the words of the disability definition itself. "Substantially" in the phrase "substantially limits" suggests "considerable" or "to a large degree." See Webster's Third New International Dictionary 2280 (1976) (defining "substantially" as "in a substantial manner" and "substantial" as "considerable in amount, value, or worth" and "being that specified to a large degree or in the main"); see also 17 Oxford English Dictionary 66–67 (2d ed. 1989) ("substantial": "relating to or proceeding from the essence of a thing; essential"; "of ample or considerable amount, quantity, or dimensions"). The word "substantial" thus clearly precludes impairments that interfere in only a minor way with the performance of manual tasks from qualifying as disabilities. Cf. Albertson's, Inc. v. Kirkingburg, supra, at 565 (explaining that a "mere difference" does not amount to a "significant restric[tion]" and therefore does not satisfy the EEOC's interpretation of "substantially limits").

"Major" in the phrase "major life activities" means important. See Webster's, supra, at 1363 (defining "major" as "greater in dignity, rank, importance, or interest"). "Major life activities" thus refers to those activities that are of central importance to daily life. In order for performing manual tasks to fit into this category—a category that includes such basic abilities as walking, seeing, and hearing—the manual tasks in question must be central to daily life. If each of the tasks included in the major life activity of performing manual tasks does not independently qualify as a major life activity, then together they must do so.

That these terms need to be interpreted strictly to create a demanding standard for qualifying as disabled is confirmed by the first section of the ADA, which lays out the legislative findings and purposes that motivate the Act. See 42 U.S.C. § 12101. When it enacted the ADA in 1990, Congress found that "some 43,000,000 Americans have one or more physical or mental disabilities." § 12101(a)(1). If Congress intended everyone with a physical impairment that precluded the performance of some isolated, unimportant, or particularly difficult manual task to qualify as disabled, the number of disabled Americans would surely have been much higher. Cf. Sutton v. United Air Lines, Inc., 527 U.S., at 487 (finding that because more than 100 million people need corrective lenses to see properly, "had Congress intended to include all persons with corrected physical limitations among those covered by the Act, it undoubtedly would have cited a much higher number than [43 million disabled persons] in the findings").

We therefore hold that to be substantially limited in performing manual tasks, an individual must have an impairment that prevents or severely restricts the individual from doing activities that are of central importance to most people's daily lives. The impairment's impact must also be permanent or long term. See 29 CFR § 1630.2(j)(2)(ii)–(iii).

It is insufficient for individuals attempting to prove disability status under this test to merely submit evidence of a medical diagnosis of an impairment. Instead, the ADA requires those "claiming the Act's protection . . . to prove a disability by offering evidence that the extent of the limitation [caused by their impairment] in terms of their own experience . . . is substantial." Albertson's, Inc. v. Kirkingburg, 527 U.S., at 567 (holding that monocular vision is not invariably a disability, but must be analyzed on an individual basis, taking into account the individual's ability to compensate for the impairment). That the Act defines "disability" "with respect to an individual," 42 U.S.C. § 12102(2), makes clear that Congress intended the existence of a disability to be determined in such a case-by-case manner. See Sutton v. United Air Lines, Inc., supra, at 483; Albertson's, Inc. v. Kirkingburg, supra, at 566; cf. Bragdon v. Abbott, 524 U.S., at 641–642 (relying on unchallenged testimony that the respondent's HIV infection controlled her decision not to have a child, and declining to consider whether HIV infection is a per se disability under the ADA); 29 CFR pt. 1630, App. § 1630.2(j) ("The determination of whether an individual has a disability is not necessarily based on the name or diagnosis of the impairment the person has, but rather on the effect of that impairment on the life of the individual"); ibid. ("The determination of whether an individual is substantially limited in a major life activity must be made on a case-by-case basis").

An individualized assessment of the effect of an impairment is particularly necessary when the impairment is one whose symptoms vary widely from person to person. Carpal tunnel syndrome, one of respondent's impairments, is just such a condition. While cases of severe carpal tunnel syndrome are characterized by muscle atrophy and extreme sensory deficits, mild cases generally do not have either of these effects and create only intermittent symptoms of numbness and tingling. Carniero, Carpal Tunnel Syndrome: The Cause Dictates the Treatment, 66 Cleveland Clinic J. Medicine 159, 161–162 (1999). Studies have further shown that, even without surgical treatment, one quarter of carpal tunnel cases resolve in one month, but that in 22 percent of cases, symptoms last for eight years or longer. See DeStefano, Nordstrom, & Uierkant, Long-Term Symptom Outcomes of Carpal Tunnel Syndrome and its Treatment, 22A J. Hand Surgery 200, 204–205 (1997). When pregnancy is the cause of carpal tunnel syndrome, in contrast, the symptoms normally resolve within two weeks of delivery. See Ouellette, Nerve Compression Syndromes of the Upper Extremity in Women, 17 J. of Musculoskeletal Medicine 536 (2000). Given these large potential differences in the severity and duration of the effects of carpal tunnel syndrome, an individual's carpal tunnel syndrome diagnosis, on its own, does not indicate whether the individual has a disability within the meaning of the ADA.

IV

The Court of Appeals' analysis of respondent's claimed disability suggested that in order to prove a substantial limitation in the major life activity of performing manual tasks, a "plaintiff must show that her manual disability involves a 'class' of manual activities," and that those activities "affect the ability to perform tasks at work." Both of these ideas lack support.

The Court of Appeals relied on our opinion in *Sutton v. United Air Lines, Inc.*, for the idea that a "class" of manual activities must be implicated for an impairment to substantially limit the major life activity of performing manual tasks. But *Sutton* said only that "*[w]hen the major life activity under consideration is that of working*, the statutory phrase 'substantially limits' requires . . . that plaintiffs allege they are unable to work in a broad class of jobs." 527 U.S., at 491 (emphasis added). Because of the conceptual difficulties inherent in the argument that working could be a major life activity, we have been hesitant to hold as much, and we need not decide this difficult question today. In *Sutton*, we noted that even assuming that working is a major life activity, a claimant would be required to show an inability to work in a "broad range of jobs," rather than a specific job. Id., at 492. But *Sutton* did not suggest that a class-based analysis should be applied to any major life activity other than working. Nor do the EEOC regulations. In defining "substantially limits," the EEOC regulations only mention the "class" concept in the context of the major life activity of working. 29 CFR § 1630.2(j)(3) ("With respect to the major life activity of working the term substantially limits means significantly restricted in the ability to perform either a class of jobs or a broad range of jobs in various classes as compared to the average person having comparable training, skills and abilities"). Nothing in the text of the Act, our previous opinions, or the regulations suggests that a class-based framework should apply outside the context of the major life activity of working.

While the Court of Appeals in this case addressed the different major life activity of performing manual tasks, its analysis circumvented *Sutton* by focusing on respondent's inability to perform manual tasks associated only with her job. This was error. When addressing the major life activity of performing manual tasks, the central inquiry must be whether the claimant is unable to perform the variety of tasks central to most people's daily lives, not whether the claimant is unable to perform the tasks associated with her specific job. Otherwise, *Sutton*'s restriction on claims of disability based on a substantial limitation in working will be rendered meaningless because an inability to perform a specific job always can be recast as an inability to perform a "class" of tasks associated with that specific job.

There is also no support in the Act, our previous opinions, or the regulations for the Court of Appeals' idea that the question of whether an impairment constitutes a disability is to be answered only by analyzing the effect of the impairment in the workplace. Indeed, the fact that the Act's definition of "disability" applies not only to Title I of the Act, 42 U.S.C. §§ 12111–12117, which deals with employment, but also to the other portions of the Act, which deal with subjects such as public transportation, §§ 12141–12150, 42 U.S.C. §§ 12161–12165, and privately provided public accommodations, §§ 12181–12189, demonstrates that the definition is intended to cover individuals with disabling impairments regardless of whether the individuals have any connection to a workplace.

Even more critically, the manual tasks unique to any particular job are not necessarily important parts of most people's lives. As a result, occupation-specific tasks may have only limited relevance to the manual task inquiry. In this case, "repetitive work with hands and arms extended at or above shoulder levels for extended periods of time," 224 F.3d, at 843, the manual task on which the Court of Appeals relied, is not an important part of most people's daily lives. The court, therefore, should not have considered respondent's inability to do such manual work in her specialized assembly line job as sufficient proof that she was substantially limited in performing manual tasks.

At the same time, the Court of Appeals appears to have disregarded the very type of evidence that it should have focused upon. It treated as irrelevant "the fact that [respondent] can . . . tend to her personal hygiene [and] carry out personal or household chores." Yet household chores, bathing, and brushing one's teeth are among the types of manual tasks of central importance to people's daily lives, and should have been part of the assessment of whether respondent was substantially limited in performing manual tasks.

The District Court noted that at the time respondent sought an accommodation from petitioner, she admitted that she was able to do the manual tasks required by her original two jobs in QCIO. In addition, according to respondent's deposition testimony, even after her condition worsened, she could still brush her teeth, wash her face, bathe, tend her flower garden, fix breakfast, do laundry, and pick up around the house. The record also indicates that her medical conditions caused her to avoid sweeping, to quit dancing, to occasionally seek help dressing, and to reduce how often she plays with her children, gardens, and drives long distances. But these changes in her life did not amount to such severe restrictions in the activities that are of central importance to most people's daily lives that they establish a manual task disability as a matter of law. On this record, it was therefore inappropriate for the Court of Appeals to grant partial summary judgment to respondent on the issue of whether she was substantially limited in performing manual tasks, and its decision to do so must be reversed. . . .

Accordingly, we reverse the Court of Appeals' judgment granting partial summary judgment to respondent and remand the case for further proceedings consistent with this opinion.

So ordered.

NOTES ON *TOYOTA MOTOR MANUFACTURING, KENTUCKY, INC. V. WILLIAMS*

1. **Effects of the ADA Amendments Act.** *Toyota Motor*'s restrictive definition of covered disabilities was specifically targeted for disapproval by Congress in the ADA Amendments Act of 2008. This restrictive definition both increased the threshold of limiting effects that a condition must have on a major life activity and narrowed the scope of affected life activities. Congress rejected both parts of *Toyota Motor*, first in the uncodified statement of the Act's purposes, § (2)(a)(5), (b)(4), (5), 42 U.S.C. § 12101(2)(a)(5), (b)(4), (5) and then in particular implementing provisions. These provisions lessened the necessary effect that an impairment must have on a major life activity and broadened the definition of such activities. § (3)(2), (4), 42 U.S.C. § 12102(2), (4).

The plaintiff in *Toyota Motor* suffered from carpal tunnel syndrome, which can take a variety of different forms, with more or less severe symptoms depending on the individual. Because of the variable nature of this condition, the Court required an individualized evaluation of its effect on the plaintiff's ability to engage in various major life activities. Out of concern that the scope of covered disabilities would expand too broadly, the Court imposed the following restrictions on them:

> We therefore hold that to be substantially limited in performing manual tasks, an individual must have an impairment

> that prevents or severely restricts the individual from doing activities that are of central importance to most people's daily lives.

In the ADA Amendments Act, Congress went in the opposite direction, clearly rejecting this analysis, although leaving less clear exactly what it accepted. Congress singled out this passage from the opinion for rejection in the uncodified statement of the Act's purposes, § (2)(a)(5), (b)(4), (5), but it did not put any alternative in its place.

2. **"Substantially Limits" a Major Life Activity.** Under *Toyota Motor*, it is necessary that the condition "prevents or severely restricts" a major life activity. The ADA now states that the definition of "disability" "shall be broadly construed in favor of coverage" and that the term "substantially limits" in this definition should be construed in light of the purposes of the ADA Amendments Act. § 3(4), 42 U.S.C. § 12102(4). Taken together, these provisions reject "prevents or severely restricts" as the interpretation of a substantial limitation on a major life activity. A further requirement from *Toyota Motor*, that the limiting effects be "permanent or long term," is not disapproved. Nevertheless the requirement that a condition be evaluated in its active state does allow temporary impairments that are the effect of continuing conditions to be sufficient for coverage. § 3(4)(D), 42 U.S.C. § 12102(4)(D).

What is put in the place of the Court's interpretation of "substantially limits" as "prevents or severely restricts"? As reported by the House Committee on the Judiciary and the House Committee on Education and Labor, the phrase "substantially limits" in the definition of covered disabilities would have been replaced by the phrase "materially restricts." H.R. Rep. 110–730 pt. 1 at 9–10, pt. 2 at 16–17 (2008). On the floor of the Senate, however, this change was abandoned on the ground that it would just introduce new terminology that would result in more litigation until it received a settled interpretation. According to the managers of the Senate bill, "using the correct standard—one that is lower than the strict or demanding standard created by the Supreme Court in Toyota—will make the disability determination an appropriate threshold issue but not an onerous burden for those seeking accommodations or modifications." 154 Cong. Rec. S8345–46 (daily ed. Sept. 11, 2008) (remarks of Sen. Harkin). What does this statement add to the rejection of *Toyota Motor* in the legislation itself? Is the test now based on the most lenient possible interpretation of the phrase "substantially limits"? Should any effect on a major life activity be sufficient if it barely satisfies the meaning of "substantially limits"? Should courts or lawyers use any other phrase to explicate what this phrase means? Are the risks of a change in meaning from any seemingly synonymous phrase too great to justify any potential benefits from clarification? The Act's uncodified statement of purposes states that "the question of whether an individual's impairment is a disability under the ADA should not demand extensive analysis." § (2)(b)(5). Does that require everyone just to stick with the phrase "substantially limits," and if it is satisfied, then to get on to the merits of whether the defendant has violated the statute?

3. "Major Life Activity." The ADA Amendments Act also undercuts the Court's analysis in another way, by including "performing manual tasks" in the list of major life activities. § (3)(2)(A), 42 U.S.C. § 12102(2)(A). There is no longer any need to consider other "activities that are of central importance to most people's daily lives," as the Court did. A substantial limit on "performing manual tasks" alone appears to be sufficient. The Act also affected the Court's analysis by resolving the question, left open in this case, whether work was a major life activity.

Addressing a limitation on Williams's ability to work would no longer be necessary to deciding that she suffered from a substantial limitation on a major life activity, but the analysis of "performing manual tasks" would still share with "work" the need to look into a range of activities. A substantial limit on "work" requires a limiting effect on a range of jobs. So, too, a substantial limit on "performing manual tasks" requires a limit on a range of manual tasks. Because Williams's impairment, carpal tunnel syndrome, can take a variety of different forms with more or less severe symptoms, the Court required an individualized inquiry into how limited her arm and hand movements were. She alleged limits on "(1) manual tasks; (2) housework; (3) gardening; (4) playing with her children; (5) lifting; and (6) working." Although she advanced all of these as separate major life activities, actual limits on "manual tasks" would affect all the others. Suppose she couldn't do housework, gardening, or lifting. Would that reveal a wide enough range of manual tasks that were limited by her impairment? Does the statement of purpose, quoted in the preceding note, preclude an extended inquiry into this question, requiring all doubts to be resolved in favor of finding a covered disability?

4. Was Williams "Regarded as" Having a Disability? If Williams encountered problems in proving that she had an actual disability, could she have claimed that she was only "regarded as" having one? Notice that if she gained coverage on this basis, she would not have been entitled to any reasonable accommodation. The ADA Amendments Act relieves employers of any duty to accommodate individuals who are only "regarded as" having a disability. § 501(g), 42 U.S.C. § 12201(g).

However, if Williams did not want an accommodation and her condition was less severe, she might have been better off claiming simply that she was "regarded as" having a disability. Suppose she had arthritis in a minor but permanent form. She would then have had an impairment under the applicable EEOC regulations. These broadly define impairments to include "[a]ny physiological disorder, or condition" affecting the "musculoskeletal" system. 29 C.F.R. § 1630.2(h)(1). Under the new Act, these regulations are now authoritative, so long as they are consistent with the new statutory definitions. § 506, 42 U.S.C. § 12206. Williams could therefore easily establish first-level coverage of her condition as a "disability," without showing any effect on a major life activity. She could also establish second-level coverage as a "qualified individual with a disability" under Title I. § 101(8), 42 U.S.C. § 12111(8). All she would have to show is that she could perform the essential functions of the job. The less severe her impairment, the easier it would be for her to make this showing. Moreover, if she succeeded, on a literal reading of the statute, the employer would have no defense to a claim that she suffered discrimination because of her impairment. If disability truly is like race, then an employer can no more take it into account under the ADA than an employer can take account of race under Title VII. The employer could not defend, for instance, on the ground that the plaintiff could no longer perform the job as efficiently as employees without arthritis. The employer would be liable simply for discriminating against her based on her impairment.

If Williams prevails on this variation of the actual case, wouldn't any employee or applicant in a similar situation? After all, the best evidence that an individual is regarded as having a disability is actually having an impairment that is obvious to the employer and that resembles an actual disability. Moreover, plaintiffs are not required to elect one basis for finding a covered disability to the exclusion of another. A plaintiff could argue both that she had an actual disability and that she was regarded as having one. If she lost on the first ground, she could still win on the second, and she might have a better chance of doing so. She would not have to prove any effect on a major life activity, which might make it easier for her to prove that she could perform the essential functions of the job. If the employer then took account of her impairment to her disadvantage, she would have suffered from discrimination in violation of the statute. Is this the right result? Does this reading of the statute call into question all relative qualifications for the job compromised by a physical or mental impairment? So long as the plaintiff can perform the essential functions of the job, the employer cannot prefer another individual free of the impairments who can perform the job better. Does this reading of the ADA transform it from a statute that prohibits discrimination into one that requires decisions based on minimal qualifications alone? Or does the answer depend upon what defenses an employer has on the merits?

5. **Bibliography.** For discussion of what constitutes a substantial limitation on a major life activity, see Cheryl L. Anderson, "Deserving Disabilities": Why the Definition of Disability Under the Americans with Disabilities Act Should Be Revised to Eliminate the Substantial Limitation Requirement, 65 Mo. L. Rev. 83 (2000).

A separate group of articles has criticized the differential treatment of nonphysical disabilities, such as psychiatric and mental conditions. Sara N. Barker, A False Sense of Security: Is Protection for Employees with Learning Disabilities Under the Americans with Disabilities Act Merely an Illusion?, 9 U. Pa. J. Lab. & Emp. L. 325 (2007); Jeffrey Swanson et al., Justice Disparities: Does the ADA Enforcement System Treat People with Psychiatric Disabilities Fairly?, 66 Md. L. Rev. 94 (2006); Elizabeth F. Emens, The Sympathetic Discriminator: Mental Illness, Hedonic Costs, and the ADA, 94 Geo. L.J. 399 (2006); Wendy F. Hensel & Gregory T. Jones, Bridging the Physical-Mental Gap: An Empirical Look at the Impact of Mental Illness Stigma on ADA Outcomes, 73 Tenn. L. Rev. 47 (2005); Ramona L. Paetzold, How Courts, Employers, and the ADA Disable Persons with Bipolar Disorder, 9 Emp. Rts. & Emp. Pol'y J. 293 (2005); Fedwa Malti-Douglas, Legal Cross-Dressing: Sexuality and the Americans with

Disabilities Act, 15 Colum. J. Gender & L. 114 (2006); Matthew G. Simon, Not All Illnesses Are Treated Equally—Does a Disability Benefits Plan Violate the ADA by Providing Less Generous Long-Term Benefits for Mentally Disabled Employees Than for Physically Disabled Employees?, 8 U. Pa. J. Lab. & Emp. L. 943 (2006); Deidre M. Smith, The Paradox of Personality: Mental Illness, Employment Discrimination, and the Americans with Disabilities Act, 17 Geo. Mason U. Civ. Rts. L.J. 79 (2006).

NOTES ON *SUTTON V. UNITED AIR LINES, INC.*

1. ***Murphy v. UPS, Inc.* and *Alberstons, Inc. v. Kirkingburg*.** In two companion cases to *Sutton*, the Supreme Court applied its holding that the existence of a disability under the ADA had to be evaluated in light of corrective measures taken by the plaintiff. In both cases, the Court also went on to consider the effect of regulations issued by the Department of Transportation (DOT) establishing minimum qualifications for drivers of commercial vehicles.

In Murphy v. UPS, Inc., 527 U.S. 516 (1999), the Court held that a plaintiff who suffered from high blood pressure was not "regarded as" disabled by his employer because the employer did not believe that his condition interfered with a "major life activity." The plaintiff's condition could be treated with medication, and although this did not make him qualified to work as a commercial driver under DOT regulations, neither did it prevent him from working at other jobs. Even assuming that work amounted to a "major life activity," the plaintiff was not disabled for purposes of the ADA because he was not disqualified from working at all jobs, but only from this one type of job.

In Albertsons, Inc. v. Kirkingburg, 527 U.S. 555 (1999), the Court held that a plaintiff who effectively could see out of only one eye had no claim under the ADA. Again, the plaintiff's condition had to be evaluated in light of the corrective glasses that he wore, but even if he were disabled within the meaning of the ADA, he still could be denied a job as a commercial driver based on DOT regulations that established minimal standards for drivers' vision. The employer was under no obligation to justify the regulations as a valid safety measure or to seek a waiver of the regulations from the DOT.

2. **The Effect of *Sutton* After the ADA Amendments Act.** This Act specifically targeted the reasoning in *Sutton* for disapproval. The uncodified statement of purpose in the Act refers to *Sutton* by name as one of the decisions that should no longer be followed. ADA Amendments Act of 2008 § (2)(a)(4), (b)(2) (reproduced in the Statutory Appendix after the ADA). The Act also contains several provisions rejecting particular arguments made by the Court in *Sutton*. In the codified findings that precede the ADA, Congress deleted the reference to "43,000,000 Americans" who have one or more disabilities and the reference to this group as "a discrete and insular minority." § 2(a)(1), 42 U.S.C. § 12101(a)(1). Detailed provisions in the ADA now greatly expand its coverage: most conditions must now be analyzed in their uncorrected or active state; "seeing" and "work" are now recognized as major life activities; coverage of impairments "regarded as" a disability must

be analyzed independently of any effect, actual or perceived, on major life activities; and the EEOC (and other administrators) are explicitly granted authority to issue regulations interpreting the statutory definition of "disability." §§ 3, 506, 42 U.S.C. §§ 12102, 12206. Nevertheless, in ironic contrast to all these provisions, Congress seemingly accepted the precise result in *Sutton*, excluding defects in eyesight that can be corrected by ordinary eyeglasses from the statutory definition of an actual "disability" sufficient for coverage. § 3(4)(E), 42 U.S.C. § 12102(4)(E).

Each of these provisions raises several technical questions of statutory interpretation, but as a whole they also raise a more general question: Did Congress try to have it both ways in the ADA Amendments Act, rejecting each step in the Supreme Court's reasoning in *Sutton*, but accepting its ultimate conclusion? Congress disagreed with the Court's reasoning for the full range of disabilities, but found it sufficient in the particular case. Or so it seems, at first glance. In a still further provision, Congress required employers to evaluate defects in eyesight in their corrected state. § 103(c), 42 U.S.C. § 12113(c). This provision presupposes that some individuals can gain coverage under the ADA for such defects, complicating the question whether Congress also rejected the ultimate result in *Sutton*. Is *Sutton* now a decision limited to its facts, like the proverbial restricted railroad ticket, "good for this day and train only," Smith v. Allwright, 321 U.S. 649, 669 (1944) (Roberts, J., dissenting)? Or is it so compromised that we do not even know what train ride it remains good for? The following notes seek to answer these questions.

3. **Impairments in Their Corrected or Uncorrected State?** The most significant holding in *Sutton* requires physical and mental conditions to be evaluated in their corrected state in order to determine whether they substantially limit a major life activity. The ADA Amendments Act rejects this approach, partly no doubt because of the perverse incentives created by *Sutton*. Under *Sutton*, a plaintiff who has counteracted the adverse effects of a disability is not disabled at all and therefore is denied any recovery under the statute. The decision gives individuals no incentives to undertake corrective measures, and if anything, penalizes them for doing so. If they take corrective measures, they lose coverage. This incentive is the opposite of the incentives created by analogous duties at common law, such as the duty to avoid contributory negligence or the duty to mitigate damages. The common law penalizes plaintiffs who do not take mitigating measures. *Sutton* penalizes plaintiffs who do. Is this the right result?

Sutton requires individuals with disabilities to help themselves instead of seeking help under the ADA. As the decision itself illustrates, such individuals are then left open to discrimination. The Sutton sisters were denied jobs as commercial airline pilots precisely because of their eyesight. They suffered for their impairment even though they had corrected it. As the dissent points out, they were denied relief even if United Air Lines had no good reason for rejecting them because of their poor eyesight. The Court's holding on coverage precluded any inquiry into the justification offered by the employer, presumably on grounds of safety, for refusing to hire the plaintiffs. Even if the plaintiffs were not entitled to any special benefits because they could correct their impairment themselves, does it follow that they can be subject to discrimination because of their impairment? Was the employer's decision particularly bad because it was self-contradictory? The employer argued both that the plaintiffs' impairment could be corrected, and so they were not disabled, and that they were disqualified precisely because of their impairment.

The ADA Amendments Act changes this result in general, although not in the particular case. Impairments are now to be evaluated "without regard to the ameliorative effects of mitigating measures." § 3(4)(E)(i), 42 U.S.C. § 12102(4)(E)(i). This subsection then goes on to list a variety of mitigating measures, such as "medication," "assistive technology," "reasonable accommodations or auxiliary aids or services," and "learned behavioral or adaptive neurological modifications." In a separate subsection, the Act also provides that an impairment "that is episodic or in remission is a disability if it would substantially limit a major life activity when active." § 3(4)(D), 42 U.S.C. § 12102(4)(D). Hence diseases such as cancer or epilepsy must be evaluated in their active state. In an abundance of caution, Congress also provided that the definition of "disability" and "substantially limits" shall be interpreted, respectively, "in favor of broad coverage" and "consistently with the findings and purposes" of the Act, and that only one major life activity needs to be affected to trigger coverage. § 3(4)(A), (B), (C), 42 U.S.C. § 12102(4)(A), (B), (C). It seems to follow that any impairment must be evaluated in its severest possible form, with all doubts resolved in favor of coverage.

Does such a presumption in favor of coverage go too far in the opposite direction from *Sutton*? Under *Sutton*, plaintiffs may have had incentives to avoid corrective measures for fear of losing coverage. Under the ADA Amendments Act, they now have incentives to take extensive corrective measures to make their uncorrected conditions appear in the worst possible light. Does this encourage plaintiffs to exaggerate their impairments? Or was this incentive there all along, created by the ADA's initial limitation on coverage to statutorily defined disabilities? How should the incentive to exaggerate disabilities be compared with the incentive to minimize disabilities to establish qualifications for the job? Note 6 below discusses this question and the quandary in which it leaves plaintiffs—to establish that they are disabled just enough, but not too much.

4. **The Exception for Ordinary Eyeglasses.** Despite all of the provisions in the ADA Amendments Act expanding coverage, Congress was content to limit coverage for the single condition directly involved in *Sutton*: impaired vision that can be corrected by "ordinary eyeglasses or contact lenses." § 3(4)(E)(ii), 42 U.S.C. § 12102(4)(E)(ii). This term itself is defined in the statute, mainly to distinguish it from "low-vision devices" that "magnify, enhance, or otherwise augment a visual image." § 3(4)(E)(iii), 42 U.S.C. § 12102(4)(E)(iii). These definitions reflect a residual concern by Congress with expanding coverage of the ADA too far, yet they distinguish common vision problems from all other impairments. Impairments that are similarly widespread, such as those in hearing (corrected by an ordinary hearing aid) or in walking (corrected by a cane), do not receive exceptional treatment. They support coverage in their uncorrected state. The reasons for treating

ordinary eyeglasses differently must be inferred from the unique characteristics of ordinary vision problems.

The opinion in *Sutton* found one such reason in Congress's original estimate that the ADA would cover 43 million Americans or about 17 percent of the population. This estimate was pointedly repealed by the ADA Amendments Act, as was the characterization of individuals with a disability as "a discrete and insular minority," eliminating these grounds for endorsing the outcome in *Sutton*. Congress substituted a statement that "many people with physical or mental disabilities" have been precluded from fully participating in all aspects of society. § 2(a)(1), 42 U.S.C. § 12101(2)(a)(1). If the limit for excess coverage is not strictly numerical, what is it? Both the majority and the dissent in *Sutton* agreed that the ADA doesn't cover everyone. By excluding impairments corrected by ordinary eyeglasses, has Congress also accepted this conclusion? Or does this exclusion confirm the newly expanded coverage of the ADA in all other respects?

The statute is premised on the need to give special protection to individuals with disabilities, but if everyone is entitled to special protection, then no one is. Not all deficiencies can count as disabilities. Even in terms of a simple prohibition against discrimination, employers must be allowed to take into account deficiencies, such as lack of skill, ability, or motivation, that do not rise to the level of disabilities. Virtually everyone suffers from these kinds of deficiencies, and they are expected to compensate for them without special legal protection. Is that because they are in a better position to do so than either the government or an employer? Or is it for a deeper reason, concerned with individual responsibility and choice, requiring people to do the best they can with the abilities they have? On either of these views, the ADA protects only people who cannot help themselves. Is that a sufficient justification for the result in *Sutton*? Are ordinary eyeglasses just a particularly clear example of a corrective step that people should be expected to take on their own?

As noted earlier, the ADA Amendments Act extends the special exception for vision problems into the prohibition against employment discrimination in Title I of the ADA, requiring employers to evaluate vision problems as corrected by ordinary eyeglasses, unless they have a good reason not to. § 103(c), 42 U.S.C. § 12113(c). Here, however, the special treatment of eyeglasses functions as an extension—not as an exception—to the substantive prohibitions in the statute. This extension presupposes some basis for coverage of individuals with correctable vision problems. The terms of the prohibition extend to all vision problems, including those that can be corrected by ordinary eyeglasses. Individuals who need ordinary eyeglasses are somehow covered by the statute, even though they do not suffer from an actual disability. They cannot obtain coverage on this ground, or on the ground of having a "record of" such a disability, but they could still obtain coverage because they are "regarded as" having a disability, as discussed in the following note.

5. **"Regarded as" Having a Disability.** *Sutton*'s narrow definition of actual disabilities also influences its interpretation of coverage of individuals who are "regarded as" having a disability. Under the statute, the plaintiff

has a covered disability if the defendant regards her as having "such an impairment," where the quoted phrase refers back to an actual impairment that substantially limits a major life activity. § 3(1)(C), 42 U.S.C. § 12102(1)(C). This form of coverage is meant to reach plaintiffs who are stigmatized as disabled even if they are not. The defendant's perceptions, even if erroneous, are still sufficient for coverage.

Sutton cut back on the scope of "regarded as" coverage, allowing reference to the defendant's perceptions, but only with respect to the existence of the condition and its immediate effects. The perceived effects are then judged by objective standards to determine whether they substantially limit a major life activity. The ADA Amendments Act changed the statute to eliminate all requirements other than a real or perceived impairment. It is no longer necessary to consider any effect beyond that necessary to create a real or perceived impairment. There is no need to consider any actual or perceived limitation on a major life activity. The plaintiff is covered simply if she has suffered discrimination in violation of the ADA "because of an actual or perceived physical or mental impairment." § 3(3)(A), 42 U.S.C. § 12102(3)(A).

In this definition, Congress plainly intended to expand "regarded as" coverage far beyond *Sutton*. The only exception to "regarded as" coverage is for impairments that are both "transitory and minor." § 3(3)(B), 42 U.S.C. § 12102(3)(B). Note that an impairment must be both "transitory" and "minor" to be exempted from coverage. All other actual and perceived impairments—for instance, those that are permanent and minor—are sufficient for coverage. The principal limitation on this form of coverage comes in the reference to the statute's substantive prohibitions. The plaintiff must have suffered discrimination in violation of the ADA because of the actual or perceived impairment. The plaintiff must establish "that he or she has been subject to an action prohibited under this chapter because of an actual or perceived impairment." § 3(3)(A), 42 U.S.C. § 12102(3)(A). This seemingly simple requirement, however, makes the analysis of covered disabilities depend upon the existence of prohibited discrimination which, in turn, depends upon the coverage of particular titles of the ADA. Title I prohibits employment discrimination only against a "qualified individual."

6. **"Qualified Individual."** Establishing the existence of a covered disability constitutes only the first level of coverage under the ADA, both in its original form and as amended. In order to recover for employment discrimination under Title I, the plaintiff must also establish a second level of coverage: that she is a "qualified individual." §§ 101(8), 102(a), 42 U.S.C. §§ 12111(8), 12112(a). The ADA Amendments Act replaced the old terminology of "qualified individual with a disability" with separate provisions, first defining "qualified individual" and then prohibiting discrimination against any such individual "on the basis of disability." Under the amended ADA, however, it is still true that having a disability alone is not enough. The plaintiff must also be qualified to perform the essential functions of the job in question. Introducing qualifications into the definition of second-level coverage creates a general problem of circularity in Title I. To state the problem starkly, although somewhat simplistically, an individual

is qualified only if the employer would violate the ADA by denying her a job, but the employer violates the ADA only if the individual is covered.

This circularity makes questions of coverage conceptually complicated because it causes them to overlap with the question on the merits whether the employer has engaged in prohibited discrimination. What it means in practice is that the plaintiff often faces a dilemma. To meet the first level of coverage under the ADA as a whole, the plaintiff must show that she has a "disability." To meet the second level of coverage under Title I, she must establish that she is a "qualified individual." And to establish a violation, she must prove that the employer had no good reason to discriminate against her. She must prove, in other words, that she is sufficiently disabled to meet the first level of coverage, but also not so disabled that she fails to meet the second level of qualifications or establish a violation of the statute. The Sutton sisters had to show both that they suffered from a disability and that they were qualified to be commercial airline pilots. Because their nearsightedness could be corrected, they did not have a covered disability, but if their nearsightedness could not have been corrected, they would not have been qualified to be commercial airline pilots. They had to show that they were disabled, but not too disabled. *Sutton* created problems for plaintiffs by narrowing the window of acceptable disabilities. It raised the threshold for showing a covered disability so high that, in many cases, plaintiffs could not also show that they were qualified.

The ADA Amendments Act solved this problem by lowering the threshold for first-level coverage, relieving the plaintiffs of the need to show a disability that could not be corrected. In doing so, however, it created other problems. The Act did not change the standards for second-level coverage, and it made both tests for coverage much more complicated, particularly for cases in which the plaintiff is "regarded as" having a disability. In these cases, the problem of circularity becomes much more acute. The first-level question of "regarded as" coverage now depends upon whether the plaintiff "has been subject to an action prohibited under this chapter because of an actual or perceived impairment." § 3(3)(A), 42 U.S.C. § 12102(3)(A). For employment discrimination plaintiffs, this requirement is met only if they meet the second-level of coverage under Title I, requiring them to be a "qualified individual."[1] Normally, qualifications are determined "with or without reasonable accommodation" because the employer has a duty of reasonable accommodation under Title I. § 102(b)(5), 42 U.S.C. § 12112(b)(5). But another change made by the ADA Amendments Act eliminates any duty on the part of employers to reasonably accommodate individuals who are covered only because they are "regarded as" having a disability. § 505(h), 42 U.S.C. § 12201(h).

This provision does not expressly apply to the definition of "qualified individual" for purposes of second-level coverage, but it probably should be

[1] There are some decisions that allow any individual to recover for violations of the employer's duty to avoid inquiries into potential disabilities, on the ground that the plaintiff should not be required to disclose a disability in litigation in order to prevent an inquiry into disability by the employer. E.g., Griffin v. Steeltek, Inc., 160 F.3d 591 (10th Cir. 1998). The authors are grateful to Jennifer Mathis of the Bazelon Center for Mental Health Law for this citation.

read into it. Otherwise, an individual "regarded as" disabled could become a "qualified individual" with the aid of reasonable accommodations that the employer was not required to make. It is more consistent with the statute as a whole to allow individuals who obtain first-level coverage because they are "regarded as" having a disability to obtain second-level coverage only if they are qualified without any reasonable accommodation. They can then establish a violation of Title I by proving that they suffered discrimination because of their impairment, not because of any failure to receive a reasonable accommodation. It follows that they can meet all three requirements for proving a violation of the ADA: first-level coverage, second-level coverage, and discrimination in violation of the statute. Although all three questions are intertwined, they can be resolved consistently. An otherwise qualified plaintiff who is regarded as disabled can satisfy both levels of coverage and recover on the merits, but only for discrimination directly based on a disability, not for failure to receive a reasonable accommodation.

7. ***Sutton* Revisited.** On the facts of *Sutton*, assuming the plaintiffs needed only ordinary eyeglass, the preceding analysis is not the end of the matter. As we have seen, the Sutton sisters are not actually disabled for purposes of first-level coverage because of the exception for ordinary eyeglasses. They could still be regarded as disabled if the following requirements were met: (1) they had an actual or perceived impairment; (2) the impairment was not "transitory and minor"; and (3) United Air Lines discriminated against them in violation of Title I because of the impairment. Requirements (1) and (2) are satisfied. Requirement (3) calls for an examination of second-level coverage to determine whether they would be qualified. (On the analysis offered in the preceding paragraph, their qualifications would be determined without any reasonable accommodation, but since they did not request any accommodation, this complication in the analysis would be irrelevant.) Their qualifications for the job would be determined according to the employer's obligations under Title I. Among these is the second special provision for vision problems, which allows employers to set qualifications "based on an individual's uncorrected vision" only if such qualifications are "shown to be job-related for the position in question and consistent with business necessity." § 103(c), 42 U.S.C. § 12113(c). If this showing could not be made, then United Air Lines would have to evaluate their qualifications with eyeglasses, and if it failed to do so, it would violate this new provision in the statute. It follows that the Sutton sisters would meet the requirements for first-level coverage because they would be "regarded as" having a disability; they would meet the requirements for second-level coverage because they would have been qualified for the job; and they would have established a violation of the statute.

The entire case, as it would be litigated under the ADA Amendments Act, would turn on the justifiability of the employer's reason for rejecting them: bad eyesight in its uncorrected state. Is this ultimately the right question to ask? If so, why does it require such a complicated path through the statute? Wouldn't it have been easier to expand coverage of the ADA to reach all individuals, as does Title VII, and then narrow the duties imposed upon employers and other covered defendants? Shorn of all of its complications, is that what the ADA Amendments Act has really accomplished?

8. **Work as a Major Life Activity.** *Sutton* assumes but does not decide that work is a major life activity. The ADA Amendments Act now resolves this question in favor of coverage. Work, along with a non-exclusive list of several other activities and "major bodily functions," is now identified as a "major life activity." Just as Congress expanded the ways in which impairments could have the requisite effect for coverage—without considering corrective measures—it also expanded the affected activities—by including several that had previously been disputed. The effect of the new list of major life activities is to expand coverage based on both actual disabilities and a record of an actual disability. Expanding coverage of impairments that constitute an actual disability automatically expands coverage based on "a record of such an impairment." An individual with a record of a condition that substantially limits any of the listed activities is covered.

Work is one of the newly listed activities. Notice, however, that Congress does not address the question of how many jobs from which the plaintiff has to be excluded. *Sutton* required the plaintiffs to prove that they were regarded as disabled because they were regarded as incapable of performing a "broad range of jobs." The "regarded as" element in this reasoning has now been transformed, as discussed in the preceding notes. The Sutton sisters would no longer have to show that their eyesight had any effect on any major life activity. Congress also resolved the Court's doubts about work as a "major life activity." Did it also reject the Court's narrow interpretation of what constitutes a substantial limitation on the ability to work? The Sutton sisters failed to prove that jobs as pilots on other kinds of aircraft were foreclosed to them, thus preventing them from proving that they were substantially limited in their ability to work.

Does the statutory language require this result because an impairment must "substantially limit" a major life activity? The inability to perform one job or a narrow range of jobs, according to this argument, does not constitute a substantial limit. Moreover, if it did, would it create another circularity in the statute: making the definition of "major life activity" depend upon plaintiff's exclusion from the very job at issue? The plaintiff's rejection from the job she sought could be used to prove that she was substantially limited in the major life activity of working. The ADA Amendments Act does not specifically address the effect necessary to substantially impair the major life activity of working. It does, however, criticize decisions that heighten the degree of impairment necessary to obtain coverage, as discussed in the notes following the next principal case. Does congressional disapproval of those decisions undermine the reasoning in *Sutton* that the plaintiff must be excluded from a wide range of jobs?

9. **Bibliography.** Almost all of the scholarship on the issues in *Sutton* was published before the ADA Amendments Act. Nevertheless, much of it was critical of the decision and anticipated the amending legislation, at least in

broad outline. For examples of such articles, see Jill C. Anderson, Just Semantics: The Lost Reading of the Americans with Disabilities Act, 117 Yale L.J. 992 (2008); Ruth Colker, The Mythic 43 Million Americans With Disabilities, 49 Wm. & Mary L. Rev. 1 (2007); Jill Elaine Hasday, Mitigation and the Americans with Disabilities Act, 103 Mich. L. Rev. 217 (2004).

For articles on the question of what constitutes discrimination against an individual "regarded as" having a disability, see Mary Crossley, The Disability Kaleidoscope, 74 Notre Dame L. Rev. 621 (1999); Alex B. Long, (Whatever Happened to) The ADA's "Record of" Prong(?), 81 Wash. L. Rev. 669 (2006); Michelle A. Travis, Perceived Disabilities, Social Cognition, and "Innocent Mistakes," 55 Vand. L. Rev. 481 (2002).

Several articles have discussed conditions such as low intelligence or an unpleasant appearance or personality, which now are more likely to receive coverage under the ADA. For instance, a significant debate has developed over whether obesity or appearance should be a prohibited ground of discrimination. See Elizabeth M. Adamitis, Appearance Matters: A Proposal to Prohibit Appearance Discrimination in Employment, 75 Wash. L. Rev. 195 (2000); Anna R. Kirkland, What's at Stake in Fatness as a Disability?, 26 Disability Stud. Q. No. 1 (2006); Jane B. Korn, Fat, 77 B.U. L. Rev. 25 (1997); Robert Post, Prejudicial Appearances: The Logic of American Antidiscrimination Law, 88 Cal. L. Rev. 1 (2000); Jennifer B. Shinall, Distaste or Disability? Evaluating the Legal Framework for Protecting Obese Workers, 37 Berkeley J. Emp. & Lab. L. 101 (2016); Yofi Tirosh, The Right to Be Fat, 12 Yale J. Health Pol'y L. & Ethics 264 (2012).

NOTES ON DISABILITIES COVERED BY OTHER STATUTES

1. ***Cleveland v. Policy Management Systems Corp.*** The Supreme Court considered the relationship between covered disabilities under the ADA and covered disabilities under the Social Security Act in Cleveland v. Policy Management Systems Corp., 526 U.S. 795 (1999).

As the Court framed the issues in that case:

> The Social Security Disability Insurance (SSDI) program provides benefits to a person with a disability so severe that she is "unable to do [her] previous work" and "cannot . . . engage in any other kind of substantial gainful work which exists in the national economy." § 223(a) of the Social Security Act, as set forth in 42 U.S.C. § 423(d)(2)(A). This case asks whether the law erects a special presumption that would significantly inhibit an SSDI recipient from simultaneously pursuing an action for disability discrimination under the Americans with Disabilities Act of 1990 (ADA), claiming that "with . . . reasonable accommodation" she could "perform the essential functions" of her job. § 101, 104 Stat. 331, 42 U.S.C. § 12111(8).
>
> We believe that, in context, these two seemingly divergent statutory contentions are often consistent, each with the other. Thus pursuit, and receipt, of SSDI benefits does not automatically estop the recipient from pursuing an ADA claim. Nor does the law

erect a strong presumption against the recipient's success under the ADA. Nonetheless, an ADA plaintiff cannot simply ignore her SSDI contention that she was too disabled to work. To survive a defendant's motion for summary judgment, she must explain why that SSDI contention is consistent with her ADA claim that she could "perform the essential functions" of her previous job, at least with "reasonable accommodation."...

The Social Security Act and the ADA both help individuals with disabilities, but in different ways. The Social Security Act provides monetary benefits to every insured individual who "is under a disability." 42 U.S.C. § 423(a)(1). The Act defines "disability" as an

> "inability to engage in any substantial gainful activity by reason of any . . . physical or mental impairment which can be expected to result in death or which has lasted or can be expected to last for a continuous period of not less than 12 months." § 423(d)(1)(A).

The individual's impairment, as we have said, must be

> "of such severity that [she] is not only unable to do [her] previous work but cannot, considering [her] age, education, and work experience, engage in any other kind of substantial gainful work which exists in the national economy. . . ." § 423(d)(2)(A).

The ADA seeks to eliminate unwarranted discrimination against disabled individuals in order both to guarantee those individuals equal opportunity and to provide the Nation with the benefit of their consequently increased productivity. See, e.g., 42 U.S.C. §§ 12101(a)(8), (9). The Act prohibits covered employers from discriminating "against a qualified individual with a disability because of the disability of such individual." § 12112(a). The Act defines a "qualified individual with a disability" as a disabled person "who . . . can perform the essential functions" of her job, including those who can do so only "with . . . reasonable accommodation." § 12111(8).

We here consider but one of the many ways in which these two statutes might interact. This case does not involve, for example, the interaction of either of the statutes before us with other statutes, such as the Federal Employers' Liability Act, 45 U.S.C. § 51 et seq. Nor does it involve directly conflicting statements about purely factual matters, such as "The light was red/green," or "I can/cannot raise my arm above my head." An SSA representation of total disability differs from a purely factual statement in that it often implies a context-related legal conclusion, namely "I am disabled for purposes of the Social Security Act." And our consideration of this latter kind of statement consequently leaves the law related to the former, purely factual, kind of conflict where we found it.

The case before us concerns an ADA plaintiff who both applied for, and received, SSDI benefits. It requires us to review a Court of Appeals decision upholding the grant of summary judgment on the ground that an ADA plaintiff's "represent[ation] to the SSA that she was totally disabled" created a "rebuttable presumption" sufficient to "judicially esto[p]" her later representation that, "for the time in question," with reasonable accommodation, she could perform the essential functions of her job. 120 F.3d, at 518–519. The Court of Appeals thought, in essence, that claims under both Acts would incorporate two directly conflicting propositions, namely "I am too disabled to work" and "I am not too disabled to work." And in an effort to prevent two claims that would embody that kind of factual conflict, the court used a special judicial presumption, which it believed would ordinarily prevent a plaintiff like Cleveland from successfully asserting an ADA claim.

In our view, however, despite the appearance of conflict that arises from the language of the two statutes, the two claims do not inherently conflict to the point where courts should apply a special negative presumption like the one applied by the Court of Appeals here. That is because there are too many situations in which an SSDI claim and an ADA claim can comfortably exist side by side. . . .

Nonetheless, in some cases an earlier SSDI claim may turn out genuinely to conflict with an ADA claim. Summary judgment for a defendant is appropriate when the plaintiff "fails to make a showing sufficient to establish the existence of an element essential to [her] case, and on which [she] will bear the burden of proof at trial." Celotex Corp. v. Catrett, 477 U.S. 317, 322 (1986). An ADA plaintiff bears the burden of proving that she is a "qualified individual with a disability"—that is, a person "who, with or without reasonable accommodation, can perform the essential functions" of her job. 42 U.S.C. § 12111(8). And a plaintiff's sworn assertion in an application for disability benefits that she is, for example, "unable to work" will appear to negate an essential element of her ADA case—at least if she does not offer a sufficient explanation. For that reason, we hold that an ADA plaintiff cannot simply ignore the apparent contradiction that arises out of the earlier SSDI total disability claim. Rather, she must proffer a sufficient explanation.

2. **Coverage and Purposes of Different Statutes.** The ADA and the Rehabilitation Act have identical terms of coverage. Other statutes, like the Social Security Act, define covered disabilities in different terms. Considered in isolation, each of these definitions makes sense. Different statutes define coverage according to the different purposes that they serve. The ADA and the Rehabilitation Act, insofar as they prohibit discrimination in employment, define covered disabilities in identical terms. The Social Security Act, because it provides for compensation instead of employment, defines covered disabilities differently. It is the divergence between these

definitions that gave rise to the issue in *Cleveland*. This difference has now been confirmed by the ADA Amendments Act, which provides that nothing in the ADA "alters the standards for determining eligibility for benefits under State worker's compensation laws or under State and Federal disability benefit programs." § 501(e), 42 U.S.C. § 12201(c). Thus, the Social Security Act provides for SSDI benefits for individuals with temporary and permanent disabilities, considered without regard to possible accommodations, so long as the individual cannot be employed in almost any job. Coverage under the ADA and the Rehabilitation Act is both narrower and broader than under the Social Security Act, excluding temporary disability, but including disabilities that result in a substantial impairment, as long as the individual will be able to perform the essential functions of her job.

As a matter of policy, does it make sense to have several wholly independent programs that provide benefits to individuals with disabilities or protect them from discrimination without any attempt at coordinated coverage? The scope of these programs need not be identical as, indeed, it is not for different parts of the ADA and the Rehabilitation Act. Title I of the ADA, as we have seen, protects only qualified individuals, not all individuals with disabilities, from employment discrimination. Yet its terms of coverage are coordinated with the general definition of disability applicable to all titles of the ADA. Could the same dependence among coverage provisions have been worked out with the Social Security Act?

By default, Congress has left the relationship among the different statutes protecting the disabled to be worked out by the courts. In *Cleveland*, the Court establishes a presumption that receipt of SSDI benefits prevents an individual from making a claim of employment discrimination under the ADA. This presumption can be overcome by the plaintiff by proof that his case is the exceptional one in which being totally disabled under Social Security Act does not bar him from claiming that he is a "qualified individual" under the ADA. Is this kind of case-by-case inquiry the best way to reconcile the coverage provisions of the two statutes?

3. **Strategic Considerations for Plaintiffs.** Individuals seek SSDI benefits in order to obtain immediate financial compensation for medical treatment of their disabilities and for loss of income resulting from their inability to work. The process of obtaining these benefits, although complicated in some cases, operates much more quickly than the adversarial process of litigation. It also costs the plaintiff much less money. Once the plaintiff obtains SSDI benefits, however, he may reconsider the long-term consequences of his disability and may seek reemployment. At that point, he would like to invoke the protection of the ADA.

In the modern law of procedure, plaintiffs are not usually required to make an election of remedies. By asserting one kind of claim, they do not usually forfeit others. Plaintiffs with claims of racial discrimination, for instance, can assert their claims under both Title VII and § 1981. The principles of res judicata or claim preclusion, however, force them to consolidate all their claims arising out of the same transaction or occurrence into a single action. These principles recognize an exception for claims, like administrative claims for SSDI benefits, that have to be brought through a special procedure that does not allow joinder of related claims, like those under the ADA. These claims can be brought separately, but they are subject to the principles of collateral estoppel or issue preclusion. A final judicial resolution of an issue involving a party in one action is usually binding on the same party in a subsequent action. *Cleveland* does not involve collateral estoppel in the usual sense, because the finding that the plaintiff was disabled for purposes of the Social Security Act was made by an administrative agency, not by a court. Moreover, as the opinion points out, this issue is not identical to the issue of coverage under the ADA. Strictly speaking, *Cleveland* involved preclusion in the form of "judicial estoppel": the inability of a party to assert in later litigation a factual assertion inconsistent with representations that he had made in earlier proceedings. This is a doctrine of equitable discretion, which a court can invoke depending on overall considerations of fairness.

Despite this flexibility in applying the doctrine, plaintiffs in cases like *Cleveland* face a difficult choice: accepting SSDI benefits may preclude relief under the ADA. How hard is it for plaintiffs to overcome the presumption established in *Cleveland*? The mere receipt of SSDI benefits, regardless of the reasons for doing so, raises a suspicion that the plaintiff is trying to have the best of both worlds: government compensation when he isn't working and government assistance in getting a job when he wants one. This suspicion is allied with an undercurrent in many disability cases, casting doubt on the plaintiff's claim on the ground that he is not genuinely disabled, but instead is malingering and attempting to obtain benefits despite his own lack of effort. How can a plaintiff overcome such suspicions? Does it involve more than showing technical compliance with the coverage provisions of both statutes?

The decision in *Cleveland* recognizes the possibility that plaintiffs can still assert a claim under the ADA despite their receipt of benefits under the Social Security Act. The presumption against coverage, however, reduces that possibility significantly. On balance, is the decision favorable or unfavorable to plaintiffs? Does it establish yet another hurdle that they must surmount in order to obtain relief under the ADA?

4. **Bibliography.** For articles on the relationship between the ADA and other statutes that benefit individuals with disabilities, see Samuel R. Bagenstos, The Americans with Disabilities Act as Welfare Reform, 44 Wm. & Mary L. Rev. 921 (2003); Matthew Diller, Dissonant Disability Policies: The Tensions Between the Americans with Disabilities Act and Federal Disability Benefits Programs, 76 Tex. L. Rev. 1003 (1998); Daniel B. Kohrman & Kimberly Berg, Reconciling Definitions of "Disability": Six Years Later, Has *Cleveland v. Policy Management Systems* Lived up to Its Initial Reviews as a Boost for Workers' Rights?, 7 Marq. Elder's Advisor 29 (2005); Francine J. Lipman, Enabling Work for People with Disabilities: A Post-Integrationist Revision of Underutilized Tax Incentives, 53 Am. U. L. Rev. 393 (2003); Mark C. Weber, Disability and the Law of Welfare: A Post-Integrationist Examination, 2000 U. Ill. L. Rev. 889.

C. DISCRIMINATION AND REASONABLE ACCOMMODATION

Southeastern Community College v. Davis

442 U.S. 397 (1979).

■ JUSTICE POWELL delivered the opinion of the Court.

This case presents a matter of first impression for this Court: Whether § 504 of the Rehabilitation Act of 1973, which prohibits discrimination against an "otherwise qualified handicapped individual" in federally funded programs "solely by reason of his handicap," forbids professional schools from imposing physical qualifications for admission to their clinical training programs.

I

Respondent, who suffers from a serious hearing disability, seeks to be trained as a registered nurse. During the 1973–1974 academic year she was enrolled in the College Parallel program of Southeastern Community College, a state institution that receives federal funds. Respondent hoped to progress to Southeastern's Associate Degree Nursing program, completion of which would make her eligible for state certification as a registered nurse. In the course of her application to the nursing program, she was interviewed by a member of the nursing faculty. It became apparent that respondent had difficulty understanding questions asked, and on inquiry she acknowledged a history of hearing problems and dependence on a hearing aid. She was advised to consult an audiologist.

On the basis of an examination at Duke University Medical Center, respondent was diagnosed as having a "bilateral, sensori-neural hearing loss." A change in her hearing aid was recommended, as a result of which it was expected that she would be able to detect sounds "almost as well as a person would who has normal hearing." But this improvement would not mean that she could discriminate among sounds sufficiently to understand normal spoken speech. Her lip-reading skills would remain necessary for effective communication: "While wearing the hearing aid, she is well aware of gross sounds occurring in the listening environment. However, she can only be responsible for speech spoken to her, when the talker gets her attention and allows her to look directly at the talker."

Southeastern next consulted Mary McRee, Executive Director of the North Carolina Board of Nursing. On the basis of the audiologist's report, McRee recommended that respondent not be admitted to the nursing program. In McRee's view, respondent's hearing disability made it unsafe for her to practice as a nurse. In addition, it would be impossible for respondent to participate safely in the normal clinical training program, and those modifications that would be necessary to enable safe participation would prevent her from realizing the benefits of the program: "To adjust patient learning experiences in keeping with [respondent's] hearing limitations could, in fact, be the same as denying her full learning to meet the objectives of your nursing programs."

After respondent was notified that she was not qualified for nursing study because of her hearing disability, she requested reconsideration of the decision. The entire nursing staff of Southeastern was assembled, and McRee again was consulted. McRee repeated her conclusion that on the basis of the available evidence, respondent "has hearing limitations which could interfere with her safely caring for patients." Upon further deliberation, the staff voted to deny respondent admission.

Respondent then filed suit in the United States District Court for the Eastern District of North Carolina, alleging both a violation of § 504 of the Rehabilitation Act of 1973, as amended, 29 U.S.C. § 794, and a denial of equal protection and due process. After a bench trial, the District Court entered judgment in favor of Southeastern. It confirmed the findings of the audiologist that even with a hearing aid respondent cannot understand speech directed to her except through lip-reading, and further found:

> "[I]n many situations such as an operation room intensive care unit, or post natal care unit, all doctors and nurses wear surgical masks which would make lip reading impossible. Additionally, in many situations a Registered Nurse would be required to instantly follow the physician's instructions concerning procurement of various types of instruments and drugs where the physician would be unable to get the nurse's attention by other than vocal means." Id., at 1343.

Accordingly, the court concluded:

> "[Respondent's] handicap actually prevents her from safely performing in both her training program and her proposed profession. The trial testimony indicated numerous situations where [respondent's] particular disability would render her unable to function properly. Of particular concern to the court in this case is the potential of danger to future patients in such situations." Id. at 1345.

Based on these findings, the District Court concluded that respondent was not an "otherwise qualified handicapped individual" protected against discrimination by § 504. In its view, "[o]therwise qualified, can only be read to mean otherwise able to function sufficiently in the position sought in spite of the handicap, if proper training and facilities are suitable and available." Because respondent's disability would prevent her from functioning "sufficiently" in Southeastern's nursing program, the court held that the decision to exclude her was not discriminatory within the meaning of § 504.

On appeal, the Court of Appeals for the Fourth Circuit reversed. It did not dispute the District Court's findings of fact, but held that the court had misconstrued § 504. In light of administrative regulations that had been promulgated while the appeal was pending, see 42 Fed. Reg. 22676 (1977), the appellate court believed that § 504 required Southeastern to "reconsider plaintiff's application for admission to the nursing program without regard to her hearing ability." It concluded that the District Court had erred in taking respondent's handicap into account in determining whether she was "otherwise qualified" for the program, rather than confining its inquiry to her "academic and technical qualifications." The Court of Appeals also suggested that § 504 required "affirmative conduct" on the part of Southeastern to modify its program to accommodate the disabilities of applicants, "even when such modifications become expensive."

Because of the importance of this issue to the many institutions covered by § 504, we granted certiorari. We now reverse.

II

As previously noted, this is the first case in which this Court has been called upon to interpret § 504. It is elementary that "[t]he starting point in every case involving construction of a statute is the language itself." Blue Chip Stamps v. Manor Drug Stores, 421 U.S. 723, 756 (1975) (POWELL, J., concurring); . . . Section 504 by its terms does not compel educational institutions to disregard the disabilities of handicapped individuals or to make substantial modifications in their programs to allow disabled persons to participate. Instead, it requires only that an "otherwise qualified handicapped individual" not be excluded from participation in a federally funded program "solely by reason of his handicap," indicating only that mere possession of a handicap is not a permissible ground for assuming an inability to function in a particular context.

The court below, however, believed that the "otherwise qualified" persons protected by § 504 include those who would be able to meet the requirements of a particular program in every respect except as to limitations imposed by their handicap. Taken literally, this holding would prevent an institution from taking into account any limitation resulting from the handicap, however disabling. It assumes, in effect, that a person need not meet legitimate physical requirements in order to be "otherwise qualified." We think the understanding of the District Court is closer to the plain meaning of the statutory language. An otherwise qualified person is one who is able to meet all of a program's requirements in spite of his handicap.

The regulations promulgated by the Department of HEW to interpret § 504 reinforce, rather than contradict, this conclusion. According to these regulations, a "[q]ualified handicapped person" is, "[w]ith respect to postsecondary and vocational education services, a handicapped person who meets the academic and technical standards requisite to admission or participation in the [school's] education program or activity. . . ." 45 CFR § 84.3(k)(3) (1978). An explanatory note states: "The term 'technical standards' refers to *all* nonacademic admissions criteria that are essential to participation in the program in question." 45 CFR pt.84, App. A, p.405 (1978) (emphasis supplied).

A further note emphasizes that legitimate physical qualifications may be essential to participation in particular programs. We think it clear, therefore, that HEW interprets the "other" qualifications which a handicapped person may be required to meet as including necessary physical qualifications.

III

The remaining question is whether the physical qualifications Southeastern demanded of respondent might not be necessary for participation in its nursing program. It is not open to dispute that, as Southeastern's Associate Degree Nursing program currently is constituted, the ability to understand speech without reliance on lip-reading is necessary for patient safety during the clinical phase of the program. As the District Court found, this ability also is indispensable for many of the functions that a registered nurse performs.

Respondent contends nevertheless that § 504, properly interpreted, compels Southeastern to undertake affirmative action that would dispense with the need for effective oral communication. First, it is suggested that respondent can be given individual supervision by faculty members whenever she attends patients directly. Moreover, certain required courses might be dispensed with altogether for respondent. It is not necessary, she argues, that Southeastern train her to undertake all the tasks a registered nurse is licensed to perform. Rather, it is sufficient to make § 504 applicable if respondent might be able to perform satisfactorily some of the duties of a registered nurse or to hold some of the positions available to a registered nurse.

Respondent finds support for this argument in portions of the HEW regulations discussed above. In particular, a provision applicable to postsecondary educational programs requires covered institutions to make "modifications" in their programs to accommodate handicapped persons, and to provide "auxiliary aids" such as sign language interpreters. Respondent argues that this regulation imposes an obligation to ensure full participation in covered programs by handicapped individuals and, in particular, requires Southeastern to make the kind of adjustments that would be necessary to permit her safe participation in the nursing program.

We note first that on the present record it appears unlikely respondent could benefit from any affirmative action that the regulation reasonably could be interpreted as requiring. Section 84.44(d)(2), for example, explicitly excludes "devices or services of a personal nature" from the kinds of auxiliary aids a school must provide a handicapped individual. Yet the only evidence in the record indicates that nothing less than close, individual attention by a nursing instructor would be sufficient to ensure patient safety if respondent took part in the clinical phase of the nursing program. Furthermore, it also is reasonably clear that § 84.44(a) does not encompass the kind of curricular changes that would be necessary to accommodate respondent in the nursing program. In light of respondent's inability to function in clinical courses without close supervision, Southeastern, with prudence, could allow her to take only academic classes. Whatever benefits respondent might realize from such a course of study, she would not receive even a rough equivalent of the training a nursing program normally gives. Such a fundamental alteration in the nature of a program is far more than the "modification" the regulation requires.

Moreover, an interpretation of the regulations that required the extensive modifications necessary to include respondent in the nursing program would raise grave doubts about their validity. If these regulations were to require substantial adjustments in existing programs beyond those necessary to eliminate discrimination against otherwise qualified individuals, they would do more than clarify the meaning of § 504. Instead, they would constitute an unauthorized extension of the obligations imposed by that statute.

The language and structure of the Rehabilitation Act of 1973 reflect a recognition by Congress of the distinction between the evenhanded treatment of qualified handicapped persons and affirmative efforts to overcome the disabilities caused by handicaps. Section 501(b), governing the employment of handicapped individuals by the Federal Government, requires each federal agency to submit "an affirmative action program plan for the hiring, placement, and advancement of handicapped individuals. . . ." These plans "shall include a description of the extent to which and methods whereby the special needs of handicapped employees are being met." Similarly, § 503(a), governing hiring by federal contractors, requires employers to "take affirmative action to employ and advance in employment qualified handicapped individuals. . . ." The President is required to promulgate regulations to enforce this section.

Under § 501(c) of the Act, by contrast, state agencies such as Southeastern are only "encourage[d] . . . to adopt and implement such policies and procedures." Section 504 does not refer at all to affirmative action, and except as it applies to federal employers it does not provide for implementation by administrative action. A comparison of these provisions demonstrates that Congress understood accommodation of the needs of handicapped individuals may require affirmative action and knew how to provide for it in those instances where it wished to do so.

Although an agency's interpretation of the statute under which it operates is entitled to some deference, "this deference is constrained by our obligation to honor the clear meaning of a statute, as revealed by its language, purpose, and history." Teamsters v. Daniel, 439 U.S. 551, 566 n.20 (1979). Here, neither the language, purpose, nor history of § 504 reveals an intent to impose an affirmative action obligation on all recipients of federal funds. Accordingly, we hold that even if HEW has attempted to create such an obligation itself, it lacks the authority to do so.

IV

We do not suggest that the line between a lawful refusal to extend affirmative action and illegal discrimination against handicapped persons always will be clear. It is possible to envision situations where an insistence on continuing past requirements and practices might arbitrarily deprive genuinely qualified handicapped persons of the opportunity to participate in a covered program. Technological advances can be expected to enhance opportunities to rehabilitate the handicapped or otherwise to qualify them for some useful employment. Such advances also may enable attainment of these goals without imposing undue financial and administrative burdens upon a State. Thus, situations may arise where a refusal to modify an existing program might become unreasonable and discriminatory. Identification of those instances where a refusal to accommodate the needs of a disabled person amounts to discrimination against the handicapped continues to be an important responsibility of HEW.

In this case, however, it is clear that Southeastern's unwillingness to make major adjustments in its nursing program does not constitute such discrimination. The uncontroverted testimony of several members of Southeastern's staff and faculty established that the purpose of its program was to train persons who could serve the nursing profession in all customary ways. This type of purpose, far from reflecting any animus against handicapped individuals is shared by many if not most of the institutions that train persons to render professional service. It is undisputed that respondent could not participate in Southeastern's nursing program unless the standards were substantially lowered. Section 504 imposes no requirement upon an educational institution to lower or to effect substantial modifications of standards to accommodate a handicapped person.

One may admire respondent's desire and determination to overcome her handicap, and there well may be various other types of service for which she can qualify. In this case, however, we hold that there was no violation of § 504 when Southeastern concluded that respondent did not qualify for admission to its program. Nothing in the language or history of § 504 reflects an intention to limit the freedom of an educational institution to require reasonable physical qualifications for admission to a clinical training program. Nor has there been any showing in this case that any action short of a substantial change in Southeastern's program would render unreasonable the qualifications it imposed.

V

Accordingly, we reverse the judgment of the court below, and remand for proceedings consistent with this opinion.

So ordered.

NOTES ON *SOUTHEASTERN COMMUNITY COLLEGE V. DAVIS*

1. **Discrimination Under the Rehabilitation Act.** The issue in *Southeastern Community College* was framed initially as whether the plaintiff was qualified "without regard to" or "in spite of" her disability. This way of posing the issue resulted from the terms of § 504, 29 U.S.C. § 794, which prohibits discrimination against any "otherwise qualified individual with a disability" "solely by reason of her or his disability." If the model for disability discrimination is equality as colorblindness, then disabilities must be entirely disregarded in determining eligibility to participate in a federally funded program. If the model is equality as merit, then the legitimate qualifications of individuals with disabilities can be taken into account. The Supreme Court chose the second of these alternatives, setting the law of disability on a different course from that developed under Title VII.

The Court's stated concern is that the plaintiff's disability would prevent her from obtaining any benefit from the training program to which she had applied. It would be pointless to require her to be admitted to a program that trained her for a job for which she would never be qualified. Between ignoring the plaintiff's disability entirely or taking it into account in some fashion, the Court had little choice but to acknowledge the relevance of her disability to legitimate requirements for the training program. The same could be said of the qualifications for the job that she ultimately wanted, and indeed, the Court seems to assume that she could be excluded from employment as a nurse in a federally funded hospital.

The immediate result in *Southeastern Community College* was favorable to the defendant, but the relevance of the plaintiff's disability to legitimate qualifications imposed by the defendant can cut both ways. It can increase, as well as decrease, the defendant's obligations. The Court's initial holding that disabilities could be taken into account does not resolve the further question of how they are taken into account. This was the more difficult question raised in *Southeastern Community College*. It has now been given renewed prominence by the ADA Amendments Act.

2. **Discrimination Under the ADA.** As discussed earlier in this chapter, the ADA Amendments Act has now resolved many, and perhaps most, questions of first-level coverage—whether the plaintiff has a covered disability. For most plaintiffs, the focus of litigation is now likely to shift to second-level questions of coverage—whether the plaintiff is a qualified individual—and whether the defendant has violated the statute. These are questions under Title I concerning the scope of the defendant's duties and the range of legitimate reasons that can be offered for a disputed employment decision. These questions are particularly acute for individuals who obtain coverage only because they are "regarded as" having a disability. The employer does not owe such individuals any duty of reasonable accommodation. § 501(h), 42 U.S.C. § 12201(h). Hence for these individuals, the question of whether they are qualified "without regard to" their disabilities or "in spite of" their disabilities remains crucial. In terms of the

employer's available defenses, it depends upon whether the employer must ignore the plaintiff's perceived disability or whether the employer can take account of its effect on performance.

Suppose, for instance, that Davis had a hearing impairment that was not so severe as to constitute an actual disability, but that an employer nevertheless regarded it as one. Could the employer take account of the same factors as Southeastern Community College did in assessing her likely performance as a nurse? Under the "without regard to" approach, the employer would have to disregard her impairment, even if it affected likely performance on the job. Assuming she could perform the essential functions of the job, she would be a "qualified individual" under § 101(8), 42 U.S.C. § 12111(8), and taking account of her impairment would then be "discrimination on the basis of disability" in violation of § 102(a), 42 U.S.C. § 12112(a). Alternatively, the employer could be allowed to take account of her likely performance "in spite of" her disability. On this view, her performance on the job would not be an impairment that constituted a disability, so that the employer would not be engaged in "discrimination on the basis of disability" in taking account of her hearing impairment. Nevertheless, the distinction between the impairment and its effect on performance might be difficult to draw, especially if the employer emphasized the latter to hide any consideration of the former. Informed employers would just rely on predicted deficiencies in performance rather than the impairment that supported those predictions. The employer would reject her, not because she had a hearing impairment, but because the hearing impairment would interfere with her work as a nurse. Shifting to an analysis of qualifications "in spite of" a disability does not eliminate the practical problems in identifying when such qualifications are legitimate—when they do not involve prohibited discrimination on the basis of disability.

For individuals with an actual disability (or a record of one), this problem would not be as severe, because it could be addressed through the duty of reasonable accommodation, as discussed in the next note. If, as in the actual case, Davis were actually disabled, the employer would owe her a duty of reasonable accommodation and her qualifications would be assessed in light of such accommodations. If she were qualified, the employer would have to make reasonable accommodations for her. The end result is that employers have a broader duty to avoid discrimination against individuals with actual disabilities than against individuals who are only regarded as disabled.

Is this the right result? Employers can invoke a narrower range of reasons against individuals who suffer from greater impairments—because they have to make reasonable accommodations for them—than they can against those who are less severely impaired. Does the difference come down to a matter of the burden of proof? The employer's burden of justifying a decision adverse to someone who is only "regarded as" having a disability is lighter than the burden for someone who is actually disabled. What are the elements of the employer's defense to a claim by a qualified individual who is "regarded as" having a disability? Is it just the burden from *McDonnell Douglas* of producing a "legitimate, nondiscriminatory reason" for a decision adverse to the plaintiff? See McDonnell Douglas Corp. v. Green, 411 U.S. 792 (1973). The Report of the House Committee on Education and Labor seems to support this view by reference to the original intent of Congress in passing the ADA:

> . . . Congress intended and believed that the fact that an individual was discriminated against because of a perceived or actual impairment would be sufficient: "if a person is disqualified on the basis of an actual or perceived physical or mental condition, and the employer can *articulate no legitimate job-related reason* for the rejection, a perceived concern about employment of persons with disabilities could be inferred and the plaintiff would qualify for coverage under the 'regarded as' test."

H.R. Rep. 110–730, pt. 1, at 13 (2008), quoting H.R. Rep. No. 101–485, pt. 3, at 30–31 (1990) (emphasis added). This report then goes on to endorse the application of *McDonnell Douglas* to claims involving indirect evidence of discrimination under Title I, reasoning that it goes to the issue whether the plaintiff is a "qualified individual" covered by that title. H.R. Rep. 110–730, pt. 1, at 16–17 (2008).

Alternatively, the employer might have the burden of proving that the decision is "job related for the position in question and consistent with business necessity" as the employer does for claims of disparate impact under Title VII. See § 703(k), 42 U.S.C. § 2000e–2(k). The ADA contains its own version of the theory of disparate impact, § 102(b)(6), 42 U.S.C. § 12112(b)(6), and as discussed in the notes after *Sutton v. United Air Lines, Inc.*, the ADA Amendments Act applied the disparate impact defense for qualifications based on uncorrected vision. See § 103(c), 42 U.S.C. § 12113(c). Has the ADA Amendments Act just taken all the problems of coverage that existed under the statute as previously interpreted and transferred them to questions about what the legitimate qualifications for the job are? What guidance does the statute give for resolving these questions? For discussion of these and similar issues, see Mark C. Weber, Intent in Disability Discrimination Law: Social Science Insights and Comparisons to Race and Sex Discrimination, 2016 U. Ill. L. Rev. 151; Mark C. Weber, Accidentally on Purpose: Intent in Disability Discrimination law. 56 B.C. L. Rev. 1417–1464 (2015).

3. **Reasonable Accommodation Under the Rehabilitation Act.** The duty of reasonable accommodation requires an individual's disability to be taken into account in some form. It is not, however, a duty imposed by the literal terms of the Rehabilitation Act, which only forbids exclusions, denial of benefits, or discrimination in § 504. This duty made its way into interpretation of the Act through regulations that defined "otherwise qualified" to be determined by reference to reasonable accommodations necessary to meet the eligibility requirements of the program in question. 29 C.F.R. § 32.13.

This connection between qualifications and accommodations was later taken up in the definition of "qualified individual" in the ADA. § 101(8), 42 U.S.C. § 12111(8). Such an individual is one "who, with or without reasonable accommodation, can perform the essential functions" of the job. The ADA, however, is more explicit than the Rehabilitation Act in defining "reasonable accommodation" in the statute itself and directly imposing a duty of reasonable accommodation on employers. §§ 101(9), 102(b)(5), 42 U.S.C. §§ 12111(9), (10), 12112(b)(5). This duty is also explicitly made subject to an exception for accommodations that impose an "undue hardship" on the employer. § 101(10), 42 U.S.C. § 12111(10).

In *Southeastern Community College*, the Court addressed the question of how to take account of the plaintiff's disabilities in terms that approach, but do not precisely follow, the duty of reasonable accommodation as subsequently formulated in the ADA. The regulations discussed by the Court concerned adjustments to the requirements of an educational program, but these regulations essentially addressed the same issue as the duty of reasonable accommodation: whether the college had to make an exception to its eligibility requirements for hearing impaired individuals like the plaintiff. The Court held that no such accommodation was necessary: "Section 504 imposes no requirement upon an educational institution to lower or to effect substantial modifications of standards to accommodate a handicapped person."

The same issue would be analyzed under the ADA in terms of the "essential functions" of the job or "undue hardship" upon the employer. In either case, the crucial inquiry is the same as in *Southeastern Community College*: whether a proposed accommodation would be too burdensome upon the ordinary operation of the employer's business. The Court held that it would be, returning again to the connection between the nurse training program and actual employment as a nurse. The plaintiff's hearing impairment affected her ability to participate in the training program less because it interfered with her ability or willingness to learn than because it interfered with clinical lessons as a nurse and ultimately with her prospects for employment in that position. Is this a matter simply of inefficiency, or does it involve risks to others? Recall that the ADA recognizes a general defense based on a "direct threat," § 103(b), 42 U.S.C. § 12113(b), and the Rehabilitation Act recognizes an exception to coverage for contagious diseases and infections that pose such a threat. § 7(20)(D), 29 U.S.C. § 705(20)(D). Did the Court implicitly rely upon a similar principle in *Southeastern Community College*?

4. Discrimination and Affirmative Action Under the Rehabilitation Act. The Court distinguishes the obligations of recipients of federal funds under § 504 from those imposed on the Federal Government under § 501 and on federal contractors under § 503. The former involve a duty not to discriminate, whereas the latter include a duty to engage in affirmative action. These duties of affirmative action survived enactment of the ADA, which has no provisions concerned specifically with employment by the federal government or by federal contractors. Federal employees are protected only by the Rehabilitation Act, and federal contractors are covered by the ADA only to the extent that they are covered employers under Title I. The ADA also does not contain any requirement that employers engage in affirmative action. The distinction between nondiscrimination and affirmative action addressed in *Southeastern Community College* thus remains one of continuing significance.

It is all the more significant because the duty of reasonable accommodation appears to require a form of individualized affirmative action: steps that the employer can take to compensate for an individual's disability. According to the Court, these steps fall short of a duty to engage in affirmative action to assure that individuals with disabilities participate in federally funded programs. But how far short? Regulations under the Rehabilitation Act require the federal government to be "a model employer" of the disabled. 29 C.F.R. § 1614.203(d). Does this imply that private employers have less onerous obligations? Presumably the federal government is better able to spread the cost of accommodating the disabilities of individuals who choose to work for it. The federal government is the nation's largest employer, and it is funded through a broad base of tax revenues. Private employers face the constraints of the market in obtaining the resources necessary to make accommodations for their employees. These constraints are all the greater for small firms whose operations are less likely to have the flexibility necessary to make individual accommodations. Do these considerations explain why the ADA does not require affirmative action generally on behalf of the disabled? Do they explain what it means for the federal government to be "a model employer" of the disabled?

These considerations certainly do not explain other features of existing law. For instance, federal contractors under § 503 are required to engage in affirmative action, but recipients of federal funds under § 504 are not. To the extent that federal funding relieves the competitive pressure of the market, it should operate more favorably for recipients of federal funds, who do not have to bid to work for the federal government, than for federal contractors. Perhaps the different obligations imposed on these entities results from the different remedies available under § 503 and § 504. Only the latter supports a private claim for damages, leaving the enforcement of affirmative action against federal contractors to be done entirely by the federal government. E.g., D'Amato v. Wisconsin Gas Co., 760 F.2d 1474, 1478 (7th Cir. 1985). Is this explanation too ad hoc to be convincing? Or is the difference between reasonable accommodation and affirmative action simply a matter of degree?

5. **Bibliography.** For discussion of the duty of reasonable accommodation as it developed under the Rehabilitation Act, see Kathryn W. Tate, The Federal Employer's Duties Under the Rehabilitation Act: Does Reasonable Accommodation or Affirmative Action Include Reassignment?, 67 Tex. L. Rev. 781 (1989); Judith Welch Wegner, The Antidiscrimination Model Reconsidered: Ensuring Equal Opportunity Without Respect to Handicap Under Section 504 of the Rehabilitation Act of 1973, 69 Cornell L. Rev. 401 (1984); Symposium, Employment Rights of the Handicapped, 27 DePaul L. Rev. 943 (1978).

For discussions of what constitutes "reasonable accommodation" and "undue hardship" under both the Rehabilitation Act and the ADA, see Jeffrey O. Cooper, Overcoming Barriers to Employment: The Meaning of Reasonable Accommodation and Undue Hardship in the Americans with Disabilities Act, 139 U. Pa. L. Rev. 1423 (1991); Steven B. Epstein, In Search of a Bright Line:

Determining When an Employer's Financial Hardship Becomes "Undue" Under the Americans with Disabilities Act, 48 Vand. L. Rev. 391 (1995); Barbara A. Lee, Reasonable Accommodation Under the Americans with Disabilities Act: The Limitations of Rehabilitation Act Precedent, 14 Berkeley J. Emp. & Lab. L. 201 (1993); Elizabeth A. Pendo, Disability, Doctors and Dollars: Distinguishing the Three Faces of Reasonable Accommodation, 35 U.C. Davis L. Rev. 1175 (2002); Frank S. Ravitch, Beyond Reasonable Accommodation: The Availability and Structure of a Cause of Action for Workplace Harassment Under the Americans with Disabilities Act, 15 Cardozo L. Rev. 1475 (1994); Laura F. Rothstein, The Employer's Duty to Accommodate Performance and Conduct Deficiencies of Individuals with Mental Impairments Under Disability Discrimination Laws, 47 Syracuse L. Rev. 931 (1997); Stewart J. Schwab & Steven L. Willborn, Reasonable Accommodation of Workplace Disabilities, 44 Wm. & Mary L. Rev. 1197 (2003); Symposium, Individual Rights and Reasonable Accommodations Under the Americans with Disabilities Act, 46 DePaul L. Rev. 871 (1997).

Both the Rehabilitation Act and the ADA apply outside of employment, as cases like *Bragdon v. Abbott* and *Southeastern Community College* illustrate. Issues of accommodation in education and testing have proved to be especially controversial. See Mark Kelman & Gillian Lester, Jumping the Queue: An Inquiry into the Legal Treatment of Students with Learning Disabilities (1997); Susan J. Adams, Because They're Otherwise Qualified: Accommodating Learning Disabled Law Student Writers, 46 J. Legal Educ. 189 (1996); W. Sherman Rogers, The ADA, Title VII, and the Bar Examination: The Nature and Extent of the ADA's Coverage of Bar Examinations and an Analysis of the Applicability of Title VII to Such Tests, 36 How. L.J. 1 (1993); Bonnie P. Tucher & Joseph F. Smith, Jr., Accommodating Law Faculty with Disabilities, 46 J. Legal Educ. 157 (1996).

U.S. Airways, Inc. v. Barnett

535 U.S. 391 (2002).

■ JUSTICE BREYER delivered the opinion of the Court.

The Americans with Disabilities Act of 1990 (ADA or Act), 42 U.S.C. § 12101 et seq., prohibits an employer from discriminating against an "individual with a disability" who, with "reasonable accommodation," can perform the essential functions of the job. §§ 12112(a) and (b). This case, arising in the context of summary judgment, asks us how the Act resolves a potential conflict between: (1) the interests of a disabled worker who seeks assignment to a particular position as a "reasonable accommodation," and (2) the interests of other workers with superior rights to bid for the job under an employer's seniority system. In such a case, does the accommodation demand trump the seniority system?

In our view, the seniority system will prevail in the run of cases. As we interpret the statute, to show that a requested accommodation conflicts with the rules of a seniority system is ordinarily to show that the accommodation is not "reasonable." Hence such a showing will entitle an employer/defendant to summary judgment on the question—unless there is more. The plaintiff remains free to present evidence of special circumstances that make "reasonable" a seniority rule exception in the particular case. And such a showing will defeat the employer's demand for summary judgment. Fed. Rule Civ. Proc. 56(e).

I

In 1990, Robert Barnett, the plaintiff and respondent here, injured his back while working in a cargo-handling position at petitioner U.S. Airways, Inc. He invoked seniority rights and transferred to a less physically demanding mailroom position. Under U.S. Airways' seniority system, that position, like others, periodically became open to seniority-based employee bidding. In 1992, Barnett learned that at least two employees senior to him intended to bid for the mailroom job. He asked U.S. Airways to accommodate his disability-imposed limitations by making an exception that would allow him to remain in the mailroom. After permitting Barnett to continue his mailroom work for five months while it considered the matter, U.S. Airways eventually decided not to make an exception. And Barnett lost his job.

Barnett then brought this ADA suit claiming, among other things, that he was an "individual with a disability" capable of performing the essential functions of the mailroom job, that the mailroom job amounted to a "reasonable accommodation" of his disability, and that U.S. Airways, in refusing to assign him the job, unlawfully discriminated against him. US Airways moved for summary judgment. It supported its motion with appropriate affidavits, Fed. Rule Civ. Proc. 56, contending that its "well-established" seniority system granted other employees the right to obtain the mailroom position.

The District Court found that the undisputed facts about seniority warranted summary judgment in U.S. Airways' favor. The Act says that an employer who fails to make "reasonable accommodations to the known physical or mental limitations of an [employee] with a disability" discriminates "*unless*" the employer "can demonstrate that the accommodation would impose an *undue hardship* on the operation of [its] business." 42 U.S.C. § 12112(b)(5)(A) (emphasis added). The court said:

> "The uncontroverted evidence shows that the US Air seniority system has been in place for 'decades' and governs over 14,000 US Air Agents. Moreover, seniority policies such as the one at issue in this case are common to the airline industry. Given this context, it seems clear that the US Air employees were justified in relying upon the policy. As such, any significant alteration of that policy would result in undue hardship to both the company and its non-disabled employees."

An en banc panel of the United States Court of Appeals for the Ninth Circuit reversed. It said that the presence of a seniority system is merely "a factor in the undue hardship analysis." 228 F.3d 1105, 1120 (CA9 2000). And it held that "case-by-case fact intensive analysis is required to determine whether any particular reassignment would constitute an undue hardship to the employer."

US Airways petitioned for certiorari, asking us to decide whether "the [ADA] requires an employer to reassign a disabled employee to a position as a 'reasonable accommodation' even though another employee is entitled to hold the position under the employer's bona fide and established seniority system." . . .

II

In answering the question presented, we must consider the following statutory provisions. First, the ADA says that an employer may not "discriminate against a qualified individual with a disability." 42 U.S.C. § 12112(a). Second, the ADA says that a "qualified" individual includes "an individual with a disability who, *with* or without *reasonable accommodation*, can perform the essential functions of" the relevant "employment position." § 12111(8) (emphasis added). Third, the ADA says that "discrimination" includes an employer's "*not making reasonable accommodations* to the known physical or mental limitations of an otherwise qualified . . . employee, *unless* [the employer] can demonstrate that the accommodation would impose an *undue hardship* on the operation of [its] business." § 12112(b)(5)(A) (emphasis added). Fourth, the ADA says that the term " 'reasonable accommodation' may include . . . reassignment to a vacant position." § 12111(9)(B).

The parties interpret this statutory language as applied to seniority systems in radically different ways. In U.S. Airways' view, the fact that an accommodation would violate the rules of a seniority system always shows that the accommodation is not a "reasonable" one. In Barnett's polar opposite view, a seniority system violation never shows that an accommodation sought is not a "reasonable" one. Barnett concedes that a violation of seniority rules might help to show that the accommodation will work "undue" employer "hardship," but that is a matter for an employer to demonstrate case by case. We shall initially consider the parties' main legal arguments in support of these conflicting positions.

A

US Airways' claim that a seniority system virtually always trumps a conflicting accommodation demand rests primarily upon its view of how the Act treats workplace "preferences." Insofar as a requested accommodation violates a disability-neutral workplace rule, such as a seniority rule, it grants the employee with a disability treatment that other workers could not receive. Yet the Act, U.S. Airways says, seeks only "equal" treatment for those with disabilities. See, e.g., 42 U.S.C. § 12101(a)(9). It does not, it contends, require an employer to grant preferential treatment. Cf. H.R. Rep. No. 101–485, pt. 2, p. 66 (1990), U.S. Code Cong. & Admin. News 1990, pp. 303, 348–349; S. Rep. No. 101–

116, pp. 26–27 (1989) (employer has no "obligation to prefer *applicants* with disabilities over other *applicants*" (emphasis added)). Hence it does not require the employer to grant a request that, in violating a disability-neutral rule, would provide a preference.

While linguistically logical, this argument fails to recognize what the Act specifies, namely, that preferences will sometimes prove necessary to achieve the Act's basic equal opportunity goal. The Act requires preferences in the form of "reasonable accommodations" that are needed for those with disabilities to obtain the same workplace opportunities that those without disabilities automatically enjoy. By definition any special "accommodation" requires the employer to treat an employee with a disability differently, i.e., preferentially. And the fact that the difference in treatment violates an employer's disability-neutral rule cannot by itself place the accommodation beyond the Act's potential reach.

Were that not so, the "reasonable accommodation" provision could not accomplish its intended objective. Neutral office assignment rules would automatically prevent the accommodation of an employee whose disability-imposed limitations require him to work on the ground floor. Neutral "break-from-work" rules would automatically prevent the accommodation of an individual who needs additional breaks from work, perhaps to permit medical visits. Neutral furniture budget rules would automatically prevent the accommodation of an individual who needs a different kind of chair or desk. Many employers will have neutral rules governing the kinds of actions most needed to reasonably accommodate a worker with a disability. See 42 U.S.C. § 12111(9)(b) (setting forth examples such as "job restructuring," "part-time or modified work schedules," "acquisition or modification of equipment or devices," "and other similar accommodations"). Yet Congress, while providing such examples, said nothing suggesting that the presence of such neutral rules would create an automatic exemption. Nor have the lower courts made any such suggestion. Cf. Garcia-Ayala v. Lederle Parenterals, Inc., 212 F.3d 638, 648 (CA1 2000) (requiring leave beyond that allowed under the company's own leave policy); Hendricks-Robinson v. Excel Corp., 154 F.3d 685, 699 (CA7 1998) (requiring exception to employer's neutral "physical fitness" job requirement).

In sum, the nature of the "reasonable accommodation" requirement, the statutory examples, and the Act's silence about the exempting effect of neutral rules together convince us that the Act does not create any such automatic exemption. The simple fact that an accommodation would provide a "preference"—in the sense that it would permit the worker with a disability to violate a rule that others must obey—cannot, in and of itself, automatically show that the accommodation is not "reasonable." As a result, we reject the position taken by U.S. Airways and Justice SCALIA to the contrary.

US Airways also points to the ADA provisions stating that a " 'reasonable accommodation' may include . . . reassignment to a *vacant* position." § 12111(9)(B) (emphasis added). And it claims that the fact that an established seniority system would assign that position to another worker automatically and always means that the position is not a "vacant" one. Nothing in the Act, however, suggests that Congress intended the word "vacant" to have a specialized meaning. And in ordinary English, a seniority system can give employees seniority rights allowing them to bid for a "vacant" position. The position in this case was held, at the time of suit, by Barnett, not by some other worker; and that position, under the U.S. Airways seniority system, became an "open" one. Moreover, U.S. Airways has said that it "reserves the right to change any and all" portions of the seniority system at will. Lodging of Respondent 2 (U.S. Air Personnel Policy Guide for Agents). Consequently, we cannot agree with U.S. Airways about the position's vacancy; nor do we agree that the Act would automatically deny Barnett's accommodation request for that reason.

B

Barnett argues that the statutory words "reasonable accommodation" mean only "effective accommodation," authorizing a court to consider the requested accommodation's ability to meet an individual's disability-related needs, and nothing more. On this view, a seniority rule violation, having nothing to do with the accommodation's effectiveness, has nothing to do with its "reasonableness." It might, at most, help to prove an "undue hardship on the operation of the business." But, he adds, that is a matter that the statute requires the employer to demonstrate, case by case.

In support of this interpretation Barnett points to Equal Employment Opportunity Commission (EEOC) regulations stating that "reasonable accommodation means . . . codifications or adjustments . . . that *enable* a qualified individual with a disability to perform the essential functions of [a] position." 29 C.F.R. § 1630(*o*)(ii) (2001) (emphasis added). See also H.R. Rep. No. 101–485, pt. 2, at 66, U.S. Code Cong. & Admin. News 1990, pp. 303, 348–349; S. Rep. No. 101–116, at 35 (discussing reasonable accommodations in terms of "effectiveness," while discussing costs in terms of "undue hardship"). Barnett adds that any other view would make the words "reasonable accommodation" and "undue hardship" virtual mirror images—creating redundancy in the statute. And he says that any such other view would create a practical burden of proof dilemma.

The practical burden of proof dilemma arises, Barnett argues, because the statute imposes the burden of demonstrating an "undue hardship" upon the employer, while the burden of proving "reasonable accommodation" remains with the plaintiff, here the employee. This allocation seems sensible in that an employer can more frequently and easily prove the presence of business hardship than an employee can prove its absence. But suppose that an employee must counter a claim of "seniority rule violation" in order to prove that an "accommodation" request is "reasonable." Would that not force the employee to prove what is in effect an absence, i.e., an absence of hardship, despite the statute's insistence that the employer "demonstrate" hardship's presence?

These arguments do not persuade us that Barnett's legal interpretation of "reasonable" is correct. For one thing, in ordinary English the word "reasonable" does not mean "effective." It is the word "accommodation," not the word "reasonable," that conveys the need for effectiveness. An ineffective "modification" or "adjustment" will not accommodate a disabled individual's limitations. Nor does an ordinary English meaning of the term "reasonable accommodation" make of it a simple, redundant mirror image of the term "undue hardship." The statute refers to an "undue hardship on the operation of the business." 42 U.S.C. § 12112(b)(5)(A). Yet a demand for an effective accommodation could prove unreasonable because of its impact, not on business operations, but on fellow employees—say because it will lead to dismissals, relocations, or modification of employee benefits to which an employer, looking at the matter from the perspective of the business itself, may be relatively indifferent.

Neither does the statute's primary purpose require Barnett's special reading. The statute seeks to diminish or to eliminate the stereotypical thought processes, the thoughtless actions, and the hostile reactions that far too often bar those with disabilities from participating fully in the Nation's life, including the workplace. See generally §§ 12101(a) and (b). These objectives demand unprejudiced thought and reasonable responsive reaction on the part of employers and fellow workers alike. They will sometimes require affirmative conduct to promote entry of disabled people into the workforce. They do not, however, demand action beyond the realm of the reasonable.

Neither has Congress indicated in the statute, or elsewhere, that the word "reasonable" means no more than "effective." The EEOC regulations do say that reasonable accommodations "enable" a person with a disability to perform the essential functions of a task. But that phrasing simply emphasizes the statutory provision's basic objective. The regulations do not say that "enable" and "reasonable" mean the same thing. And as discussed below, no circuit court has so read them. But see 228 F.3d, at 1122–1123 (Gould, J., concurring).

Finally, an ordinary language interpretation of the word "reasonable" does not create the "burden of proof" dilemma to which Barnett points. Many of the lower courts, while rejecting both U.S. Airways' and Barnett's more absolute views, have reconciled the phrases "reasonable accommodation" and "undue hardship" in a practical way.

They have held that a plaintiff/employee (to defeat a defendant/employer's motion for summary judgment) need only show that an "accommodation" seems reasonable on its face, i.e., ordinarily or in the run of cases. See, e.g., Reed v. LePage Bakeries, Inc., 244 F.3d 254, 259 (CA1 2001) (plaintiff meets burden on reasonableness by showing that, "at least on the face of things," the accommodation will be feasible for the employer); Borkowski v. Valley Central School Dist., 63 F.3d 131, 138 (CA2 1995) (plaintiff satisfies "burden of production" by showing "plausible accommodation"); Barth v. Gelb, 2 F.3d 1180, 1187 (CAD.C. 1993) (interpreting parallel language in Rehabilitation Act, stating that plaintiff need only show he seeks a "*method of accommodation* that is reasonable in the run of cases" (emphasis in original)).

Once the plaintiff has made this showing, the defendant/employer then must show special (typically case-specific) circumstances that demonstrate undue hardship in the particular circumstances. See *Reed*, supra, at 258–259 ("undue hardship inquiry focuses on the hardships imposed . . . in the context of the particular [employer's] operations' ") (quoting *Barth*, supra, at 1187); *Borkowski*, supra, at 138 (after plaintiff makes initial showing, burden falls on employer to show that particular accommodation "would cause it to suffer an undue hardship"); *Barth*, supra, at 1187 ("undue hardship inquiry focuses on the hardships imposed . . . in the context of the particular agency's operations").

Not every court has used the same language, but their results are functionally similar. In our opinion, that practical view of the statute, applied consistently with ordinary summary judgment principles, see Fed. Rule Civ. Proc. 56, avoids Barnett's burden of proof dilemma, while reconciling the two statutory phrases ("reasonable accommodation" and "undue hardship").

III

The question in the present case focuses on the relationship between seniority systems and the plaintiff's need to show that an "accommodation" seems reasonable on its face, i.e., ordinarily or in the run of cases. We must assume that the plaintiff, an employee, is an "individual with a disability." He has requested assignment to a mailroom position as a "reasonable accommodation." We also assume that normally such a request would be reasonable within the meaning of the statute, were it not for one circumstance, namely, that the assignment would violate the rules of a seniority system. See § 12111(9) ("reasonable accommodation" may include "reassignment to a vacant position"). Does that circumstance mean that the proposed accommodation is not a "reasonable" one?

In our view, the answer to this question ordinarily is "yes." The statute does not require proof on a case-by-case basis that a seniority system should prevail. That is because it would not be reasonable in the run of cases that the assignment in question trump the rules of a seniority system. To the contrary, it will ordinarily be unreasonable for the assignment to prevail.

A

Several factors support our conclusion that a proposed accommodation will not be reasonable in the run of cases. Analogous case law supports this conclusion, for it has recognized the importance of seniority to employee-management relations. This Court has held that, in the context of a Title VII religious discrimination case, an employer need not adapt to an employee's special worship schedule as a "reasonable accommodation" where doing so would conflict with the seniority rights of other employees. Trans World Airlines, Inc. v. Hardison, 432 U.S. 63, 79–80 (1977). The lower courts have unanimously found that collectively bargained seniority trumps the need for reasonable accommodation in the context of the linguistically similar Rehabilitation Act. See Eckles v. Consolidated Rail Corp., 94 F.3d 1041, 1047–1048 (CA7 1996) (collecting cases); Shea v. Tisch, 870 F.2d 786, 790 (CA1 1989); Carter v. Tisch, 822 F.2d 465, 469 (CA4 1987); Jasany v. United States Postal Service, 755 F.2d 1244, 1251–1252 (CA6 1985). And several Circuits, though differing in their reasoning, have reached a similar conclusion in the context of seniority and the ADA. See Smith v. Midland Brake, Inc., 180 F.3d 1154, 1175 (CA10 1999); Feliciano v. Rhode Island, 160 F.3d 780, 787 (CA1 1998); *Eckles*, supra, at 1047–1048. All these cases discuss collectively bargained seniority systems, not systems (like the present system) which are unilaterally imposed by management. But the relevant seniority system advantages, and related difficulties that result from violations of seniority rules, are not limited to collectively bargained systems.

For one thing, the typical seniority system provides important employee benefits by creating, and fulfilling, employee expectations of fair, uniform treatment. These benefits include "job security and an opportunity for steady and predictable advancement based on objective standards." Brief for Petitioner 32 (citing Fallon & Weiler, *Firefighters v. Stotts*: Conflicting Models of Racial Justice, 1984 S. Ct. Rev. 1, 57–58). See also 1 B. Lindemann & P. Grossman, Employment Discrimination Law 72 (3d ed. 1996) ("One of the most important aspects of competitive seniority is its use in determining who will be laid off during a reduction in force"). They include "an element of due process," limiting "unfairness in personnel decisions." Gersuny, Origins of Seniority Provisions in Collective Bargaining, 33 Lab. L.J. 518, 519 (1982). And they consequently encourage employees to invest in the employing company, accepting "less than their value to the firm early in their careers" in return for greater benefits in later years. J. Baron & D. Kreps, Strategic Human Resources: Frameworks for General Managers 288 (1999).

Most important for present purposes, to require the typical employer to show more than the existence of a seniority system might well undermine the employees' expectations of consistent, uniform treatment—expectations upon which the seniority system's benefits depend. That is because such a rule would substitute a complex case-specific "accommodation" decision made by management for the more uniform, impersonal operation of seniority rules. Such management decisionmaking, with its inevitable discretionary elements, would involve a matter of the greatest importance to employees, namely, layoffs; it would take place outside, as well as inside, the confines of a court case; and it might well take place fairly often. Cf. ADA, 42 U.S.C. § 12101(a)(1), (estimating that some 43 million Americans suffer from physical or mental disabilities). We can find nothing in the statute that suggests Congress intended to undermine seniority systems in this way. And we consequently conclude that the employer's showing of violation of the rules of a seniority system is by itself ordinarily sufficient.

B

The plaintiff (here the employee) nonetheless remains free to show that special circumstances warrant a finding that, despite the presence of a seniority system (which the ADA may not trump in the run of cases), the requested "accommodation" is "reasonable" on the particular facts. That is because special circumstances might alter the important expectations described above. Cf. *Borkowski*, 63 F.3d, at 137 ("an accommodation that imposed burdens that would be unreasonable for most members of an industry might nevertheless be required of an individual defendant in light of that employer's particular circumstances"). See also Woodman v. Runyon, 132 F.3d 1330, 1343–1344 (CA10 1997). The plaintiff might show, for example, that the employer, having retained the right to change the seniority system unilaterally, exercises that right fairly frequently, reducing employee expectations that the system will be followed—to the point where one more departure, needed to accommodate an individual with a disability, will not likely make a difference. The plaintiff might show that the system already contains exceptions such that, in the circumstances, one further exception is unlikely to matter. We do not mean these examples to exhaust the kinds of showings that a plaintiff might make. But we do mean to say that the plaintiff must bear the burden of showing special circumstances that make an exception from the seniority system reasonable in the particular case. And to do so, the plaintiff must explain why, in the particular case, an exception to the employer's seniority policy can constitute a "reasonable accommodation" even though in the ordinary case it cannot.

IV

In its question presented, U.S. Airways asked us whether the ADA requires an employer to assign a disabled employee to a particular position even though another employee is entitled to that position under the employer's "established seniority system." We answer that ordinarily the ADA does not require that assignment. Hence, a showing that the assignment would violate the rules of a seniority system warrants summary judgment for the employer—unless there is more. The plaintiff must present evidence of that "more," namely, special circumstances surrounding the particular case that demonstrate the assignment is nonetheless reasonable.

Because the lower courts took a different view of the matter, and because neither party has had an opportunity to seek summary judgment in accordance with the principles we set forth here, we vacate the Court of Appeals' judgment and remand the case for further proceedings consistent with this opinion.

It is so ordered.

[The concurring opinion of Justice Stevens is omitted.]

■ JUSTICE O'CONNOR, concurring.

I agree with portions of the opinion of the Court, but I find problematic the Court's test for determining whether the fact that a job reassignment violates a seniority system makes the reassignment an unreasonable accommodation under the Americans with Disabilities Act of 1990 (ADA or Act), 42 U.S.C. § 12101 et seq. Although a seniority system plays an important role in the workplace, for the reasons I explain below, I would prefer to say that the effect of a seniority system on the reasonableness of a reassignment as an accommodation for purposes of the ADA depends on whether the seniority system is legally enforceable. "Were it possible for me to adhere to [this belief] in my vote, and for the Court at the same time to [adopt a majority rule]," I would do so. Screws v. United States, 325 U.S. 91, 134 (1945) (Rutledge, J., concurring in result). "The Court, however, is divided in opinion," ibid., and if each member voted consistently with his or her beliefs, we would not agree on a resolution of the question presented in this case. Yet "stalemate should not prevail," ibid., particularly in a case in which we are merely interpreting a statute. Accordingly, in order that the Court may adopt a rule, and because I believe the Court's rule will often lead to the same outcome as the one I would have adopted, I join the Court's opinion despite my concerns. Cf. Bragdon v. Abbott, 524 U.S. 624, 655–656 (1998) (STEVENS, J., joined by BREYER, J., concurring); Olmstead v. L. C., 527 U.S. 581, 607–608 (1999) (STEVENS, J., concurring in part and concurring in judgment).

The ADA specifically lists "reassignment to a vacant position" as one example of a "reasonable accommodation." 42 U.S.C. § 12111(9)(B). In deciding whether an otherwise reasonable accommodation involving a reassignment is unreasonable because it would require an exception to a seniority system, I think the relevant issue is whether the seniority system prevents the position in question from being vacant. The word "vacant" means "not filled or occupied by an incumbent possessor." Webster's Third New International Dictionary 2527 (1976). In the context of a workplace, a vacant position is a position in which no employee currently works and to which no individual has a legal entitlement. For example, in a workplace without a seniority system, when an employee ceases working for the employer, the employee's former position is vacant until a replacement is hired. Even if the replacement does not start work immediately, once the replacement enters into a contractual agreement with the employer, the position is no longer vacant because it has a "possessor." In contrast, when an employee ceases working in a workplace with a legally enforceable seniority system, the employee's former position does not become vacant if the seniority system entitles another employee to it. Instead, the employee entitled to the position under the seniority system immediately becomes the new "possessor" of that position. In a workplace with an unenforceable seniority policy, however, an employee expecting assignment to a position under the seniority policy would not have any type of contractual right to the position and so could not be said to be its "possessor." The position therefore would become vacant.

Given this understanding of when a position can properly be considered vacant, if a seniority system, in the absence of the ADA, would give someone other than the individual seeking the accommodation a legal entitlement or contractual right to the position to which reassignment is sought, the seniority system prevents the position from being vacant. If a position is not vacant, then reassignment to it is not a reasonable accommodation. The Act specifically says that "reassignment to a *vacant* position" is a type of "reasonable accommodation." § 12111(9)(B) (emphasis added). Indeed, the legislative history of the Act confirms that Congress did not intend reasonable accommodation to require bumping other employees. H.R. Rep. No. 101–485, pt. 2, p. 63 (1990), U.S. Code Cong. & Admin. News 1990, pp. 303, 345 ("The Committee also wishes to make clear that reassignment need only be to a vacant position—'bumping' another employee out of a position to create a vacancy is not required"); S. Rep. No. 101–116, p. 32 (1989) (same). . . .

Although I am troubled by the Court's reasoning, I believe the Court's approach for evaluating seniority systems will often lead to the same outcome as the test I would have adopted. Unenforceable seniority systems are likely to involve policies in which employers "retain the right to change the system," and will often "permit exceptions." They will also often contain disclaimers that "reduce employee expectations that the system will be followed." Thus, under the Court's test, disabled employees seeking accommodations that would require exceptions to unenforceable seniority systems may be able to show circumstances that make the accommodation "reasonable in the particular case." Because I think the Court's test will often lead to the correct outcome, and because I think it important that a majority of the Court agree on a rule when interpreting statutes, I join the Court's opinion.

■ JUSTICE SCALIA, with whom JUSTICE THOMAS joins, dissenting.

The question presented asks whether the "reasonable accommodation" mandate of the Americans with Disabilities Act of 1990 (ADA or Act) requires reassignment of a disabled employee to a position that "another employee is entitled to hold . . . under the employer's bona fide and established seniority system." Indulging its penchant for eschewing clear rules that might avoid litigation, see, e.g., Kansas v. Crane, 534 U.S. 407, 423 (2002) (SCALIA, J., dissenting); TRW Inc. v. Andrews, 534 U.S. 19, 35–36 (2001) (SCALIA, J., concurring in judgment), the Court answers "maybe." It creates a presumption that an exception to a seniority rule is an "unreasonable" accommodation, but allows that presumption to be rebutted by showing that the exception "will not likely make a difference."

The principal defect of today's opinion, however, goes well beyond the uncertainty it produces regarding the relationship between the ADA and the infinite variety of seniority systems. The conclusion that any seniority system can ever be overridden is merely one consequence of a mistaken interpretation of the ADA that makes all employment rules and practices—even those which (like a seniority system) pose no distinctive obstacle to the disabled—subject to suspension when that is (in a court's view) a "reasonable" means of enabling a disabled employee to keep his job. That is a far cry from what I believe the accommodation provision of the ADA requires: the suspension (within reason) of those employment rules and practices that the employee's disability prevents him from observing.

■ JUSTICE SOUTER, with whom JUSTICE GINSBURG joins, dissenting.

"Reassignment to a vacant position," 42 U.S.C. § 12111(9), is one way an employer may "reasonably accommodate" disabled employees under the Americans with Disabilities Act of 1990, 42 U.S.C. § 12101 et seq. The Court today holds that a request for reassignment will nonetheless most likely be unreasonable when it would violate the terms of a seniority system imposed by an employer. Although I concur in the Court's appreciation of the value and importance of seniority systems, I do not believe my hand is free to accept the majority's result and therefore respectfully dissent.

Nothing in the ADA insulates seniority rules from the "reasonable accommodation" requirement, in marked contrast to Title VII of the Civil Rights Act of 1964 and the Age Discrimination in Employment Act of 1967, each of which has an explicit protection for seniority. See 42 U.S.C. § 2000e–2(h) ("Notwithstanding any other provision of this subchapter, it shall not be an unlawful employment practice for an employer to [provide different benefits to employees] pursuant to a bona fide seniority . . . system. . . ."); 29 U.S.C. § 623(f) ("It shall not be unlawful for an employer . . . to take any action otherwise prohibited [under previous sections] . . . to observe the terms of a bona fide seniority system [except for involuntary retirement] . . ."). Because Congress modeled several of the ADA's provisions on Title VII, its failure to replicate Title VII's exemption for seniority systems leaves the statute ambiguous, albeit with more than a hint that seniority rules do not inevitably carry the day.

With U.S. Airways itself insisting that its seniority system was noncontractual and modifiable at will, there is no reason to think that

Barnett's accommodation would have resulted in anything more than minimal disruption to U.S. Airways's operations, if that. Barnett has shown his requested accommodation to be "reasonable," and the burden ought to shift to U.S. Airways if it wishes to claim that, in spite of surface appearances, violation of the seniority scheme would have worked an undue hardship. I would therefore affirm the Ninth Circuit.

NOTES ON *U.S. AIRWAYS, INC. V. BARNETT*

1. **Burdens of Proof.** The immediate question presented in *U.S. Airways* concerned the burden of proof: whether the plaintiff had to prove that the proposed accommodation of granting him a transfer in violation of the seniority system was reasonable or whether the defendant had to prove that it involved an undue hardship. The literal terms of the ADA created this problem by requiring the plaintiff to prove that an accommodation is reasonable and requiring the defendant to prove that it causes an undue hardship. The statute, however, did not clearly distinguish between these issues, leaving for the courts the question when a reasonable accommodation could nevertheless cause an undue hardship. The statutory definitions of both "reasonable accommodation" and "undue hardship" depend upon lists of examples and factors to be taken into account, without precisely identifying what makes an accommodation "reasonable" or what makes a hardship "undue." § 101(8), (9), 42 U.S.C. § 12111(9), (10). None of these provisions were affected by the ADA Amendments Act, although the Act did restrict the duty of reasonable accommodation to individuals with actual disabilities (or a record of one) and denied the duty to individuals only "regarded as" having a disability. § 501(h), 42 U.S.C. § 12201(h).

The statutory allocation of the burden of proof corresponds to the parties' access to evidence. The plaintiff has better knowledge of what steps could be taken to compensate for his disability, and the defendant has better knowledge of what steps would be too costly for it to undertake. These generalizations need not be invariably true to be useful. They also reflect the "interactive process" that typically occurs when an employee requests an accommodation. The employee suggests a proposed accommodation, and the employer responds, accepting or rejecting it or offering its own modifications to its facilities or procedures. The statute encourages employers to engage in this process by relieving them of liability for damages if they do so. 42 U.S.C. § 1981a(a)(3). Expanding upon this provision, the lower courts have imposed on employers a kind of duty to confer, by taking their defense to claims of reasonable accommodation more seriously if they have conferred with the plaintiff about proposed accommodations. E.g., Guice-Mills v. Derwinski, 967 F.2d 794, 798 (2d Cir. 1992).

In *U.S. Airways*, the Supreme Court takes the same practical approach to allocating the burden of proof, requiring the plaintiff to prove that an accommodation is reasonable "ordinarily or in the run of cases," both in terms of effectiveness and the burdens that it places on the employer and other employees. The defendant then has the burden of proving undue hardship "in the particular circumstances" of each case. With respect to the particular accommodation at issue in this case, involving an exception to a seniority system, the defendant satisfies this burden by showing simply that it violates the seniority system. The plaintiff then has the further burden of showing exceptional circumstances that justify departing from the strict requirements of the seniority system. The Court's allocation of general and specific showings between the parties is not quite consistent because the Court requires the defendant to make a specific showing in most cases, but in this case, the plaintiff ends up making the more specific showing. Does this lack of formal consistency undermine the Court's analysis? Does it make the Court's allocation of the burden of proof unworkable?

2. **Conflicts Among the Circuits.** Before *U.S. Airways*, the federal circuits had taken varying approaches to the allocation of the burden of proof. Most of these variations involved slight differences in formulating what each party had to prove. Some, however, were more consequential. Two leading cases, one cited favorably by the Court, and the other passed over without citation, exemplify the different approaches.

a. ***Borkowski v. Valley Central School District.*** This case concerned a public school teacher who suffered from neurological disorders resulting from an automobile accident. These disorders made it difficult for her to control her class of elementary school students and she was eventually denied tenure for this reason. She resigned from her position and then filed an action under § 504 of the Rehabilitation Act, claiming that she was "otherwise qualified" if she received an accommodation in the form of a teacher's aide during class. The district court granted the defendant's motion for summary judgment, but the Second Circuit vacated this decision and remanded for reconsideration. Borkowski v. Valley Central School District, 63 F.3d 131 (2d Cir. 1995). In an opinion by Judge Calabresi, the court formulated the following standards for claims of reasonable accommodation:

> Whether a proposed accommodation is reasonable, however, is another question. "Reasonable" is a relational term: it evaluates the desirability of a particular accommodation according to the consequences that the accommodation will produce. This requires an inquiry not only into the benefits of the accommodation but into its costs as well. See Vande Zande v. Wisconsin Dep't of Admin., 44 F.3d 538, 542 (7th Cir. 1995). We would not, for example, require an employer to make a multi-million dollar modification for the benefit of a single individual with a disability, even if the proposed modification would allow that individual to perform the essential functions of a job that she sought. In spite of its effectiveness, the proposed modification would be unreasonable because of its excessive costs. In short, an accommodation is reasonable only if its costs are not clearly disproportionate to the benefits that it will produce. Id., at 542–43; cf. Barth v. Gelb, 2 F.3d 1180, 1187 (D.C. Cir. 1993), cert. denied 511 U.S. 1030 (1994) (an accommodation may be unreasonable if its costs are excessive).
>
> As to the requirement that an accommodation be reasonable, we have held that the plaintiff bears only a burden of production. Gilbert v. Frank, 949 F.2d 637, 642 (2d Cir. 1991). This burden, we have said, is not a heavy one. It is enough for the plaintiff to suggest

the existence of a plausible accommodation, the costs of which, facially, do not clearly exceed its benefits. Once the plaintiff has done this, she has made out a prima facie showing that a reasonable accommodation is available, and the risk of nonpersuasion falls on the defendant.

At this point the defendant's burden of persuading the factfinder that the plaintiff's proposed accommodation is unreasonable merges, in effect, with its burden of showing, as an affirmative defense, that the proposed accommodation would cause it to suffer an undue hardship. For in practice meeting the burden of nonpersuasion on the reasonableness of the accommodation and demonstrating that the accommodation imposes an undue hardship amount to the same thing. See, e.g., School Bd. v. Arline, 480 U.S. 273, 287 n.17 (1987) ("Accommodation is not reasonable if it either imposes 'undue financial and administrative burdens' on a grantee, or requires 'a fundamental alteration in the nature of [the] program.'" (citations omitted)); Gilbert, 949 F.2d at 642 (equating, through citation to the regulations, the employer's burden of showing that an accommodation is not reasonable with the employer's burden on undue hardship); Hall v. United States Postal Serv., 857 F.2d 1073, 1080 (6th Cir.1988) (stating that an accommodation is not reasonable if it imposes an undue hardship on the employer).

Undue hardship is not a self-explanatory concept, however. As we have already noted, the regulations implementing Section 504 go some distance in giving substance to the bare phrase. They require consideration of:

> "(1) The overall size of the recipient's program with respect to number of employees, number and type of facilities, and size of budget;
>
> "(2) The type of the recipient's operation, including the composition and structure of the recipient's workforce; and
>
> "(3) The nature and cost of the accommodation needed." 34 C.F.R. § 104.12(b); 45 C.F.R. § 84.12(b); cf. 42 U.S.C. § 12111(10) (defining undue hardship under the Americans With Disabilities Act).

But even this list of factors says little about how great a hardship an employer must bear before the hardship becomes undue. Does Section 504 require, for example, that employers be driven to the brink of insolvency before a hardship becomes too great? We think not. Cf. Jeffrey O. Cooper, Comment, Overcoming Barriers to Employment: The Meaning of Reasonable Accommodation and Undue Hardship in the Americans with Disabilities Act, 139 U. Pa. L. Rev. 1423, 1448 (1991) (noting that, during the debate over the Americans with Disabilities Act, Congress considered and rejected a provision that would have defined an undue hardship as one that threatened the continued existence of the employer). Similarly, where the employer is a government entity, Congress could not have intended the only limit on the employer's duty to make reasonable accommodation to be the full extent of the tax base on which the government entity could draw. See Vande Zande, 44 F.3d at 542–43.

What, then, does undue hardship mean? We note that "undue" hardship, like "reasonable" accommodation, is a relational term; as such, it looks not merely to the costs that the employer is asked to assume, but also to the benefits to others that will result. The burden on the employer, then, is to perform a cost/benefit analysis. In a sense, of course, that is what the plaintiff also had to do to meet her burden of making out a prima facie case that a reasonable accommodation existed. But while the plaintiff could meet her burden of production by identifying an accommodation that facially achieves a rough proportionality between costs and benefits, an employer seeking to meet its burden of persuasion on reasonable accommodation and undue hardship must undertake a more refined analysis. And it must analyze the hardship sought to be imposed through the lens of the factors listed in the regulations, which include consideration of the industry to which the employer belongs as well as the individual characteristics of the particular defendant-employer. If the employer can carry this burden, it will have shown both that the hardship caused by the proposed accommodation would be undue in light of the enumerated factors, and that the proposed accommodation is unreasonable and need not be made.

Despite the ambiguities of the statutory and regulatory language, we believe that the resulting standards should not prove difficult to apply. First, the plaintiff bears the burden of proving that she is otherwise qualified; if an accommodation is needed, the plaintiff must show, as part of her burden of persuasion, that an effective accommodation exists that would render her otherwise qualified. On the issue of reasonable accommodation, the plaintiff bears only the burden of identifying an accommodation, the costs of which, facially, do not clearly exceed its benefits. These two requirements placed on the plaintiff will permit district courts to grant summary judgments for defendants in cases in which the plaintiff's proposal is either clearly ineffective or outlandishly costly. Second, we do not at all intend to suggest that employers, in attempting to meet their burden of persuasion on the reasonableness of the proposed accommodation and in making out an affirmative defense of undue hardship, must analyze the costs and benefits of proposed accommodations with mathematical precision. District courts will not be required to instruct juries on how to apply complex economic formulae; a common-sense balancing of the costs and benefits in light of the factors listed in the regulations is all that is expected.

The plaintiff's claim in this case was under the Rehabilitation Act, but the Second Circuit analyzed the duty of reasonable accommodation in terms that apply equally to the ADA. The court cited decisions under the ADA, like the opinion of the Seventh Circuit in the following case, and the court's own decision was cited in *U.S. Airways*, which was decided under the ADA.

b. *Vande Zande v. Wisconsin Department of Administration.* In this case, a paraplegic state employee sought various accommodations, the most significant of which was working at home when complications from her disability prevented her from going to work. Her employer had granted a range of other accommodations, from modifying the bathrooms in her office to adjusting her schedule for her medical appointments. When she sued under the ADA to obtain additional accommodations, her claim was dismissed on summary judgment. The Seventh Circuit, in an opinion by Judge Posner, affirmed. Vande Zande v. Wisconsin Department of Administration, 44 F.3d 538 (7th Cir. 1995).

> The concept of reasonable accommodation is at the heart of this case. The plaintiff sought a number of accommodations to her paraplegia that were turned down. The principal defendant as we have said is a state, which does not argue that the plaintiff's proposals were rejected because accepting them would have imposed undue hardship on the state or because they would not have done her any good. The district judge nevertheless granted summary judgment for the defendants on the ground that the evidence obtained in discovery, construed as favorably to the plaintiff as the record permitted, showed that they had gone as far to accommodate the plaintiff's demands as reasonableness, in a sense distinct from either aptness or hardship—a sense based, rather, on considerations of cost and proportionality—required. On this analysis, the function of the "undue hardship" safe harbor, like the "failing company" defense to antitrust liability (on which see International Shoe Co. v. FTC, 280 U.S. 291, 302 (1930); United States v. Greater Buffalo Press, Inc., 402 U.S. 549, 555 (1971); 4 Phillip Areeda & Donald F. Turner, Antitrust Law & & 924–31 (1980)), is to excuse compliance by a firm that is financially distressed, even though the cost of the accommodation to the firm might be less than the benefit to disabled employees.
>
> This interpretation of "undue hardship" is not inevitable—in fact probably is incorrect. It is a defined term in the Americans with Disabilities Act, and the definition is "an action requiring significant difficulty or expense." 42 U.S.C. § 12111(10)(A). The financial condition of the employer is only one consideration in determining whether an accommodation otherwise reasonable would impose an undue hardship. See 42 U.S.C. §§ 12111(10)(B)(ii), (iii). The legislative history equates "undue hardship" to "unduly costly." S. Rep. No. 116, supra, at 35. These are terms of relation. We must ask, "undue" in relation to what? Presumably (given the statutory definition and the legislative history) in relation to the

> benefits of the accommodation to the disabled worker as well as to the employer's resources.
>
> So it seems that costs enter at two points in the analysis of claims to an accommodation to a disability. The employee must show that the accommodation is reasonable in the sense both of efficacious and of proportional to costs. Even if this prima facie showing is made, the employer has an opportunity to prove that upon more careful consideration the costs are excessive in relation either to the benefits of the accommodation or to the employer's financial survival or health. In a classic negligence case, the idiosyncrasies of the particular employer are irrelevant. Having above-average costs, or being in a precarious financial situation, is not a defense to negligence. Vaughan v. Menlove, 3 Bing. (N.C.) 468, 132 Eng. Rep. 490 (Comm. Pl.1837). One interpretation of "undue hardship" is that it permits an employer to escape liability if he can carry the burden of proving that a disability accommodation reasonable for a normal employer would break him. Barth v. Gelb, 2 F.3d 1180, 1187 (D.C. Cir. 1993).

This opinion imposes a heavier burden of proof on the plaintiff than does *Borkowski*. According to the Seventh Circuit, the plaintiff must show that a proposed accommodation is "reasonable in the sense both of efficacious and of proportional to costs." On the record presented in *Vande Zande*, the plaintiff had not made this showing and summary judgment was therefore properly entered against her. The accommodations that she proposed were too costly in comparison to the benefits that they conferred on both her and her employer. Does the heavier burden imposed on the plaintiff, and the fact that the plaintiff lost on summary judgment, explain why *Vande Zande* was not cited by the Supreme Court, while *Borkowski* was?

3. **The Role of Efficiency.** These decisions differ in more fundamental ways as well. *Vande Zande* gives greater prominence to efficiency in analyzing what constitutes both reasonable accommodation and undue hardship. As Judge Posner says, efficiency enters into the analysis in somewhat the same fashion as it does in tort law. Although he does not press the analogy, he would require an analysis of accommodations in the same terms as precautions against accidents: determining whether the defendant is in a good position to minimize the overall cost of the plaintiff's disability, counting the burdens on both parties and the potential accommodations that each could make. Judge Posner stops short of a full-fledged cost-benefit analysis because the ADA, unlike tort law on his view, does not aim to achieve overall efficiency. It has redistributional goals that impose costs on employers that detract from the efficiency of their operations.

In *Borkowski*, Judge Calabresi gives greater prominence to these goals, even if he uses the same terms as Judge Posner and, at some points, relies explicitly on the decision in *Vande Zande*. As Judge Calabresi elaborates in a footnote in his opinion:

> In evaluating the costs and benefits of a proposed accommodation, it must be noted that Section 504 does not require

> that the employer receive a benefit commensurate with the cost of the accommodation. The concept of reasonable accommodation, developed by regulation under Section 504, received the imprimatur of congressional approval with the passage of the Americans With Disabilities Act, 42 U.S.C. §§ 12101 et seq.; see also 29 U.S.C. § 794(d) (stating, in a 1992 amendment, that Section 504 is to be interpreted consistently with the employment-related provisions of the Americans With Disabilities Act). As set forth by statute and regulation, the concept of reasonable accommodation permits the employer to expect the same level of performance from individuals with disabilities as it expects from the rest of its workforce. See H.R. Rep. No. 485, 101st Cong., 2d Sess., pt. 2, at 55–56, reprinted in 1990 U.S.C.CAN. at 337–38. But the requirement of reasonable accommodation anticipates that it may cost more to obtain that level of performance from an employee with a disability than it would to obtain the same level of performance from a non-disabled employee. See id. And Congress fully expected that the duty of reasonable accommodation would require employers to assume more than a de minimis cost. See id., pt. 2, at 68, reprinted in 1990 U.S.C.CAN. at 350; id., pt. 3, at 40, reprinted in 1990 U.S.C.CAN. at 463. It follows that an accommodation is not unreasonable simply because it would be more efficient, in the narrow sense of less costly for a given level of performance, to hire a non-disabled employee than a disabled one.

Does it make sense to follow his position and consider efficiency only to some extent? If so, how is reliance on this concept, which usually requires all costs and benefits to be compared to reach a net result, to be limited?

For a discussion of the role of efficiency in interpreting the ADA, see Peter D. Blanck, The Economics of the Employment Provisions of the Americans with Disabilities Act: Part I—Workplace Accommodation, 46 DePaul L. Rev. 877 (1997); Heidi M. Berven & Peter D. Blanck, The Economics of the Americans with Disabilities Act: Part II–Patents and Innovations in Assistive Technology, 12 Notre Dame J.L. Ethics & Pub. Pol'y 9–120 (1998); Susan Schwochau & Peter David Blanck, The Economics of the Americans with Disabilities Act, Part III: Does the ADA Disable the Disabled?, 21 Berkeley J. Emp. & Lab. L. 271 (2000); Douglas L. Leslie, Accommodating the Employment Disabled, 17 Lab. Law. 143 (2001); Michael A. Stein, Disability, Employment Policy, and the Supreme Court, 55 Stan. L. Rev. 607 (2002); Michael A. Stein, Labor Markets, Rationality, and Workers with Disabilities, 21 Berkeley J. Emp. & Lab. L. 314 (2000); J.H. Verkerke, Is the ADA Efficient?, 50 UCLA L. Rev. 903 (2003).

4. The Social Model of Disability. The duty of reasonable accommodation can be justified on grounds independent of efficiency. The most ambitious of these invokes the "social model" of disability: that disabilities have adverse consequences only because of the socially constructed context in which individuals with disabilities must live. Their physical or mental condition alone does not make them disabled, but the social consequences attached to their condition do. The standard example concerns individuals in wheelchairs, whose mobility is impaired by man-made structures and means of transportation. On the social model of disability, their inability to get around cannot be attributed solely to their inability to walk. It also results from the failure to accommodate their condition, which is no different from putting obstacles in their way. Their disability, for all intents and purposes, results from the social response to their condition. Buildings designed for people who walk could also be designed for people in wheelchairs.

At one level, the social model is undeniable. For all but the most severe disabilities, the resulting adverse effects could be neutralized or diminished by social arrangements and technological innovations. At another level, however, the implications of the model are quite controversial. It essentially disputes whether the condition of nondisabled individuals should be taken as the baseline for determining the response to individuals with disabilities. The costs of an accommodation, on this view, are no different from the costs of standard social arrangements. Both kinds of costs should be assessed and distributed in the same manner. There is no reason to single out individuals with a disability for special treatment. It is necessary, instead, to recognize that everyone receives special treatment: the nondisabled by standard social arrangements, and individuals with a disability by the accommodations required by the law. Consequently, no special showing should be necessary to support a duty of reasonable accommodation. It does not result in special treatment of individuals with a disability, only in equal treatment.

Stated in such a stark form, the implications of the social model may not be persuasive. The model fails to take account of the cost of different social arrangements and, in particular, the economies of scale resulting from standardization around the range of abilities that most people possess. Nevertheless, it opens up the debate over the range of possible accommodations. Impairments that have been socially constructed can also be socially accommodated. The only questions are at what cost and at whose expense. These questions require a range of normative judgments that are difficult to extract from a purely causal account of the disadvantages resulting from conditions conventionally regarded as disabilities. After a thorough analysis of such accounts, Adam M. Samaha reached the following conclusion:

> The question is whether the social model can underwrite any policy, in any direction. The answer is no: the model suggests cause of disadvantage, but what we do about it is a matter of contested norms.

Adam M. Samaha, What Good Is the Social Model of Disability?, 74 U. Chi. L. Rev. 1251 (2007). Does the ADA provide such norms in the duty of reasonable accommodation? Or is this duty framed in such open-ended terms that it, too, requires further such norms?

5. **Special Protection for Seniority.** The accommodation sought in *U.S. Airways* did not compromise efficiency directly. The plaintiff sought an exception to the defendant's seniority system, which was not established through collective bargaining with a union or contained in any kind of formal

contract at all. Instead, it was unilaterally established and administered by the defendant, with a number of exceptions alleged by the plaintiff to be comparable to the one that he sought. The defendant might have established this system for reasons of efficiency, by increasing the commitment, loyalty, and morale of its employees and so improving their productivity. See Peter B. Doeringer & Michael J. Piore, Internal Labor Markets and Manpower Analysis (1971). The immediate effects of using seniority to make employment decisions, however, would have detracted from the efficiency achieved by relying only on measures of productivity. The seeming flexibility with which the defendant implemented the seniority system also indicates that it had mixed purposes, occasionally giving way to factors other than efficiency.

Unlike Title VII, the ADA does not contain a special exception for seniority systems. The closest the statute comes to such an exception is a provision identifying "reassignment to a vacant position" as a reasonable accommodation. § 101(9)(B), 42 U.S.C. § 12111(9)(B). This provision supports only a weak inference, noted in *U.S. Airways*, that reassignment to an occupied position is unreasonable. Nevertheless, the Court applies the same principles under the ADA as it does in cases under Title VII, extending some protection to the expectations of employees based on their seniority rights. As a result, the decision in *U.S. Airways* bears a surprising resemblance to the decision in Trans World Airlines v. Hardison, 432 U.S. 63 (1977), on accommodation of religious practices, discussed in Chapter 6. In both cases, the plaintiff sought accommodation by a transfer contrary to the seniority system. In *U.S. Airways*, the Court established a presumption against granting the accommodation, and in *Trans World Airlines*, the Court denied the accommodation outright. How can these similarities be explained despite the absence of any constitutional concerns under the ADA analogous to those about establishing religion under Title VII?

The added protection afforded to seniority systems obviously has to do with the burden imposed upon other employees by denying their seniority rights. Is this burden particularly onerous because these employees are innocent of any discrimination committed by the employer? Recall that this argument figured prominently in restricting awards of remedial competitive seniority, as discussed in Chapter 8. Alternatively, is this burden so onerous because it is concentrated on a few employees who cannot shift it elsewhere? Or does it undermine the cooperation that must be obtained from other employees in accepting the laws against employment discrimination? All of these arguments can be traced back directly to the special protection of seniority systems in Title VII. Why do these arguments extend beyond the specific terms of that provision to a statute without any corresponding protection for seniority?

6. **Bibliography.** For a discussion of the particular issues raised by *US Airways*, see Cheryl L. Anderson, "Neutral" Employer Policies and the ADA: The Implications of *U.S. Airways, Inc. v. Barnett* Beyond Seniority Systems, 51 Drake L. Rev. 1 (2002); Samuel R. Bagenstos, Disability Rights and Labor: Is this Conflict Really Necessary?, 92 Ind. L.J. 277 (2016); Stephen F. Befort, The Most Difficult ADA Reasonable Accommodation Issues: Reassignment

and Leave of Absence, 37 Wake Forest L. Rev. 439 (2002); Seth D. Harris, Re-Thinking the Economics of Discrimination: *U.S. Airways v. Barnett*, the ADA, and the Application of Internal Labor Market Theory, 89 Iowa L. Rev. 123 (2003); Stacy A. Hickox, Transfer as an Accommodation: Standards from Discrimination Cases and Theory, 62 Ark. L. Rev. 195 (2009); Stacy A. Hickox, Bargaining for Accommodations, 19 U. Pa. J. Bus. L. 147 (2016); Lawrence P. Postol, ADA Open Issues: Transfers to Vacant Positions, Leaves of Absence, Telecommuting, and Other Accommodation Issues, 8 Elon L. Rev. 61 (2016).

For general discussions of the duty of reasonable accommodation, see Cheryl L. Anderson, Unification of Standards in Discrimination Law: The Conundrum of Causation and Reasonable Accommodation Under the ADA, 82 Miss. L.J. 67 (2013); Cheryl L. Anderson, What Is "Because of the Disability" Under the Americans with Disabilities Act? Reasonable Accommodation, Causation, and the Windfall Doctrine, 27 Berkeley J. Emp. & Lab. L. 323 (2006); Carrie Griffin Basas, Back Rooms, Board Rooms—Reasonable Accommodation and Resistance Under the ADA, 29 Berkeley J. Emp. & Lab. L. 59 (2008); Christopher B. Brown, Incorporating Third-Party Benefits into the Cost-Benefit Calculus of Reasonable Accommodation, 18 Va. J. Soc. Pol'y & L. 319 (2011); Nicole B. Porter, *Martinizing* Title I of the Americans with Disabilities Act, 47 Ga. L. Rev. 527 (2013); Ruth Colker, Extra Time as an Accommodation, 69 U. Pitt. L. Rev. 413 (2008); Gina M. Cook, When the Duty to Provide a Reasonable Accommodation Seems Unreasonable: Accommodating and Managing Employees with Episodic Impairments or Impairments in Remission Under the ADA Amendments Act of 2008, 32 N.C. Cent. L. Rev. 1 (2009); Jeannette Cox, Reasonable Accommodations and the ADA Amendments' Overlooked Potential, 24 Geo. Mason L. Rev. 147 (2016); Elizabeth F. Emens, Integrating Accommodation, 156 U. Pa. L. Rev. 839 (2008); John E. Matejkovic & Margaret E. Matejkovic, What Is Reasonable Accommodation Under the ADA? Not an Easy Answer; Rather a Plethora of Questions, 28 Miss. C. L. Rev. 67 (2008–2009); Michael Ashley Stein & Michael Evan Waterstone, Disability, Disparate Impact, and Class Actions, 56 Duke L.J. 861 (2006); Michael Ashley Stein et al., Accommodating Every Body, 81 U. Chi. L. Rev. 689 (2014); Cass R. Sunstein, Cost-Benefit Analysis Without Analyzing the Costs or Benefits: Reasonable Accommodation, Balancing, and Stigmatic Harms, 74 U. Chi. L. Rev. 1895 (2007); Mark C. Weber, Unreasonable Accommodation and Due Hardship, 62 Fla. L. Rev. 1119 (2010).

D. OTHER CLAIMS AND DEFENSES

INTRODUCTORY NOTE ON THREATS TO SELF AND OTHERS

1. Defenses Under the ADA. Like other laws against employment discrimination, the ADA allows the employer a variety of defenses in order to serve the legitimate interests in managing an enterprise. Earlier sections have discussed the requirement of coverage that an individual be "qualified" for the position in question, §§ 101(8), 102(a), 42 U.S.C. §§ 12111(8), 12112(a), and that reasonable accommodations be made only if they do not impose "an undue hardship on the operation of the business." §§ 101(10), 102(b)(5)(A), 42 U.S.C. §§ 12111(8), 12112(b)(5)(A). The ADA also gives employers a general defense by showing that a qualification standard is "job-related and consistent with business necessity" and cannot be met "by reasonable accommodation." § 103(a), 42 U.S.C. § 12113(a). A specific version of this defense is for a qualification standard that requires "that an individual shall not pose a direct threat to the health or safety of other individuals in the workplace." § 103(a), 42 U.S.C. § 12113(a). That provision is the subject of the main case in this section, but it was preceded by several cases that raised the same issue as it related to coverage.

2. ***School Board v. Arline.*** The first of these cases arose under the Rehabilitation Act. In School Board v. Arline, 480 U.S. 273 (1987), the plaintiff alleged employment discrimination when she had been dismissed from her position as a public school teacher because she suffered from tuberculosis, a disease that can be contagious in certain circumstances. The Court held that she was a covered individual with a disability under the Rehabilitation Act, without reaching the question whether the risk posed by her disease disqualified her from the job. The crucial passage upholding coverage of her disability is as follows:

> We do not agree with petitioners [the school officials] that, in defining a handicapped individual under § 504 [of the Rehabilitation Act], the contagious effects of a disease can be meaningfully distinguished from the disease's physical effects on a claimant in a case such as this. Arline's contagiousness and her physical impairment each resulted from the same underlying condition, tuberculosis. It would be unfair to allow an employer to seize upon the distinction between the effects of a disease on others and the effects of a disease on a patient and use that distinction to justify discriminatory treatment.
>
> Nothing in the legislative history of § 504 suggests that Congress intended such a result. That history demonstrates that Congress was as concerned about the effect of an impairment on others as it was about its effect on the individual. Congress extended coverage, in 29 U.S.C. § 706(7)(B)(iii), to those individuals who are simply "regarded as having" a physical or mental impairment. The Senate Report provides as an example of a person who would be covered under this subsection "a person with some kind of visible physical impairment which in fact does not substantially limit that person's functioning." S. Rep. No. 93–1297 at 64. Such an impairment might not diminish a person's physical or mental capabilities, but could nevertheless substantially limit that person's ability to work as a result of the negative reactions of others to the impairment.
>
> Allowing discrimination based on the contagious effects of a physical impairment would be inconsistent with the basic purpose of § 504, which is to ensure that handicapped individuals are not denied jobs or other benefits because of the prejudiced attitudes or the ignorance of others. By amending the definition of

"handicapped individual" to include not only those who are actually physically impaired, but also those who are regarded as impaired and who, as a result, are substantially limited in a major life activity, Congress acknowledged that society's accumulated myths and fears about disability and disease are as handicapping as are the physical limitations that flow from actual impairment. Few aspects of a handicap give rise to the same level of public fear and misapprehension as contagiousness. Even those who suffer or have recovered from such noninfectious diseases as epilepsy or cancer have faced discrimination based on the irrational fear that they might be contagious. The Act is carefully structured to replace such reflexive reactions to actual or perceived handicaps with actions based on reasoned and medically sound judgments: the definition of "handicapped individual" is broad, but only those individuals who are both handicapped and otherwise qualified are eligible for relief. The fact that some persons who have contagious diseases may pose a serious health threat to others under certain circumstances does not justify excluding from the coverage of the Act all persons with actual or perceived contagious diseases. Such exclusion would mean that those accused of being contagious would never have the opportunity to have their condition evaluated in light of medical evidence and a determination made as to whether they were "otherwise qualified." Rather, they would be vulnerable to discrimination on the basis of mythology—precisely the type of injury Congress sought to prevent. We conclude that the fact that a person with a record of a physical impairment is also contagious does not suffice to remove that person from coverage under § 504.

In *Arline*, the Court did not reach the question whether the plaintiff's disability constituted a direct threat to others in the school where she worked, particularly the children she was teaching. That question was left for consideration on remand. Does it make sense to hold that the plaintiff is covered and then later decide that she has no claim on the merits?

3. ***Bragdon v. Abbott.*** The same set of issues came up under the ADA, in the provisions governing "public accommodations" under Title III. Public accommodations are services made available to the general public, most often by private individuals and firms. In Bragdon v. Abbott, 524 U.S. 624 (1998), the Supreme Court considered the question whether the plaintiff, who was HIV-positive, was a covered individual under the ADA. He alleged discrimination in being denied dental services, and although his case came up under Title III, it raised the same question of coverage of as would an employment discrimination case under Title I. Although the plaintiff was as yet asymptomatic, and did not have AIDS, the Court thoroughly reviewed the evidence of a compromised immune system that afflicts individuals who are HIV-positive. It concluded that these impairments substantially limited the plaintiff in the major life activity of reproduction, mainly because of the risk they posed of an infection to a sexual partner or to a child.

This holding elicited dissenting opinions at the time, but it has since been confirmed and extended by the ADA Amendments Act. The ADA now explicitly covers the "functions of the immune system" and "reproductive functions" as major life activities. § 3(2)(B), 42 U.S.C. § 12102(2)(B). Under current law, the plaintiff could have gained coverage entirely on the first issue discussed by the Court: the effect of HIV on her immune system. Because her case arose under Title III of the ADA, there would have been no further issue of coverage, in contrast to Title I, which prohibits employment discrimination only against a "qualified individual." § 102(a), 42 U.S.C. § 12112(a). For many positions, however, having a functioning immune system—one that is not substantially impaired—would not be a qualification necessary to perform the essential functions of the job. Individuals like the plaintiff in *Bragdon v. Abbott* would therefore be covered by Title I. Does the coverage of the immune system, "normal cell growth," and other "major bodily functions" listed in § 3(2)(B), greatly expand the scope of the ADA? Or is coverage for this reason no different in principle from coverage of "reproductive functions," which was already endorsed by the Supreme Court?

Having resolved this issue of coverage, the Supreme Court in *Bragdon* then went on to consider the direct threat defense. It did not itself determine whether the defense applied on the facts of the case, leaving the issue for consideration on remand, as in *Arline*. The Court's discussion of the question nevertheless reveals how sensitive these issues of safety are. The relevant passages from the opinion appear below:

> Notwithstanding the protection given respondent by the ADA's definition of disability, petitioner could have refused to treat her if her infectious condition "pose[d] a direct threat to the health or safety of others." 42 U.S.C. § 12182(b)(3). The ADA defines a direct threat to be "a significant risk to the health or safety of others that cannot be eliminated by a modification of policies, practices, or procedures or by the provision of auxiliary aids or services." Parallel provisions appear in the employment provisions of Title I. §§ 12111(3), 12113(b). . . .
>
> The existence, or nonexistence, of a significant risk must be determined from the standpoint of the person who refuses the treatment or accommodation, and the risk assessment must be based on medical or other objective evidence. Arline, supra, at 288; 28 CFR § 36.208(c) (1997); id., pt. 36, App. B, p. 626. As a health care professional, petitioner had the duty to assess the risk of infection based on the objective, scientific information available to him and others in his profession. His belief that a significant risk existed, even if maintained in good faith, would not relieve him from liability. To use the words of the question presented, petitioner receives no special deference simply because he is a health care professional. It is true that *Arline* reserved "the question whether courts should also defer to the reasonable medical judgments of private physicians on which an employer has relied." 480 U.S., at 288, n. 18. At most, this statement reserved the possibility that employers could consult with individual physicians as objective third-party experts. It did not suggest that an

individual physician's state of mind could excuse discrimination without regard to the objective reasonableness of his actions.

Our conclusion that courts should assess the objective reasonableness of the views of health care professionals without deferring to their individual judgments does not answer the implicit assumption in the question presented, whether petitioner's actions were reasonable in light of the available medical evidence. In assessing the reasonableness of petitioner's actions, the views of public health authorities, such as the U.S. Public Health Service, CDC, and the National Institutes of Health, are of special weight and authority. Arline, supra, at 288; 28 CFR pt. 36, App. B, p. 626 (1997). The views of these organizations are not conclusive, however. A health care professional who disagrees with the prevailing medical consensus may refute it by citing a credible scientific basis for deviating from the accepted norm. See W. Keeton, D. Dobbs, R. Keeton, & D. Owen, Prosser and Keeton on Law of Torts § 32, p. 187 (5th ed. 1984).

4. **Preventing Stigma or Compensating for Disabilities?** The multiple and ambiguous obligations imposed by the Rehabilitation Act and the ADA are reflected in the goals of these statutes: Are they intended to prevent actions that stigmatize and isolate individuals with disabilities, much as blacks were subjected to segregation under the regime of Jim Crow? Or are these statutes intended, like social welfare legislation, to provide compensation for the adverse consequences that directly result from having a covered disability? The ADA Amendments Act struck from the ADA's statement of findings the characterization of individuals with disabilities as "a discrete and insular minority"—probably out of concern that the ADA's coverage would otherwise be construed too narrowly—but it added a statement that individuals with disabilities have been denied the "right to fully participate in all aspects of society." § 2(a)(1), 42 U.S.C. § 12101(A)(1). As this language indicates, the different goals of the statute are not mutually exclusive, just as the obligations that implement them also are not. Yet in any particular case, one goal or another often predominates.

Nowhere is this tendency more apparent than with respect to contagious diseases. The plaintiff in *Bragdon v. Abbott* did not seek special treatment because she was HIV-positive. She only sought to be treated like other dental patients. The defendant's fear of infection, whether or not it was well-founded, appeared to stigmatize her as a dangerous individual. Yet the Court largely avoids these issues by focusing only on the first definition of a covered disability: "a physical or mental impairment that substantially limits one or more of the major life activities of such individual." By contrast, in *Arline*, the Court also relies on the additional provisions for coverage based on having "a record of" or "being regarded as having" a disability in the first sense. These expanded provisions for coverage, according to the Court, represent an attempt to counteract stereotypes about individuals with disabilities. Why does the Court avoid similar reasoning in *Bragdon v. Abbott*? Note that it explicitly refuses to address coverage under these expanded definitions of disability. Is the Court concerned about expanding coverage under the statute too far? Is it concerned about the political reaction to dismissing fears about AIDS as simply an erroneous stereotype?

5. Bibliography. For discussion of the specific disability in *Bragdon v. Abbott*, see Sharona Hoffman, AIDS Caps, Contraceptive Coverage, and the Law: An Analysis of the Federal Anti-Discrimination Statutes' Applicability to Health Insurance, 23 Cardozo L. Rev. 1315 (2002); Pamela Koehler, Using Disability Law to Protect Persons Living with HIV/AIDS: The Indian and American Approach. 19 J. Transnat'l L. & Pol'y 401 (2010); Samuel A. Marcosson, Who Is "Us" and Who Is "Them"—Common Threads and the Discriminatory Cut-Off of Health Care Benefits for AIDS Under ERISA and the Americans with Disabilities Act, 44 Am. U. L. Rev. 361 (1994); Jeffrey A. Mello, Limitations of the Americans with Disabilities Act in Protecting Individuals with HIV from Employment Discrimination, 19 Seton Hall Legis. J. 73 (1994).

Chevron U.S.A. Inc. v. Echazabal

536 U.S. 73 (2002).

■ JUSTICE SOUTER delivered the opinion of the Court.

A regulation of the Equal Employment Opportunity Commission authorizes refusal to hire an individual because his performance on the job would endanger his own health, owing to a disability. The question in this case is whether the Americans with Disabilities Act of 1990, 42 U.S.C. § 12101 et seq., permits the regulation. We hold that it does.

I

Beginning in 1972, respondent Mario Echazabal worked for independent contractors at an oil refinery owned by petitioner Chevron U.S.A. Inc. Twice he applied for a job directly with Chevron, which offered to hire him if he could pass the company's physical examination. See 48 42 U.S.C. § 12112(d)(3). Each time, the exam showed liver abnormality or damage, the cause eventually being identified as Hepatitis C, which Chevron's doctors said would be aggravated by continued exposure to toxins at Chevron's refinery. In each instance, the company withdrew the offer, and the second time it asked the contractor employing Echazabal either to reassign him to a job without exposure to harmful chemicals or to remove him from the refinery altogether. The contractor laid him off in early 1996.

Echazabal filed suit, ultimately removed to federal court, claiming, among other things, that Chevron violated the Americans With Disabilities Act in refusing to hire him, or even to let him continue working in the plant, because of a disability, his liver condition.[5] Chevron defended under a regulation of the Equal Employment Opportunity Commission permitting the defense that a worker's disability on the job

[5] Chevron did not dispute for purposes of its summary-judgment motion that Echazabal is "disabled" under the ADA, and Echazabal did not argue that Chevron could have made a " 'reasonable accommodation.' "

would pose a "direct threat" to his health, see 29 CFR § 1630.15(b)(2) (2001). Although two medical witnesses disputed Chevron's judgment that Echazabal's liver function was impaired and subject to further damage under the job conditions in the refinery, the District Court granted summary judgment for Chevron. It held that Echazabal raised no genuine issue of material fact as to whether the company acted reasonably in relying on its own doctors' medical advice, regardless of its accuracy.

On appeal, the Ninth Circuit asked for briefs on a threshold question not raised before, whether the EEOC's regulation recognizing a threat-to-self defense, ibid., exceeded the scope of permissible rulemaking under the ADA. 226 F.3d 1063, 1066, n. 3 (2000). The Circuit held that it did and reversed the summary judgment. The court rested its position on the text of the ADA itself in explicitly recognizing an employer's right to adopt an employment qualification barring anyone whose disability would place others in the workplace at risk, while saying nothing about threats to the disabled employee himself. The majority opinion reasoned that "by specifying only threats to 'other individuals in the workplace,' the statute makes it clear that threats to other persons—including the disabled individual himself—are not included within the scope of the [direct threat] defense," and it indicated that any such regulation would unreasonably conflict with congressional policy against paternalism in the workplace. The court went on to reject Chevron's further argument that Echazabal was not " 'otherwise qualified' " to perform the job, holding that the ability to perform a job without risk to one's health or safety is not an " 'essential function' " of the job.

The decision conflicted with one from the Eleventh Circuit, Moses v. American Nonwovens, Inc., 97 F.3d 446, 447 (1996), and raised tension with the Seventh Circuit case of Koshinski v. Decatur Foundry, Inc., 177 F.3d 599, 603 (1999). We granted certiorari and now reverse.

II

Section 102 of the Americans with Disabilities Act of 1990, 42 U.S.C. § 12101 et seq., prohibits "discriminat[ion] against a qualified individual with a disability because of the disability . . . in regard to" a number of actions by an employer, including "hiring." 42 U.S.C. § 12112(a). The statutory definition of "discriminat[ion]" covers a number of things an employer might do to block a disabled person from advancing in the workplace, such as "using qualification standards . . . that screen out or tend to screen out an individual with a disability." § 12112(b)(6). By that same definition, as well as by separate provision, § 12113(a), the Act creates an affirmative defense for action under a qualification standard "shown to be job-related for the position in question and . . . consistent with business necessity." Such a standard may include "a requirement that an individual shall not pose a direct threat to the health or safety of other individuals in the workplace," § 12113(b), if the individual cannot perform the job safely with reasonable accommodation, § 12113(a). By regulation, the EEOC carries the defense one step further, in allowing an employer to screen out a potential worker with a disability not only for risks that he would pose to others in the workplace but for risks on the job to his own health or safety as well: "The term 'qualification standard' may include a requirement that an individual shall not pose a direct threat to the health or safety of the individual or others in the workplace." 29 CFR § 1630.15(b)(2).

Chevron relies on the regulation here, since it says a job in the refinery would pose a "direct threat" to Echazabal's health. In seeking deference to the agency, it argues that nothing in the statute unambiguously precludes such a defense, while the regulation was adopted under authority explicitly delegated by Congress, 42 U.S.C. § 12116, and after notice-and-comment rulemaking. See United States v. Mead Corp., 533 U.S. 218, 227; Chevron U.S.A. Inc. v. Natural Resources Defense Council, Inc., 467 U.S. 837, 842–844 (1984). Echazabal, on the contrary, argues that as a matter of law the statute precludes the regulation, which he claims would be an unreasonable interpretation even if the agency had leeway to go beyond the literal text.

A

As for the textual bar to any agency action as a matter of law, Echazabal says that Chevron loses on the threshold question whether the statute leaves a gap for the EEOC to fill. Echazabal recognizes the generality of the language providing for a defense when a plaintiff is screened out by "qualification standards" that are "job-related and consistent with business necessity" (and reasonable accommodation would not cure the difficulty posed by employment). 42 U.S.C. § 12113(a). Without more, those provisions would allow an employer to turn away someone whose work would pose a serious risk to himself. That possibility is said to be eliminated, however, by the further specification that " 'qualification standards' may include a requirement that an individual shall not pose a direct threat to the health or safety of other individuals in the workplace." § 12113(b); see also § 12111(3) (defining "direct threat" in terms of risk to others). Echazabal contrasts this provision with an EEOC regulation under the Rehabilitation Act of 1973, as amended, 29 U.S.C. § 701 et seq., antedating the ADA, which recognized an employer's right to consider threats both to other workers and to the threatening employee himself. Because the ADA defense provision recognizes threats only if they extend to another, Echazabal reads the statute to imply as a matter of law that threats to the worker himself cannot count.

The argument follows the reliance of the Ninth Circuit majority on the interpretive canon, expressio unius exclusio alterius, "expressing one item of associated group or series excludes another left unmentioned." United States v. Vonn, 535 U.S. 55, 65 (2002). The rule is fine when it applies, but this case joins some others in showing when it does not. See, e.g., id., at 65; United Dominion Industries, Inc. v. United States, 532

U.S. 822, 836; Pauley v. BethEnergy Mines, Inc., 501 U.S. 680, 703 (1991).

The first strike against the expression-exclusion rule here is right in the text that Echazabal quotes. Congress included the harm-to-others provision as an example of legitimate qualifications that are "job-related and consistent with business necessity." These are spacious defensive categories, which seem to give an agency (or in the absence of agency action, a court) a good deal of discretion in setting the limits of permissible qualification standards. That discretion is confirmed, if not magnified, by the provision that "qualification standards" falling within the limits of job relation and business necessity "may include" a veto on those who would directly threaten others in the workplace. Far from supporting Echazabal's position, the expansive phrasing of "may include" points directly away from the sort of exclusive specification he claims. United States v. New York Telephone Co., 434 U.S. 159, 169; Federal Land Bank of St. Paul v. Bismarck Lumber Co., 314 U.S. 95, 100 (1941).

Just as statutory language suggesting exclusiveness is missing, so is that essential extrastatutory ingredient of an expression-exclusion demonstration, the series of terms from which an omission bespeaks a negative implication. The canon depends on identifying a series of two or more terms or things that should be understood to go hand in hand, which are abridged in circumstances supporting a sensible inference that the term left out must have been meant to be excluded. E. Crawford, Construction of Statutes 337 (1940) (expressio unius " 'properly applies only when in the natural association of ideas in the mind of the reader that which is expressed is so set over by way of strong contrast to that which is omitted that the contrast enforces the affirmative inference' ") (quoting State ex rel. Curtis v. De Corps, 134 Ohio St. 295, 299, 16 N.E.2d 459, 462 (1938)); United States v. Vonn, supra.

Strike two in this case is the failure to identify any such established series, including both threats to others and threats to self, from which Congress appears to have made a deliberate choice to omit the latter item as a signal of the affirmative defense's scope. The closest Echazabal comes is the EEOC's rule interpreting the Rehabilitation Act of 1973, as amended, 29 U.S.C. § 701 et seq., a precursor of the ADA. That statute excepts from the definition of a protected "qualified individual with a handicap" anyone who would pose a "direct threat to the health or safety of other individuals," but, like the later ADA, the Rehabilitation Act says nothing about threats to self that particular employment might pose. 42 U.S.C. § 12113(b). The EEOC nonetheless extended the exception to cover threat-to-self employment, 29 CFR § 1613.702(f), and Echazabal argues that Congress's adoption only of the threat-to-others exception in the ADA must have been a deliberate omission of the Rehabilitation Act regulation's tandem term of threat-to-self, with intent to exclude it.

But two reasons stand in the way of treating the omission as an unequivocal implication of congressional intent. The first is that the

EEOC was not the only agency interpreting the Rehabilitation Act, with the consequence that its regulation did not establish a clear, standard pairing of threats to self and others. While the EEOC did amplify upon the text of the Rehabilitation Act exclusion by recognizing threats to self along with threats to others, three other agencies adopting regulations under the Rehabilitation Act did not. See 28 CFR § 42.540(*l*)(1) (Department of Justice), 29 CFR § 32.3 (Department of Labor), and 45 CFR § 84.3(k)(1) (Department of Health and Human Services). It would be a stretch, then, to say that there was a standard usage, with its source in agency practice or elsewhere, that connected threats to others so closely to threats to self that leaving out one was like ignoring a twin.

Even if we put aside this variety of administrative experience, however, and look no further than the EEOC's Rehabilitation Act regulation pairing self and others, the congressional choice to speak only of threats to others would still be equivocal. Consider what the ADA reference to threats to others might have meant on somewhat different facts. If the Rehabilitation Act had spoken only of "threats to health" and the EEOC regulation had read that to mean threats to self or others, a congressional choice to be more specific in the ADA by listing threats to others but not threats to self would have carried a message. The most probable reading would have been that Congress understood what a failure to specify could lead to and had made a choice to limit the possibilities. The statutory basis for any agency rulemaking under the ADA would have been different from its basis under the Rehabilitation Act and would have indicated a difference in the agency's rulemaking discretion. But these are not the circumstances here. Instead of making the ADA different from the Rehabilitation Act on the point at issue, Congress used identical language, knowing full well what the EEOC had made of that language under the earlier statute. Did Congress mean to imply that the agency had been wrong in reading the earlier language to allow it to recognize threats to self, or did Congress just assume that the agency was free to do under the ADA what it had already done under the earlier Act's identical language? There is no way to tell. Omitting the EEOC's reference to self-harm while using the very language that the EEOC had read as consistent with recognizing self-harm is equivocal at best. No negative inference is possible.

There is even a third strike against applying the expression-exclusion rule here. It is simply that there is no apparent stopping point to the argument that by specifying a threat-to-others defense Congress intended a negative implication about those whose safety could be considered. When Congress specified threats to others in the workplace, for example, could it possibly have meant that an employer could not defend a refusal to hire when a worker's disability would threaten others outside the workplace? If Typhoid Mary had come under the ADA, would a meat packer have been defenseless if Mary had sued after being turned away? See 42 U.S.C. § 12113(d). Expressio unius just fails to work here.

B

Since Congress has not spoken exhaustively on threats to a worker's own health, the agency regulation can claim adherence under the rule in *Chevron*, 467 U.S., at 843, so long as it makes sense of the statutory defense for qualification standards that are "job-related and consistent with business necessity." 42 U.S.C. § 12113(a). Chevron's reasons for calling the regulation reasonable are unsurprising: moral concerns aside, it wishes to avoid time lost to sickness, excessive turnover from medical retirement or death, litigation under state tort law, and the risk of violating the national Occupational Safety and Health Act of 1970, 84 Stat. 1590, as amended, 29 U.S.C. § 651 et seq. Although Echazabal claims that none of these reasons is legitimate, focusing on the concern with OSHA will be enough to show that the regulation is entitled to survive.

Echazabal points out that there is no known instance of OSHA enforcement, or even threatened enforcement, against an employer who relied on the ADA to hire a worker willing to accept a risk to himself from his disability on the job. In Echazabal's mind, this shows that invoking OSHA policy and possible OSHA liability is just a red herring to excuse covert discrimination. But there is another side to this. The text of OSHA itself says its point is "to assure so far as possible every working man and woman in the Nation safe and healthful working conditions," § 651(b), and Congress specifically obligated an employer to "furnish to each of his employees employment and a place of employment which are free from recognized hazards that are causing or are likely to cause death or serious physical harm to his employees," § 654(a)(1). Although there may be an open question whether an employer would actually be liable under OSHA for hiring an individual who knowingly consented to the particular dangers the job would pose to him, see Brief for United States et al. as Amici Curiae 19, n. 7, there is no denying that the employer would be asking for trouble: his decision to hire would put Congress's policy in the ADA, a disabled individual's right to operate on equal terms within the workplace, at loggerheads with the competing policy of OSHA, to ensure the safety of "each" and "every" worker. Courts would, of course, resolve the tension if there were no agency action, but the EEOC's resolution exemplifies the substantive choices that agencies are expected to make when Congress leaves the intersection of competing objectives both imprecisely marked but subject to the administrative leeway found in 42 U.S.C. § 12113(a).

Nor can the EEOC's resolution be fairly called unreasonable as allowing the kind of workplace paternalism the ADA was meant to outlaw. It is true that Congress had paternalism in its sights when it passed the ADA, see § 12101(a)(5) (recognizing "overprotective rules and policies" as a form of discrimination). But the EEOC has taken this to mean that Congress was not aiming at an employer's refusal to place disabled workers at a specifically demonstrated risk, but was trying to get at refusals to give an even break to classes of disabled people, while claiming to act for their own good in reliance on untested and pretextual stereotypes.[6] Its regulation disallows just this sort of sham protection, through demands for a particularized enquiry into the harms the employee would probably face. The direct threat defense must be "based on a reasonable medical judgment that relies on the most current medical knowledge and/or the best available objective evidence," and upon an expressly "individualized assessment of the individual's present ability to safely perform the essential functions of the job," reached after considering, among other things, the imminence of the risk and the severity of the harm portended. 29 CFR § 1630.2(r) (2001). The EEOC was certainly acting within the reasonable zone when it saw a difference between rejecting workplace paternalism and ignoring specific and documented risks to the employee himself, even if the employee would take his chances for the sake of getting a job.

Finally, our conclusions that some regulation is permissible and this one is reasonable are not open to Echazabal's objection that they reduce the direct threat provision to "surplusage," see Babbitt v. Sweet Home Chapter, Communities for Great Ore., 515 U.S. 687, 698 (1995). The mere fact that a threat-to-self defense reasonably falls within the general "job related" and "business necessity" standard does not mean that Congress accomplished nothing with its explicit provision for a defense based on threats to others. The provision made a conclusion clear that might otherwise have been fought over in litigation or administrative rulemaking. It did not lack a job to do merely because the EEOC might have adopted the same rule later in applying the general defense provisions, nor was its job any less responsible simply because the agency was left with the option to go a step further. A provision can be useful even without congressional attention being indispensable.

Accordingly, we reverse the judgment of the Court of Appeals and remand the case for proceedings consistent with this opinion.

It is so ordered.

NOTES ON *CHEVRON U.S.A. INC. V. ECHAZABAL*

1. **Literal Terms of the Statute.** The defense based on a "direct threat" expressly applies only to "other individuals in the workplace." § 103(b), 42 U.S.C. § 12113(b). *Echazabal* goes beyond the literal terms of the defense and applies it to threats to the health or safety of the plaintiff himself.

---

[6] . . . Similarly, Echazabal points to several of our decisions expressing concern under Title VII, which like the ADA allows employers to defend otherwise discriminatory practices that are "consistent with business necessity," 42 U.S.C. § 2000e–2(k), with employers adopting rules that exclude women from jobs that are seen as too risky. See, e.g., Dothard v. Rawlinson, 433 U.S. 321, 335 (1977); Automobile Workers v. Johnson Controls, Inc., 499 U.S. 187, 202 (1991). Those cases, however, are beside the point, as they, like Title VII generally, were concerned with paternalistic judgments based on the broad category of gender, while the EEOC has required that judgments based on the direct threat provision be made on the basis of individualized risk assessments.

Section 103(b) does not exclude this possibility, since it provides only that a direct threat "may" justify an allowable "qualification or standard." Any such qualification or standard, however, must meet additional requirements: it must be "job-related and consistent with business necessity," and it must result in job performance that "cannot be accomplished by reasonable accommodation." § 103(a), 42 U.S.C. § 12113(a). The first of those requirements is taken from the theory of disparate impact, which is independently codified as a basis of liability in the ADA, § 102(b)(6), 42 U.S.C. § 12113(b)(6), and the second simply restates the duty of reasonable accommodation.

Reading all these provisions together, a direct threat constitutes a defense only if it is job-related and consistent with business necessity and cannot be reduced through reasonable accommodation. *Echazabal* only held that a threat to an individual's own health or safety could be a defense if it met these additional requirements. In initially granting summary judgment to the defendant in this case, the district court apparently held that these requirements were met. Is there any way, apart from refusing to hire the plaintiff, that the defendant could have protected him from exposure to chemicals that might have further damaged his liver?

2. **Effect of the EEOC Regulation.** Relying on another and better known *Chevron* case, Chevron, U.S.A., Inc. v. Natural Resources Defense Council, Inc., 467 U.S. 837 (1984), the Court finds the EEOC's regulation on the scope of the direct threat defense to be dispositive. Under this case, when a statute is ambiguous, the courts must defer to any reasonable interpretation of a statute made by an agency charged with its administration. The Court found § 103(b) to be ambiguous for the reasons discussed in the preceding note, and it then proceeded to find the EEOC regulation to be reasonable.

Would *Echazabal* have been decided the same way in the absence of this regulation? Is the EEOC regulation justifiable as an initial matter? How is this inquiry different from one into whether the regulation is reasonable? Expanding the direct threat defense to include threats to self might be justifiable entirely apart from attitudes toward individuals with disabilities in other respects. An employer might take account of threats to self not out of any stereotype about individuals with disabilities, but to reduce its own liability for injuries in the workplace. Is the prevalence of such claims based, for instance, on exposure to asbestos, sufficient to justify the EEOC regulation? Is the EEOC regulation based, in the end, on the absence of any cases of genuinely isolated threats to the disabled individual alone? The external effects of any such injury are likely to fall eventually on the employer. Even if this justification does not hold in every case, could it still be sufficient to make the EEOC regulation reasonable for most cases?

3. **Paternalism.** In the final footnote in its opinion, the Court distinguishes paternalism under Title VII from paternalism under the ADA, relying on the individualized inquiry necessary to determine whether a particular disability disqualifies an individual from a particular job. Unlike uniformly defined characteristics such as race or sex, disabilities take a wide variety of different forms. Even the same disability can take many different

forms, as the example of carpal tunnel syndrome in *Toyota* illustrates. Under the Court's analysis, the individualized inquiry presumably takes place in determining whether there is a sufficient justification for excluding individuals with disabilities because they pose a direct threat to their own health or safety. This inquiry, under § 103(a), 42 U.S.C. § 12113(a), also must consider whether a reasonable accommodation can be made to alleviate this threat.

Does it make sense to allow paternalism toward the disabled in some cases but not in others? The Court's approach seems to submerge value judgments about whether individuals with disabilities can take care of themselves into a series of indefinite and potentially inconsistent individualized assessments. Does this approach create the risk of establishing a presumption in favor of paternalism? Employers will succeed in invoking the direct threat to self as a defense only in cases in which it is well documented. As these decisions accumulate, individuals with particular disabilities will find their own assessment of their ability to work systematically discounted. Since the employer has to establish only a risk of harm, won't the courts be inclined to err on the side of safety?

The contrast with claims of sex discrimination could not be more dramatic. In narrowly interpreting the BFOQ for sex, the Supreme Court has been careful to avoid the stereotype that women cannot judge the risks of employment for themselves. These cases, discussed in Chapter 5, rely exclusively on threats to others in the workplace as the only justification for restricting the employment of women. The individualized determination in these cases is made by the individual herself, not by the employer or the court in assessing the risks to herself that she faces in a particular job. In Automobile Workers v. Johnson Controls, 499 U.S. 187 (1991), the Court went so far as to cast doubt on any form of tort liability that the employer might face by letting women assume the risks of employment and, in particular, the risks of employment while pregnant. Why couldn't the same approach work with disabilities? Is it because the forms of tort liability that would be preempted would be far more varied for disabilities than for pregnancy? For a discussion of the general connection between sex discrimination and disability discrimination, see Jennifer B. Shinall, The Substantially Impaired Sex: Uncovering the Gendered Nature of Disability Discrimination, 101 Minn. L. Rev. 1099 (2017).

Some disabilities might affect the individual's judgment about what risks are acceptable, by impairing cognitive or emotional responses to situations likely to be encountered at work. In most of these cases, however, the individual will also pose a direct threat to others, leaving only a few cases in which the direct threat to self alone arises from such impairments. Should the holding in *Echazabal* have been limited to such cases? How could these cases be distinguished from those involving physical disabilities with cognitive or emotional consequences? Does the need for paternalism in a few cases lead inevitably to the individualized approach adopted by the Court for all cases?

4. **Inquiries into Disabilities.** Some disabilities are apparent, but many are not. The plaintiff in *Echazabal* suffered from a liver condition that could

only be discovered through a physical examination. When an individual requests a reasonable accommodation, the accommodated disability must necessarily be disclosed. In other circumstances, however, the employer must find out about the disability through inquiries and examinations of its applicants and employees. Such inquiries and examinations are restricted by the ADA, in a separate prohibition designed to prevent stereotyping and other forms of unjustified discrimination. § 102(d), 42 U.S.C. § 12112(d). This prohibition applies to all medical examinations and all inquiries about disabilities, subject only to limited exceptions. Inquiries and medical examinations specifically about disabilities are allowed only if they are "job related and consistent with business necessity." Preemployment inquiries are allowed only in order to determine "the ability of an applicant to perform job-related functions." Preemployment medical examinations are subject to especially complicated restrictions: they must be given after an offer of employment has been made (although employment itself can be conditioned on the results of the examination); such examinations must be given to all new employees; and the information obtained must be kept in separate, confidential files, and used only as allowed by the ADA. See generally, Sharona Hoffman, Preplacement Examination and Job-Relatedness: How to Enhance Privacy and Diminish Discrimination in the Workplace, 49 U. Kan. L. Rev. 517 (2001).

Inquiries into mental and psychological disabilities have been particularly controversial. For an assessment of the developing doctrine and the empirical evidence, see Mental Disorder, Work Disability, and the Law (Richard J. Bonnie & John Monahan eds., 1997); Kristin Madison, Employer Wellness Incentives, the ACA, and the ADA: Reconciling Policy Objectives, 51 Willamette L. Rev. 407 (2015).

5. The Genetic Information Nondiscrimination Act of 2008. Congress greatly expanded the prohibitions against inquiries into medical and physical conditions and the use of such information in the Genetic Information Nondiscrimination Act of 2008, 42 U.S.C. § 2000ff–1 et seq. This act prohibits employment discrimination based on genetic information. It also prohibits collecting or requiring such information except in limited circumstances. Similar prohibitions apply to health insurance plans. These prohibitions are directed at the misuse of genetic tests, which have become increasingly available with advances in biotechnology, and which have a history of abuse in programs of compulsory sterilization and in forms of discrimination based on race, national origin, and sex. Like such traditional grounds of discrimination, an individual's genetic makeup is immutable, creating the risk of cumulative and uncontrolled adverse consequences if employers and health insurers can freely take genetic defects into account. Unlike discrimination on the basis of disability, an individual need not make any preliminary showing that she has a covered disability, in order to gain the benefit of this new legislation. The Act covers everyone and provides protection from discrimination on this new ground.

Genetic testing and discrimination on the basis of test results have given rise to an extensive literature. Ifeoma Ajunwa, Genetic Data and Civil Rights, 51 Harv. C.R.-C.L. L. Rev. 75 (2016); Bradley A. Areheart, GINA,

Privacy, and Antisubordination, 46 Ga. L. Rev. 705 (2012); Robert A. Bohrer, A Rawlsian Approach to Solving the Problem of Genetic Discrimination in Toxic Workplaces, 39 San Diego L. Rev. 747 (2002); Colin S. Diver & Jane M. Cohen, Genophobia: What Is Wrong with Genetic Discrimination?, 149 U. Pa. L. Rev. 1439 (2001); Henry T. Greely, Genotype Discrimination: The Complex Case for Some Legislative Protection, 149 U. Pa. L. Rev. 1483 (2001); Pauline T. Kim, Genetic Discrimination, Genetic Privacy: Rethinking Employee Protections for a Brave New Workplace, 96 Nw. U. L. Rev. 1497 (2002); Anita Silvers & Michael Ashley Stein, An Equality Paradigm for Preventing Genetic Discrimination, 55 Vand. L. Rev. 1341 (2002); Anita Silvers & Michael Ashley Stein, Human Rights and Genetic Discrimination: Protecting Genomics' Promise for Public Health, 31 J.L. Med. & Ethics 377 (2003); Jennifer K. Wagner, Sidelining GINA: The Impact of Personal Genomics and Collective Bargaining in Professional Sports, 12 Va. Sports & Ent. L.J. 81 (2012); Cynthia Nance et al., Discrimination in Employment on the Basis of Genetics: Proceedings of the 2002 Annual Meeting, Association of American Law Schools Section on Employment Discrimination Law, 6 Emp. Rts. & Emp. Pol'y J. 57 (2002); Symposium, Personal Genetic Information: Implications for the Workplace and Criminal Justice, 18 N.Y.L. Sch. J. Hum. Rts. 1 (2001).

6. **Bibliography.** For discussion of the issues raised by *Echazabal*, see Samuel R. Bagenstos, Essay, The Americans with Disabilities Act as Risk Regulation, 101 Colum. L. Rev. 1479 (2001); Steven H. Winterbauer, The Direct Threat Defense: Striking a Balance Between the Duties To Accommodate and To Provide a Safe Workplace, 23 Emp. Rel. L.J., June 1997, at 5.

For books and articles on particular disability claims, see Mark C. Weber, Disability Harassment (2007); Susannah Carr, Invisible Actors: Genetic Testing and Genetic Discrimination in the Workplace, 30 U. Ark. Little Rock L. Rev. 1 (2007); Jarod S. Gonzalez, A Matter of Life and Death—Why the ADA Permits Mandatory Periodic Medical Examinations of "Remote-Location" Employees, 66 La. L. Rev. 681 (2006); William J. McDevitt, I Dream of GINA: Understanding the Employment Provisions of the Genetic Information Nondiscrimination Act of 2008, 54 Vill. L. Rev. 91 (2009); Christine N. O'Brien, Facially Neutral No-Rehire Rules and the Americans with Disabilities Act, 22 Hofstra Lab. & Emp. L.J. 114 (2004); Lawrence D. Rosenthal, Association Discrimination Under the Americans with Disabilities Act: Another Uphill Battle for Potential ADA Plaintiffs, 22 Hofstra Lab. & Emp. L.J. 132 (2004); Sharlott K. Thompson, Hostile Work Environment Disability Harassment Under the ADA, 73 UMKC L. Rev. 715 (2005).

E. PROCEDURES AND REMEDIES

1. **Claims Under the Rehabilitation Act.** The procedures and remedies available under the Rehabilitation Act depend upon the section of the Act under which claims are brought. At one extreme, no private actions can be brought at all under § 503, 29 U.S.C. § 793, which is

enforced only by administrative and public actions. Employees of federal contractors can assert claims against their employers only under the ADA. At the opposite extreme, claims by federal employees can be brought only under § 501, 29 U.S.C. § 791. They have no claims under the ADA. Their claims under the Rehabilitation Act follow the same procedures and support the same equitable remedies as claims by federal employees under Title VII. § 505(a)(1), 29 U.S.C. § 794a(a)(1); 42 U.S.C. § 1981a(a)(2), (c). Damages and the right to jury trial are available for intentional violations of § 501 on the same terms as violations of Title VII. 42 U.S.C. § 1981a(a)(2). No punitive damages, however, are available in private actions against public entities that receive federal funds. 42 U.S.C. § 1981a(b)(1). Neither are damages available for failure to make a reasonable accommodation if the employer has made a good faith effort to provide such an accommodation in consultation with the plaintiff. 42 U.S.C. § 1981a(a)(3).

Only claims against recipients of federal funds can be brought under both the Rehabilitation Act and the ADA. Their claims under § 504, 29 U.S.C. § 794, are enforced according to the procedures and remedies under Title VI of the Civil Rights Act of 1964, which prohibits racial discrimination by recipients of federal funds. Both § 504 and Title VI cover any institution that receives federal funds for any part of its operations. 20 U.S.C. §§ 1682, 1683. Plaintiffs can recover damages and injunctive relief, but only for intentional discrimination, and against state defendants only for compensatory, not punitive, damages. See Alexander v. Sandoval, 532 U.S. 275, 282–93 (2001); Barnes v. Gorman, 536 U.S. 181 (2002).

Attorney's fees also are awarded to the prevailing party in all claims under the Rehabilitation Act. § 505(b), 29 U.S.C. § 794a(b).

2. Claims Under the ADA. Procedures and remedies under the ADA simply follow those under Title VII. § 107(a), 42 U.S.C. § 12117(a). Damages and the right to jury trial are available for intentional violations of Title I of the ADA on the same terms as violations of Title VII. 42 U.S.C. § 1981a(a)(2), (b)(1). As under § 501, no damages can be recovered for failure to make a reasonable accommodation if the employer has made a good faith effort to provide a reasonable accommodation in consultation with the plaintiff. 42 U.S.C. § 1981a(a)(3). For discussion of the substantive and remedial implications of the "interactive process" contemplated by this provision, see Sam Silverman, The ADA Interactive Process: The Employer and Employee's Duty to Work Together to Identify a Reasonable Accommodation Is More Than a Game of Five Card Stud, 77 Neb. L. Rev. 281 (1998).

The only other departure from the procedures and remedies under Title VII involves claims against state employers. Under the Eleventh Amendment, a private plaintiff cannot bring an action for damages against a state. Such claims are allowed only if the state has waived its immunity from suit or Congress has properly abrogated its immunity, usually by enacting legislation to enforce the Fourteenth Amendment. In Board of Trustees of the University of Alabama v. Garrett, 531 U.S. 356 (2001), the Supreme Court held that money damages could not be recovered against a state university under the ADA. The Court reasoned, as it had in a corresponding decision under the ADEA, that Congress could not abrogate the state's immunity by exercising its powers to enforce the Fourteenth Amendment. Disability, like age, is not a category subject to heightened constitutional review and so, according to the Court, does not justify the exercise of congressional power generally to prohibit discrimination on the basis of disability.

These restrictions on suits against the states do not, however, bar all actions against state and local government. As explained in the section on procedures and remedies under the ADEA, the ADA may still be enforced against states and their subdivisions in certain circumstances. First, the Eleventh Amendment does not apply at all to actions brought by the United States. Second, the ADA may be enforced against cities and other organs of local government because these are not "arms of the state" protected by the Eleventh Amendment. Third, the state could waive its immunity to suit, either in a particular case or by general legislation. And fourth, actions can be brought against individual state officers for injunctive relief, and it is possible that the ADA might also subject them to personal liability for damages.

3. **Bibliography.** On remedies and enforcement under the ADA, see The Americans with Disabilities Act: Empirical Perspectives (Samuel Estreicher & Michael Ashley Stein eds., 2008); Samuel R. Bagenstos, The Perversity of Limited Civil Rights Remedies: The Case of "Abusive" ADA Litigation, 54 UCLA L. Rev. 1 (2006); Scott Burris & Kathryn Moss, The Employment Discrimination Provisions of the Americans with Disabilities Act: Implementation and Impact, 25 Hofstra Lab. & Emp. L.J. 1 (2007); Roger C. Hartley, The New Federalism and the ADA: State Sovereign Immunity from Private Damage Suits After *Boerne*, 24 N.Y.U. Rev. L. & Soc. Change 481 (1998); Sharona Hoffman, Settling the Matter: Does Title I of the ADA Work?, 59 Ala. L. Rev. 305 (2008).

STATUTORY APPENDIX

THE CONSTITUTION OF THE UNITED STATES OF AMERICA

AMENDMENT V

No person shall be held to answer for a capital, or otherwise infamous crime, unless on a presentment or indictment of a Grand Jury, except in cases arising in the land or naval forces, or in the Militia, when in actual service in time of War or public danger; nor shall any person be subject for the same offense to be twice put in jeopardy of life or limb; nor shall be compelled in any criminal case to be a witness against himself, nor be deprived of life, liberty, or property, without due process of law, nor shall private property be taken for public use, without just compensation.

AMENDMENT XI

The Judicial power of the United States shall not be construed to extend to any suit in law or equity, commenced or prosecuted against one of the United States by Citizens of another State, or by Citizens or Subjects of any Foreign State.

AMENDMENT XIII

Section 1. Neither slavery nor involuntary servitude, except as a punishment for crime whereof the party shall have been duly convicted, shall exist within the United States, or any place subject to their jurisdiction.

Section 2. Congress shall have power to enforce this article by appropriate legislation.

AMENDMENT XIV

Section 1. All persons born or naturalized in the United States, and subject to the jurisdiction thereof, are citizens of the United States and of the State wherein they reside. No State shall make or enforce any law which shall abridge the privileges or immunities of citizens of the United States; nor shall any State deprive any person of life, liberty, or property, without due process of law; nor deny to any person within its jurisdiction the equal protection of the laws.

Section 2. Representatives shall be apportioned among the several States according to their respective numbers, counting the whole number of persons in each State, excluding Indians not taxed. But when the right to vote at any election for the choice of electors for President and Vice President of the United States, Representatives in Congress, the Executive and Judicial officers of a State, or the members of the Legislature thereof, is denied to any of the male inhabitants of such State, being twenty-one years of age, and citizens of the United States, or in any way abridged, except for participation in rebellion, or other crime, the basis of representation therein shall be reduced in the proportion which the number of such male citizens shall bear to the whole number of male citizens twenty-one years of age in such State.

Section 3. No person shall be a Senator or Representative in Congress, or elector of President and Vice President, or hold any office, civil or military, under the United States, or under any State, who, having previously taken an oath, as a member of Congress, or as an officer of the United States, or as a member of any State legislature, or as an executive or judicial officer of any State, to support the Constitution of the United States, shall have engaged in insurrection or rebellion against the same, or given aid or comfort to the enemies thereof. But Congress may by a vote of two-thirds of each House, remove such disability.

Section 4. The validity of the public debt of the United States, authorized by law, including debts incurred for payment of pensions and bounties for services in suppressing insurrection or rebellion, shall not be questioned. But neither the United States nor any State shall assume or pay any debt or obligation incurred in aid of insurrection or rebellion against the United States, or any claim for the loss or emancipation of any slave; but all such debts, obligations and claims shall be held illegal and void.

Section 5. The Congress shall have power to enforce, by appropriate legislation, the provisions of this article.

RECONSTRUCTION CIVIL RIGHTS ACTS

42 U.S.C. §§ 1981–83, 1985, 1988

§ 1981. Equal rights under the law

(a) Statement of equal rights

All persons within the jurisdiction of the United States shall have the same right in every State and Territory to make and enforce contracts, to sue, be parties, give evidence, and to the full and equal benefit of all laws and proceedings for the security of persons and property as is enjoyed by white citizens, and shall be subject to like punishment, pains, penalties, taxes, licenses, and exactions of every kind, and to no other.

(b) Definition

For purposes of this section, the term "make and enforce contracts" includes the making, performance, modification, and termination of contracts, and the enjoyment of all benefits, privileges, terms, and conditions of the contractual relationship.

(c) Protection against impairment

The rights protected by this section are protected against impairment by nongovernmental discrimination and impairment under color of State law.

§ 1981a. Damages in cases of intentional discrimination in employment

(a) Right of recovery

(1) Civil rights

In an action brought by a complaining party under section 706 or 717 of the Civil Rights Act of 1964 (42 U.S.C. §§ 2000e–5 or 2000e–16) against a respondent who engaged in unlawful intentional discrimination (not an employment practice that is unlawful because of its disparate impact) prohibited under section 703, 704, or 717 of the Act (42 U.S.C. §§ 2000e–2, or 2000e–16 or 2000e–3) and provided that the complaining party cannot recover under section 1981 of this title, the complaining party may recover compensatory and punitive damages as allowed in subsection (b) of this section, in addition to any relief authorized by section 706(g) of the Civil Rights Act of 1964, from the respondent.

(2) Disability

In an action brought by a complaining party under the powers, remedies, and procedures set forth in section 706 or 717 of the Civil Rights Act of 1964 (as provided in section 107(a) of the Americans with Disabilities Act of 1990 [42 U.S.C. § 12117(a)], and section 794a(a)(1) of Title 29, respectively) against a respondent who engaged in unlawful intentional discrimination (not an employment practice that is unlawful because of its disparate impact) under section 791 of Title 29 and the regulations implementing section 791 of Title 29, or who violated the requirements of section 791 of Title 29 or the regulations implementing section 791 of Title 29 concerning the provision of a reasonable accommodation, or section 102 of the Americans with Disabilities Act of 1990 [42 U.S.C. § 12112], or committed a violation of section 102(b)(5) of the Act [42 U.S.C. § 12112(b)(5)], against an individual, the complaining party may recover compensatory and punitive damages as allowed in subsection (b) of this section, in addition to any relief authorized by section 706(g) of the Civil Rights Act of 1964, from the respondent.

(3) Reasonable accommodation and good faith effort

In cases where a discriminatory practice involves the provision of a reasonable accommodation pursuant to section 102(b)(5) of the Americans with Disabilities Act of 1990 or regulations implementing section 791 of Title 29, damages may not be awarded under this section where the covered entity demonstrates good faith efforts, in consultation with the person with the disability who has informed the covered entity that accommodation is needed, to identify and make a reasonable accommodation that would provide such individual with an equally effective opportunity and would not cause an undue hardship on the operation of the business.

(b) Compensatory and punitive damages

(1) Determination of punitive damages

A complaining party may recover punitive damages under this section against a respondent (other than a government, government agency or political subdivision) if the complaining party demonstrates that the respondent engaged in a discriminatory practice or discriminatory practices with malice or with reckless indifference to the federally protected rights of an aggrieved individual.

(2) Exclusions from compensatory damages

Compensatory damages awarded under this section shall not include backpay, interest on backpay, or any other type of relief authorized under section 706(g) of the Civil Rights Act of 1964.

(3) Limitations

The sum of the amount of compensatory damages awarded under this section for future pecuniary losses, emotional pain, suffering, inconvenience, mental anguish, loss of enjoyment of life, and other nonpecuniary losses, and the amount of punitive damages awarded under this section, shall not exceed, for each complaining party—

(A) in the case of a respondent who has more than 14 and fewer than 101 employees in each of 20 or more calendar weeks in the current or preceding calendar year, $50,000;

(B) in the case of a respondent who has more than 100 and fewer than 201 employees in each of 20 or more calendar weeks in the current or preceding calendar year, $100,000; and

(C) in the case of a respondent who has more than 200 and fewer than 501 employees in each of 20 or more calendar weeks in the current or preceding calendar year, $200,000; and

(D) in the case of a respondent who has more than 500 employees in each of 20 or more calendar weeks in the current or preceding calendar year, $300,000.

(4) Construction

Nothing in this section shall be construed to limit the scope of, or the relief available under, section 1981 of this title.

(c) Jury trial

If a complaining party seeks compensatory or punitive damages under this section—

(1) any party may demand a trial by jury; and

(2) the court shall not inform the jury of the limitations described in subsection (b)(3) of this section.

(d) Definitions

As used in this section:

(1) Complaining party

The term "complaining party" means—

(A) in the case of a person seeking to bring an action under subsection (a)(1) of this section, the Equal Employment Opportunity Commission, the Attorney General, or a person who may bring an action or proceeding under title VII of the Civil Rights Act of 1964 [42 U.S.C. § 2000e et seq.]; or

(B) in the case of a person seeking to bring an action under subsection (a)(2) of this section, the Equal Employment Opportunity Commission, the Attorney General, a person who may bring an action or proceeding under section 794a(a)(1) of Title 29, or a person who may bring an action or proceeding under title I of the Americans with Disabilities Act of 1990 [42 U.S.C. § 12101 et seq.].

(2) Discriminatory practice

The term "discriminatory practice" means the discrimination described in paragraph (1), or the discrimination or the violation described in paragraph (2), of subsection (a) of this section.

§ 1982. Property rights of citizens

All citizens of the United States shall have the same right, in every State and Territory, as is enjoyed by white citizens thereof to inherit, purchase, lease, sell, hold, and convey real and personal property.

§ 1983. Civil action for deprivation of rights

Every person who, under color of any statute, ordinance, regulation, custom, or usage, of any State or Territory or the District of Columbia, subjects, or causes to be subjected, any citizen of the United States or other person within the jurisdiction thereof to the deprivation of any rights, privileges, or immunities secured by the Constitution and laws, shall be liable to the party injured in an action at law, suit in equity, or other proper proceeding for redress, except that in any action brought against a judicial officer for an act or omission taken in such officer's judicial capacity, injunctive relief shall not be granted unless a declaratory decree was violated or declaratory relief was unavailable. For the purposes of this section, any Act of Congress applicable exclusively to the District of Columbia shall be considered to be a statute of the District of Columbia.

§ 1985. Conspiracy to interfere with civil rights

(1) Preventing officer from performing duties

If two or more persons in any State or Territory conspire to prevent, by force, intimidation, or threat, any person from accepting or holding any office, trust, or place of confidence under the United States, or from discharging any duties thereof; or to induce by like means any officer of the United States to leave any State, district, or place, where his duties as an officer are required to be performed, or to injure him in his person or property on account of his lawful discharge of the duties of his office, or while engaged in the lawful discharge thereof, or to injure his property so as to molest, interrupt, hinder, or impede him in the discharge of his official duties;

(2) Obstructing justice; intimidating party, witness, or juror

If two or more persons in any State or Territory conspire to deter, by force, intimidation, or threat, any party or witness in any court of the United States from attending such court, or from testifying to any matter pending therein, freely, fully, and truthfully, or to injure such party or witness in his person or property on account of his having so attended or testified, or to influence the verdict, presentment, or indictment of any grand or petit juror in any such court, or to injure such juror in his person or property on account of any verdict, presentment, or indictment lawfully assented to by him, or of his being or having been such juror; or if two or more persons conspire for the purpose of impeding, hindering, obstructing, or defeating, in any manner, the due course of justice in any State or Territory, with intent to deny to any citizen the equal protection of the laws, or to injure him or his property for lawfully enforcing, or attempting to enforce, the right of any person, or class of persons, to the equal protection of the laws;

(3) Depriving persons of rights or privileges

If two or more persons in any State or Territory conspire or go in disguise on the highway or on the premises of another, for the purpose of depriving, either directly or indirectly, any person or class of persons of the equal protection of the laws, or of equal privileges and immunities under the laws; or for the purpose of preventing or hindering the constituted authorities of any State or Territory from giving or securing to all persons within such State or Territory the equal protection of the laws; or if two or more persons conspire to prevent by force, intimidation, or threat, any citizen who is lawfully entitled to vote, from giving his support or advocacy in a legal manner, toward or in favor of the election of any lawfully qualified person as an elector for President or Vice President, or as a Member of Congress of the United States; or to injure any citizen in person or property on account of such support or advocacy; in any case of conspiracy set forth in this section, if one or more persons engaged therein do, or cause to be done, any act in furtherance of the object of such conspiracy, whereby another is injured in his person or property, or deprived of having and exercising any right or privilege of a citizen of the United States, the party so injured or deprived may have an action for the recovery of damages occasioned by such injury or deprivation, against any one or more of the conspirators.

§ 1988. Proceedings in vindication of civil rights; attorney's fees; expert fees

(a) Applicability of statutory and common law

The jurisdiction in civil and criminal matters conferred on the district courts by the provisions of titles 13, 24, and 70 of the Revised Statutes for the protection of all persons in the United States in their civil rights, and for their vindication, shall be exercised and enforced in conformity with the laws of the United States, so far as such laws are suitable to carry the same into effect; but in all cases where they are not adapted to the object, or are deficient in the provisions necessary to furnish suitable remedies and punish offenses against law, the common law, as modified and changed by the constitution and statutes of the State wherein the court having jurisdiction of such civil or criminal cause is held, so far as the same is not inconsistent with the Constitution and laws of the United States, shall be extended to and govern the said courts in the trial and disposition of the cause, and, if it is of a criminal nature, in the infliction of punishment on the party found guilty.

(b) Attorney's fees

In any action or proceeding to enforce a provision of sections 1981, 1981a, 1982, 1983, 1985, and 1986 of this title, title IX of Public Law 92–318 [20 U.S.C. § 1681 et seq.], the Religious Freedom Restoration Act of 1993 [42 U.S.C. § 2000bb et seq.], the Religious Land Use and Institutionalized Persons Act of 2000 [42 U.S.C. § 2000cc et seq.], title VI of the Civil Rights Act of 1964 [42 U.S.C. § 2000d et seq.], or section 13981 of this title, the court, in its discretion, may allow the prevailing party, other than the United States, a reasonable attorney's fee as part of the costs, except that in any action brought against a judicial officer for an act or omission taken in such officer's judicial capacity such officer shall not be held liable for any costs, including attorney's fees, unless such action was clearly in excess of such officer's jurisdiction.

(c) Expert fees

In awarding an attorney's fee under subsection (b) of this section in any action or proceeding to enforce a provision of section 1981 or 1981a of this title, the court, in its discretion, may include expert fees as part of the attorney's fee.

TITLE VII OF THE CIVIL RIGHTS ACT OF 1964

42 U.S.C. § 2000e et seq.

§ 2000e. [§ 701 42 U.S.C. § 2000e]. Definitions

For the purposes of this subchapter—

(a) The term "person" includes one or more individuals, governments, governmental agencies, political subdivisions, labor unions, partnerships, associations, corporations, legal representatives, mutual companies, joint-stock companies, trusts, unincorporated organizations, trustees, trustees in cases under Title 11, or receivers.

(b) The term "employer" means a person engaged in an industry affecting commerce who has fifteen or more employees for each working day in each of twenty or more calendar weeks in the current or preceding calendar year, and any agent of such a person, but such term does not include (1) the United States, a corporation wholly owned by the Government of the United States, an Indian tribe, or any department or agency of the District of Columbia subject by statute to procedures of the competitive service (as defined in section 2102 of Title 5), or (2) a bona fide private membership club (other than a labor organization) which is exempt from taxation under section 501(c) of Title 26, except that during the first year after March 24, 1972, persons having fewer than twenty-five employees (and their agents) shall not be considered employers.

(c) The term "employment agency" means any person regularly undertaking with or without compensation to procure employees for an employer or to procure for employees opportunities to work for an employer and includes an agent of such a person.

(d) The term "labor organization" means a labor organization engaged in an industry affecting commerce, and any agent of such an organization, and includes any organization of any kind, any agency, or employee representation committee, group, association, or plan so engaged in which employees participate and which exists for the purpose, in whole or in part, of dealing with employers concerning grievances, labor disputes, wages, rates of pay, hours, or other terms or conditions of employment, and any conference, general committee, joint or system board, or joint council so engaged which is subordinate to a national or international labor organization.

(e) A labor organization shall be deemed to be engaged in an industry affecting commerce if

(1) it maintains or operates a hiring hall or hiring office which procures employees for an employer or procures for employees opportunities to work for an employer, or

(2) the number of its members (or, where it is a labor organization composed of other labor organizations or their representatives, if the aggregate number of the members of such other labor organization) is

(A) twenty-five or more during the first year after March 24, 1972, or

(B) fifteen or more thereafter, and such labor organization—

(1) is the certified representative of employees under the provisions of the National Labor Relations Act, as amended [29 U.S.C. § 151 et seq.], or the Railway Labor Act, as amended [45 U.S.C. § 151 et seq.];

(2) although not certified, is a national or international labor organization or a local labor organization recognized or acting as the representative of employees of an employer or employers engaged in an industry affecting commerce; or

(3) has chartered a local labor organization or subsidiary body which is representing or actively seeking to represent employees of employers within the meaning of paragraph (1) or (2); or

(4) has been chartered by a labor organization representing or actively seeking to represent employees within the meaning of paragraph (1) or (2) as the local or subordinate body through which such employees may enjoy membership or become affiliated with such labor organization; or

(5) is a conference, general committee, joint or system board, or joint council subordinate to a national or international labor organization, which includes a labor organization engaged in an industry affecting commerce within the meaning of any of the preceding paragraphs of this subsection.

(f) The term "employee" means an individual employed by an employer, except that the term "employee" shall not include any person elected to public office in any State or political subdivision of any State by the qualified voters thereof, or any person chosen by such officer to be on such officer's personal staff, or an appointee on the policy making level or an immediate adviser with respect to the exercise of the constitutional or legal powers of the office. The exemption set forth in the preceding sentence shall not include employees subject to the civil service laws of a State government, governmental agency or political subdivision. With respect to employment in a foreign country, such term includes an individual who is a citizen of the United States.

(g) The term "commerce" means trade, traffic, commerce, transportation, transmission, or communication among the several States; or between a State and any place outside thereof; or within the District of Columbia, or a possession of the United States; or between points in the same State but through a point outside thereof.

(h) The term "industry affecting commerce" means any activity, business, or industry in commerce or in which a labor dispute would hinder or obstruct commerce or the free flow of commerce and includes any activity or industry "affecting commerce" within the meaning of the Labor-Management Reporting and Disclosure Act of 1959 [29 U.S.C. § 401 et seq.], and further includes any governmental industry, business, or activity.

(i) The term "State" includes a State of the United States, the District of Columbia, Puerto Rico, the Virgin Islands, American Samoa, Guam, Wake Island, the Canal Zone, and Outer Continental Shelf lands defined in the Outer Continental Shelf Lands Act [43 U.S.C. § 1331 et seq.].

(j) The term "religion" includes all aspects of religious observance and practice, as well as belief, unless an employer demonstrates that he is unable to reasonably accommodate to an employee's or prospective employee's religious observance or practice without undue hardship on the conduct of the employer's business.

(k) The terms "because of sex" or "on the basis of sex" include, but are not limited to, because of or on the basis of pregnancy, childbirth, or related medical conditions; and women affected by pregnancy, childbirth, or related medical conditions shall be treated the same for all employment-related purposes, including receipt of benefits under fringe benefit programs, as other persons not so affected but similar in their ability or inability to work, and nothing in section 2000e–2(h) of this title shall be interpreted to permit otherwise. This subsection shall not require an employer to pay for health insurance benefits for abortion, except where the life of the mother would be endangered if the fetus were carried to term, or except where medical complications have arisen from an abortion: Provided, That nothing herein shall preclude an employer from providing abortion benefits or otherwise affect bargaining agreements in regard to abortion.

(*l*) The term "complaining party" means the Commission, the Attorney General, or a person who may bring an action or proceeding under this subchapter.

(m) The term "demonstrates" means meets the burdens of production and persuasion.

(n) The term "respondent" means an employer, employment agency, labor organization, joint labor-management committee controlling apprenticeship or other training or retraining program, including an on-the-job training program, or Federal entity subject to section 2000e–16 of this title.

§ 702. [42 U.S.C. § 2000e–1]. Applicability to foreign and religious employment

(a) Inapplicability of subchapter to certain aliens and employees of religious entities

This subchapter shall not apply to an employer with respect to the employment of aliens outside any State, or to a religious corporation, association, educational institution, or society with respect to the employment of individuals of a particular religion to perform work connected with the carrying on by such corporation, association, educational institution, or society of its activities.

(b) Compliance with statute as violative of foreign law

It shall not be unlawful under section 2000e–2 or 2000e–3 of this title for an employer (or a corporation controlled by an employer), labor organization, employment agency, or joint labor-management committee controlling apprenticeship or other training or retraining (including on-the-job training programs) to take any action otherwise prohibited by such section, with respect to an employee in a workplace in a foreign country if compliance with such section would cause such employer (or such corporation), such organization, such agency, or such committee to violate the law of the foreign country in which such workplace is located.

(c) Control of corporation incorporated in foreign country

(1) If an employer controls a corporation whose place of incorporation is a foreign country, any practice prohibited by section 2000e–2 or 2000e–3 of this title engaged in by such corporation shall be presumed to be engaged in by such employer.

(2) Sections 2000e–2 and 2000e–3 of this title shall not apply with respect to the foreign operations of an employer that is a foreign person not controlled by an American employer.

(3) For purposes of this subsection, the determination of whether an employer controls a corporation shall be based on—

(A) the interrelation of operations;

(B) the common management;

(C) the centralized control of labor relations; and

(D) the common ownership or financial control,

of the employer and the corporation.

§ 703. [42 U.S.C. § 2000e–2]. Unlawful employment practices

(a) Employer practices

It shall be an unlawful employment practice for an employer—

(1) to fail or refuse to hire or to discharge any individual, or otherwise to discriminate against any individual with respect to his compensation, terms, conditions, or privileges of employment, because of such individual's race, color, religion, sex, or national origin; or

(2) to limit, segregate, or classify his employees or applicants for employment in any way which would deprive or tend to deprive any individual of employment opportunities or otherwise adversely affect his status as an employee, because of such individual's race, color, religion, sex, or national origin.

(b) Employment agency practices

It shall be an unlawful employment practice for an employment agency to fail or refuse to refer for employment, or otherwise to discriminate against, any individual because of his race, color, religion, sex, or national origin, or to classify or refer for employment any individual on the basis of his race, color, religion, sex, or national origin.

(c) Labor organization practices

It shall be an unlawful employment practice for a labor organization—

(1) to exclude or to expel from its membership, or otherwise to discriminate against, any individual because of his race, color, religion, sex, or national origin;

(2) to limit, segregate, or classify its membership or applicants for membership, or to classify or fail or refuse to refer for employment any individual, in any way which would deprive or tend to deprive any individual of employment opportunities, or would limit such employment opportunities or otherwise adversely affect his status as an employee or as an applicant for employment, because of such individual's race, color, religion, sex, or national origin; or

(3) to cause or attempt to cause an employer to discriminate against an individual in violation of this section.

(d) Training programs

It shall be an unlawful employment practice for any employer, labor organization, or joint labor-management committee controlling apprenticeship or other training or retraining, including on-the-job training programs to discriminate against any individual because of his race, color, religion, sex, or national origin in admission to, or employment in, any program established to provide apprenticeship or other training.

(e) Businesses or enterprises with personnel qualified on basis of religion, sex, or national origin; educational institutions with personnel of particular religion

Notwithstanding any other provision of this subchapter,

(1) it shall not be an unlawful employment practice for an employer to hire and employ employees, for an employment agency to classify, or refer for employment any individual, for a labor organization to classify its membership or to classify or refer for employment any individual, or for an employer, labor organization, or joint labor-management committee controlling apprenticeship or other training or retraining programs to admit or employ any individual in any such program, on the basis of his religion, sex, or national origin in those certain instances where religion, sex, or national origin is a bona fide occupational qualification reasonably necessary to the normal operation of that particular business or enterprise, and

(2) it shall not be an unlawful employment practice for a school, college, university, or other educational institution or institution of learning to hire and employ employees of a particular religion if such school, college, university, or other educational institution or institution of learning is, in whole or in substantial part, owned, supported, controlled, or managed by a particular religion or by a particular

religious corporation, association, or society, or if the curriculum of such school, college, university, or other educational institution or institution of learning is directed toward the propagation of a particular religion.

(f) Members of Communist Party or Communist-action or Communist-front organizations

As used in this subchapter, the phrase "unlawful employment practice" shall not be deemed to include any action or measure taken by an employer, labor organization, joint labor-management committee, or employment agency with respect to an individual who is a member of the Communist Party of the United States or of any other organization required to register as a Communist-action or Communist-front organization by final order of the Subversive Activities Control Board pursuant to the Subversive Activities Control Act of 1950 [50 U.S.C. § 781 et seq.].

(g) National security

Notwithstanding any other provision of this subchapter, it shall not be an unlawful employment practice for an employer to fail or refuse to hire and employ any individual for any position, for an employer to discharge any individual from any position, or for an employment agency to fail or refuse to refer any individual for employment in any position, or for a labor organization to fail or refuse to refer any individual for employment in any position, if—

(1) the occupancy of such position, or access to the premises in or upon which any part of the duties of such position is performed or is to be performed, is subject to any requirement imposed in the interest of the national security of the United States under any security program in effect pursuant to or administered under any statute of the United States or any Executive order of the President; and

(2) such individual has not fulfilled or has ceased to fulfill that requirement.

(h) Seniority or merit system; quantity or quality of production; ability tests; compensation based on sex and authorized by minimum wage provisions

Notwithstanding any other provision of this subchapter, it shall not be an unlawful employment practice for an employer to apply different standards of compensation, or different terms, conditions, or privileges of employment pursuant to a bona fide seniority or merit system, or a system which measures earnings by quantity or quality of production or to employees who work in different locations, provided that such differences are not the result of an intention to discriminate because of race, color, religion, sex, or national origin, nor shall it be an unlawful employment practice for an employer to give and to act upon the results of any professionally developed ability test provided that such test, its administration or action upon the results is not designed, intended or used to discriminate because of race, color, religion, sex or national origin. It shall not be an unlawful employment practice under this subchapter for any employer to differentiate upon the basis of sex in determining the amount of the wages or compensation paid or to be paid to employees of such employer if such differentiation is authorized by the provisions of section 206(d) of Title 29.

(i) Businesses or enterprises extending preferential treatment to Indians

Nothing contained in this subchapter shall apply to any business or enterprise on or near an Indian reservation with respect to any publicly announced employment practice of such business or enterprise under which a preferential treatment is given to any individual because he is an Indian living on or near a reservation.

(j) Preferential treatment not to be granted on account of existing number or percentage imbalance

Nothing contained in this subchapter shall be interpreted to require any employer, employment agency, labor organization, or joint labor-management committee subject to this subchapter to grant preferential treatment to any individual or to any group because of the race, color, religion, sex, or national origin of such individual or group on account of an imbalance which may exist with respect to the total number or percentage of persons of any race, color, religion, sex, or national origin employed by any employer, referred or classified for employment by any employment agency or labor organization, admitted to membership or classified by any labor organization, or admitted to, or employed in, any apprenticeship or other training program, in comparison with the total number or percentage of persons of such race, color, religion, sex, or national origin in any community, State, section, or other area, or in the available work force in any community, State, section, or other area.

(k) Burden of proof in disparate impact cases

(1) (A) An unlawful employment practice based on disparate impact is established under this subchapter only if—

(i) a complaining party demonstrates that a respondent uses a particular employment practice that causes a disparate impact on the basis of race, color, religion, sex, or national origin and the respondent fails to demonstrate that the challenged practice is job related for the position in question and consistent with business necessity; or

(ii) the complaining party makes the demonstration described in subparagraph (C) with respect to an alternative employment practice and the respondent refuses to adopt such alternative employment practice.

(B) (i) With respect to demonstrating that a particular employment practice causes a disparate impact as described in subparagraph (A)(i), the complaining party shall demonstrate that each particular challenged employment practice causes a disparate impact, except that if the complaining party can demonstrate to the court that the elements of a respondent's decisionmaking process are not capable of separation for analysis, the decisionmaking process may be analyzed as one employment practice.

(ii) If the respondent demonstrates that a specific employment practice does not cause the disparate impact, the respondent shall not be required to demonstrate that such practice is required by business necessity.

(C) The demonstration referred to by subparagraph (A)(ii) shall be in accordance with the law as it existed on June 4, 1989, with respect to the concept of "alternative employment practice."

(2) A demonstration that an employment practice is required by business necessity may not be used as a defense against a claim of intentional discrimination under this subchapter.

(3) Notwithstanding any other provision of this subchapter, a rule barring the employment of an individual who currently and knowingly uses or possesses a controlled substance, as defined in schedules I and II of section 102(6) of the Controlled Substances Act (21 U.S.C. § 802(6)), other than the use or possession of a drug taken under the supervision of a licensed health care professional, or any other use or possession authorized by the Controlled Substances Act [21 U.S.C. § 801 et seq.] or any other provision of Federal law, shall be considered an unlawful employment practice under this subchapter only if such rule is adopted or applied with an intent to discriminate because of race, color, religion, sex, or national origin.

(*l*) Prohibition of discriminatory use of test scores

It shall be an unlawful employment practice for a respondent, in connection with the selection or referral of applicants or candidates for employment or promotion, to adjust the scores of, use different cutoff scores for, or otherwise alter the results of, employment related tests on the basis of race, color, religion, sex, or national origin.

(m) Impermissible consideration of race, color, religion, sex, or national origin in employment practices

Except as otherwise provided in this subchapter, an unlawful employment practice is established when the complaining party demonstrates that race, color, religion, sex, or national origin was a motivating factor for any employment practice, even though other factors also motivated the practice.

(n) Resolution of challenges to employment practices implementing litigated or consent judgments or orders

(1) (A) Notwithstanding any other provision of law, and except as provided in paragraph (2), an employment practice that implements and is within the scope of a litigated or consent judgment or order that

resolves a claim of employment discrimination under the Constitution or Federal civil rights laws may not be challenged under the circumstances described in subparagraph (B).

(B) A practice described in subparagraph (A) may not be challenged in a claim under the Constitution or Federal civil rights laws—

(i) by a person who, prior to the entry of the judgment or order described in subparagraph (A), had—

(I) actual notice of the proposed judgment or order sufficient to apprise such person that such judgment or order might adversely affect the interests and legal rights of such person and that an opportunity was available to present objections to such judgment or order by a future date certain; and

(II) a reasonable opportunity to present objections to such judgment or order; or

(ii) by a person whose interests were adequately represented by another person who had previously challenged the judgment or order on the same legal grounds and with a similar factual situation, unless there has been an intervening change in law or fact.

(2) Nothing in this subsection shall be construed to—

(A) alter the standards for intervention under rule 24 of the Federal Rules of Civil Procedure or apply to the rights of parties who have successfully intervened pursuant to such rule in the proceeding in which the parties intervened;

(B) apply to the rights of parties to the action in which a litigated or consent judgment or order was entered, or of members of a class represented or sought to be represented in such action, or of members of a group on whose behalf relief was sought in such action by the Federal Government;

(C) prevent challenges to a litigated or consent judgment or order on the ground that such judgment or order was obtained through collusion or fraud, or is transparently invalid or was entered by a court lacking subject matter jurisdiction; or

(D) authorize or permit the denial to any person of the due process of law required by the Constitution.

(3) Any action not precluded under this subsection that challenges an employment consent judgment or order described in paragraph (1) shall be brought in the court, and if possible before the judge, that entered such judgment or order. Nothing in this subsection shall preclude a transfer of such action pursuant to section 1404 of Title 28.

§ 704. [42 U.S.C. § 2000e–3]. Other unlawful employment practices

(a) Discrimination for making charges, testifying, assisting, or participating in enforcement proceedings

It shall be an unlawful employment practice for an employer to discriminate against any of his employees or applicants for employment, for an employment agency, or joint labor-management committee controlling apprenticeship or other training or retraining, including on-the-job training programs, to discriminate against any individual, or for a labor organization to discriminate against any member thereof or applicant for membership, because he has opposed any practice made an unlawful employment practice by this subchapter, or because he has made a charge, testified, assisted, or participated in any manner in an investigation, proceeding, or hearing under this subchapter.

(b) Printing or publication of notices or advertisements indicating prohibited preference, limitation, specification, or discrimination; occupational qualification exception

It shall be an unlawful employment practice for an employer, labor organization, employment agency, or joint labor-management committee controlling apprenticeship or other training or retraining, including on-the-job training programs, to print or publish or cause to be printed or published any notice or advertisement relating to employment by such an employer or membership in or any classification or referral for employment by such a labor organization, or relating to any classification or referral for employment by such an employment agency, or relating to admission to, or employment in, any program established to provide apprenticeship or other training by such a joint labor-management committee, indicating any preference, limitation, specification, or discrimination, based on race, color, religion, sex, or national origin, except that such a notice or advertisement may indicate a preference, limitation, specification, or discrimination based on religion, sex, or national origin when religion, sex, or national origin is a bona fide occupational qualification for employment.

§ 705. [42 U.S.C. § 2000e–4]. Equal Employment Opportunity Commission

(a) Creation; composition; political representation; appointment; term; vacancies; Chairman and Vice Chairman; duties of Chairman; appointment of personnel; compensation of personnel

There is hereby created a Commission to be known as the Equal Employment Opportunity Commission, which shall be composed of five members, not more than three of whom shall be members of the same political party. Members of the Commission shall be appointed by the President by and with the advice and consent of the Senate for a term of five years. Any individual chosen to fill a vacancy shall be appointed only for the unexpired term of the member whom he shall succeed, and all members of the Commission shall continue to serve until their successors are appointed and qualified, except that no such member of the Commission shall continue to serve (1) for more than sixty days when the Congress is in session unless a nomination to fill such vacancy shall have been submitted to the Senate, or (2) after the adjournment sine die of the session of the Senate in which such nomination was submitted. The President shall designate one member to serve as Chairman of the Commission, and one member to serve as Vice Chairman. The Chairman shall be responsible on behalf of the Commission for the administrative operations of the Commission, and, except as provided in subsection (b) of this section, shall appoint, in accordance with the provisions of Title 5 governing appointments in the competitive service, such officers, agents, attorneys, administrative law judges, and employees as he deems necessary to assist it in the performance of its functions and to fix their compensation in accordance with the provisions of chapter 51 and subchapter III of chapter 53 of Title 5, relating to classification and General Schedule pay rates: Provided, That assignment, removal, and compensation of administrative law judges shall be in accordance with sections 3105, 3344, 5372, and 7521 of Title 5.

(b) General Counsel; appointment; term; duties; representation by attorneys and Attorney General

(1) There shall be a General Counsel of the Commission appointed by the President, by and with the advice and consent of the Senate, for a term of four years. The General Counsel shall have responsibility for the conduct of litigation as provided in sections 2000e–5 and 2000e–6 of this title. The General Counsel shall have such other duties as the Commission may prescribe or as may be provided by law and shall concur with the Chairman of the Commission on the appointment and supervision of regional attorneys. The General Counsel of the Commission on the effective date of this subchapter shall continue in such position and perform the functions specified in this subsection until a successor is appointed and qualified.

(2) Attorneys appointed under this section may, at the direction of the Commission, appear for and represent the Commission in any case in court, provided that the Attorney General shall conduct all litigation to which the Commission is a party in the Supreme Court pursuant to this subchapter.

(c) Exercise of powers during vacancy; quorum

A vacancy in the Commission shall not impair the right of the remaining members to exercise all the powers of the Commission and three members thereof shall constitute a quorum.

(d) Seal; judicial notice

The Commission shall have an official seal which shall be judicially noticed.

(e) Reports to Congress and the President

The Commission shall at the close of each fiscal year report to the Congress and to the President concerning the action it has taken and the moneys it has disbursed. It shall make such further reports on the cause of and means of eliminating discrimination and such recommendations for further legislation as may appear desirable.

(f) Principal and other offices

The principal office of the Commission shall be in or near the District of Columbia, but it may meet or exercise any or all its powers at any other place. The Commission may establish such regional or State offices as it deems necessary to accomplish the purpose of this subchapter.

(g) Powers of Commission

The Commission shall have power—

(1) to cooperate with and, with their consent, utilize regional, State, local, and other agencies, both public and private, and individuals;

(2) to pay to witnesses whose depositions are taken or who are summoned before the Commission or any of its agents the same witness and mileage fees as are paid to witnesses in the courts of the United States;

(3) to furnish to persons subject to this subchapter such technical assistance as they may request to further their compliance with this subchapter or an order issued thereunder;

(4) upon the request of (i) any employer, whose employees or some of them, or (ii) any labor organization, whose members or some of them, refuse or threaten to refuse to cooperate in effectuating the provisions of this subchapter, to assist in such effectuation by conciliation or such other remedial action as is provided by this subchapter;

(5) to make such technical studies as are appropriate to effectuate the purposes and policies of this subchapter and to make the results of such studies available to the public;

(6) to intervene in a civil action brought under section 2000e–5 of this title by an aggrieved party against a respondent other than a government, governmental agency or political subdivision.

(h) Cooperation with other departments and agencies in performance of educational or promotional activities; outreach activities

(1) The Commission shall, in any of its educational or promotional activities, cooperate with other departments and agencies in the performance of such educational and promotional activities.

(2) In exercising its powers under this subchapter, the Commission shall carry out educational and outreach activities (including dissemination of information in languages other than English) targeted to—

(A) individuals who historically have been victims of employment discrimination and have not been equitably served by the Commission; and

(B) individuals on whose behalf the Commission has authority to enforce any other law prohibiting employment discrimination, concerning rights and obligations under this subchapter or such law, as the case may be.

(i) Personnel subject to political activity restrictions

All officers, agents, attorneys, and employees of the Commission shall be subject to the provisions of section 7324 of Title 5, notwithstanding any exemption contained in such section.

(j) Technical Assistance Training Institute

(1) The Commission shall establish a Technical Assistance Training Institute, through which the Commission shall provide technical assistance and training regarding the laws and regulations enforced by the Commission.

(2) An employer or other entity covered under this subchapter shall not be excused from compliance with the requirements of this subchapter because of any failure to receive technical assistance under this subsection.

(3) There are authorized to be appropriated to carry out this subsection such sums as may be necessary for fiscal year 1992.

(k) EEOC Education, Technical Assistance, and Training Revolving Fund

(1) There is hereby established in the Treasury of the United States a revolving fund to be known as the "EEOC Education, Technical Assistance, and Training Revolving Fund" (hereinafter in this subsection referred to as the "Fund") and to pay the cost (including administrative and personnel expenses) of providing education, technical assistance, and training relating to laws administered by the Commission. Monies in the Fund shall be available without fiscal year limitation to the Commission for such purposes.

(2) (A) The Commission shall charge fees in accordance with the provisions of this paragraph to offset the costs of education, technical assistance, and training provided with monies in the Fund. Such fees for any education, technical assistance, or training—

(i) shall be imposed on a uniform basis on persons and entities receiving such education, assistance, or training,

(ii) shall not exceed the cost of providing such education, assistance, and training, and

(iii) with respect to each person or entity receiving such education, assistance, or training, shall bear a reasonable relationship to the cost of providing such education, assistance, or training to such person or entity.

(B) Fees received under subparagraph (A) shall be deposited in the Fund by the Commission.

(C) The Commission shall include in each report made under subsection (e) of this section information with respect to the operation of the Fund, including information, presented in the aggregate, relating to—

(i) the number of persons and entities to which the Commission provided education, technical assistance, or training with monies in the Fund, in the fiscal year for which such report is prepared,

(ii) the cost to the Commission to provide such education, technical assistance, or training to such persons and entities, and

(iii) the amount of any fees received by the Commission from such persons and entities for such education, technical assistance, or training.

(3) The Secretary of the Treasury shall invest the portion of the Fund not required to satisfy current expenditures from the Fund, as determined by the Commission, in obligations of the United States or obligations guaranteed as to principal by the United States. Investment proceeds shall be deposited in the Fund.

(4) There is hereby transferred to the Fund $1,000,000 from the Salaries and Expenses appropriation of the Commission.

§ 706. [42 U.S.C. § 2000e–5]. Enforcement provisions

(a) Power of Commission to prevent unlawful employment practices

The Commission is empowered, as hereinafter provided, to prevent any person from engaging in any unlawful employment practice as set forth in section 2000e–2 or 2000e–3 of this title.

(b) Charges by persons aggrieved or member of Commission of unlawful employment practices by employers, etc.; filing; allegations; notice to respondent; contents of notice; investigation by Commission; contents of charges; prohibition on disclosure of charges; determination of reasonable cause; conference, conciliation, and persuasion for elimination of unlawful practices; prohibition on disclosure of informal endeavors to end unlawful practices; use of evidence in subsequent proceedings; penalties for disclosure of information; time for determination of reasonable cause

Whenever a charge is filed by or on behalf of a person claiming to be aggrieved, or by a member of the Commission, alleging that an employer, employment agency, labor organization, or joint labor-management committee controlling apprenticeship or other training or retraining, including on-the-job training programs, has engaged in an unlawful employment practice, the Commission shall serve a notice of the charge (including the date, place and circumstances of the alleged unlawful employment practice) on such employer, employment agency, labor organization, or joint labor-management committee (hereinafter referred to as the "respondent") within ten days, and shall make an investigation thereof. Charges shall be in writing under oath or affirmation and shall contain such information and be in such form as the Commission requires. Charges shall not be made public by the Commission. If the Commission determines after such investigation that there is not reasonable cause to believe that the charge is true, it shall dismiss the charge and promptly notify the person claiming to be aggrieved and the respondent of its action. In determining whether reasonable cause exists, the Commission shall accord substantial weight to final findings and orders made by State or local authorities in proceedings commenced under State or local law pursuant to the requirements of subsections (c) and (d) of this section. If the Commission determines after such investigation that there is reasonable cause to believe that the charge is true, the Commission shall endeavor to eliminate any such alleged unlawful employment practice by informal methods of conference, conciliation, and persuasion. Nothing said or done during and as a part of such informal endeavors may be made public by the Commission, its officers or employees, or used as evidence in a subsequent proceeding without the written consent of the persons concerned. Any person who makes public information in violation of this subsection shall be fined not more than $1,000 or imprisoned for not more than one year, or both. The Commission shall make its determination on reasonable cause as promptly as possible and, so far as practicable, not later than one hundred and twenty days from the filing of the charge or, where applicable under subsection (c) or (d) of this section, from the date upon which the Commission is authorized to take action with respect to the charge.

(c) State or local enforcement proceedings; notification of State or local authority; time for filing charges with Commission; commencement of proceedings

In the case of an alleged unlawful employment practice occurring in a State, or political subdivision of a State, which has a State or local law prohibiting the unlawful employment practice alleged and establishing or authorizing a State or local authority to grant or seek relief from such practice or to institute criminal proceedings with respect thereto upon receiving notice thereof, no charge may be filed under subsection (a) of this section by the person aggrieved before the expiration of sixty days after proceedings have been commenced under the State or local law, unless such proceedings have been earlier terminated, provided that such sixty-day period shall be extended to one hundred and twenty days during the first year after the effective date of such State or local law. If any requirement for the commencement of such proceedings is imposed by a State or local authority other than a requirement of the filing of a written and signed statement of the facts upon which the proceeding is based, the proceeding shall be deemed to have been commenced for the purposes of this subsection at the time such statement is sent by registered mail to the appropriate State or local authority.

(d) State or local enforcement proceedings; notification of State or local authority; time for action on charges by Commission

In the case of any charge filed by a member of the Commission alleging an unlawful employment practice occurring in a State or political subdivision of a State which has a State or local law prohibiting the practice alleged and establishing or authorizing a State or local authority to grant or seek relief from such practice or to institute criminal proceedings with respect thereto upon receiving notice thereof, the Commission shall, before taking any action with respect to such charge, notify the appropriate State or local officials and, upon request, afford them a reasonable time, but not less than sixty days (provided that such sixty-day period shall be extended to one hundred and twenty days during the first year after the effective day of such State or local law), unless a shorter period is requested, to act under such State or local law to remedy the practice alleged.

(e) Time for filing charges; time for service of notice of charge on respondent; filing of charge by Commission with State or local agency; seniority system

(1) A charge under this section shall be filed within one hundred and eighty days after the alleged unlawful employment practice occurred and notice of the charge (including the date, place and circumstances of the alleged unlawful employment practice) shall be served upon the person against whom such charge is made within ten days thereafter, except that in a case of an unlawful employment practice with respect to which the person aggrieved has initially instituted proceedings with a State or local agency with authority to grant or seek relief from such practice or to institute criminal proceedings with respect thereto upon receiving notice thereof, such charge shall be filed by or on behalf of the person aggrieved within three hundred days after the alleged unlawful employment practice occurred, or within thirty days after receiving notice that the State or local agency has terminated the proceedings under the State or local law, whichever is earlier, and a copy of such charge shall be filed by the Commission with the State or local agency.

(2) For purposes of this section, an unlawful employment practice occurs, with respect to a seniority system that has been adopted for an intentionally discriminatory purpose in violation of this subchapter (whether or not that discriminatory purpose is apparent on the face of the seniority provision), when the seniority system is adopted, when an individual becomes subject to the seniority system, or when a person

aggrieved is injured by the application of the seniority system or provision of the system.

(3) (A) For purposes of this section, an unlawful employment practice occurs, with respect to discrimination in compensation in violation of this subchapter, when a discriminatory compensation decision or other practice is adopted, when an individual becomes subject to a discriminatory compensation decision or other practice, or when an individual is affected by application of a discriminatory compensation decision or other practice, including each time wages, benefits, or other compensation is paid, resulting in whole or in part from such a decision or other practice.

(B) In addition to any relief authorized by section 1981a of this title, liability may accrue and an aggrieved person may obtain relief as provided in subsection (g)(1), including recovery of back pay for up to two years preceding the filing of the charge, where the unlawful employment practices that have occurred during the charge filing period are similar or related to unlawful employment practices with regard to discrimination in compensation that occurred outside the time for filing a charge.

(f) Civil action by Commission, Attorney General, or person aggrieved; preconditions; procedure; appointment of attorney; payment of fees, costs, or security; intervention; stay of Federal proceedings; action for appropriate temporary or preliminary relief pending final disposition of charge; jurisdiction and venue of United States courts; designation of judge to hear and determine case; assignment of case for hearing; expedition of case; appointment of master

(1) If within thirty days after a charge is filed with the Commission or within thirty days after expiration of any period of reference under subsection (c) or (d) of this section, the Commission has been unable to secure from the respondent a conciliation agreement acceptable to the Commission, the Commission may bring a civil action against any respondent not a government, governmental agency, or political subdivision named in the charge. In the case of a respondent which is a government, governmental agency, or political subdivision, if the Commission has been unable to secure from the respondent a conciliation agreement acceptable to the Commission, the Commission shall take no further action and shall refer the case to the Attorney General who may bring a civil action against such respondent in the appropriate United States district court. The person or persons aggrieved shall have the right to intervene in a civil action brought by the Commission or the Attorney General in a case involving a government, governmental agency, or political subdivision. If a charge filed with the Commission pursuant to subsection (b) of this section is dismissed by the Commission, or if within one hundred and eighty days from the filing of such charge or the expiration of any period of reference under subsection (c) or (d) of this

section, whichever is later, the Commission has not filed a civil action under this section or the Attorney General has not filed a civil action in a case involving a government, governmental agency, or political subdivision, or the Commission has not entered into a conciliation agreement to which the person aggrieved is a party, the Commission, or the Attorney General in a case involving a government, governmental agency, or political subdivision, shall so notify the person aggrieved and within ninety days after the giving of such notice a civil action may be brought against the respondent named in the charge (A) by the person claiming to be aggrieved or (B) if such charge was filed by a member of the Commission, by any person whom the charge alleges was aggrieved by the alleged unlawful employment practice. Upon application by the complainant and in such circumstances as the court may deem just, the court may appoint an attorney for such complainant and may authorize the commencement of the action without the payment of fees, costs, or security. Upon timely application, the court may, in its discretion, permit the Commission, or the Attorney General in a case involving a government, governmental agency, or political subdivision, to intervene in such civil action upon certification that the case is of general public importance. Upon request, the court may, in its discretion, stay further proceedings for not more than sixty days pending the termination of State or local proceedings described in subsection (c) or (d) of this section or further efforts of the Commission to obtain voluntary compliance.

(2) Whenever a charge is filed with the Commission and the Commission concludes on the basis of a preliminary investigation that prompt judicial action is necessary to carry out the purposes of this subchapter, the Commission, or the Attorney General in a case involving a government, governmental agency, or political subdivision, may bring an action for appropriate temporary or preliminary relief pending final disposition of such charge. Any temporary restraining order or other order granting preliminary or temporary relief shall be issued in accordance with rule 65 of the Federal Rules of Civil Procedure. It shall be the duty of a court having jurisdiction over proceedings under this section to assign cases for hearing at the earliest practicable date and to cause such cases to be in every way expedited.

(3) Each United States district court and each United States court of a place subject to the jurisdiction of the United States shall have jurisdiction of actions brought under this subchapter. Such an action may be brought in any judicial district in the State in which the unlawful employment practice is alleged to have been committed, in the judicial district in which the employment records relevant to such practice are maintained and administered, or in the judicial district in which the aggrieved person would have worked but for the alleged unlawful employment practice, but if the respondent is not found within any such district, such an action may be brought within the judicial district in which the respondent has his principal office. For purposes of sections

1404 and 1406 of Title 28, the judicial district in which the respondent has his principal office shall in all cases be considered a district in which the action might have been brought.

(4) It shall be the duty of the chief judge of the district (or in his absence, the acting chief judge) in which the case is pending immediately to designate a judge in such district to hear and determine the case. In the event that no judge in the district is available to hear and determine the case, the chief judge of the district, or the acting chief judge, as the case may be, shall certify this fact to the chief judge of the circuit (or in his absence, the acting chief judge) who shall then designate a district or circuit judge of the circuit to hear and determine the case.

(5) It shall be the duty of the judge designated pursuant to this subsection to assign the case for hearing at the earliest practicable date and to cause the case to be in every way expedited. If such judge has not scheduled the case for trial within one hundred and twenty days after issue has been joined, that judge may appoint a master pursuant to rule 53 of the Federal Rules of Civil Procedure.

(g) Injunctions; appropriate affirmative action; equitable relief; accrual of back pay; reduction of back pay; limitations on judicial orders

(1) If the court finds that the respondent has intentionally engaged in or is intentionally engaging in an unlawful employment practice charged in the complaint, the court may enjoin the respondent from engaging in such unlawful employment practice, and order such affirmative action as may be appropriate, which may include, but is not limited to, reinstatement or hiring of employees, with or without back pay (payable by the employer, employment agency, or labor organization, as the case may be, responsible for the unlawful employment practice), or any other equitable relief as the court deems appropriate. Back pay liability shall not accrue from a date more than two years prior to the filing of a charge with the Commission. Interim earnings or amounts earnable with reasonable diligence by the person or persons discriminated against shall operate to reduce the back pay otherwise allowable.

(2) (A) No order of the court shall require the admission or reinstatement of an individual as a member of a union, or the hiring, reinstatement, or promotion of an individual as an employee, or the payment to him of any back pay, if such individual was refused admission, suspended, or expelled, or was refused employment or advancement or was suspended or discharged for any reason other than discrimination on account of race, color, religion, sex, or national origin or in violation of section 2000e–3(a) of this title.

(B) On a claim in which an individual proves a violation under section 2000e–2(m) of this title and a respondent demonstrates that the respondent would have taken the same action in the absence of the impermissible motivating factor, the court—

(i) may grant declaratory relief, injunctive relief (except as provided in clause (ii)), and attorney's fees and costs demonstrated to be directly attributable only to the pursuit of a claim under section 2000e–2(m) of this title; and

(ii) shall not award damages or issue an order requiring any admission, reinstatement, hiring, promotion, or payment, described in subparagraph (A).

(h) Provisions of chapter 6 of Title 29 not applicable to civil actions for prevention of unlawful practices

The provisions of chapter 6 of Title 29 shall not apply with respect to civil actions brought under this section.

(i) Proceedings by Commission to compel compliance with judicial orders

In any case in which an employer, employment agency, or labor organization fails to comply with an order of a court issued in a civil action brought under this section, the Commission may commence proceedings to compel compliance with such order.

(j) Appeals

Any civil action brought under this section and any proceedings brought under subsection (i) of this section shall be subject to appeal as provided in sections 1291 and 1292, Title 28.

(k) Attorney's fee; liability of Commission and United States for costs

In any action or proceeding under this subchapter the court, in its discretion, may allow the prevailing party, other than the Commission or the United States, a reasonable attorney's fee (including expert fees) as part of the costs, and the Commission and the United States shall be liable for costs the same as a private person.

§ 707. [42 U.S.C. § 2000e–6]. Civil actions by the Attorney General

(a) Complaint

Whenever the Attorney General has reasonable cause to believe that any person or group of persons is engaged in a pattern or practice of resistance to the full enjoyment of any of the rights secured by this subchapter, and that the pattern or practice is of such a nature and is intended to deny the full exercise of the rights herein described, the Attorney General may bring a civil action in the appropriate district court of the United States by filing with it a complaint (1) signed by him (or in his absence the Acting Attorney General), (2) setting forth facts pertaining to such pattern or practice, and (3) requesting such relief, including an application for a permanent or temporary injunction, restraining order or other order against the person or persons responsible for such pattern or practice, as he deems necessary to insure the full enjoyment of the rights herein described.

(b) Jurisdiction; three—judge district court for cases of general public importance: hearing, determination, expedition of action, review by Supreme Court; single judge district court: hearing, determination, expedition of action

The district courts of the United States shall have and shall exercise jurisdiction of proceedings instituted pursuant to this section, and in any such proceeding the Attorney General may file with the clerk of such court a request that a court of three judges be convened to hear and determine the case. Such request by the Attorney General shall be accompanied by a certificate that, in his opinion, the case is of general public importance. A copy of the certificate and request for a three—judge court shall be immediately furnished by such clerk to the chief judge of the circuit (or in his absence, the presiding circuit judge of the circuit) in which the case is pending. Upon receipt of such request it shall be the duty of the chief judge of the circuit or the presiding circuit judge, as the case may be, to designate immediately three judges in such circuit, of whom at least one shall be a circuit judge and another of whom shall be a district judge of the court in which the proceeding was instituted, to hear and determine such case, and it shall be the duty of the judges so designated to assign the case for hearing at the earliest practicable date, to participate in the hearing and determination thereof, and to cause the case to be in every way expedited. An appeal from the final judgment of such court will lie to the Supreme Court.

In the event the Attorney General fails to file such a request in any such proceeding, it shall be the duty of the chief judge of the district (or in his absence, the acting chief judge) in which the case is pending immediately to designate a judge in such district to hear and determine the case. In the event that no judge in the district is available to hear and determine the case, the chief judge of the district, or the acting chief judge, as the case may be, shall certify this fact to the chief judge of the circuit (or in his absence, the acting chief judge) who shall then designate a district or circuit judge of the circuit to hear and determine the case.

It shall be the duty of the judge designated pursuant to this section to assign the case for hearing at the earliest practicable date and to cause the case to be in every way expedited.

(c) Transfer of functions, etc., to Commission; effective date; prerequisite to transfer; execution of functions by Commission

Effective two years after March 24, 1972, the functions of the Attorney General under this section shall be transferred to the Commission, together with such personnel, property, records, and unexpended balances of appropriations, allocations, and other funds employed, used, held, available, or to be made available in connection with such functions unless the President submits, and neither House of Congress vetoes, a reorganization plan pursuant to chapter 9 of Title 5, inconsistent with the provisions of this subsection. The Commission shall carry out such functions in accordance with subsections (d) and (e) of this section.

(d) Transfer of functions, etc., not to affect suits commenced pursuant to this section prior to date of transfer

Upon the transfer of functions provided for in subsection (c) of this section, in all suits commenced pursuant to this section prior to the date of such transfer, proceedings shall continue without abatement, all court orders and decrees shall remain in effect, and the Commission shall be substituted as a party for the United States of America, the Attorney General, or the Acting Attorney General, as appropriate.

(e) Investigation and action by Commission pursuant to filing of charge of discrimination; procedure

Subsequent to March 24, 1972, the Commission shall have authority to investigate and act on a charge of a pattern or practice of discrimination, whether filed by or on behalf of a person claiming to be aggrieved or by a member of the Commission. All such actions shall be conducted in accordance with the procedures set forth in section 2000e–5 of this title.

§ 708. [42 U.S.C. § 2000e–7]. Effect on State laws

Nothing in this subchapter shall be deemed to exempt or relieve any person from any liability, duty, penalty, or punishment provided by any present or future law of any State or political subdivision of a State, other than any such law which purports to require or permit the doing of any act which would be an unlawful employment practice under this subchapter.

§ 709. [42 U.S.C. § 2000e–8]. Investigations

(a) Examination and copying of evidence related to unlawful employment practices

In connection with any investigation of a charge filed under section 2000e–5 of this title, the Commission or its designated representative shall at all reasonable times have access to, for the purposes of examination, and the right to copy any evidence of any person being investigated or proceeded against that relates to unlawful employment practices covered by this subchapter and is relevant to the charge under investigation.

(b) Cooperation with State and local agencies administering State fair employment practices laws; participation in and contribution to research and other projects; utilization of services; payment in advance or reimbursement; agreements and rescission of agreements

The Commission may cooperate with State and local agencies charged with the administration of State fair employment practices laws and, with the consent of such agencies, may, for the purpose of carrying out its functions and duties under this subchapter and within the limitation of funds appropriated specifically for such purpose, engage in and contribute to the cost of research and other projects of mutual interest undertaken by such agencies, and utilize the services of such agencies and their employees, and, notwithstanding any other provision of law, pay by advance or reimbursement such agencies and their employees for services rendered to assist the Commission in carrying out this subchapter. In furtherance of such cooperative efforts, the Commission may enter into written agreements with such State or local agencies and such agreements may include provisions under which the Commission shall refrain from processing a charge in any cases or class of cases specified in such agreements or under which the Commission shall relieve any person or class of persons in such State or locality from requirements imposed under this section. The Commission shall rescind any such agreement whenever it determines that the agreement no longer serves the interest of effective enforcement of this subchapter.

(c) Execution, retention, and preservation of records; reports to Commission; training program records; appropriate relief from regulation or order for undue hardship; procedure for exemption; judicial action to compel compliance

Every employer, employment agency, and labor organization subject to this subchapter shall

(1) make and keep such records relevant to the determinations of whether unlawful employment practices have been or are being committed,

(2) preserve such records for such periods, and

(3) make such reports therefrom as the Commission shall prescribe by regulation or order, after public hearing, as reasonable, necessary, or appropriate for the enforcement of this subchapter or the regulations or orders thereunder. The Commission shall, by regulation, require each employer, labor organization, and joint labor-management committee subject to this subchapter which controls an apprenticeship or other training program to maintain such records as are reasonably necessary to carry out the purposes of this subchapter, including, but not limited to, a list of applicants who wish to participate in such program, including the chronological order in which applications were received, and to furnish to the Commission upon request, a detailed description of the

manner in which persons are selected to participate in the apprenticeship or other training program. Any employer, employment agency, labor organization, or joint labor-management committee which believes that the application to it of any regulation or order issued under this section would result in undue hardship may apply to the Commission for an exemption from the application of such regulation or order, and, if such application for an exemption is denied, bring a civil action in the United States district court for the district where such records are kept. If the Commission or the court, as the case may be, finds that the application of the regulation or order to the employer, employment agency, or labor organization in question would impose an undue hardship, the Commission or the court, as the case may be, may grant appropriate relief. If any person required to comply with the provisions of this subsection fails or refuses to do so, the United States district court for the district in which such person is found, resides, or transacts business, shall, upon application of the Commission, or the Attorney General in a case involving a government, governmental agency or political subdivision, have jurisdiction to issue to such person an order requiring him to comply.

(d) Consultation and coordination between Commission and interested State and Federal agencies in prescribing recordkeeping and reporting requirements; availability of information furnished pursuant to recordkeeping and reporting requirements; conditions on availability

In prescribing requirements pursuant to subsection (c) of this section, the Commission shall consult with other interested State and Federal agencies and shall endeavor to coordinate its requirements with those adopted by such agencies. The Commission shall furnish upon request and without cost to any State or local agency charged with the administration of a fair employment practice law information obtained pursuant to subsection (c) of this section from any employer, employment agency, labor organization, or joint labor-management committee subject to the jurisdiction of such agency. Such information shall be furnished on condition that it not be made public by the recipient agency prior to the institution of a proceeding under State or local law involving such information. If this condition is violated by a recipient agency, the Commission may decline to honor subsequent requests pursuant to this subsection.

(e) Prohibited disclosures; penalties

It shall be unlawful for any officer or employee of the Commission to make public in any manner whatever any information obtained by the Commission pursuant to its authority under this section prior to the institution of any proceeding under this subchapter involving such information. Any officer or employee of the Commission who shall make public in any manner whatever any information in violation of this subsection shall be guilty of a misdemeanor and upon conviction thereof, shall be fined not more than $1,000, or imprisoned not more than one year.

§ 710. [42 U.S.C. § 2000e–9]. Conduct of hearings and investigations pursuant to section 161 of Title 29

For the purpose of all hearings and investigations conducted by the Commission or its duly authorized agents or agencies, section 161 of Title 29 shall apply.

§ 711. [42 U.S.C. § 2000e–10]. Posting of notices; penalties

(a) Every employer, employment agency, and labor organization, as the case may be, shall post and keep posted in conspicuous places upon its premises where notices to employees, applicants for employment, and members are customarily posted a notice to be prepared or approved by the Commission setting forth excerpts from or, summaries of, the pertinent provisions of this subchapter and information pertinent to the filing of a complaint.

(b) A willful violation of this section shall be punishable by a fine of not more than $100 for each separate offense.

§ 712. [42 U.S.C. § 2000e–11]. Veterans' special rights or preference

Nothing contained in this subchapter shall be construed to repeal or modify any Federal, State, territorial, or local law creating special rights or preference for veterans.

§ 713. [42 U.S.C. § 2000e–12]. Regulations; conformity of regulations with administrative procedure provisions; reliance on interpretations and instructions of Commission

(a) The Commission shall have authority from time to time to issue, amend, or rescind suitable procedural regulations to carry out the provisions of this subchapter. Regulations issued under this section shall be in conformity with the standards and limitations of subchapter II of chapter 5 of Title 5.

(b) In any action or proceeding based on any alleged unlawful employment practice, no person shall be subject to any liability or punishment for or on account of

(1) the commission by such person of an unlawful employment practice if he pleads and proves that the act or omission complained of was in good faith, in conformity with, and in reliance on any written interpretation or opinion of the Commission, or

(2) the failure of such person to publish and file any information required by any provision of this subchapter if he pleads and proves that he failed to publish and file such information in good faith, in conformity with the instructions of the Commission issued under this subchapter regarding the filing of such information. Such a defense, if established, shall be a bar to the action or proceeding, notwithstanding that

(A) after such act or omission, such interpretation or opinion is modified or rescinded or is determined by judicial authority to be invalid or of no legal effect, or

(B) after publishing or filing the description and annual reports, such publication or filing is determined by judicial authority not to be in conformity with the requirements of this subchapter.

§ 714. [42 U.S.C. § 2000e–13]. Application to personnel of Commission of sections 111 and 1114 of Title 18; punishment for violation of section 1114 of Title 18; Forcibly Resisting the Commission or Its Representatives

The provisions of sections 111 and 1114, Title 18, shall apply to officers, agents, and employees of the Commission in the performance of their official duties. Notwithstanding the provisions of sections 111 and 1114 of Title 18, whoever in violation of the provisions of section 1114 of such title kills a person while engaged in or on account of the performance of his official functions under this subchapter shall be punished by imprisonment for any term of years or for life.

§ 715. [42 U.S.C. § 2000e–14]. Equal Employment Opportunity Coordinating Council; establishment; composition; duties; report to President and Congress

The Equal Employment Opportunity Commission shall have the responsibility for developing and implementing agreements, policies and practices designed to maximize effort, promote efficiency, and eliminate conflict, competition, duplication and inconsistency among the operations, functions and jurisdictions of the various departments, agencies and branches of the Federal Government responsible for the implementation and enforcement of equal employment opportunity legislation, orders, and policies. On or before October 1 of each year, the Equal Employment Opportunity Commission shall transmit to the President and to the Congress a report of its activities, together with such recommendations for legislative or administrative changes as it concludes are desirable to further promote the purposes of this section.

§ 716. [42 U.S.C. § 2000e–15]. Presidential conferences; acquaintance of leadership with provisions for employment rights and obligations; plans for fair administration; membership

The President shall, as soon as feasible after July 2, 1964, convene one or more conferences for the purpose of enabling the leaders of groups whose members will be affected by this subchapter to become familiar with the rights afforded and obligations imposed by its provisions, and for the purpose of making plans which will result in the fair and effective administration of this subchapter when all of its provisions become effective. The President shall invite the participation in such conference or conferences of (1) the members of the President's Committee on Equal Employment Opportunity, (2) the members of the Commission on Civil

Rights, (3) representatives of State and local agencies engaged in furthering equal employment opportunity, (4) representatives of private agencies engaged in furthering equal employment opportunity, and (5) representatives of employers, labor organizations, and employment agencies who will be subject to this subchapter.

§ 717. [42 U.S.C. § 2000e–16]. Employment by Federal Government

(a) Discriminatory practices prohibited; employees or applicants for employment subject to coverage

All personnel actions affecting employees or applicants for employment (except with regard to aliens employed outside the limits of the United States) in military departments as defined in section 102 of Title 5, in executive agencies as defined in section 105 of Title 5 (including employees and applicants for employment who are paid from nonappropriated funds), in the United States Postal Service and the Postal Regulatory Commission, in those units of the Government of the District of Columbia having positions in the competitive service, and in those units of the judicial branch of the Federal Government having positions in the competitive service, in the Smithsonian Institution, and in the Government Publishing Office, the Government Accountability Office, and the Library of Congress shall be made free from any discrimination based on race, color, religion, sex, or national origin.

(b) Equal Employment Opportunity Commission; enforcement powers; issuance of rules, regulations, etc.; annual review and approval of national and regional equal employment opportunity plans; review and evaluation of equal employment opportunity programs and publication of progress reports; consultations with interested parties; compliance with rules, regulations, etc.; contents of national and regional equal employment opportunity plans; authority of Librarian of Congress

Except as otherwise provided in this subsection, the Equal Employment Opportunity Commission shall have authority to enforce the provisions of subsection (a) of this section through appropriate remedies, including reinstatement or hiring of employees with or without back pay, as will effectuate the policies of this section, and shall issue such rules, regulations, orders and instructions as it deems necessary and appropriate to carry out its responsibilities under this section. The Equal Employment Opportunity Commission shall—

(1) be responsible for the annual review and approval of a national and regional equal employment opportunity plan which each department and agency and each appropriate unit referred to in subsection (a) of this section shall submit in order to maintain an affirmative program of equal employment opportunity for all such employees and applicants for employment;

(2) be responsible for the review and evaluation of the operation of all agency equal employment opportunity programs, periodically obtaining and publishing (on at least a semiannual basis) progress reports from each such department, agency, or unit; and

(3) consult with and solicit the recommendations of interested individuals, groups, and organizations relating to equal employment opportunity.

The head of each such department, agency, or unit shall comply with such rules, regulations, orders, and instructions which shall include a provision that an employee or applicant for employment shall be notified of any final action taken on any complaint of discrimination filed by him thereunder. The plan submitted by each department, agency, and unit shall include, but not be limited to—

(4) provision for the establishment of training and education programs designed to provide a maximum opportunity for employees to advance so as to perform at their highest potential; and

(5) a description of the qualifications in terms of training and experience relating to equal employment opportunity for the principal and operating officials of each such department, agency, or unit responsible for carrying out the equal employment opportunity program and of the allocation of personnel and resources proposed by such department, agency, or unit to carry out its equal employment opportunity program.

With respect to employment in the Library of Congress, authorities granted in this subsection to the Equal Employment Opportunity Commission shall be exercised by the Librarian of Congress.

(c) Civil action by employee or applicant for employment for redress of grievances; time for bringing of action; head of department, agency, or unit as defendant

Within 90 days of receipt of notice of final action taken by a department, agency, or unit referred to in subsection (a) of this section, or by the Equal Employment Opportunity Commission upon an appeal from a decision or order of such department, agency, or unit on a complaint of discrimination based on race, color, religion, sex or national origin, brought pursuant to subsection (a) of this section, Executive Order 11478 or any succeeding Executive orders, or after one hundred and eighty days from the filing of the initial charge with the department, agency, or unit or with the Equal Employment Opportunity Commission on appeal from a decision or order of such department, agency, or unit until such time as final action may be taken by a department, agency, or unit, an employee or applicant for employment, if aggrieved by the final disposition of his complaint, or by the failure to take final action on his complaint, may file a civil action as provided in section 2000e–5 of this title, in which civil action the head of the department, agency, or unit, as appropriate, shall be the defendant.

(d) Section 2000e–5(f) through (k) of this title applicable to civil actions

The provisions of section 2000e–5(f) through (k) of this title, as applicable, shall govern civil actions brought hereunder, and the same interest to compensate for delay in payment shall be available as in cases involving nonpublic parties.

(e) Government agency or official not relieved of responsibility to assure nondiscrimination in employment or equal employment opportunity

Nothing contained in this Act shall relieve any Government agency or official of its or his primary responsibility to assure nondiscrimination in employment as required by the Constitution and statutes or of its or his responsibilities under Executive Order 11478 relating to equal employment opportunity in the Federal Government.

(f) Section 2000e–5(3) of this title applicable to compensation discrimination

Section 2000e–5(e)(3) of this title shall apply to complaints of discrimination in compensation under this section.

§ 717a. [42 U.S.C. § 2000e–16a]. Short title; purpose; definition

(a) Short title

Sections 2000e–16a to 2000e–16c of this title may be cited as the "Government Employee Rights Act of 1991".

(b) Purpose

The purpose of sections 2000e–16a to 2000e–16c of this title is to provide procedures to protect the rights of certain government employees, with respect to their public employment, to be free of discrimination on the basis of race, color, religion, sex, national origin, age, or disability.

(c) "Violation" defined

For purposes of sections 2000e–16a to 2000e–16c of this title, the term "violation" means a practice that violates section 2000e–16b(a) of this title.

§ 717b. [42 U.S.C. § 2000e–16b]. Discriminatory practices prohibited

(a) Practices

All personnel actions affecting the Presidential appointees described in section 1219 of Title 2 or the State employees described in section 2000e–16c of this title shall be made free from any discrimination based on—

(1) race, color, religion, sex, or national origin, within the meaning of section 2000e–16 of this title;

(2) age, within the meaning of section 633a of Title 29; or

(3) disability, within the meaning of section 791 of Title 29 and sections 12112 to 12114 of this title.

(b) Remedies

The remedies referred to in sections 1219(a)(1) of Title 2 and 2000e–16c(a) of this title—

(1) may include, in the case of a determination that a violation of subsection (a)(1) or (a)(3) of this section has occurred, such remedies as would be appropriate if awarded under sections 2000e–5(g), 2000e–5(k), and 2000e–16(d) of this title, and such compensatory damages as would be appropriate if awarded under section 1981 or sections 1981a(a) and 1981a(b)(2) of this title;

(2) may include, in the case of a determination that a violation of subsection (a)(2) of this section has occurred, such remedies as would be appropriate if awarded under section 633a(c) of Title 29; and

(3) may not include punitive damages.

§ 717c. [42 U.S.C. § 2000e–16c]. Coverage of previously exempt State employees

(a) Application

The rights, protections, and remedies provided pursuant to section 2000e–16b of this title shall apply with respect to employment of any individual chosen or appointed, by a person elected to public office in any State or political subdivision of any State by the qualified voters thereof—

(1) to be a member of the elected official's personal staff;

(2) to serve the elected official on the policymaking level; or

(3) to serve the elected official as an immediate advisor with respect to the exercise of the constitutional or legal powers of the office.

(b) Enforcement by administrative action

(1) In general

Any individual referred to in subsection (a) of this section may file a complaint alleging a violation, not later than 180 days after the occurrence of the alleged violation, with the Equal Employment Opportunity Commission, which, in accordance with the principles and procedures set forth in sections 554 through 557 of Title 5, shall determine whether a violation has occurred and shall set forth its determination in a final order. If the Equal Employment Opportunity Commission determines that a violation has occurred, the final order shall also provide for appropriate relief.

(2) Referral to State and local authorities

(A) Application

Section 2000e–5(d) of this title shall apply with respect to any proceeding under this section.

(B) Definition

For purposes of the application described in subparagraph (A), the term "any charge filed by a member of the Commission alleging an unlawful employment practice" means a complaint filed under this section.

(c) Judicial review

Any party aggrieved by a final order under subsection (b) of this section may obtain a review of such order under chapter 158 of Title 28. For the purpose of this review, the Equal Employment Opportunity Commission shall be an "agency" as that term is used in chapter 158 of Title 28.

(d) Standard of review

To the extent necessary to decision and when presented, the reviewing court shall decide all relevant questions of law and interpret constitutional and statutory provisions. The court shall set aside a final order under subsection (b) of this section if it is determined that the order was—

(1) arbitrary, capricious, an abuse of discretion, or otherwise not consistent with law;

(2) not made consistent with required procedures; or

(3) unsupported by substantial evidence.

In making the foregoing determinations, the court shall review the whole record or those parts of it cited by a party, and due account shall be taken of the rule of prejudicial error.

(e) Attorney's fees

If the individual referred to in subsection (a) of this section is the prevailing party in a proceeding under this subsection, attorney's fees may be allowed by the court in accordance with the standards prescribed under section 2000e–5(k) of this title.

§ 718. [42 U.S.C. § 2000e–17]. Procedure for denial, withholding, termination, or suspension of Government contract subsequent to acceptance by Government of affirmative action plan of employer; time of acceptance of plan

No Government contract, or portion thereof, with any employer, shall be denied, withheld, terminated, or suspended, by any agency or officer of the United States under any equal employment opportunity law or order, where such employer has an affirmative action plan which has previously been accepted by the Government for the same facility within the past twelve months without first according such employer full hearing and adjudication under the provisions of section 554 of Title 5, and the following pertinent sections: Provided, That if such employer has deviated substantially from such previously agreed to affirmative action plan, this section shall not apply: Provided further, That for the purposes of this section an affirmative action plan shall be deemed to have been accepted by the Government at the time the appropriate compliance agency has accepted such plan unless within forty-five days thereafter the Office of Federal Contract Compliance has disapproved such plan.

THE CIVIL RIGHTS ACT OF 1991
Pub. L. No. 102–166, 105 Stat. 1071

§ 2. Findings

The Congress finds that—

(1) additional remedies under Federal law are needed to deter unlawful harassment and intentional discrimination in the workplace;

(2) the decision of the Supreme Court in Wards Cove Packing Co. v. Atonio, 490 U.S. 642 (1989) has weakened the scope and effectiveness of Federal civil rights protections; and

(3) legislation is necessary to provide additional protections against unlawful discrimination in employment.

§ 3. Purposes

The purposes of this Act are—

(1) to provide appropriate remedies for intentional discrimination and unlawful harassment in the workplace;

(2) to codify the concepts of "business necessity" and "job related" enunciated by the Supreme Court in Griggs v. Duke Power Co., 401 U.S. 424 (1971), and in the other Supreme Court decisions prior to Wards Cove Packing Co. v. Atonio, 490 U.S. 642 (1989);

(3) to confirm statutory authority and provide statutory guidelines for the adjudication of disparate impact suits under title VII of the Civil Rights Act of 1964 (42 U.S.C. 2000e et seq.); and

(4) to respond to recent decisions of the Supreme Court by expanding the scope of relevant civil rights statutes in order to provide adequate protection to victims of discrimination.

§ 116. Lawful Court-Ordered Remedies, Affirmative Action, and Conciliation Agreements Not Affected

Nothing in the amendments made by this title shall be construed to affect court-ordered remedies, affirmative action, or conciliation agreements, that are in accordance with the law.

§ 118. Alternative Means of Dispute Resolution

Where appropriate and to the extent authorized by law, the use of alternative means of dispute resolution, including settlement negotiations, conciliation, facilitation, mediation, factfinding, minitrials, and arbitration, is encouraged to resolve disputes arising under the Acts or provisions of Federal law amended by this title.

THE EQUAL PAY ACT OF 1963 and THE FAIR LABOR STANDARDS ACT

29 U.S.C. §§ 206(d), 215–17, 255, 259–60

§ 206. Minimum wage

. . .

(d) Prohibition of sex discrimination

(1) No employer having employees subject to any provisions of this section shall discriminate, within any establishment in which such employees are employed, between employees on the basis of sex by paying wages to employees in such establishment at a rate less than the rate at which he pays wages to employees of the opposite sex in such establishment for equal work on jobs the performance of which requires equal skill, effort, and responsibility, and which are performed under similar working conditions, except where such payment is made pursuant to (i) a seniority system; (ii) a merit system; (iii) a system which measures earnings by quantity or quality of production; or (iv) a differential based on any other factor other than sex: Provided, That an employer who is paying a wage rate differential in violation of this subsection shall not, in order to comply with the provisions of this subsection, reduce the wage rate of any employee.

(2) No labor organization, or its agents, representing employees of an employer having employees subject to any provisions of this section shall cause or attempt to cause such an employer to discriminate against an employee in violation of paragraph (1) of this subsection.

(3) For purposes of administration and enforcement, any amounts owing to any employee which have been withheld in violation of this subsection shall be deemed to be unpaid minimum wages or unpaid overtime compensation under this chapter.

(4) As used in this subsection, the term "labor organization" means any organization of any kind, or any agency or employee representation committee or plan, in which employees participate and which exists for the purpose, in whole or in part, of dealing with employers concerning grievances, labor disputes, wages, rates of pay, hours of employment, or conditions of work.

§ 215. Prohibited acts; prima facie evidence

(a) After the expiration of one hundred and twenty days from June 25, 1938, it shall be unlawful for any person—

. . .

(2) to violate any of the provisions of section 206 or section 207 of this title, or any of the provisions of any regulation or order of the Secretary issued under section 214 of this title;

(3) to discharge or in any other manner discriminate against any employee because such employee has filed any complaint or instituted or

caused to be instituted any proceeding under or related to this chapter, or has testified or is about to testify in any such proceeding, or has served or is about to serve on an industry committee; . . .

§ 216. Penalties

(a) Fines and imprisonment

Any person who willfully violates any of the provisions of section 215 of this title shall upon conviction thereof be subject to a fine of not more than $10,000, or to imprisonment for not more than six months, or both. No person shall be imprisoned under this subsection except for an offense committed after the conviction of such person for a prior offense under this subsection.

(b) Damages; right of action; attorney's fees and costs; termination of right of action

Any employer who violates the provisions of section 206 or section 207 of this title shall be liable to the employee or employees affected in the amount of their unpaid minimum wages, or their unpaid overtime compensation, as the case may be, and in an additional equal amount as liquidated damages. Any employer who violates the provisions of section 215(a)(3) of this title shall be liable for such legal or equitable relief as may be appropriate to effectuate the purposes of section 215(a)(3) of this title, including without limitation employment, reinstatement, promotion, and the payment of wages lost and an additional equal amount as liquidated damages. An action to recover the liability prescribed in either of the preceding sentences may be maintained against any employer (including a public agency) in any Federal or State court of competent jurisdiction by any one or more employees for and in behalf of himself or themselves and other employees similarly situated. No employee shall be a party plaintiff to any such action unless he gives his consent in writing to become such a party and such consent is filed in the court in which such action is brought. The court in such action shall, in addition to any judgment awarded to the plaintiff or plaintiffs, allow a reasonable attorney's fee to be paid by the defendant, and costs of the action. The right provided by this subsection to bring an action by or on behalf of any employee, and the right of any employee to become a party plaintiff to any such action, shall terminate upon the filing of a complaint by the Secretary of Labor in an action under section 217 of this title in which (1) restraint is sought of any further delay in the payment of unpaid minimum wages, or the amount of unpaid overtime compensation, as the case may be, owing to such employee under section 206 or section 207 of this title by an employer liable therefor under the provisions of this subsection or (2) legal or equitable relief is sought as a result of alleged violations of section 215(a)(3) of this title.

(c) Payment of wages and compensation; waiver of claims; actions by the Secretary; limitation of actions

The Secretary is authorized to supervise the payment of the unpaid minimum wages or the unpaid overtime compensation owing to any employee or employees under section 206 or section 207 of this title, and the agreement of any employee to accept such payment shall upon payment in full constitute a waiver by such employee of any right he may have under subsection (b) of this section to such unpaid minimum wages or unpaid overtime compensation and an additional equal amount as liquidated damages. The Secretary may bring an action in any court of competent jurisdiction to recover the amount of unpaid minimum wages or overtime compensation and an equal amount as liquidated damages. The right provided by subsection (b) of this section to bring an action by or on behalf of any employee to recover the liability specified in the first sentence of such subsection and of any employee to become a party plaintiff to any such action shall terminate upon the filing of a complaint by the Secretary in an action under this subsection in which a recovery is sought of unpaid minimum wages or unpaid overtime compensation under sections 206 and 207 of this title or liquidated or other damages provided by this subsection owing to such employee by an employer liable under the provisions of subsection (b) of this section, unless such action is dismissed without prejudice on motion of the Secretary. Any sums thus recovered by the Secretary of Labor on behalf of an employee pursuant to this subsection shall be held in a special deposit account and shall be paid, on order of the Secretary of Labor, directly to the employee or employees affected. Any such sums not paid to an employee because of inability to do so within a period of three years shall be covered into the Treasury of the United States as miscellaneous receipts. In determining when an action is commenced by the Secretary of Labor under this subsection for the purposes of the statutes of limitations provided in section 255(a) of this title, it shall be considered to be commenced in the case of any individual claimant on the date when the complaint is filed if he is specifically named as a party plaintiff in the complaint, or if his name did not so appear, on the subsequent date on which his name is added as a party plaintiff in such action. . . .

§ 217. Injunction proceedings

The district courts, together with the United States District Court for the District of the Canal Zone, the District Court of the Virgin Islands, and the District Court of Guam shall have jurisdiction, for cause shown, to restrain violations of section 215 of this title, including in the case of violations of section 215(a)(2) of this title the restraint of any withholding of payment of minimum wages or overtime compensation found by the court to be due to employees under this chapter (except sums which employees are barred from recovering, at the time of the commencement of the action to restrain the violations, by virtue of the provisions of section 255 of this title).

§ 255. Statute of limitations

Any action commenced on or after May 14, 1947, to enforce any cause of action for unpaid minimum wages, unpaid overtime compensation, or liquidated damages, under the Fair Labor Standards Act of 1938, as amended [29 U.S.C. § 201 et seq.] . . .—

(a) if the cause of action accrues on or after May 14, 1947—may be commenced within two years after the cause of action accrued, and every such action shall be forever barred unless commenced within two years after the cause of action accrued, except that a cause of action arising out of a willful violation may be commenced within three years after the cause of action accrued; . . .

§ 259. Reliance in future on administrative rulings, etc.

(a) In any action or proceeding based on any act or omission on or after May 14, 1947, no employer shall be subject to any liability or punishment for or on account of the failure of the employer to pay minimum wages or overtime compensation under the Fair Labor Standards Act of 1938, as amended [29 U.S.C. § 201 et seq.] . . . if he pleads and proves that the act or omission complained of was in good faith in conformity with and in reliance on any written administrative regulation, order, ruling, approval, or interpretation, of the agency of the United States specified in subsection (b) of this section, or any administrative practice or enforcement policy of such agency with respect to the class of employers to which he belonged. Such a defense, if established, shall be a bar to the action or proceeding, notwithstanding that after such act or omission, such administrative regulation, order, ruling, approval, interpretation, practice, or enforcement policy is modified or rescinded or is determined by judicial authority to be invalid or of no legal effect.

(b) The agency referred to in subsection (a) of this section shall be—

(1) in the case of the Fair Labor Standards Act of 1938, as amended [29 U.S.C. § 201 et seq.]—the Administrator of the Wage and Hour Division of the Department of Labor. . . .

§ 260. Liquidated damages

In any action commenced prior to or on or after May 14, 1947 to recover unpaid minimum wages, unpaid overtime compensation, or liquidated damages, under the Fair Labor Standards Act of 1938, as amended [29 U.S.C. § 201 et seq.], if the employer shows to the satisfaction of the court that the act or omission giving rise to such action was in good faith and that he had reasonable grounds for believing that his act or omission was not a violation of the Fair Labor Standards Act of 1938, as amended, the court may, in its sound discretion, award no liquidated damages or award any amount thereof not to exceed the amount specified in section 216[(b)] of this title.

THE AGE DISCRIMINATION IN EMPLOYMENT ACT OF 1967

29 U.S.C. §§ 621–633a

§ 2. [29 U.S.C. § 621]. Congressional statement of findings and purpose

(a) The Congress hereby finds and declares that—

(1) in the face of rising productivity and affluence, older workers find themselves disadvantaged in their efforts to retain employment, and especially to regain employment when displaced from jobs;

(2) the setting of arbitrary age limits regardless of potential for job performance has become a common practice, and certain otherwise desirable practices may work to the disadvantage of older persons;

(3) the incidence of unemployment, especially long-term unemployment with resultant deterioration of skill, morale, and employer acceptability is, relative to the younger ages, high among older workers; their numbers are great and growing; and their employment problems grave;

(4) the existence in industries affecting commerce, of arbitrary discrimination in employment because of age, burdens commerce and the free flow of goods in commerce.

(b) It is therefore the purpose of this chapter to promote employment of older persons based on their ability rather than age; to prohibit arbitrary age discrimination in employment; to help employers and workers find ways of meeting problems arising from the impact of age on employment.

§ 3. [29 U.S.C. § 622]. Education and research program; recommendation to Congress

(a) The Secretary of Labor shall undertake studies and provide information to labor unions, management, and the general public concerning the needs and abilities of older workers, and their potentials for continued employment and contribution to the economy. In order to achieve the purposes of this chapter, the Secretary of Labor shall carry on a continuing program of education and information, under which he may, among other measures—

(1) undertake research, and promote research, with a view to reducing barriers to the employment of older persons, and the promotion of measures for utilizing their skills;

(2) publish and otherwise make available to employers, professional societies, the various media of communication, and other interested persons the findings of studies and other materials for the promotion of employment;

(3) foster through the public employment service system and through cooperative effort the development of facilities of public and

private agencies for expanding the opportunities and potentials of older persons;

(4) sponsor and assist State and community informational and educational programs.

(b) Not later than six months after the effective date of this chapter, the Secretary shall recommend to the Congress any measures he may deem desirable to change the lower or upper age limits set forth in section 631 of this title.

§ 4. [29 U.S.C. § 623]. Prohibition of age discrimination

(a) Employer practices

It shall be unlawful for an employer—

(1) to fail or refuse to hire or to discharge any individual or otherwise discriminate against any individual with respect to his compensation, terms, conditions, or privileges of employment, because of such individual's age;

(2) to limit, segregate, or classify his employees in any way which would deprive or tend to deprive any individual of employment opportunities or otherwise adversely affect his status as an employee, because of such individual's age; or

(3) to reduce the wage rate of any employee in order to comply with this chapter.

(b) Employment agency practices

It shall be unlawful for an employment agency to fail or refuse to refer for employment, or otherwise to discriminate against, any individual because of such individual's age, or to classify or refer for employment any individual on the basis of such individual's age.

(c) Labor organization practices

It shall be unlawful for a labor organization—

(1) to exclude or to expel from its membership, or otherwise to discriminate against, any individual because of his age;

(2) to limit, segregate, or classify its membership, or to classify or fail or refuse to refer for employment any individual, in any way which would deprive or tend to deprive any individual of employment opportunities, or would limit such employment opportunities or otherwise adversely affect his status as an employee or as an applicant for employment, because of such individual's age;

(3) to cause or attempt to cause an employer to discriminate against an individual in violation of this section.

(d) Opposition to unlawful practices; participation in investigations, proceedings, or litigation

It shall be unlawful for an employer to discriminate against any of his employees or applicants for employment, for an employment agency to discriminate against any individual, or for a labor organization to discriminate against any member thereof or applicant for membership, because such individual, member or applicant for membership has opposed any practice made unlawful by this section, or because such individual, member or applicant for membership has made a charge, testified, assisted, or participated in any manner in an investigation, proceeding, or litigation under this chapter.

(e) Printing or publication of notice or advertisement indicating preference, limitation, etc.

It shall be unlawful for an employer, labor organization, or employment agency to print or publish, or cause to be printed or published, any notice or advertisement relating to employment by such an employer or membership in or any classification or referral for employment by such a labor organization, or relating to any classification or referral for employment by such an employment agency, indicating any preference, limitation, specification, or discrimination, based on age.

(f) Lawful practices; age an occupational qualification; other reasonable factors; laws of foreign workplace; seniority system; employee benefit plans; discharge or discipline for good cause

It shall not be unlawful for an employer, employment agency, or labor organization—

(1) to take any action otherwise prohibited under subsections (a), (b), (c), or (e) of this section where age is a bona fide occupational qualification reasonably necessary to the normal operation of the particular business, or where the differentiation is based on reasonable factors other than age, or where such practices involve an employee in a workplace in a foreign country, and compliance with such subsections would cause such employer, or a corporation controlled by such employer, to violate the laws of the country in which such workplace is located;

(2) to take any action otherwise prohibited under subsection (a), (b), (c), or (e) of this section—

(A) to observe the terms of a bona fide seniority system that is not intended to evade the purposes of this chapter, except that no such seniority system shall require or permit the involuntary retirement of any individual specified by section 631(a) of this title because of the age of such individual; or

(B) to observe the terms of a bona fide employee benefit plan—

(i) where, for each benefit or benefit package, the actual amount of payment made or cost incurred on behalf of an older worker is no less than that made or incurred on behalf of a younger worker, as permissible under section 1625.10, title 29, Code of Federal Regulations (as in effect on June 22, 1989); or

(ii) that is a voluntary early retirement incentive plan consistent with the relevant purpose or purposes of this chapter.

Notwithstanding clause (i) or (ii) of subparagraph (B), no such employee benefit plan or voluntary early retirement incentive plan shall excuse the failure to hire any individual, and no such employee benefit plan shall require or permit the involuntary retirement of any individual specified by section 631(a) of this title, because of the age of such individual. An employer, employment agency, or labor organization acting under subparagraph (A), or under clause (i) or (ii) of subparagraph (B), shall have the burden of proving that such actions are lawful in any civil enforcement proceeding brought under this chapter; or

(3) to discharge or otherwise discipline an individual for good cause.

[(g) Repealed.]

(h) Practices of foreign corporations controlled by American employers; foreign employers not controlled by American employers; factors determining control

(1) If an employer controls a corporation whose place of incorporation is in a foreign country, any practice by such corporation prohibited under this section shall be presumed to be such practice by such employer.

(2) The prohibitions of this section shall not apply where the employer is a foreign person not controlled by an American employer.

(3) For the purpose of this subsection the determination of whether an employer controls a corporation shall be based upon the—

(A) interrelation of operations,

(B) common management,

(C) centralized control of labor relations, and

(D) common ownership or financial control,

of the employer and the corporation.

(i) Employee pension benefit plans; cessation or reduction of benefit accrual or of allocation to employee account; distribution of benefits after attainment of normal retirement age; compliance; highly compensated employees

(1) Except as otherwise provided in this subsection, it shall be unlawful for an employer, an employment agency, a labor organization, or any combination thereof to establish or maintain an employee pension benefit plan which requires or permits—

(A) in the case of a defined benefit plan, the cessation of an employee's benefit accrual, or the reduction of the rate of an employee's benefit accrual, because of age, or

(B) in the case of a defined contribution plan, the cessation of allocations to an employee's account, or the reduction of the rate at which amounts are allocated to an employee's account, because of age.

(2) Nothing in this section shall be construed to prohibit an employer, employment agency, or labor organization from observing any provision of an employee pension benefit plan to the extent that such provision imposes (without regard to age) a limitation on the amount of benefits that the plan provides or a limitation on the number of years of service or years of participation which are taken into account for purposes of determining benefit accrual under the plan.

(3) In the case of any employee who, as of the end of any plan year under a defined benefit plan, has attained normal retirement age under such plan—

(A) if distribution of benefits under such plan with respect to such employee has commenced as of the end of such plan year, then any requirement of this subsection for continued accrual of benefits under such plan with respect to such employee during such plan year shall be treated as satisfied to the extent of the actuarial equivalent of in-service distribution of benefits, and

(B) if distribution of benefits under such plan with respect to such employee has not commenced as of the end of such year in accordance with section 1056(a)(3) of this title and section 401(a)(14)(C) of Title 26, and the payment of benefits under such plan with respect to such employee is not suspended during such plan year pursuant to section 1053(a)(3)(B) of this title or section 411(a)(3)(B) of Title 26, then any requirement of this subsection for continued accrual of benefits under such plan with respect to such employee during such plan year shall be treated as satisfied to the extent of any adjustment in the benefit payable under the plan during such plan year attributable to the delay in the distribution of benefits after the attainment of normal retirement age.

The provisions of this paragraph shall apply in accordance with regulations of the Secretary of the Treasury. Such regulations shall provide for the application of the preceding provisions of this paragraph to all employee pension benefit plans subject to this subsection and may provide for the application of such provisions, in the case of any such employee, with respect to any period of time within a plan year.

(4) Compliance with the requirements of this subsection with respect to an employee pension benefit plan shall constitute compliance with the requirements of this section relating to benefit accrual under such plan.

(5) Paragraph (1) shall not apply with respect to any employee who is a highly compensated employee (within the meaning of section 414(q) of Title 26) to the extent provided in regulations prescribed by the Secretary of the Treasury for purposes of precluding discrimination in favor of highly compensated employees within the meaning of subchapter D of chapter 1 of Title 26.

(6) A plan shall not be treated as failing to meet the requirements of paragraph (1) solely because the subsidized portion of any early retirement benefit is disregarded in determining benefit accruals or it is a plan permitted by subsection (m) of this section.

(7) Any regulations prescribed by the Secretary of the Treasury pursuant to clause (v) of section 411(b)(1)(H) of Title 26 and subparagraphs (C) and (D) of section 411(b)(2) of Title 26 shall apply with respect to the requirements of this subsection in the same manner and to the same extent as such regulations apply with respect to the requirements of such sections 411(b)(1)(H) and 411(b)(2).

(8) A plan shall not be treated as failing to meet the requirements of this section solely because such plan provides a normal retirement age described in section 1002(24)(B) of this title and section 411(a)(8)(B) of Title 26.

[Subdivision (9) on technical definitions for purposes of this subsection is omitted.]

(j) Employment as firefighter or law enforcement officer

It shall not be unlawful for an employer which is a State, a political subdivision of a State, an agency or instrumentality of a State or a political subdivision of a State, or an interstate agency to fail or refuse to hire or to discharge any individual because of such individual's age if such action is taken—

(1) with respect to the employment of an individual as a firefighter or as a law enforcement officer, the employer has complied with section 3(d)(2) of the Age Discrimination in Employment Amendments of 1996 if the individual was discharged after the date described in such section, and the individual has attained—

(A) the age of hiring or retirement, respectively, in effect under applicable State or local law on March 3, 1983; or

(B) (i) if the individual was not hired, the age of hiring in effect on the date of such failure or refusal to hire under applicable State or local law enacted after September 30, 1996; or

(ii) if applicable State or local law was enacted after September 30, 1996, and the individual was discharged, the higher of—

(I) the age of retirement in effect on the date of such discharge under such law; and

(II) age 55; and

(2) pursuant to a bona fide hiring or retirement plan that is not a subterfuge to evade the purposes of this chapter.

(k) Seniority system or employee benefit plan; compliance

A seniority system or employee benefit plan shall comply with this chapter regardless of the date of adoption of such system or plan.

(*l*) Lawful practices; minimum age as condition of eligibility for retirement benefits; deductions from severance pay; reduction of long-term disability benefits

Notwithstanding clause (i) or (ii) of subsection (f)(2)(B)—

(1) (A) It shall not be a violation of subsection (a), (b), (c), or (e) of this section solely because—

(i) an employee pension benefit plan (as defined in section 1002(2) of this title) provides for the attainment of a minimum age as a condition of eligibility for normal or early retirement benefits; or

(ii) a defined benefit plan (as defined in section 1002(35) of this title) provides for—

(I) payments that constitute the subsidized portion of an early retirement benefit; or

(II) social security supplements for plan participants that commence before the age and terminate at the age (specified by the plan) when participants are eligible to receive reduced or unreduced old-age insurance benefits under title II of the Social Security Act (42 U.S.C. 401 et seq.), and that do not exceed such old-age insurance benefits.

[The remaining subsections are omitted.]

(m) Voluntary retirement incentive plans

Notwithstanding subsection (f)(2)(b), it shall not be a violation of subsection (a), (b), (c), or (e) solely because a plan of an institution of higher education (as defined in section 1001 of Title 20) offers employees who are serving under a contract of unlimited tenure (or similar arrangement providing for unlimited tenure) supplemental benefits upon voluntary retirement that are reduced or eliminated on the basis of age, if—

(1) such institution does not implement with respect to such employees any age—based reduction or cessation of benefits that are not such supplemental benefits, except as permitted by other provisions of this chapter;

(2) such supplemental benefits are in addition to any retirement or severance benefits which have been offered generally to employees serving under a contract of unlimited tenure (or similar arrangement providing for unlimited tenure), independent of any early retirement or exit-incentive plan, within the preceding 365 days; and

(3) any employee who attains the minimum age and satisfies all non-age—based conditions for receiving a benefit under the plan has an opportunity lasting not less than 180 days to elect to retire and to receive the maximum benefit that could then be elected by a younger but

otherwise similarly situated employee, and the plan does not require retirement to occur sooner than 180 days after such election.

§ 5. [29 U.S.C. § 624]. Study by Secretary of Labor; reports to President and Congress; scope of study; implementation of study; transmittal date of reports

(a) (1) The Secretary of Labor is directed to undertake an appropriate study of institutional and other arrangements giving rise to involuntary retirement, and report his findings and any appropriate legislative recommendations to the President and to the Congress. Such study shall include—

(A) an examination of the effect of the amendment made by section 3(a) of the Age Discrimination in Employment Act Amendments of 1978 in raising the upper age limitation established by section 631(a) of this title to 70 years of age;

(B) a determination of the feasibility of eliminating such limitation;

(C) a determination of the feasibility of raising such limitation above 70 years of age; and

(D) an examination of the effect of the exemption contained in section 631(c) of this title, relating to certain executive employees, and the exemption contained in section 631(d) of this title, relating to tenured teaching personnel.

(2) The Secretary may undertake the study required by paragraph (1) of this subsection directly or by contract or other arrangement.

(b) The report required by subsection (a) of this section shall be transmitted to the President and to the Congress as an interim report not later than January 1, 1981, and in final form not later than January 1, 1982.

§ 6. [29 U.S.C. § 625]. Administration

The Secretary shall have the power—

(a) Delegation of functions; appointment of personnel; technical assistance

to make delegations, to appoint such agents and employees, and to pay for technical assistance on a fee for service basis, as he deems necessary to assist him in the performance of his functions under this chapter;

(b) Cooperation with other agencies, employers, labor organizations, and employment agencies

to cooperate with regional, State, local, and other agencies, and to cooperate with and furnish technical assistance to employers, labor organizations, and employment agencies to aid in effectuating the purposes of this chapter.

§ 7. [29 U.S.C. § 626]. Recordkeeping, investigation, and enforcement

(a) Attendance of witnesses; investigations, inspections, records, and homework regulations

The Equal Employment Opportunity Commission shall have the power to make investigations and require the keeping of records necessary or appropriate for the administration of this chapter in accordance with the powers and procedures provided in sections 209 and 211 of this title.

(b) Enforcement; prohibition of age discrimination under fair labor standards; unpaid minimum wages and unpaid overtime compensation; liquidated damages; judicial relief; conciliation, conference, and persuasion

The provisions of this chapter shall be enforced in accordance with the powers, remedies, and procedures provided in sections 211(b), 216 (except for subsection (a) thereof), and 217 of this title, and subsection (c) of this section. Any act prohibited under section 623 of this title shall be deemed to be a prohibited act under section 215 of this title. Amounts owing to a person as a result of a violation of this chapter shall be deemed to be unpaid minimum wages or unpaid overtime compensation for purposes of sections 216 and 217 of this title: Provided, That liquidated damages shall be payable only in cases of willful violations of this chapter. In any action brought to enforce this chapter the court shall have jurisdiction to grant such legal or equitable relief as may be appropriate to effectuate the purposes of this chapter, including without limitation judgments compelling employment, reinstatement or promotion, or enforcing the liability for amounts deemed to be unpaid minimum wages or unpaid overtime compensation under this section. Before instituting any action under this section, the Equal Employment Opportunity Commission shall attempt to eliminate the discriminatory practice or practices alleged, and to effect voluntary compliance with the requirements of this chapter through informal methods of conciliation, conference, and persuasion.

(c) Civil actions; persons aggrieved; jurisdiction; judicial relief; termination of individual action upon commencement of action by Commission; jury trial

(1) Any person aggrieved may bring a civil action in any court of competent jurisdiction for such legal or equitable relief as will effectuate the purposes of this chapter: Provided, That the right of any person to bring such action shall terminate upon the commencement of an action by the Equal Employment Opportunity Commission to enforce the right of such employee under this chapter.

(2) In an action brought under paragraph (1), a person shall be entitled to a trial by jury of any issue of fact in any such action for recovery of amounts owing as a result of a violation of this chapter,

regardless of whether equitable relief is sought by any party in such action.

(d) Filing of charge with Commission; timeliness; conciliation, conference, and persuasion

(1) No civil action may be commenced by an individual under this section until 60 days after a charge alleging unlawful discrimination has been filed with the Equal Employment Opportunity Commission. Such a charge shall be filed—

(A) within 180 days after the alleged unlawful practice occurred; or

(B) in a case to which section 633(b) of this title applies, within 300 days after the alleged unlawful practice occurred, or within 30 days after receipt by the individual of notice of termination of proceedings under State law, whichever is earlier.

(2) Upon receiving such a charge, the Commission shall promptly notify all persons named in such charge as prospective defendants in the action and shall promptly seek to eliminate any alleged unlawful practice by informal methods of conciliation, conference, and persuasion.

(3) For purposes of this section, an unlawful practice occurs, with respect to discrimination in compensation in violation of this chapter, when a discriminatory compensation decision or other practice is adopted, when a person becomes subject to a discriminatory compensation decision or other practice, or when a person is affected by application of a discriminatory compensation decision or other practice, including each time wages, benefits, or other compensation is paid, resulting in whole or in part from such a decision or other practice.

(e) Reliance on administrative rulings; notice of dismissal or termination; civil action after receipt of notice

Section 259 of this title [Portal-to-Portal Act of 1947] shall apply to actions under this chapter. If a charge filed with the Commission under this chapter is dismissed or the proceedings of the Commission are otherwise terminated by the Commission, the Commission shall notify the person aggrieved. A civil action may be brought under this section by a person defined in section 630(a) of this title against the respondent named in the charge within 90 days after the date of the receipt of such notice.

(f) Waiver

(1) An individual may not waive any right or claim under this chapter unless the waiver is knowing and voluntary. Except as provided in paragraph (2), a waiver may not be considered knowing and voluntary unless at a minimum—

(A) the waiver is part of an agreement between the individual and the employer that is written in a manner calculated to be understood by such individual, or by the average individual eligible to participate;

(B) the waiver specifically refers to rights or claims arising under this chapter;

(C) the individual does not waive rights or claims that may arise after the date the waiver is executed;

(D) the individual waives rights or claims only in exchange for consideration in addition to anything of value to which the individual already is entitled;

(E) the individual is advised in writing to consult with an attorney prior to executing the agreement;

(F) (i) the individual is given a period of at least 21 days within which to consider the agreement; or

(ii) if a waiver is requested in connection with an exit incentive or other employment termination program offered to a group or class of employees, the individual is given a period of at least 45 days within which to consider the agreement;

(G) the agreement provides that for a period of at least 7 days following the execution of such agreement, the individual may revoke the agreement, and the agreement shall not become effective or enforceable until the revocation period has expired;

(H) if a waiver is requested in connection with an exit incentive or other employment termination program offered to a group or class of employees, the employer (at the commencement of the period specified in subparagraph (F)) informs the individual in writing in a manner calculated to be understood by the average individual eligible to participate, as to—

(i) any class, unit, or group of individuals covered by such program, any eligibility factors for such program, and any time limits applicable to such program; and

(ii) the job titles and ages of all individuals eligible or selected for the program, and the ages of all individuals in the same job classification or organizational unit who are not eligible or selected for the program.

(2) A waiver in settlement of a charge filed with the Equal Employment Opportunity Commission, or an action filed in court by the individual or the individual's representative, alleging age discrimination of a kind prohibited under section 623 or 633a of this title may not be considered knowing and voluntary unless at a minimum—

(A) subparagraphs (A) through (E) of paragraph (1) have been met; and

(B) the individual is given a reasonable period of time within which to consider the settlement agreement.

(3) In any dispute that may arise over whether any of the requirements, conditions, and circumstances set forth in subparagraph (A), (B), (C), (D), (E), (F), (G), or (H) of paragraph (1), or subparagraph (A) or (B) of paragraph (2), have been met, the party asserting the validity of a waiver shall have the burden of proving in a court of competent jurisdiction that a waiver was knowing and voluntary pursuant to paragraph (1) or (2).

(4) No waiver agreement may affect the Commission's rights and responsibilities to enforce this chapter. No waiver may be used to justify interfering with the protected right of an employee to file a charge or participate in an investigation or proceeding conducted by the Commission.

§ 8. [29 U.S.C. § 627]. Notices to be posted

Every employer, employment agency, and labor organization shall post and keep posted in conspicuous places upon its premises a notice to be prepared or approved by the Equal Employment Opportunity Commission setting forth information as the Commission deems appropriate to effectuate the purposes of this chapter.

§ 9. [29 U.S.C. § 628]. Rules and regulations; exemptions

In accordance with the provisions of subchapter II of chapter 5 of Title 5, the Equal Employment Opportunity Commission may issue such rules and regulations as it may consider necessary or appropriate for carrying out this chapter, and may establish such reasonable exemptions to and from any or all provisions of this chapter as it may find necessary and proper in the public interest.

§ 10. [29 U.S.C. § 629]. Criminal penalties

Whoever shall forcibly resist, oppose, impede, intimidate or interfere with a duly authorized representative of the Equal Employment Opportunity Commission while it is engaged in the performance of duties under this chapter shall be punished by a fine of not more than $500 or by imprisonment for not more than one year, or by both: Provided, however, That no person shall be imprisoned under this section except when there has been a prior conviction hereunder.

§ 11. [29 U.S.C. § 630]. Definitions

For the purposes of this chapter—

(a) The term "person" means one or more individuals, partnerships, associations, labor organizations, corporations, business trusts, legal representatives, or any organized groups of persons.

(b) The term "employer" means a person engaged in an industry affecting commerce who has twenty or more employees for each working day in each of twenty or more calendar weeks in the current or preceding calendar year: Provided, That prior to June 30, 1968, employers having fewer than fifty employees shall not be considered employers. The term also means (1) any agent of such a person, and (2) a State or political subdivision of a State and any agency or instrumentality of a State or a political subdivision of a State, and any interstate agency, but such term does not include the United States, or a corporation wholly owned by the Government of the United States.

(c) The term "employment agency" means any person regularly undertaking with or without compensation to procure employees for an employer and includes an agent of such a person; but shall not include an agency of the United States.

(d) The term "labor organization" means a labor organization engaged in an industry affecting commerce, and any agent of such an organization, and includes any organization of any kind, any agency, or employee representation committee, group, association, or plan so engaged in which employees participate and which exists for the purpose, in whole or in part, of dealing with employers concerning grievances, labor disputes, wages, rates of pay, hours, or other terms or conditions of employment, and any conference, general committee, joint or system board, or joint council so engaged which is subordinate to a national or international labor organization.

(e) A labor organization shall be deemed to be engaged in an industry affecting commerce if (1) it maintains or operates a hiring hall or hiring office which procures employees for an employer or procures for employees opportunities to work for an employer, or (2) the number of its members (or, where it is a labor organization composed of other labor organizations or their representatives, if the aggregate number of the members of such other labor organization) is fifty or more prior to July 1, 1968, or twenty-five or more on or after July 1, 1968, and such labor organization—

(1) is the certified representative of employees under the provisions of the National Labor Relations Act, as amended [29 U.S.C. § 151 et seq.], or the Railway Labor Act, as amended [45 U.S.C. § 151 et seq.]; or

(2) although not certified, is a national or international labor organization or a local labor organization recognized or acting as the representative of employees of an employer or employers engaged in an industry affecting commerce; or

(3) has chartered a local labor organization or subsidiary body which is representing or actively seeking to represent employees of employers within the meaning of paragraph (1) or (2); or

(4) has been chartered by a labor organization representing or actively seeking to represent employees within the meaning of paragraph (1) or (2) as the local or subordinate body through which such employees may enjoy membership or become affiliated with such labor organization; or

(5) is a conference, general committee, joint or system board, or joint council subordinate to a national or international labor

organization, which includes a labor organization engaged in an industry affecting commerce within the meaning of any of the preceding paragraphs of this subsection.

(f) The term "employee" means an individual employed by any employer except that the term "employee" shall not include any person elected to public office in any State or political subdivision of any State by the qualified voters thereof, or any person chosen by such officer to be on such officer's personal staff, or an appointee on the policymaking level or an immediate adviser with respect to the exercise of the constitutional or legal powers of the office. The exemption set forth in the preceding sentence shall not include employees subject to the civil service laws of a State government, governmental agency, or political subdivision. The term "employee" includes any individual who is a citizen of the United States employed by an employer in a workplace in a foreign country.

(g) The term "commerce" means trade, traffic, commerce, transportation, transmission, or communication among the several States; or between a State and any place outside thereof; or within the District of Columbia, or a possession of the United States; or between points in the same State but through a point outside thereof.

(h) The term "industry affecting commerce" means any activity, business, or industry in commerce or in which a labor dispute would hinder or obstruct commerce or the free flow of commerce and includes any activity or industry "affecting commerce" within the meaning of the Labor-Management Reporting and Disclosure Act of 1959 [29 U.S.C. § 401 et seq.].

(i) The term "State" includes a State of the United States, the District of Columbia, Puerto Rico, the Virgin Islands, American Samoa, Guam, Wake Island, the Canal Zone, and Outer Continental Shelf lands defined in the Outer Continental Shelf Lands Act [43 U.S.C. § 1331 et seq.].

(j) The term "firefighter" means an employee, the duties of whose position are primarily to perform work directly connected with the control and extinguishment of fires or the maintenance and use of firefighting apparatus and equipment, including an employee engaged in this activity who is transferred to a supervisory or administrative position.

(k) The term "law enforcement officer" means an employee, the duties of whose position are primarily the investigation, apprehension, or detention of individuals suspected or convicted of offenses against the criminal laws of a State, including an employee engaged in this activity who is transferred to a supervisory or administrative position. For the purpose of this subsection, "detention" includes the duties of employees assigned to guard individuals incarcerated in any penal institution.

(*l*) The term "compensation, terms, conditions, or privileges of employment" encompasses all employee benefits, including such benefits provided pursuant to a bona fide employee benefit plan.

§ 12. [29 U.S.C.§ 631]. Age limits

(a) Individuals at least 40 years of age

The prohibitions in this chapter shall be limited to individuals who are at least 40 years of age.

(b) Employees or applicants for employment in Federal Government

In the case of any personnel action affecting employees or applicants for employment which is subject to the provisions of section 633a of this title, the prohibitions established in section 633a of this title shall be limited to individuals who are at least 40 years of age.

(c) Bona fide executives or high policymakers

(1) Nothing in this chapter shall be construed to prohibit compulsory retirement of any employee who has attained 65 years of age and who, for the 2-year period immediately before retirement, is employed in a bona fide executive or a high policymaking position, if such employee is entitled to an immediate nonforfeitable annual retirement benefit from a pension, profit-sharing, savings, or deferred compensation plan, or any combination of such plans, of the employer of such employee, which equals, in the aggregate, at least $44,000.

(2) In applying the retirement benefit test of paragraph (1) of this subsection, if any such retirement benefit is in a form other than a straight life annuity (with no ancillary benefits), or if employees contribute to any such plan or make rollover contributions, such benefit shall be adjusted in accordance with regulations prescribed by the Equal Employment Opportunity Commission, after consultation with the Secretary of the Treasury, so that the benefit is the equivalent of a straight life annuity (with no ancillary benefits) under a plan to which employees do not contribute and under which no rollover contributions are made.

§ 13. [29 U.S.C. § 632]. Annual report to Congress. [Omitted.]

§ 14. [29 U.S.C. § 633]. Federal-State relationship

(a) Federal action superseding State action

Nothing in this chapter shall affect the jurisdiction of any agency of any State performing like functions with regard to discriminatory employment practices on account of age except that upon commencement of action under this chapter such action shall supersede any State action.

(b) Limitation of Federal action upon commencement of State proceedings

In the case of an alleged unlawful practice occurring in a State which has a law prohibiting discrimination in employment because of age and establishing or authorizing a State authority to grant or seek relief from such discriminatory practice, no suit may be brought under section 626 of this title before the expiration of sixty days after proceedings have been commenced under the State law, unless such proceedings have been earlier terminated: Provided, That such sixty-day period shall be extended to one hundred and twenty days during the first year after the effective date of such State law. If any requirement for the commencement of such proceedings is imposed by a State authority other than a requirement of the filing of a written and signed statement of the facts upon which the proceeding is based, the proceeding shall be deemed to have been commenced for the purposes of this subsection at the time such statement is sent by registered mail to the appropriate State authority.

§ 15. [29 U.S.C. § 633a]. Nondiscrimination on Account of Age in Federal Government Employment

(a) Federal agencies affected

All personnel actions affecting employees or applicants for employment who are at least 40 years of age (except personnel actions with regard to aliens employed outside the limits of the United States) in military departments as defined in section 102 of Title 5, in executive agencies as defined in section 105 of Title 5 (including employees and applicants for employment who are paid from nonappropriated funds), in the United States Postal Service and the Postal Regulatory Commission, in those units in the government of the District of Columbia having positions in the competitive service, and in those units of the judicial branch of the Federal Government having positions in the competitive service, in the Smithsonian Institution, and in the Government Publishing Office, the Government Accountability Office, and the Library of Congress shall be made free from any discrimination based on age.

(b) Enforcement by Equal Employment Opportunity Commission and by Librarian of Congress in the Library of Congress; remedies; rules, regulations, orders, and instructions of Commission: compliance by Federal agencies; powers and duties of Commission; notification of final action on complaint of discrimination; exemptions: bona fide occupational qualification

Except as otherwise provided in this subsection, the Equal Employment Opportunity Commission is authorized to enforce the provisions of subsection (a) through appropriate remedies, including reinstatement or hiring of employees with or without backpay, as will effectuate the policies of this section. The Equal Employment Opportunity Commission shall issue such rules, regulations, orders, and instructions as it deems necessary and appropriate to carry out its responsibilities under this section. The Equal Employment Opportunity Commission shall—

(1) be responsible for the review and evaluation of the operation of all agency programs designed to carry out the policy of this section, periodically obtaining and publishing (on at least a semiannual basis) progress reports from each department, agency, or unit referred to in subsection (a);

(2) consult with and solicit the recommendations of interested individuals, groups, and organizations relating to nondiscrimination in employment on account of age; and

(3) provide for the acceptance and processing of complaints of discrimination in Federal employment on account of age.

The head of each such department, agency, or unit shall comply with such rules, regulations, orders, and instructions of the Equal Employment Opportunity Commission which shall include a provision that an employee or applicant for employment shall be notified of any final action taken on any complaint of discrimination filed by him thereunder. Reasonable exemptions to the provisions of this section may be established by the Commission but only when the Commission has established a maximum age requirement on the basis of a determination that age is a bona fide occupational qualification necessary to the performance of the duties of the position. With respect to employment in the Library of Congress, authorities granted in this subsection to the Equal Employment Opportunity Commission shall be exercised by the Librarian of Congress.

(c) Civil actions; jurisdiction; relief

Any person aggrieved may bring a civil action in any Federal district court of competent jurisdiction for such legal or equitable relief as will effectuate the purposes of this chapter.

(d) Notice to Commission; time of notice; Commission notification of prospective defendants; Commission elimination of unlawful practices

When the individual has not filed a complaint concerning age discrimination with the Commission, no civil action may be commenced by any individual under this section until the individual has given the Commission not less than thirty days' notice of an intent to file such action. Such notice shall be filed within one hundred and eighty days after the alleged unlawful practice occurred. Upon receiving a notice of intent to sue, the Commission shall promptly notify all persons named therein as prospective defendants in the action and take any appropriate action to assure the elimination of any unlawful practice.

(e) Duty of Government agency or official

Nothing contained in this section shall relieve any Government agency or official of the responsibility to assure nondiscrimination on account of age in employment as required under any provision of Federal law.

(f) Applicability of statutory provisions to personnel action of Federal departments, etc.

Any personnel action of any department, agency, or other entity referred to in subsection (a) of this section shall not be subject to, or affected by, any provision of this chapter, other than the provisions of sections 626(d)(3) and 631(b) of this title and the provisions of this section.

(g) Study and report to President and Congress by Equal Employment Opportunity Commission; scope

(1) The Equal Employment Opportunity Commission shall undertake a study relating to the effects of the amendments made to this section by the Age Discrimination in Employment Act Amendments of 1978, and the effects of section 631(b) of this title.

(2) The Equal Employment Opportunity Commission shall transmit a report to the President and to the Congress containing the findings of the Commission resulting from the study of the Commission under paragraph (1) of this subsection. Such report shall be transmitted no later than January 1, 1980.

THE REHABILITATION ACT OF 1973

29 U.S.C. §§ 705, 791, 793–94a

§ 7 [29 U.S.C. § 705]. Definitions

For the purposes of this chapter [29 U.S.C. § 701 et seq.]:

. . .

(9) Disability

The term "disability" means—

(A) except as otherwise provided in subparagraph (B), a physical or mental impairment that constitutes or results in a substantial impediment to employment; or

(B) for purposes of sections 701, 711, and 712 of this title and subchapters II, IV, V, and VII [29 U.S.C. §§ 760 et seq., 780 et seq., 790 et seq., and 796 et seq.], the meaning given it in section 12102 of Title 42 [ADA § 3].

(10) Drug and illegal use of drugs

(A) Drug

The term "drug" means a controlled substance, as defined in schedules I through V of section 202 of the Controlled Substances Act (21 U.S.C. § 812).

(B) Illegal use of drugs

The term "illegal use of drugs" means the use of drugs, the possession or distribution of which is unlawful under the Controlled Substances Act. Such term does not include the use of a drug taken under supervision by a licensed health care professional, or other uses authorized by the Controlled Substances Act or other provisions of Federal law.

(11) Employment outcome

The term "employment outcome" means, with respect to an individual—

(A) entering or retaining full-time or, if appropriate, part-time competitive employment in the integrated labor market;

(B) satisfying the vocational outcome of supported employment; or

(C) satisfying any other vocational outcome the Secretary of Education may determine to be appropriate (including satisfying the vocational outcome of customized employment, self-employment, telecommuting, or business ownership),

in a manner consistent with this chapter [29 U.S.C. § 701 et seq.]

. . .

(20) Individual with a disability

(A) In general

Except as otherwise provided in subparagraph (B), the term "individual with a disability" means any individual who—

(i) has a physical or mental impairment which for such individual constitutes or results in a substantial impediment to employment; and

(ii) can benefit in terms of an employment outcome from vocational rehabilitation services provided pursuant to subchapter I, III, or VI [29 U.S.C. §§ 720 et seq., 771 et seq., or 795 et seq.].

(B) Certain programs; limitations on major life activities

Subject to subparagraphs (C), (D), (E), and (F), the term "individual with a disability" means, for purposes of sections 701, 711, and 712 of this title and subchapters II, IV, V, and VII of this chapter [29 U.S.C. §§ 760 et seq., 780 et seq., 790 et seq., and 796 et seq.], any person who has a disability as defined in section 12102 of Title 42 [ADA § 3].

(C) Rights and advocacy provisions

(i) In general; exclusion of individuals engaging in drug use

For purposes of subchapter V [29 U.S.C. § 790 et seq.], the term "individual with a disability" does not include an individual who is currently engaging in the illegal use of drugs, when a covered entity acts on the basis of such use.

(ii) Exception for individuals no longer engaging in drug use

Nothing in clause (i) shall be construed to exclude as an individual with a disability an individual who—

(I) has successfully completed a supervised drug rehabilitation program and is no longer engaging in the illegal use of drugs, or has otherwise been rehabilitated successfully and is no longer engaging in such use;

(II) is participating in a supervised rehabilitation program and is no longer engaging in such use; or

(III) is erroneously regarded as engaging in such use, but is not engaging in such use;

except that it shall not be a violation of this chapter [29 U.S.C. § 701 et seq.] for a covered entity to adopt or administer reasonable policies or procedures, including but not limited to drug testing, designed to ensure that an individual described in subclause (I) or (II) is no longer engaging in the illegal use of drugs.

(iii) Exclusion for certain services

Notwithstanding clause (i), for purposes of programs and activities providing health services and services provided under subchapters I, II, and III [29 U.S.C. §§ 720 et seq., 760 et seq., and 771 et seq.], an individual shall not be excluded from the benefits of such programs or activities on the basis of his or her current illegal use of drugs if he or she is otherwise entitled to such services.

(iv) Disciplinary action

For purposes of programs and activities providing educational services, local educational agencies may take disciplinary action pertaining to the use or possession of illegal drugs or alcohol against any student who is an individual with a disability and who currently is engaging in the illegal use of drugs or in the use of alcohol to the same extent that such disciplinary action is taken against students who are not individuals with disabilities. Furthermore, the due process procedures at section 104.36 of title 34, Code of Federal Regulations (or any corresponding similar regulation or ruling) shall not apply to such disciplinary actions.

(v) Employment; exclusion of alcoholics

For purposes of sections 793 and 794 of this title as such sections relate to employment, the term "individual with a disability" does not include any individual who is an alcoholic whose current use of alcohol prevents such individual from performing the duties of the job in question or whose employment, by reason of such current alcohol abuse, would constitute a direct threat to property or the safety of others.

(D) Employment; exclusion of individuals with certain diseases or infections

For the purposes of sections 793 and 794 of this title, as such sections relate to employment, such term does not include an individual who has a currently contagious disease or infection and who, by reason of such disease or infection, would constitute a direct threat to the health or safety of other individuals or who, by reason of the currently contagious disease or infection, is unable to perform the duties of the job.

(E) Rights provisions; exclusion of individuals on basis of homosexuality or bisexuality

For the purposes of sections 791, 793, and 794 of this title—

(i) for purposes of the application of subparagraph (B) to such sections, the term "impairment" does not include homosexuality or bisexuality; and

(ii) therefore the term "individual with a disability" does not include an individual on the basis of homosexuality or bisexuality.

(F) Rights provisions; exclusion of individuals on basis of certain disorders

For the purposes of sections 791, 793, and 794 of this title, the term "individual with a disability" does not include an individual on the basis of—

(i) transvestism, transsexualism, pedophilia, exhibitionism, voyeurism, gender identity disorders not resulting from physical impairments, or other sexual behavior disorders;

(ii) compulsive gambling, kleptomania, or pyromania; or

(iii) psychoactive substance use disorders resulting from current illegal use of drugs.

(G) Individuals with disabilities

The term "individuals with disabilities" means more than one individual with a disability. . . .

§ 501 [29 U.S.C. § 791]. Employment of individuals with disabilities

(a) Interagency Committee on Employees who are Individuals with Disabilities; establishment; membership; co-chairmen; availability of other Committee resources; purpose and functions

There is established within the Federal Government an Interagency Committee on Employees who are Individuals with Disabilities (hereinafter in this section referred to as the "Committee"), comprised of such members as the President may select, including the following (or their designees whose positions are Executive Level IV or higher): the Chairman of the Equal Employment Opportunity Commission (hereafter in this section referred to as the "Commission"), the Director of the Office of Personnel Management, the Secretary of Veterans Affairs, the Secretary of Labor, the Secretary of Education, and the Secretary of Health and Human Services. Either the Director of the Office of Personnel Management and the Chairman of the Commission shall serve as co-chairpersons of the Committee or the Director or Chairman shall serve as the sole chairperson of the Committee, as the Director and

Chairman jointly determine, from time to time, to be appropriate. The resources of the President's Disability Employment Partnership Board and the President's Committee for People with Intellectual Disabilities shall be made fully available to the Committee. It shall be the purpose and function of the Committee (1) to provide a focus for Federal and other employment of individuals with disabilities, and to review, on a periodic basis, in cooperation with the Commission, the adequacy of hiring, placement, and advancement practices with respect to individuals with disabilities, by each department, agency, and instrumentality in the executive branch of Government and the Smithsonian Institution, and to insure that the special needs of such individuals are being met; and (2) to consult with the Commission to assist the Commission to carry out its responsibilities under subsections (b), (c), and (d) of this section. On the basis of such review and consultation, the Committee shall periodically make to the Commission such recommendations for legislative and administrative changes as it deems necessary or desirable. The Commission shall timely transmit to the appropriate committees of Congress any such recommendations.

(b) Federal agencies; affirmative action program plans

Each department, agency, and instrumentality (including the United States Postal Service and the Postal Regulatory Commission) in the executive branch and the Smithsonian Institution shall, within one hundred and eighty days after September 26, 1973, submit to the Commission and to the Committee an affirmative action program plan for the hiring, placement, and advancement of individuals with disabilities in such department, agency, instrumentality, or Institution. Such plan shall include a description of the extent to which and methods whereby the special needs of employees who are individuals with disabilities are being met. Such plan shall be updated annually, and shall be reviewed annually and approved by the Commission, if the Commission determines, after consultation with the Committee, that such plan provides sufficient assurances, procedures and commitments to provide adequate hiring, placement, and advancement opportunities for individuals with disabilities.

(c) State agencies; rehabilitated individuals, employment

The Commission, after consultation with the Committee, shall develop and recommend to the Secretary for referral to the appropriate State agencies, policies and procedures which will facilitate the hiring, placement, and advancement in employment of individuals who have received rehabilitation services under State vocational rehabilitation programs, veterans' programs, or any other program for individuals with disabilities, including the promotion of job opportunities for such individuals. The Secretary shall encourage such State agencies to adopt and implement such policies and procedures.

(d) Report to Congressional committees

The Commission, after consultation with the Committee, shall, on June 30, 1974, and at the end of each subsequent fiscal year, make a complete report to the appropriate committees of the Congress with respect to the practices of and achievements in hiring, placement, and advancement of individuals with disabilities by each department, agency, and instrumentality and the Smithsonian Institution and the effectiveness of the affirmative action programs required by subsection (b) of this section, together with recommendations as to legislation which have been submitted to the Commission under subsection (a) of this section, or other appropriate action to insure the adequacy of such practices. Such report shall also include an evaluation by the Committee of the effectiveness of the activities of the Commission under subsections (b) and (c) of this section.

(e) Federal work experience without pay; non-Federal status

An individual who, as a part of an individualized plan for employment under a State plan approved under this chapter, participates in a program of unpaid work experience in a Federal agency, shall not, by reason thereof, be considered to be a Federal employee or to be subject to the provisions of law relating to Federal employment, including those relating to hours of work, rates of compensation, leave, unemployment compensation, and Federal employee benefits.

(f) Standards used in determining violation of section

The standards used to determine whether this section has been violated in a complaint alleging nonaffirmative action employment discrimination under this section shall be the standards applied under title I of the Americans with Disabilities Act of 1990 (42 U.S.C. § 12111 et seq.) and the provisions of sections 501 through 504, and 510, of the Americans with Disabilities Act of 1990 (42 U.S.C. §§ 12201–12204 and 12210), as such sections relate to employment.

§ 503 [29 U.S.C. § 793]. Employment under Federal contracts

(a) Amount of contracts or subcontracts; provision for employment and advancement of qualified individuals with disabilities; regulations

Any contract in excess of $10,000 entered into by any Federal department or agency for the procurement of personal property and nonpersonal services (including construction) for the United States shall contain a provision requiring that the party contracting with the United States shall take affirmative action to employ and advance in employment qualified individuals with disabilities. The provisions of this section shall apply to any subcontract in excess of $10,000 entered into by a prime contractor in carrying out any contract for the procurement of personal property and nonpersonal services (including construction) for the United States. The President shall implement the provisions of this section by promulgating regulations within ninety days after September 26, 1973.

(b) Administrative enforcement; complaints; investigations; departmental action

If any individual with a disability believes any contractor has failed or refused to comply with the provisions of a contract with the United States, relating to employment of individuals with disabilities, such individual may file a complaint with the Department of Labor. The Department shall promptly investigate such complaint and shall take such action thereon as the facts and circumstances warrant, consistent with the terms of such contract and the laws and regulations applicable thereto.

(c) Waiver by President; national interest special circumstances for waiver of particular agreements; waiver by Secretary of Labor of affirmative action requirements

(1) The requirements of this section may be waived, in whole or in part, by the President with respect to a particular contract or subcontract, in accordance with guidelines set forth in regulations which the President shall prescribe, when the President determines that special circumstances in the national interest so require and states in writing the reasons for such determination.

(2) (A) The Secretary of Labor may waive the requirements of the affirmative action clause required by regulations promulgated under subsection (a) of this section with respect to any of a prime contractor's or subcontractor's facilities that are found to be in all respects separate and distinct from activities of the prime contractor or subcontractor related to the performance of the contract or subcontract, if the Secretary of Labor also finds that such a waiver will not interfere with or impede the effectuation of this chapter.

(B) Such waivers shall be considered only upon the request of the contractor or subcontractor. The Secretary of Labor shall promulgate regulations that set forth the standards used for granting such a waiver.

(d) Standards used in determining violation of section

The standards used to determine whether this section has been violated in a complaint alleging nonaffirmative action employment discrimination under this section shall be the standards applied under title I of the Americans with Disabilities Act of 1990 (42 U.S.C. § 12111 et seq.) and the provisions of sections 501 through 504, and 510, of the Americans with Disabilities Act of 1990 (42 U.S.C. §§ 12201–12204 and 12210), as such sections relate to employment.

(e) Avoidance of duplicative efforts and inconsistencies

The Secretary shall develop procedures to ensure that administrative complaints filed under this section and under the Americans with Disabilities Act of 1990 [42 U.S.C. § 12101 et seq.] are dealt with in a manner that avoids duplication of effort and prevents imposition of inconsistent or conflicting standards for the same requirements under this section and the Americans with Disabilities Act of 1990 [42 U.S.C. § 12101 et seq.].

§ 504 [29 U.S.C. § 794]. Nondiscrimination under Federal grants and programs

(a) Promulgation of rules and regulations

No otherwise qualified individual with a disability in the United States, as defined in section 705(20) of this title, shall, solely by reason of her or his disability, be excluded from the participation in, be denied the benefits of, or be subjected to discrimination under any program or activity receiving Federal financial assistance or under any program or activity conducted by any Executive agency or by the United States Postal Service. The head of each such agency shall promulgate such regulations as may be necessary to carry out the amendments to this section made by the Rehabilitation, Comprehensive Services, and Developmental Disabilities Act of 1978. Copies of any proposed regulation shall be submitted to appropriate authorizing committees of the Congress, and such regulation may take effect no earlier than the thirtieth day after the date on which such regulation is so submitted to such committees.

(b) "Program or activity" defined

For the purposes of this section, the term "program or activity" means all of the operations of—

(1) (A) a department, agency, special purpose district, or other instrumentality of a State or of a local government; or

(B) the entity of such State or local government that distributes such assistance and each such department or agency (and each other State or local government entity) to which the assistance is extended, in the case of assistance to a State or local government;

(2) (A) a college, university, or other postsecondary institution, or a public system of higher education; or

(B) a local educational agency (as defined in section 7801 of Title 20), system of career and technical education, or other school system;

(3) (A) an entire corporation, partnership, or other private organization, or an entire sole proprietorship—

(i) if assistance is extended to such corporation, partnership, private organization, or sole proprietorship as a whole; or

(ii) which is principally engaged in the business of providing education, health care, housing, social services, or parks and recreation; or

(B) the entire plant or other comparable, geographically separate facility to which Federal financial assistance is extended, in the case of any other corporation, partnership, private organization, or sole proprietorship; or

(4) any other entity which is established by two or more of the entities described in paragraph (1), (2), or (3); any part of which is extended Federal financial assistance.

(c) Significant structural alterations by small providers

Small providers are not required by subsection (a) to make significant structural alterations to their existing facilities for the purpose of assuring program accessibility, if alternative means of providing the services are available. The terms used in this subsection shall be construed with reference to the regulations existing on March 22, 1988.

(d) Standards used in determining violation of section

The standards used to determine whether this section has been violated in a complaint alleging employment discrimination under this section shall be the standards applied under title I of the Americans with Disabilities Act of 1990 (42 U.S.C. § 12111 et seq.) and the provisions of sections 501 through 504, and 510, of the Americans with Disabilities Act of 1990 (42 U.S.C. §§ 12201 to 12204 and 12210), as such sections relate to employment.

§ 505 [29 U.S.C. § 794a]. Remedies and attorney fees

(a) (1) The remedies, procedures, and rights set forth in section 717 of the Civil Rights Act of 1964 (42 U.S.C. § 2000e–16), including the application of sections 706(f) through 706(k) (42 U.S.C. § 2000e–5(f) through (k)), (and the application of section 706(e)(3) (42 U.S.C. § 2000e–5(e)(3)) to claims of discrimination in compensation) shall be available, with respect to any complaint under section 791 of this title, to any employee or applicant for employment aggrieved by the final disposition of such complaint, or by the failure to take final action on such complaint. In fashioning an equitable or affirmative action remedy under such section, a court may take into account the reasonableness of the cost of any necessary work place accommodation, and the availability of alternatives therefor or other appropriate relief in order to achieve an equitable and appropriate remedy.

(2) The remedies, procedures, and rights set forth in title VI of the Civil Rights Act of 1964 (42 U.S.C. 2000d et seq.) (and in subsection (e)(3) of section 706 of such Act (42 U.S.C. 2000e–5), applied to claims of discrimination in compensation) shall be available to any person aggrieved by any act or failure to act by any recipient of Federal assistance or Federal provider of such assistance under section 794 of this title.

(b) In any action or proceeding to enforce or charge a violation of a provision of this subchapter, the court, in its discretion, may allow the prevailing party, other than the United States, a reasonable attorney's fee as part of the costs.

THE AMERICANS WITH DISABILITIES ACT OF 1990*

42 U.S.C. § 12101 et seq.

§ 2. [42 U.S.C. § 12101]. Findings and purpose

(a) Findings

The Congress finds that—

(1) physical or mental disabilities in no way diminish a person's right to fully participate in all aspects of society, yet people with physical or mental disabilities have been precluded from doing so because of discrimination; others who have a record of a disability or are regarded as having a disability also have been subjected to discrimination;

(2) historically, society has tended to isolate and segregate individuals with disabilities, and, despite some improvements, such forms of discrimination against individuals with disabilities continue to be a serious and pervasive social problem;

(3) discrimination against individuals with disabilities persists in such critical areas as employment, housing, public accommodations, education, transportation, communication, recreation, institutionalization, health services, voting, and access to public services;

(4) unlike individuals who have experienced discrimination on the basis of race, color, sex, national origin, religion, or age, individuals who have experienced discrimination on the basis of disability have often had no legal recourse to redress such discrimination;

(5) individuals with disabilities continually encounter various forms of discrimination, including outright intentional exclusion, the discriminatory effects of architectural, transportation, and communication barriers, overprotective rules and policies, failure to make modifications to existing facilities and practices, exclusionary qualification standards and criteria, segregation, and relegation to lesser services, programs, activities, benefits, jobs, or other opportunities;

(6) census data, national polls, and other studies have documented that people with disabilities, as a group, occupy an inferior status in our society, and are severely disadvantaged socially, vocationally, economically, and educationally;

(7) the Nation's proper goals regarding individuals with disabilities are to assure equality of opportunity, full participation, independent living, and economic self-sufficiency for such individuals; and

---

* Language added or modified by the Americans with Disabilities Act Amendments Act appears in italics.

(8) the continuing existence of unfair and unnecessary discrimination and prejudice denies people with disabilities the opportunity to compete on an equal basis and to pursue those opportunities for which our free society is justifiably famous, and costs the United States billions of dollars in unnecessary expenses resulting from dependency and nonproductivity.

(b) Purpose

It is the purpose of this chapter—

(1) to provide a clear and comprehensive national mandate for the elimination of discrimination against individuals with disabilities;

(2) to provide clear, strong, consistent, enforceable standards addressing discrimination against individuals with disabilities;

(3) to ensure that the Federal Government plays a central role in enforcing the standards established in this chapter on behalf of individuals with disabilities; and

(4) to invoke the sweep of congressional authority, including the power to enforce the fourteenth amendment and to regulate commerce, in order to address the major areas of discrimination faced day-to-day by people with disabilities.

§ 3. [42 U.S.C. § 12102]. Definitions

As used in this chapter:

(1) Disability.—The term "disability" means, with respect to an individual—

(A) a physical or mental impairment that substantially limits one or more major life activities of such individual;

(B) a record of such an impairment; or

(C) being regarded as having such an impairment *(as described in paragraph (3)).*

(2) Major life activities.—

(A) In general.—For purposes of paragraph (1), major life activities include, but are not limited to, caring for oneself, performing manual tasks, seeing, hearing, eating, sleeping, walking, standing, lifting, bending, speaking, breathing, learning, reading, concentrating, thinking, communicating, and working.

(B) Major Bodily Functions.—For purposes of paragraph (1), a major life activity also includes the operation of a major bodily function, including but not limited to, functions of the immune system, normal cell growth, digestive, bowel, bladder, neurological, brain, respiratory, circulatory, endocrine, and reproductive functions.

(3) Regarded as having such an impairment.—For purposes of paragraph (1)(C):

(A) An individual meets the requirement of "being regarded as having such an impairment" if the individual establishes that he or she has been subjected to an action prohibited under this chapter because of an actual or perceived physical or mental impairment whether or not the impairment limits or is perceived to limit a major life activity.

(B) Paragraph (1)(C) shall not apply to impairments that are transitory and minor. A transitory impairment is an impairment with an actual or expected duration of 6 months or less.

(4) Rules of Construction Regarding the Definition of Disability.— The definition of "disability" in paragraph (1) shall be construed in accordance with the following:

(A) The definition of disability in this chapter shall be construed in favor of broad coverage of individuals under this chapter, to the maximum extent permitted by the terms of this Act.

(B) The term "substantially limits" shall be interpreted consistently with the findings and purposes of the ADA Amendments Act of 2008.

(C) An impairment that substantially limits one major life activity need not limit other major life activities in order to be considered a disability.

(D) An impairment that is episodic or in remission is a disability if it would substantially limit a major life activity when active.

(E) (i) The determination of whether an impairment substantially limits a major life activity shall be made without regard to the ameliorative effects of mitigating measures such as—

(I) medication, medical supplies, equipment, or appliances, low-vision devices (which do not include ordinary eyeglasses or contact lenses), prosthetics including limbs and devices, hearing aids and cochlear implants or other implantable hearing devices, mobility devices, or oxygen therapy equipment and supplies;

(II) use of assistive technology;

(III) reasonable accommodations or auxiliary aids or services; or

(IV) learned behavioral or adaptive neurological modifications.

(ii) The ameliorative effects of the mitigating measures of ordinary eyeglasses or contact lenses shall be considered in determining whether an impairment substantially limits a major life activity.

(iii) As used in this subparagraph—

(I) the term "ordinary eyeglasses or contact lenses" means lenses that are intended to fully correct visual acuity or eliminate refractive error; and

(II) the term "low-vision devices" means devices that magnify, enhance, or otherwise augment a visual image.

§ 4. [42 U.S.C. § 12103]. Additional Definitions.

As used in this Act:

(1) Auxiliary Aids and Services.—The term "auxiliary aids and services" includes—

(A) qualified interpreters or other effective methods of making aurally delivered materials available to individuals with hearing impairments;

(B) qualified readers, taped texts, or other effective methods of making visually delivered materials available to individuals with visual impairments;

(C) acquisition or modification of equipment or devices; and

(D) other similar services and actions.

(2) State.—The term "State" means each of the several States, the District of Columbia, the Commonwealth of Puerto Rico, Guam, American Samoa, the Virgin Islands of the United States, the Trust Territory of the Pacific Islands, and the Commonwealth of the Northern Mariana Islands.

TITLE I—EMPLOYMENT

§ 101. [42 U.S.C. § 12111]. Definitions

As used in this subchapter:

(1) Commission

The term "Commission" means the Equal Employment Opportunity Commission established by section 2000e–4 of this title.

(2) Covered entity

The term "covered entity" means an employer, employment agency, labor organization, or joint labor-management committee.

(3) Direct threat

The term "direct threat" means a significant risk to the health or safety of others that cannot be eliminated by reasonable accommodation.

(4) Employee

The term "employee" means an individual employed by an employer. With respect to employment in a foreign country, such term includes an individual who is a citizen of the United States.

(5) Employer

(A) In general

The term "employer" means a person engaged in an industry affecting commerce who has 15 or more employees for each working day in each of 20 or more calendar weeks in the current or preceding calendar year, and any agent of such person, except that, for two years following the effective date of this subchapter, an employer means a person engaged in an industry affecting commerce who has 25 or more employees for each working day in each of 20 or more calendar weeks in the current or preceding year, and any agent of such person.

(B) Exceptions

The term "employer" does not include—

(i) the United States, a corporation wholly owned by the government of the United States, or an Indian tribe; or

(ii) a bona fide private membership club (other than a labor organization) that is exempt from taxation under section 501(c) of Title 26.

(6) Illegal use of drugs

(A) In general

The term "illegal use of drugs" means the use of drugs, the possession or distribution of which is unlawful under the Controlled Substances Act [21 U.S.C. § 801 et seq.]. Such term does not include the use of a drug taken under supervision by a licensed health care professional, or other uses authorized by the Controlled Substances Act or other provisions of Federal law.

(B) Drugs

The term "drug" means a controlled substance, as defined in schedules I through V of section 202 of the Controlled Substances Act [21 U.S.C. § 812].

(7) Person, etc.

The terms "person," "labor organization," "employment agency," "commerce," and "industry affecting commerce," shall have the same meaning given such terms in section 2000e of this title.

(8) *Qualified individual*

The term "qualified individual" means an individual who, with or without reasonable accommodation, can perform the essential functions of the employment position that such individual holds or desires. For the purposes of this subchapter, consideration shall be given to the employer's judgment as to what functions of a job are essential, and if an employer has prepared a written description before advertising or interviewing applicants for the job, this description shall be considered evidence of the essential functions of the job.

(9) Reasonable accommodation

The term "reasonable accommodation" may include—

(A) making existing facilities used by employees readily accessible to and usable by individuals with disabilities; and

(B) job restructuring, part-time or modified work schedules, reassignment to a vacant position, acquisition or modification of equipment or devices, appropriate adjustment or modifications of examinations, training materials or policies, the provision of qualified readers or interpreters, and other similar accommodations for individuals with disabilities.

(10) Undue hardship

(A) In general

The term "undue hardship" means an action requiring significant difficulty or expense, when considered in light of the factors set forth in subparagraph (B).

(B) Factors to be considered

In determining whether an accommodation would impose an undue hardship on a covered entity, factors to be considered include—

(i) the nature and cost of the accommodation needed under this chapter;

(ii) the overall financial resources of the facility or facilities involved in the provision of the reasonable accommodation; the number of persons employed at such facility; the effect on expenses and resources, or the impact otherwise of such accommodation upon the operation of the facility;

(iii) the overall financial resources of the covered entity; the overall size of the business of a covered entity with respect to the number of its employees; the number, type, and location of its facilities; and

(iv) the type of operation or operations of the covered entity, including the composition, structure, and functions of the workforce of such entity; the geographic separateness, administrative, or fiscal relationship of the facility or facilities in question to the covered entity.

§ 102. [42 U.S.C. § 12112]. Discrimination

(a) General rule

No covered entity shall discriminate against *a qualified individual on the basis of disability* in regard to job application procedures, the hiring, advancement, or discharge of employees, employee compensation, job training, and other terms, conditions, and privileges of employment.

(b) Construction

As used in subsection (a) of this section, the term "discriminate against a qualified individual on the basis of disability" includes—

(1) limiting, segregating, or classifying a job applicant or employee in a way that adversely affects the opportunities or status of such applicant or employee because of the disability of such applicant or employee;

(2) participating in a contractual or other arrangement or relationship that has the effect of subjecting a covered entity's qualified applicant or employee with a disability to the discrimination prohibited by this subchapter (such relationship includes a relationship with an employment or referral agency, labor union, an organization providing fringe benefits to an employee of the covered entity, or an organization providing training and apprenticeship programs);

(3) utilizing standards, criteria, or methods of administration—

(A) that have the effect of discrimination on the basis of disability; or

(B) that perpetuate the discrimination of others who are subject to common administrative control;

(4) excluding or otherwise denying equal jobs or benefits to a qualified individual because of the known disability of an individual with whom the qualified individual is known to have a relationship or association;

(5) (A) not making reasonable accommodations to the known physical or mental limitations of an otherwise qualified individual with a disability who is an applicant or employee, unless such covered entity can demonstrate that the accommodation would impose an undue hardship on the operation of the business of such covered entity; or

(B) denying employment opportunities to a job applicant or employee who is an otherwise qualified individual with a disability, if such denial is based on the need of such covered entity to make reasonable accommodation to the physical or mental impairments of the employee or applicant;

(6) using qualification standards, employment tests or other selection criteria that screen out or tend to screen out an individual with a disability or a class of individuals with disabilities unless the standard, test or other selection criteria, as used by the covered entity, is shown to be job-related for the position in question and is consistent with business necessity; and

(7) failing to select and administer tests concerning employment in the most effective manner to ensure that, when such test is administered to a job applicant or employee who has a disability that impairs sensory, manual, or speaking skills, such test results accurately reflect the skills, aptitude, or whatever other factor of such applicant or employee that

such test purports to measure, rather than reflecting the impaired sensory, manual, or speaking skills of such employee or applicant (except where such skills are the factors that the test purports to measure).

(c) Covered entities in foreign countries

(1) In general

It shall not be unlawful under this section for a covered entity to take any action that constitutes discrimination under this section with respect to an employee in a workplace in a foreign country if compliance with this section would cause such covered entity to violate the law of the foreign country in which such workplace is located.

(2) Control of corporation

(A) Presumption

If an employer controls a corporation whose place of incorporation is a foreign country, any practice that constitutes discrimination under this section and is engaged in by such corporation shall be presumed to be engaged in by such employer.

(B) Exception

This section shall not apply with respect to the foreign operations of an employer that is a foreign person not controlled by an American employer.

(C) Determination

For purposes of this paragraph, the determination of whether an employer controls a corporation shall be based on—

(i) the interrelation of operations;

(ii) the common management;

(iii) the centralized control of labor relations; and

(iv) the common ownership or financial control, of the employer and the corporation.

(d) Medical examinations and inquiries

(1) In general

The prohibition against discrimination as referred to in subsection (a) of this section shall include medical examinations and inquiries.

(2) Preemployment

(A) Prohibited examination or inquiry

Except as provided in paragraph (3), a covered entity shall not conduct a medical examination or make inquiries of a job applicant as to whether such applicant is an individual with a disability or as to the nature or severity of such disability.

(B) Acceptable inquiry

A covered entity may make preemployment inquiries into the ability of an applicant to perform job-related functions.

(3) Employment entrance examination

A covered entity may require a medical examination after an offer of employment has been made to a job applicant and prior to the commencement of the employment duties of such applicant, and may condition an offer of employment on the results of such examination, if—

(A) all entering employees are subjected to such an examination regardless of disability;

(B) information obtained regarding the medical condition or history of the applicant is collected and maintained on separate forms and in separate medical files and is treated as a confidential medical record, except that—

(i) supervisors and managers may be informed regarding necessary restrictions on the work or duties of the employee and necessary accommodations;

(ii) first aid and safety personnel may be informed, when appropriate, if the disability might require emergency treatment; and

(iii) government officials investigating compliance with this chapter shall be provided relevant information on request; and

(C) the results of such examination are used only in accordance with this subchapter.

(4) Examination and inquiry

(A) Prohibited examinations and inquiries

A covered entity shall not require a medical examination and shall not make inquiries of an employee as to whether such employee is an individual with a disability or as to the nature or severity of the disability, unless such examination or inquiry is shown to be job-related and consistent with business necessity.

(B) Acceptable examinations and inquiries

A covered entity may conduct voluntary medical examinations, including voluntary medical histories, which are part of an employee health program available to employees at that work site. A covered entity may make inquiries into the ability of an employee to perform job-related functions.

(C) Requirement

Information obtained under subparagraph (B) regarding the medical condition or history of any employee are subject to the requirements of subparagraphs (B) and (C) of paragraph (3).

§ 103. [42 U.S.C. § 12113]. Defenses

(a) In general

It may be a defense to a charge of discrimination under this chapter that an alleged application of qualification standards, tests, or selection criteria that screen out or tend to screen out or otherwise deny a job or benefit to an individual with a disability has been shown to be job-related and consistent with business necessity, and such performance cannot be accomplished by reasonable accommodation, as required under this subchapter.

(b) Qualification standards

The term "qualification standards" may include a requirement that an individual shall not pose a direct threat to the health or safety of other individuals in the workplace.

(c) Qualification standards and tests related to uncorrected vision

Notwithstanding section 3(4)(E)(ii), a covered entity shall not use qualification standards, employment tests, or other selection criteria based on an individual's uncorrected vision unless the standard, test, or other selection criteria, as used by the covered entity, is shown to be job-related for the position in question and consistent with business necessity.

(d) Religious entities

(1) In general

This subchapter shall not prohibit a religious corporation, association, educational institution, or society from giving preference in employment to individuals of a particular religion to perform work connected with the carrying on by such corporation, association, educational institution, or society of its activities.

(2) Religious tenets requirement

Under this subchapter, a religious organization may require that all applicants and employees conform to the religious tenets of such organization.

(e) List of infectious and communicable diseases

(1) In general

The Secretary of Health and Human Services, not later than 6 months after July 26, 1990, shall—

(A) review all infectious and communicable diseases which may be transmitted through handling the food supply;

(B) publish a list of infectious and communicable diseases which are transmitted through handling the food supply;

(C) publish the methods by which such diseases are transmitted; and

(D) widely disseminate such information regarding the list of diseases and their modes of transmissability to the general public. Such list shall be updated annually.

(2) Applications

In any case in which an individual has an infectious or communicable disease that is transmitted to others through the handling of food, that is included on the list developed by the Secretary of Health and Human Services under paragraph (1), and which cannot be eliminated by reasonable accommodation, a covered entity may refuse to assign or continue to assign such individual to a job involving food handling.

(3) Construction

Nothing in this chapter shall be construed to preempt, modify, or amend any State, county, or local law, ordinance, or regulation applicable to food handling which is designed to protect the public health from individuals who pose a significant risk to the health or safety of others, which cannot be eliminated by reasonable accommodation, pursuant to the list of infectious or communicable diseases and the modes of transmissability published by the Secretary of Health and Human Services.

§ 104. [42 U.S.C. § 12114]. Illegal use of drugs and alcohol

(a) Qualified individual with a disability

For purposes of this subchapter, a qualified individual with a disability shall not include any employee or applicant who is currently engaging in the illegal use of drugs, when the covered entity acts on the basis of such use.

(b) Rules of construction

Nothing in subsection (a) of this section shall be construed to exclude as a qualified individual with a disability an individual who—

(1) has successfully completed a supervised drug rehabilitation program and is no longer engaging in the illegal use of drugs, or has otherwise been rehabilitated successfully and is no longer engaging in such use;

(2) is participating in a supervised rehabilitation program and is no longer engaging in such use; or

(3) is erroneously regarded as engaging in such use, but is not engaging in such use;

except that it shall not be a violation of this chapter for a covered entity to adopt or administer reasonable policies or procedures, including but not limited to drug testing, designed to ensure that an individual described in paragraph (1) or (2) is no longer engaging in the illegal use of drugs.

(c) Authority of covered entity

A covered entity—

(1) may prohibit the illegal use of drugs and the use of alcohol at the workplace by all employees;

(2) may require that employees shall not be under the influence of alcohol or be engaging in the illegal use of drugs at the workplace;

(3) may require that employees behave in conformance with the requirements established under the Drug-Free Workplace Act of 1988 (41 U.S.C. § 701 et seq.);

(4) may hold an employee who engages in the illegal use of drugs or who is an alcoholic to the same qualification standards for employment or job performance and behavior that such entity holds other employees, even if any unsatisfactory performance or behavior is related to the drug use or alcoholism of such employee; and

(5) may, with respect to Federal regulations regarding alcohol and the illegal use of drugs, require that—

(A) employees comply with the standards established in such regulations of the Department of Defense, if the employees of the covered entity are employed in an industry subject to such regulations, including complying with regulations (if any) that apply to employment in sensitive positions in such an industry, in the case of employees of the covered entity who are employed in such positions (as defined in the regulations of the Department of Defense);

(B) employees comply with the standards established in such regulations of the Nuclear Regulatory Commission, if the employees of the covered entity are employed in an industry subject to such regulations, including complying with regulations (if any) that apply to employment in sensitive positions in such an industry, in the case of employees of the covered entity who are employed in such positions (as defined in the regulations of the Nuclear Regulatory Commission); and

(C) employees comply with the standards established in such regulations of the Department of Transportation, if the employees of the covered entity are employed in a transportation industry subject to such regulations, including complying with such regulations (if any) that apply to employment in sensitive positions in such an industry, in the case of employees of the covered entity who are employed in such positions (as defined in the regulations of the Department of Transportation).

(d) Drug testing

(1) In general

For purposes of this subchapter, a test to determine the illegal use of drugs shall not be considered a medical examination.

(2) Construction

Nothing in this subchapter shall be construed to encourage, prohibit, or authorize the conducting of drug testing for the illegal use of drugs by job applicants or employees or making employment decisions based on such test results.

(e) Transportation employees

Nothing in this subchapter shall be construed to encourage, prohibit, restrict, or authorize the otherwise lawful exercise by entities subject to the jurisdiction of the Department of Transportation of authority to—

(1) test employees of such entities in, and applicants for, positions involving safety-sensitive duties for the illegal use of drugs and for on-duty impairment by alcohol; and

(2) remove such persons who test positive for illegal use of drugs and on-duty impairment by alcohol pursuant to paragraph (1) from safety-sensitive duties in implementing subsection (c) of this section.

§ 105. [42 U.S.C. § 12115]. Posting notices

Every employer, employment agency, labor organization, or joint labor-management committee covered under this subchapter shall post notices in an accessible format to applicants, employees, and members describing the applicable provisions of this chapter, in the manner prescribed by section 2000e–10 of this title.

§ 106. [42 U.S.C. § 12116]. Regulations

Not later than 1 year after July 26, 1990, the Commission shall issue regulations in an accessible format to carry out this subchapter in accordance with subchapter II of chapter 5 of Title 5.

§ 107. [42 U.S.C. § 12117]. Enforcement

(a) Powers, remedies, and procedures

The powers, remedies, and procedures set forth in sections 2000e–4, 2000e–5, 2000e–6, 2000e–8, and 2000e–9 of this title shall be the powers, remedies, and procedures this subchapter provides to the Commission, to the Attorney General, or to any person alleging discrimination on the basis of disability in violation of any provision of this chapter, or regulations promulgated under section 12116 of this title, concerning employment.

(b) Coordination

The agencies with enforcement authority for actions which allege employment discrimination under this subchapter and under the Rehabilitation Act of 1973 [29 U.S.C. § 701 et seq.] shall develop procedures to ensure that administrative complaints filed under this subchapter and under the Rehabilitation Act of 1973 are dealt with in a manner that avoids duplication of effort and prevents imposition of inconsistent or conflicting standards for the same requirements under this subchapter and the Rehabilitation Act of 1973. The Commission, the Attorney General, and the Office of Federal Contract Compliance Programs shall establish such coordinating mechanisms (similar to provisions contained in the joint regulations promulgated by the Commission and the Attorney General at part 42 of title 28 and part 1691 of title 29, Code of Federal Regulations, and the Memorandum of Understanding between the Commission and the Office of Federal Contract Compliance Programs dated January 16, 1981 (46 Fed.Reg. 7435, January 23, 1981)) in regulations implementing this subchapter and Rehabilitation Act of 1973 not later than 18 months after July 26, 1990.

TITLE V—MISCELLANEOUS PROVISIONS

§ 501. [42 U.S.C. § 12201]. Construction

(a) In general

Except as otherwise provided in this chapter, nothing in this chapter shall be construed to apply a lesser standard than the standards applied under title V of the Rehabilitation Act of 1973 (29 U.S.C. § 790 et seq.) or the regulations issued by Federal agencies pursuant to such title.

(b) Relationship to other laws

Nothing in this chapter shall be construed to invalidate or limit the remedies, rights, and procedures of any Federal law or law of any State or political subdivision of any State or jurisdiction that provides greater or equal protection for the rights of individuals with disabilities than are afforded by this chapter. Nothing in this chapter shall be construed to preclude the prohibition of, or the imposition of restrictions on, smoking in places of employment covered by subchapter I, in transportation covered by subchapter II or III, or in places of public accommodation covered by subchapter III.

(c) Insurance

Subchapters I through III of this chapter and title IV of this subchapter shall not be construed to prohibit or restrict—

(1) an insurer, hospital or medical service company, health maintenance organization, or any agent, or entity that administers benefit plans, or similar organizations from underwriting risks, classifying risks, or administering such risks that are based on or not inconsistent with State law; or

(2) a person or organization covered by this chapter from establishing, sponsoring, observing or administering the terms of a bona fide benefit plan that are based on underwriting risks, classifying risks,

or administering such risks that are based on or not inconsistent with State law; or

(3) a person or organization covered by this chapter from establishing, sponsoring, observing or administering the terms of a bona fide benefit plan that is not subject to State laws that regulate insurance.

Paragraphs (1), (2), and (3) shall not be used as a subterfuge to evade the purposes of subchapter I and III.

(d) Accommodations and services

Nothing in this chapter shall be construed to require an individual with a disability to accept an accommodation, aid, service, opportunity, or benefit which such individual chooses not to accept.

(e) Benefits under State workers' compensation laws

Nothing in this subchapter alters the standards for determining eligibility for benefits under State worker's compensation laws or under State and Federal disability benefit programs.

(f) Fundamental alteration

Nothing in this subchapter alters the provision of section 302(b)(2)(A)(ii), specifying that reasonable modifications in policies, practices, or procedures shall be required, unless an entity can demonstrate that making such modifications in policies, practices, or procedures, including academic requirements in postsecondary education, would fundamentally alter the nature of the goods, services, facilities, privileges, advantages, or accommodations involved.

(g) Claims of no disability

Nothing in this subchapter shall provide the basis for a claim by an individual without a disability that the individual was subject to discrimination because of the individual's lack of disability.

(h) Reasonable accommodations and modifications

A covered entity under title I, a public entity under title II, and any person who owns, leases (or leases to), or operates a place of public accommodation under title III, need not provide a reasonable accommodation or a reasonable modification to policies, practices, or procedures to an individual who meets the definition of disability in section 3(1) solely under subparagraph (C) of such section.

§ 502. [42 U.S.C. § 12202]. State immunity

A State shall not be immune under the eleventh amendment to the Constitution of the United States from an action in Federal or State court of competent jurisdiction for a violation of this chapter. In any action against a State for a violation of the requirements of this chapter, remedies (including remedies both at law and in equity) are available for such a violation to the same extent as such remedies are available for such a violation in an action against any public or private entity other than a State.

§ 503. [42 U.S.C. § 12203]. Prohibition against retaliation and coercion

(a) Retaliation

No person shall discriminate against any individual because such individual has opposed any act or practice made unlawful by this chapter or because such individual made a charge, testified, assisted, or participated in any manner in an investigation, proceeding, or hearing under this chapter.

(b) Interference, coercion, or intimidation

It shall be unlawful to coerce, intimidate, threaten, or interfere with any individual in the exercise or enjoyment of, or on account of his or her having exercised or enjoyed, or on account of his or her having aided or encouraged any other individual in the exercise or enjoyment of, any right granted or protected by this chapter.

(c) Remedies and procedures

The remedies and procedures available under sections 12117, 12133, and 12188 of this title shall be available to aggrieved persons for violations of subsections (a) and (b) of this section, with respect to subchapter I, subchapter II and subchapter III, respectively.

§ 505. [42 U.S.C. § 12205]. Attorney's fees

In any action or administrative proceeding commenced pursuant to this chapter, the court or agency, in its discretion, may allow the prevailing party, other than the United States, a reasonable attorney's fee, including litigation expenses, and costs, and the United States shall be liable for the foregoing the same as a private individual.

§ 506. [42 U.S.C. § 12205a]. Rule of construction regarding regulatory authority

The authority to issue regulations granted to the Equal Employment Opportunity Commission, the Attorney General, and the Secretary of Transportation under this subchapter includes the authority to issue regulations implementing the definitions of disability in section 3 (including rules of construction) and the definitions in section 4, consistent with the ADA Amendments Act of 2008.

§ 509. [42 U.S.C. § 12208]. Transvestites

For the purposes of this chapter, the term "disabled" or "disability" shall not apply to an individual solely because that individual is a transvestite.

§ 510. [42 U.S.C. § 12209]. Instrumentalities of the Congress

The Government Accountability Office, the Government Publishing Office, and the Library of Congress shall be covered as follows:

(1) In general

The rights and protections under this chapter shall, subject to paragraph (2), apply with respect to the conduct of each instrumentality of the Congress.

(2) Establishment of remedies and procedures by instrumentalities

The chief official of each instrumentality of the Congress shall establish remedies and procedures to be utilized with respect to the rights and protections provided pursuant to paragraph (1).

(3) Report to Congress

The chief official of each instrumentality of the Congress shall, after establishing remedies and procedures for purposes of paragraph (2), submit to the Congress a report describing the remedies and procedures.

(4) Definition of instrumentality

For purposes of this section, the term "instrumentality of the Congress" means the following: the Government Accountability Office, the Government Publishing Office, and the Library of Congress.

(5) Enforcement of employment rights

The remedies and procedures set forth in section 2000e–16 of this title shall be available to any employee of an instrumentality of the Congress who alleges a violation of the rights and protections under sections 12112 through 12114 of this title that are made applicable by this section, except that the authorities of the Equal Employment Opportunity Commission shall be exercised by the chief official of the instrumentality of the Congress.

(6) Enforcement of rights to public services and accommodations

The remedies and procedures set forth in section 2000e–16 of this title shall be available to any qualified person with a disability who is a visitor, guest, or patron of an instrumentality of Congress and who alleges a violation of the rights and protections under sections 12131 through 12150 or section 12182 or 12183 of this title that are made applicable by this section, except that the authorities of the Equal Employment Opportunity Commission shall be exercised by the chief official of the instrumentality of the Congress.

(7) Construction

Nothing in this section shall alter the enforcement procedures for individuals with disabilities provided in the General Accounting Office Personnel Act of 1980 and regulations promulgated pursuant to that Act.

§ 511. [42 U.S.C. § 12210]. Illegal use of drugs

(a) In general

For purposes of this chapter, the term "individual with a disability" does not include an individual who is currently engaging in the illegal use of drugs, when the covered entity acts on the basis of such use.

(b) Rules of construction

Nothing in subsection (a) of this section shall be construed to exclude as an individual with a disability an individual who—

(1) has successfully completed a supervised drug rehabilitation program and is no longer engaging in the illegal use of drugs, or has otherwise been rehabilitated successfully and is no longer engaging in such use;

(2) is participating in a supervised rehabilitation program and is no longer engaging in such use; or

(3) is erroneously regarded as engaging in such use, but is not engaging in such use;

except that it shall not be a violation of this chapter for a covered entity to adopt or administer reasonable policies or procedures, including but not limited to drug testing, designed to ensure that an individual described in paragraph (1) or (2) is no longer engaging in the illegal use of drugs; however, nothing in this section shall be construed to encourage, prohibit, restrict, or authorize the conducting of testing for the illegal use of drugs.

(c) Health and other services

Notwithstanding subsection (a) of this section and section 12212(b)(3) of this title, an individual shall not be denied health services, or services provided in connection with drug rehabilitation, on the basis of the current illegal use of drugs if the individual is otherwise entitled to such services.

(d) "Illegal use of drugs" defined

(1) In general

The term "illegal use of drugs" means the use of drugs, the possession or distribution of which is unlawful under the Controlled Substances Act [21 U.S.C. § 801 et seq.]. Such term does not include the use of a drug taken under supervision by a licensed health care professional, or other uses authorized by the Controlled Substances Act [21 U.S.C. § 801 et seq.] or other provisions of Federal law.

(2) Drugs

The term "drug" means a controlled substance, as defined in schedules I through V of section 202 of the Controlled Substances Act [21 U.S.C. § 812].

§ 512. [42 U.S.C. § 12211]. Definitions

(a) Homosexuality and bisexuality

For purposes of the definition of "disability" in section 12102(2) of this title, homosexuality and bisexuality are not impairments and as such are not disabilities under this chapter.

(b) Certain conditions

Under this chapter, the term "disability" shall not include—

(1) transvestism, transsexualism, pedophilia, exhibitionism, voyeurism, gender identity disorders not resulting from physical impairments, or other sexual behavior disorders;

(2) compulsive gambling, kleptomania, or pyromania; or

(3) psychoactive substance use disorders resulting from current illegal use of drugs.

§ 514. [42 U.S.C. § 12212]. Alternative means of dispute resolution

Where appropriate and to the extent authorized by law, the use of alternative means of dispute resolution, including settlement negotiations, conciliation, facilitation, mediation, factfinding, minitrials, and arbitration, is encouraged to resolve disputes arising under this chapter.

§ 515. [42 U.S.C. § 12213]. Severability

Should any provision in this chapter be found to be unconstitutional by a court of law, such provision shall be severed from the remainder of this chapter and such action shall not affect the enforceability of the remaining provisions of this chapter.

THE ADA AMENDMENTS ACT OF 2008

Pub. L. No. 110–325, 122 Stat. 3553

§ 2. Findings and Purposes.

(a) Findings.

Congress finds that—

(1) in enacting the Americans with Disabilities Act of 1990 (ADA), Congress intended that the Act "provide a clear and comprehensive national mandate for the elimination of discrimination against individuals with disabilities" and provide broad coverage;

(2) in enacting the ADA, Congress recognized that physical and mental disabilities in no way diminish a person's right to fully participate in all aspects of society, but that people with physical or mental disabilities are frequently precluded from doing so because of prejudice, antiquated attitudes, or the failure to remove societal and institutional barriers;

(3) while Congress expected that the definition of disability under the ADA would be interpreted consistently with how courts had applied

the definition of a handicapped individual under the Rehabilitation Act of 1973, that expectation has not been fulfilled;

(4) the holdings of the Supreme Court in Sutton v. United Air Lines, Inc., 527 U.S. 471 (1999) and its companion cases have narrowed the broad scope of protection intended to be afforded by the ADA, thus eliminating protection for many individuals whom Congress intended to protect;

(5) the holding of the Supreme Court in Toyota Motor Manufacturing, Kentucky, Inc. v. Williams, 534 U.S. 184 (2002) further narrowed the broad scope of protection intended to be afforded by the ADA;

(6) as a result of these Supreme Court cases, lower courts have incorrectly found in individual cases that people with a range of substantially limiting impairments are not people with disabilities;

(7) in particular, the Supreme Court, in the case of Toyota Motor Manufacturing, Kentucky, Inc. v. Williams, 534 U.S. 184 (2002), interpreted the term "substantially limits" to require a greater degree of limitation than was intended by Congress; and

(8) Congress finds that the current Equal Employment Opportunity Commission ADA regulations defining the term "substantially limits" as "significantly restricted" are inconsistent with congressional intent, by expressing too high a standard.

(b) Purposes.

The purposes of this Act are—

(1) to carry out the ADA's objectives of providing "a clear and comprehensive national mandate for the elimination of discrimination" and "clear, strong, consistent, enforceable standards addressing discrimination" by reinstating a broad scope of protection to be available under the ADA;

(2) to reject the requirement enunciated by the Supreme Court in Sutton v. United Air Lines, Inc., 527 U.S. 471 (1999) and its companion cases that whether an impairment substantially limits a major life activity is to be determined with reference to the ameliorative effects of mitigating measures;

(3) to reject the Supreme Court's reasoning in Sutton v. United Air Lines, Inc., 527 U.S. 471 (1999) with regard to coverage under the third prong of the definition of disability and to reinstate the reasoning of the Supreme Court in School Board of Nassau County v. Arline, 480 U.S. 273 (1987) which set forth a broad view of the third prong of the definition of handicap under the Rehabilitation Act of 1973;

(4) to reject the standards enunciated by the Supreme Court in Toyota Motor Manufacturing, Kentucky, Inc. v. Williams, 534 U.S. 184 (2002), that the terms "substantially" and "major" in the definition of disability under the ADA "need to be interpreted strictly to create a

demanding standard for qualifying as disabled," and that to be substantially limited in performing a major life activity under the ADA "an individual must have an impairment that prevents or severely restricts the individual from doing activities that are of central importance to most people's daily lives";

(5) to convey congressional intent that the standard created by the Supreme Court in the case of Toyota Motor Manufacturing, Kentucky, Inc. v. Williams, 534 U.S. 184 (2002) for "substantially limits", and applied by lower courts in numerous decisions, has created an inappropriately high level of limitation necessary to obtain coverage under the ADA, to convey that it is the intent of Congress that the primary object of attention in cases brought under the ADA should be whether entities covered under the ADA have complied with their obligations, and to convey that the question of whether an individual's impairment is a disability under the ADA should not demand extensive analysis; and

(6) to express Congress' expectation that the Equal Employment Opportunity Commission will revise that portion of its current regulations that defines the term "substantially limits" as "significantly restricted" to be consistent with this subchapter, including the amendments made by this Act.

EXECUTIVE ORDER 11246, as amended

30 Fed. Reg. 12319, 79 Fed. Reg. 42971

EQUAL EMPLOYMENT OPPORTUNITY

Under and by virtue of the authority vested in me as President of the United States by the Constitution and statutes of the United States, it is ordered as follows:

PART II—NONDISCRIMINATION IN EMPLOYMENT BY GOVERNMENT CONTRACTORS AND SUBCONTRACTORS

SUBPART A—DUTIES OF THE SECRETARY OF LABOR

§ 201. The Secretary of Labor shall be responsible for the administration of Parts II and III of this Order and shall adopt such rules and regulations and issue such orders as he deems necessary and appropriate to achieve the purposes thereof.

SUBPART B—CONTRACTORS' AGREEMENTS

§ 202. Except in contracts exempted in accordance with Section 204 of this Order, all Government contracting agencies shall include in every Government contract hereafter entered into the following provisions:

"During the performance of this contract, the contractor agrees as follows:

"(1) The contractor will not discriminate against any employee or applicant for employment because of race, creed, color, sex, sexual orientation, gender identity, or national origin. The contractor will take affirmative action to ensure that applicants are employed, and that employees are treated during employment, without regard to their race, creed, color, sex, sexual orientation, gender identity, or national origin. Such action shall include, but not be limited to the following: employment, upgrading, demotion, or transfer; recruitment or recruitment advertising; layoff or termination; rates of pay or other forms of compensation; and selection for training, including apprenticeship. The contractor agrees to post in conspicuous places, available to employees and applicants for employment, notices to be provided by the contracting officer setting forth the provisions of this nondiscrimination clause.

"(2) The contractor will, in all solicitations or advertisements for employees placed by or on behalf of the contractor, state that all qualified applicants will receive consideration for employment without regard to race, creed, color, sex, sexual orientation, gender identity, or national origin.

"(3) The contractor will send to each labor union or representative of workers with which he has a collective bargaining agreement or other contract or understanding, a notice, to be provided by the agency contracting officer, advising the labor union or workers' representative of the contractor's commitments under Section 202 of Executive Order No. 11246 of September 24, 1965, and shall post copies of the notice in conspicuous places available to employees and applicants for employment.

"(4) The contractor will comply with all provisions of Executive Order No. 11246 of Sept. 24, 1965, and of the rules, regulations, and relevant orders of the Secretary of Labor.

"(5) The contractor will furnish all information and reports required by Executive Order No. 11246 of September 24, 1965, and by the rules, regulations, and orders of the Secretary of Labor, or pursuant thereto, and will permit access to his books, records, and accounts by the contracting agency and the Secretary of Labor for purposes of investigation to ascertain compliance with such rules, regulations, and orders.

"(6) In the event of the contractor's noncompliance with the nondiscrimination clauses of this contract or with any of such rules, regulations, or orders, this contract may be cancelled, terminated or suspended in whole or in part and the contractor may be declared ineligible for further Government contracts in accordance with procedures authorized in Executive Order No. 11246 of Sept. 24, 1965, and such other sanctions may be imposed and remedies invoked as provided in Executive Order No. 11246 of September 24, 1965, or by rule, regulation, or order of the Secretary of Labor, or as otherwise provided by law.

"(7) The contractor will include the provisions of Paragraphs (1) through (7) in every subcontract or purchase order unless exempted by rule, regulations, or orders of the Secretary of Labor issued pursuant to Section 204 of Executive Order No. 11246 of Sept. 24, 1965, so that such provisions will be binding upon each subcontractor or vendor. The contractor will take such action with respect to any subcontract or purchase order as the contracting agency may direct as a means of enforcing such provisions including sanctions for noncompliance: Provided, however, That in the event the contractor becomes involved in, or is threatened with, litigation with a subcontractor or vendor as a result of such direction by the contracting agency, the contractor may request the United States to enter into such litigation to protect the interests of the United States."

§ 203. (a) Each contractor having a contract containing the provisions prescribed in Section 202 shall file, and shall cause each of his subcontractors to file, Compliance Reports with the contracting agency or the Secretary of Labor as may be directed. Compliance Reports shall be filed within such times and shall contain such information as to the practices, policies, programs, and employment policies, programs, and employment statistics of the contractor and each subcontractor, and shall be in such form, as the Secretary of Labor may prescribe.

(b) Bidders or prospective contractors or subcontractors may be required to state whether they have participated in any previous contract subject to the provisions of this Order, or any preceding similar Executive order, and in that event to submit, on behalf of themselves and their proposed subcontractors, Compliance Reports prior to or as an initial part of their bid or negotiation of a contract.

(c) Whenever the contractor or subcontractor has a collective bargaining agreement or other contract or understanding with a labor union or an agency referring workers or providing or supervising apprenticeship or training for such workers, the Compliance Report shall include such information as to such labor union's or agency's practices and policies affecting compliance as the Secretary of Labor may prescribe: Provided, That to the extent such information is within the exclusive possession of a labor union or an agency referring workers or providing or supervising apprenticeship or training and such labor union or agency shall refuse to furnish such information to the contractor, the contractor shall so certify to the contracting agency as part of its Compliance Report and shall set forth what efforts he has made to obtain such information.

(d) The contracting agency or the Secretary of Labor may direct that any bidder or prospective contractor or subcontractor shall submit, as part of his Compliance Report, a statement in writing, signed by an authorized officer or agent on behalf of any labor union or any agency referring workers or providing or supervising apprenticeship or other training, with which the bidder or prospective contractor deals, with supporting information, to the effect that the signer's practices and policies do not discriminate on the grounds of race, color, creed, sex, sexual orientation, gender identity, or national origin, and that the signer either will affirmatively cooperate in the implementation of the policy and provisions of this Order or that it consents and agrees that recruitment, employment, and the terms and conditions of employment under the proposed contract shall be in accordance with the purposes and provisions of the Order. In the event that the union, or the agency shall refuse to execute such a statement, the Compliance Report shall so certify and set forth what efforts have been made to secure such a statement and such additional factual material as the contracting agency or the Secretary of Labor may require.

§ 204. The Secretary of Labor may, when he deems that special circumstances in the national interest so require, exempt a contracting agency from the requirement of including any or all of the provisions of Section 202 of this Order in any specific contract, subcontract, or purchase order. The Secretary of Labor may, by rule or regulation, also exempt certain classes of contracts, subcontracts, or purchase orders (1) whenever work is to be or has been performed outside the United States and no recruitment of workers within the limits of the United States is involved; (2) for standard commercial supplies or raw materials; (3) involving less than specified amounts of money or specified numbers of workers; or (4) to the extent that they involve subcontracts below a specified tier. The Secretary of Labor may also provide, by rule, regulation, or order, for the exemption of facilities of a contractor which are in all respects separate and distinct from activities of the contractor related to the performance of the contract: Provided, That such an exemption will not interfere with or impede the effectuation of the purposes of this Order: And provided further, That in the absence of such an exemption all facilities shall be covered by the provisions of this Order.

SUBPART C—POWERS AND DUTIES OF THE SECRETARY OF LABOR AND THE CONTRACTING AGENCIES

§ 205. Each contracting agency shall be primarily responsible for obtaining compliance with the rules, regulations, and orders of the Secretary of Labor with respect to contracts entered into by such agency or its contractors. All contracting agencies shall comply with the rules of the Secretary of Labor in discharging their primary responsibility for securing compliance with the provisions of contracts and otherwise with the terms of this Order and of the rules, regulations, and orders of the Secretary of Labor issued pursuant to this Order. They are directed to cooperate with the Secretary of Labor and to furnish the Secretary of Labor such information and assistance as he may require in the performance of his functions under this Order. They are further directed to appoint or designate, from among the agency's personnel, compliance officers. It shall be the duty of such officers to seek compliance with the objectives of this Order by conference, conciliation, mediation, or persuasion.

§ 206. (a) The Secretary of Labor may investigate the employment practices of any Government contractor or subcontractor, or initiate such investigation by the appropriate contracting agency, to determine whether or not the contractual provisions specified in Section 202 of this Order have been violated. Such investigation shall be conducted in accordance with the procedures established by the Secretary of Labor and the investigating agency shall report to the Secretary of Labor any action taken or recommended.

(b) The Secretary of Labor may receive and investigate or cause to be investigated complaints by employees or prospective employees of a Government contractor or subcontractor which allege discrimination contrary to the contractual provisions specified in Section 202 of this Order. If this investigation is conducted for the Secretary of Labor by a contracting agency, that agency shall report to the Secretary what action has been taken or is recommended with regard to such complaints.

§ 207. The Secretary of Labor shall use his best efforts, directly and through contracting agencies, other interested Federal, State, and local agencies, contractors, and all other available instrumentalities to cause any labor union engaged in work under Government contracts or any agency referring workers or providing or supervising apprenticeship or training for or in the course of such work to cooperate in the implementation of the purposes of this Order. The Secretary of Labor shall, in appropriate cases, notify the Equal Employment Opportunity Commission, the Department of Justice, or other appropriate Federal agencies whenever it has reason to believe that the practices of any such labor organization or agency violate Title VI or Title VII of the Civil Rights Act of 1964 or other provision of Federal law.

§ 208. (a) The Secretary of Labor, or any agency, officer, or employee in the executive branch of the Government designated by rule, regulation, or order of the Secretary, may hold such hearings, public or private, as the Secretary may deem advisable for compliance, enforcement, or educational purposes.

(b) The Secretary of Labor may hold, or cause to be held, hearings in accordance with Subsection (a) of this Section prior to imposing, ordering, or recommending the imposition of penalties and sanctions under this Order. No order for debarment of any contractor from further Government contracts under Section 209(a)(6) shall be made without affording the contractor an opportunity for a hearing.

SUBPART D—SANCTIONS AND PENALTIES

§ 209. (a) In accordance with such rules, regulations, or orders as the Secretary of Labor may issue or adopt, the Secretary or the appropriate contracting agency may:

(1) Publish, or cause to be published, the names of contractors or unions which it has concluded have complied or have failed to comply with the provisions of this Order or of the rules, regulations, and orders of the Secretary of Labor.

(2) Recommend to the Department of Justice that, in cases in which there is substantial or material violation or the threat of substantial or material violation of the contractual provisions set forth in Section 202 of this Order, appropriate proceedings be brought to enforce those provisions, including the enjoining, within the limitations of applicable law, of organizations, individuals, or groups who prevent directly or indirectly, or seek to prevent directly or indirectly, compliance with the provisions of this Order.

(3) Recommend to the Equal Employment Opportunity Commission or the Department of Justice that appropriate proceedings be instituted under Title VII of the Civil Rights Act of 1964.

(4) Recommend to the Department of Justice that criminal proceedings be brought for the furnishing of false information to any contracting agency or to the Secretary of Labor as the case may be.

(5) Cancel, terminate, suspend, or cause to be cancelled, terminated, or suspended, any contract, or any portion or portions thereof, for failure of the contractor or subcontractor to comply with the non-discrimination provisions of the contract. Contracts may be cancelled, terminated, or suspended absolutely or continuance of contracts may be conditioned upon a program for future compliance approved by the contracting agency.

(6) Provide that any contracting agency shall refrain from entering into further contracts, or extensions or other modifications of existing contracts, with any noncomplying contractor, until such contractor has satisfied the Secretary of Labor that such contractor has established and will carry out personnel and employment policies in compliance with the provisions of this Order.

(b) Under rules and regulations prescribed by the Secretary of Labor, each contracting agency shall make reasonable efforts within a reasonable time limitation to secure compliance with the contract provisions of this Order by methods of conference, conciliation, mediation, and persuasion before proceedings shall be instituted under Subsection (a)(2) of this Section, or before a contract shall be cancelled or terminated in whole or in part under Subsection (a)(5) of this Section for failure of a contractor or subcontractor to comply with the contract provisions of this Order.

§ 210. Any contracting agency taking any action authorized by this Subpart, whether on its own motion, or as directed by the Secretary of Labor, or under the rules and regulations of the Secretary, shall promptly notify the Secretary of such action. Whenever the Secretary of Labor makes a determination under this Section, he shall promptly notify the appropriate contracting agency of the action recommended. The agency shall take such action and shall report the results thereof to the Secretary of Labor within such time as the Secretary shall specify.

§ 211. If the Secretary shall so direct, contracting agencies shall not enter into contracts with any bidder or prospective contractor unless the bidder or prospective contractor has satisfactorily complied with the provisions of this Order or submits a program for compliance acceptable to the Secretary of Labor or, if the Secretary so authorizes, to the contracting agency.

§ 212. Whenever a contracting agency cancels or terminates a contract, or whenever a contractor has been debarred from further Government contracts, under Section 209(a)(6) because of noncompliance with the contract provisions with regard to nondiscrimination, the Secretary of Labor, or the contracting agency involved, shall promptly notify the Comptroller General of the United States. Any such debarment may be rescinded by the Secretary of Labor or by the contracting agency which imposed the sanction. . . .

PART III—NONDISCRIMINATION PROVISIONS IN FEDERALLY ASSISTED CONSTRUCTION CONTRACTS

§ 301. Each executive department and agency which administers a program involving Federal financial assistance shall require as a condition for the approval of any grant, contract, loan, insurance, or guarantee thereunder, which may involve a construction contract, that the applicant for Federal assistance undertake and agree to incorporate, or cause to be incorporated, into all construction contracts paid for in whole or in part with funds obtained from the Federal Government or borrowed on the credit of the Federal Government pursuant to such grant, contract, loan, insurance, or guarantee, or undertaken pursuant to any Federal program involving such grant, contract, loan, insurance, or guarantee, the provisions prescribed for Government contracts by Section 202 of this Order or such modification thereof, preserving in substance the contractor's obligations thereunder, as may be approved by the Secretary of Labor, together with such additional provisions as the Secretary deems appropriate to establish and protect the interest of the United States in the enforcement of those obligations. Each such applicant shall also undertake and agree (1) to assist and cooperate actively with the administering department or agency and the Secretary of Labor in obtaining the compliance of contractors and subcontractors with those contract provisions and with the rules, regulations, and relevant orders of the Secretary, (2) to obtain and to furnish to the administering department or agency and to the Secretary of Labor such information as they may require for the supervision of such compliance, (3) to carry out sanctions and penalties for violation of such obligations imposed upon contractors and subcontractors by the Secretary of Labor or the administering department or agency pursuant to Part II, Subpart D, of this Order, and (4) to refrain from entering into any contract subject to this Order, or extension or other modification of such a contract with a contractor debarred from Government contracts under Part II, Subpart D, of this Order.

§ 302. (a) "Construction contract" as used in this Order means any contract for the construction, rehabilitation, alteration, conversion, extension, or repair of buildings, highways, or other improvements to real property.

(b) The provisions of Part II of this Order shall apply to such construction contracts, and for purposes of such application the administering department or agency shall be considered the contracting agency referred to therein.

(c) The term "applicant" as used in this Order means an applicant for Federal assistance or, as determined by agency regulation, other program participant, with respect to whom an application for any grant, contract, loan, insurance, or guarantee is not finally acted upon prior to the effective date of this Part, and it includes such an applicant after he becomes a recipient of such Federal assistance.

§ 303. (a) Each administering department and agency shall be responsible for obtaining the compliance of such applicants with their undertakings under this Order. Each administering department and agency is directed to cooperate with the Secretary of Labor, and to furnish the Secretary such information and assistance as he may require in the performance of his functions under this Order.

(b) In the event an applicant fails and refuses to comply with his undertakings, the administering department or agency may take any or all of the following actions: (1) cancel, terminate, or suspend in whole or in part the agreement, contract, or other arrangement with such applicant with respect to which the failure and refusal occurred; (2) refrain from extending any further assistance to the applicant under the program with respect to which the failure or refusal occurred until satisfactory assurance of future compliance has been received from such applicant; and (3) refer the case to the Department of Justice for appropriate legal proceedings.

(c) Any action with respect to an applicant pursuant to Subsection (b) shall be taken in conformity with Section 602 of the Civil Rights Act of 1964 (and the regulations of the administering department or agency issued thereunder), to the extent applicable. In no case shall action be taken with respect to an applicant pursuant to Clause (1) or (2) of Subsection (b) without notice and opportunity for hearing before the administering department or agency.

§ 304. Any executive department or agency which imposes by rule, regulation, or order requirements of nondiscrimination in employment, other than requirements imposed pursuant to this Order, may delegate to the Secretary of Labor by agreement such responsibilities with respect to compliance standards, reports, and procedures as would tend to bring the administration of such requirements into conformity with the administration of requirements imposed under this Order: Provided, That actions to effect compliance by recipients of Federal financial assistance with requirements imposed pursuant to Title VI of the Civil Rights Act of 1964 shall be taken in conformity with the procedures and limitations prescribed in Section 602 thereof and the regulations of the administering department or agency issued thereunder. . . .

THE LILLY LEDBETTER FAIR PAY ACT OF 2009

Pub. L. No. 111–12, 123 Stat. 5

§ 2. Findings.

Congress finds the following:

(1) The Supreme Court in Ledbetter v. Goodyear Tire & Rubber Co., 550 U.S. 618 (2007), significantly impairs statutory protections against discrimination in compensation that Congress established and that have been bedrock principles of American law for decades. The Ledbetter decision undermines those statutory protections by unduly restricting the time period in which victims of discrimination can challenge and recover for discriminatory compensation decisions or other practices, contrary to the intent of Congress.

(2) The limitation imposed by the Court on the filing of discriminatory compensation claims ignores the reality of wage discrimination and is at odds with the robust application of the civil rights laws that Congress intended.

(3) With regard to any charge of discrimination under any law, nothing in this Act is intended to preclude or limit an aggrieved person's right to introduce evidence of an unlawful employment practice that has occurred outside the time for filing a charge of discrimination.

(4) Nothing in this Act is intended to change current law treatment of when pension distributions are considered paid.

INDEX

References are to Pages